The Sunday Telegraph

GOLF COURSE GUIDE
—— TO ——
BRITAIN & IRELAND

The Sunday Telegraph

GOLF COURSE GUIDE
—— TO ——
BRITAIN & IRELAND

Introduction by Mark Reason

15th Edition

MACMILLAN

The publishers would like to acknowledge the contribution of the following:

Editorial
*Jon Ryan; Mark Reason for all his editorial work; Jim Bruce-Ball for course reviews
and all round help; Andrew Warshaw; Jim Mossop and Simon Hart.*

Text updating and checking
Elliot Littlechild; Shelley Carmichael and Anthony Pascoe (IPS)

Editorial co-ordination and typesetting
Integrated Publishing Solutions (IPS), Cape Town, South Africa

Advertising
*Enquiries about advertising in this book should be addressed to
Barry Hood on 020 8542 5051*

First published 1968 by William Collins, Sons & Co Ltd, London
This edition published 2002 by Macmillan
an imprint of Pan Macmillan Ltd
20 New Wharf Road, London N1 9RR
Basingstoke and Oxford
Associated companies throughout the world
www.panmacmillan.com

ISBN 0 333 98945 7

CONTENTS

INTRODUCTION
by Mark Reason

In 1958 a one-time naval captain stood on the steps of St Andrews, slipped a golf ball down the barrel of his gun and fired off into the yonder, comfortably carrying the Swilken Burn over 370 yards away. The sight of Tiger Woods performing similar feats with a driver and a supersonic golf ball forty years later have persuaded some that too many of our golf courses are redundant.

"We need longer courses," went up the cry. As a result whole counties were excavated in order to construct courses to accommodate Tiger's prodigious firepower. It would be unfair to be too harsh on the architects. After all this was land that might have housed shopping centres if golf hadn't come along to save us from such a terrible fate.

But in 2001 something strange occurred. The USGA decided to hold their Open championship at Southern Hills. The Royal and Ancient had chosen Royal Lytham & St Annes as the host of their Championship. Both courses were considered by many to be a little on the short side in places. Who was going to come second?

Both answers were unexpected. Mark Brooks and Niclas Fasth were not names that many people had on their shortlists. Each played far above expectations, including probably their own, but even then they could not overturn the inevitable winner who was of course, er, not Tiger Woods.

Admittedly the talented one was not at his best once he had achieved his primary target of winning the Masters and with it the 'Tiger Slam'. But even if he had been on peak form I still suspect that he would have struggled to win. No sooner had Woods won the Masters than

Peter Alliss perceptively observed that Lytham might find him out. Southern Hills and Lytham proved that length does not necessarily make a great championship golf course. US television and the new 'youf' audience might jump up and down at the prospect of a course that does not allow Tiger to unleash his 'red ass specials' on every other hole. But the rest of us were pleased to see some more shotmaking required.

Those two great courses also proved how ignorant a lot of the modern course designers are. As is discussed at greater length later on in this book, the seemingly blanket assumption that the best golfers make the best designers is absurd. Would you want David Beckham to design the new national football stadium?

Of all the modern courses in Britain and Ireland the two best are surely The European and Kingsbarns. The former was created by Pat Ruddy, a designer, a writer and a father. The latter was drawn up by a consortium (after Nick Faldo had opined that a top golf course could not be built on the land) who brought many different skills to the project. Is the absence of a big name former pro merely coincidence?

In order to reflect that might isn't necessarily right, we have featured a selection of courses that rely on all sorts of virtues. Apart from North Berwick (selected as an example of an old course with some features that the modern pro might consider heresy), The European (the modern course on our list) and Royal Worlington and Newmarket (to represent all the nine-hole courses up and down the country), the courses all fulfil at least one of the following criteria.

Either they have hosted an Open Championship, a Ryder Cup, a Walker Cup, an Amateur Championship, an English Amateur, an Irish

Close Amateur, a Scottish Amateur or a Welsh Amateur. That said we have also excluded all those courses that have been on the recent Open roster. There seemed little point in talking about places that have been frequently seen on television or described in the newspapers.

The majority of these courses are worthy of an Open (indeed some have staged the Championship in the past), but do not have the necessary infrastructure (access roads, spare land, etc) to accommodate all of the paraphernalia.

Imagine an eighteen with as good a finish as this one, a composite of some of our featured courses. The fourteenth hole belongs to Royal Portrush (although to exclude the famous 'Foxy' fourteenth at Royal Dornoch is an outrage). A suitable opening to such a finale, it is called Calamity Corner. The par is three strokes. When you look at the chasm, feel the gale and throw up a bit of grass to test how windy you are feeling, all you want is an escape clause.

The par four fifteenth at Royal St Davids is about the sea even if you never see it. The drive is from a slightly inland tee, but is worried by a sandhill to the left. The green itself is below the golfer, but it is dominated by a backdrop of massively foreboding dunes.

Just down the track from St David's is Aberdovey's sixteenth, a par four of only 288 yards. Go for it and the railway line to the left is waiting to transport your ball back to Harlech. Lay up and the second shot off an uneven stance to a narrow green is a trembler in the wind. The seventeenth at Little Aston, short but perfectly formed, is a classic inland hole bordered by trees, a sweeping downhill

dog leg that rises at the end to a heavily bunkered plateau green.

The final hole at Burnham and Berrow demands either a draw or a perfectly aimed drive. To the right of the fairway is a bank, to the left is a pit. The second shot is into a green disguised by four sneaky pot bunkers. Once on the putting surface only an agronomist would detect that there is in fact a heavy slope from front to back. Might and sleight combine to form an eighteenth as good as anywhere in the world.

The contrast of those holes in terms of length, scenery and hazard is immense, but the two short par fours are every bit as good as the two that measure over four hundred yards. A hole does not need to be a mega highway to be good.

By accident the journey between those holes, from Northern Ireland to West Wales to Birmingham to Somerset, is a logical one, although the walk from green to tee would be a bit arduous. A simpler journey for many, particularly those in the London area, is over to France.

A Londoner can be through the Channel Tunnel and sitting down to an excellent lunch in anticipation of an afternoon's golf at Hardelot in under five hours. To reflect the range of golf that modern travel has opened up there is for the first time a section on the top French courses within driving range of London. In future editions it might be possible to include their menus and wine lists.

Mark Reason, who also introduces each region, is Golf Correspondent of The Sunday Telegraph.

HOW TO USE THE GUIDE

The country is divided into regions. There are some strange anomalies which are caused primarily by some courses belonging to golf unions that do not necessarily correspond to local government boundaries.

There is a comprehensive index, if you know the name of the club you want to find out about. Each club has a phone number, postal address and relevant travel directions plus a brief description of the type of course.

There is also a separate listing of links courses. Although this is the indeterminate land on which the game originated, even now links golf is still pretty much exclusive to Britain and Ireland. We have reflected that by listing 'links courses' with their locations.

We have tried to indicate to golfers when they will be welcome at each course and whether individuals or societies are allowed. There is also a short description of the catering facilities each club provides.

It is, of course, a common courtesy to telephone any club you plan to visit to check both the availability of the date you plan to play and also any restrictions which may be placed on visitors. In the main it is recommended to make a tee-off time reservation, thus preventing any frustrating delays at the courses. Always remember to leave plenty of time to get to the course – it will improve your enjoyment and almost certainly your play!

Most clubs provide catering facilities for societies and many make a point of offering special packages that include both refreshments, food and golf. Again it is vital to ring in advance to check prices and the times that kitchens are open as well as the range of services on offer.

Prices. This is the main bone of contention with every golfer. Every care has been taken to list accurate prices for a round or a day ticket, but it is quite usual for the green fees to change from season to season and often from day to day. Some clubs offer special twilight fees, while others habitually charge more at weekends and on Bank Holidays.

Again it is vital that golfers check the prices, which can sometimes rise quite dramatically, before they step into the car or before they plan a trip. Often clubs are open to negotiating special deals but this is more likely to be achieved before rather than after arriving at the course.

All the information on green fees, club policy on visitors, societies, catering, etc has been gleaned from the secretaries, managers and professionals and *The Sunday Telegraph* thanks them for their time.

Comments. *The Sunday Telegraph* welcomes feedback on the book and comments on courses that readers visit. We would also be keen to hear of alterations, errors or extensions regarding any of the courses. Comments should be addressed to The Publisher, Telegraph Books, 1 Canada Square, Canary Wharf, London E14 5DT.

KEY TO COURSE DETAILS

 Telephone   Visitors   Societies

Email   Practice Ranges   Catering

Website   Green Fees   Hotels

Telegraph Golf Network
2 for 1 Golf

Two green fees for the price of one at over 500 courses

The **Telegraph Golf Network** is a club for readers of the *Daily* and *Sunday Telegraph*, the principal benefit of membership being **two green fees for the price of one** at over **500 courses** in the UK and abroad. Members also benefit from a range of golf-related offers and promotions, from **equipment and tickets** to golfing holidays and EGU membership, all of which are detailed in a **regular newsletter.**

Look out for the **TGN symbol** within this guide, indicating courses that currently participate in the Telegraph Golf Network **two-for-one scheme**. Membership costs **£35 for the first year** and **£30 per year after that.**

For more information and a free newsletter or to join the Telegraph Golf Network, call **08701 557 200*** between **9am and 5pm** Monday to Fridays, quoting reference ST14. Alternatively, you can email your name and postal address to tgn@telegraph.co uk

FRENCH COURSES
by Jon Ryan

Breakfast in London, coffee in Calais, eighteen holes in Normandy and back home in time for dinner.

Or perhaps the appeal of that logis you passed on that quiet little D road offering a four-course meal at 180 Euros means an overnight stay and another 18 holes in the morning.

The Channel Tunnel has opened up Northern France for golfers from London and the South-East seeking either an away-day or a short break. The drive from Calais, along the A16, then onto the chain of autoroutes – the A29, A13 and A84 – that take you across the Pas de Calais, Normandy and into Picardy.

On a drive of roughly 100 miles across the north there are fifty golf courses within easy striking distance ranging from Scottish-style links courses to tree-lined fairways reminiscent of the Home Counties.

Many were built during the height of France's golfing boom when new courses appeared on almost a monthly basis. The mad rush has now slowed and with it has come a rationalisation with an elite group of well-managed courses emerging.

Assured of a place in this elite is Hardelot, a consistent favourite with English golfers through ease of access from the Channel Ports and the tunnel and the standard of the club's two courses – the original Pines course and the newer Dunes.

The Pines is a challenging par 72, heavily wooded with a premium on accuracy off the tee. There is some respite at the far end of the course from the imposing and ever-threatening trees, but ironically the sudden change to the flatlands including, it has to be said, two slightly featureless and rather boring long

holes only leaves you yearning for the perils of the tree and sand nightmare that is the seventeenth. It is one of those innocuous looking par threes where you have a simple a choice – get on the green or get into trouble. Survive it with your mind and swing intact and the eighteenth provides a wonderful sweeping finish down towards the clubhouse.

The first at the Dunes sums up this roller-coaster of a course. An uphill par four so steep it is like going up a blue ski run and certainly not a gentle warm-up for the fragile or feeble.

Indeed the Dunes is as much a test of stamina as it is of golf with some spectacular holes, but if there is a buggy spare, don't think about the cost, grab it. But even in a buggy, life is not without its dangers and the descent from the eighteenth tee to the fairway presents a severe test of driving skill.

But while Hardelot thrives on its English clientele and can be crowded in peak season, the courses of Northern France offer a remarkable range. For a real treat, don't miss the highly scenic Belle Dune links at Fort-Mahon-Plage, a little-known and oddly under-used gem about a 30-minute drive south of Le Touquet.

Attached to the Pierre Vacances holiday complex, but open to non-residents for a green fee of around £25, this new, beautifully designed course threads its way through towering sand dunes punctuated by the occasional remains of a Second World War machine gun position.

Deep hollows, thick gorse, well-positioned water hazards, tough doglegs, elevated greens, the course packs in an array of challenges without losing sight of the wild, natural landscape. And then there is the wind. The local beaches are a haven for land yacht and kite enthusiasts and the same breezes offer plenty to think about on the more exposed holes.

Le Touquet itself has two high-quality courses: the Scottish links style Parcours de la Mer, La Foret which was opened in 1904; and the nine-hole Le Manoir. La Mer has played host to both the French Open and the French Amateur and at just under 7,000 yards is a great test of golf amid splendid scenery.

The names roll on: the splendid course at Le Champ de Bataille with the backdrop of the chateau, the hidden charms of Saint Saens with its nineteenth century clubhouse, Omaha Beach close to the scene of Second World War D-Day landings.

From Compiegne to Caen, from Dunkirk to Dieppe it is 'Le Golf' all the way.

There is a range of companies who specialise in golf trips to France and they will organise everything from ferry or Tunnel bookings to hotels, start-times and green fees. But such is the number of courses that it is fairly straightforward to arrange your own trip. Channel crossings are cheap out of season and away from school holidays and four people in a car should be able to have a decent day's golf including travel, green fees and a lunch for £50-£60 a head. For a two-day break allow around £20 a night each for accommodation at a small hotel.

Green fees tend to be between £20 and £30 on courses that are, by and large, well-kept and not crowded if you avoid the obvious summer peak times particularly the French holidays in August. Food at the clubs is generally on a much higher gastronomic level than English courses and reasonably priced.

If there is room in the car boot among the clubs, it is still worth buying wine or beer in France where prices are generally much lower and the quality of wine higher.

One of a number of companies arranging trips across the Channel is French Golf Holidays who have provided details, which follow, of our selected 20 courses within easy reach of Calais.

Jon Ryan is Sports Editor of The Sunday Telegraph

20 FRENCH COURSES WITHIN EASY REACH OF CALAIS

With 23 French courses in Europe's Top 100, France is the prime destination for quality golf in Europe. It's all very easy to get to – Northern France is served by Eurotunnel, Calais port, Dieppe, Le Havre and now the Buzz daily flights to Rouen and of course the Paris airports.

There are several old favourites near the Channel coast, but more and more British golfers are driving that little bit further to get to some great, and very much underplayed courses. I've listed the obvious and not so obvious below:

NORTHERN FRANCE

1. Wimereux: An old, classic links with a simple clubhouse, but some terrific holes. Tel: 03 21 32 43 20.

2. St Omer: A modern, parkland course that has hosted the French PGA Championship several times. Welcoming and enjoyable. Tel: 0321385990.

3. Hardelot Les Pins and Les Dunes: Where we started 20 years ago and always the 'best seller'. Manicured fairways, receptive greens, deep bunkers – all lined by mature pine trees. Rated in Europe's Top 100. Tel: 03 21 83 73 10.

4, 5 & 6 Le Touquet, La Mer and La Foret: La Mer has to be one of the toughest courses around – huge dunes, sometimes narrow fairways, cruel greens.great fun and great views. Rated in Europe's Top 100. La Foret is a flat layout carved through an oak and fir wood – a very fair challenge. Tel: 03 21 06 28 00.

7. Belle Dune: The most recent addition to Northern France, but already a firm favourite. Links in feel, but manicured to look at. Rated in Europe's Top 100. Tel: 03 22 23 45 50.

NORMANDY

8. Saint-Saens: Very friendly and a great 'loosener' – some straightforward holes and some super ones. Tel: 02 35 34 25 24.

9. Rebetz: A super inland links course with a touch of water for added fun. Tel: 03 44 49 15 54.

10. Champ de Bataille: A great course by anyone's reckoning. Cut through a forest – tranquillity and a great design guaranteed. Tel: 02 32 35 03 72.

11. Le Vaudreuil: A beautiful clubhouse and a nice golf course to boot. A fairly weak opening, but some tremendous holes later on. Tel: 02 32 59 02 60.

CHAMPAGNE

12. L'Ailette: On the way to Reims. A well put together golf course built around a lake. Big greens, lovely views, a nice day's golf. Tel: 03 23 24 83 99.

NORTH OF PARIS

13. Domaine de Raray: The clubhouse featured in the French classic film version of the Beauty and the Beast – a stunning backdrop to a very good golf course. Superb greens. Tel: 03 44 54 70 61.

14 & 15. Chantilly Vineuil and Longerese: Vineuil is rated in Europe's Top 10 and has hosted the French Open 11 times … enough said. Longeres is a fine sister course – again, parkland in style. Tel: 03 44 57 94 43.

16. Apremont: A modern, John Jacobs design – generous fairways, well-protected greens, all found within an evergreen forest. Great fun and there's a wonderful clubhouse for the post-round briefing. Tel: 03 44 25 61 11.

17. L'isle Adam: Another gem by Ronald Fream. Meandering through woodland and around streams, the course is a delight to play. Hilly in parts. Tel: 01 34 08 11 11.

18. Paris International: £26m to build and Clubcorp upgraded it when they bought it in 2000. Manicured, fair, designed by Jack Nicklaus and a fabulous golf experience. Tel: 01 34 69 90 00.

19. International Club du Lys: A traditional layout by Tom Simpson. There are two courses but Les Chenes is the one to play – shortish, flat but never out of date with well-protected greens and a lovely "upmarket" ambience. Tel: 03 44 21 26 00.

20. Dolce Chantilly: A modern course with great greens and some unusual "renaissance" style holes. A good loosener. Tel: 03 44 58 47 74.

For more information, please call French Golf Holidays on 01277 824100, fax 01277 82422, http://www.frenchgolfholidays.com/

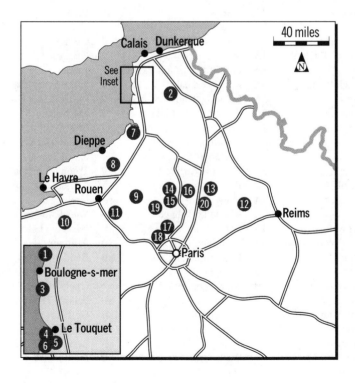

LINKS COURSES

Askernish	9D	North Wales	10	Donegal	12
Brora	9D	Prestatyn	10	Dooks	12
Buckpool (Buckie)	9D	Pyle & Kenfig	10	Dunfanaghy	12
Carnegie Club	9D	Rhyl	10	Enniscrone	12
Cruden Bay	9D	Royal St David's	10	The European	12
Cullen	9D	St David's City	10	Goldcoast	12
Durness	9D	Southerndown	10	Greencastle	12
Fortrose & Rosemarkie	9D	Swansea Bay	10	Greenore	12
Fraserburgh	9D	Tenby	10	The Island Golf Club	12
Golspie	9D	Bushfoot	11	Kilkee	12
Hopeman Golf Club	9D	Castlerock	11	Lahinch	12
Inverallochy	9D	Donaghadee	11	Laytown & Bettystown	12
Monk's Walk, Skibo		Kirkistown Castle	11	Mount Temple	12
Castle	9D	Portstewart	11	Mulranny	12
Moray	9D	Rathmore	11	Narin & Portnoo	12
Nairn	9D	Royal County Down	11	North West	12
Nairn Dunbar	9D	Royal Portrush	11	Old Head	12
Newburgh-on-Ythan	9D	Arklow	12	Portmarnock Hotel and	
Peterhead	9D	Ballybunion	12	Golf Links	12
Reay	9D	Ballyliffin	12	Portmarnock	12
Royal Aberdeen	9D	Bundoran	12	Portsalon	12
Royal Dornoch	9D	Carne Golf Links	12	Rosapenna	12
Tain Golf Club	9D	Castlegregory Golf and		Rosslare	12
Tarbat	9D	Fishing Club	12	Royal Dublin	12
Wick	9D	Ceann Sibeal (Dingle)	12	St Annes	12
Aberdovey	10	Connemara Championship		St Helen's Bay	12
Abersoch	10	Links	12	St Patricks	12
Anglesey	10	Corballis	12	Seapoint	12
Ashburnham	10	County Louth	12	Strandhill	12
Borth and Ynyslas.	10	County Sligo	12	Tralee	12
Cardigan	10	Cruit Island	12	Waterville Golf Links	12

KEY TO THE MAPS

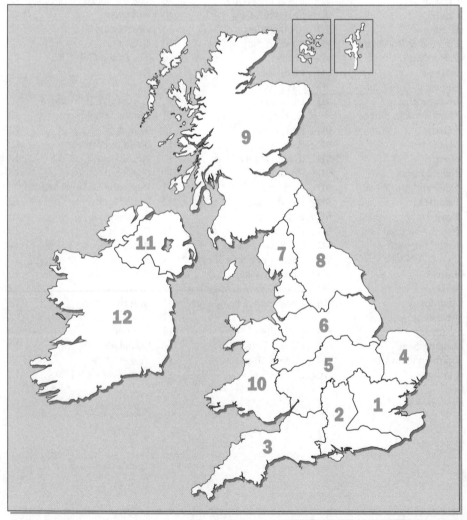

LONDON AND THE HOME COUNTIES

1A

Surrey, Kent, South London

Many people's expectations of Surrey are probably similar to those of CS Lewis when he arrived there for the first time. He had been told that Surrey was "suburban." Instead Lewis discovered, "little hills, watered valleys, and wooded commons which ranked by my Wyvernian and Irish standards as forests; bracken everywhere; a world of red and russet and yellowish greens."

It is fertile land on which to build golf courses and once people got started – Woking was founded in 1893 by "a few mad barristers" – there was no stopping them. Willie Park, JF Abercromby, James Braid and JH Taylor began designing all over the county.

Even in those years before the Great War, when men were men and women were voteless, there were limits to what was tolerable. Fed up with discrimination, one Mrs Lubbock decided that if men were so determined to keep her off Surrey's golf courses on a Sunday, then she would go ahead and build her own. West Hill was the child of her determination.

West Hill and The Addington – one of the best courses within London's immediate sprawl, although not always in top condition – are a cause of debate between two of golf's greatest writers. Henry Longhurst believed The Addington's par three thirteenth to be the best short hole on inland Britain. A perfectly struck shot into this green represented "the sweetest satisfaction that golf has to offer".

Bernard Darwin was a West Hill man. To him the par three fifteenth, flanked by trees, was the best in England. There is an obvious scenic similarity between the two holes, so perhaps Longhurst's and Darwin's difference is not as great as it might seem.

Surrey is bulging with superb holes and courses. Sunningdale, Wentworth and Walton Heath – which because of its subsoil might be described as like chalk and cheese in comparison to the other two – each has two first rate courses. Any of Worplesdon, Hindhead, St George's Hill, Coombe Hill and Hankley Common would be the feature course of a lesser golfing county.

Spare a thought, too, for Royal Mid-Surrey, the county's leading parkland course. In March 2001 a fire destroyed the friendly clubhouse and all its treasures. One theory was that some linseed oil had spontaneously combusted. While work continues to secure planning permission prior to constructing a new clubhouse, the golf still goes on. The temporary facilities are excellent and the Outer Course is always far more of a challenge than its amiable appearance would have you believe.

Kent may not have quite so many five star courses as Surrey, but the best in the county are amongst the best in the country. Royal St George's remains the only Open Championship venue south of Lancashire. It can be a swine when the wind blows, but even then you have to admire its grandeur through gritted teeth. As Bill Deedes said, "You can be in the soup at St George's, but it is delicious." So is the beer, served in proper tankards.

Neighbouring Prince's is another good test while Royal Cinque Ports has staged two Open Championships and been denied three more by war and salt water. The other Kent links not to be missed is Littlestone. It lulls you with a simple opening par four before taking ample revenge over the ensuing seventeen holes.

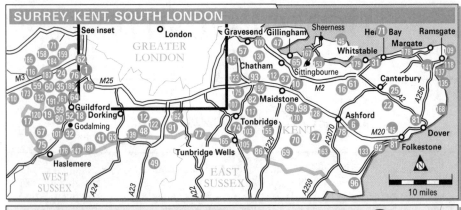

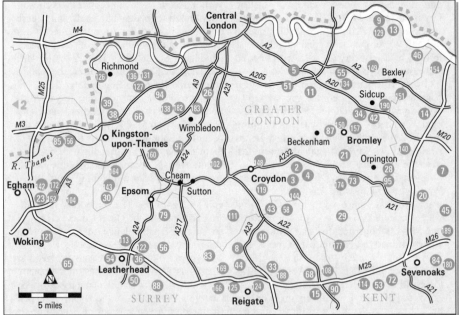

1A 1 Abbey Moor

Green Lane, Addlestone, Surrey, KT15 2XU
☎ 01932 570741, Fax 577111, Rest/Bar 570293
Leave M25 at Junction 11 and proceed on St Peter's Way towards Weybridge: take right turn at large roundabout towards Addlestone on A318, then over railway bridge; take 2nd turning right at small roundabout into Green Lane; course 0.5 mile on right.
Public parkland course.
Pro Paul Tigwell; Founded 1991
Designed by David Taylor
9 holes, 5104 yards, S.S.S. 66
♗ Welcome WD and WE; advisable to book early.
Ⅼ WD £8.00; WE £9.00.
♙ WD only; terms on application.
Ⓘ Full Bar.
⌁ White Lodge.

1A 2 The Addington

205 Shirley Church Road, Croydon, Surrey, CR0 5AB
☎ 020 8777 1055, Sec 8777 6057
Through Addington Village, 2.5 miles from East Croydon.

Heather, Bracken, Silver Birch and Pine.
Founded 1913
Designed by JF Ambercromby
18 holes, 6242 yards, S.S.S. 71
♗ WD Only.
Ⅼ WD £35.
♙ WD only; terms on application.
Ⓘ Restaurant and Bar.

1A 3 Addington Court

Featherbed Lane, Croydon, Surrey, CR0 9AA
☎ 020 8657 0281, Fax 8651 0282, Sec 8651 0282
2 miles E of Croydon off the B281 in Addington Village.
Undulating parkland course.
Pro John Good; Founded 1931
Designed by F. Hawtree Snr
Ⅼ WD £14; WE £17.
♙ Welcome by prior arrangement; catering packages available.
Ⓘ Full catering facilities.
⌁ Selsdon Park.

1A 4 Addington Palace

Gravel Hill, Addington Park, Croydon,

Surrey, CR0 5BB
☎ 020 8654 3061, Fax 8655 3632, Pro 8654 1786, Sec 8654 3061, Rest/Bar Bar 8654 2650
Rest 8655 1290
2 miles east of Croydon on the A212.
Undulating parkland course.
Pro Roger Williams; Founded 1927
Designed by JH Taylor
18 holes, 6304 yards, S.S.S. 71
♗ Welcome if accompanied by a member.
Ⅼ WD £35 everyone welcome members only at weekends no charge.
♙ Welcome Tues, Wed, Fri; details on application; £57.
Ⓘ Bar and catering facilities.
⌁ The Selsdon Park.

1A 5 Aquarius

Marmora Road, Honor Oak, London, SE22 0RY
☎ 020 8693 1626,
Pro 8693 1811
Welcome with members only
Set around a reservoir.
Pro Fred Private; Founded 1912
9 holes, 5465 yards, S.S.S. 66
♗ Welcome with members.

⌇ WD £10; WE £10.
⌁ Terms on request.
🍽 Terms on request.
⌁ Bromley Court, Queens at Crystal Palace.

1A 6 Ashford (Kent)
Sandyhurst Lane, Ashford, Kent, TN25 4NT
☎ 01233 620180, Fax 622655,
Pro 629644, Sec 622655,
Rest/Bar 620180
Welcome with handicap certs.
Parkland course.
Pro Hugh Sherman; Founded 1903
Designed by CK Cotton
18 holes, 6263 yards, S.S.S. 70
⚑ Course is 1.5 miles from Junction 9 on the M20.
⌇ WD £24; WE £40.
⌁ Tues, Thurs; packages available; £25-~£45.
🍽 Bar and restaurant.

1A 7 Austin Lodge   ⓒ
Upper Austin Lodge Road, Eynsford, Kent, DA4 OHU
☎ 01322 863000, Fax 862406
A225 to Eynsford station; course is in road behind station.
Rolling parkland course.
Pro Trevor Dungate; Founded 1991
Designed by Peter Bevan & Mike Walsh
18 holes, 7200 yards, S.S.S. 73
⚑ Welcome.
⌇ WD Mon-Wed £18; Thurs, Fri £20; WE £25.
⌁ Mon-Fri; WE after 2pm.
🍽 Meals and bar.
⌁ Castle, Eynsford.

1A 8 Banstead Downs
Burdon Lane, Belmont, Sutton, Surrey, SM2 7DD
✉ bdgc@online.co.uk
☎ 020 8642 2284, Fax 8642 5252,
Pro 8642 6884
On A217 from M25 Junction 8.
Downland course.
Pro Robert Dickman; Founded 1890
Designed by JH Taylor/J Braid
18 holes, 6194 yards, S.S.S. 69
⚑ Practice area.
⚑ Welcome WD; WE with member only.
⌇ WD £40.
⌁ Welcome, Thurs preferred; full day's golf and catering £57.
🍽 Full clubhouse facilities.

1A 9 Barnhurst
Mayplace Road East, Bexleyheath, Kent, DA7 6JU
☎ 01322 551205, Fax 528483,
Sec 523746, Rest/Bar 552952
N of Crayford town centre.
Mature inland course.
Founded 1904
Designed by James Braid
9 holes, 5474 yards, S.S.S. 68
⚑ Welcome.
⌇ WD £8.45; WE £11.55.
⌁ Welcome; terms available on application.
🍽 Full facilities and function room.
⌁ Swallow, Bexleyheath.

1A 10 Bearsted
Ware Street, Bearsted, Kent, ME14 4PQ
☎ 01622 738389, Fax 735608,
Pro 738204, Sec 738198,
Rest/Bar 738389
M20 to Junction 7 and follow Bearsted Green signs.
Parkland course.
Pro Tim Simpson; Founded 1895
Designed by Golf Landscapes
18 holes, 6486 yards, S.S.S. 71
⚑ Welcome with handicap certs.
⌇ WD £31; WE £35 with members only.
⌁ Tues-Fri; 36 holes of golf, coffee, lunch and dinner; £56.50.
🍽 Full facilities.
⌁ The Hilton, Tudor Park, Great Danes.

1A 11 Beckenham Place Park
Beckenham Hill Road, Beckenham, Kent, BR3 2BP
☎ 020 8650 2292, Fax 8663 1201,
Sec 8464 1581
1 mile from Catford towards Bromley, right at Homebase.
Parkland course.
Pro John Denham; Founded 1932
18 holes, 5722 yards, S.S.S. 68
⚑ Welcome.
⌇ WD £8; WE £12+.
⌁ Terms on application.
🍽 Meals and snacks.
⌁ Bromley Court.

1A 12 Betchworth Park
Reigate Road, Dorking, Surrey, RH4 1NZ
🖳 www.betchworthparkgc.co.uk
✉ manager@betchworthparkgc.co.uk
☎ 01306 882052, Fax 877462,
Pro 884334, Sec 882052,
Rest/Bar 889802/885929

Course is 1 mile E of Dorking on A25, entrance is opposite horticultural gardens.
Parkland course.
Pro A Tocher; Founded 1913
Designed by H Colt
18 holes, 6266 yards, S.S.S. 70
⚑ Welcome except Tues am, Sat and Sun am.
⌇ WD £34; WE £45.
⌁ Mon and Thurs; packages including meals available; terms on application.
🍽 Lunch and tea facilities available.
⌁ White Horse.

1A 13 Bexleyheath
Mount Road, Bexleyheath, Kent, DA6 8JS
☎ 020 8303 6951,
Fax 8303 6951, Sec 8303 6951,
Rest/Bar 8303 4232
1 mile from Bexleyheath station off Upton road.
Undulating course.
Founded 1907
9 holes, 5239 yards, S.S.S. 66
⚑ Welcome WD.
⌇ WD £20.
⌁ Welcome WD by appointment.
🍽 Full bar and catering facilities, except Mon.
⌁ Marriott.

1A 14 Birchwood Park   ⓒ
Birchwood Road, Wilmington, Dartford, Kent, DA2 7HJ
☎ 01322 6609554, Fax 667283
Off A20 or M25 at Swanley turn-off.
Meadowland course.
Pro Gary Orr; Founded 1990
Designed by Howard Swan
18 holes, 6364 yards, S.S.S. 71
⚑ 38.
⚑ Welcome.
⌇ WD £15; WE £19.
⌁ Welcome WD; WE limited to pm, contact Sec; terms on application.
🍽 Full facilities.
⌁ Stakis.

1A 15 Bletchingley   ⓒ
Church Lane, Bletchingley, Surrey
☎ 01883 744666, Fax 744284,
Pro 744848, Sec 744666,
Rest/Bar 744666
From M25 Junction 6 take A25; course 3 miles.
Parkland course.
Pro Alasdair Dyer; Founded 1993
18 holes, 6531 yards, S.S.S. 71
⚑ Welcome.

WD £25; WE £30.
Welcome by appointment, terms on application.
Bar and restaurant.
Priory, Redhill.

1A 16 Boughton
Brickfield Lane, Boughton, Nr. Faversham, Kent, ME13 9AJ
☎ 01227 752277, Fax 752 361,
Pro 751112, Sec 752277,
Rest/Bar 751414
At intersection of the A2/M2 follow signs for Boughton and Dunkirk.
Upland course.
Pro Trevor Dungate; Founded 1993
Designed by P Sparks
18 holes, 6551 yards, S.S.S. 71
15.
Welcome.
WD £18 WE £24.
Welcome; terms available on application.
Bar and restaurant.
White Horse Inn.

1A 17 Bowenhurst
Mill Lane, Crondall, Nr Farnham, Surrey, GU10 5RP
☎ 01252 851695, Fax 852039,
Pro 851344, Rest/Bar 851695
M3 Junction 5.4 miles on A287 to Farnham.
Parkland course.
Pro Adrian Carter; Founded 1994
Designed by N Finn/G Baker
9 holes, 4210 yards, S.S.S. 60
20.
Welcome.
WD £11; WE £14.
Welcome by arrangement with Sec.
Function facilities.

1A 18 Bramley
Bramley, Nr Guildford, Surrey, GU5 0AL
Secreterty@bramleygolfclub.co.uk
☎ 01483 893042, Fax 894673,
Pro 893685, Sec 892696,
Rest/Bar 893042
3 miles S of Guildford on A281.
Parkland course.
Pro Gary Peddie; Founded 1914
Designed by Charles Mayo (redesigned by James Braid)
18 holes, 5990 yards, S.S.S. 69
Members only 10.
Welcome with member.
WD £28; WE Members only.
Round 36 holes £35.
Contact Sec; full bar and catering

with driving range and practice area; £43-£58.
Full catering and grill menu.
Harrow, Compton; Parrot, Shalford.

1A 19 Broadwater Park
Guildford Road, Farncome, Nr Godalming, Surrey, GU7 3BU
☎ 01483 429955, Fax 429955,
Pro 429955, Sec 429955,
Rest/Bar 429955
On A3100 between Godalming and Guildford.
Par 3 parkland course.
Pro K Milton; Founded 1989
Designed by KD Milton
9 holes,1301 yards, S.S.S. 27
16.
Welcome
WD £4.95; WE £5.75.
Not available.
Bar and snacks.
The Manor Inn.

1A 20 Broke Hill
Sevenoaks Road, Halstead, Kent, TN14 7HR
www.brokehillgolf.co.uk
☎ 01959 533225, Fax 532880,
Pro 533810, Rest/Bar 533810
Close to M25 Junction 4 opposite Knockholt station.
Parkland course/downland.
Pro Chris West; Founded 1993
Designed by D Williams
18 holes, 6374 yards, S.S.S. 71
Welcome WD.
WD £35.
Societies welcome Mon to Fri but not weekends.
Full clubhouse facilities.
Post House, Borough Green; Bromley Court Hotel; Brands Hatch.

1A 21 Bromley
Magpie Hall Lane, Bromley, Kent, BR2 8JF
☎ 020 8462 7014
A21 2 miles S of Bromley.
Public parkland course.
Pro Alan Hodgson
9 holes, 5158 yards, S.S.S. 67
Welcome; no restrictions.
WD £5.60; WE £7.35.
Welcome by appointment; terms on application.
Limited.

1A 22 Broome Park CC
Broome Park Estate, Barham, Canterbury, Kent, CT4 6QX

www.broomepark.co.uk
broomeparkgolf@compuserve.com
☎ 01227 831701, Fax 832591,
Pro 831126, Sec 830728
Just off A2 E of Canterbury.
Parkland course.
Pro Tienie Britz; Founded 1982
Designed by Donald Steel
18 holes, 6610 yards, S.S.S. 72
6.
Welcome.
WD £30 WE £35.
Welcome by prior arrangement; terms on application.
Full facilities.

1A 23 Burhill
Walton-On-Thames, Surrey, KT12 4BL
☎ 01932 227345, Fax 267159,
Pro 221729
M25 Junction 10; off A3 London-bound towards Byfleet on the A245.
Parkland course.
Pro Lee Johnson; Founded 1907
Designed by Willie Park
2 x 18 holes, 6179/6597 yards, S.S.S. 71/72
6 plus grass range.
Welcome weekdays only.
£75 per day; £60 per round.
By prior arrangement only; terms on application.
Full facilities.
Oatlands Park Hotel, Weybridge.

1A 24 Camberley Heath
Golf Drive, Camberley, Surrey, GU15 1JG
info@
camberleyheathgolfclub.co.uk
☎ 01276 23258, Fax 692505,
Pro 27905, Sec 23258,
Rest/Bar 23258
Off A325 Portsmouth road between Bagshot and Frimley.
Pine and heather course.
Pro Glenn Ralph; Founded 1913
Designed by HS Colt
18 holes, 6637 yards, S.S.S. 70
Welcome WD only.
WD £48.
Welcome weekdays by appointment; terms available on application.
Full facilities.
Frimley Hall Hotel.

1A 25 Canterbury
Scotland Hills, Canterbury, Kent, CT1 1TW
canterburygolf@hotmail.com
☎ 01227 453532, Fax 784277,

Pro 462865, Sec 453532,
Rest/Bar 781871
1 mile from town centre on A257 road
to Sandwich.
Parkland course.
Pro Paul Everard; Founded 1927
Designed by HS Colt
18 holes, 6249 yards, S.S.S. 70
† Welcome if carrying handicap
certs.
⌇ WD £30; WE £36.
⌁ Welcome Tues and Thurs;
minimum 12, 36 holes, light lunch, 3-
course evening meal, £50 per person
Discounts for larger groups.
◉ Full facilities and bar.
⤱ Many in Canterbury, recommend
County Hotel.

1A 26 Central London GC
Burntwood Lane, Wandsworth,
London, SW17 0AT
⤱ www.clgc.co.uk
☎ 020 8871 2468, Fax 8874 7447,
Pro 8871 2468, Rest/Bar 8871 2468
Take Garratt Lane from A3 in
Wandsworth, Burntwood Lane is off
Garratt Lane after Earlsfield.
Parkland course.
Pro Jeremy Robson; Founded 1992
Designed by Patrick Tallack
9 holes, 4468 yards, S.S.S. 62
⫾ 14.
† Welcome anytime.
⌇ WD £8.50; WE £10.50.
⌁ By arrangement.
◉ Function and conference facilities.
⤱ In Wimbledon.

1A 27 Chart Hills
Weeks Lane, Biddenden, Kent, TN27
8JX
☎ 01580 292222, Fax 292233
M20 to Junction 8; follow signs to
Leeds Castle before turning on to A274
through Sutton Valence; 7 miles turn
into Weeks Lane.
Parkland course.
Pro Danny French; Founded 1993
Designed by Nick Faldo
18 holes, 7086 yards, S.S.S. 72
† Welcome any day other than
Sat.
⌇ WD £65; WE £75.
⌁ Restricted; full facilities including
lunch and coffee; £75-£105.
◉ Full facilities.
⤱ Great Danes; Forstal B&B.

1A 28 Chelsfield Lakes
Court Road, Orpington, Kent, BR6 9BX
⤱ www.chelsfieldgolf.co.uk

📧 cdo@chelsfieldgolf.co.uk
☎ 01689 896266, Fax 824577,
Rest/Bar 896266
From M25 Junction 4 follow signs to
Orpington; course 300 yds from 2nd
roundabout.
Parkland course.
Pro Nigel Lee; Founded 1993
Designed by MRM Leisure
18 holes, 6110 yards, S.S.S. 69
⫾ Full driving range facilities.
† Welcome.
⌇ WD £17; WE £22. 18-hole course
WD £4; WE £5 9-hole course.
⌁ Welcome by prior application;
minimum 8; golf and catering packages
available; terms on application.
◉ Full clubhouse facilities.
⤱ Recommend Brandshatch Thistle
Hotel.

1A 29 Cherry Lodge ♛
Jail Lane, Biggin Hill, Kent, TN16 3AX
⤱ www.cherrylodgegc@aol.com
☎ 01959 572250, Fax 540672,
Pro 572989, Sec 572250,
Rest/Bar 572250
3 miles N of Westerham off A233.
Parkland course.
Pro Nigel Child; Founded 1970
Designed by John Day
18 holes, 6652 yards, S.S.S. 73
† WD by prior arrangement; with a
member only at WE.
⌇ WD £20; WE £20.
⌁ Welcome by arrangement.
Packages from £44.
◉ Full bar and restaurant facilities
available.
⤱ Kings Arms, Westerham.

1A 30 Chessington ♛
Garrison Lane, Chessington, Surrey,
KT9 2LW
⤱ www.chessingtongolf.co.uk
☎ 020 8391 0948, Fax 8397 2068,
Pro 8391 0948, Sec 8391 0948,
Rest/Bar 8391 0948
Opposite Chessington South station,
very near Chessington Zoo.
Parkland course.
Pro Mark Janes; Founded 1983
Designed by Patrick Tallack
9 holes, 1761 yards, S.S.S. 30
⫾ 18.
† Everyone welcome.
⌇ WD £7.50; WE £9.
⌁ Welcome; terms on application.
◉ Full facilities.
⤱ Seven Hills; Oatlands Park.

1A 31 Chestfield ♛
103 Chestfield Road, Whitstable, Kent,
CT5 3LU
⤱ www.chestfield/golfclub.co.uk
📧 secretary@
chestfield/golfclub.co.uk
☎ 01227 794411, Fax 794454,
Pro 793563, Sec 794411
0.5 mile S of A299 at Chestfield
station.
Parkland course, with sea views.
Pro John Brotherton; Founded 1924
18 holes, 6200 yards, S.S.S. 70
⫾ Practice green.
† WD Call for availability.
⌇ WD £22 Round; £30 day.
⌁ Welcome WD; packages available;
terms on application.
◉ Facilities available.
⤱ Marine, Tankerton.

1A 32 Chiddingfold ♛
Petworth Road, Chiddingfold, Surrey,
GU8 4SL
☎ 01428 685888, Fax 685939,
Pro 8681381
Take A283 off A3 and course is 10
minutes away, 50 yards S of
Chiddingfold
Downland course
Pro Gary Wallace; Founded 1994
Designed by J Gaunt & P Alliss
18 holes, 5568 yards, S.S.S. 67
⫾ 4.
† Welcome.
⌇ WD £16; WE £22 summer/WD
£13; WE £20 winter.
⌁ Welcome, packages available;
terms on application.
◉ Full facilities; conference suite.
⤱ Lythe Hill.

1A 33 Chipstead ♛
How Lane, Coulsden, Surrey, CR5 3LN
⤱ www.chipsteadgolf.co.uk
📧 office@
chipsteadgolf.freeserve.co.uk
☎ 01737 555781, Fax 555404,
Pro 554939
Follow signs to Chipstead from the
A217. M25 take Junction 7 or 8.
Undulating parkland course.
Pro Gary Torbett; Founded 1906
18 holes, 5504 yards, S.S.S. 67
† Welcome WD.
⌇ WD £30 per round, after 4pm £20.
⌁ Welcome WD by appointment;
terms on application.
◉ Lunch served; booking required.
Bar snacks.
⤱ Reigate Manor, hotel heathside in
Burgh heath.

Coulsdon Manor
Golf Centre

Set in 140 acres of parkland with many rare and beautiful trees, this 18 hole, 6037 yards, par 70 course was designed by Harry S Colt - designer of many of the greatest courses.

Add to this a 35 bedroom, 4 star hotel built as a home for Thomas Byron in the 1850's and sympathetically restored and extended, with a perfect 19th hole in The Terrace Bar, and you have the perfect venue for a gold society day, a relaxing weekend or a golfing holiday.

Coulsdon Manor also has a two rosette restaurant and Reflections Leisure Club with a well equipped gymnasium, and facilities for a variety of racket sports as well as a sauna and steam room for relaxing after a day out on the golf course.

Players must be competent and have a knowledge of the rules and etiquette of golf, however whatever your skill level you may wish to take the opportunity of tuition from our Professionals and visit the well stocked shop. Club repair is also available.

USEFUL INFORMATION

Society Packages: From £33.50 per person - contact Coulsdon Manor
Green Fees: Contact club for details. **Visitors Restrictions:** Handicap and golf dress code
How to get there: From M23/25 Junction 7, A23 for 2.5 miles then B2030
Accommodation: 4 star hotel on site
E-mail: coulsdonmanor@marstonhotels.com **Web:** www.marstonhotels.com

MARSTON HOTELS

Coulsdon Manor Golf Centre, Couldson Court Road, Old Coulsdon, Nr. Croydon, Surrey CR5 2LL
Tel: 020 8668 0414 (hotel) Fax: 020 8668 3118 Tel: 020 8660 6083 (club)

1A 34 Chislehurst
Camden Place, Camden Park Road,
Chislehurst, Kent, BR7 5HJ
☎ 020 8467 055, Fax 8295 0874,
Pro 8467 6798, Sec 8467 2782,
Rest/Bar 8467 2888
0.5 miles from Chislehurst station.
Parkland course.
Pro Jon Bird; Founded 1894
18 holes, 5106 yards, S.S.S. 65
♦ Welcome WD; with a member at
WE.
Ⅰ WD £25; WE £25.
⚘ Welcome Mon-Fri; 36 holes
available Thurs; £33.
🍴 Full facilities.

1A 35 Chobham   ☞
Chobham Road, Knaphill, Woking,
Surrey, GU21 2TZ
☎ 01276 855584, Fax 855663,
Pro 855748
Take the A322 from the M3 Junction 3
towards Guildford; at the first
roundabout take the A319 to
Chobham, course is 2 miles on right
towards Knaphill.
Wooded parkland with lakes.
Pro Tim Coombes; Founded 1994
Designed by Clive Clark & Peter Alliss
18 holes, 5959 yards, S.S.S. 69
♦ Members' guests welcome only in
midweek.
Ⅰ WD £16.50 before 2.00pm.
⚘ Welcome by appointment; terms
on application.
🍴 Restaurant, bar and function
rooms.

1A 36 Clandon Regis
Epsom Road, West Clandon, Nr
Guildford, Surrey, GU4 7TT
☎ 01483 224888, Fax 211781,
Pro 223922
Course is four miles E of Guildford on
the A246.
Parkland course.
Pro Steve Lloyd; Founded 1994
Designed by D Williams
18 holes, 6412 yards, S.S.S. 71
♦ Welcome by prior arrangement.
Ⅰ WD £25; WE £35.
⚘ Welcome by prior arrangement;
terms on application.
🍴 Full bar and restaurant.

1A 37 Cobtree Manor Park
Chatham Road, Maidstone, Kent,
ME14 3AZ
☎ 01622 753276, Rest/Bar 751881
Take A229 from M20.
Municipal parkland course.

Pro Paul Foston; Founded 1984
Designed by F Hawtree
18 holes, 5611 yards, S.S.S. 67
♦ Welcome.
Ⅰ Guest rate WD £15.50; WE
£18.50. If registered WE £15 and WD
£11.
⚘ Terms on application.
🍴 Available.
🏨 Holiday Inn, Rochester;
Bridgewood Manor Hotel, Rochester;
Maidstone Hilton, Maidstone.

1A 38 Coombe Hill
Golf Club Drive, Kingston, Surrey,
KT27DF
☎ 020 8336 7600, Fax 8336 7601,
Pro 8949 3713, Sec 8336 7600,
Rest/Bar 8942 2284
1 mile W of New Malden on A238.
Undulating, tree-lines.
Pro Craig Defoy; Founded 1911
Designed by JF Abercromby
18 holes, 6293 yards, S.S.S. 71
♦ WD by prior arrangement.
Ⅰ WD £65, Summertime. WD £50
Wintertime weekdays only.
⚘ Welcome by prior arrangement
with Sec; terms on application.
🍴 Restaurant and bar.
🏨 Kingston Lodge.

1A 39 Coombe Wood
George Road, Kingston Hill, Kingston-
On-Thames, Surrey, KT2 7NS
🖥 www.coombewoodgolf.com
✉ cwoodgc@ukonline.co.uk
☎ 020 8942 0388, Fax 8942 5665,
Pro 8942 6764, Rest/Bar 8942 3828
From the A3 take the A308 (E) or the
A238 (W).
Mature parkland course.
Pro David Butler; Founded 1904
Designed by Tom Williamson
18 holes, 5299 yards, S.S.S. 66
♦ Visitors welcome 7 days
(weekends pm only).
Ⅰ WD £25; WE £35.
⚘ Welcome Wed, Thurs, Fri;
packages available from £22.50.
🍴 Full bar and restaurant facilities
available.
🏨 Kingston Lodge.

1A 40 Coulsdon Manor
Coulsdon Court Road, Old Coulsdon,
Surrey, CR5 2LL
🖥 www.marstonhotels.com
✉ coulsdonmanor@
marstonhotels.com
☎ 020 8668 0414, Fax 8668 3118,
Pro 8660 6083, Sec 8660 6083,

Rest/Bar 866080414
Just off A23, 2 miles S of Croydon, 2
miles N of M25 and M23.
Parkland course.
Pro James Leaver; Founded 1926
Designed by H S Buck
18 holes, 6037 yards, S.S.S. 68
♦ Welcome.
Ⅰ WD £15.50; WE £19.00.
⚘ Welcome by prior arrangement;
terms on application.
🍴 Full facilities.
🏨 Coulsdon Manor.

1A 41 The Cranleigh Golf   ☞
and Leisure Club
Barhatch Lane, Cranleigh, Surrey, GU6
7NG
🖥 www.cranleighgolfandleisure.co.uk
☎ 01483 268855, Fax 267251
Take A281 out of Guildford, 1 mile
through Cranleigh take Ewhurst road,
then turn into Barhatch Road and
Barhatch Lane.
Parkland course.
Pro Trevor Longmuir; Founded 1985
18 holes, 5648 yards, S.S.S. 67
♦ Welcome WD; restrictions WE.
Ⅰ WD £27; WE £30.
⚘ Welcome WD, WE subject to
availability; terms on application.
🍴 Bar, restaurant, snacks, banquets.
🏨 The Cranley Hotel, The Random
Hall.

1A 42 Cray Valley
Sandy Lane, St Paul's Cray, Orpington,
Kent, BR5 3HY
☎ 01689 839677, Fax 891428,
Pro 837909, Rest/Bar 871490
Leave the A20 off Ruxley roundabout;
course is on Sandy Lane, 0.5 miles on
left.
Parkland course.
Pro Stephen Lee, Raphael
Piannandrea; Founded 1972
Designed by Golf Centres Ltd
18 holes, 5669 yards, S.S.S. 67
♦ Pay and play.
Ⅰ WD £16.75; WE £22.
⚘ Bookings requested 7 days in
advance.
🍴 Bar and restaurant.

1A 43 Croham Hurst
Croham Road, South Croydon, Surrey,
CR2 7HJ
☎ 020 8657 5581, Fax 8657 3229,
Pro 8657 7705, Sec 8657 5581,
Rest/Bar 8657 2075
1 mile from S Croydon; from M25 exit
6 N on to A22, take B270 to

Warlingham at roundabout, then B269 to Selsdon; at traffic lights turn left into Farley Road, clubhouse is 1.75 miles on left.
Parkland course.
Pro Eric Stillwell; Founded 1911
Designed by Hawtree & Sons
18 holes, 6290 yards, S.S.S. 70
♦ Welcome, handicap certs required; with member only at WE.
[WD £37; WE £46.
♪ Welcome Wed, Thurs, Fri by arrangement; terms on application.
◉ Full facilities every day 10am-6pm; banqueting.
⌁ Selsdon Park.

1A 44 Cuddington
Banstead Road, Banstead, Surrey, SM7 1RD
✉ cuddingtongc@aol.com
☎ 020 8393 0952, Fax 8786 7025, Pro 8393 5850, Sec 8393 0952
200 yards from Banstead station.
Parkland course.
Pro Mark Warner; Founded 1929
Designed by H S Colt
18 holes, 6394 yards, S.S.S. 70
♦ Welcome if carrying handicap certs.
[WD £35; WE £35.
♪ Welcome Thurs; full day's golf and meals, including dinner; £60.
◉ Full catering service.
⌁ Heathside; Driftbridge.

1A 45 Darenth Valley
Station Road, Shoreham, Kent, TN14 7SA
⌨ www.darenth-valley.co.uk
✉ darenthvalleygolfcourse@ shoreham2000.fsbuisness.co.uk
☎ 01959 522922, Fax 525089, Pro 522922, Rest/Bar 522944
Along A225 Sevenoaks – Dartford Road, 4 miles N of Sevenoaks.
Parkland course.
Pro David Copsey; Founded 1973
18 holes, 6394 yards, S.S.S. 71
♦ Welcome; bookings daily. No members.
[WD £17.50; WE £25.
♪ Welcome by prior arrangement with manager; terms available on application, societies welcome Mon-Fri.
◉ Bar meals, society catering, functions (up to 100 persons).

1A 46 Dartford
Dartford Heath, Dartford, Kent, DA1 2TN
✉ dartfordgolf@hotmail.com

☎ 01322 223616, Pro 226409, Sec 226455, Rest/Bar 223616
0.5 miles from A2 Dartford-Crayford turn-off.
Park/heathland course.
Pro John Gregory; Founded 1897
Designed by James Braid
18 holes, 5591 yards, S.S.S. 69
♦ WD with handicap certs; with member only at WE.
[WD £21.
♪ Mon and Fri by prior arrangement; full day's package of golf and catering, including evening meal; £50.
◉ Full clubhouse facilities.
⌁ Swallow, Bexleyheath; The Stakis, Dartford Bridge.

1A 47 Deangate Ridge
Hoo, Rochester, Kent, ME3 8RZ
☎ 01634 251180, Fax 250537, Pro 251180, Sec 251950, Rest/Bar 254481
A228 from Rochester to Isle of Grain, then road signposted to Deangate.
Municipal parkland course.
Pro Richard Fox; Founded 1972
Designed by Hawtree & Sons
18 holes, 6300 yards, S.S.S. 71
∫ 11.
♦ Welcome anytime; bookings essential at WE.
[WD £12.10; WE £16.
♪ Welcome; terms available on application.
◉ Lunch and dinner served.

1A 48 Dorking
Chart Park, Dorking, Surrey, RH5 4BX
⌨ www.dorkinggolfclub.co.uk
✉ dorklinggolfclub@ukgateway.net
☎ 01306 886917, Rest/Bar 885914
1 mile S of Dorking on A24.
Parkland course.
Pro Paul Napier; Founded 1897
Designed by James Braid
9 holes, 5163 yards, S.S.S. 65
♦ Welcome WD only.
[WD £15.
♪ Welcome by prior arrangement.
◉ Restaurant and bar.
⌁ Burford Bridge, Boxhill.

1A 49 The Drift
The Drift, East Horsley, KT24 5HD
✉ info@driftgolfclub.co.uk
☎ 01483 284641, Fax 284642, Pro 284772, Rest/Bar 284641
On B2039 East Horsley road off A3.
Woodland course.
Liam Greasley; Founded 1975

Designed by H Cotton/R Sandow
18 holes, 6425 yards, S.S.S. 72
♦ WD only unless member's guest.
[Terms on application.
♪ Mon-Fri by appointment.
◉ Full restaurant and bar.
⌁ Jarvis Thatcher Hotel, E Horsley; Hautboy, Ockham.

1A 50 Duke's Dene Golf Course
Haliloo Valley Road, Woldingham, Surrey, CR3 7HA
☎ 01883 653501, Fax 653502, Pro 653541
From M25 Junction 6 towards Caterham; at roundabout take Woldingham exit.
Valley course, we guarantee no tempgreen.
Pro Nick Bradley; Founded 1996
18 holes, 6393 yards, S.S.S. 70
∫ Practice range.
♦ Welcome except after 12 at WE.
[WD £25; WE £35.
♪ Welcome WD.
◉ Bar and brasserie.

1A 51 Dulwich & Sydenham Hill
Grange Lane, College Road, London, SE21 7LH
✉ dulwichgc@hotmail.com
☎ 020 8693 3961, Fax 8693 2481, Pro 8693 8491, Sec 8693 3961, Rest/Bar 8693 3961
Off S Circular road at Dulwich College and College Road.
Parkland course.
Pro David Baillie; Founded 1894
18 holes, 6008 yards, S.S.S. 69
♦ Welcome all week with handicap certs.
[WD £25; WE £35.
♪ Welcome WD by prior arrangement; terms available on application.
◉ Lunch daily, dinner by appointment.

1A 52 Dunsfold Aerodrome
British Aerospace, Dunsfold Aerodrome, Nr Godalming, Surrey, GU8 4BS
☎ 01483 265403
12 miles S of Guildford on A281.
Parkland course.
Founded 1965
Designed by John Sharkey
9 holes, 6099 yards, S.S.S. 69
♦ With member only.
[Member's responsibility.
♪ Welcome from British Aerospace.
◉ Bar and snacks.

1A 53 **Edenbridge G & CC**
Crouch House Road, Edenbridge,
Kent, TN8 5LQ
☎ 01732 865097, Fax 867029,
Pro 865097, Sec 867381,
Rest/Bar 867381
Traveling N through Edenbridge High
Street, turn left into Stangrove Road
(30 yds before railway station), at end
of the road turn right, course is on the
left.
Undulating meadowland course.
Founded 1975
2 x 18-hole and 1 x 9-hole,
5605 yards, S.S.S. old course 72
new course 68
⚲ Practice 14.
♦ Welcome.
⚲ WD £12; WE £19; Blue £5
⚬ Welcome by appointment;
packages available; terms on
application.
⚬⚬ Clubhouse bar and catering
facilities available.
⚲ Langley Arms, Tonbridge.

1A 54 **Effingham**
Guildford Road, Effingham, Surrey,
KT24 5PZ
⚲ www.effinghamgolfclub.com
⚲ secretary@effinghamgolfclub.com
☎ 01372 452203, Fax 459959,
Pro 452606
On A246 8 miles E of Guildford.
Downland course.
Pro Stephen Hoatson; Founded 1927
Designed by HS Colt
18 holes, 6524 yards, S.S.S. 71
♦ WD only by arrangement;
handicap certs required.
⚲ WD £35.
⚬ Welcome Wed, Thurs and Fri;
terms on application.
⚬⚬ Lunch, tea, evening meal, snacks,
etc.
⚲ Thatchers (East Horsley); Preston
Cross (Great Bookham).

1A 55 **Eltham Warren**
Bexley Road, Eltham, London, SE9
2PE
⚲ www.elthamwarrangolfclub.co.uk
⚲ secretary@
elthamwarren.idps.co.uk
☎ 020 8850 1166, Pro 8859 7909,
Sec 8850 4477, Rest/Bar 8850 1166
0.5 miles from Eltham Station on A210.
Parkland course.
Pro Gary Brett; Founded 1890
9 holes, 5840 yards, S.S.S. 68
♦ Welcome on WD.
⚲ WD £25, WE £25.
⚬ Thurs only; green fees, morning

coffee, ploughman's lunch, evening
meal; £42.
⚬⚬ Full bar and catering.
⚲ Swallow, Bexleyheath.

1A 56 **Epsom** ⚯
Longdown Lane South, Epsom, Surrey,
KT17 4JR
⚲ www.epsomgolfclub.co.uk
⚲ enquires@epsom golfclub.co.uk
☎ 01372 721666, Fax 817183,
Pro 741867, Rest/Bar 723363
Course is 0.5 miles south of Epsom
Downs Station on the road to Epsom
College.
Downland course.
Pro Ron Goudie; Founded 1889
18 holes, 5658 yards, S.S.S. 68
♦ Welcome except before noon on
Tues, Sat and Sun.
⚲ WD £26; WE £30.
⚬ Welcome WD except Tues, and
WE pm; min 12, max 40; packages
available; terms on application.
⚬⚬ Full clubhouse facilities.
⚲ Heathside hotel.

1A 57 **Falcon Valley**
Gay Dawn Farm, Fawkham, Longfield,
Kent, DA3 8LY
☎ 01474 707144, Fax 707911,
Pro 707144, Sec 707144,
Rest/Bar 707144
Take A20 off Junction 3 of M25
towards Brands Hatch and turn left
towards Fawkham/Longfield.
Wooded parkland course.
Pro Cameron McKillop; Founded 1986
Designed by Greg Turner
9 holes, 6547 yards, S.S.S. 72
⚲ Large practice area.
♦ Welcome WD, after 1pm at WE.
⚲ WD £20; WE £27.50.
⚬ Welcome midweek; packages
available; terms on application.
⚬⚬ Bar and restaurant.
⚲ Brands Hatch Hotel; Brands Hatch
Thistle.

1A 58 **Farleigh Court**
Old Farleigh Road, Farleigh, Surrey,
CR6 9PX
⚲ enq @farleighcourt.co.uk
☎ 01883 627711, Fax 627722,
Pro 627733, Sec 627711,
Rest/Bar 627711
Ten minutes from Croydon town
centre.
Parkland course.
Pro Scott Graham; Founded 1996
Designed by John Jacobs
18 (Visitors 9) holes, 6409 (Visitors

3255) yards, S.S.S. 72
⚲ 20.
♦ Welcome 7 days.
⚲ Terms available on application.
⚬ Welcome WD.
⚬⚬ Restaurant, bar and function
rooms.

1A 59 **Farnham**
The Sands, Farnham, Surrey, GU10
1PX
⚲ www.grahamecowlishaw.co.uk
⚲ grahameproshop@aol.com
☎ 01252 783163, Fax 781185,
Pro 782198, Sec 782109,
Rest/Bar 782342
On A31 from Runfold.
Heathland, pines, parkland course.
Pro Grahame Cowlishaw; Founded 1896
18 holes, 6447 yards, S.S.S. 71
♦ Welcome WDs.
⚲ WD £35.
⚬ Wed, Thurs, Fri only; 2 rounds of
golf, coffee and roll on arrival, snack
lunch and evening meal; golf clinics
available; £58.50.
⚬⚬ Bar and restaurant facilities
available.
⚲ Hogs Back Hotel.

1A 60 **Farnham Park**
Folly Hill, Farnham, Surrey, GU9 0AU
☎ 01252 715216, Rest/Bar 715216
On A287 next to Farnham Castle.
Parkland course.
Pro Darren Bryant; Founded 1966
Designed by Henry Cotton
9 holes, 2326 yards, S.S.S. 54
♦ Public pay and play.
⚲ WD £4.25; WE £4.75.
⚬ By prior arrangement.
⚲ The Bush Hotel, Farnham.

1A 61 **Faversham**
Belmont Park, Faversham, Kent, ME13
0HB
⚲ www.faversham.co.uk
☎ 01795 890561, Fax 890760,
Pro 890275, Sec 890561,
Rest/Bar 890251
Leave M2 at Junction 6, A251 to
Faversham, then A2 Sittingbourne for
0.5 mile, turn left at Brogdale Road,
and then follow signs.
Parkland course.
Pro Stuart Rokes; Founded 1902
18 holes, 6030 yards, S.S.S. 69
♦ WD; only with member WE and
BH and with handicap cert.
⚲ WD £30; WE £30.
⚬ By arrangement; terms on
application.

🍽 By arrangement with Steward.
🛒 Granary; Porch House.

1A 62 Foxhills
Stonehill Road, Ottershaw, Surrey,
KT16 0EL
💻 www.foxhills.co.uk
📧 events@foxhills.co.uk
☎ 01932 872050, Fax 874762,
Pro 873961, Sec 704513,
Rest/Bar 704480
From the M25 Junction 11 follow the
signs for Woking; at the 2nd
roundabout take the 3rd exit into
Foxhills Road.
Treelined course.
Pro A Good; Founded 1972
Designed by F Hawtree
Bernard Hunt 18; Longcross 18 holes,
Bernard Hunt 6883; Longcross 6743
yards, S.S.S. Bernard Hunt 73;
Longcross 72
† Welcome WD if carrying handicap
certs.
ɪ WD £55.
⬦ WD only; packages available;
driving range facilities; £85-£140.
🍽 Full clubhouse facilities.
🛒 Accommodation on site.

1A 63 Gatton Manor   ☎
Ockley, Dorking, Surrey, RH5 5PQ
💻 www.gattonmanor.co.uk
📧 gattonmanor@enterprize.net
☎ 01306 627555, Fax 627713,
Pro 627557
Course is 1.5 miles SW of Ockley on
the A29.
Parkland course.
Pro Rae Sergeant; Founded 1969
Designed by DB & DG Heath
18 holes, 6653 yards, S.S.S. 72
ɪ 5 mats.
† Welcome except Sun until 10.15am.
ɪ WD £23; WE £30.
⬦ Welcome WD; coffee, lunch, dinner,
36 holes of golf; conference facilities,
tennis with gym and health suite; £30-£59.
🍽 Bar and restaurant.
🛒 Gatton Manor.

1A 64 Goal Farm Par 3
Gole Road, Pirbright, Surrey, GU24
0PZ
☎ 01483 473183
1 mile from Brookwood station off A322
towards Pirbright.
Parkland course.
Founded 1977
9 holes, 1128 yards, S.S.S. 48
† Welcome except Thurs am or Sat
am.

ɪ WD £4.50; WE £4.75.
⬦ Welcome.
🍽 Bar and bar snacks.
🛒 Lakeside.

1A 65 Guildford
High Path Road, Merrow, Guildford,
Surrey, GU1 2HI
☎ 01483 563941, Fax 453228,
Pro 566765, Rest/Bar 531842
Course is 2 miles E of Guildford on the
A246.
Downland course.
Pro PG Hollington; Founded 1886
Designed by James Braid
18 holes, 6090 yards, S.S.S. 70
† Welcome WD; members' guests
only at WE.
ɪ WD £30; WE £30.
⬦ Welcome by prior arrangement;
packages including practice areas and
indoor practice rooms and snooker;
terms available on application.
🍽 Full bar and catering facilities
available.
🛒 White Horse; Angel.

1A 66 Hampton Court Palace Golf Club
Hampton Wick, Kingston-Upon-
Thames, KT1 4AD
📧 Hamptoncourtpalace@
americangolf.uk.com
☎ 020 8977 2423, Fax 8977 4414,
Pro 8977 2658, Rest/Bar 8977 6645
Entrance to Home Park is through
Kingston Gate at Hampton Wick
roundabout.
Parkland course/links.
Pro Len Roberts; Founded 1895
18 holes, 6611 yards, S.S.S. 71
† Welcome.
ɪ WD £22; WE £27.50.
⬦ Welcome with prior appointment;
packages available; terms on
application.

1A 67 Hankley Commom
Tilford Road, Tilford, Farnham, Surrey,
GU10 2DD
☎ 01252 792493, Fax 795699,
Pro 793761
Off M3 or A3 to Farnham, along A31
Farnham by-pass to lights; left to
Tilford.
Heathland course.
Pro P Stow; Founded 1896
Designed by James Braid
18 holes, 6438 yards, S.S.S. 71
ɪ Practice ground.
† Welcome only with telephone
booking and handicap certs.

ɪ WD £50; WE £65.
⬦ Tues, Wed; packages available;
£75/£85.
🍽 Full catering and bar.
🛒 Bush, Farnham; Frensham Ponds;
Pride of Valley, Churt.

1A 68 Happy Valley Golf Club
Rook Lane, Chaldon, Surrey, CR3 5AA
💻 www.happyvalley.co.uk
📧 cgm.wells@virgin.net
☎ 01883 344555
3 miles from Junction 7/8 M23/M25.
Part hilly, part flat.
18 holes, 6333 yards
† Yes.
ɪ WD £20, WE £25.
⬦ Yes.
🍽 Bar/restaurant.
🛒 Hotels in Croydon, 5 miles away.

1A 69 Hawkhurst   ☎
High Street, Hawkhurst, Cranbrook,
Kent, TN18 4JS
☎ 01580 752396, Pro 753600,
Sec 429664
On A268 3 miles from A21 at Flimwell,
0.5 mile from junction with A229.
Undulating parkland course.
Pro Tony Collins; Founded 1968
Designed by Rex Baldock
9 holes, 5791 yards, S.S.S. 68
† Welcome weekdays; only with
member at weekends.
ɪ WD £18; WE £20 after noon.
⬦ Welcome by prior arrangement;
mostly Fri; £18.
🍽 By arrangement.
🛒 Royal Oak, Tudor Court; Queens.

1A 70 Hemsted Forest
Golford Road, Cranbrook, Kent, TN17
4AL
💻 www.hemstedforest.co.uk
📧 golf@hemstedforest.co.uk
☎ 01580 712833, Fax 714274,
Pro 712833, Sec 712833,
Rest/Bar 715771
Off A262 at Sissinghurst; turn right at
Bull towards Beneden; 1 mile on left.
Tree-lined parkland course.
Pro Karl Steptoe; Founded 1969
Designed by John D Harris
18 holes, 6295 yards, S.S.S. 70
† Welcome except Mon.
ɪ WD £25; WE £30.
⬦ Welcome Tues-Fri; packages
available from £19.50.
🍽 Full clubhouse facilities.
🛒 Kennel Holt; The George.

1A 71 Herne Bay
Eddington, Herne Bay, Kent, CT6 7PG
☎ 01227 373964, Pro 374727,
Rest/Bar 374097
Off A299 Thanet road at Herne Bay –
Canterbury Junction.
Parkland course/links.
Pro F Scott; Founded 1895
Designed by James Braid
18 holes, 5567 yards, S.S.S. 66
⏐ Practice green.
✝ Welcome WD, and afternoons at
WE.
⎰ WD £18; WE £28.
↺ By prior arrangement; terms on
application.
⦿⎸ Full facilities.

1A 72 Hever
Hever, Edenbridge, Kent, TN8 7NP
⚘ www.hever.com
📧 golf@hever.com
☎ 01732 700771, Fax 700775,
Pro 700771, Sec 700771,
Rest/Bar 700016
Course is off the A21 between
Sevenoaks and Edenbridge adjacent
to Hever Castle.
Parkland course, with water hazards.
Pro Peter Parks; Founded 1992
Designed by Dr Peter Nicholson
18 holes, 7002 yards
✝ Welcome.
⎰ WD £35; WE £55.
↺ By prior appointment; coffee, golf,
dinner, use of gymnasium included.
Also on site: sauna, spa, snooker,
tennis; £38-68.
⦿⎸ Restaurant and bar.
⎘ Hotel on site.

1A 73 High Elms
High Elms Road, Downe, Kent, BR6 7SI
☎ 01689 858175, Pro 853232,
Rest/Bar 861813
5 miles out of Bromley off the A21 to
Sevenoaks.
Public parkland course.
Pro Peter Remy; Founded 1969
Designed by Fred Hawtree
18 holes, 6221 yards, S.S.S. 70
⏐ Practice ground.
✝ Welcome.
⎰ WD £11.80; WE £15.30.
↺ Welcome WD only; terms on
application.
⦿⎸ Full meals and snacks.
⎘ Bromley Court.

1A 74 Hilden
Rings Hill, Hildenborough, Kent, TN11
8LX ☎

☎ 01732 833607, Fax 834484,
Pro 833607, Sec 833607,
Rest/Bar 838577
Course is off the A21 towards
Tunbridge Wells adjacent to
Hildenborough station.
Parkland course.
Pro Nicky Way; Founded 1994
9 holes, 1558 yards, S.S.S. 54
⏐ 36.
✝ Welcome.
⎰ WD £5.95; WE £7.50.
↺ Welcome; terms on application.
⦿⎸ Full facilities.

1A 75 Hindhead
Churt Road, Hindhead, Surrey, GU26
6HX
☎ 01428 604614, Fax 608508,
Pro 604458, Sec 604614,
Rest/Bar 604614
1.5 miles N of Hindhead on the A287.
Heathland course.
Pro Neil Ogilvy; Founded 1908
18 holes, 6373 yards, S.S.S. 70
✝ Welcome WD; by appt WE.
⎰ WD £36; WE £47.
↺ Wed, Thurs only; 36 holes of golf,
coffee, snack lunch, evening meal;
£65.
⦿⎸ Full catering and bar.
⎘ Mariners, Farnham; Devils Punch
Bowl, Hindhead; Frensham Pond.

1A 76 Hoebridge Golf Centre
Old Woking Road, Old Woking, Surrey,
GU22 8JH
⚘ www.hoebridge.co.uk
📧 info@hoebridge.co.uk
☎ 01483 722 611, Fax 740369,
Pro 722611, Sec 720256,
Rest/Bar 722611
On B382 between Old Woking and
West Byfleet.
Public parkland one par 3 course; one
18-hole course; one 9-hole course.
Pro Tim Powell; Founded 1982
Designed by John Jacobs
Hoebridge 18 holes; Sheycopse 9
holes; Maybury 18 holes,
Hoebridge 6536; Sheycopse 2294
holes; Maybury 2280 Yards, S.S.S.
Hoebridge 71; Sheycopse 31;
Maybury 54
⏐ Practice range 36 floodlit bays.
✝ Welcome 7 days per week.
⎰ Hoebridge WD £18 WE £22.50;
Sheycopse WD £9.50 WE £10.50;
Maybury WD £7.20 WE £8.00.
↺ WD by prior arrangement, Health
and Fitness terms on application.
⦿⎸ Restaurant and bar facilties.
⎘ Travel Inn nearby.

1A 77 Holtye
Holtye Common, Cowden, Kent, TN8
7ED
☎ 01342 850635, Fax 850576,
Pro 850957, Sec 850576
On the A264 1 mile S of Cowden.
Forest/heathland course.
Pro K Hinton; Founded 1893
9 holes, 5325 yards, S.S.S. 66
⏐ 3/4 bays under cover.
✝ Welcome Mon, Tues, Fri;
Restrictions Wed and Thurs
mornings.
⎰ WD £16; WE £18.
↺ By prior arrangement; terms on
application.
⦿⎸ Catering and bar facilities.
⎘ White Horse Inn (next door).

1A 78 Homelands Bettergolf Centre
Ashford Road, Kingsnorth, Kent, TN26
1NJ
📧 isj@bettergolf.invictornet.co.uk
☎ 01233 661620, Fax 720553
M20 Junction 10 following signs for
International station until 2nd
roundabout where course is
signposted.
Parkland course.
Pro Tony Bowers; Founded 1995
Designed by D Steel
9 holes, 4410 yards, S.S.S. 64
⏐ 14.
✝ Public pay as you play.
⎰ WD £7 for 9 holes £11 for 18; WE
£10 for 9 holes £18 for 18.
↺ Welcome; bar snacks, driving
range, academy pitch and putt; terms
on application.
⦿⎸ Bar with drinks and snacks; BBQs
can be arranged.
⎘ Many in area, contact golf club for
details.

1A 79 Horton Park Country Club
Hook Road, Epsom, Surrey, KT19 8QG
☎ 020 8393 8400, Fax 8394 1369
M25 Junction 9; follow signs to
Chessington, turning right at Malden
Rushett lights. 2 miles, then left into
Horton Lane.
Parkland course.
Pro Martyn Hurst/Stewart Walker/ John
Terrill; Founded 1987
18; 9 holes, 6028; 1637 yards, S.S.S.
70
⏐ Practice area/Floodlit driving bays.
✝ Bookings WD; WE.
⎰ Terms on application.
↺ Welcome; packages include golf
and lunch/dinner.

🎦 Restaurant, bar, private suites.
⤸ Chalk Lane Hotel, Epsom.

1A 80 Hurtmore
Hurtmore Road, Hurtmore, Surrey,
GU7 2RN
☎ 01483 426492, Fax 426121,
Sec 424440
6 miles S of Guildford on A3 at
Hurtmore exit.
Parkland course.
Pro Maxine Burton; Founded 1992
Designed by Peter Alliss & Clive Clark
18 holes, 5514 yards, S.S.S. 67
♦ Public pay and play.
[WD £12; WE £16.
⟳ Welcome by appointment; from
£12.
🎦 Full facilities available.
⤸ Squirrel.

1A 81 Hythe Imperial
Princes Parade, Hythe, Kent, CT21
6AE
🖳 www.hytheimperialgolfclub.co.uk
☎ 01303 267554, Fax 264610,
Pro 233745
Turn off M20 to Hythe, to E end of
seafront.
Seaside links course.
Pro Gordon Ritchie; Founded 1950
9 holes, 5560 yards, S.S.S. 68
🏌 Practice area, chipping and putting
green.
♦ Welcome; handicap certificate
required.
[WD £15; WE £20.
⟳ Welcome by prior appointment;
terms on application.
🎦 Hotel/club bar.
⤸ Hythe Imperial 4 star on site with
full leisure facilities.

1A 82 Kings Hill
Kings Hill, West Malling, Kent, ME19
4AF
🖳 www.kingshill-golfclub.com
🖳 khatkhgolf@aol.com
☎ 01732 875040, Fax 875019,
Pro 842121, Sec 875040,
Rest/Bar 875040
From M20 Junction 4 take A228
towards Tonbridge.
Heathland course.
Pro David Hudspith; Founded 1996
Designed by David Williams
18 holes, 6622 yards, S.S.S. 72
🏌 6.
♦ Welcome WD; WE with member.
[WD £30.
⟳ Welcome by appointment; £37-53.
🎦 Full bar and catering.

1A 83 Kingswood Golf & CC
Sandy Lane, Tadworth, Surrey, KT20
6NE
☎ 01737 832188, Fax 833920,
Pro 832334, Rest/Bar 832316
From A217 take Bonsor Drive (A2032)
to Kingswood Arms. Club 0.25 miles
down Sandy Lane.
Parkland course.
Pro Terry Sims; Founded 1938
Designed by James Braid
18 holes, 6904 yards, S.S.S. 73
🏌 Driving range, practice area.
♦ Welcome but WE restrictions.
[WD £36; WE £50.
⟳ Welcome; terms on application.
🎦 Bar and restaurant.
⤸ Club will provide list.

1A 84 Knole Park
Seal Hollow Road, Sevenoaks, Kent,
TN15 0HJ
🖳 www.kentgolf.co.uk/
knolepark/knoleparkl.htm
☎ 01732 452150, Fax 463159,
Pro 451740, Sec 452150,
Rest/Bar 740221
0.5 miles from Sevenoaks town centre.
Parkland course.
Pro Phil Sykes; Founded 1924
Designed by JA Abercromby
18 holes, 6266 yards, S.S.S. 70
♦ Welcome after 9am WD.
[WD £40.
⟳ Tues, Thurs, Fri by appt. £73.
🎦 Full facilities.
⤸ Donnington Manor Hotel, Dunton
Green.

1A 85 Laleham
Laleham Reach, Chertsey, Surrey,
KT16 8RP
🖳 www.laleham-golf.co.uk
🖳 secretary@laleham-golf.co.uk
☎ 01932 564211, Fax 564448,
Pro 562877, Sec 564211,
Rest/Bar 502188
From M25 Junction 11 take A320 to
Thorpe Park roundabout then to
Penton Marina and signposted.
Parkland course.
Pro Hogan Scott; Founded 1908
18 holes, 6211 yards, S.S.S. 70
♦ Welcome with handicap certs.
[WD £22.
⟳ Mon, Tues, Wed; catering facilities;
£21-£48.50.
🎦 Full facilities.

1A 86 Lamberhurst Golf Club
Church Road, Lamberhurst, Kent, TN3
8DT

🖳 www.lamberhurstgolfclub.com
🖳 secretary@
amberhurstgolfclub.com
☎ 01892 890241, Fax 891140,
Pro 890552, Sec 890591
6 miles S of Tunbridge Wells on A21;
turning on to B2162 at Lamberhurst.
Parkland course.
Pro Brian Impett; Founded 1890
Designed by Fran Pennik
18 holes, 6275 yards, S.S.S. 70
♦ Welcome WD, and pm at WE.
[Summer rate WD £25 per round;
WE £40 per round – winter rates WD
£25 per round WE £25 per round.
⟳ Welcome Tues, Wed and Thurs,
April to October; 36 holes, coffee,
lunch and 3-course dinner; min 16,
max 36; £49.
🎦 Full clubhouse facilities.
⤸ Pembury Resort, Pembury;
George & Dragon, Lamberhurst.

1A 87 Langley Park
Barnfield Wood Road, Beckenham,
Kent, BR3 6SZ
☎ 020 8658 6849, Fax 8658 6310,
Pro 8650 1663, Sec 8658 6849,
Rest/Bar 8650 2090
1 mile from Bromley South station.
Parkland course.
Pro Colin Staff; Founded 1910
Designed by JH Taylor
18 holes, 6488 yards, S.S.S. 71
♦ Welcome WD by arrangement with
Pro shop. WE only with member.
[WD £20 for a round £35 for the
day; WE members only.
⟳ Wed and Thurs only; maximum 24
Thurs; 36 holes of golf, lunch and
dinner; £52.
🎦 Full bar and restaurant.
⤸ Bromley Court Hotel.

1A 88 Leatherhead
Kingston Road, Leatherhead, Surrey,
KT22 0EE
🖳 www.lgc/golf.co.uk
🖳 professional@lgcgolf.co.uk
☎ 01372 843966, Fax 842241,
Pro 843956
From M25 Junction 9 take A243
towards London, course entrance 500
yards.
Parkland course.
Pro Simon Norman; Founded 1903
18 holes, 6203 yards, S.S.S. 70
🏌 Practice area.
♦ Welcome by appointment; WE not
before 12 noon.
[WD £37.50; WE £47.50.
⟳ Welcome; terms available on
application.

🍴 Restaurant, brasserie, bar.
🍺 Woodlands Park (Oxshott).

1A 89 Leeds Castle
Leeds Castle, Maidstone, Kent, ME17
1PL
🖥 www.leeds-castle.co.uk
📧 stevepurvis@leeds-castle.co.uk
☎ 01622 880467, Fax 735616,
Pro 880467, Sec 880467
M20 Junction 8 and follow signs to
Leeds Castle on A20.
Parkland course.
Pro Steve Purvis; Founded 1933
Designed by Neil Coles
9 holes, 2681 yards, S.S.S. 33
† Can book 6 days ahead; no jeans
please.
[WD £11; WE £12.
🌀 WD only; terms on application.
🍺 Tudor Park, Maidstone.

1A 90 Limpsfield Chart
Limpsfield, Oxted, Surrey, RH8 0SL
☎ 01883 722106, Sec 723405,
Rest/Bar 722106
Course is on the A25 between Oxted
and Westerham, over the traffic lights
300 yards on right, east of Oxted.
Heathland course.
Founded 1889
9 holes, 5718 yards, S.S.S. 69
⚑ Practice net.
† WD welcome; WE by prior
arrangement or with member.
[WD £18; WE £20.
🌀 Can be arranged; terms on
application.
🍴 Meals served.
🍺 Kings Arms (Westerham).

1A 91 Lingfield Park ⚑
Racecourse Road, Lingfield, Surrey,
RH7 6PQ
☎ 01342 834602, Fax 836077,
Pro 832659, Sec 834602
From A22 at E Grinstead take the B
2028 to Lingfield.
Parkland course.
Pro Chris Morley; Founded 1987
18 holes, 6487 yards, S.S.S. 72
⚑ 20.
† Welcome WD, WE by appt.
[WD £38; WE £52.
🌀 Welcome by prior arrangement;
packages include golf and catering;
call for information.
🍴 Full facilities available.
🍺 Felbridge; Copthorne.

1A 92 Littlestone
St Andrew's Road, Littlestone, New
Romney, Kent, TN28 8RB
☎ 01797 363355, Fax 362740,
Pro 362231, Rest/Bar 362310
In New Romney on A259 between
Brenzett and Hythe; 15 miles S of
Ashford.
Links course.
Pro Andrew Jones; Founded 1888
Designed by Laidlaw Purves
18 holes, 6486 yards, S.S.S. 72; Blue
Course: 18 holes, 6676 yards, S.S.S.
73
† Welcome by prior arrangement
WD and WE.
[WD £35; WE £45.
🌀 Welcome WD; golf and catering
packages; from £36.
🍴 Full facilities.
🍺 Romney Bay House; Broadacre;
Rose and Crown; White House B&B.

1A 93 The London
South Ash Manor Estate, Ash, Nr
Sevenoaks, Kent, TN15 7EN
☎ 01474 879889, Fax 879912
Off A20 near Brands Hatch at W
Kingsdown.
Parkland course.
Pro K Morgan/Paul Way (touring);
Founded 1993
Designed by Jack Nicklaus
Heritage 18; International 18 holes,
Heritage 7208; Int 7005 yards, S.S.S.
Heritage 72; Int 74
† Welcome only if accompanied by a
member.
[Heritage WD £50; WE £60.
International WD £40; WE £45.
🌀 Corporate days arranged.
🍴 Restaurant bar, function rooms
and coffee shop.
🍺 Brands Hatch Thistle; Brands
Hatch Place.

1A 94 The London Scottish
Windmill Enclosure, Wimbledon
Common, London, SW19 5NQ
🖥 www.lsgc.co.uk
📧 secretary@lsgc.co.uk
☎ 020 8789 1207, Fax 8789 7517,
Pro 8789 1207, Rest/Bar 8788 0135
1 mile from Putney station.
Heathland course.
Pro Steve Barr; Founded 1865
Designed by Tom Dunn
18 holes, 5458 yards, S.S.S. 66
† Welcome WD, except BH; must
wear red upper garment.
[WD from £10.
🌀 Welcome except WE; terms on
application.

🍴 Lunch served, dinner if ordered.
🍺 Wayfarer.

1A 95 Lullingstone Park
Park Gate, Chelsfield, Orpington, Kent,
BR6 7PX
☎ 01959 533793, Fax 533795,
Rest/Bar 532928
Signposted from M25 Junction 4.
Municipal parkland course.
Pro Mark Watt; Founded 1923
Designed by Fred Hawtree
18 holes, 6779 yards, S.S.S. 72
⚑ 32.
† Welcome.
[WD £12.25 WE £16.50.
🌀 Welcome by prior arrangement;
terms on application.
🍴 Bar and restaurant.
🍺 Thistle (Brands Hatch).

1A 96 Lydd ⚑
Romney Road, Lydd, Romney Marsh,
Kent, TN29 9LS
🖥 www.lyddgolfclub.co.uk
📧 info@lyddgolfclub.co.uk
☎ 01797 320808, Fax 321482,
Pro 321201
Take Ashford exit off M20 and follow
A2070 signs to Lydd Airport. At
Brenzett turn left and take B2075, club
is on left.
Links type course.
Pro Miss Stuwart; Founded 1993
Designed by M Smith
18 holes, 6517 yards, S.S.S. 71
⚑ 25 flood lit.
† Welcome.
[WD £17; WE £25.
🌀 Welcome only by prior
appointment; terms available on
application.
🍴 Bar and restaurant.

1A 97 Malden
Traps Lane, New Malden, Surrey, KT3
4RS
📧 moldongc@lwcdial.net
☎ 020 8942 0654, Fax 8936 2219,
Pro 8942 6009, Sec 8942 0645,
Rest/Bar 8942 3266
0.5 miles from New Malden station,
close to the A3 between Wimbledon
and Kingston.
Parkland course.
Pro Robert Hunter; Founded 1926
Designed by Alex Herd
18 holes, 6295 yards, S.S.S. 70
† Welcome WD; WE restrictions.
[WD £27.50; WE £50.
🌀 Available, subject to availability
midweek.

⁑ Full clubhouse facilities.
⌂ Kingston Lodge.

1A 98 Marriott Tudor Park ☏ Hotel & CC
Ashford Road, Bearsted, Maidstone, Kent, ME14 4NQ
🖧 www.marriotthotels.co.uk/tudorpark
☎ 01622 734334, Fax 735360,
Pro 739412, Sec 739412,
Rest/Bar 734334
Follow A20 Ashford road; 3 miles from Maidstone centre.
Parkland course.
Pro Nick McNally; Founded 1988
Designed by Donald Steel
18 holes, 6041 yards, S.S.S. 69
⚐ 6 bays.
♦ Welcome with handicap certs.
£ WD £25; WE £35.
⟳ Welcome WD by appointment.
⁑ Hotel and restaurant.
⌂ Marriott Tudor Park.

1A 99 Merrist Wood ☏
Coombe Lane, Worplesdon, Guildford, Surrey, GU3 3PE
🖥 mwgc@merristwood.co,uk
☎ 01483 238890, Pro 884050,
Rest/Bar 884048
Off A323 at Worplesdon.
Parkland/woodland course.
Pro Andrew Kirk; Founded 1997
Designed by David Williams
18 holes, 6909 yards, S.S.S. 73
♦ Welcome WDs.
£ WD £35.
⟳ Welcome by appointment.
⁑ Bar and restaurant facilities.
⌂ Worplesdon Place.

1A 100 Mid-Kent
Singlewell Road, Gravesend, Kent, DA11 7RB
☎ 01474 568035, Fax 564218,
Pro 332810, Rest/Bar 352387
On A227 after leaving A2 signposted Gravesend.
Parkland course.
Pro Mark Foreman; Founded 1909
Designed by Frank Pennink
18 holes, 6218 yards, S.S.S. 70
♦ Welcome WDs if members of a club with handicap certs; WE with member only.
£ WD £25; WE not available.
⟳ Terms on application.
⁑ Full facilities.
⌂ Manor; Tolgate.

1A 101 Milford
Milford, Nr Guildford, Surrey, GU8 5HS
🖧 www.americangolf.com
🖥 milford@americangolf.uk.com
☎ 01483 419200, Fax 419199,
Pro 416291
From A3 take Milford exit and head for station.
Parkland course.
Pro Paul Creamer; Founded 1993
Designed by Peter Alliss, Clive Clark
18 holes, 5960 yards, S.S.S. 69
⚐ 8.
♦ Welcome.
£ WD £20; WE £25 after 12 noon.
⟳ Welcome; from £35.
⁑ Full clubhouse facilities.
⌂ Inn on the Lake.

1A 102 Mitcham
Carshalton Road, Mitcham Junction, Surrey, CR4 4HN
☎ 020 8648 1508, Fax 8648 4197,
Pro 8640 4280, Sec 8648 4197
A237 off A23, by Mitcham Junction station.
Meadowland course.
Pro Jeff Godfrey; Founded 1886
18 holes, 5935 yards, S.S.S. 68
♦ Welcome by appointment WD; pm only at WE.
£ WD £16; WE £16.
⟳ Terms on application.
⁑ Full facilities.
⌂ Hilton, Sutton Croydon.

1A 103 Moatlands ☏
Watermans Lane, Brenchley, Kent, TN12 6ND
🖧 www.moatlands.com
🖥 moatlandsgolf@btconnect.com
☎ 01892 724400, Fax 723300,
Pro 724252, Rest/Bar 724555
From A21 take B2160 to Paddock Wood traveling through Matfield.
Parkland course.
Pro Simon Wood; Founded 1993
Designed by K Saito
18 holes, 7060 yards, S.S.S. 74
⚐ 15.
♦ Welcome WD; pm at WE.
£ WD £29; WE £39.
⟳ Welcome Mon, Tues, Thurs, Fri, terms on application.
⁑ Clubhouse bar and restaurant.
⌂ Ramada Jarvis Resort.

1A 104 Moore Place
Portsmouth Road, Esher, Surrey, KT10 9LN
🖧 www.moore-place.co.uk
☎ 01372 463533, Fax 463533,

Pro 463533, Rest/Bar 463532
On A3 Portsmouth road, 0.5 mile from centre of Easher towards Cobham.
Public undulating parkland course.
Pro Nick Gadd; Founded 1926
Designed by Harry Varden
9 holes, 2078 yards, S.S.S. 61
♦ Welcome.
£ WD £6.30; WE £8.00.
⟳ Welcome WD; terms on application.
⁑ Full facilities.
⌂ The Haven Hotel.

1A 105 Nevill
Benhall Mill Road, Tunbridge Wells, Kent, TN2 5JW
🖧 www.nevillgolfclub.co.uk
🖥 manager@nevillgolfclub.co.uk
☎ 01892 525818, Fax 517861,
Pro 532941, Rest/Bar 527820
S of Tunbridge Wells on A21.
Parkland course.
Pro Paul Huggett; Founded 1914
Designed by CK Cotton
18 holes, 6349 yards, S.S.S. 70
♦ Welcome with handicap certs.
£ WD £25; WE £32.50.
⟳ Welcome Wed, Thurs; terms on application.
⁑ Full facilities.
⌂ Spa Hotel, Tunbridge Wells.

1A 106 New Zealand Golf Club
Woodham Lane, Addlestone, Surrey, KT15 3QD
☎ 01932 345049, Fax 342891,
Pro 349619
On A245 from W Byfleet to Woking.
Wooded heathland course.
Pro V Evelvidge; Founded 1895
Designed by Muir-Ferguson/Simpson
18 holes, 6012 yards, S.S.S. 69
♦ Welcome by appointment.
£ Terms on application.
⟳ Welcome by appointment; terms on application.
⁑ Full facilities.

1A 107 Nizels
Nizels Lane, Hildenborough, Nr Tonbridge, Kent, TN11 8NU
☎ 01732 833138, Fax 835492,
Pro 838926
Take the A21 southbound from M25 Junction 5; then take the B245 towards Tonbridge. At roundabout head for Hildenborough and the first right is Nizels Lane.
Parkland course.
Pro Ally Mellor; Founded 1992
Designed by Paul Way

18 holes, 6297 yards, S.S.S. 71
♦ Welcome except am WE.
[Summer WD £40; WE £45. Winter
WD £20 WE £25.
⌒ Welcome by prior arrangement;
minimum 12.
⦿ Full facilities and bar.
⤳ Rose & Crown, Tonbridge; Philpots
Manor, Hildenborough.

1A 108 North Downs
Northdown Road, Woldingham, Surrey,
CR3 7AA
⤸ www.northdownsgolfclub.co.uk
☎ 01883 652057, Fax 652832,
Pro 653004, Sec 652057,
Rest/Bar 653298
Travel 2 miles north of the M25 Junction
6 to the roundabout, take the 5th exit to
Woldingham (2 miles); the clubhouse is
0.5 mile through village on left.
Parkland course.
Pro Mike Homewood; Founded 1899
Designed by JJ Pennink
18 holes, 5843 yards, S.S.S. 68
♦ Welcome WD with handicap certs
or prior enquire to manager.
[WD £20; WE £12 (with member).
⌒ WD, half or full day (half-day only
Thurs); terms available on application.
⦿ Restaurant, snacks.
⤳ Travel Lodge(M25).

1A 109 North Foreland
Convent Road, Broadstairs, Kent,
CT10 3PU
✉ Bpre342845@aol.com
☎ 01843 862140, Fax 862663,
Pro 604471
A28 from Canterbury, or A2/M2/A299
from London to Kingsgate via
Broadstairs; course 1.5 miles from
Broadstairs station.
Seaside/clifftop course; links course.
Pro Neil Hansen; Founded 1903
Designed by Fowler and Simpson
18 holes, 6430 yards, S.S.S. 71; Short
course: 18 holes, 1752 yards, par 3
♦ Prior booking, not Sun, Mon, Tues
am; handicap certs required; short
course unrestricted.
[WD £30; WE £40; Short: WD £6;
WE £7.50.
⌒ Welcome by appointment; terms
on application.
⦿ Full clubhouse facilities.
⤳ Castle Keep.

1A 110 Oak Park
Heath Lane, Crondall, Nr Farnham,
Surrey, GU10 5PB
☎ 01252 850850, Fax 850851,

Pro 850066
Course is 1.25 miles off the A287
Farnham-Oldham road; and 5 miles
from M3 Juntion 5.
Woodland course; also 9-hole Village
Parkland course.
Pro Gary Murton; Founded 1984
Designed by Patrick Dawson
18 holes, 6318 yards, S.S.S. 70
♦ Welcome.
[WD £20; WE £28; 9-hole course:
WD £10; WE £12.
⌒ Welcome by appointment.
⦿ Conservatory bar, restaurant with
cocktail bar.
⤳ Bishops Table; Bush, both Farnham.

1A 111 Oaks Sports Centre
Woodmansterne Road, Carshaton,
Surrey, SM5 4AN
⤸ www.oaksportscentre.co.uk
☎ 020 8643 8363, Fax 8770 7303,
Pro 8643 8363, Sec 8642 7103,
Rest/Bar 8643 8363
Course is on the B2032 past
Carshalton Beeches station, the Oaks
Sports Centre signposted N of the
A2022, halfway between the A217 and
the A237.
Public parkland course.
Pro Craig Mitchell/Michael Pilkington;
Founded 1972
Designed by Alphagreen
18 holes, 6033 yards, S.S.S. 69
𝍎 16 bays.
♦ Welcome.
[WD £15.25; WE £18.
⌒ Welcome by appointment; terms
on application.
⦿ Restaurant and bar.
⤳ The Post House,Croydon.

1A 112 Oastpark
Malling Road, Snodland, Kent, ME6
5LG
☎ 01634 242818, Fax 240744,
Pro 242661, Sec 242818,
Rest/Bar 242659
On A228 close to M20 Junction 4 and
M2 Junction 2.
Parkland course.
Pro David Porthouse; Founded 1992
Designed by Terry Cullen
9 holes, 2833 yards, S.S.S. 68
♦ Welcome.
[WD 9 £7. WD 18 £12. WE 9 £8
WE 18 £14.
⌒ Welcome WD and after 11am at
WE; minimum 8; from £15.
⦿ Full clubhouse facilities.
⤳ Swan; Larkfield Priory; Forte Crest.

1A 113 Pachesham Golf Centre
Oaklawn Road, Leatherhead, Surrey,
KT22 0BT
✉ philktaylor@hotmail.com
☎ 01372 843453, Fax 844076
M25 Junction 9; A244 towards Esher.
Parkland course.
Pro Phil Taylor; Founded 1991
Designed by Phil Taylor
9 holes, 5608 yards, S.S.S. 67
𝍎 33 bays.
♦ Welcome; book 48 hours ahead.
[WD £9; WE £10.50.
⌒ Welcome by appointment; terms
on application.
⦿ Full facilities.
⤳ Woodlands Park.

1A 114 Park Wood
Chestnut Avenue, Westerham, Kent,
TN16 2EG
⤸ www.parkwoodgolf.co.uk
✉ mail@parkwoodgolf.co.uk
☎ 01959 577744, Fax 572702,
Pro 577177, Sec 577744,
Rest/Bar 577740
From the centre of Westerham take
Oxted Road then turn right onto the
B2024, go under M25 to the top of the
hill; course is right and immediate right
again.
Parkland and lakes course.
Pro Nick Terry; Founded 1993
Designed by L Smith & R Goldsmith
18 holes, 6835 yards, S.S.S. 72
♦ Welcome.
[WD £36; WE £50.
⌒ Welcome Mon-Fri.
⦿ 120-seat restaurant, Full bar.
⤳ Kings Arms (Westerham).

1A 115 Pedham Place Golf Club
London Road, Swanley, Kent, BR8 8PP
⤸ www.ppgc.co.uk
✉ golf@ppgc.co.uk
☎ 01322 867000
Junction 3 M25, A20 towards Brands
Hatch.
Links style course.
♦ Yes, pay and play course.
[Par 2: WD £5.50, WE £6.75;
18-hole: WD £15, WE £20.
⌒ Welcome.
⦿ Restaurant.
⤳ Travel inns off M25.

1A 116 Pine Ridge Golf Centre
Old Bisley Road, Frimley, Camberley,
Surrey, GU16 5NX
⤸ www.pineridgegolf.co.uk
✉ enquiry@pineridgegolf.co.uk
☎ 01276 675444, Fax 678837,

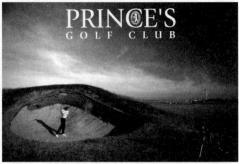
Pro 675444, Rest/Bar 675444
5 mins from M3 Junction 3; location map available on request.
Public pine-forested course.
Pro Peter Sefdon; Founded 1992
Designed by Clive D Smith
18 holes, 6012 yards, S.S.S. 72
ǁ 36.
† Welcome.
Ɩ WD £20; WE £26.
⟳ Welcome WD, min 12; terms on application.
🍽 Bar and restaurant, all day.
↩ Lakeside; Frimley Hall.

1A 117 Poult Wood
Higham Lane, Tonbridge, Kent, TN11 9QR
☎ 01732 364039, Fax 353781, Sec 364039, Rest/Bar 366180
Course is 1 mile N of Tonbridge off the A227.
Municipal wooded course.
Pro Chris Miller; Founded 1972
Designed by Fred Hawtree
18 holes, 5569 yards, 9 holes, S.S.S. 67; 9 holes, 1281 yards
† Welcome; booking required for 18.
Ɩ Prices on application.
⟳ Welcome WD by appointment; terms on application.

🍽 Restaurant and bar.
↩ Langley; Rose & Crown.

1A 118 Prince's Golf Club   ☿
Sandwich Bay, Sandwich, Kent, CT13 9QB
🖧 www.princes-leisure.co.uk
📧 golf@princes-leisure.co.uk
☎ 01304 611118, Fax 612000, Pro 613797, Sec 611118, Rest/Bar 611118
M2, A2 to A256 then follow signs for Sandwich; course signposted.
3 loops of 9 holes; Links course.
Pro Derek Barbour; Founded 1906
Designed by Sir Guy Campbell & John Morrison
18 holes, 6947 yards, S.S.S. 73
† Welcome.
Ɩ WD £55; WE £60.
⟳ Welcome by appointment.
Packages available from £45.
🍽 Spike bar; restaurant (shirt and tie required).
↩ The Bell; The Blazing Donkey, Ham; Royal, Deal.

1A 119 Purley Downs
106 Purley Downs Road, South Croydon, Surrey, CR2 0RB

🖧 www.parlydownsgolfclub.co.uk
📧 info@pearlydownsgolfclub.co.uk
☎ 020 8657 1231, Fax 8651 5044, Pro 8651 0819, Sec 8657 8347, Rest/Bar 8657 1231/8657 8142
3 miles S of Croydon on A235.
Downland course.
Pro Graham Wilson; Founded 1894
18 holes, 6275 yards, S.S.S. 70
† Welcome WD. WE with members.
Ɩ WD £30; WE £15 with a member.
⟳ Welcome Mon, Thurs; terms on application.
🍽 19th hole bar, lounge bar and restaurant.
↩ Selsdon Park; Trust House Forte; Croydon Hilton.

1A 120 Puttenham
Heath Road, Puttenham, Guildford, Surrey, GU3 1AL
☎ 01483 810609, Fax 810988, Pro 810277, Sec 810498, Rest/Bar 811087
Off A31 Hogs Back at Puttenham sign (B3000).
Tight heathland course.
Pro Gary Simmons; Founded 1894
18 holes, 6211 yards, S.S.S. 70
† Welcome WD by prior arrangement; with a member only at WE.

WD £25; WE no green fees invitation with members only.
Welcome Wed, Thurs, Fri; terms on application.
Full catering and bar.
Hogs Back Hotel.

1A 121 Pyrford
Warren Lane, Pyrford, Woking, Surrey, GU22 8XR
pyrford@americangolf.uk.com
01483 723555, Fax 729777, Pro 751070, Sec 723555
From A3 take Ripley/Wisley exit (B2215) through Ripley, follow signs for Pyrford.
Parkland course.
Pro Darren Brewer; Founded 1993
Designed by Peter Alliss & Clive Clark
18 holes, 6230 yards, S.S.S. 70
Welcome.
WD £36; WE £52.
Welcome; from £45.
Full bar and catering.
Cobham Hilton.

1A 122 Redhill & Reigate 𝕿
Clarence Lodge, Pendleton Road, Redhill, Surrey, RH1 6LB
redhillandreigategolfclub@btopenworld.com
01737 240777, Fax 242117, Pro 244433, Sec 240777(office), Rest/Bar 244626
1 mile S of Redhill between A23 and A25.
Wooded parkland course.
Pro Warren Pike; Founded 1887
Designed by James Braid
18 holes, 5272 yards, S.S.S. 68
Welcome WD and after 11am at WE.
WD £15; WE £25.
Welcome by prior arrangement; packages available from £37.50.
Full facilities.
Reigate Manor.

1A 123 Redlibbets
Manor Lane, West Yoke, Ash, Sevenoaks, Kent, TN15 7HT
www.golfandsport.co.uk
redllibbets@golfandsport.com
01474 872278, Fax 879290, Pro 4872278, Sec 4 879190
Take the A20 exit from the M25 towards Brands Hatch, course is on Paddock side next to Fawkham Manor Hospital, 8 miles from Sevenoaks.
Parkland course.
Pro Ross Taylor; Founded 1996
Designed by J Gaunt
18 holes, 6639 yards, S.S.S. 72
Welcome. With a member weekends only.
WD £30.00 (without a member), WD £15; WE £25.
Mon,Tues, Thurs; terms available on application.
Full facilities.
Brands Hatch Place.

1A 124 Reigate Heath
Reigate Heath, Reigate, Surrey, RH2 8QR
reigateheath@surreygolf.co.uk
01737 242610, Fax 249226, Sec 226793, Rest/Bar 242610
1.5 miles W of Reigate on Flanchford Road off A25.
Heathland course.
Pro Barry Davies; Founded 1895
9 holes, 5658 yards, S.S.S. 67
Welcome in midweek.
WD £20; WE n/a.
Wed, Thurs; max 30; terms on application.
Full facilities.
Cranleigh Hotel, Reigate.

1A 125 Reigate Hill 𝕿
Gatton Bottom, Reigate, Surrey, RH2 0TU
www.reigatehillgolfclub.co.uk
01737 646070, Fax 642650, Pro 646070, Sec 645577, Rest/Bar 64577
Course is 1 mile from Junction 8 of the M25.
Parkland course.
Pro Christopher Forsyth; Founded 1995
Designed by D Williams
18 holes, 6175 yards, S.S.S. 70
12.
WD, WE after 12 noon.
WD £25; WE £35.
Welcome by appointment; terms on application.
Full facilities.
Bridge House, Reigate Hill; The Priory, Nutfield.

1A 126 Richmond
Fulwood Court, Long Lane, Staines, Middx, TW19 7AS
020 8940 1463, Fax 8332 7914, Pro 8940 7792, Sec 8940 4351
On A307 1 mile S of Richmond, look for Sudbrook Lane on left.
Parkland course.
Pro Nick Job; Founded 1891
Designed by Tom Dunn
18 holes, 5785 yards, S.S.S. 69
WD by appointment. WE with members.
WD £27; WE £25.
Tues, Thurs, Fri by appointment; terms on application.
Bar snacks, lunches every day.
Petersham; Richmond Gate.

1A 127 Richmond Park
Roehampton Gate, Richmond Park, London, SW15 5JR
020 8876 3205, Fax 8878 1354, Pro 8876 1795
Inside Richmond Park; enter through Roehampton Gate off Priory Lane.
Parkland courses.
Pro David Bown; Founded 1923
Designed by Hawtree & Sons
Duke's 18. Prince's 18 holes, Duke's 6036 Prince's 5868 yards. S.S.S. Duke's 68. Prince's 69
18 not floodlit.
Pay and play course.
WD £15; WE £18.
Welcome.
None.
Richmond Gate Hotel.

1A 128 The Ridge
Chartway Street, East Sutton, Maidstone, Kent, ME17 3JB
ridge@americangolf.uk.com
01622 844382, Fax 844168, Pro 844243
From M20 Junction 8 take B2163 to Sutton Valence.
Old apple orchards.
Pro James Cornish; Founded 1993
Designed by Tryton Design Ltd
18 holes, 6214 yards, S.S.S. 70
Handicap certs required; midweek only.
WD £30; WE £18 (pm, with members only).
Tues, Thurs, welcome by prior appointment; golf and catering; £35-£57.
Full catering facilities.

1A 129 Riverside
Summerton Way, Thamesmead, SE28 8PP
enquiries@thamesview-golf.fsnet.co.uk
020 8310 7975, Pro 07855864485, Sec 8310 7975, Rest/Bar 8310 7975
Course is off the A1, 10 mins from Blackheath, 15 mins from Bexleyheath; near Woolwich.
Pay-as-you-play on reclaimed marshland.
Pro Graeme Wilson; Founded 1991
Designed by Heffernan & Heffernan

9 holes, 5482 yards, S.S.S. 66
⚑ 30.
✝ Welcome subject to reasonable standard of golf.
⌨ WD £6.50; WE £8.50.
✎ Welcome by appointment WD, only small societies WE; terms on application.
🍽 2 bars, à la carte.
↩ Black Prince (Bexleheath); Swallow.

1A 130 Rochester & Cobham Park

Park Pale By Rochester, Kent, ME2 3UL
🖳 www.rochesterandcobhamgc.co.uk
📧 rcpgc@talk21.com
☎ 01474 823411, Fax 824446,
Pro 823658, Sec 823411,
Rest/Bar 823412
3 miles E of Gravesend east exit off A2.
Parkland course.
Pro Iain Higgins; Founded 1891/1997
Designed by Donald Steel
18 holes, 6596 yards, S.S.S. 71
⚑ 8.
✝ WD with handicap certs; WE with member only.
⌨ WD £30 per round £40 per day; WE members only.
✎ Tues and Thurs; packages available; £39-60.
🍽 Full catering facilities.
↩ Inn on the Lake, A2; Tolgate Motel, Gravesend.

1A 131 Roehampton

Roehampton Lane, London, SW15 5LR
🖳 www.roehamptonclub.co.uk
📧 james.tucker@ roehamptonclub.co.uk
☎ 020 8480 4200, Fax 8480 4265,
Pro 8876 3858, Sec 8480 4200,
Rest/Bar 8480 4200
Just off the South Circular road between Sheen and Putney.
Private members parkland course.
Pro Alan Scott; Founded 1901
18 holes, 6065 yards, S.S.S. 69
✝ Members' guests only.
⌨ WD £22; WE £30.
✎ Welcome by members' Introduction only; terms available on application.
🍽 Restaurant, buttery, bar and 3 function rooms.

1A 132 Roker Park

Holly Lane, Aldershot Road, Guildford, Surrey, GU3 3PB

☎ 01483 236677, Fax 232324,
Pro 236677, Sec 232324,
Rest/Bar 237700
2 miles W of Guildford on A323.
Parkland course.
Pro Kevin Warn; Founded 1992
Designed by WV Roker
9 holes, 6074 yards, S.S.S. 72
⚑ 12.
✝ Public pay and play course.
⌨ WD £8.50; WE £10 and BH for 9 holes £17.50 for 18 holes. WD £14.50 for 18 holes. £12.50 unlimited use in winter.
✎ WD preferable; minimum 12; WD £12; WE £15.
🍽 Facilities available.
↩ Worpelson Hotel.

1A 133 Romney Warren

St Andrew's Road, Littlestone, New Romney, Kent, TN28 8RB
☎ 01797 362231, Fax 363511,
Pro 362231, Sec 362231,
Rest/Bar 366613
Take A259 to New Romney, turn right into Littlestone Road and after 0.5 miles into St Andrew's Road.
Links course.
Pro Andrew Jones; Founded 1993
Designed by JD Lewis, BM Evans
18 holes, 5126 yards, S.S.S. 65
⚑ Practice ground.
✝ Welcome with booking.
⌨ WD £15; WE £20.
✎ Apply at Pro shop; from £14.

1A 134 Royal Blackheath

Court Road, Eltham, London, SE9 0LR
🖳 www.rbgc.com
📧 jan@rbgc.com
☎ 020 8850 1795, Fax 8859 0150,
Pro 8850 1763, Rest/Bar 8850 1042
Junction 3 M25-A25 to London; 2nd lights turn right; club is 600 yards on right.
Parkland course; oldest known in world.
Pro Ian McGregor; Founded 1608
Designed by James Braid
18 holes, 6219 yards, S.S.S. 70
✝ Welcome midweek by arrangement with handicap cert; WE only with member.
⌨ WD £40, £60 (for the day); WE no fees.
✎ Welcome Wed-Fri by appointment; from £65.
🍽 Full catering and bar facilities.
↩ Bromley Court, Bromley Clarendon, Blackheath.

1A 135 Royal Cinque Ports *(see overleaf)*

Golf Road, Deal, Kent, CT14 6RF
📧 rcpgcsec@aol
☎ 01304 374007, Fax 379530,
Pro 374170, Sec 367856,
Rest/Bar 374007
Follow coast road through Deal to end and turn left on to Godwyn Road, at the end turn right on to Golf Road.
Seaside links course.
Pro Andrew Reynolds; Founded 1892
Designed by Tom Dunn, Guy Campbell, James Braid
18 holes, 6754 yards, S.S.S. 71
✝ Welcome WD except Weds; WE by appointment; handicap certs required.
⌨ WD £60; WE £70.
✎ Welcome WD by prior appointment; terms available on application.
🍽 Full facilities; dress code required.
↩ Royal; Kings Head, both Deal; Bell, Sandwich.

1A 136 Royal Mid-Surrey

Old Deer Park, Richmond, Surrey, TW9 2SB
🖳 www.rmsgc.co.uk
📧 secretary@rmsgc.co.uk
☎ 020 8940 1894, Fax 8332 2957,
Pro 8940 0459, Sec 8940 1894
On A316 300 yards before the Richmond roundabout heading to London.
Parkland courses.
Pro Phillip Talbot; Founded 1892
Designed by JH Taylor
Inner: 18; Outer: 18 holes, Inner: 5544; Outer 6345 yards, S.S.S. Inner: 68; Outer: 69
✝ WDs with handicap cert; WE only with a member.
⌨ WD £68; WE (for member's guests only) £23.50.
✎ Contact Sec; terms available on application.
🍽 Lunches served every day except Mon; bar and snacks available.
↩ Richmond Hill; Richmond Gate.

1A 137 Royal St George's

Sandwich, Kent, CT13 9PB
☎ 01304 613090, Fax 611245,
Pro 615236, Sec 613090,
Rest/Bar 617308
2 miles E of Sandwich on road to Sandwich Bay.
Open Championship 1993; Links.
Pro Andrew Brooks; Founded 1887
Designed by Dr Laidlaw Purves
18 holes, 6947 yards, S.S.S. 72
✝ Welcome midweek but with

maximum 18 handicap; cert required.
⚐ WD £75-£110 per day.
⚑ Mon, Tues, Wed, but not mid-July to end of August; £115.
🏵 Full facilities.

1A 138 Royal Wimbledon
29 Camp Road, Wimbledon, SW19 4UW
🖧 www.rwgc.co.uk
✉ secretary@rwgc.co.uk
☎ 020 8946 2125, Fax 8944 8652,
Pro 8946 4606, Sec 8946 2125,
Rest/Bar 8946 0055
0.75 mile from War Memorial in Wimbledon Village.
Parkland course.
Pro Hugh Boyle; Founded 1865
Designed by Harry Colt
18 holes, 6348 yards, S.S.S. 70
† Members only.
⚐ £55.
⚑ Wed, Thurs only; terms on application.
🏵 Full facilities.
⌁ Cannizaro House Hotel.

1A 139 Rusper   ⚷
Rusper Road, Newdigate, Surrey, RH5 5BX
☎ 01293 871871
M25 exit 9 and A24 towards Dorking, follow signs to Newdigate and Rusper.
Parkland course.
Pro Janice Arnold; Founded 1992
Designed by S Hood
18 holes, 6218 yards, S.S.S. 69
† Welcome.
⚐ WD £11.50; WE £15.50.
⚑ Welcome with prior arrangement.
🏵 Bar and meals.
⌁ Ghyll Manor, Rusper.

1A 140 Ruxley
Sandy Lane, St Paul's Cray, Orpington, Kent, BR5 3HY
🖧 www.americangolf.co.uk
☎ 01689 839677, Fax 891428,
Pro 871490, Sec 839677,
Rest/Bar 871490
M20 exit 1, follow signs to St Paul's Cray and then signs to course.
Parkland course.
Pro Stephen Lee; Raphael Giannandrea; Founded 1973
Designed by Gilbert Lloyd
18 holes, 5712 yards, S.S.S. 68
⚑ 30.
† Public pay and play.
⚐ WD £16.75; WE £22.
⚑ Welcome; terms available on application.
🏵 Facilities available.

1A 141 St Augustine's
Cottington Road, Cliffsend, Ramsgate, Kent, CT12 5JN
☎ 01843 590333, Fax 590444,
Pro 590222
On B2048 off Ramsgate to Sandwich road.
Parkland course.
Pro Derek Scott; Founded 1907
Designed by Tom Vardon
18 holes, 5282 yards, S.S.S. 66
† Welcome with handicap certs.
⚐ WD £21.50; WE £23.50.
⚑ Welcome by appointment; from £25-£40.
🏵 Clubhouse facilities.
⌁ Jarvis Marine, Ramsgate; Blazing Donkey, Ham.

1A 142 St George's Hill
St George's Hill, Weybridge, Surrey, KT13 0NL
✉ admin@stgeorgeshillgolfclub.co.uk
☎ 01932 847758, Fax 821564,
Pro 843523
B374 towards Cobham, 0.5 miles from station.
Wooded heathland courses.
Pro AC Rattue; Founded 1913
Designed by HS Colt
27 holes, 6513 yards, S.S.S. 71
† Welcome Wed, Thurs, Fri by prior appointment.
⚐ WD £70 per round £95 per day.
⚑ Wed, Thurs, Fri only £125 to £140.
🏵 Full facilities available.
⌁ Oatlands Park Hotel; Hilton, Cobham.

1A 143 Sandown Golf Centre
More Lane, Esher, Surrey, KT10 8AN
☎ 01372 461234, Pro 461234,
Sec 461234, Rest/Bar 461234
In centre of Sandown Park racecourse.
Parkland course.
Cranfield Golf Academy; Founded 1967
Designed by John Jacobs
9 holes, 5656 yards, S.S.S. 68
† Welcome.
⚐ WD £6.75; WE £8.50.
⚑ Welcome.
🏵 Facilities available.
⌁ Haven Hotel, Sandown.

1A 144 Selsdon Park Hotel   ⚷
& GC
Addington Road, Sanderstead, South Croydon, Surrey, CR2 8YA
🖧 www.principalhotels.co.uk
☎ 020 8657 8811 ext 659,
Fax 8657 3401, Pro 8657 8811 ext 694,

Sec 86578811, Rest/Bar 86578811
Take A2022 towards Selsdon. Hotel entrance is 0.5 miles opposite Junction with Upper Selsdon Road.
Parkland/downland course.
Pro Malcolm Churchill; Founded 1929
Designed by JH Taylor
18 holes, 6473 yards, S.S.S. 71
⚑ 6.
† Welcome by prior arrangement.
⚐ WD £27.50; WE £32.50.
⚑ Welcome by prior arrangement; terms on application.
🏵 Catering in hotel.
⌁ Selsdon Park.

1A 145 Sene Valley
Sene, Folkestone, Kent, CT18 8BL
🖧 www.sceneatsene.cwc.net
☎ 01303 268513, Fax 237513,
Pro 268514, Sec 268513,
Rest/Bar 268513
M20 Junction 12, take A20 towards Ashford and left at 1st roundabout.
Downland course.
Pro Nick Watson; Founded 1888
Designed by Henry Cotton
18 holes, 6196 yards, S.S.S. 70
† Welcome with handicap certs.
⚐ WD £25; WE £30.
⚑ Welcome with prior arrangement.
🏵 Catering and bar facilities.
⌁ Sunny Bank House.

1A 146 Sheerness
Power Station Road, Sheerness, Kent, ME12 3AE
☎ 01795 662585, Fax 668180,
Pro 583060, Sec 662585,
Rest/Bar 662585
M2/M20 to A249 to Sheerness.
Seaside course.
Pro Leon Stanford; Founded 1906
18 holes, 6460 yards, S.S.S. 71
† WD welcome; WE with a member.
⚐ WD £18; WE £18.
⚑ Welcome WD by prior arrangement; from £34.
🏵 Clubhouse bar and catering facilities available.
⌁ Kingsferry GH, Isle of Sheppey.

1A 147 Shillinglee Park   ⚷
Chiddingfold, Godalming, Surrey, GU8 4TA
🖧 www.shillinglee.co.uk
☎ 01428 653237, Fax 644391,
Sec 6532377
Leave A3 at Milford, S on A283 to Chiddingfold; at top end of green turn left along local road, then after 2 miles turn right signposted Shillinglee;

Royal Cinque Ports

In 1920, Walter Hagen swept into Deal in the certain knowledge that he was about to win his first Open Championship. Everyone said that he was unbeatable, forgetting that they were merely repeating what Hagen had already told them. He finished in 55th place, 26 shots behind the joint winners – George Duncan and Royal Cinque Ports.

The spectators got to see Hagen play all manner of shots, although rather too many of them were not exactly what the great man had in mind. He failed to break 80 in any of his four rounds and is reputed to have had a side bet with his partner over the final eighteen holes as to which of them would finish last.

The local mullahs stroked their beards. They said that Hagen hit the ball too high to prevail on a windy links like Deal. Hagen retorted, "There are no bunkers in the air." After he was undone he added, "I tried too hard, just like any duffer might play. Guess I figured the boys were tougher than they were." Even Hagen wasn't taken in by that one.

It was the second and the last Open Championship to be held at Deal. The course was scheduled to stage the Open again in both 1938 and 1949, but high tides damaged the greens beforehand. The waters will have saved a few more Hagen's from ritual humiliation. Although Deal has hosted the Amateur and English Amateur in recent years, the Open is now unlikely ever to return.

Deal is a sadist. It opens up with a simple par four alongside the clubhouse. The second shot has to carry a ditch, but it would take a pretty dismal shot to get wet. The hole has claimed one notable victim. Abe Mitchell began the third round of the 1920 Open leading the field by six shots. He then left his eighteen-inch putt on the first green twelve inches short, a blow from which he never recovered.

Abe apart, the remainder of the outward nine continues to flatter the golfer who is anywhere near on top of his game. The tenth and eleventh should do little to dissipate the sense of self-satisfaction although neither is by any means a pushover. And then you turn for home. Only the lucky few will make it.

Having buttered you up for eleven holes, Deal then exposes you to the world as an abject hacker. Played into the prevailing southwesterly wind, the final seven holes comprise six unrelenting par fours and a long par three. You know how George Foreman must have felt when Muhammad Ali belted him on the button after all those rounds of rope-a-dope.

It is easy to imagine the mood of Henry Cotton when he said of Deal, "It is possible at nearly every hole to place a ball bang in the middle of the fairway and then find yourself in such an awkward position that a successful second can scarcely be played." It is not really true. I rather more suspect that Cotton had just come off the eighteenth green when he gave vent to such feelings.

There is only one thing more certain about Deal than a sense of outrage at the injustice of the finish. You will be back. — **Mark Reason**

entrance to course on left after 0.5 mile.
Public undulating parkland course.
Pro Mark Dowdell; Founded 1981
Designed by Roger Mace
9 holes, 2516 yards, S.S.S. 64
♱ Welcome, book in advance.
♣ WD £8.50; WE £9.50.
♧ Welcome; terms on application.
♒ Bar and restaurant 8.30am-6pm
(3pm Sun); evening meals and parties
by arrangement.
♞ Lythe Hill.

1A 148 Shirley Park
194 Addiscombe Road, Croydon,
Surrey, CR0 7LB
♒ www.shirleyparkgolfclub.co.uk
✉ secretary@
shirleyparkgolfclub.co.uk
☎ 020 8654 1143, Fax 8654 6733,
Pro 8654 8767, Sec 8654 1143,
Rest/Bar 8654 1143
On A232 1 mile E of E Croydon
station.
Parkland course.
Pro Raith Grant; Founded 1914
Designed by Tom Simson/Herbert
Fowler
18 holes, 6210 yards, S.S.S. 70
♱ Welcome WD; with a member only
at WE.
♣ WD £35; Sun £40.
♧ Various packages available.
♒ Full catering and bar.
♞ Croydon Park Hotel.

1A 149 Shooters Hill
Lowood, Eaglesfield Road, London,
SE18 3DA
☎ 020 8854 6368, Fax 8854 0469,
Pro 8854 0073, Sec 8854 6368,
Rest/Bar 8854 1216
Just past water tower on A207
Shooters Hill.
Hilly parkland/woodland course.
Pro Dave Brotherton; Founded 1903
Designed by Willie Park
18 holes, 5721 yards, S.S.S. 68
♱ Welcome WD with handicap cert.
♣ WD £22; £27 all day Mon-Fri.
♧ Tues, Thurs only; terms on
application.
♒ Full clubhouse facilities.
♞ Clarendon, Blackheath.

1A 150 Shortlands
Meadow Road, Shortlands, Kent, BR2
0PB
☎ 020 8460 2471, Pro 8464 6182
2 miles S of Bromley.
Parkland course.
Pro Mick; Founded 1894

10 holes, 5261 yards, S.S.S. 66
♱ With member only and handicap
cert.
♣ £10.
♧ By arrangement; terms on
application.
♒ Bar and catering.
♞ Bromley Court.

1A 151 Sidcup
7 Hurst Road, Sidcup, Kent, DA15 9AE
☎ 020 8300 2864, Pro 8309 0679,
Sec 8300 2150, Rest/Bar 8302 8661
A222 off A2, 400 yards N of station.
Parkland course.
Pro Nigel Willis; Founded 1891
Designed by James Braid and H Myrtl
9 holes, 5571 yards, S.S.S. 68
♱ Welcome; WE with member only;
handicap certs required, smart casual
dress.
♣ WD £18.
♧ Welcome; terms on application.
♒ Bar, restaurant, except Mon.
♞ Brickley Arms; Mariot Bexley
Heath.

1A 152 Silvermere
Redhill Road, Cobham, Surrey, KT11
1EF
✉ claire@silvermere.freeserve.uk
☎ 01932 867275, Fax 868259,
Pro 866894, Rest/Bar 864988
At Junction 10 of M25 and A3 take
A245 to Byfleet; Silvermere is 0.5 mile.
Parkland course.
Pro Doug McClelland; Founded 1976
18 holes, 6404 yards, S.S.S. 71
♣ 32.
♱ Welcome WD; WE by appointment
from Apr-Oct.
♣ WD £20; WE £30.
♧ Welcome WD; terms on application.
♒ Bar, restaurant.
♞ Bickley Arms; Swallow.

**1A 153 Sittingbourne & Milton
Regis**
Wormdale, Newington, Sittingbourne,
Kent, ME9 7PX
✉ sittingbourne@
golfclub.totalserve.co.uk
☎ 01795 842261, Fax 844117,
Pro 842775, Sec 842261,
Rest/Bar 842261
1 mile N of exit 5 off M2 on A249.
Undulating course.
Pro John Hearn; Founded 1929
Designed by Harry Hunter
18 holes, 6291 yards, S.S.S. 70
♱ Welcome WD if carrying handicap
certs.

♣ WD £25.
♧ Welcome Tues and Thurs; terms
on application.
♒ Facilities available.
♞ Coniston, Sittingbourne;
Newington Manor.

**1A 154 Southern Valley Golf
Course**
Thong Lane, Shorne, Gravesend;
Kent, DA12 4LF
♒ www.southernvalley.co.uk
✉ info@southernvalley.co.uk
☎ 01474 7400026
1/3 mile off A2 south of Gravesend.
Exit signposted to Chalk/Thong.
Links style.
18 holes, 6100 yards
♱ Yes.
♣ WD £16, WE £19.
♧ Yes.
♒ Yes.
♞ Manor Hotel, Gravesend; Inn on
the Lake, Gravesend.

1A 155 Staplehurst Golf Centre
Craddock Lane, Staplehurst, Kent,
TN12 0DR
☎ 01580 893362, Fax 893373
Course lies 9 miles south of Maidstone
on the A229 Hastings Road, turning on
to Headcorn Road at Staplehurst and
then right into Craddock Lane.
Parkland course.
Pro Colin Jenkins; Founded 1993
Designed by John Sayner
9 holes, 6114 yards, S.S.S. 70
♱ Open Range.
♱ Welcome.
♣ WD £12; WE £13.
♧ Welcome terms on application.
♒ Bar and snacks.
♞ Bell Inn, The George at Cranbrook.

**1A 156 American Golf at
Sunbury**
Charlton Lane, Shepperton, Middlesex,
TW17 8QA
✉ sunbury@americangolf.uk.com
☎ 01932 770298, Fax 789300,
Pro 771414
2 miles from M3 Junction 1.
Public parkland course.
Pro Alistair Hardaway; Founded 1992
Designed by Clive Clark/Peter Alliss
27 holes, 5103 yards, S.S.S. 65
♱ Welcome; golf shoes must be worn.
♣ WD £14; WE £20.
♧ Welcome by appointment; terms
on application.
♒ Bar and restaurant facilities in 16th
century clubhouse.

THE SELSDON PARK HOTEL & GOLF COURSE

SANDERSTEAD, NEAR SOUTH CROYDON, SURREY CR2 8YA

Pay & play parkland course, designed by J H Taylor. 18 holes, 6473 yards, Par 73, S.S.S. 71. Practice ground. Buggy hire. Pre-bookable tee times. Green fees: on application. Corporate Golf Days. Society Meetings. Golfing Breaks. Eating facilities: restaurant, grill and private dining. 204 de luxe en suite bedrooms. Superb conference/meeting facilities. PGA Professional: Malcolm Churchill

Golf Enquiries: **020-8657-8811**
Pro Shop: **020-8768-3116** • *Fax:* **020-8651-6174**
★★★★ De luxe ○○ AA/RAC

◦ Warren Lodge Hotel, Moat House.

1A 157 Sundridge Park
Garden Road, Bromley, Kent, BR1 3NE
⌂ www.spgc.co.uk
✉ secretary@spgc.co.uk
☎ 020 8460 0278, Fax 8289 3050,
Pro 8460 5540, Sec 8460 0278,
Rest/Bar 8460 1822/8289 3060
N of Bromley on A2212.
Parkland courses.
Pro Bob Cameron; Founded 1901
Designed by Willie Park
East 18. West 18 holes, East 6538.
West 6019 yards, S.S.S. East 71. West 69.
† Welcome WD; WE only with a member.
Ⅰ WD £50; WE £50 with a member only.
⌀ Welcome WD by prior appointment; terms available on application.
⦿ Full catering and bar.
◦ Bromley Court.

1A 158 Sundingdale *(see overleaf)*
Ridgemount Road, Sunningdale, Surrey, SL5 9RR
⌂ www.sunningdale-golfclub.co.uk
☎ 01344 621681, Fax 624154,
Pro 620128, Sec 621681,
Rest/Bar 621681
From M3 Junction 3 or M25 Junction 13; take A30.
Heathland courses.
Pro Keith Maxwell; Founded 1900
Designed by HS Colt
New 18. Old 18 holes, New 6703 Old 6609 yards, S.S.S. New 70. Old 72
† Mon-Thurs only; with max 18 handicap and letter of introduction.
Ⅰ WD £85 (New); £120 (Old); £145 WE (Both).
⌀ Tues, Wed, Thurs only; min 20 players, max 20 handicap; £205.

⦿ Full catering and bar.
◦ Berystede Hotel.

1A 159 Sunningdale Ladies
Cross Road, Sunningdale, Surrey, SL5 9RX
✉ ladiesgolf@lineone.net
☎ 01344 620507, Sec 620507,
Rest/Bar 620507
S of A30 600 yards W of Sunningdale level crossing.
Heathland course.
Founded 1902
Designed by Edward Villiers/HS Colt
18 holes, 3616 yards, S.S.S. 60
† Welcome with handicap certs but not before 11am at WE.
Ⅰ WD £22(men £22); WE £25 (men £25).
⌀ Societies; terms on application.
⦿ Full facilities, not Sun.

1A 160 Surbiton
Woodstock Lane, Chessington, Surrey, KT9 1UG
☎ 020 8398 3101, Fax 8339 0992,
Pro 8398 6619, Rest/Bar 8398 2056
From the A3 westbound take the Esher/Chessington turn-off, turn left to Claygate, and the club is 400 yards on right.
Parkland course.
Pro Paul Milton; Founded 1895
18 holes, 6055 yards, S.S.S. 69
† Welcome WD only; handicap certs required; members' guests only at WE.
Ⅰ WD £30; WE £17.
⌀ Welcome by prior arrangement; terms on application.
⦿ Full facilities.
◦ Haven, Esher; Travelodge.

1A 161 Sutton Green ⚲
New Lane, Sutton Green, Nr Guildford, Surrey, GU4 7QF
☎ 01483 747989, Fax 750289,

Pro 766849
Midway between Guildford and Woking on A320.
Parkland with water features.
Pro Tim Dawson; Founded 1994
Designed by Laura Davies and D Walker
18 holes, 6400 yards, S.S.S. 70
Ⅰ Grass covered.
† WD; after 1pm at WE.
Ⅰ WD £30; WE £40.
⌀ Welcome WD; packages available; from £29.50.
⦿ Full catering and bar.
◦ Forte Post House, Guildford; Cobham Hilton; Worplesdon Place.

1A 162 Tandridge
Oxted, Surrey, RH8 9NQ
⌂ www.tandridgegolfclub.com
✉ info@tandridge.fsnet.co.uk
☎ 01883 712274, Fax 730537,
Pro 713701, Sec 712274,
Rest/Bar 712273
From M25 Junction 6, take A22 and the A25.
Parkland course.
Pro Chris Evans; Founded 1924
Designed by H S Colt
18 holes, 6250 yards, S.S.S. 70
† Welcome Mon, Wed, Thurs.
Ⅰ WD £52, after 12 noon £40.
⌀ Welcome Mon, Wed, Thurs; £78.
⦿ Full clubhouse facilities.

1A 163 Tenterden
Woodchurch Road, Tenterden, Kent, TN30 7DR
⌂ www.tenterdengolfcourse.co.uk
✉ tenterden-golf-club@lineone.net
☎ 01580 763987, Fax 763987
Take A28 to Tenterden and at St Michaels take B2067.
Woodland course.
Pro Kyle Kelsall; Founded 1905
18 holes, 6152 yards, S.S.S. 69
† Welcome by appointment; with

member at WE.
 WD £22.50; WE £15.50.
⟁ Contact secretary; terms on application.
⦿ Catering facilities and bar.
⌁ White Lion; Little Silver.

1A 164 Thames Ditton & Esher
Scilly Isles, Portsmouth Road, Esher, Surrey, KT10 9AI
⧈ www.tdandegc.co.uk
☎ 0208 3981551
Off A3 by Scilly Isles roundabout (0.25 mile from Sandown Park Race Course).
Parkland course.
Pro Robert Jones; Founded 1892
9 holes, 2537 yards, S.S.S. 33
 Practice green 2 Driving nets
† Welcome Mon-Sat and Sun pm.
 WD £12; WE £14.
⟁ Max 28 booked in advance with Sec; terms on application.
⦿ Bar and snacks available.

1A 165 Tunbridge Wells ☽
Langton Road, Tunbridge Wells, Kent, TN4 8XH
☎ 01892 536918, Pro 541386, Sec 536918, Rest/Bar 523034
Behind Marchants Garage next to Spa Hotel.
Undulating parkland course.
Pro Mike Barton; Founded 1889
9 holes, 4725 yards, S.S.S. 62
† Welcome.
 WD £15.75; WE £26.25.
⟁ Contact Sec; terms on application.
⦿ By arrangement.
⌁ Spa; Periquito, Royal Wells.

1A 166 Tyrrell's Wood
The Drive, Tyrrell's Wood, Leatherhead, Surrey, KT22 8QP
☎ 01372 376025, Fax 360836, Pro 375200, Sec 376025, Rest/Bar 360702
2 miles SE of Leatherhead off the A24; M25 Junction 9, 1 mile.
Undulating course.
Pro Simon Defoy; Founded 1924
Designed by James Braid
18 holes, 6063 yards, S.S.S. 70
† Welcome WD.
 WD £34.
⟁ Welcome by appointment; from £40.
⦿ Full clubhouse facilities.
⌁ Burford Bridge Hotel.

1A 167 Upchurch River Valley
Oak Lane, Upchurch, Sittingbourne, Kent, ME9 7AY

☎ 01634 360626, Fax 387784, Pro 379592, Rest/Bar 378116
From M2 Junction 4 take A278 Gillingham road; then A2 for 2.5 miles towards Rainham.
Moorland/seaside courses.
Pro Roger Cornwell; Founded 1991
Designed by David Smart
18 holes, 6237 yards, S.S.S. 70;
 9 holes, 3192 yards, par 60
 24.
† Welcome; book 2 days in advance.
 WD £11.45; WE £14.45.
⟁ Welcome WD; min of 12 in party; terms on application.
⦿ Restaurant and bar facilities available.
⌁ Newington Manor; Rank Motor Lodge.

1A 168 Walmer & Kingsdown ☽
The Leas, Kingsdown, Deal, Kent, CT14 8EP
✉ kingsdown.golf@gtwiz.co.uk
☎ 01304 373256, Fax 382336, Pro 363017, Sec 373256, Rest/Bar 373256
Off A258 Dover to Deal road; follow signs to Kingsdown from Ringwould, signposted thereon.
Downland with views of English Channel.
Pro M Paget; Founded 1909
Designed by James Braid
18 holes, 6444 yards, S.S.S. 71
† Welcome by appointment with Pro.
 WD £25; WE £30.
⟁ Welcome by appointment; terms on application.
⦿ Full catering and bar.

1A 169 Walton Heath *(see overleaf)*
Off Deans Lane, Walton-On-The-Hill, Tadworth, Surrey, KT20 7TP
☎ 01737 812380, Fax 814225, Pro 812152, Sec 812380, Rest/Bar 813777
From the M25 exit at Junction 8 and take the A217, London bound. After the 2nd roundabout turn left into Mill Road and at the next junction left into Dorking Road. Deans Lane is 1.5 miles on right.
Heathland course.
Pro Ken MacPherson; Founded 1903
Designed by Herbert Fowler/James Braid
Old: 18. New: Old: 6817.
New: 6613 yards, S.S.S. Old: 73. New 72.
† By appointment only.
 WD £76 (before 10.30am), £65

(after 10.30am); WE £85.
⟁ By prior arrangement only; terms on application.
⦿ Full facilities in clubhouse.
⌁ Club can provide list.

1A 170 Weald of Kent
Maidstone Road, Headcorn, Kent, TN27 9PT
☎ 01622 890866, Fax 891793, Sec 891793, Rest/Bar 891793
7 miles from Maidstone on A274.
Parkland course.
Founded 1991
Designed by John Millen
18 holes, 5954 yards, S.S.S. 70
† Public pay and play course.
 WD £16; WE £20.
⟁ Welcome; from £15.
⦿ Catering and bar facilities.
⌁ Chilston Park; Great Danes; Shant.

1A 171 Wentworth
Wentworth Drive, Virginia Water, Surrey, GU25 4LS
⧈ www.wentworthclub.com
☎ 01344 842201, Fax 842804, Pro 846306, Sec 842201, Rest/Bar 846300
21 miles SW of London on A30/A329 Junction.
Heathland courses.
Pro D Rennie; Founded 1924
Designed by HS Colt
East: 18 holes, 6198 yards, S.S.S. 70;
West: 18 holes, 6957 yards, S.S.S. 74;
Edinburgh: 18 holes, 6979 yards, S.S.S. 73
† Welcome WD by appointment.
 WD.
⟁ Welcome by appointment Mon-Thurs; min 20; from £115. Driving range, caddies, buggies and golf clinics.
⦿ Top-class catering facilities available.
⌁ 16 rooms available at course.

1A 172 West Byfleet
Sheerwater Road, West Byfleet, Surrey, KT14 6AA
☎ 01932 345230, Fax 340667, Pro 346584, Sec 343433
On A245 in West Byfleet.
Woodland course.
Pro David Regan; Founded 1906
Designed by Cuthbert Butchart
18 holes, 6211 yards, S.S.S. 70
† Welcome by appointment, no WE.
 WD £33.
⟁ Welcome Mon, Tues, Wed; £67.

Sunningdale

George VI was once captain here and a day at Sunningdale is still something of a regal experience. The Old and the New (that will be eighty years young next year) courses offer two very different challenges, but both possess abundant charm.

The New Course is arguably tougher than the Old. Designed in 1923 by Harry Colt, it is not too arboreal, but it is still savage to anything weak off the tee, fiercely bunkered and full of mobile doglegs. Sunningdale actually encourages its members to allow their dogs to share a walk around what was once Chobham Common. For every foursome or fourball you come across, a black Labrador is more than likely to be in tow, watching its master, but refraining from criticism of his backswing.

The first is good preparation for what is in store; a long par four where the optimum tee shot is required. That shot is a well hit ball up the left, avoiding the slope that continues all the way down the right hand side. Keep left and a good start is on the cards. Fade it and fade away.

Two par threes quickly follow, but then the most demanding stretch begins. The par five sixth, at 485 yards, is short but is stroke index No.2 for a reason.

The drive must negotiate trees, heather and a couple of ditches and it doesn't get any easier after that. Two lakes obstruct a path to the two-tiered green which is also protected by many bunkers. Whatever the result, the hole will stick in your memory.

After another, and possibly the most tricky par three at the tenth, the wooden lodge that caters to both courses is an inviting sight. Maybe seduced by the thought of sausage sandwiches, mugs of coffee or a nip of whisky, Karrie Webb nearly visited it a little early in the 2001 Weetabix Women's Open when she thinned her bunker shot through the green.

It may not be quite as demanding as the New, but the Old course possesses something a little extra in terms of charm and history. It was here that Bobby Jones played his 'perfect' round in 1926, when qualifying for the Open which he won at Royal Lytham. He hit 66 shots; 33 on the front nine, 33 on the back. He also struck 33 shots from off the green and 33 putts. He had no score worse than a four although on ten of the holes his second had to be played with a wood or a 2-iron.

That says a great deal about how modern equipment has emasculated many of our great courses. These days the Old Course is a tad short to host a men's professional tournament. From the yellow tees it has three par fours of well under three hundred yards.

But for the rest of us it is a joy. The par threes test a wide range of shots, there is a sequence of par fours in the middle of the front nine that are both beautiful and bothersome and there is a really tough finish. If you can walk off the eighteenth green having negotiated the previous four holes in par, then you are almost bound to have scored well.

The famous old oak tree that looms behind the 18th has seen many fail in the attempt. As I headed for home, another of those black labradors was sitting under the oak as his master shook his head and cursed his luck at the three putts with which he had just concluded his round. Loping off to the clubhouse, the dog appeared less surprised. — **Jim Bruce-Ball**

🍴 Full clubhouse facilities.
🛏 Holiday Inn,Woking.

1A 173 West Hill
Bagshot Road, Brookwood, Surrey,
GU24 0BH
💻 www.westhill/golfclub.co.uk
💻 secretary@
westhill/golfclub.co.uk
☎ 01483 474365, Fax 474252,
Pro 473172, Rest/Bar 472110/474365
5 miles W of Woking on A322.
Heathland course.
Pro John Clements; Founded 1909
Designed by Willie Park/Jack White
18 holes, 6368 yards, S.S.S. 70
✝ Welcome WD with handicap certs;
WE only with member.
ℂ WD £60 day in summer; £25 per
round in winter.
⟳ WD except Wed, by prior
arrangement; packages available.
🍴 Full facilities and bar; jacket and
tie required in dining room.
🛏 Worplesdon Place, Perry Hill.

1A 174 West Kent
West Hill, Downe, Orpington, Kent,
BR6 7JJ
💻 www.wkgc. co.uk
☎ 01689 851323, Fax 858693,
Pro 856863, Sec 851323,
Rest/Bar 853737
A21 to Orpington, head for Downe
village; leave on Luxted Lane for 300
yards then right into West Hill.
Woodland course.
Pro Roger Fidler; Founded 1916
18 holes, 6385 yards, S.S.S. 70 Men
74 Women
✝ Welcome WD with letter from Sec
or handicap cert; must phone in
advance.
ℂ WD £30.
⟳ Welcome by appointment; terms
on application.
🍴 Full facilities.
🛏 Kings Arms Westrum.

1A 175 West Malling
London Road, Addington, Maidstone,
Kent, ME19 5AR
☎ 01732 844785, Fax 844795,
Pro 844022, Sec 844785
Course is off the A20, 8 miles NW of
Maidstone.
Parkland courses.
Pro Duncan Lambert; Founded 1974
Hurricane: 18. Spitfire: 18 holes,
Hurricane 6256. Spitfire 6142 yards,
S.S.S. Hurricane 70. Spitfire 70
ℐ 13.

✝ Welcome WD; WE afternoon.
ℂ WD £25; WE £30.
⟳ Welcome by appointment; terms
on application.
🍴 Full facilities.
🛏 Larkfield.

1A 176 West Surrey
Enton Green, Godalming, Surrey, GU8
5AF
💻 www.wsgc.co.uk
💻 westsurreygolfclub@
btinternet.com
☎ 01483 421275, Fax 415419,
Pro 417278, Sec 421275,
Rest/Bar 419786
0.5 miles SE of Milford Station.
Wooded parkland course.
Pro A Tawse; Founded 1910
Designed by Herbert Fowler
18 holes, 6300 yards, S.S.S. 70
ℐ 1 range for members only.
✝ By appointment with Sec.
ℂ WD £40 WE £50.
⟳ Welcome Wed, Thurs, Fri by
appointment; £65.
🍴 Full catering facilities.
🛏 Inn on the Lake.

1A 177 Westerham
Valence Park, Brasted Road,
Westerham, Kent, TN16 1LJ
💻 www.Golfbreaks.com
☎ 01959 567100, Fax 567101
On A25 between Brasted and
Westerham Village.
Woodland course.
Pro Robert Sturgeon; Founded 1997
Designed by David Williams
18 holes, 6272 yards, S.S.S. 72
ℐ Driving range; buggies available.
✝ Welcome.
ℂ WD £26; WE £35.
⟳ Welcome WD by appointment.
🍴 Restaurant, bar and function room.
🛏 Jarvis Fellbridge.

1A 178 Westgate & Birchington
176 Canterbury Road, Westgate-On-
Sea, Kent, CT8 8LT
☎ 01843 831115, Pro 831115,
Sec 831115, Rest/Bar 833905
0.25 miles from Westgate station off
A28.
Parkland by the sea.
Pro Roger Game; Founded 1892
18 holes, 4889 yards, S.S.S. 64
✝ Welcome after 10am Mon-Sat;
after 11am Sun.
ℂ WD £15.00; WE £17.00 both
prices inclusive of insurance.
⟳ Welcome by appointment; Thurs

preferred; terms on application.
🍴 Clubhouse facilities.
🛏 The Promenade Travel Lodge.

1A 179 Whitstable & Seasalter
Collingwood Road, Whitstable, Kent,
CT5 1EB
💻 wsgc@tinyworld.co.uk
☎ 01227 272020, Fax 280822,
Sec 272020, Rest/Bar 272020
On A290 to Whitstable.
Seaside links course.
Founded 1910
9 holes, 5357 yards, S.S.S. 63
✝ By arrangement.
ℂ WD £15; WE £15.
⟳ Not welcome.
🍴 Full catering facilities.
🛏 Marine Hotel, Tankerton.

1A 180 Wildernesse
Seal, Sevenoaks, Kent, TN15 0JE
💻 www.wildernesse.co.uk
☎ 01732 761526, Fax 763809,
Pro 761527, Sec 761199,
Rest/Bar 761526
Off A25 in Seal village.
Rolling parkland course.
Pro Craig Walker; Founded 1890
Designed by W Park
18 holes, 6448 yards, S.S.S. 72
✝ Letter of introduction is required;
not WE.
ℂ WD £40.
⟳ Apply to Sec; terms on application.
🍴 Bar and restaurant.

1A 181 Wildwood Country Club
Horsham Road, Alfold, Cranleigh,
Surrey, GU6 8JE
💻 www.wildwoodgolf.co.uk
💻 enquiries@wildwoodgolf.co.uk
☎ 01403 753255, Fax 752005
On A281 Guildford to Horsham road 10
miles from Guildford.
Parkland course.
Pro Simon Andrews; Founded 1992
Designed by Martin Hawtree
18 holes, 6655 yards, S.S.S. 72
ℐ 7 mat and 9-hole par 3 course.
✝ Welcome.
ℂ WD £30; WE £45.
⟳ Welcome WD; packages available;
from £26.
🍴 Full catering and bar.
🛏 Random Hall, Slinfold.

1A 182 Wimbledon Common
19 Camp Road, Wimbledon Common,
London, SW19 4UW
💻 www.wcgc.co.uk

Walton Heath

The club's official website states that "Walton Heath Golf Club was founded by Sir Cosmo Bonsor and his son and the courses were designed by Sir Herbert Fowler who was related to them by marriage." There must be a lot of people who wish that they were related by marriage to the Old and the New courses at Walton Heath and I am certainly one of them.

The first live golf event that I ever saw was at Walton Heath and it wasn't a bad place or a bad match to begin with. It was the 1981 Ryder Cup, when Europe was understandably trounced by an American team comprising of Lee Trevino, Tom Kite, Bill Rogers (probably the best golfer in the world that year), Larry Nelson, Ben Crenshaw, Bruce Lietzke, Jerry Pate, Hale Irwin, Johnny Miller, Tom Watson, Ray Floyd and Jack Nicklaus. The Americans were simply breathtaking, but so too was the golf course.

Wild and exposed Walton Heath's Old Course is the most extraordinary of Surrey's heathland courses. Set on chalk, the ball can bound on forever; the twists and turns and ups and downs never fail to surprise you and the wind can play havoc. When discussing the merits of inland and links golf, Peter Dobereiner wrote: "There is no reconciling the opposing views, but if ever the twain should meet, it would surely be at Walton Heath."

The course insists on placement all the way round and the wonderful greens can be deceptive on first sight. Even on a recent visit I was completely fooled by the way my playing partner's chip checked and apparently failed to roll out. Assuming the green to be a little woolly, I nearly sent my twelve-foot putt off the putting surface altogether. Mind you, that won't surprise those who have seen me putt.

Pragmatic changes to the course mean that the start is perhaps not all that it once was, but once you get into your stride, there is a procession of wonderful par fours before you hit a finish that Tom Weiskopf described as amongst the best he had seen.

There are three par fives in the final six holes of which the best is probably the sixteenth. The tee shot must avoid the heather on either side before, turning the corner slightly; the second is to a green on a crest protected by an ogreish bunker. If you lay up, the green's elevation makes judgement of the third extremely difficult. Turning at right angles from the green is the par three seventeenth over a valley and with a cluster of bunkers to embrace a misclubbed tee shot. The eighteenth is a longish four with a bunker running across the fairway before the green and a hedge behind.

Apart from the greatness of the Old Course, the delights of the New Course and a fabulous practice putting green that must be the best in England, there is something else to Walton Heath. I don't know whether it is because it was once owned by the News of the World or because David Lloyd George and Winston Churchill were once members, but there is a raffish charm to the place.

Henry Longhurst used to love to tell the story of an incident at Walton Heath involving Wash Carr, a friend of his from Cambridge. "Wash Carr hit a drive right up the middle, only to find the ball deep in a divot mark. 'That'd be a nice one to get in the Medal,' he said to his caddie. 'You'd never 'ave 'ad it in the Medal,' said the man darkly."

Maybe that was what Bernard Darwin meant when he said, "If there is anything that golfers want and do not get at Walton Heath I do not know what it can be."— **Mark Reason**

✉ secretary@wcgc.co.uk
☎ 020 8946 0294, Fax 8947 8697,
Pro 8946 0294, Sec 8946 7571,
Rest/Bar 8946 0294
1 mile NW of War Memorial past Fox
and Grapes.
Links type wooded course.
Pro J S Jukes; Founded 1908
Designed by Tom and Willie Dunn
18 holes, 5438 yards, S.S.S. 66
† Welcome WD.
Ⓘ WD £15 (Mon £10).
⌂ Welcome Tues-Fri by appointment;
terms on application.
Ⓘ Full facilities.
↪ Canizaro House.

1A 183 Wimbledon Park
Home Park Road, Wimbledon, London,
SW19 7HR
🖥 www.wpgc.co.uk
☎ 020 8946 1002, Fax 8944 8688,
Pro 8946 4053, Sec 8946 1250
Near Wimbledon Park District Line
tube.
Parkland course.
Pro Dean Wingrove; Founded 1898
Designed by Willie Park Jnr
18 holes, 5492 yards, S.S.S. 66
† Welcome WD with handicap certs.
Ⓘ WD £40.
⌂ Welcome Tues, Thurs by
appointment; terms available on
application.
Ⓘ Full facilities available except Mon.
↪ Canizaro House.

1A 184 Windlemere
Windlesham Road, West End, Woking,
Surrey, GU24 9QL
☎ 01276 858727, Pro 858727,
Sec 858727, Rest/Bar 858727
Take A322 from Bagshot towards
Guildford; turn left on A319 towards
Chobham, course is on left opposite
Gordon Boys School.
Gently undulating public parkland
course.
Pro David Thomas; Founded 1978
Designed by Clive D Smith
9 holes, 2673 yards, S.S.S. 34
Ⓘ 13.
† Open to public on payment of
green fees.
Ⓘ WD £9; WE £10.50.
⌂ By appointment with Pro; terms on
application.
Ⓘ Bar snacks always available.

1A 185 Windlesham   ⚷
Grove End, Bagshot, Surrey, GU19 5HY
🖥 www.windleshamgolf.com

☎ 01276 452220, Fax 452290
At Junction of A30 and A322.
Parkland course.
Pro Lee Mucklow; Founded 1994
Designed by Tommy Horton
18 holes, 6650 yards, S.S.S. 72
Ⓘ 3 covered bays. 10 outdoor.
† Welcome except before noon at
WE; handicap certs required.
Ⓘ WD £25; WE £35.
⌂ Welcome Mon-Fri by prior
appointment; terms available on
application.
Ⓘ Bar and restaurant.
↪ Berrystead.

1A 186 The Wisley
Mill Lane, Ripley, Nr Woking, Surrey,
GU23 6QU
☎ 01483 211022, Fax 211622,
Pro 211213
Exit A3 at Ockham, Send and Ripley,
3rd exit from the roundabout and first
left into Mill Lane.
Parkland course 3 x 9 holes.
Pro Hugh Marr; Founded 1991
Designed by Robert Trent Jones, Jr.
27 holes, 6858 yards, S.S.S. 73
Ⓘ Large practice ground.
† Private members' club.
⌂ None.
Ⓘ Full clubhouse catering and bar
facilities.

1A 187 Woking
Pond Road, Hook Heath, Woking,
Surrey, GU22 0JZ
☎ 01483 760053, Fax 772441,
Pro 769582, Sec 760053,
Rest/Bar 760053
Off A322 after West Hill GC.
Oldest heathland course in Surrey.
Pro Carl Bianco; Founded 1893
Designed by Tom Dunn
18 holes, 6340 yards, S.S.S. 70
† WD with a handicap cert; WE only
with member.
Ⓘ WD £58.
⌂ By appointment with 12 months'
notice.
Ⓘ Full facilities.
↪ Glen Court, Woking; Worplesdon
Place, Worplesdon.

1A 188 Woodcote Park
Meadow Hill, Bridleway, Coulsden,
Surrey, CR5 2QQ
☎ 020 8668 2788, Fax 8660 0918,
Pro 8668 1843,
Rest/Bar 8660 0176
2 miles N of Purley on Coulsdon-
Wallington road.

Parkland course.
Pro Ian Golding; Founded 1912
Ⓘ Practice Area.
† Welcome by appointment and with
handicap certs, not WE.
Ⓘ WD £30.
⌂ Welcome by appointment; Varied
society prices.
Ⓘ Catering and bar facilities.

1A 189 Woodlands Manor
Tinkerpot Lane, Sevenoaks, Kent,
TN15 6AB
☎ 01959 523805, Pro 524161,
Sec 523806
Off A225, 4 miles NE of Sevenoaks, 5
miles S of M25 Junction 3.
Undulating parkland course.
Pro Phil Womack; Founded 1928
Designed by N Coles, J Lyons
18 holes, 6037 yards, S.S.S. 68
† Welcome WD; not WE.
Ⓘ WD £21.
⌂ Welcome Mon-Fri by appointment;
terms on application.
Ⓘ Meals served.
↪ Thistle (Brands Hatch).

**1A 190 World of Golf (Jack
Nicklaus Golf Centre)**
Sidcup by-pass, Chislehurst, Kent,
BR7 6RP
🖥 www.World of Golf-uk.co.uk
✉ SC.World of golf@line1.net
☎ 020 8309 0181, Fax 8308 1691
Course is on the main A20 London
Road.
Parkland course.
Pro David Bailey
Designed by M Gillet
9 holes, 1055 yards
Ⓘ Practice range 54 bays floodlit.
† Welcome only if accompanied by a
member. Driving range open to public
course members.
Ⓘ WD £3.50; WE £3.50.
⌂ Welcome Terms on Application.
Ⓘ Cafe Bar.
↪ Stakis Nr Dartford Tunnel.

1A 191 Worplesdon
Heath House Road, Woking, Surrey,
GU22 0RA
☎ 01483 472277, Fax 473303,
Pro 473287, Sec 472277
Leave Guildford on A322 to Bagshot,
6 miles turn right into Heath House
Road.
Heathland course.
Pro Jim Christine; Founded 1908
Designed by JF Abercromby
18 holes, 6440 yards, S.S.S. 71

✝ Welcome WD only by prior arrangement.

ɪ WD £46 (Nov-Feb £30).

⌂ Welcome WD by prior appointment (except Tues); terms on application.

🍽 Bar and Catering Facilities Daily.

🛌 Worplesdon Place.

1A 192 Wrotham Heath
Seven Mile Lane, Borough Green, Sevenoaks, Kent, TN15 8QZ

☎ 01732 884800, Fax 887370

Off A20 near junction with A25.

Woodland/heathland course.

Pro Harry Dearden; Founded 1906

Designed by Donald Steel

18 holes, 5954 yards, S.S.S. 69

✝ Welcome WD with handicap certs, not WE or BH without member.

ɪ WD £25.

⌂ Welcome Fri only; terms on application.

🍽 Full catering by arrangement with Steward, except Mon.

🛌 Post House.

1B

Hertfordshire, Essex, Middlesex, North London

Henry Cotton, the winner of three Open Championships, wore "silk monogrammed shirts and drove a large motor car, which he had a tendency to park opposite a sign saying 'No parking'." His exhibitionism did much to put Ashridge on the map when he was employed as the club's professional in 1937, five years after its foundation.

The four woods that he used to win the Open Championship at Carnoustie that same year are on display in the clubhouse, although they will soon have to move home as Ashridge expands from its current modest building. Cotton would doubtless have been pleased to see the club barging its way into the twenty-first century. His professional's shop went about its business as immodestly as possible.

When you survey the par four ninth hole at Ashridge, the line of the drive is not an obvious one and the green does not come into consideration until hopefully the second shot. Unless you are Cotton. He devised a low hooker to take maximum advantage of the downslope, kicking onto the green over 350 yards away.

With three reachable par fives in the final six holes Ashridge offers an encouraging finish to those who have so far held their score together.

Berkhamsted has some unusual hazards to overcome. Accuracy off the tee is a prerequisite although there are no bunkers to bother about. An ancient earthwork called Grim's Dyke provides the natural obstacle on seven of the holes, once again raising a finger at those who like to scatter sand all over the place.

Several such American-style courses have reared their ugly heads around Colchester in Essex. They are far too long for most amateurs, far too sandy and full of artificial lakes. But there is more to Essex than these modern monstrosities.

Thorpe Hall has been the home club of Sir Michael Bonallack for several years and Thorndon Park, designed by Harry Colt, is a lush course with lots of intrigue once the nondescript opening hole is out of the way.

For some bizarre reason many of these courses to the north of London are dominated by huge houses. Thorndon Park has a neo-classical mansion; Hanbury Manor is the site of a former convent now a luxury hotel; and Moor Park is the home of a grade 1 listed historic building that is inconceivably grand. Happily Moor Park's two golf courses are rather better conceived than the attack on Arnhem – the subject of the film 'A Bridge Too Far' – which was planned here.

The High Course is considered to be the better of the two courses. Unusually it finishes with a par three, but the real scandal was caused by the pond beside the eighth green, inserted long before water features became all the rage. Just up the road Sandy Lodge also finishes with a par three. There is some fierce bunkering on the opening two holes of Sandy Lodge, although the name of the club did not apparently derive from the amount of balls that tended to plug in the face.

North London's principal courses are Highgate, Hampstead, Hendon, Fulwell and Mill Hill. Soft spikes are recommended for Mill Hill, not because the course has a reputation for aridity, just the opposite in fact, but to negotiate the scuttle across a busy dual carriageway necessary to reach the first tee.

1B 1 **Abbey View**

Holywell Hill, Westminster Lodge, St
Albans, Herts, AL1 2DJ
☎ 01727 868227, Pro 868227,
Sec 868227
In centre of St Albans.
Public parkland course.
Pro Roddy Watkins; Founded 1990
Designed by Jimmy Thomson
9 holes, 1383 yards
† Open to public at all times.
[WD £5.50; WE £5.50.
⟲ Welcome; terms on application.
⦿ Tea/coffee on site; cafe in main
centre.

1B 2 **Abridge G & CC**

Epping Lane, Stapleford Tawney,
Essex, RM4 1ST
⬚ www.abridgegolfclub.co.uk
✉ lynn@abridgegolf.freeserve.co.uk
☎ 01708 688396, Fax 688550,
Pro 688333, Sec 688396,
Rest/Bar 688367
M11 from London exit 5 via Abridge;
from the N, M11 exit 7 via Epping.
Parkland course.
Pro Stuart Layton; Founded 1964
Designed by Henry Cotton
18 holes, 6686 yards, S.S.S. 72
† Welcome WD only; handicap certs
required.
[WD £33.
⟲ Mon, Wed and Fri; terms on
application.
⦿ Available every day.
↵ Post House, Epping.

1B 3 **Airlinks**

Southall Lane, Hounslow, Essex, TW5
9PE
☎ 020 8561 1418, Fax 8813 6284,
Pro 8561 1418,
Rest/Bar 8561 1418
M4 Junction 3 on to A312 and A4020;
part of David Lloyd Tennis Centre.
Public meadowland/parkland course.
Pro Tony Martin; Founded 1984
Designed by P Alliss
18 holes, 5813 yards, S.S.S. 68
𝄃 24.
† Welcome; some restrictions at
weekends.
[WD £12; WE £18.
⟲ Welcome Mon-Fri; fees negotiable.
⦿ Bar snacks, hot and cold meals
available.
↵ London Airport hotels nearby.

1B 4 **Aldenham G & CC**   ₡

Church Lane, Aldenham, Nr Watford,
Herts, WD25 8NN

✉ aldenhamgolf@ukonline.co.uk
☎ 01923 853929, Fax 858472,
Pro 857889
M1 Junction 5 on to A41, left at
roundabout to A462 and then into
Church Road.
Parkland course.
Pro Tim Dunstan; Founded 1975
18; 9 holes, 6480; 2350 yards,
S.S.S. 71
† Welcome WD but afternoon only at
WE.
[WD £25; WE £32.
⟲ Welcome WD and WE afternoons;
Full catering packages and 36 holes of
golf; from £54.
⦿ Full facilities.
↵ Watford Hilton National; Jarvis
International.Premier Lodge; Red Lion;
Elstree Inn.

1B 5 **Aldwickbury Park**   ₡

Piggottshill Lane, Harpenden, Herts,
AL5 1AB
⬚ www.aldwickburyparkgolfclub.com
✉ enquiries@
aldwiclkburyparkgolfclub.com
☎ 01582 760112, Fax 760113,
Pro 760112, Sec 765112,
Rest/Bar 766463
10 mins from M1 Junction 9 on road
between Harpenden and
Wheathampstead.
Parkland course.
Pro James Jones; Founded 1995
Designed by K Brown/M Gillett
18 holes, 6352 yards, S.S.S. 70
† Welcome WD; after 1pm WE.
[WD £24; WE £30.
⟲ Welcome WD; 36 holes, coffee and
biscuits, lunch, 3-course dinner; other
packages available; £49.
⦿ Full catering and bar.
↵ Harpenden House.

1B 6 **Arkley**

Rowley Green Road, Barnet, Herts,
EN5 3HL
⬚ www.arkleygolfclub.co.uk
✉ secretary@arkleygolfclub.co.uk
☎ 020 8449 0555, Fax 8440 5214,
Pro 8440 8473, Sec 8449 0394,
Rest/Bar 8449 0394
Off A1 at Arkley.
Parkland course.
Pro Martin Porter; Founded 1909
Designed by James Braid
9 holes with 18 tees, 6117 yards,
S.S.S. 69
† Welcome WD but with members
only at WE.
[WD £22.
⟲ Welcome Wed and Fri; terms on

application.
⦿ Full catering facilities except Mon.

1B 7 **Ashford Manor**   ₡

Fordbridge Road, Ashford, Middx,
TW15 3RT
⬚ www.amgc.co.uk
✉ postmaster@amgc.co.uk
☎ 01784 257687, Fax 420355,
Pro 255940, Sec 424644,
Rest/Bar 424641/424642
Off A308 between Staines and Sunbury.
0.5 miles from Fordbridge roundabout.
Wooded parkland course.
Pro Ian Partington; Founded 1898
18 holes, 6352 yards, S.S.S. 70
† Welcome WD with handicap certs.
[WD £30 £35 for the day.
⟲ Welcome WD by prior
arrangement; golf, morning coffee,
lunch, afternoon tea, dinner.
⦿ Full catering facilities.
↵ Shepperton Moathouse; The Ship,
Shepperton.

1B 8 **Ashridge**

Little Gaddesden, Berkhamsted, Herts,
HP4 1LY
⬚ www.ashridgegolfclub.ltd.uk
☎ 01442 842244, Fax 843770,
Pro 842307, Sec 842307,
Rest/Bar 842379
4 miles N of Berkhamstead on B4506.
Parkland course.
Pro Andrew Ainsworth; Founded 1932
Designed by Sir Guy Campbell/Colonel
Hotchkin
18 holes, 6547 yards, S.S.S. 71
𝄃 14.
† Welcome WD only.
[WD £47.
⟲ WD only; terms on application.
⦿ Full facilities.

1B 9 **Ballards Gore**   ₡

Gore Road, Canewdon, Essex, SS4 2DA
☎ 01702 258917, Fax 258571,
Pro 258924, Sec 258917
From London via A127 to Southend
Airport, then through Rochford on to
Great Stambridge road; course 1.5
miles from Rochford centre.
Parkland course.
Pro Richard Emery; Founded 1980
Designed by D and JJ Caton
18 holes, 6845 yards, S.S.S. 73
† Welcome WD; guest of member
only at WE, Sun after 2pm.
[WD £25.
⟲ WD by arrangement with Sec,
subject to availability; terms on
application.

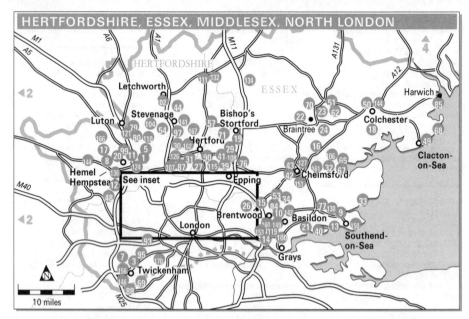

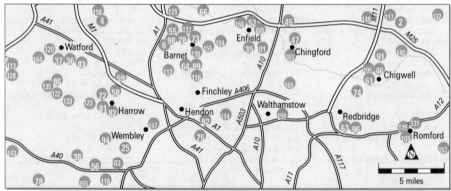

🍽 Bar and restaurant; private functions.
🥢 Renouf.

1B 10 **Basildon**
Clay Hill Lane, Basildon, Essex, SS16 5JP
☎ 01268 533297, Fax 533849, Pro 533352
On A176 S of Basildon via either A127 or A13.
Undulating wooded parkland.
Pro Mike Oliver; Founded 1967
Designed by A H Cotton
18 holes, 6236 yards, S.S.S. 70
† Welcome.
ʃ WD £9; WE £15.
⌂ Welcome, packages by prior

arrangement; terms on application.
🍽 Restaurant and bar.
🥢 Haywain; Campanile, Basildon.

1B 11 **Batchwood Hall**
Batchwood Tennis And Golf Centre, St Albans, Herts, AL3 5XA
☎ 01727 833349, Fax 850586, Pro 844250
NW corner of St Albans; 5 miles S of M1 Junction 9.
Parkland course.
Pro Mark Flitton; Founded 1935
Designed by J H Taylor
18 holes, 6509 yards, S.S.S. 71
ʃ 18-hole putting green.
† Welcome.

ʃ WD £10; WE £13.
⌂ Welcome by prior arrangement; packages available; tennis courts; 2 squash courts; fitness gym; dance studio.
🍽 Bar and restaurant.
🥢 Aubry Park.

1B 12 **Batchworth Park**
London Road, Rickmansworth, Herts, WD3 1JS
🖧 www.crownsportplc.com
🖥 bpgc@crownsportplc.com
☎ 01923 711400, Fax 710200, Pro 714922
From M 25 Junction 17 towards Rickmansworth to the Batchworth

KEY					
		35 Bush Hill Park	70 Gosfield Lake	104 Little Hay Golf Complex	139 Stanmore
1	Abbey View	36 Bushey G & CC	71 Great Hadham	105 Loughton	140 Stapleford Abbotts
2	Abridge G & CC	37 Bushey Hall	72 Grim's Dyke	106 Maldon	141 Stevenage
3	Airlinks	38 C & L Golf & CC	73 Hadley Wood	107 Malton	142 Stock Brook Manor
4	Aldenham G & CC	39 Canons Brook	74 Hainault Forest	108 Manor of Groves G & CC	143 Stockley Park
5	Aldwickbury Park	40 Castle Point	75 Hampstead	109 Maylands Golf & CC	144 Stocks Hotel & CC
6	Arkley	41 Chadwell Springs	76 Hanbury Manor G& CC	110 Mid-Herts	145 Stoke-by-Nayland
7	Ashford Manor	42 Channels	77 Hanover	111 Mill Green	146 Strawberry Hill
8	Ashridge	43 Chelmsford	78 Harefield Place	112 Mill Hill	147 Sudbury
9	Ballards Gore	44 Chesfield Downs	79 Harpenden	113 Moor Park	148 Theydon Bois
10	Basildon	45 Cheshunt	80 Harpenden Common	114 Muswell Hill	149 Thorndon Park
11	Batchwood Hall	46 Chigwell	81 Harrow Hill	115 The Nazeing	150 Thorpe Hall
12	Batchworth Park	47 Chingford	82 Harrow School	116 North Middlesex	151 Three Rivers Golf & CC
13	Belfairs Park	48 Chorleywood	83 Hartsbourne G & CC	117 North Weald Golf Club	152 Toothill
14	Belhus Park (Thurrock)	49 Clacton-on-Sea	84 Hartswood	118 Northwood	153 Top Meadow
15	Bentley	50 Colchester	85 Harwich & Dovercourt	119 Orsett	154 Trent Park
16	Benton Hall	51 Colne Valley (Essex)	86 Haste Hill	120 Oxhey Park	155 Tudor Park Sports Gd
17	Berkhamsted	52 Crews Hill	87 Hatfield London CC	121 Panshanger	156 Twickenham Park
18	Birch Grove	53 Crondon Park	88 Hazelwood	122 Perivale Park	157 Upminster
19	Bishop's Stortford	54 Danesbury Park	89 Hendon	123 Pinner Hill	158 Verulam
20	Boxmoor	55 Dyrham Park	90 The Hertfordshire	124 Porters Park	159 Wanstead
21	Boyce Hill	56 Ealing	91 High Beech	125 Potters Bar	160 Warley Park
22	Braintree	57 East Herts	92 Highgate	126 Redbourn	161 Warren
23	Braintree Towerlands	58 Edgewarebury	93 Hillingdon	127 Regiment Way	162 Welwyn Garden City
24	Braxted Park	59 Elstree	94 Horsenden Hill	128 Rickmansworth	163 West Essex
25	Brent Valley	60 Enfield	95 Hounslow Heath	129 Risebridge (Havering)	164 West Herts
26	Brentwood	61 Epping Forest Golf & CC	96 Ilford	130 Rochford Hundred	165 West Middlesex
27	Brickendon Grange	62 Essex Golf & CC	97 Knebworth	131 Romford	166 Whipsnade Park
28	Bridgedown	63 Fairlop Waters	98 Laing Sports Club	132 Royston	167 Whitehill
29	Briggens House Hotel	64 Finchley	99 Lamerwood	133 Ruislip	168 Whitewebbs
30	Brocket Hall	65 Five Lakes Hotel	100 Langdon Hills	134 Saffron Walden	169 Woodford
31	Brookmans Park	66 Forest Hills	101 Lee Valley	135 Sandy Lodge	170 Wyke Green
32	Bunsay Downs	67 Forrester Park	102 Letchworth	136 Shendish Manor	
33	Burnham-on-Crouch	68 Frinton	103 Limetrees Park Golf	137 Simpson Golf Club	
34	The Burstead	69 Fulwell	Course	138 South Herts	

roundabout; course 400 yards.
Parkland course.
Pro Steven Proudfoot; Founded 1996
Designed by Dave Thomas
18 holes, 6723 yards, S.S.S. 72
⚲ Practice range for members and
guests.
♦ Private; members and guests only.
⌶ Not available.
⦿ Bar and restaurant.
↰ Jarvis Watford.

1B 13 Belfairs Park (Southend-on-Sea)

Starter's Hut, Eastwood Road North,
Leigh-On-Sea, Essex, SS9 4LR
☎ 01702 252345, Pro 520202
4.5 miles from Southend centre;
Eastwood Rd links A127 and A13. Set
in Belfairs Park.
Parkland/Woodland course.
Pro Martin Foreman; Founded 1926
Designed by HS Colt
18 holes, 5840 yards, S.S.S. 68
♦ Unrestricted; bookings every day,
week in advance or on day.
⌶ WD £10; WE £15.80.
⌔ Welcome; terms available on
application.
⦿ Public restaurant.
↰ Westcliff Hotel.

1B 14 Belhus Park (Thurrock)

Belhus Park, South Ockendon, Essex,
RM15 4QR
☎ 01708 854260, Fax 854260,
Pro 854260, Sec 852907,
Rest/Bar 852907
A13 to Avely.
Public parkland course.
Pro Gary Lunn; Founded 1972
Designed by Frank Pennink
18 holes, 5589 yards, S.S.S. 69
⚲ 12; floodlit.
♦ Bookings can be made at course
WD; in advance by phone WE
(booking card required).
⌶ WD £10.00; WE £15.
⌔ Welcome; terms on application.
⦿ Bar and restaurant.
↰ Thurrock Hotel.

1B 15 Bentley

Ongar Road, Brentwood, Essex, CM15
9SS
☎ 01277 373179, Fax 375097,
Pro 372933, Sec 373179,
Rest/Bar 373179
On A128 between Brentwood and
Ongar.
Parkland course with water hazards.
Pro Nick Garrett; Founded 1972
Designed by Alec Swan
18 holes, 6709 yards, S.S.S. 72
♦ Welcome WD.
⌶ WD £22.

⌔ Welcome WD; terms on
application.
⦿ Full catering facilities.
↰ The Holiday Inn Brentwood.

1B 16 Benton Hall

Wickham Hill, Witham, Essex, CM8 3LH
⣀ www.clubhaus.com
☎ 01376 502454, Fax 521050
Off A12 at Witham; course is well
signposted.
Woodland course.
Pro C Fairweather; Founded 1993
Designed by Alan Walker and Charlie
Cox
18 holes, 6495 yards, S.S.S. 72
♦ Welcome by prior arrangement.
⌶ Terms on application.
⌔ Welcome WD by prior
arrangement; packages available; from
£37.50.
⦿ Clubhouse facilities.

1B 17 Berkhamsted

The Common, Berkhamsted, Herts,
HP4 2QB
☎ 01442 865832, Fax 863730,
Pro 865851, Rest/Bar 870965
1 mile N of Berkhamsted.
Heathland course.
Pro Basil Proudfoot; Founded 1890
Designed by GH Gowring (1890-92
Founder)

18 holes, 6605 yards, S.S.S. 72
♦ Welcome with handicap certificate.
⟨ WD £30; WE £40.
⟨⟩ Welcome Wed and Fri; maximum £50.
⟨●⟩ Meals and bar facilities.
⟨⟩ Hemel Hempstead Post House.

1B 18 Birch Grove

Layer Road, Colchester, Essex, CO2 0HS
☎ 01206 734276, Fax 734276, Pro 734276, Sec 734103
On B1026 3 miles S of Colchester.
Parkland course.
Pro C Laitt; Founded 1970
Designed by Course owners
9 holes, 4038 yards, S.S.S. 66
♦ Welcome.
⟨ £9 9 holes; £12 18 holes.
⟨⟩ Welcome by arrangement; golf and 4-course dinner, bar, dining area; £15-21.
⟨●⟩ Full facilities.
⟨⟩ Kingsford Park Hotel.

1B 19 Bishop's Stortford

Dunmow Road, Bishop's Stortford, Herts, CM23 5HP
⟨⟩ www.bsgc.co.uk
✉ bishopstortfordgc@hotmail.com
☎ 01279 654715, Fax 655215, Pro 651324, Sec 654715, Rest/Bar 461779
From M11 Junction 8 follow signs to Bishop's Stortford; course is 1.5 miles on left.
Well-established, undulating, parkland.
Pro Steve Bryan; Founded 1910
Designed by James Braid
18 holes, 6404 yards, S.S.S. 71
♦ Welcome with handicap certs; not at WE.
⟨ WD £27 (round), £35 (day); WE guest of members only.
⟨⟩ Welcome by prior arrangement; varied packages available (minimum 12); Tues (Ladies' day) exc; special winter deals; from £35-65.
⟨●⟩ Full restaurant and bar bistro.
⟨⟩ Stansted Airport; Downhall, Hatfield Heath.

1B 20 Boxmoor

18 Box Lane, Hemel Hempstead, Herts, HP3 0DJ
☎ 01442 242434
On A41 0.75 miles from Hemel Hempstead station.
Undulating parkland course.
Founded 1890
9 holes, 4812 yards, S.S.S. 64
♦ Welcome except Sun.

⟨ WD £10; WE £15.
⟨⟩ Welcome with month's notice.
⟨●⟩ Limited service; meals available by prior arrangement.
⟨⟩ Boxmoor Lodge.

1B 21 Boyce Hill

Vicarage Hill, South Benfleet, Essex, SS7 1PD
✉ boycehill@hotmail.com
☎ 01268 793625, Fax 750497, Pro 752565, Sec 793625, Rest/Bar 793102
7 miles W of Southend-on-Sea; A127 to Rayleigh Weir (3 miles from course); A13 to Victoria House Corner (1 mile from course).
Undulating parkland course.
Pro Graham Burroughs; Founded 1922
Designed by James Braid
18 holes, 6003 yards, S.S.S. 68
♦ Welcome WD; WE with member; handicap certs required and 24 hours notice.
⟨ WD £25.
⟨⟩ Thurs only; terms available on application.
⟨●⟩ Service 7.30am-8pm.
⟨⟩ Crest Maisonwyck.

1B 22 Braintree ☞

Kings Lane, Stisted, Braintree, Essex, CM7 8DA
⟨⟩ www.braintreegolfclub.freeserve.uk
✉ manager@braintreegolfclub.freeserve.co.uk
☎ 01376 346079, Fax 348677, Sec 346079, Rest/Bar 346079
A120 eastbound after Braintree by-pass, 1st left, 1 mile to course, signposted.
Parkland course.
Pro Tony Parcell; Founded 1891
Designed by Hawtree and Son
18 holes, 6191 yards, S.S.S. 69
♦ Welcome; handicap certs required Sat and Sun pm.
⟨ WD £20; WE £40.
⟨⟩ By arrangement all WD except Tues am.
⟨●⟩ Meals served.
⟨⟩ White Hart.

1B 23 Braintree Towerlands

Panfield Rd, Braintree, Essex, CM7 5BJ
⟨⟩ www.towlands.co.uk
☎ 01376 326802, Fax 552487
Course is 1 mile NW of Braintree on the B1053.
Picturesque parkland course.
Founded 1985
Designed by GR Shiels/Golf Landscapes

9 holes, 5559 yards, S.S.S. 68
⟨ Practice range.
♦ Welcome.
⟨ WD £10; WE £12.
⟨⟩ Welcome by appointment; contact C W Hunnable or J C Sillett; terms on application.
⟨●⟩ Clubhouse facilities.
⟨⟩ Old House; Old Court, Hare and Hounds.

1B 24 Braxted Park

Braxted Park, Witham, Essex, CM8 3EN
☎ 01376 572372, Fax 892840, Pro 572372, Sec 572372, Rest/Bar 572372
1.5 miles off A12 near Kelvedon.
Parkland course.
Pro John Hudson; Founded 1953
Designed by Sir Allen Clark
9 holes, 5704 yards, S.S.S. 68
♦ Public pay as you play WD; members only WE.
⟨ WD £13.
⟨⟩ Welcome WD; terms on application.
⟨●⟩ Restaurant, bar.
⟨⟩ Braxted Park; Rivenhall.

1B 25 Brent Valley

Church Road, Hanwell, London, W7 3BE
☎ 020 8567 4230, Pro 8567 1287, Sec 8567 4230
A4020 Uxbrdige Road, Hanwell, on to Greenford Ave then on to Church Rd.
Public meadowland course.
Pro Peter Bryant; Founded 1938
Designed by P Alliss and D Thomas
18 holes, 5446 yards, S.S.S. 66
♦ Welcome.
⟨ WD £10; WE £14.95.
⟨⟩ Organised via the Pro; terms on application.
⟨●⟩ Restaurant from 8am.
⟨⟩ Ealing Common.

1B 26 Brentwood Golf Centre

Ingrave Road, Brentwood, Essex, CM14 5AE
⟨⟩ www.discountgolfstore.co.uk
☎ 01277 214830, Fax 200601, Pro 218714, Sec 218850, Rest/Bar 218850
Take M25 Junction 29 then take A127 to Southend. Turn up the A128 towards Brentwood. Then go over 2 round-abouts. Course is 100 yards on the left.
Parkland course.
Pro Steve Cole; Founded 1965
18 holes, 6192 yards, S.S.S. 69

✝ Municipal course.
▯ WD £10; WE £15.
⟲ Welcome WD; meals and 18 or 36 holes, coffee on arrival; £25-£35.
🍴 Facilities available.
⌂ Brentwood Post House.

1B 27 Brickendon Grange ☕
Brickendon, Nr Hertford, Herts, SG13 8PD
🖥 www.brickendongrangegc.co.uk
✉ genman@brickendongrangegc.co.uk
☎ 01992 511258, Fax 511411,
Pro 511218, Sec 511258,
Rest/Bar 511228
3 miles S of Hertford near Bayford Br station.
Undulating parkland course.
Pro G Tippett; Founded 1968
Designed by CK Cotton
18 holes, 6394 yards, S.S.S. 70
✝ Welcome WD; handicap certs required.
▯ WD £35.
⟲ WDs except Wed; terms on application.
🍴 Bar lunches.
⌂ White Horse.

1B 28 Bridgedown
St Albans Road, Barnet, Herts, EN5 4RE
☎ 020 8441 7649, Fax 8440 2757,
Pro 8440 4009
1.5 miles from M25 Junction 23 at South Mimms exit.
Parklands course.
Pro Lee Jones; Founded 1994
Designed by Seve Ballesteros
18 holes, 6626 yards, S.S.S. 72
✝ Welcome.
▯ WD £15; WE £17.
⟲ Welcome by prior arrangement; terms on application.
🍴 Bar and catering facilities available.
⌂ Travel Lodge, J23 off M25.

1B 29 Briggens House Hotel
Stanstead Road, Stanstead Abbots, Ware, Herts, SG12 8LD
🖥 www.corushotels.com/briggenshouse
☎ 01279 829955, Fax 793685,
Pro 793742, Sec 793742,
Rest/Bar 793742
Situation on A414 between Harlow and A10.
Parkland course.
Pro Alan Battle; Founded 1988
9 holes, 5582 yards, S.S.S. 69

✝ Welcome at all times.
▯ WD £11 for 9 holes £15 for 18 holes; WE £14 for 9 holes, £18 for 18 holes. Discounts for on site hotel residents.
⟲ Terms on application.
🍴 Full Facilities available, recent refurbishment completed October 2001.
⌂ On site.

1B 30 Brocket Hall
Brockett Hall, Welwyn Garden City, Herts, AL8 7XG
🖥 www.Brockethall.co.uk
☎ 01707 390055, Fax 390052,
Pro 390063, Sec 368808
On B653 to Wheathampstead off A1 (M) Junction 4.
Parkland course.
Pro Keith Wood; Founded 1992
Designed by Peter Alliss/Clive Clark
18 holes, 6616 yards, S.S.S. 72
▯ 15.
✝ Members' guests only.
⟲ Corporate days can be arranged; terms on application.
🍴 Clubhouse restaurant and bar facilities.
⌂ Melbourne Lodge.

1B 31 Brookmans Park
Golf Club Road, Hatfield, Herts, AL9 7AT
☎ 01707 652487, Fax 661851,
Pro 652468, Sec 652487
10 min from M25 through Potters Bar.
Parkland course.
Pro Ian Jelley; Founded 1930
Designed by Hawtree & Taylor
18 holes, 6460 yards, S.S.S. 71
✝ Welcome by prior arrangement not WE.
▯ WD £30.
⟲ Welcome WD, terms on application.
🍴 Full facilities, bar and catering.
⌂ Brookmans Park Hotel.

1B 32 Bunsay Downs
Little Baddow Road, Woodham Walter, Nr Maldon, Essex, CM9 6RW
☎ 01245 222648, Sec 222648,
Rest/Bar 222369
Leave A414 at Danbury towards Woodham Water; course 0.5 W of village.
Gently undulating meadowland.
Pro Henry Roblin; Founded 1982
9 holes, 5864 yards, S.S.S. 68. Also Badgers course: 9 holes, 5864 yards, par 27.
▮ Practice facilities.
✝ Welcome.

▯ WD £11; WE £13.00.
⟲ Welcome WD except BH; packages available.
🍴 Full facilities all week.
⌂ Blue Boar in Mouden, Pondlands Park.

1B 33 Burnham-on-Crouch ☕
Ferry Road, Creeksea, Burnham-On-Crouch, Essex, CM0 8PQ
✉ burnhamgolf@hotmail.com
☎ 01621 782282, Fax 784489,
Pro 782282, Sec 782282,
Rest/Bar 785508
1 mile before entering Burnham on B1010.
Undulating parkland course.
Founded 1923
Designed by Howard Swan (2nd 9)
18 holes, 6056 yards, S.S.S. 69
✝ Welcome WD.
▯ WD £26.
⟲ Welcome WD except Thurs; Full catering facilities; from £30.
🍴 Full bar and restaurant facilities.

1B 34 The Burstead
Tye Common Road, Little Burstead, Billericay, Essex, CM12 9SS
☎ 01277 631171, Fax 632766
Leave A127 at Research Centre/Laindon exit; 1st exit at roundabout and then right into Dunton Road; left into Rectory Road.
Parkland course.
Pro Keith Bridges; assisted by D Bullock; Founded 1993
Designed by Patrick Tallack
18 holes, 6275 yards, S.S.S. 70
✝ Welcome WD and Sat, Sun pm.
▯ WD £19; WE £25.
⟲ Welcome WD by prior arrangement; packages available; from £19.
🍴 Clubhouse bar and restaurant facilities.
⌂ Trust House Forte and Camponile, both A127; Hill House.

1B 35 Bush Hill Park
Bush Hill, Winchmore Hill, London, N21 2BU
🖥 www.bushhillgolfclub.co.uk
☎ 020 8360 5738, Fax 8360 5583,
Pro 8360 4103
0.5 mile S of Enfield town.
Parkland course.
Pro Adrian Andrews; Founded 1895
18 holes, 5767 yards, S.S.S. 68
✝ Welcome WD except Wed am.
▯ WD £27.
⟲ On application, except Wed.

🍽 Bar snacks, restaurant service.
🛏 West Lodge.

1B 36 Bushey Golf & CC ♛
High Street, Bushey, Herts, WD23 1TT
☎ 020 8950 2283, Fax 8386 1181,
Pro 8950 2215, Rest/Bar 8950 2283
On A411, 1.5 miles from M1/A411
Junction.
Parkland course.
Pro Graham Atkinson; Founded 1980
Designed by Donald Steel
9 holes, 6120 yards, S.S.S. 69
⚑ 30.
♦ Welcome WD except Wed, Thurs
am; WE and Bank Holidays after
3.30pm.
£ WD £11 WE £13.
⟳ Maximum 50 by arrangement; not
available Wed or Thurs mornings;
terms on application.
🍽 Meals served.
🛏 The Hilton.

1B 37 Bushey Hall ♛
Bushey Hall Drive, Bushey, Herts,
WD23 2EP
🖳 www.golfclubuk.co.uk
📧 busheyhallgolf@aol.com
☎ 01923 222253, Fax 229759,
Pro 225802, Sec 222253,
Rest/Bar 222253
1 mile SE of Watford.
Undulating parkland course.
Pro Ken Wickham; Founded 1886
Designed by Robert Stewart Clouston
18 holes, 6099 yards, S.S.S. 69
♦ Welcome; must book at reception.
£ WD £25 WE £35.
⟳ Welcome WD; terms on
application.
🍽 Full facilities.

1B 38 C & L Golf & Country Club
West End Road, Northolt, Middlesex,
UB5 6RD
☎ 020 8845 5662, Fax 8841 5515
Junction of West End Road and A40,
travelling from London; opposite
Northolt Airport.
Parkland course.
Pro Richard Kelly; Founded 1991
Designed by Patrick Tallack
9 holes, 2251 yards
♦ Welcome; no jeans or T-shirts; golf
shoes only.
£ WD £4.50; WE £7.00.
⟳ Welcome WD; terms on application.
🍽 Bar restaurant, banqueting hall
available.
🛏 Master Brewer.

1B 39 Canons Brook
Elizabeth Way, Harlow, Essex, CM19
5BE
🖳 www.canonsbrook.co.uk
📧 sjl.canonsbrook@btclick.com
☎ 01279 421482, Fax 626393,
Pro 418357, Sec 421482,
Rest/Bar 425142
1 mile W of Harlow Town station.
Parkland course.
Pro A McGinn; Founded 1963
Designed by Sir Henry Cotton
18 holes, 6763 yards, S.S.S. 73
♦ Welcome WD.
£ WD £24.
⟳ Welcome Mon, Wed, Fri; golf and
catering; £45.
🍽 Full catering facilities.
🛏 Churchgate Hotel; Moat House.

1B 40 Castle Point
Sommes Avenue, Canvey Island,
Essex, SS8 9FG
☎ 01268 510830, Pro 510830,
Rest/Bar 511149
A13 to Southend right on A130 to canvey
Island at Saddlers Farm roundabout over
Waterside farm roundabout to Sommes
Ave, course on left.
Public seaside links course.
Pro Michael Otleridge; Founded 1988
Designed by Golf Landscapes
18 holes, 6096 yards, S.S.S. 69
⚑ 24 bays floodlit.
♦ No restrictions booking required;
WE smart attire.
£ WD £10; WE £14.30.
⟳ On request telephone in advance
terms on application.
🍽 Bar and Restaurant facilities
available.
🛏 Crest; Basildon; Oyster Fleet.

1B 41 Chadwell Springs
Hertford Road, Ware, Herts, SG12 9LE
☎ 01920 461447, Pro 462075
On A119 halfway between Hertford and
Ware.
Parkland course.
Pro Mark Wall; Founded 1975
Designed by J H Taylor
9 holes, 3209 yards, S.S.S. 71
♦ Welcome WD: WE by arrangement.
£ WD £10; WE £15.
⟳ Welcome Mon; terms on application.
🍽 Full facilities.
🛏 Salisbury, Hertford; Moat House,
Ware.

1B 42 Channels ♛
Belsteads Farm Lane, Little Waltham,
Chelmsford, Essex, CM3 3PT

🖳 www.channelsgolf.co.uk
📧 info@channelsgolf.co.uk
☎ 01245 440005, Fax 442032,
Pro 441056, Sec 440005,
Rest/Bar 440005
Course is two miles NE of Chelmsford
off the A130.
Undulating parkland course.
Pro Ian Sinclair; Founded 1974
Designed by Henry Cotton
Belsteads: 9. Channels: 18 holes,
Belsteads: 4779. Channels: 6376 yards,
S.S.S. Belsteads: 63. Channels: 71
♦ Welcome anytime.
£ Belsteads course: WD £18, WE
£20; Channels course: WD £28 .
⟳ Welcome WD; packages involve
playing both Channels and Belsteads
courses; £26-60.
🍽 Full catering facilities.
🛏 County Hotel, Chelmsford.

1B 43 Chelmsford
Widford Road, Chelmsford, Essex,
CM2 9AP
🖳 www.chelmsfordgc.co.uk
📧 office@
chelmsfordgc.sagehost.co.uk
☎ 01245 256483, Fax 256483,
Pro 257079, Sec 256483,
Rest/Bar 250555
Off A414 Chelmsford road.
Parkland course.
Pro Mark Welch; Founded 1893
Designed by Harry Colt (1924)
18 holes, 5981 yards, S.S.S. 69
♦ Welcome WD only.
£ WD £35.
⟳ Welcome Wed and Thurs only;
terms on application.
🍽 Full facilities.
🛏 South Lodge, Chelmsford.

1B 44 Chesfield Downs
Jack's Hill, Graveley, Herts, SG4 7EQ
☎ 01462 482929, Fax 485753
From A1M follow signs on B197 to
Graveley. Southbound exit A1m at
Junction 8 and head for B197
northbound.
Parkland course.
Pro Jane Fernley/Henry Arnott;
Founded 1991
Designed by Jonathan Gaunt
18 holes, 6646 yards, S.S.S. 71
♦ Everyone welcome.
£ WD £16; WE £24.
⟳ Welcome; various packages
available; terms on application.
🍽 Full facilities.
🛏 Balckmore Hotel, Little
Wymondley.

1B 45 Cheshunt

Park Lane, Cheshunt, Herts, EN7 6QD
🏧 www.broxbourne.gov.uk
🖳 refer to website
☎ 01992 624009, Fax 636403,
Sec 624009, Rest/Bar 633610
From M25 Junction 25 towards
Cambridge. 2nd junction 1st set of
traffic lights take left filter.
Municipal parkland course.
Pro David Banks; Founded 1976
⌇ Practice area with 10 bays
specifically for irons use/nets-both.
⸶ Visitors welcome at any time
advisable to phone for availability at
weekends.
⌐ WD £12 (pm £8); WE £16.50.
⊘ By arrangement; terms on
application.
⫶⦿⫶ Cafe service all day.
⤳ Marriott.

1B 46 Chigwell ☜

High Road, Chigwell, Essex, IG7 5BH
🏧 www.chigwellgolfclub.co.uk
🖳 info@chigwellgolfclub.co.uk
☎ 020 8500 2059, Fax 8501 3410,
Pro 8500 2384
On A113, 13.5 miles NE of London or
M25,Juntion 26.
Undulating parkland course.
Pro Ray Beard; Founded 1925
Designed by Hawtree Taylor
18 holes, 6279 yards, S.S.S. 70
⸶ Welcome Mon-Thurs with handicap
certs; only with member at WE.
⌐ WD £35.
⊘ Welcome Mon, Wed and Thurs by
prior arrangement; terms on application.
⫶⦿⫶ Bar and catering facilities.
⤳ Prince Regent; Roebuck Holiday
Inn Express.

1B 47 Chingford

Bury Road, Chingford, London, E4 7QJ
☎ 0208 5292107, Pro 85295708,
Sec 85292107
In Station Road, 150 yards S of
Chingford station.
Public Forest course.
Pro John Francis; Founded 1888
Designed by James Braid
18 holes, 6342 yards, S.S.S. 69
⸶ Welcome; red outer garment must
be worn.
⌐ WD £10.40; WE £14.25.
⊘ Welcome by appointment; terms
on application.
⫶⦿⫶ Snacks, no bar; cafe available next
to club.
⤳ Ridgeway (Chingford).

1B 48 Chorleywood

Common Road, Chorleywood, Herts,
WD3 5LN
☎ 01923 282009
0.5 mile from Chorleywood station near
Sportsman Hotel.
Wooded heathland course on common
land.
Founded 1890
9 holes, 5712 yards, S.S.S. 67
⸶ Welcome WD except Tues am.
WE restrictions apply.
⌐ WD £16; WE £20.
⊘ Small societies; terms on application.
⫶⦿⫶ Bar and catering.

1B 49 Clacton-on-Sea

West Road, Clacton-On-Sea, Essex,
C015 1AJ
🏧 www. clactongolf.com
☎ 01255 421919, Fax 424602,
Pro 426304, Sec 421919,
Rest/Bar 424793
On the seafront at Clacton.
Parkland course.
Pro Stuart Levermore; Founded 1892
Designed by Jack White
18 holes, 6532 yards, S.S.S. 71
⸶ Welcome WD; WE restrictions
apply.
⌐ WD £20; WE £25.
⊘ Welcome WD; full day of golf plus
lunch and dinner; £45.
⫶⦿⫶ Full facilities and bar.
⤳ Kingcliff; Plaza; Chudleigh.

1B 50 Colchester

Braiswick, Colchester, Essex, C04 5AV
☎ 01206 852946, Fax 852698,
Pro 853920, Sec 853396
0.75 miles NW of Colchester North
station on the B1508.
Parkland course.
Pro Mark Angel; Founded 1907
Designed by James Braid
18 holes, 6307 yards, S.S.S. 70
⸶ Welcome with handicap certs.
⌐ WD £20; WE £30.
⊘ Welcome by arrangement; terms
on application.
⫶⦿⫶ Full facilities.
⤳ George Hotel; Rose & Crown; both
Colchester.

1B 51 Colne Valley (Essex) ☜

Station Road, Earls Colne, Essex, C06
2LT
🏧 www.club-noticeboard.co.uk/
colnevalley
🖳 enquiries@colnevalleygolfclub.co.uk
☎ 01787 224343, Fax 224126,
Pro 224343, Sec 224343,

Rest/Bar 224343
10 miles W from A12/A1124 Junction.
Parkland course.
Pro James Gurry/Robert Taylor;
Founded 1991
Designed by Howard Swan
18 holes, 6301 yards, S.S.S. 70
⸶ Welcome midweek and after
11.00am at WE with prior arrangement.
no earlier than 7 days.
⌐ WD £25; WE £30.
⊘ Welcome; in-house catering
corporate days for up to 200; football
table; terms available on application.
⫶⦿⫶ Restaurant and bar.
⤳ Bull Hotel; Forte Posthouse; Marks
Tey Hotel.

1B 52 Crews Hill

Cattlegate Road, Crews Hill, Enfield,
Middx, EN2 8AZ
☎ 020 8363 6674, Fax 8364 5641,
Pro 8366 7422, Sec 8363 6674,
Rest/Bar 8363 6674
Off A1005 Enfield to Potters Bar road
into East Lodge Lane, turn right into
Cattlegate Road.
Parkland course.
Pro Neil Wichelow; Founded 1921
Designed by H Colt
18 holes, 6244 yards, S.S.S. 70
⸶ Must be members of a recognised
golf club; WE and BH only with a
member.
⌐ WD £25.
⊘ Welcome with advance booking;
terms on application.
⫶⦿⫶ Full facilities, except Mon.
⤳ Royal Chase.

1B 53 Crondon Park ☜

Stock Road, Stock, Essex, CM4 9DP
☎ 01277 841115, Fax 841356,
Pro 841887, Rest/Bar 841386
Off the B1007 outside the village of
Stock.
Parkland course.
Pro Paul Barham/Freddy Sunderland;
Founded 1984
Designed by M Gillett
18 holes, 6585 yards, S.S.S. 71
⸶ Welcome.
⌐ WD £20; WE £30.
⊘ WDs only, full clubhouse facilities;
POA.
⫶⦿⫶ Full bar and restaurant.
⤳ South Lodge; County Hotel; Miami
Hotel, all Chelmsford.

1B 54 Danesbury Park

Codictoe Road, Welwyn Garden City,
Herts

☎ 01438 840100, Fax 846109
0.5 miles from A1M Junction 6 on
B656 to Hitchin.
Parkland course.
9 holes, 4150 yards, S.S.S. 60
† Restrictions at weekends; by prior
arrangement only.
㋁ WD £12.
⌂ By arrangement only.
🍴 Facilities; meals by arrangement.

1B 55 Dyrham Park
Galley Lane, Barnet, Herts, EN5 4RA
☎ 020 8440 3904, Pro 8440 3904,
Sec 8440 3361
2 miles outside Barnet near Arkley, off
A1 and M25.
Parkland course.
Pro Bill Large; Founded 1963
Designed by C K Cotton
18 holes, 6428 yards, S.S.S. 71
† Only as guest of member or
member of golf society.
㋁ Golf society rate: WD £25; WE £35.
⌂ Wed only; two rounds golf, light
lunch and dinner or lunch and afternoon
tea; terms available on application.
🍴 Full restaurant facilities.
🛏 Post House.

1B 56 Ealing Golf Club 1923 Ltd
Perivale Lane, Greenford, Middx, UB6
8SS
✉ junemackison@hotmail.com.
☎ 020 8997 0937, Fax 8998 0756,
Pro 8997 3959
Off A40 W opposite Hoover building.
Parkland course.
Pro Ian Parsons; Founded 1898
Designed by H Colt
18 holes, 6216 yards, S.S.S. 70
† Welcome WD only, phone for
advance booking.
㋁ WD £35.
⌂ Advanced booking only; terms on
application.
🍴 Full facilities.
🛏 Travel Inn (Metro) Greenford.

1B 57 East Herts
Hamels Park, Buntingford, Herts, SG9
9NA
☎ 01920 821923, Fax 823700,
Pro 821922, Sec 821978,
Rest/Bar 821923
On A10 N of Puckeridge.
Parkland course.
Pro Glen Culmer; Founded 1899
18 holes, 6456 yards, S.S.S. 71
† WDs with handicap certs; WE with
member only.
㋁ WD £35.

⌂ Terms available on application; 18
holes of golf, bar, catering; £60.00.
🍴 Full facilities.

1B 58 Edgewarebury
Edgeware Way, Edgeware, Middlesex,
AL4 0BR
☎ 020 8958 3571, Fax 958 2000,
Sec 8905 3393
On A41 between Edgeware and
Elstree.
Pitch and putt course.
Founded 1946
9 holes, 2090 yards, S.S.S. 27
† Welcome 9am until dusk; no
booking necessary.
㋁ WD £4; WE £4.50.
⌂ Welcome; terms on application.
🍴 No facilities.
🛏 Edgewarebury Hotel.

1B 59 Elstree
Watling Street, Elstree, Herts, WD6
3AA
☎ 020 8953 6115, Fax 8207 6390
On A5183 between Elstree and
Radlett.
Parkland course.
Pro Marc Warwick; Founded 1984
18 holes, 6556 yards, S.S.S. 72
㋁ 60.
† Welcome WD and after midday at
WE. Conference rooms available. Also
functions, weddings, bar mitzvahs etc.
㋁ WD £20; WE £25.
⌂ Welcome WD except Wed, by prior
arrangement; minimum 8 players in
party; golf and catering packages
available; In golf Simulator room; from
£15.
🍴 Full catering and bar.
🛏 Edgwarebury Hotel, Elstree;
Oaklands, Boreham Wood; North Me.

1B 60 Enfield
Old Park Road South, Enfield, Middx,
EN2 7DA
☎ 020 8366 4492, Fax 8342 0381,
Sec 8363 3970, Rest/Bar 8363 3970
Leave the M25 at Junction 24; take the
A1005 to Enfield, turn right at the
roundabout in Slades Hill, then the first
left into Old Park View, at the end of the
road turn right into Old Park Road South.
Parkland course.
Pro Lee Fickling; Founded 1893
Designed by James Briad
18 holes, 6154 yards, S.S.S. 70
† WD, except Tue.
㋁ WD £25.
⌂ WD only with references; full
clubhouse facilities; from £50.

🍴 Full catering facilities.
🛏 West Lodge Park, Cockforsters;
Royal Chase, Enfield.

1B 61 Epping Forest G & CC
Woolston Manor, Abridge Road,
Chigwell, Essex, IG7 6BX
☎ 020 8500 2549, Fax 8501 5452,
Pro 8559 8272
From M11 Junction 5 take the A113;
course is 1 mile on between Abridge
and Chigwell.
Parkland course.
Pro Paul Eady; Founded 1994
Designed by Neil Coles
18 holes, 6408 yards, S.S.S. 71
㋁ 18 floodlit.
† Welcome.
㋁ WD £27.50 after 10.30; WE £35
after 11.30.
⌂ WD welcome by prior
arrangement; terms on application.
🍴 Full catering and bar facilities.
🛏 Marriott Hotel, Waltham Abbey.

1B 62 Essex Golf & CC
Earls Cone, Nr Colchester, Essex,
Plumbridge, CO6 2NS
🖳 www.clubhaus.com
☎ 01787 224466, Fax 224410
On B1024 2 miles N of A120 at
Coggeshall.
Parkland course.
Pro Lee Cocker; Founded 1990
Designed by Reg Plumbridge
18 holes, 6982 yards, S.S.S. 73
㋁ 20.
† Also 9-hole academy course, par
34. Welcome by prior arrangement.
㋁ WD £25; WE £30.
⌂ Welcome WD by prior
arrangement; packages available;
health and beauty facilities; terms on
application.
🍴 Restaurant and bar, also has
poolside cafe.
🛏 The Lodge.

1B 63 Fairlop Waters
Forest Rd, Barkingside, Ilford, Essex,
IG6 3HN
🖳 www.wigginsplc.co.uk
☎ 020 8501 1881, Pro 8500 9911
Signposted from M11 along the A12;
near fairlop station (Central Line).
Public Heathland course.
Pro Paul Davies; Founded 1968
Designed by John Jacobs
18 holes, 6281 yards, S.S.S. 69
㋚ Practice range 36 bays; floodlit.
† Welcome; tidy dress required.
㋁ WD £10.95; WE £15.50.

ENFIELD GOLF CLUB
Old Park Road South, Enfield, Middlesex EN2 7DA
A warm welcome awaits you at Enfield. Course designed by James Braid.
Casual green fees and Society Days welcome.
Call Professional shop for details: **020 8366 4492.**

1893

⟲ Welcome WD prior arrangement; sailing; childrens play area; country parks, terms available on application.
🍴 Bar;Daitons American Diner; 2 Banqueting suites.
🛏 Granada Travel Inn (Redbridge).

1B 64 Finchley
Nether Court, Frith Lane, Mill Hill, London, NW7 1PU
🖥 www.finchleygolfclub.co.uk
✉ secretary@finchleygolfclub.co.uk
☎ 020 8346 2436, Fax 8343 4205,
Pro 8346 5086
2 miles from M1 Junction 2.
Parkland course.
Pro David Brown; Founded 1929
Designed by James Braid
18 holes, 6411 yards, S.S.S. 71
🏌 Practice Area.
† By prior arrangement only.
🎫 WD £25; WE £34.
⟲ Terms on application.
🍴 Full facilities.

1B 65 Five Lakes Hotel ⓒ
Colchester Rd, Tolleshunt Knight, Maldon, Essex, CM9 8HX
🖥 www.fivelakes.co.uk
✉ inquires@fivelakes.co.uk
☎ 01621 862326, Fax 862320,
Pro 862307
Off A12 at Kelvedon take B1023 to Tiptree following tourist signs.
Links style course.
Pro Gary Carter; Founded 1991
Designed by N Coles MBE
2 x 18 holes, 6751 lakes course; 6181 links course yards, S.S.S. 73/70
🏌 10 Bay driving range.
† Welcome.
🎫 WD £29; WE £37.50, lakes course; WD £20; WE £28, links course.
⟲ By arrangement packages available.
🍴 Three restaurants available.
🛏 Five Lakes Hotel.

1B 66 Forest Hills
Newgate Street Village, Herts, SG13 8EW
☎ 01707 876825
5 mins from M25 jct 25 at Cuttley.

Hilly parkland course.
Pro Craig Easton; Founded 1994
Designed by Mel Flannagan
9 holes, 6440 yards, S.S.S. 71
† Welcome.
🎫 WD £15; WE £20.
⟲ By arrangement packages available.
🍴 Chinese Restaurant available in clubhouse.

1B 67 Forrester Park
Beckingham Road, Great Totham, Near Maldon, Essex, CM9 8EA
☎ 01621 891406, Fax 891406,
Pro 891406, Sec 891406,
Rest/Bar 891406
Off A12 at Rivenhall End, follow signs to Great Braxted until B1022. Turn right to Maldon, course is 1.8 miles on left.
Undulating woodland course.
Pro Gary Pike; Founded 1968
Designed by DAH. Everett & TR Forrester-Muir
18 holes, 6073 yards, S.S.S. 69
† Welcome by arrangement.
🎫 WD £18; WE £20; twilight rates available £12. WD after midday and at WE.
⟲ Societies welcome. Pre booking essential. Prices may vary.
🍴 Full facilities available.
🛏 Rivenhall Hotel.

1B 68 Frinton ⓒ
1 The Esplanade, Frinton-On-Sea, Essex, CO13 9EP
☎ 01255 674618, Fax 674618,
Pro 671618
On B1033 in Frinton.
Seaside course not traditional links.
Pro PeterTaggart; Founded 1895
Designed by Tom Dunn (1895)/Willie Park Jnr (1904)
18 holes, 6265 yards, S.S.S. 70
† Welcome by prior arrangement with Sec.
🎫 WD £28; WE £28.
⟲ Welcome Wed, Thurs and some Fri by arrangement with Sec; catering by arrangement; £25-45.
🍴 Facilities available.
🛏 Maplin Hotel; Rock Hotel; Glenco Hotel.

1B 69 Fulwell
Wellington Road, Hampton Hill, Middlesex, TW12 1JY
🖥 www.fulwellgolfclub.co.uk
✉ secretary@fulwellgolfclub.co.uk
☎ 020 8977 3844, Fax 8977 3844,
Pro 8977 3844, Sec 8977 2733,
Rest/Bar 8977 2733
2 miles S of Twickenham on A311 opposite Fulwell bus station.
Meadowland course.
Pro Nigel Turner; Founded 1904
Designed by JT Morrison
18 holes, 6544 yards, S.S.S. 71
† Welcome WD; book via Pro shop.
🎫 WD £30.
⟲ Welcome by prior arrangement; terms on application.
🍴 By arrangement.
🛏 The Winning Post.

1B 70 Gosfield Lake
The Manor House, Hall Drive, Gosfield, Halstead, Essex, CO0 1SE
☎ 01787 474747, Fax 476044,
Pro 474488, Rest/Bar 474400
7 miles N of Braintree on A1017;
1 mile W of Gosfield village.
Parkland course.
Pro Richard Wheeler; Founded 1988
Designed by Sir Henry Cotton; Howard Swan
18 holes, 6756 yards, S.S.S. 72
† Welcome.
🎫 WD £25; WE £30.
⟲ Welcome; 36 holes; lunch carvery; from £42.
🍴 Full catering facilities.
🛏 Bull in Halstead.

1B 71 Great Hadam
Great Hadam Rd, Much Hadam, Herts, SG10 6JE
☎ 01279 843558
5 mins on the B1004 off the A120 and M11 at Junction 8.
Meadowland course.
Pro Kevin Lunt; Founded 1993
18 holes, 6854 yards, S.S.S. 73
🏌 All-weather driving range, 15 bays, 3 practice holes, practice bunker. Hadam Health Club; Kevin Lunt Golf College.
† Welcome every day except before noon at WE.

Call for details.
Welcome WD except Wed; packages available from £19.
Two bars, fully licensed dining area.
Down Hall, Hatfield Heath; Hilton International.

1B 72 Grim's Dyke
Oxhey Lane, Hatch End, Pinner, Middx, HA5 4AL
☎ 020 8428 4539, Fax 8421 5494, Pro 8428 7484
On the A4008 between Hatch End and Watford.
Gently undulating parkland.
Pro N Stephens; Founded 1910
Designed by James Braid
18 holes, 5590 yards, S.S.S. 67
Practice green.
Welcome WD.
WD £26.
Welcome Tues-Fri; 36 holes 2 meals; £54.
Full catering facilities.

1B 73 Hadley Wood
Beech Hill, Barnet, Herts, EN4 0JJ
☎ 020 8449 4328, Fax 8364 8633, Pro 8449 3285
Off A111 Cockfosters road a mile from M25 Junction 24.
Parkland course.
Pro Peter Jones; Founded 1922
Designed by A MacKenzie
18 holes, 6457 yards, S.S.S. 71
Welcome WD with handicap certs.
WD £36.
Welcome Mon, Thurs and Fri; terms on application.
Full catering and bar facilities available.
West Lodge Park, Cockfosters.

1B 74 Hainault Forest
Chigwell Row, Hainault, Essex, IG7 4QW
www.essexgolfcentres.com
info@essexgolfcentres.com
☎ 020 8500 0385, Pro 8500 2131, Sec 8500 2131, Rest/Bar 8500 8333
Off the A12.
Parkland course.
Pro Chris Hope; Founded 1912
Designed by JH Taylor
2 x18 hole courses, 6545/5886 yards, S.S.S. 72/69
22 bay range.
Welcome pay and play course.
WD £15.00; WE £19.00.
Welcome by prior arrangement; packages available.
Meals and bar service.

1B 75 Hampstead
Winnington Rd, Hampstead, London, N2 0TU
☎ 020 8455 0203, Fax 8731 6194, Pro 8455 7089
400 yards down Winnington Road near Kenwood House.
Undulating parkland course with mature trees.
Pro Peter Brown; Founded 1893
Designed by Tom Dunn
9 holes, 5822 yards, S.S.S. 68
Welcome with handicap certs or letter of introduction; restrictions Tues and WE.
WD £30; WE £35.
Not available.
Not available.

1B 76 Hanbury Manor
Ware, Hertfordshire, SG12 0SD
www.marriotthotels.com/stngs
brian@hanburymanor.fsnet.co.uk
☎ 01920 487722, Fax 487692, Pro 885000, Sec 885000, Rest/Bar 487722
Junction 25 off M25 and take A10 N for 12 miles.
Parkland course.
Pro Brian Alderson, Jonathan Dove; Founded 1990
Designed by Jack Nicklaus
18 holes, 7016 yards, S.S.S. 74
Welcome if hotel resident or member's guest.
Hotel residents: WD/WE £75, Summertime. WD/WE £55 Wintertime.
Welcome by prior arrangement with the golf co-ordinator; terms on application.
Hotel and clubhouse facilities.
Marriott Hanbury Manor.

1B 77 Hanover
Hullbridge Rd, Rayleigh, Essex, SS6 9QS
☎ 01702 232377, Fax 231811
Down A130 past Carpenters Arms Roundabout. Right down Rawreth Lane.
Undulating course.
Pro Tony Blackburn; Founded 1991
Designed by Reg Plumbridge
18 holes, 3700 yards, S.S.S. 61
Welcome.
WD £12.50; WE £17-£50.
Welcome midweek; afternoons at WE; terms on application.
Full catering facilities including carvery and bar.
Master Brewer Hillingdon.

1B 78 Harefield Place
The Drive, Harsfield Place, Uxbridge, Middlesex, UB10 8AQ
☎ 01895 272457, Fax 810262, Pro 237287, Sec 272457, Rest/Bar 272457
B467 towards ruislip off off at A40 1st left down The Drive.
Undulating parkland.
Pro Cameron Smillie
18 holes, 5677 yards, S.S.S. 68
Welcome.
WD £12.50; WE £18.50.
Welcome midweek afternoons; at WE terms on application.
Full catering facilities; including carvery and Bar.
Master Brewe.

1B 79 Harpenden
Hammonds End, Redbourn Lane, Harpenden, Hertfordshire, AL5 2AX
harpgolf@ hammonds94.freeserve.co.uk
☎ 01582 712580, Fax 712725, Pro 767124, Sec 817520, Rest/Bar 817520
On A487 Redbourn road.
Parkland course.
Pro Mr Peter Cherry; Founded 1894/1931
Designed by Hawtree & Taylor
18 holes, 6232 yards, S.S.S. 70
Welcome WD except Thurs; with a member at WE.
WD £26.
Welcome WD except Thurs; £55-£60.
Full facilities.
Gleneagles Harpenden; Harpenden House Hotel.

1B 80 Harpenden Common
Cravells Road, East Common, Harpenden, Hertfordshire, AL5 1BL
hcgc@hcommon.freeserve.co.uk
☎ 01582 712856, Fax 715959, Pro 460655, Sec 715959, Rest/Bar
Course is 4 miles N of St Albans on the A1081.
Parkland course.
Pro D Fitzsimmons; Founded 1931
Designed by Ken Brown (1995)
18 holes, 6214 yards, S.S.S. 70
Welcome WD.
WD £25.
Welcome on Thurs and Fri; £50.
Full facilities.
Gleneagles Harpenden.

1B 81 Harrow Hill
Kenton Road, Harrow, Middlesex, HA1 2BW

🖥 www.harrowhillgolfcourse.co.uk
☎ 020 8864 3754, Pro 8864 3754,
Sec 8864 3754
Off main Harrow by-pass near
Northwick Park roundabout.
Simon Bishop; Founded 1982
Designed by S Teahan
9 holes, 850 yards
† Public beginners par 3.
♀ WD £4; WE £5.
🍴 Cold soft drinks and sweets
available.

1B 82 Harrow School
Harrow School, 5 High St, Harrow-on-
the-Hill, Middlesex, HA1 3JE
☎ 020 8872 8000
Parkland course.
Founded 1979
Designed by Donald Steel
9 holes, 3690 yards, S.S.S. 57
† Members guests' only.
♀ WD £20; WE £30.
☝ Welcome WD only; catering
packages available.
🍴 Full catering and bar facilities.
🛏 Hilton National.

**1B 83 Hartsbourne Golf and
Country Club**
Hartsbourne Ave, Bushey Heath,
Herts, WD23 1JW
🖥 www.hartsbournegolfclub.co.uk
📧 GM@hartsbournegolfclub.co.uk
☎ 20 894 217 272, Fax 2 089 505 357
Turn off A411 at entrance to Bushey
Heath village 5 miles SE of Watford.
Parkland course.
Pro Alistair Cardwell; Founded 1946
Designed by Hawtree and Taylor
18 and 9 holes, 6385 and 5773 yards,
S.S.S. 70 Par 70
† Members' guests only.
♀ WD £20 WE £30.
☝ Welcome WD only catering
packages available.
🍴 Full catering and bar facilities.
🛏 Hilton National.

1B 84 Hartswood
King George's Playing Fields, Ingrave
Road, Brentwood, Essex, CME14 5AE
☎ 01277 214830, Pro 218714,
Sec 218850
On A128 Ingrave Rd, 1 mile from
Brentwood.
Parkland course.
Pro Steve Cole; Founded 1965
18 holes, 6192 yards, S.S.S. 69
† Municipal course.
♀ WD £10; WE £15.
☝ Welcome WD, minimum 20; meals

and 18 or 36 holes, coffee on arrival;
£25–£35.
🍴 Full facilities.

1B 85 Harwich & Dovercourt
Station Rd, Parkeston, Harwich,
Essex, CO12 4NZ
☎ 01255 503616, Fax 503323
Turn left off the A120 roundabout for
Harwich International Port; course is
100 yards.
Parkland course.
Founded 1906
9 holes, 5900 yards, S.S.S. 69
† WD welcome if carrying handicap
certs; WE welcome only if guests of a
member.
♀ WD £20.
☝ Welcome by prior arrangement;
catering by prior arrangement.
🍴 Clubhouse facilities.
🛏 Tower; Cliff both at Dovercourt.
Pier Hotel, Harwich.

1B 86 Haste Hill
The Drive, Northwood, Middx, HA6
1HN
☎ 01923 829808, Fax 826485,
Pro 822877, Sec 825224,
Rest/Bar 822877
On A404 at Northwood.
Tree-lined parkland course.
Pro Cameron Smilie; Founded 1933
18 holes, 5797 yards, S.S.S. 68
† Welcome; book in advance.
♀ WD £12.50; WE £18.50.
☝ Welcome; terms on application.
🍴 Facilities available.
🛏 Tudor Lodge, Eastcote.

1B 87 Hatfield London CC
Bedwell Park, Essendon, Hatfield,
Herts, AL9 6JA
☎ 01707 642624, Fax 646187,
Pro 642624
A1000 from Potters Bar B158 towards
Essendon.
Undulating parkland course.
Pro Norman Greer; Founded 1976
Designed by Fred Hawtree
18 holes, 6385 yards, S.S.S. 70
♀ Practice area. Par 3 pitch and putt.
Practice green.
† Welcome by advance booking.
♀ WD £17; WE £27.
☝ Welcome; terms on application.
🍴 Full facilities.

1B 88 Hazelwood
Croysdale Ave, Sunbury-On-Thames,
Middlesex, TW16 6QU

☎ 01932 770981, Fax 770933,
Pro 770932
1 mile from M3 Junction 1.
Parkland course.
Pro Francis Sheridan; Founded 1993
Designed by Jonathan Gaunt
9 holes, 5660 yards, S.S.S. 68
♀ 36 bay driving range.
† Welcome.
♀ WD £7; WE £8.50.
☝ Welcome Tues-Fri by
arrangement; terms on application.
🍴 Snacks only Mon; other days lunch
12-3pm.
🛏 Holiday Inn (Brent Cross); Hendon
Hall.

1B 89 Hendon
Ashley Walk, Devonshire Rd, Nill Hill,
London, NW 7 1DG
☎ 020 8346 6023, Fax 8343 1974,
Pro 8346 8990, Sec 8346 6023,
Rest/Bar 8349 0728
From Hendon Central take Queens Rd
through Brent St continue to
roundabout take 1st exit on left club
0.5 miles on left in Devonshire Rd.
Parkland course.
Pro Matt Deal; Founded 1903
Designed by HS Colt
18 holes, 6266 yards, S.S.S. 70
† WD advise to book in Summer.
♀ WD £30 WE £35.
☝ By arrangement.
🍴 Bar/Rest.
🛏 Holiday Inn (Brent Cross).

1B 90 The Hertfordshire
Broxbournebury Mansion, White
Stubbs Lane, Broxbourne, Herts, EN10
7PY
🖥 www.americangolf.com
📧 hertfordshire@
americangolf.uk.com
☎ 01992 466666
M25 Junction 25 take A10 towards
Cambridge. Take A10 exit for Turnford
and then A1170 to Bell Lane. Turn left
Bell Lane becomes White Stubbs
Lane. Course is on the right.
Parkland course.
Pro Adrian Shearn; Founded 1995
Designed by Jack Nicklaus (his first
pay and play course In Europe)
18 holes, 6388 yards, S.S.S. 70
♀ Practice range, 30 bays floodlit.
† Welcome WE 7.30-11.30 am
members only.
♀ WD £30; WE £35.
☝ Welcome; corporate days available;
health club, indoor swimming pool,
tennis club, golf academy with chipping
green; terms available on application.

🍽 Restaurant and bar.
🛏 The Cheshunt Marriott.

1B 91 High Beech
Wellington Hill, Loughton, Essex,
IG10 4AH
☎ 020 8508 7323, Pro 8508 7323,
Sec 8508 7323, Rest/Bar 8508 7323
5 mins from M25 Junction 26 at
Waltham Abbey.
Parkland course.
Pro Clark Baker; Founded 1963
Two 9-hole courses, 1477/847 yards,
S.S.S. par 3
⚑ Practice nets.
† Public pay and play.
[WD £3.70; WE £4.70.
⌁ Everyone welcome.
🍽 No facilities.
🛏 The Swallow, Waltham Abbey.

1B 92 Highgate
Denewood Road, London, N6 4AH
🖳 www.highgategolfclub.
freeserve.co.uk
📧 secretary@
highgategolfclub.freeserve.co.uk
☎ 020 8340 1906, Fax 8348 9152,
Pro 8340 5467, Sec 8340 3745,
Rest/Bar 8240 1906
Off Hampstead Lane near Kenwood
House, turn into Sheldon Ave then 1st
left into Denewood Rd.
Parkland course.
Pro RobinTurner/DarrenTurner;
Founded 1904
18 holes, 5985 yards, S.S.S. 69
† Welcome WD (after noon on Wed);
no visitors at WE.
[WD £30.
⌁ Welcome Tues, Thurs, Fri; terms
on application.
🍽 Full facilities 12-8pm.

1B 93 Hillingdon
18 Dorset Way, Hillingdon, Middx,
UB10 0JR
📧 hillingdongolfclub@lineone.net
☎ 01895 233956
Turn off A40 to Uxbridge past
RAF station up Hillingdon Hill, turn
left at Vine Public House into Vine
Lane.
Undulating parkland course.
Pro Phil Smith; Founded 1892
Designed by Harry Woods & Chas E
Stevens
9 holes, 5490 yards, S.S.S. 68
† Welcome WD except Thurs pm;
WE with a member only after 12.30pm.
[WD £15.
⌁ Welcome Mon by prior

arrangement; special golf and catering
packages available; from £25.
🍽 Bar and catering facilities available.
🛏 Master Brewer; Old Cottage.

1B 94 Horsenden Hill
Woodland Rise, Greenford, Middx,
UB6 0RD
☎ 020 8902 4555
Signposted off Whitton Ave East at the
rear of Sudbury Golf club.
Public undulating parkland course.
Pro Jeff Quarshie; Founded 1935
9 holes, 1632 yards, S.S.S. 28
⚑ Practice area.
† Welcome no restrictions.
[WD £4.40; WE £7.40.
⌁ Welcome any time by prior
arrangement.
🍽 Bar and restaurant.

1B 95 Hounslow Heath
Staines Rd, Hounslow, Middx, TW4
5DS
☎ 020 8570 5271, Fax 8570 5205
A315 main road between Hounslow
and Bedfont on left hand side.
Heathland course.
Pro Jo Smith; Founded 1979
Designed by Fraser Middleton
18 holes, 5901 yards, S.S.S. 68
⚑ Practice green, Putting area.
† Welcome.
[WD £8.80; WE £12.70.
⌁ Welcome by arrangement; terms
on application.
🍽 No bar; snacks and soft drinks
available.
🛏 Several available in Hounslow or
Heathrow.

1B 96 Ilford
291 Wanstead Park Rd, Ilford, Essex,
IG1 3TR
☎ 020 8554 0094
0.5 mile from Ilford railway station.
Parkland course.
Pro Stuart Dowsett; Founded 1908
18 holes, 5297 yards, S.S.S. 66
⚑ Practice area.
† Welcome with advance booking;
restricted Tues and Thurs; Sat
10.30am-12.30pm Sun 12.30pm-
1.30pm.
[WD £15; WE £19.
⌁ Welcome WD by prior
arrangement with Sec; terms available
on application.
🍽 Restaurant available most days.
🛏 Woodford Moat House.

1B 97 Knebworth
Deards End Lane, Knebworth, Herts,
SG3 6NL
☎ 01438 812752, Fax 815216
1 mile S of Stevenage on B197 leave
A1M at Junction 7.
Undulating parkland.
Pro Garry Parker; Founded 1908
Designed by Willie Park
18 holes, 6492 yards, S.S.S. 71
† Welcome WD.
[WD £30.
⌁ Welcome Mon, Tues and Thurs
only; terms on application.
🍽 Full catering and bar.

1B 98 Laing Sports Club
Rowley Lane, Arkley, Barnet, Herts,
EN5 3HW
☎ 020 8441 6051
Off A1 S at Borehamwood.
Parkland course.
Designed by Employees of John Laing
and members
9 holes, 4178 yards, S.S.S. 60
† Welcome by prior arrangement;
weekend restrictions.
[WD £8; WE £8.
⌁ Packages available.
🍽 Bar and English and Japanese
restaurant.

1B 99 Lamerwood Country Club
Codicote Rd, Wheathampstead, Herts,
AL4 8GB
🖳 www.Lamerwood.Humax.UK
☎ 01582 833013, Fax 832604,
Pro 833013, Sec 833013,
Rest/Bar 833013
5 miles W of A1 jct 4 on B653.
Woodland/parkland course.
Pro Matthew Masters; Founded 1996
Designed by Mr Sinclair
18 holes, 6588 yards, S.S.S. 73
⚑ 11 floodlit bays.
† Welcome by prior arrangement.
[WD £25; WE £37.
⌁ Packages available.
🍽 Bar and English and Japanese
restaurant.

1B 100 Langdon Hills Golf ♔
And Country Club
Lower Dunton Road, Bulphan, Essex,
RM14 3TY
☎ 01268 548444, Fax 490084,
Pro 544300, Sec 548444,
Rest/Bar 548444
Course is 8 miles from M25 Junction 30;
take the A13 E towards Tilbury after
approx 7 miles turn off on the B1007

towards Horndon on the Hill; after approx 1 mile turn left into Lower Dunton Rd. Parkland course.
Pro Terry Moncur; Founded 1991
Designed by MRM Sandow
27 holes, 9558 yards, S.S.S. 71
ℐ Practice range 22 bays; floodlit.
✝ Welcome WD; not before 10.30am WE.
ℐ WD £20 approx; WE £22 approx.
Pre-booking required 5 days in advance maximum with pro shop.
↺ Welcome WD by prior arrangement; European School of golf; special packages; function suite; terms on application.
|●| Bar and restaurant.
↵ Langdon Hills.

1B 101 Lee Valley
Edmonton, London, N9 0AS
☎ 020 8803 3611, Fax 8884 4975,
Pro 8803 3611, Sec 8364 7782,
Rest/Bar 8345 6666
1 mile N of North Circular Road Junction with Montagu Rd.
Public parkland course with large lake and river.
Pro Richard Gerken; Founded 1974
18 holes, 4902 yards, S.S.S. 64
ℐ Practice range 20 bays; floodlit.
✝ Open to public every day no restrictions.
ℐ WD £12.00; WE £15.00.
↺ Welcome WD only; max 30 persons; sporting facilities at leisure centre; terms on application.
|●| Breakfast until midday, bar and bar snacks daily.
↵ Holt Whites Hotel Enfield.

1B 102 Letchworth
Letchworth Lane, Letchworth, Herts, SG6 3NQ
☎ 01462 683203, Fax 484567
1 mile S of Letchworth off A505. Parkland course.
Pro Steve Allen; Founded 1905
Designed by Harry Vardon
18 holes, 6181 yards, S.S.S. 69
ℐ Large practice area with open driving range bays.
✝ Welcome WD; restrictions Tues.
ℐ WD £28.
↺ Welcome Wed, Thurs and Fri; 36 holes of golf snack lunch and dinner; £58.
|●| Full clubhouse facilities.
↵ Ambassador, Letchworth; Letchworth Hall.

1B 103 Limetrees Park Golf Course
Ruislip Rd, Northolt, Middx, UB5 6QZ
☎ 020 8845 3180, Fax 8842 0542,
Pro 087074590289
0.5 miles S of Polish War Memorial on A4180.
Parkland course.
Pro Neil MacDonald/Michael Stanger;
Founded 1982
9 holes, 5836 yards, S.S.S. 69
ℐ Driving range 20 floodlit bays
✝ Welcome.
ℐ WD £7.25; WE £8.75.
↺ Welcome WD; unlimited golf 2-course lunch.
|●| Bar and catering facilities.

1B 104 Little Hay Golf Complex
Box Lane, Bovingdon, Hemel Hempstead, Herts, HP3 0QD
✉ chrisgordon@decoram.gov.uk
☎ 01442 833798, Fax 831399,
Pro 833798, Rest/Bar 831378
Just off A41 turn left at first traffic lights past Hemel Hempstead station turn right up hill at lights; 1.5 miles up hill, complex on right.
Public parkland pay and play course.
Pro Nick Allen
Designed by Hawtree & Son
18 holes, 6311 yards, S.S.S. 70
ℐ Practice range 22 bays; floodlit.
✝ Welcome.
ℐ WD £12; WE £16.30.
↺ Welcome by prior arrangement; bookings accepted on the day after 8.30am by phone; golf and catering packages available on request; terms on application.
|●| Full meals.
↵ Bobsleigh.

1B 105 Loughton
Clay's Lane, Debden Green, Loughton, Essex, IG10 2RZ
☎ 020 8502 2923
From M25 Junction 26 take A121 towards Loughton; 3rd exit at roundabout; first turning on left.
Undulating parkland course.
Pro Richard Layton; Founded 1982
9 holes, 4652 yards, S.S.S. 63
ℐ Practice field.
✝ Welcome.
ℐ WD £6.50 (9) £11 (18); WE £7.50 (9) £13 (18).
↺ Terms available on application.
|●| Facilities available but limited.
↵ The Bell, Epping; The Swallow, Watham Abbey.

1B 106 Maldon
Beeleigh, Langford, Maldon, Essex, CM9 6LL
✉ maldon.golf@virgin.net
☎ 01621 853212
2 miles NW of Maldon on B1019. Turn off at Essex waterworks.
Parkland course.
Founded 1891
9 holes, 6253 yards, S.S.S. 70
ℐ Practice area.
✝ Welcome WD; with a member only at WE.
ℐ WD £15.
↺ Welcome; maximum of 32; packages; terms on application.
|●| Clubhouse catering and bar.
↵ Blue Boar, Maldon.

1B 107 Malton
Malton Lane, Meldreth, Royston, Hertfordshire, SG8 6PE
⚲ www.maltongolf.co.uk
✉ info@maltongolf.co.uk
☎ 01763 262200, Fax 262209,
Rest/Bar 262662
A10 towards Cambridge turn at Melbourne towards Meldreth; 4 Miles.
Parkland course.
Pro Graham Harvey; Founded 1994
18 holes, 6708 yards, S.S.S. 72
ℐ Driving range; 10 bays.
✝ Everyone welcome.
ℐ WD £10; WE £16.
↺ Welcome; packages available; from £10.
|●| Bar and bar snacks.
↵ Cambridge Motel.

1B 108 Manor of Groves Hotel Golf Country Club   ℭ
High Wych, Sawbridgeworth, Herts, CM21 0JU
⚲ www.monorofgroves.com
✉ info@manorofgroves.com
☎ 01279 722333, Fax 726972,
Pro 721486
On A1184 to High Wych; leave M11 at Junction 7 on A414.
Parkland course.
Founded 1991
Designed by S Sharer
18 holes, 6228 yards, S.S.S. 71
ℐ Putting green, constructing a 72 bed hotel plus bar. Health complex Gym and Pool. Due end 2002.
✝ Welcome WD; pm at WE.
ℐ WD £20; WE £25 During summer.
↺ Welcome WD; packages arranged for parties; from £26.
|●| Full hotel facilities.
↵ Manor of Groves Hotel.

1B 109 Maylands Golf & CC
Colchester Road, Harold Park,
Romford, Essex, RM3 0AZ
☎ 01708 342055, Fax 373080,
Pro 346466, Sec 342055,
Rest/Bar 342055
1 mile W of M25 Junction 28.
Parkland course.
Pro S Hopkin/R Cole Touring;
Founded 1936
Designed by Colt Alison and Morrison
18 holes, 6361 yards, S.S.S. 70
♦ WD Welcome with prior
arrangement and handicap certs.
Ⅰ WD £20.
♦ Mon, Wed and Fri; packages
available; terms on application.
♦ Full catering facilities.
♦ Brentwood Post House; Mary
Green Manor.

1B 110 Mid-Herts　　　♛
Lamer Lane Gustard Wood,
Wheathampstead, St Albans, Herts,
AL4 8RS
♣ www.mid-hertsgolfclub.co.uk
✉ secretary@mid-hertsgolfclub.co.uk
☎ 01582 832242, Fax 834834
6 miles N of St Albans on B651.
Parkland course.
Pro Barney Puttick; Founded 1892
18 holes, 6060 yards, S.S.S. 69
Ⅰ Practice area.
♦ Welcome except Tues morning
and Wed afternoon.
Ⅰ WD £25, day pass £35.
♦ Welcome Thurs and Fri; terms on
application.
♦ Catering and bar facilities.
♦ Hatfield Lodge Hotel.

1B 111 Mill Green
Gypsy Lane, Welwyn Garden City,
Hertfordshire, AL7 4TY
♣ www.americangolf.com
✉ millgreen@americangolf.uk.com
☎ 01707 276900, Fax 276898,
Pro 270542, Sec 276900,
Rest/Bar 276900
Off A100 Welwyn Garden City, past
Bush Hall, at lights turn left, 2nd right
and then into Gypsy Lane.
Parkland/woodland course.
Pro Ian Parker; Founded 1993
Designed by Peter Alliss & Clive Clark
18 holes, 6615 yards, S.S.S. 72
Ⅰ Practice range grass.
♦ Everyone welcome.
Ⅰ WD £19 (Mon £15); WE £25.
♦ Welcome by prior arrangement;
packages available; par 3 course;
terms on application.
♦ Full catering and bar.

♦ Jarvis Comet Hatfield.

1B 112 Mill Hill　　　♛
100 Barnet Way, Mill Hill, London,
NW7 3AL
☎ 020 8959 2282, Fax 8906 0731,
Pro 8959 7261
From Junction of A1/A41 going N
immediately filter right and cross into
Marsh Lane after 0.5 mile turn left into
Hankins Lane leading to club-house;
going S 1 mile from Stirling Corner.
Parkland course.
Pro David Beal; Founded 1925
Designed by JF Abercromby (1931
remodelled by HS Colt)
18 holes, 6247 yards, S.S.S. 70
Ⅰ Practice area with driving area.
♦ Welcome WD; WE reservations
only.
Ⅰ WD £25; WE £30.
♦ Welcome Mon, Wed, Fri (except
BH); terms on application.
♦ Facilities daily.
♦ Jarvis; Hilton National; Welcome
Lodge.

1B 113 Moor Park
Rickmansworth, Hertfordshire, WD3
1QN
✉ moorparkgolfclub@aol.com
☎ 01923 773146, Fax 777109,
Pro 774113, Sec 773146,
Rest/Bar 773146
1 mile SE of Rickmansworth off
Batchworth roundabout on A4145.
Parkland course.
Pro L Farmer; Founded 1923
Designed by H.S. Colt
High: 18 holes, 6713 yards, S.S.S. 72;
West: 18 holes, 5815 yards, S.S.S. 68
♦ WDs only with handicap certs.
Ⅰ WD West £35; High £60.
♦ Welcome WD only; packages
available; terms on application.
♦ Full restaurant facilities.

1B 114 Muswell Hill
Rhodes Ave, Wood Green, London,
N22 7UT
☎ 020 8888 1764, Fax 8889 9380
1 mile from Bounds Green tube station
1.5 miles from N Circular Rd.
Undulating parkland course.
Pro David Wilton; Founded 1893
18 holes, 6432 yards, S.S.S. 70
Ⅰ Limited practice area.
♦ WD; WE and BH limited bookings
through Pro.
Ⅰ WD £30.
♦ Welcome WD by arrangement;
packages available; terms on application.

♦ Meals and snacks bar.
♦ Raglan Hall.

1B 115 The Nazeing
Middle Street, Nazeing, Essex, EN9
2LW
☎ 01992 893915, Fax 893882,
Pro 893798, Sec 893798,
Rest/Bar 893915
On B194 in Nazeing.
Parkland course.
Pro Robert Green; Founded 1992
Designed by Martin Gillett
18 holes, 6598 yards, S.S.S. 72 off the
whites
Ⅰ 18.
♦ Welcome after 8.30am WD and 12
at WE.
Ⅰ WD £20; WE £28 PMs only. Mon
£16 only.
♦ Welcome WD with a minimum of
12 players; packages involving
breakfast lunch and dinner and 18, 27
or 36 holes can be arranged.
♦ Full catering and bar.
♦ Swallow Hotel; Waltham Abbey.

1B 116 North Middlesex
The Manor House, Friern Barnet Lane,
Whetstone, London, N20 0NL
♣ www.northmiddlesexgc.co.uk
✉ manager@northmiddlesexgc.co.uk
☎ 020 8445 1604, Fax 8445 5023,
Pro 8445 3060, Sec 8445 1604,
Rest/Bar 020 8445 1732
Course is 5 miles south of M25
Junction 23 between Barnet and
Finchley.
Parkland course.
Pro Freddy George; Founded 1905
Designed by Willie Park Jnr
18 holes, 5594 yards, S.S.S. 67
♦ Welcome by prior arrangement.
WE after 12.30 pm.
Ⅰ WD £23; WE £29 summer. WD
£20; WE £25.
♦ Welcome WD by prior
arrangement with Secretary.
♦ Full clubhouse facilities available.

1B 117 North Weald GC
Rayley Lane, North Weald, Essex,
CM16 6AR
☎ 0199 2522118, Fax 522881
On A414 Chelmsford road from M11
Junction 7.
Parkland course.
Pro David Rawlings; Founded 1996
Designed by D Williams
18 holes, 6311 yards, S.S.S. 70
Ⅰ Driving range and practice areas.
♦ Welcome; book with Pro.

WD £20; WE £27.50.
Welcome by prior arrangement with Sec; bar and restaurant facilities.
Bar and restaurant.

1B 118 Northwood
Rickmansworth Rd, Northwood, Middx, HA6 2QW
jenny@ngcnorthwood.co.uk
01923 821384, Fax 840150, Pro 820112
0.25 miles S of Northwood on A404.
Parkland course.
Pro C Holdsworth; Founded 1891
Designed by James Braid
18 holes, 6535 yards, S.S.S. 73
Practice area.
Welcome WD.
WD £28.
Welcome Mon and Thurs; packages available; terms on application.
Full catering facilities.
Tudor Lodge, Eastcote; The Barn, Ruislip.

1B 119 Orsett
Brentwood Rd, Orsett, Essex, RM16 3DS
OrsettGC@aol.com
01375 891226, Fax 892471, Pro 891797, Sec 891352
4 miles NE of Grays on the A128.
Heathland/parkland course.
Pro Paul Joiner; Founded 1899
Designed by James Braid
18 holes, 6603 yards, S.S.S. 72
Practice area, netted bays.
Welcome with member.
WD £35.
Welcome, Mon, Tues and in afternoon on Wed; packages include all meals.
Full catering and bar facilities.
Orsett Hall; Stifford Moat House Near Grays.

1B 120 Oxhey Park
Prestwick Rd, South Oxhey, Watford Herts, WD1 6DT
01923 248312
2 miles SW of Watford.
9 holes, 1637 yards, S.S.S. 58
Welcome.
£10.00.

1B 121 Panshanger
Old Herns Lane, Welwyn Garden City, Hertfordshire, AL7 2ED
01707 333350, Fax 390010, Pro 323443, Sec 333312,

Rest/Bar 333312
Off B1000 close to A1 1 mile NE of town.
Municipal undulating parkland course.
Pro Mick Corlass/Bryan Lewis; Founded 1975
18-hole main course 9-hole pitch and put holes, 6347 yards, S.S.S. 70
2.
Welcome; no restrictions.
WD £13.30; WE £18.50.
Welcome by prior arrangement; terms on application.
Lunch every day.
Tewinbury Farm, Beefeater, Stanborough.

1B 122 Perivale Park
Stockdove Way, Argyle Road, Greenford, Middx, UB6 8TJ
020 8575 7116
On Ruislip Rd East between Greenford and Perivale, entrance from Argyle Rd.
Public parkland course.
Pro Peter Bryant; Founded 1932
9 holes, 2733 yards, S.S.S. 67
Practice area.
Welcome.
WD £5; WE £7.85.
No societies.
Café serving meals, tea, coffee, etc; no bar.
Kenton Hanger Hill.

1B 123 Pinner Hill
South View Rd, Pinner Hill, Middx, HA5 3YA
www.pinnergc.co.uk
pinnerhillgc@uk2.net
020 8866 0963, Fax 8868 4817, Pro 8866 2109
1 mile W of Pinner Green.
Parkland course.
Pro Mark Grieve; Founded 1928/47
Designed by JH Taylor/Hawtree
18 holes, 6388 yards, S.S.S. 70
Putting greens and practice area.
Welcome WD particularly Wed and Thurs.
WD £30; Wed & Thurs £15; WE £30
Welcome WD for groups of 12-40 players; package of full meals and full day's golf; £40-£42.
Full facilities.
Barn House Eastcote; Harrow Hotel; Frithwood GH Northwood.

1B 124 Porters Park
Shenley Hill, Radlett, Herts, WD7 7AZ
www.porterspark.com
info@porterspark.fsnet.co.uk
01923 854127, Fax 855475,

Pro 854366, Rest/Bar 856262
From M25 Junction 22 to Radlett via A5183 turn at railway station 0.5 mile to top of Shenley Hill.
Undulating parkland course.
Pro David Gleeson; Founded 1899
18 holes, 6313 yards, S.S.S. 70
Practice area.
Welcome WD; handicap certs required, phone 24 hours in advance; member guest only at WE.
WD £30.
Wed, Thurs only; min 20 max 50; £68 inc. Full catering available for societies.
Breakfast (pre-ordered), bar menu.
Red Lion.

1B 125 Potters Bar
Darkes Lane, Potters Bar, Herts, EN6 1DE
www.pottersbargolfclub.com
info@pottersbargolfclub.com
01707 652020, Fax 655051
1 mile N of M25 Junction 24 close to Potters Bar station.
Parkland course.
Pro G A'ris/J Harding; Founded 1924
Designed by James Braid
18 holes, 6291 yards, S.S.S. 70
Welcome WD with handicap certs.
WD £27.50.
Welcome WD except Wed; full lunch and dinner with 36 holes of golf.
Full clubhouse facilities.

1B 126 Redbourn
Kinsbourne Green Lane, Redbourn, Herts, AL3 7QA
www.redbourngolfclub.com
golfclubsecretary@redbourngolfclub.com
01582 793493, Fax 794362, Sec 794888
Off A5183 turn into Luton Lane and club is 0.5 miles.
Parkland course.
Pro Stephen Hunter; Founded 1971
Designed by H Stovin
18 holes, 6506 yards, S.S.S. 71
Practice range, 20 bay target range.
Welcome with prior bookings accepted 3 days in advance.
WD £24; WE £30.
Welcome WD; full golfing day on 18-hole course; Golf clinics golf ranger buggies; £26-£53.
Full restaurant and bar facilities.

1B 127 Regiment Way
Pratts Farm Lane, Little Waltham, Chelmsford, Essex, CM3 3PR

☎ 01245 361100
On A130 off the A12 at Boreham.
Parkland course.
Pro D March; Founded 1995
Designed by Richard Stubbings
9 holes, 4887 yards, S.S.S. 64
Ⓘ Practice range, 16 bays floodlit.
† Welcome; pay and play.
Ⓘ WD £11; WE £12.
⟁ Welcome by arrangement.
Ⓘ Snack facilities. Restaurant and bar.

1B 128 **Rickmansworth**
Moor Lane, Rickmansworth, Herts,
WD3 1QL
☎ 01923 775278
0.5 miles S of Rickmansworth on A4145.
Undulating parkland course.
Pro Alan Dobbins; Founded 1944
Designed by HS Colt
18 holes, 4493 yards, S.S.S. 62
† Welcome.
Ⓘ WD £9.60; WE £13.80.
⟁ Welcome with prior appointment;
terms on application.
Ⓘ Available in the Fairway Inn.
⌁ Long Island Hotel.

1B 129 **Risebridge (Havering)**
Risebridge Chase, Off Lower Bedfords
Road, Romford, Essex, RM1 4DG
☎ 01708 741429, Pro 741429,
Sec 727376, Rest/Bar 727376
From A12 Gallows Corner; left and
then left again.
Parkland course.
Pro Paul Jennings; Founded 1972
Designed by FW Hawtree
18 holes, 6271 yards, S.S.S. 71
Ⓘ Driving Range; 15 bays; 9-hole
pitch and putt.
† Welcome anytime.
Ⓘ WD £11.00; WE £14.50.
⟁ Welcome by prior arrangement
with Pro; packages available; terms on
application.
Ⓘ Full clubhouse catering.
⌁ Forte Lodge Brentwood.

1B 130 **Rochford Hundred**
Rochford Hall, Hall Rd, Rochford,
Essex, SS4 1NW
☎ 01702 544302, Fax 541343
On B1013 off the A127.
Parkland course.
Pro Graham Hill; Founded 1893
Designed by James Braid
18 holes, 6176 yards, S.S.S. 71
† Welcome with handicap certs,
except Sun.
Ⓘ WD £30; WE £40.
⟁ Welcome; packages available

include 36 holes of golf and meals.
Ⓘ Full clubhouse facilities.

1B 131 **Romford**
Heath Drive, Gidea Park, Romford,
Essex, RM2 5QB
☎ 01708 740986, Fax 752157
1.5 miles from Romford centre off A12.
Parkland course.
Pro Chris Goddard; Founded 1894
Designed by James Braid
18 holes, 6185 yards, S.S.S. 69
Ⓘ Practice field.
† WD with handicap certs and by
arrangement with Pro; with member
only at WE.
Ⓘ WD £27.50.
⟁ Welcome by prior arrangement;
packages available; terms on
application.
Ⓘ Facilities available.
⌁ Coach House.

1B 132 **Royston**   ☡
Baldock Road, Royston, Hertfordshire,
SG8 5BG
⚏ www.roystongolfclub.co.uk
▤ roystongolf@btconnect.com
☎ 01763 242696, Fax 246910,
Pro 243476, Sec 242696,
Rest/Bar 242696
On A505 on outskirts of town to W
course on Therfield Heath.
Heathland course.
Pro Sean Clark; Founded 1892
18 holes, 5959 yards, S.S.S. 69
Ⓘ Practice area.
† Welcome WD; WE with member
only.
Ⓘ WD £25.
⟁ By prior arrangement with Sec;
packages available; terms on
application.
Ⓘ Full clubhouse dining facilities.
⌁ Old Bull Inn; The Banyers.

1B 133 **Ruislip**
Ickenham Rd, Ruislip, Middx, HA4 7DQ
☎ 01895 638835
Course is opposite West Ruislip Tube
station.
Parkland course.
Pro Paul Glozier/Paul Hendrick;
Founded 1936
Designed by Sandy Herd
18 holes, 5571 yards, S.S.S. 67
† Public pay and play.
Ⓘ WD £12.50; WE £17.50.
⟁ Terms on application: contact
01923 825224.
Ⓘ Facilities available.
⌁ Barn Ruislip.

1B 134 **Saffron Walden**
Windmill Hill, Saffron Walden, Essex,
CB10 1BX
⚏ www.philipdavis.co.uk
▤ golf@philipdavis.co.uk
☎ 01799 527728, Sec 527728
Take the B184 from Stumps Cross
roundabout on the M11 (exit at
Junction 9) course entrance is just
before entering town.
Parkland course.
Pro Philip Davis; Founded 1919
18 holes, 6606 yards, S.S.S. 72
Ⓘ Practice range, 9 bays.
† Welcome WD with handicap certs;
with member WE and BH.
Ⓘ WD £35.
⟁ Welcome Mon, Wed, Thurs; terms
on application.
Ⓘ Lunch available WD; evening
meals for societies.
⌁ Saffron.

1B 135 **Sandy Lodge**
Sandy Lodge Lane, Northwood, Middx,
HA6 2JD
⚏ www.sandylodge.com
☎ 01923 825429, Fax 824319,
Pro 825321, Sec 825429,
Rest/Bar 825429
Off A404 adjacent to Moor Park
underground station.
Inland links.
Pro J Pinsent; Founded 1910
Designed by Harry Vardon
18 holes, 6328 yards, S.S.S. 71
Ⓘ 17 bays.
† Welcome WD by prior arrangement.
Ⓘ WD £25 till April; May-October £35.
⟁ Welcome Mon and Thurs; full
catering and bar facilities; £28-£40.
Ⓘ Full clubhouse facilities.
⌁ Hilton National, Watford; Bedford
Arms, Rickmansworth.

1B 136 **Shendish Manor**
Shendish Manor, London Road,
Apsley, Hemel Hempstead, Herts, HP3
0AA
☎ 01442 251806, Fax 230683
3 miles from M25 Junction 20 on
A4251. M1 Junction 8 is 5 miles away.
Parkland course.
Pro Murray White; Founded 1984/96
Designed by Henry Cotton
18 holes, 5660 yards, S.S.S. 67
Ⓘ Pitch and Putt area.
† Welcome by prior arrangement.
Ⓘ WD £15; WE £20.
⟁ Welcome WD and by special
arrangement at WE; packages
available include 18-hole course,
health club, 9-hole pitch and putt,

ROYSTON GOLF CLUB Founded 1892

Baldock Road, Royston, Hertfordshire SG8 5BG   Tel: 01763 242696   Fax: 01763 246910
E-mail: roystongolf@btconnect.com   Website: www.roystongolfclub.co.uk
"A 109 year old Heathland cracker which will test anybody's game to the limit..." - **Todays Golfer**
"It's over a hundred years old and it's terrific" - **Fore Magazine**
"It's like a links in the middle of Hertfordshire" - **Fore Magazine**

---

conference and banqueting rooms. Lessons also available; from £21.
🍽 Full clubhouse facilities with private function rooms.

1B 137 Simpson Golf Club
Old Ford Lane, Hadley Green, Barnet, Herts, EN5 4QN
☎ 020 8449 1650, Fax 8441 4863, Pro 8440 7488, Sec 8440 9185
On A1000 1 mile N of Barnet close to M25 Junction 23.
Heathland course.
Pro Gary Potter; Founded 1910
18 holes, 6260 yards, S.S.S. 71
🏌 Welcome with handicap certs.
⌊ WD £20; WE £20.
⌒ Welcome Thurs and Fri; packages for golf and catering available; £51.50.
🍽 Full clubhouse facilities.
↩ Hadley Hotel; West Lodge.

1B 138 South Herts
Links Drive, Totteridge, London, N20 8QU
♒ www.southherts.co.uk
☎ 020 8445 0117, Fax 8445 7569, Pro 8445 4633, Sec 8445 2035, Rest/Bar 8445 0117/8446 3951
On Totteridge Lane 2.5 miles E of A1M at Mill Hill.
Parkland course.
Pro R Mitchell; Founded 1899
Designed by Harry Vardon
18 holes, 6432 yards, S.S.S. 71
🏌 Welcome with handicap of 24 or less.
⌊ WD £30; WE £30.
⌒ Welcome Wed, Thurs and Fri; terms on application.
🍽 Full clubhouse catering and bar facilities.
↩ Queens Moat House Boreham Wood; South Mimms Post House.

1B 139 Stanmore
Gordon Avenue, Stanmore, Middlesex, HA7 2RL
☎ 020 8954 2599, Fax 8954 6418, Pro 8954 2646, Sec 8954 2599, Rest/Bar 8954 4661
Between Stanmore and Belmont off Old Church Lane.

Parkland/woodland course.
Pro VR Law; Founded 1893
18 holes, 5860 yards, S.S.S. 68
🏌 Welcome WD – reduced rates on Mon and Fri.
⌊ £15 Mon and Fri; £18 Tue, Wed, Thu; £25 Sat/Sun.
⌒ Welcome Mon-Fri. Various packages available from £36.50.
🍽 Full catering service and bar.

1B 140 Stapleford Abbotts
Horseman's Side, Tysea Hill, Stapleford Abbotts, Essex, RM4 1JU
✉ staplefordabbotts@americangolf.uk.com
☎ 01708 381108, Fax 386345, Pro 381278
Course is 3 miles from M25 Junction 28 off the B175 Romford to Ongar road; left at Stapleford Abbots, up Tysea Hill.
Parkland course.
Pro Alan Hall; Founded 1972
Designed by Howard Swan
18 holes, 6501 yards, S.S.S. 72
🏌 Practice ground x 2.
🏌 Welcome.
⌊ Terms on application.
⌒ Welcome by prior arrangement; packages available; sauna; function room; also Friars course: 2280 yards par 3; Priors course: 5720 yards.
🍽 Full bar and restaurant facilities.
↩ Post House Harlow.

1B 141 Stevenage
Aston Lane, Aston, Stevenage, Hertfordshire, SG2 7EL
☎ 01438 880424, Fax 880040, Pro 438424, Sec 880322, Rest/Bar 880223
Leave A1(M) Stevenage South then on A602 to Hertford, course signposted about 1.5 miles.
Parkland course.
Pro Steve Barker; Founded 1967
Designed by John Jacobs
18 holes, 6341 yards, S.S.S. 71
🏌 Practice range 24 bays; floodlit.
🏌 Welcome every day; book in advance.
⌊ WD £11.80; WE £15.50.
⌒ Welcome WD; packages available;

terms available on application.
🍽 Full meals and bar snacks.
↩ Roebuck.

1B 142 Stock Brook Manor Golf & CC
Queens Park Avenue, Stock, Billericay, Essex, CM12 0SP
✉ events@stockbrook.com
☎ 01277 653616, Fax 633063
M25 Junction 28 then A12 to Gallywood/Billericay exit following the B1007 to Stock.
Parkland course.
Pro Kevin Merry; Founded 1992
Designed by Martin Gillett
27 holes, 6728 yards, S.S.S. 72
🏌 Driving range and practice areas.
🏌 Welcome.
⌊ WD £25; WE £30.
⌒ Welcome by prior arrangement; country club facilities; bowls; tennis; gym facilities. swimming pool.
🍽 Full clubhouse facilities.
↩ Trust House; Basildon.

1B 143 Stockley Park
Uxbridge, Middx, UB11 1AQ
♒ www.stockleyparkgolf.com
✉ l.newell@TGACTC.co.uk
☎ 020 8813 5700, Fax 8813 5655, Rest/Bar 8813 5701
Course is 5 mins from Heathrow airport and 2 mins from the M4 Junction 4 towards Uxbridge.
Hilly parkland American style championship course.
Pro Alex Knox/Martin Hulse; Founded 1993 Opened by Nick Faldo
Designed by Robert Trent Jones Snr
18 holes, 6754 yards, S.S.S. 71
🏌 Welcome, pay as your play, correct attire required.
⌊ Summer WD £25; WE £35; reductions in winter.
⌒ Welcome WD; booked in advance packages available; terms available on application; limited WE.
🍽 Bar and Restaurant .
↩ Novotel; Crowne Plaza; Many in Heathrow area.

1B 144 Stocks Hotel And Golf Club
Stocks Road, Aldbury, Near Tring, Hertfordshire, HP23 5RX
🖳 www.stockshotel-golf.co.uk
📧 rdarling@
stockshotel-golf.demon.co.uk
☎ 01442 851341, Fax 851253,
Pro 851341, Sec 851341,
Rest/Bar 851341
From either Junction 20 of M25 or Junction 11 of M1 follow signs to Tring. Then follow signs to Aldbury.
Parkland course.
Pro Peter Lane; Founded 1993
Designed by Mike Billcliff
18 holes, 7016 yards, S.S.S. 74
† Welcome WD any time, WE after 12 noon; handicap certs required.
Ⅰ WD £30; WE £40.
⟳ WD by prior arrangement; terms on application.
🍴 Full club and hotel facilities available.
⌐ Stocks Hotel Golf & Country Club.

1B 145 Stoke-by-Nayland
Keepers Lane
Leavenheath, Colchester, Essex, CO6 4PZ
☎ 01206 262836, Fax 263356
Off A134 on B1068 between Colchester and Sudbury.
Parkland with lake features.
Pro Kevin Lovelock; Founded 1972
Designed by W Peake
18 holes, 6498 yards, S.S.S. 71
Ⅰ Practice range 20 bays.
† Welcome at all times with handicap certs.
Ⅰ WD £22; WE £27.50.
⟳ Welcome WD; 36 holes of golf on 2 courses plus driving range and full facilities; from £30.
🍴 Full clubhouse facilities available.
⌐ Stoke by Nayland Club Hotel.

1B 146 Strawberry Hill
Wellesley Rd, Strawberry Hill, Twickenham, Middx, TW2 5SD
☎ 020 8894 0165,
Fax 8894 0165, Pro 8898 2082,
Sec 8894 0165,
Rest/Bar 8894 0165
Near Strawberry Hill BR station.
Parkland course.
Pro Peter Buchan; Founded 1900
Designed by JH Taylor
9 holes, 4762 yards, S.S.S. 62
† Welcome WD only.
Ⅰ WD £21 per round; £26 all day; April to October; £11 per round with a member; £15 all day.

⟳ Fri only; maximum 25; terms on application.
🍴 Bar and catering facilities available.

1B 147 Sudbury ♺
Bridgewater Rd, Wembley, Middx, HA0 1AL
☎ 020 8903 2966, Fax 8903 2966,
Pro 8902 7910, Sec 8902 3713,
Rest/Bar 8902 0218
At Junction of Bridgewater Rd (A4005) and Whitton Ave East (A4090).
Undulating parkland course.
Pro Neil Jordan; Founded 1920
Designed by H Colt
18 holes, 6277 yards, S.S.S. 70
† Welcome WD with handicap certs; Mon open day (no handicap certs required); WE as a guest of member only.
Ⅰ WD £30.
⟳ Welcome Tues pm, Wed and Fri; package includes coffee, Fri by appointment; terms on application.
🍴 Full catering service bar.
⌐ The Cumberland Harrow.

1B 148 Theydon Bois ♺
Theydon Rd, Epping, Essex, CM16 4EH
📧 theydongolf@aol.com
☎ 01992 813054, Pro 812460,
Sec 813054
1 mile S of Epping on B1721.
Woodland course; no par 5s.
Pro Richard Hall; Founded 1897
Designed by James Braid
18 holes, 5487 yards, S.S.S. 68
Ⅰ Practice area.
† Welcome with handicap certs.
Ⅰ WD £26; WE £22 after 2pm.
⟳ Welcome Mon, Tues, Fri; £35.
🍴 Full clubhouse facilities available.
⌐ The Bell, Theydon Bois.

1B 149 Thorndon Park
Ingrave, Brentwood, Essex, CM13 3RH
📧 tpgc@btclick.com
☎ 01277 811666, Fax 810645,
Pro 810736, Sec 810345,
Rest/Bar 811666
Course is 2 miles SE of Brentwood on the A128.
Parkland course.
Pro Brian White; Founded 1920
Designed by H Colt
18 holes, 6492 yards, S.S.S. 71
† Welcome WD and Sun after 1.00pm; with member WE; handicap certs required.

Ⅰ WD £40.
⟳ Welcome Mon, Tues and Fri; terms on application.
🍴 Meals served WD.
⌐ Post House.

1B 150 Thorpe Hall
Thorpe Hall Ave, Thorpe Bay, Essex, SS1 3AT
📧 thgc@hotmail.com
☎ 01702 585331, Fax 584498,
Pro 588195, Sec 582205,
Rest/Bar 582205
4 miles E of Southend on Sea, on seafront at Thorpe Bay.
Parkland/meadowland course.
Pro Bill McColl; Founded 1907
18 holes, 6319 yards, S.S.S. 71
† Welcome on WD by prior arrangement.
Ⅰ WD £40.
⟳ Fri only; maximum party of 40; catering by arrangement; terms available on application.
🍴 Full catering facilities available.
⌐ Rosylin Hotel.

1B 151 Three Rivers Golf & Country Club
Purleigh, Nr Chelmsford, Essex, CM3 6RR
🖳 www.clubhaus.com
☎ 01621 828631, Fax 828060,
Pro 828631, Sec 828631,
Rest/Bar 828631
From the M25 Junction 29 take the A127 and then the A132 to South Woodham Ferrers. Follow the signs for Cold Norton. Course is 4 miles.
Parkland/new heathland course.
Pro Phil Green; Founded 1973
Designed by Fred Hawtree
18 holes, 6500 yards, S.S.S. 71
† Welcome.
Ⅰ WD £20; £15 as a guest; WE £25. £18 as a guest.
⟳ Welcome by prior arrangement; combination of 18, 27, 36 holes, video analysis, clubhouse and private rooms; squash and tennis; from £20.
🍴 Full facilities.
⌐ Three Rivers.

1B 152 Toothill
School Road, Toot Hill, Ongar, Essex, CM5 9PU
☎ 01277 365523, Fax 364509,
Pro 365747, Sec 365523,
Rest/Bar 366221
2 miles off A414 between N Weald and Ongar.
Parkland course.

Pro Mark Bishop; Founded 1991
Designed by Martin Gillett
18 holes, 6053 yards, S.S.S. 69
⚑ 5.
† Welcome, WE after 1.30pm by
prior arrangement.
[WD £25; after 1.30pm WE £30.
⚘ Welcome Tues and Thurs; packages
include lunch and/or dinner; from £34.
🍴 Full catering facilities.
⌖ Post House, Epping

1B 153 Top Meadow
Fen Lane, North Ockendon, Essex,
RM14 3PR
⚲ www.topmeadow.co.uk
✉ info@topmeadow.co.uk
☎ 01708 859545
Off B186 in North Ockendon.
Parkland course.
Pro Roy Porter; Founded 1986
18 holes, 6227 yards, S.S.S. 72
⚑ Practice range.
† Welcome WD; only with member
at WE.
[WD £12 inc breakfast.
⚘ Welcome WD by advance booking;
terms on application.
🍴 Bar and restaurant.
⌖ On site hotel.

1B 154 Trent Park
Bramley Road, Southgate, London,
N14 4UW
✉ trentpark@americangolf.uk.com
☎ 020 8367 4653, Fax 8366 4581,
Pro 8367 4653, Sec 8367 4653,
Rest/Bar 8367 4653
200 yards from Oakwood underground
station between Barnet and Enfield on
A110.
Parkland course.
Pro Ray Stocker; Founded 1973
18 holes, 6200 yards, S.S.S. 69
⚑ Practice range; video teaching bay
and range heaters.
† Public course (booking available).
[WD £13; WE £16.50. Different
rates for members.
⚘ Welcome; restaurant and bar
facilities; driving range; buggies; video
analysis; terms on application.
🍴 Full facilities available.

1B 155 Tudor Park Sports
Clifford Rd, New Barnet, Herts,
EN5 9ND
☎ 020 8449 0282
Off Potters road.
Public parkland course.
9 holes, 3772 yards, S.S.S. 58
⚑ Driving range and practice area.

† Welcome.
[WE & WD £4 (9) £7 (18).
⚘ Apply for details.
🍴 Clubhouse for members only.

1B 156 Twickenham Park
Staines Rd, Twickenham, Middx, TW2
5JD
☎ 020 8941 9134
On A305 near Hope and Anchor
roundabout.
Municipal parkland course.
Pro Suzy Watt; Founded 1977
Designed by Charles Lawrie
9 holes, 6076 yards, S.S.S. 69
⚑ Practice range 24 bays; floodlit.
† Welcome.
[WD £6.50; WE £7.
⚘ Welcome by arrangement; catering
packages available; terms on
application.
🍴 Full licensed bar, snacks, function
room.
⌖ Richmond Gate.

1B 157 Upminster
114 Half Lane, Upminster, Essex,
RM14 1 AU
☎ 01708 222788, Pro 220000,
Rest/Bar 220249
On A127 towards Southend from M25
Jct 29.
Parkland course.
Pro Neil Carr; Founded 1927
Designed by HA Colt
18 holes, 6013 yards, S.S.S. 69
† Welcome WD prior arrangement.
[WD £25.
⚘ Welcome Wed- Fri by prior
arrangement some small societies
possible Mon and Tues.
🍴 Full clubhouse facilities.
⌖ Post House Brentwood.

1B 158 Verulam ♛
London Rd, St Albans, Herts, AL1 1JG
⚲ www.verulamgolf.co.uk
✉ genman@verulamgolf.co.uk
☎ 01727 853327, Fax 812201,
Pro 861401, Sec 853327,
Rest/Bar 839016
Turn off London Road A1081 at railway
bridge.
Parkland course.
Pro Nick Burch; Founded 1905
Designed by James Braid/upgrade by
D Steel
18 holes, 6448 yards, S.S.S. 71
† Welcome WD; WE with member.
[WD £25 (Mon £17.50).
⚘ Tues and Thurs only by
arrangement with Sec; Full day golf

and catering packages available; from
£61.
🍴 Full facilities.
⌖ Apple Hotel; Sopwell House.

1B 159 Wanstead ♛
Overton Drive, Wanstead, London, E11
2LW
⚲ www.wanstead.golf.org.uk
✉ wgclub@aol.com
☎ 020 8989 3938, Fax 8532 9138,
Pro 8989 9876, Sec 8989 3938,
Rest/Bar 8530 1315/8989 0604
Close to Wanstead Tube station.
Parkland/heathland course.
Pro David Hawkins; Founded 1893
Designed by James Braid
18 holes, 6015 yards, S.S.S. 69
† Welcome Mon, Tues and Fri.
[WD £30.
⚘ Welcome Mon, Tues and Fri;
facilities include 36 holes of golf, lunch
and dinner.
🍴 Full clubhouse facilities.

1B 160 Warley Park ♛
Magpie Lane, Little Warley, Brentwood,
Essex, CM13 3DX
✉ enquiries@worleyparkgc.co.uk
☎ 01277 224891, Fax 200679,
Pro 200441, Sec 224891,
Rest/Bar 231352
Off B186.
Parkland course.
Pro Jason Groat; Founded 1975
Designed by R Plumbridge
27 holes, 6232 yards, S.S.S. 69
† Welcome WD only.
[WD £30.
⚘ Welcome WD; packages available;
terms available on application.
🍴 Restaurant and spike bar.
⌖ Holiday Inn; New World Inn;
Marygreen Manor.

1B 161 Warren
Woodham Walter, Maldon, Essex, CM9
6RW
⚲ www.warrengolfclub.co.uk
✉ warrengolfclub@hotmail.com
☎ 01245 223258, Fax 223989,
Pro 224662
A414 6 miles E of Chelmsford towards
Maldon.
Undulating parkland course.
Pro David Brooks; Founded 1934
18 holes, 6263 yards, S.S.S. 70
⚑ Practice ground.
† Welcome WD; booking essential.
[WD £30.
⚘ Mon, Tues, Thurs, Fri; packages
available; terms available on application.

🍽 Full facilities 7 days.
🛏 Pontlands Park; Blue Boar.

1B 162 Welwyn Garden City
Mannicotts, High Oaks Rd, Welwyn Garden City, Herts, AL8 7BP
📧 dharvey@btconnect.com
☎ 01707 322722, Fax 393213, Pro 325525
1 mile N of Hatfield from A1M Junction 4.
Parkland course.
Pro Richard May; Founded 1922
Designed by Hawtree & Son
18 holes, 6074 yards, S.S.S. 69
⚑ Practice area.
† Welcome by arrangement.
⌾ WD £25; WE £35.
⚘ Welcome Wed and Thurs; 36 holes, coffee, lunch and dinner; £57.
🍽 Full clubhouse bar and catering.
🛏 Homestead Court, Welwyn; Bush Hall Hotel, Hatfield.

1B 163 West Essex ☮
Bury Rd, Sewardstonebury, Chingford, Essex, E4 7QL
🖳 www.westessexgolfclub.co.uk
📧 sec@westessexgolfclub.co.uk
☎ 020 8529 7558, Fax 8524 7870, Pro 8529 4367, Sec 8529 7558, Rest/Bar 8529 1029/8529 0517
1.5 miles N of Chingford station.
Parkland course.
Pro Robert Joyce; Founded 1900
Designed by James Braid
18 holes, 6289 yards, S.S.S. 70
† Welcome WD except Tues am and Thurs pm.
⌾ WD £28.
⚘ Welcome Mon, Wed and Fri; package includes coffee, lunch, dinner and 36 holes of golf plus driving range; £50.
🍽 Bar and catering facilities.
🛏 Swallow Hotel Waltham Abbey.

1B 164 West Herts
Cassiobury Park, Watford, Herts, WD1 7SL
☎ 01923 236484, Fax 222300, Pro 220352, Sec 236484
Off A412 between Watford and Rickmansworth.
Parkland course.
Pro Charles Gough
Designed by Tom Morris & Harry Vardon
18 holes, 6528 yards, S.S.S. 71
⚑ 2.
† Welcome.
⌾ WD £26; WE £32.

⚘ Welcome Wed, Fri; Full facilities; £50.
🍽 Full facilities.

1B 165 West Middlesex
Greenford Rd, Southall, Middx, UB1 3EE
📧 westmid.gc@virgin.net
☎ 020 8574 3450, Fax 8574 2383, Pro 8574 1800
At Junction of Greenford and Uxbridge road.
Parkland course.
Pro IP Harris; Founded 1891
Designed by James Braid
18 holes, 6119 yards, S.S.S. 69
⚑ Practice area.
† Welcome.
⌾ WD £24 (Mon £12 Wed £14).
⚘ Welcome; coffee, lunch, evening meal, 2 rounds of golf.
🍽 Full catering and bar.
🛏 Bridge Hotel. Greenford.

1B 166 Whipsnade Park
Studham Lane, Dagnall, Herts, HP4 1RH
🖳 www.whipsnadeparkgc.co.uk
📧 whipsnadeparkgc@talk21.com
☎ 0144 2842330, Fax 842090, Pro 842310
Between Studham and Dagnall.
Parkland course.
Pro Matthew Green; Founded 1974
18 holes, 6704 yards, S.S.S. 72
⚑ Practice ground.
† Welcome WD; WE with member.
⌾ WD £27.
⚘ Welcome Tues, Wed, Thurs, Fri; coffee, 2 rounds of golf with lunch and 4-course dinner.
🍽 Full catering facilities.
🛏 Post House Hemel Hempstead.

1B 167 Whitehill
Dane End, Ware, Herts, SG12 0JS
📧 whitehillgolfcentre@btinternet.com
☎ 01920 438702, Fax 438891, Pro 438326, Sec 438495
4 miles N of Ware just off A10.
Parkland course.
Pro M Belsham; Founded 1990
Designed by Golf Landscapes
18 holes, 6681 yards, S.S.S. 72
⚑ 25 bay floodlit driving range.
† Welcome with handicap certs.
⌾ WD £21; WE £25.50.
⚘ Welcome WD; maximum 16 at WE; golf and catering packages available; £20-40.
🍽 Full facilities.
🛏 County Ware; Vintage Corner, Puckeridge.

1B 168 Whitewebbs
Whitewebbs Lane, Enfield, EN2 9HH
☎ 020 8363 4454, Fax 8366 2257, Pro 8363 4454, Sec 8363 2951, Rest/Bar 8363 2951
1.5 miles from M25 Junction 25.
Public parkland course.
Pro Gary Sherriff; Founded 1932
18 holes, 5507 yards, S.S.S. 68
† Welcome; book 6 days in advance.
⌾ WD £12.50; WE £15.50.
⚘ Welcome by arrangement; café on site; nature trails and horse riding; packages available on application.
🍽 Public café on site.
🛏 Royal Chase.

1B 169 Woodford ☮
2 Sunset Ave, Woodford Green, Essex, IG8 0ST
📧 office@ woodfordgolfclub.fsnet.co.uk
☎ 020 8504 0553, Fax 8559 0504, Pro 8504 4254, Sec 8504 3330, Rest/Bar 8504 0553
11 miles northeast of London; 2 miles N of North Circular Road on A11.
Forest course.
Pro Richard Layton; Founded 1890
Designed by Tom Dunn
9 holes, 5867 yards, S.S.S. 68
† Welcome except Tues am; Sat or Sun am; red clothing must always be worn.
⌾ WD £15; WE £15 (£10 twilight).
⚘ Welcome by prior arrangement with Sec; packages including meals can be arranged; terms available on application.
🍽 Dining facilities bar.
🛏 Packfords, Woodford Green.

1B 170 Wyke Green
Syon Lane, Isleworth, Middx, TW7 5PT
🖳 www.wykegreengolfclub.co.uk
📧 office@wykegreen.golfagent.co.uk
☎ 020 8560 8777, Fax 8569 8392, Pro 8847 0585, Rest/Bar 8847 1956
0.5 miles N of A4 near Gillettes corner.
Flat parkland course.
Pro Neil Smith; Founded 1928
Designed by FG Hawtree
18 holes, 6211 yards, S.S.S. 70
† Welcome on WD only.
⌾ WD £28; WE £30.
· ⚘ Welcome Tues, Thurs; 3 different packages available; minimum 12 players.
🍽 Full catering facilities and bar.
🛏 Four Pillars at Osterley.

THE SOUTH

2A

Hampshire, Sussex, Isle of Wight

Many of the courses in this part of the country combine charm with snobbery, a blend that is perhaps exemplified by Rye, an exclusive course that can be hard to get onto unless you are related to a member or bare an uncanny resemblance to the Duke of York. The club used to boast a steward who was the rudest man in Sussex. A day at Rye is far from just a golfing experience.

If three of you turn up to play you may be asked to play a Rye threesome, whereby each of you plays his own ball over six holes while the other two join forces playing alternate shots against the single. But whatever game you play, Rye is a course worth playing it on, perhaps the most varied and surprising of all the English links.

The course is a mix of classic and quirky seaside golf with a loop of holes around the turn that are a little more inland in character. It is the home of the Presidents Putter, an Oxbridge competition of past and present Blues, played early in the year preferably with a scattering of snow on the ground and a mild gale in the air.

Perhaps the eighteenth best sums up Rye's character. The tee shot is difficult enough to an elevated fairway. Then further along the hole the lesser golfers amongst us can stand trembling in fear of a pull hook, a shot that threatens to shatter the windows of the clubhouse and the glasses of pink gin inside. The daunting finish only loses its peril when the visitor is informed (usually at the end of his round) that the windows are made from bulletproof glass.

Another peculiarity of Sussex is Royal Ashdown Forest, a golf course with no bunkers. Bernard Darwin wrote, "Nature had been kind in supplying a variety of pits and streams to carry." It also left a fair bit of thick grass and heather behind. This is Winnie the Pooh country, although being "a bear of very little brain", it is hard to imagine Pooh breaking par around Ashdown Forest.

An absorbing course, Ashdown Forest is a severe rebuttal of those people who smear golf courses with vast sandy beaches, seemingly unaware that these no longer present a hazard to the half-decent player. Liphook, in Hampshire, is another course that makes a point about golf architecture. Arguably the outstanding course in the county, Liphook was designed by AC Croome, a man who was schoolteacher, golfer, writer and many things besides.

The assumption that the best golfers make great course designers seems as sensible as the notion that master bricklayers make great architects. It is a point rather well made by Liphook and Croome.

Some of the other courses in this region that are well worth a visit are North Hants, the home of Justin Rose; Osborne, a nine-hole parkland course on the Isle of Wight that runs through the grounds of Osborne House, Queen Victoria's favourite royal retreat; East Sussex National, a course slightly in the American-style that offers a big welcome; West Sussex, a much shorter traditional course with several stunning par threes.

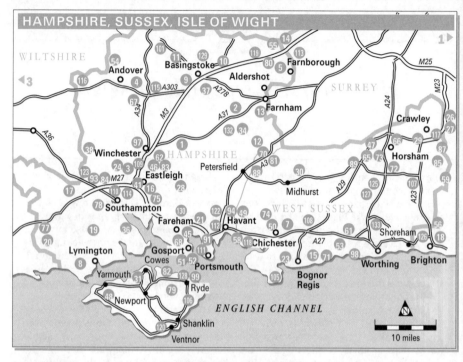

HAMPSHIRE, SUSSEX, ISLE OF WIGHT

2A 1 Alresford

Cheriton Road, Tichborne Down,
Alresford, Hants, SO24 0PN
www.alresfordgolf.com
secretary@alresford-
golf.demon.co.uk
01962 733746, Fax 736040,
Pro 733998, Sec 735735,
Rest/Bar 733067
One mile S of Alresford.
Downland/parkland course.
Pro Malcolm Scott; Founded 1890
Designed by Scott Webb Young
18 holes, 5622 yards, S.S.S. 68
Covered practice area.
Anytime Mon-Fri, after 12 pm WE.
WD £25, WE £40, full day £35.
Welcome by prior arrangement
with sec, terms on application.
Full facilities.
The Swan Alresford.

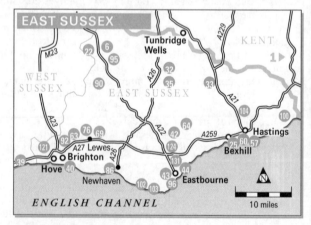

EAST SUSSEX

2A 2 Alton

Old Odiham Road, Alton, Hants, GU34
4BU
01420 82042, Pro 86518
On B3349 Alton to Odiham road, turn
off at Golden Pot.
Parkland course.
Pro Paul Brown; Founded 1908
Designed by James Braid

9 holes, 5744 yards, S.S.S. 68
Welcome, restrictions on Sun.
WD £15, WE £18.
Welcome by prior arrangement,
bar catering, PGA professional,
practice area; terms on application.
Full facilities.
Wheatsheef Inn, Alto House,
Grange Hotel.

2A 3 Ampfield

Winchester Road, Ampfield, Romsey,
Hants, SO51 9BQ
01794 368480, Pro 368750
A31 Winchester to Romsey Road
opposite Keats restaurant, next stop
White Horse Public House.
Parkland course.
Pro Richard Benfield; Founded 1965
Designed by Henry Cotton

KEY							
		Park	55	Hartley Wintney GC	82	Osborne	109 South Winchester
1	Alresford	28 Corhampton	56	Hassocks Golf Club	83	Otterbourne GC	110 Southampton
2	Alton	29 Cottesmore	57	Hastings	84	Paultons Golf Centre	111 Southsea
3	Ampfield Par 3 G & CC	30 Cowdray Park	58	Hayling Golf Club	85	Paxhill Park	112 Southwick Park
4	Andover	31 Cowes	59	Haywards Heath GC	86	Peacehaven	113 Southwood
5	Army Golf Club	32 Crowborough Beacon	60	Highwoods	87	Pease Pottage GC	114 Stoneham
6	Ashdown Forest Hotel	33 Dale Hill Hotel	61	Hill Barn		& Driving Range	115 Test Valley
7	Avisford Park	34 Dean Farm (Kingsley)	62	Hockley	88	Petersfield	116 Tidworth Garrison
8	Barton-on-Sea	35 Dewlands Manor GC	63	Hollingbury Park	89	Petworth Golf Club	117 Tilgate Forest Golf
9	Basingstoke	36 Dibden	64	Horam Park	90	Piltdown	Centre
10	Basingstoke Golf Centre	37 Dummer	65	Horsham Golf Park	91	Portsmouth	118 Tournerbury
11	Bishopswood	38 Dunwood Manor GC	66	Ifield G & Country Club	92	Pyecombe	119 Tylney Park
12	Blackmoor	39 The Dyke Golf Club	67	Leckford & Longstock	93	Romsey	120 Ventnor
13	Blacknest	40 East Brighton	68	Lee-on-the-Solent	94	Rowlands Castle	121 Waterhall
14	Blackwater Valley	41 East Horton Golf Centre	69	Lewes	95	Royal Ashdown Forest	122 Waterlooville
15	Bognor Regis	42 East Sussex	70	Liphook	96	Royal Eastbourne	123 Wellow
16	Botley Park Hotel	43 Eastbourne Downs	71	Littlehampton	97	Royal Winchester	124 Wellshurst Golf &
	& Country Club	44 Eastbourne Golfing Park	72	Mannings Heath	98	Rustington Golf Centre	Country Club
17	Bramshaw	45 Fleetlands	73	Mannings Heath Hotel	99	Ryde	125 West Chiltington
18	Brighton & Hove	46 Fleming Park	74	Marriott Goodwood Park	100	Rye	126 West Hove
19	Brockenhurst Manor	47 Foxbridge		Golf & Country Club	101	Sandford Springs	127 West Sussex
20	Burley	48 Freshwater Bay	75	Meon Valley Hotel	102	Seaford	128 Westridge
21	Cams Hall Estates Golf	49 Furzeley		Golf & Country Club	103	Seaford Head	129 Weybrook Park
22	Chartham Park	50 Goodwood	76	Mid-Sussex	104	Sedlescombe	130 Wickham Park
23	Chichester Golf Centre	51 Gosport & Stokes Bay	77	Moors Valley Golf Centre		(Aldershaw)	131 Willingdon
24	Chilworth Golf Centre	Golf Club	78	New Forest	105	Selsey	132 Worldham Park
25	Cooden Beach	52 Great Salterns GC	79	Newport	106	Shanklin & Sandown	133 Worthing
26	Copthorne	53 Ham Manor Golf Club	80	North Hants	107	Singing Hills Golf Course	
27	Copthorne Effingham	54 Hampshire	81	Old Thorns	108	Slinfold Park G & CC	

EST 1905

Mannings Heath
G O L F   C L U B

Mannings Heath Golf Club is set within 500 glorious acres of the Sussex South Downs and it offers not one, but two challenging championship courses together with practice facilities. What's more, an exquisite clubhouse provides perfect facilities for the most discerning golfer.

A visit here promises to provide an experience like no other.
We look forward to welcoming visitors and members alike.

Mannings Heath Golf Club Hammerpond Road, Mannings Heath, Horsham, West Sussex RH13 6PG
tel **01403 210228**   *fax* 01403 270974   *email* enquiries@manningsheath.com
www.manningsheath.com

---

18 holes, 2478 yards, S.S.S. 53
† Welcome but advisable to telephone first.
⟁ WD £9 WE £15.50.
⟁ Welcome by arrangement; function room; terms on application.
⦿ Bar and catering by arrangement.
⤳ Potters Heron, Ampfield.

2A 4 Andover
51 Winchester Road, Andover, Hants, SP10 2EF
☎ 01264 358040, Fax 358040, Pro 324151, Rest/Bar 323980
Turn off A303 at Wherwell/Stockbridge turning; take Andover direction, golf course 0.5 mile on right.
Downland course.
Pro Derrick Lawrence; Founded 1907
Designed by JH Taylor
9 holes holes, 6096 yards, S.S.S. 69
† Welcome.

⟁ Terms on application.
⟁ Welcome.
⦿ Full facilities .
⤳ White Hart Hotel, Andover.

2A 5 Army Golf Club
Laffans Road, Aldershot, Hants, GU11 2HF
⦿ www.whichgolfclub.com/army
✉ agc@ic24.net
☎ 01252 337272, Fax 337562, Pro 336722, Sec 337272, Rest/Bar 336776
Access from Eelmoor Bridge off A323 Aldershot – Fleet Rd.
Heathland course.
Pro Graham Cowley; Founded 1883
18 holes, 6550 yards, S.S.S. 71
† Welcome on WD by prior arrangement; WE members and guests only.
⟁ WD £26; WE Visitors with a

member only.
⟁ Welcome by prior arrangement.
⦿ Facilities available.
⤳ Trust House Forte, Farnborough Potters International, Farnborough.

2A 6 Ashdown Forest Hotel   ☏
Chapel Lane, Forest Row, E Sussex, RH18 5BB
☎ 01342 824866, Fax 824869
3 miles S of East Grinstead on A22 in village of Forest Row, East on B2110, Chapel Lane 4th on the right.
Heathland/Woodland course.
Pro Martyn Landsborough; Founded 1985
Designed by Horace Hutchinson (1930s) Henry Luff (1965)
18 holes, 5606 yards, S.S.S. 67
† Welcome but advisable to phone first, particularly at WE.
⟁ WD £16; WE £21.

⌐ Welcome by prior arrangement; full facilities; terms on application.
◖ Full restaurant service; bar snacks; banqueting facilities for up to 100.
⌐ Ashdown Forest.

2A 7 **Avisford Park Hilton**
Yapton Lane, Walberton, Arundel, W Sussex, BN18 0LS
☎ 01243 554611, Fax 552485
On A27 4 miles W of Arundel, 6 miles E of Chichester.
Parkland course.
Pro Niel Georges; Founded 1985/1997
18 holes, 5390 yards, S.S.S. 67
Ⅰ Practice area.
↑ Welcome, pay as you play.
Ⅰ WD £15 WE £18.
⌐ Welcome by prior arrangement.
◖ Bar and catering.
⌐ Hilton, Arundel.

2A 8 **Barton-on-Sea**
Milford Road, New Milton, Hants, BH25 5PP
⌐ www.barton-on-sea-golf.co.uk
☎ 01425 615308, Fax 621457,
Pro 611210, Sec 615308,
Rest/Bar 610189
From New Milton take B3058 towards Milford on Sea; club is signposted about 0.75 miles on the right.
Cliff Top Links course.
Pro Peter Rodgers; Founded 1897
Designed by J Hamilton Stutt
27 holes, 6296 yards, S.S.S. 70
↑ Welcome with handicap certificates by prior arrangement.
Ⅰ WD £35 WE £40.
⌐ Welcome by arrangement.
◖ Snacks and teas available, other catering by arrangement.
⌐ Chewton Glen.

2A 9 **Basingstoke**
Kempshott Park, Kempshott, Basingstoke, Hants, RG23 7LL
☎ 01256 465990, Fax 331793, Pro 351332
3 miles West of Basingstoke on A30 M3 Junction 7.
Parkland course.
Pro Guy Shoesmith; Founded 1928
Designed by James Braid
18 holes, 6334 yards, S.S.S. 70
Ⅰ Practice area for members only.
↑ Welcome WD, WE with a member.
Ⅰ Prices on application.
⌐ Welcome Wed and Thur packages available.
◖ Full clubhouse facilities available.

⌐ Wheatsheaf.

2A 10 **Basingstoke Golf Centre**
Worting Road, West Ham, Basingstoke, Hampshire, RG22 6PG
☎ 01256 350054, Pro 350054
M3 Junction 7, 0.5 miles from Basingstoke town centre.
Public parkland course.
Pro Matthew Skinner; Founded 1985
9 holes, 908 yards
Ⅰ Practice range 24 bays.
↑ Everyone welcome.
Ⅰ WD £2.70 WE £3.20.
⌐ No societies. Course is open to public only.
◖ Confectionery Machine.
⌐ Travel Inn in leisure park next door.

2A 11 **Bishopswood**
Bishopswood Lane, Tadley, Hampshire, RG26 4AT
⌐ www.bishopswoodgolfcourse.co.uk
✉ david@bishopswoodgolfcourse.co.uk
☎ 0118 9815213, Fax 9408606,
Rest/Bar 9408603
6 miles North of Basingstoke.
Proprietary parkland course.
Pro Stephen Ward; Founded 1976
Designed by Blake and Phillips
9 holes, 6474 yards, S.S.S. 71
Ⅰ Practice range 12 bays.
↑ Welcome WD.
Ⅰ WD £11, for 9; WD £16.50 for 18. Reduced rates for OAPs and juniors.
⌐ Welcome WD by arrangement, full facilities.
◖ Bar snacks and restaurant.
⌐ Romans.

2A 12 **Blackmoor**
Firgrove Road, Whitehill, Bordon, Hants, GU35 9EH
☎ 01420 472775, Fax 487666, Pro 472345
Located on A325 between Petersfield and Farnham, at Whitehill crossroads turn left into Firgrove Rd, Blackmoor is 1000 yards on right.
Parkland/heathland course.
Pro Steve Clay; Founded 1913
Designed by HS Colt
18 holes, 6164 yards, S.S.S. 69
Ⅰ Practice ground.
↑ Welcome WD, members' guests only at WE.
Ⅰ WD £34.
⌐ Welcome Mon/Wed/Thurs and Fri by arrangement, packages available.
◖ Full facilities.

2A 13 **Blacknest**
Binstead Road, Binstead, Alton, Hants, GU34 4QL
☎ 01420 22888, Fax 22001,
Pro 22888, Rest/Bar 22888
Take A31 to Bentley, then the Bordon road, course is immediately on right.
Parkland/heathland course.
Pro Tony Cook; Founded 1994
Designed by P Nicholson
18 holes, 6038 yards, S.S.S. 69
Ⅰ Practice range, 13 bays, gym.
↑ Welcome; no jeans.
Ⅰ WD £16; WE £18.
⌐ Welcome by arrangement; full facilities.
◖ Bar and restaurant.
⌐ Alton House; The Bush; The Farnham Park.

2A 14 **Blackwater Valley**
Chandlers Lane, Yateley, Hants, GU46 7SZ
☎ 01252 874 725, Fax 874725,
Pro 874725, Sec 874725,
Rest/Bar 874725
5 miles from Camberley on the Reading road.
Parkland course with Lake.
Pro James Rodger; Founded 1994
Designed by Harry Allenby
9 holes, 2372 yards, S.S.S. 66
Ⅰ Practice range 30 bays.
↑ Welcome.
Ⅰ WD £8, WE £9.
⌐ Welcome by arrangement; full facilities.
◖ Full facilities.

2A 15 **Bognor Regis GC**
Downview Road, Felpham, Bognor Regis, W Sussex, PO22 8JD
⌐ www.bognorgolfclub.co.uk
☎ 01243 821929, Fax 860719,
Pro 865209, Sec 821929,
Rest/Bar 865867
A259 Bognor Littlehampton road at Felpham traffic lights turn left into Downview Road.
Parkland course.
Pro Stephen Bassil; Founded 1892
Designed by James Braid
18 holes, 6238 yards, S.S.S. 70
Ⅰ Practice ground; indoor teaching room with golftek and sports coach system.
↑ Welcome with handicap certs WD, with member at WE during summer. Terms on application.
Ⅰ WD £25, WE £30. Call for information.
⌐ Welcome by arrangement, tee-off times allocated, full facilities available

£45 package.
🍽 Restaurants and bar.
⛳ The Beachcroft, Felpham.

2A 16 Botley Park Hotel and CC
Winchester Road, Botley,
Southampton, Hants, SO32 2UA
☎ 01489 780888, Fax 789242, Pro
789771
NW of Botley on B3354 Winchester
Rd, within easy reach of M27 Junction
7 or M3/A33.
Parkland course.
Pro Matt Robins; Founded 1990
Designed by Charles Potterton
18 holes, 6341 yards, S.S.S. 70
🏌 Practice range 10 bays.
† Welcome by arrangement,
handicap certs or letter of introduction
required.
🔲 WD £30, WE £30.
⌛ Welcome Mon, Weds and Thurs by
arrangement, full facilities.
🍽 Full facilities, banqueting service.
⛳ Hotel in complex.

2A 17 Bramshaw
Brook, Lyndhurst, Hants, SO43 7HE
☎ 0203 8081 3433, Fax 8081 3958,
Pro 8081 3434, Rest/Bar 8081 4628
10 miles from Southampton 1 mile
from Junction 1 M27.
Open New Forest course.
Pro Clive Bonner; Founded 1880
Forest: 18 holes, 5774 yards, S.S.S.
69; Manor: 18 holes, 6517 yards,
S.S.S. 71
† Welcome WD, members' guests
only WE.
🔲 Terms on application.
⌛ Welcome Mon–Fri; packages
available.
🍽 Catering and bar facilities.
⛳ Bell Inn, Brook.

2A 18 Brighton and Hove ☎
Dyke Road, Brighton, E Sussex, BN1
8YJ
🖥 www.bhgolf.net
☎ 01273 556482, Fax 554247,
Pro 540560, Rest/Bar 507861
A23/A27 NW Brighton.
Downland course.
Pro P Bonsall; Founded 1887
Designed by James Braid
9 holes, 5710 yards, S.S.S. 68
🏌 Practice ground/chipping green.
† Welcome with some restrictions.
🔲 WD £17; WE £25.
⌛ Welcome by arrangement
restaurant facilities.
🍽 Full facilities available.

2A 19 Brockenhurst Manor
Sway Road, Brockenhurst, Hants,
SO42 7SG
☎ 01590 623092, Fax 623332,
Pro 624140, Sec 623092
A337 to Brockenhurst then B3055
S from village centre, club 1 mile
on right.
Undulating forest/parkland course.
Pro Bruce Parker; Founded 1919
Designed by HS Colt alterations by
J Hamilton
18 holes, 6222 yards, S.S.S. 70
† Welcome on Thur by prior
arrangement, must have handicap
certificates.
🔲 WD £36 WE £46.
⌛ Welcome on Thursday by prior
arrangement, also small parties
welcome Mon,Wed and Fri by prior
arrangement.
🍽 Full facilities.

2A 20 Burley
Cot Lane, Burley, Ringwood, Hants,
BH24 4BB
☎ 01425 402431, Fax 402431,
Rest/Bar 403737
From A31 through Burley towards New
Milton/Brockenhurst turn immediately
after cricket pitch.
Open Heathland course.
Founded 1905
9 holes, 6149 yards, S.S.S. 69
† Welcome with handicap certs
preferred.
🔲 WD £16;WE £20.
⌛ Groups up to 14 people welcome
but phone in advance.
🍽 Bar and limited food available.
⛳ Burley Manor, Moorhill, White Buck.

2A 21 Cams Hall Estates Golf
Cams Hall, Fareham, Hants,
PO16 8UP
🖥 camshall@
americangolf.uk.com
☎ 01329 827222, Fax 827111,
Pro 827732
Close to M27, Junction 11.
18-hole links course, 9-hole parkland
course.
Pro Jason Neve; Founded 1993
Designed by Peter Allis & Clive Clark
18 holes, 6244 yards, S.S.S. 71;
9 holes, 3197 yards, S.S.S. 36
🏌 Practice range; £2 bucket of balls.
† Welcome.
🔲 WD £20; WE £27.50.
⌛ Welcome, subject to availability;
full facilities; £21-£47 for range of

packages.
🍽 Full facilities available.
⛳ Marriott Hotel, Cosham; Holiday
Inn, Fareham; Solent Hotel, Whiteley.

2A 22 Chartham Park
Felcourt Road, Felcourt, East
Grinstead, West Sussex, RH19 2JT
🖥 www.clubhaus.com
☎ 01342 870340, Fax 870719, Pro
870008, Sec 870340, Rest/Bar 870340
1 mile out of E Grinstead town centre
on the Lingfield road.
Mature parkland course.
Pro David Hobbs; Founded 1992
Designed by N Coles
18 holes, 6680 yards, S.S.S. 72
† Welcome but not before 12 noon
at WE.
🔲 WD £30; WE £35.
⌛ Welcome WD; full facilities.
🍽 Full facilities.
⛳ Felbridge.

2A 23 Chichester Golf Centre ☎
Hoe Farm, Hunston, Chichester, W
Sussex, PO20 6AX
🖥 www.chichestergolf.com
📧 enquiries@chchestergolf.com
☎ 01243 533833, Fax 539922, Pro
528999, Sec 536666, Rest/Bar 530777
3 miles S of Chichester (A27) on
B2145 to Selsey, on left after Hunston.
Public Florida-style course with
membership.
Pro John Slinger/Emma Fields;
Founded 1990
Designed by Philip Sanders
Cathedral: 18 holes; Tower: 18 holes,
Cathedral: 6442; Tower: 6109 yards,
S.S.S. Cathedral 71;Tower 71
🏌 Practice range, 27 bays; floodlit;
academy hole; par 3 course.
† Welcome; tee reservations
required; handicap certs required for
Cathedral.
🔲 Cathedral WD £21, WE £29; Tower
WD £16, WE £18.
⌛ Welcome by prior arrangement;
society clubroom available; terms on
application.
🍽 Full catering/refreshments.
⛳ Millstream (Bosham); Hunston Mill
B&B (Hunston); Posthouse (Hayling
Island).

2A 24 Chilworth Golf Centre
Main Road, Chilworth, Southampton,
Hants, SO16 7JP
☎ 023 8074 0544, Fax 8073 3166
On A27 between Romsey and
Southampton

Dale Hill The Four Star **Dale Hill Hotel** has two 18 hole golf courses, suitable for players of all abilities - we are very proud of it's reputation as of one of Kent and Sussex's finest courses. Our new course, designed to USGA standards by former US Masters champion **Ian Woosnam**, is challenging, even for the more experienced golfer and demands and rewards accuracy off the tee. Additional on site facilities include a covered driving range, two putting greens and a practice area; our Pro Shop offers an extensive range of golfing accessories.

Dale Hill Hotel, Ticehurst, Wadhurst, East Sussex TN5 7DQ   *e-mail:* **info@dalehill.co.uk**
tel: **(01580) 200 112**   *fax:* **(01580) 201 249**   *golf office:* **(01580) 201 800**

Parkland course.
Pro C Aby; Founded 1989
18 holes, 5740 yards, S.S.S. 69
⌸ 35 bays.
♦ Welcome.
⌶ WD £12; WE £15.
⌀ Welcome by prior arrangement; terms on application.
⍟ Catering facilities available.
⌁ Trusthouse Forte.

2A 25 Cooden Beach ♛
Cooden Sea Road, Cooden, Nr Bexhill On Sea, E Sussex, TN39 4TR
▤ manager@ coodenBgolfclub.force9.co.uk
☎ 01424 842040, Fax 842040, Pro 843938, Sec 842040, Rest/Bar 843936
From the A259 Eastbourne-Hastings road; follow Cooden Beach sign at Little Common roundabout; course is 1 mile further on.
Wetland course.
Pro Jeffrey Sim; Founded 1912
Designed by Herbert Fowler
18 holes, 6500 yards, S.S.S. 71
⌸ 4.
♦ Welcome with handicap certs, telephone first.
⌶ WD £29; WE £35.
⌀ Welcome by arrangement; full facilities; £49 package.
⍟ Full facilities available.
⌁ Jarvis Cooden Resort; Brickwall Hotel, Lansdowne Hotel.

2A 26 Copthorne
Copthorne Golf Club, Borers Arms Road, Copthorne, Crawley, W Sussex, RH10 3LL
⌨ www.copthornegolfclub.co.uk
▤ info@copthornegolfclub.co.uk
☎ 01342 712033, Fax 717682, Pro 712405, Sec 712033, Rest/Bar 712508
M23 Junction 10; follow A264 to East Grinstead; course 3 miles on left.
Heathland course.
Pro Joe Burrell; Founded 1892
Designed by James Braid
18 holes, 6505 yards, S.S.S. 71
♦ Welcome with handicap certs. WE only after 1pm.
⌶ WD £32; WE £34.

⌀ Mon-Fri by arrangement with Sec; full facilities available; £45-£60 packages.
⍟ Full facilities available.
⌁ Copthorne; Effingham Park.

2A 27 Copthorne Effingham Park
West Park Road, Copthorne, Crawley, W Sussex, RH10 3EU
☎ 01342 716528, Fax 716039, Sec 716528, Rest/Bar 714994
From M23 Junction 10 on to A264.
Parkland course.
Pro Mark Root; Founded 1980
Designed by Francisco Escario
9 holes, 3644 yards, S.S.S. 57
♦ Welcome with prior booking, bookings are 2 weeks in advance.
⌶ WD £9; WE £10.
⌀ Welcome by prior arrangement; terms on application.
⍟ Two restaurants and bar facilities available.
⌁ Copthorne Effingham Park; Copthorne Gatwick.

2A 28 Corhampton
Sheeps Pond Lane, Droxford, Southampton, Hants, SO32 1LP
▤ corhamptongc@ netscapeonline.co.uk
☎ 01489 877279, Fax 877680, Pro 877638, Sec 877279, Rest/Bar 878749
Right off A32 at Corhampton on B3135 for 1 mile.
Downland course.
Pro Ian Roper; Founded 1891
18 holes, 6444 yards, S.S.S. 71
⌸ Practice area.
♦ Welcome WD; with member at WE.
⌶ WD £24; WE £24.
⌀ Welcome by arrangement Mon&Thurs; full facilities; terms on application.
⍟ Lunch, teas and dinners available.
⌁ The Uplands Hotel; Little Uplands.

2A 29 Cottesmore
Buchan Hill, Pease Pottage, Crawley, W Sussex, RH11 9AT

▤ Cottagemoor@americangolf.com
☎ 01293 528256, Fax 522819, Pro 535399
Take M23 Junction 11 and follow signs for Pease Pottage Services; course 1.5 miles on right.
Undulating meadowland course; start and finish par 5.
Pro Calum Callam; Founded 1975
Designed by MD Rogerson
Griffin: 18 holes; Phoenix: 18 holes, Griffin: 6248; Phoenix: 5514 yards, S.S.S. Griffin: 69; Phoenix: 67
⌸ Practice area, 2 putting greens.
♦ Welcome WD, WE and BH.
⌶ Griffin WD £22.50 Fri £26, WE £32.50; Phoenix WD £12, WE £16.
⌀ Welcome; packages to suit all needs; health club and tennis facilities; conference and function facilities.
⍟ Full restaurant, coffee shop and bar, including spike bar, facilities.
⌁ Country club has 12 bedrooms on site.

2A 30 Cowdray Park ♛
Midhurst, W Sussex, GU29 0BB
☎ 01730 813599, Fax 815900, Pro 812091, Sec 813599
About 1 mile E of Midhurst on A272.
Parkland course.
Pro Richard Gough; Founded 1920
18 holes, 6212 yards, S.S.S. 70
♦ Welcome but handicap certs essential.
⌶ WD £35; WE £35.
⌀ Welcome by arrangement; full facilities; terms on application.
⍟ Bar snacks daily, evening meals by arrangement. New Clubhouse under construction, completion May 2002.
⌁ Angel; Spread Eagle.

2A 31 Cowes
Crossfield Avenue, Cowes, Isle Of Wight, PO31 8HN
☎ 01983 280135, Pro 280135, Sec 292303, Rest/Bar 280135
Next to Cowes High school.
Parkland course.
Founded 1909
9 holes, 5923 yards, S.S.S. 68
♦ Welcome.
⌶ WD £15; WE £18.

Welcome; packages available; from £12.
🍽 Full clubhouse facilities.
💬 New Holmwood; Fountain.

2A 32 **Crowborough Beacon GC**
Beacon Road, Crowborough, E Sussex, TN6 1UJ
🖥 www.crowboroughbeacongolfclub.co.uk
✉ cbgc@eastsxxray.fsnet.co.uk
☎ 01892 661511, Fax 667339, Pro 653877, Sec 661511, Rest/Bar 654016
8 miles S of Tunbridge Wells on A26.
Heathland course.
Pro Dennis Newnham; Founded 1895
18 holes, 6256 yards, S.S.S. 70
🚩 Welcome WD; handicap certs or letter of introduction required.
£ WD £27.50; WE £32.50.
💬 Welcome WD by arrangement; not Thurs; terms on application.
🍽 For up to 60; breakfast available by prior arrangement.

2A 33 **Dale Hill Hotel** ☎
Dale Hill, Ticehurst, Wadhurst, E Sussex, TN5 7DQ
🖥 www.dalehill.co.uk
✉ golf@dalehill.co.uk
☎ 01580 200112, Fax 201880, Pro 201090, Sec 201800, Rest/Bar 200112
On A21 from Tonbridge Wells.
Parkland course with lake features. Ian Woosnam course.
Pro Paul Charman; Founded 1973
Old: 18; Woosnam: 18 holes, Old: 5856; Woosnam: 6512 yards, S.S.S. Old: 68; Woosnam: 71
🏌 4.
🚩 Welcome by arrangement.
£ Old: WD £25, WE restricted; Woosnam: WD £50, WE £60 including compulsory buggy.
💬 Welcome by prior arrangement; restaurant, golf clinics, pool and leisure facilities; terms on application.
🍽 Restaurant and full facilities.
💬 Dale Hill.

2A 34 **Dean Farm (Kingsley)**
Main Road, Kingsley, Bordon, Hants, GU35 9NG
☎ 01420 489478, Pro 489478, Sec 489478, Rest/Bar 489478
On B3004 between Alton and Bordon on W side of Kingsley.
Parkland course.
Founded 1984
Designed by GW Doggrell

9 holes, 1399 yards, S.S.S. 29
🚩 Public pay and play.
£ WD £5; WE £5.
💬 Not available.

2A 35 **Dewlands Manor Golf Course**
Cottage Hill, Rotherfield, Crowborough, E Sussex, TN6 3JN
☎ 01892 852266, Fax 853015, Pro 852266, Sec 853015
0.5 mile S of village of Rotherfield just off B2101 to Five Ashes, 10 miles from Tunbridge Wells.
Parkland/woodland course.
Pro Nick Godin; Founded 1991
Designed by RM and Nick Goding
9 holes, 3186 yards, S.S.S. 70
🚩 Welcome all year; 15 minute tee intervals.
£ WD £14; WE £16. Concessions apply.
💬 Small business groups welcome, maximum 24 persons; full facilities; terms on application. Corporate days also available.
🍽 Bar, light snacks at all times, special orders by arrangement.
💬 Spa; Royal Wells (Tunbridge Wells); Winston Manor (Crowborough).

2A 36 **Dibden**
Main Road, Dibden, Southampton, Hants, SO45 5TB
🖥 www.nfdc.gov.uk/golf
☎ 023 80207508, Pro 80845596, Sec 80207508, Rest/Bar 80845060
Turn off A326 at Dibden roundabout, course situated 0.5 mile on right.
Public parkland course.
Pro John Slade; Founded 1974
Designed by J Hamilton Stutt
18 and 9 holes, 5931 yards, S.S.S. 69
🏌 Practice range, 20 bays; floodlit (also 9-hole par 3 course).
🚩 Welcome; no restrictions.
£ WD £10.75; WE £13.50.
💬 Welcome by arrangement with Pro; full facilities; terms on application.
🍽 Full facilities.
💬 Four Seasons; Pilgrim; Fountain Court.

2A 37 **Dummer** ☎
Basingstoke, Hants, RG25 2AR
🖥 www.dummergc.co.uk
✉ golf@dummergc.co.uk
☎ 01256 397888, Fax 397889, Pro 397950, Sec 397888
M3 exit 7.
Parkland course.
Pro A Fannon and D Chivers; Founded

1993
Designed by Peter Alliss and Clive Clark
18 holes, 6407 yards, S.S.S. 71
🏌 11 bays covered.
🚩 Welcome.
£ WD £28; WE £34 no visitors between April and September.
💬 Welcome by arrangement; full facilities; terms on application.
🍽 Full facilities.
💬 Audley's Wood; Hilton National (Basingstoke), The Wheatsheaf.

2A 38 **Dunwood Manor Golf Club**
Danes Road, Awbridge, Romsey, Hants, SO51 0GF
🖥 www.dunwood-golf.co.uk
✉ admin@duwood-golf.co.uk
☎ 01794 340549, Fax 341215, Pro 340663, Sec 340549, Rest/Bar 340549
Off A27 Romsey to Salisbury road; after 2 miles turn right at Shootash crossroads into Danes Road; club is 800 yards on left.
Undulating parkland course.
Pro Heath Teschner; Founded 1972
18 holes, 5474 yards, S.S.S. 68
🏌 Practice area.
🚩 Welcome WD by arrangement.
£ WD £24 Summer.
💬 Welcome Mon/Tues/Thurs/Fri all day and Wed pm; packages available.
🍽 Facilities available.
💬 Luxury farmhouse and lodge accommodation available; details on request. Abbey Hotel; Bell Inn.

2A 39 **The Dyke Golf Club**
Devil's Dyke, Dyke Road, Brighton, E Sussex, BN1 8YJ
🖥 www.sussexgolf.co.uk
✉ secretary@dykegolfclub.org.uk
☎ 01273 857296, Fax 857078, Pro 857260, Sec 857296, Rest/Bar 857230
A27 Brighton by-pass; follow directions for Devil's Dyke; course 2.5 miles west of by-pass.
Downland course.
Pro Richard Arnold; Founded 1906
Designed by Fred Hawtree
18 holes, 6611 yards, S.S.S. 72
🏌 Practice area and net.
🚩 Welcome by prior arrangement; Suns not before 12 noon.
£ WD £28; WE £35.
💬 Welcome by prior arrangement; full facilities available; £48 package.
🍽 Full facilities.

↪ Tottington Manor, nr Henfield.

2A 40 East Brighton ♌
Roedean Road, Brighton, E Sussex, BN2 5RA
☎ 01273 604838, Fax 680277, Pro 603989, Sec 604838, Rest/Bar 621461
1.5 miles east of Palace Pier, just off A259 behind Brighton Marina.
Undulating downland course.
Pro Mark Stewart-William; Founded 1894
Designed by James Braid
18 holes, 6020 yards, S.S.S. 69
♦ Welcome WD except Tues am; WE and Bank Holidays after 11am.
Ⅼ WD from £25; WE from £30.
♺ Welcome Mon-Fri, except for Tues am, by arrangement.
|●| Full facilities available.
↪ Old Ship; Grand; Metropole.

2A 41 East Horton Golfing Centre
Mortimers Lane, Fair Oak, Eastleigh, Hants, SO50 7EA
☎ 023 80602111, Fax 80696280
From M27 Junction 7 follow signs for Fair Oak.
Parkland course.
Pro Trevor Pearce; Founded 1993
Greenwood:18; Parkland:18 holes, Greenwood: 5920; Parkland: 5097 yards, S.S.S. Greenwood: 70; Parkland: 70
Ⅰ Practice range, 15 bays; floodlit.
♦ Welcome; 7 day advance booking system.
Ⅼ WD £13; WE £16.
♺ Welcome everyday by prior arrangement.
|●| Bar and restaurant facilities.
↪ Marwell Lodge; Botley Grange.

2A 42 East Sussex National
Little Horsted, Uckfield, E Sussex, TN22 5ES
❧ www.eastsussexnational.co.uk
❧ golf@eastsussexnational.co.uk
☎ 01825 880088, Fax 880066, Pro 880256, Sec 880233, Rest/Bar 880224
Situated on the A22 between East Grinstead and Eastbourne just outside Uckfield.
American style layout in English countryside.
Pro Sarah Maclennan; Founded 1989
Designed by Bob Cupp
East:18; West:18 holes, East: 7138; West: 7154 yards, S.S.S. East 74; West 74
Ⅰ 8 covered, 2 covered with video

room.
♦ Welcome.
Ⅼ Terms on application.
♺ Welcome with handicap certs.
|●| Full catering and entertaining as well as bar facilities, sauna and steam rooms.
↪ Club will provide comprehensive list of hotels and B&B.

2A 43 Eastbourne Downs
East Dean Road, Eastbourne, E Sussex, BN20 8ES
☎ 01323 720827, Fax 412506, Pro 732264, Sec 720827, Rest/Bar 730809
0.5 miles W of Eastbourne on the A259.
Downland course.
Pro Terry Marshall; Founded 1908
Designed by JH Taylor
18 holes, 6601 yards, S.S.S. 72
Ⅰ Practice range.
♦ Welcome.
Ⅼ Terms on application.
♺ Welcome WD; some WE by arrangement; packages available.
|●| Full clubhouse facilities.
↪ Landsdown.

2A 44 Eastbourne Golfing Park ♌
Lottbridge Drove, Eastbourne, E Sussex, BN23 6QJ
☎ 01323 520400, Fax 520400, Pro 506500, Rest/Bar 504134
East side of Eastbourne, turn left at Tesco.
Parkland course.
Pro Barrie Finch, Phil Lewin and Ben Porter; Founded 1993
Designed by David Ashton
9 plus blue tees for back 9 holes, 5046 yards, S.S.S. 63 Par 66
Ⅰ Practice range, 24 bays, floodlit all-weather driving range; £2 for 42 balls, Range cards available with great discounts.
♦ Welcome.
Ⅼ 9 holes £9, 18 holes £14. All day golf £18. Junior, OAP & students £7 for 9 holes, £11 for 18 holes. WE no concessions.
♺ Welcome by arrangement; full facilities; terms on application.
|●| Full facilities.
↪ Wish Tower Hotel.

2A 45 Fleetlands
Naval Aircraft Repair Organisation, Fleetlands Division, Fareham Road, Gosport, Hants, PO13 0AA
☎ 023 92544384
Off A32 2 miles S of Fareham.

Parkland course.
Founded 1963
9 holes, 4852 yards, S.S.S. 64
♦ Welcome with a member.
Ⅼ WD £5; WE £7.
♺ None.
|●| Bar.

2A 46 Fleming Park
The New Club House, Paffield Avenue, East Leigh, Hampshire, SO50 9NL
☎ 023 80512797, Fax 80651686
A27/M27, turn off at Eastleigh sign, 1 mile to course.
Parkland course.
Pro Chris Strickett; Founded 1973
Designed by Charles Lawrie
18 holes, 4380 yards, S.S.S. 61
♦ Welcome.
Ⅼ Terms on application.
♺ Terms on application to Sec; full facilities; packages available.
|●| Bar snacks and meals.
↪ Holiday Inn Gateway.

2A 47 Foxbridge
Foxbridge Lane, Plaistow Road, Kirdford, nr Billingshurst, West Sussex, RH14 0LB
☎ 01403 753303, Pro 01798 872218
Take B2133 from Billingshurst to Lockswood; then take Plaistow road and course is signposted.
Parkland course.
Pro Steven Hall; Founded 1991
Designed by P Clark
9 holes, 6236 yards, S.S.S. 70
♦ Welcome.
Ⅼ WD £18; WE £25.
♺ Welcome WD by arrangement; full facilities; terms on application.
|●| Full facilities and bar available.
↪ Lythe Hill Hotel; Checkers Blue.

2A 48 Freshwater Bay
Afton Down, Freshwater Bay, Isle Of Wight, PO40 9TZ
▤ fbgc_iow@yahoo.co.uk
☎ 01983 752955
3 miles from Yarmouth on A3055 overlooking Freshwater Bay.
Seaside downland course.
Founded 1893
18 holes, 5725 yards, S.S.S. 68
Ⅰ Practice area.
♦ Welcome after 9.30am on WD and 10:30am on Sun.
Ⅼ WD £22; WE £26.
♺ Welcome by arrangement; after 9.30am on WD and 10:30am on Sun; full facilities; terms on application.
|●| Full catering facilities; licensed

bar.
🗪 Albion, Country Garden, Farringford.

2A 49 **Furzeley**
Furzeley Road, Denmead, Hants, PO7 6TX
☎ 023 92231180, Fax 92230921, Pro 92231180, Sec 92231180, Rest/Bar 92231180
2 miles NW of Waterlooville.
Parkland course.
Pro Derek Brown; Founded 1993
Designed by M Sale
18 holes, 4454 yards, S.S.S. 61
✝ Welcome, bookings taken 2 days in advance.
[WD £11; WE £12.50.
⟳ Welcome; packages available; terms on application.
🍽 Available.

2A 50 **Goodwood**
Kennell Hill, Goodwood, Chichester, W Sussex, PO18 0PN
☎ 01243 785012, Fax 781741, Pro 774994, Sec 774968, Rest/Bar 774504
3 miles NE of Chichester on road to racecourse.
Downland course.
Pro Keith Macdonald; Founded 1892
Designed by James Braid
18 holes, 6434 yards, S.S.S. 71
✝ Welcome with handicap certs.
[WD £32 (£16 with a member); WE £42 (£21 with member).
⟳ Welcome Wed/Thurs only; minimum 16; full facilities.
🍽 Full facilities available.

2A 51 **Gosport & Stokes Bay**
Fort Road, Alverstoke, Gosport, Hants, PO12 2AT
☎ 023 92581625, Fax 92527941, Pro 92587423, Sec 92527941, Rest/Bar 92580226
M27 to Fareham; A32 Gosport; Haslar Bridge to Haslar Road to Fort Road.
Links course.
Founded 1885
9 holes, 5999 yards, S.S.S. 69
✝ Welcome.
[Terms on application.
⟳ Welcome by arrrangement; full facilities.
🍽 Full facilities.
🗪 The Old Lodge; The Alverbank; The Anglesey (all in Alverstoke).

2A 52 **Great Salterns Golf Course**
Burrfields Road, Portsmouth, Hants, PO3 5HH
☎ 023 92664549, Fax 92650525, Sec 92668667
2 miles off M27/A27/A3 on A2030 road into Portsmouth.
Municipal meadowland course.
Pro Terry Healy; Founded 1935
18 holes, 5575 yards, S.S.S. 67
[Practice range, 24 bays; floodlit.
✝ Welcome.
[WD £10.50; WE £13.50.
⟳ Welcome by arrangement; catering available in adjacent farmhouse pub; terms on application.
🍽 Available in adjacent farmhouse pub.

2A 53 **Ham Manor Golf Club**
West Drive, Angmering, Littlehampton, W Sussex, BN16 4JE
📧 secretary.ham.manor@tinyonline.co.uk
☎ 01903 783288, Fax 850886, Pro 783732, Rest/Bar 775653
Off A259 between Littlehampton and Worthing.
Parkland course.
Pro Simon Buckley; Founded 1936
Designed by HS Colt
18 holes, 6267 yards, S.S.S. 70
✝ Welcome with handicap certs.
[WD £30; WE £40.
⟳ Welcome Wed/Thurs/Fri by arrangement; full facilities; packages available.
🍽 Full facilities.
🗪 Arundel Hotel; Lamb Inn, Angmering.

2A 54 **Hampshire Golf Club** ℂ
Winchester Road, Goodworth Clatford, Andover, Hants, SP11 7TB
☎ 01264 357555, Fax 356606
From Andover take the Stockbridge road on the A3057, course is 0.5 mile S of Andover.
Downland course.
Pro Stuart Cronin; Founded 1993
Designed by T Fiducia & A Mitchell
18 holes, 6376 yards, S.S.S. 70
[Practice range, covered bays.
✝ Welcome.
[WD £15, WE £25.
⟳ Welcome by arrangement; full facilities; packages available; terms on application.
🍽 Full facilities.
🗪 White Hart (Andover).

2A 55 **Hartley Wintney**
London Road, Hartley Wintney, Hook, Hants, RG27 8PT
☎ 01252 844211, Pro 843779, Sec 844211, Rest/Bar 842214
A30 between Camberley (5 miles) and Basingstoke (12 miles).
Parkland course.
Pro Martin Smith; Founded 1891
18 holes, 6240 yards, S.S.S. 71
[Driving range.
✝ Welcome, WE/Bank Holiday only with member.
[WD £25.
⟳ Tues/Thurs only by arrangement with Sec; full facilities.
🍽 Comprehensive menu available.
🗪 Lismoyne Hotel, Fleet.

2A 56 **Hassocks**
London Road, Hassocks, W Sussex, BN6 9NA
☎ 01273 846630, Fax 846070, Pro 846990, Rest/Bar 846949
Take A273 towards Hassocks from Brighton; club is between Hassocks and Burgess Hill.
Parkland course.
Pro Charles Ledger; Founded 1995
Designed by P Wright
18 holes, 5439 yards, S.S.S. 68
✝ Welcome anytime; tee time booking recommended.
[WD £14.25; WE £17.50.
⟳ Welcome by arrangement with Sec; full facilities.
🍽 Full facilities.
🗪 The Birch Hotel, Haywards Heath; Hickstead Hotel, Bolney.

2A 57 **Hastings**
Battle Rd, St Leonards-on-Sea, E Sussex, TN37 7BP
⚐ www.hastingsgolfclub.com
📧 mark@hastingsgolfclub.com
☎ 01424 852981, Fax 854244
A2100 from Battle to Hastings, 3 miles NW of Hastings.
Municipal undulating parkland course.
Pro Charles Giddings/Sean Creasy; Founded 1973
Designed by Frank Pennink
18 holes, 6248 yards, S.S.S. 70
[Practice range, 14 bays; floodlit.
✝ Welcome; no restrictions WD; booking system in use at WE 7am-10.30am.
[WD £14; WE £17.50.
⟳ Welcome Mon-Fri; full facilities; terms on application.
🍽 Full facilities.
🗪 Beauport Park.

IFIELD GOLF & COUNTRY CLUB

75 years old this year, Ifield is the course to play with its
beautiful tree-lined fairways.
Society days from only £21.50 per head.
Phone David Knight for details on 01293 520222.

2A 58 Hayling Golf Club
Links Lane, Hayling Island, Hants,
PO11 0BX
☎ 023 92464446, Fax 92464446,
Pro 92464491, Sec 92464446,
Rest/Bar 92463712
From Havant Junction on A27 take
A3023 to SW corner of Hayling Island.
Links course.
Pro R Gadd; Founded 1883
Designed by JH Taylor/Tom Simpson
18 holes, 6521 yards, S.S.S. 71
⚐ Practice range, putting green; 2
covered driving nets.
† Welcome with handicap certs.
Ⅼ WD £36; WE £50.
⟳ Welcome Tues/Wed by prior
arrangement; full facilities.
🍽 Full facilities.
⌁ Newton House Hotel; Broad Oak
Country Hotel.

2A 59 Haywards Heath
High Beech Lane, Haywards Heath, W
Sussex, RH16 1SL
✉ haywardsheath.golfclub@virgin.net
☎ 01444 414457, Fax 458319, Pro
414866, Sec 414457, Rest/Bar 414310
1.5 miles north of Haywards Heath on
the Ardingly road.
Parkland course.
Pro Michael Henning; Founded 1922
Designed by Donald Steel
18 holes, 6204 yards, S.S.S. 70
⚐ 8.
† Welcome with handicap certs.
Ⅼ WD £26; WE £36.
⟳ Welcome by prior arrangement
with the secretary; packages from £38.
🍽 Full facilities.

2A 60 Highwoods
Ellerslie Lane, Bexhill On Sea, E
Sussex, TN39 4LJ
🖳 www.highwoodsgolfclub.co.uk
✉ secretary@
highwoodsgolfclub.co.uk
☎ 01424 212625, Pro 212770,
Rest/Bar 21262
Off A259 from Eastbourne or Hastings;
2 miles from Bexhill; from Battle, A269
via Ninfield, turn right in Sidley.
Parkland course.
Pro Mike Andrews; Founded 1925

Designed by JH Taylor
18 holes, 6218 yards, S.S.S. 70
† Welcome with handicap certs; no
visitors Sun before 12 noon unless
with member.
Ⅼ WD £28; WE £33.
⟳ Welcome by prior arrangement; full
facilities; terms on application.
🍽 Full facilities.
⌁ Cooden Resort.

2A 61 Hill Barn
Excess Cottages, Hill Barn Lane,
Worthing, W Sussex, BN14 9QE
☎ 01903 237301, Fax 217613,
Rest/Bar 233918
N of Worthing off Norwich union
roundabout on A27, take last exit
before the Brighton exit; course is
signposted.
Municipal downland course.
Pro Simon Blanchard; Founded 1935
Designed by Hawtree & Son
18 holes, 6224 yards, S.S.S. 70
† Welcome.
Ⅼ WD £13.50; WE £14.50.
⟳ Welcome WD only; minimum 12;
terms on application.
🍽 Breakfasts, snacks, hot meals
available all day.
⌁ Beach; Ardington & Chatsworth.

2A 62 Hockley
Twyford, Winchester, Hants, SO21 1PL
☎ 01962 713165, Fax 713612, Pro
713678, Rest/Bar 714572
Leave M3 at Junction 11 and follow
signs for Twyford.
Downland course.
Pro Mr T Lane; Founded 1914
Designed by James Braid
18 holes, 6296 yards, S.S.S. 70
† Welcome anytime.
Ⅼ WD £30; WE £40.
⟳ Welcome Wed/Fri by prior
arrangement; full facilities.
🍽 Full facilities every day except
Mon.
⌁ Winchester Royal Hotel; Harestock
Lodge; Potters Heron.

2A 63 Hollingbury Park
Ditchling Road, Brighton, E Sussex,

BN1 7HS
🖳 www.hollingburypark.co.uk
☎ 01273 552010, Fax 500086,
Pro 500086, Sec 552010,
Rest/Bar 552010
1 mile from Brighton, astride the
Downs between A23 London Rd and
A27 Lewes Rd.
Public undulating downland course.
Pro Graeme Crompton; Founded 1908
Designed by J Braid and J H Taylor
18 holes, 6400 yards, S.S.S. 71
† Welcome anytime.
Ⅼ WD £12; WE £17.
⟳ Welcome WD; full facilities; terms
on application.
🍽 Full restaurant facilities.
⌁ Old Ship; Preston Resort.

2A 64 Horam Park
Chiddingly Road, Horam, Heathfield, E
Sussex, TN21 0JJ
🖳 www.holramparkgolf.co.uk
✉ angie@holramgolf.freeserve.co.uk
☎ 01435 813477, Fax 813677
Off M25 at Junction 6; A22 to
Eastbourne; A267 to Heathfield; before
reaching Horam, take Chiddingly road,
200 yards on right.
Parkland course with lakes.
Pro Giles Velvick; Founded 1985
Designed by Glen Johnson
9 holes, 6128 yards, S.S.S. 69
† Welcome 7 days a week.
Ⅼ WD £9-£15.50; WE £9.50-£17.
⟳ Welcome by arrangement.
🍽 Full facilities.
⌁ The Boship Hotel, Hialsham.

2A 65 Horsham Golf Park
Denne Park, Horsham, W Sussex,
RH13 7AX
☎ 01403 271525, Fax 274528
A24 between Horsham and
Southwater; off Hop-Oast roundabout.
Parkland course.
Pro Guy Hovil; Founded 1993
9 holes, 4122 yards, S.S.S. 60
⚐ Practice range; £2.50 bucket of balls.
† Welcome at all times except before
11am Sat.
Ⅼ WD £7; WE £8.
⟳ Welcome by arrangement except
before 11am Sat; full facilities.

🍽 Full facilities.

2A 66 Ifield Golf and Country Club
Rusper Road, Ifield, Crawley, West Sussex, RH11 0LN
☎ 01293 520222, Fax 612973,
Pro 523088, Sec 520222,
Rest/Bar 520222
M23 Junction on the outskirts of Crawley near Gossops Green.
Parkland course.
Pro Jon Earl; Founded 1927
Designed by Bernard Darwin
18 holes, 6330 yards, S.S.S. 70
† Welcome WD but should phone in advance.
ℐ WD £26 per day.
⟁ Society Bookings taken for 16 people or more; coffee, buffet lunch, 3-course dinner in carvery and 36 holes of golf; £55.
🍽 Full Facilities.
⤳ Ifield Court Hotel.

2A 67 Leckford and Longstock
Leckford, Stockbridge, Hants, SO20 6JF
☎ 01264 810320
2.5 miles north of Stockbridge on Andover road.
Parkland course.
Pro Tony Ashton
9:9 holes, 6394:4562 yards, S.S.S. 72:66
† Employees of John Lewis Partnership and guests only.
ℐ WD £10; WE £14.
⟁ Welcome by prior arrangement.
🍽 None.

2A 68 Lee-on-the-Solent
Brune Lane, Lee-on-the-Solent, Hants, PO13 9PB
⬚ www.leegolfclub.plus.uk
✉ leegolfclub@yahoo.com
☎ 023 92550207, Fax 92554233,
Pro 92551181, Sec 92551170,
Rest/Bar 92550207
3 miles South of M27 Junction 11.
Heathland course.
Founded 1905
Designed by JH Taylor
18 holes, 5933 yards, S.S.S. 69
ℐ Practice range.
† Welcome WD.
ℐ WD £30.
⟁ Welcome Thur by prior arrangement.
🍽 Full Clubhouse facilities.
⤳ Belle Vue.

2A 69 Lewes
Chapel Hill, Lewes, E Sussex, BN7 2BB
☎ 01273 483474, Fax 483474,
Pro 473245, Rest/Bar 473245
East of town centre on A27.
Downland course.
Pro Paul Dobson; Founded 1896
18 holes, 6220 yards, S.S.S. 70
† Welcome weekdays and after 2pm at weekends.
ℐ WD £25; WE £36.
⟁ Welcome; terms on application.
🍽 Full bar and restaurant facilities.
⤳ White Hart Hotel, Lewes.

2A 70 Liphook
Wheatsheaf Enclosure, Liphook, Hants, GU30 7EH
☎ 01428 723271, Fax 724853
I mile south of Liphook on B2070 (old A3).
Heath and heather course.
Pro Geoffrey Lee; Founded 1922
Designed by Arthur Croome
18 holes, 6167 yards, S.S.S. 69
† Welcome with handicap certs but not on Tue and only PM at WE.
ℐ WD £35 Sat £45 Sun £53.
⟁ Welcome Wed, Thur, Fri; min 16, max 36; terms on application.
🍽 Bar, bar snacks and restaurant facilities.

2A 71 Littlehampton
Rope Walk, Riverside West, Littlehampton, W Sussex, BN17 5DL
✉ lgc@talk21.com
☎ 01903 717170, Fax 726629,
Pro 716369, Sec 717170,
Rest/Bar 717170
From Littlehampton take the A259 Bognor Regis Road; take the first left after New River Bridge, follow signs for the golf club.
Seaside links course.
Pro Guy Mc Quitty; Founded 1889
18 holes, 6226 yards, S.S.S. 70
† Welcome at any time; after 12 noon on Sun with handicap certificates.
ℐ WD £28; WE £35.
⟁ Welcome WD; full facilities; terms on application.
🍽 Full facilities.
⤳ Bailiff's Court; Norfolk Arms.

2A 72 Mannings Heath
Fullers, Hammerpond Road, Mannings Heath, Horsham, W Sussex, RH13 6PG
⬚ www.manningsheath.com
✉ enquiries@manningsheath.com
☎ 01403 210228, Fax 270974,
Sec 210228, Rest/Bar 210228
2 miles south of Horsham on A281 from Junction 11 on the M23; 4 miles along Grouse Road; turn right at T junction.
Undulating wooded course.
Pro Clive Tucker; Founded 1905
Kingfisher course, Designed by D Williams
† Visitors with handicaps preferred but everyone welcome.
ℐ Waterfall WD £42, Kingfisher £34. WE; Waterfall £56, Kingfisher £40 Day Tickets available from £37 in week and £45 for weekend. Prices on application after April 2002.
⟁ Welcome; full catering available, tennis, steam rooms and practice facilities; Societies from £65.
🍽 Full facilities.
⤳ South Lodge.

2A 73 Manningsheath Hotel
Winterpit Lane, Lower Beeding, Horsham, West Sussex, RH13 6LY
⬚ www.manningsheathhotel.com
✉ info@manningsheathhotel.com
☎ 01403 891191, Fax 891499,
Sec 891191, Rest/Bar 891191
From the M23 take A2110 to Handcross, through village and right at Red Lion Pub, approx 2 miles past garage on right (Church Lane) then 1st left into Winterpit Lane.
Public parkland course.
Founded 1991
Designed by P Webster
9 holes, 4000 yards
† Welcome at all times.
ℐ WD £10 WE £10.
⟁ Welcome, corporate days available.
🍽 Bar, lounge and restaurants.
⤳ Mannings Heath Hotel on site.

2A 74 Marriott Goodwood Park Golf & CC
Goodwood, Nr Chichester, W Sussex, PO18 0QB
☎ 01243 775537, Fax 520120,
Pro 520117, Sec 520117,
Rest/Bar 520117
3 miles north of Chichester.
Parkland course.
Pro Adrian Wratting; Founded 1989
Designed by Donald Steel
18 holes, 6579 yards, S.S.S. 72
ℐ 6.
† Welcome.
ℐ WD £28, WE £35.

⚲ Welcome; packages available for golf, catering and hotel; aerobic studio, swimming pool, tennis, gym, driving range; from £55.
🍽 Full facilities, restaurant and sports cafe bar.
⌁ Marriott Goodwood Park.

2A 75 Meon Valley Hotel ⚉
Golf & CC
Sandy Lane, Shedfield, Southampton, Hants, SO32 2HQ
🖥 www.marriotthotels.co.uk
✉ golf.meonvalley@
marriotthotels.co.uk
☎ 01329 833455, Fax 834411,
Pro 832184, Sec 833455,
Rest/Bar 836826
Off M27 at Junction 27, take Botley exit A334 towards Wickham; course is on Sandy Lane.
Wooded parkland course.
Pro Rod Cameron; Founded 1978
18 holes, 6520 yards, S.S.S. 71;
9-hole Valley Course, 2879 yards
⚐ 8 covered,7 uncovered.
† Book in advance.
⌶ WD £36; WE £42.
⚲ Welcome; parties catered for; terms on application.
🍽 Full facilities.
⌁ Meon Valley Country Club.

2A 76 Mid Sussex ⚉
Spatham Lane, Ditchling, East Sussex, BN6 8XJ
🖥 www.midsussexgolfclub.co.uk
✉ admin@midsussexgolfclub.co.uk
☎ 01273 846567, Fax 845767,
Pro 846567, Sec 841835,
Rest/Bar 845644
1 mile east of Ditchling on Lewes Road.
Parkland course.
Founded 1995
Designed by D Williams Partnership
18 holes, 6446 yards, S.S.S. 71
⚐ Practice range, grass tees available.
† Welcome WD and afternoons at WE.
⌶ WD £22; WE £22.
⚲ Welcome on WD; restaurant and practice facilities.
🍽 Full Facilities.
⌁ Many in the Brighton area.

2A 77 Moors Valley Golf Course
Horton Road, Ashley Heath, Ringwood, Hants, BH24 2ET
🖥 www.moors-valley.co.uk
✉ mvalley@eastdorset.gov.uk
☎ 01425 479776, Fax 472057,

Pro 479776, Rest/Bar 480448
A31 through Ringwood, right at roundabout to Ashley Heath, course 2 miles on the right.
Parkland/heathland course.
Coaching Pro Michael Torrens;
Founded 1988
Designed by Martin Hawtree
18 holes, 6337 yards, S.S.S. 70
⚐ Full practice facilities.
† Welcome.
⌶ WD £12.50; WE £15.
⚲ Welcome after 11am.
🍽 Full bar and catering facilities.
⌁ Struan, St Leonards.

2A 78 New Forest ⚉
Southampton Road, Lyndhurst, Hants, SO43 7BU
☎ 0123 80282752
On the A 35 between Ashurst and Lyndhurst.
Forest heathland course.
Founded 1888
Designed by Peter Swann
18 holes, 5772 yards, S.S.S. 68
† Welcome.
⌶ WD £10; WE £12.
⚲ Welcome but must book in advance; bar and lounge facilities.
🍽 Full facilities.

2A 79 Newport
Near Shide, Newport, Isle Of Wight, PO30 3BA
☎ 01983 525076
On A 3056 Newport Sandown Road half a mile from Newport.
Downland course.
Founded 1896
Designed by Guy Hunt
9 holes, 5660 yards, S.S.S. 68
† Welcome with Handicap certs.
⌶ Terms on application.
⚲ Welcome by arrangement; catering packages available by special arrangement with caterer; from £12.
🍽 Bar and catering facilities.

2A 80 North Hants
Minley Road, Fleet, Hants, GU51 1RF
☎ 01252 616443, Fax 811627,
Pro 616655
Half a mile north of Fleet station on B3013, Junction 4A on M3
Heathland course.
Pro Steve Porter; Founded 1904
Designed by James Braid
18 holes, 6519 yards, S.S.S. 72
† Welcome by prior arrangement with Sec; letter off introduction and handicap certs required.

⌶ WD £32.
⚲ Welcome Mon to Fri by arrangement with Sec; full facilities; packages available; terms on application.
🍽 Lunch, tea, dinner; pre-booking required.
⌁ Various in Fleet, Camberley and Farnborough.

2A 81 Old Thorns
Old Thorns, Weavers Down, Longmoor Road, Liphook, Hants, GU30 7PE
✉ info@oldthorns.com
☎ 01428 724555, Fax 725063
Signposted from A3 at Griggs Green.
Parkland course.
Pro Keiran Stevensons; Founded 1982
Designed by Commander John Harris; adapted by Peter Alliss and Dave Thomas
18 holes, 6533 yards, S.S.S. 71
⚐ 2.
† Welcome.
⌶ WD £35; WE £40.
⚲ Welcome any day; corporate and society days can be arranged; packages available; function rooms.
🍽 European and Japanese restaurants.
⌁ Old Thorns.

2A 82 Osborne
Osborne House Estate, East Cowes, Isle Of Wight, PO32 6JX
☎ 01983 295421
1 mile from Red Funnel Terminal in grounds of Osborne House.
Parkland course.
Founded 1903
2 holes opened for Royal household in 1892; extended to 9 by Osborne House Governor in 1904
9 holes, 6398 yards, S.S.S. 70
⚐ Practice nets, practice green.
† Welcome by prior arrangement except Tues, Sat and Sun am.
⌶ Terms on application.
⚲ Welcome by arrangement but a maximum of 24; bar and restaurant facilities; terms on application.
🍽 Facilities available.
⌁ Memories, East Cowes;
Wheatsheaf, Newport Albert Cottage York Avenue.

2A 83 Otterbourne Golf Club
Poles Lane, Otterbourne, Nr Winchester, Hants, SO21 1DZ
☎ 01962 775225
On A31 between Hursley and

Otterbourne villages.
Parkland course.
Founded 1995
9 holes, 1939 yards, S.S.S. 30
⚲ Open practice range.
♦ Public pay and play.
⚏ WD £4; WE £5.
⚘ None.
⚉ None.

2A 84 Paultons Golf Centre

Salisbury Road, Ower, Romsey, Hants,
SO51 6AN
☎ 023 8081 3345
Exit 2 off M27 in direction of Ower, left
at 1st roundabout, then right at
Heathlands Hotel, then signposted.
Parkland course.
Pro Rod Park; Founded 1993
18 holes, 6238 yards, S.S.S. 70
⚲ Practice range 24 bays; floodlit.
♦ All welcome at all times.
⚏ Available on request.
⚘ Welcome by arrangement; full
facilities; terms on application.
⚉ Bars and restaurant.
⚐ Heathlands (500 yards).

2A 85 Paxhill Park

East Mascalls Lane, Lindfield,
Haywards heath, W Sussex, RH16 2QN
⚏ www.paxhillpark.com
⚏ johnbowen@paxhillpark.fsnet.com
☎ 01444 484467, Fax 482709, Pro
484000
2 miles outside Haywards Heath on
Lindfield Road.
Parkland course.
Pro Marcus Green; Founded 1990
Designed by Patrick Tallack
18 holes, 6117 yards, S.S.S. 69
⚲ 5.
♦ Welcome WD and after 12 noon at
WE.
⚏ WD £17; WE £22.
⚘ Welcome Mon-Fri; full facilities but
no food on Mon evenings; from £45.
⚉ Full facilities except evenings
unless prior arranged.
⚐ Birch Hotel, Haywards Heath.

2A 86 Peacehaven

Brighton Road, Newhaven, E Sussex,
BN9 9UH
⚏ golf@peacehaven.freeserve.co.uk
☎ 01273 514049, Pro 512602
On A259 1 mile W of Newhaven.
Undulating downland course.
Pro Ian Pearson; Founded 1895
Designed by James Braid
9 holes, 5488 yards, S.S.S. 67
♦ Welcome WD; after 11.30am WE

and BH.
⚏ WD £12; WE £18.
⚘ Welcome WD; full facilities; terms
on application.
⚉ Available WE; by prior
arrangement WD.

2A 87 Pease Pottage Golf Club

Buchan Hill, Horsham Road, Crawley,
W Sussex, RH11 9SG
☎ 01293 521706, Fax 518428
Leave M23 at Junction 11, then course
is signposted from large roundabout.
Public parkland course.
Pro David Blair; Founded 1986
Designed by Adam Lazar
9 holes, 3511 yards, S.S.S. 60
⚲ Practice range, 26 bays; floodlit.
♦ Welcome.
⚏ WD £8.50; WE £11.
⚘ Welcome by arrangement; full
facilities; terms on application.
⚉ No Restaurant.
⚐ Cottismore Hotel.

2A 88 Petersfield

Tankerdale Lane, Liss, Hants, GU33
7QY
⚏ greghughes@18global.com
☎ 01730 895216, Fax 894713, Pro
895216, Sec 895165, Rest/Bar 895324
Off A3 between Petersfield/Midhurst &
Liss exit.
Parkland course.
Pro Greg Hughes; Founded 1892; New
course 1997
New course designed by Martin
Hawtree
18 holes, 6387 yards, S.S.S. 71
♦ Welcome with handicap certificates.
⚏ WD £25; WE £30.
⚘ Welcome Mon, Wed and Fri;
modern new clubhouse facilities; terms
on application.
⚉ Full facilities.
⚐ Concord Hotel.

2A 89 Petworth Golf Club

London Road, Petworth, W Sussex,
GU28 9LX
☎ 01798 344097, Fax 342528,
Pro 07932 163 941, Sec 1730 817707
1.5 miles N of Petworth on A283.
Parkland course over farmland.
Pro Mr Little; Founded 1989
Designed by Chris Duncton
18 holes, 6191 yards, S.S.S. 69
♦ Welcome.
⚏ WD £10; WE £10.
⚘ Welcome; new clubhouse opened
1999 with full facilities; terms on
application.

⚉ Full facilities in new clubhouse.
⚐ B&B on course; Stonemasons
Arms, Petworth.

2A 90 Piltdown

Piltdown, Uckfield, E Sussex, TN22 3XB
☎ 01825 722033, Fax 724192, Pro
722389
1 mile W of Maresfield on the A272.
Heathland course.
Pro J Partridge & A Milligan; Founded
1904
Designed by J Rowe, GM Dodd, Frank
Pennink
18 holes, 6070 yards, S.S.S. 69
♦ Welcome by arrangement.
⚏ WD £30 & WE £30.
⚘ Welcome Mon, Wed and Fri;
packages available; terms on
application.
⚉ Full facilities.

2A 91 Portsmouth

Crookhorn Lane, Widley Waterlooville,
Hants, PO7 5QL
☎ 023 92372210, Fax 92200766,
Pro 92372210, Sec 92201827,
Rest/Bar 92375999
1.5 miles from A3(M), junction of
Purbrook/Leigh Park.
Parkland course.
Pro Jason Banting; Founded 1972
Designed by Hawtree
18 holes, 5760 winter card summer
card yardage6139 yards, S.S.S. 70
♦ Welcome with prior booking.
⚏ WD £10.50; WE £13.50.
⚘ Welcome at any time by prior
arrangement; packages available.
⚉ Bar and restaurant facilities.
⚐ Innlodge Hotel.

2A 92 Pyecombe

Clayton Hill, Pyecombe, Brighton, E
Sussex, BN45 7FF
⚏ pyecombegc@btopenworld.com
☎ 01273 845372, Fax 843338, Pro
845398, Sec 845372
Off A23 at Hassocks and Pyecombe.
Turn left on to A273 and course is 300
yds on right.
Downland course.
Pro Chris White; Founded 1894
18 holes, 6204 yards, S.S.S. 70
⚲ Practice green. Practice nets.
♦ Welcome.
⚏ WD £25; WE £30.
⚘ Welcome by prior arrangement;
terms on application.
⚉ Full facilities.
⚐ Club can advise.

2A 93 Romsey
Romsey Road, Nursling, Southampton, Hants, SO16 0XW
🖳 www.romseygolfclub.com
📧 barbra@romseygolf.co.uk
☎ 023 80734637, Fax 80741036, Pro 80736673,
Rest/Bar 80732218
2 miles SE of Romsey on A3057 Southampton Road, near M27/M271 Junction 3.
Wooded parkland course.
Pro Mark Desmond; Founded 1900
Designed by Charles Lawrie
18 holes, 5856 yards, S.S.S. 68
† Welcome WD.
Ⅰ WD £23.
⚘ Welcome by arrangement Mon, Tues and Thurs; full facilities; terms on application.
🍽 Full facilities.
⌂ White Horse (Romsey); Travel Inn (Nursling); Novotel (Southampton).

2A 94 Rowlands Castle ♔
Links Lane, Rowlands Castle, Hants, PO9 6AE
☎ 023 92412784, Fax 92413649, Pro 92412785, Rest/Bar 92412216
3 miles on the B2149 off Junction 2 of the A3M.
Parkland course.
Pro P Klepacz; Founded 1902
Designed by HS Colt
18 holes, 6612 yards, S.S.S. 72
† Welcome except for Sat.
Ⅰ WD £30; WE £35.
⚘ Welcome Tues and Thurs by prior arrangement; packages include 36 holes plus lunch and dinner; £41-£45.
🍽 Full facilities.
⌂ Brook Fields hotel, Emsworth.

2A 95 Royal Ashdown Forest
Chapel Lane, Forest Row, E Sussex, RH18 5LR
🖳 www.royalashdownforest.com
☎ 01342 822018, Fax 825211, Pro 822247, Sec 822018, Rest/Bar 823014
A22 East Grinstead-Eastbourne Road,4.5 miles S of East Grinstead turn left in Forest Row opposite church on to B2110, after 0.5 mile turn right into Chapel Lane, top of hill turn left, over heath to clubhouse.
Undulating heathland course with views over forest.
Pro Martyn Landsborough; Founded 1888
2 x 18 holes, 6477 yards, S.S.S. 70
† Welcome by arrangement only; restrictions at WE and BH.
Ⅰ WD £45; WE £60.

⚘ Welcome by prior arrangement; catering; full facilities, except Mon.
🍽 Lunch, tea; casual visitors requested to book in advance or before teeing off.
⌂ Ashdown Forest; Brambletye (E Grinstead); Chequers.

2A 96 Royal Eastbourne ♔
Paradise Drive, Eastbourne, E Sussex, BN20 8BP
☎ 01323 729738, Fax 729738, Pro 736986, Rest/Bar 730412
0.5 miles from Town Hall.
Downland course.
Pro Alan Harrison; Founded 1887
18 holes, 6118 yards, S.S.S. 69
Ⅰ 9-hole course, 4294 yards, S.S.S. 61.
† Welcome but handicap certs needed on the Devonshire course.
Ⅰ WD £25; WE £30.
⚘ Welcome on WD only; golf, lunch and 3-course dinner; £40-£50.
🍽 Full facilities.
⌂ Grand; Lansdowne; Chatsworth, all in Eastbourne.

2A 97 Royal Winchester ♔
Sarum Road, Winchester, Hants, SO22 5QE
📧 Royalwincestergolfclub.com
☎ 01962 852462, Fax 865048, Pro 862473, Sec 852462, Rest/Bar 851694
Take M3 to Junction 11 and at Pitt roundabout follow sign to Winchester until roundabout, first turn off into Chilbolton Ave, first turning left into Sarum Road, mile up the road on the right is the golf club.
Downland course.
Pro Steve Hunter; Founded 1888
Designed by HS Colt and AP Taylor
18 holes, 6216 yards, S.S.S. 70
† Welcome WD; with a member only at WE. Not bank holidays.
Ⅰ WD £33.
⚘ Mon, Tues afternoon £42 and Wed only by prior arrangement; £55.
🍽 Full facilities.

2A 98 Rustington Golf Centre ♔
Golfers Lane, Angmering, Littlehampton, W Sussex, BN16 4NB
🖳 www.slicetheprice.com
☎ 01903 850790, Fax 850982
A259 at Rushington, between Worthing and Chichester.
Public parkland course, membership avail.
Pro D Moxham/C Rotar/M Pulman/ I Williams; Founded 1995

Designed by David Williams P'ship
9 holes, 5735 yards, S.S.S. 68
Ⅰ Practice range, 30 covered bays, 6 outdoor bays.
† Welcome 8:30am to 9pm 7 days a week; bookings taken.
Ⅰ 18 holes £16.50. 9 Holes £10.50.
⚘ Welcome by arrangement; full facilities; terms on application.
🍽 Coffee shop serving hot and cold lunches; licensed bar.

2A 99 Ryde
Binstead Road, Ryde, Isle Of Wight, PO33 3NF
🖳 www.rydegolf.co.uk
📧 seceratary@ rydegolfclub.freeserve.co.uk
☎ 01983 614809, Fax 567418, Sec 614809, Rest/Bar 614809
Main Ryde-Newport road.
Parkland course.
Founded 1895
9 holes, 5287 yards, S.S.S. 66
† Welcome; not Wed pm or Sun am.
Ⅰ WD £15; WE £20.
⚘ Welcome WD except Wed; contact Sec; facilities and packages by arrangement; terms on application.
🍽 By arrangement.
⌂ Newlands.

2A 100 Rye
New Lydd Road, Camber, Rye, E Sussex, TN31 7QS
☎ 01797 225241, Fax 225460, Pro 225218, Sec 225241
From Rye take the A259 to New Romney; 2 miles out of town turn right towards Camber; course is 1.5 miles on right.
Links course.
Pro Micheal Lee; Founded 1894
Designed by HS Colt
27 holes, 6308 yards, S.S.S. 71
† Welcome, but only with a member.
Ⅰ Not available.
⚘ None.
🍽 Full facilities.
⌂ Hope; Anchor; Mermaid, all in Rye.

2A 101 Sandford Springs ♔
Wolverton, Tadley, Hants, RG26 5RT
☎ 01635 296800, Fax 296801, Pro 296808
Off the A339 at Kingsclere between Basingstoke and Newbury.
Picturesque varied course overlooking 5 counties.
Pro Gary Edmunds; Founded 1988
Designed by Hawtree & Son
27 holes, 3 courses (Parks, Woods,

Lakes). Parks 6143 yards, S.S.S. 69; Woods 6222 yards, S.S.S. 70; Lakes 6005 yards, S.S.S. 69
♦ Welcome WD, booking system in operation; WE subject to availability.
⌐ WD £23.
♤ Society and Company days welcome by prior arrangement.
🍽 Full bar and restaurant facilities.
⌐ Hilton National, Basingstoke & Newbury.

2A 102 Seaford Golf Club
Firle Road, Seaford, E Sussex, BN25 2JD
🖳 www.seafordgolfclub.co.uk
✉ secretary@seafordgolfclub.co.uk
☎ 01323 892442, Fax 894113, Pro 894160
1 mile N of Seaford on A259.
Downland course.
Pro D Mills; Founded 1887
Designed by JH Taylor
18 holes, 6551 yards, S.S.S. 71
♦ Open.
♦ Welcome by arrangement.
⌐ WD £28; WE £33.
♤ By arrangement; terms on request.
🍽 Full facilities available.
⌐ Dormy House.

2A 103 Seaford Head
Southdown Road, Seaford, East Sussex, BN25 4JS
☎ 01323 894843, Pro 890139, Sec 894843, Rest/Bar 894843
S of A259, 12 miles from Brighton.
Public seaside course.
Pro Tony Lowles; Founded 1887
18 holes, 5848 yards, S.S.S. 68
♦ Welcome at all times.
⌐ WD £15; WE £18 and bank holidays £18.
♤ Welcome; full facilities; terms on application Mon-Fri.
🍽 Light snacks.
⌐ Traslyn, Clear View.

2A 104 Sedlescombe
Kent Street, Sedlescombe, Battle, E Sussex, TN33 0SD
☎ 01424 870898
On main A21 near Sedlescombe.
Parkland course.
Pro James Andrews; Founded 1991
18 holes, 6321 yards, S.S.S. 70
♦ Practice range, 25 bays; floodlit.
♦ Welcome.
⌐ WD £16; WE £20.
♤ Full facilities; terms on application.
🍽 Bar and snacks.
⌐ Brickwall.

2A 105 Selsey
Selsey Country Club Ltd, Golf Links Lane, Selsey, Chichester, W Sussex, PO20 9DR
🖳 www.energylinks.co.uk/selsey
☎ 01243 607101, Fax 602203
On B2145 7 miles S of Chichester.
Seaside course.
Pro Peter Grindley; Founded 1909
9 holes, 5848 yards, S.S.S. 68
♦ Welcome.
⌐ WD £12; WE £15.
♤ Small societies welcome; full facilities; terms on application.
🍽 Lunch and snacks.
⌐ Chichester Ship (Bedford).

2A 106 Shanklin & Sandown
The Fairway, Sandown, Isle Of Wight, PO36 9PR
☎ 01983 403217, Fax 403217, Pro 404424, Rest/Bar 403170
Off main Sandown & Shanklin road at Lake (A3055).
Sandy parklan,d course with some steep slopes.
Pro Peter Hammond; Founded 1900
Designed by Dr J Cowper, James Braid
18 holes, 6083 yards, S.S.S. 69
♦ Welcome with handicap certs; restrictions at WE before lunch.
⌐ WD £25; WE £30.
♤ Welcome on WD except Tues by prior arrangement; packages available; terms on application.
🍽 Full facilities available.

2A 107 Singing Hills Golf Course
Albourne, Hassocks, W Sussex, BN6 9EB
☎ 01273 835353, Fax 835444
On the B2117 off the A23.
Parkland course with 3 x 9 holes (River, Valley & Lake).
Pro Wallace Street; Founded 1992
Designed by Richard Hurd (Sandow)
27 holes, 6079 yards, S.S.S. 71
♦ Practice range, 15 bays.
♦ Welcome.
⌐ WD £23; WE £31 (18 holes).
♤ Welcome for groups of more than 12; prices and packages vary each day.
🍽 Restaurant and bar facilities available.
⌐ Hickstead Hotel, Bolney; Birch Hotel, Haywards Heath.

2A 108 Slinford Park Golf & Country Club   ☾
Stane Street, Slinfold, Horsham, W

Sussex, RH13 7RE
☎ 01403 791154, Fax 791465, Pro 791555
4 miles W of horesham, with direct access from A29, there also fast road connections from the N via the M25 and the A24. Slinford Park is also convieniently situated from the South coast or in either direction via the A272.
Parkland course.
Pro Tony Clingan; Founded 1992
Designed by John Fortune
27 holes, 6418 yards, S.S.S. 71
♦ Practice range, 19 bays floodlit.
♦ Welcome.
⌐ WD £25; WE £25.
♤ Welcome Mon-Fri although some restrictions on Tues; full facilities; from £25.
🍽 Full facilities.
⌐ Ramson Hall, Slinford.

2A 109 South Sea
Burrfields Road, Portsmouth, Hants, PO3 5HH
☎ 023 92664549, Fax 92650525, Sec 92668667
2 miles off M27/A27/A3 on A2030 road into Portsmouth.
Municipal meadowland course.
Pro Terry Healy; Founded 1935
18 holes, 5575 yards, S.S.S. 67
♦ Practice range, 24 bays; floodlit.
♦ Welcome.
⌐ WD £10.50; WE £13.50.
♤ Welcome by arrangement; catering available in adjacent farmhouse pub; terms on application.
🍽 Available in adjacent farmhouse pub.

2A 110 South Winchester
Pitt, Winchester, Hants, SO22 5QW
🖳 www.southwinchester.com
☎ 01962 877800, Fax 877900, Pro 840469, Sec 877800, Rest/Bar 877800
S of Winchester on Romsey road.
Championship style links course.
Pro Richard Adams; Founded 1993
Designed by D Thomas, P Alliss, C Clark
18 holes, 7100 for men 5981 for ladies yards, S.S.S. par 72 men par 74 women
♦ Practice range for teaching and members only.
♦ Guests of members only.
⌐ Visitors £25 WD £40 WE.
♤ Welcome; terms on application.
🍽 Full bar and dining facilities. Bistro and Carvery open to visitors.

Lainstone Hotel; Royal Hotel; Hotel du Vin.

2A 111 Southampton
Golf Course Road, Bassett, Southampton, herts, SO16 7AY
☎ 023 80760546, Pro 80768407, Rest/Bar 80767996
N end of city, off Bassett Ave, halfway between Chilworth roundabout and Winchester Rd roundabout.
Municipal parkland course.
Pro Jon Waring; Founded 1935
18 holes, 6213 yards, S.S.S. 70
⌁ Also a 9-hole course.
† Welcome.
⌂ WD £8.20; WE £11.30.
⌁ Welcome by arrangement; full facilities; terms on application.
🍽 Breakfast, lunch, bar snacks.
⌁ Hilton (Chilworth).

2A 112 Southwick Park
Pinsley Drive, Southwick, Fareham, Hants, PO17 6EL
☎ 023 92370683, Fax 92210289, Pro 92380442, Sec 92380131
B2177 to Southwick village.
Parkland course.
Pro J Green; Founded 1977
Designed by Charles Lawrie
18 holes, 5992 yards, S.S.S. 69
† Strictly by prior arrangement.
⌂ Not available.
⌁ Welcome by prior arrangement; 36 holes with coffee, lunch and dinner; £20-£35.
🍽 Full bar and dining facilities.

2A 113 Southwood
Ively Road, Farnborough, Hants, GU14 0LJ
☎ 01252 548700, Pro 548700, Sec 548700,
Rest/Bar 515139
0.5 miles W of Farnborough.
Parkland course.
Pro Scott Shibley; Founded 1976
Designed by Hawtree & Son
18 holes, 5738 yards, S.S.S. 68
† All Welcome.
⌂ Terms on application.
⌁ Welcome on WD; full facilities available; terms on application.
🍽 Full facilities.
⌁ Potters International, Aldershot. The Monkey Puzzle, Farnborough.

2A 114 Stoneham
Monks Wood Close, Southampton, Hants, SO16 3TT

www.stonehamgolfclub.org.uk
✉ stonehamgc@stoneham09.freereserve.co.uk
☎ 023 80768151, Fax 80766320, Pro 80768397, Sec 80769272,
Rest/Bar 8076 6510
Close to M3 and M27.
Undulating parkland course with heather.
Pro Ian Young; Founded 1908
Designed by Willie Park
18 holes, 6387 yards, S.S.S. 70
† Welcome by arrangement.
⌂ Terms on application.
⌁ Welcome Mon, Thurs and Fri; 36 holes, coffee, lunch and dinner; golf clinic, video analysis; from £52.
🍽 Full facilities.
⌁ Hilton, Southampton.

2A 115 Test Valley ⌑
Micheldever Road, Overton, Basingstoke, Hants, RG25 3DS
www.testgolf.com
✉ testvalley@testvalleygolf.com
☎ 01256 771737, Fax 08707 459023, Rest/Bar 772080
2 miles S of Overton village junction with B3400, or 1.5 miles N of A303 from Overton turn-off.
Inland links course.
Pro Alastair Briggs; Founded 1992
Designed by D Wright
18 holes, 6883 yards, S.S.S. 72
⌁ 6.
† Welcome WD and WE; advisable to phone first.
⌂ WD £18; WE £24.
⌁ Welcome 7 days; full facilities.
🍽 Full bar and dining facilities; dining room for up to 100.
⌁ White Hart Overton.

2A 116 Tidworth Garrison
Bulford Road, Tidworth, Hants, SP9 7AF
✉ tidworth@garrison-golfclub.ffnet.co.uk
☎ 01980 842301, Fax 842301, Pro 842393, Rest/Bar 842321
A338 Salisbury to Marlborough into Bulford Road.
Tree-lined downland course.
Pro Terry Gosden; Founded 1908
Designed by Donald Steel
18 holes, 6320 yards, S.S.S. 70
† Welcome.
⌂ WD £29; WE £29.
⌁ Welcome Tues and Thurs; full facilities and packages on application.
🍽 Full catering facilities.
⌁ Red House Hotel, Parkhouse Motel.

2A 117 Tilgate Forest Golf Centre
Titmus Drive, Crawley, W Sussex, RH10 5EU
☎ 01293 530103, Fax 523478
M23 Junction 11 for Pease Pottage, follow main road to Crawley, at 1st roundabout turn right, follow signs.
Public parkland course.
Pro Shaun Trussll; Founded 1983
Designed by Huggett and Coles
18 holes, 6359 yards, S.S.S. 70
⌁ Practice range, 36 bays. Also a 9-hole course.
† Welcome.
⌂ WD £14; WE £18.50.
⌁ Welcome Mon-Thurs; full facilities; terms on application.
🍽 Restaurant and bar all day.
⌁ Holiday Inn(Crawley).

2A 118 Tournerbury
Tournerbury Lane, Hayling Island, Hants, PO11 9DL
☎ 023 9246 2266, Pro 92462266, Sec 92462266
Off A27 on Hayling Island.
Seaside course.
Pro Robert Brown; Founded 1994
Designed by Robert Brown
9 holes, 5912 yards, S.S.S. 68
⌁ Practice range, 16 bays; floodlit.
† Welcome; pay and play.
⌂ WD £8.00 WE £9.30 9 HOLES; WD£12.50 WE£15 for 18 holes.
⌁ Welcome by arrangement.
🍽 None; local pub.
⌁ Forte Post House.

2A 119 Tylney Park
Rotherwick, Hook, Hampshire, RG27 9AY
☎ 01256 762079, Fax 763079, Pro 762079, Sec 762079,
Rest/Bar 762079
Take M3 to Junction 5 amd then 2 miles to Rotherwick via Hook or Newnham. Take M4 Junction 11 and then A33 and B3349 to Rotherwick.
Mature parkland course; fine specimen trees; practice areas.
Pro Chris de Bruin; Founded 1974
Designed by W Wiltshire
18 holes, 6200 yards, S.S.S. 69
† Welcome on WD; WE telephone for availability.
⌂ WD £25; WE £32.
⌁ Welcome Mon to Thurs inc; 36 holes of golf plus coffee, lunch and dinner max £49; alternative packages available throughout golfing year.
🍽 Full facilities.
⌁ Tylney Hall; AA hotels in Hook.

2A 120 **Ventnor**
Ventnor Golf Club, Steephill Down
Road, Ventnor, Isle Of Wight, PO38
1BP
☎ 01983 853326
On A3055 to Ventnor.
Undulating downland course.
Founded 1892
12 holes, 5767 yards, S.S.S. 68
† Welcome; not before 1pm Sun.
Tees closed until 12pm Mon. Mon 11 til
1pm closed.
⌊ WD £17; WE £20.
⌂ Welcome by arrangement.
🍴 Bar and bar snacks.
🛌 Eversly; Bonchurch Manor;
Mayfair, Shanklin.

2A 121 **Waterhall**
Waterhall Road, Brighton, E Sussex,
BN1 8YN
☎ 01273 508658
3 miles N of Brighton off A27.
Hilly downland course.
Pro Graham Crompton; Founded 1923
18 holes, 5713 yards, S.S.S. 68
† Welcome.
⌊ WD £12; WE £17.
⌂ Welcome; full catering facilities and
packages on request; terms on
application.
🍴 Restaurant and bar.

2A 122 **Waterlooville**
Cherry Tree Avenue, Waterlooville,
Hants, PO8 8AP
☎ 023 92263388, Fax 92347513,
Pro 92256911
A3(M) Junction 3 take B2150 to
Waterlooville; at 1st roundabout take
exit for Hurstwood.
Parkland course.
Pro John Hay; Founded 1907
Designed by Henry Cotton
18 holes, 6602 yards, S.S.S. 72
† Welcome WD.
⌊ WD £30.
⌂ Welcome Thurs with prior
arrangement with Sec.; 36 holes of
golf; coffee on arrival, light lunch and
evening meal; other packages also
available; £46.
🍴 Full catering and bar facilities.
🛌 Hilton National.

2A 123 **Wellow**
Ryedown Lane, East Wellow, Romsey,
Hants, SO51 6BD
☎ 01794 322872, Fax 323832,
Pro 323833
Take M27 to Junction 2 then A36 for 2
miles to Whinwhistle road, then 1.5

miles to Ryedown Road.
Parkland course; 27 holes, three 9s:
Ryedown, Embley, Blackwater.
Pro Neil Bratley; Founded 1991
Designed by W Wiltshire
27 holes, 5966 yards
† Welcome.
⌊ WD £16; WE £20.
⌂ Welcome on WD; 27 holes, full
catering; terms on application.
🍴 Full catering available.
🛌 Vine Hotel, Ower Romsey;
Bramble Hill, Bramshaw.

2A 124 **Wellhurst Golf &
Country Club**
North Street, Hellingly, Hailsham, E
Sussex, BN27 4EE
📧 info@wellhurst.com
☎ 01435 813636, Fax 812444,
Pro 813456
From the A22, Take A267 Heathfield on
the left 2/3 miles is the golf course.
Parkland course.
Pro M Jarvis; Founded 1992
Designed by Golf Corporation
18 holes, 5771 yards, S.S.S. 70
⌊ Practice range, 8 bays and 2
bunker bays.
† Public pay and play.
⌊ WD £18; WE £22.
⌂ Welcome; packages available. Full
fitness room and gym, sauna etc.
🍴 Available.
🛌 Boship Farm Hotel, Hailsham.

2A 125 **West Chiltington Golf
Club**
Broadford Bridge Road, West
Chiltington, Pulborough, W Sussex,
RH20 2YA
☎ 01798 812115, Fax 812631, Pro
812115
On A29 proceed south and turn left at
Advesane.
Undulating parkland course.
Pro George Mackay; Founded 1988
Designed by Brian Barnes and Max
Faulkner
18 (additional short course of 9 holes)
holes, 5877 yards, S.S.S. 69
† Welcome.
⌊ WD £15; WE £17.50.
⌂ Welcome by arrangement; terms
on application.
🍴 Full facilities.
🛌 Roundabout Hotel, W Chiltington;
Chequers Hotel, Pulborough.

2A 126 **West Hove**
Church Farm, Hangleston Valley Drive,
Hove, E Sussex, BN3 8AN

📧 info@westhovegolf.co.uk
☎ 01273 419738, Fax 439988, Pro
413494, Rest/Bar 413411
On A27 Brighton by-pass at the
Hangleton Interchange.
Downland course relocated in 1990.
Pro Darren Cook; Founded 1910/1991
Designed by Hawtree
18 holes, 6216 yards, S.S.S. 70
⌊ Practice range, 18 bays.
† Welcome.
⌊ WD £25; WE £30.
⌂ Welcome; packages available for
groups; terms on application.
🍴 Full bar and catering.
🛌 Grand Hotel.

2A 127 **West Sussex**
Golf Club Lane, Pulborough, W
Sussex, RH20 2EN
🖥 www.westsussexgolf.co.uk
📧 secretary@westsussexgolf.co.uk
☎ 01798 872563, Fax 872033, Pro
872426, Sec 872563, Rest/Bar 874019
1.5 miles E of Pulborough on A283.
Heathland course.
Pro Tim Packham; Founded 1931
Designed by Sir Guy Campbell, Major
CK Hutchison
18 holes, 6221 yards, S.S.S. 70
⌊ Practice range, 12 bays.
† Welcome WD only.
⌊ WD £47.50.
⌂ Welcome Wed and Thurs; full
facilities; terms available on application.
🍴 Lunch and tea.
🛌 Amberley Castle; Roundabout.

2A 128 **Westridge**   ☂
Brading Road, Ryde, Isle Of Wight,
PO33 1QS
🖥 www.westridgegc.co,uk
📧 westgc@aol.com
☎ 01983 613131, Fax 567017
A3054 Ryde to Dandown road 2 miles
S of Ryde.
Flat parkland course.
Pro Mark Wright; Founded 1992
9 holes, 3554 yards, S.S.S. 58
⌊ Practice range, 19 bays floodlit.
† Welcome.
⌊ WD £8.50; WE £9.50 (9 holes).
⌂ Welcome by arrangement; terms
on application.
🍴 Bar and food available.
🛌 Several in area.

2A 129 **Weybrook Park**
Rooksdown Lane, Basingstoke, Hants,
RG24 9NT
☎ 01256 320347, Fax 812973,
Pro 333232, Rest/Bar 331159

2 miles NW of town centre between A339 and A340.
Parkland course.
Pro Anthony Dillon; Founded 1971
18 holes, 6468 yards, S.S.S. 70
⚑ Practice range, grass.
⚑ Welcome by arrangement.
⚑ POA.
⚑ Welcome by prior arrangement.
⚑ Available.

2A 130 **Wickham Park**
Titchfield Lane, Wickham, Fareham, Hants, PO17 5PJ
⚑ www.crownsportsplc.com
☎ 01329 833342, Fax 834798
2 miles N of Fareham off M27 Junction 10.
Parkland course.
Pro Robynn Gordon; Founded 1995
Designed by J Payne
18 holes, 6022 yards, S.S.S. 69
⚑ Public pay and play.
⚑ WD £12; WE £15.
⚑ Welcome by prior arrangement WD; packages available; society room.
⚑ Clubhouse facilities.

2A 131 **Willingdon**
Southdown Road, Eastbourne, E Sussex, BN20 9AA
⚑ www.wgc.demon.co.uk
✉ secretary@wgc.demon.co.uk
☎ 01323 410981, Fax 411510, Pro 410984, Sec 410981, Rest/Bar 410983
2 miles N of Eastbourne off A22.
Downland course.
Pro Troy Moore; Founded 1898
Designed by JH Taylor; modernised by Dr MacKenzie 1925
18 holes, 6044 yards, S.S.S. 69
⚑ Welcome WD.
⚑ WD £25 WE £28.
⚑ By prior arrangement WD except Tues; packages available; terms on application.
⚑ By arrangement.
⚑ Grand; Queens; Lansdown.

2A 132 **Worldham Park**
Blanket Street, East Worldham, Alton, Hants, GU34 3AG
☎ 01420 543151, Sec 544606
Take A31, then A3004 to Bordon; course on right.
Parkland course.
Pro Jon Le Roux; Founded 1994
Designed by F Whidborne

18 holes, 5897 yards, S.S.S. 68
⚑ Pay and play.
⚑ WD £11; WE £14.
⚑ Welcome Mon to Fri; terms on application.
⚑ Full bar and catering.
⚑ Alton Hotel; Swan Hotel.

2A 133 **Worthing**
Links Road, Worthing, W Sussex, BN14 9QZ
⚑ www.worthinggolf.co.uk
✉ worthinggolf@easynet.co.uk
☎ 01903 260801, Fax 694664, Pro 260718, Sec 260801, Rest/Bar 01903 260801
On A27 near Junction with A24.
Downland courses.
Pro Stephen Rolley; Founded 1905
Designed by H Vardon
18/18 holes, 6530/5243 yards, S.S.S. 72/66
⚑ Welcome except at WE April-Oct.
⚑ WD £40; WE £40.
⚑ Welcome by arrangement; full day's golf and catering arrangements; from £59.
⚑ Full facilities.
⚑ Winsor House; Rosedale GH; Ardington Hotel.

Berkshire, Buckinghamshire, Oxfordshire

For far too long the people in these three shires thought that they had far better things to be getting on with in life than golf. The game was regarded as the unspeakable in pursuit of the unhittable. Their resistance was futile. Little by little courses began to appear. Now, like Surrey, the land is fertile with golf.

It would be hard to think of a more pleasant place on which to spend a summer's day than the Berkshire, near Ascot. The Berkshire has two courses, the Red and the Blue. Primary courses named after primary colours because the powers-that-were did not want to imply that one was superior to the other.

If someone took a popular vote, however, the Red would just about nudge it. It is most unusual in consisting of six par threes, six par fives and six par fours. The Red does not have even a hint of monotony about it and keeps you honest right through to a punishing finish.

The Blue opens with a majestic par three that is carry all the way, but is perhaps not quite so consistently fascinating as the Red thereafter. However, the demands on driving accuracy are just as great. It is not just the quality of the Berkshire's courses that make for such a wonderful day out, the club is also renowned for its lunches.

Swinley Forest really is a hidden gem. The heathland course is a joy, but perhaps the most memorable part of the experience is the clubhouse atmosphere. You are very clearly a guest, although a most welcome one, but many of the members lurk like "pot plants left over from the Edwardian era", seemingly reluctant to come out into the vulgar sunlight of the twenty-first century.

Oxfordshire has many excellent clubs. It would be hard to pick a favourite out of Frilford Heath, Tadmarten and Huntercombe. Frilford has three courses, colour-coded like the Berkshire. Again, the Red probably just shades it.

Tadmarten, according to Harry Vardon, has a divine spark. When Vardon was asked if a golf course could be built on Wiggington Hill he replied, "God made it to be a golf course." It is a short course, but a tight course. A ball missing the fairway has not that much hope of an instant recovery. It is more than likely to finish in the gorse or broom under penalty of a drop.

Huntercombe opens with an ordinary looking par three down the hill, although clubbing can be deceptive, but after that gets better and better. Just out of Frilford's and Tadmarten's earshot, Huntercombe is a favourite of the three.

Although opened as recently as 1976 Woburn is now the best known course in Buckinghamshire. In 2001, the Victor Chandler British Masters was played on the Marquess course, the most recent addition. The course held up very well to all the attention, even when Thomas Levet of France went on his hilarious victory lap around the seventeenth green after winning a multiple play-off. The Duke's, the oldest of the three, starts and finishes well, but can be a little humdrum in the middle. The Duchess is slightly easier, but still very popular.

Amongst other Buckinghamshire courses worth a mention are Stoke Poges, the course at which the golfing sequence of 'Goldfinger' was filmed, Denham, with its beautiful sequence of holes just after the turn, and Burnham Beeches.

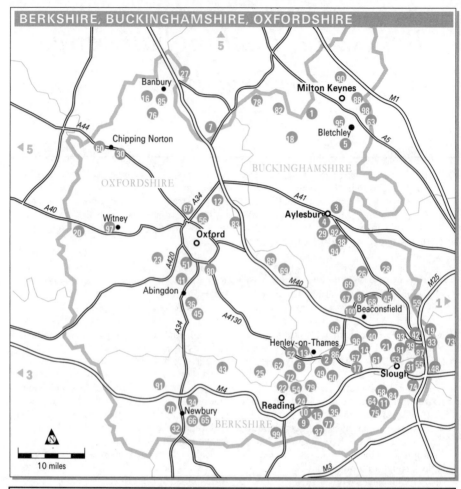

BERKSHIRE, BUCKINGHAMSHIRE, OXFORDSHIRE

KEY				
1 Abbey Hill	19 The Buckinghamshire	40 Flackwell Heath	60 Lyneham	80 Southfield
2 Aspect Park	20 Burford	41 Frilford Heath	61 Maidenhead Golf Club	81 Stoke Poges Golf Club
3 Aylesbury	21 Burnham Beeches	42 Gerrards Cross	62 Mapledurham	82 Stowe
4 Aylesbury Park	22 Calcot Park	43 Goring & Streatley	63 Marquess Course at	83 Studley Wood
5 Aylesbury Vale	23 Carswell Golf & CC	44 Hadden Hill	Woburn	84 Swinley Forest
6 Badgemore Park	24 Castle Royle	45 Harewood Downs	64 Mill Ride	85 Tadmarton Heath
7 Banbury	25 CavershamHeath GC	46 Harleyford Golf	65 Newbury & Crookham	86 Temple
8 Beaconsfield	26 Chartridge Park	47 Hazlemere Golf &	66 Newbury Golf Centre	87 Thorney Park
9 Bearwood	27 Cherwell Edge	Country Club	67 North Oxford	88 Three Locks
10 Bearwood Lakes	28 Chesham & Ley Hill	48 Heathpark GC	68 Oakland Park	89 Waterstock
11 The Berkshire	29 Chiltern Forest	49 Henley Golf Club	69 The Oxfordshire	90 Wavendon Golf Centre
12 Biecester Golf and	30 Chipping Norton	50 Hennerton	70 Parasampia Golf and	91 West Berks
Country Club	31 Datchet	51 Hinksey Heights	Country Club	92 Weston Turville
13 Billingbear Park	32 Deanwood Park	52 Huntercombe	71 Princes Risborough	93 Wexham Park
14 Bird Hills	33 Denham	53 Huntswood	72 Reading	94 Whiteleaf
(Hawthorn Hill)	34 Donnington Valley	54 Hurst	73 Rectory Park	95 Windmill Hill
15 Blue Mountain Golf	Hotel	55 Iver	74 Richings Park	96 Winter Hill
Centre	35 Downshire	56 Kirtlington	75 Royal Ascot	97 Witney Lakes
16 Braires	36 Drayton Park	57 Lambourne	76 Rye Hill	98 Woburn
17 Braywick	37 East Berkshire	58 Lavender Park Golf	77 Sandmartins	99 Wokefield Park
18 Buckingham	38 Ellesborough	Centre	78 Silverstone	100 Wycombe Heights
	39 Farnham Park (Bucks)	59 Little Chalfont	79 Sonning	Golf Centre

BADGEMORE PARK GOLF CLUB
Badgemore, Henley-on-Thames, Oxon RG9 4NR
In the heart of the Chilterns, superb challenging 18 hole mature parkland course. Offering a friendly welcome to all golfers. S.S.S. 69, chipping green, 2 putting greens, practice nets and bunkers. Visitors and Societies welcome. ℂ19th Clubhouse with restaurant, spike bar; en suite accommodation available. PGA Professional Jonathan Dunn (01491 574175). Large car park. Ideally located close to M4 & M40.
Tel: 01491 572206   Fax: 01491 576899   Email: info@badgemorepark.com

---

2B 1 Abbey Hill Golf Centre ℂ
Two Mile Ash, Milton Keynes, Bucks, MK8 8AA
☎ 01908 562566, Fax 569538, Pro 563845
2 miles S of Stony Stratford.
Parkland course.
Pro K Bond/M Booth; Founded 1982
⌁ Practice range, 21 bays floodlit.
† Public pay and play.
⌁ Available on application.
⌁ Welcome WD; golf and catering packages; £19-£25.
⦿ Available.
⌁ Friendly Hotel, Milton Keynes.

2B 2 Aspect Park ℂ
Remenham Hill, Remenham, Henley On Thames, Oxon, RG9 3EH
☎ 01491 578306, Fax 578306, Pro 577562, Sec 578306, Rest/Bar 578306
On A4130 Henley-Maidenhead road 0.75 miles from Henley.
Historic parkland course.
Pro Terry Notley; Founded 1988
Designed by Tim Winsland
18 holes, 6559 yards, S.S.S. 71
⌁ 6 bays.
† Welcome WD; limited WE.
⌁ WD £20; WE £25.
⌁ Welcome WD; terms on application.
⦿ Facilities available.
⌁ Red Lion.

2B 3 Aylesbury Golf Centre
Hulcott Lane, Bierton, Aylesbury, Bucks, HP22 5GA
☎ 01296 393644
1 mile N of Aylesbury on the A418 Leighton Buzzard road.
Parkland course.
Pro Mitch Kierstenson; Founded 1992
Designed by TS Benwell
18 holes, 5965 yards, S.S.S. 69
⌁ Practice range, 30 floodlit bays.
† Welcome.
⌁ WD £10; WE £12.
⌁ Welcome at all times; terms on application.
⦿ Facilities available.
⌁ Forte Crest; Holiday Inn.

2B 4 Aylesbury Park
Aylesbury Park Golf Club, Andrew's Way, Aylesbury, Bucks, HP17 8QQ
☎ 01296 399196, Fax 336830
Just off A418.
Parkland course.
Founded 1996
Designed by Hawtree & Son
18 holes, 6150 yards, S.S.S. 69
† Welcome at all times.
⌁ WD £14; WE £20.
⌁ Welcome at all times; terms on application.
⦿ Bar and servery.
⌁ Forte Post House; Hartwell House.

2B 5 Aylesbury Vale ℂ
Stewkley Road, Wing, Leighton Buzzard, Beds, LU7 0UJ
⌁ www.avgc.co.uk
📧 info@www.avgc.co.uk
☎ 01525 240196, Fax 240848, Pro 240197, Sec 240196, Rest/Bar 240196
Course lies three miles W of Leighton Buzzard between Wing and Stewkley.
Parkland course.
Pro Guy Goble; Founded 1990
Designed by D Wright/Mick Robinson
18 holes, 6612 yards, S.S.S. 72
⌁ 9.
† Welcome with prior booking.
⌁ WD £15; WE £28.
⌁ Welcome midweek.
⦿ Meals and bar facilities.

2B 6 Badgemore Park ℂ
Badgemore, Henley On Thames, Oxon, RG9 4NR
⌁ www.badgemorepark.com
📧 info@badgemorepark.com
☎ 01491 573667, Fax 576899, Pro 574175, Sec 572206, Rest/Bar 573667
1 mile North West from centre of Henley-on-Thames.
Parkland course.
Pro J Dunn; Founded 1972
Designed by Bob Sandow
18 holes, 6129 yards, S.S.S. 69
† Welcome WD and WE afternoons only.
⌁ Fees on request from Pro

Shop/Secretary.
⌁ Welcome WD; full catering facilities for lunch and dinner; £34-£59.
⦿ Full facilities, management training centre, overnight accommodation available.

2B 7 Banbury ℂ
Aynho Road, Adderbury, Banbury, Oxon, OX17 3NT
☎ 01295 810419, Fax 810056, Pro 812880, Sec 812880, Rest/Bar 812880
5 miles S of Banbury on the B4100; 10 mins from M40 Junction 10.
Parkland course.
Pro Stuart Kier; Founded 1994
27 holes, 2872/3066/5938 yards, S.S.S. 71
† Welcome.
⌁ WD £14; WE £20 (18 holes).
⌁ Welcome by prior arrangement; terms available on application.
⦿ Clubhouse facilities.

2B 8 Beaconsfield Golf Club
Seer Green, Beaconsfield, Bucks, HP9 2UR
☎ 01494 676545, Fax 681148, Pro 676616
Off M40 on to A355 Amersham road adjacent to Seer Green/Jordans railway station.
Parkland course.
Pro Michael Brothers; Founded 1914
Designed by HS Colt
18 holes, 6493 yards, S.S.S. 71
⌁ Practice range, 6 bays.
† Welcome WD with handicap certificates.
⌁ WD £35.
⌁ Welcome Tues and Wed.
⦿ Full facilities.
⌁ Bellhouse.

2B 9 Bearwood
Mole Road, Sindlesham, Berks, RG11 5DB
☎ 0118 9761330, Pro 9760156, Sec 9760060
On B3030 1.5 miles N of Arborfield Cross.
Parkland course.

Pro Bayley Tustin; Founded 1986
Designed by B Tustin
9 holes, 5600 yards, S.S.S. 68
✴ 10 bay covered driving range,
two chipping greens and practice
bunkers.
✝ Welcome WD; with member at WE.
✉ WD £18; WE £22 (18 holes).
⟳ Small societies welcome by prior
arrangement.
▮●▮ Facilities and special packages
available.
⤴ Reading Moat House.

2B 10 **Bearwood Lakes**
Keepers Cottage, Bearwood Road,
Wokingham, Berks, RG41 4SJ
⬚ www.bearwoodlakes.co.uk
⬚ golf@bearwoodlakes.co.uk
☎ 0118 9797900, Fax 97972911,
Pro 9783030, Sec 9797900,
Rest/Bar 9797900
Half a mile S of M4 Junction 10 for
Wokingham & Sindlesham.
Parkland course.
Pro Euan Inglis; Founded 1995
Designed by Martin Hawtree
18 holes, 6857 yards, S.S.S. 72
✴ 11.
✝ Members and guests only.
✉ WD £30; WE £35.
⟳ Not allowed.
▮●▮ Full facilities for members and
guests.
⤴ The Moat House.

2B 11 **The Berkshire**
Swinley Road, Ascot, Berks, SL5
8AY
☎ 01344 621495, Pro 622351
On A332 between Ascot and Bagshot.
Heathland course.
Pro Paul Anderson; Founded 1928
Designed by Herbert Fowler
2 x 18 holes, 6379/6260 yards, S.S.S.
71/71
✴ Lessons by arrangement with Pro.
✝ Welcome WD by prior
arrangement with the secretary.
✉ WD £70 1 round, £90 for two.
⟳ Welcome by prior arrangement;
packages available.
▮●▮ Full clubhouse facilities.
⤴ Beryststede; Cricketers; Royal
Foresters.

2B 12 **Bicester Golf and Country Club**
Chesterton, Bicester, Oxon, OX26 1TE
⬚ bicestergolf@ukonline.co.uk
☎ 01869 241204, Fax 240754, Pro
242023

1 mile from M40 exit 9 by A41 towards
Bicester, 2nd left, left again at Red
Cow, 150 yards on right.
Meadowland course.
Pro Julian Goodman; Founded 1973
Designed by RR Stagg
18 holes, 6229 yards, S.S.S. 70
✴ Practice ground.
✝ Welcome.
✉ Prices on application.
⟳ By arrangement; min 16 persons;
full facilities.
▮●▮ Bar and bar snacks and full
restaurant.
⤴ Littlebury (Bicester).

2B 13 **Billingbear Park Golf Course**
The Straight Mile, Wokingham, Berks,
RG40 5SJ
☎ 01344 869259, Fax 869259,
Pro 869259, Sec 869259,
Rest/Bar 869259
From M4 Junction 10 take A329M to
Binfield; after Coppid Beech
roundabout, left at Travelodge lights;
then into Foxley Lane; left at T junction
to mini roundabout, then right for 1 mile.
Parkland course; second 9-hole course
planned.
Pro Martin Blainey; Founded 1994
9 holes, 5750 yards, S.S.S. 68
✝ Pay and play; advance booking
available.
✉ Terms on application.
⟳ Welcome by arrangement only.
▮●▮ None; clubhouse planned.
⤴ Coppid Beech.

2B 14 **Bird Hills**
Drift Road, Maidenhead, Berks, SL6 3ST
⬚ www.infoabirdshill.co.uk
⬚ info@birdshill.oc.ul
☎ 01628 771030, Fax 631023, Pro
07973324203/635153
M4 Junction 8/9; take A330 towards
Bracknell for 2.5 miles; course on right
at crossroads.
Parkland course.
Pro Nick Slimming; Founded 1984
Designed by Clive D Smith
18 holes, 6176 yards, S.S.S. 69
✴ Practice range, 36 floodlit bays.
✝ Welcome subject to club
competitions; pay as you play.
✉ WD £7; WE £12.
⟳ Welcome WD; packages available;
terms on application.
▮●▮ Extensive facilities including
baronial function room.
⤴ Holiday Inn, Maidenhead;
Frederick's Maidenhead; Thames
Riviera, Maidenhead.

2B 15 **Blue Mountain Golf Centre**
Wood Lane, Binfield, Bracknell, Berks,
RG42 4EX
☎ 01344 300200, Fax 360960
At Binfield on the A322 off the A329.
Parkland course with lake features.
Founded 1992
18 holes, 6097 yards, S.S.S. 70
✴ Practice range, 33 bays; floodlit
with video and tuition.
✝ Welcome any day.
✉ WD £16; WE £22.
⟳ Welcome.
▮●▮ Full restaurant and hospitality
facilities.

2B 16 **Brailes**   ☎
Sutton Lane, Lower Brailes, Banbury,
Oxon, OX15 5BB
⬚ www.brailes-golf-club.co.uk
☎ 01608 685633, Pro 685633, Sec
685336, Rest/Bar 685611
On B4035 4 miles from Shipston on
Stour towards Banbury.
Parkland/meadowland course.
Pro Alastair Brown; Founded 1992
Designed by Brian A Hull
18 holes, 6304 yards, S.S.S. 70
✴ Practice area, 14 bays.
✝ Welcome.
✉ WD £18; WE £28.
⟳ Welcome Mon, Tues, Fri and
afternoons on Wed and Thurs; lunch
and dinner available; from £30.
▮●▮ Full facilities and bar.
⤴ The George, at Lower Brailes.

2B 17 **Braywick**
Braywick Road, Maidenhead, Berks,
SL6 1DH
☎ 01628 676910
On A308 Maidenhead-Windsor road.
Parkland course.
Pro Mike Upcott; Founded 1992
Designed by Mike Upcott
9 holes, 2514 yards, S.S.S. 55
✴ Practice and driving range.
✝ With member only.
✉ £8 Full Day.
⟳ Terms on Application.
▮●▮ By arrangement.
⤴ Oakley Court.

2B 18 **Buckingham**
Tingewick Road, Tingewick,
Buckingham, Bucks, MK18 4AE
☎ 01280 815566, Fax 821812, Pro
815210, Rest/Bar 813282
2 miles SW of Buckingham on A421.
Parkland course.
Pro Tom Gates; Founded 1914

18 holes, 6068 yards, S.S.S. 69
♦ Welcome WD.
⌐ WD £28 (day ticket).
⟳ Welcome Tues and Thurs; bar, restaurant, conference facilities, full day's golf.
⦿ Full facilities.
⤳ Four Pillars; Villiers.

2B 19 The Buckinghamshire
Denham Court Drive, Denham, Bucks, UB9 5PG
⊞ www.buckingshire-golfclub.co.uk
✉ golf@bucks.dircon.co.uk
☎ 01895 835777, Fax 835210, Pro 836814, Sec 836800
Follow signs to Denham Country Park from M40 Junction 1 or M25 Junction 16.
Gently undulating parkland course.
Pro John O'Leary Dir of Golf; Founded 1992
Designed by John Jacobs
18 holes, 6880 yards, S.S.S. 73
⫽ Up to 12 grass driving, extensive short game practice area.
♦ Members' guests only.
⌐ WD £70; WE £80 and Bank Holidays.
⟳ By prior arrangement only; full catering and bar facilities; lunch and dinner; £90-£130.
⦿ Catering and clubhouse bar and Restaurant Herring Fine Dining.
⤳ The Bull Hotel and the Bellhouse both in Gerrards Cross.

2B 20 Burford
Burford, Oxon, OX18 4JG
☎ 01993 822583, Fax 822801, Pro 822344, Sec 822583, Rest/Bar 822149
19 miles W of Oxford at junction of A40 and A361 at Burford roundabout.
Parkland course.
Pro Michael Ridge; Founded 1936
18 holes, 6432 yards, S.S.S. 71
♦ By arrangement.
⌐ Apply for details.
⟳ By arrangement.
⦿ Full facilities.
⤳ several.

2B 21 Burnham Beeches
Green Lane, Burnham, Slough, Berks, SL1 8EG
⊞ www.bbgc.co.uk
✉ enquiries@bbgc.co.uk
☎ 01628 661448, Fax 668968, Pro 661661, Sec 661448, Rest/Bar 661150
M40 exit Beaconsfield Junction 2, follow signs to Slough, A355 as far as Farnham Royal at second mini

roundabout, turn right and follow Burnham signs (not Burnham Beeches) to Green Lane.
Parkland course.
Pro Ronnie Bolton; Founded 1891
18 holes, 6449 yards, S.S.S. 71
♦ Welcome WD; at WE only with member.
⌐ WD £35.
⟳ Welcome Wed, Thurs, Fri; full catering facilities; from £62.
⦿ Full facilities except Mon.

2B 22 Calcot Park
Bath Road, Calcot, Reading, Berks, RG31 7RN
✉ info@calcotpark.com
☎ 0118 9427124, Fax 9453373, Pro 9427797, Rest/Bar 9414952
1.5 miles from M4 Junction 12 on A4.
Parkland course.
Pro I J Campbell; Founded 1930
Designed by HS Colt
18 holes, 6283 yards, S.S.S. 70
♦ Welcome WD.
⌐ WD £36.
⟳ Welcome WD; minimum of 15 with £100 deposit; coffee, lunch, dinner, 36 holes, trolley hire, course planners and refreshment hut: £60.
⦿ Full facilities.

2B 23 Carswell Golf & Country Club
Carswell Home Farm, Carswell, Faringdon, Oxon, SN7 8PU
✉ info@carswellcountryclub.co.uk
☎ 01367 870422, Pro 870505
Off A420 near Faringdon.
Parkland course.
Pro Steve Parker; Founded 1993
Designed by Ely Brothers
18 holes, 6183 yards, S.S.S. 70
⫽ Practice range, 19 bays covered floodlit.
♦ Welcome at all times.
⌐ WD £18; WE £25.
⟳ Welcome WD only; full facilities; terms on application.
⦿ Facilities available.
⤳ Sudbury House.

2B 24 Castle Royle Golf Club
Bath Road, Knowl Hill, Reading, Berks, RG10 9XA
⊞ www.clubhouse.com
☎ 01628 829252, Fax 829299
From M4 Junction 8/9 follow A4 signs to Reading and course is 2.5 miles.
Inland links course.
Founded 1992
Designed by Neil Coles

18 holes, 6828 yards, S.S.S. 73
⫽ Function room available for hire, golf tuition for non members, 24000sq ft health and fitness cub, driving range.
♦ Members and their guests only.
⌐ Not applicable.
⦿ Facilities available.
⤳ Bird in Hand; Holiday Inn, Maidenhead.

2B 25 Caversham Heath Golf Club
Mapledurham, Reading
⊞ www.cavershamgolf.co.uk
✉ golf@cavershamgolf.co.uk
☎ 0118 9478600
In Mapledurham on Oxfordshire/Reading border, just outside Reading.
Slightly hilly.
♦ Yes.
⌐ WD £28, WE £38.
⟳ Yes.
⦿ Restaurant.
⤳ In Caversham.

2B 26 Chartridge Park   ⓒ
Chartridge, Chesham, Bucks, HP5 2TF
⊞ www.cpgc.co.uk
☎ 01494 791772
From M25 Junction 19 take A41 W to Aylesbury until Chesham sign.
Parkland course.
Pro Peter Gibbins; Founded 1989
Designed by John Jacobs
18 holes, 5580 yards, S.S.S. 67
♦ Welcome with booking.
⌐ WD £30; WE £35.
⟳ Welcome by arrangement; unlimited golf and catering.
⦿ Full catering facilities.
⤳ Club can recommend.

2B 27 Cherwell Edge   ⓒ
Chacombe, Banbury, Oxon, OX17 2EN
⊞ www.cegc.co.uk
✉ cegc@ukonline.co.uk
☎ 01295 711591, Fax 713674, Pro 711591, Sec 711591, Rest/Bar 711591
3 miles E of Banbury, A442 to Northampton; 1.5 miles E of M40 Junction 11.
Parkland course.
Founded 1983
Designed by Richard Davies
18 holes, 5947 yards, S.S.S. 68
⫽ Practice range, 18 bays; floodlit.
♦ Welcome any time.
⌐ WD £12; WE £16.
⟳ Welcome by arrangement; full facilities; £48 full day.

🍴 Lunches, bar snacks, evening meals.
🍸 Whatley Arms.

2B 28 Chesham & Ley Hill
Ley Hill, Chesham, Bucks, HP5 1UZ
🖥 www.lhgc.com
☎ 01494 784541, Fax 785506
Course is off the A41 on the B4504 to Ley Hill.
Parkland course.
Founded 1900
9 holes, 5296 yards, S.S.S. 66
† Welcome Mon and Thurs all day; afternoon Wed and after 4pm Fri.
⌇ WD £13.
⌁ Welcome on Thurs by prior arrangement; full catering facilities and 36 holes of golf; various menus; from £39.
🍴 Restaurant and packages.
🍸 Crown, Old Amersham.

2B 29 Chiltern Forest   ⓣ
Aston Hill, Halton, Aylesbury, Bucks, HP22 5NQ
🖥 www.chilternforest.co.uk
📧 secratary@chilternforest.co.uk
☎ 01296 631267, Fax 631817, Pro 631817, Sec 631267, Rest/Bar 630899
Between Aylesbury, Tring and Wendover.
Wooded hilly course.
Pro Andy Lavers; Founded 1920
18 holes, 5760 yards, S.S.S. 70
† Welcome WD; with member at WE.
⌇ WD £25; £30 2-for-1 with a Telegraph ticket.
⌁ Welcome Tue, Wed and Thurs; full day of golf, lunch and dinner; £45.
🍴 Full facilities.
🍸 Red Lion, Wendover; Forte, Aylesbury.

2B 30 Chipping Norton
Southcombe, Chipping Norton, Oxon, OX7 5QH
📧 Chipping.nortongc@virgin.net
☎ 01608 641150, Fax 645422, Pro 643356, Sec 642383, Rest/Bar 644321
Follow A44 to Evesham from Oxford and turn left at Chipping Norton sign; club 50 yards.
Downland course.
Pro Neil Rowlands; Founded 1890
18 holes, 6241 yards, S.S.S. 70
⚑ Practice area.
† Welcome WD; with members at WE.
⌇ WD £27; WE £12 with a member.
⌁ Welcome WD by prior arrangement; morning coffee, buffet

lunch and evening meal with full day of golf (27 or 36 holes).
🍴 Full facilities.
🍸 Crown & Cushion; White Hart; Fox, all Chipping Norton.

2B 31 Datchet G & CC   ⓣ
Buccleuch Road, Datchet, Slough, Berks, SL3 9BP
☎ 01753 5438872
Close to Slough and Windsor, easy access from M4.
Parkland course.
Pro to be appointed; Founded 1890
9 holes, 6087 yards, S.S.S. 70
† Welcome WD, 9am-3pm.
⌇ WD £16; WE £16.
⌁ Small societies welcome by prior arrangement; full facilities.
🍴 Bar snacks and lunches available.
🍸 The Manor.

2B 32 Deanwood Park
R Snook And Son, Deanwood Farm Baydon Road, Stockcross, Newbury, Berks, RG20 8JS
📧 deanwood@newburyweb.net
☎ 01635 48772, Fax 48772
From the A4 take the B4000 towards Stockcross; the course lies 500 yards on the right.
Parkland course.
Pro James Purton; Founded 1995
Designed by Dion Beard
9 holes, 4228 yards, S.S.S. 60
⚑ 10 bays.
† Welcome with prior booking.
⌇ WD £14.50; WE £17.50.
⌁ Welcome by prior arrangement; full practice, clubhouse facilities; packages available; terms on application.
🍴 Bar and restaurant facilities available.
🍸 Elcot Park; Folley Lodge.

2B 33 Denham
Tilehouse Lane, Denham, Uxbridge, Middx, UB9 5DE
📧 club.secretary@denhamgolfclub.co.uk
☎ 01895 832022, Fax 835340, Pro 832801
From M40 take Uxbridge/Gerrards Cross turn off on to A40 towards Gerrards Cross; right on to A412 towards Watford; 2nd turning left.
Parkland course.
Pro Stuart Campbell; Founded 1910
Designed by HS Colt
18 holes, 6462 yards, S.S.S. 71
† Welcome Mon-Thurs by prior arrangement.

⌇ WD £48 Day £65.
⌁ Welcome Tues, Wed, Thurs by prior arrangement; from £91 for full day's package and £69 for half a day.
🍴 Full facilities; lunches served daily.
🍸 Bull, Gerrards Cross .

2B 34 Donnington Valley Hotel
Donnington Valley Golf Club, Snells Moore Common, Newbury, Berks, RG14 3BG
🖥 www.Donnigtonvalley. co.uk
☎ 01635 568140, Fax 568141, Pro 568142, Sec 568140
Off the Old Oxford Road N of Newbury.
Parkland course.
Pro Martin Balfour; Founded 1985
Designed by Mike Smith
18 holes, 6358 yards, S.S.S. 71
† Welcome.
⌇ WD £22; WE £28.
⌁ Welcome by prior arrangement; packages on request.
🍴 Full facilities.
🍸 Donnington Valley Hotel (on site).

2B 35 Downshire
Easthampstead Park, Wokingham, Berks, RG11 3DH
📧 downshiregc@brecknell\forest.golf.uk
☎ 01344 302030, Fax 301020
Between Bracknell and Wokingham off Nine Mile Ride.
Municipal parkland course.
Pro Wayne Owers/Will Alsop; Founded 1973
Designed by F Hawtree
18 holes, 6416 yards, S.S.S. 71
⚑ Practice range, 30 bays covered, floodlit.
† Welcome.
⌇ WD £12.80; WE £17.20.
⌁ Welcome by arrangement.
🍴 Full bar and restaurant.
🍸 Ladbroke Mercury; St Annes Manor.

2B 36 Drayton Park
Stevington Rd, Abingdon, Oxon, OX14 4LA
📧 draytonpark@btclick.com
☎ 01235 528989, Fax 525731, Pro 550607, Rest/Bar 539339
2 miles S of Abingdon off A34.
Parkland course.
Pro Martin Morbey; Founded 1992
Designed by Hawtree & Co
18 holes, 5503 yards, S.S.S. 67
⚑ Practice range, 21 bays; floodlit
Also 9 holes, 776 yards, par 3.
† Welcome.

⌐ WD from £17.95; WE from £19.95.
⌒ Welcome; packages available.
⬤ Full bar and dining facilities.
↝ Abingdon Four Pillows, Milton Travel Lodge.

2B 37 East Berkshire

Ravenswood Avenue, Crowthorne, Berks, RG45 6BD
☎ 01344 772041, Fax 777378, Pro 774112
M3 Junction 3 towards Bracknell and follow Crowthorne signs to Railway station.
Heathland course.
Pro Jason Brant; Founded 1903
Designed by P Paxton
18 holes, 6344 yards, S.S.S. 70
⬥ Welcome WD.
⌐ WD £40.
⌒ Welcome Thurs and Fri only; golf, lunch and dinner; £65.
⬤ Clubhouse facilities.
↝ Waterloo.

2B 38 Ellesborough

Wendover Road, Butlers Cross, Aylesbury, Bucks, HP17 0TZ
☎ 01296 622114, Pro 623126, Rest/Bar Bar 622375 Rest.623514
On B4010 1 mile W of Wendover.
Undulating downland course.
Pro Mark Squire; Founded 1906
Designed by James Braid
18 holes, 6283 yards, S.S.S. 71
⬥ Welcome WD except Tues.
⌐ Terms on application.
⌒ Welcome by prior arrangement; packages available for full day's golf and catering; from £62.
⬤ Full clubhouse facilities available.
↝ Red Lion, Wendover.

2B 39 Farnham Park

Park Road, Stoke Poges, Slough, Berks, SL2 4PJ
☎ 01753 647065, Pro 643332, Rest/Bar 643335
M4 Junction 5 take A355 to Farnham Pump; at first roundabout turn right into Park Road.
Parkland course.
Pro Paul Warner; Founded 1977
Designed by Hawtree & Sons
18 holes, 6172 yards, S.S.S. 69
⬥ Public pay and play.
⌐ WD £10; WE £13.50.
⌒ Welcome Tues and Thurs; terms on application.
⬤ Full clubhouse facilities available.
↝ Burnham Beeches.

2B 40 Flackwell Heath

Treadaway Road, Flackwell Heath, High Wycombe, Bucks, HP10 9PE
☎ 01628 520027, Fax 530040, Pro 523017, Sec 520929
Off A40 High Wycombe-Beaconsfield road at Loudwater roundabout; 1.5 miles from M40 Junction 3 or 4.
Undulating heathland course.
Pro Paul Watson; Founded 1905
18 holes, 6211 yards, S.S.S. 70
⬩ Practice facilities are available.
⬥ Welcome WD with handicap certs.
⌐ WD £24.
⌒ Welcome Wed & Thurs only.
⬤ Full facilities Tues-Sun; limited Mon.
↝ Bellhouse; Crest; Paper Makers.

2B 41 Frilford Heath

Oxford Road, Frilford Heath, Abingdon, Oxon, OX13 5NW
☎ 01865 390864, Fax 390823, Pro 390887, Sec 390866
3 miles W of Abingdon on A338.
Parkland/heathland course.
Pro Derek Craik; Founded 1908
Designed by JH Taylor, CK Cotton and S Gidman
3 x 18 holes, 6884; 6006; 6728 yards, S.S.S. 73; 69; 72
⬥ Welcome with handicap certs.
⌐ WD £45; WE £60.
⌒ Welcome WD; packages using 3 golf courses available; £70-£80.
⬤ Full clubhouse facilities available.
↝ Four Pillars; Upper Reaches, both Abingdon.

2B 42 Gerrards Cross

Chalfont Park, Chalfont St Peter, Gerrards Cross, Bucks, SL9 0QA
✉ inger@gxgolf.demon.co.uk
☎ 01753 883263, Fax 883593, Pro 885300, Rest/Bar 278513
Off A413 at Gerrards Cross.
Wooded parkland course.
Pro Matthew Barr; Founded 1922
Designed by Bill Pedlar
18 holes, 6212 yards, S.S.S. 70
⬥ Welcome WD with handicap certs.
⌐ WD £35.
⌒ Welcome on Thurs and Fri with handicap certs; terms on application.
⬤ Full facilities.
↝ Bull; Bellhouse Gerrards Cross The Ethorpe.

2B 43 Goring & Streatley

Rectory Road, Streatley, Reading, Berks, RG8 9QA
☎ 01491 873229, Fax 875224, Pro 873715

On A417 Wantage Road 0.25 miles from the Streatley crossroads.
Parkland course.
Pro Jason Hadland; Founded 1895
18 holes, 6320 yards, S.S.S. 70
⬥ Welcome WD; WE with member.
⌐ WD £35.
⌒ Welcome by prior arrangement; packages available; from £55.
⬤ Full restaurant facilities.
↝ Swan Diplomat, Streatley; Miller at Mansfield, Goring.

2B 44 Hadden Hill

Hadden Hill, North Moreton, Didcot, Oxon, OX11 9BJ
☎ 01235 510410, Fax 811539, Pro 510410, Sec 510410, Rest/Bar 510656
On A4130 E of Didcot.
Parkland course.
Pro Adrian Waters; Founded 1990
Designed by Michael V Morley
18 holes, 6563 yards, S.S.S. 71
⬩ Practice range, 20 bays; floodlit.
⬥ Welcome; start times are bookable.
⌐ WD £15; WE £20.
⌒ Welcome WD by arrangement; packages available.
⬤ Full bar and restaurant.
↝ George; Springs, both Wallingford; George; White Hart, both Dorchester.

2B 45 Harewood Downs

Cokes Lane, Chalfont St Giles, Bucks, HP8 4TA
✉ secretary@hdgc.co.uk
☎ 01494 762184, Fax 766869, Pro 764102, Sec 762184
Course lies 2 miles E of Amersham on the A413.
Rolling tree-lined parkland course.
Pro GC Morris; Founded 1903
18 holes, 5958 yards, S.S.S. 69
⬥ Welcome with advance application.
⌐ WD £30, £40 per day; WE £35: £45.
⌒ Welcome; 2 rounds of golf and full day's catering with refreshment hut; £62.50.
⬤ Full clubhouse facilities are available.

2B 46 Harleyford Golf Club

Harleyford estate, Henley Road, Marlow, Bucks, SL7 2SP
🖳 www.harleyfordgolf.org
✉ info@harleyfordgolf.org
☎ 01628 402300, Fax 487434, Pro 402149, Sec 420110
Course is on the A4155 Marlow-Henley road two miles from Marlow town

centre.
Downland course.
Pro Lee Jackson; Founded 1996
Designed by Donald Steel
18 holes, 6604 yards, S.S.S. 72
⚑ Driving range for the use of
members.
† Welcome by arrangement.
⌊ Terms on application.
⟳ Welcome by prior arrangement;
minimum 12 maximum 60; winter and
summer packages available; terms on
application.
⚑ Full clubhouse facilities.
⤳ Danesfield House.

2B 47 Hazlemere Golf Club ⚏
Penn Road, Hazlemere, High
Wycombe, Bucks, HP15 7LR
⚏ www.Hazlemeregolfclub.co.uk
✉ enquiry@hazlemeregolfclub.co.uk
☎ 01494 719300, Fax 713914, Pro
710396
B474 between Beckham Field and
Hazlemere.
Parkland course.
Pro P Harrison; Founded 1982
Designed by Terry Murray
18 holes, 5807 yards, S.S.S. 69
⚑ Practice area for members.
† Welcome.
⌊ WD £30; WE £40. Limited
availability at WE.
⟳ Welcome; packages available;
from £45.
⚑ Full restaurant and bar facilities.
⤳ White Harte, Beaconsfield;
Bellhouse; Bull, Gerrards Cross;
Crown, Amersham.

2B 48 Heathpark GC
Stockley Rd, West Drayton, Middx,
UB7 8BQ
☎ 01895 444232, Fax 445122
In carpark of Crowne Plaza Hotel at
M4 Junction 4.
Undulating heath/parkland course.
9 holes, 3856 yards, S.S.S. 62
† Welcome.
⌊ Pay and play: £7.
⟳ Limited facilities.
⚑ Tea and snacks only; hotel close
by with full bar and restaurant facilities.

2B 49 Henley
The Flat, Henley Golf Club, Harpsden,
Henley On Thames, Oxon, RG9 4HG
☎ 01491 575742, Fax 412179, Pro
575710, Rest/Bar 575781
1 mile SW of Henley; off A4155
Henley-Reading road.
Parkland course.

Pro Mark Howell; Founded 1907
Designed by James Braid
18 holes, 6239 yards, S.S.S. 70
† Welcome WD with handicap certs
and prior arrangement; WE with member.
⌊ WD £30.
⟳ Wed and Thurs only; packages
available; £57.50.
⚑ Full clubhouse facilities.

2B 50 Hennerton ⚏
Crazies Hill Road, Wargrave, Reading,
Berks, RG10 8LT
⚏ www.hennertongolfclub.co.uk
☎ 0118 9401000, Fax 9401042,
Pro 9404778
Off A321 into Wargrave village; club
signposted.
Parkland course.
Pro William Farrow; Founded 1992
Designed by Col.Dion Beard
9 holes, 5460 yards, S.S.S. 67
⚑ Practice range, 7 bays.
† Welcome with prior booking.
⌊ WD £15; WE £18.
⟳ Welcome; terms on application.
⚑ Full bar and restaurant facilities.

2B 51 Hinksey Heights ⚏
South Hinksey, Oxford, Oxon, OX1
5AB
⚏ www.oxford'golf.co.uk
✉ clay@oxford'golf.co.uk
☎ 01865 327 775, Fax 736930
Off the A34 at Oxford between the
Botley and Hinksey Hill interchanges.
Heathland and links type course with
water coming into play.
Pro David Bolton; Founded 1996
Designed by David Heads
18 (also 9-hole par 3), 7023 yards,
S.S.S. 74
† Welcome any time.
⌊ WD £15; WE and BH £20.
⟳ Welcome any time by prior
arrangement.
⚑ Fully licensed bar providing home
cooked meals and snacks.
⤳ Oxford Holiday Inn.

2B 52 Huntercombe
Huntercombe, Nuffield, Henley On
Thames, Oxon, RG9 5SL
☎ 01491 641207, Fax 642060,
Pro 641241
On A4130 6 miles from Henley towards
Oxford.
Woodland/heathland course.
Pro David Ressin; Founded 1901
Designed by Willie Park Jnr
18 holes, 6311 yards, S.S.S. 70
† Welcome WD; no 3 or 4 balls.

⌊ WD £28/40.
⟳ Welcome Tues and Thurs only.
⚑ Restaurant and bar facilities.
⤳ White Hart, Nettlebed.

2B 53 Huntswood Golf Course
Taplow Common Road, Burnham,
Slough, Berks, SL1 8LS
☎ 01628 667144, Fax 663145
Off M4 Junction 7; turn left at round-
about and then right at next mini-
roundabout; straight on for 1.5 miles
and course is just past Grovefield Hotel.
Wooded valley course.
Pro Steve Weston; Founded 1996
9 holes, 5258 yards, S.S.S. 65
† Welcome.
⌊ WD £12; WE £14.
⟳ Welcome by prior arrangement with
club manager Mark Collard; packages
available; terms on application.
⚑ Full bar and catering; Sun lunches.
⤳ Grovefield.

2B 54 Hurst
Hurst Grove, Sandford Lane, Hurst,
Reading, Berks, RG10 0SQ
☎ 0118 9344355, Sec 9344355
Between Reading and Twyford
signposted from Hurst village.
Parkland course.
Pro Justin Hennesey; Founded 1977
9 holes, 6308 yards, S.S.S. 70
⚑ Practice green.
† Welcome.
⌊ WD £6.50; WE £8 OAP £4 Mon-Fri
⟳ Welcome by prior arrangement.
⚑ Bar facilities.

2B 55 Iver
Hollow Hill Lane, Iver, Bucks, SL0 0JJ
☎ 01753 655615, Fax 654225
Near Langley station.
Parkland course.
Pro Karl Teschner; Founded 1984
Designed by David Morgan
⚑ Practice range, 18 bays, 9 covered.
† Welcome.
⌊ WD £11; WE £14.50.
⟳ Welcome; packages available;
terms on application.
⚑ Full facilities.
⤳ Marriott.

2B 56 Kirtlington
Glen Andrews Golf Courses Ltd,
Vicarage Farm, Kirtlington, Kidlington,
Oxon, OX5 3JY
☎ 01869 351133, Fax 351143
On A34 to Kirtlington off M40 Junction 9.
Parkland course.

Founded 1995
Designed by Graham Webster
18 holes, 6084 yards, S.S.S. 69
✪ Practice range, 12 bays.
✝ Welcome.
Ⅼ WD £17; WE £22.
⚘ Welcome; packages available;
terms on application.
◉ Full facilities.

2B 57 **Lambourne**
Dropmore Road, Burnham, Slough,
Berks, SL1 8NF
☎ 01628 666755, Fax 663301, Pro
662936, Rest/Bar 606716
From M4 Junction 7 to Slough and
Burnham; M40 Junction 2 to Burnham.
Parkland course.
Pro David Hart; Founded 1991
Designed by Donald Steel
18 holes, 6771 yards, S.S.S. 72
✪ Practice range, grass.
✝ Welcome WD with handicap certs.
Ⅼ Terms on application.
⚘ Not welcome.
◉ Full clubhouse facilities available.
⌁ Burnham Beeches.

2B 58 **Lavender Park**
Swinley Road, Ascot, Berks, SL5 8BD
⚎ www.lavenderparkgolf.co.uk
✉ lavenderparkgolf@yahoo.co.uk
☎ 01344 893344, Pro 893344, Sec
893344, Rest/Bar 893344
On A329 opposite the Royal Foresters
Hotel.
Parkland course.
Pro David Johnson; Founded 1974
9 holes, 2248 yards, S.S.S. 56
✪ Practice range, 26 bays; floodlit.
✝ Welcome any time.
Ⅼ WD from £5; WE from £8.
⚘ Welcome by prior arrangement.
◉ Full bar and catering facilities
available.
⌁ Royal Foresters.

2B 59 **Little Chalfont**
Lodge Lane, Chalfont St Giles, Bucks,
HP8 4AJ
☎ 01494 764877, Fax 762860, Pro
762942, Sec 764877, Rest/Bar 764877
From M25 Junction 18 take A404
towards Amersham; course first left
after garden centre.
Parkland course.
Pro Mike Dunne; Founded 1982
Designed by James Dunne
9 holes, 5852 yards, S.S.S. 70
✝ Welcome by prior arrangement.
Ⅼ WD £11.50; WE £13.50.
⚘ Welcome by arrangement;

package includes day's golf and full
catering; £30.
◉ Bar and clubhouse.
⌁ White Hart.

2B 60 **Lyneham** ☂
Lyneham, Chipping Norton, Oxon, OX7
6QQ
✉ golf@lynehamgc.freeserve.co.uk
☎ 01993 831841, Fax 831775, Pro
831841, Sec 831841, Rest/Bar 832011
1 mile off A361 Chipping Norton to
Burford Road.
Parkland course with water hazards.
Pro James Fincher; Founded 1992
Designed by D Carpenter, A Smith
18 holes, 6707 yards, S.S.S. 72
✪ 15.
✝ Welcome; after 11am at weekends;
booking 3 days in advance.
Ⅼ WD £20; WE £24.
⚘ Welcome; full day's golf and
catering; scorecard and scoreboard
administration available; terms on
application.
◉ Full facilities.
⌁ Mill, Kingham; Crown & Cushion;
Kings Arms, both Chipping Norton.

2B 61 **Maidenhead Golf Club**
Shoppenhangers Road, Maidenhead,
Berks, SL6 2PZ
☎ 01628 624693, Fax 624693, Pro
624067, Sec 624693, Rest/Bar 620545
Off A404 signposted Henley.
Parkland course.
Pro S Geary; Founded 1896
18 holes, 6364 yards, S.S.S. 70
✝ Welcome WD; not afternoons on
Fri. WE by prior arrangement.
Ⅼ WD £30; WE £35.
⚘ Welcome Wed and Thurs; terms
on application; winter society.
Packages are £27.50 for food and golf
on Mon-Thurs.
◉ Full catering and bar facilities.
⌁ Fredericks; Holiday Inn.

2B 62 **Mapledurham**
Chazey Heath, Mapledurham,
Reading, Berks, RG4 7UD
☎ 0118 9463353, Fax 9463363
Off A4074 NW of Reading 1.5 miles
from Mapledurham village.
Undulating parkland course.
Pro Simon O'Keefe; Founded 1992
Designed by MRM Sandow
18 holes, 5621 yards, S.S.S. 67
✪ Practice range.
✝ Welcome.
Ⅼ WD £15; WE £18.
⚘ Welcome by prior arrangement;

packages available; terms on
application.
◉ Bar and restaurant facilities
available.
⌁ Holiday Inn, Caversham.

2B 63 **Marquess Course; Woburn Town and Country Club**
Little Brickhill, Milton Keynes
⚎ www.woburngolf.com
✉ enquiries@woburngolf.com
☎ 01908 370756
From South – Junction 13 off M1,
through Ashby Guise for 1 mile then
turn right; From North – Junction 14 off
M1 towards Woburn Sands, follow signs
to Woburn for 1 mile and then turn right.
Not hilly, not flat.
✝ WD. Must be member of another
club and have current handicap.
Ⅼ Enquire.
⚘ Yes WD.
◉ Restaurant/breakfast bar.
⌁ Bedford Arms in Bedford. B&Bs in
surrounding villages.

2B 64 **Mill Ride**
Mill Ride Estate, Mill Ride, Ascot,
Berks, SL5 8LT
☎ 01344 891494, Fax 886820, Pro
886777
From Ascot take A329 until lights, then
right into Fernbank Road, which leads
to Mill Ride.
Blend of parkland and links course.
Pro to be appointed; Founded 1991
Designed by Donald Steel
18 holes, 6762 yards, S.S.S. 72
✝ Welcome by prior arrangement.
Ⅼ WD £35; WE £50.
⚘ Welcome; terms on application.
◉ Full catering and club facilities.
⌁ Royal Berkshire, Ascot; Berystede,
Sunningdale.

2B 65 **Newbury & Crookham** ☂
Burys Bank Road, Greenham,
Thatcham, Berks, RG19 8BZ
☎ 01635 40035, Fax 40045, Pro
31201
2 miles SE of Newbury.
Wooded parkland course.
Pro David Harris; Founded 1873
Designed by JH Turner
18 holes, 5940 yards, S.S.S. 68
✝ Welcome WD.
Ⅼ WD £20.
⚘ Welcome by prior arrangement;
terms on application.
◉ Full clubhouse facilities.
⌁ Hilton, Newbury.

2B 66 Newbury Golf Centre
Newbury Racecourse Plc, Newbury
Racecourse, Newbury, Berks, RG14
7NZ
⌨ www.mitchgolf@ukf.net
▦ mitchgolf@ukf.net
☎ 01635 551464
Signposted off the A34 for
racecourse/conference centre.
Parkland course.
Pro Nick Mitchell; Founded 1994
18 holes, 6500 yards, S.S.S. 70
⚐ Practice range, 20 floodlit bays.
† Welcome.
⌧ WD £14; WE £18.
⟁ Welcome by prior arrangement.
⦿ Full catering facilities available.
⌁ Hilton National.

2B 67 North Oxford Golf Club
Banbury Road, Oxford, Oxon, OX2
8EZ
☎ 01865 554924, Fax 515921, Pro
553977
Between Kidlington and N Oxford 2.5
miles N of the city centre.
Parkland course.
Pro Robert Harris; Founded 1907
18 holes, 5456 yards, S.S.S. 67
† Welcome WD.
⌧ WD £25.
⟁ Welcome by prior arrangement;
packages available; terms on
application.
⦿ Full facilities.
⌁ Moat House; Linton Lodge;
Randolph.

2B 68 Oakland Park
Bowles Farm, Three Households,
Chalfont St Giles, Bucks, HP8 4LW
☎ 01494 876293, Fax 874692
Beaconsfield Junction off M40; course
is off A413 Amersham road.
Parkland course.
Pro Alistair Thatcher; Founded 1994
Designed by J Gaunt
18 holes, 5208 yards, S.S.S. 66
⚐ Driving range.
† Welcome WD.
⌧ WD £20.
⟁ Welcome WD; terms on application.
⦿ Facilities available.

2B 69 The Oxfordshire
Rycote Lane, Thame, Oxon, OX9 2PU
☎ 01844 278300, Fax 278003, Pro
278505
M40 Junction 7 turn right on to A329;
club is 1.5 miles on right.
Championship parkland course; hosts
B&H Masters.

Pro Neil Pike; Founded 1993
Designed by Rees Jones
18 holes, 7187 yards, S.S.S. 76
† Members' guests only.
⌧ WD £35; WE £55.
⟁ None.
⦿ Outstanding clubhouse bar and
catering facilities.
⌁ Manoir aux Quat Saisons, Great
Milton; Oxford Belfry, Milton Common.

**2B 70 Parasampia Golf &
Country Club**
Donnington Grove, Donnington,
Newbury, Berks, RG14 2LA
⌨ www.Parasampia.com
▦ enquiry@parasampia.com
☎ 01635 581000, Fax 552259, Pro
551975
Follow signs to Donnington Castle off
A34; after 2.5 miles, Grove Road is on
the right.
Moorland/parkland course.
Pro Gareth Williams; Founded 1993
Designed by Dave Thomas
18 holes, 7108 yards, S.S.S. 74
⚐ Practice area (Bring your own
balls).
† Must become day member.
⌧ WD £30; WE £35.
⟁ Welcome; full facilities, tennis
courts, lake fishing; from £36.
⦿ Japanese and English restaurant.
⌁ Donnington Grove Hotel (onsite).

2B 71 Princes Risborough
Lee Road, Saunderton Lee, Princes
Risborough, Bucks, HP27 9NX
☎ 01844 346989, Pro 274567
7 miles NW of High Wycombe on
A4010.
Parkland course.
Pro Simon Lowry; Founded 1990
Designed by Guy Hunt
9 holes, 5440 yards, S.S.S. 66
⚐ Practice ground, tuition with Pro
available by prior arrangement.
† Welcome.
⌧ WD £14; WE £18.
⟁ Welcome by prior arrangement;
packages available; terms on
application.
⦿ Full clubhouse facilities available.
⌁ Rose and Crown, Saunderton.

2B 72 Reading
Kidmore End Road, Emmer Green,
Reading, Berks, RG4 8SG
⌨ www.readinggolfclub.com
▦ secretary@readinggolfclub.com
☎ 0118 9472909, Fax 9464468,
Pro 9476115, Sec 9472909,

Rest/Bar 9472169
2 miles N of Reading off Peppard
Road.
Parkland course.
Pro Scott Fotheringham; Founded 1910
Designed by James Baird
18 holes, 6212 yards, S.S.S. 70
† Welcome Mon-Thurs.
⌧ WD £30.
⟁ Welcome Tues-Thurs; catering
packages available; terms on
application.
⦿ Full catering and bar facilities
available.
⌁ Holiday Inn.

2B 73 Rectory Park
Northolt Golf Club Ltd, Huxley Close,
Northolt, Middx, UB5 5UL
☎ 020 88415550, Fax 88424735,
Pro 88458555, Sec 88415550,
Rest/Bar 88415550
Course is off the Target roundabout on
the M40, then the fourth turning on the
left.
Parkland course.
9 holes, 3000 yards, S.S.S. 52
† Welcome.
⌧ Pay and play; £5.
⟁ No facilities.
⦿ Snack bar.

2B 74 Richings Park
North Park, Iver, Bucks, SL0 9DL
⌨ www.richingspark.co.uk
☎ 01753 655370, Fax 655409,
Pro 655352, Sec 655370,
Rest/Bar 655370
From M4 Junction 5 head towards
Colnbrook; turn left at the lights to Iver.
Parkland course.
Pro Ryan Kirby; Founded 1995
Designed by Alan Higgins
18 holes, 6094 yards, S.S.S. 69
⚐ Practice range, 12 bays; academy
course, tuition available.
† Welcome WD.
⌧ WD £22.
⟁ Welcome by arrangement;
packages available; terms on
application.
⦿ Restaurant and function room
available.
⌁ Marriott.

2B 75 Royal Ascot
Winkfield Road, Ascot, Berks, SL5 7LJ
▦ golf@royalascotgc.fsnet.co.uk
☎ 01344 625175, Fax 872330, Pro
624656, Sec 625175, Rest/Bar 622923
Inside Ascot racecourse.
Heathland course.

Pro Alastair White; Founded 1887
Designed by JH Taylor
18 holes, 5716 yards, S.S.S. 68
⚑ Yes.
† Members' guests only.
⚲ Welcome Wed and Thurs by prior arrangement; 36 holes, lunch and dinner; £47.
🍴 Restaurant.
⌁ Royal Berkshire; Berystede.

2B 76 Rye Hill ☎
Milcombe, Banbury, Oxon, OX15 4RU
☎ 01295 721818, Fax 720089, Pro 721818, Sec 721818, Rest/Bar 721818
Off A361 between Banbury and Chipping Norton, take road signposted Bloxham.
Links style hillside course; 2 holes redesigned in late 1998.
Pro Tony Pennock; Founded 1993
18 holes, 6916 yards, S.S.S. 73
† Welcome.
⌶ WD £20; WE £25.
⚲ Welcome by prior arrangement; packages available; terms on application.
🍴 Full facilities.
⌁ White Horse.

2B 77 Sandmartins ☎
Finchampstead Road, Finchampstead, Wokingham, Berks, RG40 3RQ
⌨ www.sandmartins.com
✉ sandmartins@sandmartins.com
☎ 0118 9792711, Fax 9770282, Pro 9770265, Sec 9792711, Rest/Bar 9792711
1 mile S of Wokingham & 4 miles from Reading on B3016.
Parkland first 9; links style back 9.
Pro Andrew Hall; Founded 1993
Designed by ET Fox
18 holes, 6212 yards, S.S.S. 70
† Welcome WD.
⌶ WD £30.
⚲ Welcome; minimum 12 in summer; various packages available with dining facilities in the Georgian style clubhouse; terrace; video analysis; terms on application.
🍴 Full clubhouse catering and bar facilities.
⌁ Stakis St Annes Manor.

2B 78 Silverstone
Silverstone Road, Stowe, Buckingham, Bucks, MK18 5LH
☎ 01280 850005, Fax 850156
1.5 miles beyond race track on Silverstone road from Buckingham and Stowe.

Farmland course.
Pro Rodney Holt; Founded 1992
Designed by David Snell
18 holes, 6213 yards, S.S.S. 71
⚑ Practice range, 11 bays.
† Welcome.
⌶ WD £14; WE £18.
⚲ Welcome WD by prior arrangement; private dining room; 9-hole pitching course; swing analysis; terms on application.
🍴 Full bar and restaurant facilities.
⌁ White Hart, Buckingham; Green Man, Syresham; Travelodge, Towcester.

2B 79 Sonning
Duffield Road, Sonning, Reading, Berks, RG4 6GJ
✉ secretary@sonning-golf-club.co.uk
☎ 0118 9693332, Fax 9448409, Pro 9692910, Rest/Bar 9272055
S of A4 between Reading and Maidenhead.
Parkland course.
Pro Richard MacDougall; Founded 1914
18 holes, 6366 yards, S.S.S. 70
† Welcome WD if carrying handicap certs.
⌶ WD £30-£40.
⚲ Welcome Wed; terms on application.
🍴 Full clubhouse catering facilities available.
⌁ The Great House-Sonning.

2B 80 Southfield Golf Club
Hill Top Road, Oxford, Oxon, OX4 1PF
⌨ www.southfieldgolfclub.co.uk
✉ southfieldgolfclub@btinternet.com
☎ 01865 242158, Pro 244258
1.5 miles SE of Oxford city centre off B480.
Undulating parkland course.
Pro Tony Rees; Founded 1875
Designed by James Braid (1875),
Redesigned H Colt (1923)
18 holes, 6320 yards, S.S.S. 70
† Welcome WD; with a member WE.
⌶ Terms on application.
⚲ Welcome but must make prior arrangement in writing; the home of Oxford University GC, Oxford City and Oxford Ladies; terms available on application.
🍴 Full catering facilities are available in Southfield restaurant and 19th bar.
⌁ Randolph Hotel; Eastgate Hotel, both Oxford; Travel Inn, Cowley.

2B 81 Stoke Poges
Park Road, Stoke Poges, Slough, Berks, SL2 4PG

⌨ www.stokepark.com
✉ info@stokepark.com
☎ 01753 717171, Fax 717181, Pro 717172, Sec 717172, Rest/Bar 717172
Take the exits from the M4 or A4 into Slough, head for Stoke Poges Lane, then into Park Road.
Parkland course.
Pro Stuart Collier; Founded 1909
Designed by HS Colt
27 holes, 6721 yards, S.S.S. 71
⚑ 15.
† Welcome.
⌶ WD £110; WE £180 (18 holes); winter prices on application.
⚲ Society and corporate days welcomed; various packages and prices available on application to the events organiser; terms on application.
🍴 Full facilities.
⌁ Bellhouse; Bull Gerrards Cross; Copthorne, Slough; Chequers Inn, Wooburn Common.

2B 82 Stowe
Stowe School, Buckingham, Bucks, MK18 5EH
☎ 01280 816264, Sec 813650
At Stowe school.
Parkland course.
Founded 1974
9 holes, 4573 yards, S.S.S. 63
† Private; members only.
⌶ WD £10; WE £10.

2B 83 Studley Wood Golf Club ☎
Straight Mile Road, Horton-cum-Studley, Oxford, Oxon, OX33 1BF
⌨ www.studleywoodgolf.cc.uk
✉ admin@swgc.co.uk
☎ 01865 351144, Fax 351166, Pro 351122, Sec 351144, Rest/Bar 351144
From M40 Junction 8 take A40 to Headington roundabout; follow signs to Horton-cum-Studley.
Woodland course.
Pro Tony Williams; Founded 1996
Designed by Simon Gidman
18 holes, 6315 yards, S.S.S. 71
⚑ Practice range, 13 bays.
† Welcome.
⌶ WD £30; WE £40; winter fees on application.
⚲ Welcome only by prior arrangement.
🍴 Restaurant and function room;spike bar.
⌁ Studley Priory.

2B 84 Swinley Forest
Bodens Ride, Ascot, Berks, SL5 9LE
☎ 01344 620197, Fax 874733, Pro

874811, Sec 620197
2 miles S of Ascot.
Heathland course.
Pro RC Parker; Founded 1909
Designed by HS Colt
18 holes, 5952 yards, S.S.S. 69
♦ Members' guests only.
[WD £65; WE £65.
⌒ By introduction of a member only;
packages £120.
⦿ Clubhouse bar and catering.
⌐ Royal Berkshire; Highclere;
Berystede.

2B 85 **Tadmarton Heath**
Banbury, Oxon, OX15 5HL
☎ 01608 737278, Fax 730548, Pro
730047, Sec 737278, Rest/Bar 737278
Off A361 at Broughton Castle on
B4035 for 5 miles to Tadmarton.
Heathland course.
Pro Tom Jones; Founded 1922
Designed by Major C K Hutchison
18 holes, 5917 yards, S.S.S. 69
♦ Welcome WD by prior
arrangement.
[WD £38.
⌒ Welcome WD except Thurs by
arrangement; 36 max; full day's golf,
coffee, lunch and dinner; £60.
⦿ Full facilities.
⌐ Banbury Manor; Wheatley Hall;
Cromwell Lodge.

2B 86 **Temple**
Henley Road, Hurley, Maidenhead,
Berks, SL6 5LH
☎ 01628 824795, Fax 828119, Pro
824254, Rest/Bar 824248
Off A4130 Maidenhead to Henley Road
or A404.
Parkland course.
Pro James Whiteley; Founded 1908
Designed by Willie Park Jnr
18 holes, 6248 yards, S.S.S. 70
▮ Practice area.
♦ By appointment only.
[WD £36; WE £44.
⌒ By prior appointment; packages
available on request; coffee, lunch,
dinner all available.
⦿ Full clubhouse catering facilities.
⌐ Compleat Angler, Marlow; Bell Inn,
Hurley.

2B 87 **Thorney Park**
Thorney Mill Road, Iver, Bucks, SL0
9AL
☎ 01895 422095
Off A4 at Langley into Parlaunt Road.
Parkland course.
Pro Andrew Killing; Founded 1993

Designed by Grundon Leisure Ltd
9 holes, 5668 yards, S.S.S. 67
▮ Practice area.
♦ Welcome.
[WD £13; WE £16 (18 holes).
⌒ Welcome; terms on application.
⦿ Restaurant.
⌐ Any Heathrow hotel.

2B 88 **Three Locks**
Partridge Hill, Great Brickhill, Milton
Keynes, Bucks, MK17 9BH
⌐⌐ www.threelocks.com
☎ 01525 270470, Fax 270470, Pro
270050, Sec 270470, Rest/Bar 270696
3 miles from Leighton Buzzard on
A4146.
Parkland course with several water
hazards.
Pro Gareth Harding; Founded 1992
Designed by MRM Sandow/P Critchley
18 holes, 6025 yards, S.S.S. 68
♦ Welcome; booking strongly
recommended.
[WD £15.00; WE £18.
⌒ Welcome with prior booking;
various packages available to cover
day's golf and catering; terms on
application.
⦿ Full catering facilities available.
⌐ Limited accommodation on site.

2B 89 **Waterstock Golf Club** ⌒
Thame Road, Waterstock, Oxford,
Oxon, OX33 1HT
⌐⌐ www.waterstockgolfltd.com
✉ wgc-oxfordgolf@btinternet.com
☎ 01844 338093, Fax 338036
Direct access from M40 Junction 8 and
Junction 8a on to A418 Thame road.
Parkland course.
Pro Paul Bryant; Founded 1994
Designed by Donald Steel
18 holes, 6535 yards, S.S.S. 71
▮ 22 bays and floodlit.
♦ Welcome.
[WD £15.50; WE £18.50.
⌒ Welcome by prior arrangement;
packages available for groups of up to
70; terms on application.
⦿ Bar and grill facilities.
⌐ Belfry (01844 279381), Milton;
County Inn; Travelodge, both
Wheatley. Days Inn-Junction 8a M40
(0800 0280 400).

2B 90 **Wavendon Golf Centre** ⌒
Lower End Road, Wavendon, Milton
Keynes, Bucks, MK17 8DA
✉ jackbarker@btinternet.com
☎ 01908 281811, Fax 281257, Pro
281011, Sec 281297

M1 Junction 13 to A421, 1st left at
roundabout; take first left into Lower
End Road.
Parkland course.
Pro Greg Iron; Founded 1989
Designed by John Drake/Nick Elmer
18 holes, 5570 yards, S.S.S. 69
▮ Driving range; 9-hole par 3 course.
2x9 hole pitch and putt. 9-hole
academy course.
♦ Public pay & play.
[WD £12; WE £17.50.
⌒ Contact events co-ordinator.
⦿ Facilities; carvery, bar and bar
snacks.
⌐ The Bell-Woburn.

2B 91 **West Berks**
Chaddleworth, Newbury, Berks, RG16
0HS
☎ 01488 638574, Fax 638781, Pro
638851
M4 Junction 14 follow signs to RAF
Welford.
Downland course
Pro Paul Simpson; Founded 1975
Designed by R Stagg
18 holes, 7001 yards, S.S.S. 73
▮ Yes and practice area.
♦ Welcome; afternoons only at WE.
[WD £25; WE £35.
⌒ Welcome by prior arrangement;
packages available; terms on
application.
⦿ Full facilities.
⌐ Queens, E Gaston; Blue Boar,
Chiveley; Littlecote House, Hungerford.

2B 92 **Weston Turville** ⌒
New Road, Weston Turville, Aylesbury,
Bucks, HP22 5QT
☎ 01296 424084, Fax 395376, Pro
425949
2 miles from Aylesbury between Aston
Clinton and Wendover.
Parkland course.
Pro Gary George; Founded 1975
18 holes, 6008 yards, S.S.S. 69
♦ Welcome except Sun am.
[Terms on application.
⌒ Welcome WD, some WE, by prior
appointment; terms available on
application.
⦿ Lunches and evening snacks.
⌐ Holiday Inn.

2B 93 **Wexham Park**
Wexham Street, Wexham, Slough,
Berks, SL3 6ND
⌐⌐ www.europro.com
☎ 01753 663271, Fax 663318
2 miles from Slough towards Gerrards

Cross; follow signs to Wexham Park Hospital; 200 yrds from hospital. Parkland course. Pro John Kennedy; Founded 1976 Designed by Emil Lawrence and David Morgan
18 holes, 5251 yards, S.S.S. 66; 9 holes, 2727 yards, S.S.S. 34; 9 holes, 2219 yards, S.S.S. 32
⚑ 36.
♸ Welcome.
⌱ £16 WE, £12.50 WD.
⚘ Welcome; full catering facilities; terms on application.
🍽 Bar and catering facilities.
⚑ Wexham Park Hall.

2B 94 **Whiteleaf**

Upper Icknield Way, Whiteleaf, Bucks, HP27 0LY
⚎ Whiteleaf@tiscali.co.uk
☎ 01844 343097, Fax 275551, Pro 345472, Sec 274058, Rest/Bar 343097
From Monks Risborough turn right into Casden Road and 100 yards on turn right into Whiteleaf village; course 0.25 miles on left.
Hilly Chilterns course.
Pro Ken Ward; Founded 1904
9 holes, 5391 yards, S.S.S. 66
♸ Welcome WD and with member at WE.
⌱ WE £12 only with member.
⚘ Welcome on Thurs by prior arrangement; special packages available.
🍽 Full facilities.
⚘ Red Lion; Whiteleaf; Rose & Crown, Saunderton.

2B 95 **Windmill Hill**

Tattenhoe Lane, Bletchley, Milton Keynes, Bucks, MK3 7RB
☎ 01908 631113, Fax 630034, Pro 378623, Sec 366457, Rest/Bar 630660 main number
Off A421 through Milton Keynes towards Buckingham, M1 Junction 13 northbound 14 southbound.
Parkland course.
Pro Colin Clinghan; Founded 1972 Designed by Henry Cotton
18 holes, 6720 yards, S.S.S. 72
⚑ Practice range; 23 indoor, 6 outdoor bays, 3 putting greens, all year round greens.
♸ Welcome.
⌱ WD £11; WE £15.
⚘ Welcome WD and after 11am at

WE; packages available for catering and golf; from £10.50.
🍽 Full clubhouse facilities available.
⚘ Forte Crest, Milton Keynes; Shenley, Bletchley.

2B 96 **Winter Hill**

Grange Lane, Cookham, Maidenhead, Berks, SL6 9RP
☎ 01628 527613, Fax 527479, Pro 527610, Rest/Bar 527811
M4 Junction 8/9 through Maidenhead to Cookham; club signposted.
Parkland course.
Pro Roger Frost; Founded 1976 Designed by Charles Lawrie
18 holes, 6408 yards, S.S.S. 71
♸ Welcome WD; with members at WE afternoons.
⌱ Terms on application; £29.00 around.
⚘ Welcome Wed and Fri; packages can be arranged; terms on application.
🍽 Full facilities.
⚘ Spencers, Cookham.

2B 97 **Witney Lakes**

Downs Road, Witney, Oxon, OX29 0SY
⚎ www.witney-reit.co.uk
✉ resort@witney-reit.co.uk
☎ 01993 893000, Fax 778866, Pro 893011
Course is W of Witney on the B4047 Burford road, 1.5 miles from town centre.
Lakeland style course.
Pro Adam Souter; Founded 1994 Designed by Simon Gidman
18 holes, 6675 yards, S.S.S. 71
⚑ Practice range, 24 bays; floodlit.
♸ Welcome.
⌱ WD £16; WE £22.
⚘ Welcome; various packages available; £17-£44.
🍽 Full clubhouse facilities.
⚘ Four Pillars, Witney.

2B 98 **Woburn Golf And Country Club**

Little Brickhill, Milton Keynes, Bucks, MK17 9LJ
⚎ www.woburngolf.com
✉ enquiries@woburngolf.com
☎ 01908 370756, Fax 378436, Pro 626600
Course is four miles W of M1 Junction 13; one mile E of Little Brickhill Junction.

Woodland course.
Pro Luther Blacklock; Founded 1976 Designed by Charles Lawrie
Duchess course: 18 holes, 6651 yards, S.S.S. 72; Dukes Course: 18 holes, 6961 yards, S.S.S. 74
⚑ Practice range.
♸ Welcome WD by prior arrangement.
⌱ Terms on application.
⚘ Welcome WD by prior arrangement; terms available on application.
🍽 Full clubhouse catering, restaurant and bar facilities.
⚘ Bedford Arms.

2B 99 **Wokefield Park** ♛

Mortimer, Reading, Berkshire, RG7 3AG
☎ 01189 334072
Exit from the M4 at Junction 11 and take the A33 towards Basingstoke. At first roundabout, take first exit, golf course is 2.5 miles down this road on the right.
Mature parkland course built in an American style.
Founded 1998
Designed by Jonathan Gaunt
18 holes, 7000 yards, S.S.S. 73
♸ Welcome any time.
⌱ WD £36; WE £19.50+.
⚘ Welcome by prior arrangement.
🍽 3 restaurants.
⚘ Own accommodation: 300 rooms and full leisure facilities for residents.

2B 100 **Wycombe Heights** ♛ **Golf Centre**

Mobile Home Park, Rayners Avenue, Loudwater, High Wycombe, Bucks, HP10 9SW
☎ 01494 816686, Fax 816728
Exit M40 at Junction 3, A40 to High Wycombe, right in Rayner Avenue after half a mile.
Parkland course.
Pro Joseph Awuku; Founded 1991 Designed by John Jacobs
18 holes, 6253 yards, S.S.S. 72
⚑ Practice range, 24 floodlit bays.
♸ Pay and play.
⌱ Terms on application.
⚘ Welcome WD by prior arrangement; packages available.
🍽 Bar, restaurant, family room.
⚘ Post House Forte; Cressex; Alexandria.

THE SOUTH WEST

3A

Cornwall, Devon, Channel Islands

The royal, the ancient and the new can each be found in the region, occasionally even on the same golf course. Royal North Devon, aka Westward Ho!, is the oldest seaside course in England. Yet despite all that tradition, in 1934 a lady called Gloria Minoprio shocked the Western world by turning up to play golf at Westward Ho! in a pair of trousers, an event that Henry Longhurst recorded for posterity.

More recently Westward Ho! and neighbouring Saunton devised a match between the two clubs. The players teed up on the first at Saunton, played along the beach until they reached the narrowest part of the estuary, a carry of 170 yards, entered Westward Ho! near the eighth green and holed out on the eighteenth green. A tee peg was allowed for each shot or, in the case of the rocks along the shore, three polo mints. The 'hole' stretched seven miles and the winning pairing required just 61 strokes.

Golf in the area has come a long way since the pre-Monoprio days at Westward Ho! when players used to solve the problem of deteriorating holes by cutting a new one with a dinner knife and marking it with a gull's feather. Jack Nicklaus used rather more up to date equipment to build St Mellion in Cornwall, a course that is politely described as challenging.

Among the most loved of Cornish courses is St Enedoc. Sir John Betjeman once composed a poem on the subject of a birdie he achieved there. But if ever he hit his ball into the Himalayas that protect St Enedoc's sixth hole, alleged to be the largest sand dune on a British course, he was not moved to verse by that experience.

With 326 miles of coastline and a climate that wavers between temperate and extremely cross, Cornwall is full of first rate golf courses. Trevose and West Cornwall (often called Lelant) are amongst the best of them.

An even severer hazard than the Himalayas is the belief of some Cornish folk that everyone originating outside the county border is a foreigner.

When one holidayer told an inquisitive local that he was from London, the overheard reply was, "Then either you are a pixie or a homosexual." A seldom used phrase, the golf clubs tend to be a bit more broadminded.

Moving on to the Channel Islands and in particular to Jersey, the birthplace of Harry Vardon and Ted Ray – it seems extraordinary that two winners of the US Open should both hail from an island more famous for its tomatoes than its golf courses.

Another US Open winner Tony Jacklin, who had found the British mainland rather too taxing, was made an honorary member of La Moye after he took up residency on the island. La Moye and Royal Jersey are both excellent links courses, although they can get pretty congested in the summer. Over the water, Royal Guernsey is another fine course that has been known to suffer from the same problem.

Devon has its perils too – "they were the footprints of a gigantic hound" – but the crowds should be slightly less intense. There is an abundance of good courses to choose from. The East Course at Saunton is the most highly regarded, but East Devon (described by Donald Steel as "a sort of elevated Sunningdale"), Thurlestone and Yelverton each has its admirers.

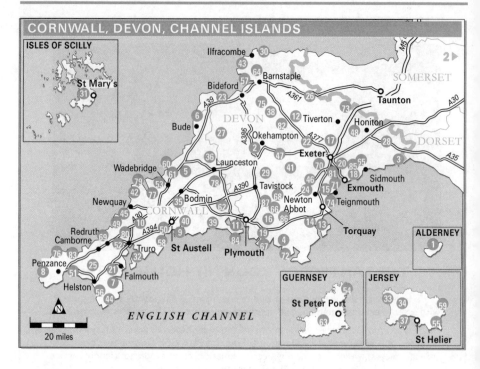

A beautiful 18-hole course overlooking the sea in South Devon

BIGBURY GOLF CLUB

Bigbury-on-sea, South Devon TQ7 4BB; Club Pro (01548) 810412, Secretary (01548) 810557

No golfer visiting the South Hams should miss the opportunity of playing at Bigbury. It's an ideal holiday course - challenging enough for low handicappers but not too daunting for the average golfer. There are outstanding views from almost everywhere on the course - with Dartmoor to the North, the river Avon running near a number of holes and breathtaking scenes of Bantham beach and Burgh Island.

3A 1 Alderney
Route Des Carrieres, Alderney, Guernsey, Channel Islands, GY9 3YD
☎ 01481 822835
1 Mile E of St Annes.
Undulating seaside course.
Designed by Frank Pennink
9 holes, 4964 yards, S.S.S. 65
♦ Welcome at all times; except competition days.
⌐ WD from £12; WE from £17.50.
⌐ Welcome by arrangement WD and WE; for special events catering available.
🍽 All day; arrangement for large parties.
⌐ Seaview. Reduced green fees if you stay there.

3A 2 Ashbury
Higher Maddaford, Southcott, Okehampton, Devon, EX20 4NL
☎ 01837 55453, Fax 55468, Pro 55453, Sec 55453, Rest/Bar 55453
Leaving Okehampton, take Okehampton-Holsworthy Road A3079 and turn right to Ashbury; course half mile on right.
Hilly parkland course.
Pro Reg Cade; Founded 1991
Designed by DJ Fensom Ashbury course
27 holes, 4300/5880/5300 yards, S.S.S. 68
⌐ 8 Bays.
♦ Welcome; normal dress codes apply; half-price if playing with a member; booking essential.
⌐ WD £20; WE £25.
⌐ Essential to book at least 2 weeks in advance; no societies April – October; March packages available; terms on application.
🍽 Full facilities lunch available.
⌐ Manor House Hotel, Okehampton; golf free to hotel guests.

3A 3 Axe Cliff
Squires Lane, Axmouth, Seaton, Devon, EX12 4AB
☎ 01297 24371, Pro 21754, Rest/Bar 20499
Off A3052 Axmouth-Seaton Road.

Coastal/parkland course.
Pro Mark Dack; Founded 1884
Designed by James Briade
18 holes, 5969 yards, S.S.S. 70
♦ Welcome.
⌐ WD £18; WE £22.
⌐ Welcome by prior arrangement; packages available; terms on application.
🍽 Bar and restaurant facilities.
⌐ Seaton Heights Hotel, Anchor Hotel, Dolfin Hotel, Peer Galands Hotel at Peer.

3A 4 Bigbury
Bigbury-On-Sea, Bigbury, South Devon, TQ7 4BB
🖥 www.bigburygolfclub.com
☎ 01548 810412, Fax 810207, Pro 810412, Sec 810557
Turn off the A379
Kingsbridge/Plymouth road near Modbury, on to the B3392; follow signs to Bigbury-on-Sea which lead to the course.
Seaside/parkland course.
Pro Simon Lloyd; Founded 1923
Designed by JH Taylor
18 holes, 6061 yards, S.S.S. 69
⌐ Practice ground and practice green.
♦ Welcome, but essential to belong to a golf club, handicap certs preferred.
⌐ WD £27; WE £30.
⌐ Bookings taken in advance for Tues and Thurs; handicap places preferred, prices from £17.50 (winter) £28 (summer).
🍽 Full Facilities.
⌐ Cottage Hotel, Hope Cove; Thurlestone Hotel, Thurlestone; Pickwick Inn, St Ann's Chapel; Royal Oak, Bigbury.

3A 5 Bowood
Lanteglos, Camelford, Cornwall, PL32 9RF
☎ 01840 213017, Fax 212622
3A39 through Camelford to Valley Truckle, then right on to B3266 Boscastle-Tintagel road, 1st left after garage towards Lanteglos; entrance 0.5 mile on left.
Parkland course with woodland, lakes.
Pro Alan Johnston; Founded 1992

18 holes, 6692 yards, S.S.S. 72
⌐ Practice range available.
♦ Welcome with handicap certs.
⌐ WD £25; WE £25.
⌐ Welcome anytime by arrangement; full facilities available; day ticket £35; terms on application.
🍽 Full facilities.
⌐ Lanteglos Country House Hotel; Bowood Park Hotel.

3A 6 Bude and North Cornwall Golf Club
Burn View, Bude, Cornwall, EX23 8DA
🖥 www.budegolf.co.uk
🖥 secretary@budegolf.co.uk
☎ 01288 352006, Fax 356855, Pro 353635, Rest/Bar 353176
Through the Bude one-way system on A39 and turn right and right again to the Golf Club; 1 minute from town centre.
Seaside links course.
Pro John Yeo; Founded 1891
Designed by Tom Dunn
18 holes, 6057 yards, S.S.S. 70
♦ Welcome.
⌐ WD £25; WE £30.
⌐ Some societies are welcome but not at WE; available depending on numbers; terms on application.
🍽 Wide selection of meals available throughout the day.
⌐ Many in local area.

3A 7 Budock Vean Hotel
Budock Vean, Mawnan Smith, Falmouth, Cornwall, TR11 5LG
🖥 relax@budockvein.co.uk
☎ 01326 250288, Pro 252102
On main road between Falmouth and Helston; head for Mawnan Smith approx 1.5 miles on left.
Undulating parkland course.
Founded 1932
Designed by James Braid, D. Cook and PH Whiteside
9 holes, 5222 yards, S.S.S. 65
♦ Welcome with handicap certs; phone for start time am only.
⌐ Day Ticket: Mon-Sat £18; Sun £20.
⌐ Welcome; full facilities; phone prior.
🍽 Full facilities available.
⌐ Budock Vean.

3A 8 **Cape Cornwall Golf and Country Club**
Cape Cornwall, St Just, Penzance, Cornwall, TR19 7NL
🖳 www.capecornwall.com
🖳 info@capecornwall.com
☎ 01736 788611, Fax 788611
3A3071 to St Just-in-Penwith, turn left at memorial clock, 1 mile down road on left.
Coastal parkland course.
Founded 1990
Designed by Bob Hamilton
18 holes, 5650 yards, S.S.S. 68
♦ Welcome 7 days a week.
Ⅰ WD £20; WE £20.
⌀ Welcome by arrangement; full bar all weekend, lunch 12am-2pm, dinner 7-10pm.
🍴 Full facilities.
🛏 The Boswedden Hotel/B&B.

3A 9 **Carlyon Bay Hotel**
Carlyon Bay Hotel, Sea Road, Carlyon Bay, St Austell, Cornwall, PL25 3RD
🖳 info@carlyonbay.com
☎ 01726 812304, Fax 814938, Sec 814250
Main Plymouth -Truro road, 1 mile W of St Blazey.
Parkland course.
Pro Mark Rowe; Founded 1926
Designed by J Hamilton Stutt
18 holes, 6578 yards, S.S.S. 71
♦ Handicap certs required; phone for start times.
Ⅰ Varies from £25-£37 depending on season.
⌀ Welcome by arrangement.
🍴 Full facilities available.
🛏 Carlyon Bay.

3A 10 **Carvynick Golf & Country Club**
Summercourt, Newquay, Cornwall, TR8 5AF
🖳 www.carynick.co.uk
🖳 info@carynick.co.uk
☎ 01872 510716, Fax 510172, Rest/Bar 510544
Off A30 at Summercourt exit on the road towards Newquay.
Parkland course.
Pro Eric Randle
9 holes, 2492 yards, S.S.S. 66
♦ Welcome at all times.
Ⅰ 9 holes £5; 18 holes £8; reduced rates for players staying in the cottages.
⌀ Welcome.
🍴 Evenings only after 6.30 pm.

3A 11 **China Fleet Country Club**
North Pill, Saltash, Cornwall, PL12 6LJ
🖳 www.china-fleet.co.uk
🖳 sales@china-fleet.co.uk
☎ 01752 848668, Fax 848456
1 mile from Tamar Bridge, leave A38 before tunnel and follow signs.
Parkland course.
Pro Nick Cook; Founded 1991
Designed by Martin Hawtree
18 holes, 6551 yards, S.S.S. 72
♦ Welcome by prior arrangement only.
Ⅰ WD £25; WE £30.
⌀ By arrangement with Sec; full facilities available.
🍴 Full Facilities.
🛏 Accommodation available, telephone for details.

3A 12 **Chulmleigh** ♉
Leigh Road, Chulmleigh, Devon, EX18 7BL
🖳 www.chumleygolf.co.uk
🖳 howard@chumleygolf.co.uk
☎ 01769 580519
From Barnstaple follow Tourist Route Exeter signs; from Exeter follow A377 Crediton road, continue through Crediton, after approx 12 miles turn right into Chulmleigh.
Meadowland course.
Founded 1976
Designed by JWD Goodban OBE
Dec-March 9 hole; 1450 yards, April-Nov 18 holes; 2310 yards, S.S.S. 54
Ⅰ Practice areas.
♦ Welcome.
Ⅰ WD £6.50; WE £6.50.
⌀ Welcome by arrangement; bar and light snacks available.
🍴 Bar and light snacks.
🛏 Cottage for rent, phone for details; Thelbridge Cross Inn.

3A 13 **Churston Golf Club**
Dartmouth Road, Churston Ferrers, Brixham, Devon, TQ5 0LA
🖳 www.Churstongolfclublimited.co.uk
☎ 01803 842751, Fax 845738, Pro 843442, Sec 842751
5 miles south of Torquay along the main road towards Brixham.
Clifftop course.
Pro Neil Holman; Founded 1890
Designed by HS Colt
18 holes, 6208 yards, S.S.S. 70
♦ Welcome with handicaps certs.
Ⅰ WD £30; WE £35; concessions apply.
⌀ Mon, Thurs and Fri only; minimum 12; reductions for 50+; bar, restaurant, pro shop, function and conference

room; terms on application.
🍴 Restaurant facilities.
🛏 Grand Hotel, Torquay; Imperial Hotel, Torquay; Redcliffe Hotel, Paignton; Berry Head Hotel, Brixham.

3A 14 **Dainton Park**
Totnes Road, Ipplepen, Newton Abbot, Devon, TQ12 5TN
☎ 01803 813812
2 miles south of Newton Abbot on the A381.
Parkland course.
Pro Martin Tyson; Founded 1993
Designed by Adrian Stiff
18 holes, 6207 yards, S.S.S. 70
Ⅰ Practice range, 12 bays; floodlit.
♦ Unrestricted access.
Ⅰ WD £15; WE £18.
⌀ Groups of 15 or more welcome; bar and catering available as well as practice ground; £15.
🍴 Full bar and catering service.
🛏 Passagehouse, Kingsteignton; Coppa Dolla, Broadhempston; Sea Trout Inn, Totnes.

3A 15 **Dartmouth Golf & Country Club** ♉
Blackawton, Totnes, Devon, TQ9 7DE
🖳 info@dgcc.co.uk
☎ 01803 712686, Fax 712628, Pro 712650
Off A3122 between Totnes and Dartmouth, 5 miles W of Dartmouth.
Moorland/parkland course.
Pro Steve Dougan; Founded 1992
Designed by Jeremy Pern
18 holes, 6663 yards, S.S.S. 74
Ⅰ 18.
♦ Welcome; phone for starting times.
Ⅰ WD £27; WE £35.
⌀ Welcome by arrangement; full facilities available. Also a 9-hole course; terms on application.
🍴 Bar meals, restaurant, function room.
🛏 Fingals (Dittisham).

3A 16 **Dinnaton Sporting And Country Club** ♉
Blachford Road, Ivybridge, Devon, PL21 9HU
☎ 01752 892512, Fax 698334, Pro 690020
Leave A38 at Ivybridge and head to town centre; follow signs to club from roundabout.
Parkland course.
Pro David Ridyard; Founded 1987
Designed by Cotton & Pink
9 holes, 4089 yards, S.S.S. 59

✝ Welcome.
⌾ WD £7.50; WE £7.50 (9 holes).
⟳ Welcome.
🍽 Snacks available.
⌁ Accommodation on site.

3A 17 Downes Crediton ☏
The Clubhouse, Hookway, Crediton, Devon, EX17 3PT
☎ 01363 773991, Fax 775060, Pro 774464, Sec 773025
Leave A377 Exeter to Crediton road, 8 miles NW of Exeter at Crediton station; turn left at crossroads to Hookway.
Parkland course with water.
Pro Howard Finch; Founded 1976
18 holes, 5954 yards, S.S.S. 69
✝ By arrangement and with handicap certs.
⌾ WD £24; WE £27.
⟳ Welcome by arrangement; catering facilities available; terms on application.
🍽 Meals and snacks with coffee available.

3A 18 East Devon
North View Rd, Budleigh Salterton, Devon, EX9 6DQ
☎ 01395 443370, Pro 445195, Rest/Bar 442018
M5 junction 30; follow signs to Exmouth and the course is on the right as you enter Budleigh Salterton.
Clifftop, heathland course.
Pro Trevor Underwood; Founded 1902
18 holes, 6239 yards, S.S.S. 70
⌁ Long practice area.
✝ Welcome by prior arrangement and with handicap certs.
⌾ £30 for 18 holes; £40 for 36.
⟳ Welcome on Thurs only; bar and restaurant as well as practice facilities; £30 per round.
🍽 Restaurant and bar.
⌁ Recommendations available from secretary.

3A 19 Elfordleigh Hotel Golf ☏ And Country Club
Colebrook, Plympton, Plymouth, Devon, PL7 5EB
📧 Elfordleigh@btinternet.com
☎ 01752 336428, Fax 344581, Pro 348425
Off A38 5 miles NE of Plymouth, 2 miles from Marsh Mills roundabout.
Parkland course.
Pro John Nolan; Founded 1932
Designed by JH Taylor
9 holes, 5664 yards, S.S.S. 67
✝ Welcome with handicap certs.

⌾ WD £25; WE £30.
⟳ Terms on application.
🍽 Full facilities available.
⌁ Elfordleigh Hotel.

3A 20 Exeter Golf & CC ☏
Countess Wear, Topsham Road, Exeter, Devon, EX2 7AE
📧 info@exetergcc.fsnet.co.uk
☎ 01392 874139, Pro 875028, Rest/Bar 874139
Exit 30 off M5; follow road marked Topsham; course is 4 miles south east of Exeter.
Parkland course.
Pro Mike Rowett; Founded 1895
Designed by James Braid
18 holes, 6008 yards, S.S.S. 69
✝ Welcome with handicap certs; not on Tues mornings, Sats booking advisable.
⌾ WD £30; WE £35 per round.
⟳ Welcome on Thurs only; function room, four bars and spike bars; players' guests welcome; terms on application.
🍽 Full catering facilities available from 8.00am.
⌁ Buckerell Lodge; Countess Wear Lodge; Devon Motel.

3A 21 Falmouth
Swanpool Road, Goldenbank, Falmouth, Cornwall, TR11 5BQ
☎ 01326 314296, Fax 317783, Pro 311262
Half a mile west of Swanpool beach on the road to Maenporth.
Seaside parkland course.
Pro Bryan Patterson; Founded 1894
18 holes, 6061 yards, S.S.S. 70
⌁ Practice range; driving range.
✝ Welcome.
⌾ WD £25; WE £25.
⟳ Welcome by prior arrangement; bar, lunch and tea facilities; terms on application.
🍽 Available.
⌁ Royal Duchy; Meudon Vean; Park Grove.

3A 22 Fingle Glen Golf Hotel
Tedburn St Mary, Exeter, Devon, EX6 6AF
🌐 www.UKgolfer.com/fingle
📧 fingle.glen@btinternet.com
☎ 01647 61817, Fax 61135, Pro 61718, Sec 61817,
Rest/Bar 61817
4 miles from Exeter on the A30 to Okehampton, 400 yards from Fingle Glen Junction.

Parkland course.
Pro K Pitts; Founded 1989
Designed by W Pile
9 holes, 4747 yards, S.S.S. 63
⌁ 12.
✝ Welcome.
⌾ WD £8.50; WE £10 (9 holes).
WD £13.50; WE £16 (18 holes).
⟳ Welcome; golfing packages can be arranged; terms on application.
🍽 Bar, lounge and restaurant.
⌁ Own accommodation on site.

3A 23 Hartland Forest Golf & Leisure Parc ☏
Woolsery, Bideford, Devon, EX39 5RA
☎ 01237 431442, Fax 431734
6 miles S of Clovelly off A39.
Parkland course.
Founded 1987
Designed by John Hepplewhite
18 holes, 6015 yards, S.S.S. 69
✝ No restrictions except acceptable standard of golf; dress code applies.
⌾ WD £20; WE £20; booking advisable.
⟳ Welcome by arrangement; full facilities available.
🍽 Full facilities.
⌁ 34 units of accommodation available on site sleeping 130.

3A 24 Hele Park
Ashburton Road, Newton Abbot, Devon, TQ12 6JN
☎ 01626 336060, Fax 332661, Pro 336060
On edge of Newton Abbot on the A383 Newton Abbot-Ashburton road.
Parkland course.
Pro J Lamgmead; Founded 1992
Designed by M Craig/N Stanbury
9 holes, 5168 yards, S.S.S. 65
⌁ Practice range, floodlit driving range and outdoor grass tees.
✝ Welcome.
⌾ WD from £9.50; WE from £10.50.
⟳ Welcome on application to the secretary; terms on application.
🍽 Full facilities.
⌁ Passage House, Kingsteignton, Newton Abbot.

3A 25 Helston Golf and Leisure
Wendron, Coverack Bridges, Helston, Cornwall, TR13 0LX
☎ 01326 572228, Rest/Bar 565103
1 mile N of Helston on B3297 Redruth road.
Short park and downland course.
Founded 1988
18 holes, 2100 yards, S.S.S. 54

Welcome anytime.
WD £5; WE £5.
Welcome by prior arrangement.
Full facilities available at Whealdream Bar.
Lyndale Guesthouse, Helston.

3A 26 Highbullen Hotel

Chittlehamholt, Umberleigh, Devon, EX37 9HD
www.Highbullen.co.uk
info@Highbullen.co.uk
01769 540561, Fax 540492, Pro 540 530
10 mins west on A361 from South Molton.
Parkland course.
Pro Paul Weston; Founded 1960
Designed by Hugh Neil. New Extension by M Neil & H Stutt Desi
18 holes, 5455 yards, S.S.S. 66
Welcome; free for hotel guests.
WD £16; WE £18.
By arrangement.
Restaurant open everyday; Bar snacks also.
Highbullen Hotel.

3A 27 Holsworthy Golf Club ☎

Killatree, Holsworthy, Devon, EX22 6LP
www.holsworthygolfclub.co.uk
hgcsecretary@aol.com
01409 253177, Fax 253177, Pro 254771, Sec 253177, Rest/Bar 253177
1.5 miles out of Holsworthy on the A3072 Bude Road.
Parkland course.
Pro Grasham Webb; Founded 1937
18 holes, 6062 yards, S.S.S. 69
Very welcome.
WD up to £15; WE up to £20.
By arrangement; packages available; terms on application.
Clubhouse facilities.
Court Barn, Clawton.

3A 28 Honiton

Middlehills, Honiton, Devon, EX14 9TR
01404 44422, Fax 46383, Pro 42943, Sec 44422, Rest/Bar 47167
1 mile S of Honiton off the A35.
Parkland course.
Pro A Cave; Founded 1896
18 holes, 5902 yards, S.S.S. 68
Welcome by arrangement.
WD £23; WE £28.
Welcome on Thurs; terms on application.
Bar facilities available.

Space for 10 touring caravans available.

3A 29 Hurdwick

Tavistock Hamlets, Tavistock, Devon, PL19 OLL
01822 612746
Signposted from centre of Tavistock; course is one mile N of Tavistock on Brentor road.
Parkland course.
Founded 1988
Designed by Hawtree
18 holes, 5217 yards, S.S.S. 67
Welcome at any times; dress code applies.
WD £15; WE £15.
Welcome; packages available; 36 holes of golf and lunch available from £18.
Lunch and snacks.
Bedford Hotel, Tavistock; Castle Inn, Lydford.

3A 30 Ilfracombe

Hele Bay, Ilfracombe, North Devon, EX34 9RT
www.ilfracombegolfclub.com
ilfracombe.golfclub@virgin.net
01271 862050, Fax 867731, Pro 863328, Sec 862176, Rest/Bar 862675
Course is one mile from Ilfracombe towards Combe Martin on the A399 coast road.
Undulating heathland course with spectacular views.
Pro Mark Davis; Founded 1892
Designed by TK Weir
18 holes holes, 5893 yards yards, S.S.S. 69
Welcome by prior arrangement, particularly in the summer.
WD £20; WE £25.
Welcome by prior arrangement with the secretary; terms on application.
Full clubhouse facilities.
Club can recommend in local area.

3A 31 Isles of Scilly

St Mary's, Isle Of Scilly, TR21 0NF
01720 422692, Sec 423103
1.5 miles from Hugh Town in St.Mary's.
Heathland/seaside course.
Founded 1904
Designed by Horace Hutchinson
9 holes, 6001 yards, S.S.S. 69
Welcome; phone one hour before on Sunday.
WD £19; WE £19. twilight golf £10.
Available.

Star Castle Hotel.

3A 32 Killiow Park

Killiow, Kea, Truro, Cornwall, TR3 6AG
office@killiow.fsnet.co.uk
01872 270246, Fax 240915, Sec 240915, Rest/Bar 270246
Leave Truro on A39 Truro/Falmouth road, turn right at first roundabout 3 miles from Truro, clearly signposted thereafter.
Picturesque parkland course.
Founded 1987
18 holes, 5274 yards, S.S.S. 68
8 indoor and 3 outdoor.
Welcome after 8.30am; advisable to book in high season.
WD £15.50; WE £15.50.
Welcome.
Bar and Restaurant.
The Alverton Manor.

3A 33 La Grande Mare Country Club

Vazon Coast Road, Castel, Guernsey, Channel Islands, GY5 7LL
01481 53544, Fax 55194, Pro 53432, Rest/Bar 56576
On the west coast of Guernsey at Vazon Bay.
Parkland course.
Pro Matt Groves; Founded 1994
Designed by Hawtree
18 holes, 5112 yards, S.S.S. 66
Welcome.
WD £25; WE £28.
Book in advance; restaurant and bar; hotel has 5 crowns; terms on application.
Bar, restaurant and hotel.
La Grande Mare Hotel.

3A 34 La Moye

La Moye, La Route Orange, St Brelade, Jersey, Channel Islands, JE3 8GQ
01534 743401, Fax 747289, Pro 743130, Sec 743401, Rest/Bar 742701
2 miles W of airport off Route des Orange.
Links course.
Pro Mike Deeley; Founded 1902
Designed by James Braid
18 holes, 6664 yards, S.S.S. 72
1 driving range.
Welcome by prior arrangement.
WD £45; WE and bank holidays £50.
Welcome by prior arrangement WD only; £5 booking fee per person; Restaurant facilities available.

Lower Polscoe, Lostwithiel,
Cornwall, PL22 0HQ

 ETB
★★★ ★★★ ★★★

LOSTWITHIEL

Hotel ·

GOLF & COUNTRY CLUB

Tel: 01208 873550
Fax: 01208 873479
E-mail:
reception@golf-hotel.co.uk
Website:
www.golf-hotel.co.uk

With magnificent views and in a peaceful setting, Lostwithiel's 18-hole undulating parkland course in richly wooded hill country is a joy to play. It's situated alongside the river Fowey and overlooked by Restormel Castle in the heart of the beautiful Cornish countryside, close to the Eden Project.

Plus we've got a superb golf and leisure hotel boasting 18 charming bedrooms, tennis, indoor swimming pool, gym, bar and restaurant, with the stunning Cornish coast just a short drive away.

🍴 Full clubhouse restaurant and bar facilities.
🛏 Atlantic; L'Horizon, both St Brelade.

3A 35 Lanhydrock ☏
Lostwithiel Rd, Bodmin, Cornwall,
PL30 5AQ
🖳 www.lanhydrock-golf.co.uk
📧 postmaster@lanhydrock-golf.
co.uk
☎ 01208 73600, Fax 77325,
Pro 73600, Sec 73600,
Rest/Bar 73600
1 mile south of Bodmin.
Parkland course.
Pro Jason Broadway; Founded 1992
Designed by J Hamilton Stutt
18 holes, 6100 yards, S.S.S. 70
† Welcome.
⌊ WD £30; WE £35.
⌒ Welcome; packages available for groups of 16 and above players; private suite available with own bar facility.
🍴 Full facilities.
🛏 Lanhydrock Golfing Lodge adjacent to first tee.

3A 36 Launceston ☏
St Stephen's, North Street,
Launceston, Cornwall, PL15 8HF
☎ 01566 773442, Fax 777506,
Pro 775359, Sec 773442,
Rest/Bar 773442
1 mile N of Launceston on Bude road (B3254).
Parkland course.
Pro John Tozer; Founded 1927
Designed by J. Hamilton Stutt
18 holes, 6415 yards, S.S.S. 71
† Welcome by arrangement.
⌊ WD £20; WE £20.
⌒ Welcome WD by arrangement; full facilities; terms on application.
🍴 Available by prior arrangement.
🛏 White Hart.

3A 37 Les Ormes Golf and Leisure
Le Mont A La Brune, St Brelade,
Jersey, Channel Islands, JE3 8FL
🖳 www.lesormes.je
📧 mikegraham@localdial.com
☎ 01534 744464, Fax 499122, Pro 497000, Sec 497006, Rest/Bar 497010
Course is five minutes from Jersey Airport following the signs for St Brelade.
Parkland course.
Pro Andrew Chamberlain; Founded 1996
9 holes, 5018 yards, S.S.S. 66
🏌 Practice range, 17 bays, 4 very modern indoor tennis courts.
† Welcome.
⌊ WD £13; WE £16.
⌒ Welcome by prior arrangement.
🍴 Full catering facilities.
🛏 Many in Jersey; contact local tourist board.

3A 38 Libbaton
High Bickington, Umberleigh, Devon,
EX37 9BS
☎ 01769 560269, Fax 560342,
Pro 560167, Sec 560269,
Rest/Bar 560260
A377 to Atherington and then B3217 to High Bickington.
Parkland course.
Pro Sarah Burnell; Founded 1988
Designed by Col P Badham
18 holes, 6494 yards, S.S.S. 72
🏌 Practice range.
† Visitors and societies welcome at all times. Advanced booking for tees advisable.
⌊ WD £18; WE £22.
⌒ Welcome Mon, Wed, Fri; golf, coffee, snack lunch, evening meal; £25.
🍴 Full catering facilities available all day.
🛏 Northcote Manor, Umberleigh;
Exeter Inn, Chittlehamholt.

3A 39 Looe
Bin Down, Looe, Cornwall, PL13 1PX
☎ 01503 240239, Fax 240864
Course is three miles E of Looe just off the B3253.
Parkland/downland course.
Pro A MacDonald; Founded 1933
Designed by Harry Vardon
18 holes, 5940 yards, S.S.S. 68
† Welcome.
⌊ Price on application.
⌒ Welcome but minimum of 8 players; catering packages available; from £18; special society weekend rates available; details on application.
🍴 Facilities available.
🛏 Call club for details.

3A 40 Lostwithiel Hotel ☏
Golf & Country Club
Lower Polscoe, Lostwithiel, Cornwall,
PL22 0HQ
🖳 www.golf-hotel.co.uk
📧 reception@golf-hotel.co.uk
☎ 01208 873550, Fax 873479,
Pro 873822
On the A390 from Plymouth to Lostwithiel.
Parkland course.
Pro Tony Nash; Founded 1991
Designed by Stewart Wood
18 holes, 5984 yards, S.S.S. 72
🏌 Practice range, 6 undercover bays; floodlit.
† Welcome.
⌊ WD £25; WE £29.
⌒ Welcome; golf only £15; coffee and lunch, evening meal and day's golf £28; terms on application.
🍴 Full facilities.
🛏 18 country-style bedrooms on site with tennis courts, indoor swimming pool and gym.

3A 41 Manor House Hotel & Golf Course
Moretonhampstead, North Bovey, Newton Abbot, Devon, TQ13 8RE
☎ 01647 445000, Fax 440961, Pro 440998, Rest/Bar 440355
On B3212 towards Mortonhampstead. Parkland built around 2 rivers.
Pro Richard Lewis; Founded 1921
Designed by JF Abercrombie
18 holes, 6016 yards, S.S.S. 69
† Welcome but must book start time.
Ɩ WD £30; WE £37.
♢ Welcome by prior arrangement; packages can be arranged; terms on application.
🍽 Hotel Facilities.
↩ Manor House Hotel.

3A 42 Merlin   ₢
Mawgan Porth, Newquay, Cornwall, TR8 4DN
☎ 01841 540222, Fax 541031
On coast road between Newquay and Padstow. After Mawgan Porth take St Eval Road.
Heathland course.
Founded 1991
Designed by Ross Oliver
18 holes, 5305 yards, S.S.S. 67
Ɩ Practice range, 6 covered bays.
† No restrictions.
Ɩ WD £12; WE £12.
♢ Welcome by prior arrangement; includes unlimited golf only; lunch and dinner are available at special rates; £10.
🍽 Bar and Restaurant.
↩ Bedruthan Steps; Merrymoor Inn; Whitelodge; Sea Vista, all Mawgan Porth; Falcon, St Mawgan.

3A 43 Mortehoe & Woolacombe
Easewell, Mortehoe, Devon, EX34 7EH
🖳 www.easewellfarm.co.uk
☎ 01271 870225, Fax 870225, Pro

870566
1 mile before Mortehoe on the Ilfracombe road.
Parkland with superb sea views.
Founded 1992
Designed by Hans Ellis/David Hoare
9 holes, 4638 yards, S.S.S. 63
† Welcome.
Ɩ WD £7; WE £7; £12 for 18 holes.
♢ Welcome with pre-booking; terms on application.
🍽 Bar and restaurant
↩ Woolacombe Bay; Watersmeet; Lundy House; Rockham Bay.

3A 44 Mullion   ₢
Cury Cross Lanes, Helston, Cornwall, TR12 7BP
🖳 secretary@ mulliongolfclub.plus.com
☎ 01326 240276, Fax 240685, Pro 241176, Sec 240685, Rest/Bar 241231
S of Helston on A3083 towards The Lizard past Culdrose Naval Air station.
Parkland/links course.
Pro P Blundell; Founded 1895
Designed by W Sich
18 holes, 6037 yards, S.S.S. 70
† Welcome with handicap certs.
Ɩ WD £25; WE £30.(or bank holidays).
♢ Welcome with prior arrangement; packages available; terms on application.
🍽 Full catering and bar available.
↩ Polurrian; Mullion Cove; Angel.

3A 45 Newquay Golf Club
Tower Road, Newquay, Cornwall, TR7 1LT
🖳 newquaygolfclub@ smartone.co.uk
☎ 01637 874354, Fax 874066, Pro 874830, Sec 874354, Rest/Bar 872091
Adjacent to Fistral Beach.signpostsed.
Seaside links course.
Pro Mark Bevan; Founded 1890

Designed by HS Colt
18 holes, 6150 yards, S.S.S. 69
† Welcome; handicap certificates required.
Ɩ WD £25; WE £25.
♢ By arrangement only; full facilities; terms on application.
🍽 Bar and restaurant.
↩ Bristol; Esplanade, Narrowcliff.

3A 46 Newton Abbot (Stover Golf Club)   ₢
The Club House, Stover, Newton Abbot, Devon, TQ12 6QQ
☎ 01626 352460, Fax 330210, Pro 362078, Sec 352460, Rest/Bar 352460
Off A38 at Drumbridges and turn towards Newton Abbot on the A382; course is 500 yards on right.
Wooded parkland course.
Pro Malcolm Craig; Founded 1931
Designed by James Braid
18 holes, 5764- 5527 yards, S.S.S. 68
† Welcome with handicap certs unless with a member.
Ɩ WD £25 or £30 per day; WE £28 or £32 per day.
♢ Thurs only; full catering facilities to order; terms on application.
🍽 Bar and restaurant.
↩ Dolphin; Edgemoor, both Bovey Tracey.

3A 47 Okehampton   ₢
Tors Road, Okehampton, Devon, EX20 1EF
☎ 01837 52113, Fax 52734, Pro 53541, Sec 52113, Rest/Bar 659334
Enter town centre from A30 and follow signs from the main lights.
Parkland course.
Pro Simon Jefferies; Founded 1913
Designed by JH Taylor
18 holes, 5281 yards, S.S.S. 67
† Welcome but only by prior arrangement; booking essential.

ROSERROW GOLF & COUNTRY CLUB   Tel: 01208 863000

Roserrow, St Minver, Wadebridge, Cornwall PL27 6QT   www.roserrow.co.uk   e-mail: mail@roserrow.co.uk

Nestling in over 400 acres of unspoilt countryside near Rock and the Camel Estuary, Roserrow's 6507 yard 18-hole course offers a congenial atmosphere of quiet seclusion against a beautiful backdrop. Considered one of Cornwall's favourite society venues, both visitors and societies are warmly welcomed. Additionally, Roserrow boasts extensive self-catering accommodation, tennis courts, heated indoor swimming pool, sauna, steam room, spa and fitness suite.

⅃ WD and Sunday £17-20; WE £20.
⟳ Welcome by prior arrangement; Group discounts available; terms on application.
⚞ Available.
⤣ Fox and Hounds, Bridestowe; White Hart, Okehampton.

3A 48 Padbrook Park   ☜
Cullompton, Devon, EX15 1RU
☎ 01884 38286, Fax 34359
Exit 28 of the M5; follow signs through Okehampton; across roundabout and then first on right.
Parkland course.
Pro Stewart Adwick/Ross Troke; Founded 1991
Designed by Bob Sandow
9 holes, 6108 yards, S.S.S. 69
† Welcome but must pre-book tee time.
⅃ WD £13; WE £17.
⟳ Welcome with prior arrangements; full catering for society and corporate packages; terms on application.
⚞ Bar and restaurant.
⤣ Exeter Inn, Brampton.

3A 49 Perranporth
Budnic Hill, Perranporth, Cornwall, TR6 0AB
☎ 01872 573701, Fax 573701, Pro 572317, Sec 573701, Rest/Bar 572454
Take Perranporth road off the A30; course is on the right when entering town.
Links course with panoramic views.
Pro Derek Mitchell; Founded 1929
Designed by James Braid
18 holes, 6286 yards, S.S.S. 72
† Welcome with prior booking.
⅃ Day ticket: WD £25; WE £30.
⟳ Welcome with booking; packages can be arranged; terms on application.
⚞ Bar and restaurant.
⤣ Ponsmere, Perranporth; White Lodge, Mawgan Porth.

3A 50 Porthpean
Porthpean, St Austell, Cornwall, PL26 6AY
☎ 01726 64613

Off A390 2 miles from St Austell.
Parkland course.
Founded 1992
Designed by R Oliver/A Leather
18 holes, 5184 yards, S.S.S. 67
⅃ Practice range, 9 bays; floodlit range.
† Welcome.
⅃ WD £12; WE £12.
⟳ Welcome by prior arrangement; packages available; terms on application.
⚞ Clubhouse facilities.
⤣ Cliff Head; Pier House; Porth Avallen.

3A 51 Praa Sands   ☜
Germoe Crossroads, Praa Sands, Penzance, Cornwall, TR20 9TQ
✉ praasandsgolf@aol.co.uk
☎ 01736 763445, Fax 763399
7 miles east of Penzance on A394 to Helston.
Seaside parkland course.
Founded 1971
2 x 9 holes, 4122 yards, S.S.S. 60
† Welcome except Sun mornings.
⅃ 9 holes £10; 18 holes £15; day ticket £20.
⟳ By arrangement; packages available; terms on application.
⚞ Meals and snacks.
⤣ Praa Sands Hotel; Queens, Penzance.

3A 52 Radnor Golf Centre
Radnor Road, Redruth, Cornwall, TR16 5EL
🖳 www.radnorgolfski.fsnet.co.uk
☎ 01209 211059, Fax 211059, Pro 211059, Sec 211059, Rest/Bar 211059
Take A30 from Redruth to Porthtowan; after 200 yards turn right; golf centre on left after 1 mile.
Heathland course with gorse.
Pro Gordon Wallbank; Founded 1988
Designed by Gordon Wallbank
9 holes, 1312 yards, S.S.S. men 52 ladies 56
⅃ 4 indoor,3 outdoor.
† Pay and play.
⅃ WD £8.00; WE £8.00 (18 holes). £5.00 (9 holes;).

⟳ Welcome.
⚞ None.
⤣ The Inn for all Seasons.

3A 53 Roserrow Golf &   ☜
Country Club
Roserrow, St Minver, Wadebridge, Cornwall, PL27 6QT
✉ Mail@roserrow.co.uk
☎ 01208 863000, Fax 863002
From Wadebridge take the B3314 towards Polzeath.
Parkland course.
Pro Andrew Cullen; Founded 1997
18 holes, 6951 yards, S.S.S. 72
⅃ 13.
† Welcome anytime.
⅃ £25 any time.
⟳ Welcome by prior arrangement.
⚞ Full bar meals and brasserie.
⤣ Own accommodation.

3A 54 Royal Guernsey
L'Ancresse Vale, Guernsey, Channel Islands, GY3 5BY
☎ 01481 47022, Fax 43960, Pro 45070, Sec 46523
3 miles north of St Peter Port.
Seaside links course.
Pro Noramn Wood; Founded 1890
Designed by MacKenzie Ross
18 holes, 6206 yards, S.S.S. 70
† Welcome; restricted times on Thurs and Sat morning; no visitors on Sun.
⅃ WD £36; WE £36.
⟳ Not welcome.
⚞ Coffee, afternoon teas and meals available.
⤣ Pembroke Bay; L'Ancresse Hotel.

3A 55 Royal Jersey
Le Chemin Au Greves, Grouville, Jersey, Channel Islands, JE3 9BD
🖳 www.royaljersey.com
☎ 01534 854416, Fax 854684, Pro 852234, Rest/Bar 851042
4 miles east of St Helier on road to Gorey.
Links course.
Pro David Morgan; Founded 1878
18 holes, 6100 yards, S.S.S. 70
† Welcome between 10am-12 noon

and 2pm-4pm on WD and after 2.30pm at WE.
[WD £45; WE £45.
⌒ Apply in writing to Sec; full catering by prior arrangement with Steward.
⦿ Bar and catering facilities.

3A 56 Royal Navy Air Station Culdrose
RNAS Culdrose, Helston, Cornwall, TR12 8QY
☎ 01326 552413, Sec 573929
3A3083 1 mile from Helston towards Lizard.
Flat parkland course built around part of airfield.
Founded 1962
14 holes holes, 6132 yards yards, S.S.S. 70
† Must be accompanied by club member.
[Terms on application.
⌒ Welcome by arrangement.
⦿ Clubhouse bar and hot/cold snacks available.

3A 57 Royal North Devon
Golf Links Road, Westward Ho,
Bideford, Devon, EX39 1HD
☎ 01237 473817, Fax 423456,

Pro 477598, Rest/Bar 473824
Take M5 to A361 and go through Northam Village to Sandymere road and then into Golf Links Road.
Links course.
Pro Richard Herring; Founded 1864
Designed by Tom Morris
18 holes holes, 6653 yards, S.S.S. 72
† Welcome with handicap certs.
[WD £30; WE £36.
⌒ Welcome; bar, restaurant, snooker room; terms on application.
⦿ Full facilities.
⌐ Anchorage Hotel; Durrant House, Northam; Riversford Hotel, Northam.

3A 58 St Austell ☎
Tregongeeves Lane, St Austell, Cornwall, PL26 7DS
☎ 01726 72649, Fax 71978,
Pro 68621, Sec 74756,
Rest/Bar 72649
1 mile out of St Austell on the A390 Truro road; signposted.
Heathland/parkland course.
Pro Tony Pitts; Founded 1911
18 holes, 6089 yards, S.S.S. 69
[Practice range, opening 1998.
† Must be a member of a golf club and hold handicap cert.
[WD £20; WE £22.

⌒ Welcome by appointment except on WE; restaurant and lounge bar; meals to be arranged with the caterer; £20.
⦿ Full catering facilities.
⌐ The White Hart.

3A 59 St Clements
Jersey Recreation Grounds Co Ltd, Plat Douet Road, St Clement, Jersey, Channel Islands, JE2 6PN
☎ 01534 721938, Fax 721012
Close to St Helier.
Meadowland course.
Founded 1913
9 holes, 4138 yards
† Welcome every day except before 11.30 Tues and 1.30pm Sun.
[WD £10; WE £10.
⌒ Welcome by arrangement.
⦿ Buffet bar and restaurant.
⌐ Hotel de Normandy, Merton.

3A 60 St Enodoc
Rock, Wadebridge, Cornwall, PL27 6LD
☎ 01208 863216, Fax 862976, Pro 862402, Sec 862200
6 miles NW of Wadebridge.
Links course.
Pro Nick Williams; Founded 1890

St Mellion

Deep in the Cornish countryside a few years ago two farming brothers, steeped in the businesses of rearing pigs and growing potatoes, had a dream. They looked at 450 acres of woodland and pasture and visualised unique golfing territory.

Martin and Hermon Bond never did anything in a small way, but few could have imagined the outcome once they began to chase that dream. Suddenly the greatest of them all, Jack Nicklaus, was among them in Wellington boots and a four-wheel drive, creating the course that is now St Mellion.

Not long after its opening, the Benson and Hedges International made St Mellion its home for six years producing such outstanding champions as Jose-Maria Olazabal, Bernhard Langer, Peter Senior, Paul Broadhurst, Seve Ballesteros and Peter O'Malley.

A hotel, lodge and leisure centre were added to the complex and golfers from all over Europe travelled to play the difficult, but beautiful Nicklaus course of 6,626 yards (par 72).

They found water, long carries, intriguing par three holes and a countryside teeming with wild life. That St Mellion always produced true and worthy champions was testimony to the examination it provided.

The Bond brothers began with the Old Course – it is still there and excellent indeed – but when they saw the success of that they decided they wanted "the best course in Cornwall." That's when they bought 200 acres of adjoining woodland from the Duchy of Cornwall and hired the Golden Bear to create the course everyone was soon talking about.

It has been described as the 'Augusta of Cornwall', while others have said it is the toughest course in Britain, while Eamonn Darcy, playing the 1995 Benson and Hedges said: "It's a bitch. It's an animal. If you try to steer it around you'll end up in a straitjacket."

The Nicklaus course abounds with intriguing holes. The third (a par four of 356 yards) gives you a taste of what is to come. The drive is one of the tightest shots on the course with a very deep drop to the right. The ball needs to be held towards the left hand side or you could be faced with a seriously difficult uphill shot over the ravine to a well-guarded green.

The fifth appears on the card as a relatively short and simple par four of 315 yards and then the danger presents itself. The tee shot has to carry water and land perfectly as there is a stream running across 40 yards in front of a severely sloping green. There is no scope for error.

And so the course meanders tantalisingly on and it is easy to see why the eleventh and twelfth have been compared to the last two holes in Augusta's famous Amen Corner – a par three followed by a par five

The 11th is probably the most photographed hole on the course and Nicklaus admits it was created almost by accident. They were missing out that particular corner of real estate, but as Nicklaus says: "We had not anticipated this hole at all, but then I took another look and saw an opportunity for a great short hole. We damned the stream to make a lake, built the green into the hillside and put in some stepped down tees."

The hole is both brilliant and cruel. It has wrecked many a card. The twelfth, the longest hole on the course, stretches for 525 yards and runs through a valley, demanding accuracy all the way.

The Augusta illusion disappears when you take in the unmistakable Cornish surroundings. There are rolling pastures, brooks that tumble along with the occasional blue dart of a kingfisher brightening the scene. There are sentinel trees that look as if they have been standing for centuries.

St Mellion may seem a distant place as it nestles near the town of Saltash, but it is well worth the journey. — **Jim Mossop**

Saunton

Regarded by some as worthy of an Open Championship, Saunton has accommodated some very famous names over the years. Francis Ouimet, who defeated Harry Vardon and Ted Ray in a play-off to win the US Open in 1913, took away a very high opinion of the East course after taking 80 shots to get round.

Nearly one hundred years later, Sergio Garcia won the Boys' Amateur Championship at Saunton while the members grumbled about being forced onto the West Course unaware of the talent that they were missing.

In 2001, Nick Faldo was happy to show any member who was interested the wonders of his range finder. Fanny Sunesson might be alarmed to know that equipped with this gadget and an uncluttered mind, Faldo took just 65 strokes to complete his round.

The only professional to have been rather sniffy about Saunton was Brian Barnes. He called it a pitch and putt course that needed only a drive and a nine iron. The next day he went out and shot 81 much to the amusement of the locals who wondered if he had lost his nine iron.

Barnes was certainly a most gifted striker of the golf ball, but the wind must have been in a very funny place if he needed only a nine iron. The first hole is a 478-yard par four that requires two fair blows. The third and fourth are also testing par fours between spectacular banks of dunes.

Worried that the par five second offers too much respite in the midst of such a start, the club is considering pushing the green 40 yards further back into the dunes. The middle of the course is full of twists and turns and is where a player hopes to make his score. The ninth hole is typical. A dogleg par four of moderate length it has a fiendishly sloped green that is more devilish to read than the mind of Fu Manchu. The finish is justly famous, particularly the sixteenth hole, a plunging dogleg left that requires a gamble off the tee to facilitate the second.

Those who get past this hole without blowing up are still not quite safe. The bomb disposal unit has been called in many times over the years. During the second world war, Saunton was used as a military training ground in preparation for the Normandy landings. The troops had to leave so quickly that they just buried everything as best they could. It is a toss up whether you will be impeded by explosives or a Harley Davidson rising to the surface.

Most people come to Saunton to play the East Course, but they would be well advised to try out the West. It is just as spectacular, requires precision rather than length off the tee and generally has better greens than the East now that they have been relaid. The turn for home from the thirteenth is one of the most beautiful stretches of golfing country in the land.

Saunton is an unusual experience, not least because the high volume of rain in recent years means that it sometimes veers from traditional links towards something more parkland in nature. The quality of both courses means that Saunton is excellent value for the day, although the price has gone up a little since the original annual subscription of 10/6d. — **Mark Reason**

SAUNTON GOLF CLUB
Two Championship Links Course

Visitors and Societies Welcome (Handicap Certificates **are** required)
Excellent Bar and Restaurant facilities (all green fees include a complimentary meal voucher)
Venue for the 2002 PGA Club Professionals Championship
Tel: **01271 812436**   Email: **info@sauntongolf.co.uk**   **www.sauntongolf.co.uk**

Designed by James Braid
18 holes, 6243 yards, S.S.S. 70
⏴ Basic driving range.
† Welcome; max handicap 24 on Church course. No restrictions on other course.
[WD £38; WE £45 for Church course: £15 for Holywell course.
⏚ Welcome by prior arrangement; meals can be arranged through restaurant.
⏺ Full restaurant and bar.

3A 61 St Kew
St Kew Highway, Nr Wadebridge, Bodmin, Cornwall, PL30 3EF
☎ 01208 841500, Fax 841500
Main A30 Wadebridge to Camelford road; course two and a half miles north of Wadebridge.
Parkland course.
Pro Nick Rogers; Founded 1993
Designed by D Derry
9 holes holes, 4543 yards, S.S.S. 62
⏴ Practice range, covered.
† Welcome at all times.
[WD £13; WE £13.
⏚ Welcome by arrangement; discounts on application; catering available; terms on application.
⏺ Full facilities.
⏚ Bodare Hotel, Daymer Bay; Molesworth Arms, Wadebridge; St Moritz, Trebetherick.

3A 62 St Mellion International ⏾
(see page 109)
St Mellion Hotel Golf And Country Club, St Mellion, Saltash, Cornwall, PL12 6SD
⏿ www.st-mellion.co.uk
✉ stmellion@americangolf.uk.com
☎ 01579 351351, Fax 350537, Pro 352002, Rest/Bar 352005
3 miles south of Callington on A388.
Parkland course; former home of Benson & Hedges Masters.
Pro D Moon; Founded 1976
Designed by Jack Nicklaus; old course designed by J Hamilton Stutt
Nicklaus course: 18 holes, 6651 yards, S.S.S. 72; Old course: 18 holes, 5782 yards, S.S.S. 68
⏴ 6 undercover, 30 turf bays.

---

† Welcome.
[Nicklaus: WD £50, WE £50 Old Course; WD £35, WE £35.
⏚ Welcome subject to availability; coffee, 18 holes of golf, 3-course club meal packages available.
⏺ Full catering, coffee shop, grill room.
⏚ Own lodge and hotel.

3A 63 St Pierre Park Hotel
Rohais Road, St Peter Port, Guernsey, Channel Islands, GY1 1FD
☎ 01481 727039, Fax 712041, Rest/Bar 428282
1 mile west of St Peter Port on Rohais Road.
Hilly course with water hazards.
Pro Roy Corbet; Founded 1982
Designed by Tony Jacklin
9 holes, 2610 yards, S.S.S. 50
† Welcome.
[WD £12; WE £14 (9 holes).
⏚ Welcome; packages available, terms on application.
⏺ Full facilities at the hotel.
⏚ St Pierre Park Hotel.

3A 64 Saunton
Braunton, Devon, EX33 1LG
⏿ www.sauntongolf.co.uk
✉ trevor@sauntongolf.co.uk
☎ 01271 812436, Pro 812013, Sec 812436, Rest/Bar 812436
On B3231 from Braunton to Croyde, 7 miles from Barnstaple.
Traditional links course.
Pro Albert MacKenzie; Founded 1897
Designed by Herbert Fowler
⏴ 4-6.
† Welcome with handicap certificates.
[WD £45, WE £50 (18 holes); WD £65, WE £75 (36 holes); All inclusive of a meal voucher.
⏚ Welcome by arrangement; full facilities available.
⏺ Full restaurant facilities.
⏚ Saunton Sands; Kittiwell House; Preston House; Croyde Bay House, Woolacombe Bay.

3A 65 Sidmouth
Cotmaton Road, Sidmouth, Devon,

EX10 8SX
☎ 01395 516407, Rest/Bar 513023
Take station road to Woodlands Hotel and then turn right into Cotmaton Road.
Undulating parkland course.
Pro Gaele Tapper; Founded 1889
18 holes, 5068 yards, S.S.S. 65
† Welcome by prior arrangement with the Pro.
[WD £20, WE £20; packages on request.
⏚ Welcome – terms on application.
⏺ Full Facilities.

3A 66 Sparkwell
Welbeck Manor Hotel, Sparkwell, Plymouth, Devon, PL7 5DF
☎ 01752 837219, Fax 837219, Rest/Bar 837374
From Plymouth take A38, turn left at Plympton and then signposted to Sparkwell.
Parkland course.
Founded 1993
9 holes, 5772 yards, S.S.S. 68
† Welcome; pay as you play course.
[WD £6; WE £7.
⏚ Welcome; full facilities available.
⏺ Full bar and restaurant facilities.
⏚ Welbeck Manor.

3A 67 Staddon Heights
Plymouth, Devon, PL9 9SP
☎ 01752 402475
Club is five miles south of the city near the Royal Navy aerials.
Parkland cliff-top course; no par fives.
Pro Ian Marshall; Founded 1904
18 holes, 5845 yards, S.S.S. 68
† Welcome if carrying handicap certificates.
[WD £18, WE £22.
⏚ Welcome with prior arrangement and handicap certificates; catering available; £25.
⏺ Bar Available.

3A 68 Tavistock
Down Road, Tavistock, Devon, PL19 9AQ
✉ tavygolf@hotmail.com
☎ 01822 612049, Fax 612344, Pro 612316, Sec 612344

From town centre take Whitchurch Road, turn left at Down Road. Moorland course.
Pro Dominic Rehaag; Founded 1890
18 holes, 6495 yards, S.S.S. 71
♦ Welcome on weekdays by prior arrangement; must be accompanied by member at weekend.
⌊ WD £24 WE £30.
⌃ Welcome by prior arrangement; minimum 20; terms on application.
⦿ Full clubhouse facilities.
⌐ Bedford.

3A 69 Tehidy Park
Tehidy, Camborne, Cornwall, TR14 0HH
☎ 01209 842208, Fax 843680,
Pro 842914, Rest/Bar 842557
Off A30 at Camborne exit; follow Portreath signs to club; 2 miles north-east of Camborne.
Parkland course.
Pro James Dumbreck; Founded 1922
18 holes, 6241 yards, S.S.S. 71
⌐ Practice Area.
♦ Welcome with handicap certificates; day ticket, WD £25.50, WE £30.50.
⌊ WD £22.50 WE £27.50.
⌃ Welcome with handicap certificates; packages available.
⦿ Full bar snacks and meals available.

3A 70 Teign Valley Golf Club
Christow, Exeter, Devon, EX6 7PA
☎ 01647 253026, Pro 253127,
Sec 253026, Rest/Bar 253026
From M5 to A38 Plymouth road taking exit marked Teign Valley.
Parkland course.
Pro Scott Amiet; Founded 1995
Designed by David Nicholson
18 holes, 5913 yards, S.S.S. 68
♦ Welcome.
⌊ WD from £17, WE from £20.
⌃ Welcome; packages available; discounts for larger groups; catering packages arranged; terms on application.
⦿ Full bar and catering facilities.
⌐ Ilsington; Passage House; club manager can arrange local B&Bs.

3A 71 Teignmouth
Teignmouth Golf Club Ltd, Teignmouth, Devon, TQ14 9NY
☎ 01626 774194, Pro 772894,
Sec 777070
2 miles from Teignmouth on Exeter road B3192.

Heathland course.
Pro Peter Ward; Founded 1924
Designed by Dr Alister MacKenzie
18 holes, 6083 yards, S.S.S. 69
♦ Must be members of a club and have handicap certificates.
⌊ WD from £25 WE from £27.50.
⌃ Welcome Tuesday/Thursday by arrangement; full facilities available.
⦿ Full facilities available.
⌐ London; The Bay Hotel.

3A 72 Thurlestone Golf Club
Thurlestone, Kingsbridge, Devon, TQ7 3NZ
☎ 01548 560405, Fax 560405,
Pro 560715, Sec 560405,
Rest/Bar 560405
Seaward side of A379 Kingsbridge-Salcombe road.
Downland links course; all par fives on back nine.
Pro Peter Laugher; Founded 1897
18 holes, 6340 yards, S.S.S. 70
♦ Welcome with booking and handicap certificates.
⌊ WD £30 WE £30.
⌃ None.
⦿ Available.
⌐ Thurstone Hotel; Cottage Hotel, Hope Cove.

3A 73 Tiverton
Post Hill, Tiverton, Devon, EX16 4NE
☎ 01884 252187, Fax 251607,
Pro 254836, Rest/Bar 252114
5 miles from Junction 27 on M5 towards Tiverton on A373; take first exit left on dual carriageway through Samford Peverell to Halberton.
Parkland/meadow course.
Pro Michael Hawton; Founded 1931
Designed by James Braid
18 holes, 6236 yards, S.S.S. 71
♦ Welcome with letter of introduction or handicap certificates, not Wednesday, weekends, Bank Holidays or competition days.
⌊ WD £21, WE £33.
⌃ By prior arrangement.
⦿ Lunch and teas available.
⌐ Parkway Hotel; Tiverton; Hartnol.

3A 74 Torquay
Petitor Road, Torquay, Devon, TQ1 4QF
▫ www.torquaygolfclub.com
✉ torquaygolfclub@skynow.net
☎ 01803 314591, Pro 329113,
Sec 314591, Rest/Bar 327471
North of Torquay on A379 Teignmouth

road on outskirts of town.
Parkland course.
Pro Martin Ruth; Founded 1910
18 holes, 6175 yards, S.S.S. 70
⌐ Practice nets.
♦ Welcome with handicap certificates.
⌊ WD £25 WE £30.
⌃ Welcome by prior arrangement.
⦿ Full Facilities.

3A 75 Torrington
Weare Trees, Torrington, Devon, EX38 7EZ
☎ 01805 622229
Between Bideford and Torrington.
Heathland course.
Founded 1895/1932
9 holes, 4429 yards, S.S.S. 62
♦ Welcome.
⌊ WD£12; WE £12.
⌃ Welcome by prior arrangement to secretary; terms on application.
⦿ Facilities available.

3A 76 Tregenna Castle Hotel ⚇
St Ives, Cornwall, TR26 2DE
☎ 01736 795254, Fax 796066,
Sec 797381
In grounds of Treganna Castle Hotel, signposted to left just before St Ives on A3074 from Hayle.
Parkland course.
Founded 1982
18 holes, 3478 yards, S.S.S. 58
♦ Welcome.
⌊ WD£13.50; WE £13.50.
⌃ Welcome by prior arrangement; full facilities; terms on application.
⦿ Full bar and restaurant.
⌐ Treganna Castle.

3A 77 Treloy
Newquay, Cornwall, TR8 4JN
☎ 01637 878554, Fax 871710
On A3059 St Columb Major-Newquay road, 3 miles from Newquay.
Public heathland/parkland course.
Founded 1991
Pro Designed by MRM Sandow
9 holes, 4286 yards, S.S.S. 62
♦ Welcome.
⌊ WD £12.50; WE £12.50.
⌃ Welcome.
⦿ Bar, full facilities.
⌐ Barrowfield; California Hotel, Newquay.

3A 78 Trethorne Golf Club ⚇
Kennards House, Launceston, Cornwall, PL15 8QE
▫ www.trethornegolfclub.com

TREVOSE GOLF & COUNTRY CLUB

Constantine Bay, Padstow, Cornwall. Tel: **(01841) 520208** Fax: **(01841) 521057**

Email: **info@trevose-gc.co.uk**   **http://www.trevose-gc.co.uk**

- Championship Golf Course of 18 holes, S.S.S.71. Fully automatic watering on all greens.
- 2 x 9-hole courses. One 3100 yards, par 35; the other 1369 yards, par29.
- Excellent appointed Clubhouse with Bar and Restaurant providing full catering facilities. A/C throughout.

- Superior accommodation in 18 flats, 7 chalets, 6 bungalows and 4 cabins. Daily rates available. Mid-week bookings encouraged.
- **OPEN ALL YEAR.**
- 3 hard tennis courts.
- Heated swimming pool open from mid May to mid September.

- In addition to Membership for Golf and tennis, Social Membership of the Club is also available with full use of the Clubhouse facilities.
- 6 glorious sandy bays within about a mile of the Clubhouse, with pools, open sea and surf bathing.
- 8 miles from Civil Airport.
- Daily flights to and from London Gatwick.
- **SOCIETIES WELCOME.**

---

jen@trethornegolfclub.com
☎ 01566 86903, Fax 86981,
Pro 86903, Sec 86903,
Rest/Bar 86903
2 miles west of Launceston, 200 yards off the A30 on the A395.
Parkland course.
Pro Mark Boundy; Founded 1993
Designed by F Frayne
18 holes, 6432 yards, S.S.S. 71
🏌 Practice range, floodlit driving range and 9 bays.
♦ Welcome.
🍸 WD £28; WE £28.
🛒 Welcome; £15 for 18 holes.
🍽 Available.
🛏 Guest House on site.

3A 79 **Trevose Golf And Country Club** ☎
Constantine Bay, Padstow, Cornwall, PL28 8JB
🖥 www.trevose-gc.co.uk
✉ info@trevose-gc.co.uk
☎ 01841 520208, Fax 521057,
Pro 520261
Course is four miles west of Padstow off the B3276.
Seaside links course.
Pro Gary Allis; Founded 1925
Designed by HS Colt
18 holes, 6435 yards, S.S.S. 71
♦ Welcome; 3 and 4 ball matches restricted; phone first.
🍸 WD £38; WE £38 (summer).
🛒 Welcome anytime, except from July to September; full facilities available.
🍽 Full facilities.
🛏 Own self-contained accomodation available; phone for details.

3A 80 **Truro** ☎
Tresawls Road, Truro, Cornwall, TR1 3LG
☎ 01872 272640, Fax 278684,
Pro 276595, Sec 278684,

Rest/Bar 272640
On edge of Truro adjacent to Treliske Hospital on the A390 Truro to Redruth road.
Undulating parkland overlooking Truro; no par fives.
Pro Nigel Bicknell; Founded 1937
Designed by Colt, Alison & Morrison
18 holes, 5306 yards, S.S.S. 66
♦ Welcome if carrying handicap certificates.
🍸 WD £20, WE £25.
🛒 Welcome; inclusive price on application.
🍽 Two bars and a restaurant.
🛏 The Brookdale: The golf view.

3A 81 **Warren**
Dawlish Warren, Dawlish, Devon, EX7 0NF
☎ 01626 862255, Fax 888005,
Pro 864002, Sec 862255,
Rest/Bar 862493
12 miles south of Exeter off the A379.
Links course.
Pro Darren Prowse; Founded 1892
Designed by J Braid & Sir Guy Campbell
18 holes, 5965 yards, S.S.S. 69
♦ Welcome.
🍸 WD £21.50; WE £24.50.
🛒 Welcome by application; terms on application.
🍽 Bar and meals available.
🛏 Langstone Cliff; Sea Lawn Lodge.

3A 82 **Waterbridge**
Down St Mary, Copplestone, Crediton, Devon, EX17 5LG
🖥 www.waterbridge.fsnet.co.uk
☎ 01363 85111, Pro 83406,
Sec 85111
Off A377 Barnstaple road, 1 mile after Copplestone.
Parkland course.
Pro David Ridyard; Founded 1992
Designed by David Taylor

9 holes, 3910 yards, S.S.S. 63
🏌 WD £6; WE £7 (9 holes).
🍸 As above.
🛒 Welcome by arrangement; packages available; terms on application.
🍽 light snacks.
🛏 New Inn, Crediton.

3A 83 **West Cornwall**
Church Lane, Lelant, St Ives, Cornwall, TR26 3DZ
☎ 01736 753401, Pro 753177,
Rest/Bar 753319
Take A30 to Lelant, turn right at Badger Inn.
Links course.
Pro Paul Atherton; Founded 1889
Designed by Rev Tyack
18 holes, 5884 yards, S.S.S. 69
🏌 Practice ground.
♦ Welcome with handicap certificates.
🍸 Prices on application.
🛒 Welcome; catering to be negotiated; snooker.
🍽 Restaurant, snack bar and bar.
🛏 Badger Inn, Lelant.

3A 84 **Whitsand Bay Hotel** ☎
Seaview Cottage, Finnygook Lane, Portewrinkle, Cornwall, PL11 3BU
🖥 www.cornish-golf.hotels.co.uk
✉ carlehotels@btconnect.com
☎ 01503 230276, Fax 230329,
Pro 230788, Sec 230276
On B3247 6 miles off A38 from Plymouth.
Clifftop course.
Pro S Poole; Founded 1905
Designed by William Fernie of Troon
18 holes, 5885 yards, S.S.S. 69
♦ Handicap certificates except for residents.
🍸 WD £20; WE £22.50.
🛒 Welcome; bar and leisure facilities; terms on application.
🛏 Whitsand Bay.

3A 85 **Woodbury Park Golf and Country Club**
Woodbury Castle, Woodbury, Exeter, Devon, EX5 1JJ
✉ golfbookings@woodburypark.co.uk
☎ 01395 233382, Fax 233384
From M5 Junction 30, take A3052 Sidmouth road, turn right onto B3180, after approximately 1 mile turn right to Woodbury, then immediately turn right to course.
Parkland/moorland/heathland course.
Founded 1992
Designed by J Hamilton Stutt
18 holes, 6626 yards, S.S.S. 72
⚑ 16 bays (covered).
♦ Welcome with handicap certificates.
✐ Prices on application.
◔ Welcome by prior arrangement; catering packages by arrangement; 9-hole Acorn course: 4582 yards, par 65; terms on application.
🍽 Full facilities.
⌂ Swiss style lodges on site with leisure complex.

3A 86 **Wrangaton**
Golf Links Road, Wrangaton, South Brent, Devon, TQ10 9HJ
☎ 01364 72229, Pro 72161
Turn off A38 between South Brent and Bittaford at Wrangaton Post Office.
Moorland/parkland course.
Pro Glenn Richards; Founded 1895
Designed by Donald Steel
18 holes, 6083 yards, S.S.S. 69
⚑ Practice area.
♦ Welcome with handicap certificates or member of recognised club; no beginners.
✐ WD £20; WE £20.
◔ Welcome by arrangement.
🍽 Bar and catering (except Monday in winter).
⌂ The Coach House Inn; Glazebrook.

3A 87 **Yelverton**
Golf Links Road, Yelverton, Devon, PL20 6BN
☎ 01822 852824, Fax 854869, Pro 853593, Sec 852824, Rest/Bar 852824
Off A386, 8 miles north of Plymouth.
Moorland course.
Pro Tim McSherry; Founded 1904
Designed by Herbert Fowler
18 holes, 6351 yards, S.S.S. 71
♦ Welcome with handicap certificates.
✐ WD £30; WE £40.
◔ Welcome with handicap certificates; full bar and restaurant facilities.
🍽 Restaurant and bar.
⌂ Moorland Links Hotel: Burrator Inn; Rosemount Guest House.

3B

Somerset, Dorset, Wiltshire and South Avon

When Bath became England's leading rugby club in the 1980s, county golf was not high on the list of Somerset's sporting priorities. Burnham and Berrow remained one of the country's finest links courses, but after that, there was plenty of pause for thought.

But when David Dixon won the silver medal for the leading amateur at the 2001 Open Championship, he reminded everyone of the progress the game has made in some of the less well-known golfing parts of the country.

Dixon emerged from Enmore Park Golf Club near Bridgewater. Boosted by a gentleman who made a small fortune out of keeping central heating systems quiet, Enmore Park is typical of many a less famous club that now has a flourishing junior section.

Wiltshire is another county without a great golf reputation that is starting to attract investment. Peter Green, a friend and adviser to Dixon, is the affable professional at Manor House Golf Club. The course was designed by Peter Alliss and Clive Clark and is located in one of England's most picturesque towns. Apart from its beauty, Castle Combe is remarkable for its absence of television aerials. They were all replaced by cable when the 1967 film 'Dr Doolittle' was shot in the town.

Another relatively new course to the area is Bowood. With one par five of 600 yards, it is unsociably long off the back tees, particularly in winter when it can get a bit boggy. But on the holes where the designers didn't get overly excited, there are challenges and views to absorb the golfer. The course is set beside the Great Park, 2,000 acres that were originally laid out by Capability Brown.

The modernist fingers of Alliss have done much progressive prodding in this part of England, but they began their golfing activities at Ferndown in Dorset where his father was the professional. In contrast to Bowood, you don't have to be a mighty hitter to cope with Ferndown, just a good golfer. The heather, birch and pines are reminiscent of some of Surrey's lovelier courses.

Dorset is the richest golfing land in the region. Parkstone, a course which like Ashridge has five par fives and five par threes, and Broadstone are well thought of. Queen's Park is one of the best public courses in England and the Isle of Purbeck has some of the finest views.

The finish to one of the most exposed of the courses in the area, Came Down's eighteenth hole has views of Egdon Heath, the "great inviolate" hero of Thomas Hardy's 'Return of the Native'. "The sea changed, the fields changed, the rivers, the villages, and the people changed, yet Egdon remained." It has even proved fairly resistant to golf course designers.

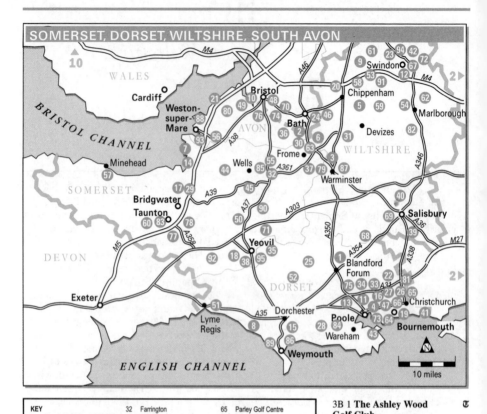

SOMERSET, DORSET, WILTSHIRE, SOUTH AVON

KEY		32	Farrington	65	Parley Golf Centre
1	The Ashley Wood Golf Club	33	Ferndown	66	Queen's Park
2	Bath Golf Club	34	Ferndown Forest		(Bournemouth)
3	Blue Circle	35	Folke	67	RMCS Shrivenham
4	Bournemouth & Meyrick	36	Fosseway Country Club	68	Rushmore Park
	Park	37	Frome	69	Salisbury & South Wiltshire
5	Bowood Golf & Country	38	Halstock	70	Saltford
	Club	39	Hamptworth Golf & Country	71	Sherborne
6	Bradford-on-Avon		Club	72	Shrivenham Park
7	Brean	40	High Post	73	Solent Meads Par 3
8	Bridport & West Dorset	41	Highcliffe Castle	74	Stockwood Vale
9	Brinkworth	42	Highworth Golf Centre	75	Sturminster Marshall
10	Bristol & Clifton	43	Isle of Purbeck	76	Tall Pines
11	Broadstone	44	Isle of Wedmore	77	Taunton & Pickeridge
12	Broome Manor	45	King Weston	78	Taunton Vale
13	Bulbury	46	Kingsdown	79	Thoulstone Park
14	Burnham & Berrow	47	Knighton Heath	80	Tickenham
15	Came Down	48	Knowle	81	Two Riversmeet
16	Canford Magna	49	Long Ashton	82	Upavon (RAF)
17	Cannington	50	Long Sutton	83	Vivary
18	Chedington Court	51	Lyme Regis	84	Wareham
19	Chichester	52	Lyons Gate	85	Wells (Somerset)
20	Chippenham	53	Manor House Golf Club	86	Wessex Golf Centre
21	Clevedon		(at Castle Combe)	87	West Wilts
22	Crane Valley	54	Marlborough	88	Weston-super-Mare
23	Cricklade Hotel & Country	55	Mendip	89	Weymouth
	Club	56	Mendip Spring	90	Wheathill
24	Cumberwell Park	57	Minehead & West Somerset	91	The Wiltshire Golf Club
25	Dorset Heights	58	Monkton Park Par 3	92	Windwhistle
26	Dudmoor Farm	59	North Wilts	93	Worlebury
27	Dudsbury	60	Oake Manor	94	Wrag Barn Golf & Country
28	East Dorset	61	Oaksey Park		Club
29	Enmore Park	62	Ogbourne Downs	95	Yeovil
30	Entry Hill	63	Orchardleigh		
31	Erlestoke Sands	64	Parkstone		

3B 1 The Ashley Wood ☏
Golf Club
Wimborne Road, Blandford Forum,
Dorset, DT11 9HN
📧 ashleywoodgolfclub@hotmail.com
☎ 01258 452253, Fax 450590,
Pro 480379, Sec 452253,
Rest/Bar 450190
Half a mile from Blandford.
Parkland course; two par fives in first
three holes.
Pro John Shimmons; Founded 1896
Designed by Patrick Tallack
18 holes, 6276 yards, S.S.S. 70
† Welcome weekdays.
⚡ WD £20.
⌒ Welcome Weekdays by prior
application to Secretary.
⌂ Anville (Pimperne).

3B 2 Bath Golf Club
Sham Castle, North Road, Peasedown
St John, Bath, Avon, BA2 6JG
☎ 01225 425182, Fax 331027,
Pro 466953, Sec 463834,
Rest/Bar 425182
One and a half miiles south east off
A36 Warminster road.
Downland course.

BOWOOD
GOLF & COUNTRY CLUB

Set in the heart of 'Capability' Brown's Great Park and the 2,000 acre estate of Bowood House and Gardens.

- Corporate Golf Events
- Society Golf Days
- Conferencing/Activities
- Queenwood Golf Lodge
- Host of European Challenge Tour Championships.

Bowood Golf and Country Club, Derry Hill, Calne SN11 9PQ
Tel: **01249 822228**   Fax: **01249 822218**
E-mail: **golfclub@bowood.org**   Website: **www.bowood.org**

Pro Peter Hancox; Founded 1880
Designed by HS Colt
18 holes, 6438 yards, S.S.S. 71
⚐ 4.
† Welcome, handicap certificates required.
⌷ WD £25; WE £33.
↻ Welcome Wed and Fri only; coffee, 18 holes, soup and sandwiches, £25; 18 holes, 3-course dinner, £40.
⦿ restaurant, bar snacks.
⌁ Bath; Beafort, Dukes; Spa.

3B 3 **Blue Circle**
Trowbridge Road, Westbury, Wilts, BA13 3AY
☎ 01373 828489
Part of Blue Circle Works Sport Complex.
Parkland course.
9 holes, 5600 yards, S.S.S. 66
† With members only or on county card system.
⌷ Terms on application.
↻ Welcome by prior arrangement; terms on application.
⦿ By prior arrangement.

3B 4 **Bournemouth & Meyrick Park**
Central Drive, Meyrick Park, Bournemouth, Dorset, BH2 6LH
☎ 01202 292425, Fax 290233
In centre of Bournemouth.
Picturesque parkland course (Meyrick Park).
Founded 1890
18 holes, 5461 yards, S.S.S. 69
† Welcome; advisable to book up to 7 days in advance.
⌷ WD £13.40; WE £14.60.
↻ Welcome by prior arrangement; packages available; full facilities.
⦿ Bars and restaurant.

3B 5 **Bowood Golf and Country Club**   ☎
Derry Hill, Bowood, Calne, Wilts, SN11 9PQ
⌨ www.bowood.org
☎ 01249 822228, Fax 822218
Off the A4 between Chippenham and Calne.
Parkland course.
Pro Max Taylor; Founded 1992
Designed by Dave Thomas
18 holes, 7317 yards, S.S.S. 72
⚐ Practice range, 10 bays; floodlit.
† Welcome on weekdays and after 12 noon weekends.
⌷ Prices on application.
↻ Welcome by prior arrangement; special rates on Monday (£20 for 18 holes); coffee & bacon roll, 9 holes, Ploughman's lunch, 18 holes, 3-course dinner; £51.
⦿ Full facilities.
⌁ Queenwood Golf Lodge; Bowood Golf and CC; Luckham Park Hotel, Colerne.

3B 6 **Bradford-on-Avon**
Avon Close, Bradford On Avon, Wilts, BA15 1JJ
☎ 01225 868268
From Bardford towards Trowbridge on left near Police Station.
Picturesque parkland course next to River Avon.
Founded 1991
9 holes, 2109 yards, S.S.S. 61
† Welcome anytime; pay and play.
⌷ £6 for 9 holes; £10 for 18 holes.
↻ Welcome by prior arrangement.
⦿ None.

3B 7 **Brean**   ☎
Coast Road, Berrow, Burnham On Sea, Somerset, TA8 2QY
⌨ www.brean.com
✉ admin@brean.com
☎ 01278 751595, Fax 752102,

Pro 752111, Sec 751570,
Rest/Bar 751595
Follow tourist signs for Brean Leisure Park from Junction 22 off M5.
Meadowland course.
Pro David Hanes; Founded 1973
Designed by Brean Leisure Park
18 holes, 5715 yards, S.S.S. 68
† Welcome at all times except competition days.
⌷ WD £15; WE £18.
↻ Welcome weekdays and after 1pm at weekends; packages available from £14-£16.
⦿ Facilities available.
⌁ Accomodation available on the Brean Leisure Park.

3B 8 **Bridport and West Dorset**   ☎
East Cliff, West Bay, Bridport, Dorset, DT6 4EP
☎ 01308 421095, Fax 421095,
Pro 421591, Rest/Bar 422597
One and a half miles south of Bridport at West Bay.
Clifftop links course.
Pro David Parsons; Founded 1891
Designed by CSP Salmon/1996 modified by F Hawtree
18 holes, 6028 yards, S.S.S. 69
† Welcome; dress codes apply.
⌷ WD £22; WE £22.
↻ Welcome; bookings must be made in advance; packages can be arranged to meet individual requirements; terms on application.
⦿ Full facilities.
⌁ Haddon House, West Bay.

3B 9 **Brinkworth**
Longmans Farm, Brinkworth, Chippenham, Wilts, SN15 5DG
☎ 01666 510277
Between Swindon and Malmesbury on B4042.
Meadowland course.

Pro Charles Pears; Founded 1984
18 holes, 6000 yards, S.S.S. 70
† Welcome anytime.
[WD £8; WE £10.
♿ Welcome by arrangement.
📷 Full facilities.

3B 10 Bristol and Clifton
Beggar Bush Lane, Failand, Bristol,
Avon, BS8 3TH
🖳 www.bristolgolf.co.uk
✉ mansec@bristolgolf.co.uk
☎ 01275 393474, Fax 394611,
Pro 393031, Sec 393474,
Rest/Bar 393117
Junction 19 off M5, 4 miles along A369
to Bristol, turn right at traffic lights, then
further 1.5 miles.
Parkland course.
Pro Peter Mawson; Founded 1891
18 holes, 6316 yards, S.S.S. 70
† Welcome weekdays with handicap
certificates; restrictions at weekends.
[WD £32; WE £35.
♿ Welcome by arrangement on
Thurs only; full facilities available.
📷 Full facilities.
☜ Redwood Lodge.

3B 11 Broadstone
Broadstone Dorset Golf Club,
Wentworth Drive, Broadstone, Dorset,
BH18 8DQ
🖳 www.broadstonegolfclub.com
✉ admin@broadstonegolfclub.com
☎ 01202 692595, Fax 692595,
Pro 692835, Sec 692595,
Rest/Bar 693363
Take A349 from Poole to the village;
the club is signposted off the main
roundabout.
Heathland course.
Pro Nigel Tokley; Founded 1898
Designed by George Dunn (1898) &
HS Colt (1925)
18 holes, 6315 yards, S.S.S. 70
† Members may introduce one guest
per round.
[WD £35. WE subject to
booking/availability.
♿ Welcome but there are restricted
times so it is essential to phone in
advance.
📷 Full bar and restaurant facilities.

3B 12 Broome Manor
Pipers Way, Swindon, Wilts, SN3 1RG
☎ 01793 495761, Fax 433255,
Pro 532403, Rest/Bar 490939
Take junction 15 off M4 and follow
signs; course 2 miles off motorway.
Parkland course.

Pro Barry Sandry; Founded 1976
Designed by Hawtree & Son
18 & 9 holes, 6283 & 2690 yards,
S.S.S. 70 & 33
╱ Practice range and 34 bays.
† Pay and play course.
[9 holes £7.20; 18 holes £12.
♿ Welcome Monday to Friday; 27
holes, driving range and most
packages include first tee video and
analysis; £15-£40.
📷 Full facilities.

3B 13 Bulbury Woods Golf Club
Halls Road, Lytchett Matravers, Poole,
Dorset, BH16 6EP
☎ 01929 459574, Fax 459000, Sec
459100
On main A35, 3 miles from Poole.
Parkland course set in ancient
woodlands.
Pro David Adams; Founded 1989
Designed by J Sharkey
18 holes, 6313 yards, S.S.S. 70
† Welcome.
[WD £15; WE £20.
♿ Welcome; full catering packages
available on application; terms on
application.
📷 Full à la carte and bistro menu.
☜ On site accomodation.

3B 14 Burnham & Berrow
St Christopher's Way, Burnham-On-
Sea, Somerset, TA8 2PE
🖳 www.bunhamandberrowgc.
2-golf.com
✉ secretary@
burnhamandberrowgc.2-golf.com
☎ 01278 783137, Fax 795440, Pro
784545, Sec 785760, Rest/Bar 783137
M5 Junction 22; 1 mile N of Burnham.
Seaside links; also has a 9-hole course.
Pro Mark Crowther-Smith; Founded
1890
18 holes, 6759 yards, S.S.S. 73
╱ Practice area (own balls required).
† Must be members of golf clubs
with handicaps of 22 and under.
[WD £40; WE £60.
♿ Terms on application.
📷 Full facilities.
☜ Batch Farm, Lympsham; Lulworth
GH; Warren GH both Burnham on Sea.

3B 15 Came Down
Dorchester, Dorset, DT2 8NR
☎ 01305 812531, Fax 813494
2 miles S of Dorchester off A354.
Undulating downland course.
Pro David Holmes; Founded 1896
Designed by JH Taylor

18 holes, 6244 yards, S.S.S. 71
† Welcome by arrangement with
handicap certs; midweek after 9am;
Sun after 11am.
[Terms on application.
♿ Welcome by arrangement on Wed;
packages available approx £32; full
facilities.
📷 Bar and restaurant.
☜ Rembrandt (Weymouth); Junction
Hotel (Dorchester).

3B 16 Canford Magna
Knighton Lane, Wimborne, Dorset,
BH21 3AS
☎ 01202 592552, Fax 592550,
Sec 503902
Off the A341 Magna road near the
Bearcross roundabout on the main
A348 Ringwood road.
Parkland course.
Pro Roger Tuddenham; Founded 1994
Designed by Howard Swan & Trevor
Smith
2 x 18 holes, 6695 and 6034 yards,
S.S.S. 70 and 71
╱ 6-hole Academy course and
driving range; 9-hole par 3 course.
† Welcome.
[Prices on application.
♿ Welcome by prior arrangement;
Cygnet Suite available for corporate
hire.
📷 Two bars and a restaurant.
☜ Contact local tourist board.

3B 17 Cannington
Cannington College, Nr Bridgewater,
Somerset, TA5 2LS
☎ 01278 655050
Leave the M5 at Junction 23. Take the
A38 to Bridgewater; course is 4 miles
from Bridgewater on the A39 road to
Minehead.
Links/parkland course.
Pro Ron Macrow; Founded 1993
Designed by Martin Hawtree
9 holes 18 tees, 6072 yards,
S.S.S. 68
╱ New Driving Range10 floodlit bays.
Two-piece balls.
† Welcome.
[Terms on application.
♿ Apply to Pro; 25% off for groups of
12+; terms on application.
📷 Clubhouse facilities.

3B 18 Chedington Court
South Perrott, Beaminster, Dorset, DT8
3HU
✉ chedingtoncourtgolfclub@
waitrose.com

Burnham and Berrow

When Mark O'Meara won the Open Championship at Birkdale in 1998, a denizen of that historic Lancashire club observed that the members of Burnham and Berrow would be putting on better greens on Monday morning than the Open champion had enjoyed on that final Sunday. When Christie O'Connor won the Seniors Championship at Burnham he said of the greens, "I wish I could dig them up and take them back to Royal Dublin."

Burnham has smoother surfaces than Omar Sharif. There are those, of course, who have felt like digging up the eighteenth green having just taken three putts to complete their round. The trick is in knowing that an apparently flat green slopes three foot from front to back.

Burnham is deceptively difficult. That difficulty comes into play right from the start. There should not be too much worry about a 380-yard par four, except that it has a nasty habit of pointing right into what is known as the Burnham breeze. The club professional gives an idea of the differing conditions that come into play when he owns up to having driven the first. But normally the only way that you would get there with a drive is by car. It can be brutal.

Burnham's opening holes plunge dramatically through vast dunes and the second is rated by Tony Jacklin as one of his favourite holes in golf. He wanted to include it in a best eighteen, but restricted to only one hole per course, he eventually plumped for the seventeenth. The seventeenth is a 200-yard carry to an elevated green that is protected at the front by a bunker called Sansom, probably the deepest on the course. It reflects the strength of Burnham's short holes, each cleverly protected in its own way, whether by crafty pot bunkers, exposure to the elements or multi-tiered greens.

Like a photographer's portfolio, the start and finish represent the best of Burnham, which is to say the best of the excellent. The eighteenth must be one of the strongest finishing holes in golf. At 445 yards long, it really requires a draw off the tee, but overdo it and you fall into some pits, undercook it and the ball finishes in the side of a bank. If you do find the fairway, the second shot has to be precise because there are four sneakily placed pot bunkers protecting the green. The second shot was even more difficult in days past because the Burnham fairways could get a little ragged, but a computerised irrigation system has taken care of that problem.

The course has staged many premier events, but it is worthy of an Open Championship. As a test of golf it is magnificent, as a walk on the wild side it is just as good.

On the inward nine the church and the lighthouse are marker points on the way home towards the Somerset hills. On the way out there are views of the islands of Steep Holm and Flat Holm proud in the Bristol Channel against the background of the Welsh coastline. The course is part of a protected area of wild flowers that includes several varieties of orchid of which the bee orchid is the most famous.

With a very tricky nine-hole course as well, Burnham would be a lovely place to spend a few days. Happily you can. The club has its own dormie house and the going rates for a day's golf plus bed and breakfast are extremely competitive. — **Mark Reason**

☎ 01935 891413, Fax 891217,
Pro 891413, Sec 891413,
Rest/Bar 891413
0.5 mile E of South Perrott on A356
Crewkerne-Dorchester road.
Parkland course.
Founded 1991
Designed by D Hemstock; D Astill
18 holes, 5924 yards, S.S.S. 70
⌔ Driving range and practice area.
† Welcome; properly dressed.
⌔ WD £16; WE £20.
⟲ Welcome by arrangement; terms
on application.
⍩⍢ Bar and Catering facilities
available all day.
⌁ The Stage Coach, Crewekerne.

3B 19 Chichester
Iford Bridge Sports Centre, Barrack
Rd, Christchurch, Dorset, BH23 2BA
☎ 01202 473817
Off the A35 between Bournemouth and
Christchurch.
Parkland course.
Pro Laurence Moxon; Founded 1977
9 holes, 4360 yards, S.S.S. 61
⌔ Practice range.
† Welcome.
⌔ WD £6.40; WE £7.25.
⟲ Welcome by prior arrangement;
also tennis, bowling.
⍩⍢ Full bar facilities.
⌁ Contact local tourist board.

3B 20 Chippenham
Malmesbury Road, Chippenham,
Wiltshire, SN15 5LT
☎ 01249 652040, Fax 446681,
Pro 655519, Sec 652040,
Rest/Bar 443481
From M4 Junction 17 take A350
towards Chippenham; course on right
before town.
Parkland course.
Pro Bill Creamer; Founded 1896
18 holes, 5600 yards, S.S.S. 67
† Everyone Welcome.
⌔ WD £20; WE £25.
⟲ Welcome Tues Thurs Fri by prior
arrangement; full day of golf and
catering packages available.
⍩⍢ Clubhouse facilities.

3B 21 Clevedon
Castle Road, Clevedon, North
Somerset, BS21 7AA
▤ clevedongc.sec@virgin.net
☎ 01275 874057, Fax 341228,
Pro 874704, Sec 874057,
Rest/Bar 341443
Leave the M5 at Junction 20 and follow

the signs to Portishead; turn right into
Walton Road then Holly Lane.
Hilltop course overlooking Bristol
Channel.
Pro Robert Scanlan; Founded 1891
Designed by JH Taylor
18 holes, 6557 yards, S.S.S. 72
† Welcome with handicap certs.
⌔ WD £25; WE £40.
⟲ Welcome except Fri; must book in
advance and minimum of 12; terms on
application.
⍩⍢ Facilities and bar.
⌁ Walton Park; Highcliffe House.

3B 22 Crane Valley   ☜
The Club House, Verwood, Dorset,
BH31 7LE
▤ crane-valley@hoburne.com
☎ 01202 814088, Fax 813407,
Pro 814088, Sec 814088,
Rest/Bar 814088
On B3081 0.5 miles after Verwood.
Parkland course.
Pro Darrel Ranson; Founded 1992
Designed by Donald Steel
1x18 hole/1x9 hole, 6424 yards,
S.S.S. 71
⌔ Practice range 12 Bays; floodlit.
† Welcome with handicap certs.
⌔ Terms on application.
⟲ Welcome WD; packages available.
⍩⍢ Clubhouse facilities.
⌁ St Leonards Hotel.

3B 23 Cricklade Hotel &
Country Club
Common Hill, Cricklade, Near
Swindon, SN6 6HA
⌨ www.crickladehotel.co.uk
▤ info@crickladehotel.co.uk
☎ 01793 750751, Fax 751767,
Rest/Bar 750751
B4040 Cricklade-Malmesbury road 15
mins from M4 Junctions 15/16.
Parkland course.
Pro Ian Bolt; Founded 1990
Designed by Ian Bolt/C Smith
9 holes, 3660 yards, S.S.S. 57
† Welcome Mon-Fri; WE must be
accompanied by a member.
⌔ WD £16 WE must be guest of
member £10 charge.
⟲ Welcome; terms available on
application.
⍩⍢ Full bar and restaurant facilities.

3B 24 Cumberwell Park
Bradford On Avon, Wiltshire, BA15
2PQ
⌨ www.cumberwellpark.co.uk
▤ john@cumberwellpark.co.uk

☎ 01225 863322, Fax 868160,
Pro 862332, Sec 863322,
Rest/Bar 863322
M4 Junction 18; take A46 to Bath and
Then A363 to Bradford-on-Avon.
Parkland course.
Pro John Jacobs; Founded 1994
Designed by Adrian Stiff
27 holes, Park 6123, Wood 6405, Lake
6040 yards, S.S.S. Park 71 Wood 70
Lake 71
⌔ 8 undercover 10 outdoor teaching
facilities also.
† Welcome.
⌔ WD £25; WE £30.
⟲ Welcome Mon-Fri; 27 holes of golf
plus 3-course private dinner and coffee
on arrival; prices on application.
⍩⍢ Bar and restaurant.
⌁ Bath Spa Hotel; Homewood Park;
Swan Hotel Bradford-on-Avon.

3B 25 Dorset Heights
Belchalwell, Blandford Forum, Dorset,
DT11 0EG
☎ 01258 861386
On A357 Sturminster Newton-
Blandford road.
Woodland course.
Founded 1991
Designed by Project Golf (DW Asthill)
18 holes, 6138 yards, S.S.S. 70
† Welcome with prior arrangement.
⌔ Terms on application.
⟲ Welcome by prior arrangement;
packages available; restaurant; terms
on application.
⍩⍢ Restaurant and bar.
⌁ Crown Hotel Blandford.

3B 26 Dudmoor Farm
Dudmoor Farm Rd, Christchurch,
Dorset, BH23 6AQ
☎ 01202 483980
Off A35 W of Christchurch.
Woodland course.
Founded 1974
9 holes, 1428 yards
† Welcome anytime.
⌔ Terms on application.
⟲ Welcome by arrangement.
⍩⍢ Snacks and soft drinks.
⌁ Avon Causeway.

3B 27 Dudsbury   ☜
64 Christchurch Road, Ferndown,
Dorset, BH22 8ST
⌨ www.thedudsbury.co.uk
▤ giles@dudsbury.demon.co.uk
☎ 01202 593499, Fax 594555,
Pro 594488, Sec 593499,
Rest/Bar 593499

On B3073 off A348 from Ferndown.
Parkland course.
Pro Kevin Spurgeon; Founded 1992
Designed by Donald Steel
18 holes, 6904 yards, S.S.S. 73
⚑ 8.
† Welcome with prior booking.
£ WD £32; WE £37.
⚐ Welcome; packages available from
secretary; restaurant lounge bar 6-
hole par 3 course; terms on
application. Spikes and lounge bar.
⚐ function room and restaurant.
⌂ Dormy Hotel; Bridge House.

3B 28 **East Dorset** ☏
Bere Regis, Nr Poole, Dorset, BH20
7NT
⌨ www.golf.co.uk
✉ edgc@dorsetshiregolf.co.uk
☎ 01929 472244, Fax 471294
A35 or A31 50 Bere Regis take Wool
road and signs to the club.
Parkland course.
Pro Derwyn Honan; Founded 1978
Designed by Martin Hawtree
18 holes, 7029 yards, S.S.S. 74;
9 holes, 5032 yards, S.S.S. 64
⚑ Practice range; floodlit and
covered.
† Welcome with prior reservation.
£ Lakeland: WD £30 WE £35;
Woodland: WD £21 WE £23.
⚐ Welcome any day with reservation;
combination of courses and catering
on application; from £20.
🍴 Full facilities.
⌂ Own accommodation the
Dorsetshire Golf Lodge includes free
Golf.

3B 29 **Enmore Park**
Enmore, Bridgewater, Somerset, TA5
2AN
⌨ www.golfdirector.com/enmore
✉ golfclub@enmore.fsnet.co.uk
☎ 01278 671481, Fax 671740, Pro
671519
M5 to Junction 23 or 24; follow A38 to
Bridgewater; A39 to Minehead then left
to Spaxton/Durleigh; left at reservoir
and course is 2 miles on the right.
Parkland course.
Pro Nigel Wixon; Founded 1906
Designed by Hawtree and Son
18 holes, 6411 yards, S.S.S. 71
⚑ Practice ground.
† Welcome but handicap certs
required at WE.
£ WD £20; WE £30.
⚐ Mon, Thurs or Fri with advance
booking; 27-hole packages available;
from £25.

🍴 Full facilities.

3B 30 **Entry Hill Golf Course**
Entry Hill, Somerset, BA2 5NA
☎ 01225 834248
Take A367 Wells road from city centre;
fork left into Entry Hill Road after 1
mile; course is 0.5 mile on right.
Parkland course.
Pro Tim Tapley; Founded 1984
9 holes, 2078 yards, S.S.S. 61
† Welcome; book up to 7 days in
advance for WE, Bank Holidays and
peak periods.
£ WD and WE 9 holes £6.50 18
holes £10; concessions for juniors and
seniors.
⚐ Welcome.
⌂ Sienna; Hautecombe.

3B 31 **Erlestoke Sands**
Erlestoke, Devizes, Wiltshire, SN10
5UB
☎ 01380 831069, Fax 831069, Pro
831027
On B3098 off A350 at Westbury
signposted Bratton; course 6 miles on
left before village of Erlestoke, (3
miles) on right after Erlestoke village.
Pro Adrian Marsh Founded 1992.
Designed by Adrian Stiff
18 holes, 6406 yards, S.S.S. 71
† Welcome.
£ WD £18; WE £25.
⚐ Preferably WD by prior
arrangement; full facilities.
🍴 Full facilities.

3B 32 **Farrington** ☏
Marsh Lane, Farrington Gurney,
Bristol, BS39 6TS
⌨ www.farringtongolfclub.net
✉ info@farringtongolfclub.net
☎ 01761 451596, Fax 451021, Pro
451046
Course is 12 miles S of Bristol on the
A37.
Parkland course with lakes.
Pro Jon Cowgill; Founded 1993
Designed by Peter Thompson
18 holes, 6716 yards, S.S.S. 72
⚑ Practice range 16 bays covered;
floodlit.
† Welcome; advisable to phone in
advance for weekends.
£ WD £22; WE £28.
⚐ Welcome WD only; 2 courses
driving range, spikes bar, restaurant
and private suite seating 150; BBQ
area; terms on application.
🍴 Bar and restaurant.
⌂ Country ways-Marsh Lane;

🍴 Full facilities.

Hunstrete House Hunstrete;
Harnham House Paulton; Stown
Easton.

3B 33 **Ferndown**
119 Golf Links Rd, Ferndown, Dorset,
BH22 8BU
☎ 01202 874602, Fax 873926
A31 to Trickett's Cross and A348 to
Ferndown.
Heathland course.
Pro Ian Parker; Founded 1913
Designed by Harold Hilton (Old
Course)
18 holes, 6452 yards, S.S.S. 71
† With prior permission.
£ Handicap certs required; limited
WE. WD £42; WE £50.
⚐ Tues and Fri only; full facilities;
9-hole course: 5604 yards.
🍴 Full facilities all week.
⌂ Coach House Motel; Dormy;
Bridge House.

3B 34 **Ferndown Forest**
Forest Links Road, Ferndown, Dorset,
BH22 9QE
☎ 01202 876096, Fax 894095,
Pro 876096, Sec 876096,
Rest/Bar 894990
Midway between Ringwood and
Wimborne directly off the Ferndown
by-pass A31.
Parkland course.
Pro Mike Dodd; Founded 1993
Designed by G Hunt & R Grafham
18 holes, 5094 yards, S.S.S. 65
⚑ Practice range floodlit bays with
targets.
† Everyone welcome.
£ WD £11; WE £13.
⚐ Welcome; catering facilities; £8-
£10.
🍴 Full bar and restaurant facilities
available.
⌂ Dormy House on course; Coach
House Motel Ferndown.

3B 35 **Folke Golf Centre**
Alweston, Sherborne, Dorset, DT9 5HR
☎ 01963 23330
From Sherborne head towards
Sturminster Newton; 2 miles from
Sherborne turn off towards Alweston;
course is 200 yards away.
Parkland course.
Founded 1991
9 holes, 2847 yards, S.S.S. 66
⚑ Practice range 10 covered bays;
floodlit.
† Welcome.
£ WD £11; WE £13.

Welcome by prior arrangement; terms on application.
Sandwiches, snacks; bar.

3B 36 Fosseway Country ☻
Charlton Lane, Midsomer Norton, Bath, Somerset, BA3 4BD
www.centurionhotel.com
centurion@centurionhotel.demon.co.uk
☎ 01761 412214, Fax 418357, Rest/Bar 417711
10 miles S of Bath on the A367.
Parkland course.
Founded 1971
Designed by CK Cotton and F Pennink
9 holes, 4565 yards, S.S.S. 67
† By prior arrangement.
WD £15; WE £15.
Terms on application.
Facilities.
Centurion Hotel (on site).

3B 37 Frome
Critchill Manor, Frome, Somerset, BA11 4LJ
☎ 01373 453410, Fax 453410
Take A361 from Frome towards Shepton Mallet; at Nunney Catch roundabout follow signs to course.
Parkland course.
Founded 1994
18 holes holes, 4890 yards, S.S.S. 64
† Welcome.
WD £10.50; WE £12.50.
Welcome; contact club for details.
Available.

3B 38 Halstock Golf Enterprises
Common Lane, Nr Yeovil, Somerset, BA22 9SF
☎ 01935 891689
300 yards from centre of Halstock village turn right at green, signposted.

Parkland course.
Founded 1988
18 holes, 4351 yards, S.S.S. 63
† Welcome.
WD £11 (18) £6.50 (9); WE £13 (18) £8 (9).
Welcome by arrangement; terms on application.
Light refreshments available.

3B 39 Hamptworth Golf ☻
Hamptworth Rd, Landford, Nr Salisbury, Wilts, SP5 2DU
www.hamptworthgolf.co.uk
info@hamptworthgolf.co.uk
☎ 01794 390155, Fax 390022, Rest/Bar 399970
6 miles from M27 Junctions 1 and 2 off the A36 to Salisbury; follow Landford and then Downton road signs. Parkland course among ancient woodlands lakes and river.
Pro K Kuffam/M White/L Blake; Founded 1994
18 holes, 6512 yards, S.S.S. 71
Full practice facilities covered bay driving range.
† Welcome by arrangement; handicap certs not always required.
WD £30; WE £30.
Welcome by arrangement.
Full facilities.
Devere Grand Harbour.

3B 40 High Post
Great Durnford, Salisbury, Wilts, SP4 6AT
☎ 01722 782356, Fax 782356
Halfway between Salisbury and Amesbury on the A345 opposite the Inn at High Post.
Downland course.
Pro Ian Welding; Founded 1922
18 holes, 6305 yards, S.S.S. 70
† Welcome WD without restriction; handicap certs required at WE.
WD £25; WE £30.

Welcome WD by arrangement; full facilities available.
Full facilities.
The Inn; High Post; Milford Hall (Salisbury).

3B 41 Highcliffe Castle
107 Lymington Rd, Highcliffe On Sea, Dorset, BH23 4LA
☎ 01425 272953
1 mile W of Highcliffe on A337.
Parkland course.
Founded 1913
18 holes, 4776 yards, S.S.S. 63
† Welcome if member of recognised golf club.
WD £15.50(Winter) £25.50 (Summer); WE £20.50 (Winter) £30.50 (Summer).
By prior arrangement with the secretary; terms on application.
Clubhouse facilities.

3B 42 Highworth Golf Centre
Swindon Road,, Highworth, Wiltshire, SN6 7SJ
☎ 01793 766014, Fax 766014, Pro 766014, Sec 762446
Take A361 from Swindon.
Parkland course.
Pro Barry Sandry; Founded 1990
Designed by Swindon Council
9 holes, 3120 yards, S.S.S. 35
† Pay as you play.
£7.90 per round.
Pay as you play.
Jesmond Hotel.

3B 43 Isle Of Purbeck
Studland, Swanage, Dorset, BH19 3AB
☎ 01929 450361, Fax 450501
3 miles north of Swanage on the B3351 Corfe Castle road.
Heathland course set in a nature reserve.
Pro Ian Brake; Founded 1892
Designed by HS Colt

18 holes, 6295 yards, S.S.S. 71
† Welcome.
Ⱡ WD £30; WE £35.
♻ Welcome; morning coffee;
Ploughman's lunch 2 rounds of golf
two course dinner; £47.50-£50.
🍴 Bar snacks and restaurant.

3B 44 Isle of Wedmore ♛
Lineage, Lascots Hill, Wedmore,
Somerset, BS28 4QT
♨ www.wedmoregolfclub.com,
✉ office@wedmoregc.
junglelink.co.uk
☎ 01934 713649, Fax 713696,
Pro 712452
Junction 22 off M5; take A38 north to
Bristol after 5 miles turn right in Lower
Weare; follow signposts to Wedmore.
Parkland course.
Pro Graham Coombe; Founded 1992
Designed by Terry Murray
18 holes, 6009 yards, S.S.S. 68
Ⅰ Practice area.
† Welcome but after 9.30am at WE.
Ⱡ WD £18; WE £22.
♻ Welcome; packages available;
private function room and professional
lessons; £24-£32.
🍴 Bar and restaurant.

3B 45 King Weston
Millfield Enterprises Sports &
Recreation, Nr Glastonbury, BA16
0YD
☎ 01458 448300
1 mile SE of Butleigh.
Parkland course.
Founded 1970
9 holes, 4434 yards, S.S.S. 62
† Welcome with member when not
required by school.
Ⱡ Terms on application.
♻ Limited.

3B 46 Kingsdown
Corsham, Wilts, SN13 8BS
☎ 01225 742530, Fax 743472,
Pro 742634
5 miles E of Bath on A365.
Downland course.
Pro Andrew Butler; Founded 1880
18 holes, 6445 yards, S.S.S. 71
Ⅰ Practice area.
† Welcome Mon-Fri; handicap certs
required.
Ⱡ WD £26.
♻ Welcome Mon-Fri; full bar and
catering facilities.
🍴 Bar and catering facilities.

3B 47 Knighton Heath
Francis Ave, Bournemouth, Dorset,
B11 8NX
☎ 01202 572633, Fax 590774,
Pro 578275, Sec 572633,
Rest/Bar 572633
Course is signposted from the junction
of the A348/A3049 (at Mountbatten
Arms).
Heathland course.
Pro Norman Flindale; Founded 1976
Designed by Bill Freeman
18 holes, 6094 yards, S.S.S. 69
† Welcome after 9.30 WD; member's
guests at WE.
Ⱡ WD £25; WE £18 with member.
♻ Welcome by arrangement;
minimum 12 players; packages
available; from £35.
🍴 Full catering facilities.
🛏 Many in Bournemouth.

3B 48 Knowle ♛
Fairway, West Town Lane, Brislington,
Bristol, BS4 5DF
♨ www.knowlegolfclub.co.uk
☎ 0117 9776341, Fax 9720615,
Pro 9779193, Sec 9770660,
Rest/Bar 9776341
3 miles S of City Centre on A4 to Bath
or A37 to Shepton Mallett.
Parkland course.
Pro Rob Hayward; Founded 1905
Designed by Hawtree & JH Taylor
18 holes, 6016 yards, S.S.S. 69
Ⅰ Practice area, putting green.
† Welcome with handicap certs.
Ⱡ WD £22; WE £27.
♻ Welcome on Thurs; coffee lunch;
evening meal available.
🍴 Full facilities.

3B 49 Long Ashton
Clarken Combe, Long Ashton, Bristol,
BS18 9DW
☎ 01275 392316, Fax 394395,
Pro 392265
Leave M5 at Junction 19, take A369 to
Bristol, turn right into B3129 at traffic
lights and then left on to B3128; club is
0.5 mile on right.
Undulating moorland/downland course.
Pro Denis Scanlan; Founded 1893
Designed by Hawtree & Taylor
18 holes holes, 6177 yards, S.S.S. 70
† Welcome with official club
handicap certs.
Ⱡ WD £30; WE £35.
♻ Welcome by arrangement; full
facilities available.
🍴 Full facilities daily until 6pm;
evening meals by arrangement.
🛏 Redwood Lodge.

3B 50 Long Sutton ♛
Long Load, Nr Langport, Somerset,
TA10 9JU
♨ www.longsuttongolf.co.uk
✉ reservations@longsuttongolf.co.uk
☎ 01458 241017, Fax 241022,
Pro 241017, Sec 241017,
Rest/Bar 241017
Course after Long Sutton village.
Parkland course.
Pro Andrew Hayes; Founded 1990
Designed by Patrick Dawson
18 holes, 6329 yards, S.S.S. 70
Ⅰ 8.
† Welcome with advance tee
reservation.
Ⱡ WD £16; WE £20.
♻ Welcome by prior arrangement; full
facilities; terms on application.
🍴 Bar restaurant and function rooms.
🛏 List can be provided.

3B 51 Lyme Regis ♛
Timber Hill, Lyme Regis, Dorset,
DT7 3HQ
✉ bwheeler@ic24.net
☎ 01297 442963, Pro 443822,
Sec 442963, Rest/Bar 442043
Off A3052 Charmouth road 1 mile E
of town.
Clifftop course.
Pro Andrew Black; Founded 1893
18 holes, 6283 yards, S.S.S. 70
Ⅰ Practice green.
† Welcome with handicap certificates
or proof of membership of recognised
club; restrictions Thurs and Sun
afternoons.
Ⱡ WD £30; WE £23. All day £30.
Morning only £25. After 2pm £20.
♻ Welcome by arrangement not
Thurs or Sun am; full facilities available.
🍴 Hot and cold snacks all day; full
restaurant.
🛏 Alexander; Bay; Buena Vista;
Devon; Fairwater Head; Tudor House.
Fern Hill Hotel.

3B 52 Lyons Gate Farm
Lyons Gate, Dorchester, DT2 7AZ
♨ www.lyonsgategolfclub.co.uk
☎ 01300 345239, Sec 345239,
Rest/Bar 245239
4 miles N of Cerne Abbas on A352
Sherborne-Dorchester road.
Wooded farmland/parkland course.
Founded 1991-club 1990-course
Designed by Ken Abel
9 holes,18 tees, 3834 yards, S.S.S. 60
† Welcome; no restrictions.
Ⱡ WD £5.00 for 9 holes. £9.00 for 18
holes.; WE £6.00 for 9 holes, £10.00
for 18 holes.

Welcome by arrangement.
⦿ Light refreshments available.
Meals by arrangement.
↵ The Hunter's Moon, The Antelope.

3B 53 The Manor House at Castle Coombe
Castle Combe, Wilts, SN14 7PL
⬡ www.exclusivehotels.co.uk
☎ 01249 782982, Fax 782992, Pro 782982, Sec 782982, Rest/Bar 782982
On B4039 to N of Castle Combe village.
Ancient woodland/parkland course.
Pro Peter Green; Founded 1992
Designed by Peter Alliss and Clive Clark
18 holes, 6286 yards, S.S.S. 71
Ⓘ 10.
† Welcome anytime with handicap certs and by making prior tee reservation.
Ⓛ WD £37.50; WE £60.
↷ Welcome by arrangement; full facilities. Two bars restaurant private dining facilities.
⦿ Bar snacks available all day.
↵ Manor House.

3B 54 Marlborough
The Common, Marlborough, Wilts, SN8 1DU
☎ 01672 512147, Fax 513164, Pro 512493, Sec 512147, Rest/Bar 512147
On the A346 1 mile north of Marlborough; 7 miles south of M4 exit 15.
Downland course.
Pro Simon Amor; Founded 1888
Designed by T Simpson/upgraded by H Fowler
18 holes, 6491 yards, S.S.S. 71
† Welcome with prior arrangement.
Ⓛ WD £25; WE £30.
↷ Welcomed midweek particularly Tues and Thurs; packages available; day's golf coffee light lunch and dinner from £25.
⦿ Full facilities.
↵ Castle and Ball Hotel; Ivy House Hotel both Marlborough.

3B 55 Mendip
Gurney Slade, Radstock, Somerset, BA3 4UT
⬡ www.mendipgolfclub.co.uk
✉ secretary@mendipgolfclub.co.uk
☎ 01749 840570, Fax 841439, Pro 840793, Sec 840570, Rest/Bar 840570
3 miles N of Shepton Mallett off A37.
Undulating downland course.
Pro Adrian Marsh; Founded 1908
Designed by H Vardon with extension

by F. Pennink
18 holes, 6381 yards, S.S.S. 71
† Welcome.
Ⓛ WD £24; WE £35.
↷ Welcome by arrangement Mon & Thurs; full facilities.
⦿ Full facilities.
↵ Stone Easton Park Hotel.

3B 56 Mendip Spring
Honeyhall Lane, Congresbury, North Somerset, BS49 5JT
☎ 01934 852322, Fax 853021, Pro 852322, Sec 852322, Rest/Bar 853080
Take A370 from M5 Junction 21 to Congresbury.
Parkland/water features; also 9-hole lakeside course.
Pro John Blackburn/Robert Moss; Founded 1991
Designed by Terry Murray
18 holes, 6334 yards, S.S.S. 70
Ⓘ 14 bays.
† Welcome by prior arrangement.
Ⓛ WD £24; WE £27.
↷ Welcome; full catering facilities; halfway house facilities for refreshments buggies; terms on application.
⦿ Full facilities.

3B 57 Minehead and West Somerset
The Warren, Minehead, Somerset, TA24 5SJ
⬡ www.mineheadgolf.co.uk
✉ secretary@mineheadgolf.co.uk
☎ 01643 702057, Fax 705095, Pro 704378
Course at end of seafront.
Links course.
Pro Ian Read; Founded 1882
Designed by Johnny Alan
18 holes, 6228 yards, S.S.S. 71
Ⓘ Practice green.
† Welcome.
Ⓛ WD £26; WE £30.
↷ Welcome on written application; full facilities.
⦿ By prior arrangement with caterer; snacks always available.
↵ York; Northfield; Marshfield.

3B 58 Monkton Park Par 3
Chippenham, Wilts, SN15 3PE
⬡ www.pitchandputtgolf.com
☎ 01249 653928, Pro 653928, Sec 653928
Into Chippenham, past railway station, turn right.
Parkland course.
Pro Mel Dawson; Founded 1960
Designed by M Dawson

9 holes, 990 yards, S.S.S. 27
† Welcome.
Ⓛ WD £4.00; WE £4.00; concessions apply.
↷ Welcome.
⦿ Refreshments available.

3B 59 North Wilts
Bishops Cannings, Devizes, Wilts, SN10 2LP
☎ 01380 860257, Fax 860877, Pro 860330, Sec 860627, Rest/Bar 860257
Take A361 Devizes to Swindon road and after 3 miles turn to Calne.
Downland course.
Pro Graham Laing; Founded 1890/1972
Designed by K Cotton
18 holes, 6414 yards, S.S.S. 71
† Welcome by prior arrangement.
Ⓛ WD £21; WE £24.
↷ Welcome WD by prior arrangement; brochure and price list available; terms available on application.
⦿ Clubhouse facilities.
↵ Bear Devizes; Landsdown Calne.

3B 60 Oake Manor
Oake, Taunton, Somerset, TA4 1BA
⬡ www.oakemanor.com
▤ gardner.golf
☎ 01823 461993, Fax 461995, Pro 461993, Sec 461993, Rest/Bar 461992
5 minutes from Junction 26 off M5.
Parkland course with water features on 10 of 18 holes, breathtaking views of the Quantock and Blackdown hills.
Pro Russell Gardner; Founded 1993
Designed by Adrian Stiff
18 holes, 6109 yards, S.S.S. 70
† Welcome by prior arrangement.
Ⓛ WD £20; WE £25.
↷ Welcome; contact golf manager Russell Gardner; from £20. Function rooms.
⦿ bar and restaurant, function suites for up to 250 people, air conditioned clubhouse.
↵ Rumwell Manor.

3B 61 Oaksey Park
Oaksey, Nr Malmesbury, Wilts, SN16 9SB
▤ johnscooper@btinternet.com
☎ 01666 577995, Fax 577174
Off A419 between Swindon and Cirencester W of Cotswold Water Park.
Public parkland course.
Pro David Carrol; Founded 1991
Designed by Chapman & Warren
9 holes, 2904 yards, S.S.S. 69

⚐ 8 Driving bays.
† Welcome.
[WD £8; WE £10. 18 Holes WD
£12 WE £15.
⟳ Welcome; full facilities; terms on
application.
🍽 Full facilities.
↵ Oaksey Park Country Cottages
Hotel (10 farm cottages).

3B 62 Ogbourne Downs ☎
Ogbourne St George, Marlborough,
Wilts, SN8 1TB
☎ 01672 841327, Fax 841327, Pro
841287, Sec 841327, Rest/Bar 841327
Junction 15 off M4; course on A345.
Downland course.
Founded 1907
Designed by Taylor; Hawtree and
Cotton
18 holes, 6363 yards, S.S.S. 71
† Welcome with handicap certs.
[WD £25; WE £35.
⟳ Terms on application from
secretary; bar; dining room; ball hire;
buggy hire.
🍽 Full Bar and restaurant facilities.
↵ Parklands Hotel; Ogbourne St
George.

3B 63 Orchardleigh ☎
Frome, Somerset, BA11 2PH
☎ 01373 454200, Fax 454202,
Pro 454206, Rest/Bar 454200
On the A362.
Parkland course.
Pro Ian Ridsdale; Founded 1995
Designed by Brian Huggett
18 holes, 6810 yards, S.S.S. 73
⚐ 2 practice 2 putting greens and
grass practice range.
† Welcome.
[WD £22; WE £30.
⟳ Welcome; terms available on
application.
🍽 Bar and restaurant.
↵ The Full Moon at Rudge.

3B 64 Parkstone ☎
49a Links Road, Parkstone, Poole,
Dorset, BH14 9QS
☐ www.parkstonegolfclub.co.uk
☎ 01202 707138, Fax 706027,
Pro 708092, Sec 707138,
Rest/Bar 708025
On A35 between Bournemouth and
Poole; signposted left off Bournemouth
road.
Links course.
Pro Martyn Thompson; Founded 1910
Designed by Willie Park and James
Braid

18 holes, 6250 yards, S.S.S. 70
⚐ 1 bay for members' use only.
† Welcome with handicap
certificates.
[Terms on application.
⟳ Welcome but booking is essential.
🍽 Full catering facilities.

3B 65 Parley Court
Parley Green Lane, Hurn,
Christchurch, Dorset, BH23 6BB
☎ 01202 591600, Fax 591600,
Pro 593131, Rest/Bar 591600
Opposite Bournemouth International
Airport.
Parkland course.
Pro Jane Miles Chris Brook; Founded
1992
Designed by Paul Goodfellow
9 holes, 4584 yards, S.S.S. 62
⚐ Practice range, 23 bays floodlit,
2 teaching bays.
† Everyone welcome.
[WD £5.50 for 9 holes, £7.80 for
18 holes; WE £6 for 9 holes, £8.80 for
18 holes.
⟳ Welcome by arrangement; full
facilities.
🍽 Full catering facilities.
↵ Avon Causeway, Dormy Hotel.

**3B 66 Queen's Park
(Bournemouth)**
Queens Park West Drive,
Bournemouth, Dorset, BH8 9BY
☎ 01202 396198, Fax 396817,
Pro 396817, Sec 302611,
Rest/Bar 394466
Off Wessex Way in Bournemouth.
Parkland course.
Pro R Hill; Founded 1906
18 holes, 6319 yards, S.S.S. 70
⚐ Putting green.
† Welcome.
[WD £15; WE £16.50; concessions
apply.
⟳ Welcome, prior booking essential.
🍽 Full catering.
↵ Embassy; Wessex; Marsham Court.

3B 67 RMCS Shrivenham
Swindon, Wilts, SN6 8LA
☎ 01793 785725
In the grounds of Royal Military
College of Science on A420 1 mile NE
of Shrivenham.
Parkland course.
Founded 1953
18 holes, 5684 yards, S.S.S. 69
⚐ Practice green.
† Restricted access; welcome with
member.

[WD £10; WE £10.
⟳ Welcome WD subject to
availability.
🍽 Coffee and soft drinks.

3B 68 Rushmore Park ☎
Tollard Royal, Salisbury, Wiltshire, SP5
5QB
☐ rushmore.golfclub@
rushmore-estate.co.uk
☎ 01725 516326, Fax 516437,
Pro 516326, Sec 516391,
Rest/Bar 516391
12 miles from Salisbury off the A354
Blandford road through Sixpenny
Handley; course is just before Tollard
Royal.
Parkland course.
Pro Sean McDonagh; Founded 1994
18 holes, 6200 yards, S.S.S. 67
⚐ 6 bays.
† Welcome.
[terms on application.
⟳ Welcome by prior arrangement.
🍽 Full menu available.

**3B 69 Salisbury & South
Wiltshire**
Netherhampton, Salisbury, Wilts, SP2
8PR
☐ www.salisburygolf.co.uk
☐ mail@salisburygolf.co.uk
☎ 01722 742645
On A3094 2 miles from Salisbury and
from Wilton.
Downland course.
Pro John Cave; Founded 1888
Designed by JH Taylor; extra 9 holes
by S Gidman 1991
27 holes, 6485 yards, S.S.S. 71
† Welcome.
[WD £25; WE £40.
⟳ Welcome by arrangement; full
facilities.
🍽 Full facilities.
↵ Rose & Crown Kings Arm,
both Salisbury; Pembroke Arms,
Wilton.

3B 70 Saltford ☎
Golf Club Lane, Saltford, Bristol, BS31
3AA
☎ 01225 873513, Fax 873525,
Pro 872043, Sec 873513,
Rest/Bar 873220
Off A4 between Bath and Bristol.
Meadowland course.
Pro Dudley Millensted; Founded 1904
18 holes, 6046 yards, S.S.S. 70
⚐ Practice ground.
† Welcome with handicap certs.
[WD £24; WE £32.

↪ Welcome Mon and Thurs by arrangement; full facilities.
🍽 Full facilities.
🚪 Grange (Keynsham); Crown; Tunnel House.

3B 71 Sherborne
Higher Clatcombe, Sherborne, Dorset, DT9 4RN
📧 info@sherbournegolfclub.com
☎ 01935 814431, Fax 814218, Pro 812274, Sec 814431, Rest/Bar 812475
1 miles N of Sherborne off B3145.
Parkland course.
Pro Alistair Tresidder; Founded 1894
Designed by James Braid
18 holes, 6446 yards, S.S.S. 72
⚑ Practice area members only.
† Welcome with handicap certs.
〖 WD £30; WE £35.
↪ Welcome Tues and Wed only; full playing practice and dining facilities; terms available on application.
🍽 Full facilities.
🚪 Sherborne Hotel; Eastbury; Antelope.

3B 72 Shrivenham Park
Pennyhooks, Shrivenham, Swindon, Wilts, SN6 8EX
📧 angie@freeserve.co.uk
☎ 01793 783853, Fax 782999, Pro 783853, Sec 783853, Rest/Bar 783853
Off A420 between Swindon and Oxford.
Parkland course.
Pro Stuart Ash; Founded 1969
Designed by Glen Johnson
18 holes, 5769 yards, S.S.S. 69
† All Welcome.
〖 WD £12; WE £15.
↪ Welcome anytime with prior booking; packages available.
🍽 Facilities available.
🚪 Blunsdon House.

3B 73 Solent Meads Par 3
Rolls Drive, Nr Hengistbury Head, Bournemouth, Dorset, BH6 5NX
☎ 01202 420795, Pro 396198, Rest/Bar 420795
Off Broadway at Hengistbury Head.
Seaside course.
Pro Richard Hill; Founded 1968
18 holes, 2182 yards
⚑ Practice range 10 bays.
† All Welcome; pay and play.
〖 WD £7; WE £7 (includes club hire); concessions apply.
↪ Limited.
🍽 Light refreshments and snacks.

3B 74 Stockwood Vale
Stockwood Lane, Keynsham, Bristol, BS18 2ER
🖳 www.stockwoodvale.com
📧 stockwoodvalegc@netscapeonline.co.uk
☎ 0117 9866505, Fax 9868974, Pro 9866505, Sec 9860509, Rest/Bar 9866505
In Stockwood Lane off A4.
Undulating parkland course.
Pro John Richards; Founded 1991
Designed by J Wade & M Ramsay
18 holes, 6031 yards, S.S.S. 71
⚑ 16.
† Welcome with prior reservation.
〖 WD £15; WE £17.
↪ Welcome by prior arrangement; terms on application.
🍽 Restaurant and Bar snacks available.
🚪 Grange Hotel, Keynesham.

3B 75 Sturminster Marshall
Moor Lane, Sturminster Marshall, Dorset, BH21 4AH
☎ 01258 858444
In village centre on the A350 midway between Blandford and Poole.
Parkland course.
Pro Graham Howell; Founded 1992
Designed by John Sharkey
9 holes, 4882 yards, S.S.S. 65
⚑ New driving range for 2002.
† Welcome.
〖 WD £12 £8 (9 holes); WE £12 (18 holes) £8 (9 holes).
↪ Welcome with prior bookings accepted 7 days in advance; terms on application.
🍽 Full facilities.

3B 76 Tall Pines Golf Club ℂ
Cooks Bridle Path, Downside, Backwell, Bristol, BS48 3DJ
☎ 01275 472076, Fax 474869, Pro 472076, Rest/Bar 474889
Take A38 or A370 from Bristol and course is next to Bristol International Airport.
Woodland/parkland.
Pro Alex Murray; Founded 1990
Designed by Terry Murray
18 holes, 6067 yards, S.S.S. 69
† Welcome; no restrictions.
〖 WD £16; WE £16.
↪ Welcome; full facilities; terms on application.
🍽 Bar and restaurant.
🚪 Town and Country Lodge.

3B 77 Taunton & Pickeridge
Corfe, Taunton, Somerset, TA3 7BY
☎ 01823 421537, Fax 421742, Pro 421790, Sec 421537, Rest/Bar 421876/421840
B3170 4 miles S of Taunton through Corfe village then first left.
Undulating course.
Pro Gary Milne; Founded 1892
Designed by Hawtree
18 holes, 5926 yards, S.S.S. 68
† Welcome WD; handicap certs required.
〖 WD £20; WE £28.
↪ Welcome by arrangement; full facilities.
🍽 Full facilities.
🚪 Castle.

3B 78 Taunton Vale
Creech Heathfield, Taunton, Somerset, TA3 5EY
☎ 01823 412220, Fax 413583
Just off A361 junction with A38 exits 24 or 25 from the M5.
Parkland course.
Pro Martin Keitch; Founded 1991
Designed by John Pyne
18 holes, 6142 yards, S.S.S. 69
† Welcome; dress code applies.
〖 WD £16; WE £24.
↪ Welcome WD; terms on application.
🍽 Full facilities.
🚪 Walnut Tree (North Petherton); Castle (Taunton); Falcon (Henlade); Tudor (Bridgwater).

3B 79 Thoulstone Park
Chapmanslade, Nr Westbury, Wilts, BA13 4AQ
☎ 01373 832825, Fax 832821, Pro 832808, Sec 832825, Rest/Bar 832825
3 miles NW of Warminster on the A36.
Parkland course.
Pro Tony Isaacs; Founded 1991
Designed by MRM Sandow
18 holes, 6312 yards, S.S.S. 70
⚑ 20.
† All welcome.
〖 WD £10; WE £20.
↪ Welcome; terms on application.
🍽 Full facilities.
🚪 Granada Lodge, Warminster. Travel Lodge, Beckington.

3B 80 Tickenham
Clevedon Rd, Tickenham, N Somerset, BS21 6RY
🖳 www.tichenhamgolf.co.uk
📧 info@tichenhamgolf.co.uk

☎ 01275 856626
Take M5 Junction 20 and follow signs for Nailsea; course on left after Tickenham.
Pro Andrew Sutcliffe; Founded 1994.
Designed by A Sutcliffe
9 holes, 3836 yards, S.S.S. 58
ℐ Practice range 24 bays floodlit.
♦ Welcome.
ℐ WD £6; WE and after 4pm £8 (9 holes).
⚐ Welcome by arrangement; catering and bar facilities; driving range; teaching academy; terms on application.
🍴 Bar club room.
⚒ Redwood Lodge.

3B 81 Two Riversmeet
Stony Lane South, Christchurch, Dorset, BH23 1HW
☎ 01202 477987, Fax 470853, Sec 477987, Rest/Bar 477987
Signposted from the centre of Christchurch.
Public seaside course.
Founded 1986
Designed by local authority
18 holes, 1591 yards
♦ Pay and play.
ℐ WD £5.10; WE £5.10.
⚐ Welcome; terms on application.
🍴 Bar and restaurant.
⚒ Many by the seaside; list available from the club.

3B 82 Upavon (RAF)
Andover Rd, Upavon, Nr Pewsey, Wilts, SN9 6BQ
☎ 01980 630787, Fax 630787, Pro 630281
On the A342 1.5 miles SE of Upavon village.
Undulating chalk downland course.
Pro Richard Blake; Founded 1918/1997
18 holes, 6407 yards, S.S.S. 71
ℐ Practice range.
♦ Welcome on WD and afternoon at WE.
ℐ WD £22; WE £25.
⚐ Welcome WD; from £18 per head.
🍴 Bar and restaurant.

3B 83 Vivary
Vivary Park, Taunton, Somerset, TA1 3JW
☎ 01823 289274, Pro 333875
Centre of Taunton in Vivary Park.
Parkland course.
Pro Mike Steadman; Founded 1928
Designed by Herbert Fowler

18 holes, 4620 yards, S.S.S. 63
♦ Welcome.
ℐ WD £8.50; WE £8.50.
⚐ Welcome on WD only; contact Pro; terms on application. Catering on application.
🍴 Full restaurant and bar facilities.
⚒ Corner House; Castle.

3B 84 Wareham ♛
Sandford Rd, Wareham, Dorset, BH20 4DH
⚎ www.warehamgolfclub.com
✉ admin@warehamgolfclub.com
☎ 01929 554147, Fax 557993, Rest/Bar 557995
N of Wareham off A351 between Sandford and Wareham.
Mixture of parkland and heathland course; fine views.
Pro Gary Prince; Founded 1908
Designed by C Whitcome
18 holes, 5753 yards, S.S.S. 68
ℐ Practice area.
♦ Welcome WD after 9.30am; WE after 1pm.
ℐ WD £22, £28 day pass; WE £25.
⚐ Welcome WD; packages available; group prices negotiable; full facilities for dining.
🍴 Full bar and catering.
⚒ Worgret Manor; Springfield; Priory; Kemps.

3B 85 Wells (Somerset)
East Horrington Rd, Wells, Somerset, BA5 3DS
✉ secretary@wellsgolfclub99.freeserve.co.uk
☎ 01749 675005, Fax 675005, Pro 679059, Sec 679059, Rest/Bar 672868
E of Wells off B3139.
Parkland course.
Pro Adrian Bishop; Founded 1893
18 holes, 6015 yards, S.S.S. 69
ℐ Practice range 10 bays floodlit.
♦ Welcome.
ℐ WD £20; WE £25.
⚐ Welcome on Tues and Thurs by prior arrangement; packages available; from £33.
🍴 Full facilities.
⚒ Swan; White Hart both Wells; Charlton House Shepton Mallet.

3B 86 Wessex Golf Centre
Radipole Lane, Weymouth, Dorset, DT4 9HX
☎ 01305 784737
Off Weymouth bypass behind the football club.

Parkland course.
Pro N Statham; Founded 1980
9 holes, 1432 yards, S.S.S. 30
ℐ Practice range available.
♦ Public pay and play.
ℐ WD £4.20; WE £4.20.
⚐ No restrictions.
🍴 None at all.

3B 87 West Wilts
Elm Hill, Warminster, Wilts, BA12 0AU
☎ 01985 213133, Fax 219809, Pro 212110
Course is in Warminster off the Westbury road.
Downland course.
Pro Andy Lamb; Founded 1891
Designed by JH Taylor
18 holes, 5709 yards, S.S.S. 68
♦ Welcome with handicap certs or as members' guests.
ℐ WD £20; WE £36.
⚐ Welcome but advance booking essential.
🍴 Full facilities.
⚒ Bishopstrow; Old Bell.

3B 88 Weston-super-Mare
Uphill Rd North, Weston-Super-Mare, N Somerset, BS23 4NQ
✉ Karen@wsngolfclub.net.co.uk
☎ 01934 66968, Fax 621360, Pro 633360, Sec 626968
M5 to Junction 21 and then follow road to seafront.
Links course.
Pro M Laband; Founded 1892
Designed by T Dunn, A McKenzie
18 holes, 6208 yards, S.S.S. 70
♦ Welcome; handicap certs required at WE.
ℐ WD £24; WE £35. 2 for 1 offer.
⚐ Welcome; terms on application.
🍴 Full bar and restaurant facilities.
⚒ Beachlands; Commodore; Rozel; Timbertops.

3B 89 Weymouth
Links Rd, Weymouth, Dorset, DT4 0PF
⚎ www.weymouthgc.co.uk
✉ weymouth'gc@line1.net
☎ 01305 784994, Fax 788029, Pro 773997, Sec 773981, Rest/Bar 773981
1 mile from Weymouth town centre.
Parkland course.
Pro Des Lochrie; Founded 1909
Designed by James Braid
18 holes, 5976 yards, S.S.S. 69
ℐ Practice area.
♦ Welcome if carrying handicap certs.
ℐ WD £24; WE £30.

⌕ Welcome WD; catering by arrangement.
🍽 Full facilities.

3B 90 **Wheathill**
Somerton, Somerset, TA11 7HG
☎ 01963 240667, Fax 240230,
Pro 240667, Sec 240667,
Rest/Bar 240667
Take A37 towards Yeovil; at village of Lydford Cross turn left; course 1 mile on right.
Parkland course.
Pro Andrew England; Founded 1993
Designed by J Payne
18 holes, 5351 yards, S.S.S. 66
† Welcome.
Ⅼ WD £15; WE £20.
⌕ Welcome by arrangement; full facilities.
🍽 Full facilities.
⊸ George (Castle Cary).

3B 91 **The Wiltshire Golf Club**☎
Vastern, Wootton Basset, Swindon, Wilts, SN4 7PB
✉ tracey@vthe-wiltshire.co.uk
☎ 01793 849999, Fax 849988
Course is on the A3102 one mile S of Wootton Bassett close to the M4 Junction 16.
Pro Paul Grevel; Founded 1990
Designed by Peter Alliss/Clive Clark
18 holes, 6522 yards, S.S.S. 72
⌇ Practice range; practice ground.
† Welcome by prior arrangement.
Ⅼ WD £20.00; WE £30.
⌕ Welcome by arrangement; golf and catering packages can be arranged; terms on application.
🍽 Full clubhouse facilities.
⊸ Marsh Farm.

3B 92 **Windwhistle** ☎
Cricket St Thomas, Near Chard,
Somerset, TA20 4DG
☎ 01460 30231, Fax 30055,
Pro 30231, Sec 30231,
Rest/Bar 30231
Course is on the north side of the A30 five miles from Crewkerne; three miles from Chard; opposite a wildlife park; follow signs from the M5 Junction 5.
Downland/parkland course.
Pro Duncan Driver; Founded 1932
Designed by JH Taylor (1932) and Leonard Fisher (1992)
18 holes, 6470 yards, S.S.S. 71
⌇ 12.
† Welcome but best to phone first.
Ⅼ WD £18; WE £22.
⌕ Welcome by arrangement; full facilities.
🍽 Full facilities.

3B 93 **Worlebury** ☎
Monks Hill, Worlebury, Weston-Super-Mare, Avon, BS22 9SX
🖳 www.worleburygc.co.uk
✉ secretary@worburygc.co.uk
☎ 01934 625789, Fax 621935,
Pro 623932, Sec 625789,
Rest/Bar 623214
From M5 Junction 21 follow old road to Weston-super-Mare; turn right at Milton Church.
Hilltop parkland course.
Pro Gary Marks; Founded 1908
Designed by W Hawtree & Son
18 holes, 5936 yards, S.S.S. 69
† Everyone welcome.
Ⅼ WD £20; WE £30.
⌕ Welcome by prior arrangement; terms on application.
🍽 Bar and restaurant facilities.
⊸ Commodore; Beachlands.

3B 94 **Wrag Barn Golf** ☎
Shrivenham Rd, Highworth, Wilts, SN6 7QQ
🖳 www.wragbarn.com

✉ info@wragbarn.com
☎ 01793 861327, Fax 861325
10 miles from M4 Junction 15; take A419 towards Cirencester left turn to Highworth; follow A361 to Highworth; then 3rd exit at roundabout on to B4000 to Shrivenham; course is 0.5 miles to the right.
Parkland course.
Pro Barry Loughrey; Founded 1990
Designed by Hawtree & Sons
18 holes, 6348 yards, S.S.S. 72
⌇ Driving range, covered.
† Welcome; restrictions apply in afternoon at WE so it is advisable to phone first.
Ⅼ WD £25; WE £30.
⌕ Welcome WD by arrangement.
🍽 Full bar and restaurant, catering for companies, parties, receptions.
⊸ Blunsden House Hotel; Jesmond House (Highworth).

3B 95 **Yeovil**
Sherborne Road, Yeovil, Somerset, BA21 5BW
☎ 01935 475949, Fax 411283,
Pro 473763, Sec 422965,
Rest/Bar 431130
1 mile from town centre towards Sherborne on A30.
Parkland course; also 9-hole course available.
Pro Geoff Kite; Founded 1919
Designed by Fowler & Alison (18 holes); Sports Turf Rese (9 holes)
18 holes holes, 6144 yards, S.S.S. 70
† Welcome but ring for tee times.
Ⅼ WD £25; WE £30.
⌕ Welcome Mon, Wed, Thurs and Fri; packages available to be arranged.
🍽 Full facilities.
⊸ Ludgate House, Ilchester.

EAST ANGLIA

4

Suffolk, Norfolk

This is Bernard Darwin country. He learned to play golf at Felixstowe Ferry, a bleak links course dominated by its Martello tower. He is said to have hit his last shots at Aldeburgh before declaring, "Now I can retire gracefully from this unspeakable game." Between the two events he wrote and travelled great distances.

This is his description of the journey to Royal West Norfolk, more commonly called Brancaster. "We get out at Hunstanton station and drive a considerable number of miles along a nice, flat, dull east country road till we get to the tranquil little village, with a church and some pleasant trees. In front of the village is a stretch of grey-green marsh, and beyond the marsh is a range of sandhills, and that is where the golf is."

That is where the golf is. He could not have put it better. Sand dunes, railway sleepers, salt marsh, marram grass, Brancaster makes you feel as if you have been playing a century of golf on this same spot without ever wanting to leave. The clubhouse, dressed in a wooden wind cheater, is one of the cosiest in the country.

Also mentioned in Darwin's journey, Hunstanton is a championship course that runs between the sea and the river Hun. It is an out-and-back links with superlative greens. It is also the course where Robert Taylor, a visitor from Scraptoft in Leicestershire, holed in one at the 188 yards 16th hole with a one iron. Nothing too remarkable in that, except that he had a hole-in-one at the same hole on the following day, this time with a six iron. The next day he was offered rather skinny odds of a million to one to repeat the feat and promptly plonked it in the hole again.

Along the coast, Royal Cromer and Sheringham are both excellent courses, but their greens are not as reliable as Hunstanton's. Sheringham is where Joyce Wethered, one of the game's greatest players, is reputed to have said "What train?" after holing a winning putt to the background accompaniment of a locomotive. The same story, but with a different cast, is often attached to Lytham. They are probably both true.

If Suffolk does not quite match the splendour of Norfolk, it still has a lot of good golf about it. Aldeburgh, a heathland course with deep bunkers and nine par fours over four hundred yards, would be an appropriate setting for one of Benjamin Britten's more fiendish works such as 'The Turn of the Screw'.

Woodbridge and Thorpeness are also good tracks, but Suffolk's most famous course is according to some just half a course. The nine holes of Royal Worlington were described by Darwin as "the sacred nine". Nine holes zig-zagging through a giant field might not seem a recipe for a great golf course, so try it for yourself. And while you are at it, see if the superb chocolate cake is as rich as ever. But be warned, a second piece used to bring on wheezing and serious chest pains.

4 1 Aldeburgh

Saxmundham Road, Aldeburgh,
Suffolk, IP15 5PE
☎ 01728 452408, Fax 452937,
Pro 453309, Sec 452890,
Rest/Bar 452408
From the A12 N of Ipswich take the
A1094 to Aldeburgh; course is six
miles E of the A12.
Open heathland course; no par 5s
Pro Keith Preston; Founded 1884
Designed by John Thompson/Willie
Fernie
27 holes, 6350 yards, S.S.S. 71
⚑ Practice green.
† Welcome by prior arrangement.
Ⅰ WD £45; WE £60 before 12 am;
After 12 WD, £35 WE £40.
⟳ Welcome by prior arrangement;
terms on application. Also a 2114-yard,
9-hole course with SSS 62.
🍴 Clubhouse facilities.
⌂ Wentworth; White Lion; Brudewell;
Uplands.

4 2 Alnesbourne Priory

Priory Park, Nacton Road, Ipswich,
Suffolk, IP10 0JT
☎ 01473 727393, Fax 278372
From A14 take Ransomes Europark
exit and follow signs to Prior Park.
Parkland course.
Founded 1987
9 holes, 1760 yards, S.S.S. 58
† Public pay and play (closed Tues).
Ⅰ WD £10; Sat £11; Sun £12.
⟳ Course available for hire every
Tues; packages available, adventure
playground; terms on application.
🍴 Bar and restaurant.
⌂ Lodge cabins on site.

4 3 Barnham Broom ℭ

Honingham Road, Barnham Broom,
Norwich, Norfolk, NR9 4DD
🖧 www.barnham-broom.co.uk
☎ 01603 759393, Fax 758224
9 miles SW of Norwich.
River valley setting
Pro Simon Dicksee; Founded 1977
Designed by Frank Pennink (Valley),
Donald Steel (Hill)
Hill: 18. Valley: 18 holes, Hill: 6495.
Valley 6483 yards, S.S.S. Hill: 72.
Valley 71
† Welcome by prior arrangement.
Ⅰ WD £40; WE £40.
⟳ Many golfing breaks and corporate
packages available; complete hotel,
conference and golfing leisure breaks
available at the hotel.
🍴 Full club and hotel facilities.
⌂ Barnham Broom Hotel.

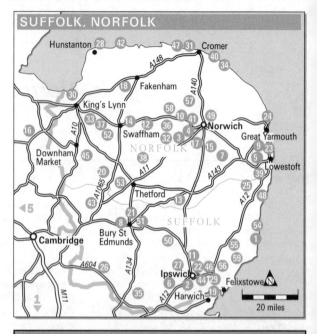

SUFFOLK, NORFOLK

KEY					
1	Aldeburgh	20	Feltwell	41	Royal Norwich
2	Alnesbourne Priory	21	Flempton	42	Royal West Norfolk
3	Barnham Broom	22	Fynn Valley	43	Royal Worlington &
4	Bawburgh	23	Gorleston		Newmarket
5	Beccles	24	Great Yarmouth & Caister	44	Rushmere
6	Brett Vale	25	Halesworth	45	Ryston Park
7	Bungay & Waveney Valley	26	Haverhill	46	Seckford
8	Bury St Edmunds	27	Hintlesham Hall	47	Sheringham
9	Caldecott Hall	28	Hunstanton	48	Southwold
10	Costessey Park	29	Ipswich	49	Sprowston Park
11	Cretingham	30	King's Lynn	50	Stowmarket
12	Dereham	31	Links Country Park	51	Suffolk Golf & Country Club
13	Diss	32	Mattishall	52	Swaffham
14	Dunham Golf Club	33	Middleton Hall	53	Thetford
	(Granary)	34	Mundesley	54	Thorpeness
15	Dunston Hall	35	Newton Green	55	Ufford Park Hotel
16	Eagles	36	Norfolk Golf & Country Club	56	Waldringfield Heath
17	Eaton	37	RAF Marham	57	Wensum Valley
18	Fakenham	38	Richmond Park	58	Weston Park
19	Felixstowe Ferry	39	Rookery Park	59	Woodbridge
		40	Royal Cromer		

4 4 Bawburgh ℭ

Glen Lodge, Marlingford Road,
Bawburgh, Norfolk, NR9 3LU
🖧 www.bawburgh.com
📧 info@bawburgh
☎ 01603 740404, Fax 740403,
Pro 742323, Sec 740404,
Rest/Bar 740404
Off the Norwich southern by-pass
(A47) at the Royal Norfolk Showground
Junction; follow road to Bawburgh.
Parkland/heathland course
Pro Chris Potter; Founded 1978
Designed by S Manser
18 holes, 6231 yards, S.S.S. 70
⚑ 14 floodlit.

† Welcome.
Ⅰ WD £22; WE £25.
⟳ Welcome by prior arrangement;
normal packages involve 18-36 holes;
lunch and evening meal; terms on
application.
🍴 Full clubhouse facilities.
⌂ Park Farm, Hethersett.

4 5 Beccles

The Common, Beccles, Suffolk, NR34
9BX
☎ 01502 712244, Sec 714616
Leave A146 Norwich-Lowestoft road at
Sainsbury's roundabout.

Parkland course; formerly Wood Valley.
Founded 1899
9 holes, 5562 yards, S.S.S. 67
† Welcome; with a member on Sun
am.
ℂ WD £8; WE £10.
⟳ Welcome with prior notice; terms
on application.
🍽 Clubhouse facilities.
⌁ King's Head; Waveney House,
both Beccles.

4 6 Brett Vale
Noaks Road, Raydon, Ipswich, Suffolk,
IP7 5LR
✉ info@brettvalegolf.com
☎ 01473 310718, Fax 312270,
Pro 310718, Sec 310718,
Rest/Bar 310718
Course is 8 miles from Ipswich off the
A12.
Parkland;stunningly beautiful.
Pro Paul Bate; Founded 1993
Designed by Howard Swan
18 holes, 5797 yards, S.S.S. 70
ℐ 7.
† Welcome preferably by prior
arrangement.
ℂ WD £20, WE £25, £20 after 2pm.
⟳ Welcome by prior arrangement;
terms on application.
🍽 Full clubhouse facilities.
⌁ The County Hotel, Copdock.

4 7 Bungay & Waveney Valley
Outney Common, Bungay, Suffolk,
NR35 1DS
🖳 www.club'noticeboard.co.uk
✉ bungeygolf@aol.com
☎ 01986 892337, Fax 892222,
Pro 892337
Signposted from Bungay by-pass.
Heathland course.
Pro N Whyte; Founded 1889
Designed by James Braid
18 holes, 6044 yards, S.S.S. 69
ℐ Practice area.
† Welcome by arrangement.
ℂ Terms on application.
⟳ Welcome by prior arrangement;
discounted day rates and green fees
for groups of more than 20.
🍽 Clubhouse facilities.
⌁ Ersham Park Farm.

4 8 Bury St Edmunds
Tuthill, Bury St Edmunds, Suffolk, IP28
6LG
🖳 www.club-noticeboard.co.uk/
burystedmunds
✉ bury.golf@talk21.com
☎ 01284 755979, Fax 763288,

Pro 755978
1st exit off A14 for Bury St Edmunds;
0.25 miles down B1106 to Brandon.
Parkland course.
Pro Mark Jillings; Founded 1924
Designed by Hawtree (9 holes); Ray
(18 holes)
18 holes, 6678 yards, S.S.S. 72
† Welcome WD; WE with a member.
ℂ WD £25.
⟳ Welcome WD by arrangement;
also a pay and play 9-hole course;
terms on application.
🍽 Full clubhouse facilities.
⌁ Butterfly.

4 9 Caldecott Hall
Caldecott Hall, Beccles Road, Fritton,
Norfolk, NR31 9EY
🖳 www.caldecotthall.com
☎ 01493 488488, Fax 488561
5 miles SW of Great Yarmouth on
A143 Beccles Road.
Parkland course.
Pro Syer Shulver; Founded 1994
18 holes, 6318 yards, S.S.S. 70
ℐ 20.
† Welcome by prior arrangement.
ℂ WD £20; WE £25.
⟳ Welcome by prior arrangement;
discounts available for groups of 10 or
more; terms available on application.
Also a 9-hole par 3 course.
🍽 Full clubhouse facilities.
⌁ Caldecott Hall Hotel.

4 10 Costessey Park   ℭ
Old Costessy, Norwich, Norfolk, NR8
5AL
🖳 www.costesseypark.com
✉ cpgc@ljgroup.com
☎ 01603 746333, Fax 746185,
Pro 747085, Sec 746333,
Rest/Bar 746333
Course is off the A1074 at the Round
Well public house three miles W of
Norwich.
Parkland/river valley course.
Pro Andrew Young; Founded 1983
Designed by Frank MacDonald
18 holes, 5900 yards, S.S.S. 69
† Welcome; only after 11am at WE.
Handicaps required.
ℂ WD £22; WE £28.
⟳ Welcome by prior arrangement;
terms on application.
🍽 Full catering and bar facilities
available.

4 11 Cretingham
Cretingham, Woodbridge, Suffolk, IP13
7BA

☎ 01728 685275, Fax 685037
2 miles from the A1120 at Earl Soham;
10 miles N of Ipswich.
Parkland course.
Pro Neil Jackson; Founded 1984
9 holes, 4380 yards, S.S.S. 64
† Welcome.
ℂ WD £7; WE £9.
⟳ Welcome by arrangement; catering
packages available; snooker; pitch &
putt; swimming pool; tennis; caravan
park.
🍽 Full restaurant and licensed bar
available.

4 12 Dereham
Quebec Road, Dereham, Norfolk,
NR19 2DS
☎ 01362 695900, Fax 695904,
Pro 695631, Sec 695900
0.5 miles out of Dereham on B1110.
Parkland course.
Pro R Curtis; Founded 1934
9 holes, 6225 yards, S.S.S. 70
† Welcome by prior arrangement.
ℂ Terms on application.
⟳ Welcome by arrangement;
packages available; terms on
application.
🍽 Clubhouse facilities.
⌁ Phoenix; Kings Head; George.

4 13 Diss
Stuston Common, Diss, Norfolk, IP21
4AA
🖳 www.club-noticeboard.co.uk\diss
✉ sec.dissgolf@virgin.net
☎ 01379 642847, Fax 644586,
Pro 644399, Sec 641025
Course is one mile W of the A140 at
Scole, half-way between Norwich and
Ipswich.
Commonland course.
Pro Nigel Taylor; Founded 1903
18 holes, 6262 yards, S.S.S. 70
† Welcome; WE only as the guest of
a member.
ℂ WD £25; £30 per day.
⟳ Welcome WD by prior
arrangement.
🍽 Full facilities available.
⌁ Park Hotel, Diss. Cornwallis
Country Hotel, Broome.

4 14 Dunham Golf Club
Little Dunham, Nr Swaffham, King
Lynn, Norfolk, PE32 2DF
🖳 www.dunhamgolfclub.com
☎ 01328 701718, Sec 701906,
Rest/Bar 701906
On A47 at Necton/Dunham crossroads.
Parkland with lakes.

Pro Gary Potter; Founded 1987
Designed by Mr Jim Harris
9 holes, 4852 yards, S.S.S. 67
▮ Indoor practice facility available.
† Welcome.
▯ Terms on application. WE 18-holes
£16, WD 18-holes £12.
↻ Welcome by prior arrangement.
Weekends included.
▮●▮ Full bar and snack facilities
available.

---

4 15 Dunston Hall ♛
Dunston Hall, Ipswich Road, Norwich,
Norfolk, NR14 8PQ
☎ 01508 470178
On the main A140 Ipswich road; 10
minutes drive from Norwich city centre.
Meadowlands course.
Pro Peter Briggs; Founded 1994
Designed by M Shaw (1998 extension)
18 holes, 6319 yards, S.S.S. 70
▮ 22.
† Welcome but booking essential,
priority to members and hotel guests.
▯ WD £25; WE £30.
↻ Welcome by prior arrangement;
catering packages; conference
facilities; leisure and health centre.
▮●▮ Full clubhouse facilities.
↵ Dunston Hall on site.

---

4 16 Eagles
28 School Road, Tilney All-Saints,
King'S Lynn, Norfolk, PE34 4RS
🖳 www.eagles-golf.co.uk
🖳 shop@eagles-golf.co.uk
☎ 01553 827147, Fax 829777,
Pro 827147, Sec 829777,
Rest/Bar 829000
Off A47 between King's Lynn and
Wisbech.
Parkland course.
Pro Nigel Picerell; Founded 1992
Designed by David Horn
9 holes and a par 3 course, 4284
yards, S.S.S. 61
▮ 20.
† Welcome. 2 floodlit tennis courts
on astro turf, also for 5-a-side football.
▯ WD £7.50 9 holes; £11.00 18
holes; WE £8.50 9 holes £14.50 18
holes.
↻ Welcome by arrangement; catering
facilities available by negotiation; terms
on application.
▮●▮ Facilities available.
↵ Bufferfly; Park View, both King's
Lynn.

---

4 17 Eaton
Newmarket Road, Norwich, Norfolk,

NR4 6SF
🖳 www.eatongc.co.uk
🖳 administator@eatongc.co.uk
☎ 01603 451686, Fax 451686,
Pro 452478, Sec 451686,
Rest/Bar 452881
Off A11 1 mile S of Norwich.
Predominantly parkland course.
Pro Mark Allen; Founded 1910
18 holes, 6114 yards, S.S.S. 70
† Welcome WD; only after 11.30 on
WE.
▯ WD £30; WE £40.
↻ Welcome by arrangement; terms
on application.
▮●▮ Bar and catering facilities.
↵ Norwich; Nelson and Holiday Inn.

---

4 18 Fakenham Sports Centre
The Race Course, Fakenham, Norfolk,
NR21 7NY
🖳 brian.watson6@btinternet.com
☎ 01328 862867, Pro 863534,
Sec 855665
Course is on the B1146 from Dereham
or the A1067 from Norwich.
Parkland course.
Pro Martyn Clarke; Founded 1981
Designed by Charles Lawrie
9 holes, 6245 yards, S.S.S. 69
† Welcome; restrictions Sat and Sun
morning.
▯ WD £20; WE £25.
↻ Welcome by arrangement.
▮●▮ Bar and restaurant in Sports
Centre.
↵ Wensum Lodge; Crown; Limes.

---

4 19 Felixstowe Ferry
Ferry Road, Felixstowe, Suffolk, IP11
9RY
☎ 01394 286834, Fax 283975
A14 to Felixstowe, following signs for
the yacht centre.
Links course.
Pro Ian MacPherson; Founded 1880
Designed by Henry Cotton & Sir Guy
Campbell
18 holes, 6272 yards, S.S.S. 70
▮ Practice.
† Welcome WD.
▯ Terms on application.
↻ Welcome Tues, Wed and Fri by
arrangement; catering packages; also
9-hole Kingsfleet course opened in
April 1997: 5980 yards, par 70.
▮●▮ Full catering facilities.
↵ Orwell House; self-catering flats
above clubhouse for rent.

---

4 20 Feltwell
Thor Ave, Feltwell, Thetford, Norfolk,

IP26 4AY
☎ 01842 827644, Pro 827666
Off B1112 Lakenheath-Feltwell road
just before Feltwell village.
Inland links course.
Pro Neil Mitchell; Founded 1972
9 holes, 6256 yards, S.S.S. 70
† Welcome.
▯ WD £15; WE £24.
↻ Welcome WD; by arrangement;
terms on application.
▮●▮ Bar and catering except Mon.
↵ Brandon House, Brandon.

---

4 21 Flempton
Flempton, Bury St Edmunds, Suffolk,
IP28 6EQ
☎ 01284 728291
4 miles NE of Bury St Edmunds on
A1101 to Mildenhall.
Breckland course.
Pro Mark Jillings; Founded 1895
Designed by JH Taylor
9 holes, 6240 yards, S.S.S. 70
† Welcome WD with handicap certs;
with member at weekend.
▯ WD £30 all day.
↻ Limited availability.
▮●▮ By arrangement.
↵ Priory & Angel, Bury St.Edmunds;
The Riverside, Mildenhall.

---

4 22 Fynn Valley ♛
Witnesham, Ipswich, Suffolk, IP6 9JA
🖳 www.fynn'valley.co.uk
🖳 enquiries@fynn'valley.co.uk
☎ 01473 785267, Fax 785632,
Pro 785463, Sec 785267,
Rest/Bar 785202
From A14 or A12 take A1214 and then
B1077 to N of Ipswich.
Parkland course.
Pro P Wilby/K Vince/A Lucas; Founded
1991
Designed by Tony Tyrrell
18 holes, 6310 yards, S.S.S. 70
▮ 22 Driving range bays and 18
putting greens.
† Welcome except before 10.30am
Sun; Ladies day Wed.
▯ WD £22; WE £25.
↻ Welcome WD; catering and golf
packages available; also 9-hole par 3
course; special offer between Nov-Feb
£17.50 – 18 holes of golf & 2 course
lunch.
▮●▮ Excellent restaurant.
↵ Novotel, Ipswich; Travel Lodge,
Claydon; Marlborough Hotel.

---

4 23 Gorleston
Warren Road, Gorleston, Great

Yarmouth, Norfolk, NR32 6JT
☎ 01493 661911, Fax 611911,
Pro 662103, Rest/Bar 441922
Off A12 between Great Yarmouth and
Lowestoft.
Clifftop course.
Pro N Brown; Founded 1906
Designed by JR Taylor
18 holes, 6391 yards, S.S.S. 71
♦ Welcome with handicap certs.
⌇ WD £21; WE £25.
♦ Welcome by prior arrangement; full
golf and catering package; terms on
application.
◉ Full clubhouse catering facilities.
↩ Cliffs, Gorleston; Potters HH,
Hopton.

4 24 Great Yarmouth & Caister
Beach House, Caister-On-Sea, Great
Yarmouth, Norfolk, NR30 5DT
☎ 01493 728699, Fax 728699,
Pro 720421, Sec 728699,
Rest/Bar 720214
From Yarmouth N to Caister-on-Sea.
Links course.
Pro James Hill; Founded 1882
Designed by T Dunn/HS Colt
18 holes, 6330 yards, S.S.S. 70
♦ Welcome; handicap certs
preferred.
⌇ WD £30; WE £35.
♦ Welcome by prior arrangement;
packages available; dining room, TV
lounge, snooker; terms available on
application.
◉ Full catering and bar facilities
available.
↩ Imperial; Burlington; Caister Old
Hall.

4 25 Halesworth   🌣
Bramfield Road, Halesworth, Suffolk,
IP19 9XA
▤ info@halesworthgc.co.uk
☎ 01986 875567, Fax 874565,
Pro 875697, Sec 875567,
Rest/Bar 875567
On A144 off the A12 1 mile N of
Darsham.
Parkland; formerly St Helena GC.
Pro S. Harrison; Founded 1990
Designed by JW Johnson
27 holes, 6580 yards, S.S.S. 72
♦ Welcome.
⌇ WD £15, WE £15.
♦ Welcome by prior arrangement;
Full day packages available; company
days organised; also 9-hole par 33
course available; terms on application.
◉ Full clubhouse facilities.
↩ The Angel.

4 26 Haverhill   🌣
Coupals Road, Haverhill, Suffolk, CB9
7UW
⌨ www.club-noticeboard.co.uk
▤ haverhillgolf@
coupalsroad.fsnet.co.uk
☎ 01440 761951, Fax 761951,
Pro 712628, Rest/Bar 710311
Leave Haverhill on A1307 towards
Colchester and turn second left after
railway viaduct; first right into Coupals
Road.
Parkland course; new 18 opened April
1998.
Pro Nick Duc; Founded 1973
Designed by Charles Lawrie
18 holes, 5929 yards, S.S.S. 69
⌇ Practice range.
♦ Welcome.
⌇ WD £22; WE £28.
♦ Welcome by prior arrangement.
◉ Bar facilities and catering
available.
↩ Woodlands.

4 27 Hintlesham Hall   🌣
Hintlesham, Ipswich, Suffolk, IP8 3NS
⌨ www.hintleshamhallgolfclub.co.uk
▤ office@hintleshamhallgolfclub.com
☎ 01473 652761, Fax 652750,
Pro 656006
4 miles W of Ipswich; 10 mins from
A12 or A14.
Parkland course.
Pro Alistair Spink; Founded 1991
Designed by Hawtree & Sons
18 holes, 6062 off yellows 6602 off
whites yards, S.S.S. 72
♦ Welcome with handicap
certificates.
⌇ WD£30; WE £38.
♦ Welcome WD by prior
arrangement with the secretary;
packages available; spa; sauna; steam
room.
◉ Full bar and restaurant service.
↩ Hintlesham Hall.

4 28 Hunstanton *(see overleaf)*
Golf Course Road, Old Hunstanton,
Norfolk, PE36 6JQ
▤ hunstanton.golf@eidosnet.co.uk
☎ 01485 532811, Fax 532319,
Pro 532751, Sec 532811,
Rest/Bar 533932
On the North Norfolk coast; take
the A149 Cromer Road through
Old Hunstanton and follow signs to
club.
Links course; 2 ball only.
Pro James Dodds; Founded 1891
Designed by George Fernie; updated
by J Braid

18 holes, 6759 yards, S.S.S. 72
♦ Welcome from 9.30am to
11.30am and after 2pm on WD in
summer; 10.30am-11am and after 2pm
at WE.
⌇ WD £55; WE £65 summer. WD
£35; WE £45 winter.
♦ Welcome by prior arrangement,
but 2 ball play only; packages
available; Full facilities; terms on
application.
◉ Full catering facilities from 11am to
4.30pm Otherwise by prior
arrangement.
↩ The Lodge; Le Strange Arms,
Hunstanton; Lifeboat Inn, Thornham.

4 29 Ipswich
Purdis Heath, Bucklesham Road,
Ipswich, Suffolk, IP3 8UQ
⌨ www.ipswichgolfclub.com
▤ mail@ipswichgolfclub.com
☎ 01473 728941, Fax 715236,
Pro 724017, Rest/Bar 713030
3 miles E of Ipswich off A14.
Heathland course with pine trees.
Pro S Whymark; Founded 1895/1927
Designed by James Braid, Hawtree &
Taylor
27 holes, 6435 yards, S.S.S. 71
♦ Welcome WD by arrangement; WE
as member's guest only.
⌇ WD £30; WE £35.
♦ Welcome by prior arrangement;
packages including breakfast, lunch
and dinner available.
◉ Full catering facilities.
↩ Marriott Courtyard.

4 30 King's Lynn
Castle Rising, King's Lynn, Norfolk,
PE31 6BD
▤ klgc@eidosnet.co,uk
☎ 01553 631654, Fax 631036,
Pro 631655, Sec 631654,
Rest/Bar 631656
On A149 King's Lynn to Hunstanton,
turn at Castle Rising.
Parkland course.
Pro John Reynolds; Founded 1923/1975
Designed by Alliss & Thomas
18 holes, 6609 yards, S.S.S. 73
♦ Welcome with handicap certificate
by prior arrangement.
⌇ WD £40; WE £50.
♦ Welcome Thurs and Fri
only; catering available from society
menu; minimum 16. Enquiries
welcome.
◉ Full facilities.
↩ Knights Hill Hotel, Grimston
Road/Grange Hotel (Wooton Rd).

Hunstanton

Hunstanton is a golfer's golf course. It is not blessed with the spectacular scenery of a Royal St Davids or a Turnberry and it does not deal in the aching, nostalgic charm of its near neighbour Brancaster. It is simply crammed with top class golf holes.

The finish is as severe as any in the land. The par three sixteenth is renowned for Bob Taylor's extraordinary feat of a hole-in-one on three consecutive days, but his achievement belies the trickiness of the hole.

Freshly measured at 191 yards, the tee shot is played to a narrow green squeezed between seven bunkers. When Malcolm Gregson set his course record of 65 he dropped a shot here.

The seventeenth was hard enough before they added another 17 yards in 2001. On the championship card it is now listed at 464, but by the time you add on the prevailing wind, half the distance of a 38 yard long green for a back pin placement, the narrowness of the target and a maliciously sloping fairway, the total is far more terrifying.

The eighteenth isn't much easier. The colourful beach huts to the right of the fairway and the lights on its left, warning of beach bound pedestrians, are amusing distractions. But the long second shot to a sharply banked green requires absolute concentration and skill.

When Peter McEvoy tied with Ronan Rafferty, then just sixteen years old, in the 1980 Brabazon he finished six, six. The previous day Rafferty had run up an eight on the seventeenth.

The start is much gentler although the opening tee shot is intimidating enough. It is played from right in front of the clubhouse windows and requires a carry - although not admittedly a long one - over a huge bunker, recently shored up by the addition of some sleepers.

Some reckon that the course doesn't truly get going until the sixth - although there are a couple of testing par fours to be played before then - which is a shortish four to a wickedly elevated green. The seventh is a fine par three over a gully and a solitary front bunker and from now on the problems come thick and fast.

The ninth demands an intimidating carry to reach the fairway, the eleventh has no need of a single bunker to deepen its sadistic inquisition, the thirteenth requires a well-struck second over a lump of rough ground and the fourteenth is a blind par three of 222 yards.

Huge changes were made to these last two holes on 'professional advice' in the eighties, but the members soon had the sense to restore them.

They also revolted when the rough was grown trendily long. A Mr Roddis wrote that it was depriving members and visitors of their enjoyment. "The majority of people playing...have long handicaps and it is the majority upon whom the very existence of the club depends." Well said.

The greens at Hunstanton are sacrosanct being some of the smoothest and most puzzling in the country. They are also well protected.

When James Braid departed in 1907 after adding more sand to the course, in the words of Darwin "he left a cunning trail of bunkers behind him". Then there is the wind. One comment in the suggestions book calls for deeper holes to prevent the flags from being carried away into the Wash.

The clubhouse offers some excellent home cooked ham and the drink is much improved since 1921 when one member noted, "As regards the whiskey, to ask a defeated opponent to partake thereof is practically an unfriendly act." And that would never do at Hunstanton. — **Mark Reason**

4 31 The Links Country ☏
Park Golf Course
Sandy Lane, West Runton, Cromer,
Norfolk, NR27 9QH
🖳 www.links-hotel.co.uk
✉ sales@links-hotel.co.uk
☎ 01263 838383, Fax 838264,
Pro 838215, Sec 838383,
Rest/Bar 838383
Off the A149 road.
Coastal course with heath; 300 yards
from sea.
Pro Andrew Collison; Founded
1899/1903
Designed by JH Taylor (1903 when 18
holes)
9 holes, 4842 yards, S.S.S. 64
† Welcome.
[WD £22.50; WE £27.50 summer
WD £15 WE £20 winter.
⟁ Welcome with prior arrangement;
full catering and golf packages; hotel
on site with pool, sauna, sun bed and
tennis course; terms on application.
🍽 Full catering facilities.
⟲ ETB 4 Crown Links Country Park
Hotel.

4 32 Mattishall
South Green, Mattishall, Dereham,
Norfolk, NR20 3JZ
☎ 01362 850111, Sec 850464
B1063 to Mattishall; right at church;
course 1 mile on left from Dereham. If
one comes from Norwich turn left at
church and course is 1.5 miles on left.
Parkland course.
Peter Briggs; Founded 1990
Designed by Mr Todd
9 holes, 18 tees, 6170 yards, S.S.S.
69, par 70 men, par 72 ladies
⫟ Pitch and putt.
† Welcome.
[Terms on application.
⟁ Limited availability.
🍽 Limited.
⟲ Phoenix, E Dereham, Wensum
Valley Golf Club, Taverham.

4 33 Middleton Hall
Hall Orchards, Middleton, Nr King's
Lynn, Norfolk, PE32 1RH
🖳 www.middletonhall.co.uk
✉ middleton/hall@btclick.com
☎ 01553 841800, Fax 841800,
Pro 841801, Sec 841800,
Rest/Bar 841800
On A47 between King's Lynn and
Swaffham.
Parkland course.
Steve White; Founded 1989
Designed by D Scott

18 holes, 6007 yards, S.S.S. 69
⫟ 6.
† Welcome.
[WD £25; WE and BH £30.
⟁ Welcome by prior arrangement;
golfing and catering packages available;
carvery available for 30 or more players.
🍽 Full catering and bar facilities
available.
⟲ Butterfly; Knight's Hill, both King's
Lynn.

4 34 Mundesley
Links Road, Mundesley, North Norfolk,
NR11 8ES
☎ 01263 720279, Fax 720279,
Sec 720095, Rest/Bar 720279
Turn off Mundersley-Cromer road at
Mundersley church.
Undulating parkland with fine views.
Pro Terry Symmons; Founded 1903
Designed by Harry Vardon (in part)
9 holes, 5377 yards, S.S.S. 66
† Welcome WD except Weds; after
11.30am at WE.
[WD £18 per round £20 per day;
WE £25 after 11.30.
⟁ Welcome as with guests; catering
by prior arrangement; terms on
application.
🍽 Clubhouse bar and catering
facilities.
⟲ Manor House, Mundersley.

4 35 Newton Green
Newton Green, Sudbury, Suffolk, CO10
0QN
✉ tcoopergolf@aol.com
☎ 01787 377217, Fax 377549,
Pro 313215, Sec 377217,
Rest/Bar 377501
Course is on the A134 three miles E of
Sudbury.
Moorland course.
Pro Tim Cooper; Founded 1907
18 holes, 5947 yards, S.S.S. 68
† Welcome 7 Days.
[Terms on application.
⟁ Welcome by prior arrangement;
packages available; from £15.
🍽 Bar and restaurant facilities.
⟲ Mill Hotel, Sudbury.

4 36 Norfolk Golf & CC
Hingham Road, Reymerston, Norwich,
Norfolk, NR9 4QQ
🖳 www.the-norfolk.co.uk
☎ 01362 850297, Fax 850614,
Pro 850297, Rest/Bar 850297
Signposted from B1135.
Parkland course; was Reymerston GC.

Pro T Varney; Founded 1993
Designed by Adas
18 holes, 6609 yards, S.S.S. 72
⫟ Practice range, golf academy.
† Welcome with prior arrangement.
[WD £19; WE £23.
⟁ Welcome WD; full golf, catering
and leisure packages; terms on
application.
🍽 Full facilities; function room.
⟲ White Hare, Hingham; Mill,
Yaxham.

4 37 RAF Marham
King's Lynn, Norfolk, PE33 9NP
🖳 www.rafmarham.co,uk
☎ 01760 337261, Sec 337261
EXT7422
7 miles SE of King's lynn near
Narborough.
9 holes, 5244 yards, S.S.S. 66
† Restricted; apply on ext 7262.
⟁ Restricted access, MOD land,
apply on 01760337261 ext7062.

4 38 Richmond Park ☏
Saham Road, Watton, Thetford,
Norfolk, IP25 6EA
🖳 www.richmondpark.co.uk
☎ 01953 881803, Fax 881817,
Pro 886104, Sec 881803,
Rest/Bar 881803
Course is at bottom of Watton High
Street.
Parkland course.
Pro Alan Hemsley; Founded 1990
Designed by R Jessup, R Scott
18 holes, 6289 yards, S.S.S. 70
⫟ 4 bay driving range available, call
for details.
† All welcome, special offers at
selected times.
[WD £22.50 per round, WE £30
then £20 after 2pm.
⟁ Welcome WD by prior
arrangement; coffee on arrival, light
lunch and 3-course dinner; other
packages available.
🍽 Full facilities.
⟲ Accommodation on site.

4 39 Rookery Park
Carlton Colville, Lowestoft, Suffolk,
NR33 8HJ
☎ 01502 560380, Fax 560380,
Pro 515103, Sec 560380,
Rest/Bar 574009
Course is two miles W of Lowestoft on
the A146.
Parkland course.
Pro Martin Elsworthy; Founded 1975

Designed by Charles Lawrie
18 holes, 6714 yards, S.S.S. 72
† Only visitors with handicaps
welcome.
⌇ WD £30; WE £35.
⌁ Welcome by prior arrangement
except Tues; packages by
arrangement; also 9-hole par 3 course;
snooker.
⦿ Full facilities.
⌁ Carlton Manor, Broadlands.

4 40 Royal Cromer
145 Overstrand Road, Cromer, Norfolk,
NR27 0JH
⌁ www.royalcromergolfclub.com
✉ general.manager@
royal-cromer.com
☎ 01263 512884, Fax 512430,
Pro 512267, Sec 512884,
Rest/Bar 512884
1 mile E of Cromer on the B1159 coast
road close to the Cromer lighthouse.
Undulating seaside links course.
Pro Lee Patterson; Founded 1888
Designed by James Braid
18 holes, 6508 yards, S.S.S. 72
† Welcome WD and after 11am most
WE.
⌇ Terms available on application.
⌁ Welcome WD by prior
arrangement.
⦿ Daily facilities.
⌁ Cliftonville; Roman Camp Inn;
Anglia Court; Red Lion; Virginia Crt.

4 41 Royal Norwich
Drayton High Road, Hellesdon,
Norwich, NR6 5AH
⌁ www.royalnorwichgolf.co.uk
✉ mail@royalnorwichgolf.co.uk
☎ 01603 429928, Fax 417954,
Pro 408459, Sec 429928,
Rest/Bar 429928
On A1067 3 miles from Norwich on
Fakenham road.
Mature undulating Parkland course.
Pro Dean Futter; Founded 1893
Designed by JJW Deuchar 1893;
J Braid 1924
18 holes, 6603 yards, S.S.S. 72
† Welcome; bookings necessary at
WE.
⌇ Available upon request.
⌁ Welcome; book through general
manager; packages available; catering
and golf facilities; from £40.
⦿ Bar and restaurant facilities
available.
⌁ Norwich Sports Village; Hotel
Norwich; Stakis Hotel.

4 42 Royal West Norfolk
Brancaster, King's Lynn, Norfolk, PE31
8AX
☎ 01485 210223, Fax 210087,
Pro 210616, Sec 210087
Course is seven miles E of
Hunstanton; in Brancaster village turn
at the Beach/Broad Lane Junction with
the A149; course one mile.
Historic links course.
Pro S Rayner; Founded 1892
Designed by Holcombe Ingleby
18 holes, 6428 yards, S.S.S. 71
⌇ Practice range.
† Welcome at secretary's discretion;
deposit needed to confirm booking; not
last week of July or August or first
week of September.
⌇ WD £50; WE £60.
⌁ Welcome but prior booking
essential.
⦿ Full facilities.
⌁ Hoste Arms, Burnham Market;
Titchwell Manor, Titchwell.

4 43 Royal Worlington & Newmarket
Golf Links Road, Worlington, Bury St
Edmunds, Suffolk, IP28 8SD
☎ 01638 712216, Fax 717787,
Pro 715224, Sec 717787,
Rest/Bar 712216
6 miles NE of Newmarket on A14 then
A11 towards Thetford; follow signs to
Worlington.
Inland links course.
Pro Malcolm Hawkins; Founded 1893
Designed by HS Colt
9 holes, 6210 yards, S.S.S. 70
† WD only.
⌇ WD £48 before 12pm, £35 after
12pm. No WE.
⌁ Welcome Tues and Thurs by
arrangement; catering packages; limit
24 players, from £50.
⦿ Full clubhouse facilities.
⌁ Worlington Hall; Riverside,
Mildenhall.

4 44 Rushmere ⚷
Rushmere Heath, Ipswich, Suffolk, IP4
5QQ
⌁ www.club-noticeboard.co.uk
✉ rushmeregolfclub@talk21.com
☎ 01473 725648, Fax 273852,
Pro 728076, Sec 725648,
Rest/Bar 719034
3 miles E of Ipswich off A1214
Woodbridge road.
Heath and commonland course.
Pro NTJ McNeill; Founded 1927
18 holes, 6262 yards, S.S.S. 70
† Welcome WD and after 2.30pm

WE; handicap certs required and proof
of membership of another club.
⌇ WD £25; WE £25.
⌁ Welcome by arrangement;
packages available; terms on
application.
⦿ Full clubhouse facilities.
⌁ Marriott; Posthouse.

4 45 Ryston Park
Ely Road, Denver, Downham Market,
Norfolk, PE38 0HH
☎ 01366 382133, Sec 383834
On A10 1 mile S of Downham Market.
Parkland course.
Founded 1933
Designed by J Braid
9 holes, 6310 yards, S.S.S. 70
† Welcome WD; with members at
WE.
⌇ Terms on application.
⌁ Welcome; maximum 45; catering
packages available from the steward;
terms on application.
⦿ Full facilities.
⌁ Castle Hotel, Downham Market.

4 46 Seckford
Seckford Hall Road, Great Bealings,
Woodbridge, Suffolk, IP13 6NT
☎ 01394 388000, Fax 382818,
Rest/Bar 384588
Off A12 at Woodbridge Junction.
Parkland course; Mizuno golf academy.
Pro Simon Jay; Founded 1991
Designed by Johnny Johnson
18 holes, 5303 yards, S.S.S. 66
⌇ Practice course.
† Welcome with prior arrangement.
⌇ WD £16; WE £18.50.
⌁ Welcome by prior arrangement;
special leisure and golf breaks can be
arranged in old Many House Hotel with
34 rooms; spa pool, swimming pool;
packages available; terms on
application.
⦿ Bar, bistro, terrace and hotel
restaurant.
⌁ Seckford Hall.

4 47 Sheringham
Weybourne Road, Sheringham,
Norfolk, NR26 8HG
⌁ www.shernamgolfclub.co.uk
✉ sgc@seccare43.net
☎ 01263 823488, Fax 825189,
Pro 822980, Sec 823488,
Rest/Bar 822038
From the A148 follow the signs into
Sheringham; left at roundabout; club
0.5 miles.
Clifftop links course.

Royal Worlington and Newmarket Golf Club

One of the attractions of a nine-hole course is that you get a second chance at every hole. The converse is that the second time around, you know much more, and your mind has the opportunity to magnify the difficulties. This, however, is said to be the best nine-hole course in the world and the truth of this dictum makes it worth playing again and again.

Royal Worlington and Newmarket Golf Club was created in 1890 and founded officially in 1893. It achieved royal patronage in 1895, when the then Prince of Wales agreed to be President of the club. Many Cambridge undergraduates remember it fondly as the course where they cut their competitive teeth in the game, though they sometimes refer to it sentimentally as 'Mildenhall' rather than give it its full title.

Patric Dickinson stoutly defended the reputation of 'the sacred nine'. He wrote, "If ever a man declares: 'nine holes are not enough; real golf requires 18', let him be reminded of Mildenhall, for there is no more difficult feat of real golf in this country, probably anywhere in the world."

It is difficult to exaggerate a nine-hole course. Worlington is set on heathland, with stands of pine trees forming natural divisions between some of the fairways. The opening par five might unkindly be described as nondescript, but at least it allows the golfer to get swinging in preparation for what is to follow.

The second is an oxymoron, 'a long short hole' that can make or break the good bad golfer. Dickinson described the difficulty of finding the green to being "like pitching onto a policeman's helmet". It is well over 200 yards long and made all the more difficult by the green sloping away on all sides. Even the truest of drives to the heart of the green is sometimes not enough to score well.

The greens are quick too, aided by the sandy Suffolk soil that allows a round to be played all the year round here. One of the more popular topics of conversation in the clubhouse after an afternoon's golf is generally how many putts each golfer made. To keep in the twenties is something to brag about - so long as you are playing the nine holes twice.

The fifth is one of the most memorable holes on the course. At 155 yards, it seems innocuous enough, but the three-level green is long and narrow, set on a promontory with steep slopes on either side. A former captain of the club is said to have driven the green and walked off with an eight on his card. Astute bunkering and awkward swales around some greens offer a challenge to all standards of golfer. Peter Alliss recalls that four Ryder Cup players played an exhibition match here some forty years ago, and the best round among them was a 74.

This is the sort of course where the inclusion on the card of the bogey for each hole, as well as par, strikes you not as an affectation, but as a reminder that this is a club which prides itself on tradition and propriety. There is nothing stuffy about the club, and every aspect of its clubhouse exhibits the same mixture of warmth and austerity. Visitors are provided with a standard issue tankard and a ration of IPA.

Henry Longhurst once wrote a piece entitled 'Golftopia'. In it he described his ideal, and imaginary, course. The more you see of Worlington, and Longhurst saw it a fair bit, the more you imagine that he had this famous nine-hole course in mind. — **Jim Bruce-Ball**

Pro M W Jubb; Founded 1891
Designed by Tom Dunn
18 holes, 6464 yards, S.S.S. 71
� Practice green.
† Welcome with prior booking.
⌂ WD £40; WE £45.
⌀ Welcome with prior arrangement;
terms on application.
⦿ Clubhouse facilities.

---

4 48 Southwold
The Common, Southwold, Suffolk,
IP18 6TB
☎ 01502 723234, Fax 723635,
Pro 723790, Sec 723248,
Rest/Bar 723234
From A12 Henham to Blythborough;
take A1095 to Southwold.
Heathland course.
Pro Brian Allen; Founded 1884
Designed by J Braid
9 holes, 6052 yards, S.S.S. 69
⌀ Practice green.
† Welcome.
⌂ WD £22; WE £24. Daily rate £35.
⌀ Welcome by arrangement;
packages available; terms on
application.
⦿ Clubhouse facilities.
⌲ Swan; Crown; Cricketers; Pier
Avenue Hotel.

---

4 49 Sprowston Manor
(Marriott)
Wroxham Road, Sprowston, Norwich,
NR7 8RP
🖳 www.marriotthotels.com
☎ 01603 254290, Fax 788884,
Pro 254290, Rest/Bar 254292
On A1551 Norwich to Wroxham road;
10 minutes from city centre.
Parkland course.
Pro G Ireson; M Borrett, C Jefferson,
R Lewis; Founded 1980
18 holes, 5763 yards, S.S.S. 68
⌀ 27.
† Welcome.
⌂ WD £21; WE £27.
⌀ Welcome by prior arrangement;
Full package of golf and catering,
including morning coffee, lunch and
dinner. Inclusive golf breaks.
⦿ Full catering facilities.
⌲ Sprowston Manor.

---

4 50 Stowmarket
Lower Road, Onehouse, Stowmarket,
Suffolk, IP14 3DA
🖳 www.club'noticeboard.co.uk
☎ 01449 736733, Fax 736826,
Pro 736392, Sec 736473,
Rest/Bar 736473

Course is 2.5 miles south-west of
Stowmarket off the B1115 Stowmarket-
Bidlestone road.
Parkland course.
Pro Duncan Burl; Founded 1962
18 holes, 6107 yards, S.S.S. 69
⌀ 12.
† Welcome after 9.15am with
handicap certs, except Wed.
⌂ WD £25; WE £31.
⌀ Welcome Thurs and Fri.
⦿ Full facilities.
⌲ Cedars.

---

4 51 Suffolk Golf & CC
St John's Hill Plantation, Fornham All
Saints, Bury St Edmunds, Suffolk, IP28
6JQ
☎ 01284 706777, Fax 706721
From A14 take B1106 to Fornham.
Parkland course; was Fornham Park.
Pro Steven Hall; Founded 1969
18 holes, 6077 yards, S.S.S. 70
† Welcome by prior arrangement.
⌂ WD £20; WE £25.
⌀ Welcome WD; packages with golf,
catering and leisure on request; terms
on application.
⦿ Full clubhouse catering facilities
available.

---

4 52 Swaffham
Cley Road, Swaffham, Norfolk, PE37
8AE
☎ 01760 721611, Fax 725485,
Pro 721611, Sec 721621
1 mile out of town on Cockley Cley
road; signposted in market place.
Heathland course.
Pro Peter Field; Founded 1922
18 holes, 6539 yards, S.S.S. 71
⌀ Practice green.
† Welcome WD; with member at
WE.
⌂ WD £25.
⌀ Welcome WD by arrangement.
⦿ Full catering except Mon and Tues;
snacks.
⌲ George.

---

4 53 Thetford
Brandon Road, Thetford, Norfolk, IP24
3NE
🖳 www.club'noticeboard.co.uk
☎ 01842 752258, Fax 752662,
Pro 752662, Sec 752169
Just off A11 on B1107.
Wooded heathland course.
Pro Gary Kitley; Founded 1912
Designed by CH Mayo, Donald Steel
18 holes, 6879 yards, S.S.S. 73
⌀ Practice green.

† Welcome WD with handicap certs;
weekend with member only.
⌂ Terms on application. Without
member £34.
⌀ Welcome Wed, Thurs, Fri only;
packages available; terms on
application.
⦿ Full facilities.
⌲ Bell; Thomas Paine; Wereham
House.

---

4 54 Thorpeness   ⌶
Thorpeness Hotel & Golf Club,
Lakeside Avenue, Thorpeness, Suffolk,
IP16 4NH
🖳 www.thorpeness.co.uk
📧 info@thorpeness.co.uk
☎ 01728 452176, Fax 453868,
Pro 454926, Sec 452176,
Rest/Bar 452176
25 miles N of Ipswich on A12; then
B1094 to Aldeburgh and then B1069 to
Thorpeness.
Coastal heathland course.
Pro Frank Hill; Founded 1922
Designed by James Braid
18 holes, 6241 yards, S.S.S. 71
⌀ 3.
† Welcome if carrying handicap
certs.
⌂ WD £25; WE £30.
⌀ Welcome; packages available;
catering facilities, snooker; lounge,
function room; tennis courts; terms on
application.
⦿ Restaurant, patio bar, lounge.
⌲ 30-room hotel on site; guests have
priority tee-times.

---

4 55 Ufford Park Hotel   ⌶
Yarmouth Road, Ufford, Woodbridge,
Suffolk, IP12 1QW
☎ 01394 382836, Fax 383582,
Pro 382836
Course is two miles N of Woodbridge
on the B1438.
Parkland with ponds.
Pro S Robertson; Founded 1991
Designed by Phil Pilgrim
18 holes, 6300 yards, S.S.S. 70
⌀ Practice; driving nets.
† Welcome by arrangement.
⌂ WD £20; WE £30.
⌀ Welcome on WD; packages
available; leisure facilities inc pool,
spa, sauna, gym; terms on application.
⦿ Full facilities.
⌲ Ufford Park Hotel on site.

---

4 56 Waldringfield Heath
Newbourne Road, Waldringfield,
Woodbridge, Suffolk, IP12 8PT

Ufford Park Hotel, Golf & Leisure

Best Western

Woodbridge, Nr. Ipswich, Suffolk

Voted one of the best 40 Winter Golf Courses in Britain

• Challenging Par 71: 6485 yards • 50 Ensuite Bedrooms • Modern Conference Facilities
• Gymnasium, Deck Level Pool, Sauna, Steam & Jacuzzi • Weddings • Parties

Tel: **01394 383555**   Fax: **01394 383582**   email: **uffordparkltd@btinternet.com**   **www.uffordpark.co.uk**

🖧 www.club-noticeboard.co.uk/
walderingfield
☎ 01473 736426, Fax 736 436,
Pro 736417, Sec 736768,
Rest/Bar 736768
3 miles NE of Ipswich.
Heathland course.
Founded 1983
Designed by P Pilgrim
18 holes, 7863 yards, S.S.S. 70
⚑ Welcome WD; after 11am WE.
Ⓘ WD £15; WE £18.
🖊 Welcome WD by prior arrangement;
day tickets are available from £22.50
and £25 on WE. Terms on application.
🍽 Full facilities.
⌂ Marlborough, Ipswich.

4 57 Wensum Valley
Beech Avenue, Taverham, Norwich,
Norfolk, NR8 6HP
☎ 01603 261012, Fax 261664,
Pro 261012, Sec 261012,
Rest/Bar 261012
Take the A1067 Fakenham to
Taverham road.
Parkland course; golf school.
Pro Peter Whittle; Founded 1989
Designed by BC Todd
Valley course; 6223 yards; S.S.S. 70; 9

holes, 5812 yards; S.S.S. 68
⚑ Welcome.
Ⓘ WD £20; WE £20 (day ticket that
includes a bar meal of up to £5).
🖊 Welcome; packages on request;
TV lounge, pool table; bowling green.
Other leisure facilities can be
organised; conference facilities; golfing
breaks available; terms on application.
🍽 Clubhouse facilities; Morton
Restaurant; Wensum suite; bars.
⌂ Hotel on site.

4 58 Weston Park
Weston Longville, Norwich, Norfolk,
NR9 5JW
🖧 www.weston'park.co.uk
☎ 01603 872363, Fax 873040,
Pro 872998, Rest/Bar 871842
9 miles NW of Norwich off A1067
Norwich-Fakenham road.
Parkland course.
Pro Michael Few; Founded 1993
Designed by Golf Technology
18 holes, 6603 yards, S.S.S. 72
Ⓘ Practice green.
⚑ Welcome.
Ⓘ WD £28.50; WE £45.
🖊 Welcome with a minimum of 12
players; packages available £25-£45;

group lessons; snooker room;
conference room.
🍽 Full restaurant facilities.
⌂ Wensum Country Hotel.

4 59 Woodbridge
Bromeswell Heath, Woodbridge,
Suffolk, IP12 2PF
🖧 www.woodbridgegolfclub.com
✉ woodbridgegolfclub.co.uk
☎ 01394 382038, Fax 382392,
Pro 383213, Sec 382038,
Rest/Bar 383212
2 miles E of Woodbridge on A1152.
Heathland course.
Pro A Hubert; Founded 1893
Designed by F Hawtree
27 holes, 6299 yards, S.S.S. 70
⚑ Welcome WD with handicap
certs. 9-hole course open all week to
visitors.
Ⓘ WD £33 18-hole course, £16 9-
hole course.
🖊 Welcome WD by prior
arrangement; maximum 36; packages
available; from £32.
🍽 Catering facilities available 9am to
5.30pm or by prior arrangement.
⌂ Crown & Castle, Orford; The Bull
Hotel, Woodbridge.

SOUTH MIDLANDS

5A

Bedfordshire, Northamptonshire, Cambridgeshire, Leicestershire

Henry Longhurst learned his golf at Bedford Golf Club, or the Bedfordshire as it now more grandly known. He wrote, "It was a flat, lush hundred-acre meadow, bounded by the Midland Railway, the River Ouse, the Girls High School hockey field, the allotments, a cornfield and Mr Somebody's garden." As it happened all these boundaries were to the golfer's left, so in years to come, when someone hit a shot with a touch of involuntary fade, it was said "to have a bit of Bedfordshire on it."

The Bedfordshire is greatly improved from those muddy days, indeed Longhurst called its advancement a "miracle", but his description makes the point about a lot of the golf in the area. Flat and muddy, much of the Midlands makes for mundane golf.

Dunstable Downs is the exception that proves the rule. Because of its elevation and chalky subsoil it has some of the best fairways in Britain. It can be a testing walk, but it has several dramatically elevated tees. Standing on the eleventh you can see six counties. There is a gliding school nearby, so do not be surprised to see your ball carried off on a thermal.

John O'Gaunt is another decent course, although it leans rather heavily in favour of par fours (there are 13 of them), and Aspley Guise & Woburn Sands, just over the county border from Woburn, is a well-maintained heathland course.

Cambridgeshire is not blessed with too many top golf courses and many a stymie (the name for a Cambridge second team golfer) has crossed the Suffolk border to play their golf at Royal Worlington. But Gog Magog, three-and-a-half miles outside Cambridge and with over a

hundred years of history, is well worth a visit. Named after some rare bumps in the fen landscape, the Gogs has a hilly start and a hilly finish with a flat stretch between.

Northamptonshire is another of those counties that has welcomed a big name with a big design in order to raise its golfing profile. Johnny Miller excavated a lake to shape the land to create Collingtree Park. It is another of those long, American-style courses designed to accommodate championships more than the average golfer.

More to many people's taste is Northamptonshire County, often used for regional qualifying into the Open Championship. A Harry Colt heathland design it opens with a 450 yard par four, but mellows out after that.

Leicestershire has received a little more recognition as a golfing county following the emergence of Gary Wolstenholme, the only Briton to have played on three winning Walker Cup teams. Having left it late to learn his golf in Leicestershire Wolstenholme is helping to raise the profile of Kilworth Springs, a course that is nearly always open for play, quite a recommendation in a county that often has to turn to the dreaded rubber mat in winter.

Tree-lined Longcliffe is the most highly regarded of Leicestershire's courses, but The Leicestershire itself is a good place for spotting county cricketers and international rugby players out for a hack. It has a couple of severe dog legs, a feature that seems something of a regional trait as Peterborough Milton and Hinckley are also remembered for their doglegs.

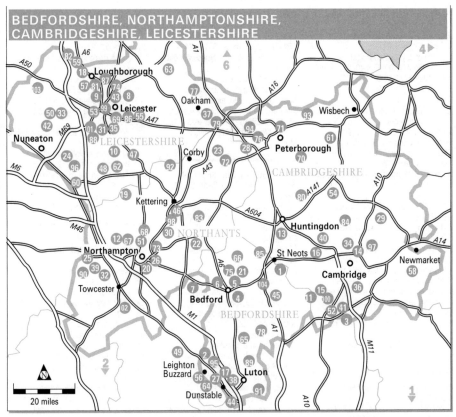

BEDFORDSHIRE, NORTHAMPTONSHIRE, CAMBRIDGESHIRE, LEICESTERSHIRE

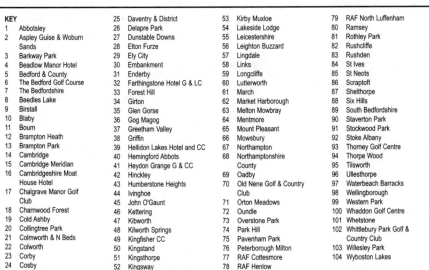

KEY			
1	Abbotsley	25	Daventry & District	53	Kirby Muxloe	79	RAF North Luffenham
2	Aspley Guise & Woburn	26	Delapre Park	54	Lakeside Lodge	80	Ramsey
	Sands	27	Dunstable Downs	55	Leicestershire	81	Rothley Park
3	Barkway Park	28	Elton Furze	56	Leighton Buzzard	82	Rushcliffe
4	Beadlow Manor Hotel	29	Ely City	57	Lingdale	83	Rushden
5	Bedford & County	30	Embankment	58	Links	84	St Ives
6	The Bedford Golf Course	31	Enderby	59	Longcliffe	85	St Neots
7	The Bedfordshire	32	Farthingstone Hotel G & LC	60	Lutterworth	86	Scraptoft
8	Beedles Lake	33	Forest Hill	61	March	87	Shelthorpe
9	Birstall	34	Girton	62	Market Harborough	88	Six Hills
10	Blaby	35	Glen Gorse	63	Melton Mowbray	89	South Bedfordshire
11	Bourn	36	Gog Magog	64	Mentmore	90	Staverton Park
12	Brampton Heath	37	Greetham Valley	65	Mount Pleasant	91	Stockwood Park
13	Brampton Park	38	Griffin	66	Mowsbury	92	Stoke Albany
14	Cambridge	39	Hellidon Lakes Hotel and CC	67	Northampton	93	Thorney Golf Centre
15	Cambridge Meridian	40	Hemingford Abbots	68	Northamptonshire	94	Thorpe Wood
16	Cambridgeshire Moat	41	Heydon Grange G & CC		County	95	Tilsworth
	House Hotel	42	Hinckley	69	Oadby	96	Ullesthorpe
17	Chalgrave Manor Golf	43	Humberstone Heights	70	Old Nene Golf & Country	97	Waterbeach Barracks
	Club	44	Ivinghoe		Club	98	Wellingborough
18	Charnwood Forest	45	John O'Gaunt	71	Orton Meadows	99	Western Park
19	Cold Ashby	46	Kettering	72	Oundle	100	Whaddon Golf Centre
20	Collingtree Park	47	Kibworth	73	Overstone Park	101	Whetstone
21	Colmworth & N Beds	48	Kilworth Springs	74	Park Hill	102	Whittlebury Park Golf &
22	Colworth	49	Kingfisher CC	75	Pavenham Park		Country Club
23	Corby	50	Kingstand	76	Peterborough Milton	103	Willesley Park
24	Cosby	51	Kingsthorpe	77	RAF Cottesmore	104	Wyboston Lakes
		52	Kingsway	78	RAF Henlow		

5A 1 Abbotsley Golf Hotel and Country Club

Eynesbury Hardwicke, St Neots, Cambs, PE19 4XN
🖳 abbotsley@americangolf.uk.com
☎ 01480 474000, Fax 403280, Pro Abbotsley 477669, Cromwell
Pro 215153, Sec 474000,
Rest/Bar 474000
2 Miles SE of St Neots leaving A428 at Tesco roundabout.
Parkland course.
Pro Steve Connolly; Founded 1976
Designed by Derek Young, Vivien Saunders, Jenny Wisson
Abbotsley: 18 holes, 6311 yards, S.S.S. 72; cromwell: 18 holes, 6087 yards, S.S.S. 69
🏌 21-bay floodlit driving range.
† Welcome; restrictions at WE (Abbotsley); 7-day bookings availability for tee times.
Ⅼ Terms on application.
⌕ Welcome by prior arrangement; packages available; tailored to suit individual needs, prices on request; residential packages; residential golf schools: Denise Hastings and Vivian Saunders.
🍽 The Garden restaurant and choice of bars.
⌂ Hotel on site; 40 well-appointed, en suite bedrooms.

5A 2 Aspley Guise & Woburn Sands

West Hill, Aspley Guise, MK17 8DX
☎ 01908 583596, Fax 583596,
Pro 582974, Sec 583596
2 Miles W of M1 Junction 13 between Aspley Guise and Woburn Sands
Undulating parkland course.
Pro Colin Clingan; Founded 1914
Designed by Sandy Herd
18 holes, 6079 yards, S.S.S. 70
† Welcome WD; WE as member's guest.
Ⅼ WD £37 per day £28 for 18 holes; WE £37 per round £52 per day by prior arrangement only.
⌕ Welcome Wed and Fri; April to October; catering and golf packages available; from £55.00 for an all day package.
🍽 Full catering facilities 7 days a week.
⌂ Moore Place.

5A 3 Barkway Park ☏

Barkway Park Golf Club,
Nuthampstead Road, Barkway,
Royston, Herts, SG8 8EN
☎ 01763 848215, Pro 849070
On B1368 5 miles S of Royston

Gently undulating links course.
Pro Jamie Bates; Founded 1992
Designed by Vivien Saunders
18 holes, 6997 yards, S.S.S. 74
† Welcome; WE tee times cannot be booked until Fri pm.
Ⅼ WD £10; WE £15.
⌕ Welcome by prior arrangement; packages available; function room; pool table and darts; terms on application.
🍽 Full facilities. Practice area.
⌂ Vintage Puckeridge; Flintcroft Motel.

5A 4 Beadlow Manor Hotel

Beadlow, Nr Shefford, Beds, SG17 5PH
🖳 beadlow@kbnet.co.uk
☎ 01525 860800, Fax 861345,
Pro 861292
On the A507 between Ampthill and Shefford; 1.5 miles W of Shefford.
Parkland course.
Pro G Dixon; Adrienne Englemann;
Founded 1973
Designed by Baron Manhattan
18 holes, 6072 yards, S.S.S. 69
🏌 Practice range, 25 bays floodlit; buggies and clubs for hire.
† Welcome.
Ⅼ Terms on application.
⌕ Welcome by prior arrangement; several golf and catering packages available; health club; conference rooms; terms on application.
🍽 Bar, restaurants.
⌂ 33 room hotel on site.

5A 5 Bedford and County

Green Lane, Clapham, Bedford, Beds, MK41 6ET
🖳 olga@bedcounty.fsnet.co.uk
☎ 01234 352617, Fax 357195, Pro 359189, Sec 352617, Rest/Bar 354010
Off the A6 N of Bedford before Clapham village.
Parkland course.
Pro Roger Tattersall; Founded 1912
18 holes, 6399 yards, S.S.S. 70
† Welcome WD; with a member at WE.
Ⅼ WD £24.
⌕ Welcome WD except Wed; all day golf packages available; from £50.
🍽 Full facilities.
⌂ Woodlands Manor.

5A 6 The Bedford Golf Course

Kanussi Drive, Great Denham Golf village, Biddenham, Bedford, MK40 4FF
🖳 www.kolengolf.com
🖳 Thebedford1@ukonline.co.uk
☎ 01234 320022, Fax 320023,

Pro 353653, Sec 330559,
Rest/Bar 348822
1.5 miles W of Bedford A248
Northampton Road.
American design well bunkered, many lakes.
Pro Zac Thompson; Founded 1998
Designed by David Pottidge*
18 holes, 6305 yards, S.S.S. 72
🏌 Grass driving range, up to thirty people.
† Welcome WD; as members' guests at WE.
Ⅼ WD £24-£28; WE £40-50
⌕ Welcome WD; full clubhouse facilities; green fee plus catering.
Moving Sept 2000, upgraded facilities.
🍽 Full clubhouse facilities.
⌂ Shakespeare; Swan; Moat House.

5A 7 Bedfordshire Golf Club

Spring Lane, Stagsden, Bedford, MK43 8SR
🖳 www.bedfordshiregolf.com
🖳 david@bedfordshiregolf.com
☎ 01234 822555
On A422 between Milton Keynes and Bedford.
Hilly, crossways.
18 holes – 6565 yards, 9-hole par 3
† Yes but not a WE unless with member; 9-hole at all times.
Ⅼ Enquire for fees.
⌕ Yes.
🍽 Dining room, function suite.
⌂ Shakespeare Hotel, Bedford; Swan Revived, Newport Pagnell; Post House, Newport Pagnell Road.

5A 8 Beedles Lake

Broome Lane, East Goscote, Leics, LE7 3NQ
☎ 0116 2606759, Fax 2604414,
Pro 2606759, Sec 2606759,
Rest/Bar 2607086
Between A46 Leicester-Newark road and A607 Leicester-Melton Mowbray.
Parkland course.
Pro Sean Bryne; Founded 1993
Designed by D Tucker
18 holes, 6625 yards, S.S.S. 71
🏌 17.
† Welcome at all times.
Ⅼ WD £10; WE £13.
⌕ Welcome any time; terms on application.
🍽 Clubhouse facilities. Practice range.

5A 9 Birstall ☏

Station Road, Birstall, Leicester, Leics, LE4 3BB

Beedles Lake Golf Centre
170 Broome Lane • East Goscote • Leicestershire LE7 3WQ
Tel: **0116 260 6759** (Pro)   Tel: **0116 260 7080** (Steward)   Tel/Fax: **0116 260 4414** (Golf Manager)
MEMBERSHIPS AVAILABLE
SOCIETY PACKAGES AVAILABLE (Mon - Fri from £16.00; Sat & Sun from £19.00)
VISITORS WELCOME

☎ 0116 2674322, Fax 2674322, Pro 2675245
Off A6 3 miles N of town.
Parkland course.
Pro David Clarke; Founded 1901
18 holes, 6222 yards, S.S.S. 70
† Welcome except WE.
Ⅰ WD £25-£30.
⟋ Welcome Wed and Fri by prior arrangement; reductions for groups of more than 20; snooker; billiards; prices on application.
🍽 Full facilities except Mon.
🛏 Contact club for details.

5A 10 Blaby
Lutterworth Road, Blaby, Leics., LE8 3DP
🕸 www.blabygolfcourse.com
☎ 0116 2784804
From Leicester through Blaby village; course on the left-hand side.
Parkland course.
Pro Matt Fisher; Founded 1991
9 holes, 5312 yards, S.S.S. 66
Ⅰ Practice range, 27 floodlit bays; crazy golf course.
† Welcome; pay and play.
Ⅰ WD and WE 9 holes £5, 18 holes £7
⟋ Welcome; special company days available; terms on application.
🍽 Bar.

5A 11 Bourn
Toft Road, Bourn, Cambridge, Cambs, CB3 7TT
☎ 01954 718057, Fax 718908, Pro 718958, Sec 718088, Rest/Bar 718057
6 miles W of Cambridge off A14 through Bourn village.
Parkland course.
Pro Craig Watson; Founded 1991
Designed by J Hull and S Bonham
18 holes, 6417 yards, S.S.S. 71
† Welcome.
Ⅰ WD £16; WE £22.
⟋ Welcome; full clubhouse facilities available; terms on application.
Practice area, bring own balls; buggies for hire.
🍽 Clubhouse facilities.
🛏 Many in Cambridge.

5A 12 Brampton Heath
Sandy Lane, Church Brampton, Northampton, Northants, NN6 8AX
🕸 www.bhgc.co.uk
✉ slawrence@bhgc.co.uk
☎ 01604 843939, Fax 843885
3 miles N of Northampton just off A5119
Undulating heathland course.
Pro R Hudson; Founded 1995
Designed by D Snell
18 holes, 6366 yards, S.S.S. 70
† Welcome at all times.
Ⅰ WD £14; WE £18.
⟋ Welcome WD and WE; packages from only £14 arranged to suit. PGA-approved short course; driving range.
🍽 Full facilities.

5A 13 Brampton Park   ♛
Buckden Road, Brampton, Huntingdon, Cambs, PE28 4NF
☎ 01480 434700, Fax 411145, Pro 434705
Take A1 or A14 to RAF Brampton; club is opposite airbase.
Meadowland course.
Pro A Currie; Founded 1991
Designed by Simon Gidman (Hawtree & Sons)
18 holes, 6403 yards, S.S.S. 73
† Welcome.
Ⅰ Winter: WD £15, WE £35; Summer: WD £25, WE £35.
⟋ Welcome WD; function room; practice area; trolleys for hire; full facilities; from £29.75.
🍽 Clubhouse facilities.
🛏 Limited accomodation on site.

5A 14 Cambridge Golf Club   ♛
Station Road, Longstanton, Cambridge, Cambs, CB4 5DR
☎ 01954 789388
10 mins N of Cambridge on B1050 off A14.
Parkland course.
Pro G Huggett/A Engelman; Founded 1992
Designed by G Huggett
18 holes, 6736 yards, S.S.S. 74
Ⅰ Floodlit covered driving range and play off grass allowed.
† Welcome.
Ⅰ WD £10; WE £13.

⟋ Welcome at all times; various packages and reductions available; terms on application.
🍽 Full clubhouse facilities.

5A 15 Cambridge Meridian   ♛
Comberton Road, Toft, Cambridge, Cambs, CB3 7RY
🕸 www.golfsocieties.com
✉ meridian@golfsocieties.com
☎ 01223 264700, Fax 264701, Pro 264702, Sec 264700, Rest/Bar 264700
On B1046 at Toft 3 miles W of M11 Junction 12.
Parkland course.
Pro Michael Clemons; Founded 1994
Designed by P Alliss/C Clark
18 holes, 6651 yards, S.S.S. 72
† Welcome with telephone booking.
Ⅰ WD £19; WE £25.
⟋ Welcome WD and after 1pm WE; range of packages available; £19-£49.
🍽 Full clubhouse catering facilities.
Practice range, large practice facilities.
🛏 University Arms Hotel; Abbotsley Golf Hotel.

5A 16 Cambridgeshire Moat   ♛
House Hotel
Bar Hill, Cambridge, Cambridgeshire, CB3 8EU
🕸 www.cambridgeshiregolf.co.uk
☎ 01954 780098, Fax 780010, Pro 780098, Sec 249971, Rest/Bar 249988
On A14 5 miles N of Cambridge.
Parkland course.
Pro Paul Simpson; Founded 1974
Designed by F Middleton
18 holes, 6734 yards, S.S.S. 72
† Everyone welcome.
Ⅰ Unconfirmed as yet for 2002.
⟋ Welcome; day packages can be organised; terms on application.
🍽 Full hotel and clubhouse facilities.
Practice area, buggies and clubs for hire; group tuition available.
🛏 Cambridgeshire Moat House, 134 en suite rooms; just undergone a four million pound refurbishment.

5A 17 Chalgrave Manor   ♛
Dunstable Road, Toddington, Dunstable, Beds, LU5 6JN

Collingtree Park Golf Club

- American Style golf course Designed by British Open Champion Johnny Miller
- A Championship Golf Course having twice held the British Masters & also several Senior Tour events
- Water comes into play on at least 10 holes
- A Covered Floodlit Driving Range
- A three hole Academy Course
- Bar & Restaurant catering for up to 100 people at any one time
- Corporate, Society & Casual Green fees taken

Collingtree Park Golf Club, Windingbrook Lane, Northampton NN4 0XN   Tel: **01604 700 000**   Fax: **01604 702 600**
e-mail : **mailto:j.hammond@pgaetc.co.uk   j.hammond@pgaetc.co.uk**

☎ 01525 876556, Fax 876556, Pro 876554, Sec 876556, Rest/Bar 876556
2 miles W of M1 Junction 12 on A 5120 between Toddington and Houghton Regis.
Undulating parkland course.
Pro Terry Bunyan; Founded 1994
Designed by Mike Palmer/S Rumble
18 holes, 6022 yards, S.S.S. 72
✝ Welcome.
Ⅼ WD £15; WE £30.
⌂ Welcome midweek; full golf and catering packages can be arranged; £21-£37.
⑨ Full catering facilities.

5A 18 Charnwood Forest
Breakback Road, Woodhouse Eaves, Loughborough, Leics, LE12 8TA
☎ 01509 890259, Fax 890925, Sec 890259, Rest/Bar 890259
Close to M1 Junctions 22/23.
Heathland course with heather, gorse.
Founded 1890
Designed by James Braid
9 holes, 5960 yards, S.S.S. 69
Ⅰ Practice green.
✝ Handicapped certificates required.
Ⅼ WD £20; WE £25.
⌂ Welcome Wed, Thurs and Fri; full catering packages plus 27 holes of golf Details on application.
⑨ Full catering facilities; limited catering Mon.
⌁ Friendly Hotel.

5A 19 Cold Ashby
Stanford Road, Cold Ashby, Northampton, Northants, NN6 6EP
⌁ www.coldashbygolfclub.co.uk
▤ coldashby.golfclub@virgin.net
☎ 01604 740548, Fax 740548, Pro 740099
11 miles N of Northampton near A5199/A14 Junction 1.
Undulating parkland course.
Pro Shane Rose; Founded 1974
Designed by John Day extension by

D Croxton 1995
27 holes, 6308 yards, S.S.S. 70
Ⅰ Practice Area.
✝ Welcome; some WE restrictions.
Ⅼ WD £14; WE £16.50.
⌂ Welcome any day by prior arrangement; full day's golf and catering packages available; 27-hole course; 3 loops of 9; Winwick/Ashby par 70; Ashby/Elkington par 72; Elkington/Winwick par 70; dining room facilities; £37 WD £42 WE.
⑨ Full clubhouse facilities. Extensive practice area, buggies and clubs for hire.
⌁ Pytchley, W Haddon; Crick; Broomhill, Spratton.

5A 20 Collingtree Park　　☎
Windingbrook Lane, Northampton, Northants, NN4 0XN
⌁ www.collingtreeparkgolf.com
☎ 01604 700000, Fax 702600, Pro 701202, Rest/Bar 700000
M1 Junction 15 just past Stakis Hotel
Championship course; owned by European PGA.
Pro Henry Bareham; Geoff Pook, Alan Carter; Founded 1990
Designed by Johnny Miller
18 holes, 6908 yards, S.S.S. 73
Ⅰ 26.
✝ Welcome with 7- day advance booking; handicap certs required.
Ⅼ Mon-Thu £20, Fri-Sun £25.
⌂ Welcome with prior arrangement; full clubhouse facilities and driving range and practice ground; terms on application.
⑨ Full facilities in clubhouse.
⌁ Stakis Hotel; Swallow Hotel; Midway Hotel.

5A 21 Colmworth & N Beds
New Road, Colmworth, Bedford, Beds, MK44 2NN
☎ 01234 378181, Fax 376235,

Pro 378822, Sec 378181, Rest/Bar 378181
From Bedford just off B660.
Links style course.
Pro Steve Bonham; Founded 1991
Designed by John Glasgow
18 holes, 6435 yards, S.S.S. 71
✝ Welcome after 9.30 am WD and with booking at WE.
Ⅼ WD £12; WE £18.
⌂ Welcome every day; packages can be arranged; restaurant facilities until 2.30pm; terms on application.
⑨ Full restaurant and bar. Driving range, putting green, Holiday Homes.
⌁ Holiday Homes inquire at the Bar.

5A 22 Colworth
Unilever Research Laboratory, Colworth House, Sharnbrook, Bedford, Beds, MK44 1LQ
☎ 01234 781781
10 miles N of Bedford off A6 through village of Shambrook.
Parkland course.
Founded 1985
9 holes, 5000 yards, S.S.S. 64
✝ Private members only.
Ⅼ Terms on application.

5A 23 Corby
Stamford Road, Weldon, NN17 3JH
☎ 01536 260756, Fax 260756, Sec 743829
A43 Corby to Stamford road 2 miles E of Weldon.
Parkland course.
Pro Jeff Bradbrook; Founded 1965
Designed by Fred Hawtree
18 holes, 6677 yards, S.S.S. 72
✝ Welcome.
Ⅼ WD £10.60; WE £13.70.
⌂ Welcome anytime; large golf shop; packages for golf and catering available; from £9.35.
⑨ Snacks and meals available.
⌁ Hilton.

5A 24 Cosby ☡

Chapel Lane, Off Broughton Road, Cosby, Leicester, Leics, LE9 1RG
🖳 www.cosby-golf-club.co.uk
📧 secretary@cosby-golf-club.co.uk
☎ 0116 2864759, Fax 2864484, Pro 2848275, Sec 2864759, Rest/Bar 2864759
From M1 Junction 21 take B4114 for 3 miles until Cosby turning.
Parkland course.
Pro Martin Wing; Founded 1895
Designed by C Sinclair
18 holes, 6410 yards, S.S.S. 71
⚑ Practice Range.
† Welcome midweek; member's guest only at WE.
⌊ WD £22 per round; £29 per day.
⟁ Welcome, maximum 80 with prior arrangement; various packages available.
🍽 Full clubhouse facilities available.
⌕ Stakis Leicester, Mill on the Soar, Broughton Astley.

5A 25 Daventry & District

Norton Road, Daventry, Northants, NN11 5LS
☎ 01327 702829, Fax 702829, Sec 702829
1 mile N of the town next to the BBC station.
Undulating meadowland course.
Founded 1922
9 holes, 5812 yards, S.S.S. 68
† Welcome; except before Sunday noon.
⌊ WD £10; WE £15.
⟁ Welcome by prior arrangement with the Sec; packages by arrangement; discounts for more than 16 players; terms on application.
🍽 Bar and restaurant.
⌕ Britannia; Hanover.

5A 26 Delapre Park

John Corby Golf Ltd, Delapre Golf Complex, Eagle Drive, Northampton, Northants, NN4 7DU
📧 ruth@delaprenorthhampton.golf.uk
☎ 01604 764036, Fax 706378, Sec 763957
M1 Junction 15 then 4 miles on A45.
Parkland course; also has 9-hole Hardingstone course.
Pro J Corby/J Cuddihy; Founded 1976
Designed by J Jacobs/J Corby
⚑ Practice range 40 bays also grass tees; 2 par 3 courses; pitch & putt course; senior PGA professional tutor; 3 teaching pros; club hire available.
† Welcome at all times.
⌊ WD 9 holes £6.50, 18 holes £8.50; WE 9 holes £7.50, 18 holes £12.50

⟁ Welcome one per day but also welcome WE; packages can be arranged; terms on application.
🍽 Full clubhouse catering and bar facilities.
⌕ Swallow; Stakis; Northampton Moat House; Courtyard by Marriott.

5A 27 Dunstable Downs

Whipsnade Road, Dunstable, Beds, LU6 2NB
🖳 www.dunstable-golf.co.uk
📧 ddgc@btconnect.com
☎ 01582 604472, Fax 478700, Pro 662806, Sec 604472, Rest/Bar 604472
2 miles from Dunstable on Whipsnade road B4541.
Downland course.
Pro M Weldon; Founded 1907
Designed by James Braid
18 holes, 6251 yards, S.S.S. 70
† Welcome WD; member's guests at WE.
⌊ WD £25 per round; £40 per day.
⟁ Welcome WD except Wed; full golf and catering package including lunch and dinner; half-day packages also available. Terms on application.
🍽 Full clubhouse facilities.
⌕ Old Palace Lodge; Hertfordshire Moat House.

5A 28 Elton Furze

Bullock Road, Haddon, Peterborough, Cambs, PE7 3TT
🖳 www.eltonfurzegolfclub.co.uk
📧 secretary@eltonfurzgolfclub.co.uk
☎ 01832 280189, Fax 280299, Pro 280614, Sec 280189, Rest/Bar 280118
4 miles W of Peterborough on old A606; leaving A1 at the Alwalton/Showground exit.
Parkland course.
Pro Frank Kiddie; Founded 1993
Designed by Roger Fitton
18 holes, 6279 yards, S.S.S. 71
⚑ 4 bays, practice range, practice ground; buggies for hire; tuition available.
† Welcome by prior arrangement; handicap certs. preferred; dress codes apply.
⌊ WD £22; WE £32.
⟁ Welcome by prior arrangement with the secretary WD; golf and catering packages available; terms on application.
🍽 Full facilities.
⌕ Swallow, Peterborough.

5A 29 Ely City ☡

Cambridge Road, Ely, Cambs, CB7 4HX

🖳 www.elygolf.co.uk
📧 elygolf@line1.net
☎ 01353 662751, Fax 668636, Pro 663317, Sec 662751, Rest/Bar 662751
1 mile S of City Centre on old A10.
Parkland course.
Pro Andrew George; Founded 1961
Designed by Henry Cotton
18 holes, 6627 yards, S.S.S. 72
† Welcome with handicap certs.
⌊ WD £28; WE £34.
⟁ Welcome Tues-Fri in official organised groups; full packages available; also practice area; snooker; terms on application.
🍽 Full bar and restaurant facilities.
⌕ Nyton Hotel; Lamb Hotel.

5A 30 Embankment Golf club

The Embankment, Wellingborough, Northants, NN8 1LD
☎ 01933 228465, Sec 224997, Rest/Bar 228465
In the embankment area of the City alongside the river.
Parkland course.
Founded 1977
9 holes, 3562 yards, S.S.S. 57
† Welcome with members only.
⌊ WD and WE £5 – must be accompanied by a club member.
⟁ None.
🍽 Bar and limited food.
⌕ The Hind Hotel, Sheep St-Wellingborough.

5A 31 Enderby

Mill Lane, Enderby, Leicester, Leics, LE9 5LH
☎ 0116 2849388, Fax 2849388, Pro 2849388, Sec 2849388, Rest/Bar 2849388
From M1 Junction 21 to Enderby and then follow the signs to Leisure Centre
Municipal heathland course.
Pro Chris d'Araujo; Founded 1986
9 holes, 5712 yards, S.S.S. 72
⚑ 10.
† Welcome.
⌊ WD 9 holes £5.30, 18 holes £6.50; WE 9 holes £6.30, 18 holes £8.75.
⟁ Welcome by arrangement.
🍽 Bar and bar snacks.
⌕ The Stakis.

5A 32 Farthingstone Hotel ☡ Golf & LC

Everdon Road, Farthingstone, Towcester, Northants, NN12 8HA
🖳 www.farthingstone.co.uk
☎ 01327 361291, Fax 361645,

Pro 361533, Sec 361291,
Rest/Bar 361560
M1 Junction 16; take signs to Weedon,
then Everdon and Farthingstone.
Woodland course.
Pro Greg Lunn; Founded 1972
Designed by M Gallagher
18 holes, 6299 yards, S.S.S. 70
⌁ Practice range and nets; buggies
for hire.
† Welcome at all times.
⌑ WD £17; WE £25.
⌁ Welcome any time by prior
arrangement; packages available; also
pool and snooker tables; squash court;
hotel facilities; terms on application.
⦿ Full bar; restaurant and hotel
facilities.
⌁ Farthingstone 16 en-suite twin-
bedded rooms.

5A 33 Forest Hill
Markfield Lane, Botcheston, Leicester,
Leics, LE9 9FJ
☎ 01455 824800, Fax 828522, Pro
824800, Sec 824800, Rest/Bar 824800
2 miles from Botcheston; 3 miles SW
of the A50.
Well-wooded parkland course.
Pro Philip Harness; Founded 1991/1995
Designed by Alan York
18 holes, 6039 yards, S.S.S. 69
⌁ 20 bays floodlit, electric trolleys
and clubs for hire; tuition available.
† Welcome.
⌑ WD £16; WE £22.
⌁ Welcome WD by arrangement;
packages for golf and catering
available; terms on application.
⦿ Bar; restaurant and function room.
⌁ Forest Lodge.

5A 34 Girton   ☾
Dodford Lane, Girton, Cambridge,
Cambs, CB3 0QE
⬚ www.girtongolfclub.co.uk
✉ secretary@girtongolfclub.co.uk
☎ 01223 276169, Fax 277150, Pro
276991, Sec 276169, Rest/Bar 276169
Course is 3 miles N of Cambridge on
the A14.
Flat open course.
Pro Scott Thomas; Founded 1936
Designed by Alan Gow
18 holes, 6012 yards, S.S.S. 69
† Welcome WD; with member at WE.
⌑ WD £20.
⌁ Welcome Tues-Fri by prior
arrangement; packages available;
terms on application.
⦿ Lunches and dinners served
except Mon.
⌁ Post House, Impington.

5A 35 Glen Gorse
Glen Road, Oadby, Leicester, Leics,
LE2 4RF
☎ 0116 2712226, Fax 2714159,
Pro 2713748, Sec 2714159,
Rest/Bar 2714159
On A6 Leicester- Market Harborough
road between Oadby and Great Glen,
5 miles S of Leicester.
Parkland course.
Pro Dominic Fitzpatrick; Founded 1933
18 holes, 6648 yards, S.S.S. 72
⌁ Practice area; tuition available.
† Welcome WD by arrangement; WE
with member.
⌑ WD £25; WE £10.50 with member.
⌁ Tues-Fri by arrangement with
secretary; full golf and catering
facilities; terms on application.
⦿ Full catering facilities.
⌁ Hermitage, Oadby.

5A 36 Gog Magog
Shelford Bottom, Cambridge, Cambs,
CB2 4AB
⬚ www.gogmagog.co.uk
✉ secretary@gogmagog.co.uk,
media@gogmagog.co.uk
☎ 01223 247626, Fax 414990,
Pro 246058
On A1307 5 miles from Cambridge. Nr
Adenbrook's hospital.
Chalkdownland course.
Pro Ian Bamborough; Founded 1901
Designed by Hawtree
⌁ 10 for members only.
† Welcome WD; booking required
Wed.
⌑ WD £35 for 18 holes (without
member) £17.50(with member) WD
£42 day rate without member & with
member £21. Juniors 1/2 price.
Handicap certs required.
⌁ Welcome WD Tues and Thurs; full
day's golf and catering package; prices
on application.
⦿ Full clubhouse facilities available.
⌁ Duxford Lodge, Duxford; many in
Cambridge.

5A 37 Greetham Valley   ☾
Wood Lane, Greetham, Oakham,
Leics, LE15 7NP
✉ gvgc@rutnet.co.uk
☎ 01780 460004, Fax 460623,
Pro 460666, Sec 460004,
Rest/Bar 460444
1 mile from A1 off the B668,
signposted Greetham.
Parkland course with water.
Pro John Pengelly; Founded 1991
Designed by Ben Stevens Course
Design

⌁ Driving range, Par 3 and golf video
academy; buggies available only £12
per round.
† Welcome.
⌑ 18 holes: WD £28, WE £32; WD
£40, WE £48 All Day Tickets.
⌁ Welcome WD in groups of 12 or
more.
⦿ Full restaurant and bar facilities.
⌁ Barnsdale Lodge; Barnsdale CC;
Hambleton Hall; Stapleford Park.

5A 38 Griffin
Chaul End Road, Caddington Village,
Luton, Beds, LU1 4AX
☎ 01582 415573, Fax 415314
10 mins from M1 Junction 10 or 11 via
A5 or A5056.
Parkland course.
Founded 1982
18 holes, 6240 yards, S.S.S. 70
⌁ Practice green within 2 min of the
1st tee.
† Welcome WD after 9am; by
arrangement at WE.
⌑ WD £13; Fri £15.50; WE £18.
⌁ Welcome WD; packages can be
arranged for full day's catering and
golf; from £29.
⦿ Full catering facilities.

5A 39 Hellidon Lakes Hotel   ☾
& Country Club
Hellidon, Daventry, Northants, NN11 6LN
⬚ www.marston hotels.com
✉ stay@hellidon.demon.co.uk
☎ 01327 262550, Fax 262559,
Pro 262551
15 miles from M1 Junction 16 by A45
and A361 Banbury road; turn right
before village of Charwelton.
Undulating parkland course.
Pro Gary Wills; Founded 1991
Designed by David Snell
18-hole course & 9-hole course holes,
18-hole course 6587; 9-hole course
2791 yards, S.S.S. 18-hole course 72;
9-hole course 35
⌁ Practice range; buggies and clubs
for hire; tuition available with prior
arrangement.
† Welcome; handicap certs. needed
WE.
⌑ WD £15; WE £25.
⌁ Welcome by arrangement;
packages available through the hotel;
conference facilities can be arranged; fly
fishing; tennis; health studio; swimming
pool; 4-lane tenpin bowling alley; smart
golf simulator; terms on application.
⦿ Full bar and restaurant facilities: The
Lakes Restaurant; The Brunswick Bar.
⌁ 4 – star hotel on site.

5A 40 **Hemingford Abbots**   �
Cambridge Road, Hemingford Abbots,
Huntingdon, Cambs, PE28 9HQ
.ᴸ www.astroman8.co.uk
▤ ray/george@
astroman8.freeserve.co.uk
☎ 01480 495000, Fax 496000
Alongside A14 between Huntingdon
and St Ives.
Public parkland course.
Founded 1991
Designed by Advanced Golf Services
9/18 holes, 5414 yards, S.S.S. 68
⌇ Practice range; clubs for hire;
tuition available.
† Welcome.
⌐ WD £12.50; WE £17.
⌒ Small groups welcome by prior
arrangement.
⦿ Full catering facilities; bar and
restaurant.
↳ St Ives; The Bridge.

5A 41 **Heydon Grange Golf &
Country Club**
Fowlmere Road, Heydon, Royston,
Herts, SG8 7NS
.ᴸ www.heydongrange.co.uk
▤ heydon-grange@compuserve.com
☎ 01763 208988, Fax 208926
Leave M11 at Junction 10 on to the
A505 towards Royston; take third left
to Heydon.
Downland/parkland courses with lakes.
Pro Stuart Smith; Founded 1994
Designed by Alan Walker
Combs/Essex: 18 holes, 6336 yards.
S.S.S. 71; Combs/Herts: 18 holes,
6503 yards, S.S.S. 72; Herts/Essex: 18
holes, 6193 yards, S.S.S. 71
⌇ Practice range and practice
ground; buggies and clubs for hire;
tuition available.
† Welcome; book in advance.
⌐ Winter: 18 holes + food WD
£12.50; WE £17.50. Summer:18 holes
WD £12.50; WE £17.50.
⌒ Welcome by prior arrangement;
company days arranged; packages
available; conferences and functions
available; terms on application.
⦿ Lounge, cocktail and wine bar;
restaurants; carvery on Sun; full Indian
menu.

5A 42 **Hinckley**
Leicester Road, Hinckley, Leics, LE10
3DR
.ᴸ hinckleygolfclub.com
▤ proshop@hinckleygolfclub
☎ 01455 615124, Fax 890841,
Pro 615014
From Hinckley Town Centre follow

signs for Earl Shinton.
Lakeland parkland course; (Burbage
Green until 1983).
Pro Richard Jones; Founded 1894/1983
Designed by Southern Golf
18 holes, 6517 yards, S.S.S. 71
† Welcome WD; members of guests
WE.
⌐ WD £25; WE £30.
⌒ Welcome WD with handicap certs;
packages available; terms on application.
⦿ Full catering facilities.
↳ Sketchley Grange.

5A 43 **Humberstone Heights**
Gipsy Lane, Leicester, Leics, LE5 0TB
☎ 0116 27619805, Fax 299569,
Pro 2995570, Rest/Bar 2761905
Off Uppingham Road opposite Towers
Hospital.
Parkland course.
Pro Phillip Highfield; Founded 1978
Designed by Hawtree & Son
18 holes, 6343 yards, S.S.S. 70
⌇ Practice range, 30 bays; buggies
and clubs for hire, tuition available; 9-
hole par 3 course.
† Pay and play.
⌐ Winter WD £7.99; WE £9.99;
Summer WD £8.99 WE £10.99.
⌒ Terms on application.
⦿ Clubhouse facilities.
↳ City-centre hotels in Leicester.

5A 44 **Ivinghoe**
Wellcroft, Ivinghoe, Leighton Buzzard,
Beds, LU7 9EF
☎ 01296 668696, Fax 662755,
Pro 668696, Sec 668696,
Rest/Bar 661186
4 miles from Tring and 6 miles from
Dunstable behind the Kings Hed in
Ivinghoe village.
Meadowland course.
Pro Bill Garrad; Founded 1967
Designed by R Garrad & Sons
9 holes, 4508 yards, S.S.S. 62
⌇ Tuition available
† Welcome after 9am WD; after 8am
WE.
⌐ WD £9; WE £9.
⌒ Welcome WD by arrangement;
includes 36 holes of golf; coffee; light
lunch and evening meal; from £25.
⦿ Full facilities.
↳ Rose & Crown, Tring; Stocks,
Aldbury.

5A 45 **John O'Gaunt**
John Ogaunt Golf And Country Club
1962 Ltd, Biggleswade Road, Sutton,
Sandy, Beds, SG19 2LY

☎ 01767 260360, Fax 262834,
Pro 260094, Sec 260360,
Rest/Bar 261469
Between Biggleswade and Potten on
B1040.
Parkland course.
Pro Lee Scarbrow; Founded 1948
Designed by Hawtree
Carthagena: 18; The John O'Gaunt: 18
holes, Carthagena: 5869; The John
O'Gaunt: 6513 yards, S.S.S.
Carthagena: 69; The John O'Gaunt: 71
⌇ Tuition available through pro;
buggies for hire.
† Welcome with handicap certs and
by prior arrangement.
⌐ WD £45; WE £50.
⌒ Welcome WD by prior arrangement
through administrators office; package
for catering and green fees on
application; terms on application.
⦿ Full clubhouse catering.
↳ Holiday Inn; Stratton House,
Biggleswade; Rose & Crown, Potten.

5A 46 **Kettering**
Headlands, Kettering, Northants, NN15
6XA
☎ 01536 511104, Fax 511104,
Pro 481014, Rest/Bar 512074
S of Kettering, adjacent to A14.
Parkland course.
Pro K Theobald; Founded 1891
Designed by Tom Morris
18 holes holes, 6081 yards, S.S.S. 69
† Welcome WD; with member at WE.
⌐ WD £15-22.
⌒ Welcome Wed and Fri; full catering
and golf packages; from £40.
⦿ Full clubhouse facilities.
↳ Kettering Park; George; Royal .

5A 47 **Kibworth**   ☐
Weir Road, Kibworth, Leicester, Leics,
LE8 0LP
☎ 0116 2796172, Fax 2792301,
Pro 2792283, Sec 2792301,
Rest/Bar 2796172
Course is 10 miles S of Leicester off
A6.
Flat woodland/parkland course.
Pro Bob Larratt; Founded 1904/62
18 holes, 6338 yards, S.S.S. 70
⌇ Practice grass range; trolleys for
hire; tuition available from PGA
qualified professional.
† Welcome WD; WE with a member.
⌐ £22-£30 Wed.
⌒ Welcome by arrangement; golf and
catering available; from £20.
⦿ Full catering facilities.
↳ Angel, Market Harborough.

5A 48 Kilworth Springs
South Kilworth Road, North Kilworth,
Lutterworth, Leics, LE17 6HJ
☎ 01858 575082, Fax 575078,
Pro 575974, Sec 575082,
Rest/Bar 575082
Course is 5 miles from the M1 Junction
20.
Front 9: Inland links; Back 9: parkland
course.
Pro Anders Mankert; Founded 1993
Designed by Ray Baldwin
18 holes, 6718 yards, S.S.S. 72
⚑ 18.
† All Welcome. Practice ground, 2
putting greens, practice bunker, also
available video swing facilities.
Ⓛ WD £18; WE £21.
⚙ Welcome WD and after 12 at WE;
catering and golf packages; bar, spike
bar, private 20-seat boardroom,
restaurant, driving range; prices on
application.
🍴 Full clubhouse bar, spikes bar and
restaurant facilities.
💤 Club can supply list.

5A 49 Kingfisher CC
Buckingham Road, Deanshanger,
Northants, Bucks, MK19 6DG
☎ 01908 562332, Fax 260557,
Sec 560354
Course is on th A422 Buckingham road
seven miles from Milton Keynes
opposite the village of Deanshanger.
Parkland course with lake features.
Pro Brian Mudge; Founded 1994
9 holes, 5066 yards, S.S.S. 65
⚑ Practice range, 10 bays.
† Welcome; pay and play.
Ⓛ WD 9 holes £6.50, 18 holes £10;
WE 9 holes £9, 18 Holes £13.
⚙ Welcome by prior arrangement;
corporate days organised; fishing;
model steam railway; function room;
terms on application.
🍴 Full facilities; 2 restaurants and 2
bars.
💤 Shires.

5A 50 Kingstand
Beggars Lane, Leicester Forest East,
Leicester, Leics, LE3 3NQ
☎ 0116 2387908, Fax 2388087
Off main A47 Hinkley Road; 5 mins
from M1 Junction 21.
Parkland course.
Pro Simon Sherrit; Founded 1991
Designed by S.Chenia
9 holes, 5380 yards, S.S.S. 66
⚑ Practice range, 16 bays floodlit.
† Welcome.
Ⓛ WD £9; WE £10.

⚙ Welcome by prior arrangement
with the professional; packages and
discounts available; gymnasium.
🍴 Indian restaurant on site.
💤 Red Cow.

5A 51 Kingsthorpe ♛
Kingsley Road, Northampton,
Northants, NN2 7BU
✉ kingsthorpe.gc@lineone.net
☎ 01604 719602, Fax 719602,
Pro 719602, Sec 710610,
Rest/Bar 711173
Off A508 2 miles N of Northampton
town centre.
Parkland course.
Pro Paul Armstrong; Founded 1908
Designed by Charles Alison
18 holes, 5918 yards, S.S.S. 69
† Welcome with handicap certs.
Ⓛ WD £25; WE £25, with member.
⚙ Welcome; catering facilities and
golf packages available; from £20.
🍴 Clubhouse catering facilities
available.
💤 Westone Hotel; Broom Hill.

5A 52 Kingsway
Cambridge Road, Melbourn, Royston,
Herts, SG8 6EY
☎ 01763 262727, Fax 263298,
Pro 262727
On A10 N of Royston.
Landscape farmland.
Pro Steve Brown; Founded 1991
9 holes, 4910 yards, S.S.S. 64
⚑ Practice range, 36 bays floodlit;
crazy golf.
† Welcome.
Ⓛ WD £9 (18 holes); WE £12 (18
holes).
⚙ Welcome by prior arrangement;
corporate days arranged; 9-hole pitch
and putt; terms on application.
🍴 Bar and restaurant facilities.
💤 Sheene Mill Hotel.

5A 53 Kirby Muxloe
Station Road, Kirby Muxloe, Leicester,
LE9 9EN
☎ 0116 2393457, Fax 2393457,
Pro 2392813, Rest/Bar 2396577
From M1 Junction 21A follow signs to
Kirby Muxloe.
Parkland course.
Pro Bruce Whipham; Founded 1893
18 holes, 6279 yards, S.S.S. 70
† Welcome Mon, Wed and Fri,
handicap cert required.
Ⓛ £25.
⚙ Welcome with handicap certs only;
all day and individual round packages

available; from £40.
🍴 Full clubhouse catering facilities.
💤 Travel Inn; Red Cow.

5A 54 Lakeside Lodge
Fen Road, Pidley, Huntingdon, Cambs,
PE28 3DD
🖳 www.lakeside-lodge.co.uk
✉ info@lakeside-lodge.co.uk
☎ 01487 740540, Fax 740852,
Pro 741541, Rest/Bar 740968
From A14 Cambridge-St Ives road take
B1040 to Pidley.
Open parkland with 8 lakes and 15,000
trees.
Pro Scott Waterman; Founded 1991
Designed by Alister Headley
The Lodge: 18; Manor: 9; Church: 6
holes, Lodge: 6865; Manor: 2601;
Church: 3290 yards, S.S.S. The
Lodge: 73; Manor: 33
⚑ Floodlit covered driving range,
buggies for hire, 9-hole pitch and putt
course, tuition available.
† Welcome.
Ⓛ The Lodge course: WD £12, WE
£19; The Manor course: WD £6, WE
£8. The Church course: for 12 holes
WD £6, WE £8.
⚙ Welcome any time; golf, catering
and other corporate activities can be
arranged (ten pin bowling); terms on
application.
🍴 Full catering facilities.
💤 On-site accommodation, 5 en suite
twin rooms.

5A 55 Leicestershire
Evington Lane, Leicester, Leics, LE5 6DJ
✉ lecistergolfclub@hotmail.com
☎ 0116 2738825, Fax 2731900,
Pro 2736730, Rest/Bar 2731307
2 miles east of Leicester.
Parkland course; no par 5s.
Pro Darren Jones; Founded 1890
Designed by James Braid
18 holes, 6326 yards, S.S.S. 70
† Welcome with handicap certs and
prior arrangement.
Ⓛ WD £24; WE £30.
⚙ Welcome with handicap certs;
packages can be arranged; terms
available on application.
🍴 Full clubhouse facilities.
💤 Gables Hotel.

5A 56 Leighton Buzzard
Plantation Road, Leighton Buzzard,
Beds, LU7 3JF
☎ 01525 244800, Fax 244801,
Pro 244815, Rest/Bar 244805, 244810
1 mile N of Leighton Buzzard.

Parkland/woodland course.
Pro Lee Scarbrow; Founded 1925
18 holes, 6101 yards, S.S.S. 70
♦ Welcome WD with handicap certs;
WE with member.
⌊ WD £24.
⌃ Welcome WD except Tues (ladies
day); day's golf and catering from
morning coffee to evening meals; from
£39 and member from £55.
◉ Full clubhouse catering facilities.
⌁ Cock Horse Hotel.

5A 57 Lingdale
Joe Moores Lane, Woodhouse Eaves,
Loughborough, Leics, LE12 8TF
☎ 01509 890703, Pro 890684,
Sec 890703, Rest/Bar 890035
2 miles off M1 Junction 22 towards
Woodhouse Eaves.
Parkland course.
Pro P Sellears; Founded 1967
Designed by DW Tucker & G Austin
18 holes, 6545 yards, S.S.S. 71
⌊ Practice range, practice ground;
tuition available.
♦ Welcome.
⌊ WD £22; WE £32.
⌃ Welcome by prior arrangement
with secretary; minimum 12; day's golf
and catering packages available;
prices on application.
◉ Full clubhouse facilities.

5A 58 Links Golf Course
The Links, Cambridge Road,
Newmarket, Suffolk, CB8 0TG
☎ 01638 663000, Fax 661476,
Pro 662395, Rest/Bar 662708
On A1304 1 mile S of Newmarket
midway between racecourse entrances.
Parkland course.
Pro John Sharkey; Founded 1902
Designed by Col. Hotchkin
18 holes, 6582 yards, S.S.S. 71
♦ Welcome with handicap certs; not
before 11.30am Sun.
⌊ WD £32; WE £36. Special winter
rates WD £20; 18 holes £24W WD's
36 holes £32 WD. WE £36.
⌃ Welcome by prior arrangement;
booking fee of £35; catering packages;
maximum 60; prices on application.
◉ Full restaurant and bar.
⌁ Bedford Lodge.

5A 59 Longcliffe
Snells Nook Lane, Nanpantan,
Loughborough, Leicestershirse, LE11
3YA
✉ longcliffegolf@btconnect.com
☎ 01509 239129, Fax 231286,

Pro 231450, Sec 239129,
Rest/Bar 216321
1 mile from M1 Junction 23 off A512
towards Loughborough.
Heathland course.
Pro David Mee; Founded 1904
18 holes, 6611 yards, S.S.S. 72
♦ Welcome WD 9am-4.30pm except
Tues; WE with a member.
⌊ WD £29 per round, WD £39 per
day No weekend play.
⌃ Welcome WD except Tues (ladies
day); packages available for groups of
12 or more; from £29 and £39 for day.
◉ Bar, restaurant and snacks.
⌁ Quality Hotel.

5A 60 Lutterworth
Rugby Road, Lutterworth, Leics, LE17
4HN
🖳 www.lutterworthgc.co.uk
☎ 01455 552532, Fax 553586,
Pro 557199, Sec 552532,
Rest/Bar 557141
On A426 0.5 miles from M1 Junction 20.
Parkland course.
Pro Roland Tisdall; Founded 1904
Designed by D Snell
18 holes, 6226 yards, S.S.S. 70
⌊ Practice range.
♦ Welcome WD; guests of members
only at WE.
⌊ 18 holes £22 all week.
⌃ Welcome Mon,Wed and Thurs all
day and Tues pm and Fri am; indoor
academy; terms on application.
◉ Clubhouse facilities.
⌁ The Denby Arms; The Greyhound,
both Lutterworth.

5A 61 March
Froggs Abbey, Grange Road, March,
Cambs, PE15 0YH
☎ 01354 652364, Fax 652364,
Pro 657255, Sec 652364,
Rest/Bar 652364
Course is on the A141 West of the
March bypass.
Parkland course.
Pro Stuart Brown; Founded 1920
9 holes, 6204 yards, S.S.S. 70
♦ Welcome WD; guests of members
only at weekends.
⌊ WD £16.50, £8.50 with a member.
⌃ Welcome WD by prior booking.
◉ Bar facilities; meals by prior
booking.
⌁ Griffin,The Oliver Cromwell.

5A 62 Market Harborough
Harborough Road, Great Oxendon,
Market Harborough, Leics, LE16 8NB

☎ 01858 46384, Fax 432906
Course is one mile S of Market
Harborough on the A508 towards
Northampton.
Parkland course.
Pro F Baxter; Founded 1898
Updated by H Swan
18 holes, 6022 yards, S.S.S. 69
♦ Welcome WD; WE guests of
members only.
⌊ WD £20.
⌃ Welcome WD by arrangement;
inclusive packages available; from £35.
◉ Clubhouse facilities.
⌁ Three Swans, Market Harborough;
George, Oxendon.

5A 63 Melton Mowbray ♛
Waltham Road, Thorpe Arnold, Melton
Mowbray, Leics, LE14 4SD
🖳 www.mmgc.org
☎ 01664 562118, Pro 569629,
Sec 562118, Rest/Bar 562118
2 miles NE of Melton Mowbray on A607.
Undulating parkland course.
Pro James Hetherington; Founded 1925
18 holes, 6222 yards, S.S.S. 70
♦ Welcome before 3pm.
⌊ WD £20; WE and BH £23.
⌃ Welcome WD by prior
arrangement; golf and lunch, dinner
packages can be organised; from £21.
◉ Full catering, bar and dining
facilities.
⌁ Sysonsby Knoll; George;
Harborough; Stapleford Park.

5A 64 Mentmore ♛
Mentmore, Leighton Buzzard, Beds,
LU7 0UA
🖳 www.clubhaus.co.uk
☎ 01296 662020, Fax 662592,
Pro 660500, Sec 662020,
Rest/Bar 662020
1 mile from Cheddington, E of A41 to
Aylesbury.
Parkland course.
Pro Rob Davies; Founded 1992
Designed by Bob Sandow
⌊ 12.
♦ Welcome WD; WE booking
allowed 7 days in advance.
⌊ Call to confirm.
⌃ Welcome WD; max 120; facilities;
also pool, sauna, 2 tennis courts, sports
bar, fitness room, Jacuzzi; £55-£75.
◉ Full bar, restaurant facilities.
⌁ Pendley Manor; Rose and Crown,
both Tring.

5A 65 Mount Pleasant ℭ
Station Road, Lower Stondon, Henlow,
Beds, SG16 6JL
🖳 www.mountpleasantgolfclub.co.uk
☎ 01462 850999, Fax 850257,
Pro 850999, Sec 850999,
Rest/Bar 850999
0.75 miles W of Stondon-Henlow
Camp roundabout off A600 Hitchin to
Bedford road; 4 miles N of Hitchin.
Undulating meadowland course.
Pro Mike Roberts; Founded 1992
Designed by Derek Young
9 holes,18 tees, 6003 yards,
S.S.S. 68
🏌 Practice facilities available,
buggies, shoes and clubs for hire; PGA
tuition available.
🏌 Welcome at all times; booking
advisable; can be made up to 2 days in
advance.
⌊ WD 9 holes £7.50, 18 holes £13;
WE 9 holes £10, 18 holes £17; OAPs:
discounts of £1.50 for 9 holes; Juniors:
discounts of £2.
⌀ Welcome WD; packages available;
24 maximum for full catering, 36 for
buffet; terms on application.
🍽 Clubhouse bar facilities.
🛌 Sun, Hitchin.

**5A 66 Mowsbury Golf and
Squash Complex**
Cleat Hill, Kimbolton Road,
Ravensden, Bedford, MK41 8DQ
☎ 01234 771493, Fax 267040,
Pro 216374, Sec 771041,
Rest/Bar 771493
On B660 at northern limit of city
boundary.
Parkland course.
Pro M Summers; Founded 1975
Designed by Hawtree
18 holes, 6514 yards, S.S.S. 71;72 is
par for the course
🏌 14.
🏌 Welcome.
⌊ wd £10; WE £13.50.
⌀ Welcome anytime; golf and
catering packages; driving range,
squash court; terms on application.
🍽 Full facilities.
🛌 in town centre.

5A 67 Northampton
Harlestone, Northampton, Northants,
NN7 4EF
🖳 www.northamptongolfclub.
co.uk
📧 golf@
northamprongolfclub.co.uk
☎ 01604 845155, Fax 820262,
Pro 845167, Sec 845155,

Rest/Bar 845102/821905
On A428 Rugby road 4 miles from
Northampton.
Parkland course.
Pro Kevin Dickins; Founded 1893
Designed by Donald Steel
18 holes, 6615 yards, S.S.S. 72
🏌 Welcome WD; members and
member's guests at WE.
⌊ WD £35.
⌀ Welcome by prior arrangement
WD except Wed; packages for golf and
catering available; snooker;
banqueting; terms on application.
🍽 Full facilities.
🛌 Northampton Moat House; Heyford
Manor.

**5A 68 Northamptonshire
County**
Golf Lane, Church Brampton,
Northampton, NN6 8AZ
📧 office@ncgc.fsworld.co.uk
☎ 01604 843025, Fax 843463,
Pro 842226, Sec 843025,
Rest/Bar 842170
5 miles NW of Northampton in village
of Church Brampton.
Heathland course with woods, gorse
and streams.
Pro Tim Rouse; Founded 1909
Designed by HS Colt
18 holes, 6505 yards, S.S.S. 72
🏌 Welcome by arrangement, with
handicap certs.
⌊ WD £45; WE £45.
⌀ Large groups on Wed; smaller
groups Thurs; terms on application.
🍽 Full catering facilities.
🛌 Broomhill; Limetrees.

5A 69 Oadby
Leicester Road, Oadby, Leicester,
Leics, LE2 4AB
☎ 0116 2709052, Sec 2703828,
Rest/Bar 2700215
On A6 from Leicester inside Leicester
racecourse.
Meadowland municipal course; 9 holes
inside adjacent Leicester racecourse.
Pro Andrew Wells; Founded 1975
18 holes, 6311 yards, S.S.S. 72
🏌 2 nets.
🏌 Everybody welcome.
⌊ Prices on application.
⌀ Welcome by prior application to the
professional; welcome WD and after 12
noon WE; terms on application.
🍽 Bar meals and snacks; meals on
request.
🛌 The Chase Hotel: adjacent hotel
and leisure complex.

5A 70 Old Nene Golf & ℭ
Country Club
Muchwood Lane, Ramsey, Huntingdon,
Cambs, PE26 2XQ
☎ 01487 813519, Pro 710122,
Sec 813519, Rest/Bar 815622
1 mile N of Ramsey.
Parkland course with water hazards.
Pro Ian Gallaway; Founded 1992
Designed by Richard Edrich
9 holes, 5675 yards, S.S.S. 68
🏌 Practice range, floodlit; 2 piece
balls; tuition available.
🏌 Pay and play.
⌊ WD 9 holes £7, 18 holes £11; WE
9 holes £9, 18 holes £16.
⌀ Welcome; reductions for 10 or
more players WD; packages available;
terms available on application.
🍽 Bar and bar snacks available.
🛌 Several in area.

5A 71 Orton Meadows
Ham Lane, Orton Waterville,
Peterborough, Cambs, PE2 5UU
🖳 www.ortonmeadowscourse.co.uk
☎ 01733 237478
On the A605 Peterborough-Oundle
road 2 miles W of Peterborough.
Parkland course.
Pro Jason Mitchell; Founded 1987
Designed by Dennis & Roger Fitton
18 holes, 5613 yards, S.S.S. 68
🏌 Welcome; advance bookings
available.
⌊ WD £11.20; WE £14.75.
⌀ Prior bookings for societies.
🍽 In adjoining steakhouse, The
Granary.
🛌 Travelodge.

5A 72 Oundle ℭ
Benefield Road, Oundle,
Peterborough, Cambs, PE8 4EZ
☎ 01832 273267, Fax 273267,
Pro 272273, Rest/Bar 274882
On A427 Oundle-Corby road, 1.5 miles
from Oundle.
Parkland course.
Pro Richard Keys; Founded 1893
18 holes, 6235 yards, S.S.S. 70
🏌 Practice range, 2 practice areas;
trolleys for hire; contact Pro about tuition.
🏌 Welcome WD, after 10.30am WE.
⌊ WD £25.50; WE £35.50.
⌀ Welcome WD except Tues; golf and
catering packages available; from £35.
🍽 Full clubhouse facilities.
🛌 Talbot, Oundle; Travel Lodge,
Thrapston.

Park Hill Golf Club

Park Hill Golf Club is one of Leicestershire's finest 18 hole Championship length golf courses. Nestled in the heart of the Leicestershire countryside, Park Hill combines the land's natural contours and water features with precisely positioned bunkers to create a challenging course with excellent playing conditions all year round.

PARK HILL
Seagrave

• Championship Length Course 7219 yards Par 73
• Society and corporate golf packages available
• Restaurant serving home cooked food

• Extensive practice facilities
• Golf cart and trolley hire available
• Conference and training facilities

Located just off the A46 north of Leicester, 10 minutes from J21a of the M1.

Park Hill Golf & Leisure Limited, Park Hill, Seagrave, Leicestershire LE12 7NG   Tel: **01509 815454**   Fax: **01509 816062**
E-mail: **mail@parkhillgolf.co.uk**   Website: **www.parkhillgolf.co.uk**

5A 73 Overstone Park ☺
Billing Lane, Overstone, Northampton, Northants, NN6 0AP
💻 www.overstonepark.co.uk
📧 enquiries@overstonepark
☎ 01604 647666, Fax 642635,
Pro 647666, Sec 647666,
Rest/Bar 647666
Take A45 Northampton road to Billing Lane.
Parkland course in walled Victorian estate.
Pro Brian Mudge; Founded 1993
Designed by Donald Steel
18 holes, 6602 yards, S.S.S. 72
⏐ Practice range and practice area.
♦ Welcome WD from 11am; WE only after 2pm.
⌊ Green fees available on application.
⟳ Welcome by prior arrangement; packages; health and leisure club.
🍽 Bar and Brasserie.
⌁ Hotel on site; 27 en suite bedrooms.

5A 74 Park Hill ☺
Park Hill Lane, Seagrave, Loughborough, Leics, LE12 7NG
💻 www.parkhillgolf.co.uk
☎ 01509 815454, Fax 816062,
Pro 815775, Sec 815 454,
Rest/Bar 815885
Off A46 from Leicester; turn left at Seagrave.
Parkland course; five par 5's more than 500 yards.
Pro David Mee; Founded 1995
18 holes, 7219 yards, S.S.S. 74
♦ Welcome.
⌊ WD £20; WE and BH £24.
⟳ Welcome; terms on application.
🍽 Clubhouse catering facilities.
⌁ Rothley Court; Willoughby.

5A 75 Pavenham Park ☺
High Street, Pavenham, Bedford, Beds, MK43 7PE
☎ 01234 822202, Fax 826602
Course is on the A6 six miles N of

Bedford.
Parkland course.
Pro Zac Thompson; Founded 1994
Designed by Derek Young/Z Thompson
18 holes, 6353 yards, S.S.S. 71
⏐ Practice range, practice area; buggies and clubs for hire.
♦ Welcome WD; guests of members only at WE.
⌊ WD £20.
⟳ Welcome WD; full catering and golf packages; from £16.
🍽 Clubhouse facilities.

5A 76 Peterborough Milton
Milton Ferry, Peterborough, Cambridgeshire, PE6 7AG
💻 www.peterboroughmiltongolfclub. co.uk
☎ 01733 380489, Fax 380489,
Pro 380793, Sec 380489,
Rest/Bar 380204
Course is two miles W of Peterborough on the A47.
Parkland course.
Pro Mike Gallagher; Founded 1938
Designed by James Braid
18 holes, 6463 yards, S.S.S. 72
⏐ Practice range, large practice area.
♦ Welcome with handicap certs.
⌊ WD £30; WE £30.
⟳ Welcome Tues-Fri; full catering facilities and golf packages; prices on application.
🍽 Full facilities.
⌁ Haycock, Wansford; Swallow; Butterfly, both Peterborough.

5A 77 RAF Cottesmore
Royal Air Force, Cottesmore, Oakham, Leics, LE15 7BL
☎ 01572 812241 EX 6706
Course is seven miles N of Oakham off the B668.
Parkland course.
Founded 1980
9 holes, 5622 yards, S.S.S. 67

♦ With members only.
⌊ Terms on application.

5A 78 RAF Henlow
R A F S E E, Raf Henlow, Henlow, Beds, SG16 6DN
☎ 01462 851515 EX 7083
3 miles SE of Shefford on A505, follow signs to RAF Henlow.
Meadowland course.
Founded 1985
9 holes, 5618 yards, S.S.S. 67
♦ Only with a member.
⌊ Terms on application.
⟳ Can be arranged through Sec.
🍽 Light refreshments available.
⌁ Bird in Hand.

5A 79 RAF North Luffenham
St George's Barracks, North Luffenham, Oakham, Leics, LE15 8RL
☎ 01780 720041 ext 7523
Follow signposts for MOD North Luffenham from A606, station is close to Rutland Water.
Meadowland course.
Founded 1975
12 holes 18 Tees holes, 5910 yards, S.S.S. 69
⏐ Open driving range.
♦ With member.
⌊ Terms on application.
⟳ Can be arranged through Sec.
🍽 Bar and restaurant facilities.
⌁ George; Crown.

5A 80 Ramsey
Abbey Terrace, Ramsey, Huntingdon, Cambs, PE26 1DD
📧 ramseyclub@ramsey.uk.com
☎ 01487 812600, Fax 815746, Pro 813022, Sec 812600, Rest/Bar 813573
Off B660 Ramsey road from the A1 between Huntingdon and Peterborough
Parkland course.
Pro Stuart Scott; Founded 1964

Designed by J Hamilton Stutt
18 holes, 6163 yards, S.S.S. 70
⚑ Practice range, 4 large practice
areas; PGA tuition available.
☂ Welcome WD; WE as member's
guest.
ℓ WD £25.
⌁ Welcome WD only; minimum 20;
18 holes of golf and catering packages
available; from £25; large well stocked
pro shop, offering society prizes.
Bowling green.
🍽 Clubhouse facilities.
⌐ George, Huntingdon; Bell, Stilton;
Dolphin, St Ives.

5A 81 **Rothley Park** ♱
Westfield Lane, Rothley, Leicester,
Leics, LE7 7LH
⌖ www.rothleypark.com
✉ secretary@rothleypark.co.uk
☎ 0116 2302809, Fax 2302809,
Pro 2303023, Sec 2302809,
Rest/Bar 2302019
Off A6 N of Leicester
Parkland course
Pro Andrew Collins; Founded 1912
Designed by Hawtree
18 holes, 6476 yards, S.S.S. 71
⚑ Practice ground, tuition available
☂ Welcome WD except Tues;
handicap certs required
ℓ WD £25
⌁ Welcome Mon, Wed, Thurs, Fri;
10 % discount for more than 40
players; full catering available; terms
on application.
🍽 Full clubhouse facilities.
⌐ Rothley Court; Quorn Country
Hotel; Quorn Grange.

5A 82 **Rushcliffe**
Stocking Lane, East Leake,
Loughborough, Leics, LE12 5RL
✉ rushcliffegc@netscapeonline.co.uk
☎ 01509 852959, Fax 852688, Pro
852701, Sec 852959, Rest/Bar 852209
From M1 Junction 24 take A453
towards West Bridgford; turn at
Gotham, East Leake signs
Parkland course
Pro Chris Hall; Founded 1910
18 holes, 6013 yards, S.S.S. 69
⚑ 4
☂ Welcome
ℓ WD £25 (per round) £30 per day;
WE £30
⌁ Welcome WD; packages available;
prices available on application; enquire
with Sec. for details.
🍽 Clubhouse facilities.

5A 83 **Rushden**
Kimbolton Road, Chelveston,
Wellingborough, Northants, NN9 6AN
☎ 01933 312581, Sec 418511,
Rest/Bar 312581
Course is on the A45 two miles E of
Higham Ferrers.
Undulating meadowland course.
Founded 1919
10 holes, 6350 yards, S.S.S. 70
☂ Welcome WD except Wed pm; WE
with member.
ℓ WD £18, £12 with a member.
⌁ Welcome WD, except Wed pm, by
prior arrangement.
🍽 Full facilities except Mon.

5A 84 **St Ives**
Westwood Road, St Ives, Cambs,
PE27 6RS
☎ 01480 468392, Fax 468392,
Pro 466067, Rest/Bar 464459
Course is on the B1040 off the A45 in
St Ives.
Parkland course.
Pro Darren Glasby; Founded 1923
9 holes, 6100 yards, S.S.S. 69
⚑ Practice ground; tuition available.
☂ Welcome WD; with member WE.
ℓ WD £20; WE £20.
⌁ Welcome Wed and Fri by prior
arrangement; packages available; from
£20.
🍽 Full clubhouse facilities.
⌐ Slepe Hall.

5A 85 **St Neots** ♱
Crosshall Road, Eaton Ford, St Neots,
Cambs, PE19 7GE
⌖ www.stneots.golfclub.co.uk
✉ office@stnoets.golfclub.co.uk
☎ 01480 472363, Fax 472363, Pro
476513, Sec 472363, Rest/Bar 474311
On B1048 off the A1.
Parkland course with water hazards.
Pro Graham Bithrey; Founded 1890
Designed by Harry Vardon
18 holes, 6026 yards, S.S.S. 69
⚑ Practice area available.
☂ Welcome WD; WE with member;
handicap certs preferred.
ℓ WD £25.
⌁ Welcome Tues, Wed, Thurs by
prior arrangement; packages available;
snooker; function room; terms on
application.
🍽 Full clubhouse facilities.
⌐ Eaton Oak; Kings Head.

5A 86 **Scraptoft** ♱
Beeby Road, Scraptoft, Leicester,
Leics, LE7 9SJ

☎ 0116 2418863, Fax 2418863,
Pro 2419138, Sec 2419000,
Rest/Bar 2419000
Turn off A47 main Peterborough-
Leicester road at Scraptoft at Thurnby.
Meadowland course.
Pro Simon Wood; Founded 1928
18 holes, 6151 yards, S.S.S. 70
☂ Welcome; dress code applies after
7pm.
ℓ WD £20; we £25.
⌁ Welcome WD by prior arrangement;
packages available; terms on application.
🍽 Full facilities.
⌐ White House.

5A 87 **Shelthorpe**
Poplar Road, Loughborough
☎ 01509 267766
From Leicester on A6 turn left at first
traffic lights, over island and then 2nd
left.
Municipal parkland course.
18 holes holes, 2054 yards yards,
S.S.S. 54
☂ Welcome.
ℓ WD £3.30; WE £3.30.

5A 88 **Six Hills**
Six Hills Road, Six Hills, Melton
Mowbray, Leics, LE14 3PR
☎ 01509 881225, Rest/Bar 889347
From M1 take A46 N; course 0.5 mile
from A46.
Parkland course.
Pro Tony Westward; Founded 1986
18 holes, 5758 yards, S.S.S. 69
⚑ 12 bays.
☂ Welcome; pay and play.
ℓ WD £10; WE £13.
⌁ Welcome but no advance booking
system.
🍽 Bar and restaurant.
⌐ Ragdale Hall.

5A 89 **South Bedfordshire**
Warden Hill Road, Luton, Beds, LU2
7AE
☎ 01582 591500, Fax 495381,
Pro 591209, Rest/Bar 596486
3 miles N of Luton on A6, signposted
into Warden Hill Road.
Undulating course with trees and
hawthorn hedges.
Pro Eddie Cogle; Founded 1892
18 holes, 6389yards, S.S.S. 71; 9
holes, 4914 yards, par 64
⚑ Practice area; tuition available.
☂ Welcome WD; WE by prior
arrangement.
ℓ Prices on application.
⌁ Welcome mainly Wed and Thurs by

prior arrangement; packages available; snooker; prices on application.
|◉| Restaurant and bar facilities available.
↩ Chiltern; Strathmore.

5A 90 Staverton Park   ☎
Daventry Road, Staverton, Daventry, Northants, NN11 6JT
↪ www.initialstyle.co.uk
☎ 01327 302000, Fax 311428,
Pro 705506, Sec 302000,
Rest/Bar 302000
Course is on the A425 Daventry to Leamington road; one mile S of Daventry.
Undulating meadowland course.
Pro Richard Mudge; Founded 1978
Designed by Comm. John Harris
18 holes, 6100 yards, S.S.S. 73
⌁ 11 bays floodlit; practice range; tuition available; buggy hire £20; club hire individually £1, set £7.50.
† Welcome.
⌁ WD £30; WE £35 (Friday inclusive)
↻ Welcome WD by prior arrangement; snooker; solarium; sauna; banqueting suites; terms on application.
|◉| Full facilities at all times.
↩ Staverton Park offers golfing weekends.

5A 91 Stockwood Park Golf Centre
London Road, Luton, Beds, LU1 4LX
☎ 01582 413704, Fax 481001,
Rest/Bar 731421
Leave the M1 at Junction 10; go 10 A, head towards the town centre and then turn left at the first traffic lights.
Parkland course.
Pro Glyn McCarthy; Founded 1973
Designed by Charles Lawrie
18 holes, 6077 yards, S.S.S. 69
⌁ 24 bays floodlit; 9-hole pitch & putt; clubs and trolleys.
† Welcome.

⌁ WD £9.10; WE £12.25
↻ Welcome Mon, Tues and Thurs by prior arrangement with Pro; packages for catering and golf by arrangement; 9-hole pitch and putt; terms on application.
|◉| Full facilities.
↩ Strathmore; The Hertfordshire Moathouse (full leisure facilities).

5A 92 Stoke Albany
Ashley Road, Stoke Albany, Market Harborough, Leics, LE16 8PL
☎ 01858 535208, Fax 535505
Course is off the A427 Market Harborough-Corby road just through Stoke Albany.
Parkland course.
Pro Adrian Clifford; Founded 1995
⌁ Practice ground and bunker, chipping green and putting green; trolleys for hire.
† Welcome.
⌁ WD £13; WE £17.
↻ Welcome by prior arrangement; packages for golf and catering available; terms on application.
|◉| Fairways Bar and Restaurant; spike bar.
↩ Three Swans, Market, Harborough; Rockingham Forest, Corby.

5A 93 Thorney Golf Centre
English Drove, Thorney, Peterborough, Cambs, PE6 0TJ
☎ 01733 270570, Fax 270842
On A47 E of Peterborough
Parkland course
Pro Mark Templeman; Founded 1991/1995
Designed by A Dow
The Lakes:18 holes, The Fen: 18 holes; The Lakes: 6402 yards; The Fen: 6104 yards; S.S.S. lakes 71; Fen 69; plus a 9-hole par 3 course
⌁ 12 bays floodlit; lessons available; buggies, trolleys and clubs for hire.
† Welcome.

⌁ The Lakes Course: WD £12, WE £19; The Fens Course: WD £7.50, WE £9.50; Par 3 course: £2.95 all week.
↻ Welcome WD; anytime on Fen; packages available; terms on application.
|◉| Bar and restaurant.

5A 94 Thorpe Wood
Thorpe Wood Golf Course, Thorpe Wood, Peterborough, Cambs, PE3 6SE
↪ www.thorpewoodgolfcourse.co.uk
✉ enquiries@ thorpewoodgolfcourse.co.uk
☎ 01733 267701, Fax 332774,
Rest/Bar 267601
On A47 to Leicester 2 miles W of Peterborough.
Parkland course.
Pro Roger Fitton/Gary Casey; Founded 1975
Designed by Peter Alliss and Dave Thomas
18 holes, 7086 yards, S.S.S. 74
⌁ Tuition available.
† Welcome.
⌁ WD £11.20; WE £14.75.
↻ Welcome by arrangement up to a year in advance.
|◉| The Woodman Public House (next door).
↩ Moat House.

5A 95 Tilsworth
Dunstable Road, Tilsworth, Leighton Buzzard, Beds, LU7 9PU
☎ 01525 210721, Fax 210465,
Pro 210722, Rest/Bar 210722
2 miles N of Dunstable on A5; take Tilsworth/Stanbridge turning.
Parkland course.
Pro Nick Webb; Founded 1977
18 holes, 5306 yards, S.S.S. 69
⌁ Practice range, open all week; tuition available; buggy and club hire.
† Welcome except before 10am Sun
⌁ Prices on application.
↻ Welcome WD; terms on application

🍽 Full facilities.
🛏 Travel Lodge.

5A 96 **Ullesthorpe Court**
Frolesworth Road, Ullesthorpe,
Lutterworth, Leics, LE17 5BZ
🖳 www.ullesthorpecourt.co.uk
📧 bookings@ullesthorpecourt.co.uk
☎ 01455 209023, Fax 202537,
Pro 209150
Close to the M1 and M69, just off the
A5.
Parkland course.
Pro David Bowring; Founded 1976
18 holes, 6650 yards, S.S.S. 72
† Welcome WD; with members at WE.
Ⅰ WD £20.
⟳ Golf day packages and overnight
accommodation can be organised
through the hotel; full clubhouse and
hotel facilities for both corporate and
society golf days; from £25..
🍽 Full hotel and clubhouse facilities
available.
🛏 On-site hotel Ullesthorpe Court.

5A 97 **Waterbeach Barracks**
39 Engineer Regiment, Waterbeach
Barracks, Waterbeach, Cambridge,
Cambs, CB5 9PA
☎ 01223 860681, Fax 440007,
Rest/Bar 440007
Fenland course.
Founded 1972
9 holes, 6237 yards, S.S.S. 70
† HM Forces welcome; civilians must
be introduced by and play with a member.
Ⅰ Terms on application.
🍽 Limited bar available.

5A 98 **Wellingborough**
The Slips, Great Harrowden,
Wellingborough, Northants, NN9 5AD
☎ 01933 677234, Fax 679379, Pro
678752, Sec 677234, Rest/Bar 402612
Course is two miles N of
Wellingborough on the A509.
Undulating parkland course.
Pro David Clifford; Founded 1893/1975
Designed by Hawtree & Sons
18 holes, 6617 yards, S.S.S. 72
† Welcome WD.
Ⅰ WD £40 per round.
⟳ Welcome WD except Tues; full
day's golf, bar, restaurant, snooker;
tuition available.
🍽 Full clubhouse facilities available.
🛏 Foxford Tudor Gate, Finedon;
Kettering Park; Oak House and Hind,
both Wellingborough.

5A 99 **Western Park**
Scudamore Road, Leicester, Leics,
LE3 1UQ
☎ 0116 2995566, Fax 2995568,
Rest/Bar 875211
Off A47 2 miles W of city centre.
Parkland course.
Pro David Butler; Founded 1920
Designed by FW Hawtree
18 holes, 6518 yards, S.S.S. 70
† Welcome; must book at WE.
Ⅰ Winter: WD £8.99, WE £11.50;
Summer: WD £9.99, WE £12.50;
discount rate for juniors and OAPs.
⟳ Welcome by prior arrangement;
catering and golf packages available;
terms on application.
🍽 Full clubhouse facilities.
🛏 Hilton Hotel.

5A 100 **Whaddon Golf Centre**
Church Street, Whaddon, Royston,
Herts, SG8 5RX
☎ 01223 207325, Fax 207325, Pro
207325, Sec 207325, Rest/Bar 207325
4 miles N of Royston off A1198
Parkland course.
Pro G Huggett; Founded 1990
Designed by Richard Green
9 holes, 905 yards, S.S.S. par 3
Ⅰ 14.
† Public pay and play.
Ⅰ WD £3; WE £3.50.
⟳ Welcome; terms on application.
🍽 Bar snacks.

5A 101 **Whetstone**
Cambridge Road, Cosby, Leicester,
LE9 5SH
☎ 0116 2861424, Fax 2861424,
Pro 2861424, Sec 2861424,
Rest/Bar 2861424
4 miles from M1 Junction 21 SE of
Leicester; take A46 to Narborough then
signposts for Whetstone.
Wooded parkland course with water
features.
Pro David Raitt; Founded 1963
Designed by Nick Leatherland
18 holes, 5795 yards, S.S.S. 68
Ⅰ 20 bays, Practice range.
† Welcome.
Ⅰ WD £15; WE £16.
⟳ Welcome by arrangement.
🍽 Full bar and catering facilities.
🛏 Time Out, Blaby.

5A 102 **Whittlebury Park Golf and Country Club**
Kennels Road, Whittlebury, Towcester,
Northants, NN12 8XW

☎ 01327 858092, Fax 858009, Pro
858588, Sec 858092, Rest/Bar 858092
Course is on the A413 15 mins from the
M1 Junction 15A, three miles S of
Towcester.
Parkland/lakeland course.
Pro Tom Jones; Founded 1992
Designed by Cameron Sinclair
36 holes, 6662 yards, S.S.S. 72
Ⅰ 16.
† Welcome.
Ⅰ Winter: Mon £10, Tues-Fri am £20,
WE am £30; 7 days a week pm £10;
Summer rates: prices on application.
⟳ Welcome at all times by prior
arrangement; 4 x 9 loops (1905, Royal
Whittlewood, Grand Prix, Wedgewood);
indoor course; clay pigeon shooting;
archery; cricket ground; croquet lawn;
corporate hospitality; function suites;
terms on application.
🍽 Bars, bistros, restaurant.
🛏 On site Whittlebury Hall Hotel; 124
en-suite rooms.

5A 103 **Willesley Park**
Measham Road, Ashby-de-la-Zouch,
Leics, LE65 2PF
☎ 01530 411532, Fax 414596,
Pro 414820, Sec 414596
2 miles S of Ashby-de-la-Zouch on
B5006.
Parkland/heathland course.
Pro CJ Hancock; Founded 1921
Designed by CK Cotton
18 holes, 6304 yards, S.S.S. 70
Ⅰ Tuition available.
† Welcome with handicap certs.
Ⅰ WD £30; WE £35.
⟳ Welcome Wed, Thurs, Fri; terms
on application; from £30.
🍽 Clubhouse facilities.
🛏 Royal; Fallen Knight.

5A 104 **Wyboston Lakes**
Great North Road, Wyboston, Bedford,
Beds, MK44 3AL
☎ 01480 223004, Fax 407330
Off A1 at St Neots.
Public parkland with lake features.
Pro Paul Ashwell; Founded 1981
Designed by Neil Oackden
18 holes, 5955 yards, S.S.S. 70
Ⅰ 12 bays floodlit; practice range;
lessons available.
† Welcome; bookings taken 7 days
in advance for WE.
Ⅰ WD £11; WE £15.
⟳ Welcome WD by prior
arrangement.
🍽 Full catering facilities.
🛏 Hotel on site offers golf packages.

5B

Gloucestershire, Warwickshire, Herefordshire and Worcestershire

Hereford must have a very good claim to being England's most beautiful county. To the south lies Symonds Yat, where Anthony Hopkins and Debra Winger in the parts of CS Lewis and Joy Gresham came to film the golden valley scene of 'Shadowlands'. Symonds Yat looks over the River Wye meandering its way along the valley below. A view that inspires joy, humility and Englishness, it's the sort of spot where William Blake might have written 'Jerusalem'. North west of Symonds Yat is the true golden valley lying in the shadow of the Black Mountains. To the east are the Malvern Hills from which Sir Edward Elgar derived much of his inspiration.

Many of Britain's greatest golf courses are not laid out in such beautiful countryside. That is rather the point of them. They are good at turning a scrubby bit of decaying coastal land into something useful and lovely. So finding a suitable spot to build a golf course in Hereford has been known to present quite a problem.

In a previous edition of this book Donald Steel wrote of the difficulties Ross-on-Wye had in relocating from their previous nine-hole course. Originally the designer Ken Cotton wouldn't countenance building a course on the suggested site, but following a personal visit from the club committee he relented. His task entailed hacking a path through acres of woodland. Steel wrote, "My first memory was the sight of the head woodsman, then in his eighties, fuelling a woodland fire with fresh scrub and branches and cooking a lunch of bacon and eggs on the back of a carefully cleaned shovel." Given all the woodland that had to be cleared it is not surprising that Ross-on-Wye has such narrow fairways – one professional observed that the tee shot from the tenth could only be negotiated with a rifle – but what an achievement the course is in an area almost devoid of golf for many years.

For a long while Minchinhampton, in Gloucestershire, remained just about the only course between Westward Ho! and the Worcestershire, the first of the Midlands golf clubs. Like Minchinhampton, the Worcestershire had to move from its original site on common land because all the non-golfing activity going on – from grazing sheep to picnickers – made concentration rather hazardous. There is no document of what Elgar, a member of the club, had to say about it all, but it is recorded that he once holed his second shot on the fourth hole.

Kington, the highest course in the country and devoid of bunkers, Blackwell, Abbey Park, Worcester Golf and County and Cotswold Hills are other courses of some reputation in the counties that are better known for being home to the Three Choirs Festival.

Warwickshire has a louder golfing voice if not necessarily as tuneful a one. The Forest of Arden is the home of the English Open and the Belfry will forever be associated with the Ryder Cup. The tenth and eighteenth holes across the lake are exciting for just those associations, but overall it is a bit of a field despite the recent modifications to the third and the fourth. Many in the Birmingham area regard Sandwell Park or King's Norton as much better value.

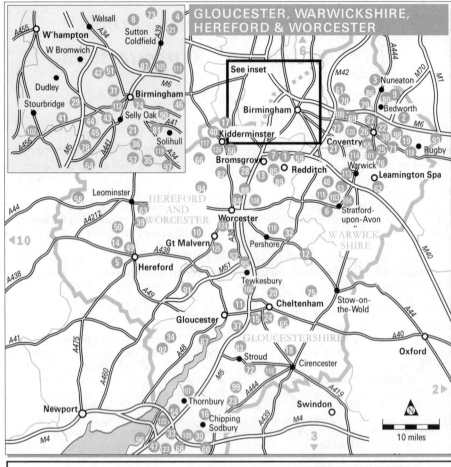

KEY
1	Abbey Hotel G & CC	24	Cotswold Hills	49	Hereford Municipal	75	Naunton Downs	101	Stoneleigh Deer Park

1	Abbey Hotel G & CC
2	Ansty Golf Centre
3	Atherstone
4	The Belfry
5	Belmont Lodge and GC
6	Bidford Grange
7	Blackwell
8	Boldmere
9	Bramcote Waters
10	Bransford at Bank House Hotel
11	Brickhampton Court
12	Broadway
13	Bromsgrove Golf Centre
14	Burghill Valley
15	Canons Court
16	Chipping Sodbury
17	Churchill & Blakedown
18	Cirencester
19	City of Coventry (Brandon Wood)
20	Cleeve Hill
21	Cocks Moor Woods
22	Copt Heath
23	Cotswold Edge
24	Cotswold Hills
25	Coventry
26	Coventry Hearsall
27	Cromwell Course at Nailcote Hall
28	Droitwich G & CC
29	Dudley
30	Dymock Grange
31	Edgbaston
32	Evesham
33	Filton
34	Forest Hills
35	Fulford Heath
36	Gay Hill
37	Gloucester
38	Grange (GPT Golf Club)
39	Grove Golf Centre
40	Habberley
41	Hagley Country Club
42	Halesowen
43	Handsworth
44	Harborne
45	Harborne Church Farm
46	Hatchford Brook
47	Henbury
48	Henley Golf & CC
49	Hereford Municipal
50	Herefordshire
51	Hill Top
52	Hilton Puckrup Hall (98)
53	Ingon Manor G & CC
54	The Kendleshire
55	Kenilworth
56	Kidderminster
57	Kings Norton
58	Kington
59	Ladbrook Park
60	Lansdown
61	Lea Marston Hotel
62	Leamington & County
63	Leominster
64	Lickey Hills (Rose Hill)
65	Lilley Brook
66	Little Lakes
67	Lydney
68	Mangotsfield
69	Marriott Forest of Arden
70	Maxstoke Park
71	Memorial Park
72	Minchinhampton
73	Moor Hall
74	Moseley
75	Naunton Downs
76	Newbold Comyn
77	North Warwickshire
78	North Worcestershire
79	Nuneaton
80	Oakridge
81	Olton
82	Ombersley
83	Painswick
84	Perdiswell
85	Pitcheroak
86	Purley Chase G & CC
87	Pype Hayes
88	Ravenmeadow
89	Redditch
90	Robin Hood
91	Ross-on-Wye
92	Royal Forest of Dean
93	Rugby
94	Sapey
95	Sherdons
96	Shirehampton Park
97	Shirley
98	Sphinx
99	Stinchcombe Hill
100	Stonebridge
101	Stoneleigh Deer Park
102	Stourbridge
103	Stratford Oaks
104	Stratford-upon-Avon
105	Sutton Coldfield
106	Tewkesbury Park Hotel
107	Thornbury Golf Centre
108	Tolladine
109	Tracy Park Country Club
110	Vale Golf & CC
111	Walmley
112	Warley
113	Warwick
114	Warwickshire
115	Welcombe Hotel
116	Westonbirt
117	Wharton Park
118	Whitefields
119	Widney Manor
120	Windmill Village Hotel
121	Wishaw
122	Woodlands
123	Woodspring
124	Worcester G & CC
125	Worcestershire
126	Wyre Forest

5B 1 Abbey Hotel Golf & Country Club

Dagnell End Road, Redditch, Worcs, B98 7BD
☎ 01527 63918, Fax 584112,
Pro 68006
On A441 Redditch to Birmingham road.
Parkland course.
Pro Spencer Edwards; Founded 1985
Designed by Donald Steel
18 holes, 6561 yards, S.S.S. 71
† Welcome subject to course availability.
Ⅰ WD 18 holes £14; WE 18 holes £19.
⌒ Welcome by prior arrangement; special packages available for members of golf club and guests of hotel; snooker; gym; swimming pool; sauna.
🍽 The Nineteenth Hole Bar and the Brambling's restaurant.
↩ Abbey Hotel on site.

5B 2 Ansty Golf Centre

Brinklow Road, Ansty, Coventry, Warwicks, CV7 9JH
☎ 024 76621341, Fax 76602568
From M6 Junction 2 take B4065 to Ansty; turning on to B4029 to Brinklow.
Parkland course.
Pro C Phillips; Founded 1990
Designed by D Morgan
18 holes, 6079 yards, S.S.S. 69
Ⅰ 18 bays; 9-hole academy course; tuition available 7 days a week; buggies and clubs for hire.
† Pay and play.
Ⅰ WD £9; WE £13.
⌒ Welcome with 24 hours notice.
🍽 Full facilities.
↩ Ansty Hall; Hanover at Hinckley.

5B 3 Athersone

The Outwoods, Mancetter, Atherstone, Warks, CV9 2RL
☎ 01827 713110
On A5 in town centre on Coleshill Road.
Parkland course.
Founded 1894
18 holes, 6006 yards, S.S.S. 70
† Welcome; guests of members at WE.
Ⅰ WD £20.
⌒ Welcome by arrangement; packages available; full catering facilities; terms on application.
🍽 Full catering and bar.
↩ Chapel House; Mancetter Manor, both Atherstone.

5B 4 The Belfry ♛

The Belfry, Lichfield Road, Wishaw, Sutton Coldfield, W Midlands, B76 9PR
🖳 www.devereonline.co.uk
✉ golf.reception@thebelfry.com
☎ 01675 470301, Fax 470174,
Pro 470301, Sec 470301
M42 Junction 9 follow A446 towards Lichfield and course is 1 mile on left.
Parkland course 2001 Ryder Cup course.
Pro Peter McGovern; Founded 1977
Designed by Peter Alliss & Dave Thomas
Brabazon: 18 holes, 6393 yards, S.S.S. 71; Derby: 18 holes, 6009 yards, S.S.S. 69; PGA national: 18 holes, 6153 yards, S.S.S. 70
Ⅰ Practice ground; buggies (seasonal only) and clubs for hire; tuition available, group lessons available; caddies and bag carriers available.
† Welcome.
Ⅰ WD £130, WE £130 (Brabazon); WD £35, WE £35 (Derby); WD £65, WE £65 (PGA National).
⌒ Welcome; full championship course, clubhouse and hotel facilities; terms on application.
🍽 First-class clubhouse and hotel facilities; choice of three restaurants.
↩ The Belfry.

5B 5 Belmont Lodge And ♛ Golf Club

Belmont, Hereford, Herefordshire, HR2 9SA
🖳 www.belmont-hereford.co.uk
✉ info@belmont-hereford.co.uk
☎ 01432 352666, Fax 358090,
Pro 352717
1.5 miles from the centre of Hereford just off A465 Abergavenny road.
Parkland course with back 9 bordering the river.
Pro Mike Welsh; Founded 1983
Designed by R Sandow
18 holes, 6511 yards, S.S.S. 71
Ⅰ Practice ground; tuition available; caddy cars for hire £16.50 per round.
† Welcome.
Ⅰ Prices on application.
⌒ Welcome; packages can be organised; terms on application.
🍽 Full club and hotel facilities.
↩ Belmont Lodge; self catering accomodation on site.

5B 6 Bidford Grange Golf Complex and Hotel

Bidford Grange, Stratford Road, Bidford-on-Avon, Alcester, Warks, B50 4LY
🖳 www.ukgolfer/bidfordgrange.co.uk
☎ 01789 490319, Fax 490998,
Pro 491376
Course is off the A439 Evesham-Stratford road.
Parkland course with last 4 holes close to River Avon.
Pro Simon Leahy; Founded 1992
Designed by Howard Swan and Paul Tillman
18 holes, 7233 yards, S.S.S. 72
Ⅰ 16 bays, practice range.
† Welcome.
Ⅰ WD £15; WE £18.
⌒ Welcome; various packages available, including golf, catering, dinner and accommodation; minimum 12; from £20 – £50.
🍽 New clubhouse with spikes bar, restaurant and hotel facilities.
↩ Bidford Grange.

5B 7 Blackwell

Agmore Road, Blackwell, Bromsgrove, Worcs, B60 1PY
☎ 0121 4451994, Fax 4454911,
Pro 4453113, Rest/Bar 4451781
3 miles E of Bromsgrove close to Blackwell village centre.
Parkland course.
Pro Nigel Blake; Founded 1893
Designed by H Fowler and T Simpson
18 holes, 6230 yards, S.S.S. 71
† Welcome WD; with member at WE.
Ⅰ WD £50.
⌒ Welcome Wed, Thurs, Fri by prior arrangement with Sec.
🍽 Full clubhouse facilities.
↩ Pery Hall; Bromsgrove.

5B 8 Boldmere

Boldmere Municipal Golf Course, Monmouth Drive, Sutton Coldfield, West Midlands, B73 6JL
☎ 0121 354 3379, Fax 3554534, Rest/Bar 3211476
Off A452 Chester Road, 6 miles NE of Birmingham.
Parkland course.
Pro Trevor Short; Founded 1936
Designed by Bretherton
18 holes, 4474 yards, S.S.S. 62
† Everyone welcome.
Ⅰ WD £9.50; WE £11.
⌒ Welcome WD only.
🍽 Bar and Catering.
↩ Parson & Clerk.

5B 9 Bramcote Waters

Bazzard Road, Bramcote, Nuneaton, Warks, CV11 6QJ
☎ 01455 220 807

5 miles SE of Nuneaton off the B4114.
Parkland course.
Pro Nic Gilks; Founded 1995
9 holes, 2491 yards, S.S.S. 64
⚑ Pay and play.
☰ 18 holes WD £12, WE £13; 9
holes WD £67, WE £8.
⟲ None.
🍽 Full clubhouse.
⟿ The Hanover International.

5B 10 **Bransford at Bank House Hotel** ☙

Bransford, Worcester, Worcs, WR6
5JD
✉ info@bankhousehotel.co.uk
☎ 01886 833545, Fax 832461,
Pro 833621, Rest/Bar 833754
Course is three miles W of Worcester
on the A4013 Hereford road in
Bransford village.
Florida-style course with 14 lakes and
2 island greens.
Pro Craig George/Lysa Jones;
Founded 1993
Designed by Bob Sandow
18 holes, 6204 yards, S.S.S. 70
☰ 20-bay, practice range; buggies
and clubs for hire; tuition and golf
clinics available.
⚑ Welcome.
☰ Terms on application.
⟲ Welcome; various packages
including 2-night golfing break for
£160; hotel and clubhouse facilities,
outdoor pool, fitness centre; prices on
application.
🍽 Bars, restaurants.
⟿ On site Bank House Hotel.

5B 11 **Brickhampton Court**

Cheltenham Road East, Gloucester,
Glos, GL2 9QF
☎ 01452 859444, Fax 859333
On B4063 between Cheltenham and
Gloucester; 3 miles from Junction 11
off the M5.
Parkland course.
Pro Bruce Wilson; Founded 1995
Designed by S Gidman
18 holes, 6387 yards, S.S.S. 31
☰ 26-bay floodlit range; Mizuno
teaching academy; buggies for hire.
⚑ Welcome.
☰ WD £16; WE £22.50.
⟲ Welcome WD; golf and catering
packages; also 9-hole Glevum course;
on-course refreshments; welcome
packs and golf clinics; £21-£37.50.
🍽 Clubhouse facilities, bar restaurant,
⟿ Golden Valley; Hatherley Manor;
White House.

5B 12 **Broadway**

Broadway Golf Club, Willersey Hill,
Willersey, Broadway, Worcs, WR12
7LG
☎ 01386 853275, Fax 858643,
Pro 853275, Sec 853683,
Rest/Bar 853561
1.5 miles E of Broadway on A44.
Inland Links.
Pro M Freeman; Founded 1895
Designed by James Braid
18 holes, 6228 yards, S.S.S. 70
☰ 4.
⚑ Welcome by prior arrangement
except before 3pm on Sat in summer.
☰ WD £30; WE £37.
⟲ Welcome Wed, Thurs, Fri; terms
on application.
🍽 Clubhouse facilities.
⟿ Dormy House next door; Lygon
Arms, Broadway.

5B 13 **Bromsgrove Golf Centre**

Stratford Road, Bromsgrove,
Worcestershire, B60 1LD
🖳 www.bromsgrovegolfcentre.co.uk
☎ 01527 570505, Fax 570964,
Pro 575886, Sec 575886,
Rest/Bar 579179
1 mile from Bromsgrove at junction of
A38 and A448.
Gently undulating parkland course.
Pro G Long/D Wall; Founded 1992
Designed by Hawtree & Sons
18 holes, 5869 yards, S.S.S. 68
☰ 41-bay covered floodlit practice
range; large practice bunker; putting
green; tuition available; equipment for
hire.
⚑ Pay and play.
☰ WD £14.50; WE £19.
⟲ Welcome by prior arrangement;
group and society packages available;
terms on application.
🍽 Full facilities with bar and lounge.
⟿ List available on request.

5B 14 **Burghill Valley** ☙

Tillington Road, Burghill, Hereford,
HR4 7RW
🖳 www.bvgc.co.uk
✉ golf@bvgc.co.uk
☎ 01432 760456, Fax 761654,
Pro 760808
4 miles NW of Hereford. Built around
cider orchards.
2 lakes and woods.
Pro Nigel Clarke; Founded 1991
18 holes, 6239 yards, S.S.S. 70
☰ Practice ground; tuition and golf
clinics available; buggies and clubs for
hire.
⚑ Welcome.

☰ WD £20; WE £25.
⟲ Welcome; golf and catering
packages available; from £25.
🍽 Clubhouse facilities.

5B 15 **Canons Court**

Canons Court Farm, Bradley,
Wotton-under-Edge, Glos, GL12 7PN
☎ 01453 843128
3 miles from M5 Junction 14 on
Wotton-under-Edge to N Nibley road.
Parkland course.
Founded 1982
9 holes, 5323 yards, S.S.S. 68
⚑ Public pay and play.
☰ WD £8; WE £10.
⟲ Welcome WD; terms on
application.
🍽 Bar and bar snacks.

5B 16 **Chipping Sodbury**

Chipping Sodbury, Bristol, Gloucs,
BS17 6PU
🖳 www.breathmail.net
✉ csgc@breathmail.net
☎ 01454 319042, Pro 314087,
Rest/Bar 315822
Leave M4 Junction 18 or M5 Junction
14 and from Chipping Sodbury take
the Wickwar road; first right turn.
Parkland course; also 9 holes 1076
yards.
Pro Mike Watts; Founded 1906
Designed by Fred Hawtree
18 holes, 6786 yards, S.S.S. 73
☰ Practice ground; tuition available;
buggies and clubs for hire.
⚑ Welcome; after 12 noon at WE.
☰ Terms on application.
⟲ Welcome WD by prior
arrangement.
🍽 Full bar and meal service.
⟿ Moda; Cross Hands.

5B 17 **Churchill & Blakedown**

Churchill Lane, Blakedown,
Kidderminster, Worcester,
DY10 3NB
☎ 01562 700018
Off A456 3 miles NE of Kidderminster;
turn under railway viaduct in village of
Blakedown.
Undulating parkland course.
Pro Keith Wheeler; Founded 1926
9 holes, 6472 yards, S.S.S. 71
⚑ Welcome WD; WE with a member.
☰ WD £17.50; WE £10.
⟲ Welcome by prior arrangement;
from £15.
🍽 Full facilities except Mon.
⟿ Cedars.

COPT HEATH GOLF

1220 WARWICK ROAD • KNOWLE • SOLIHULL • WEST MIDLANDS • B93 9LN

- Enjoy a game at a well known Midlands venue.
- Within half a mile of Junction 5 on the M42, the course, basically flat and parkland by nature, is a challenging one.
- Bar and catering facilities are available throughout the day.

Telephone: Professional (01564) 776155 • Secretary (01564) 772650

5B 18 Cirencester
Cheltenham Rd, Bagendon,
Cirencester, Glos, GL7 7BH
☎ 01285 652465, Fax 650665,
Pro 656124, Rest/Bar 6539390
Off A435 Cirencester-Cheltenham road
1.5 miles from Cirencester.
Undulating course.
Pro Peter Garratt; Founded 1893
Designed by James Braid
18 holes, 6055 yards, S.S.S. 69
† Welcome.
[WD £25; WE £30.
⌁ Welcome by arrangement.
🔘 Full facilities.
🛏 King's Head.

**5B 19 City of Coventry
(Brandon Wood)**
Brandon Lane, Wolston, Coventry,
CV8 3GQ
☎ 024 7654 3133, Sec 76543141
6 miles S of Coventry off A45.
Parkland course.
Pro Chris Gledhill
Designed by Frank Pennink
18 holes, 6610 yards, S.S.S. 72
† Welcome.
[WD £8.45; WE £11.25.
⌁ Welcome on application to
professional; terms on application.
🔘 Clubhouse facilities.
🛏 Brandon Hall Hotel.

5B 20 Cleeve Hill
Cleeve Hill, Cheltenham, Glos,
GL52 3PW
☎ 01242 672025, Fax 672025
6 miles N of M5; 4 miles from
Cheltenham off A46.
Municipal heathland course.
Pro Dave Finch; Founded 1891
18 holes, 6411 yards, S.S.S. 71
† Welcome WD; some restrictions
WE.
[WD £11; WE £13.
⌁ Welcome by prior arrangement;

catering packages; skittles alley.
🔘 Bar snacks.
🛏 Rising Sun.

5B 21 Cocks Moor Woods
Alcester Rd South, Kings Heath,
Birmingham, W Midlands,
B14 6ER
☎ 0121 4443584
On A435 near city boundary.
Public parkland course.
Pro Steve Ellis; Founded 1924
18 holes, 5769 yards, S.S.S. 68
† Welcome.
[WD £9; WE £10.
⌁ Welcome by arrangement.
🔘 Full clubhouse facilities.

5B 22 Copt Heath
1220 Warwick Rd, Knowle, Solihull,
Warwickshire, B93 9LN
☎ 01564 772650, Fax 771022,
Pro 776155
From M42 Junction 5 take A4141;
course 0.5 miles.
Parkland course.
Pro BJ Barton; Founded 1910
Designed by H Vardon
18 holes, 6508 yards, S.S.S. 71
† Welcome WD.
[WD £40 all day.
⌁ Welcome by prior arrangement
with secretary; maximum 36; terms on
application; from £40.
🔘 Clubhouse facilities.
🛏 Greswolde Arms; St Johns.

5B 23 Cotswold Edge
Upper Rushmire, Wotton-under-Edge,
Gloucestershire, GL12 7PT
☎ 01453 844167, Fax 845120
On B4058 Wotton-under-Edge/Tetbury
road 8 miles from M5 Junction 14.
Meadowland course.
Pro David Gosling; Founded 1980
18 holes, 6170 yards, S.S.S. 71

† Welcome WD; WE with member.
[WD £15; WE £20.
⌁ Welcome WD by prior
arrangement; packages available; from
£30.
🔘 Full clubhouse facilities.
🛏 Hunters Hall; Calcot Manor.

5B 24 Cotswold Hills
Ullenwood, Cheltenham, Glos, GL53
9QT
☎ 01242 515264, Fax 515264,
Pro 515263
3 miles S of Cheltenham.
Parkland course on limestone;
1981 English Ladies Amateur.
Pro Norman Allen; Founded 1902/1976
Designed by MD Little
18 holes, 6750 yards, S.S.S. 72
† Welcome by prior arrangement.
[WD £25; WE £30.
⌁ Welcome Wed and Thurs;
packages available; from £25.
🔘 Clubhouse facilities.
🛏 Crest Motel; George Hotel;
Lilleybrook; Golden Valley.

5B 25 Coventry
St Martin's Rd, Finham Park, Coventry,
Warwicks, CV3 6PJ
☎ 024 7641 1452, Fax 76690131,
Pro 76411298, Sec 76414152
Close to A45/A46 Junction; take A45
towards Birmingham and left at
island.
Parkland course.
Pro Phil Weaver; Founded 1887
Designed by Tom Vardon
18 holes, 6601 yards, S.S.S. 73
† Welcome WD; with member WE.
[WD £35.
⌁ Welcome Wed and Thurs;
packages available; from £50-£55.
🔘 Clubhouse facilities.
🛏 Chesford Grange; Old Mill.

5B 26 Coventry Hearsall
Beechwood Ave, Earlsdon, Coventry, CV5 6DF
☎ 024 7667 2935, Fax 76691534, Pro 76713156, Sec 76713470
From A45/A429 towards city centre turn into Beechwood Avenue.
Parkland course.
Pro Mike Tarn; Founded 1894/1921
18 holes, 6005 yards, S.S.S. 69
♦ Welcome with member.
⌐ Terms on application.
⌂ Welcome Tues and Thurs.
|●| Clubhouse facilities.
↩ Hylands Hotel.

5B 27 Cromwell Course
Nailcote Hall Hotel, Nailcote Lane, Berkswell, Warwickshire, CV7 7DE
⌨ www.nailcotehall.co.uk
✉ info@nailcotehall.co.uk
☎ 024 7646 6174, Fax 76470720
Take A452 Balsall Common Junction from B4101 and follow brown signs towards Tile Hall, hotel 1.5 miles on right.
Parkland course.
Pro Sid Mouland; Founded 1994
Designed by Short Course Golf Ltd
9 holes, 1023 yards, S.S.S. 27
⌐ Practice putting green, tution available, leisure facilities (swimming pool, croquet lawn, tennis, sauna).
♦ Welcome.
⌐ WD £10; WE £10.
⌂ Welcome by prior arrangement; terms on application.
|●| Full hotel facilities.
↩ Nailcote Hall on site.

5B 28 Droitwich Golf & Country Club
Westford House, Ford Lane, Droitwich, WR9 0BQ
☎ 01905 774344, Fax 797290, Pro 770207
Off A38 1 mile N of town.
Undulating meadowland course.
Pro Chris Thompson; Founded 1897
18 holes, 5976 yards, S.S.S. 69
♦ Welcome WD with handicap certs; with member at WE.
⌐ WD £26.
⌂ Welcome Wed and Fri.
|●| Bar meals and restaurant.
↩ The Chateau Impney; Raven.

5B 29 Dudley
Turners Hill, Rowley Regis, Warley, W Midlands, B65 9DP
☎ 01384 254020, Sec 233877

1 mile S of town centre.
Undulating parkland course.
Pro Paul Taylor; Founded 1893
18 holes, 5714 yards, S.S.S. 68
♦ Welcome WD.
⌐ WD £18.
⌂ Welcome by prior arrangement; packages available for 20 or more; 10% reduction; from £25.
|●| Lunch and evening meals.
↩ Travelodge.

5B 30 Dymock Grange
The Old Grange, Dymock, Glos, GL18 2AN
☎ 01531 890840
On A4172 off the A449 Ledbury-Ross-on-Wye Rd.
Parkland course.
Pro Sara Foster (touring);
Founded 1995
18 holes, 4600 yards, S.S.S. 65
♦ Welcome with prior reservation.
⌐ WD £10; WE £14.
⌂ Welcome by prior arrangement.
|●| Bar.
↩ Restaurant; fitness centre.

5B 31 Edgbaston
Edgbaston Hall, Church Rd, Edgbaston, Birmingham, B15 3TB
☎ 0121 454 1736, Fax 4542395, Pro 4543226
From city centre take A38 Bristol road; after 1.5 miles turn right into Priory Road (B4217); after mini roundabout club 100 yards.
Parkland course; woods and lake.
Pro J Cundy; Founded 1896/1935
Designed by HS Colt
18 holes, 6106 yards, S.S.S. 69
⌐ Practice range, practice areas and nets.
♦ Welcome except Sat comp days before 2pm and Sun before 11.15am.
⌐ WD £37.50; WE £50.
⌂ Welcome WD except Thurs; packages available including private function room, changing rooms, golf and catering; minimum 20 maximum 100.
|●| Extensive clubhouse facilities; restaurant, bars and private rooms.
↩ Copperfield House; Portland House; Apollo; Plough & Harrow; Swallow.

5B 32 Evesham
Craycombe Links, Fladbury Cross, Pershore, Worcs, WR10 2QS
☎ 01386 860395, Fax 861356, Pro 861144

3 miles W of Evesham towards Worcester on A4538.
Parkland course.
Pro Charles Haynes; Founded 1894
9 holes, 6415 yards, S.S.S. 71
⌐ One practice ground; Two practice greens; PGA tuition.
♦ Welcome with prior arrangement WD; WE with a member.
⌐ WD non members £20, guests of members £10.
⌂ Welcome with prior arrangement; terms on application.
|●| Clubhouse facilities.

5B 33 Filton
Golf Course Lane, Filton, Bristol, BS34 7QS
☎ 0117 9692021, Fax 9314359, Pro 9694158
M5 Junction 16 to A38 at Filton roundabout turn right then first right at lights.
Parkland course with views of Brecon Beacons.
Pro Nicky Lums; Founded 1909
Designed by F Hawtree & Son
18 holes, 6318 yards, S.S.S. 69
♦ Welcome WD only; guests of members at WE.
⌐ WD £20.
⌂ Welcome by prior arrangement; terms on application.
|●| Full clubhouse facilities.
↩ Aztec; Stakis; Premier.

5B 34 Forest Hills
Mile End Road, Coleford, Gloucestershire, GL16 7QD
☎ 01594 810620
Course is on the B4028 towards Gloucester, 0.5 miles from Coleford town centre.
Meadowland course.
Pro Richard Ballard; Founded 1992
Designed by Adrian Stiff
18 holes, 5674 yards, S.S.S. 67
♦ Welcome.
⌐ WD £15; WE £20.
⌂ Welcome by prior arrangement; terms on application. Driving range; buggies and clubs for hire; tuition available 7 days a week; junior academy Sat morning; new juniors always welcome.
|●| Full clubhouse facilities.

5B 35 Fulford Heath
Tanners Green Lane, Wythall, Birmingham, B47 6BH
☎ 01564 822930, Fax 822629, Pro 822930, Sec 824758
8 miles S of Birmingham.

Parkland course.
Pro David Down; Founded 1933
18 holes, 5959 yards, S.S.S. 69
† Welcome WD; with member WE.
[WD £34.
⌔ Welcome by arrangement on Tues
and Thurs possibly one other day; golf
and catering packages available;
prices on application.
|●| Clubhouse facilities.

5B 36 Gay Hill
Hollywood Lane, Hollywood,
Birmingham, W Midlands, B47 5PP
☎ 0121 4308544, Fax 4367796,
Pro 4746001, Sec 4308544
On A435 7 miles from Birmingham city
centre and 3 miles from Junction 3 of
the M42.
Meadowland course.
Pro Andrew Potter; Founded 1913
18 holes, 6532 yards, S.S.S. 71
† Welcome WD; WE with member
but not before 12.30pm Sun.
[WD £28.50.
⌔ Welcome Thurs by arrangement.
|●| Full facilities.
⌐ George.

5B 37 Gloucester   ☎
Jarvis Hotel & CC, Robinswood Hill,
Matson Lane, Gloucester,
Gloucestershire, GL4 9EA
☎ 01452 411331, Fax 307212
2 miles S of Gloucester on B4073 to
Painswick.
Parkland course.
Pro Peter Darnell; Founded 1976
Designed by Donald Steel
18 holes, 6170 yards, S.S.S. 69
† Welcome.
[WD £19; WE £25.
⌔ Welcome; terms on application.
|●| Full hotel and clubhouse facilities.
⌐ Jarvis Gloucester Hotel & CC.

5B 38 Grange (GPT GC)
Copsewood, Coventry, W Midlands,
CV3 1HS
☎ 024 76562336
2.5 miles from Coventry on A428
Binley Rd.
Meadowland course.
Founded 1924
9 holes, 6100 yards, S.S.S. 71
† Welcome WD before 2pm; except
Wed; not Sat; Sun after 11am.
[WD £10; Sun £15.
⌔ Welcome by arrangement with
secretary.
|●| By arrangement only.
⌐ Hilton.

5B 39 Grove Golf Centre
Fordbridge, Leominster, Herefordshire,
HR6 0LE
☎ 01568 610602, Fax 615333
3 miles S of Leominster on A49.
Wooded parkland course.
Pro Phil Brooks; Founded 1994
Designed by J Gaunt/R Sandow
9 holes, 3560 yards, S.S.S. 60
⌘ Practice range, floodlit bays;
putting green.
† Public pay and play.
[WD £4; WE £5.
⌔ Welcome any time; terms on
application.
|●| Full bar and restaurant.

5B 40 Habberley
Low Habberley, Kidderminster, Worcs,
DY11 5RG
☎ 01562 745756
2 miles NW of Kidderminster.
Parkland course.
Founded 1924
9 holes, 5481 yards, S.S.S. 69
† Welcome WD if member of
recognised club; WE and BH with
member only.
[WD £10; WE £10.
⌔ Welcome by prior arrangement;
terms on application.
|●| Clubhouse facilities.
⌐ Gainsborough; Heath Hotel.

5B 41 Hagley Country Club
Wassell Grove, Hagley, W Midlands,
DY9 9JW
☎ 01562 883701
4 miles S of Birmingham on A456.
Undulating parkland course.
Pro Ian Clark; Founded 1979
18 holes, 6353 yards, S.S.S. 72
† Welcome WD; WE with a member,
after 10am.
[WD £22.50.
⌔ Welcome WD by prior
arrangement with club manager;
packages available; also squash.
|●| Bar and restaurant facilities.

5B 42 Halesowen
The Leasowes, Halesowen, W
Midlands, B62 8QF
☎ 0121 5501041, Pro 5030593,
Sec 5013606
M5 Junction 3; A456 Kidderminster, 2
miles.
Parkland course.
Pro J Nicholas; Founded 1907
18 holes, 5754 yards, S.S.S. 68
† Welcome; WE with member only;
BH by arrangement.

[WD £18; WE £18.
⌔ Welcome by prior arrangement
with Sec; packages available for
groups of 25 or more; from £18.
|●| Clubhouse facilities except Mon
evening.

5B 43 Handsworth
11 Sunningdale Close, Handsworth,
Birmingham, W Midlands, B20 1NP
☎ 0121 5540599, Fax 5543387,
Pro 5233594
Course is close to either Junction 1 of
the M5 or Junction 7 of the M6 off
Hamstead Hill.
Parkland course.
Pro Lee Bashford; Founded 1895
18 holes, 6267 yards, S.S.S. 70
⌘ Practice range; practice ground;
squash; tuition available.
† Welcome WD with handicap certs;
guests of members at WE.
[WD £30.
⌔ Welcome WD by arrangement;
special packages available.
|●| Full clubhouse facilities except
Mon.
⌐ Post House.

5B 44 Harborne
40 Tennal Rd, Birmingham, W
Midlands, B32 2JE
☎ 0121 4271728, Pro 4273512,
Sec 4273058
2 miles SW of city centre adjacent to
M5 Junction 3.
Parkland course.
Pro Alan Quarterman; Founded 1893
Designed by HS Colt
18 holes, 6235 yards, S.S.S. 70
† Welcome WD.
[WD £35; WE £35.
⌔ Welcome by prior arrangement;
terms on application; £30.
|●| Clubhouse facilities.

5B 45 Harborne Church Farm
Vicarage Rd, Harborne, Birmingham,
B17 0SN
☎ 0121 427 1204
5 miles SW of Birmingham city centre.
Parkland course.
Pro Paul Johnson; Founded 1926
9 holes, 4882 yards, S.S.S. 64
† Welcome with prior booking.
[WD £8; WE £8.50.
⌔ Welcome by prior arrangement;
terms on application.
|●| Full facilities.

5B 46 Hatchford Brook
Coventry Rd, Sheldon, Birmingham, B26 3PY
☎ 0121 743 9821, Fax 7433420, Sec 7793780
On A45 Birmingham to Coventry road, close to Birmingham airport.
Parkland course.
Pro Mark Hampton; Founded 1969
18 holes, 6120 yards, S.S.S. 69
† Welcome.
✑ WD £9; WE £10.
⌀ Welcome by prior arrangement; terms on application.
⦿ Full facilities.
⌁ Metropole; Arden Motel.

5B 47 Henbury
Henbury Hill, Westbury-on-Trym, Bristol, Gloucs, BS10 7QB
☎ 0117 9500044, Fax 9591928, Pro 9502121
Leave M5 Junction 17 2nd exit from roundabout into Crow Lane; course at top of hill.
Pro Nick Riley; Founded 1891
18 holes, 6007 yards, S.S.S. 70
† Welcome WD with handicap certs.
✑ WD and WE: non-members £25 guests of members £15.
⌀ Welcome Tues and Fri by arrangement. Tuition available club and trolley hire.
⦿ Full facilities.
⌁ Many in local area.

5B 48 Henley Golf & CC
Crockett's Manor, Birmingham Rd, Henley in Arden, Warwicks, B95 5QA
☎ 01564 793715
On A3400 4 miles N of Stratford-on-Avon.
Parkland course.
18 holes, 6933 yards, S.S.S. 73
† Welcome by prior arrangement.
✑ WD £20; WE £25.
⌀ Full packages available via Pro shop.
⦿ Full Country Club facilities.

5B 49 Hereford Municipal
The Racecourse, Holmer Road, Hereford, HR4 9UD
☎ 01432 344376
A49 towards Leominster, in centre of race track.
Public parkland course.
Pro Gary Morgan; Founded 1983
9 holes, 6120 yards, S.S.S. 69
⌁ Practice range, practice ground; club hire £2.50; trolley hire £1.20; tuition available.

† Welcome except race days.
✑ 9 holes: WD £4.25, WE £5.25; 18 holes: WE £6.50, WE £8.00; reduced green fees available for juniors and OAPs.
⌀ Welcome by prior arrangement; packages include 18 holes, coffee and 2-course meal; please ring for details.
⦿ Bar and restaurant facilities.
⌁ Starling Gate; Travel Inn.

5B 50 Herefordshire Golf Club ☎
Ravens Causeway, Wormsley, Hereford, HR4 8LY
☎ 01432 830219, Pro 830465, Sec 830817
Off Roman Road from Hereford in direction of Weobley.
Parkland course.
Pro D Hemming; Founded 1898
Designed by Major Hutchison
18 holes, 6078 yards, S.S.S. 69
† Welcome WD; WE by arrangement.
✑ WD £19; WE £22.
⌀ Welcome; terms available on application.
⦿ Clubhouse facilities.
⌁ The Burton Hotel; The Pilgrim Hotel.

5B 51 Hill Top
Park Lane, Handsworth, Birmingham, W Midlands, B21 8LJ
☎ 0121 5544463
From M5 Junction 1 follow signs for Handsworth.
Parkland course.
Pro Kevin Highfield; Founded 1980
18 holes, 6208 yards, S.S.S. 69
† Welcome; link card service, book 8 days in advance.
✑ WD £8.50; WE £9.
⌀ Welcome WD by prior arrangement with the professional; packages available.
⦿ Full clubhouse facilities.
⌁ Post House, W Bromwich.

5B 52 Hilton Puckrup Hall ☎
Puckrup, Tewkesbury, Glos, GL20 6EL
☎ 01684 296200, Fax 850788
M50 Junction 1 towards Tewkesbury on the A38.
Parkland course.
Pro Kevin Pickett; Founded 1992
Designed by Simon Gidman
18 holes, 6189 yards, S.S.S. 70
⌁ Practice area; tuition available; full leisure facilities (gym, pool, jacuzzi, beauty rooms etc).
† Welcome.

✑ WD £25; WE and BH £30.
⌀ Welcome by prior arrangement; full day and half-day packages can be arranged; £19.50-£45.
⦿ Full clubhouse facilities; restaurant for 50, licensed bar.
⌁ 112-room hotel on site.

5B 53 Ingon Manor Golf & Country Club
Ingon Lane, Snitterfield, Nr Stratford-upon-Avon, Warwickshire, CV37 0QE
☎ 01789 731857, Fax 731657, Pro 731938
Course is signposted from the M40 Junction 15.
Parkland course.
Pro Rob Greer; Founded 1993
Designed by David Hemstock Associates & Colin Geddes
18 holes, 6623 yards, S.S.S. 71
⌁ Driving range; club; buggy; trolley and shoe hire; tuition for adults and juniors; group tuition available; practice putting green
† Welcome.
✑ WD £20; WE £25.
⌀ Welcome by prior arrangement; terms on application; packages available.
⦿ Full clubhouse and hotel, restaurant and bar facilities.
⌁ On site Ingon Manor Hotel.

5B 54 The Kendleshire
Henfield Rd, Coalpit Heath, Bristol, Glos, BS17 2TG
☎ 0117 9567007, Fax 573433, Pro 9567000
1 mile from M32.
Parkland course with soft spikes.
Pro Paul Barrington; Founded 1997
Designed by A Stiff
18 holes, 6507 yards, S.S.S. 71
⌁ Grass practice range; 6 hole short course; tuition available; childrens club 'Kendlshire Kubs'; buggies; shoes and clubs for hire
† Welcome WD; WE by arrangement.
✑ WD £18; WE £24.
⌀ Welcome by prior arrangement; packages on request; function room for 250.
⦿ Bar and restaurant facilities available.
⌁ Post House; Emerson Green Beefeater.

5B 55 Kenilworth

Crewe Lane, Kenilworth, Waricks, CV8
2EA
☎ 01926 854296, Fax 864453,
Pro 512732, Sec 858517
6 miles from Coventry.
Undulating parkland course.
Pro Steve Yates;
Founded 1889/1936
Designed by Hawtree
18 holes, 6400 yards, S.S.S. 71
⚐ 6-hole par 3 course; tuition and
golf clinics available; contact pro for
details.
⚑ Welcome by arrangement.
⌞ WD £30; WE £37.
⚐ Welcome Wed; packages
available; small conferance room;
terms on application.
⦿ Clubhouse facilities.
⌁ Chesford Grange; DeMontfort.

5B 56 Kidderminster

Russell Rd, Kidderminster, Worcs,
DY10 3HT
☎ 01562 822303
Course signposted off A449 within 1
mile of town centre.
Parkland course.
Pro Nick Underwood; Founded 1909
18 holes, 6405 yards, S.S.S. 71
⚑ Welcome WD only; WE with
member.
⌞ WD £30.
⚐ Welcome Thurs by prior
arrangement.
⦿ Full facilities except Mon.
⌁ The Gainsborough; Collingdale;
Stone Manor.

5B 57 Kings Norton

Brockhill Lane, Weatheroak,
Alvechurch, Birmingham, B48 7ED
☎ 01564 826706, Fax 826955,
Pro 822635, Sec 826789
1 miles N of M42 Junction 3, just off
A435.
Parkland course; 3 x 9 combinations.
Pro Kevin Hayward; Founded 1892
Designed by F Hawtree & Son
18 holes, 7019 yards, S.S.S. 74
⚐ Practice range, 12-hole par 3 short
course, PGA tuition available.
⚑ Welcome WD.
⌞ WD £30.
⚐ Welcome by prior arrangement; full
catering and golf packages; separate
reception room bar; 100-seater ball
room; use of club starter; from £30.
⦿ Full clubhouse facilities.
⌁ Inkford Cottage; Pine Lodge.

5B 58 Kington

Bradnor Hill, Kington, Herefordshire,
HR5 3RE
☎ 01544 230340, Fax 340270,
Pro 231320
From A44 take the B4355 Presteigne
road for 100 metres and then left to
Bradnor Hill.
Mountain links: highest 18-hole course
in England.
Pro Dean Oliver; Founded 1925
Designed by CK Hutchinson
18 holes, 5228 yards, S.S.S. 68
⚑ Welcome with prior arrangement.
⌞ WD £15; WE £20.
⚐ Welcome by prior arrangement
with Pro shop; extensive menu and
facilities available; winter packages
available; prices on application.
⦿ Full catering and bar facilities.
⌁ Royal George.

5B 59 Ladbrook Park

Poolhead Lane, Tamworth-in-Arden,
Warwicks, B94 5ED
☎ 01564 742264, Pro 742581
Take A435 to Tamworth/Portway; left
into Penn Lane; then left into Broad
Lane and left into Poolhead Lane.
Parkland course.
Pro Richard Mountford;
Founded 1908
Designed by HS Colt
18 holes, 6427 yards, S.S.S. 71
⚑ Welcome WD; except Tues am.
⌞ WD £25.
⚐ Welcome by prior arrangement
with the Secretary; full golfing and
catering packages; terms on
application.
⦿ Restaurant and bar facilities.
⌁ Regency; Plough Inn.

5B 60 Lansdown   ℭ

Lansdown, Bath, Avon, BA1 9BT
☎ 01225 420242, Fax 339252,
Pro 420242, Sec 422138
From M4 Junction 18 take A46 towards
Bath; at roundabout take A420 towards
Bristol; take first left and club is 2 miles
on right
Parkland course.
Pro Terry Mercer; Founded 1894
Designed by Harry Colt
18 holes, 6316 yards, S.S.S. 70
⚑ Welcome; handicap certs preferred.
⌞ WD £20; WE £20.
⚐ Welcome by prior arrangement;
from £20.
⦿ Clubhouse snacks and meals.
⌁ Hilton.

5B 61 Lea Marston Hotel & Leisure Complex

Haunch Lane, Lea Marston,
Warwickshire, B76 0BY
⌨ www.leamarstonhotel.co.uk
✉ info@leamarstonhotel.co.uk
☎ 01675 470468, Fax 470871,
Pro 470707
1 mile from M42 Junction 9 on A4097
Kingsbury road; 1.5 miles from The
Belfry.
Parkland course.
Pro Andrew Stokes; Founded 1983
Designed by JR Blake
9 holes, 7750 yards, S.S.S. 30
⚐ Practice range, 26 bays floodlit;
golf simulator; tuition available.
⚑ Welcome.
⌞ WD £4.25; WE £5; discounts for
juniors and OAPs.
⚐ Welcome by prior arrangement;
tennis; pool table; health club;
swimming pool.
⦿ Bar and restaurant facilities.
⌁ Lea Marston Hotel on site; golf
breaks call reservations for details.

5B 62 Leamington & County

Golf Lane, Whitnash, Leamington Spa,
Warwicks, CV31 2QA
☎ 01926 425961, Fax 425961,
Pro 428014
6 mins from M40 towards Leamington
Spa and then take Whitnash signs.
Parkland course.
Pro Iain Grant; Founded 1908
Designed by HS Colt
18 holes, 6437 yards, S.S.S. 71
⚑ Welcome with handicap certs.
⌞ WD £30; WE £40.
⚐ Welcome Mon, Wed, Thurs; full
golf and catering facilities; from £28.
⦿ Clubhouse facilities.
⌁ Marriott Courtyard.

5B 63 Leominster   ℭ

Ford Bridge, Leominster, Hereford,
HR6 0LE
☎ 01568 610055, Fax 610055,
Pro 611402
3 miles S of Leominster on A49.
Undulating parkland course running
alongside River Lugg.
Pro Andrew Ferriday; Founded
1903/67/90
Designed by Bob Sandow
18 holes, 6026 yards, S.S.S. 69
⚐ Practice range 18 bays.
⚑ Welcome by arrangement.
⌞ WD £17; WE £23.
⚐ Welcome WD except Mon; 36
holes of golf; coffee, light lunch and 3-
course dinner; fishing on river also

available; from £31.
🍴 Full bar and bar snacks; restaurant every day except Mon.
🛏 Talbot; Royal Oak.

5B 64 Lickey Hills (Rose Hill)
Lickey Hills, Rednal, Birmingham, W Midlands, B45 8RR
☎ 0121 453 3159
M5 Junction 4 or M42 Junction 1 signposted to Lickey Hills Park.
Public parkland course.
Pro Joe Kelly; Founded 1927
Designed by Carl Bretherton
18 holes, 5835 yards, S.S.S. 68
🏌 Welcome.
🍴 WD £9; WE £10.
🎁 Welcome by arrangement.
🍴 Snacks.
🛏 Westmead.

5B 65 Lilley Brook
Cirencester Rd, Charlton Kings, Cheltenham, Glos, GL53 8EG
☎ 01242 526785, Fax 256880,
Pro 525201
2 miles SE of Cheltenham on A435 Cirencester road.
Parkland course.
Pro Forbes Hadden; Founded 1922
Designed by MacKenzie
18 holes, 6212 yards, S.S.S. 70
🏌 Welcome with handicap certs.
🍴 WD £25; WE £30.
🎁 Welcome WD by arrangement; packages available; terms on application.
🍴 Full clubhouse facilities.
🛏 Cheltenham Park; Charlton Kings.

5B 66 Little Lakes ℭ
Lye Head, Rock, Beweley, Worcs, DY12 2UZ
☎ 01299 266385
Course is on the A456 2 miles W of Beweley; turn left at Greenhouse and Garden Centre.
Undulating parkland course.
Pro Mark Laing; Founded 1975
Designed by Michael Cooksey
18 holes, 5644 yards, S.S.S. 68
🏌 Practice range, buggies for hire, tuition and golf clinics available individually and on a group basis.
🏌 Welcome.
🍴 WD £14; WE £19.
🎁 Welcome by prior arrangement; packages available; from £28.
🍴 Lunches available.
🛏 Heath.

5B 67 Lydney
Lakeside Ave, Lydney, Glos, GL15 5QA
☎ 01594 842614
Entering Lydney on A48 from Gloucester turn left at bottom of Highfield Hill and look for Lakeside Ave on left.
Parkland course.
Founded 1909
9 holes, 5298 yards, S.S.S. 66
🏌 Welcome; WE with member.
🍴 WD £10.
🎁 Small societies by arrangement; packages can be arranged.
🍴 Bar lunch and dinners.
🛏 Speech House.

5B 68 Mangotsfield
Carson's Rd, Mangotsfield, Bristol, Glos, BS16 9LW
☎ 0117 9565501
From M32 leave at Junction for Filton/Downend; follow signs for Downend and Mangotsfield.
Hilly meadowland course.
Pro Craig Trewin; Founded 1975
18 holes, 5290 yards, S.S.S. 66
🏌 Welcome.
🍴 WD £10; WE £12.
🎁 Welcome by prior arrangement; packages available.
🍴 Full clubhouse facilities.
🛏 Post House.

5B 69 Marriott Forest of Arden ℭ
Maxstoke Lane, Meriden, Coventry, Warwicks, CV7 7HR
☎ 01676 526113, Fax 526125,
Pro 0958632170, Sec 522335
Off A45 close to M42 Junction 6 or M6 South Junction 4.
Championship parkland course; site of English Open 2000.
Pro Kim Thomas; Founded 1970/91
Designed by Donald Steel
18 holes, 7134 yards, S.S.S. 71
🏌 Practice range, 6 undercover bays; teaching facility.
🏌 Residents and visitors welcome.
🍴 Terms on application.
🎁 Corporate packages can be booked through golf office; 27 holes, coffee, buffet lunch, dinner, strokesaver and driving range prices; £135.
🍴 Clubhouse and hotel facilities.
🛏 Marriott Forest of Arden.

5B 70 Maxstoke Park
Castle Lane, Coleshill, Warwicks, B46 2RD
☎ 01675 466743, Fax 466743,
Pro 464915
From M6 take Coleshill road and at high street lights turn towards Nuneaton; club 2 miles.
Parkland course.
Pro Neil McEwan; Founded 1898/45
Designed by Tom Marks
18 holes, 6442 yards, S.S.S. 71
🏌 Practice range; lessons available from Pro.
🏌 Welcome with handicap certs.
🍴 WD £25; WE £27.50.
🎁 Welcome Tues and Thurs; packages on application; from £25.
🍴 Clubhouse facilities.
🛏 Lea Marston Hotel.

5B 71 Memorial Park
Memorial Park Golf Office, Kenilworth Rd, Coventry, W Midlands
☎ 024 76675415
1 mile from the city centre.
Municipal parkland course.
Designed by John Bredemus
18 holes, 2840 yards, S.S.S. 60
🏌 Welcome.
🍴 WD £3.45; WE £3.45.
🎁 Welcome; tennis courts; playground; bowling greens.
🍴 Café in park in summer.

5B 72 Minchinhampton ℭ
Old Course, Minchinhampton Common, Stroud, Glos, GL6 9AQ
☎ 01453 833866, Pro 833860
Old course is on Minchinhampton Common 3 miles SE of Stroud; New course between Avening and Minchinhampton off B4014.
Parkland course.
Pro C Steele; Founded 1889 (Old); 1975 (New)
Designed by R Wilson (Old); FW Hawtree (New)
Old 18 holes, 6019 yards, S.S.S. 70; New Avening: 18 holes, 6279 yards, S.S.S. 70; Cherington: 18 holes, 6520 yards, S.S.S. 70
🏌 Welcome (Old); Welcome by prior arrangement (New).
🍴 WD £12, WE £15 (Old); WD £26, WE £30 (New).
🎁 Welcome by prior arrangement; full range of packages available; terms on application.
🍴 Both clubs provide clubhouse bar and catering facilities.
🛏 Amberley Inn; Bear of Rodborough; Burleigh House.

5B 73 Moor Hall
Moor Hall Drive, Sutton Coldfield, W
Midlands, B75 6LN
☎ 0121 3086130, Pro 3085106
From M42 take A446 to Bassets Pole
roundabout; follow Sutton Coldfield road,
at first lights course 200 yards on left.
Parkland course.
Pro Alan Partridge; Founded 1932
18 holes, 6249 yards, S.S.S. 70
† Welcome WD; after 12.30pm Thurs
Ⅰ WD £30.
🕹 Welcome Tues and Wed by prior
arrangement.
🍴 Full facilities.
🛏 Moor Hall.

5B 74 Moseley
Springfield Rd, Kings Heath,
Birmingham, B14 7DX
✉ admin@mosgolf.freeserve.co.uk
☎ 0121 4442115, Fax 4414662
On Birmingham ring road 0.5 miles E
of Alcester road.
Parkland course.
Pro Gary Edge; Founded 1892
18 holes, 6300 yards, S.S.S. 70
† Welcome WD with letter of
introduction/handicap certs.
Ⅰ WD £37.
🕹 Welcome Wed only by prior
arrangement with secretary.
🍴 Full facilities.
🛏 The Strathallan; Edgbaston;
Oxford Hotel, Mosely; St John's
Swallow, Solihull.

5B 75 Naunton Downs ⓣ
Naunton, Cheltenham, Gloucs, GL54
3AE
☎ 01451 850090, Fax 850091,
Pro 850092
On B4068 Stow-on-the-Wold to
Cheltenham road near Naunton.
Downland course.
Pro Martin Seddon; Founded 1993
Designed by Jacob Pott
18 holes, 6078 yards, S.S.S. 69
† Welcome; WE by prior arrangement.
Ⅰ WD £19.95; WE £25.
🕹 Welcome by prior arrangement;
new conference room open; three
astroturf tennis courts; terms on
application.
🍴 Lounge; spike bars; restaurant
facilities; limited Mon.
🛏 Washbourne Court; The Manor;
local hotels in Stow-on-the-Wold.

5B 76 Newbold Comyn
Newbold Terrace East, Leamington
Spa, Warwicks, CV32 4EW

☎ 01926 421157
Off B4099 Willes road.
Parkland course.
Pro R Carvell; Founded 1972
18 holes, 6259 yards, S.S.S. 70
† Welcome.
Ⅰ WD £8.75; WE £11.75.
🕹 Welcome by prior arrangement;
packages on request.
🍴 Newbold Comyn Arms (next door).

5B 77 North Warwickshire
Hampton Lane, Meriden, W Midlands,
CV7 7LL
☎ 01676 522259, Fax 522915
Off A45 between Coventry and
Birmingham.
Parkland course.
Pro Andrew Bownes; Founded 1894
9 holes, 6390 yards, S.S.S. 71
† WD only by prior arrangement.
Ⅰ WD £18.
🕹 Welcome WD by arrangement;
maximum 30 players; meals available
in restaurant; terms available on
application.
🍴 Restaurant and bar facilities
available.
🛏 Manor Hotel; Strawberry Bank.

5B 78 North Worcestershire
Frankley Beeches Rd, Northfield,
Birmingham, B31 5LP
☎ 0121 475 1026, Fax 4768681,
Pro 4755721
On A38 from Birmingham.
Parkland course.
Pro Finlay Clark; Founded 1907
Designed by James Braid
18 holes, 5950 yards, S.S.S. 68
† Welcome WD.
Ⅰ WD £18.50.
🕹 Welcome Tues and Thurs; terms
on application.
🍴 Full facilities available.
🛏 Norwood, Kings Norton.

5B 79 Nuneaton ⓣ
Golf Drive, Whitestone, Nuneaton,
Warwicks, CV11 6QF
☎ 024 7634 7810, Fax 76327563
Leave M6 Junction 3 on A444 2 miles
S of Nuneaton.
Wooded undulating meadowland course.
Pro Steve Bainbridge; Founded 1906
18 holes, 6480 yards, S.S.S. 71
† Welcome WD; WE with member.
Ⅰ WD £25.
🕹 Welcome by prior arrangement;
terms on application.
🍴 Full facilities except Mon.
🛏 Long Shoot; Chase.

5B 80 Oakridge
Arley Lane, Ansley Village, Nuneaton,
Warwicks, CV10 9PH
☎ 01676 541389, Fax 542709
Off B4112 3 miles W of Nuneaton.
Parkland course.
Pro Tony Harper; Founded 1993
18 holes, 6242 yards, S.S.S. 70
† Welcome WD; WE with member.
Ⅰ WD £15.
🕹 Welcome Mon-Thurs and Fri am.
🍴 Full meals and bar except Mon.
🛏 Marriott Forest of Arden.

5B 81 Olton
Mirfield Rd, Solihull, W Midlands, B91
1JH
☎ 0121 705 1083, Fax 7112010
2 miles from M42 Junction 5 on A41
towards Birmingham.
Parkland course.
Pro Craig Phillips; Founded 1893
18 holes, 6623 yards, S.S.S. 71
† Welcome by arrangement.
Ⅰ WD £30; WE £30.
🕹 Welcome WD by prior
arrangement; terms on application.
🍴 Clubhouse facilities.
🛏 Ingon Manor.

5B 82 Ombersley
Bishops Wood Road, Lineholt,
Ombersley, Droitwich, Worcs, WR9
0LE
☎ 01905 620747, Fax 620047,
Sec 620047
Off A449 Kidderminster to Worcester
road at A4025.
Rural parkland setting.
Pro Graham Glenister; Founded 1991
Designed by On Course Design (David
Morgan)
18 holes, 6139 yards, S.S.S. 69
Ⅰ Practice range 36 bays (20
covered); chipping green; putting
green; tuition available from PGA
professionals; custom fit club maker
Debbie Hall; open from 5am in
summer; buggies and clubs for hire.
† Welcome; pay and play.
Ⅰ WD £14.70; WE £19.60.
🕹 Welcome; society and corporate
packages; prices on application.
🍴 Restaurant bar terrace.
🛏 Hadley Bowling Green Inn.

5B 83 Painswick ⓣ
Painswick Beacon, Painswick, Stroud,
Glos, GL6 6TL
☎ 01452 812180
On the A46 one mile N of Painswick.
Commonland course.

Founded 1891
18 holes, 4680 yards, S.S.S. 64
⫻ Practice range practice ground.
† Welcome WD and Sat; with member Sun.
Ⅼ WD £15, Sat £20.
⟡ Welcome by prior arrangement with Sec; special packages.
▮●▮ Bar and catering facilities.
⛛ The Painswick Hotel.

5B 84 **Perdiswell**
Bilford Road, Worcester, Worcs, WR3 8DX
☎ 01905 457189, Fax 756608, Pro 754668
Off main Droitwich road, N of Worcester.
Meadowland course (extention; opened 2000).
Pro Mark Woodward; Founded 1981
18 holes, 5297 yards, S.S.S. 68
⫻ Teaching Area; lesons available; leisure centre adjacent to course.
† Welcome.
Ⅼ Prices on application.
⟡ Welcome by prior arrangement; catering packages available.
▮●▮ Bar and snacks.

5B 85 **Pitcheroak**
Plymouth Rd, Redditch, Worcs, B97 4PB
☎ 01527 541054, Pro 541054
Signposted from centre of Redditch.
Municipal parkland course.
Pro David Stewart; Founded 1973
18 holes, 4561 yards, S.S.S. 62
⫻ Practice range; practice area; putting green; tuition available; hire equipment available.
† Welcome.
Ⅼ WD £7.85; WE £9.10.
⟡ Welcome by prior arrangement.
▮●▮ Licensed clubhouse; bar and restaurant.
⛛ Mont Ville.

5B 86 **Purley Chase G & Country Club**
Ridge Lane, Nr Nuneaton, Warwickshire, CV10 0RB
☎ 024 7639 3118, Fax 76398015, Pro 76395348
From A5 Mancetter to Atherstone road; follow signs.
Parkland course.
Pro Gary Carver; Founded 1977
Designed by B Tomlinson
18 holes, 6772 yards, S.S.S. 72
† Welcome WD; WE afternoons only.
Ⅼ WD £15; WE £25.

⟡ Welcome WD; various packages available; terms on application.
▮●▮ Full clubhouse facilities.
⛛ Hanover International; Bosworth Hall.

5B 87 **Pype Hayes**
Eachelhurst Rd, Walmley, Sutton Coldfield, W Midlands, B76 8EP
☎ 0121 351 1014
Off M6 Junction 6 on to Tyburn Rd; 1 mile to Eachelhurst Rd.
Public parkland course.
Pro Jim Bayliss; Founded 1932
18 holes, 5927 yards, S.S.S. 68
† Welcome with prior booking.
Ⅼ WD £8.50; WE £9.
⟡ Welcome WD by prior arrangement.
▮●▮ Cafeteria.
⛛ Pens Hall.

5B 88 **Ravenmeadow**
Hindlip Lane, Claines, Worcester, Worcs, WR3 8SA
☎ 01905 757525, Fax 759184, Sec 759183
4 miles N of Worcester off the A38.
Parkland course.
Pro Dean Davis; Founded 1996
9 holes, 5435 yards, S.S.S. 68
⫻ Practice range 10 bays floodlit; smart golf simulator; junior academy; adult and junior tuition.
† Welcome.
Ⅼ 9 holes: WD £7.75, WE and BH £9.75; 18 holes: WD £10.75, WE and BH £14.75.
⟡ Welcome by prior arrangement; packages available; terms on application.
▮●▮ Bar and restaurant facilities.
⛛ The Founds; Star.

5B 89 **Redditch**
Lower Grinsty Lane, Callow Hill, Redditch, Worcs, B97 5JP
☎ 01527 543309, Fax 543079, Pro 546372
2 miles W of Redditch.
Parkland course.
Pro Frank Powell; Founded 1913/72
Designed by F Pennink
18 holes, 6671 yards, S.S.S. 72
† Welcome; WE with members.
Ⅼ WD £20-£27.50.
⟡ Welcome by prior arrangement; catering packages and reductions available; terms on application.
▮●▮ Full clubhouse facilities.
⛛ The Quality Hotel; Mont Ville.

5B 90 **Robin Hood**
St Bernards Rd, Solihull, W Midlands, B92 7DJ
✉ robin.hood.golf.club@dial.pipex.com
☎ 0121 706 0061, Fax 7060061, Pro 7060806, Sec 7060061
2 miles S of M42 Junction 4 & 5.
Parkland course.
Pro A J Harvey; Founded 1893
Designed by HS Colt
18 holes, 6635 yards, S.S.S. 72
† Welcome WD.
Ⅼ WD £29-£35; WE £12 with member.
⟡ Welcome Tues, Thurs, Fri, with handicap certs; packages available; from £40.
▮●▮ Clubhouse facilities.
⛛ Arden Hotel.

5B 91 **Ross-on-Wye**
Two Park, Gorsley, Ross-on-Wye, Hereford, HR9 7UT
☎ 01989 720267, Fax 720212, Pro 720439
5 miles N of Ross-on-Wye; close to M50 Junction 3.
Parkland course.
Pro Nick Catchpole; Founded 1903
Designed by CK Cotton
18 holes, 6451 yards, S.S.S. 73
⫻ Practice range; practice area; tuition.
† Welcome.
Ⅼ WD £32-42; WE £32-42.
⟡ Welcome Wed, Thurs, Fri; packages available for 20+; deposit required; snooker tables; from £28.
▮●▮ Clubhouse facilities; bar and restaurant.
⛛ Chase Hotel; Royal Hotel.

5B 92 **Royal Forest Of Dean**
Lord's Hill, Coleford, Glos, GL16 8BD
☎ 01594 832583, Fax 832584
4 miles from Monmouth; 8 miles from Ross and Chepstow.
Parkland/meadowland course.
Pro John Hansel; Founded 1973
Designed by John Day of Alphagreen Ltd
18 holes, 5813 yards, S.S.S. 69
† Welcome.
Ⅼ Winter WD and WE £10; Summer WD and WE £18.
⟡ Welcome by prior arrangement with the hotel; packages available for golf; catering and hotel; tennis; bowls; prices on application.
▮●▮ Full bar and restaurant service.
⛛ Bells on site.

5B 93 **Rugby**
Clifton Rd, Rugby, Warwicks, CV21
3RD
☎ 01788 575134, Fax 542306,
Pro 575134, Sec 542306
On Rugby-Market Harborough road on
right just past railway bridge.
Parkland course.
Pro Nathanial Summers;
Founded 1891
18 holes, 5614 yards, S.S.S. 67
⌁ Practice range; practice area;
tuition available with two teaching pros;
trolleys for hire.
† Welcome WD; WE with a member.
⌶ WD £20; WE £10 with a member .
⌔ Welcome WD by arrangement;
packages available; minimum 12.
⦿ Full catering except Sun and Tues.
⌁ Carlton; Grosvenor.

5B 94 **Sapey**　　　　　　　　　☎
Upper Sapey, Nr Worcester, Worcs,
WR6 6XT
☎ 01886 853288, Fax 853485,
Pro 853567/853288, Sec 853506
On B4203 between Bromyard and
Stourport.
Parkland course.
Pro Chris Knowles; Founded 1990
18 holes, 5935 yards, S.S.S. 68
† Welcome.
⌶ Rowan: WD £16; WE £22. Oaks:
WD £4; WE £5.
⌔ Welcome by prior arrangement;
terms on application.
⦿ Clubhouse facilities.
⌁ Hundred House; The Granary.

5B 95 **Sherdons**
Manor Farm, Tredington, Tewkesbury,
Gloucs, GL20 7BP
☎ 01684 274782
2 miles out of Tewkesbury on the A38;
turn off at the Odessa Inn.
Parkland course.
Pro Philip Clark/John Parker; Founded
1995
9 holes, 2618 yards, S.S.S. 66
⌁ Practice range 26 floodlit bays.
† Welcome; pay and play.
⌶ 9 holes: WD £6, WE £7.50; 18
holes: WD £11, WE £14.
⌔ Welcome WD; WE by
arrangement.
⦿ Soft drinks, coffee, snacks.
⌁ Gubshill Manor.

5B 96 **Shirehampton Park**　　　☎
Park Hill, Shirehampton, Bristol, BS11
0UL
☎ 0117 9823059, Fax 9822083,

Pro 9822488
2 miles from M5 Junction 18 on B4054
through Shirehampton.
Undulating parkland course.
Pro Brent Ellis; Founded 1907
18 holes, 5430 yards, S.S.S. 67
† Welcome.
⌶ WD £18; WE £25.
⌔ Welcome; snacks lunch available;
dinner by appointment; from £18.
⦿ Clubhouse facilities.

5B 97 **Shirley**
Stratford Rd, Monkspath, Shirley,
Solihull, W Midlands, B90 4EW
☎ 0121 744 6001, Fax 7458220,
Pro 7454979
Towards Birmingham off M42
Junction 4.
Parkland course.
Pro S Botterill; Founded 1956
18 holes, 6507 yards, S.S.S. 71
† Welcome WD; with member at
WE.
⌶ WD £25; WE £25.
⌔ Welcome by arrangement;
packages available; terms on
application.
⦿ Restaurant and bar facilities.
⌁ Regency Hotel.

5B 98 **Sphinx Club**
Siddeley Ave, Coventry, Warwicks,
CV3 1FZ
☎ 024 7645 1361
4 miles S of Coventry close to main
Binley Road.
Parkland course.
Founded 1948
9 holes, 4262 yards, S.S.S. 60
† Welcome WD; with member at
WE.
⌶ Terms on application.
⌔ Welcome by arrangement.
⦿ Bar and bar meals.

5B 99 **Stinchcombe Hill**　　　　☎
Stinchcombe Hill, Dursley, Glos, GL11
6AQ
☎ 01453 542015, Fax 549545
From A38 at Dursley; right past
post office.
Downland course.
Pro Paul Bushell; Founded 1889
Designed by Arthur Hoare
18 holes, 5734 yards, S.S.S. 68
⌁ Practice range, putting green and
practice net, Pros available for tuition.
† Welcome.
⌶ WD £20; WE £25.
⌔ Welcome Mon, Wed and Fri;
catering packages available for 12 or

more players; terms on application.
⦿ Full facilities and bar.
⌁ Club can provide full list.

5B 100 **Stonebridge**
Somers Rd, Meriden, Warwicks, CV7
7PL
☎ 01676 522442
2 miles from M42 Junction 6.
Parkland course.
Pro Steve Harrison; Founded 1995
18 holes, 6240 yards, S.S.S. 70
⌁ Practice range, 21 bays floodlit.
† Welcome; bookings taken 9 days
in advance.
⌶ Mon-Thur £14, Fri £15; WE £16.
⌔ Welcome Mon to Thurs by prior
arrangement; from £20.
⦿ 2 bars, restaurant and conference
facilities.
⌁ Strawberry Bank.

5B 101 **Stoneleigh Deer Park**
The Old Deer Park, Coventry Rd,
Stoneleigh, Warwicks, CV8 3DR
☎ 024 7663 9991, Fax 76511533,
Pro 76639912
Off A46 or A454 at Stoneleigh village.
Parkland course.
Pro Matt McGuire; Founded 1991
Designed by K Harrison/Brown
18 holes, 5846 yards, S.S.S. 68
⌁ Practice area.
† Welcome.
⌶ WD £14.50; WE £22.50.
⌔ Welcome with prior arrangement;
packages available; catering from
8am-9pm; also 9-hole 1251-yard par 3
course; from £14.50.
⦿ Catering and bar facilities.
⌁ Club can recommend.

5B 102 **Stourbridge**
Worcester Lane, Pedmore,
Stourbridge, Glos, DY8 2RB
☎ 01384 393129, Fax 444660,
Pro 393129, Sec 395566
Course is one mile S of Stourbridge on
the B4147.
Parkland course.
Pro Mark Male; Founded 1892
18 holes, 6231 yards, S.S.S. 70
† Welcome WD; with member WE.
⌶ WD £28.
⌔ Welcome Tues and Thurs;
packages available; from £25.
⦿ Restaurant and bar facilities.
⌁ Limes, Pedmore; Travelodge,
Hagley.

5B 103 **Stratford Oaks**
Bearley Road, Snitterfield, Stratford-upon-Avon, Warwicks, CV37 0EZ
☎ 01789 731982
On A34 to Stratford following signs to Snitterfield.
Parkland course.
Pro Andrew Dunbar; Founded 1989
Designed by Howard Swan
18 holes, 6121 yards, S.S.S. 69
⌘ Practice range 22 floodlit covered bays.
♦ Welcome with booking.
⌐ WD £20; WE £25.00.
⌒ Welcome WD by arrangement; catering packages available.
⦿ Bar and restaurant facilities.
⌁ Arden Valley; Alveston Manor.

5B 104 **Stratford-upon-Avon**
Tiddington Rd, Stratford-upon-Avon, Warwicks, CV37 7BA
☎ 01789 205749, Fax 414909,
Pro 205677, Rest/Bar Bar297296
Rest 414546
On B4089 0.5 miles from river bridge.
Parkland course.
Pro David Sutherland; Founded 1894
18 holes, 6303 yards, S.S.S. 70
♦ Welcome WD; WE by prior arrangement.
⌐ WD £29.50; WE £35.
⌒ Welcome Tues and Thurs by arrangement; catering packages available.
⦿ Full bar and catering.
⌁ Many in Stratford.

5B 105 **Sutton Coldfield**
110 Thornhill Rd, Streetly, Warwicks, B74 3ER
☎ 0121 3539633, Fax 3535503,
Rest/Bar 3532014
On B4138 9 miles NE of Birmingham.
Heathland course.
Pro Jerry Hayes; Founded 1889
18 holes, 6541 yards, S.S.S. 71
⌘ Practice area.
♦ Welcome WD; WE with member
⌐ WD £25.
⌒ Welcome WD by arrangement.
⦿ Full clubhouse facilities.
⌁ Sutton Court; Post House.

5B 106 **Tewkesbury Park Hotel**   ☾
Lincoln Green Lane, Tewkesbury, Glos, GL20 7DN
⌁ www.chorushotels.com
☎ 01684 295405, Fax 292386,
Pro 294892, Sec 299452
0.5 miles S of Tewkesbury on A38; 2

miles from M5 Junction 9.
Parkland course.
Pro Robert Taylor; Founded 1976
Designed by Frank Pennink
18 holes, 6533 yards, S.S.S. 72
♦ Welcome.
⌐ WD £15; WE £25.
⌒ Welcome WD; packages available; terms on application.
⦿ Clubhouse & hotel facilities.
⌁ 75-bedroom Tewkesbury Park Hotel on site.

5B 107 **Thornbury Golf Centre**
Bristol Rd, Thornbury, BS35 3XL
☎ 01454 281144, Fax 281177,
Pro 416543, Rest/Bar 281166
Off A38 at Berkeley Vale Motors; 5 miles from M4/M5.
Parkland course.
Pro Simon Hubbard; Founded 1992
Designed by Hawtree
18 holes, 6154 yards, S.S.S. 69
⌘ Floodlit driving range; 2 piece balls; 18-hole; par 3 course; Europro teaching centre.
♦ Welcome; pay and play.
⌐ WD £14.50; WE £17.
⌒ Welcome; packages available; conference and function rooms; terms on application.
⦿ Full catering facilities.
⌁ 11-bedroom lodge on site.

5B 108 **Tolladine**
The Fairways, Tolladine Rd, Worcester, WR4 9BA
☎ 01905 21974
M5 Junction 6 towards Warndon; club towards Worcester city centre.
Parkland course; steep in parts.
Founded 1898
9 holes, 5432 yards, S.S.S. 67
♦ Welcome WD except after 4pm Wed; with member at WE.
⌐ WD £10; WE £8.
⌒ Welcome by prior arrangement; terms on application.
⦿ By prior arrangement.

5B 109 **Tracy Park Country Club**
Bath Rd, Wick, Bristol, BS15 5RN
☎ 0117 9372251, Fax 9374288
From Junction 18 on M4 head S on the A46 towards Bath; then right on the A420 to Bristol 4 miles.
Parkland course.
Pro Tim Thompson-Green; Founded 1975
Designed by Grant Aitken
18 holes, 6430 yards, S.S.S. 71

♦ Welcome.
⌐ 18 holes WD £24 WE £30; 36 holes WD £30 WE £35.
⌒ Welcome; packages available; terms on application.
⦿ Clubhouse facilities; two restaurants.
⌁ On site hotel wth 18 en suite bedrooms.

5B 110 **Vale Golf & CC**
Hill Furze Rd, Bishampton, Pershore, Worcs, WR10 2LZ
⌁ www.gch.co.uk
✉ thevale@btinternet.com
☎ 01386 462781, Fax 462597,
Pro 462520
5 miles from Evesham on A4538; take Bishampton turn.
Parkland course.
Pro Caroline Griffiths; Founded 1991
Designed by M R M Sandow
18 holes, 7114 yards, S.S.S. 74
⌘ Practice range, 20 bays floodlit; 9-hole par 35 course; tuition available; equipment hire.
♦ Welcome.
⌐ WD £20; WE £25.
⌒ Welcome WD; terms on application; corporate packages can be arranged; conference and hospitality suites; terms on application.
⦿ Clubhouse and country club.
⌁ Club can recommend.

5B 111 **Walmley**
Brooks Rd, Wylde Green, Sutton Coldfield, Warwickshire, B72 1HR
☎ 0121 373 0029, Fax 3777272,
Pro 3737103
6 miles N of Birmingham.
Parkland course.
Pro Chris Wicketts; Founded 1902
18 holes, 6559 yards, S.S.S. 72
♦ Welcome WD; with member WE.
⌐ WD £30.
⌒ Welcome WD; discounts available for 30+ players; from £30.
⦿ Clubhouse facilities.
⌁ Penns Hall.

5B 112 **Warley**
Lightwoods Hill, Smethwick, Warley, W Midlands, B67 5ED
☎ 0121 4292440, Fax 4344430
Off A465 4.5 miles W of Birmingham behind the Cock & Magpie.
Municipal parkland course; part of link card system.
Pro David Owen; Founded 1921
9 holes, 5370 yards, S.S.S. 66
♦ Welcome.
⌐ WD £8; WE £9; with a link card

£1.50 off 18 holes; juniors WD £2-£3.25 WE £2.20-£4; discount with passports to leisure.
⚲ None.
🍴 Café.

5B 113 **Warwick**
The Racecourse, Warwick, Warwicks, CV34 6HW
☎ 01926 494316
In centre of Warwick racecourse.
Parkland course.
Pro Philip Sharp; Founded 1886
Designed by D.G. Dunkley
9 holes, 5364 yards, S.S.S. 66
⚑ Practice range, 26 floodlit covered bays.
† Welcome except on race days.
[WD £4.50; WE £5.
⚲ Welcome by arrangement.
🍴 Bar (open from 7pm).
⌂ Tudor House.

5B 114 **Warwickshire**
Leek Woolton, Warwick, Warwickshire, CV35 7QT
☎ 01926 409409
M49 Junction 15 take A46 towards Coventry; turn at signs for Leek Wootton on B4115.
Parkland course.
Pro Danny Peck; Founded 1993
Designed by K Litten
18 holes, 7407 yards, S.S.S. 74
⚑ Practice range, 30 bays, 9 covered; leisure complex.
† Welcome.
[Summer: WD £45, WE £45;
Winter: WD £25, WE £25.
⚲ Welcome; minimum 12; packages available; private function suites; buggies; coaching clinics; terms on application.
🍴 Full restaurant and bar facilities.
⌂ Chesford Grange; Alveston Hall; Charlecote Pheasant; Walton Hall.

5B 115 **Welcombe Hotel**
Warwick Rd, Stratford-upon-Avon, Warwicks, CV37 0NR
⌨ www.welcombe.co.uk
✉ sales@welcombe
☎ 01789 299012, Fax 262665,
Sec 262665
5 miles from M40 Junction 15; 1.5 miles from Stratford on A439.
Parkland course; being upgraded and remeasured.
Pro Carl Mason/Karen Thatcher;
Founded 1956/80
Designed by TJ McCauley
18 holes, 6288 yards, S.S.S. 70

† Welcome by prior arrangement.
[Summer: WD £40, WE £50;
Winter: WD £25, WE £25.
⚲ Welcome; packages available; discounts available; golf clinics; floodlit tennis courts; corporate days; snooker; fitness room; solarium; conference facilities; terms on application.
🍴 Full clubhouse and hotel facilities including Trevelyan Restaurant.
⌂ Welcombe Hotel; 63 en-suite rooms.

5B 116 **Westonbirt Girls School**
Tetbury, Glos, GL8 8QG
☎ 01666 880242
From A433 Tetbury to Bath road turn into Westonbirt village; opposite Arboretum.
Parkland course.
Founded 1934
Designed by Monty Hearn
9 holes, 4504 yards, S.S.S. 61
† Welcome.
[WD £8; WE £16.
⚲ None.
⌂ Hare and Hounds.

5B 117 **Wharton Park**   ♛
Long Bank, Bewdley, Worcs, DY12 2QW
☎ 01299 405222, Fax 405121
On A456 at west end of Bewdley by-pass.
Parkland course.
Pro Angus Hoare; Founded 1992
18 holes, 6603 yards, S.S.S. 72
† Welcome.
[WD £20; WE £25.
⚲ Welcome by prior arrangement; packages available; terms on application.
🍴 Clubhouse facilities.
⌂ Heath Hotel.

5B 118 **Whitefields**   ♛
Coventry Rd, Thurlaston, Nr Rugby, Warwicks, CV23 9JR
☎ 01788 815555, Fax 521695,
Sec 521800
Course is on the A45 close to junction with the M45.
Parkland course overlooking Draycote Water.
Founded 1992
Designed by R Mason
18 holes, 6223 yards, S.S.S. 70
⚑ Practice range, 16 bays floodlit; 18-hole putting green; tuition available.
† Welcome by prior arrangement.
[WD £18; WE £25.
⚲ 3 packages available; terms on application.

🍴 Hotel facilities.
⌂ Whitefields; 50-room hotel on site.

5B 119 **Widney Manor**
Saintbury Drive, Widney Manor, Solihull, W Midlands, B91 3SZ
☎ 0121 7113646
Off M42 Junction 4 take Stratford road and then turn right into Monkshall Path Road; signposted for Widney Manor.
Parkland course.
Pro Tim Atkinson; Founded 1993
Designed by Golf Design Group
18 holes, 5001 yards, S.S.S. 64
⚑ Practice range, practice area.
† Welcome.
[WD £10; WE £13.50.
⚲ Welcome WD but not before 10am at WE; terms on application.
🍴 Full facilities.

5B 120 **Windmill Village Hotel**
Birmingham Road, Allesley, Coventry, Warwicks, CV5 9AL
⌨ www.windmillvillage.co.uk
✉ windmillvillage@compuserve.com
☎ 024 76404041, Fax 76407016
On A45 westbound Coventry-Birmingham road.
Part flat part hilly course.
Pro Robert Hunter; Founded 1990
Designed by Robert Hunte & John Harrhy
18 holes, 5169 yards, S.S.S. 68
† Welcome.
[WD £9.95; WE £14.95.
⚲ Welcome by arrangement; packages available; swimming pool; tennis courts; gym; sauna; conference suites.
🍴 Bar and restaurant facilities.
⌂ Windmill Village on site.

5B 121 **Wishaw**
Bulls Lane, Wishaw, W Midlands, B76 9QW
☎ 0121 3513221
From M42 Junction 9 take second left at The Belfry to the Cock at Wishaw; course 0.75 miles.
Parkland course.
Pro Alan Partridge; Founded 1993
18 holes, 5481 yards, S.S.S. 70
† Welcome.
[WD £10; WE £15.
⚲ Welcome WD by arrangement; packages available; terms on application.
🍴 Restaurant and bar facilities available.
⌂ Belfry; Moor Hall.

Widney Manor Golf Club

- 18 hole Golf Course
- Driving Range
- Buggies
- Societies welcome
- Pro Shop & Tuition
- Membership

Saintbury Drive, Solihull, West Midlands B91 3SZ Telephone 0121 704 0704

5B 122 Woodlands
Woodlands Lane, Almondsbury, Bristol,
BS32 4JZ
✉ woodlands@tracypark.com
☎ 01454 619319, Fax 619397,
Sec 619319
Off A38 at the Aztec roundabout
turning left into Woodlands Lane.
Parkland course.
Pro Andy Lowen/Nigel Warburton;
Founded 1989
Designed by C Chapman
18 holes, 6068 yards, S.S.S. 69
♉ Welcome.
☒ WD £12; WE £14.
⟳ Welcome by prior arrangement;
terms on application.
⦿ Full clubhouse facilities.
↝ The Range; Stakis.

**5B 123 Woodspring Golf and
Country Club**
Yanley Lane, Long Ashton, Bristol,
Avon, BS18 9LR
☎ 01275 394378
On A38 near Bristol Airport.
Parkland course;
Pro Nigel Beer; Founded 1994
Designed by P Alliss & C Clark/D Steel
27 holes, 6587 yards, S.S.S. 70
♉ Practice range 25 bays floodlit;

sauna jacuzzi snooker.
♉ Welcome.
☒ WD £20; WE £28.50.
⟳ Welcome; catering packages
available; contact Kevin Pitts; 3 x 9
courses: Avon Brunel Severn; terms on
application.
⦿ Full clubhouse facilities.
↝ Swallow Royal; Redwood Lodge;
Town & Country Lodge; Marriott.

**5B 124 Worcester Golf &
Country Club**
Boughton Park, Bransford Road,
Worcester, Worcester, WR2 4EZ
☎ 01905 422555, Fax 749090,
Pro 422044
From M5 Junction 7 follow signs for
Worcester West.
Parkland course.
Pro Colin Colenso; Founded 1898
Designed by Dr A MacKenzie (1926)
18 holes, 6251 yards, S.S.S. 70
♉ Welcome WD; guests of members
only at WE.
☒ WD £25.
⟳ Welcome with 12 months prior
booking; catering and golf packages
can be arranged; jacket and tie
required in dining room; tennis;
squash; from £33.

⦿ Full clubhouse, restaurant and bar
facilities.

5B 125 Worcestershire
Wood farm, Malvern Wells, Worcs,
WR14 4PP
☎ 01684 575992, Fax 575992,
Pro 564428, Sec 575992,
Rest/Bar 573905
Course is two miles south of Great
Malvern; turn off the A449 on to the
B4209.
Parkland course.
Pro Richard Lewis; Founded 1879
Designed by Colt; Mackenzie; Braid
amended by Jiggins and Hawtree
18 holes, 6470 yards, S.S.S. 71
♉ Welcome; handicap certs required;
no visitors before 10am WE.
☒ Prices on application.
⟳ Welcome Thurs and Fri; package
includes coffee, light lunch and 3-
course dinner; £45.
⦿ Full catering facilities.
↝ Abbey; Foley; Cottage in the
Woods.

5B 126 Wyre Forest
Zortech Avenue, Kidderminster, Worcs,
DY11 7EX

☎ 01299 822682, Fax 879433,
Pro 822682
Take A451 towards Stourport and
course is signposted.
Parkland course.
Pro Simon Price; Founded 1994

Designed by Golf Design Group
18 holes holes, 5790 yards, S.S.S. 68
╱ Driving range, buggies and clubs
for hire; tuition available.
♦ Welcome.
Ⅰ WD £12; WE £16.

╱ Welcome; terms on application;
from £18.
🍴 Clubhouse facilities.
↩ Heath; Gainsborough; Severn
Manor.

Shropshire, Staffordshire, Cheshire

Ian Woosnam and Sandy Lyle played their junior golf for Shropshire before remembering that they were Welsh and Scottish respectively.

Woosie's club was Llanymynech, a course that evokes the blue remembered hills of AE Housman. Constructed high on limestone outcrops, Llanymynech offers views for miles around as it leads you back and forth between England and Wales. On the fourth hole the golfer drives off in Wales and holes out in England.

Sandy Lyle was raised at Hawkestone Park where later he became the touring pro. Hawkestone provides the large-scale hotel golf experience without being punitively expensive. It has been an inn since 1790, although the first golf course wasn't built until the 1930s and the second added much later.

Bridgnorth is a cheerful club with a course admired by Donald Steel, but Shropshire is not exactly congested with golf. It is astonishing that two such players – Ballesteros rated Lyle as the most talented in the world and the quality of Woosnam's iron play is incontrovertible – should come up through such a relatively minor golfing county at around the same time.

Neighbouring Staffordshire has its own claim to fame – aside from the sort of high quality beer that Woosie disposes of by the jugful. Diane Bailey, who grew up at Enville, was the first to captain a winning Curtis Cup team in America and Geoff Marks, a stalwart of Trentham, was the first captain of a winning Walker Cup team in America. Marks did it the hard way in 1989, having to lead his anchor man by the arm to the final tee after watching a six-point lunchtime lead all but evaporate in the Georgia heat of the final afternoon singles. Jim Milligan's bogey on the last was enough to secure the half required for victory.

Enville has two courses set in woodland, the Highgate and the Lodge. The Highgate is the better thought of, an interesting contrast between some heathland holes and others dominated by trees. Trentham is a parkland course and neighbour to Trentham Park, David Gilford's old club.

Little Aston is Staffordhire's top course, but Beau Desert has been used for Regional qualifying into the Open. It is a moorland course flanked by fir and heather that requires a few carries from the tee. Whittington Heath is the other pick of the county, or Whittington Barracks as it used to be known. A member of Hankley Common in Surrey became so fond of Whittington's thinning, close-cropped fairways, which he likens to those at his home course, that he now refers to the club as Hankley Barracks. High praise indeed.

A vote would not be required to single out Cheshire's leading course. Hoylake, or Royal Liverpool as it is more correctly known, has just returned to the Open roster. But the links of Wallasey, the club associated with Dr Frank Stableford and his scoring system, Wilmslow, where crows used regularly to pick off golf balls over the final holes leading to the club emblem of a crow picking up a ball, Delamere Forest, a club that reviles the gratuitous use of trees to line fairways, and Carden Park, a fully kitted out Nicklaus project, might all win election in another constituency.

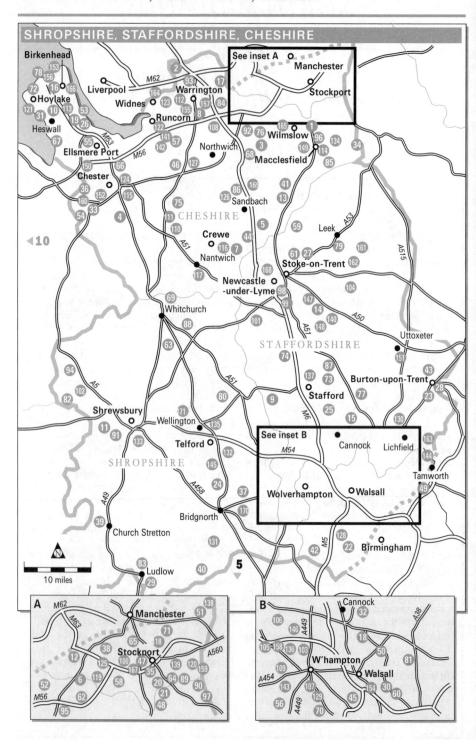

KEY		34	Chapel-en-le-Frith		Club	104	Parkhall	139	Stockport
1	Adlington Golf Centre	35	Cheadle	70	Himley Hall Golf Centre	105	Patshull Park Hotel Golf	140	Stone
2	Alder Root Golf Club	36	Chester	71	Houldsworth		and Country Club	141	Styal
3	Alderley Edge	37	Chesterton Valley GC	72	Hoylake Municipal	106	Penkridge G & CC	142	Sutton Hall
4	Aldersey Green Golf	38	Chorlton-cum-Hardy	73	Ingestre Park	107	Penn	143	Swindon
	Club	39	Church Stretton	74	Izaak Walton	108	Peover	144	Tamworth Municipal
5	Alsager Golf & Country	40	Cleobury Mortimer GC	75	Knights Grange Sports	109	Perton Park Golf Club	145	Telford Moat House
	Club	41	Congleton		Complex	110	Portal G & Country Club	146	Three Hammers Golf
6	Altrincham	42	Corngreaves	76	Knutsford	111	Portal G & Country Club		Complex
7	Alvaston Hall Golf Club	43	The Craythorne	77	Lakeside (Rugeley)		Premier Course	147	Trentham
8	Antrobus Golf Club	44	Crewe	78	Leasowe	112	Poulton Park	148	Trentham Park
9	Aqualate	45	Dartmouth	79	Leek	113	Prenton	149	The Tytherington
10	Arrowe Park	46	Delamere Forest	80	Lilleshall Hall	114	Prestbury	150	Upton-by-Chester
11	Arscott	47	Didsbury	81	Little Aston	115	Pryors Hayes Golf Club	151	Uttoxeter
12	Ashton on Mersey	48	Disley	82	Llanymynech	116	Queen's Park	152	Vicars Cross
13	Astbury	49	Drayton Park	83	Ludlow	117	Reaseheath	153	Wallasey
14	Barlaston	50	Druids Heath	84	Lymm	118	Reddish Vale	154	Walsall
15	Beau Desert	51	Dukinfield	85	Macclesfield	119	Ringway	155	Walton Hall
16	Bidston	52	Dunham Forest Golf &	86	Malkins Bank	120	Romiley	156	Warren
17	Birchwood		Country Club	87	The Manor Golf Club	121	Royal Liverpool	157	Warrington
18	Bloxwich	53	Eastham Lodge		(Kingstone) Ltd	122	Runcorn	158	Wergs
19	Brackenwood	54	Eaton	88	Market Drayton	123	St Michael Jubilee	159	Werneth Low
20	Bramall Park	55	Ellesmere Port	89	Marple	124	St Thomas's Priory GC	160	Westminster Park
21	Bramhall	56	Enville	90	Mellor & Townscliffe	125	Sale	161	Westwood (Leek)
22	Brand Hall	57	Frodsham	91	Meole Brace	126	Sandbach	162	Whiston Hall
23	Branston Golf & CC	58	Gatley	92	Mere Golf & CC	127	Sandiway	163	Whittington Heath
24	Bridgnorth	59	Goldenhill	93	Mersey Valley	128	Sandwell Park	164	Widnes
25	Brocton Hall	60	Great Barr	94	Mile End	129	Sedgley Golf Centre	165	Wilmslow
26	Bromborough	61	Greenway Hall	95	Mobberley	130	Seedy Mill	166	Wirral Ladies
27	Burslem	62	Hale	96	Mottram Hall Hotel	131	Severn Meadows	167	Withington
28	Burton-on-Trent	63	Hawkstone Park Hotel	97	New Mills	132	Shifnal	168	Wolstanton
29	Cadmore Lodge	64	Hazel Grove	98	Newcastle Municipal	133	Shrewsbury	169	Woodside
30	Calderfields	65	Heaton Moor	99	Newcastle-under-Lyme	134	Shrigley Hall Hotel	170	Worfield
31	Caldy	66	Helsby	100	Northenden	135	The Shropshire	171	Wrekin
32	Cannock Park	67	Heswall	101	Onneley	136	South Staffordshire		
33	Carden Park Hotel, Golf	68	Heyrose	102	Oswestry	137	Stafford Castle		
	Resort & Spa	69	Hill Valley Golf & Country	103	Oxley Park	138	Stamford (Stalybridge)		

6A 1 Adlington Golf Centre

Sandy Hey Farm, Adlington,
Macclesfield, Cheshire, SK10 4NG
⊕ www.adlingtongolfcentre.com
☎ 01625 850660, Fax 850960,
Sec 878468
Course is one mile South of Poynton
on the A523 Stockport-Macclesfield
road.
Par 3 course.
Pro John Watson; Founded 1995
Designed by Hawtree
9 holes, 635 yards
⌇ Driving range and golf academy.
† Public pay and play.
⌇ WD £4.50; WE £4.50.
⌁ Not available.
⦿ Vending machines.

6A 2 Alder Root Golf Club ☎

Alder Root Lane, Winwick, Warrington,
Cheshire, WA2 8RZ
☎ 01925 291919, Pro 291932
M62 Junction 9 then N on A49, turn left
at first set of lights; then 1st right into
Alder Root Lane.
Parkland course.
Pro Chris McKevitt; Founded 1993
Designed by Mr EM Millington
9 holes with 18 tees, 5834 yards,
S.S.S. 69

† Welcome by arrangement.
⌇ WD £16; WE £18.
⌁ Welcome WD by prior
arrangement; full catering and 27 holes
of golf; from £24.
⦿ Bar and snacks.
⌒ Winwick Quay.

6A 3 Alderley Edge

Brook Lane, Alderley Edge, Cheshire,
SK9 7RU
⊕ www.aegc.co.uk
✉ jerry.dickson@breathemail.net.
☎ 01625 585583, Pro 584493
From Alderley Edge turn off A34 to
Mobberley/Knutsford on B5085.
Undulating parkland course.
Pro Peter Bowring; Founded 1907
Designed by TG Renouf
9 holes, 5823 yards, S.S.S. 68
† Welcome with handicap certs;
restrictions WE. Ladies day Tues.
⌇ WD £20; WE £25.
⌁ Welcome Thurs by prior
arrangement; from £30.
⦿ Full catering except Mon.
⌒ De Trafford Arms.

6A 4 Aldersey Green Golf Club

Aldersey, Chester, Cheshire, CH3 9EH

☎ 01829 782157, Pro 782157,
Rest/Bar 782453
On A41 Whitchurch road.
Parkland course.
Pro Stephen Bradbury; Founded 1993
18 holes, 6159 yards, S.S.S. 69
† Welcome.
⌇ WD £12; WE £15.
⌁ Welcome by prior arrangement; 2
packages available WD; 1 at WE;
terms on application.
⦿ Bar and bar meals.
⌒ Calverley Arms.

6A 5 Alsager Golf & ☎ Country Club

Audley Road, Alsager, Stoke-on-Trent,
Staffs, ST7 2UR
⊕ www.alsagerclub.com
✉ business@alsagergolfclub.com
☎ 01270 875700, Fax 882207,
Pro 877432, Sec 875700,
Rest/Bar 875700
Leave M6 Junction 16 taking A500
towards Stoke for 1 mile; first left turn
for Alsager.
Parkland course.
Pro Richard Brown; Founded 1976
18 holes, 6225 yards, S.S.S. 70
† Welcome WD; WE with member.
⌇ WD £25.

⟡ Welcome Mon, Wed and Thurs; 3 packages available for societies; snooker; bowls; from £27.50.
⦿ Clubhouse facilities; banqueting available.
⊷ Manor Hotel.

6A 6 Altrincham
Stockport Road, Timperley, Altrincham, Cheshire, WA15 7LP
✉ scott-partington@hotmail.com
☎ 0161 9280761, Fax 9288542
On A560 1 mile W of Altincham.
Undulating parkland course.
Pro Scott Partington; Founded 1935
18 holes, 6385 yards, S.S.S. 71
† Welcome; advance booking at all times.
ⅼ WD £8.50; WE £11.50.
⟡ Welcome.
⦿ No catering; facilities at adjacent restaurant.
⊷ Cresta Court; Woodlands Park.

6A 7 Alvaston Hall GC ♛
Middlewich Road, Nantwich, Cheshire, CW5 6PD
☎ 01270 628473, Fax 623395,
Pro 628473, Rest/Bar 624341
1 mile from Nantwich on A530 to Middlewich.
Meadowland course.
Pro Kevin Valentine; Founded 1989
Designed by Kevin Valentine
9 holes, 3708 yards, S.S.S. 59
ⅼ 16.
† Welcome.
ⅼ WD £7.50; WE £10.00.
⟡ Welcome WD; terms on application.
⦿ Full facilities.
⊷ Alvaston Hall Hotel.

6A 8 Antrobus Golf Club ♛
Foggs Lane, Antrobus, Northwich, Cheshire, CW9 6JQ
☎ 01925 730890, Fax 730100,
Pro 730900
From A559 road off M56 Junction 10; take second left after Birch and Bottle; left into Foggs Lane.
Parkland course with water features.
Pro Paul Farrance; Founded 1993
Designed by Mike Slater
18 holes, 6220 yards, S.S.S. 71
† Welcome.
ⅼ WD £18; WE £20.
⟡ Welcome every day; packages available.
⦿ Full clubhouse facilities.
⊷ Park Royal, Stretton; Lord Daresbury, Warrington.

6A 9 Aqualate
Stafford Road, Newport, Shropshire, TF10 9JT
☎ 01952 825343
300 yds E of junction of A41 Newport bypass and A518 Newport to Stafford Road.
Heathland course.
Pro K Short; Founded 1995
Designed by MD Simmons/T Juhre
18 holes, 5659 yards, S.S.S. 67
† Welcome.
ⅼ WD £12; WE £15.
⟡ Welcome by arrangement; terms on application.
⦿ Coffee shop.

6A 10 Arrowe Park
Woodchurch, Birkenhead, Cheshire, CH49 5LW
☎ 0151 6771527, Pro 6771527, Sec 6771527, Rest/Bar 6771527
3 miles from town centre; 1 mile from M53 Junction 3 opposite Landicon Cemetery.
Municipal parkland course.
Pro Colin Disbury; Founded 1932
18 holes and a 9-hole par 3 course, 6435 yards, S.S.S. 71
† Welcome.
ⅼ WD £7.70; WE £7.70; seniors and juniors £3.85.
⟡ Welcome by prior arrangement with club Pro.
⦿ Restaurant facilities.
⊷ The Cherry Tree Hotel.

6A 11 Arscott ♛
Pontesbury, Shropshire, SY5 0XP
⌨ www.askatgolfclub.co.uk
☎ 01743 860114, Fax 860114,
Pro 860881, Sec 860114
1 mile past Hanwood on the A488 road from Shrewsbury to Bishops Castle; signposted at Lea Cross.
Parkland course.
Pro G Sadd; Founded 1992
Designed by Martin Hamer
18 holes, 6178 yards, S.S.S. 69
ⅼ Practice green.
† Welcome by prior arrangement.
ⅼ WD £16; WE £20.
⟡ Welcome WD; packages including golf and catering available; from £20.
⦿ Clubhouse facilities.
⊷ Prince Rupert; Boards Head.

6A 12 Ashton on Mersey
Church Lane, Sale, Cheshire, M33 5QQ
✉ golf@aomgc.fsnet.co.uk
☎ 0161 9764390, Pro 973 3727,

Sec 9764390, Rest/Bar 9733220
2 miles from Sale station.
Parkland course.
Pro Michael Williams; Founded 1897
9 holes, 6115 yards, S.S.S. 71
† Welcome except Tues after 3pm (Ladies Day).
ⅼ WD £20.50; WE £20.50.
⟡ Welcome by arrangement; terms on application.
⦿ Bar snacks and evening meals.
⊷ Mersey Farm Travelodge.

6A 13 Astbury
Peel Lane, Astbury, Nr Congleton, Cheshire, CW12 4RE
☎ 01260 272772, Fax 291300,
Pro 298663, Sec 291300,
Rest/Bar 272772
1 mile S of Congleton off A34.
Parkland course.
Pro Ashley Salt; Founded 1922
18 holes, 6296 yards, S.S.S. 70
† Welcome with handicap certs WD; WE with a member.
ⅼ WD £30 (day ticket).
⟡ Thurs only May-October; catering by prior arrangement.
⦿ Facilities available.
⊷ The Edgerton Star (0.5 mile from the golf course).

6A 14 Barlaston
Meaford Road, Stone, Staffs, ST15 8UX
☎ 01782 372795, Fax 372867,
Sec 372867
Between M6 Junction 14-15 just off A34 outside Barlaston village.
Picturesque parkland course with water hazards.
Pro Ian Rogers; Founded 1982
Designed by Peter Alliss
18 holes, 5801 yards, S.S.S. 68
ⅼ Practice area.
† Welcome midweek; some WE restrictions.
ⅼ WD £18; WE £22.50.
⟡ Welcome WD; packages for golf (maximum 27 holes), catering and prizes available; terms on application.
⦿ Bar and restaurant facilities.
⊷ Moat House; Stakis Grand, both Stoke; Stone House, Stone.

6A 15 Beau Desert
Rugeley Road, Hazel Slade, Cannock, Staffs, WS12 5PJ
☎ 01543 22626, Fax 451137,
Pro 422492, Sec 422626
On A460 between Rugeley and Cannock near Hednesford.

Heathland course.
Pro Barrie Stevens; Founded 1921
Designed by H Fowler
18 holes, 6310 yards, S.S.S. 71
⚑ 20.
† Welcome by arrangement.
⌐ WD £40; WE £50.
⌂ Welcome Mon-Thurs by prior
arrangement; packages available; from
£56.
⦿ Facilities available.
⌱ Little Barrow Hotel.

6A 16 Bidston
Bidston Link Road, Wallasey,
Merseyside, L46 2HR
☎ 0151 6383412, Pro 6306650
Course is close to Junction 1 on the
M53.
Parkland course/links.
Pro Seil Macsarlane; Founded 1913
18 holes, 6140 yards, S.S.S. 70
† Welcome WD.
⌐ WD £18. WE £25.00.
⌂ Welcome by prior arrangement;
packages available; terms on
application.
⦿ Full clubhouse facilities.
⌱ The Bowler Hat; The Leasowe
Castle.

6A 17 Birchwood
Kelvin Close, Birchwood, Warrington,
Cheshire, WA3 7PB
⌨ www.virtuagolfclub.com
✉ birchwoodgolfclub.com@
lineone.net
☎ 01925 818819, Fax 822403,
Pro 816574, Rest/Bar 818819
Off M62 at Junction 11 taking A574
road to Leigh and Science Park North;
club entrance just past Science Park
North.
Parkland course; natural water
hazards.
Pro Paul McEwan; Founded 1979
Designed by TJ MacAuley
18 holes, 6727 yards, S.S.S. 73
† Welcome; restrictions on
competition days.
⌐ WD £26; WE £34.
⌂ Welcome Mon, Wed, Thurs;
packages can be arranged; from £23.
⦿ Full catering facilities.
⌱ Garden Court, Woolston.

6A 18 Bloxwich
136 Stafford Road, Bloxwich, Walsall,
W Midlands, WS3 3PQ
✉ bloxwich.golf-club@virgin.net
☎ 01922 476593, Fax 476593
1 mile N of Bloxwich on A34 off M6 at

Junction 10 or 11.
Parkland course.
Pro RJ Dance; Founded 1924
Designed by J Sixsmith
18 holes, 6273 yards, S.S.S. 71
† Welcome midweek; members
guests at WE only.
⌐ WD £30; WE £35.
⌂ Welcome by prior arrangement;
reductions for groups; packages
available.
⦿ Facilities available.
⌱ Many in local area.

6A 19 Brackenwood
Bracken Lane, Bebington, Wirral,
Merseyside, CH63 2LY
☎ 0151 6083093
M53 Junction 4 to Clatterbridge and
Bebington.
Public parkland course.
Pro Kent Lamb; Founded 1933
18 holes, 6285 yards, S.S.S. 70
† Welcome.
⌐ WD £7.70; WE £7.70.
⌂ Welcome by arrangement.
⦿ Thornton Hall; Village.

6A 20 Bramall Park
Manor Road, Bramall, Stockport, SK7
3LY
☎ 0161 4853119, Fax 4857101,
Pro 4852205, Sec 4857101,
Rest/Bar 4853119
8 miles S of Manchester (club can
provide directions from M56 and M60).
Parkland course.
Pro M Proffitt; Founded 1894
Designed by J Braid
18 holes, 6214 yards, S.S.S. 70
⚑ Practice green.
† Welcome by arrangement.
⌐ Terms on application.
⌂ Welcome Tues and Thurs by prior
arrangement; packages available;
terms on application.
⦿ Clubhouse catering facilities
available.
⌱ County, Bramhall; Belfry;
Handforth.

6A 21 Bramhall
Ladythorn Road, Bramhall, Stockport,
Cheshire, SK7 2EY
⌨ www.bramhallgolfclub.com
☎ 0161 4394057, Fax 4390264,
Pro 4391171, Sec 4394057
Off A5102 S of Stockport.
Parkland course.
Pro R Green; Founded 1905
18 holes, 6340 yards, S.S.S. 70
† Welcome; restrictions Thurs.

⌐ WD £30; WE £37.
⌂ Welcome on Wed by prior
arrangement; golf and catering
packages can be arranged; from £30.
⦿ Clubhouse facilities.
⌱ County Hotel, Bramhall.

6A 22 Brand Hall
Heron Road, Oldbury, Warley, W
Midlands, B68 8AQ
☎ 0121 5522195, Fax 5445088,
Rest/Bar 5527475
6 miles NW of Birmingham, 1.5 miles
from M5 Junction 2.
Public parkland course.
Pro Carl Yates; Founded 1901
18 holes, 5734 yards, S.S.S. 68
⚑ Practice area.
† Welcome; pay and play.
⌐ Terms on application.
⌂ Welcome by arrangement.
⦿ Cafe, clubhouse bar.

6A 23 Branston Golf and   ♔
Country Club
Burton Road, Branston, Burton-On-
Trent, Staffs, DE14 3DP
⌨ www.bryanston/golf/club.co.uk
✉ golfacadamedy@
bryanston/golf/club.co.uk
☎ 01283 512211, Fax 566984,
Sec 543207
On A5121 off A38 at Burton South.
Parkland banks of River Trent; water
on 13 holes.
Pro Jacob Sture; Founded 1975
18 holes, 6697 yards, S.S.S. 72
⚑ 20.
† Welcome WD and afternoons at
WE. April-November soft spikes only.
⌐ WD £28; WE £40.
⌂ Welcome by arrangement; terms
on application.
⦿ Full catering facilities.
⌱ Dog and Partridge.

6A 24 Bridgnorth
Stanley Lane, Bridgnorth, Shropshire,
WV16 4SF
☎ 01746 763315, Fax 761381,
Pro 762045, Sec 763315,
Rest/Bar 763315/ 765735
On road to Broseley, 0.5 miles from
Bridgnorth.
Parkland course.
Pro Paul Hinton; Founded 1889
18 holes, 6650 yards, S.S.S. 73
† Welcome.
⌐ WD £26; WE £32.
⌂ Welcome Tues; Thurs, Fri;
reserved tee times and packages
available; from £30.

🍽 Clubhouse facilities.
↳ Parlours Hall; Falcon; Croft.

6A 25 Brocton Hall
Sawpit Lane, Brocton, Staffs, ST17 0TH
☎ 01785 662627, Fax 661591,
Pro 661485, Sec 661901
4 miles S of Stafford off A34.
Parkland course.
Pro RG Johnson; Founded 1894/1923
Designed by Harry Vardon
18 holes, 6064 yards, S.S.S. 69
† Welcome.
↧ WD £33; WE £40.
☘ Welcome Tues and Thurs by prior arrangement and with handicap certs; packages for golf and catering by prior arrangement.
🍽 Full clubhouse bar and restaurant facilities.
↳ Tillington Hall; Garth Hotel, both Stafford.

6A 26 Bromborough
Raby Hall Road, Bromborough, Wirral, Merseyside, CH63 0NW
🖳 www.bromborough-golf-club.freeserve.co.uk
📧 sec@bromborough-golf-club.freeserve.co.uk
☎ 0151 3342155, Fax 3347300,
Pro 3344499
Close to M53 Junction 5, 0.75 miles from A41 Birkenhead to Chester road; 0.5 miles from Bromborough station.
Parkland course.
Pro Geoff Berry; Founded 1904
18 holes, 6603 yards, S.S.S. 73
† Welcome WD; by arrangement WE.
↧ WD £35; WE £35.
☘ Welcome Wed; early booking essential.
🍽 Extensive catering and bar facilities.
↳ Thornton Hall; Village.

6A 27 Burslem
Wood Farm, High Lane, Tunstall, Stoke-on-Trent, ST6 7JT
☎ 01782 837006
4 miles N of Hanley.
Parkland course.
Founded 1907
11 holes, 5360 yards, S.S.S. 66
† Welcome WD only by prior arrangement.
↧ Terms on application.
☘ WD by prior arrangement; catering to be arranged with the steward; terms on application.

🍽 By arrangement with the steward.

6A 28 Burton-on-Trent
Ashby Road East, Burton-on-Trent, Derbyshire, DE15 0PS
📧 burtongolfclub@btinternet.com
☎ 01283 568708, Fax 544551,
Pro 562240, Sec 544551
On A511 3 miles E of Burton-on-Trent.
Undulating woodland course.
Pro G Stafford; Founded 1894
Designed by HS Colt
18 holes, 6579 yards, S.S.S. 71
† Welcome with handicap certs.
↧ WD £28; WE £32.
☘ Welcome WD; catering packages available except Mon; snooker; terms on application.
🍽 Full facilities except Mon.
↳ Stanhope Arms; Riverside, both Burton-on-Trent; Newton Park, Newton Solney.

6A 29 Cadmore Lodge
Berrington Green, Tenbury Wells, Worcester, Worcs, WR15 8TQ
📧 info@cadmore.demon.co.uk
☎ 01584 810044
Off A456.
Parkland course with lakes.
Founded 1990
Designed by John Weston
9 holes, 5132 yards, S.S.S. 65
† Welcome.
↧ WD £10; WE £14.
☘ Welcome by prior arrangement; packages can be arranged; bowls; tennis; fishing.
🍽 Full facilities.
↳ Hotel on site.

6A 30 Calderfields
Aldridge Road, Walsall, W Midland, WS4 2JS
☎ 01922 632243, Fax 638787,
Pro 613675, Sec 640540,
Rest/Bar 646888
On A454 off M6 Junctions 7 or 10.
Parkland course with lakes.
Pro David Williams; Founded 1981
Designed by Roy Winter
18 holes, 6509 yards, S.S.S. 71
↧ 27 floodlit; floodlit bunker and putting green.
† Welcome.
↧ WD £18; WE £18.
☘ Welcome every day; packages available; from £18.
🍽 Bar and restaurant facilities.
↳ Boundary; Fairview; County.

6A 31 Caldy
Links Hey Road, Caldy, Wirral, Merseyside, CH48 1NB
🖳 www.caldygolf.co.uk
☎ 0151 6255660, Fax 6257394,
Pro 6251818, Sec 6255660,
Rest/Bar 6255515
A540 from Chester, turn left from Caldy crossroads.
Seaside/parkland course.
Pro Kevin Jones; Founded 1907
Designed by James Braid, John Salvesen
18 holes, 6668 yards, S.S.S. 73
† Welcome WD; Tues Ladies Day; WE with a member.
↧ WD £42 all day; £37 one round.
☘ Welcome Thursday by arrangement; winter packages available.
🍽 Bar snacks all day; dinner by arrangement.
↳ Thornton Hall in Thornton Hough.

6A 32 Cannock Park
Stafford Road, Cannock, Staffs, WS11 2AL
☎ 01543 578850, Fax 578850,
Pro 578850, Sec 572800,
Rest/Bar 578850
Half a mile N of Cannock on A34
Parkland course.
Pro David Dunk; Founded 1990
Designed by John Mainland
18 holes, 5048 yards, S.S.S. 65
† Welcome; telephone in advance.
↧ WD £9; WE £11.
☘ Welcome by prior arrangement; packages available; terms on application.
🍽 Cafeteria within leisure complex.
↳ Roman Way; Hollies.

6A 33 Carden Park Hotel, Golf Resort & Spa
Carden Park, Chester, Cheshire, CH3 9DQ
🖳 www.carden-park.co.uk
📧 reservations@carden-park.co.uk
☎ 01829 731600, Fax 731636,
Pro 731600, Sec 731594,
Rest/Bar 731633
On A534 east of Wrexham; 1 and a half miles from junction with A41.
Parkland course.
Founded 1993
Designed by Course; redesigned several times
36 holes and a par 3 9-hole course, Nicklaus course 7010; Cheshire 6800 yards, S.S.S. 72

At **Cleobury Mortimer Golf Club** we believe that your whole experience - from the friendly welcome in the golf shop to your drinks and meal in our relaxed clubhouse - should all be part of a day that you'll remember. You will also have our 27 holes - set out in 3 very individual 9 hole loops and covering 200 acres of Shropshire's most beautiful countryside - to look forward to.

Wyre Common, Cleobury Mortimer, Shropshire DY14 8HQ
Tel: 01299 271112   **Fax:** 01299 271468
Email: enquiries@cleoburygolfclub.com   **Website:** www.cleoburygolfclub.com

---

⌘ Practice range, also 9-hole course available, par 3 £5; short game practice area.
† Welcome with handicap certs.
⌐ WD £40 – £60; WE £40 – £60.
⌐ Welcome with handicap certs and by prior arrangement; packages available for golf and catering; full first class hotel leisure and catering facilities; terms on application.
⦿ Full first class hotel facilities.
⌐ Carden Park Hotel on site with 192 rooms.

6A 34 Chapel-en-le-Frith
Manchester Road, Chapel-en-le-Frith, High Peak, Derbyshire, SK23 9UH
⌐ www.chapelgolf.co.uk
▣ info@chapelgolf.co.uk
☎ 01298 812118, Fax 813943,
Pro 812118, Sec 813943,
Rest/Bar 812118
On the road between Whaley Bridge and Chapel.
Parkland course with water hazards.
Pro D Cullen; Founded 1905
18 holes, 6462 yards, S.S.S. 71
† Welcome by prior arrangement.
⌐ Terms on application.
⌐ Welcome by prior arrangement; 36 holes of golf; coffee and biscuits on arrival, lunch and 5-course meal; from £35.
⦿ Full clubhouse facilities.

6A 35 Cheadle
Cheadle Road, Cheadle, Cheshire, SK8 1HW
☎ 0161 428 9878, Fax 428 9878,
Sec 491 3873, Rest/Bar 491 3873
One and a half miles from M63 Junction 11 follow signs for Cheadle; 1 mile south of Cheadle village.
Undulating parkland course.
Founded 1885
Designed by R Renouf
9 holes, 5006 yards, S.S.S. 65
† Welcome with handicap certs except Tues and Sat.
⌐ WD £20; WE £25.
⌐ Welcome by prior arrangement Mon, Wed, Thurs, Fri; catering packages can be arranged through the steward; no lunchtime catering on

Thurs; snooker; terms available on application.
⦿ Bar and catering facilities, except Thurs.
⌐ Village, Cheadle.

6A 36 Chester
Curzon Park North, Chester, Cheshire, CH4 8AR
☎ 01244 677760, Fax 676667
1 mile from Chester off the A55 behind Chester racecourse.
Parkland course.
Pro George Parton; Founded 1901
18 holes, 6508 yards, S.S.S. 71
† Welcome by arrangement.
⌐ WD £25; WE £30.
⌐ Welcome by arrangement.
⦿ Full facilities.
⌐ Many in Chester.

6A 37 Chesterton Valley Golf Club
Chesterton, Nr Worfield, Bridgnorth, Shropshire, WV15 5NX
☎ 01746 783682
On B4176 Dudley Telford Road.
Heathland course.
Pro Phil Hinton; Founded 1993
Designed by L Veines & M Davis
18 holes, 5671 yards, S.S.S. 67
† Pay and play.
⌐ WD £14.50; WE £15.50.
⌐ Welcome by prior arrangement; terms on application.
⌐ The Parlors Hall-Bridgenorth.

6A 38 Chorlton-cum-Hardy
Barlow Hall Road, Chorlton-Cum-Hardy, Manchester, Lancs, M21 7JJ
☎ 0161 8813139, Fax 8814532,
Pro 8819911, Sec 8815830
4 miles S of Manchester close to A5103/A5145 Junction.
Parkland course.
Pro David Valentine; Founded 1902
18 holes, 5980 yards, S.S.S. 69
⌐ Yes.
† Welcome by arrangement.
⌐ WD £25; WE £30.
⌐ Welcome on Thurs & Fri by prior arrangement; booking form available; terms on application.

⦿ Clubhouse facilities.
⌐ Post House, Britannia, both Northenden.

6A 39 Church Stretton   ⌦
Hunters Moon, Trevor Hill, Church Stretton, Shropshire, SY6 6JH
☎ 01694 722281
From A49 into Church Stretton; right at top of town; first left into Cardinmill Valley; 100 yards to Trevor Hill.
Hillside course.
Pro Peter Seal; Founded 1898
Designed by James Braid
18 holes, 5020 yards, S.S.S. 65
† Welcome.
⌐ Terms on application.
⌐ Welcome by arrangement; some WE available; golf and catering packages by arrangement; from £12.
⦿ Clubhouse facilities.
⌐ Denehurst; Longmynd, both Church Stretton; Stretton Hall, All Stretton.

6A 40 Cleobury Mortimer   ⌦
Golf Club
Wyre Common, Cleobury Mortimer, Kidderminster, Worcs, DY14 8HQ
☎ 01299 271112, Fax 271468,
Pro 271628, Rest/Bar 271320
2 miles E of Cleobury Mortimer just off A4117; halfway between Kidderminster and Ludlow.
Parkland course.
Founded 1993
Designed by EGU
27 holes, 6438 yards, S.S.S. 71
⌘ Practice range; nets; putting green; chipping area; digital golf coaching; please call club for information regarding courses available with the latest technology.
† Welcome by arrangement.
⌐ WD £20; WE £30 for 18 holes Mon madness offer; Winter £10 unlimited golf; Summer £15 unlimited golf; terms on application.
⌐ Welcome by arrangement; packages involving 18, 27 and 36 holes; catering plus private function room for 90; snooker.
⦿ Spike bar, lounge bar and restaurant facilities.
⌐ Redfern Hotel.

6A 41 Congleton
Biddulph Road, Congleton, Cheshire,
CW12 3LZ
✉ congletongolfclub@
hotmail.com
☎ 01260 273540, Fax 290902,
Pro 273540, Sec 273540,
Rest/Bar 273540
1 mile SE of Congleton station on
A527; Congleton Biddulph road.
Parkland course.
Pro John Colclough; Founded 1898
9 holes, 5119 yards, S.S.S. 65
† Welcome; Tues Ladies Day.
Ⅰ WD £21; WE £31.
♂ Welcome Mon and Thurs by prior
booking.
⦿ Full facilities except Mon.
↘ Lion & Swan; Bulls Head.

6A 42 Congreaves
Corngreaves Road, Cradley Heath, W
Midlands, B64 7NL
☎ 01384 567880
2 miles E of Dudley.
Public parkland course.
Pro Carl Yates; Founded 1985
18 holes, 3979 yards, S.S.S. 61
† Welcome.
Ⅰ Terms on application.
♂ Welcome by arrangement.
⦿ Full facilities.

6A 43 The Craythorne Golf Club
Craythorne Road, Stretton, Burton On
Trent, Staffs, DE13 0AZ
🖳 www.craythorne.co.uk
☎ 01283 564329, Fax 511908
300 yards from village after leaving
A38 at Stretton.
Parkland course.
Pro S Hadfield; Founded 1974
Designed by Cyril Johnson/AA Wright
18 holes, 5306 yards, S.S.S. 67
† Welcome by prior arrangement;
handicap certs required.
Ⅰ WD £22; WE £28.
♂ Welcome by prior arrangement;
packages available; terms on
application.
⦿ Full facilities.
↘ The Brook House.

6A 44 Crewe
Fields Road, Haslington, Crewe,
Cheshire, CW1 5TB
🖳 www.crewegolfclub.co.uk
✉ secretary@crewegolfclub.co.uk
☎ 01270 584227, Fax 584099,
Pro 585032, Sec 584099
2 miles NE of Crewe station off A534.

Parkland course.
Pro Michael Booker; Founded 1911
18 holes, 6424 yards, S.S.S. 71
† Welcome WD; WE with a member.
Ⅰ WD £27.
♂ Welcome Tues; golf and catering
packages available.
⦿ Clubhouse facilities.
↘ Hunter Lodge, Crewe Arms.

6A 45 Dartmouth
Dartmouth Golf Club, Vale Street, West
Bromwich, W Midlands, B71 4DW
☎ 0121 588 2131
One and a half miles from M5/M6
Junction.
Undulating meadowland/parkland
course.
Pro Simon Joyce; Founded 1910
9 holes, 6036 yards, S.S.S. 69
† Welcome WD with handicap certs,
with member only at WE.
Ⅰ WD £15 (day ticket).
♂ By arrangement with Pro;
packages available; snooker.
⦿ Full facilities.
↘ Moat House, Albion.

6A 46 Delamere Forest
Delamere, Northwich, Cheshire, CW8
2JE
✉ delamere@btconnet.com
☎ 01606 883264, Fax 889444,
Pro 883307, Sec 883800
From A556 take B5152 towards
Frodsham; lane to club is 1 mile, next
to Delamere station.
Undulating heathland course.
Pro Ellis Jones; Founded 1910
Designed by Herbert Fowler
18 holes, 6305 yards, S.S.S. 71
† Welcome; restrictions at WE and
bank holidays.
Ⅰ WD £35 for a round. Day rate £50.
WE £50 a round from 1 Jan 2002.
♂ Welcome by arrangement.
⦿ Bar snacks; restaurant.
↘ Hartford Hall; Swan; Willington
Hall, Blue Cap Motel.

6A 47 Didsbury
Ford Lane, Northenden, Manchester,
M22 4NQ
🖳 www.didsburygolfclub.com
✉ golf@didsburygolfclub.com
☎ 0161 998 9278, Fax 998 9278,
Pro 998 2811, Rest/Bar 998 2743
6 miles S of Manchester.
Parkland course.
Pro P Barber; Founded 1891
Designed by G Lowe (1891); G
MacKenzie (1921); D Thomas an P

Alliss (1973)
18 holes, 6273 yards, S.S.S. 70
† Welcome with handicap certs.
Ⅰ WD £28; WE £32.
♂ Welcome Thurs Fri; restricted
availability Sun and Mon; catering and
golf packages available minimum 12
maximum 80.
⦿ Full clubhouse facilties.
↘ Post House; Brittania both
Northend.

6A 48 Disley
Stanley Hall Lane, Jackson'S Edge,
Disley, Stockport, Cheshire, SK12 2JX
☎ 01663 762071, Fax 762678,
Pro 762884, Sec 764001
Off A6 in Disley village.
Open hillside/parkland course.
Pro Andrew Esplin; Founded 1889
Designed by James Braid
18 holes, 6015 yards, S.S.S. 69
† Welcome WD by prior arrangement.
Ⅰ WD £25.
♂ Welcome WD by prior
arrangement; catering and golf
packages available; from £35.
⦿ Clubhouse facilities except
Mondays.
↘ Stakis Moorside.

6A 49 Drayton Park
Drayton Park Golf Club Ltd, Drayton
Manor Drive, Tamworth, Staffs, B78
3TN
☎ 01827 251139, Fax 284035,
Pro 251478, Rest/Bar 287481
On A4091 at Drayton Leisure Park.
Parkland course.
Pro MW Passmore; Founded 1897
Designed by James Braid
18 holes, 6401 yards, S.S.S. 71
† Welcome weekdays, except
Wednesday.
Ⅰ WD £34.
♂ Welcome Tues and Thurs
throughout the year by prior
arrangement with Secretary, minimum
of 12 players; catering packages can
be arranged; from £26.
⦿ Full facilities available.
↘ Gungate; Beefeater, both in
Tamworth.

6A 50 Druids Heath
Stonnall Road, Walsall, W Midlands
WS9 8JZ
☎ 01922 455595, Fax 452887,
Pro 459523
Off A452 6 miles NW of Sutton
Coldfield.
Undulating course.

Pro Glenn Williams; Founded 1973
18 holes, 6659 yards, S.S.S. 73
† Welcome WD and after 2pm on
WE.
Ɪ WD £25; WE £33.
⚷ WD by prior arrangement.
🍽 By prior arrangement.
⚲ Barons Court; Fairlawns.

6A 51 Dukinfield
Yew Tree Lane, Dukinfield, Cheshire,
SK16 5DB
📧 dgc@telinco.co.uk
☎ 0161 3382340, Fax 3030205,
Pro 3382340, Sec 3382340,
Rest/Bar 3382340
From Ashton Road 1 mile then right
into Yew Tree Lane; club 1 mile on
right on hill behind Senior Service
factory.
Hillside course.
Pro Andrew Jowett; Founded 1913
18 holes, 5338 yards, S.S.S. 66
† Welcome WD by prior
arrangement.
Ɪ WD £16.50.
⚷ Welcome by prior arrangement
with Sec.
🍽 Full clubhouse facilities except
Mon.
⚲ Village, Hyde.

6A 52 Dunham Forest Golf &
Country Club
Oldfield Lane, Altrancham, Cheshire,
WA14 4TY
📧 dunham@absonline.net
☎ 0161 9282605, Fax 9298975,
Pro 9282727
2 miles N of M56 Junction 7 towards
Manchester and course on left.
Woodland course.
Pro Ian Wrigley; Founded 1961
18 holes, 6636 yards, S.S.S. 72
Ɪ Practice range.
† Welcome.
Ɪ WD £40; WE £45. out of season
WD:30. WE:35.
⚷ Welcome WD except Wed;
discounts for groups of more than 20;
packages available.
🍽 Bar and restaurant facilities
available.
⚲ Bowdon; Cresta Court.

6A 53 Eastham Lodge
Ferry Road, Wirral, Merseyside, CH62
0AP
☎ 0151 3273003, Fax 3277574,
Pro 3273008, Sec 3273003,
Rest/Bar 3271483
M53 Junction 5 to A41; follow signs for

Eastham Country Park.
Parkland course; was Port Sunlight GC
from 1932-76.
Pro Nick Sargent; Founded 1976
Designed by Hawtree & Sons, and
David Hemstock
18 holes, 5706 yards, S.S.S. 68
† Welcome WD; with a member only
at WE.
Ɪ £22.50.
⚷ Welcome Tues by prior
arrangement; some Mon and Fri dates
available; golf and catering packages
available. Other days by arrangement
with secretary.
🍽 Full clubhouse bar and catering
facilities.
⚲ Raby House, Willaston,Village
Hotel & Leisure Centre.

6A 54 Eaton
Guy Lane, Waverton, Chester,
Cheshire, CH3 7PH
🖥 www.eatongolfclub.co.uk
📧 office@eatongolfclub.co.uk
☎ 01244 335885, Fax 335782, Pro
335826
3 miles SE of Chester off the A41
through the village of Waverton.
Parkland course.
Pro Bill Tye; Founded 1965
Designed by Donald Steel
18 holes, 6562 yards, S.S.S. 71
Ɪ Practice range.
† Welcome with handicap certs.
Ɪ WD £30; WE £35.
⚷ Welcome WD except Wed by prior
arrangement; full golf and catering
packages available; from £25.
🍽 Full clubhouse facilities available.
⚲ Rowton Hall.

6A 55 Ellesmere Port
Chester Road, Childer Thornton,
Ellesmere Port, Merseyside, CH66 1QH
☎ 0151 3397689
On M53 W to A41 turn S to Chester for
2 miles; club at rear of St Paul's
Church, Hooton.
Municipal parkland/meadowland
course.
Pro Anthony Roberts; Founded 1971
Designed by Cotton, Pennink, Lawrie &
Partners
18 holes, 6432 yards, S.S.S. 71
† Welcome.
Ɪ WD £6.70; WE £7.40; concessions
apply.
⚷ Welcome with booking fee of £1.40
per head; winter packages available.
🍽 Full bar and restaurant.
⚲ Brook Meadow; Chimney; Village.

6A 56 Enville
Highgate Common, Enville,
Stourbridge, W Midlands, DY7 5BN
🖥 www.envillegolf.co.uk
📧 enville@egolfclub.freeserve.co.uk
☎ 01384 872074, Fax 873396, Pro
872585, Sec 872074, Rest/Bar 872551
6 miles W of Stourbridge on the A458
to Bridgnorth.
Woodland/heathland course.
Pro Sean Power; Founded 1935
18 holes, 6275 yards, S.S.S. 72:70
† Welcome WD only.
Ɪ WD £30 (18 holes).
⚷ Welcome by prior arrangement
and payment of £10 per player deposit;
minimum 12 players; 10 per cent
reduction for 30 or more; terms on
application.
🍽 Full clubhouse catering.
⚲ The Anchor Inn, The Blakelands at
Bobbington.

6A 57 Frodsham   ☿
Simons Lane, Frodsham, Cheshire,
WA6 6HE
🖥 www.froghamgolfclub.co.uk
📧 offir@frodshamgc.golfagent.co.uk
☎ 01928 732159, Fax 734070, Pro
739442
Close to M56 Junction 12; turn left at
lights in Frodsham centre on to B5152.
Parkland course.
Pro Graham Tonge; Founded 1990
Designed by John Day
18 holes, 6298 yards, S.S.S. 70
† Welcome WD except for
competition days; tee times booked
through the shop.
Ɪ WD £30.
⚷ Welcome WD by prior
arrangement with golf office; packages
available; terms on application.
🍽 Full bar and catering facilities
available.
⚲ Forest Hills.

6A 58 Gatley
Waterfall Farm, Styal Road, Heald
Green, Cheadle, Cheshire, SK8 3TW
☎ 0161 4372091, Pro 4362830,
Rest/Bar 4372091
Off Yew Tree Grove and Styal Road, 2
miles from Cheadle and 1 mile from
Manchester Airport.
Parkland course.
Pro James Hopley; Founded 1912
9 holes, 5934 yards, S.S.S. 68
† Welcome except Tues and Wed.
Ɪ Terms on application.
⚷ Welcome by prior arrangement
with Sec or Pro.
🍽 Full facilities except Mon.

✈ Pymgate Lodge, Travel Inn at Heald Green.

6A 59 **Goldenhill**
Mobberley Road, Stoke On Trent, Staffs, ST6 5SS
☎ 01782 234200, Fax 234303
On A50 between Tunstall and Kidsgrove.
Parkland/meadowland course in old mine basin.
Founded 1983
18 holes, 5957 yards, S.S.S. 69
Ⅰ Practice range, practice ground; putting green.
♦ Welcome; booking system available.
Ⅰ WD £7.00; WE £7.50.
♂ Welcome by arrangement.
⦿ Bar and restaurant.

6A 60 **Great Barr**
Chapel Lane, Great Barr, Birmingham, W Midlands, B43 7BA
☎ 0121 3571232, Pro 3575270, Sec 3584376
Close to M6 Junction 7, 6 miles NW of Birmingham.
Parkland course.
Pro Richard Spragg; Founded 1961
Designed by J Hamilton Stutt
18 holes, 6523 yards, S.S.S. 71
♦ Welcome WD.
Ⅰ WD £30, £36 for the day.
♂ Welcome Tues and Thurs by prior arrangement.
⦿ Full clubhouse facilities.
✈ Post House, The Holiday Inn.

6A 61 **Greenway Hall**
Stanley Road, Stockton Brook, Stoke On Trent, Staffs, ST9 9LJ
☎ 01782 503158, Fax 504259
Off A53 Stoke-Leek road at Stockton Brook.
Parkland course/heathland.
Pro Mark Armitage; Founded 1909
18 holes, 5681 yards, S.S.S. 67
♦ Welcome.
Ⅰ WD £10; WE £12.50.
♂ Welcome by prior arrangement; packages available; terms on application.
⦿ Clubhouse facilities.
✈ Moat House, Quality Inn.

6A 62 **Hale Golf Club**
Rappax Road, Hale, Altrincham, Cheshire, WA15 0NU
☎ 0161 9804225, Pro 9040835
2 miles SE of Altrincham; near

Altrincham Priory.
Parkland course.
Pro Alec Bickerdike; Founded 1903
9 holes, 5780 yards, S.S.S. 68
Ⅰ Practice ground.
♦ Welcome WD except Thurs; with member only at WE.
Ⅰ WD £20.
♂ Welcome by prior arrangement; catering available for coffee and lunch; evening meals by prior arrangement with the steward; from £20.
⦿ Clubhouse facilities.
✈ Four Seasons, Manchester Airport.

6A 63 **Hawkstone Park**   ♨
Weston High Castle, Shrewsbury, Shropshire, SY4 5UY
🖳 www.Hawkstone.co.uk
🖳 info @ hawkstone.co.uk
☎ 01939 200611, Fax 200311
Off A49 12 miles N of Shrewsbury or A442 12 miles N of Telford.
Parkland course.
Founded 1920
Two 18-hole and one 6-hole course, 6491/6476 yards, S.S.S. 72/72
Ⅰ Practice range, 15 bays; also 6-hole par 3 academy course; putting and pitching green.
♦ Welcome with prior booking; handicap certs required.
Ⅰ WD £32; WE £40.
♂ Welcome by prior arrangement with golf reservation office; terms on application.
⦿ Full bar and restaurant facilities.
✈ Hawkstone Park on site; golfing breaks available.

6A 64 **Hazel Grove**
Occupiers Lane, Buxton Road, Hazel Grove, Stockport, Cheshire, SK7 6LU
☎ 0161 4833978, Pro 4837272, Rest/Bar 4833217 Club house/ 4874399 catering
Off A6 Stockport-Buxton road.
Parkland course.
Pro Malcolm Hill; Founded 1913
18 holes, 6263 yards, S.S.S. 71
♦ Welcome by prior arrangement.
Ⅰ WD £30; WE £35.
♂ Welcome Thurs and Fri by prior arrangement; package includes full day of golf and catering; £38.
⦿ Full clubhouse bar and restaurant facilities.

6A 65 **Heaton Moor Golf Club**
Mauldeth Road, Stockport, Cheshire, SK4 3NX
🖳 hmgc@ukgateway.net

☎ 0161 4322134, Pro 4320846
From M63 Junction 12 follow Didsbury signs and Mauldeth Rd is 1.5 miles on right.
Flat, tree-lined parkland course.
Pro Simon Marsh; Founded 1892
18 holes, 5968 yards, S.S.S. 69
♦ Welcome by prior arrangement.
Ⅰ Terms on application.
♂ Welcome by prior arrangement; Thurs and Fri preferred; golf and catering packages available; from £33.
⦿ Full clubhouse facilities.
✈ Rudyard, Heaton Chapel.

6A 66 **Helsby**
Towers Lane, Helsby, Frodsham, Cheshire, WA6 0JB
☎ 01928 722021, Fax 725384, Pro 725457, Sec 722021
From M56 Junction 14; follow sign to Helsby and then right turn into Primrose lane, first right into Towers Lane.
Parkland course.
Pro M Jones; Founded 1901
Designed by James Braid
18 holes, 6229 yards, S.S.S. 70
♦ Welcome WD.
Ⅰ WD £22; WE £22.
♂ Welcome Tues and Thurs; packages include full day's golf and catering; £25.00 for 27 holes.
⦿ Full clubhouse facilities available.

6A 67 **Heswall**
Cottage Lane, Wirral, Merseyside, CH60 8PB
☎ 0151 3421237, Pro 3427431
M53 Junction 4; from roundabout, turn into Well Lane; leads into Cottage Lane.
Parkland course.
Pro Alan Thompson; Founded 1901
18 holes, 6554 yards, S.S.S. 72
♦ Welcome except Tues.
Ⅰ WD £35; WE £40.
♂ Welcome Wed and Fri only; winter packages available.
⦿ Full facilities.
✈ Mollington Banastre; Thornton Hall; Parkgate; Travelodge (Gayton); Woodhey; Victoria.

6A 68 **Heyrose**
Budworth road, Tabley, Knutsford, Cheshire, WA16 0HY
☎ 01565 733664, Pro 734267
4 miles W of Knutsford 0.5 miles along Budworth road off Pickmere Lane; M6 Junction 19, 1 mile.
Parkland course with ancient woodland.

Pro Colin Hiddon; Founded 1990 Designed by ELCN Bridge 18 holes, 6515 yards, S.S.S. 71 ⌇ Practice range, practice ground; practice bunkers; putting green; driving net.
† Welcome except before 2pm on Sat.
⌇ WD £19; WE £24.
⚑ Welcome WD by prior arrangement; from £36.
🍽 Clubhouse bar and restaurant.
⌁ Cottons, Knutsford; Swan, Bucklow Hill; Old Vicarage, Tabley; Travelodge.

From M60 Junction 13 turn left up to roundabout then take road to Reddish; turn left at Houldsworth pub.
Parkland course.
Pro David Naylor; Founded 1910 Designed by TG Renouf 18 holes, 6247 yards, S.S.S. 69 ⌇ 1.
† Welcome WD (Ladies Day Tues).
⌇ WD £24; WE £30.
⚑ Welcome by prior arrangement.
🍽 Full facilities.
⌁ Bredbury Hall, Bredbury Travel Lodge, Denton.

☎ 01785 760900 On B5026 between Stone and Eccleshall.
Parkland course.
Pro Julie Brown; Founded 1992 Designed by Mike Lowe 18 holes, 6281 yards, S.S.S. 72 † Welcome.
⌇ WD £15; WE £20.
⚑ Welcome by prior arrangement; packages for catering and golf available; full facilities; terms on application.
🍽 Full clubhouse facilities.
⌁ Stone House, Stone.

6A 69 Hill Valley Golf & Country Club
Terrick, Whitchurch, Shropshire, SY13 4JZ
⌁ www.hill-valley.co.uk
✉ reception@hill-valley.co.uk
☎ 01948 663584, Fax 665927, Pro 663032
Off A49/A41 Whitchurch by-pass. Undulating parkland course.
Pro Tony Minshall; Founded 1975 Designed by P Alliss & D Thomas 36 holes, S.S.S. 73
† Welcome.
⌇ WD on application.
⚑ Welcome by prior arrangement; packages available; also East course, 5280 yards, par 66; health and leisure centre; snooker.
🍽 Full clubhouse facilities.
⌁ Motel accommodation at club; Dodington Lodge; Terrick Hall.

6A 70 Himley Hall Golf Centre
Himley Park, Himley, Dudley, W Midlands, DY3 4DF
☎ 01902 895207
From A449 Wolverhampton-Kidderminster road to Dudley on B4176; then into Himley Hall Park.
Public parkland course.
Pro Jeremy Nicholls; Founded 1980 Designed by DA Baker 9 holes, 6215 yards, S.S.S. 70
† Welcome.
⌇ WD £6.00; WE £6.50/£9.50 Winter prices.
⚑ Welcome by arrangement.
🍽 Cafe and hot meals.
⌁ Himley House; Park Hall.

6A 71 Houldsworth
Houldsworth Street, Stockport, Cheshire, SK5 6BN
☎ 0161 4429611, Fax 9479678, Pro 4421714, Sec 4421712, Rest/Bar 4429611

6A 72 Hoylake Municipal
Carr Lane, Hoylake, Wirral, Merseyside, CH47 4BG
⌁ www.hoylake-golf.org.uk
☎ 0151 632 2956, Rest/Bar 6326357 Off M53 10 miles SW of Liverpool following signs for Hoylake; 100 yards beyond Hoylake station.
Municipal parkland course.
Pro Simon Hooton; Founded 1933 Designed by James Braid 18 holes, 6321 yards, S.S.S. 70
† Welcome; book in advance at WE; Sat from 8.30am.
⌇ WD £6.50; WE £6.50.
⚑ Welcome by prior arrangement; after 1.30pm at WE.
🍽 Hot snacks, meals and bar.
⌁ Green Lodge.

6A 73 Ingestre Park ⌖
Ingestre, Stafford, Staffs, ST18 0RE
✉ ipgc@lineone.net
☎ 01889 270845, Fax 270845, Pro 270304, Rest/Bar 270061 Course is six miles E of Stafford off the A51 via Great Haywood and Tixall.
Parkland course in former estate of Earl of Shrewsbury.
Pro D Scullion; Founded 1977 Designed by Hawtree & Son 18 holes, 6268 yards, S.S.S. 70 ⌇ Practice area.
† Welcome WD with handicap certs; with member at WE.
⌇ WD £25.
⚑ Welcome WD except Wed with prior arrangement; special packages available for 15 or more; snooker room; lounge; from £34.
🍽 Bar and restaurant facilities available.
⌁ Ingestre; Garth, Tillington Hall, both Stafford.

6A 74 Izaak Walton
Norton Bridge, Stone, Staffs, ST15 0NS

6A 75 Knights Grange Sports Complex
Grange Lane, Winsford, Cheshire, CW7 2PT
✉ Knightsgrangewinsford@royalmail.co .uk
☎ 01606 552780 Course in centre of Winsford.
Public meadowland course.
Pro Graham Moore; Founded 1983 18 holes, 6010 yards, S.S.S. 67 ⌇ Practice area; tennis; bowls.
† Welcome.
⌇ WD £5.50 WE £6.50 concessions apply.
⚑ Welcome by prior arrangement in writing.
🍽 Hot drinks and snacks.

6A 76 Knutsford
Mereheath Lane, Knutsford, Cheshire, WA16 6HS
☎ 01565 633355, Pro 633355 2 miles from M6 Junction 19; make for Knutsford entrance to Tatton Park.
Parkland course.
Pro Granville Ogden; Founded 1891 10 holes, 6203 yards, S.S.S. 70 † Welcome WD except Wed.
⌇ Terms on application; £25.00 wd.
⚑ Welcome Thurs by prior arrangement.
🍽 Full facilities.
⌁ Angel; Cottons; Rose & Crown; Swan.

6A 77 Lakeside
Eastern Generation, Rugeley Power Station, Rugeley, Staffs, WS15 1PR
☎ 01889 575567 Between Lichfield and Stafford.
Parkland course.
Founded 1969 18 holes, 5534 yards, S.S.S. 67 † Welcome with a member.
⌇ WD on application.
🍽 Evening service.

6A 78 Leasowe
Leasowe Road, Moreton, Wirral,
Merseyside, CH46 3RD
☎ 0151 6775852, Fax 6041448, Pro
678 5460
Off M53 1 mile after tunnel; 1 mile W
of Wallasey village.
Links course.
Pro Andrew Ayre; Founded 1891
Designed by John Bull Jnr
18 holes, 6263 yards, S.S.S. 70
⚑ Practice area.
† Welcome WD; WE by prior
arrangement.
⌇ WD £20.50 WE £25.50.
⌒ Welcome by arrangement;
minimum 16 players; not Sat.
🍽 Restaurant, bar and snacks.
↩ Leasowe Castle.

6A 79 Leek
Cheddleton Road, Leek, Staffs, ST13
5RE
☎ 01538 384779, Pro 384767, Sec
384779, Rest/Bar 381983
On A520 0.75 miles S of Leek.
Parkland course.
Pro Ian Benson; Founded 1892
18 holes, 6240 yards, S.S.S. 70
⚑ Practice facilities.
† Welcome with handicap certs.
⌇ WD £26; WE £32.
⌒ Welcome Wed; golf and catering
packages available. contact secretary.
🍽 Full clubhouse facilities.
↩ Bank End Farm; Horse Shoes at
Blacksham Moor.

6A 80 Lilleshall Hall
Lilleshall Hall Drive, Lilleshall, Newport,
Shropshire, TF10 9AS
☎ 01952 604776, Fax 604776, Pro
604104, Rest/Bar 603840
Between A41 and A5 at Sherrifhales.
Parkland course.
Pro S McKane; Founded 1937
Designed by HS Colt
18 holes, 5789 yards, S.S.S. 68
† Welcome WD and WE with a
member.
⌇ WD £20; WE £15.
⌒ Welcome WD by prior
arrangement; terms available on
application.
🍽 Clubhouse facilities.

6A 81 Little Aston
Roman Road, Sutton Coldfield, W
Midlands, B74 3AN
⚙ www.ne.quik.co.uk/lagolf
✉ manager@littleastongolf.co.uk
☎ 0121 3532942, Fax 5808387,

Pro 3530330, Sec 3532942
4 miles NW of Sutton Coldfield off
A454.
Parkland course.
Pro John Anderson; Founded 1908
Designed by Harry Vardon
18 holes, 6670 yards, S.S.S. 73
† Welcome by arrangement.
⌇ Terms on application; round £50,
day £60.
⌒ Welcome Mon, Tues, Wed and Fri
by prior arrangement; catering and golf
packages available.
🍽 Full clubhouse.

6A 82 Llanymynech
Pant, Oswestry, Shropshire, SY10 8LB
☎ 01691 830542, Pro 830879, Sec
830983
6 miles S of Oswestry on A483; take
turning at Cross Guns Inn at Pant.
Hilltop; 4th hole tee in Wales, green in
England.
Pro Andrew Griffiths; Founded 1933
18 holes, 6114 yards, S.S.S. 69
† Welcome by arrangement.
⌇ WD £20 £25 day price; WE £25.
⌒ Welcome WD except Thurs;
catering available by prior arrangement.
🍽 Bar and restaurant facilities.
↩ Many in Oswestry area.

6A 83 Ludlow
Bromfield, Ludlow, Shropshire, SY8 2BT
✉ ludlowgo@barboxnet.co.uk
☎ 01584 856285, Fax 856366, Pro
856366
Course is one mile N of Ludlow off the
A49.
Heathland course.
Pro Russell Price; Founded 1889
18 holes, 6277 yards, S.S.S. 70
† Welcome.
⌇ WD £20; WE £25 and bank
holidays.
⌒ Welcome by prior arrangement;
terms on application.
🍽 Clubhouse facilities.
↩ Feathers, Ludlow.

6A 84 Lymm
Lymm Golf Club, Whitbarrow Road,
Lymm, Cheshire, WA13 9AN
☎ 01925 755054, Sec 755020,
Rest/Bar 752177
5 miles SE of Warrington.
Parkland course.
Pro Steve McCarthy; Founded 1907
18 holes, 6304 yards, S.S.S. 70
† Welcome WD; Thurs ladies day, no
visitors before 2.30pm; with members
at WE.

⌇ WD £22.
⌒ Welcome, usually on Wed; winter
packages.
🍽 Full meals facilities.
↩ Lumm; Statham Lodge.

6A 85 Macclesfield   ℭ
Hollins Road, Macclesfield, Cheshire,
SK11 7EA
☎ 01625 423227, Fax 260061, Pro
616952, Sec 615845
From the southern end of the A523
(Silk Road), turn into Windmill St.
Parkland/heathland course.
Pro Tony Taylor; Founded 1889/1901
Designed by Hawtree & Son
18 holes, 5769 yards, S.S.S. 68
† Welcome.
⌇ WD £20; WE £25.
⌒ Welcome by arrangement;
packages available; contact Sec; terms
on application.
🍽 Full clubhouse facilities.
↩ Sutton Hall.

6A 86 Malkins Bank
Betchton Road, Malkins Bank,
Sandbach, Cheshire, CW11 4XN
☎ 01270 765931, Fax 764730,
Sec 873904, Rest/Bar 767878
1.5 miles from M6 Junction 17.
Municipal parkland course.
Pro David Wheeler; Founded 1980
18 holes, 5971 yards, S.S.S. 69
⚑ Practice area.
† Welcome; booking system in
operation.
⌇ WD £8.80; WE £10.30 Adults. WD
£5.30; WE £5.30 Juniors (9 holes WE
adults £7 WD £6, Juniors WD £3.90
WE £3.90).
⌒ Welcome.
🍽 Bar and catering daily.
↩ Old Hall; Saxon Cross Motel.

**6A 87 The Manor Golf Club
(Kingstone)**
Leese Hill, Kingstone, Uttoxeter, Staffs,
ST14 8QT
☎ 01889 563234
On the main Uttoxeter to Stafford road
Parkland course.
Founded 1992
Designed by David Gough
18 holes, 5360 yards, S.S.S. 69
⚑ Practice range, 5-bay driving
range, putting green.
† Welcome.
⌇ Terms on application.
⌒ Welcome and catering facilities.
🍽 Bar and catering facilities.

Little Aston

No matter what direction you approach Little Aston from, it always comes as something of a surprise. It is set in a pocket of reproduction suburbia worthy of Surrey and buffeted by Birmingham to the south, Wolverhampton to the west, Stoke to the north and Leicester to the east. The drive is often an arduous one not helped by a succession of speed bumps at the end of the journey. Then all at once you come upon Little Aston and remember why you set off in the first place.

It is one of Britain's finest parkland courses, a former deer park that was laid out for golf by Harry Vardon early in the twentieth century. Vardon did not design all that many courses, so maybe he gave of his best to the ones that attracted him. The only quibble was that there were too many testing carries from the tee, so Harry Colt was brought in to make it a bit more member friendly.

It is usually in superb condition. Only if you are very unlucky will you occasionally encounter a little bit of boggy ground on the lower part of the course around the turn. Henry Cotton said, "The course must have the best fairways in the world – I naturally have not seen them all, but I have never seen better and more weed-free turf – dry all the year round, too. Ganton, Gleneagles and Hoylake are in the running for top places, but even they must be runners up alongside Little Aston."

Another famous feature of the club is the practice putting green. It is a first rate surface, but perhaps its proximity to the clubhouse, the eighteenth green and the first tee persuaded the twitchier putters amongst the members to have it surrounded with heather and shrubs.

The opening two holes aren't particularly special, the first being a fairly short downhill par four and the second, turning at right angles away from the first, a slightly tedious slog up a minor gradient. But standing on the third tee the golfer has the first taste of what is to come. The hole is a par five, violently downhill to begin with, with a wood to the left and more trees to the right, before it climbs severely up to the green. The surprising undulations of Little Aston are part of what marks it out.

At the end of the nine is a par three beautifully framed by the trees, but I have always thought that it is the second nine that really makes the course. It is the longer of the two nines, but the presence of an extra par five and only the one par three pretty much accounts for that.

The tenth is a terrific dog legging par four, arguably the hardest hole on the course. The left front of the green on the par five twelfth is well hidden by a lake and the fourteenth is an ingenious little par four with a diagonal set of bunkers to challenge the drive. The showpiece of a daunting finish is the seventeenth, a dogleg right to a green protected by the course's second lake and a necklace of bunkers. The bunkering at Little Aston is frustratingly good.

In the past the only aspect that let Little Aston down was a deserved reputation for male chauvinism. But they have done much to get rid of that image in the past fifteen years, staging many women's tournaments of which the culmination was the British Open Amateur in 1998. It is now a much more friendly place to visit. — **Mark Reason**

6A 88 **Market Drayton**
Sutton, Market Drayton, Shropshire,
TF9 2HX
☎ 01630 652266
1.5 miles S of Market Drayton.
Undulating meadowland course.
Pro Russell Clewes; Founded 1911
18 holes, 6290 yards, S.S.S. 71
† Welcome WD except Tues which
is Ladies Day; Sat with a member; Sun
members only.
[WD £24.
⟋ Welcome by arrangement.
|●| Full facilities.
⤳ Bungalow at course(sleeps six);
Bear; Corbet Arms.

6A 89 **Marple** ☯
Barnsfold Road, Marple, Stockport,
Cheshire, SK6 7EL
☎ 0161 4272311, Fax 4271125,
Pro 4271195, Sec 4271125,
Rest/Bar 4272311
Signposted from Hawk Green.
Parkland course.
Pro David Myers; Founded 1892
18 holes, 5552 yards, S.S.S. 67
† Welcome except comp days.
[WD £20; WE £30.
⟋ Welcome by prior arrangement;
golf and catering packages available;
from £34.50.
|●| Clubhouse facilities.
⤳ Bredbury Hall Hotel.

6A 90 **Mellor & Towncliffe**
Mellor And Towncliffe Golf Club Ltd,
Gibb Lane, Mellor, Stockport,
Cheshire, SK6 5NA
⬡ www.mandtgc@demon.co.uk
☎ 0161 4279700, Pro 4275759,
Sec 4472208
Off A626 opposite Devonshire Arms on
Longhurst Lane, Mellor.
Parkland/moorland course.
Pro Gary Broadley; Founded 1894
22 holes, 5925 yards, S.S.S. 69
† Welcome except Sat.
[WD £20; WE £27.50; Summer
Special £30 full day and meal.
⟋ Welcome by prior arrangement;
winter packages available.
|●| Full facilities except Tues.
⤳ Pack Horse Inn.

6A 91 **Meole Brace**
Municipal Golf Course, Oteley Road,
Shrewsbury, Shropshire, SY2 6QQ
☎ 01743 364050
At Junction of A5/A49 S of Shrewsbury.
Parkland course.
Pro Nigel Bramall; Founded 1976

12 holes, 3400 yards, S.S.S. 43
⚐ 9-hole pitch and putt.
† Welcome; pay as you play.
[WD £4.70; WE £5.70
⟋ Welcome by prior arrangement.
|●| Drinks and confectionery machines.

6A 92 **Mere Golf & Country** ☯
Club
Mere Golf And Country Club, Chester
Road, Mere, Knutsford, Cheshire,
WA16 6LJ
⬡ www.meregolf.co.uk
☎ 01565 830155, Fax 830713, Pro
830219
1 mile E of M6 Junction 19 on A556; 2
miles W of M56 Junction 7.
Parkland course.
Pro Peter Eyre; Founded 1934
Designed by George Duncan and
James Braid
18 holes, 6817 yards, S.S.S. 73
⚐ 6 bays open March to October.
† Welcome Mon, Tues and Thurs by
prior arrangement.
[WD £70.
⟋ Welcome Mon, Tues and Thurs by
arrangement; full range of clubhouse
facilities; golf days and golf packages;
terms on application.
|●| Bar and restaurant service.
⤳ Cottons.

6A 93 **Mersey Valley** ☯
Warrington Road, Bold Heath, Widnes,
Cheshire, WA8 3XL
⬡ www.merseyvalleygolfclub.co.uk
☎ 0151 424 6060, Fax 2579097
Leave M62 Junction 7; 1.5 miles on
A57 towards Warrington.
Parkland course.
Pro Andy Stevenson; Founded 1995
Designed by St Mellion Leisure
18 holes, 6374 yards, S.S.S. 70
⚐ Practice area.
† Welcome.
[WD £18; WE £20.
⟋ Welcome by arrangement; deposit
required; packages available for 18
and 27 holes of golf with meals; from
£26.
|●| Bar and bar snacks; function suite
available.
⤳ Hillcrest, Widnes.

6A 94 **Mile End**
Shrewsbury Road, Oswestry,
Shropshire, SY11 4JE
✉ mileendgc@aol.com
☎ 01691 670580, Pro 671246
1 mile SE of Oswestry; signposted
from A5.

Parkland course (converted farmland).
Pro Scott Carpenter; Founded 1992
Designed by Michael Price/D Gough
18 holes, 6194 yards, S.S.S. 69
⚐ Practice range, 12 bays floodlit.
† Welcome.
[WD £15; WE £20.
⟋ Welcome WD by prior
arrangement; terms on application.
|●| Full clubhouse facilities.
⤳ Wynnstay; Sweeney Hall, Moreton
Lodge.

6A 95 **Mobberley** ☯
Mobberley Golf Club, Burleyhurst
Lane, Mobberley, Knutsford, Cheshire,
WA16 7JZ
☎ 01565 880178, Fax 880178,
Pro 880188
From M56 Junction 6 head towards
Wilmslow and after Moat House turn
right.
Parkland course.
Pro Steve Dewhurst; Founded 1995
9 holes, 5542 yards, S.S.S. 67
⚐ Practice range, practice area;
indoor teaching facilities.
† Welcome.
[WD £12.50; WE £16.
⟋ Welcome by prior arrangement.
|●| Bar and restaurant.
⤳ Moat House; Boddington Arms.

6A 96 **Mottram Hall Hotel** ☯
Wilmslow Road, Mottram St Andrew,
Macclesfield, Cheshire, SK10 4QT
☎ 01625 820064, Fax 829135
From M56 Junction 6 follow A538
through Wilmslow; follow signposts.
Parkland/woodland course.
Pro Tim Rastall; Founded 1991
Designed by David Thomas
18 holes, 7006 yards, S.S.S. 74
⚐ 8 bays.
† Welcome with handicap certs.
[WD £45; WE £50 (residents
receive a £5.00 reduction on fees).
⟋ Welcome by arrangement;
packages available; on-course
drink/food buggy; leisure centre.
|●| Full clubhouse and hotel facilities.
⤳ Mottram Hall on site (133 beds).

6A 97 **New Mills**
Shaw Marsh, New Mills, Derbyshire,
SK22 4QE
⬡ www.newmillsgolfclub.co.uk
✉ carlpcross@aol.com
☎ 01663 743485, Pro 746161
0.75 miles from centre of New Mills on
St Mary Road.
Moorland course.

Pro Carl Cross; Founded 1907
Designed by David Williams
18 holes, 5665 yards, S.S.S. 68
🏌 Small practice range.
† Welcome WD and Sat mornings
except on competition days.
🍴 POA.
🛒 Welcome WD by prior
arrangement.
🍽 Bar and clubhouse catering.
🛏 Pack Horse; Sportsman; Moorside.

6A 98 Newcastle Municipal

Keele Road, Newcastle, Staffs, ST5
5AB
☎ 01782 617006, Rest/Bar 616583
Off M6 Junction 15, on A525 for 2
miles.
Public parkland course.
Pro Colin Smith; Founded 1975
18 holes, 6396 yards, S.S.S. 70
🏌 Practice range, 26 bays floodlit.
† Welcome; book any time.
🍴 Terms on application.
🛒 Welcome on application to local
council.
🍽 Bar and meals.
🛏 Keele Hospitality Inn.

6A 99 Newcastle-under-Lyme

Golf Lane, Newcastle, Staffs, ST5 2QB
🖥 www.newcastlegolfclub.co.uk
☎ 01782 618526, Sec 617006
1.5 miles SW of Newcastle-under-
Lyme on A53.
Parkland course.
Pro Paul Symonds; Founded 1908
18 holes, 6331 yards, S.S.S. 71
† Welcome WD.
🍴 WD £26.
🛒 Welcome on Mon all day and Thurs
pm; packages on application; snooker.
🍽 Bar and restaurant.
🛏 Post House; Borough Arms.

6A 100 Northenden

Palatine Road, Manchester, Lancs,
M22 4FR
☎ 0161 9984738, Fax 9455592,
Pro 9453386, Rest/Bar 9984079
0.5 miles from M56 Junction 9; M60
Junction 5.
Parkland course.
Pro James Curtis; Founded 1913
Designed by T Renouf
18 holes, 6503 yards, S.S.S. 71
† Welcome by arrangement.
🍴 WD £28; WE £32.
🛒 Welcome Tues and Fri; packages
include 27 holes of golf; coffee and
bacon sandwich on arrival; light lunch
and dinner; from £45.

🍽 Full clubhouse facilities.
🛏 Britannia Country House; Post
House, Northenden.

6A 101 Onneley

Crewe, Cheshire, CW3 5QF
☎ 01782 750577, Sec 846759
1 mile from Woore on A51 to Newcastle
Undulating meadowland course.
Founded 1968
Designed by Jeff Marks
13 holes, 5535 yards, S.S.S. 68
† Welcome on application.
🍴 WD on application.
🛒 Welcome by prior arrangement
with Sec; from £18.
🍽 Clubhouse facilities.
🛏 Wheatsheaf.

6A 102 Oswestry Golf Club

Aston Park, Oswestry, Shropshire,
SY11 4JJ
🖥 www.oswestrygolfclub.co.uk
☎ 01691 610221, Fax 610535, Pro
610448, Sec 610535, Rest/Bar 610221
3 miles SE of Oswestry on A5.
Undulating parkland course.
Pro David Skelton; Founded 1903
Designed by James Braid
18 holes, 6038 yards, S.S.S. 69
🏌 Practice area.
† Welcome with handicap certs.
🍴 WD £24; WE £32.
🛒 Welcome Wed and Fri; packages
available; from £31.
🍽 Full clubhouse facilities.
🛏 Morten Park Lodge, the Wynstay
Hotel.

6A 103 Oxley Park

Stafford Road, Wolverhampton, W
Midlands, WV10 6DE
☎ 01902 420506, Pro 425445, Sec
425892
On A449 1 mile N of Wolverhampton.
Parkland course.
Pro Les Burlison; Founded 1913
18 holes, 6222 yards, S.S.S. 70
† Welcome; only with a member at
WE in winter.
🍴 WD £25; WE £25.
🛒 Welcome Wed by arrangement;
snooker.
🍽 Full clubhouse catering.
🛏 Mount; Goldthorn; Park Hall.

6A 104 Parkhall

Hulme Lane, Hulme, Stoke on Trent,
Staffs, ST3 5BH
☎ 01782 599584
1 mile outside Longton on A50.

Public moorland course.
Founded 1989
18 holes, 4770 yards, S.S.S. 54
† Welcome.
🍴 WD £6; WE £7.
🛒 Welcome by arrangement.
🍽 None.

6A 105 Patshull Park Hotel Golf & Country Club

Patshull Park, Burnhill Green,
Wolverhampton, W Midlands, WV6 7HR
🖥 www.patshull-park.co.uk
☎ 01902 700100, Fax 700874, Pro
700342
From A41 Wolverhampton-Whitchurch
Road follow signs to Pattingham.
Parkland course.
Pro Peter Baker; Founded 1972
Designed by John Jacobs
18 holes, 6412 yards, S.S.S. 70
🏌 Practice ground.
† Welcome with handicap certs.
🍴 WD £30; WE £40.
🛒 Welcome by prior arrangement;
packages including catering from
£29.95 per person.
🍽 Full clubhouse and hotel facilities.
🛏 Patshull Park Hotel on site.

6A 106 Penkridge Golf & CC

Pottal Pool Road, Penkridge, Stafford,
Staffs, ST19 5RN
🖥 www.leadingedgegolfacademy.com
☎ 01785 716455
Off A34 at Penkridge/Rugeley cross
roads; turn to Penkridge and course is
0.75 miles on left; from M6 Junction
12, take A5 towards Telford, then A449
followed by B5102 towards Cannock,
turning left in Pottal Pool Rd after
Wolgarston School.
Parkland course.
Pro Andrew Preston; Founded 1995
Designed by John Reynolds
18 holes, 6613 yards, S.S.S. 72
🏌 Practice range, 20 bay, teaching
academy, putting green, chipping green.
† Welcome.
🍴 WD £14.50; WE £19.50.
🛒 Welcome by arrangement; deposit
required; discounts for larger groups;
video analysis; from £16.
🍽 Full clubhouse facilities.
🛏 Hatherton Country Hotel.

6A 107 Penn

Penn Common, Wolverhampton, W
Midlands, WV4 5JN
☎ 01902 341142, Fax 620504,
Pro 330472
On A449 2.5 miles W of

Wolverhampton at Penn.
Heathland course.
Pro B Burlison; Founded 1908
18 holes, 6487 yards, S.S.S. 72
† Welcome WD; with member at WE.
[WD £20 round £25 day ticket.
◇ Welcome Mon, Wed, Fri;
reductions for groups of 20+; catering
packages available; from £17.
|●| Full clubhouse facilities.

6A 108 **Peover**
Plumley Moor Road, Lower Peover,
Knutsford, Cheshire, WA16 9SE
⚒ www. peovergolfclub.co.uk
✉ mail@peovergolfclub.co.uk
☎ 01565 723337, Fax 723311
Leave M6 Junction 19 to A556; follow
signs to Plumley and Lower Peover on
Plumley Moor Rd; course is 1.5 miles.
Parkland course.
Pro Bobby Young; Founded 1996
Designed by P Naylor
18 holes, 6702 yards, S.S.S. 72
[Practice area.
† Welcome.
[WD £20 WE £25.
◇ Welcome WD; packages available
on application; from £22.50.
|●| Full clubhouse catering facilities
available.
↘ Belle Park.

6A 109 **Perton Park Golf Club**
Wrottesley Park Road, Perton,
Wolverhampton, W Midlands, WV6 7HL
☎ 01902 380103, Fax 326219, Pro
380073, Sec 897031
Just off the A454 Bridgnorth to
Wolverhampton Road.
Meadowland course.
Pro Jeremy Harrold; Founded 1990
18 holes, 6620 yards, S.S.S. 72
[Practice range, 18-bay range.
† Welcome with tee time from starter.
[WD £12; WE £18.
◇ Welcome by prior arrangement;
golf and catering packages available;
from £15.
|●| Full clubhouse catering facilities
available.

6A 110 **Portal Golf & Country Club**
The Champion Course, Cobblers Craft
Lane, Tarporley Cheshire, CW6 0DJ
⚒ www.porthallgolf@aol.com
✉ porthallgolf@aol.com
☎ 01829 733933, Fax 733928
11 miles SE of Chester off A49 near
Tarporley.
Parkland course; 3rd: Haddington's

Ground, 602 yards.
Pro Adrian Hill; Founded 1989
Designed by Donald Steel
45 holes, 7037 yards, S.S.S. 74
[UK largest indoor golf academy.
† Welcome by arrangement.
[WD £50; WE £50.
◇ Welcome by arrangement; packages
available; also Arderne course, par 71;
from £35 playing on the Premiere and
the Championship course Arderne
course is Par 30 and is £10 a round.
|●| Restaurant and bar facilities.
↘ The Swan, Tarporley; Wild Boar,
Beeston; Nunsmere Hotel.

6A 111 **Portal Golf & Country Club Prem. Course**
Forest Road, Tarporley, Cheshire, CW6
0JA
⚒ www.portlandspremier.co.uk
✉ july@
portlandspremier.totalserve.co.uk
☎ 01829 733884, Fax 733666, Pro
733703
1 mile S of Tarporley between Chester
and Northwich.
Parkland course.
Pro Judy Statham; Founded 1990
Designed by T Rouse
18 holes, 6508 yards, S.S.S. 72
† Welcome.
[WD £30; WE £35.
◇ Welcome WD by prior
arrangement; on application; from £29.
|●| Full clubhouse facilities.
↘ Swan, Tarporley; Wild Boar, Beeston.

6A 112 **Poulton Park**
Dig Lane, Croft, Warrington, Cheshire,
WA2 0SH
☎ 01925 812034, Pro 825220, Sec
822802
3 miles from Warrington off A574.
Parkland course.
Pro Andrew Matthews; Founded 1978
9 holes, 4978 yards, S.S.S. 67
† Welcome by arrangement.
[WD £17; WE £19.
◇ Welcome by prior arrangement;
packages for golf and catering
available; minimum 8; £20-£26.
|●| Clubhouse facilities.

6A 113 **Prenton**
Golf Links Road, Birkenhead,
Merseyside, CH42 8LW
✉ nigelbrown@pentongolfclub.co.uk
☎ 0151 6081461, Fax 6091580, Pro
6081636, Sec 6081053
From M53 Junction 2 take A552
towards Birkenhead.

Parkland course.
Pro Robin Thompson; Founded 1905
Designed by Colt MacKenzie & Co
18 holes, 6429 yards, S.S.S. 71
[Practice range, two practice areas.
† Welcome by arrangement.
[WD £30; WE £35.
◇ Welcome by prior arrangement;
golf and catering packages available;
from £24.
|●| Full clubhouse bar and catering
facilities.

6A 114 **Prestbury Golf Club**
Macclesfield Road, Prestbury,
Macclesfield, Cheshire, SK10 4BJ
✉ office@prestburygolfclub.com
☎ 01625 829388, Fax 828241, Pro
828242, Sec 828241, Rest/Bar 829388
Course is two miles NW of
Macclesfield.
Parkland course.
Pro Nick Summerfield; Founded 1920
Designed by Colt & Morrison
18 holes, 6359 yards, S.S.S. 71
† Welcome by prior arrangement on
WD; with a member at WE.
[WD £38.
◇ Welcome Thurs; minimum 20; from
£34 pp.
|●| Full clubhouse bar and catering
facilities.
↘ Bridge; White House, both Prestbury.

6A 115 **Pryors Hayes Golf Club** ♛
Willington Road, Oscroft, Tarvin,
Chester, Cheshire, CH3 8NL
✉ info@Pryors-Hayes.co.uk
☎ 01829 741250, Fax 749077, Pro
740140
5 miles from Chester near Tarvin
between A54 and A51.
Parkland course.
Founded 1993
Designed by John Day
18 holes, 6074 yards, S.S.S. 69
† Welcome by prior booking.
[WD £20; WE £25.
◇ Welcome every day by prior
arrangement; catering and golf
packages available.
|●| Clubhouse facilities.
↘ Willington Hall.

6A 116 **Queen's Park**
Queen's Park Drive, Crewe, Cheshire,
CW2 7SB
☎ 01270 662378, Pro 666724, Sec
580424
1.5 miles from town centre off Victoria
Avenue.

Parkland course.
Pro Jamie Lowe; Founded 1985
9 holes, 4922 yards, S.S.S. 64
⌁ Small practice area.
† Pay and play; restrictions on Wed,
Sun, Thurs so call in advance.
⌾ WD £6.50; WE £8.50 (18 holes).
⌁ Welcome.
◉ Clubhouse facilities.

6A 117 Reaseheath
Reaseheath College, Reaseheath,
Nantwich, Cheshire, CW5 6DF
⌁ www.reaseheath.ac.uk
✉ enquiries@reaseheath.ac.uk
☎ 01270 625131, Fax 625665,
Sec 613201
1 mile from Nantwich on A51 Chester
road.
Research course used for greenkeeper
training.
Founded 1987
Designed by D Mortram
9 holes, 3729 yards, S.S.S. 54
† Limited availability for non-
members; phone in advance.
⌾ WD £7; WE £7.
⌁ Small groups; prior booking essential.
◉ Restaurant on site WD.
⌁ Alvaston Hall Hotel.

6A 118 Reddish Vale   ⅏
Southcliffe Road, Stockport, Cheshire,
SK5 7EE
⌁ www.reddishvalegolfclub.co.uk
☎ 0161 480 2359, Fax 4778242,
Pro 4803824, Rest/Bar 4761521
1 mile N of Stockport off B6167
Reddish road.
Undulating course in valley.
Pro Bob Freeman; Founded 1912
Designed by Dr A MacKenzie
18 holes, 6086 yards, S.S.S. 69
† Welcome WD (lunchtime
restrictions); with a member at WE.
⌾ Terms on application.
⌁ Welcome WD by prior
arrangement; packages available.
◉ Restaurant and bar service.
⌁ Bradbury Hall.

6A 119 Ringway
Hale Road, Halebarns, Altrincham,
Cheshire, WA15 8SW
☎ 0161 9808432, Fax 9804414,
Pro 9808432, Sec 9802630,
Rest/Bar 9049609
8 miles S of Manchester 1 mile from
M56 Junction 6 on the A538 towards
Altrincham through Hale Barns.
Parkland course.
Pro Nick Ryan; Founded 1909

Designed by Harry Colt and James Braid
18 holes, 6482 yards, S.S.S. 71
⌁ Practice Range available.
† Welcome except Fri; Tues & Sat
are club competition days.
⌾ WD £35; WE £45.
⌁ Welcome Thurs in summer by prior
arrangement; packages available;
corporate days organised; snooker.
◉ Full facilities.
⌁ Cresta Court; Marriott.

6A 120 Romiley
Goosehouse Green, Romiley,
Stockport, Cheshire, SK6 4LJ
☎ 0161 4302392, Fax 4307258,
Pro 4307122
On B6104 off A560 0.75 miles from
Romiley station.
Undulating parkland course.
Pro Robert N Giles; Founded 1897
18 holes, 6454 yards, S.S.S. 71
† Welcome except Thurs (Ladies Day).
⌾ WD £30; WE £40.
⌁ Welcome Tues and Wed by prior
arrangement.
◉ Full clubhouse service.

6A 121 Royal Liverpool Golf
Club (see overleaf)
30 Meols Drive, Hoylake, Wirral,
Merseyside, CH47 4AL
⌁ www.royal-liverpoll-golf.com
✉ bookings@royal-liverpoll-golf-com
☎ 0151 6323101, Fax 6326737,
Pro 6325868, Sec 6323101,
Rest/Bar 6323102
On A540 between Hoylake and West
Kirby, off Junction 2 of the M53.
Championship links course.
John Heggarty; Founded 1869
Designed by Robert Chambers & Pro
George Morris
18 holes, 7165 yards, S.S.S. 75
⌁ Practice ground.
† Welcome by appointment only; WE
very restricted.
⌾ WD £95; WE £120 (for 18 holes
and lunch).
⌁ Welcome by prior arrangement
only; from £95, including snack lunch;
full facilities.
◉ Full restaurant (12-2) and
clubhouse facilities.
⌁ Thornton Hall, Thornton-le-Hough;
Crabwell Manor, Mollington, Craxton
Wood, Kings Gap Court.

6A 122 Runcorn   ⅏
The Heath, Clifton Road, Runcorn,
Cheshire, WA7 4SU
☎ 01928 572093, Pro 564791, Sec

574214
M56 Junction 12; signposted off A557.
Parkland course.
Pro A Franklyn; Founded 1909
18 holes, 6035 yards, S.S.S. 69
† Welcome WD except Tues; WE
with member.
⌾ WD £20.
⌁ Welcome Mon and Fri; includes
coffee, lunch and dinner for groups of
12 or more; from £31.
◉ Clubhouse facilities.
⌁ Lord Daresbury, Warrington.

6A 123 St Michael Jubilee
Dundalk Road, Widnes, Cheshire,
WA4 8BS
☎ 0151 4245636, Fax 4952124,
Pro 4246230, Sec 4246461
Close to centre of Widnes off the
Runcorn Bridge.
Public parkland course.
Pro Darren Chapman; Founded 1977
18 holes, 5667 yards, S.S.S. 68
⌁ Practice area.
† Welcome WD; with bookings at WE.
⌾ Available on request.
⌁ Welcome by arrangement.
◉ Full facilities.
⌁ Hillcrest.

6A 124 St Thomas's Priory Golf
Club
Armitage Lane, Rugeley, Staffs, WS15
1ED
⌁ www.st-thomass-golfclub.com
☎ 01543 491116, Fax 492244, Pro
492096, Sec 491911
1 mile SE of Rugeley on A513;
opposite Ash Tree Inn.
Parkland course; 14th is 601 yards.
Pro R O'Hanlon; Founded 1995
Designed by Paul Mulholland
18 holes, 5969 yards, S.S.S. 70
† Welcome.
⌾ WD £20; WE £25.
⌁ Welcome by prior arrangement;
terms on application.
◉ Full clubside facilities.
⌁ Riverside Inn; Holiday Inn Express,
both Branston.

6A 125 Sale
Sale Lodge, Golf Road, Sale,
Cheshire, M33 2XU
☎ 0161 9731730, Fax 9624217,
Sec 9731638, Rest/Bar 9733404
Close to M60 Junction 6.
Parkland course.
Pro Mike Stewart; Founded 1913
18 holes, 6126 yards, S.S.S. 69
† Welcome WD.

Royal Liverpool

Known as Hoylake by its many friends, Royal Liverpool is one of golf's great eccentrics. The holes potter around an undistinguished, flat piece of land, sometimes only finding definition through an internal out of bounds. Yet Hoylake is blissfully unaware that anybody could consider it ugly. It lives in a world of its own.

Golfers who require a reasonably sized freight train to transport their equipment, a wardrobe lady and a briefcase of yardage charts, probably won't like Hoylake. The Xanadu Country Club up the road, with its sacred rivers and immeasurable caverns, is altogether a lovelier place. They are missing out. Hoylake is not as well-known as it should be.

Since 1967, a lack of surrounding space on which to pitch all the attendant paraphernalia has forced Hoylake off the Open roster. But the recent purchase of some school land led to its reinstatement in 2001. Bernard Darwin, fine golfer and finer writer, once wrote, "This dear flat historic expanse of Hoylake, blown upon by mighty winds, has been a breeder of mighty champions." He omits to mention rain and snow. The local fire brigade was summoned to pump water out of the bunkers during the 1932 Varsity match. They failed. Four years later the Open lost a day's play due to snow. In the middle of July.

Darwin is bound to have liked the place because in 1921 he reached the semi-final of the Amateur here. On the eve of that Championship, Bill Fownes led a team of Americans to victory over the British, scotching the rather sniffy presumption of the time that American golf was somehow inferior.

The contest presaged the inaugural Walker Cup. The locals were so shocked by this defeat that Darwin was hailed as a hero when he beat the last two remaining Americans in the ensuing Amateur. One gentleman accosted him in the street to say, "I would like to thank you for the way in which you saved your country."

Hoylake hums with history. Bobby Jones won the second leg of his Grand Slam on the course. John H Taylor, Walter Hagen and Peter Thomson won Open Championships here. James Braid, Harry Vardon and Jack Nicklaus have each been a runner up. The first Amateur Championship was played at Hoylake.

Jones said of Hoylake, "This is a tight course. You can't get up there and slam away and trust to freedom of action to take care of the shot. You simply have to exercise some control of the ball." And a great deal of control of yourself. When Jamie Anderson placed a third ball down on the first tee, having put the previous two out of bounds, he said, "Ma God, it's like playing up a spout."

The members reflect the course. Their eccentric charm has gone way beyond the philosophical. In their early days they might suffer Hoylake's outrageous slings and arrows with a Gallic shrug. Perhaps it is no great surprise that Arnaud Massy, still the only Frenchman to have won the Open, triumphed at Hoylake. But after a while the shrug becomes a twitch, then a flail, then a rant, before finally a sort of lunatic calm takes over.

Each year the former captains of the club assemble in an upstairs room to agree upon next year's captain. When the decision is made they come among the waiting membership below and lay a hand upon the new incumbent's shoulder.

Not so very long ago the intended got rather drunk whilst watching England defeat Wales at rugby. As he reenacted one of the tries in the bar, various bits of his body parted company. Naturally enough the outgoing captain grabbed a bunch of flowers, headed to the hospital and after a few well-chosen words about the virtues of drink, laid his hand upon the shoulder.

I am not quite sure what the story is all about, but then that's rather the point of Hoylake. — **Mark Reason**

WD £28.
Welcome by arrangement with the Sec/Manager; golf and food packages available on application; terms on application.
Clubhouse facilities.
Dane Lodge, Sale.

6A 126 Sandbach
117 Middlewich Road, Sandbach, Cheshire, CW11 1FH
☎ 01270 762117, Rest/Bar 759227
Course is one mile N of Sandbach on the A53.
Meadowland course.
Founded 1895
9 holes, 5295 yards, S.S.S. 67
Welcome WD; WE by invitation.
£20.00 or £10.00 with a member.
Limited; by prior arrangement; terms on application.
Full facilities except Mon and Thurs.
Saxon Cross Motel; Old Hall.

6A 127 Sandiway Golf Club Ltd
Chester Road, Sandiway, Northwich, Cheshire, CW8 2DJ
☎ 01606 88327, Fax 888548, Pro 883180
On B556 14 miles E of Chester, 4 miles from Northwich.
Undulating parkland course.
Pro Bill Laird; Founded 1921
Designed by Ted Ray
18 holes, 6404 yards, S.S.S. 72
Welcome WD except Thurs (ladies day); WE by prior arrangement.
WD £35; WE £40.
Welcome Tues by prior arrangement; packages available; terms on application.
Full clubhouse facilities.
Hartland Hall; Oaklands.

6A 128 Sandwell Park
Birmingham Road, West Bromwich, W Midlands, B71 4JJ
www.sandwellpark.co.uk
☎ 0121 5534637, Fax 5251651, Pro 5534384, Rest/Bar 5254151
On A41 Birmingham Road, 200 yards from M5 Junction 1.
Heathland course.
Pro Nigel Wylie; Founded 1985
Designed by H S Colt
18 holes, 6468 yards, S.S.S. 73
Welcome WD.
WD £35.
Welcome WD by prior arrangement; reductions for bigger parties; catering facilities available; from £26.

Full restaurant facilities and two bars.
West Bromwich Moat House.

6A 129 Sedgley Golf Centre
Sandyfields Road, Dudley, W Midlands, DY3 3DL
☎ 01902 880503
Off A463 0.5 miles from Sedgley town centre near Cotwell End Nature Reserve.
Parkland course on the side of a valley with mature trees.
Pro Garry Mercer; Founded 1989
Designed by WG Cox
9 holes, 6294 yards, S.S.S. 70
Practice range, 16 bays covered and floodlit.
Pay and play course.
Terms on application.
Welcome by arrangement; snacks available; terms on application.
Snacks.

6A 130 Seedy Mill
Elmhurst, Lichfield, Staffs, WS13 8HE
www.clubhouse.com
☎ 01543 417333, Fax 418098
3 miles N of Lichfield off A51.
Parkland course with lakes, ponds and streams.
Pro Chris Stanley; Founded 1991
Designed by Hawtree & Sons
18 holes and a 9-hole par 3 course, 6305 yards, S.S.S. 70
Practice range, 26 bays floodlit.
Welcome.
WD £22; WE £27.
Welcome by prior arrangement; limited WE access; packages available for food and golf ranging packing available; corporate days available; also 9-hole Spires course, par 3; from £24.
Full clubhouse bar and restaurant.
Little Barrow, Lichfield.

6A 131 Severn Meadows
Highley, Bridgnorth, Shropshire, WV16 6HZ
☎ 01746 862212
10 miles N of Bewdley; 8 miles S of Bridgenorth.
Hilly parkland course in Severn valley.
Pro Martin Payne; Founded 1989
9 holes, 5258 yards, S.S.S. 67
Welcome WD; pay and play; must book WE.
Terms on application.
Welcome by arrangement.
Clubhouse facilities.
Bull, Chelmarsh.

6A 132 Shifnal
Decker Hill, Shifnal, Shropshire, TF11 8QL
www.shifnalgolfclub.co.uk
secretary@shifnalgolfclub.co.uk
☎ 01952 460330, Fax 461127, Pro 460457, Sec 460330
1 mile N of Shifnal close to M54 Junction 4.
Parkland course.
Pro J Flanagan; Founded 1929/1963
Designed by Frank Pennink
18 holes, 6468 yards, S.S.S. 71
2 practice areas.
Welcome WD; members only WE.
WD £25.
Welcome Tues, Wed and Fri; reductions for groups of 20 or more; terms on application.
Full clubhouse bar and catering facilities except Mondays.
Park House.

6A 133 Shrewsbury
Condover, Shrewsbury, Shropshire, SY5 7BL
☎ 01743 872976, Pro 873751, Sec 872977
S of Shrewsbury off A49.
Parkland course.
Pro Peter Seal; Founded 1890/1972
Designed by CK Cotton, Pennink, Lawrie & Partners
18 holes, 6205 yards, S.S.S. 70
Welcome WD; after 2pm Wed; WE between 10am-12 noon and after 2pm.
WD £19; WE £23.
Welcome Mon and Fri; limited availability Tues, Thurs and Sun am; packages can be arranged through the professional; terms on application.
Full clubhouse facilities.
Shrewsbury Hotel.

6A 134 Shrigley Hall Hotel
Pott Shrigley, Macclesfield, Cheshire, SK10 5SB
www.paramount'hotels.co.uk
☎ 01625 575757, Fax 573323, Pro 575626
Off A523 Macclesfield road; follow Pott Shrigley from Adlington.
Parkland course.
Pro Tony Stevens; Founded 1989
Designed by Donald Steel
18 holes, 6281 yards, S.S.S. 71
Practice range.
Welcome by arrangement.
WD £30; Fri £35; WE £35.
Welcome WD by prior arrangement; packages can be arranged; terms on application.

🍽 Full clubhouse and hotel facilities.
🛏 150-room Shrigley Hall Hotel on site.

6A 135 Shropshire ⚓
Muxton Lane, Muxton, Telford,
Shropshire, TF2 8PQ
☎ 01952 677800, Fax 677622, Pro
677866
From M54/A5 take B5060, turning right
at Granville roundabout; course
opposite equestrian centre.
Parkland course; 3 loops of 9 holes.
Pro Steve Marr; Founded 1992
Designed by Martin Hawtree
27 holes, 6637 yards, S.S.S. 72
🏌 Practice range, 30 bays covered
floodlit.
🚶 Welcome.
💰 WD £16; WE £22.
⤴ Welcome everyday; minimum 8;
catering and golf packages available;
private room; from £20.
🍽 Restaurant and three bars.
🛏 White House, Muxton; Telford Moat
House.

6A 136 The South Staffordshire
Golf Club Ltd
Danescourt Road, Wolverhampton, W
Midlands, WV6 9BQ
☎ 01902 751065, Pro 754816
On A41 from Wolverhampton in
Tettenhall; clubhouse and course
behind cricket club.
Parkland course.
Pro Mark Sparrow; Founded 1892
Designed by Harry Vardon/HS Colt
18 holes, 6513 yards, S.S.S. 71
🚶 Welcome except Tues am.
💰 WD £34; WE £45.
⤴ Welcome except Tues am and WE.
🍽 Clubhouse catering and bar.
🛏 Mount; Connaught.

6A 137 Stafford Castle Golf Club
Newport Road, Stafford, Staffs, ST16 1BP
☎ 01785 223821, Pro 212200
On A518 1 mile from Stafford Castle.
Parkland course.
Founded 1907
Designed by local lady in 1900s
9 holes, 6382 yards, S.S.S. 70
🏌 Longest 9-hole course in the
Midlands.
🚶 Welcome by arrangement.
💰 Terms on application.
⤴ Welcome WD by arrangement;
terms on application.
🍽 Clubhouse restaurant and bar
facilities.
🛏 Tillington Hall.

6A 138 Stamford Golf Club
(Stalybridge)
Huddersfield Road, Carrbrook,
Stalybridge, Cheshire, SK15 3PY
📧 stamford.golfclub@totalise.co.uk
☎ 01457 834829, Pro 834829,
Rest/Bar 834829
On B6175 NE of Stalybridge.
Parkland/moorland course.
Pro Brian Badger; Founded 1901
18 holes, 5701 yards, S.S.S. 68
🚶 Welcome WD.
💰 WD £20; WE £25.
⤴ Welcome by prior arrangement,
min 12; packages include 27 holes of
golf, lunch and dinner; from £30.
🍽 Clubhouse facilities.
🛏 The Village, in Hyde.

6A 139 Stockport
Offerton Road, Stockport, Cheshire,
SK2 5HL
📧 stockportgolf@genie.co.uk
☎ 0161 4272001, Fax 4498293,
Pro 4272421, Sec 4278369,
Rest/Bar 4274425
Take A627 Torkington road from A6;
course 1.5 miles on right.
Parkland course.
Pro Mike Peel; Founded 1906
18 holes, 6326 yards, S.S.S. 71
🚶 Welcome by arrangement.
💰 WD £35; WE £45.
⤴ Welcome Wed and Thurs;
minimum 20 players; catering and golf
packages available.
🍽 Full clubhouse bar and restaurant
service.
🛏 Moorside, Disley; Britannia,
Offerton; Alma Lodge, Stockport.

6A 140 Stone
The Fillybrooks, Stone, Staffs, ST15
0NB
☎ 01785 813103, Sec 284875
1 mile NW of Stone on A34.
Parkland course.
Founded 1896
9 holes, 6299 yards, S.S.S. 70
🚶 Welcome WD; WE only with a
member.
💰 WD on application.
⤴ Welcome by arrangement; catering
packages available; terms on
application.
🍽 Clubhouse catering facilities.
🛏 Stone House.

6A 141 Styal
Styal Golf Club, Station Road, Styal,
Wilmslow, Cheshire, SK9 4JN
🔗 www.stylegolf.co.uk

☎ 01625 530063, Fax 530063
Off M56 Junction 5 at Manchester
Airport; straight on at roundabout instead
of turning to Airport; at end of Ringway
road turn right into Styal Road; after 1 mile
turn left into station road, club on right.
Parkland course.
Pro G Traynor; Founded 1995
Designed by T Holmes
18 holes, 6172 yards, S.S.S. 70
🏌 Practice range, 24 bays; driving
range also has 9-hole par 3 golf course.
🚶 Welcome.
💰 WD £18; WE £22.
⤴ Welcome by prior arrangement;
packages available; from £19.
🍽 Clubhouse catering and bar.
🛏 Stanneylands; Hilton at
Manchester Airport.

6A 142 Sutton Hall
Aston Lane, Sutton Weaver, Runcorn,
Cheshire, WA7 3ED
☎ 01928 715530, Fax 759174, Pro
714872, Sec 790747
M56 Junction 12, follow signs to
Frodsham; turn left at Swinbridge for
course.
Parkland course.
Pro Ian Smith; Founded 1995
Designed by S Wundke
18 holes, 6547 yards, S.S.S. 71
🚶 Welcome.
💰 WD £18; WE £22.
⤴ Welcome WD; some at WE;
packages for catering and golf
available for groups of more than 10;
groups up to 100 can be catered for.
🍽 Full catering and bar.
🛏 Forte Crest, Beechwood.

6A 143 Swindon
North road, Swindon, Dudley, W
Midlands, DY3 4Pu
☎ 01902 897031, Fax 326219, Pro
896191
On B4176 Dudley to Bridgnorth road; 3
miles off A449 at Himley.
Wooded parkland course with
exceptional views.
Pro Phil Lester; Founded 1974
Designed by Phil Lester
27 holes, 6091 yards, S.S.S. 69
🏌 Practice range, 27 bays; also 9-
hole course, par 3.
🚶 Welcome.
💰 WD £18; WE £27.
⤴ Welcome by arrangement with
J Smith; terms on application.
🍽 Clubhouse facilities.
🛏 Himley Country Club, Himley.

6A 144 **Tamworth Municipal**
Eagle Drive, Tamworth, Staffs, B77 4EG
☎ 01827 709303, Fax 709304, Rest/Bar 709306
From M42 Junction 10 proceed towards Tamworth; course is signposted off the B5000 Polesworth road.
Municipal parkland course.
Pro Wiyna Illcock; Founded 1975
18 holes, 6525 yards, S.S.S. 72
Welcome.
WD £10; WE £10.
Welcome WD by appointment.
Bar and daily catering.
Canada Lodge.

6A 145 **Telford Golf and Country Club** 𝕿
Great Hay Drive, Sutton Heights, Telford, Shropshire, TF7 4DT
www.regalhotels.co.uk/telfordgolfandcountry
☎ 01952 429977, Fax 586602
Off A442 at Sutton Hill S of Telford.
Parkland course.
Pro Daniel Bateman; Founded 1975
Designed by John Harris
18 holes, 6761 yards, S.S.S. 72
8 bays, floodlit.
Welcome.
WD £25; WE £30.
Welcome by prior arrangement.
Hotel facilities.
Telford Moat House on site.

6A 146 **Three Hammers Golf Complex**
Old Stafford Road, Cross Green, Wolverhampton, W Midlands, WV10 7PP
☎ 01902 790428, Pro 790940
From M54 Junction 2 travel N on A449 course 1 mile on right.
Parkland course.
Pro Shaun Ball and Ted Large
Designed by Henry Cotton
18 holes, 1438 yards, S.S.S. 54
Practice range, 23-bay floodlit range.
Welcome.
WD £6; WE £7.
Welcome Mon-Sat.
Bar, bistro, restaurant and private dining facilities.

6A 147 **Trentham Golf Club** 𝕿
14 Barlaston Old Road, Stoke On Trent, Staffs, ST4 8HB
secretery@trenthamgolf.org
☎ 01782 642347, Fax 644024, Pro 657309, Sec 658109, Rest/Bar 643623
Off A34 from Stoke to Stone, turn left at Trentham Gardens.
Parkland course.
Pro Sandy Wilson; Founded 1894
18 holes, 6619 yards, S.S.S. 72
Practice ground.
Welcome by prior arrangement.
WD £40; WE £50.
Welcome Mon – Fri by prior arrangement; terms available on application.
Clubhouse facilities.
Trentham Hotel; Post House Hotel; Tollgate Leisure.

6A 148 **Trentham Park**
Stoke-on-Trent, Staffs, ST4 8AE
☎ 01782 642245, Fax 658800, Pro 642125, Sec 658800, Rest/Bar 644130
Course is on the A34 four miles S of Newcastle; one mile from the M6 Junction 15.
Parkland course.
Founded 1936
18 holes, 6425 yards, S.S.S. 71
Welcome by arrangement.
WD £22.50; WE £30.
Welcome Wed and Fri by prior arrangement; packages for golf and catering available; from £22.50.
Clubhouse facilities.

6A 149 **Tytherington**
Dorchester Way, Macclesfield, Cheshire, SK10 2JP
☎ 01625 506000, Fax 506040, Pro 506003
2 miles from Macclesfield on the A523 Stockport Road.
Parkland course; one of WPGA European Tour.
Pro Neil Coulson – Golf Operations Manager; Founded 1986
Designed by Dave Thomas and Patrick Dawson
18 holes, 6765 yards, S.S.S. 73
Welcome with handicap certs.
WD £28; WE £34.
Welcome WD by prior arrangement; full facilities for golf and catering packages; private rooms; snooker and pool; health club; tennis; terms on application.
Restaurant, bars and full catering facilities.
Contact club for details.

6A 150 **Upton-by-Chester**
Upton Lane, Upton, Chester, Cheshire, CH2 1EE
☎ 01244 381183, Fax 376955
Off A41 Chester-Liverpool road near Chester Zoo.
Parkland course.
Pro Peter Gardener; Founded 1934
Designed by Bill Davis
18 holes, 5850 yards, S.S.S. 68
Putting green.
Welcome except on competition days.
£20 Full day £30.
Welcome Wed, Thurs and Fri by prior arrangement.
Full clubhouse facilities.
Dene; Euromill; Mollington Banastre.

6A 151 **Uttoxeter**
Wood Lane, Uttoxeter, Staffs, ST14 8JR
☎ 01889 5666552, Fax 567501, Pro 564884, Sec 566552, Rest/Bar 01889 565108
Off B5017 Uttoxeter-Marchington road, 0.5 miles along Wood Lane just past the race course.
Parkland course with views over Dove Valley.
Pro Adam McCandless; Founded 1972
18 holes, 5801 yards, S.S.S. 70
Welcome by arrangement.
WD £20, WE £30, 50% discount with a member.
Welcome by prior arrangement; packages available for groups of 10; from £21.50.
Catering and restaurant facilities.
White Hart; Bank House Hotel, both Uttoxeter.

6A 152 **Vicars Cross**
Tarvin Road, Christleton, Chester, Cheshire, CH3 7HN
☎ 01244 335174, Pro 335595
On A51 4 miles E of Chester.
Undulating parkland course.
Pro J Forsythe; Founded 1939
Designed by E Parr
18 holes, 6243 yards, S.S.S. 72
8 indoors, 8 outdoors, floodlit bays.
Welcome except on competition days.
WD £25; WE £25.
Welcome Tues and Thurs, April-October except June; full golf and catering packages; from £31.50.
Full clubhouse facilities.

6A 153 **Wallasey**
Wallasey Golf Club Ltd, Bayswater Road, Wallasey, Wirral, CH45 8LA
www.wallaseygc.com
wallaseygc@aol.com
☎ 0151 6911024, Fax 6388988, Pro 6383888
Leave the M53 at Junction 1; follow the A554 towards New Brighton, course is 0.25 miles on left.
Links course.
Pro Mike Adams; Founded 1891

Designed by Tom Morris Snr
18 holes, 6607 yards, S.S.S. 72
⚑ Practice area.
† Welcome by arrangement.
ℐ WD £45; WE £60.
⌂ Welcome by prior arrangement;
packages for groups of 16 or more;
catering available.
🍽 Clubhouse facilities.
⌐ Grove House, Wallasey.

6A 154 Walsall
Broadway, Walsall, W Midlands, WS1
3EY
🖳 www.walsallgolf.freeserve.co.uk
✉ golfclub@walsallgolf.
freeserve.co.uk
☎ 01922 613512
Off A34 1 mile S of Walsall.
Wooded parkland course.
Pro R Lambert; Founded 1907
Designed by Dr MacKenzie
18 holes, 6257 yards, S.S.S. 70
† Welcome WD; WE as a members
guest.
ℐ WD £33; WE £33.
⌂ Welcome WD by prior arrangement;
catering and golf packages available for
minimum 16; from £30.
🍽 Clubhouse facilities.
⌐ Boundary; County Hotel.

6A 155 Walton Hall
Warrington Road, Higher Walton,
Warrington, Cheshire, WA4 5LU
☎ 01925 266775, Pro 263061
Course is one mile from the M56
Junction 11.
Scenic parkland course.
Pro John Jackson; Founded 1972
Designed by Dave Thomas
18 holes, 6647 yards, S.S.S. 73
† Welcome.
ℐ WD £9; WE £11.
⌂ Welcome by prior arrangement with
the Pro shop; terms on application.
🍽 Full catering facilities in season;
limited in winter.
⌐ Lord Daresbury.

6A 156 Warren
Grove Road, Wallasey, Merseyside,
CH45 0JA
☎ 0151 6398323, Pro 6395730
500 yards up Grove Rd at Wallasey
Grove Rd station on left before traffic
lights.
Municipal links course.
Pro Stephen Konrad; Founded 1911
9 holes, 5714 yards, S.S.S. 70
† Welcome.
ℐ Prices on application.

⌂ Welcome by prior arrangement.
⌐ Grove House.

6A 157 Warrington
London Road, Appleton, Warrington,
Cheshire, WA4 5HR
🖳 www.warrington-golf-club.co.uk
☎ 01925 261620, Fax 265933, Pro
265431, Sec 261775
On A49 1 mile from M56 Junction 10.
Parkland course.
Pro Reay Mackay; Founded 1903
Designed by James Braid
18 holes, 6210 yards, S.S.S. 70
⚑ Practice ground.
† Welcome by prior arrangement.
ℐ WD £27; WE £32.
⌂ Welcome on Wed by prior
arrangement; summer and winter
packages for golf and catering.
🍽 Full clubhouse facilities.
⌐ Birchdale Hotel, Stockton Heath.

6A 158 Wergs
Keepers Lane, Wolverhampton, W
Midlands, WV6 8UA
☎ 01902 742225, Fax 744748
Off A41, 2.5 miles from Wolverhampton
Open parkland course.
Pro Bryan Berlison; Founded 1990
Designed by CW Moseley
18 holes, 6949 yards, S.S.S. 73
† Welcome.
ℐ WD £13.50; WE £17.
⌂ Welcome WD; after 10am at WE;
catering packages available; from £13.50.
🍽 Clubhouse catering facilities available.

6A 159 Werneth Low
Werneth Low Road, Hyde, Cheshire,
SK14 3AF
☎ 0161 3682503, Pro 3679376
Course is two miles from Hyde town
centre via Gee Cross and Joel Lane.
Hilltop course.
Pro Tony Bacchus; Founded 1912
Designed by Peter Campbell
11 holes, 6113 yards, S.S.S. 70
† Welcome, except Sun.
ℐ WD £18; WE £24.
⌂ WD by prior arrangement.
🍽 Full catering facilities available.
⌐ The Village, Hyde.

6A 160 Westminster Park
Hough Green, Chester, Cheshire, CH4
8JQ
☎ 01244 680231, Fax 680231
Course is two miles W of Chester city
centre.
Parkland course.

Founded 1980
9 holes, 963 yards, S.S.S. 27
† Pay and play.
ℐ WD £2.50; WE £2.50 discounts for
OAPs and juniors.
⌂ None.
🍽 Limited soft drinks.
⌐ Hotel Hough Green.

6A 161 Westwood (Leek)
Newcastle Road, Leek, Staffs, ST13 7AA
☎ 01538 398385, Fax 382485, Pro
398897
On A53 1 mile S of Leek.
Heathland/parkland course.
Pro Neale Hyde; Founded 1923
18 holes, 6214 yards, S.S.S. 69
⚑ Practice area.
† Welcome by prior arrangement.
ℐ WD £18; WE £20.
⌂ Welcome by prior arrangement;
packages available including golf and
catering; games/snooker room; from
£27.50.
🍽 Full clubhouse facilities.
⌐ The Hatcheries; Bank End Farm;
Abbey Inn.

6A 162 Whiston Hall Golf Club
Whiston, Stoke On Trent, Staffs, ST10
2HZ
🖳 www.whistonhall.com
☎ 01538 266260, Fax 266820
On A52 midway between Stoke-on-
Trent and Ashbourne; 3 miles from
Alton Towers.
Parkland/heathland course.
Pro Derry Goodman; Founded 1971
Designed by Thomas Cooper
18 holes, 5784 yards, S.S.S. 69
† Welcome.
ℐ WD £10; WE £10.
⌂ Welcome by prior arrangement;
packages available both WD and WE;
from £12.95.
🍽 Full clubhouse facilities.
⌐ Mansion Court Hotel.

6A 163 Whittington Heath
Tamworth Road, Lichfield, Staffs,
WS14 9PW
☎ 01543 432317, Fax 433962, Pro
432261
On A51 Lichfield to Tamworth road.
Heathland course.
Pro A Sadler; Founded 1886
Designed by HS Colt
18 holes, 6490 yards, S.S.S. 71
† Welcome WD with handicap certs.
ℐ WD £35.
⌂ Welcome Wed and Thurs by
arrangement; packages for golf and

The Wilmslow Golf Club

Founded 1889

Enjoy a warm, friendly welcome at our superb 18 hole (6, 607 yd) parkland course set in the heart of the Cheshire countryside.

Great Warford
Mobberley
Knutsford
WA16 7AY

VISITORS WELCOME Special rates for Society, Corporate & Charity events

Tel: **01565 872148**   Email: **wilmslowgolfclub@ukf.net**   Website: **www.wilmslowgolfclub.ukf.net**

---

catering; maximum 40.
🍴 Full clubhouse facilities.
🛏 Little Barrow, Lichfield.

6A 164 Widnes
Highfield Road, Widnes, Cheshire, WA8 7DT
🖥 www.widnes-golfclub.co.uk
📧 arudder.wgc@uku.co.uk
☎ 0151 4242995, Fax 4952849, Pro 4207467
Signposted from the town centre. Take signs to autoquest stadium, take highfield road and 20 yards on the left through the lights.
Parkland course.
Jason O'Brien; Founded 1924
18 holes, 5729 yards, S.S.S. 68
† Welcome WD except Tues.
Ⅼ WD £18; WE £24.
⌔ Welcome Thurs by prior arrangement; from £30.
🍴 Catering and bar facilities.
🛏 Hillcrest; Everglades.

6A 165 Wilmslow
Warford Lane, Mobberley, Knutsford, Cheshire, WA16 7AY
☎ 01565 873620, Fax 872172, Sec 872148
From the A34 Wilmslow-Alderley Edge road take the B5085 signposted for Knutsford; Warford Lane is three miles.
Parkland course.
Pro John Nowicki; Founded 1889
Designed by Alexander Herd
18 holes, 6607 yards, S.S.S. 72
† Welcome by arrangement.
Ⅼ WD £40; WE £50.
⌔ Welcome Tues and Thurs by prior arrangement; packages for golf and catering available; minimum 24; from £30.
🍴 Full clubhouse facilities.

6A 166 Wirral Ladies
93 Bidston Road, Prenton, Merseyside,

CH43 6TS
☎ 0151 6521255, Pro 6522468
On A41 adjacent to M53 Junction 3.
Heathland course.
Pro Angus Law; Founded 1894
Designed by H Hilton
18 holes, 5185 (mens), 4948 (ladies) yards, S.S.S. 65 (mens), 69 (ladies)
ↆ Practice area.
† Welcome.
Ⅼ WD £25.50; WE £25.50.
⌔ Welcome by arrangement.
🍴 Full facilities.
🛏 Bowler Hat.

6A 167 Withington
Palatine Road, Manchester, Lancs, M20 2UE
📧 withingtongc@lineone.net
☎ 0161 4459544, Fax 4455210, Pro 4454861
S of Manchester on B5166.
Parkland course.
Pro Bob Ling; Founded 1892
18 holes, 6364 yards, S.S.S. 71
† Welcome by arrangement.
Ⅼ Terms on application.
⌔ Welcome by prior arrangement; 27-hole packages available; from £42.
🍴 Full clubhouse facilities.

6A 168 Wolstanton
Hassam Parade, Newcastle, Staffs, ST5 9DR
☎ 01782 622413, Fax 622718, Pro 622718, Rest/Bar 616995
0.5 miles off A34, 3 miles from Newcastle, turn right at McDonalds.
Parkland course.
Pro Simon Arnold; Founded 1904
18 holes, 5807 yards, S.S.S. 68
† Welcome WD; with member at WE.
Ⅼ WD £20.
⌔ Welcome WD except Tues; catering packages can be arranged.
🍴 Clubhouse facilities.
🛏 Friendly Hotel on A34 at Newcastle.

6A 169 Woodside
Knutsford Road, Cranage, Holmes Chapel, Crewe, Cheshire, CW4 8HT
☎ 01477 532 388
Off M6 at Junction 18.
† Pay and play.
Ⅼ WD £5.
⌔ Limited facilities.
🍴 Limited.

6A 170 Worfield
Roughton, Bridgnorth, Shropshire, WV15 5HE
🖥 www.worfieldgolf.co.uk
☎ 01746 716541, Fax 716302, Sec 716372
3 miles outside Bridgnorth on A454, Wolverhampton road.
Parkland course.
Pro Stephen Russell; Founded 1991
Designed by T Williams/D Gough
18 holes, 6801 yards, S.S.S. 73
ↆ Practice area.
† Welcome WD; after 2pm at WE.
Ⅼ WD £20; WE £25.
⌔ Welcome by arrangement; packages arranged through secretary/manager; terms on application.
🍴 Full clubhouse facilities.
🛏 Old Vicarage, Bridgnorth.

6A 171 Wrekin
Ercall Woods, Wrekin, Telford, Shropshire, TF6 5BX
☎ 01952 244032, Pro 223101
Course is off the M54; take the B5061 to Golf Links Lane.
Parkland course.
Pro Keith Housden; Founded 1905
18 holes, 5570 yards, S.S.S. 67
† Welcome WD.
Ⅼ WD £20; WE £28.
⌔ Welcome WD.
🍴 Clubhouse facilities.

6B

Derbyshire, Nottinghamshire, Lincolnshire

The trio of Lord Alfred Tennyson, herb sausages and Margaret Thatcher ought to say something about Lincolnshire, but as to what it is I haven't the faintest idea. The golf courses seem to be an altogether more eloquent description of the character of this county.

On the coast, just up the road from Skegness, is Seacroft Golf Club which is one of the most pleasant surprises in golf. You can park your car in a car park a little way from the course, but it is rather easier to stick it on the road behind the first tee. It is an unprepossessing beginning, not altogether alleviated by the sight of the club buildings, begun in 1904 and apparently still unfinished.

But the course is an unexpected wonder. The front nine, with the exception of the sixth, heads south towards the Gibraltar Point nature reserve. A road to the right threatens out of bounds on several holes – in fact there are fourteen holes where out of bounds to the right is a possibility – but often that is the least of the golfer's worries. The inward nine is even better, with two excellent par threes and a par five that is perhaps the signature hole. From the tee you can see the outline of Hunstanton across the Wash. Take it in whilst you can, because once started on this dog leg par five, with thorn trees and bushes left and right and a well bunkered ridge across the fairway, you will need all your wits about you.

Driving inland from Seacroft past fields that seem a cross between the fens and Romney marshes eventually you will reach Woodhall Spa. At the home of the English Golf Union everything is thoroughly well-prepared. At around the time in the mid nineties when Woodhall was getting a second course, Forest Pines was opened and in just a few years has become one of Lincolnshire's best.

On past Stamford lies Luffenham Heath. Its members will say that it is not in Lincolnshire at all, but in Rutland. The wood-panelled clubhouse is full of royal portraits, maybe because it lies within a conservation area. There is plenty of gorse, heather and shrubbery into which to stick your ball from the tee and the slippery greens maintain the challenge.

Notts Golf Club is more usually called Hollinwell, a name derived from Holy Well. It lies within the boundaries of Sherwood Forest so it is not surprising that there should be a fair bit of oak and silver birch about. It is a stiff test, but does not quite have the romance that you might suspect from a course with a rock called Robin Hood's Chair behind its second green.

Sherwood Forest is the preferred venue of some in the county. It is not quite so exacting as Hollinwell, but it feels more intimate and has a memorable back nine. If the first nine was as good, Sherwood Forest would be indisputably the county's best. Coxmoor is also highly-rated and Worksop is renowned as the home territory of Lee Westwood.

Derbyshire is not quite such lush land for golf and there are so many good walks to be had that it might be better not to spoil them. But Cavendish, designed by Alister Mackenzie of Augusta fame, is worth a visit with its recessed tees, meandering greens and huge swales. So too is Kedleston Park, although it is not the finest of James Braid's work and isn't always in the best of nick.

KEY

1 Alfreton	23 Cavendish	46 Humberston Park	68 Maywood	91 Sherwood Forest
2 Allestree Park	24 Chatsworth	47 Ilkeston Borough (Pewit)	69 Mickleover	92 Shirland
3 Ashbourne	25 Chesterfield	48 Immingham	70 Millfield	93 Sickleholme
4 Ashby Decoy	26 Chevin	49 Kedleston Park	71 Newark	94 Sleaford
5 Bakewell	27 Chilwell Manor	50 Kenwick Park	72 New Mills Golf Club	95 South Kyme
6 Beeston Fields	28 Cleethorpes	51 Kilton Forest	73 Normanby Hall	96 Southview
7 Belton Park	29 College Pines	52 Kingsway	74 North Shore	97 Spalding
8 Belton Woods Hotel	30 Cotgrave Place G & CC	53 Kirton Holme	75 Norwood Park	98 Springwater
9 Birch Hall	31 Coxmoor	54 Leen Valley	76 Nottingham City	99 Stanedge
10 Blankney	32 Derby	55 Lincoln	77 Notts	100 Stanton-on-the-Wolds
11 Bondhay Golf & CC	33 Edwalton Municipal	56 The Lincolnshire (43)	78 Oakmere Park	101 Stoke Rochford
12 Boston	34 Elsham	57 Lindrick	79 Ormonde Fields CC	102 Sudbrook Moor
13 Boston West	35 Erewash Valley	58 Louth Golf Club	80 Pastures	103 Sutton Bridge
14 Brailsford	36 Forest Pines	59 Luffenham Heath	81 Pottergate	104 Tapton Park Municipal
15 Bramcote Hills GC	37 Gainsborough	60 The Manor Golf Course	82 Radcliffe-on-Trent	105 Tetney
16 Breedon Priory	38 Gedney Hill	61 Mansfield Woodhouse	83 RAF Waddington	106 Toft Hotel
17 Bulwell Forest	39 Glossop & District	62 Mapperley	84 Ramsdale Park GC	107 Trent Lock Golf Centre
18 Burghley Park	40 Grange Park	63 Market Rasen & District	85 Retford	108 Waltham Windmill
19 Buxton & High Peak	41 Grassmoor Golf Centre	64 Market Rasen Race Course	86 Riverside	109 Welton Manor
20 Canwick Park	42 Grimsby	65 Marriott Breadsall Priory	87 Ruddington Grange	110 Wollaton Park
21 Carholme	43 Holme Hall	66 Martin Moor	88 Rutland County	111 Woodhall Spa
22 Carsington Water	44 Horncastle	67 Matlock	89 Sandilands	112 Woodthorpe Hall
	45 Horsley Lodge		90 Seacroft	113 Worksop

6B 1 Alfreton

Highfields, Wingfield Rd, Oakthorpe,
Alfreton, Derbys, DE5 7DH
☎ 01773 832070
On Matlock Road 1 mile W of Alfreton.
Parkland course.
Pro Julian Mellor; Founded 1892
11 holes, S.S.S. 66
† Welcome WD; with member at WE.
Ⅰ WD £16; WE £8.
♨ Welcome by prior arrangement;
max 36; terms available on
application.
⦿ Clubhouse facilities.
↴ Swallow, South Normanton.

6B 2 Allestree Park

Allestree Hall, Allestree Park, Derby,
Derbyshire, DE22 2EU
☎ 01332 550616, Fax 541195, Pro
550616, Sec 552971, Rest/Bar 552971
4 miles N of Derby; 1 mile N of A38/A6
Junction.
Undulating parkland course.
Pro Leigh Woodward; Founded 1947
18 holes, 5806 yards, S.S.S. 68
† Welcome.
Ⅰ Terms on application.
♨ Welcome by prior arrangement;
various 18, 27, 36-hole packages
available; catering; golf clinics; terms
on application.
⦿ Clubhouse facilities.
↴ International, Hotel Derby.

6B 3 Ashbourne

The Clubhouse Wyaston Road,
Ashbourne, Derbys, DE6 1NB
⬚ www.ashbournegolfclub.co.uk
✉ sec@ashbournegc.fsnet.co.uk
☎ 01335 342078, Fax 347930,
Pro 347960, Sec 343457
On A515 2 miles W of Ashbourne. A52
Derby Leek road, turn off on to to Old
Derby road.
Parkland course.
Pro Andrew Smith; Founded
1886/1999 redeveloped
Designed by Frank Pennink
18 holes, 6365 yards, S.S.S. 72
Ⅰ Practice round.
† Welcome WD.
Ⅰ WD £20; WE £30.
♨ Welcome WD; by arrangement
with professional; prices on application.
⦿ Clubhouse catering and bar.
↴ Green Man; Hanover International
both Ashbourne.

6B 4 Ashby Decoy

Burringham Rd, Scunthorpe, Lincs,
DN17 2AB

⬚ www.ashbydecoy.co.uk
✉ ashby.decoy@btclick.com
☎ 01724 866561, Fax 271708,
Pro 868972, Rest/Bar 842913
From M181 turn right at first three
roundabouts; course is 400 yards on left
course.
Pro A Miller; Founded 1936
Designed by Members
18 holes, 6250 yards, S.S.S. 70
† Welcome WD except Tues; with a
member WE.
Ⅰ Summer WD £18; Winter WD £13.
♨ Welcome WD except Tues by prior
arrangement; various packages on
application; from £22-£37.
⦿ Full clubhouse facilities.
↴ Royal; Wortley both Scunthorpe.

6B 5 Bakewell

Station Road, Bakewell, Derbyshire,
DE45 1GB
☎ 01629 812307,
Rest/Bar 812307
0.75 miles from Bakewell Square;
cross River Wye on A619 Sheffield-
Chesterfield Road; up Station Rd
turning right before Industrial estate.
Hilly parkland course.
Founded 1899
Designed by George Low
9 holes, 5240 yards, S.S.S. 66
† Welcome WD; Ladies priority
Thurs; WE by prior arrangement.
Ⅰ Prices on application.
♨ Welcome by arrangement.
⦿ Meals and bar except Mon.
↴ Rutland Arms.

6B 6 Beeston Fields

Old Drive, Beeston Fields, Nottingham,
NG9 3DD
⬚ www.beestonfields.com
✉ beestonfieldsgolfclub@
supernet.com
☎ 0115 9257062, Fax 9254280, Pro
9220872
1 mile from Beeston, 5 miles W of
Nottingham on S side of A52.
Parkland course.
Pro Alun Wardle; Founded 1923
Designed by Tom Williamson
18 holes, 6404 yards, S.S.S. 71
Ⅰ Practice area.
† Welcome WD (after 3pm Tues);
some restrictions at WE.
Ⅰ WD £26-£36; WE £31.
♨ Welcome Mon and Wed by prior
arrangement; packages available for
catering contact steward; separate
dining room.
⦿ Clubhouse facilities.
↴ Priory Hotel.

6B 7 Belton Park ☎

Belton Lane, Londonthorpe Rd,
Grantham, Lincs, NG31 9SH
☎ 01476 567399, Fax 592078,
Pro 563911, Sec 567399,
Rest/Bar 563355
From A607 Grantham-Sleaford Road;
turn right to Londonthorpe; course 1
mile on left.
Parkland course.
Pro Brian McKee; Founded 1890
Designed by T Williamson/Dave
Thomas and Peter Alliss
Ⅰ Practice range, 2 practice areas.
† Welcome with handicap certs
except Tues.
Ⅰ WD £30, WE £36.
♨ Welcome WD except Tues; by
prior arrangement; terms on
application.
⦿ Full clubhouse facilities.
↴ Angel & Royal/Kings/Marriot.

6B 8 Belton Woods Hotel ☎

Belton, Nr Grantham, Lincolnshire,
NG32 2LN
⬚ www.deveronline.com
✉ belton.woods@dever-online.com
☎ 01476 593200, Fax 574547,
Pro 514332, Sec 514332,
Rest/Bar 593200
2 miles E of A1 via Gonerby Moor; 2
miles N of Grantham on A607 Lincoln
Road.
Parkland course with mature trees and
ancient woodland.
Pro Steven Sayers
36 holes and a par-3 9-hole,
6831/6623 yards, S.S.S. 73
Ⅰ Practice range, 24 bays floodlit.
† Welcome; bookings taken 10 days
in advance.
Ⅰ WD £27; WE £30.
♨ Welcome WD by prior
arrangement; packages available;
company days organised; reductions
for residents; banqueting facilities for
240; health and sports leisure centres;
conference facilities; also Spitfire 9-
hole course 1184 yards par 3.
⦿ Full bar and restaurant facilities.
↴ Belton Woods on site.

6B 9 Birch Hall

Sheffield Rd, Unstone Green,
Sheffield, S18 5DH
☎ 01246 291979, Rest/Bar 291087
Off A61.
Moorland course.
Pro Pete Ball; Founded 1992
Designed by David Tucker
18 holes, 6505 yards, S.S.S. 73
Ⅰ Practice area.

A beautiful 9 hole golf course situated on the edge of the Peak District, Derbyshire.

9 Holes - PAR 36.   18 Holes - PAR 72.

- Superb floodlit under cover driving range   • A warm welcome to visitors and societies
- Buggy, trolleys and golf clubs available for hire   • Modest green fees
- Golfing competitions can be arranged together with full hospitality facilities.

Pools Heath Lane, Brailsford, Ashbourne, Derbyshire DE6 3BU   Tel: **01335 360096**

---

† Welcome; prior arrangement at WE.
⌊ WD £10; WE £10.
⟳ Welcome WD and afternoons at WE; catering on application; from £10.
⚑ Clubhouse facilities.
↩ Sandpiper.

6B 10 **Blankney**
Blankney, Lincoln, Lincs, LN4 3AZ
☎ 01526 320263, Fax 322521
Course is on the B1188 10 miles S of Lincoln.
Parkland course.
Pro Graham Bradley; Founded 1903
Designed by Cameron Sinclair (updated Design)
18 holes, 6638 yards, S.S.S. 73
† Welcome by prior arrangement.
⌊ WD £20; WE £30.
⟳ Welcome by prior arrangement with general manager; from £20.
⚑ Clubhouse facilities available.
↩ Dower House; Golf Hotel.

6B 11 **Bondhay Golf & Country Club**
Bondhay Lane, Whitwell, Worksop, Notts, S80 3EH
☎ 01909 723608, Fax 720226
Just off A619; 5 minutes from M1 Junction 30.
Parkland course.
Pro David Cox; Founded 1991
Designed by Donald Steel
18 holes, 6720 yards, S.S.S. 74
⚐ Practice range 15-bay floodlit covered range.
† Welcome; advance booking.
⌊ Winter WD £16.00; WE £21.00; Summer WD £15 WE £20.
⟳ Welcome by prior arrangement; catering packages by arrangement; function rooms available; also family course; from £3.
⚑ Full bar and restaurant facilities available.
↩ Vandykes, Whitwell, Beeches, Rotherham.

6B 12 **Boston**
Cowbridge, Honcastle Rd, Boston, Lincs, PE22 7EL
✉ steveshaw@bostongc.co.uk

☎ 01205 350589, Fax 350589,
Pro 362306, Rest/Bar 352533
Course is on the B1183 two miles N of Boston.
Parkland course with water on 8 holes.
Pro Terry Squires; Founded 1900
Designed by BS Cooper; Extended by Donald Steel
18 holes, 6490 yards, S.S.S. 71
† Welcome by arrangement.
⌊ WD £18; WE £24.
⟳ Welcome WD except Tues; packages available for 18-36 holes; lunch and dinner; from £27.50 – £37.50.
⚑ Clubhouse facilities.
↩ New England; White Hart; Kings Arms all Boston.

6B 13 **Boston West**
Hubbert's Bridge, Boston, Lincs, PE20 3QX
🖳 www.bostonwestgolfclub.co.uk
✉ info@bostonwestgolfclub.co.uk
☎ 01205 290670, Fax 290725,
Pro 290540
At junction of A1121/B1192 2 miles W of Boston.
Parkland course.
Pro Andrew Hare/Paul Creasey; Founded 1995
Designed by KMB
18 holes, 6333 yards, S.S.S. 71
† Welcome.
⌊ Terms on application.
⟳ Welcome at all times; golf and catering packages can be arranged; terms on application.
⚑ Full catering facilities.
↩ Boston Lodge.

6B 14 **Brailsford**   ⚑
Pools Head Lane, Brailsford, Ashbourne, Derbys, DE6 3BU
☎ 01335 360096
Signposted off A52 just before Ashbourne. 6 miles from Derby city centre along the A52 on the left hand side.
Parkland course.
Pro David McCarthy; Founded 1994
9 holes, 6292 yards, S.S.S. 70
⚐ Practice range 15 bays floodlit; Under coverpractice bunker and

putting green; new clubhouse.
† Welcome.
⌊ POA.
⟳ Welcome by prior arrangement; reductions for groups of 16 or more of 20%; terms on application.
⚑ Full catering facilities and bar.
↩ Mackwith Hotel, Mundy Arms Hotel.

6B 15 **Bramcote Hills Golf Course**
Thoresby Rd, off Derby Rd, Bramcote, Nottingham, Notts, NG9 3EP
☎ 0115 9281880
Leave M1 Junction 25, take A52 towards Nottingham, past Bramcote Leisure Centre; left after 0.25 miles.
Parkland course.
Founded 1981
18 holes, 1501 yards, S.S.S. 31
† Welcome; pay and play.
⌊ WD £6.50; WE and BH £7.00;
Discounts for juniors, OAPs and students (£5.50 all week).
⟳ Welcome.
⚑ None.
↩ Novtel hotel.

6B 16 **Breedon Priory**
The Clubhouse, Green Lane, Wilson, Nr Derby, DE73 1LG
🖳 www.breedongolf.co.uk
☎ 01332 863081, Sec 864046
On A453 3.5 miles W of M1 Junction 23A.
Parkland course.
Pro Jim Broughton; Founded 1991
Designed by D Snell
18 holes, 5777 yards, S.S.S. 70
† Welcome.
⌊ Prices on application.
⟳ Welcome by prior arrangement; catering and golf packages available; terms on application.
⚑ Full clubhouse facilities. Golf Simulator.

6B 17 **Bulwell Forest**
Hucknall Rd, Bulwell, Nottingham, NG6 9LQ
☎ 0115 9770576, Fax 9763172,
Pro 9763172, Sec 9608435
On A611 close to M1 Junction 26.

Heathland course.
Pro Lee Rawlings; Founded 1870/1902
Designed by John Dolman
18 holes, 5561 yards, S.S.S. 67
† Welcome; restrictions at WE.
[WD £11; WE £13.
↻ Welcome WD; after 11am Tues;
2pm Sat and 12 noon Sun; full day
packages available; £25.
⦿ Clubhouse catering facilities.
↩ Moat House; Gateway both
Nottingham.

6B 18 Burghley Park
St Martins Without, Stamford, PE9 3JX
▤ burley.golf@lineone.net
☎ 01780 753789, Fax 753789
On B1081 1 mile S of Stamford.
Parkland course.
Pro Glenn Davies; Founded 1890
18 holes, 6236 yards, S.S.S. 70
∤ Practice area.
† Welcome WD with handicap certs.
[WD £25 day pass.
↻ Welcome WD by prior
arrangement; full golf and catering
package including insurance; £42.
⦿ Clubhouse facilities.
↩ The George at Stamford; Garden
House; Lady Annes; Crown; Royal Oak
Duddington.

6B 19 Buxton & High Peak
Waterswallows Rd, Fairfield, Buxton,
Derbyshire, SK17 7EN
⬚ www.buxtonandhighpeakgolfclub.
co.uk
▤ sec@bhpgc.fsnet.co.uk
☎ 01298 23453, Fax 26333,
Pro 23112
On A6 Manchester-Derby Road just N
of Buxton.
Parkland course.
Pro Gary Brown; Founded 1887
Designed by J Morris
18 holes, 5966 yards, S.S.S. 69
∤ Driving range located next door.
† Welcome by prior arrangement.
[WD £23; WE £29.
↻ Welcome by prior arrangement; full
golf and catering packages available;
£35.
⦿ Full clubhouse facilities.
↩ Palace Hotel; Hawthorn Farm.

6B 20 Canwick Park   ♋
Washingborough Road, Lincoln,
Lincoln, LN4 1EF
⬚ www.canwickpark.co.uk
▤ info@canwickpark.co.uk
☎ 01522 542912, Fax 526997,
Pro 536870, Sec 542912

On B1190 Washingborough Road 2
miles W of Lincoln.
Parkland course.
Pro SJ Williamson; Founded 1893/1975
Designed by Hawtree & Partners
18 holes, 6257 yards, S.S.S. 69
† Welcome WD; after 3pm at WE.
Between 10am and 12 pm and 2-4pm
£10 per round.
[WD £16; WE £21; reduced green
fees at certain times; phone for details.
↻ Welcome by prior arrangement;
packages available for catering and
golf; from £17.
⦿ Clubhouse catering facilities.
↩ Travel Inn; Branston Hall; Grand
Lincoln.

6B 21 Carholme
Carholme Road, Lincoln, LN1 1SE
⬚ www.carholme-golf-club.co.uk
▤ info@carholme-golf-club.co.uk
☎ 01522 523725, Fax 533733,
Pro 536811, Rest/Bar 523725
On A57 Worksop Road, 1 mile from
Lincoln city centre.
Parkland course.
Pro Richard Hunter; Founded 1906
18 holes, 6215 yards, S.S.S. 70
† Welcome by prior arrangement
except Sun.
[Summer £18 per round £22 per
day. Winter £11 per round £13 per day.
↻ Welcome by prior arrangement;
catering and golf packages available;
terms on application.
⦿ Bar and restaurant (except Mon).
↩ Delph GH.

6B 22 Carsington Water
Carsington, Wirksworth, Derbyshire
☎ 01403 784864
8 miles NE of Ashbourne off B5035.
Parkland course.
9 holes, 3000 yards, S.S.S. 33
† Welcome.
[Pay and play £9.
↻ Terms on application.
⦿ Limited.

6B 23 Cavendish
Gadley Lane, Buxton, Derbyshire,
SK17 6XD
☎ 01298 23494, Fax 79708, Pro
25052, Sec 79708, Rest/Bar 23494
On outskirts of Buxton off the ring road
in direction of A53 Leek.
Moorland/parkland course.
Pro P Hunstone; Founded 1925
Designed by Dr Alister MacKenzie
18 holes, 5721 yards, S.S.S. 68
∤ Practice area.

† Everyone welcome.
[WD/WE £26-£35.
↻ Welcome by prior arrangement;
minimum 16; 27 holes £25; for catering
contact stewardess.
⦿ Full clubhouse facilities available.
↩ Leewood; Buckingham; Palace;
Portland all Buxton.

6B 24 Chatsworth
Chatsworth Park, Bakewell,
Derbyshire, DE45 1PP
☎ 01246 582204, Fax 583536
On Chatsworth Estate on B6012 onto
Chatsworth Estate.
Parkland course.
9 holes, 5248 yards, S.S.S. 66
† Private; for estate workers and
members only.
[Terms on application.
⦿ No clubhouse.

6B 25 Chesterfield
Walton, Chesterfield, Derbyshire, S42
7LA
☎ 01246 279256, Fax 276622,
Pro 276297, Sec 279256,
Rest/Bar 232035
Course is 2 miles W of town centre on
A632 to Matlock.
Parkland course.
Pro Mike McLean; Founded 1897
18 holes, 6261 yards, S.S.S. 70
† Welcome WD; with member at
WE.
[WD £26 per round, £35 per day.
WE Sun pm £30 or with member £13
anytime in week.
↻ Welcome WD by prior application;
packages available; from £36 including
meals.
⦿ Full clubhouse facilities.
↩ Chesterfield Hotel; Swallows;
Normanton, Ibis Hotel Chesterfield.

6B 26 Chevin
Golf Lane, Duffield, Derbys,
DE56 4EE
☎ 01332 841864
On A6 5 miles N of Derby outside
Duffield.
Hilly parkland course.
Pro Willie Bird; Founded 1894
Designed by W Braid
18 holes, 6057 yards, S.S.S. 69
∤ Practice area.
† Welcome WD except before
9.30am and between 12.30pm and
2pm; WE with member.
[WD £25; day ticket £30.
↻ Welcome WD by prior
arrangement with Sec.*

🍴 Full facilities, except Mon.
↪ Strutt Arms adjacent.

6B 27 Chilwell Manor
Meadow Lane, Chilwell, Nottingham,
Notts, NG9 5AE
☎ 0115 9258958, Fax 9257050,
Sec 9257050, Rest/Bar 9257050
4 miles W of Nottingham on A6005
near Beeston.
Parkland course.
Pro Paul Wilson; Founded 1906
18 holes, 6395 yards, S.S.S. 70
† Welcome after 9am WD; after
11am WE.
Ⅰ WD £18; WE £20.
☺ Welcome Mon, Wed, Fri. Full
clubhouse facilities available.
↪ Post House; Novotel; Village.

6B 28 Cleethorpes ⓣ
Kings Road, Cleethorpes, N E
Lincolnshire, DN35 0PN
☎ 01472 816110, Fax 814060,
Pro 814060, Sec 816110,
Rest/Bar 812059
2 miles SE of Cleethorpes.
Mature coastal course.
Pro Paul Davies; Founded 1894
Designed by Harry Vardon (now vastly
altered)
18 holes, 6356 yards, S.S.S. 70
Ⅰ Practice area.
† Visitors welcome Mon, Thurs, Fri
and Sun.
Ⅰ WD £20; WE £25.
☺ Welcome by prior arrangement.
🍴 Full facilities.
↪ Kingsway; Wellow.

6B 29 College Pines ⓣ
Worksop College Drive, Worksop,
Nottingham, S80 3AP
⬛ www.collegepinesgolfclub.co.uk
☎ 01909 501431, Fax 481227,
Pro 501431, Sec 501431,
Rest/Bar 488785
Half mile S of Worksop on B6034; just
off A57 Worksop by-pass.
Heathland course.
Pro Charles Snell; Founded 1994
Designed by David Snell
18 holes, 6663 yards, S.S.S. 72
Ⅰ 20 grass bays.
† Welcome by prior arrangement.
Ⅰ WD £12; WE £18.
☺ Packages available.
🍴 Bar food/Restaurant.
↪ Lion Hotel, Worksop Travel Lodge.

6B 30 Cotgrave Place ⓣ
Stragglethorpe, Nr Radcliffe On Trent,
Nottingham, NG12 3HB
☎ 0115 9333344
Off A52 5 miles SE of Nottingham.
Parkland course with lake features.
Pro R Smith; Founded 1992
Designed by P Alliss/J Small
2 x 18 holes, 6303 yards, S.S.S. 70
Ⅰ Floodlit driving range.
† Welcome.
Ⅰ WD £18: £17; WE £22: £21.
☺ Welcome by prior arrangement;
catering and golf packages available
by prior arrangement; banqueting
facilities available; prices on
application.
🍴 Full clubhouse facilities available.
↪ Hilton; Moat House; Langar Hall.

6B 31 Coxmoor
Coxmoor Rd, Sutton-In-Ashfield, Notts,
NG17 5LF
⬛ www.coxmoor.freeuk.com
⬛ coxmoor@freeuk.com
☎ 01623 557359, Fax 557359,
Pro 559906
Course is on the A611 1.5 miles S of
Mansfield.
Heathland course.
Pro D Ridley; Founded 1913
18 holes, 6589 yards, S.S.S. 72
Ⅰ Practice area.
† Welcome WD; with member at
WE.
Ⅰ WD £37-£48.
☺ Welcome WD except Tues, by
prior arrangement; golf and catering
available.
🍴 Clubhouse, catering and bar
facilities.
↪ Pine Lodge, Mansfield.

6B 32 Derby
Wilmore Road, Sinfin, Derby, DE24
9HD
☎ 01332 766323, Fax 769004,
Pro 766462
2 miles from city centre off Wilmore
Road.
Parkland course.
Pro John Siddons; Founded 1923
18 holes, 6163 yards, S.S.S. 69
Ⅰ Practice green.
† Welcome by prior arrangement.
Ⅰ Terms on application.
☺ Welcome by prior arrangement;
packages available; terms on
application.
🍴 Full clubhouse facilities available.
↪ International, Derby.

6B 33 Edwalton Municipal
Edwalton Village, Nottingham, Notts,
NG12 4AS
☎ 0115 9234775
Off A606 from Nottingham at Edwalton
Hall, on Welling Lane.
Municipal parkland course; also 9-hole
par 3.
Pro J Staples; Founded 1981
Designed by Frank Pennink
9 holes, 3336 yards, S.S.S. 36
† Welcome.
Ⅰ WD £6.50; WE (am) £7.20. Loyalty
card holders WD £5.50; WE (am)
£6.20. Pensioners £3.90.
Unemployed/Students £4.00.
☺ Welcome WD.
🍴 Lunches and meals available.
↪ Many in local area.

6B 34 Elsham ⓣ
Barton Rd, Elsham, Brigg, Lincs, DN20
0LS
☎ 01652 680291, Pro 680432
3 miles N of Brigg on B1206 Road.
Parkland course.
Pro Stewart Brewer; Founded 1901
18 holes, 6406 yards, S.S.S. 71
† Welcome WD; with member at
WE.
Ⅰ WD £24; WE £18.
☺ Welcome WD; full packages of golf
and catering available; from £40.
🍴 Full clubhouse catering facilities
available.
↪ Arties Mill Castlethorpe; Red lion
Hotel Redbourne; Jolly Miller Wrawby.

6B 35 Erewash Valley
Golf Club Road, Stanton-By-Dale,
Ilkeston, Derbys, DE7 4QR
⬛ www.evgc.com
⬛ secretary@evgc.com
☎ 0115 9323258, Fax 9322984,
Pro 9324667, Sec 9323258,
Rest/Bar 9323258
Course is 3 miles from the M1 Junction
25.
Parkland course.
Pro Mike Ronan; Founded 1905
Designed by Hawtree
18 holes, 6557 yards, S.S.S. 71
† Welcome WD and pm at WE.
Practice ground & 9-hole par 3 course.
Ⅰ WD £24.50; WE £29.50.
☺ Welcome Mon, Wed, Fri by prior
arrangement; catering packages
available; from £24.50.
🍴 Restaurant and bar facilities.
↪ Post House; Novotel.

6B 36 Forest Pines
Ermine Street, Nr Brigg, Lincs, DN20
0AQ
🖳 www.forestpines.co.uk
📧 enquires@forestpines.co.uk
☎ 01652 650756, Fax 650495,
Pro 650756, Sec 650756,
Rest/Bar 650756
Take M180 Junction 4 and then A15
towards Scunthorpe; club at first
roundabout.
Forest course.
Pro David Edwards; Founded 1996
Designed by J Morgan
27 holes; Forest 3291 yards; Pines
3591 yards; Beeches 3102 yards.
🏌 15 Bay grass driving range &
practice ground. chipping area &
putting green.
♦ Welcome by prior arrangement.
🎫 Both WD and WE £30; £40 for day.
♨ Welcome by prior arrangement;
coffee, bacon roll, 18 holes of golf &
dinner, accommodation packages; golf
schools;corporate packages from
season £45.
🍽 Restaurant & bar snacks available
on site.
↵ Forest Pines Golf Course Hotel &
Spa 86-bed hotel on site.

6B 37 Gainsborough
The Belt Road, Thonock,
Gainsborough, Lincs, DN21 1PZ
☎ 01427 613088, Fax 810172
Signposted off A631 Gainsborough-
Grimsby Rd.
US Style course with lakes and many
bunkers.
Pro Stephen Cooper; Founded 1997
(Karsten Lakes) 1894/1985 (Thonock
Park)
Designed by N Coles (Karsten Lakes)
B Waites (Thonock Park)
Karsten Lakes 18; Thonock Park 18
holes, Karsten Lakes 6900; Thonock
Park 6266 yards, S.S.S. Karsten Lakes
70; Thonock Park 70
🏌 20 floodlit bays.
♦ Welcome at WE with member
(Thonock Park).
🎫 Karsten Lakes £25 – £30; Thonock
Park £18 – £25.
♨ Welcome (WD for Thonock Park);
packages for golf and catering can be
arranged; snooker tables; menus
available for societies in restaurant;
prices on application.
🍽 Full catering and bar service
including coffee shop and restaurant.
↵ Hickman Hill Gainsborough.

6B 38 Gedney Hill
West Drove, Gedney Hill, Nr Spalding,
Lincs, PE12 0NT
☎ 01406 330922, Fax 330323,
Pro 330922
On B1166 6 miles from Crowland.
Links style course.
Pro David Hutton; Founded 1989
Designed by C Britton
18 holes, 5285 yards, S.S.S. 66
🏌 10 Driving bays and a practice
green.
♦ Welcome.
🎫 WD £6.50; WE £11.
♨ Welcome by prior arrangement;
catering available; snooker; terms on
application.
🍽 Clubhouse catering.

6B 39 Glossop & District
Hurst Lane, off Sheffield Rd, Glossop,
Derbys, SK13 9PU
☎ 01457 865247, Pro 853117
Off A57 1.5 miles outside Glossop; turn
at Royal Oak pub.
Moorland course.
Pro Daniel Marsh; Founded 1894
11 holes, 5800 yards, S.S.S. 68
🏌 Practice area.
♦ Welcome; restrictions on Sat.
🎫 Terms on application.
♨ Welcome by prior arrangement;
terms on application.
🍽 Clubhouse facilities.
↵ Wind in the Willows, Glossop.

6B 40 Grange Park
Butterwick Rd, Messingham,
Scunthorpe, N Lincs, DN17 3PP
📧 info@grangepark.uk.com
☎ 01724 762945, Pro 762945
5 miles S of Scunthorpe between
Messingham and E Butterwick; 4 miles
S of M180 Junction 3.
Parkland course.
Pro Mark Thornly; Founded 1991
Designed by Ray Price
13 holes, 4141 yards, S.S.S. 49
🏌 Practice range floodlit; also par 3
9-hole course (£3). 20 bays.
♦ Welcome.
🎫 WD £6.50; WE £8.50.
♨ Welcome by prior arrangement;
from £6.50.
🍽 By prior arrangement.

6B 41 Grassmoor Golf Centre
North Wingfield Rd, Grassmoor,
Chesterfield, Derbys, S42 5EA
☎ 01246 856044, Pro 856044,
Sec 856044, Rest/Bar 856044
2 miles S of Chesterfield close to M1

Junction 29.
Moorland course.
Pro Gary Hagues; Founded 1992
Designed by Michael Shattock
18 holes, 5723 yards, S.S.S. 69
🏌 Practice range 25 bays floodlit.
♦ Welcome WE; by prior
arrangement.
🎫 WD £10; WE £12.
♨ Welcome.
🍽 Full facilities.
↵ Chesterfield

6B 42 Grimsby
Littlecoates Rd, Grimsby, Ne Lincs,
N34 4LU
☎ 01472 342823, Fax 342630,
Pro 356981
1 mile W of Grimsby town centre; turn
left off A18 at first roundabout; course
is 0.75 miles on left.
Pro Richard Smith; Founded 1922
18 holes, 6057 yards, S.S.S. 70
🏌 Practice ground.
♦ Welcome if member of a golf club;
Ladies Day Tues.
🎫 WD £22-£28; WE £28.
♨ Welcome Mon and Fri by prior
arrangement.
🍽 Full facilities.
↵ Post House.

6B 43 Holme Hall
Holme Lane, Bottesford, Scunthorpe,
DN16 3RF
☎ 01724 851816, Fax 278150,
Pro 851816, Sec 862078,
Rest/Bar 282053
Close to M180 Junction 4 for
Scunthorpe East.
Heathland course.
Pro R McKiernan; Founded 1908
18 holes, 6404 yards, S.S.S. 71
♦ Welcome WD; only with member
at WE.
🎫 WD £20 per round £25 per day.
Members and guests only at WE.
♨ Welcome WD by arrangement; on
application; from £20.
🍽 Clubhouse facilities.
↵ Club can provide list.

6B 44 Horncastle
West Ashby, Horncastle, Lincolnshire,
LN9 5PP
☎ 01507 526800, Pro 526800,
Sec 526800, Rest/Bar 526800
Off A158 W of Horncastle.
Parkland course with water hazards.
Pro EC Wright; Founded 1990
Designed by Ernie Wright
18 holes, 5717 yards, S.S.S. 70

- **6438 yards, SSS 71**
- **Venue for Lincolnshire Amateur Championship and Lincolnshire County Championships**
- **Putting green**
- **Large practice area**
- **3-hole pitch and putt**
- **Golf shop**

Lincoln Golf Club

TORKSEY · LINCOLN · LN1 2EG

Founded in 1891, Lincoln is a mature, testing, championship standard course built on sandy subsoil offering a variety of holes from links-style to parkland with mature trees and some water features. We offer golfing packages in summer and winter, including a wide range of excellent snacks and meals.

Manager: Derek B Linton Tel/fax: 01427 718721.
Pro: Ashley Carter Tel/fax: 01427 718273. E-mail: info@lincolngc.co.uk
Web page: www.lincolngc.co.uk

Practice range, 24 bays floodlit.
Everyone welcome.
WD £18 per round, £25 per day. WE/Bank holidays £20 per round, £27 per day.
Welcome; packages for golf and catering available; from £10.
Clubhouse facilities.
Admiral Rodney.

6B 45 Horsley Lodge
Smalley Mill Road, Horsley, Derbys, DE21 5BL
www.horsleylodge.co.uk
enquiries@horsleylodge.co.uk
01332 780838, Fax 781118, Pro 781400
Course is off the A38 four miles N of Derby.
Meadowland course.
Pro Graham Myall; Founded 1990
Designed by Peter McEvoy
18 holes, 6400 yards, S.S.S. 71
Driving range.
Welcome WD, after 2pm WE.
WD £35; WE £35; half-price for members; guests; hotel guests and holders of Derbyshire union card £15.
Welcome Tues; Thurs or Fri by prior arrangement; packages available; conference facilities; from £22.
Clubhouse and à la carte restaurant available; bars in 1840 clubhouse.
Horsley Lodge on site.

6B 46 Humberston Park
Humberston Ave, Humberston, NE Lincs, DN36 4SJ
chriscrookes@lineone.net
01472 210404
Off Humberstone Ave behind the Cherry Garth Scouts Field.
Parkland course; leased by consortium of 8 members.
Founded 1970
9 holes, 3672 yards, S.S.S. 58

Putting green.
Welcome.
WD 18 holes £9, 9 holes £7; WE 18 holes £11, 9 holes £8; discounts for guests.
Welcome by arrangement.
Bar facilities and snacks.

6B 47 Ilkeston Borough (Pewit)
West End Drive, Ilkeston, Derbyshire, DE7 5GH
0115 9307704, Sec 9327021, Rest/Bar 9304550
0.5 miles E of Ilkeston.
Municipal meadowland course.
Founded 1920
9 holes, 4072 yards, S.S.S. 60
Everyone welcome.
18 holes WD £6.95; WE £6.95; 9 holes WD £4.00; WE £4.00.
Concession rates Mon-Frid. £3.20 for 18 holes. Junior rate £2.35 all week for 18 holes.
Welcome weekends only by prior arrangement.
The Post House Motel,Sandiacre, near M1 motorway.

6B 48 Immingham
Church Lane, Immingham, Grimsby, NE Lincolnshire, DN40 2EU
www.immgc.com
admin@immgc.com
01469 575298, Fax 577636, Pro 575493, Sec 575298, Rest/Bar 575298
2 miles off M180 behind St Andrew's Church.
Flat parkland course.
Pro Nick Harding; Founded 1975
Designed by Hawtree & Son (front 9); F Pennink (back 9)
18 holes, 6215 yards, S.S.S. 70
Practice area.
Everyone welcome.
WD £12; WE £18. Societies welcome.

6B 49 Kedleston Park
Kedleston, Quarndon, Derby, DE22 5JD
www.kedlestonparkgolf.com
secretary@ keddlestonpark.sagehost.co.uk
01332 840035, Fax 840035, Pro 841685, Sec 840335, Rest/Bar 840634
4 miles N of Derby; from A38 follow signs to Kedleston Hall.
Parkland course.
Pro Paul Wesselingh; Founded 1947
Designed by James Braid and Morrison & Co
18 holes, 6675 yards, S.S.S. 72
Welcome by arrangement.
WD £35; WE £35.
Welcome Mon and Fri; catering packages can be arranged; from £40.
Full catering facilities.
Kedleston House; Midland Hotel; Mundy Arms.

6B 50 Kenwick Park
Kenwick, Nr Louth, Lincs, LN11 8NY
www.louthnet.com
golfatkenwick@nascr.net
01507 605134, Fax 606556, Pro 607161, Sec 605134, Rest/Bar 608210
1 mile S of Louth.
Rolling parkland course.
Pro Eric Sharp; Founded 1992
Designed by Patrick Tallack
18 holes, 6782 yards, S.S.S. 73
8 bays; members and guests only.
Welcome by prior arrangement.
WD £27; WE £35.
Welcome by prior arrangement;

Welcome; packages available; special winter packages from £12.00: coffee; round of golf & meal: book in advance/ring for details; company days welcome; new clubhouse.
Full clubhouse facilities.
Stallingborough Grange

catering and golf packages can be arranged; terms on application.
🍽 Clubhouse facilities.
🛏 Kenwick Park Hotel on site.

6B 51 Kilton Forest
Blyth Rd, Worksop, Notts, S81 0TL
☎ 01909 486563, Fax 486563,
Sec 479199, Rest/Bar 479199
Course is one mile from Worksop on the Blyth Road.
Parkland course.
Pro Stuart Betteridge; Founded 1977
18 holes, 6424 yards, S.S.S. 71
🏌 Chipping and putting area.
† Welcome; bookings required at WE.
🍴 WD £9; WE £12.
🕗 Welcome by prior arrangement; catering packages available; terms on application.
🍽 Restaurant and bar facilities.
🛏 Regency; Lion both Worksop.

6B 52 Kingsway
Kingsway, Scunthorpe, N Lincs, DN15 7ER
☎ 01724 840945
Between Berkeley and Queensway roundabouts S of A18.
Undulating parkland course.
Pro Chris Mann; Founded 1971
Designed by RD Highfield
9 holes, 1915 yards, S.S.S. 59
† Welcome.
🍴 WD £3.70; WE £4.35
🕗 None.

6B 53 Kirton Holme
Holme Rd, Kirton Holme Nr Boston, Lincs, PE20 1SY
☎ 01205 290669
Off A52 4 miles W of Boston.
Parkland course.
Founded 1992
Designed by DW Welberry
9 holes, 5778 yards, S.S.S. 68
† Pay and play.
🍴 WD £5; WE £6.
🕗 Welcome by prior arrangement; maximum 30; meals available; terms on application.
🍽 Full clubhouse facilities.
🛏 Poacher Inn.

6B 54 Leen Valley ☕
Wigwam Lane, Hucknall, Notts, NG15 7TA
☎ 0115 9642037, Fax 9642724
On B6011 off A611 from Hucknall.
Parkland course; was Hucknall GC.
Pro John Lines; Founded 1994

Designed by Tom Hodgetts
18 holes, 6233 yards, S.S.S. 72
🏌 Practice putting green; 9-hole par 3 course also available.
† Welcome.
🍴 WD £9.50; WE £13.50.
🕗 Welcome; packages can be arranged; terms on application.
🍽 Full clubhouse facilities.
🛏 Premier Lodge Hucknall.

6B 55 Lincoln Golf Club
Torksey, Lincoln, LN1 2EG
🖥 www.lincolngc.co.uk
📧 lincolngolfclub@btinternet.com
☎ 01427 718721, Fax 718721,
Pro 718273, Rest/Bar 718210
Course is on the A156, 7 miles S of Gainsborough, 10 miles W of Lincoln.
Inland links course.
Pro A Carter; Founded 1891
18 holes, 6438 yards, S.S.S. 71
🏌 Large practice area.
† Welcome.
🍴 WD £26; WE £26.
🕗 Welcome WD by prior arrangement; catering packages available.
🍽 Full clubhouse facilities.
🛏 Hume Arms.

6B 56 The Lincolnshire
Near Crowle, Scunthorpe, DN17 4BU
☎ 01724 711619, Fax 711619,
Sec 711619, Rest/Bar 711621
Off A1161 Crowle to Goole Road from M180 Junction 2.
Parkland course.
Founded 1994
18 holes, 6400 yards, S.S.S. 71
† Everyone welcome.
🍴 Summer WD £10.00, WE £14.00; Winter WD £10.00, WE £14.00.
🕗 Welcome at all times.
🍽 Full facilities available.
🛏 Red Lion Epworth.

6B 57 Lindrick
Lindrick Common, Worksop, Notts, S81 8BH
🖥 www.lindrickgolf.com
☎ 01909 485802, Fax 488685,
Pro 475820, Sec 475282
On A57 4 miles NW of Worksop.
Heathland course; 1957 Ryder Cup; 1960 Curtis Cup.
Pro John R King; Founded 1891
Designed by Tom Dunn; Willie Parks and H Fowler
18 holes, 6606 yards, S.S.S. 72
🏌 Practice range; 2 practice areas.
† Welcome WD except Tues.

🍴 WD £48; WE £48.
🕗 Welcome by prior arrangement; packages available; from £48.
🍽 Full clubhouse facilities.
🛏 Red Lion; Todwick.

6B 58 Louth Golf Club
Crowtree Lane, Louth, Lincs, LN11 9LJ
📧 louthgolfclub1992@btinternet.com
☎ 01507 602554, Fax 608501,
Pro 604648, Sec 603681,
Rest/Bar 611087
W of Louth, close to Hubbards Hills.
Undulating parkland course.
Pro A J Blundell; Founded 1965
Designed by CK Cotton
18 holes, 6430 yards, S.S.S. 71
🏌 Practice ground.
† Welcome by arrangement.
🍴 WD £20; WE £30.
🕗 Welcome by prior arrangement; discounts for groups of more than 25; catering packages available.
🍽 All day catering and bar facilities.
🛏 Masons Arms; Beaumont; Priory; Kings Head; Brackenborough Arms Hotel.

6B 59 Luffenham Heath
Ketton, Stamford, Lincs, PE9 3UU
☎ 01780 720205, Fax 720298,
Pro 720298, Sec 720205
On A6121 5 miles W of Stamford.
Heathland course.
Pro Ian Burnett; Founded 1911
Designed by James Braid
18 holes, 6315 yards, S.S.S. 70
† Welcome by arrangement.
🍴 WD £35; WE £40.
🕗 Welcome by prior arrangement with Sec; packages and catering available on application; terms on application.
🍽 Full clubhouse facilities.
🛏 The George at Stamford; Monkton Arms, Glaston.

6B 60 The Manor Golf ☕
Laceby Manor, Laceby, Grimsby, Lincolnshire, DN37 7EA
☎ 01472 873468, Fax 276706,
Sec 873469, Rest/Bar 873470
On A16 0.5 miles past Oaklands Hotel.
Parkland course.
Founded 1992
Designed by Sir Charles Nicholson and Rushton
18 holes, 6343 yards, S.S.S. 70
🏌 Practice area.
† Welcome by arrangement.
🍴 WD £18 WE £20.
🕗 Welcome by prior arrangement; terms on application.

🍴 Full clubhouse facilities.
🚩 Oaklands.

6B 61 Mansfield Woodhouse
Leeming Lane North, Mansfield
Woodhouse, Notts, NG19 9EU
☎ 01623 623521
On A60 Mansfield-Worksop road, 2
miles N of Mansfield.
Public parkland course.
Pro L Highfield; Founded 1973
Designed by F Horseman and
A Highfield
9 holes, 4892 yards, S.S.S. 65
† Welcome except before 11am Sat.
⌐ £3.80 9 holes, £5.80 18.
🕊 None.
🍴 Clubhouse bar facilities.

6B 62 Mapperley
Central Ave, Plains Rd, Mapperley,
Nottingham, NG3 5RH
☎ 0115 9556672, Fax 9556670,
Pro 9556673, Sec 9556672,
Rest/Bar 9556672
Off B684 3 miles NE of Nottingham.
Undulating parkland course.
Pro Jason Barker; Founded 1903
18 holes, 6307 yards, S.S.S. 70
† Welcome by prior arrangement.
⌐ WD £17; WE £22.
🕊 Welcome by arrangement with
secretary; packages available; terms
on application.
🍴 Full clubhouse facilities.
🚩 Many in Nottingham.

6B 63 Market Rasen & District
Legsby Road, Market Rasen,
Lincolnshire, LN8 3DZ
☎ 01673 842319, Pro 842416,
Sec 842319, Rest/Bar 842319
On A361 1 mile E of Market Rasen.
Heathland course.
Pro AM Chester; Founded 1922
Designed by Hawtree Ltd
18 holes, 6209 yards, S.S.S. 70
† Welcome with handicap certs; with
member at WE.
⌐ WD £20 per round. £29 per day.
🕊 Welcome Tues and Fri; packages
for catering available; from £11.
🍴 Full clubhouse facilities.
🚩 Limes Hotel.

6B 64 Market Rasen Race Course
Legsby, Market Rasen, Lincs, LN8 3EA
☎ 01673 843434
At Market Rasen racecourse; follow
signs to golf course from entrance.

Founded 1989
Designed by Racecourse/Peter Alliss
9 holes, 2377 yards, S.S.S. 45
† Welcome.
⌐ Terms on application.
🕊 Welcome with advance booking.

6B 65 Marriott Breadsall ♛
Moor Rd, Morley, Derbys, DE7 6DL
🖳 www.marriothotel.com/emags
📧 golf.breadsallpriory@
marriothotel.co.uk
☎ 01332 832235, Fax 833509
3 miles NE of Derby off A61 towards
Breadsall.
Parkland and Moorland course.
Pro Darren Steeles; Founded 1977
18 holes, 6028 yards, S.S.S. 68
† Welcome by prior arrangement.
⌐ Terms on application.
🕊 Welcome by prior arrangement;
packages available; tennis swimming
pool; gym and leisure facilities; terms
on application.
🍴 Full hotel and clubhouse facilities;
5 bars and 2 restaurants.
🚩 On site, Marriott Breadsall Priory.

6B 66 Martin Moor
Martin Moore Course, Martin Lane,
Blankney, Lincs, LN4 3BE
☎ 01526 378243
On B1189 2 miles E of Metheringham.
Parkland course.
Pro A Hare; Founded 1992
Designed by S Harrison
9 holes, 6325 yards, S.S.S. 70
⎂ Practice ground.
† Welcome.
⌐ WD £6 for 9 £8 for 18; WE £7 for 9
£9.50 for 18.
🕊 Welcome by prior arrangement;
packages available; terms on
application.
🍴 Bar snacks.
🚩 Eagle Lodge; Golf Hotel; Petwood
Hotel all Woodhall Spa.

6B 67 Matlock
Chesterfield Rd, Matlock, Derbys, DE4
5LZ
☎ 01629 582191, Fax 582135,
Pro 584934
On Chesterfield Road 1, mile from
Matlock.
Moorland course.
Pro Mark Whithorn; Founded 1907
Designed by Tom Williamson
18 holes, 5996 yards, S.S.S. 69
† Welcome WD by prior
arrangement.
⌐ WD £25; WE by prior

arrangement.
🕊 Welcome by prior arrangement;
parties of more than 12; catering
available; £25.
🍴 Clubhouse facilities.
🚩 Red House, Darley Dale.

6B 68 Maywood
Rushy Lane, Risley, Draycott,
Derbyshire, DE72 3SW
☎ 0115 9392306, Pro 9490043,
Rest/Bar 9392306
Course is off the A52 to Risley from the
M1 Junction 25 at the Post House
Hotel.
Wooded course with water features.
Pro Simon Sherrat; Founded 1990
Designed by Peter Moon
18 holes, 6424 yards, S.S.S. 72
† Everyone welcome.
⌐ WD £15; WE £20.
🕊 Welcome by prior arrangement; full
day's golf and coffee light lunch and 4-
course evening meal; from £30.
🍴 Full bar and catering facilities
available.
🚩 Post House; Novotel; Risley Park.

6B 69 Mickleover ♛
Uttoxeter Rd, Mickleover, Derbyshire,
DE3 5AD
☎ 01332 513339, Fax 512092,
Pro 518662, Sec 512092,
Rest/Bar 513339
Course is on the A516/B5020 three
miles W of Derby.
Undulating parkland course.
Tim Coxon; Founded 1923
18 holes, 5708 yards, S.S.S. 68
† Welcome.
⌐ WD £22; WE £30.
🕊 Welcome Tues and Thurs;
packages can be arranged; from £22.
🍴 Clubhouse facilities.
🚩 Mickleover Court; International
Derby.

6B 70 Millfield
Laughterton, Torksey, Nr Lincoln,
Lincs, LN1 2LB
☎ 01427 718473, Fax 718473
On A113 between A57 and A158 8
miles from Lincoln; 10 miles from
Gainsborough.
Inland links course.
Pro Richard Hunter; Founded 1984
18 holes, 6001 yards, S.S.S. 71
† Welcome.
⌐ WD £7; WE £7.
🕊 Welcome WD by prior
arrangement; tennis, bowls; second
18-hole course (4500 yards par 65)

NEWARK GOLF CLUB
Founded 1901

On the Notts/Lincs border only 3 miles from the A1, Newark Golf Club is set within its own peaceful grounds away from main roads.

A tree-lined, parkland course with easy walking over 6458 yards with a large practice area and putting green. The large clubhouse with restaurant serves wholesome food, in pleasant surroundings, with good wines and beers. There is a spike bar plus a snooker table. The well-stocked pro's shop provides golfers with all their requirements. The halfway house is adjacent to the clubhouse with toilets and small kitchen. Societies and groups are very welcome during the week. The Secretary can be contacted on **01636 626282** for any further details.

---

and a 9-hole course (1500 yards par 3); terms on application.
🍽 Light refreshments; bar meals available.
⌂ Holiday chalets and log cabins on site.

6B 71 New Mills Golf Club
High Peak, Derbyshire, SK22 4QE
🖳 www.newmillsgolfclub.co.uk
✉ carltcross@aol.com
☎ 01663 743408
1 mile off A6, through New Mills Town
Flat, moorland.
18 holes from end Apr 2002 yards
† Yes, by prior arrangement.
£20 approx.
⌖ Yes.
🍽 Bar/Restaurant.
⌂ In New Mills Town Centre.

6B 72 Newark
Kelwick, Coddington, Newark, Notts, NG24 2QX
☎ 01636 626282, Fax 626497,
Pro 626492, Sec 626282
On A17 between Newark and Sleaford just past Coddington roundabout.
Parkland course.
Pro Peter Lockley; Founded 1901
18 holes, 6457 yards, S.S.S. 71
⌖ Practice ground.
† Welcome with handicap certs; Ladies Day Tues.
⌖ WD £22; WE £27.
⌖ Welcome WD by prior arrangement; catering packages; snooker; indoor coaching facilities; terms on application.
🍽 Bar and meals.
⌂ George Inn Leadenham; Travelodge.

6B 73 Normanby Hall
Normanby Park, Normanby, Scunthorpe, N Lincs, DN15 9HU

☎ 01724 720226, Fax 853183,
Pro 720226, Sec 720226,
Rest/Bar 720252
5 miles N of Scunthorpe adjacent to Normanby Hall.
Municipal parkland course.
Pro Chris Mann; Founded 1978
Designed by HF Jiggens; Hawtree and Sons
18 holes, 6548 yards, S.S.S. 71
⌖ Practice range; practice area.
† Welcome; telephone for bookings.
⌖ WD £8.00; WE £10.00.
⌖ Welcome by prior arrangement with the local council.
🍽 Full facilities including banqueting at Normanby Hall.
⌂ Royal; Wortley House.

6B 74 North Shore   ☎
North Shore Rd, Skegness, Lincs, PE25 1DN
🖳 www.north-shore.co.uk
✉ golf@north-shore.co.uk
☎ 01754 763298, Fax 761902,
Pro 764822
Just off A52 Inglemels. 1 mile N of Skegness town centre on the outskirts.
Parkland/links course.
Pro John Cornelius; Founded 1910
Designed by James Braid
18 holes, 6257 yards, S.S.S. 71
† Welcome.
⌖ WD £22; WE £31.
⌖ Welcome by prior arrangement; packages and hotel rates available; from £29.
🍽 Full clubhouse catering and bar facilities.
⌂ On site North Shore.

6B 75 Norwood Park   ☎
Norwood Park, Southwell, Nottinghamshire, NG25 0PF
🖳 www.norwoodpark.org.uk
✉ norwoodgolf@mail.com
☎ 01636 816626, Fax 815702,

Pro 816626, Sec 813226,
Rest/Bar 816626
Half a mile W of Southwell on the road to Kirklington.
Parkland course set in the grounds of a stately home.
Pro Paul Thornton; Founded 1999
Designed by Clyde B Johnston
9 holes, 6666 yards, S.S.S. 71
⌖ 8.
† Welcome at any time.
⌖ 9 holes: WD £7.50 WE £10; 18 holes: WD £14 WE £17.50.
⌖ Welcome by prior arrangement.
🍽 Snacks available.
⌂ The Saracen's Head.

6B 76 Nottingham City
Lawton Drive, Bulwell, Nottingham, NG6 8BL
☎ 0115 9276916, Fax 9276916,
Pro 9272767, Sec 9276916,
Rest/Bar 9278021
2 miles from M1 Junction 26, follow signs to Bulwell.
Municipal parkland course; private club.
Pro Cyril Jepson; Founded 1910
Designed by H Braid
18 holes, 6218 yards, S.S.S. 70
† Welcome.
⌖ WD £11; WE £13.
⌖ Welcome by prior arrangement; 18 and 36-hole packages with catering available; terms on application.
🍽 Clubhouse facilities.
⌂ The Gateway; Station Hotel.

6B 77 Notts
Hollinwell, Derby Rd, Kirkby-In-Ashfield, Notts, NG17 7QR
✉ nottsgolfclub@hollinwell.fsnet.co.uk
☎ 01623 753225, Fax 753655,
Pro 753087
Course is three miles from the M1 Junction 27 off the A611.

Heathland course with gorse/heather; lake at Hollinwell.
Pro Alasdair Thomas; Founded 1901
Designed by Willie Park Jnr
18 holes, 7098 yards, S.S.S. 75
🏌 Covered driving range.
♦ Welcome by prior arrangement; guests of members only at WE and BH.
🍴 WD £50-£75.
♻ Welcome WD except Fri morning by prior arrangement.
🍽 Clubhouse facilities.
🛌 Pine Lodge Mansfield; Swallow S Normanton; The Holly Lodge, Ravenshead.

6B 78 Oakmere Park ♛

Oaks Lane, Oxton, Notts, NG25 0RH
🖳 www.ukgolf.net/oakmerepark
📧 oakmere@ukgolf.net
☎ 0115 9653545, Fax 9655628,
Pro 9653545, Sec 9653545,
Rest/Bar 9653545
Course lies between Blidworth and Oxton.
Parkland course; also Commanders course: 9 holes, 6573 yards, par 72.
Pro Daryl St John Jones; Founded 1977
Designed by Frank Pennink
27 holes, 6612 yards, S.S.S. 72
🏌 25.
♦ Welcome.
🍴 WD £18; WE £24.
♻ Welcome; restrictions at WE; packages available; terms on application.
🍽 Full clubhouse facilities.
🛌 Moat House, Nottingham.

6B 79 Ormonde Fields ♛

Nottingham Rd, Codnor, Ripley, Derbys, DE5 9RG
☎ 01773 742987
On A610 towards Ripley, 2 miles from M1 Junction 26.
Undulating course.
Pro Peter Buttifant; Founded 1906
18 holes, 6011 yards, S.S.S. 69
♦ Welcome WD; by prior arrangement WE.
🍴 WD £17.50; WE £22.50.
♻ Welcome by arrangement.
🍽 Full facilities.

6B 80 Pastures ♛

Merlin Way, Mickleover, Derby, Derbys, DE3 5UJ
☎ 01332 521074, Sec 516700, Rest/Bar 521074
Course is on the A516 four miles W of Derby.

Undulating meadowland course.
Founded 1969
Designed by Frank Pennink
9 holes, 5004 yards, S.S.S. 65
♦ Welcome with handicap certs.
🍴 Prices on application.
♻ Welcome by prior arrangement; packages include lunch and evening meal; from £22.
🍽 Limited catering.

6B 81 Pottergate

Moor Lane, Branston, Near Lincoln, Lincolnshire, LN4 1JA
☎ 01522 794867, Pro 794867, Sec 794867, Rest/Bar 794867
On B1188 in Branston.
Parkland course.
Pro Lee Tasker; Founded 1993
Designed by W Bailey
9 holes, 5164 yards, S.S.S. 65
♦ Everyone welcome.
🍴 Prices on application.
♻ Everyone welcome.
🍽 Bar and snacks available.
🛌 Moor Lodge, Branston.

6B 82 Radcliffe-on-Trent

Dewberry Lane, Cropwell Rd, Radcliffe-on-Trent, Notts, NG12 2JH
📧 les.rotgc@talk21.com
☎ 0115 9333000, Fax 9116991, Pro 9332396
From A52 follow signs to Cropwell Butler.
Wooded parkland course.
Pro to be arranged; Founded 1909
Designed by Tom Wilkinson
18 holes, 6381 yards, S.S.S. 71
🏌 2 large practice grounds.
♦ Welcome by arrangement.
🍴 WD £23; WE £28.
♻ Welcome Wed only; packages available; from £23.
🍽 Full clubhouse catering and bar facilities.
🛌 Westminster Hotel.

6B 83 RAF Waddington

Waddington, Lincoln, Lincs, LN5 9NB
☎ 01522 720271, Sec 957716854
Off A15 at Bracebridge Heath 3 miles S of Lincoln. On RAF airfield.
Founded 1972
9 holes, 5558 yards, S.S.S. 69
♦ Must be accompanied by RAF Waddington member.
🍴 Prices on application.
♻ By arrangement with captain or secretary; terms available on application.
🍽 Terms on application.

🛌 Moor Lodge; Mill Lodge.

6B 84 Ramsdale Park Golf Centre

Oxton Road, Calverton, Nottinghamshire, NG14 6NU
🖳 www.burhillgolf.net
📧 ramsdale@burhillgolf.net
☎ 0115 9655600, Fax 9654105, Pro 9655600, Sec 9655600, Rest/Bar 9655600
Club is off the A614 betwwen Mansfield and Nottingham.
Undulating course.
Pro Robert Macey; Founded 1992
Designed by Hawtree & Son
18 holes, 6546 yards, S.S.S. 71
🏌 30.
♦ Pay and play.
🍴 WD £15; WE £18.50.
♻ Welcome by prior arrangement; packages and catering available; also par 3 course; prices on application.
🍽 Clubhouse facilities.
🛌 Many in local area.

6B 85 Retford

Ordsall, Retford, Notts, DN22 7UA
☎ 01777 703733, Fax 710412, Pro 703733, Sec 711188, Rest/Bar 703733
Off A620 midway between Worksop and Gainsborough.
Parkland course.
Pro C Morris; Founded 1920
18 holes, 6409 yards, S.S.S. 72
🏌 Practice ground.
♦ Welcome by prior arrangement WD, visitors after 12.30 at WE; BH by prior arrangement.
🍴 Winter WD and WE £15; £10 with a member; Summer WD £20 per round; £28 for the day; with a member £12.
♻ Welcome WD by prior arrangement; golf and catering packages available; prices on application.
🍽 New clubhouse facilities.
🛌 West Retford; The Mill House both Retford; Ye Olde Bell, Barnby Moor.

6B 86 Riverside

Trentside, Lenton Lane, Notts, NG7 2SA
☎ 0115 9862220
2 miles from city centre off A52 Ruddington road.
Parkland course.
3 x Pro, call for info
9 holes, 2001 yards, S.S.S. 31
🏌 Practice area.

THE SHERWOOD FOREST GOLF CLUB LTD

EAKRING ROAD, MANSFIELD, NOTTS NG18 3EW

Secretary:	Mrs. P. Davies	Tel: 01623 626689
Professional/Golf Mgr.	Mr. K. Hall	Tel: 01623 627403
Head Chef	Mr. W. Britten	Tel: 01623 623327
		Fax: 01623 420412

Full catering service available with dining for up to 100 persons at one sitting. Course is heathland, set in the very heart of Robin Hood country, and was designed by James Braid. Yellow markers distance is 6294 yds. S.S.S. 71. White markers distance is 6714 yds. S.S.S. 73. Championship Tees 6849 yds. S.S.S. 74.

The course was the venue for the **Midland region Qualifying Round for the Open Championship 1990 - 1995; British Open Amateur Seniors Championship 1997**, and the **English Open Amateur Seniors Championship 2001**.

Green fees on application to the Golf Manager.
Within a few miles of places of interest - such as the Major Oak (Robin Hood's larder). Newstead Abbey, Thoresby Hall, Clumber Oark, and 14 miles from the centre of Nottingham.

---

† Welcome.
Ⅼ WD £6.80; WE £7.50.
⟂ Packages available.
⏣ Full bar and restaurant facilities.

6B 87 Ruddington Grange ☎
Wilford Road, Ruddinton, Nottingham, Notts, NG11 6NB
⛆ www.ruddingtongrange.com
✉ info@ruddingtongrange.com
☎ 0115 9846141, Fax 9405165, Pro 9211951, Sec 9214139, Rest/Bar 9846141
Off A52 Grantham Road S of Nottingham.
Parkland course.
Pro Robert Simpson; Founded 1988
Designed by Eddie McCausland; David Johnson
18 holes, 6543 yards, S.S.S. 72
† Welcome with handicap certs.
Ⅼ WD £16; WE £23.50.
⟂ Welcome WD by arrangement.
⏣ Full facilities and function room.
⬫ Cottage; Ruddington.

6B 88 Rutland County
Hardwick Farm, Great Casterton, Stamford, Lincolnshire, PE9 4AQ
✉ pat@rutlandcounty.freeserve.co.uk

☎ 01780 460239, Fax 460437, Pro 460239, Sec 460330, Rest/Bar 460330
4 miles N of Stamford on A1.
Inland Links course.
Pro James Darroch; Founded 1992
Designed by Cameron Sinclair
18 holes, 6401 yards, S.S.S. 71
⌁ 20.
† Welcome with prior arrangement.
Ⅼ WD £25; WE £30.
⟂ Packages available.
⏣ Bar and restaurant.

6B 89 Sandilands ☎
Roman Bank, Sandilands, Sutton-on-Sea, Mablethorpe, Lincs, LN12 2RJ
☎ 01507 441432, Fax 441617
Course is on the A52 three miles S of Mablethorpe.
Links course.
Founded 1901
18 holes, 5995 yards, S.S.S. 69
† Welcome; some WE restrictions.
Ⅼ Winter WD £12-£15, WE £15; Summer WD £15-£20, WE £18-£25.
⟂ Welcome by prior arrangement.
⏣ Clubhouse facilities.
⬫ Grange and Links.

6B 90 Seacroft
Drummond Road, Skegness, Lincolnshire, PE25 3AU
⛆ www.seacroft-golfclub.co.uk
✉ richard@seacroftgolfclub.co.uk
☎ 01754 763020, Fax 763020, Pro 769624, Sec 763020, Rest/Bar 763020
S of Skegness towards Seacroft and Gibraltar Point nature reserve.
Links course.
Pro Robin Lawie; Founded 1895
Designed by Tom Dunn
18 holes, 6479 yards, S.S.S. 71
† Welcome with handicap certs.
Ⅼ WD £27; WE £32.
⟂ Welcome by prior arrangement; deposit required; catering and golf days can be arranged; from £27.
⏣ Full clubhouse facilities.
⬫ Crown; Vine; Links.

6B 91 Sherwood Forest
Eakring Rd, Mansfield, Notts, NG18 3EW
✉ sherwood@forest43.freeserve.co.uk
☎ 01623 626689, Fax 420412, Pro 627403, Sec 626689, Rest/Bar 623327
Off A617 at Oak Tree Lane to roundabout; second exit; 1 mile to junction; right; club is 500 yards.

Heathland course.
Pro Ken Hall; Founded 1895
Designed by HS Colt; Redesigned:
James Braid
18 holes, 6849 yards, S.S.S. 74
✝ Welcome by prior arrangement
with Sec; members' guests only at WE.
£ WD £40-£55.
⟳ Terms on application.
⦿ Full clubhouse facilities.
⤳ Pine Lodge; Swallow; Fringe.

6B 92 Shirland Lower Delves
Shirland, Nr Alfreton, Derbys, DE55
6AU
☎ 01773 834935, Sec 832515
Course is off the A61 Chesterfield
Road; turn opposite the church in
Shirland village.
Parkland course with views over
Derbyshire countryside.
Pro Neville Hallam; Founded 1977
18 holes, 6072 yards, S.S.S. 69
✝ Practice area.
✝ Welcome WD; by prior
arrangement at WE.
£ WD £15; WE £20.
⟳ By prior arrangement with
professional; golf and catering packages
can be arranged; terms on application.
⦿ Full clubhouse facilities.
⤳ Riber Hall; Swallow Hotel; Higham
Farm.

6B 93 Sickleholme
Saltergate Lane, Bamford, Sheffield,
S33 0BN
☎ 01433 651306, Fax 659498,
Rest/Bar 651252
On A625 14 miles W of Sheffield.
Undulating parkland course.
Pro Patrick Taylor; Founded 1898
18 holes, 6064 yards, S.S.S. 69
✝ Practice area.
✝ Welcome by prior arrangement;
except Wed am.
£ WD £29; WE £32.
⟳ Welcome by prior arrangement;
golf and catering packages can be
arranged; from £32.
⦿ Restaurant and bar facilities
available.
⤳ George; Plough, both Hathersage;
Yorkshire Bridge, Bamford.

6B 94 Sleaford   ☏
Willoughby Rd, South Rauceby,
Sleaford, Lincs, NG34 8PL
✉ sleafordgolfclub@btinternet.com
☎ 01529488273, Fax 488326
2 miles W of Sleaford at South
Rauceby, S of the A153 Sleaford to

Grantham Road.
Inland links with trees and scrubland.
Pro James Wilson; Founded 1905
Designed by Tom Williamson
18 holes, 6443 yards, S.S.S. 71
✝ Practice area.
✝ Welcome by prior arrangement.
£ Prices on application.
⟳ Welcome WD by prior
arrangement; packages can be
arranged; terms on application.
⦿ Restaurant and bar facilities.
⤳ Carre Arms; Lincolnshire Oak; Tally
Ho Motel.

6B 95 South Kyme   ☏
Skinners Lane, South Kyme, Lincoln,
LN4 4AT
🖥 www.skgc.co.uk
☎ 01526 861113, Fax 861080,
Pro 861113, Sec 861113,
Rest/Bar 861113
Course is on the B1395 four miles off
the A17, midway between Boston and
Sleaford.
Fenland course.
Pro Peter Chamberlain; Founded 1990
Designed by Graham Bradley
18 holes, 6597 yards, S.S.S. 71
✝ Practice ground and 6-hole course.
✝ All welcome.
£ WD £15; WE £18.
⟳ Terms on application.
⦿ Clubhouse facilities (Restaurant &
Bar snacks available).
⤳ The Leagate, Coningsby.

6B 96 Southview
Burgh Rd, Skegness, Lincs, PE25 2LA
✉ spence.golfshop@spalding2000.
freeserve.co.uk
☎ 01754 760589
On the A158 on the outskirts of
Skegness signposted to Southview
Leisure Park.
Parkland course.
Pro Peter Cole; Founded 1990
9 holes, 4816 yards, S.S.S. 64
✝ Welcome.
£ WD £6 per day; WE £6 per round.
⟳ Welcome at all times; tuition;
swimming pool; sauna; sunbeds;
snooker.
⦿ Full bar and catering in leisure
park.
⤳ North Shore; Crown; Links.

6B 97 Spalding
Surfleet, Spalding, Lincs, PE11 4EA
☎ 01775 680474, Sec 680386
Off A16 Spalding to Boston Road, 4
miles N of Spalding.

Parkland course.
Pro John Spencer; Founded 1908
Designed by Spencer/Price/Ward
extension 1993
18 holes, 6478 yards, S.S.S. 71
✝ Practice ground.
✝ Welcome by prior arrangement.
£ WD £20; WE £30.
⟳ Welcome Tues pm and Thurs;
catering packages can be arranged;
from £18.
⦿ Full catering and bar facilities
except Tues.

6B 98 Springwater
Moor Lane, Calverton, Notts, NG14
6FZ
☎ 0115 9652129,
Rest/Bar 9654946
Off A6097 between Lowdham and
Oxton. Extended 1998.
Parkland course.
Pro Paul Drew; Founded 1991
18 holes, 6224 yards, S.S.S. 71
✝ 6 bays, floodlit.
✝ Welcome.
£ Pay and play; WD £15; WE £20.
⟳ Packages available.
⦿ Full clubhouse facilities.

6B 99 Stanedge
Walton Hay Farm, Stanedge,
Chesterfield, Derbys, S45 0LW
☎ 01246 566156, Sec 566156
5 miles W of Chesterfield off the
A632 and the B5057 Near the Red
Lion Pub.
Moorland course.
Founded 1934
9 holes, 5786 yards, S.S.S. 69
✝ Practice area.
✝ Welcome WD (Fri before 2pm);
WE with a member.
£ WD £15.
⟳ Welcome by arrangement with
Sec; catering packages can be
arranged; terms on application.
⦿ Snacks at the bar.
⤳ Chesterfield Hotel; Olde House,
both Chesterfield.

6B 100 Stanton-on-the-Wolds
Stanton-on-the-Wolds, Keyworth,
Notts, NG12 5BH
☎ 0115 9372044, Pro 9372390,
Rest/Bar 9372264
Off A606 8 miles SE of Nottingham.
Meadowland course.
Pro Nick Hernon; Founded 1906
Designed by Tom Williamson
18 holes, 6437 yards, S.S.S. 71
✝ Practice range, Practice area;

chipping green.
† Welcome WD; WE with a member.
Ⅰ WD £20.
♢ Welcome by prior arrangement with Sec.
⦿ Full bar and catering facilities.
⌐ Edwalton Nottingham.

6B 101 **Stoke Rochford**
Stoke Rochford, Grantham, Lincs, NG33 5EW
☎ 01476 530275, Fax 530237, Pro 530218, Sec 01572 756305, Rest/Bar 530275
6 miles S of Grantham off Northbound A1.
Parkland course.
Pro Angus Dow; Founded 1926/1936
Designed by Major Hotchkin/C. Turner
18 holes, 6256 yards, S.S.S. 70
† Welcome by prior arrangement.
Ⅰ WD £22-£30, £12 with a member; WE £28-£40, £14 with a member.
♢ Welcome by prior arrangement; catering packages available; snooker; terms on application.
⦿ Full clubhouse bar and restaurant facilities.
⌐ Many in Grantham.

6B 102 **Sudbrook Moor**
Charity Street, Carlton Scroop, Near Grantham, Lincolnshire, NG32 3AT
⌨ www.sudbrookmoor.co.uk
☎ 01400 250796, Pro 250796, Sec 250796, Rest/Bar 250876
On A607 6 miles NE of Grantham.
Meadowland course in picturesque valley.
Pro Tim Hutton; Founded 1986
Designed by Tim Hutton
9 holes, 4800 yards, S.S.S. 64
† Pay and play.
Ⅰ Winter WD £5, WE £7; Summer WD £7, WE £9.
♢ None.
⦿ Coffee shop only.

6B 103 **Sutton Bridge**
New Rd, Sutton Bridge, Spalding, Lincs, PE12 9RQ
☎ 01406 350323, Pro 351422
Off A17 Long Sutton to King's Lynn road at Sutton Bridge.
Parkland course.
Pro Alison Johns; Founded 1914
9 holes, 5822 yards, S.S.S. 69
† Welcome WD only.
Ⅰ WD £18.
♢ Welcome WD by prior arrangement; minimum group 6; catering can be arranged.

⦿ Bar and restaurant facilities.
⌐ The Anchor Inn & numerous other small inns in the area.

6B 104 **Tapton Park Municipal**
Murray House, Crow Lane, Chesterfield, Derbyshire, S41 0EQ
☎ 01246 273887, Fax 558024, Pro 239500
Signposted in Chesterfield centre.
Municipal parkland course.
Pro Andrew Carnall; Founded 1934
18 holes, 6005, S.S.S. 69; 9 holes, 2613 yards, par 34
Ⅰ Pitch and putt course, practice area.
† Welcome; can book 6 days in advance.
Ⅰ WD £6.80; WE £8.40.
♢ Welcome by prior arrangement; packages available; terms on application.
⦿ Bar and restaurant facilities available. Function room available.

6B 105 **Tetney**
Station Rd, Tetney, Grimsby, Lincs, DN36 5HY
☎ 01472 211644, Fax 211644, Rest/Bar 811344
Off A16 at Tetney; 1.5 miles down Station Rd.
Parkland course.
Pro Jason Abrams; Founded 1994
Designed by The Caswell Family & Stuart Grant
18 holes, 6245 yards, S.S.S. 69
Ⅰ Driving range, 12 bays.
† Welcome.
Ⅰ WD £10; WE £10.
♢ Welcome, packages available for all-day catering and golf; from £25.
⦿ Bar and restaurant facilities available.

6B 106 **Toft Hotel**
Toft, Nr Bourne, Lincs, PE10 0XX
☎ 01778 590616, Pro 590616, Sec 590616, Rest/Bar 590614
6 miles E of Stamford on A6121.
Undulating parkland course with water features.
Pro Mark Jackson; Founded 1988
Designed by Derek and Roger Fitton
18 holes, 6486 yards, S.S.S. 71
† Welcome; tees bookable 14 days ahead.
Ⅰ WD £20; WE £25.
♢ Welcome by arrangement.
⦿ Full bar and restaurant facilities and function room in hotel.
⌐ On site Toft Hotel; golfing packages available.

6B 107 **Trent Lock Golf Centre**
Lock Lane, Sawley, Long Eaton, Notts, NG10 2FY
☎ 0115 9464398, Fax 9461183, Pro 9464398, Rest/Bar 9461184
2 miles from M1 Junction 25.
Parkland course.
Pro Mark Taylor; Founded 1991
Designed by E.W. McCausland
18 holes, 5900 yards, S.S.S. 68; 9 holes 2911, par 36
Ⅰ Practice range; 24 bays floodlit.
† Welcome; must book at WE.
Ⅰ WD £10; WE £12. £5 for the 9-hole, no bookings.
♢ Welcome by prior arrangement; from £24.95.
⦿ Bar snacks; restaurant; private functions room.

6B 108 **Waltham Windmill**
Cheapside, Waltham, Grimsby, NE Lincs, DN37 0HT
☎ 01472 824109, Pro 823963
In village of Waltham.
Parkland course.
Pro Nigel Burkitt; Founded 1997
Designed by Jim Payne
18 holes, 6442 yards, S.S.S. 71
Ⅰ Practice ground.
† Welcome.
Ⅰ WD £18; WE £25.
♢ Welcome WD by prior arrangement; restrictions at WE; packages available.
⦿ Catering bar and function room.
⌐ Brackenborough Arms.

6B 109 **Welton Manor**   ☎
Hackthorn Rd, Welton, Lincs, LN2 3PD
☎ 01673 862827
Off A46 Lincoln-Grimsby road.
Undulating parkland course.
Pro Gary Leslie; Founded 1995
18 holes, 5601 yards, S.S.S. 67
Ⅰ Driving range, 10 bays floodlit.
† Welcome; pay and play.
Ⅰ WD £12; WE £15.
♢ Welcome any time by prior arrangement.
⦿ Bar, restaurant and function facilities.
⌐ Four Seasons.

6B 110 **Wollaton Park**
Lime Tree Avenue, Wollaton Park, Nottingham, NG8 1BT
☎ 0115 9784834, Fax 9787574, Sec 9787574
Off slip road from A52 at junction with Nottingham ring road.
Parkland course.

Woodhall Spa

It has been said that the Hotchkin course at Woodhall Spa has hosted more amateur championships than any other course in England. If a test of a course is a list of its champions, then the Hotchkin is a very good course indeed. The four men to have won an English Amateur Championship here are Sir Michael Bonallack, Mark James, David Gilford and Ian Garbutt.

The original layout goes back to 1905 when a nine-hole course designed by Harry Vardon was opened on the land. JH Taylor and James Braid joined Vardon in playing the course in, but it wasn't long before Harry Colt came along and extended the course to eighteen holes.

Presumably someone didn't think very much of the architecture because in the early 1920s Colonel SV Hotchkin MC completely redesigned it. The only thing that he left from Colt's original ideas was a solitary green. The course today is virtually unaltered since then and has been described by the American magazine 'Golf' as, "the best in England and the 27th in the world".

That might seem like excessive praise to many people, but certainly the Hotchkin has a great deal to recommend it. It is rightly famed for its bunkers. I have been in enough of them to know - purely the fault of my foursomes partner, of course - but by my reckoning there were 112 of them in all.

This is not the gratuitous use of sand so beloved of many American designers who believe that a course is incomplete without at least one bunker large enough to accommodate a drive-in movie. They vary considerably in circumference, but not so much in depth. If you lose your footing and tumble down into one, you are very likely to find yourself in the sort of buried lie that even Phil Mickelson wouldn't have a wedge for.

Moreover, the bunkers are not just cavernous, they are so well-placed that the golfer's thinking is influenced on nearly every shot.

The Hotchkin's two nines are very different in character. The outward nine is more heathland in nature and feels quite roomy compared to what is to follow. At the right time of year it is a beautiful spot to be. Purple heather, yellow gorse, the rhododendrons for which the resort is famed, pine and silver birch, all combine to colour the day.

After a gentle opening par four the course throws in three par fours that can be really testing off the back tees. Then comes the first of the three par threes that are another part of the course's reputation. Each one is likely to test a different club and each one is visually very different to the others. Henry Cotton and Henry Longhurst were admirers of the short holes, but perhaps so much has been made of them now that the quality of the par fives is sometimes overlooked.

After the relative openness of the front nine - not that the fairways are particularly generous - the second nine can feel rather claustrophobic.

The par four eleventh presents a particularly deceptive second due to the presence of a bunker sixty yards short of the green and the hole to follow scarcely offers much relief. The choice, however, is straightforward enough - hit the green or face an intimidating bunker shot, followed possibly by another, and another.

The home of the English Golf Union, who bought the course in 1995, Woodhall Spa has tremendous facilities that include a second course designed by Donald Steel. Because the owners are intent on promoting golf there is none of the aloofness associated with some clubs.

— **Mark Reason**

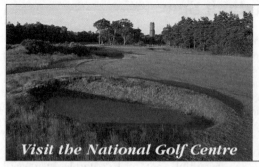

For a copy of our information booklet contact
Woodhall Spa Golf Management Co Ltd
The National Golf Centre • The Broadway
Woodhall Spa • Lincolnshire LN10 6PU
Telephone 01526 352511 • Fax 01526 351817
e-mail booking@englishgolfunion.org
www.englishgolfunion.org

Woodhall Spa

Visit the National Golf Centre

The National Golf Centre

Pro John Lower; Founded 1927
Designed by T Williamson
18 holes, 6445 yards, S.S.S. 71
† Welcome.
⌇ WD £26; WE £31.
⌀ Welcome by prior arrangement on Tues and Fri; golf and catering packages available on application to secretary; from £27.
|●| Clubhouse catering facilities available.
� Toby Lodge, Nottingham.

6B 111 **Woodhall Spa** *(see previous page)*
The Broadway, Woodhall Spa, Lincs, LN10 6PU
⌂ www.englishgolfunion.org
✉ booking@englishgolfunion.org
☎ 01526 352511, Fax 351817,
Pro 351803
Course is on the B1191, 19 miles SE of Lincoln.
Heathland course.
Pro Campbell C Elliott; Founded 1905
Designed by Col SV Hotchkin

Pro course: 18 holes, 7080yards, S.S.S. 75; Bracken course: 18 holes, 6735 yards, S.S.S. 74
⌇ Driving Range; teaching Academy; Pitch and putt.
† Welcome by prior arrangement; discount for EGU members.
⌇ WD £45; WE £45. EGU £30 on bracken course.
⌀ Welcome by prior arrangement; golf and catering by arrangement.
|●| Full clubhouse facilities.
� Golf; Petwood Hotel; Eagle Lodge.

6B 112 **Woodthorpe Hall**
Woodthorpe, Alford, Lincs, LN13 0DD
⌂ www.woodthorpehall.co.uk
✉ info@woodthorpehall.co.uk
☎ 01507 450000
Course is off the B1371 three miles N of Alford.
Parkland course.
Founded 1986
18 holes, 5140 yards, S.S.S. 65
⌇ Practice nets.

† Welcome.
⌇ WD £10; WE £10.
⌀ Welcome WD by prior arrangement; four weeks' notice needed; packages can be arranged for a minimum of 8; from £20.
|●| Inn on site.

6B 113 **Worksop**
Windmill Lane, Worksop, Notts, S80 2SQ
☎ 01909 472696, Fax 477731,
Pro 477732, Sec 477731,
Rest/Bar 472513
Off the B6034 road to Edwinstowe off the A57.
Heathland course with woods and gorse.
Pro C Weatherhead; Founded 1914
18 holes, 6660 yards, S.S.S. 73
† Welcome by prior arrangement.
⌇ WD £26; WE £35.
⌀ Welcome WD by prior arrangement; catering packages can be arranged; terms on application.
|●| Full clubhouse facilities.

Lancashire, Isle of Man, Cumbria

The Mersey beat is the toughest and most famous cluster of golf courses in England. Royal Birkdale is the Open Championship venue amongst them. On a still day it is a challenge, on a normal day it can be a nightmare. During practise for the 1998 Open, Tiger Woods asked a local when the weather was going to pick up. "You never know, last year summer fell on a Tuesday," was the reply. The only easy thing about Birkdale is that most of the stances are flat.

After shooting 82 in his third round in 1998, the defending Open champion Justin Leonard couldn't wait to get back to his hotel room so that he could watch the leaders on television and laugh his head off. Lee Trevino once said that Birkdale looked like the moon, but lunar conditions tend to be much more conducive to low scoring.

Some of the surrounding courses can be just as hard. In attempting to qualify for that 1998 Open, Jose Coceres, a winner on both sides of the Atlantic, shot 105 at Hesketh. Hillside is a very fine course, the last of Tony Jacklin's hurrahs when he won the PGA there in 1982. Birkdale is visible from its eleventh tee. Nearby Southport & Ainsdale is good enough to have hosted two Ryder Cups. And Formby is simply a joy.

Along the coast from Blackpool lies another astonishingly rich piece of golfing country. Royal Lytham and St Annes, the venue of the 2001 Open, is a masterpiece. Set on a scrubby piece of land with no views of the sea and flanked by a railway and red Victorian houses, it is not the world's most beautiful course, but it demands some of its most beautiful golf.

Seve Ballesteros rated the twelfth as the best par three in Britain, Jack Nicklaus thought the fifteenth one of the most difficult par fours in the world and the seventeenth would feature on many an all time top eighteen holes. Up the road is Fairhaven, where Les Dawson was a member, often said to have a bunker for every day of the year, Lytham Green Drive and St Annes Old Links.

The Isle of Man's foremost course is Castletown. On a clear day you can see the Cumbrian Hills, but this is an exposed primal course consisting of gorse, bracken, rough, rocks and beach with scarcely a tree in sight. The fifth hole is the first big challenge and it usually come from the hotel manager who will offer a wager of a bottle of champagne for a par. He seldom loses. The tenth hole is known as the racecourse because it was the original site of the derby. On the seventeenth the golfer is faced with a drive across the Irish sea which is a long carry in anyone's language.

Cumbria has a number of decent courses. Silloth-on-Solway was built by the North British railway company as a way of encouraging people to take the train. It is well worth the journey and perhaps Richard Branson should consider taking up such a scheme with Virgin. Brampton, sometimes called Talkin Tarn, has the Newcastle to Carlisle railway running along the side of its third hole, but is a fell course of rare beauty. Other courses have the scenery, but not necessarily the quality of golf.

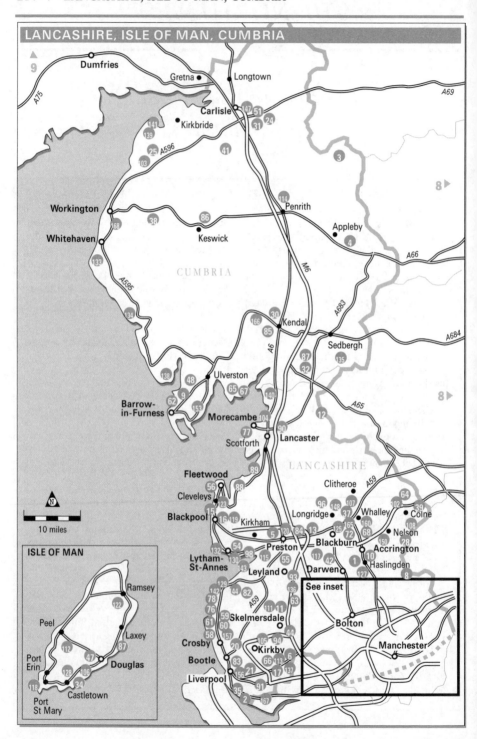

LANCASHIRE, ISLE OF MAN, CUMBRIA

KEY								
		36	Chorley	71	Greenmount	105	Mossack Hall	139	Silloth on Solway
1	Accrington & District	37	Clitheroe	72	Haigh Hall	106	Mount Murray	140	Silverdale
2	Allerton Municipal	38	Cockermouth	73	Harwood	107	Mytton Fold	141	Solway Village
3	Alston Moor	39	Colne	74	Haydock Park	108	Nelson	142	Southport & Ainsdale
4	Appleby	40	Crompton & Royton	75	Heaton Park	109	North Manchester	143	Southport Municipal
5	Ashton & Lea	41	Dalston Hall	76	Hesketh	110	Oldham	144	Southport Old Links
6	Ashton-in-Makerfield	42	Darwen	77	The Heysham	111	Ormskirk	145	Stand
7	Ashton-under-Lyne	43	Davyhulme Park	78	Hillside Golf Club	112	Peel	146	Standish Court Golf Club
8	Bacup	44	Dean Wood	79	Hindley Hall	113	Pennington	147	Stonyholme Municipal
9	Barrow	45	Deane	80	Horwich	114	Penrith	148	Stonyhurst Park
10	Baxenden & District	46	Denton	81	Houghwood	115	Penwortham	149	Swinton Park
11	Beacon Park	47	Douglas	82	Hurlston Hall	116	Pike Fold	150	Towneley
12	Bentham	48	Dunnerholme	83	Huyton & Prescot	117	Pleasington	151	Tunshill
13	Blackburn	49	Dunscar	84	Ingol Golf & Squash	118	Port St Mary Golf	152	Turton
14	Blackley	50	Duxbury Park		Club		Pavilion	153	Ulverston
15	Blackpool North Shore	51	Eden	85	Kendal	119	Poulton-le-Fylde	154	Walmersley
16	Blackpool Park	52	Ellesmere	86	Keswick	120	Preston	155	Werneth (Oldham)
17	Blundells Hill	53	Fairfield Golf & Sailing	87	Kirkby Lonsdale	121	Prestwich	156	West Derby
18	Bolton		Club	88	Knott End	122	Ramsey	157	West Lancashire
19	Bolton Old Links	54	Fairhaven	89	Lancaster	123	Reach	158	Westhoughton
20	Bootle	55	Fishwick Hall	90	Lansil	124	Regent Park (Bolton)	159	Westhoughton Golf
21	Bowring	56	Fleetwood	91	Lee Park	125	Rishton		Centre
22	Boysnope Park	57	Flixton	92	Leigh	126	Rochdale	160	Whalley
23	Brackley	58	Formby	93	Leyland	127	Rossendale	161	Whitefield
24	Brampton	59	Formby Golf Centre	94	Liverpool Municipal	128	Rowany	162	Whittaker
25	Brayton Park	60	Formby Hall		(Kirkby)	129	Royal Birkdale	163	Wigan
26	Breightmet	61	Formby Ladies	95	Lobden	130	Royal Lytham & St	164	William Wroe
27	Brookdale	62	Furness	96	Longridge		Annes	165	Wilpshire
28	Burnley	63	Gathurst	97	Lowes Park	131	Saddleworth	166	Windermere
29	Bury	64	Ghyll	98	Lytham Green Drive	132	St Annes Old Links	167	Woolton
30	Caras Green	65	Grange Fell	99	Manchester	133	St Bees	168	Workington
31	Carlisle	66	Grange Park	100	Manor (Bolton)	134	Seascale	169	Worsley
32	Casterton	67	Grange-over-Sands	101	Marland Park	135	Sedbergh	170	Worsley Park Marriot
33	Castle Hawk	68	Great Harwood	102	Marsden Park	136	Shaw Hill Hotel G & CC		
34	Castletown Golf Links	69	Great Lever & Farnworth	103	Maryport	137	Sherdley Park		
35	Childwall	70	Green Haworth	104	Morecambe	138	Silecroft		

7 1 Accrington & District Golf Club
Devon Avenue, Oswaldtwistle, Accrington, Lancs, BB5 4LS
www.Accrington/golf/club.fsnet.co.uk
acgolf@globalnet.co.uk
01254 232734, Fax 233423, Pro 231091, Sec 381614, Rest/Bar 232734
On A679 5 miles from Blackburn
Parkland-moorland course.
Pro Bill Harling; Founded 1893
Designed by James Braid
18 holes, 6060 yards, S.S.S. 69
Practice ground.
Welcome.
WD £22; Fri, Sat, Sun, BH £28.
Welcome by arrangement.
Full facilities except Mon & Thurs.
County; Duncan House.

7 2 Allerton Municipal Golf Course
Allerton Road, Mossley Hill, Liverpool,
Merseyside, L18 3JT
0151 4287490, Fax 4287490,
Pro 4281046, Rest/Bar 4288510
From end of M62 S on to Queens Drive, on to the ring road to Yewtree Road, signposted on Allerton Road.
Parkland course; also 9-hole.
Pro B Large; Founded 1923
18 holes, 5494 yards, S.S.S. 67
Beginners 9-hole course.
Welcome.
Terms on application.
Welcome WD and WE pm by arrangement with the professional; terms on application.
No facilities; light refreshments available.
Redbourne; Grange.

7 3 Alston Moor
The Hermitage, Alston, Cumbria, CA9 3DB
01434 381675
Course is on the B6277 1.5 miles
south of Alston; signposted from the top of the town.
Parkland and fell course.
Founded 1906/1969
Designed by Members
10 holes, 5518 yards, S.S.S. 67
Welcome.
WD £9; WE £11.
Welcome by prior arrangement; packages for golf and catering can be provided; prices on application.
Bar and catering facilities from May to October.
Secretary can provide details.

7 4 Appleby
Brackenber Moor, Appleby In Westmorland, Cumbria, CA16 6LP
017683 51432, Fax 52773,
Pro 52922, Sec 51432,
Rest/Bar 51432
Course is on the A66 two miles E of Appleby.
Moorland course.

Pro Gary Key, James Taylor; Founded 1903
Designed by Willie Fernie of Troon
18 holes, 5901 yards, S.S.S. 68
⚑ Practice ground.
⚑ Welcome.
⚑ WD £18 per round £20 per day; WE £22 per round £25 per day.
⚑ Welcome by prior arrangement.
⚑ Full catering and bar except Tuesdays when menu is limited.
⚑ Tufton Arms; Royal Oak; Appleby Manor; The Gate.

7 5 Ashton & Lea ⚒
Tudor Avenue, Off Blackpool Road, Lea, Preston, PR4 0XA
⚑ www.ashtonleagolf@supanet.com
⚑ ashtonleagolf@supernet.com
⚑ 01772 726480, Fax 735762, Pro 720374, Sec 735282, Rest/Bar 726480 bar 736936 restaurant
Course is on the A5085 three miles W of Preston.
Parkland course with water features.
Pro M Greenough; Founded 1913
Designed by J Steer
18 holes, 6370 yards, S.S.S. 70
⚑ Welcome by prior arrangement.
⚑ WD £23; WE £25.
⚑ Welcome by prior arrangement; Training/conference rooms available; packages include golf and catering; from £33.
⚑ Full clubhouse facilities available.
⚑ Travel Inn, Lea; Marriott, Broughton.

7 6 Ashton-in-Makerfield
Garswood Park, Liverpool Road, Ashton In Makerfield, Wigan, Lancs, WN4 0YT
⚑ 01942 719330, Fax 719330, Pro 724229, Sec 719330
Off A58 from M6 0.5 miles to course.
Parkland course.
Pro Peter Alan; Founded 1902
Designed by FW Hawtree
18 holes, 6205 yards, S.S.S. 70
⚑ Welcome WD except Wed; WE only with member.
⚑ WD £28.
⚑ Welcome Mon, Tues and Thurs, Fri by prior arrangement.
⚑ Full facilities except Mon (not applicable for societies).
⚑ Thistle, Haydock.

7 7 Ashton-under-Lyne ⚒
Gorsey Way, Ashton-under-Lyne,

Lancshire, OL6 9HT
⚑ 0161 3301537, Fax 3306673, Pro 3082095, Sec 3301537, Rest/Bar 3301537
3 miles from town centre.
Semi-parkland course.
Pro Colin Boyle; Founded 1913
18 holes, 6209 yards, S.S.S. 70
⚑ Welcome by prior arrangement; guests of members only at WE.
⚑ WD £25; play only allowed with a member at weekends; Sat £25 with member; Sun £10 with member.
⚑ Welcome Tues, Thurs and Fri; packages for golf and catering available; terms on application.
⚑ Clubhouse facilities.
⚑ Broadoak Hotel.

7 8 Bacup
Maden Road, Bacup, Lancs, OL13 8HY
⚑ 01706 873170, Fax 877726, Sec 873170, Rest/Bar 873170
Off A671 7 miles N of Rochdale, 0.5 miles from Bacup centre.
Meadowland course.
Founded 1911
9 holes, 6008 yards, S.S.S. 67
⚑ Welcome Wed, Thurs and Fri, and after competitions at WE.
⚑ Prices on application.
⚑ Welcome Wed, Thurs and Fri by prior arrangement.
⚑ Full clubhouse facilities available.
⚑ Royal, Waterfoot.

7 9 Barrow
Rakesmoor Lane, Hawcoat, Barrow In Furness, Cumbria, LA14 4QB
⚑ 01229 825444, Pro 825444, Sec 825444, Rest/Bar 825444
From M6 Junction 36 take A590 to Barrow; 3 miles before town follow Industrial route turning left into Bank Lane.
Parkland course.
Pro J McLeod; Founded 1922
18 holes, 6200 yards, S.S.S. 70
⚑ Welcome with handicap certs and by prior arrangement.
⚑ WD £20; WE £20.
⚑ Welcome by prior arrangement with the professional; packages include a full day's golf and catering; snooker table; from £26.
⚑ Full clubhouse facilities.
⚑ Club can recommend local hotels.

7 10 Baxenden & District
Top-O'-The Meadow, Wooley Lane, Baxenden, Accrington, Lancs, BB5 2EA

⚑ 01254 234555
Take M65 Accrington exit and follow the signs for Baxenden; course signposted in village.
Moorland course.
Founded 1913
9 holes, 5717 yards, S.S.S. 68
⚑ Welcome WD; with member only WE.
⚑ Prices on application.
⚑ Welcome WD by prior arrangement with the Secretary; packages include coffee, light lunch, 3-course meal and 27 holes of golf; from £22.
⚑ Bar and snacks available; meals to order.
⚑ Syke Side House; Haslingden.

7 11 Beacon Park
Beacon Lane, Dalton, Wigan, Lancs, WN8 7RU
⚑ 01695 622700, Fax 622700, Pro 622700, Sec 726298, Rest/Bar 625551
Off A577 in Up Holland.
Parkland course.
Pro Gary Nelson; Founded 1982
Designed by Donald Steel
18 holes, 5931 yards, S.S.S. 69
⚑ Practice range, 24 bays floodlit.
⚑ Pay and play.
⚑ Terms on application.
⚑ Welcome by prior arrangement; payment required 10 days in advance; terms on application.
⚑ Clubhouse facilities.
⚑ Lancashire Lodge.

7 12 Bentham
Robin Lane, Bentham, Lancaster, Lancs, LA2 7AG
⚑ trev.tudor@virginnet.com
⚑ 015242 62455, Fax 62455, Sec 62455, Rest/Bar 61018
Between Lancaster and Settle on B6480 13 miles E of M6 Junction 34.
Undulating meadowland course.
Founded 1922
9 holes, 5820 yards, S.S.S. 69
⚑ Everyone welcome.
⚑ WD £15; WE £15.
⚑ Welcome by arrangement.
⚑ Bar snacks and meals.
⚑ Bridge, Ingleton; Post House, Lancaster.

7 13 Blackburn
Beardwood Brow, Blackburn, Lancashire, BB2 7AX
⚑ sec@blackburngolfclub.com
⚑ 01254 51122, Fax 665578,

Pro 55942, Sec 51122,
Rest/Bar 51122
Off A677 at W end of Blackburn.
Parkland course.
Pro A Rodwell; Founded 1894
18 holes, 6144 yards, S.S.S. 70
🏌 Practice ground, putting green,
indoor practice area.
† Welcome by prior arrangement.
🔒 WD £24; WE £28; guests of
members £7.50 all week; juniors WD
£5-£9, WE £7.50-£9.
🍴 Welcome WD except Tues;
catering and golf packages can be
arranged; terms on application.
🍽 Clubhouse facilities except Mon.

7 14 Blackley

Victoria Avenue East, Blackley,
Manchester, M9 7HW
☎ 0161 6432980, Fax 6538300,
Pro 6433912, Sec 6547770,
Rest/Bar 6432980
5 miles N of City centre.
Parkland course.
Pro Craig Gould; Founded 1907
Designed by Gaunt & Marlet
18 holes, 6217 yards, S.S.S. 70
† Welcome WD; with member at
weekend.
🔒 WD £15 with member, £24 without.
🍴 Welcome WD except Thurs; golf
and catering packages available; from
£20.
🍽 Full clubhouse catering facilities
available.
🛏 Bower Hotel, Chadderton, The
Royal Toby.

7 15 Blackpool North Shore

Devonshire Road, Blackpool, Lancs,
FY2 0RD
☎ 01253 352054, Fax 591240, Pro
354640, Rest/Bar 351017
From M55 Junction 4 take Preston
New Road to Whitegate Drive and
Devonshire Road.
Moorland course with upper seaside
elements.
Pro Brendan Ward; Founded 1904
Designed by Harry Colt
18 holes, 6431 yards, S.S.S. 71
🏌 Practice green.
† Welcome by prior arrangement;
tees reserved for members until
9.30am & 12.30-1.30pm; not before
2pm Thurs and 4pm Sat.
🔒 WD £30; WE and BH £35.
🍴 Welcome WD except Thurs; golf
and catering packages available; terms
on application.
🍽 Catering and bar facilities daily.
🛏 Many in Blackpool.

7 16 Blackpool Park Golf Club

North Park Drive, Blackpool, Lancs,
FY3 8LS
☎ 01253 393960, Fax 397916, Pro
391004, Sec 397916, Rest/Bar 396683
2 miles E of Blackpool signposted off
M55.
Parkland course.
Pro B Purdie; Founded 1926
Designed by Dr MacKenzie
18 holes, 6192 yards, S.S.S. 69
🏌 Practice nets, practice putting
green, practice chipping.
† Welcome; tee reservations through
Blackpool Borough Council.
🔒 WD £12; WE £14.
🍴 Welcome by prior arrangement
with Blackpool Borough Council; terms
on application.
🍽 Clubhouse facilities.
🛏 Many in Blackpool.

7 17 Blundells Hill

Blundells Lane, Rainhill, Liverpool,
Merseyside, L35 6NA
🖥 www.blundellshill.co.uk
✉ info@blundellshill.demon.co.uk
☎ 0151 4309551, Fax 4265256,
Pro 4300100, Sec 4309551,
Rest/Bar 4269040
From M62 Junction 7 take A57 towards
Prescot; turn left after garage; then
2nd left into Blundells Lane.
Parkland course.
Pro R Burbidge; Founded 1994
Designed by S Marnoch
18 holes, 6256 yards, S.S.S. 70
† Welcome by arrangement.
🔒 WD £25, WE £30.
🍴 Welcome Mon to Thurs; catering
and golf packages for a minimum of 12
people; £33-£42.
🍽 Full clubhouse facilities.
🛏 Ship Inn, Rainhill; The Hilton, St
Helens; The Village, Whiston; Hillcrest,
Cronton.

7 18 Bolton

Chorley New Road, Lostock, Bolton,
Lancs, BL6 4AJ
☎ 01204 843278, Fax 843067,
Pro 843073, Sec 843067 office/fax
3 miles W of Bolton, Junction 6 of the
M61.
Hilly course.
Pro Robert Longworth; Founded
1891/1912
18 holes, 6237 yards, S.S.S. 70
† Welcome between 10am-12noon
and after 2pm.
🔒 WD £30-£36; WE £33-£40.
🍴 Welcome Mon, Thurs and some
Fri; discount available for larger

groups; packages for golf and catering
available; terms on application.
🍽 Clubhouse facilities.
🛏 Devere Whites Hotel, Reebok
Stadium.

7 19 Bolton Old Links Golf Club

Chorley Old Road, Bolton, Lancs, BL1
5SU
🖥 www.boltonoldlinks.co.uk
✉ mail@boltonoldlinks.co.uk
☎ 01204 842307, Fax 842307,
Pro 843089, Sec 842307,
Rest/Bar 840050
On B6226 N of A58 from Junction 5 on
M61.
Moorland course.
Pro Paul Horridge; Founded 1891
Designed by Dr A MacKenzie
18 holes, 6469 yards, S.S.S. 71
🏌 Practice ground; indoor practice
facilities.
† Welcome except on competition
days; phone in advance to make booking
🔒 WD £30; WE £40.
🍴 Welcome WD by prior
arrangement.
🍽 Full clubhouse facilities available
except Mon (possible by prior
arrangement).
🛏 Crest; Pack Horse; Last Drop;
Moat House.

7 20 Bootle

Bootle Golf Course, Dunnings Bridge
Road, Bootle, Merseyside, L30 2PP
☎ 0151 9281371, Fax 9491815,
Rest/Bar 9286196
On A565 5 miles from Liverpool.
Municipal seaside links course.
Pro Alan Bradshaw; Founded 1934
Designed by F Stephens
18 holes, 6242 yards, S.S.S. 70
† Welcome.
🔒 WD £7.20; WE £9.20.
🍴 Welcome by prior arrangement.
🍽 Full clubhouse facilities available.
🛏 The Park Hotel.

7 21 Bowring Park Golf Course

Roby Road, Huyton, Liverpool,
Merseyside, L36 4HD
☎ 0151 4891901
6 miles N of Liverpool.
Municipal parkland course.
Founded 1913
18 holes, 6147 yards, S.S.S. 70
† Welcome.
🔒 Adults WD £7.20, WE £8; OAP
WD £3.55, WE £3.85; juniors WD
£2.25, WE £3.60.

♂ Welcome by prior arrangement.
🍴 Snacks; bar for members only.

---

7 22 Boysnope Park
Liverpool Road, Barton Moss, Eccles,
Manchester, Lancs, M30 7RF
☎ 0161 7076125, Pro 70186685
Off M60 at Junction 11 on A57 towards
Irlam.
Parkland course.
Pro Scott Curry; Founded 1998
9 holes, 2975 yards, S.S.S. 34
♦ Welcome.
[WD £6; WE £7.
♂ Welcome by prior notice.
🍴 Limited to snacks.

---

7 23 Brackley
Bullows Road, Little Hulton, Worsley,
Manchester, Lancs, M38 9TR
☎ 0161 7906076
9 miles from Manchester on A6; turn
right at White Lion Hotel into Highfield
Rd; left into Captain Fold Rd; left into
Bullows Rd.
Parkland course.
Founded 1976
9 holes, 6006 yards, S.S.S. 69
♦ Welcome; book at WE.
[WD £4; WE and BH 9 holes £4, 18
holes £7; OAP WD £3; juniors WD
£2.50.
♂ Welcome by prior arrangement;
from £7.00.
🍴 None.

---

7 24 Brampton (Talkin Tarn) ☏
Tarn Road, Brampton, Cumbria, CA8
1HN
☎ 016977 2255, Fax 41487,
Pro 2000, Sec 2255,
Rest/Bar 2255
1.75 miles from Brampton on B6413
Castle Carrock Road.
Moorland course.
Pro Stewart Wilkinson; Founded 1907

Designed by James Braid
18 holes, 6407 yards, S.S.S. 71
♦ Practice ground/Driving range for
irons only.
♦ Welcome; tee booked 9.30am-
10.30am Mon, Wed, Thurs.
[WD £22; WE £30.
♂ Welcome by prior arrangement
WD; limited at WE.
🍴 Full facilities in refurbished
clubhouse.
↪ Details of local guest houses and
hotels offering reduced fees from club
or pro.

---

7 25 Brayton Park Golf Course
Brayton, Aspatria, Carlisle, Cumbria,
CA7 3PY
☎ 016973 20840, Fax 20854
Off A596 W of Carlisle.
Parkland course.
Pro Graham Batey; Founded 1978
Designed by Barry Ward
9 holes, 5042 yards, S.S.S. 64
♦ Welcome.
[WD £5 for 9 holes £7 for 18.
♂ Welcome by prior arrangement;
terms on application.
🍴 Bar Restaurant.
↪ Kelsey; Wheyrigg; Green Hill.

---

7 26 Breightmet
Red Lane, Red Bridge, Bolton, Lancs,
BL2 5PA
☎ 01204 527381
Off Bury Road in Bolton.
Moorland/parkland course.
Founded 1911
9 holes, 6416 yards, S.S.S. 72
♦ Welcome by prior arrangement;
some restrictions Sat and Wed.
[WD £15; WE £18.
♂ Welcome WD; some Suns;
packages include full day's golf and
catering; snooker; £25-£30.
🍴 Full clubhouse facilities.
↪ In Bolton town centre.

---

7 27 Brookdale
Medlock Road, Failsworth,
Manchester, Lancs, M35 9WQ
🖳 www.brookdalegolfclub.co.uk
✉ info@brookdalegolfclub.co.uk
☎ 0161 6814534, Fax 6886872,
Pro 6812655, Sec 6854534
From Manchester take A62 turning
right at Ashton Rd East; 1 mile turn
right into Failsworth Rd; 0.25 miles into
Medlock Road.
Parkland course.
Pro Tony Cupello; Founded 1896
18 holes, 5874 yards, S.S.S. 68
♦ Practice area.
♦ Welcome WD only.
[WD £22.
♂ Welcome Wed, Thurs, Fri;
packages include golf and catering
from £34.
🍴 Clubhouse facilities.
↪ Smokies Park; Bower Hotel, avant
hotel.

---

7 28 Burnley Golf Club
Glen View Road, Burnley, Lancs, BB11
3RW
🖳 www.burnley-golf.co.uk
✉ burnleygolf@currantbun.com
☎ 01282 421045, Fax 451281, Pro
455266, Sec 451281
Glen View road is off Manchester Road
Moorland course.
Pro Paul MacAvoy; Founded 1905
18 holes, 5911 yards, S.S.S. 69
♦ Welcome with handicap certs.
[WD £20; WE £25.
♂ Welcome everyday except Sat;
handicap certs required; 36 holes of
golf plus meals; £30.
🍴 Full facilities.
↪ Rosehill House Hotel.

---

7 29 Bury
Unsworth Hall. Blackford Bridge,
Manchester Road. Bury, Lancs, BL9
9TJ

☎ 0161 7664897, Fax 7963480, Pro 7662213
On A57 1.5 miles from M62 Junction 17
Undulating moorland course.
Pro D Proctor; Founded 1890
Designed by Dr A Mackenzie
18 holes, 5927 yards, S.S.S. 69
♌ Welcome except on club competition days.
⌇ WD £26; WE £30.
⟳ Welcome Wed-Fri; packages include full day's golf and catering £35.
🍽 Full clubhouse facilities.
⌂ Red Hall; Rostrevor.

7 30 Caras Green

Burneside Road, Kendal, Cumbria, LA9 6EB
☎ 01539 72107, Fax 72107
From roundabout at N end of Kendal follow A591 to Burnside.
Designed by W Adamson
18 holes, 5961 yards, S.S.S. 68
♌ Welcome; some WE restrictions.
⌇ Terms on application.
⟳ Contact secretary for packages.
🍽 Full clubhouse catering.

7 31 Carlisle

Aglionby, Carlisle, Cumbria, CA4 8AG
☎ 01228 513029, Fax 513303, Pro 513241, Sec 513303
Course is on the A69 0.25 miles E of M6 Junction 43.
Parkland course (Open Championship).
Pro Martin Heggie; Founded 1908, moved 1940
Designed by MacKenzie Ross
18 holes, 6223 yards, S.S.S. 70
⌇ Practice area.
♌ Welcome except Tues and Sat.
⌇ WD £25-£40; Sun £40.
⟳ Welcome Mon, Wed, Fri by prior arrangement; packages available; club can administer competitions; private dining facilities; terms on application.
🍽 Full clubhouse facilities.
⌂ Cumbrain Hotel, Carlisle; Crown Hotel, Wetherall.

7 32 Casterton ☜

Sedburgh Road, Casterton, Carnforth, Lancs, LA6 2LA
✉ castertongc@hotmail.com
☎ 01524 271592, Fax 274387
On A683 Sebergh Road.
Picturesque undulating parkland course.
Pro Roy Williamson; Founded 1946/1993
Designed by W Adamson
9 holes, 5726 yards, S.S.S. 68
♌ Welcome by prior arrangement;

weekend reservations essential.
⌇ WD £10; WE £14.
⟳ Welcome by arrangement; maximum 20; terms available on application.
🍽 Light refreshments only.
⌂ Pheasant, Casterton; Royal, Kirkby Lonsdale.

7 33 Castle Hawk

Chadwick Lane, Heywood Rd, Rochdale, Lancs, OL11 3BY
✉ teeoff@castlehawk.freeserve.co.uk
☎ 01706 640841, Fax 860587, Pro 633855, Rest/Bar 710020
Leave Rochdale on the Manchester Road towards Castleton; turn right for the course directly before Castleton station.
Undulating parkland/meadowland course.
Pro Frank Accleton; Founded 1965
Designed by T Wilson
· 18 holes, 5398 yards, S.S.S. 68
9 holes, 3036 yards, S.S.S. 55
♌ Welcome.
⌇ Mon-Sat £9 Sun £11. Paying guests unable to play 9-hole course on Sat.
⟳ Welcome by prior arrangement.
🍽 Restaurant and bar facilities.
⌂ Royal Toby.

7 34 Castletown Golf Links

Fort Island, Castletown, Derbyhaven, Isle Of Man, IM9 1UA
🖳 www.castletowngolflinks.co.uk
☎ 01624 822201, Fax 824633
3 miles from airport.
True links course.
Pro Murray Crowe; Founded 1892
Designed by MacKenzie Ross
18 holes, 6711 yards, S.S.S. 72
⌇ Practice ground.
♌ Welcome; residents have priority at WE.
⌇ WD £25; WE £30.
⟳ Welcome by prior arrangement; discounts for residents; catering packages available; snooker, sauna, indoor pool; from £25.
🍽 Full club and hotel catering restaurant and bar facilities.
⌂ On site hotel.

7 35 Childwall

Naylor's Rd, Liverpool, Merseyside, L27 2YB
☎ 0151 4870654, Fax 4870882, Pro 4879871
5 miles from Liverpool, 2 miles from M62 Junction 6.

Parkland course.
Pro Nigel Parr; Founded 1913
Designed by James Braid
18 holes, 6470 yards, S.S.S. 71
⌇ Practice ground.
♌ Welcome WD except Tues between 9.45am and 2pm.
⌇ WD £26; WE £35.
⟳ Welcome WD except Tues by prior arrangement.
🍽 Bar and restaurant facilities available.
⌂ Village; Derby Lodge.

7 36 Chorley

Chorley Road, Heath Charnock, Chorley, Lancs, PR6 9HX
🖳 www.chorleygolfclub.co.uk
✉ secretary@chorleygolfclub.freeserve.co.uk
☎ 01257 480263, Fax 480722, Pro 481245
Course is on the A673 100 yds south of the A6 Junction at Skew Bridge traffic lights.
Heathland course.
Pro Mark Bradley; Founded 1897
Designed by JA Steer
18 holes, 6307 yards, S.S.S. 70
♌ Welcome WD except Mon by prior arrangement.
⌇ WD £29.
⟳ Welcome Tues to Fri by prior arrangement.
🍽 Full bar and restaurant facilities available.
⌂ Yarrow Bridge; Parkville; Hartwood Hall; Gladmar.

7 37 Clitheroe

Whalley Road, Pendleton, Clitheroe, Lancs, BB7 1PP
☎ 01200 422292, Fax 422292, Pro 424242, Sec 422292, Rest/Bar 442494
2 miles S of Clitheroe on the Clitheroe-Whalley Road.
Parkland course.
Pro JE Twissell; Founded 1891/1932
Designed by James Braid
18 holes, 6323 yards, S.S.S. 71
⌇ Practice area.
♌ Welcome by prior arrangement.
⌇ WD £28; WE £34, full day WD £33; WE £39.
⟳ Welcome by prior arrangement; packages can be arranged for golf and catering from £33.
🍽 Full clubhouse facilities.

7 38 Cockermouth Golf Club ☜

Embleton, Cockermouth, Cumbria,

CA13 9SG
☎ 017687 76223, Fax 76941, Sec 76941
3 miles E of Cockermouth.
Fell land course.
Founded 1896
Designed by James Braid
18 holes, 5496 yards, S.S.S. 67
♦ Welcome by prior arrangement.
▐ Summer WD £15, WE £20; Winter WD £10, WE £15.
♫ Welcome; terms on application; from £15.
|●| Clubhouse facilities.
♫ Trout; Derwent Lodge, both Cockermouth.

---

7 39 **Colne**
Law Farm, Skipton Old Road, Colne, Lancs, BB8 7EB
☎ 01282 863391, Fax 870547
From the end of M65 E travel one mile to roundabout, then take first exit left for course.
Moorland course with trees.
Founded 1901
Designed by club members
9 holes, 6053 yards, S.S.S. 69
⚑ Practice ground, practice green, putting green.
♦ Welcome except competition days; 2 balls only on Thurs.
▐ WD £16; WE £20.
♫ Welcome WD; snooker; function room; terms on application; from £16.
|●| Full clubhouse facilities except Mons.
♫ The Oaks, Burnley; The Old Stone Trough, Colne.

---

7 40 **Crompton & Royton**
High Barn Street, Royton, Oldham, Lancs, OL2 6RW
☎ 0161 6240986, Fax 6524711, Pro 6242154,
Rest/Bar 624 9867
Off A627 at Royton centre.
Moorland course.
Pro David Melling; Founded 1908
18 holes, 6214 yards, S.S.S. 70
♦ Welcome; restrictions at WE and on Tues and Wed.
▐ WD £24; WE £30; reductions for guests of members.
♫ Welcome Mon, Thurs and Fri; terms on application.
|●| Clubhouse facilities.
♫ Peraquito, Oldham.

---

7 41 **Dalston Hall**
Dalston, Carlisle, Cumbria, CA5 7JX
☎ 01228 710165

From M6 Junction 42 to Dalston Village; course 0.5 miles on right.
Parkland course.
Founded 1990
Designed by David Pearson
9 holes, 5103 yards, S.S.S. 65
♦ Welcome; tee booking required at WE and after 4pm WD.
▐ WD 9 holes £6.50, 18 holes £10; WE 9 holes £7.50,18 holes £13.
♫ Welcome by arrangement; packages on application.
|●| Bar and restaurant.
♫ Dalston Hall caravan park on site; Dalston Hall Hotel adjacent.

---

7 42 **Darwen**
Winter Hill, Duddon Avenue, Darwen, Lancs, BB3 0LB
✉ admin@darwengolfclub.com
☎ 01254 701287, Pro 776370, Sec 704367
1.5 miles from Darwen centre.
Moorland/parkland course.
Pro W Lennon; Founded 1893
18 holes, 5863 yards, S.S.S. 68
♦ Welcome.
▐ Prices on application.
♫ Welcome by prior arrangement; terms on application.
|●| Clubhouse facilities.
♫ Whitehall Hotel & CC.

---

7 43 **Davyhulme**
Gleneagles Road, Urmston, Manchester, Lancs, M41 8SA
☎ 0161 7482260, Fax 7474067, Pro 7483931
Course is eight miles S of Manchester adjacent to Trafford Hospital in Davyhulme.
Parkland course.
Pro Dean Butler; Founded 1910
18 holes, 6237 yards, S.S.S. 70
⚑ Two practice putting greens, practice area with green and bunker, two indoor practice nets, tuition available, group and individual; pro shop caters for society prizes (giftware/glassware, etc).
♦ Welcome WD and WE.
▐ WD £24-£30; WE £33.
♫ Welcome Mon, Tues, Thurs by arrangement.
|●| Full facilities.
♫ The Manor Hey Hotel; The Tulip.

---

7 44 **Dean Wood**
Lafford Lane, Upholland, Skelmersdale, Lancs, WN8 0QZ
☎ 01695 622219, Fax 622245, Pro 622980, Rest/Bar 622980

1.5 miles from M6 Junction 26 following Up Holland signs.
Hilly parkland course.
Pro S Danchin; Founded 1922
Designed by James Braid
18 holes, 6137 yards, S.S.S. 70
⚑ Practice area; practice nets.
♦ Welcome by prior arrangement.
▐ WD £30; WE £33.
♫ Welcome Mon, Thurs and Fri; terms on application.
|●| Clubhouse facilities.
♫ Holland Hall; Travel Inn.

---

7 45 **Deane**
Broadford Road, Bolton, Lancs, BL3 4NS
☎ 01204 61944, Fax 651808, Sec 651808
Course is one mile from Junction 5 on the M61.
Undulating parkland course.
Pro David Martindale; Founded 1908
18 holes, 5652 yards, S.S.S. 67
♦ Welcome by arrangement.
▐ WD £20; WE £25.
♫ Welcome Tues, Thurs, Fri by prior arrangement; full day package of golf and catering; £31.
|●| Clubhouse facilities.
♫ Beaumont Hotel.

---

7 46 **Denton**
Manchester Road, Wilton Paddock, Denton, Manchester, Lancs, M34 2GG
☎ 0161 3363218, Fax 3364751, Pro 3362070
5 miles SE of Manchester off the A57; also close to the M60 Denton roundabout.
Parkland course.
Pro Michael Hollingworth; Founded 1909
18 holes, 6541 yards, S.S.S. 71
♦ Welcome WD; WE only with a member.
▐ WD £25; WE £30.
♫ Welcome Wed to Fri.
|●| New clubhouse facilities.
♫ Stable Gate Travelodge; Diamond Hotels.

---

7 47 **Douglas Golf Club**
Pulrose Road, Douglas, Isle Of Man, IM2 1AE
☎ 01624 675952, Pro 661558
1 mile from Douglas town centre, clubhouse near Power Station cooling tower.
Municipal parkland course.
Pro Mike Vipond; Founded 1927
Designed by Dr A MacKenzie
18 holes, 5922 yards, S.S.S. 68

✝ Welcome; advisable to phone in advance.
⌶ WD £8; WE £13.
⌔ Welcome by prior arrangement.
⦿ Full meals and bar snacks throughout season.
⌁ Contact local tourist board.

7 48 **Dunnerholme**
Duddon Road, Askam-in-Furness, Cumbria, LA16 7AW
☎ 01229 462675
Take A590 to Askam, turn left over railway into Duddin Rd, continue down towards the seashore over the cattle grid.
Links course.
Founded 1905
10 holes, 6154 yards, S.S.S. 70
✝ Welcome except before 4.30pm Sun.
⌶ Prices on application.
⌔ Welcome by prior arrangement; few restrictions.
⦿ Bar and catering facilities.
⌁ Railway; White Water; Clarence; Wellington; Abbey House.

7 49 **Dunscar**
Longworth Lane, Bromley Cross, Bolton, Lancs, BL7 9QY
☎ 01204 598228, Pro 592992, Sec 303321, Rest/Bar 598228
Off A666 3 miles N of Bolton.
Moorland course.
Pro Gary Treadbold; Founded 1908
Designed by George Lowe
18 holes, 6085 yards, S.S.S. 69
⌶ Practice range.
✝ Welcome by prior arrangement.
⌶ WD £20; WE £30.
⌔ Welcome by prior arrangement; terms on application.
⦿ Clubhouse facilities.
⌁ Egerton House; Last Drop.

7 50 **Duxbury Park**
Duxbury Hall Road, Chorley, Lancs, PR7 4AT
☎ 01257 265380, Fax 241378, Sec 241634, Rest/Bar 277049
1.5 miles S of Chorley on A5106 from A6.
Municipal parkland course.
Pro Simon Middleham; Founded 1970
18 holes, 6390 yards, S.S.S. 71
✝ Welcome; booking system.
⌶ Terms on application.
⌔ Welcome WD by prior arrangement.
⦿ Limited at club; facilities available close by.

⌁ Hartwood Hall; Kilhey Court.

7 51 **Eden** ♣
Crosby-on-Eden, Carlisle, Cumbria, CA6 4RA
⌕ www.edengolf.co.uk
☎ 01228 573003, Fax 818435, Pro 573003, Sec 573003, Rest/Bar 573013
From M6 Junction 44 take A689 to Low Crosby and Crosby-on-Eden.
Parkland course.
Pro Steve Harrison; Founded 1991
Designed by E MacCauslin
18 holes, 6368 yards, S.S.S. 72
⌶ 16.
✝ Welcome; prior booking is advisable.
⌶ Winter WD £22; WE £28; Summer WD £28; WE £32.
⌔ Welcome by prior arrangement; discounts are available for larger groups; practice area; driving range; catering packages; terms available on application.
⦿ Full clubhouse bar and restaurant facilities.
⌁ Wall Foot Hotel; Crosby Lodge; Crown Hotel.

7 52 **Ellesmere**
Old Clough Lane, Worsley, Manchester, M28 5HZ
⌕ www.Ellesmeregolf.co.uk
⌨ Honsec@Ellesmeregolf.fs net.co.uk
☎ 0161 7908591, Fax 7908591, Pro 7998594, Sec 7990554, Rest/Bar 7902122
Off A580 adjacent to M60 Ring road.
Parkland course.
Pro Terry Morley; Founded 1913
18 holes, 6265 yards, S.S.S. 70
✝ Welcome except on competition days and BH.
⌶ WD £22 per round; WE £28 per day.
⌔ Welcome Mon, Tues and Fri; Wed also in winter: 27 holes of golf plus catering; from £33.
⦿ Full clubhouse facilities available.
⌁ Novotel, Worsley.

7 53 **Fairfield Golf & Sailing Club**
Boothdale, Booth Road, Audenshaw, Manchester, Lancs, M34 5GA
⌕ www.fairfieldgolf.co.uk
☎ 0161 3702292, Fax 3702292, Sec 3014528, Rest/Bar 3701641
On A635 5 miles E of Manchester.
Parkland course around reservoir.
Pro SA Pownell; Founded 1892

18 holes, 5664 yards, S.S.S. 68
✝ Welcome WD; Thurs ladies day; some weekend restrictions; telephone in advance.
⌶ WD £20; WE £25..
⌔ Welcome by prior arrangement with the secretary; terms on application.
⦿ Full facilities by prior arrangement.
⌁ Village, Hyde; York, Ashton-under-Lyne.

7 54 **Fairhaven**
Lytham Hall Park, Blackpool Road, Ansdell, Lytham-St-Annes, Lancs, FY8 4JU
⌨ nugent@fairhaven-golfclub.co.uk
☎ 01253 736976, Fax 731461, Pro 736976, Sec 736741, Rest/Bar 734787
Course is on the B5261 two miles from Lytham.
Semi links; Open Championship qualifying course.
Pro Brian Plucknett; Founded 1895
Designed by James Braid
18 holes, 6883 yards, S.S.S. 73
⌶ Practice area.
✝ Welcome by arrangement; restrictions at WE.
⌶ WD £35; WE £40.
⌔ Welcome by arrangement.
⦿ Full facilities except Mon; banqueting room.
⌁ Clifton Arms; Grand; Dalmeney; Fearnlea.

7 55 **Fishwick Hall**
Glenluce Drive, Farringdon Park, Preston, Lancs, PR1 5TD
⌕ www.fishwickhallgolfclub.co.uk
⌨ fishwickhallgolfclub@supanet.com
☎ 01772 798300, Fax 704600, Pro 795870, Sec 798300, Rest/Bar 798300
From M6 Junction 31 take A59 past Tickled Trout; Glenluce Drive is first left at top of the hill.
Undulating meadowland/parkland course.
Pro Martin Watson; Founded 1912
18 holes, 6045 yards, S.S.S. 69
✝ Welcome.
⌶ WD £26; WE £31.
⌔ Welcome WD by prior arrangement.
⦿ Full catering facilities.
⌁ Tickled Trout.

7 56 **Fleetwood Golf Club**
Princes Way, Fleetwood, Lancs, FY7 8AF
☎ 01253 873661, Fax 773573, Pro 873661, Sec 773573, Rest/Bar 873114

Off A587 0.5 miles from Fleetwood, follow signs for Fleetwood Freeport. Links course.
Pro S McLaughlin; Founded 1932
Designed by Edwin Steer
18 holes, 6557 yards, S.S.S. 71 Par 72
⚑ Practice area.
† Welcome WD; some restrictions WE.
Ⅰ WD £24; WE £30. Day tickets WD £30; WE £40.
⌀ Welcome by prior arrangement; discounts available for larger groups; from £24.
⦿ Full clubhouse facilities.
⌂ North Euston; New Boston; Briardene.

7 57 Flixton
Church Road, Urmston, Manchester, Lancs, M41 6EP
☎ 0161 7482116, Pro 7467160, Sec 7483456, Rest/Bar 7498834
Course is on the B5213 five miles SW of Manchester.
Parkland course.
Pro Danny Proctor; Founded 1893
9 holes, 6410 yards, S.S.S. 71
† Welcome by prior arrangement; WE only with a member.
Ⅰ WD £16; WE £16.
⌀ Welcome by prior arrangement; packages available; terms on application.
⦿ Clubhouse facilities.

7 58 Formby
Formby Gents Golf Club, Golf Road, Formby, Liverpool, Lancs, L37 1LQ
🖳 www.formbygolfclub.co.uk
🖳 info@formbygolfclub.co.uk
☎ 01704 872164, Fax 833028, Pro 873090
1 mile W of A565 adjacent to Freshfield station.
Championship links course.
Pro Gary Butler; Founded 1884
Designed by Willie Park
18 holes, 6993 yards, S.S.S. 72
⚑ Practice area.
† By prior arrangement only.
Ⅰ WD £75 per round WE £85.
⌀ By prior arrangement only; terms on application.
⦿ Full clubhouse facilities.
⌂ Tree Tops.

7 59 Formby Golf Centre
Moss Side, Formby, Liverpool, Merseyside, L37 0AF
☎ 01704 875952
Just off the Formby by-pass.

Parkland course.
Pro Mike Mawdsley; Founded 1985
9 pitch and putt holes, 1510 yards, S.S.S. 54
⚑ Practice range, 20 bays floodlit, putting green.
† Welcome; pay and play.
Ⅰ WD £3; WE £3 for 18 holes.
⦿ Coffee, tea and light refreshments.
⌂ Club can provide list of local hotels.

7 60 Formby Hall
Southport Old Road, Formby, Liverpool, Merseyside, L37 0AB
☎ 01704 875699, Fax 832134, Pro 875699, Sec 875699, Rest/Bar 875699
Off Formby by-pass opposite Woodvale Aerodrome.
Parkland course with 11 lakes.
Pro David Lloyd; Founded 1996
Designed by PSA/Alex Higgins
18 holes, 6731 yards, S.S.S. 72
⚑ Practice range, 31 bays floodlit; academy.
† Welcome WD; restrictions at WE.
Ⅰ WD £35; WE £40.
⌀ Welcome by prior arrangement; corporate days available; from £40.
⦿ 5 bars and 2 restaurants open from 7.30am-11pm.
⌂ Treetops; many B&B's can be recommended.

7 61 Formby Ladies
Golf Road, Formby, Liverpool, Merseyside, L37 1YH
☎ 01704 873493, Fax 873493, Pro 873090, Rest/Bar 874127
Course is off the A565 five miles S of Southport.
Seaside links course.
Pro Gary Butler; Founded 1896
18 holes, 5374 yards, S.S.S. 71
† Welcome by arrangement.
Ⅰ WD £35; WE £40.
⌀ Welcome by arrangement; full golf and catering available; terms on application.
⦿ Bar snacks available.
⌂ Treetops; selection in Southport.

7 62 Furness
Furness Golf Club, Central Drive, Walney Island, Barrow-In-Furness, Cumbria, LA14 3LN
☎ 01229 471232
Off A590 to Walney Island; 0.5 miles after end of bridge.
Seaside links course.
Pro Andrew Whitehall; Founded 1872
18 holes, 6363 yards, S.S.S. 71
† Welcome by prior arrangement;

some restrictions apply on Wed and WE.
Ⅰ WD £20; WE £25.
⌀ Welcome by prior arrangement; must be members of recognised golf clubs; discounts for groups of more than 10; from £17.
⦿ Clubhouse facilities.
⌂ White House; Infield GH.

7 63 Gathurst
Miles Lane, Shevington, Wigan, Lancs, WN6 8EW
🖳 gathurst.golfclub@genie.co.uk
☎ 01257 255235, Fax 255953, Pro 255882, Rest/Bar 252861
1 mile S of M6 Junction 27.
Parkland course.
Pro D Clarke; Founded 1913
Designed by N Pearson
18 holes, 6016 yards, S.S.S. 69
⚑ Practice area.
† Welcome WD except Wed; WE with member.
Ⅰ WD £24.
⌀ Welcome WD except Wed; 27 holes, full day's catering; from £33.
⦿ Bar and restaurant facilities available.
⌂ Almond Brook Moathouse (offers reductions for club visitors).

7 64 Ghyll
Ghyll Brow, Barnoldswick, Lancs, BB18 6JQ
☎ 01282 842466
A56 to Thornton-in-Craven turn left on B6252; 1 mile on left opposite Rolls Royce factory.
Scenic parkland course.
Founded 1907
9/11 holes, 5770 yards, S.S.S. 67
† Welcome except Tues am; Fri after 4.30 or Sun.
Ⅰ Prices on application.
⌀ Welcome as with visitors; reductions for parties of more than 8; from £14.
⦿ Bar catering by arrangement.
⌂ Stirk House, Gisburn; Tempest, Elslack.

7 65 Grange Fell
Grange Fell Road, Grange-over-Sands, Cumbria, LA11 6HB
☎ 01539 532536, Sec 532021
From Junction 36 of the M6 follow the signs to Barrow until Grange turn-off; through the town in direction of Cartmel Hillside.
Parkland course.
Founded 1952

FORMBY

While the 'big game' hunters flock to Lancashire to play Birkdale and Lytham, Formby offers discerning golfers a welcome and challenging surprise.

Quietly tucked away within the residential calm of one of Merseyside's more affluent areas, the course opens with a long, sharp shock.

Those who have knocked a ball around here for a few years tell visitors that the hardest hole is invariably the first – chiefly because of the absence of a practice range at the club. Visitors stroll out of the glowing shelter of the stately clubhouse and straight onto the first tee where the prevailing wind sweeps across them, from left to right, towards a line of firs and the coastal railway. Allow your tee shot to drift into trouble on the right and you will turn back to the member's bar to see the sages shake their heads knowingly at your undoing.

Willie Park designed the course in 1884 to wind its way from the first – with frequent changes of direction – out to the coastline of the Irish Sea.

Too far, as it happens: in 1972 it was adjudged that, owing to the proximity of the seventh, eighth and ninth to the shore, the holes were being eroded and had to be redesigned. The replacements that cut back inland, and are flanked by pine trees, are yet to meet with universal approval from the members, particularly as the changes also affected the tenth, once renowned for being the region's best par three.

The woodland of Formby is startlingly unusual in the context of links golf and makes the course all the more deceptive. On the back nine some of this protection disappears and you are left in no doubt that reaching the twelfth and fifteenth in regulation will be a challenge if the wind is up. James Braid redesigned holes 15-18 in 1922 to add extra length, but it seems unlikely that any more will be put on them now. It would almost be cruel.

Unsurprisingly, therefore, it is the fourth, one of the shorter par fours, that remains one of the most popular holes with members and visitors alike. It is just over 300 yards, but, as ever, the drive must be spot on if one is to have a decent chance of making par. Owing to the strategically placed sand-traps and natural lie of the land, the approach is one of the most demanding shots of the day, even from the middle of the fairway, and can be played with anything from a 3-wood to a 9-iron depending on the wind. But it is also one of the most satisfying to hit well.

The pine trees also serve to cut golfers off completely from the other course built on this land: the Ladies. The Ladies Club, formed two years after the Men's, is independent of it. It is the only course in the UK that is owned and run by women. The ethos at Formby is not 'segregation', but 'self-determination' and both clubs seem more than happy with an arrangement that has stood for over a century. The clubs' separate lives, however, do not entail that the twain shall never meet and the two co-hosted the 1998 Junior Open and will also host the 2004 Curtis Cup.

After your round one more surprise awaits within the clubhouse: 'Hippo'.

A hippopotamus head is mounted on a wall in the bar. It was shot at the turn of the century by a former member, Mr ME Storey, and its presence remains as a reminder that, when you visit this golf club, you will always get something a bit different. — **Jim Bruce-Ball**

9 holes, 5278 yards, S.S.S. 66
♦ Welcome.
▯ WD £12; WE £17.
⚲ None.
▭ Netherwood; Grange, both in Grange-over-Sands; Aynsome, Cartmel.

7 66 Grange Park
Prescot Road, St Helens, Merseyside, WA10 3AD
▯ www.uk.golfer.org
▭ gpgc@ic24.net
☎ 01744 26318, Fax 26318, Pro 28785, Rest/Bar 22980
M62 Junction 7.
Heathland course.
Pro Paul Roberts; Founded 1891
18 holes, 6422 yards, S.S.S. 71
♦ Welcome WD except Tues; restrictions at WE.
▯ WD £26 WE £33.00.
⚲ Welcome WD except Tues; packages including all-day food and up to 36 holes of golf available; from £39.00.
▯◉▮ Full clubhouse facilities.
▭ Hilton; Haydock Thistle; Haydock Moathouse; St Helens.

7 67 Grange-over-Sands
Meathop Road, Grange-over-Sands, Cumbria, LA11 6QX
☎ 015395 33180, Fax 33754, Pro 35937, Sec 33754, Rest/Bar 33810
Off A590 course is located just before entering town just as you get to 30mph sign.
Parkland course.
Pro Andrew Pickering; Founded 1919
Designed by A MacKenzie
18 holes, 5958 yards, S.S.S. 69
▮ Practice area.
♦ Welcome with handicap certs.
▯ WD £20, £25 for the day; WE £25, £30 for the day.
⚲ Welcome by appointment; packages available; prices on application.
▯◉▮ Full clubhouse facilities.
▭ Grange Hotel; Graythwaite Manor; Clare House.

7 68 Great Harwood
Harwood Bar, Whalley Road, Great Harwood, Blackburn, Lancs, BB6 7TE
☎ 01254 884391
Easy access from Clitheroe by-pass.
Parkland course.
Founded 1896
9 holes, 6456 yards for 18 holes, S.S.S. 71
♦ Welcome WD; restrictions at WE.

▯ WD £16; WE £22.
⚲ Welcome by prior arrangement, catering packages can be arranged; snooker; prices on application.
▯◉▮ Clubhouse facilities.
▭ Dunkenhalgh, Clayton-le-Moors.

7 69 Great Lever & Farnworth
Off Plodder Lane, Farnworth, Bolton, Lancs, BL4 0LQ
☎ 01204 656137, Fax 652780, Pro 656650, Rest/Bar 656493
From M61 Junction 4 take Watergate Lane to Plodder Lane.
Parkland course.
Pro Tony Howarth; Founded 1917
18 holes, 6064 yards, S.S.S. 69
▮ Practice area.
♦ Welcome WD with handicap certs; restrictions at WE.
▯ WD £16.50; WE £27.
⚲ Welcome WD by arrangement; full day packages available for golf and catering except Mon; £29.50.
▯◉▮ Full facilities except Mon.

7 70 Green Haworth
Green Haworth, Accrington, Lancs, BB5 3SL
▯ www.GreenHaworth.freeserve.co.uk
▭ Golf@greenhaworth.freeserve.co.uk
☎ 01254 237580, Sec 382510
From Accrington town centre take main road to Blackburn; turn left on Willows Lane; follow road for 2-3 miles; signposted after Red Lion Hotel.
Moorland course.
Founded 1914
9 holes, 5556 yards, S.S.S. 68
♦ Welcome WD; some restrictions apply on Wed; Sat by prior arrangement.
▯ WD £15; Sat £20.
⚲ Allow societies on the course by prior arrangement.
▯◉▮ Full facilities; restaurant can be pre-booked.

7 71 Greenmount
Greenhalgh Fold Farm, Greenmount, Bury, Lancs, BL8 4LH
☎ 01204 883712, Pro 888616
Leave M66 at Bury follow signs to Tottington, once in Tott. centre, turn right at Carmelios, 1st left.
Undulating parkland course.
Pro Jason Seed; Founded 1920
9 holes, 4980 yards, S.S.S. 64
♦ Welcome WD; with member at WE, Tues ladies day.

▯ Prices on application.
⚲ Welcome WD except Tues by prior arrangement.
▯◉▮ Full service except Mon; function suite available.
▭ Red Hall; Old Mill; Red Lion, Victoria.

7 72 Haigh Hall
Haigh Country Park, Aspull, Wigan, Lancs, WN2 1PE
☎ 01942 833337, Fax 831081, Pro 831107, Sec 01942 833337
Take Junction 27 off the M6 and the B5239 to Standish; course is six miles NE of Wigan.
Municipal parkland course.
Pro Ian Lee; Founded 1973
18 and a 9-hole course, 6500 yards, S.S.S. 71
▮ 6.
♦ Welcome any time by arrangement; telephone bookings via professional.
▯ Prices on application.
⚲ Welcome with prior arrangement with the professional.
▯◉▮ Full restaurant and cafe service.
▭ Brocket; Oak; Almond Brook; Moathouse.

7 73 Harwood
Springfield, Roading Brook Road, Bolton, Lancs, BL2 4JD
☎ 01204 522878, Fax 524233, Pro 362834, Sec 524233
4 miles NE of Bolton.
Parkland course extended to 18 holes.
Pro Paul Slater; Founded 1926/1998
Designed by Whole New Concept
18 holes, 5851 yards, S.S.S. 69
▮ Practice area.
♦ Welcome WD; with member at WE.
▯ WD/WE £20.
⚲ Welcome by arrangement; terms on application.
▯◉▮ Clubhouse facilities.
▭ Last Drop, Bromley Cross; The Bolholt Hotel & Conference Leisure Centre.

7 74 Haydock Park
Haydock Park Golf Club Co Ltd, Newton Lane, Newton Le Willows, Merseyside, WA12 0HX
☎ 01925 224389, Fax 228525, Pro 226944, Sec 228525, Rest/Bar 291020
1 mile E of the M6 off A580.
Parkland course.
Pro Peter Kenwright; Founded 1877
18 holes, 6058 yards, S.S.S. 69
▮ Practice area, putting green.

† Welcome WD except Tues.
Ⅰ WD £28.
♪ Welcome WD except Mon and
Tues; from £42.
⦿ Full clubhouse facilities.
↝ Kirkfiled; Post House; Thistle.

7 75 Heaton Park ℃
Middleton Road, Heaton Park,
Prestwich, Manchester, Lancs, M25
2SW
☎ 0161 6549899, Fax 6532003
M60 Junction 19.
Undulating parkland course.
Pro Karl Morris/Gary Durmott;
Founded 1912
Designed by JH Taylor
18 holes, 5755 yards, S.S.S. 68
Ⅰ Driving range, par 3 course, golf
academy.
† Welcome; pre book all tee times.
Ⅰ WD £10; WE £12.50; special
twilight rates.
♪ Welcome by prior arrangement.
⦿ Bar and catering in cafe.
↝ Heaton Park Hotel.

7 76 Hesketh
Cockle Dick's Lane, off Cambridge
Road, Southport, Merseyside, PR9
9QQ
⸿ www.ukgolfer.org
✉ secretary@
heskethgolf.freeserve.co.uk
☎ 01704 536897, Fax 539250, Pro
530050, Rest/Bar 530226/531055
Course is on the A565 one mile N of
Southport.
Seaside links course with some
parkland.
Pro John Donoghue; Founded 1885
Designed by JOF Morris
18 holes, 6522 yards, S.S.S. 72
† Welcome by prior arrangement.
Ⅰ WD £40-£50; WE £50.
♪ Welcome by prior arrangement;
inclusive packages for catering and
golf available for groups of 12 or more;
from £50.
⦿ Bar and dining facilities.
↝ Prince of Wales; Scarisbrick.

7 77 The Heysham ℃
Trumacar, Park Middleton Road,
Middleton, Morecambe, Lancs, LA3
3JH
☎ 01524 852000, Fax 853030, Sec
851011, Rest/Bar 859154
Off A683 5 miles from M6 Junction 34.
Parkland course with wooded areas.
Pro Ryan Done; Founded 1929
Designed by Alec Herd

18 holes, 6258 yards, S.S.S. 70
Ⅰ 8-bay range; practice areas.
† Welcome with handicap certs.
Ⅰ Prices on application.
♪ Welcome by arrangement with
Sec; discounts for groups of 12 or
more; from £22.
⦿ Full clubhouse facilities.
↝ Strathmore, Morecambe.

7 78 Hillside Golf Club
Hastings Road, Southport, Merseyside,
PR8 2LU
⸿ www.ukgolfer.org
✉ hillside@ukgolfer.org
☎ 01704 567169, Fax 563192, Pro
568360, Rest/Bar 568682
Course is on the A565 three miles S of
Stockport.
Outstanding championship links course.
Pro B Seddon; Founded 1911/1923
Designed by Fred Hawtree
18 holes, 6850 yards, S.S.S. 74
Ⅰ Practice ground.
† Restricted WD, no visitors Sat or
BH; contact Sec.
Ⅰ WD £55-£70; Sun £70 (one round
only).
♪ Restricted; contact Sec; special
approval needed for groups of more
than 24; terms on application.
⦿ Full bar and restaurant seating 100
↝ Scarisbrick; Prince of Wales;
Metropole.

7 79 Hindley Hall
Hall Lane, Hindley, Wigan, Lancs,
WN2 2SQ
☎ 01942 255131, Fax 253871, Pro
255991
Off A6 from M61 Junction 6 then take
Dicconson Lane; after 1 mile into Hall
Lane; club just after lake.
Moorland course.
Pro Neil Brazell; Founded 1895
18 holes, 5913 yards, S.S.S. 68
Ⅰ Practice area.
† Welcome if member of a club;
check with Sec in advance.
Ⅰ WD £20; WE £27.
♪ Welcome by prior arrangement;
terms on application.
⦿ Clubhouse facilities.
↝ Georgian House.

7 80 Horwich
Victoria Road, Horwich, Bolton, Lancs,
BL6 5PH
☎ 01204 696980
Close to M61 Junction 6.
Parkland course.
Founded 1895

9 holes, 5286 yards, S.S.S. 67
† Welcome with member or by prior
arrangement with Sec..
Ⅰ Terms on application.
♪ Welcome WD and occasional Sun
by prior arrangement.
⦿ Full bar and catering facilities.
↝ Swallowfield; Holiday Inn Express
The Devire Whites Hotel.

7 81 Houghwood
Billinge Hill, Crank Road, St Helens,
Merseyside, WA11 8RL
☎ 01744 894754, Fax 894754, Pro
894444
From M6 Junction 26 follow signs to
Billinge; course 1 mile from Billinge
Hospital.
Parkland course with USGA standard
greens.
Pro Paul Dickenson; Founded 1996
Designed by N Pearson
18 holes, 6202 yards, S.S.S. 70
Ⅰ Practice area; new snooker room;
indoor golf simulator for all-year use.
† Welcome.
Ⅰ WD £17.50; WE £25; Deals
available.
♪ Welcome by arrangement; from
£17-£30.
⦿ Bar and restaurant facilities.
↝ Post House, Haydock; Stakis, St
Helens.

7 82 Hurlston Hall ℃
Hurlston Lane, Moorfield Lane,
Scarisbrick, Ormskirk, Lancs, L40 8JD
⸿ www.hurlstonhall.co.uk
☎ 01704 840400, Fax 841404, Pro
841120, Sec 840400, Rest/Bar 840400
On A570 8 miles from M58 6 miles
from Southport and 2 miles from
Ormskirk.
Parkland course with two brooks.
Pro John Esclapez; Founded 1994
Designed by Donald Steel
18 holes, 6746 yards, S.S.S. 72
Ⅰ Practice range, 18 bays floodlit, 2
teaching bays.
† Welcome by prior arrangement;
handicap certs may be required.
Ⅰ Summer WD £27.50, WE £33;
Winter WD £21, WE £26.
♪ Registered golf societies welcome
by prior arrangement with club office;
packages including 36 holes, catering
and gourmet dinner can be arranged;
satellite TV; golf academy; terms on
application.
⦿ Full catering facilities available with
70-seat restaurant; balcony and patio.
↝ Beaufort Hotel; Scarisbrick; Prince
of Wales.

7 83 Huyton & Prescot
Hurst Park, Huyton Lane, Huyton,
Liverpool, Merseyside, L36 1UA
☎ 0151 4893948, Fax 4893948,
Pro 4892022, Sec 4893948,
Rest/Bar 4891138
Course is 10 miles from Liverpool just
off the M57.
Parkland course.
Pro John Fisher; Founded 1905
18 holes, 5839 yards, S.S.S. 68
♦ Practice bay.
♦ Welcome WD; WE with member
£13.
↳ WD £24.
⌒ By arrangement WD.
◉ Full facilities.
↳ Derby Lodge; Hillcrest; Bell Tower.

7 84 Ingol Golf Club　☞
Tanterton Hall Road, Ingol, Preston,
Lancs, PR2 7BY
⌂ www.golfers.net
▤ ingolfclub@btconnect.com
☎ 01772 734556, Fax 729815, Pro
769646
Leave M6 Junction 32 and turn
towards Preston; follow signs for Ingol.
Parkland course.
Pro Ryan Grimshaw; Founded 1980
Designed by Cotton, Pennink, Lawrie &
Partners
18 holes, 6294 yards, S.S.S. 70
♦ Practice grounds.
♦ Welcome.
↳ Winter WD £15, WE £20; Summer
WD £20, WE £25.
⌒ Welcome by arrangement but not
before 1.30pm on Sun; from £18-39.
◉ Full facilities; bar and function
rooms.
↳ Marriott Broughton Park; Barton
Grange.

7 85 Kendal　☞
The Heights, High Tenterfell, Kendal,
Cumbria, LA9 4PQ
☎ 01539 723499, Fax 733708, Sec
733708, Rest/Bar 736466
To Kendal on A6 signposted in town.
Moorland course; redesigned in late
1998.
Pro Peter Scott; Founded 1891
18 holes, 5800 yards, S.S.S. 68
♦ Welcome any time except Sat
competition days; by prior arrangement
WE.
↳ WD £22; WE £27.50.
⌒ Welcome anytime subject to
availability and by prior arrangement;
from £27.
◉ Full facilities except Mon.
↳ County; Woolpack.

7 86 Keswick　☞
Threlkeld Hall, Threlkeld, Keswick,
Cumbria, CA12 4SX
⌂ www. Keswickgolfclub.com
☎ 017687 79010, Sec 79324,
Rest/Bar 79013
Course is off the A66 four miles E of
Keswick.
Moorland/parkland course.
Pro Garry Watson; Founded 1975
Designed by Eric Brown
18 holes, 6225 yards, S.S.S. 72
♦ Welcome, even most WE.
↳ WD £20; WE £25.
⌒ Welcome by prior arrangement
with Sec; some WE available;
packages for 12 or more; prices on
application.
◉ Bar and dining facilities.
↳ The Horse and Farrier; Lodore
Swiss; Keswick; Borrowdale;
Wordsworth; Middle Ruddings.

7 87 Kirkby Lonsdale　☞
Scalebar Lane, Barbon, Carnforth,
Lancs, LA6 2LJ
⌂ www.klgolf.dial.pipex.com
▤ kl.golf@dial.pipex.com
☎ 015242 76365, Fax 76503, Pro
76366, Rest/Bar 76367
On A683 Sedbergh Road 3 miles from
Kirkby Lonsdale.
Parkland course.
Pro Chris Barrett; Founded 1991
Designed by Bill Squires
18 holes, 6481 yards, S.S.S. 71
♦ Practice ground.
♦ Welcome.
↳ WD £25; WE £30.
⌒ Welcome by arrangement
◉ Clubhouse facilities.
↳ Whoop Hall, Cowan Bridge;
Pheasant, Casterton.

7 88 Knott End
Wyreside, Knott End-on-Sea, Poulton,
Lancs, FY6 0AA
▤ knottendgolfclub.co.uk.
☎ 01253 810576, Fax 813446
A588 to Knott End.
Links course.
Pro Paul Walker; Founded 1911
Designed by James Braid
18 holes, 5843 yards, S.S.S. 68
♦ Practice ground and net.
♦ Welcome WD not before 9.30am
or between 12.30pm-1.30pm.
↳ WD £22; WE £25.
⌒ Welcome by prior arrangement;
terms on application
◉ Full facilities.
↳ Bourne Arms; Springfield House
Hotel.

7 89 Lancaster
Ashton Hall, Ashton-with- Stodday,
Lancaster, Lancs, LA2 0AJ
⌂ www.lancastergc.co.uk
▤ sec@lancastergc.co.uk
☎ 01524 751247, Fax 752742, Pro
751802, Rest/Bar 751105
On A588 2 miles S of Lancaster.
Parkland course.
Pro David Sutcliffe; Founded 1933
Designed by James Braid
18 holes, 6500 yards, S.S.S. 71
♦ Welcome by prior arrangement
with handicap certs.
↳ WD £32; WE £32.
⌒ Welcome by prior arrangement on
WD; handicap certs required; catering
and golf packages available; from £42.
◉ Full clubhouse facilities.
↳ Dormy House with accommodation
for 18 on site,11 bedrooms en-suite.

7 90 Lansil
Caton Road, Lancaster, Lancs, LA1
3PE
☎ 01524 39269, Sec 39269,
Rest/Bar 39269
Junction 34 off M6 head to Lancaster
A683 2nd left turn after Holiday inn.
Parkland/meadowland course.
Founded 1947
9 holes, 5608 yards, S.S.S. 67
♦ Welcome but not before 1pm Sun.
↳ WD £12; WE £12.
⌒ Welcome WD by arrangement;
catering packages organised with
steward.
◉ Meals and bar snacks available.
↳ Holiday Inn & Lancaster Town
House.

7 91 Lee Park
Childwall Valley Road, Liverpool,
Merseyside, L27 3YA
☎ 0151 4873882, Fax 4984666,
Rest/Bar 4879861
On B5171 off A562 next to Lee Manor
High School.
Parkland course.
Founded 1950
Designed by Frank Pennink
18 holes, 6095 yards, S.S.S. 69
♦ Welcome.
↳ Prices on application.
⌒ Welcome Mon, Thurs and Fri by
prior arrangement with Sec; terms on
application.
◉ Bar snacks and meals.
↳ Gateacre Hall.

7 92 Leigh Golf Club
Broseley Lane, Culcheth, Warrington,

Cheshire, WA3 4BG
🌐 www.leighgolf.co.uk
☎ 01925 763130, Fax 765097, Pro 762013, Sec 762943, Rest/Bar 763130
Off B5217 in Culcheth village.
Parkland course.
Pro Andrew Baguley; Founded 1906
Designed by James Braid
18 holes, 5884 yards, S.S.S. 68
Ⓘ Practice range: 3 practice areas; 2 putting greens.
✝ Welcome with handicap certs or letter of introduction.
Ⓛ WD £30; WE £40.
Ⓓ Welcome Mon, except BH, and Tues; catering packages available; snooker room; from £23.
🍴 Full clubhouse facilities.
🛏 Greyhound, Leigh; Thistle, Haydock.

7 93 Leyland
Wigan Road, Leyland, Lancs, PR25 5UD
☎ 01772 436457, Pro 423425
On A49 0.25 miles from M6 Junction 28.
Meadowland course.
Pro Colin Burgess; Founded 1924
18 holes, 6123 yards, S.S.S. 69
Ⓘ Practice area adjacent to first tee; Brand new clubhouse opens June 2002.
✝ Welcome WD; WE only with a member.
Ⓛ WD £25; WE £25.
Ⓓ Welcome by prior arrangement with Sec; packages available on request.
🍴 Full facilities.
🛏 Jarvis.

7 94 Liverpool Municipal
Ingoe Lane, Liverpool, Merseyside, L32 4SS
☎ 0151 5465435
M57 Junction 6, 300 yards on right of B5192.
Municipal meadowland course.
Pro David Weston; Founded 1966
18 holes, 6706 yards, S.S.S. 72
Ⓘ Practice ground.
✝ Welcome.
Ⓛ WD £7.30; WE £8.30.
Ⓓ Welcome every day; tee booking required 1 week in advance.
🍴 Bar and cafeteria.
🛏 Golden Eagle.

7 95 Lobden
Lobden Moor, Whitworth, Rochdale, Lancs, OL12 8XJ

☎ 01706 343228, Fax 643241, Sec 643241
Take A671 from Rochdale to Whitworth
Moorland course.
Founded 1888
9 holes, 5697 yards, S.S.S. 68
✝ Welcome except Sat.
Ⓛ WD £10; WE £12.
Ⓓ Welcome by prior arrangement; terms on application.
🍴 By arrangement with steward.

7 96 Longridge
Fell Barn, Jeffrey Hill, Longridge, Preston, Lancs, PR3 2TU
☎ 01772 783291, Fax 783022
From M6 Junction 31a follow signs to Longridge.
Moorland course with panoramic views.
Pro Stephen Taylor; Founded 1877
18 holes, 5969 yards, S.S.S. 69
Ⓘ Practice area/pitching area.
✝ Welcome.
Ⓛ Prices on application.
Ⓓ Welcome by written prior arrangement with Sec; summer and winter packages available.
🍴 Full facilities available except Mon.
🛏 Shireburn Arms; Gibbon Bridge; Black Moss GH.

7 97 Lowes Park
Hill Top, Lowes Road, Bury, Lancs, BL9 6SU
☎ 0161 7641231, Fax 7639503, Sec 7639503, Rest/Bar 7641231
On A56 1 mile N of Bury; turn at Bury General Hospital into Lowes Road.
Moorland course.
Founded 1930
9 holes, 6014 yards, S.S.S. 69
Ⓘ Small practice area.
✝ Welcome by prior arrangement.
Ⓛ Prices on application.
Ⓓ Welcome by prior arrangement; package deals available; ladies only on Wed; terms available on application.
🍴 Full clubhouse facilities except Mon.
🛏 Red Hall.

7 98 Lytham Green Drive
Ballam Road, Lytham St Annes, Lancs, FY8 4LE
🌐 www.ukgolfer.com
✉ green@greendrive.fsnet.co.uk
☎ 01253 737390, Fax 731350, Pro 737379, Rest/Bar 376087
1 mile from Lytham centre.
Parkland course.
Pro Andrew Lancaster; Founded 1913
Designed by A Herd

18 holes, 6163 yards, S.S.S. 69
Ⓘ Large practice area.
✝ Welcome WD by prior arrangement.
Ⓛ WD £27-£37.
Ⓓ Welcome WD except Wed; coffee on arrival, soup and sandwiches, 3-course meal, 27 holes of golf; £40.
🍴 Full clubhouse facilities available.
🛏 Clifton Arms, Lytham; Fernlea, St Anne's.

7 99 Manchester
Hopwood Cottage, Rochdale Road, Middleton, Manchester, Lancs, M24 2QP
☎ 0161 6433202, Fax 6432472, Pro 6432638, Sec 6433202, Rest/Bar 6432718/6553073
From A627 (M) take the A664 for Middleton.
Parkland-moorland course.
Pro Brian Connor; Founded 1882
Designed by HS Colt
18 holes, 6519 yards, S.S.S. 72
Ⓘ Practice area and driving range available to members, guests and visitors only.
✝ Welcome by arrangement.
Ⓛ WD £30; WE £45.
Ⓓ Welcome by prior arrangement; packages of golf and catering available on application; £40-£47.
🍴 Full clubhouse facilities.
🛏 Norton Grange; Royal Toby.

7 100 Manor
Moss Lane, Kearsley, Bolton, Lancs, BL4 8SF
✉ manorsports@
netscapeonline.co.uk
☎ 01204 701027, Fax 796914
1 mile from M62 Junction 17.
Parkland course.
Founded 1995
18 holes, 4914 yards, S.S.S. 66
Ⓘ Driving range next door.
✝ Welcome; pay and play.
Ⓛ WD £8; WE £10.
Ⓓ Welcome by arrangement.
🍴 Bar and restaurant; function suites.
🛏 Clifton Park Country House.

7 101 Marland Park
Springfield Park, Rochdale, Lancs, OL11 4RE
🌐 www. Appleonline.net/dwillspga
☎ 01706 649801, Pro 649801
3 miles from M62.
Parkland course.
Pro David Wills; Founded 1927
18 holes, 5237 yards, S.S.S. 66

† Welcome.
[WD £8; WE £10.
⌂ Welcome by prior arrangement with the Professional; WE booking in advance, WD pay and play.
|●| None.
⌐ Midway, Rochdale.

7 102 Marsden Park

Town House Road, Nelson, Lancs, BB9 8DG
☎ 01282 661912, Rest/Bar 661915
From M65 Junction 13 and take B5446 on to Leeds Road and right at second roundabout.
Parkland course.
Pro Martin Ross; Founded 1968/1976
Designed by CK Cotton & Partners
18 holes, 5669 yards, S.S.S. 68
[Practice area.
† Pay and play.
[WD Adults £9.50, OAPs £5.50, juniors £2.50; WE peak (7.30am-2pm) £12.50; off-peak (2pm-dusk) £10.50; special 9-hole ticket (twilight hours only) £8.50.
⌂ Welcome by prior arrangement; golf and catering packages available on application; from £15.
|●| Catering facilities.
⌐ The Oaks, Burnley; Great Marsden, Nelson.

7 103 Maryport

Bank End, Maryport, Cumbria, CA15 6PA
☎ 01900 812605, Fax 815626, Sec 815626, Rest/Bar 812605
N of Maryport turn left off A596 on to the B5300 (Silloth Road).
Seaside links course.
Founded 1905
18 holes, 6088 yards, S.S.S. 69
[Practice area.
† Welcome.
[WD £17; WE £22 summer. Winter fees are WD £11 WE £16.
⌂ Welcome by prior arrangement; discounts available for groups of nine or more.
|●| Full clubhouse facilities.
⌐ Ellenbank; Skimberness Hotel.

7 104 Morecambe

Marine Road East, Morecambe, Lancs, LA4 6AJ
☎ 01524 412841, Fax 412841, Pro 415596, Sec 412841, Rest/Bar 418050
On road to Morecambe from A6.
Parkland/links course; superb views over Morcombe Bay; no par fives.
Pro Simon Fletcher; Founded 1922

Designed by Dr Clegg
18 holes, 5770 yards, S.S.S. 67
† Welcome by arrangement.
[Prices on application.
⌂ Welcome by prior arrangement; terms on application.
|●| Full clubhouse facilities.
⌐ The Strathmore; The Elm.

7 105 Mossack Hall

Liverpool Road, Bickerstaffe, Ormskirk, Lancs, L39 0EE
☎ 01695 421717, Fax 424961, Pro 424969
From M58 Junction 3 take first left to Stanley Gate Pub; turn left and follow road for 2 miles; club on right.
Meadowland course.
Pro Liam Kelly; Founded 1996
Designed by Steve Marnoch
18 holes, 6375 yards, S.S.S. 70
† Welcome by prior arrangement with professional.
[WD £25; WE £30.
⌂ Welcome by prior arrangement with golf course manager.
|●| Full catering facilities including restaurant; catering for private functions.

7 106 Mount Murray Hotel and CC ☞

Santon, Ballacutchel Road. Mount Murray, Douglas, Isle of Man, IM4 2HT
⌂ www.mountmurray.com
■ hotel@enterprise.net
☎ 01624 661111, Fax 611116, Pro 695308, Sec 695308, Rest/Bar 6611111
On the Castletown road 2 miles from Douglas.
Parkland course.
Pro Andrew Dyson; Founded 1994
Designed by Bingley Sports Turf Research
18 holes, 6715 yards, S.S.S. 73
[Chipping area, 24 bays floodlit, 2 putting greens.
† All Welcome.
[WD £20; WE £26.
⌂ Welcome by prior arrangement; hotel's facilities (gym, etc) tennis courts and squash courts available for use.
|●| Bistro and restaurant facilities available.
⌐ On site Mount Murray Hotel (golf packages available).

7 107 Mytton Fold ☞

Whalley Road, Langho, Blackburn, Lancs, BB6 8AB
⌂ www.myttonfold.co.uk

☎ 01254 245392, Fax 248119, Pro 245392, Rest/Bar 240662
9 miles N of Blackburn off A59.
Parkland course.
Pro Garry Coope; Founded 1994
18 (Championship course) holes, 6217 yards, S.S.S. 70
† Welcome by prior arrangement.
[WD £14; WE £16.
⌂ Welcome by prior arrangement.
|●| Full hotel facilities.
⌐ Mytton Fold.

7 108 Nelson ☞

King's Causeway, Brierfield, Nelson, Lancs, BB9 0EU
☎ 01282 614583, Fax 606226, Pro 617000, Sec 614583, Rest/Bar 614583
On B6248 off A682 at Brierfield from M65 Junction 12.
Moorland course.
Pro Nigel Sumner; Founded 1902
Designed by Dr A MacKenzie
18 holes, 5977 yards, S.S.S. 69
† Welcome.
[WD £26; WE £30.
⌂ Welcome by prior arrangement; catering and golf packages available; from £25.
|●| Full clubhouse facilities available.
⌐ Higher Trapp Country House.

7 109 New North Manchester

Rhodes House, Manchester Old Road, Middleton, Manchester, Lancs, M24 4PE
■ sectretary@nmgc.co.uk
☎ 0161 6439033, Fax 6437775, Pro 6437094, Sec 6439033, Rest/Bar 6432941
0.25 mile from Junction 19 off M60.
Moorland/parkland course.
Pro Jason Peel; Founded 1894
Designed by H Braid
18 holes, 6542 yards, S.S.S. 72
[Small practice area.
† Welcome WD; by arrangement WE through course pro.
[WE £25; WE £30.
⌂ Welcome WD except Thurs; terms on application.
|●| Full catering and bar service.
⌐ Bower, Oldham; Birch, Heywood.

7 110 Oldham

Lees New Road, Oldham, Lancs, OL4 5PN
☎ 0161 624498, Pro 6268346, Sec 624498, Rest/Bar 6244986
Off A669 turning right at Lees.
Moorland/parkland course.
Pro David Green; Founded 1891

18 holes, 5122 yards, S.S.S. 65
† Welcome by prior arrangement.
Ⲓ WD £18; £10 with member; WE and BH £24; £13 with member.
⚑ Welcome by arrangement; packages for all day golf and catering; terms on application.
⬤ Full facilities.
⚐ Many hotels in 2-mile radius.

7 111 Ormskirk
Cranes Lane, Lathom, Ormskirk, Lancs, L40 5UJ
☎ 01695 572112, Fax 572227, Pro 572074, Sec 572227, Rest/Bar 572112/5722781
2 miles E of Ormskirk.
Parkland course.
Pro Jack Hammond; Founded 1899
18 holes, 6480 yards, S.S.S. 71
† Welcome.
Ⲓ WD £35; WE & Wed £40.
⚑ Welcome by prior arrangement; terms on application.
⬤ Full facilities.
⚐ Briars Hall.

7 112 Peel
Rheast Lane, Peel, Isle Of Man, IM5 1BG
☎ 01624 843456, Fax 843456, Pro 844232, Sec 843456, Rest/Bar 842227
On A1 signposted on outskirts of Peel.
Moorland course.
Pro Murray Crowe; Founded 1895
Designed by A Herd
18 holes, 5874 yards, S.S.S. 69
† Welcome WD; WE by arrangement. Also available practice ground and putting green.
Ⲓ WD £18; WE & Bank Holidays £25
⚑ Welcome on application to Sec; packages on request.
⬤ Meals and snacks to order; bar.
⚐ Stakis, Douglas.

7 113 Pennington
St Helens Road, Leigh, Lancs, WN7 3PA
☎ 01942 682852, Fax 682852, Pro 682852
Off A572 to S of Leigh.
Parkland course with ponds and streams.
Pro Tim Kershaw; Founded 1975
9 holes, 2895 yards, S.S.S. 34
† Welcome.
Ⲓ WD £3.50; WE £4.60.
⚑ Welcome by prior arrangement.
⬤ Snack bar.
⚐ Thistle, Haydock.

7 114 Penrith
Salkeld Road, Maidenhill, Penrith, Cumbria, CA11 8SG
☎ 01768 891919, Fax 891919, Rest/Bar 865429
From Junction 41 on the M6 follow the signs for Penrith and turn left when entering town.
Parkland course.
Pro Garry Key; Founded 1890
18 holes, 6047 yards, S.S.S. 69
Ⲓ 8 bays.
† Welcome by arrangement.
Ⲓ WD £20; WE £25.
⚑ Welcome by prior arrangement with Sec; golf and catering packages available; terms on application.
⬤ Clubhouse facilities.
⚐ George, Penrith.

7 115 Penwortham
Blundell Lane, Penwortham, Preston, Lancs, PR1 0AX
⚑ www.penwortham-ukgolfer.org
✉ penworthamgolfclub@supernet.com
☎ 01772 744630, Fax 740172, Pro 742345, Sec 744630, Rest/Bar 743207
Off A59 1.5 miles W of Preston.
Parkland course.
Pro Steve Holden; Founded 1908
18 holes, 6056 yards, S.S.S. 69
Ⲓ Practice area.
† Welcome WD except Tues and WE.
Ⲓ WD £25 for a round and £30 for the day; WE £33.
⚑ Welcome WD except Tues by prior arrangement; tee available between 10am-12.30pm and after 2pm; golf and catering packages available; from £41.
⬤ Full clubhouse facilities.
⚐ Carleton; Forte Posthouse, both Preston.

7 116 Pike Fold
Hills Lane, Unsworth, Bury, Manchester, BL9 8QP
☎ 0161 7663561, Fax 7963569, Pro 7663561, Rest/Bar 7667653
4 miles N of Manchester off Rochdale Road.
Undulating meadowland course.
Pro Andrew Cory; Founded 1909
9 holes, 6307 yards, S.S.S. 72
Ⲓ Practice green.
† Welcome Mon-Sat; members only Sun.
Ⲓ Mon-Sat £20.
⚑ Welcome by appointment; catering packages by arrangement with

Manager.
⬤ Full facilities by prior arrangement.
⚐ Villiage Hotel.

7 117 Pleasington
Pleasington Lane, Pleasington, Blackburn, Lancs, BB2 5JF
☎ 01254 202177, Fax 201028, Pro 201630, Sec 202177, Rest/Bar 207346
3 miles SW of Blackburn; from A674 turn north on to road signposted Pleasington Station.
Undulating heathland/parkland course.
Pro GJ Furey; Founded 1891
18 holes, 6423 yards, S.S.S. 71
† Welcome by prior arrangement Mon, Wed, Fri and WE.
Ⲓ WD £36, WE £40.
⚑ Welcome Mon, Wed, Fri; some discounts and packages available; £40
⬤ Full clubhouse facilities.
⚐ The Millstone Hotel, Mellor, Blackburn.

7 118 Port St Mary Golf Pavilion
Kallow Point Road, Port St Mary, Isle Of Man, IM9 5EJ
☎ 01624 834932
Just outside Port St Mary; course signposted.
Public seaside links course.
Pro Murray Crowe; Founded 1936
Designed by George Duncan
9 holes, 5418 yards, S.S.S. 66
Ⲓ Practice green.
† Welcome but not before 10.30am at WE.
Ⲓ WD £13.50; WE £14.
⚑ Welcome by arrangement; discounts for 10 or more players.
⬤ Bar, cafe and restaurant.
⚐ Port Erin; Bay View.

7 119 Poulton-le-Fylde
Myrtle Farm, Breck Road, Poulton-le-Fylde, Lancs, FY6 7HJ
☎ 01253 892444, Fax 892444, Sec 893150
0.5 miles N of Poulton town centre.
Municipal meadowland course.
Pro Lewis Ware; Founded 1974
9 holes, 6056 yards, S.S.S. 70
Ⲓ Practice range, indoor two-bay range; tuition available.
† Welcome.
Ⲓ WD £11; WE £13.
⚑ Welcome by prior arrangement; packages available.
⬤ Bar and catering facilities.
⚐ Singleton Lodge.

METROPOLE HOTEL, SOUTHPORT

Portland Street, Southport PR8 1LL   Tel: (01704) 536836   Fax: (01704) 549041
Web: *www.btinternet.com/~metropole.southport*   Email: *metropole.southport@btinternet.com*

RAC/AA 2-star hotel. Centrally situated and close to Royal Birkdale and 5 other championship courses. Fully licensed with late bar facilities for residents. Full sized snooker table. Proprietors will assist with tee reservations.

---

7 120 Preston
Fulwood Hall Lane, Fulwood, Preston, Lancs, PR2 8DD
☎ 01772 700011, Fax 794234, Pro 700022, Rest/Bar 700436
From M6 Junction 32 turn towards Preston and after 1.5 miles into Watling St Rd and then into Fulwood Hall Road.
Parkland course.
Pro Andrew Greenbank; Founded 1892
Designed by James Braid
18 holes, 6312 yards, S.S.S. 71
† Welcome WD; some restrictions Tues but only as a guest of member WE.
[WD £27-£32.
⌂ Welcome WD except Tues; golf and catering packages can be arranged; parties of more than 48 by special arrangement only; from £27.
🍽 Bar and restaurant facilities.
↩ Broughton Marriott; Barton Grange.

7 121 Prestwich
Hilton Lane, Prestwich, Manchester, Lancs, M25 9XB
☎ 0161 7732544, Fax 7731404, Pro 7731404, Rest/Bar 7732544
On A6044 1 mile from Junction with A56.
Parkland course.
Pro Simon Wakefield; Founded 1908
18 holes, 4806 yards, S.S.S. 63
▮ Practice green.
† Welcome WD if carrying handicap certs.
[WD £20.
⌂ Welcome on WD by prior arrangement with professional; 27-hole golf and catering packages available; from £29.95.
🍽 Full clubhouse facilities.
↩ Village Hotel.

7 122 Ramsey
Golf Professionals Shop, Ramsey Golf Club Brookfield Avenue, Ramsey, Isle Of Man, IM8 2AH
✉ ramseypro@iofm.net
☎ 01624 814736, Fax 814736, Pro 814736, Sec 812244, Rest/Bar 813365
12 miles N of Douglas; 5 mins from

town centre.
Parkland course.
Pro Calum Wilson; Founded 1890
Designed by James Braid
18 holes, 5960 yards, S.S.S. 69
▮ Practice area.
† Welcome; please telephone in advance.
[WD £22; WE £25.
⌂ Welcome by arrangement.
🍽 Lunches and full facilities available.
↩ Grand Island.

7 123 Reach
De Vere Hotel, East Park Drive, Blackpool, Lancs, FY3 8LL
✉ db.golfshop@deverehotels.com
☎ 01253 766156, Fax 798800, Pro 766156, Sec 766156, Rest/Bar 838866
From M55 Junction 4, follow signs for Blackpool on A583; at fourth set of lights turn right into South Park Drive; follow signs for zoo.
Parkland course with links characteristics.
Pro Dominik Naughton; Founded 1993
Designed by Peter Alliss and Clive Clark
18 holes, 6628 yards, S.S.S. 72
▮ Practice range, 18 bays floodlit.
† Welcome; after 10am Fri.
[WD £40; WE £45.
⌂ Welcome all year round by prior arrangement; packages available; leisure club; swimming pool; tennis; squash courts.
🍽 Full facilities; spikes bar; 3 restaurants.
↩ De Vere Blackpool on site.

7 124 Regent Park Municipal Golf Course
Links Road, Lostock, Bolton, Lancs, BL6 4AF
☎ 01204 844170, Pro 495201, Sec 844170, Rest/Bar 844170
1 mile from M61 Junction 6.
Municipal parkland course.
Pro Bob Longworth; Founded 1932
18 holes, 6130 yards, S.S.S. 69
† Welcome; restrictions on Sat.
[WD £;9.50 WE £11.50.
⌂ Welcome WD by arrangement.

🍽 Bar, restaurant, take away.
↩ Forte Crest; Swallowfield.

7 125 Rishton
Station Road, Rishton, Blackburn, Lancs, BB1 4HG
☎ 01254 884442
3 miles E of Blackburn signposted from church in village.
Meadowland course.
Founded 1928
9 holes, 6097 yards for 18 holes, S.S.S. 69
† Welcome WD; WE with a member.
[WD £12.
⌂ Welcome with prior arrangement with Sec.
🍽 Bar and catering available except Mon.
↩ Dunkenhalgh.

7 126 Rochdale
Edenfield Road, Rochdale, Lancs, OL11 5YR
☎ 01706 646024, Fax 643818, Pro 522104, Sec 643818
On A680 3 miles from M62 Junction 20.
Parkland course.
Pro Andrew Laverty; Founded 1888
18 holes, 6050 yards, S.S.S. 69
† Welcome by arrangement.
[Prices on application.
⌂ Welcome by prior arrangement; terms on application.
🍽 Full clubhouse facilities.

7 127 Rossendale
Ewood Lane, Haslingden, Rossendale, Lancs, BB4 6LH
☎ 01706 831686, Fax 228669, Pro 213616, Sec 831339
16 miles from Manchester off the M66.
Meadowland course.
Pro Stephen Nicholls; Founded 1903
18 holes, 6293 yards, S.S.S. 71
▮ Practice green.
† Welcome except Sat.
[WD £25.50; members only Sat; Sun £30.
⌂ Welcome by prior arrangement.
🍽 Full facilities; banqueting facilities; brand new clubhouse.

🏕 Red Hall; Sykeside, both Haslingden.

7 128 Rowany
Rowany Drive, Port Erin, Isle Of Man, IM9 6LN
✉ rowany@iommail.net
☎ 01624 834072, Fax 834072,
Pro 834108, Sec 834072,
Rest/Bar 834108
4 miles W of Castletown; located at end of Port Erin promenade.
Parkland/seaside course.
Pro Founded 1895
18 holes, 5803 yards, S.S.S. 69
⚐ Outdoor practice area; pitch and putt course.
⚑ Welcome.
£ WD £16; WE £20.
⚐ Welcome by arrangement with the Manager.
🍴 Full bar, snacks and restaurant facilities.
🏕 Cherry Orchard; The Ocean Castle.

7 129 Royal Birkdale
Waterloo Road, Southport, Merseyside, PR8 2LX
🌐 www.royalbirkdale.com
✉ royalbirkdalegc@dial.pipex.com
☎ 01704 567920, Fax 562327,
Pro 568857, Sec 567920,
Rest/Bar 567920
Course is 1.5 miles south of Southport on the A565.
Open Championship venue 1998; links course.
Pro Brian Hodgkinson; Founded 1889
Designed by Hawtree & Taylor
18 holes, 6690 yards, S.S.S. 73
⚑ Handicap certs required; not Sat; limited Fri and Sun am.
£ WD £108; WE £125.
⚐ Welcome Mon, Wed and Thurs by prior arrangement; from £98.
🍴 Full catering facilities.
🏕 Local tourist board can provide detailed list.

7 130 Royal Lytham & St Annes
Links Gate, Lytham St Annes, Lancs, FY8 3LQ
☎ 01253 724206, Fax 780946
1 mile from centre of Lytham.
Links course; Open Championship venue 2001.
Pro Eddie Birchenough; Founded 1886
18 holes, 6685 yards, S.S.S. 74
⚑ Welcome Mon and Thurs only; WE Dormy guests only.
£ WD £100 (including lunch).
⚐ Welcome by prior arrangement.

🍴 Full catering and bar facilities available.
🏕 Dormy House on site: 9 single, 4 twin-bedded rooms (no en suite facilities).

7 131 Saddleworth
Mountain Ash, Ladcastle Road, Uppermill, Oldham, Lancs, OL3 6LT
☎ 01457 873653, Fax 820647,
Pro 810412, Sec 873653,
Rest/Bar 872059
5 miles from Oldham, signposted off the A670 Ashton-Huddersfield Road at the bend where road crosses railway.
Scenic moorland course.
Pro Robert Johnson; Founded 1904
Designed by Dr A Mackenzie
18 holes, 5992 yards, S.S.S. 69
⚑ All welcome.
£ WD £23; WE £30.
⚐ Welcome WD by prior arrangement; package deals from £35 inclusive of 3- course meal.
🍴 Full facilities.
🏕 La Pergola, Denshaw.

7 132 St Annes Old Links
Highbury Road East, Lytham St, Annes, Lancs, FY8 2LD
✉ info@saolgc.uk.com
☎ 01253 723597, Fax 781506,
Pro 722432, Sec 723597,
Rest/Bar 721826 Bar,
Catering 712863
Course is off the A584 coast road at St Anne's.
Championship links course.
Pro Daniel Webster; Founded 1901
Designed by James Herd
18 holes, 6684 yards, S.S.S. 72
⚐ Practice ground.
⚑ Welcome except before 9.30am or between 12 noon-1.30pm WD.
£ WD £38; WE £50.
⚐ Welcome by prior arrangement WD only; packages available; menus on request; separate changing rooms; snooker; from £38.
🍴 Full clubhouse dining and bar facilities.
🏕 Contact local tourist board.

7 133 St Bees
Peck Mill, St Bees, Cumbria, CA27 0EJ
☎ 01946 824300, Sec 822515
Course is on the B5345 four miles S of Whitehaven.
Seaside course.
Founded 1942
9 holes, 5122 yards, S.S.S. 65

⚑ Welcome except on comp days.
£ Prices on application.
⚐ Welcome by arrangement with the school.
🍴 No facilities.
🏕 Queens.

7 134 Seascale
The Banks, Seascale, Cumbria, CA20 1QL
🌐 www.seascalegolfclub.org
☎ 01946 728202, Fax 728202, Pro 721779
Course is off the A595 at NW edge of Seascale.
Links course.
Pro Shean Rudd; Founded 1893
Designed by Willie Campbell
18 holes, 6416 yards, S.S.S. 71
⚐ Practice area for members and green fee paying visitors only.
⚑ Welcome.
£ WD £24-29; WE £27-£32. Winter £14.
⚐ Welcome by prior arrangement; discounts of 10 per cent for 12 or more and 15 per cent for 20 or more; from £20.
🍴 Clubhouse facilities.
🏕 Lutwidge Arms, Holmnook; Calder House, Seascale; Horse & Groom, Gosforth.

7 135 Sedbergh Golf Club
Dent Road, Sedbergh, Cumbria, LA10 5SS
✉ sedbergc@btinternet.com
☎ 01539 621551, Fax 20993,
Sec 20993, Rest/Bar 621551
1 mile from Sedbergh on road to Dent and 5 miles E of M6 Junction 37.
Mature parkland course in Yorkshire Dales National Park.
Founded 1896
Designed by W.G.Squires
9 holes, 5624 yards, S.S.S. 68 White, 67 Yellow, 70 Red (Ladies)
⚐ Practice ground.
⚑ Welcome by prior arrangement at WE.
£ WD £16; WE £18.
⚐ Welcome by prior arrangement; various packages can be arranged; from £30.
🍴 Full catering facilities.
🏕 George & Dragon, Dent; Bull, Sedbergh; Sec can assist with stay and play breaks.

7 136 Shaw Hill Hotel Golf ☕ **& Country Club**
Shaw Hill, Whittle Le Woods, Chorley,

Lancs, PR6 7PP
📧 Info@shaw-hill.co.uk
☎ 01257 269221, Fax 261223, Pro
279222, Sec 791164, Rest/Bar 226825
Course is one mile N of M61 Junction
8 and two miles from M6 Junction 28.
Parkland course with water hazards.
Pro David Clarke; Founded 1925
Designed by T McCauley
18 holes, 6239 yards, S.S.S. 73
♦ Welcome WD only with handicap
certs; residents of hotel only at WE.
[Prices available on application;
subject to weather condition and time
of year.
♂ Welcome WD with handicap certs;
golf and catering packages can be
arranged; terms available on
application.
🍽 Bar, restaurant and à la carte
menus available.
⌖ Club has 30 rooms; leisure centre
with extensive facilities (available for
guests of hotel).

7 137 Sherdley Park
Sherdley Road, St Helens,
Merseyside, WA9 5DE
☎ 01744 813149/817967, Fax
817967, Rest/Bar 815518
M62 Junction 7 A570 Signposted St
Helens at second roundabout third exit;
second left into park.
Public undulating parkland course.
Pro Daniel Jones; Founded 1973
Designed by PR Parkinson
18 holes, 5974 yards, S.S.S. 69
❚ Practice range, 12 bays floodlit.
♦ Welcome.
[Prices on application; concessions
for pensioners and juniors.
♂ Welcome by prior arrangement;
terms on application.
🍽 Bar and cafeteria.
⌖ Hilton, St Helens.

7 138 Silecroft
Silecroft, Millom, Cumbria, LA18
4NX
☎ 01229 77434, Rest/Bar 774250
On A5093 three miles N of Millom
through Silecroft village towards shore.
Seaside course.
Founded 1903
9 holes, 5877 yards, S.S.S. 68
♦ Welcome WD; restricted access
WE and BH.
[WD £15; WE £15.
♂ Welcome by arrangement.
🍽 Limited; Miners Arms provides
food.
⌖ Bankfield; Miners Arms.

7 139 Silloth on Solway ☪
Station Road, Silloth, Wigton, Cumbria,
CA7 4BL
⌨ www.sillothgolfclub.co.uk
📧 silloth.g.c@btinternet.com
☎ 016973 31304, Fax 31782, Pro
32404, Sec 31304, Rest/Bar 32442
From Wigton follow B5302 to Silloth.
Championship links course; 1997
British women's strokeplay.
Pro Johnathan Graham; Founded 1892
Designed by Willie Park Jnr
18 holes, 6614 yards, S.S.S. 71
♦ Welcome by prior arrangement.
[WD £28 per day; WE £37 per
round.
♂ Welcome by prior arrangement; full
day packages of golf and catering
available; Mon catering only by prior
arrangement; from £42.
🍽 Full bar and catering facilities,
except Mon.
⌖ Wheyrigg Hall, Wigton; Golf Hotel;
Queens; Skinburness, all Silloth-on-
Solway.

7 140 Silverdale
Red Bridge Lane, Silverdale,
Carnforth, Lancs, LA5 0SP
☎ 01524 702074, Fax 702074, Sec
702074, Rest/Bar 701300
3 miles NW of Carnforth by Silverdale
station.
Heathland/parkland course.
Founded 1906
12 holes, 5559 yards, S.S.S. 67
♦ Welcome by prior arrangement;
some Sun summer restrictions.
[WD £15; WE £18.
♂ Welcome by prior arrangement
with Sec, WD and WE packages
available; from £22.
🍽 Clubhouse facilities.
⌖ Silverdale Hotel.

7 141 Solway Village Golf Centre
Solway Holiday Village, Skinburness
Drive, Silloth, Wigton, Cumbria,
CA7 4QQ
☎ 016973 31236, Fax 32553
Easy to locate in village of Silloth.
Scenic parkland course.
Founded 1988
9 holes, 4001 yards, S.S.S. 3
♦ Welcome.
[WD and WE £5 for daily pass.
♂ Welcome by arrangement.
🍽 Bar and restaurant.
⌖ Self-catering log cabins and
caravans.

7 142 Southport & Ainsdale
Bradshaws Lane, Ainsdale, Southport,
PR8 3LG
⌨ www.sandagolfclub.co.uk
📧 secretary@sandagolfclub.co.uk
☎ 01704 578000, Fax 570896, Pro
577316, Rest/Bar 579422
Course is on the A565 three miles S of
Southport, 0.5 miles from Ainsdale
station.
Links course.
Pro Jim Payne; Founded 1906
Designed by James Braid
18 holes, 6583 yards, S.S.S. 73
♦ Welcome WD between 10am-12
noon and 1:00pm-4.00pm.
[WD £45-£50; WE £60 for a round.
♂ Welcome WD; terms on
application; from £45.
🍽 Full clubhouse facilities.
⌖ Scarisbrick, Southport.

7 143 Southport Municipal
Park Road West, Southport,
Merseyside, PR9 0JS
☎ 01704 530133, Pro 535286
N end of Promenade.
Public seaside course.
Pro Bill Fletcher; Founded 1914
18 holes, 5953 yards, S.S.S. 69
♦ Welcome.
[WD £6.50; WE £9.90.
♂ Welcome by prior booking at least
six days in advance.
🍽 Meals and bar facilities.
⌖ Scarisbrick; Prince of Wales.

7 144 Southport Old Links
Moss Lane, Churchtown, Southport,
Merseyside, PR9 7QS
📧 secretary@solgc.freeserve.co.uk
☎ 01704 228207, Fax 505353, Pro
228207, Sec 228207, Rest/Bar 228207
Off Manchester Rd into Roe Lane and
then into Moss Lane; close to town
centre.
Seaside course.
Pro Gary Copeman; Founded 1920
9 holes, 6244 yards, S.S.S. 71
♦ Welcome except Wed and
restrictions at WE.
[WD £22; WE £30.
♂ Welcome by prior arrangement if
party is more than 12; terms on
application.
🍽 Full facilities except Mon.
⌖ Richmond House.

7 145 Stand Golf Club ☪
Ashbourne Grove, Whitefield,
Manchester, Lancs, M45 7NL
📧 Mark.Dance@bt.com

0161 7662214, Fax 7963234, Sec 7663197, Rest/Bar 7662388
1 mile N of M60 ring road Junction 17.
Undulating parkland course.
Pro Mark Dance; Founded 1904
Designed by Alex Herd
18 holes, 6426 yards, S.S.S. 71
Welcome WD; restricted WE and Tues due to ladies day.
WD £25; WE £30 + 50p for insurance.
Welcome Wed and Fri; winter packages.
Full facilities except Mon.
Hawthorn; Travel Inn.

7 146 **Standish Court Golf Club** 𝕿
Rectory Lane, Standish, Wigan, Lancs, WN6 0XD
www.standishgolf.co.uk
info@standishgolf.co.uk
01257 425777, Fax 425888, Pro 425777, Rest/Bar 425777
5 mins off M6 Junction 27 following signs for Standish village.
Parkland course.
Pro Mike Halliwell; Founded 1995
Designed by Patrick Dawson
18 holes, 5750 yards, S.S.S. 66
Welcome by arrangement.
WD £10; WE £15.
Welcome by prior arrangement; full day packages available from £15-£35.
Full clubhouse facilities available.
Kilbey Court; Wigan Moat House.

7 147 **Stonyholme Municipal**
St Aidans Rd, Carlisle, Cumbria, CA1 1LF
01228 625511, Fax 625511, Rest/Bar 625512
Course is off the A69 one mile W of M6 Junction 43.
Flat meadowland course.
Pro Stephen Ling; Founded 1974
Designed by Frank Pennink
18 holes, 5787 yards, S.S.S. 69
Practice area; practice range, 16 bays floodlit and 9-hole short course adjacent.
Welcome.
WD £8.30; WE £10.40; day tickets available all week.
Welcome by prior arrangement.
Clubhouse facilities.
Post House; numerous B&Bs in the area.

7 148 **Stonyhurst Park**
c/o The Bayley Arms, Avenue Road, Hurst Green, Clitheroe, Lancs, BB7 9QB
01254 826478, Fax 826797
On B6243 Clitheroe-Longridge road.
Parkland course.
Founded 1979
9 holes, 5529 yards, S.S.S. 67
Welcome except WE; contact The Bayley Arms.
WD £15.
Limited and by prior arrangement only.
None.
The Bayley Arms.

7 149 **Swinton Park**
East Lancashire Road, Swinton, Manchester, Lancs, M27 5LX
golfer@swintongolf.freeserve.co.uk
0161 7940861, Fax 2810698, Pro 7938077, Sec 7277061, Rest/Bar 7941785
On A580 5 miles from Manchester on East Lancs.
Parkland course.
Pro Jim Wilson; Founded 1926
Designed by Braid & Taylor
18 holes, 6726 yards, S.S.S. 72
Welcome WD except Thurs.
WD £25.
Welcome by arrangement Mon, Tues, Wed and Fri.
Bar and restaurant facilities; function and conference rooms.
Large selection in Manchester city centre.

7 150 **Towneley**
Todmorden Road, Burnley, Lancs, BB11 3ED
01282 438473/421517, Sec 414555, Rest/Bar 451636
From M65, Junction 9, follow signs for Halifax.
Parkland course.
Founded 1932
Designed by Burnley Council
The Townley course:18 holes, 5811 yards, S.S.S. 69; The Brunshaw course: 9 holes, par 3
Small practice ground, two tennis courts, two bowling greens, 18-hole pitch and putt.
Welcome.
WD 9 holes £5.30, 18 holes £9.55; WE 9 holes £6.10, 18 holes £10.60. Concessions for OAPs during week. Concessions for unemployed and school children during week.
Welcome by prior arrangement; catering can be arranged with steward; from £8, not at WE during Summer.
Bar and restaurant facilities available
Alexander.

7 151 **Tunshill**
Tunshill Lane, Milnrow, Rochdale, Lancs, OL16 3TS
01706 759320
From M62 Junction 21 take road to Milnrow and follow Kiln Lane out of town to narrow lane for clubhouse.
Moorland course.
Founded 1943
9 holes, 5743 yards, S.S.S. 68
Welcome WD except Tues evening; by prior arrangement WE
Terms on application.
Welcome WD by prior arrangement; terms available on application.
Restaurant and bar facilities.
John Milne, Milnrow.

7 152 **Turton** 𝕿
Chapeltown Road, Bromley Cross, Bolton, Lancs, BL7 9QH
01204 852235
4 miles NW of Bolton behind Last Drop Hotel and country club, Last Drop Village.
Moorland course.
Founded 1908
Designed by James Braid
18 holes, 6159 yards, S.S.S. 68
Welcome except Wed 11.30am-3pm and WE only by prior arrangement.
WD £20; WE £25.
Welcome by arrangement.
Full catering facilities.
Last Drop; Egerton House.

7 153 **Ulverston**
Bardsea, Ulverston, Cumbria, LA12 9QJ
ulverston@bardseapark.freeserve.co.uk
01229 582824, Fax 588910, Pro 582800
From M6 Junction 36 follow signs for Barrow on A590 and take A5087 to Bardsea.
Parkland course.
Pro MR Smith; Founded 1895/1909
Designed by A Herd
18 holes, 6201 yards, S.S.S. 71
Practice chipping green, practice grounds adjacent to course.
Welcome by prior arrangement.
WD £25; WE £30.
Welcome by prior arrangement; packages for golf and catering can be arranged; terms on application.
Full clubhouse catering and bar facilities.
The Fisherman's Arms; The Swan; Lansdale House.

7 154 Walmersley ♛
White Carr Lane, Bury, Lancs, BL9 6TE
☎ 0161 7647770, Fax 01706827618, Pro 7639050, Rest/Bar 7641429
Off A56 3 miles N of Bury.
Moorland course.
Pro P Thorpe; Founded 1906
18 holes, 5341 yards, S.S.S. 67
† Welcome.
�︎ WD £20; WE £20.
⏶ Welcome Wed-Fri; 27 holes golf, coffee, light lunch and 4-course meal; from £26.
🍽 Full clubhouse facilities.
🛏 Red Hall, Bury.

7 155 Werneth (Oldham)
Green Lane, Oldham, Lancs, OL8 3AZ
⏓ www.wernethgolfclub.co.uk
✉ sales@the'golf'centre.co.uk
☎ 0161 6287136, Fax 6287136, Rest/Bar 6241190
Course is five miles from Manchester, take the A62 to Hollinwood and then the A6104.
Moorland course.
Pro Roy Penney; Founded 1908
18 holes, 5364 yards, S.S.S. 66
⏶ Practice green.
† Welcome WD; guests of members only at WE.
⏎ WD £18.50.
⏶ Welcome Mon, Wed and Fri by arrangement.
🍽 Lunch and meals served except Mon.
🛏 Smokeys, Oldham.

7 156 West Derby
Yew Tree Lane, Liverpool, Merseyside, L12 9HQ
✉ pmilne@westderbygc.freeserve.co.uk
☎ 0151 2281540, Fax 2590505, Pro 2205478, Sec 2541034
Follow signs for Knotty Ash to roundabout and then into Blackmoor Drive, right into Yew Tree Lane.
Flat parkland course with trees.
Pro Andrew Witherup; Founded 1896
18 holes, 6277 yards, S.S.S. 70
† Welcome WD; except Tues.
⏎ WD £26; WE £36.
⏶ Welcome WD except Tues; full golf and catering packages available; from £26.
🍽 Bar and restaurant.
🛏 Derby Lodge, Huyton; Bell Tower, Knowsley.

7 157 West Lancashire
Hall Road West, Liverpool, Merseyside, L23 8SZ
⏓ www.westlancashiregolf.co.uk
✉ golf@wlgc.lancastrian.co.uk
☎ 0151 9241076, Fax 9314448, Pro 9245662, Rest/Bar 9244115
M57 to Aintree then A5036 to Seaforth and A565 to Crosby; signposted close to Hall Rd Station.
Links course.
Pro Gary Edge; Founded 1873
Designed by CK Cotton/D Steel
18 holes, 6767 yards, S.S.S. 73
⏶ Practice ground; tuition available; equipment for hire.
† Welcome by arrangement.
⏎ WD (not Tues) £50; WE £70 per round.
⏶ Welcome WD except Tues; packages available; green fees for groups of 12 or more include soup and sandwich lunch and 3-course meal; £45-£55.
🍽 Full clubhouse facilities.
🛏 Southport.

7 158 Westhoughton
School Street, Westhoughton, Bolton, Lancs, BL5 2BR
☎ 01942 811085, Fax 811085, Pro 840545, Sec 608958
Course is off School Lane, adjacent to the Parish Church in Westhoughton.
Parkland course.
Pro Jason Seed; Founded 1929
9 holes, 5772 yards, S.S.S. 68
⏶ Practice area.
† Welcome.
⏎ WD £16; WE £16; £8 with a member.
⏶ Welcome; packages of 18 holes, available with catering; from £25.
🍽 Full clubhouse facilities available.
🛏 Large selection available in Bolton.

7 159 Westhoughton Golf Centre
Wigan Road, Westhoughton, Nr Bolton, Lancs, BL8 2BX
☎ 01942 813195, Rest/Bar 818445
M61 Junction 5; travel through Westhoughton towards Hindley.
Parkland course; home to Hart Common GC.
Pro Gareth Benson; Founded 1996
Designed by Mike Sattock
18 holes, 6188 yards, S.S.S. 72
⏶ Practice range, 26 bays floodlit covered; also 9-hole par 3 course is now open.
† Welcome.

⏎ Prices on application.
⏶ Welcome by prior arrangement; terms on application.
🍽 Clubhouse facilities.

7 160 Whalley ♛
Portfield Lane, Clerk Hill Road, Whalley, Clitheroe, Lancs, BB7 9DR
⏓ www.whalleygolfcourse.co.uk
☎ 01254 822236, Pro 824766
Course is off the A671 one mile SE of Whalley following the signs for Sabden.
Parkland course.
Pro Jamie Hunt; Founded 1912
9 holes, 6258 yards, S.S.S. 70
⏶ Practice ground.
† Welcome except Thurs pm and Sat in summer.
⏎ WD £16; WE £20.
⏶ Welcome by arrangement with secretary; catering and packages on application; from £15.
🍽 Clubhouse facilities.
🛏 Higher Trapp, Simonstone; Old Stone Manor,Mytton.

7 161 Whitefield ♛
Higher Lane, Whitefield, Manchester, Lancs, M45 7EZ
☎ 0161 3512700, Fax 3512712, Pro 3512709, Rest/Bar 3512710
On A665 near Whitefield exit from M60.
Parkland course.
Pro Paul Reeves; Founded 1932
18 holes, 6045 yards, S.S.S. 69
⏶ Practice putting green and practice.
† Welcome by arrangement.
⏎ WD £25; WE £35.
⏶ Welcome WD except Tues; also some Sat afternoons; groups of more than 12 players should contact the club for rates.
🍽 Full clubhouse facilities.
🛏 The Village; Travel Lodge.

7 162 Whittaker
Shore Lane, Littleborough, Lancs, OL15 0LH
☎ 01706 378310
On Blackstone Edge Old Road, 1.5 miles out of Littleborough; turn right at High Peak Hamlet.
Moorland course.
Founded 1906
9 holes, 5606 yards, S.S.S. 67
⏶ Practice ground.
† Welcome except Tues pm and Sun.
⏎ Prices on application.
⏶ Welcome by prior arrangement with Sec; limited catering on application with Sec; limited catering on application; prices on application.

⚫ Bar can be arranged.

7 163 Wigan

Arley Hall, Arley Lane, Haigh, Wigan, Lancs, WN1 2UH
www.wigangolfclub.co.uk
☎ 01257 421360, Sec 01942 244429
From M6 Junction 27 through Standish on B5239; turn left at Canal Bridge lights and course is opposite Crawford Arms.
Parkland course.
Founded 1898
18 holes, 6020 yards, S.S.S. 70
† Welcome any day except Tues and Sat.
[WD £25 18 holes, £30 all day; WE £30 18 holes, £35 all day.
 Welcome by prior arrangement; special packages available; terms on application.
⚫ Full catering.
 Bellingham; Brockett Arms; Kilhey Court.

7 164 William Wroe

Penny Bridge Lane, Urmston, Manchester, Lancs, M41 5DX
☎ 0161 7488680, Fax 7488680,
Pro 0161 9288542
Leave M63 Junction 4 and take B5124 then B5158 to Flixton; 12 miles SW of Manchester.
Municipal parkland course.
Pro Scott Partington; Founded 1974
18 holes, 4395 yards, S.S.S. 64
† Welcome: bookings taken 7 days in advance.
[WD £8.30; WE £11.50 and bank holidays.
 Welcome with booking.
⚫ Clubhouse facilities.
 Manor Hey.

7 165 Wilpshire

Whalley Road, Wilpshire, Blackburn, Lancs, BB1 9LF
☎ 01254 248260, Fax 246745,
Pro 249558
Course is on the A666 four miles N of Blackburn.
Moorland/parkland course.

Pro Walter Slaven; Founded 1890
18 holes, 5802 yards, S.S.S. 69
† Welcome WD; by arrangement at WE.
[WD £25.50; WE £30.50.
 Welcome by prior appointment.
⚫ Full facilities.
 County; Swallow, Salmesbury.

7 166 Windermere

Cleabarrow, Windermere, Cumbria, LA23 3NB
☎ 015394 43123, Fax 43123,
Pro 43550
On B5284 1.5 miles from Bowness towards Kendal.
Undulating parkland course.
Pro Stephen Rook; Founded 1891
Designed by George Low
18 holes, 5132 yards, S.S.S. 65
† Welcome by arrangement.
[WD £24; WE £28.
 Welcome by arrangement; packages can be arranged; from £25.
⚫ Bar and Licensed Restaurant.
 The Wild Boar Hotel (golf discounts available).

7 167 Woolton

Doe Park Speke Road, Woolton, Liverpool, Merseyside, L25 7TZ
☎ 0151 4862298, Fax 4861664,
Pro 4861298, Rest/Bar 4861601
6 miles from city centre on road to Liverpool Airport.
Parkland course.
Pro Alan Gibson; Founded 1901
18 holes, 5724 yards, S.S.S. 68
† Welcome.
[WD £24; WE £35.
 Welcome; packages can be arranged; terms available on application.
⚫ Clubhouse facilities.
 Redbourne.

7 168 Workington

Branthwaite Road, Workington, Cumbria, CA14 4SS
☎ 01900 603460, Fax 607122,
Pro 67828
Off A595 2 miles SE of Workington.

Undulating meadowland.
Pro Adrian Drabble; Founded 1893
Designed by James Braid/Howard Swan
18 holes, 6247 yards, S.S.S. 70
 Practice ground.
† Welcome if carrying handicap certs.
[Summer WD £20, WE and BH £25; Winter WD £15, WE and BH £20.
 Welcome by prior arrangement with Pro.
⚫ Full facilities, 7 days a week if prior booked.
 Washington Central; Westlands (adjacent to course), Melbreak Hotel.

7 169 Worsley

Stableford Avenue, Eccles, Manchester, Lancs, M30 8AP
☎ 0161 7894202, Fax 7893200
Follow signs to Monton Green, Eccles from M60, Junction 13 then to Stableford Ave.
Parkland course.
Pro C Cousins; Founded 1894
Designed by James Braid
18 holes, 6252 yards, S.S.S. 70
† Welcome by prior arrangement.
[WD £30; WE £35.
 Welcome Wed and Thurs; tees available 10.15am and 1.35pm.
⚫ Clubhouse facilities.
 Wendover, Monton.

7 170 Worsley Park Marriott

Marriott Manchester Hotel and Country Club, Worsley, Manchester, M28 2QT
http://www.marriotthotels.com/MANGS
✉ golf.worsleypark@marriotthotels.co.uk
☎ 0161 9752000
Junction M13 off M62 to Worsley. Signposted Marriott Hotel.
Parklands to USGA specifications.
18 holes, 6611 yards yards
† Yes.
[Enquire for green fees.
 Yes.
⚫ Restaurant/cafe.
 Worsley Park Marriott

THE NORTH EAST

8A

Yorkshire

Strange how one man's life can touch so many others. Dr Alister Mackenzie was a Cambridge medic who went on to become a field surgeon in the Boer War. Subsequently he became an adviser to the British government on camouflage and then in 1914 won first prize in a Country Life golf design competition.

He went on to influence the architecture of courses as far ranging as Augusta, Cypress Point, Royal Melbourne, even Titirangi in New Zealand, a name that means 'fringe of heaven'.

There are a few fringes of heaven in the Leeds area where Mackenzie made his home. He had a hand in the Leeds courses of Alwoodley, Moortown, Sand Moor and further down the road at York he also designed Fulford.

He was particularly fond of Alwoodley where he became the club's first secretary in the days when they had a liveried butler. It is a course of great variety, a difficult finish and a par five eighth that Longhurst rated one of the best in the country.

Sand Moor is quite a hilly course with some fine par threes and Moortown is notable as the venue of the first Ryder Cup to be played in Britain. It also boasts a 'Tin Cup' type story when a competitor in the Brabazon chipped back to the eighteenth green via the open window of the bar.

The one famous course in this cluster not to bear the fingerprints of Mackenzie is Moor Allerton, the first Robert Trent Jones course in Britain.

It has fine views over the Vale of York and typically cavernous bunkers, rolling greens and an assortment of lakes.

Completing the York-Leeds triangle are the courses around Harrogate. Pannal is an exposed moorland course of quality, Harrogate, overlooked by Knaresborough Castle, is well thought of, but the pick is perhaps Ilkley.

Situated in a valley below the moor, a river runs through it and is a vibrant feature of the opening seven holes. River, Bridge and Island are the names of the first three holes in acknowledgement of the influence of the Wharfe. Colin Montgomerie honed his game here.

To the north Ganton, lying in the Vale of York, is one of England's most treasured courses. It is the only inland course to have hosted the Amateur Championship and is very much looking forward to hosting the Walker Cup in 2003. The omens are good because past winners of the Amateur at Ganton include Peter McEvoy and Gary Wolstenholme, such influential figures in the previous two Walker Cup victories. The 14th and 17th, both short par fours, are a feature of the course and nicely balance out the relative scarcity of par threes. Just to the north east of Ganton is Scarborough, which has two good courses in the North Cliff and the South Cliff, the latter yet another Mackenzie design.

In truth, the south of Yorkshire is not particularly blessed by outstanding golf courses. Woodsome Hall, near Huddersfield, has a good course that could not possibly live up to the historic clubhouse. Rotherham has a mansion for its clubhouse guarded by a vast beech, equally impressive oak by the first tee and a user friendly golf course.

Part of Lindrick also lies in South Yorkshire, but for a golfing trip of rich diversity you really need to be heading north.

8A 1 Abbeydale ♣
Twentywell Lane, Dore, Sheffield,
S Yorks, S17 4QA
🖳 www.abbeydalegolf.co.uk
📧 abbeygolf@compuserve.com
☎ 0114 2360763, Fax 23607632,
Pro 2365633
Course is off the A621 five miles S of
Sheffield.
Parkland course
Pro Nigel Perry; Founded 1895
Designed by Herbert Fowler.
18 holes, 6407 yards, S.S.S. 71
† Welcome by arrangement but not
before 9.30am or between 12 noon
and 1.30pm.
Ⅰ WD £35; WE £40.
⟳ Welcome by prior arrangement;
terms on application.
🍽 By prior arrangement; bar and
restaurant facilities.
⌁ Beauchief; Sheffield Moat
House.

8A 2 Aldwark Manor
Aldwark, Alne, York, YO61 1UF
☎ 01347 838353, Fax 830007,
Pro 838353, Sec 838353,
Rest/Bar 838146
Course is off the A1 five miles SE of
Boroughbridge; 13 miles NW of York
off the A19.
Easy walking parkland around River
Ure.
Founded 1978
18 holes, 1671 yards, S.S.S. 70
Ⅰ Practice green x 2
† Welcome WD; some WE
restrictions.
Ⅰ WD £26; WE £32.
⟳ Welcome WD; some restrictions;
various packages available from £32.
🍽 Full catering in the Victorian Manor
House built in 1856; minimum 12;
private dining rooms available; full
restaurant and bar facilities.
⌁ Aldwark Manor (60 bedrooms).

8A 3 Allerthorpe Park
Allerthorpe Park, Allerthorpe, York,
Yorks, YO42 4RL
☎ 01759 306686, Fax 304308
Off the A1079 York-Hull road 2 miles W
of Pocklington.
Parkland course
Founded 1994
Designed by J G Hatcliffe & Partners.
18 holes, 5506 yards, S.S.S. 66
† Welcome.
Ⅰ WD £18; WE £18.
⟳ Welcome by prior arrangement;
terms on application.
🍽 Clubhouse facilities.

8A 4 Alwoodley
Wigton Lane, Alwoodley, Leeds, W
Yorks, LS17 8SA
🖳 www.alwoodley.co.uk
📧 julie@
alwoodleygolfclub.freeserve.co.uk
☎ 01132 681680, Fax 2939458,
Pro 689603, Sec 681680,
Rest/Bar 681680
On A61 5 miles N of Leeds.
Heathland/moorland course
Pro John Green; Founded 1907
Designed by Dr A MacKenzie and
H Colt.
18 holes, 6666 yards, S.S.S. 72
† Welcome by prior arrangement;
terms on application.
Ⅰ WD £55; WE £75.
⟳ Welcome by prior arrangement;
terms on application.
🍽 Bar and restaurant facilities;
catering packages available by prior
arrangement.
⌁ Harewood Arms; Jarvis Porter,
Headingley.

8A 5 Ampleforth College
Gilling East, York, York, YO5 5AE
☎ 01653 628555
Entrance oppostie church in the centre
of Gilling East.
Parkland course
Founded 1972
Designed by Ampleforth College
9 holes, 5567 yards, S.S.S. 69
† Welcome but restrictions between
2pm-4pm for pupils on WD.
Ⅰ WD £9; WE £12.
⟳ Club will consider applications.
🍽 None; public house next door.
⌁ Worsley Arms, Hovingham.

8A 6 Baildon
Moorgate, Baildon, Shipley, Yorkshire,
BD17 5PP
🖳 www.baildongolfclub.com
☎ 01274 584266, Fax 530551,
Pro 595162, Sec 530551
3 miles N of Bradford off the Bradford-
Ilkley road.
Moorland course laid out as links
course
Pro Richard Masters; Founded 1896
Designed by T Morris – modified by J
Braid.
18 holes, 6231 yards, S.S.S. 70
Ⅰ Large practice area
† Welcome by prior arrangement.
Ⅰ WD £16; WE £20.
⟳ Welcome by prior arrangement;
discounts for larger groups; terms on
application.
🍽 Clubhouse facilities, catering

packages available.
⌁ Many in local area.

8A 7 Barnsley
Wakefield Road, Staincross, Nr
Barnsley, S Yorkshire, S75 6JZ
☎ 01226 382856, Fax 382856,
Pro 380358, Sec 382856,
Rest/Bar 382856
Course is on A61 three miles from
Barnsley.
Undulating meadowland course.
Pro Sean Wyke; Founded 1928
18 holes, 5951 yards, S.S.S. 69
Ⅰ Practice range 50 yards from
club/driving range next door
† Welcome.
Ⅰ WD £10; WE £12.
⟳ Welcome by prior arrangement;
terms on application. All bookings are
via the professional.
🍽 Bar meals.
⌁ Queens; Ardley Moat House.

8A 8 Bawtry Golf and Country Club
Cross Lane, Austerfield, Doncaster,
Yorkshire, DN10 6RF
☎ 01302 710841, Fax 710841,
Pro 710841
Take A614 towards Fourn; Cross Lane
is on right at first roundabout.
Parkland course.
Pro Hayden Selby-Green/Steve Pool;
Founded 1974
Designed by E & M Baker Ltd
18 holes, 6900 yards, S.S.S. 73
Ⅰ 10 bays floodlit and practice green.
† Welcome.
Ⅰ WD £14 WE £18; per day WD £18
or WE £22.
⟳ Welcome by prior arrangement;
terms on application. Includes WE.
🍽 Clubhouse facilities.
⌁ Crown, Bawtry. Mount Pleasent
Doncaster.

8A 9 Beauchief
Abbey Lane, Sheffield, S Yorks, S8 0DB
☎ 01142 367274, Pro 367274
From M1 Junction 33 towards city
centre and follow signs A612 to
Bakewell for 4 miles, turning left into
Abbeydale Road at lights.
Parkland course
Pro Mark Trippett; Founded 1925
18 holes, 5469 yards, S.S.S. 66
† Municipal pay and play.
Ⅰ WD £8.50; WE £10.
🍽 Meals served daily.
⌁ Beauchief adjacent to court.

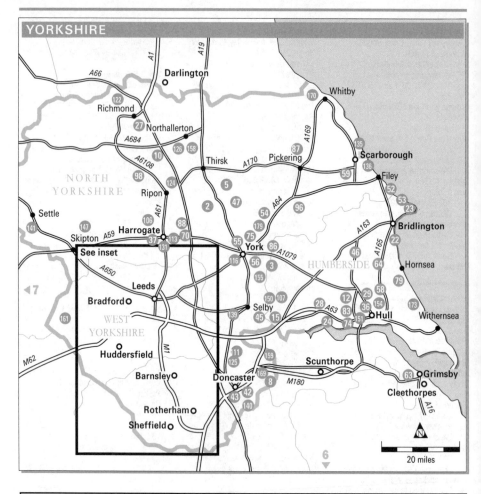

KEY		23	Bridlington Links	47	Easingwold	71	Headingley	95	Low Laithes
1	Abbeydale	24	Brough	48	East Bierley	72	Headley	96	Malton & Norton
2	Aldwark Manor	25	Calverley	49	Elland	73	Hebden Bridge	97	Marsden
3	Allerthorpe Park	26	Castle Fields	50	Fardew	74	Hessle	98	Masham
4	Alwoodley	27	Catterick	51	Ferrybridge 'C'	75	Heworth	99	Meltham
5	Ampleforth College	28	Cave Castle Hotel	52	Filey	76	Hickleton	100	Mid Yorkshire
6	Baildon	29	Cherry Burton	53	Flamborough Head	77	Hillsborough	101	Middleton Park
7	Barnsley	30	City Golf (153)	54	Forest of Galtres	78	Hollins Hall Golf Centre	102	Moor Allerton
8	Bawtry Golf and Country	31	City of Wakefield	55	Forest Park	79	Hornsea	103	Moortown
	Club (6)	32	Clayton	56	Fulford	80	Horsforth	104	Normanton
9	Beauchief	33	Cleckheaton & District	57	Fulneck	81	Howley Hall	105	Northcliffe
10	Bedale	34	Cocksford	58	Ganstead Park	82	Huddersfield (Fixby)	106	Oakdale
11	Ben Rhydding	35	Concord Park	59	Ganton	83	Hull	107	The Oaks
12	Beverley & East Riding	36	Cottingham	60	Garforth	84	Ilkley	108	Otley
13	Bingley St Ives	37	Crimple Valley	61	Gott's Park	85	Keighley	109	Oulton Park
14	Birley Wood	38	Crookhill Park	62	Grange Park	86	Kilnwick Percy	110	Outlane
15	Boothferry Park	39	Crosland Heath	63	Great Grimsby	87	Kirkbymoorside	111	Owston Park
16	Bracken Ghyll	40	Crows Nest Park	64	Hainsworth Park	88	Knaresborough	112	Painthorpe House Golf
17	Bradford	41	Dewsbury District	65	Halifax	80	Leeds (Cobble Hall)		& Country Club
18	Bradford Moor	42	Doncaster	66	Halifax Bradley Hall	90	Leeds Golf Centre	113	Pannal
19	Bradley Park	43	Doncaster Town Moor	67	Hallamshire	91	Lees Hall	114	Phoenix
20	Brandon	44	Dore & Totley	68	Hallowes	92	Lightcliffe	115	Phoenix Park
21	Branshaw	45	Drax	69	Hanging Heaton	93	Lofthouse Hill	116	Pike Hills
22	Bridlington	46	Driffield	70	Harrogate	94	Longley Park	117	Pontefract & District

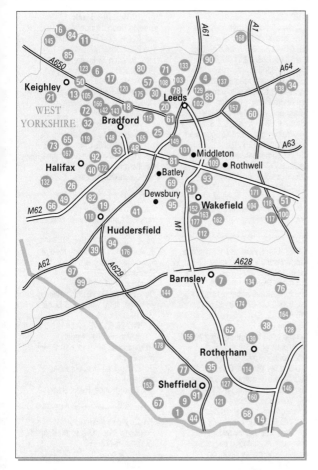

8A 10 Bedale

Leyburn Road, Bedale, N Yorkshire, DL8 1EZ
⌨ www.bedalegolfclub.com
✉ bedalegolfclub@aol.com
☎ 01677 422568, Fax 427143, Pro 422443, Sec 422451, Rest/Bar 422568
From A1 take A684 through Bedale; course 400 yards from town centre.
Parkland course
Pro Tony Johnson; Founded 1894
18 holes, 6610 yards, S.S.S. 72
⚐ Welcome with handicap certs.
🏌 WD £20; WE £30.
↻ Welcome by prior arrangement; catering and golfing packages available; terms available on application.
🍴 Clubhouse facilities.
🛏 Nags Head, Pickhill; White Rose, Leeming Bar.

8A 11 Ben Rhydding

High Wood, Ben Rhydding, Ilkley, W Yorkshire, LS29 8SB
☎ 01943 608759, Sec 600342
From A65 to Ilkley turn up Wheatley Lane and then into Wheatley Grove, left on to High Wood, club signposted.
Moorland course; mix of light park/links.
Founded 1890/1947
Designed by W Dell
9 holes, 4711 yards, S.S.S. 64
🏌 2.
⚐ Welcome WD; limited access with member at WE.
🏌 WD £12; WE £17.
↻ Very limited; access to small parties; terms available on application.
🍴 Very limited/self catering.
🛏 Local tourise office can supply details.

8A 12 Beverley & East Riding

Anti Mill, Westwood, Beverley, E Yorks, HU17 8PJ
☎ 01482 8671980, Fax 868757, Pro 869519, Sec 868757
On B1230 Walkington road 0.5 miles W of town centre.
Common pastureland.
Pro Ian Mackie; Founded 1889
Designed by Dr JJ Fraser
18 holes, 5972 yards, S.S.S. 69
⚐ Welcome.
🏌 WD £13; WE £17.
↻ Welcome WD; catering packages can be arranged; from £13.
🍴 Clubhouse facilities.
🛏 Lairgate, Beverley.

8A 13 Bingley St Ives
The Golf Clubhouse, Harden, Bingley, BD16 1AT
☎ 01274 562436, Fax 511788, Pro 562506, Sec 511788
Course is close to A650 Keighley to Bradford road and A629 Bingley to Denholme.
Parkland/moorland/woodland course.
Pro Ray Firth; Founded 1932
Designed by A MacKenzie .
18 holes, 6485 yards, S.S.S. 71
† Welcome by arrangement.
[WD £24; WE £28.
⌁ Welcome by prior arrangement; all day golf and catering packages available; from £36.
◉ Clubhouse facilities.
↶ Bankfield; Five Flags; Three Sisters.

8A 14 Birley Wood
Birley Lane, Sheffield, S Yorks, S12 3BP
☎ 0114 2647262, Fax 2647262, Pro 2394285, Sec 2653784
Course is off the A616 four miles S of Sheffield.
Public open course.
Pro Peter Ball; Founded 1974
18 holes, 5647 yards, S.S.S. 68
† Welcome.
[WD £8.50; WE £10.00.
⌁ Welcome by prior arrangement with the Sheffield Recreation Department. Please book through the manager, Andy Carnell.
◉ Catering at Fairways Inn adjacent to course.

8A 15 Boothferry Park
Spaldington Lane, Howden, Goole, E Yorkshire, DN14 7NG
☎ 01430 430364, Pro 430364, Rest/Bar 430371
On B1228 between Howden and Bubwith off M62 Junction 37.
Meadowland with ponds and ditches.
Pro N Bundy; Founded 1981
Designed by Donald Steel
18 holes, 6651 yards, S.S.S. 72
† Welcome at all times.
[WD £10; WE £15. Summer rates. Please telephone for Winter rates.
⌁ Welcome by prior arrangement with the professional; packages can be arranged; terms on application.
◉ Clubhouse facilities.
↶ Cave Castle.

8A 16 Bracken Ghyll
Skipton Road, Addingham, Yorkshire,
LS29 0SL
↶ www.bracken.ghyll.com
✉ office@brackenghyll.com
☎ 01943 831207, Fax 839453, Pro 831207, Sec 831207,
Rest/Bar 830691
Off A65 Skipton road in Addingham.
Undulating parkland course.
Pro Andrew Hall; Founded 1993
Designed by OCM Associates
18 holes, 5310 yards, S.S.S. 66
† Welcome by prior arrangement.
[WD £18; WE £20.
⌁ Welcome; catering and golf packages available; video tuition; indoor practice area; terms on application.
◉ Full clubhouse facilities.
↶ Craiglands; Devonshire Country House; Randells.

8A 17 The Bradford Golf Club ♨
Hawksworth Lane, Guiseley, Leeds, W Yorks, LS20 8NP
✉ manager@
bradfordgolfclub.sagehost.co.uk
☎ 01943 875570, Fax 875570, Pro 873719, Sec 875570,
Rest/Bar 873817
Course is off the A6038 3.5 miles NE of Shipley.
Moorland/parkland course.
Pro Sydney Welden; Founded 1862
Designed by Fowler and Simpson
18 holes, 6303 yards, S.S.S. 71
† Welcome WD by prior arrangement; not Sat; limited Sun.
[WD £30; WE £35.
⌁ Welcome WD by prior arrangement; catering packages available; terms available on application.
◉ Full clubhouse facilities.
↶ Marriott Hollins Hall; Chevin Lodge Others available on request.

8A 18 Bradford Moor
Scarr Hall, Pollard Lane, Bradford, W Yorks, BD2 4RW
☎ 01274 771716
2 miles from Bradford town centre on Harrogate Rd.
Moorland course.
Founded 1906
9 holes, 5900 yards, S.S.S. 68
† Welcome WD; discount before 1.30pm.
[WD £10.
⌁ Welcome WD by prior arrangement; catering and golf packages available; from £16.
◉ Clubhouse facilities.

8A 19 Bradley Park
Bradley Road, Huddersfield, HD2 2PJ
☎ 01484 223772, Fax 451613, Pro 223772
M62 Junction 26 in direction of Huddersfield; right at first lights.
Parklands course.
Pro Parnell Reilly; Founded 1973
Designed by Donald Steel
18 holes, 6284 yards, S.S.S. 70
／ 18 floodlit; 9-hole par 3 course.
† Welcome by prior arrangement.
[WD £12; WE £14.
⌁ Welcome WD; catering packages can be arranged; from £10.
◉ Clubhouse facilities.

8A 20 Brandon
Holywell Lane, Shadwell, Leeds, W Yorks, LS17 8EZ
☎ 0113 2737471, Sec 2737471
1 mile from N Leeds ring road at Roundhay Park.
Parkland course.
Founded 1967
Designed by George Eric Allamby
18 holes, 4800 yards, S.S.S. 62
† All welcome.
[WD £6.50; WE £7.50.
⌁ Welcome WD by prior arrangement; 10 days' notice required; from £6.50.
◉ Clubhouse snack facilities available.
↶ White House; Rydal Bank.

8A 21 Branshaw
Branshaw Moor, Oakworth, Keighley, W Yorks, BD22 7ES
☎ 01535 643235, Pro 647441, Rest/Bar 643235
Course is on the B6143 two miles SW of Keighley.
Moorland course.
Pro Mark Tyler; Founded 1912
Designed by James Braid
18 holes, 5870 yards, S.S.S. 69
† Welcome WD; restrictions at WE.
[WD £20; WE £30.
⌁ Welcome WD by prior arrangement.
◉ Clubhouse catering facilities available.
↶ Three Sisters, Haworth; Newsholme Manor, Oakworth.

8A 22 Bridlington
Belvedere Road, Bridlington, E Yorks, YO153NA
↶ www.bridlingtongolfclub.co.uk
✉ golfbrid@aol.com
☎ 01262 672092, Fax 606367,

Pro 674721, Sec 606367,
Rest/Bar 672092
Off A165 S of town on Bridlington-Hull road.
Open parkland course.
Pro ARA Howarth; Founded 1905
Designed by James Braid
18 holes, 6577 yards, S.S.S. 72
† Welcome by prior arrangement.
丨 WD £18; WE £25.
⟋ Welcome by prior arrangement; golf and catering packages available; terms on application.
⦿ Full clubhouse facilities available.
⌇ Club can provide list on request.

8A 23 Bridlington Links
Flamborough Road, Marton, Bridlington, E Yorks, YO15 1DW
☎ 01262 401584, Fax 401702,
Pro 401584, Sec 401584,
Rest/Bar 401584
Course is on the B1255 just N of Bridlington towards Flamborough Head.
Clifftop links course.
Pro Steve Raybould; Founded 1993
Designed by Howard Swan
18 holes, 6719 yards, S.S.S. 72
丨 24 covered floodlit.
† All welcome.
丨 WD £12; WE £15 (This includes lunch in winter months).
⟋ Welcome; summer and winter packages available; driving range; short course; terms available on application.
⦿ Full clubhouse facilities.
⌇ Rags Hotel; Manor Court; Sewerby Grange; North Star, Flambor.

8A 24 Brough
Cave Road, Brough, E Yorks, HU15 1HB
☎ 01482 667374, Fax 669823,
Pro 667483, Sec 667291
Off A63, 10 miles W of Hull.
Parkland course.
Pro G W Townhill; Founded 1893
18 holes, 6134 yards, S.S.S. 69
† Welcome WD except Wed; WE by prior arrangement.
丨 WD £30; WE £40.
⟋ Welcome by prior arrangement; full golf and catering packages available; terms available on application.
⦿ Full clubhouse facilities.
⌇ Beverley Arms; Walkington Manor.

8A 25 Calverley
Woodhall Lane, Pudsey, Yorks, LS28 5QY

☎ 0113 2569244, Fax 2564362,
Sec 2569244
Close to M1 & M62 motorways 4 miles from Bradford, 7 miles from Leeds.
Parkland course.
Pro Niel Wendal-Jones; Founded 1983
18 holes, 5590 yards, S.S.S. 67
丨 Large practice ground + 9-hole course.
† Welcome; restrictions Sat and Sun am.
丨 WD £12; WE £17.
⟋ Welcome by arrangement; catering packages available for groups up to 30; terms available on application.
⦿ Full clubhouse facilities.
⌇ Marriott.

8A 26 Castle Fields
Rastrick Common, Rastrick, Brighouse, W Yorks, HD6 3HI
☎ 01484 713276, Sec 713276
On A643 1 mile out of Brighouse.
Parkland course.
Founded 1903
6 holes, 2406 yards, S.S.S. 50
† Welcome only as a guest of a member.
丨 WD £5.50; WE £7.50.
⟋ Welcome only by prior arrangement with Sec.
⦿ Facilities at local Inns within 0.25 miles.

8A 27 Catterick ☎
Leyburn Road, Catterick Garrison, N Yorks, DL9 3QE
☎ 01748 833401, Fax 833268,
Pro 833671, Sec 833268,
Rest/Bar 833268
On B6136 6 miles SW of Scotch Corner.
Parkland/moorland course.
Pro Andy Marshall; Founded 1930
Designed by Arthur Day (1938)
18 holes, 6329 yards, S.S.S. 71
† Welcome by prior arrangement.
丨 Terms on application.
⟋ Welcome by prior arrangement; packages can be arranged; 2 practice areas; billiards room; satellite TV.
⦿ Lounge bar, restaurant, bar snacks, snooker room.
⌇ Several.

8A 28 Cave Castle Hotel
South Cave, Brough, E Yorks, HU15 2EU
☎ 01430 421286, Rest/Bar 422245
10 miles from Kingston upon Hull.
Parkland course.

Pro Stephen MacKinder; Founded 1989 ·
18 holes, 6524 yards, S.S.S. 71
† Welcome.
丨 WD £12.50; WE £18.
⟋ Welcome WD and after 10.30am at WE; special packages available; conference facilities for 250; à la carte restaurant; practice facilities; terms on application.
⦿ Full hotel facilities.
⌇ Cave Castle.

8A 29 Cherry Burton
Leconfield Road, Cherry Burton, Beverley, Yorks, HU17 7RB
☎ 01964 550924
On the B1248 close to Beverley.
Parkland course.
Pro to be appointed; Founded 1993
Designed by W Adamson
9 holes, 6480 yards, S.S.S. 71
丨 Practice area.
† Welcome.
丨 WD £9; WE £10.
⟋ Welcome by prior arrangement.
⦿ Bar and catering facilities available.
⌇ Beverley; Lairgate.

8A 30 City Golf
Redcote Lane, Leeds, W Yorks, LS4 2AW
☎ 0113 2633040, Fax 2633044
1.5 miles W of Leeds town centre off Kirkstall Road.
Parkland course.
Founded 1996
9 holes, 1800 yards, par 30
† Welcome.
丨 WD £5; WE £5.
⟋ Welcome with prior booking.
⦿ Full facilities.

8A 31 City of Wakefield
Lupset Park, Horbury Road, Wakefield, W Yorkshire, WF2 8QS
☎ 01924 367442, Pro 360282,
Sec 367442, Rest/Bar 367442
Course is on the A642 two miles W of Wakefield.
Parkland course.
Pro Roger Holland; Founded 1936
Designed by JSF Morrison
18 holes, 6319 yards, S.S.S. 70
† Everybody welcome.
丨 WD £10 per round; WE £12 per round.
⟋ Welcome on WD by prior arrangement; packages can be arranged through the stewardess; terms on application.

Clubhouse facilities.
Cedar Court, Forte Post House, Wakefield.

8A 32 Clayton
Thornton View Road, Clayton, Bradford, W Yorks, BD14 6JX
☎ 01274 880047
On A647 from Bradford following signs for Clayton.
Moorland course.
Founded 1906
9 holes, 5467 yards, S.S.S. 67
† Welcome WD and Sat unless comps.
WD £10; WE £12.
Welcome by arrangement with Sec; catering packages by arrangement; snooker; terms on application.
Bar and bar snacks.
Pennine Hilton.

8A 33 Cleckheaton & District
Bradford Road, Cleckheaton, W Yorks, BD19 6BU
www.cleckheatongolfclub.co.uk
info@ cleckheatongolf.fsnet.co.uk
☎ 01274 851267, Fax 871382, Pro 851267, Sec 851266, Rest/Bar 874118
On A638 from M62 Junction 26 towards Bradford.
Parkland course.
Pro Mike Ingham; Founded 1900
18 holes, 5860 yards, S.S.S. 68
† Welcome.
WD £25; WE £30.
Welcome WD by arrangement; catering packages by arrangement; terms on application.
Clubhouse catering and bar facilities.
Novotel.

8A 34 Cocksford
Stutton, Tadcaster, N Yorks, LS24 9NG
☎ 01937 834253, Fax 834253, Rest/Bar 530346
Course is in village of Strutton close to the A64.
Parkland course with Cock Beck running through it.
Pro Graham Thompson; Founded 1991
Designed by Townend/Brodigan
27 holes, 5632 yards, S.S.S. 69
† Welcome by arrangement.
WD £17; WE £23.
Welcome by prior arrangement; 27 holes golf; all-day catering high season

only; 3rd nine added in 1995 to form Plews and Quarry high courses; £29.
Clubhouse facilities, including bistro and Sparrows restaurant all year round.
Club have cottages to rent.

8A 35 Concord Park
Shiregreen, Sheffield, S Yorks, S5 6AE
☎ 0114 2577378, Pro 577378, Sec 2349802, Rest/Bar 577378
Course is off the A6135 3.5 miles N of Sheffield.
Parkland course.
Pro Warren Allcroft; Founded 1952
18 holes, 4872 yards, S.S.S. 64
20 bays, floodlit and under cover.
† Welcome by prior arrangement.
WD £7.50; WE £8.
Welcome; from £7.50.
Full clubhouse facilities.

8A 36 Cottingham
Woodhill Way, Cottingham, E Yorks, HU16 5RZ
☎ 01482 842394, Fax 8459332, Sec 846030, Rest/Bar 846030
Off A164 4 miles off the M62/A63.
Parkland course.
Pro Chris Gray; Founded 1994
Designed by J Wiles/T Litten
18 holes, 6230 yards, S.S.S. 69
Ranges available.
† Welcome by prior arrangement.
WD £16; WE £24.
Welcome by prior arrangement; WD and WE packages available; from £30.
Fully licensed bar and restaurant.
Willerby Manor; Jarvis Grange.

8A 37 Crimple Valley
Hookstone Wood Road, Harrogate, Yorks, HG2 8PN
☎ 01423 883485, Pro 883485, Sec 883485, Rest/Bar 883485
Course is off the A61 one mile S of town centre.
Parkland course.
Founded 1976
Designed by R Lumb
9 holes, 5000 yards
† Public pay and play.
WD £5; WE £6 (9 holes).
Welcome by arrangement.
Fully licensed bar and restaurant.

8A 38 Crookhill Park
Carr Lane, Conisbrough, Nr Doncaster, S Yorks, DN12 2AH

☎ 01709 862979, Sec 863566, Rest/Bar 862974
Off A630 Doncaster to Rotherham road.
Parkland course.
Pro R Swaine; Founded 1976
18 holes, 5849 yards, S.S.S. 68
† Welcome by prior arrangement.
WD £9.25; WE £10.50.
Welcome by prior arrangement with the professional; discounts available depending on group size; terms on application.
Clubhouse facilities.

8A 39 Crosland Heath
Felks Stile Road, Crosland Heath, Huddersfield, HD4 7AF
☎ 01484 653216, Pro 653877, Sec 653262
Take A62 Huddersfield-Oldham road and follow signs for Countryside Leisure.
Moorland course
Pro John Jeyre; Founded 1913
18 holes, 6004 yards, S.S.S. 69
Practice fields.
† By prior arrangement only; handicap certs required.
Terms on application.
Welcome except Sat by prior arrangement; catering packages by arrangement; terms on application.
Full facilities available except Mon.
Dryclough, Crosland Moor; Durker Roods, Meltham.

8A 40 Crows Nest Park
Coach Road, Hove Edge, Brighouse, W Yorks, HD6 2LN
☎ 01484 401121, Pro 01484 401121, Rest/Bar 01484 401152
Off M62 at Brighouse follow signs for Bradford; turn left at Ritz.
Parkland course.
Pro Paul Everitt; Founded 1985
Designed by W Adamson
9 holes, 6020 yards, S.S.S. 69
8 bays, floodlight.
† Welcome.
WD £10; WE £10.
Welcome; golf and catering packages available; terms on application.
Clubhouse facilities available.
Lane Head.

8A 41 Dewsbury District
The Pinnacle, Sands Lane, Mirfield, W Yorks, WF14 8HJ
☎ 01924 492399, Fax 492399, Pro 496030, Rest/Bar 491928

Course is two miles W of Dewsbury off the A644; three miles from the M62 Junction 25.
Parkland/moorland course.
Pro N Hirst; Founded 1891
Designed by T Morris/P Alliss
18 holes, 6360 yards, S.S.S. 71
♣ Welcome WD and after 2.30pm WE.
⌐ WD £17.50; WE £12.50.
⟳ Welcome WD and Sun after 2.30pm; full packages of 27 holes of golf and catering available; from £32.
⦿ Full clubhouse facilities.
↵ Four Arches.

8A 42 Doncaster
278 Bawtry Road, Bessacarr, Doncaster, S Yorks, DN4 7PD
▤ GBDoncaster.g.c@ic24.net
☎ 01302 865632, Fax 865994, Pro 868404
On A638 between Doncaster and Bawtry.
Undulating heathland course.
Pro Graham Bailey; Founded 1894
18 holes, 6220 yards, S.S.S. 70
♣ Welcome.
⌐ WD £27.50; WE £33.00.
⟳ Welcome WD by prior arrangement with Sec; packages by arrangement; terms available on application.
⦿ Full clubhouse facilities.
↵ Punches; Danum.

8A 43 Doncaster Town Moor
Bawtry Road, Belle Vue, Doncaster, S Yorks, DN4 5HU
☎ 01302 533778, Pro 535286, Sec 533778, Rest/Bar 533167
Next to Doncaster Rovers FC and close to racecourse.
Moorland course.
Pro Steve Shaw; Founded 1895
18 holes, 6001 yards, S.S.S. 69
⊺ Practice ground.
♣ Welcome; restrictions Sun.
⌐ WD £17; WE £18.
⟳ Welcome by arrangement; full days golf and catering by arrangement, prices on application.
⦿ Clubhouse facilities.
↵ Royal St Ledger; Earl of Doncaster.

8A 44 Dore & Totley
Bradway Road, Sheffield, S Yorks, S17 4QR
⬚ www.doreandtotleygolf.co.uk
▤ dtgc@lineone.net
☎ 0114 2360492, Fax 2353436,

Pro 2366844, Sec 2369872, Rest/Bar 2360492
6 miles S of Sheffield on the B6054 for Bradway.
Parkland course.
Pro Greg Roberts; Founded 1913
18 holes, 6256 yards, S.S.S. 70
♣ Welcome by prior arrangement except Sat; restrictions apply on Sun and Wed.
⌐ WD £26; WE £26.
⟳ Welcome except Wed and Sat; summer and winter packages can be arranged through Pro; terms on application.
⦿ Full clubhouse facilities.

8A 45 Drax
Drax, Nr Selby, N Yorks, YO8 8PQ
☎ 01405 860533
Corse is off the A1041 six miles south of Selby opposite the Drax power station.
Tree-lined parkland course.
Founded 1989
9 holes, 5510 yards, S.S.S. 67
♣ Only with a member.
⌐ Not available.
⦿ At Drax Sports and Social Club.

8A 46 Driffield
Sunderlandwick, Beverley Road, Driffield, E Yorks, YO25 7AD
☎ 01377 253116, Fax 240599, Pro 241224, Sec 253116, Rest 255211 Bar 240448
Off A164 Beverley to Driffield road off the first main roundabout.
Mature parkland course.
Pro Kenton Wright; Founded 1934
18 holes, 6215 yards, S.S.S. 70
♣ Welcome with club or society handicap certs WD 9.30am-12noon & 1.30pm-30m; WE between 9.30am-11am.
⌐ WD £20; WE £30 per round.
⟳ Welcome by prior arrangement with handicap certs; catering packages available; practice area; terms on application.
⦿ Clubhouse facilities.
↵ Bell, Driffield.

8A 47 Easingwold
Stillington Road, Easingwold, York, N Yorkshire, YO 13ET
▤ brian@easingwold-golf.club. fsnet.co.uk
☎ 01347 821486, Fax 822474, Pro 821964, Sec 822474
On A19 12 miles N of York; 1 mile down Stillington road at S end of

Easingwold.
Parkland course.
Pro J Hughes; Founded 1930
Designed by Hawtree
18 holes, 6705 yards, S.S.S. 72
⊺ Large practice area.
♣ Welcome by prior arrangement.
⌐ WD £25; WE £30.
⟳ Welcome by prior arrangement; golf and full catering packages; £38.
⦿ Clubhouse facilities.
↵ The George.

8A 48 East Brierley
South View Road, Bierley, Bradford, W Yorkshre, BD4 6PP
☎ 01274 681023, Sec 683666, Rest/Bar 680450
4 miles S of Bradford.
Parkland course.
Founded 1904/28
9 holes, 4692 yards, S.S.S. 63
♣ Welcome. Except Sun.
⌐ WD £14; WE £17.
⟳ Welcome by prior arrangement; terms on application.
⦿ Full catering facilities.

8A 49 Elland
Hammerstones, Leach Lane, Elland, W Yorks, HX5 0TA
☎ 01422 372505, Pro 374886
From M62 Junction 24 in direction of Blackley.
Parkland course.
Pro N Kryzwicki; Founded 1910
9 holes, 5630 yards, S.S.S. 66
♣ Welcome.
⌐ Terms on application.
⟳ Welcome Tues, Wed, Fri; catering packages available; from £14.
⦿ Clubhouse facilities.
↵ Rock Hotel, Holywell Green.

8A 50 Fardew
Nursery Farm, Carr Lane, East Morton, Keighley, W Yorks, BD20 5RY
▤ fardewgc@btclick.com
☎ 01274 561229, Fax 561229
1.25 miles from Bingley, then to E Morton.
Parkland course.
Pro Ian Bottomley; Founded 1993
Designed by W Adamson
9 holes, 6208 yards, S.S.S. 70
⊺ Open practice ground.
♣ Pay and play.
⌐ WD £14; WE £16 (18 holes); £2 per 18 holes reduction if booked in advance.
⟳ Welcome by prior arrangement; terms on application.

🍴 Café.
🏌 Beeches, Keighley.

8A 51 **Ferrybridge 'C'**
Ferrybridge 'C' P.S. Golf Club,
Knottingley, WF11 8SQ
☎ 01977 884165
On Castleford-Knottingley road 200
yards from A1.
Parkland course.
Founded 1976
Designed by NE Pugh
9 holes, 5138 yards, S.S.S. 65
🏌 Welcome as the guest of a
member.
⌊ Terms on application.
🏌 Welcome by arrangement.
🏌 Darrington Hotel; Golden Lion.

8A 52 **Filey**
West Ave, Filey, N Yorks, YO14 9BQ
☎ 01723 513116, Fax 514952,
Pro 513134, Sec 513293,
Rest/Bar 513293
1 mile S of Filey.
Links/parkland course.
Pro Gary Hutchinson; Founded 1897
Designed by J Braid
18 holes, 6112 yards, S.S.S. 69
🏌 Practice facilities.
🏌 Welcome by arrangement.
⌊ WD £22; WE £29.
🏌 Welcome with prior arrangement;
catering packages available; from
£21.
🍴 Clubhouse facilities.
🏌 White Lodge; Hallam.

8A 53 **Flamborough Head**   ☎
Lighthouse Road, Flamborough,
Bridlington, E Yorkshire, YO15 1AR
☎ 01262 850333, Sec 850683
5 miles NE of Bridlington situation on
Flamborough headland.
Clifftop course.
Founded 1931
18 holes, 6189 yards, S.S.S. 69
🏌 Practice area.
🏌 Welcome.
⌊ WD £20; WE £25.
🏌 Welcome by arrangement; full day
golf and catering available.
🍴 Clubhouse facilities.
🏌 North Star; Flaneburg.

8A 54 **Forest of Galtres**
Moorlands Road, Skelton, York, Yorks,
YO32 2RF
☎ 01904 766198, Fax 766198,
Pro 766198, Sec 769400,
Rest/Bar 750287

Just off A19 Thirsk road through
Skelton; 1.5 miles from B1237 York
ring road.
Parkland in ancient Forest of Galtres.
Pro Phil Bradley; Founded 1993
Designed by S Gidman
18 holes, 6412 yards, S.S.S. 70
🏌 12
🏌 Welcome.
⌊ WD £20; WE £27.
🏌 Welcome by prior arrangement
only; discounts for groups of 12 or
more; from £27.
🍴 Full clubhouse facilities.
🏌 Beechwood Close; Jacobean
Lodge; Fairfield Manor.

8A 55 **Forest Park**
Stockton on Forest, York, YO32 9UW
☎ 01904 400425
Course is 2.5 miles from E end of York
by-pass.
Flat parkland course.
Founded 1991
18 holes, 6660 yards, S.S.S. 72
🏌 Welcome.
⌊ WD £16; WE £22.
🏌 Welcome; all-day golf and catering
packages available; also 9-hole West
Course: 6372 yards, par 70; from £33.
🍴 Full clubhouse facilities.
🏌 B&B in Stockton-on-Forest.

8A 56 **Fulford**
Heslington Lane, York, Yorks, YO10
5DY
☎ 01904 413579, Fax 416918,
Pro 412882, Sec 413579,
Rest/Bar 411503
Off A19 1 mile S of York following signs
to University.
Parkland/heathland course.
Pro Martin Brown; Founded 1909
Designed by Major C MacKenzie
18 holes, 6775 yards, S.S.S. 72
🏌 Welcome by arrangement.
⌊ WD £37; WE £48.
🏌 Welcome by prior arrangement;
not Tues am; packages can be
arranged through manager; terms on
application.
🍴 Full clubhouse facilities.
🏌 Pavilion, Hilton, Poste House,The
swallow, The Viking.

8A 57 **Fulneck**
The Clubhouse, Fulneck, Pudsey, W
Yorks, LS28 8NT
☎ 0113 2565191, Sec 256519,
Rest/Bar 2565191
Between Leeds and Bradford; at
Pudsey cenotaph turn left then turn

right at T-junction and take the first left
at Bankhouse lane.Turn left at the
Bankhouse Pub.
Undulating wooded parkland course.
Founded 1892
9 holes, 5456 yards, S.S.S. 66
🏌 Welcome all week. Prior booking
for Saturdays.
⌊ £15 per day all week, £8 with a
member.
🏌 Welcome by prior arrangement
with Sec; catering packages by
arrangement; terms available on
application.
🍴 By arrangement.
🏌 Stakis Hotel, Tong village.

8A 58 **Ganstead Park**
Longdales Lane, Coniston, Hull, E
Yorks, HU11 4LB
☎ 01482 874754, Fax 817754,
Pro 811121, Rest/Bar 811280
On A165 Hull-Bridlington road at
Ganstead.
Parkland course with water.
Pro Mike Smee; Founded 1976
Designed by Peter Green
18 holes, 6801 yards, S.S.S. 73
🏌 Welcome by prior arrangement.
⌊ Terms on application.
🏌 Welcome by prior arrangement;
special packages can be arranged;
terms on application.
🍴 Full clubhouse facilities.
🏌 Kingstown, Hedon; Tickton
Grange, Beverley.

8A 59 **Ganton**
Ganton, Scarborough, N Yorks, YO12
4PA
✉ secretray@
gantongolfclub.fsnet.co.uk
☎ 01944 710329, Fax 710922,
Pro 710260, Sec 710329,
Rest/Bar 712806
On A64 11 miles W of Scarborough.
Heathland/links course.
Pro Gary Brown; Founded 1891
Designed by Dunn, Vardon, Colt, CK
Cotton
18 holes, 6734 yards, S.S.S. 73
🏌 13 acre practice range and short
game area.
🏌 Welcome by prior arrangement.
⌊ WD round or day £60; WE round
or day and public holidays £70.
🏌 Welcome by prior agreement;
packages can be organised; terms on
application.
🍴 Full clubhouse facilities.
🏌 Crescent, Scarborough; Ganton
Greyhound.

Ganton

Ganton can be proud of the fact that very little appears to have altered over the past 110 years in this restful nook of north Yorkshire. Founded in 1891, Harry Vardon joined as professional in 1896 and immediately charmed the locals when he won his first Open at Muirfield.

Feasting on port and Ganton Cake (another club legend) before the log fire, misty-eyed members – of which there are only 250 – return from their labours on this handsome inland links and speak of Vardon as the standard-bearer for their way of life there.

Vardon, together with Ted Ray, another Open champion, was influential in redesigning the course in 1905 and it is surely no coincidence that it became strongly reminiscent of the site of Vardon's first of six Opens; most notably for its deep revetted bunkers.

Nowhere is this more pronounced than at the 16th where a cross bunker, 30 yards wide and looking almost as deep, confronts the tee. Today it is only a 150-yard carry to clear the trap, but hitting a guttie with hickory-shafted clubs at the turn of the century would have been a different story.

Sometimes the bunkers challenge you to take them on (at the driveable 280-yard par four fourteenth for instance), other times they loiter innocuously on the fringes of fairways (the glorious dog-leg seventh) but, owing to the subtle contours of the land around them, they will always gather in your ball. The secretary, Major Robert Woolsey, admits he has never avoided a trap during a round.

Gorse – thick, wild and always in bloom on some part of the course – is a relative innovation at Ganton; it was planted in the late 1930s. As you might expect the three par threes – all intriguing holes – demand you play over it. The fifth is the shortest (144 yards) with a pond to the left, a stream to the right, and a couple more monstrous bunkers surrounding the green.

The Scarborough sea-breeze blowing in from eight miles away with bunkers short and long make club selection crucial at the tenth while the 252-yard seventeenth is, somewhat controversially, a short par four from medal tees – but a damn difficult par three for everyone else.

The course keeps you thinking until your last shot has been holed. A blind drive at the eighteenth must come to rest in the centre of the fairway if you do not want the additional challenge of carrying fir trees to another guarded, and deceptively undulating green. When Ganton hosted the thirty-first Curtis Cup in 2001, members took heart as they witnessed a procession of the world's finest ladies golfers fail to master the final test. They now anticipate the world's best amateurs struggling when the Walker Cup arrives in 2003.

While the glory of hosting the 1949 Ryder Cup will never return, modern golf events and modern golfers are still drawn here.

As is right and proper, 'the mobile' is outlawed here; but the decree is stressed in the visitor's changing-room where a notice reads: "A golf course is a place where members and visitors expect to find peaceful recreation and good fellowship in the enjoyment of the game of golf. The advent of the personal telephone may be regarded by some as an important addition to their personal efficiency, but to take their equipment onto the golf course destroys for others much of the enjoyment of the game." Mr Vardon would have approved. — **Jim Bruce-Ball**

8A 60 Garforth
Long Lane, Garforth, Leeds, LS25 2DS
☎ 0113 2862021, Pro 2862063,
Sec 2863308
6.5 miles E of Leeds off A642 1 mile
from Wass Garage.
Parkland course.
Pro Ken Finlater; Founded 1913
18 holes, 6304 yards, S.S.S. 70
† Welcome WD.
Ⓛ WD on application.
♨ Welcome WD by prior
arrangement; terms available on
application.
Ⓘ Full facilities.
↝ Hilton.

8A 61 Gott's Park
Armley Ridge Road, Leeds, W Yorks,
LS12 2QX
☎ 0113 2311896, Rest/Bar 2310492
3 miles W of the city centre.
Parkland course.
Founded 1933
18 holes, 4978 yards, S.S.S. 65
† Welcome.
Ⓛ WD £7.25; WE £8.75.
♨ Welcome by arrangement.
Ⓘ Cafe facilities; bar in evenings and
WE.

8A 62 Grange Park
Upper Wortley Road, Rotherham, S
Yorks, S61 2SJ
☎ 01709 558884, Pro 559497
On A629 2 miles W of Rotherham.
Municipal parkland; private clubhouse
Pro Eric Clark; Founded 1971
18 holes, 6421 yards, S.S.S. 71
Ⓘ 36 two-tier floodlit covered.
† Welcome.
Ⓛ WD £9; WE £11.
♨ Welcome by prior arrangement
with Sec; special catering and golf
packages available; terms on
application.
Ⓘ Full bar and catering facilities
Tues-Sun; limited Mon.
↝ Swallow.

8A 63 Great Grimsby Golf Centre
Cromwell Road, Grimsby, DN31 2BH
🖳 www.greatgrimsbygolfcentre.
co.uk
☎ 014722 50555, Fax 67447,
Pro 50555
From A180 follow signs for Auditorium
and Leisure centre.
Parkland course.
Pro Stephen Bennett; Founded 1995
9 holes, 4652 yards, S.S.S. 32

Ⓘ Practice ground/27 driving bays.
† Public pay and play.
Ⓛ WD £5.50; WE £6.50.
♨ None.
Ⓘ Limited.
↝ Millfields Hotel, Grimsby.

8A 64 Hainsworth Park
Brandesburton, Driffield, E Yorks,
YO25 8RT
✉ hainsworth@hemscott.net
☎ 01964 542362
Just off A165 8 miles N of Beverley.
Parkland course.
Pro Paul Binnington; Founded 1983
18 holes, 6362 yards, S.S.S. 69
† Welcome by prior arrangements.
Ⓛ Terms on application.
♨ Welcome by prior arrangement;
day tickets available (WD £20, WE
£25); from £14.
Ⓘ Full catering and restaurant
facilities.
↝ Burton Lodge on course.

8A 65 Halifax
Union Lane, Ogden, Halifax, W Yorks,
HX2 8XR
☎ 01422 244171, Fax 241459,
Pro 240047, Rest/Bar 248108
Course is on the A629 four miles from
Halifax.
Moorland course.
Pro Michael Allison; Founded 1895
Designed by WH Fowler, James
Braid
18 holes, 6037 yards, S.S.S. 70
Ⓘ 2 miles away.
† Welcome WD; limited at WE.
Ⓛ WD £25; WE £35.
♨ Welcome WD by prior
arrangement with Sec; packages
available with catering; fees by prior
arrangement.
Ⓘ Full clubhouse facilities.
↝ Windmill Court; Holdsworth House;
Moorlands.

8A 66 Halifax Bradley Hall
Stainland Road, Holywell Green,
Halifax, W Yorks, HX4 9AN
☎ 01422 374108, Pro 370231
On B6112 off A629 Halifax-
Huddersfield Road.
Moorland/parkland course.
Pro Peter Wood; Founded 1905/24
18 holes, 6213 yards, S.S.S. 70
† Welcome with handicap certs.
Ⓛ WD £18; WE £28.
♨ Welcome with handicap certs and
by prior arrangement; golf and catering
packages; £33.

Ⓘ Full clubhouse facilities.
↝ Rock Inn, Holywell Green.

8A 67 Hallamshire
The Clubhouse, Sandygate, Sheffield,
S Yorks, S10 4LA
☎ 0114 2301007, Fax 2302153,
Pro 2305222, Sec 2302153
3 miles W of Sheffield off A57 at
Crosspool.
Moorland course.
Pro Geoff Tickell; Founded 1897
Designed by Various including Dr A
MacKenzie
18 holes, 6359 yards, S.S.S. 71
† Welcome; some restrictions at WE.
Ⓛ Terms on application.
♨ Welcome by arrangement with
Sec; packages available; terms on
application.
Ⓘ Full clubhouse facilities.
↝ Beauchef; Trust House Forte.

8A 68 Hallowes
Hallowes Lane, Dronfield, Sheffield, S
Yorks, S18 1UA
☎ 01246 413734, Fax 411196,
Pro 411196, Sec 413734,
Rest/Bar 410394
Take A61 Sheffield-Chesterfield road
into Dronfield and turn sharp right
under railway bridge.
Undulating moorland course.
Pro Philip Dunn; Founded 1892
18 holes, 6342 yards, S.S.S. 71
† Welcome WD. Visitors
accompanied by members WE.
Ⓛ WD £30, WE £15 with member.
♨ Welcome WD by arrangement; day
ticket WD £35; catering by
arrangement; terms available on
application.
Ⓘ Full clubhouse facilities.
↝ Chantry.

8A 69 Hanging Heaton
White Cross Road, Bennett Lane,
Dewsbury, W Yorks, WF12 7DT
☎ 01924 461606, Fax 430100,
Pro 467077, Sec 430100
On A653 Dewbury-Leeds road 0.75
miles from town centre.
Parkland course.
Pro G Moore; Founded 1922
9 holes, 5902 yards, S.S.S. 69
† Welcome WD; with member at
WE.
Ⓛ WD £11 with member £16 without.
♨ Welcome by arrangement with
Sec; full day packages available; terms
on application.
Ⓘ Full clubhouse facilities.

8A 70 **Harrogate**
Forest Lane Head, Harrogate, N Yorks, HG2 7TF
☎ 01423 863158, Fax 860073, Pro 862547, Sec 862999, Rest/Bar 863158
On A59 betwen Knaresborough and Harrogate.
Parkland course.
Pro Paul Johnson; Founded 1892
Designed by Sandy Herd; revised by Dr A McKenzie
19 holes, 6241 yards, S.S.S. 70
† Welcome by arrangement.
[WD £30 per round £35 for the day; WE £40.
⟁ Welcome by prior arrangement; packages can be arranged; min 12.
|●| Bar and restaurant.
⤷ Local tourist board can provide brochures.

8A 71 **Headingley**
Back Church Lane, Adel, Leeds, LS16 8DW
☎ 0113 2679573, Fax 2817334, Pro 2675100, Sec 2679573, Rest/Bar 2673052
Course is off the A660 Leeds to Otley road.
Undulating parkland course.
Pro Steve Foster; Founded 1892
18 holes, 6298 yards, S.S.S. 70
⫯ Practice area.
† Welcome by prior arrangement.
[WD £30; WE £40.
⟁ Welcome by arrangement with the manager; day ticket WD £35; snooker; terms available on application.
|●| Full facilities.
⤷ Village Hotel.

8A 72 **Headley**
Headley Lane, Thornton, Bradford, W Yorks, BD13 3LX
☎ 01274 833481, Fax 833481
4 miles W of Bradford on B6145 in Thornton village.
Moorland course.
Founded 1907
9 holes, 5253 yards, S.S.S. 64
⫯ Practice range and green
† Welcome WD.
[WD £15.
⟁ Welcome by arrangement with Sec; special golf and catering packages available.
|●| Dining room and bar.
⤷ Guide Post.

8A 73 **Hebden Bridge**
Wadsworth, Hebden Bridge, HX7 8PH

☎ 01422 842896, Sec 842732
In Hebden Bridge, cross Keighley road until Mount Skip Inn.
Upland course on edge of moor.
Founded 1930
9 holes, 5242 yards, S.S.S. 65
† Welcome by prior arrangement.
[WD £12; WE £15.
⟁ Welcome, preferably on Wed; from £12.
|●| Clubhouse facilities.
⤷ Carlton; White Lion.

8A 74 **Hessle**
Westfield Road, Cottingham, Hull, E Yorks, HU16 5YI
☎ 01482 650171, Fax 652679, Pro 650190, Sec 650171, Rest/Bar 659187 Bar Caterers 659457
Course is 3 miles SW of Cottingham off the A164.
Undulating meadowland; new course 1975.
Pro Grahame Fieldsend; Founded 1906
Designed by Peter Alliss & Dave Thomas
18 holes, 6604 yards, S.S.S. 72
† Welcome except Tues 9.am-1pm or before 11.30am at WE.
[WD £25; WE £30.
⟁ Welcome by prior arrangement with Sec; catering packages by arrangement except Mon; terms on application.
|●| Catering except Mon.
⤷ Grange Park; Willoughby Manor.

8A 75 **Heworth**
Muncaster House, Muncastergate, York, Yorks, YO31 9JX
☎ 01904 422389, Fax 422389, Pro 422389, Sec 426156
On 1036 Scarborough Malton road 1.5 miles NE of City centre.
Parkland course.
Pro G Roberts; Founded 1911
11 holes, 6141 yards, S.S.S. 69
⫯ Practice area.
† Welcome.
[WD £14, WE£18. £10 with member.
⟁ Welcome by prior arrangement; full catering packages available except Mon; terms available on application.
|●| Full clubhouse bar and catering except Mon.

8A 76 **Hickleton**
Lidget Lane, Hickleton, Nr Doncaster, S Yorks, DN5 7BE
☎ 01709 896081, Fax 896083, Pro 888436, Sec 896081,

Rest/Bar 896081
On B6411 Thurnscoe road off the A635 Barnsley road; 4.5 miles from A1 (M) Junction 37.
Parkland course.
Pro Paul Audsley; Founded 1909
Designed by Huggett, Coles & Dyer
18 holes, 6418 yards, S.S.S. 71
† Welcome by prior arrangement.
[WD £20; WE £27.
⟁ Welcome by prior arrangement; summer packages available; terms on application.
|●| Bar, with cask beers, and restaurant available.
⤷ Ardsley House, Barnsley; Doncaster Moat House.

8A 77 **Hillsborough**　　　　♛
Worrall Road, Sheffield, S Yorks, S6 4BE
⬚ www.hillsboroughgolfclub.co.uk
✉ louis.horsman@line1.net
☎ 0114 2349151, Fax 2349151, Pro 2332666, Sec 2349151, Rest/Bar 2349151
Off A6102 Sheffield to Manchester road NW of the city just past Sheffield Wed's football ground, turning right at Horse and Jockey pub.
Undulating wooded parkland and heathland.
Pro Louis Horsman; Founded 1920
Designed by T Williamson
18 holes, 6216 yards, S.S.S. 70
† Welcome WD and after 2pm at WE.
[WD £30; WE £35.
⟁ Welcome by prior arrangement with Sec; larger groups can negotiate rates; snooker; catering packages; driving range; terms on application.
|●| Full restaurant and bar service.
⤷ Queens Ground, Hillsborough; Grosvenor,Tankersley; Manor,Tankersley.

8A 78 **Hollins Hall Golf Course**
Marriott Hollins Hall and Country Club, Baildon, Shipley; W Yorks, BD17 7QW
⬚ www.marriotthotels.com/LBAGS
☎ 01274 530053
On A6038, main road from Shipley to Otley. 10 miles from Leeds, 6 miles from Bradford.
First 9 holes flat, 2nd 9 holes hilly.
18 holes, blue 6671, white 6354, yellow 6051, red 5433 yards
† Yes.
[£35.
⟁ Yes.
|●| Café/restaurant.
⤷ Hollins Hall Hotel.

8A 79 Hornsea
Rolston Road, Hornsea, E Yorks,
HU18 1XG
⅏ www.hornseagolfclub.cwc.net
☎ 01964 532020, Fax 532080,
Pro 534989, Sec 532020
Follow signs to Hornsea Free Port
Club, 300 yards past port.
Parkland course.
Pro Stretton Wright; Founded 1898
Designed by Harry Vardon/Dr
McKenzie/J Braid
18 holes, 6421 yards, S.S.S. 72
† Welcome WD and after 3pm Sat
and 2pm Sun.
Ⅼ WD £22 or £30 for the day; Sat
£30 and Sun £22 per round.
⟳ Welcome by prior arrangement;
packages available prices on
application.
▣ Full clubhouse facilities.
↩ Burton Lodge, Brandesburton;
Merlstead, Hornsea.

8A 80 Horsforth   ☎
Layton Rise, Horsforth, Leeds, W
Yorkshire, LS18 5EX
☎ 0113 2581703, Fax 2586819,
Pro 2585200, Sec 2586819,
Rest/Bar 2581703
Off A65 towards Ilkley 6 miles from city
centre.
Upland/parkland course.
Pro DeanStokes/Simon Booth;
Founded 1907
18 holes, 6205 yards, S.S.S. 70
Ⅰ Large practice ground.
† Welcome WD; WE by prior
arrangement.
Ⅼ WD £25; WE £35. Mon-Fri 2 for 1
on golf and Daily Telegraph.
⟳ Welcome WD by prior
arrangement; full packages of golf and
catering available.
▣ Full clubhouse facilities.
↩ The Parkway.

8A 81 Howley Hall
Scotchman Lane, Morley, Leeds, W
Yorks, LS27 0NX
⅏ www.howleyhall.co.uk
▤ office@howleyhall.co.uk
☎ 01924 350100, Fax 350104,
Pro 350102, Sec 478417
Course is on the B6123 0.75 miles
from junction with the A650 at Halfway
House pub.
Parkland course.
Pro Gary Watkinson; Founded 1900
18 holes, 6346 yards, S.S.S. 71
† Welcome.
Ⅼ WD £29; WE £39.
⟳ Welcome by prior arrangement;

catering packages available on
application; from £29.
▣ Full clubhouse facilities.

8A 82 Huddersfield (Fixby)
Fixby Hall, Lightridge Road,
Huddersfield, West Yorkshire, HD2
2EP
⅏ www.huddersfield-golf.co.uk
▤ secretary@huddersfield-golf.co.uk
☎ 01484 426203, Fax 424623,
Pro 426463, Sec 426203,
Rest/Bar 420110
From M62 Junction 24 follow signs to
Brighouse; turn right at traffic lights.
Parkland course.
Pro Paul Carman; Founded 1891
Designed by Herbert Fowler,
amendments by Hawtree.
18 holes, 6467 yards, S.S.S. 71
† Welcome; handicap certs required.
Ⅼ WD £37; WE £47.
⟳ Welcome WD except Tues;
catering can be organised; from £45.
▣ Full clubhouse bar and restaurant
facilities.
↩ Cedar Court.

8A 83 Hull
The Hall, 27 Packman Lane, Kirkella,
Hull, East Yorkshire, HU10 7TJ
☎ 01482 658919, Fax 658919,
Pro 653074, Sec 658919,
Rest/Bar 653026
5 miles W of Hull.
Parkland course.
Pro David Jagger; Founded 1904
Designed by James Braid
18 holes, 6246 yards, S.S.S. 70
† Welcome by prior arrangement;
with member at WE.
Ⅼ WD £26.50 per round, £32 per full
day.
⟳ Welcome Tues and Thurs by prior
arrangement; terms available on
application.
▣ Full clubhouse facilities.
↩ Willerby Manor; Grange Park.

8A 84 Ilkley
Nesfield Road, Myddleton, Ilkley, W
Yorks, LS29 0BE
⅏ www.ilkleygolfclub.co.uk
▤ honsec@ilkleygolfclub.co.uk
☎ 01943 600214, Fax 816130,
Pro 607463, Sec 600214,
Rest/Bar 607277
15 miles N of Bradford.
Parkland course.
Pro John Hammond; Founded 1890
Designed by Alistair Mackenzie
18 holes, 6262 yards, S.S.S. 70

† Welcome by arrangement;
handicap certs required.
Ⅼ WD £37; WE £42 and BH.
⟳ Welcome WD by arrangement;
catering packages can be arranged;
£35.
▣ Full clubhouse facilities.
↩ Devonshire Arms Country Hotel.

8A 85 Keighley
Howden Park, Utley, Keighley, West
Yorkshire, BD20 6DH
⅏ www.keighleygolfclub.co.uk
▤ golf@keighleygolfclub.co.uk
☎ 01535 604778, Fax 604833,
Pro 665370, Sec 604778,
Rest/Bar 604778
1 mile W of Keighley on the old
Keighley-Skipton road.
Parkland course.
Pro Mike Bradley; Founded 1904
18 holes, 6141 yards, S.S.S. 70
† Welcome except before 9.30am
and between 12 00pm-1.30pm WD;
Ladies day Tues; not Sat; by prior
arrangement Sun.
Ⅼ WD £28; WE and BH £32.
⟳ Welcome by prior arrangement
with the manager; day rates available;
catering by arrangement; terms on
application.
▣ Full bar and catering facilities
available every day; à la carte menu.
↩ Dales Gate.

8A 86 Kilnwick Percy   ☎
Pocklington, East Yorkshire, YO42 1UF
☎ 01759 303090, Pro 303090,
Sec 303090, Rest/Bar 303090
1 mile E of Pocklington off the
B1246.
Parkland course.
Pro Jill Townhill; Founded 1994
Designed by John Day
18 holes, 6214 yards, S.S.S. 70
† Welcome any time.
Ⅼ WD £15; WE £18; full day: WD
£21, WE £25.
⟳ Welcome by prior arrangement;
terms on application.
▣ Snack menu, full catering service
available for societies by prior
arrangement.
↩ Yorkway Motel.

8A 87 Kirkbymoorside   ☎
Manor Vale, Kirkbymoorside, York,
YO62 6EG
⅏ www.kirkbymoorsidegolf.co.uk
▤ enqs@kmsgolf.fsnet.co.uk
☎ 01751 431525, Fax 433190,
Pro 430402, Sec 431525

Course is on the A170 N of Kirkbymoorside. Parkland course; club moved to site 1953.
Pro Chris Tyson; Founded 1905/53
Designed by TK Cotton
18 holes, 6101 yards, S.S.S. 69
† Welcome after 9.00am.
[WD £20; WE £27.
⌂ Welcome by prior arrangement; packages available for golf and catering; £29.50.
|●| Full clubhouse facilities available.
↳ George & Dragon; Kings Head, both Kirkbymoorside.

8A 88 **Knaresborough**
Butterhills, Boroughbridge Road, North Yorkshire, HG5 0QQ
☎ 01423 862690, Fax 869345,
Pro 864865, Sec 862690,
Rest/Bar 863219
On A6055 Boroughbridge Road 2 miles outside Knaresborough.
Parkland course with extensive trees.
Pro Gary J Vickers; Founded 1920
Designed by Hawtree & Son
18 holes, 6507 yards, S.S.S. 71
† Welcome after 9.30am WD and noon WE; during winter season visitors must be accompanied by a member on WE.
[WD £28.50; WE £35.50.
⌂ Welcome by prior arrangement between April 1 and Oct 31; parties of 12 or more welcome; full day golf and catering packages available from £42.
|●| Full restaurant and bar facilities.
↳ Newton House Hotel, Knaresborough Dower House, Knaresborough; Crown Hotel, Boroughbridge.

8A 89 **Leeds (Cobble Hall)** ☾
Elemete Lane, Leeds, W Yorks, LS8 2LJ
⌨ www.leedsgolfclub.com
☎ 0113 2658775, Fax 2323369,
Pro 2658786, Sec 2659203
On A58 Leeds-Wetherby road.
Parkland course, views of Roundhay Park.
Pro Simon Longster; Founded 1896
18 holes, 6092 yards, S.S.S. 69
† Welcome WD by prior arrangement.
[WD £30; £35 for day.
⌂ Welcome by prior arrangement; packages available; terms on application.
|●| Full catering facilities.
↳ Holiday Inn, special rates available.

8A 90 **Leeds Golf Centre**
Wike Ridge Lane, Shadwell, Leeds, West Yorkshire, LS17 9JW
⌨ www.leedsgolfcentre.co.uk
☎ 0113 2886000, Fax 2886185,
Pro 2886000, Rest/Bar 2886160
Just off A61 Harrogate Road, 5 miles N of Leeds.
Open heathland course.
Pro N Harvey, M Pinkett; Founded 1993
Designed by Donald Steel
18 holes, 6482 yards off the white
5963 yards off the yellow, S.S.S. 71
[20 covered floodlit.
† Everyone welcome.
[WD £14.50; WE £16.50.
⌂ Welcome; restricted numbers at WE; golf and catering packages are available; also the 12-hole Oaks course.
|●| Full facilities.
↳ Harewood Arms; Weetwood Hall, both Leeds.

8A 91 **Lees Hall**
Hemsworth Road, Norton, Sheffield, S8 9LI
☎ 0114 2554402, Fax 2552900,
Pro 2507868, Sec 2552900,
Rest/Bar 2551526
3 miles S of Sheffield.
Parkland course.
Pro Simon Berry; Founded 1907
18 holes, 6171 yards, S.S.S. 70
† Welcome.
[WD £20; WE £30.
⌂ Welcome WD by prior arrangement; catering packages by arrangement; snooker; terms on application.
|●| Full facilities except Mon.
↳ Grosvenor; Holiday Inn; Sheffield Moat House.

8A 92 **Lightcliffe**
Knowle Top Road, Lightcliffe, Halifax, W Yorks, HX3 8SE
☎ 01422 202459, Pro 204081, Sec 204081
Course is on the A58 Leeds-Halifax road.
Parkland course.
Pro Robert Kershaw; Founded 1907
9 holes, 5826 yards, S.S.S. 68
[Practice green.
† Welcome except on Wed and competition days.
[WD £10; WE £15.
⌂ Welcome by prior arrangement; terms on application.
|●| Full clubhouse facilities.
↳ Trust House, Brighouse.

8A 93 **Lofthouse Hill**
Leeds Road, Lofthouse, Wakefield, WF3 3LR
⌨ www.lhgc.co.uk
☎ 01924 823703, Fax 823703,
Pro 823703, Sec 823703,
Rest/Bar 823703
Course is off the A61 four miles from Wakefield.
Parkland course.
Pro Derek Johnson; Founded 1994
Designed by BJ Design
18 holes, 5933 yards, S.S.S. 68
[8 floodlit.
† Welcome.
[WD £15; WE £17.50.
⌂ Welcome.
|●| Bar and catering facilities available.
↳ The Fir Tree Hotel.

8A 94 **Longley Park**
Maple Street, Off Somerset Rd, Huddersfield, West Yorkshire, HD5 9AX
☎ 01484 426932, Pro 422303, Sec 426932, Rest/Bar 426932
0.5 miles from Town centre.
Parkland course.
Pro Nick Leeming; Founded 1911
9 holes, 5269 yards, S.S.S. 66
† Welcome WD; restricted WE.
[WD £13; WE £16.
⌂ Welcome by arrangement except Thurs and Sat; catering by arrangement; terms available on application.
|●| Full facilities except Mon.
↳ George, Huddersfield

8A 95 **Low Laithes**
Parkmill Lane, Flushdyke, Ossett, W Yorks, WF5 9AP
⌨ www.lowlaithes.com
☎ 01924 273275, Fax 266067,
Pro 274667, Sec 266067,
Rest/Bar 273275/ 267517
Close to M1 Junction 40 off A638 towards Dewsbury; turn right at end of slip road.
Parkland course.
Pro Paul Browning; Founded 1925
Designed by MacKenzie
18 holes, 6463 yards, S.S.S. 71
† Welcome WD after 9.30am and not between 12.30pm-1.30pm; WE by prior arrangement with the club Professional.
[WD £20 per round, £25 per day. WE £32.
⌂ Welcome WD by prior arrangement; package includes 27 holes and full catering; £33.

🍴 Full clubhouse facilities.
🛏 Post House; Mews House, both Ossett.

8A 96 Malton & Norton
Welham Park, Malton, North Yorkshire, YO17 9QE
📧 maltonandnorton@golfcl.fsnet.co.uk
☎ 01653 697912, Fax 697912, Pro 693882, Sec 697912, Rest/Bar 692959
From York take the A64 to the centre of Malton, right at traffic lights and right at rail crossing; club is 0.75 miles.
Parkland course.
Pro SI Robinson; Founded 1910
Designed by Hawtree & Son
27 (3 loops of 9) holes, Welham: 6456. Park: 6251. Derwent: 6295 yards; S.S.S. Welham: 71. Park 70. Derwent 70
🏌 Welcome.
[WD £25; WE £30.
🔄 Welcome by prior arrangement; full catering packages available. All day catering package available from £15.50.
🍴 Full clubhouse facilities.
🛏 Many in local area.

8A 97 Marsden
Mount Rd, Hemplow, Marsden, Huddersfield, W Yorks, HD7 6NN
☎ 01484 844253, Sec 844253, Rest/Bar 844253
Course is off the A62 eight miles from Huddersfield.
Moorland course.
Pro Nick Kryswicki; Founded 1920
Designed by Dr A MacKenzie
9 holes, 5702 yards, S.S.S. 68
🏌 Welcome WD.
[WD £10.
🔄 Welcome WD by arrangement; packages available; terms on application.
🍴 Clubhouse facilities except Tues.
🛏 Durker Roods, Meltham.

8A 98 Masham
Burnholme, Swinton Rd, Masham, Ripon, N Yorkshire, HG4 4HT
☎ 01765 689379
Off A6108 10 miles N of Ripon.
Meadowland course.
Founded 1895
9 holes, 6068 yards, S.S.S. 70
🏌 Welcome WD; with a member at WE.
[WD £15 (18 holes), £20 for the

day, up to 3 guests with a member only £10 each.
🔄 Welcome by arrangement with Sec; catering packages available; from £15.
🍴 Full clubhouse facilities.
🛏 Swinton Park Hotel,Kings Head; Bay Horse; White Bear; Bruce Arms,all in Marsham.

8A 99 Meltham
Thick Hollins Hall, Meltham, Huddersfield, W Yorks, HD9 4DQ
☎ 01484 850227, Fax 859051, Pro 851521, Sec 850227, Rest/Bar 850227
On B6107 6 miles SW of Huddersfield.
Parkland course.
Pro PF Davies; Founded 1908
21 holes, 6305 yards, S.S.S. 70
🏌 Welcome except Wed and Sat.
[WD £22; WE £27.
🔄 Welcome by prior arrangement; full catering packages available; terms on application.
🍴 Full clubhouse facilities.
🛏 Durker Roods Hall.

8A 100 Mid Yorkshire
Havercroft Lane, Darrington, Nr Pontefract, Yorks, WF8 3BP
☎ 01977 704522, Fax 600823, Pro 600844, Sec 704522, Rest/Bar 704522
400 yards on A1 S from the M62/A1 intersection.
Parkland course.
Pro James Major; Founded 1993
Designed by Steve Marnoch
18 holes, 6466 yards, S.S.S. 71
🏌 22 floodlit.
🏌 Welcome WD; restrictions on WE mornings.
[WD £15 per round, day tickets available. WE £25.
🔄 Welcome WD; WE between 1pm-4.30pm by prior arrangement; conference facilities; catering packages by arrangement; golf clinic; terms on application.
🍴 Bar and restaurant facilities available.
🛏 Darrington.

8A 101 Middleton Park
Ring Road, Beeston, Leeds, W Yorks, LS10 3TN
☎ 0113 2700449, Pro 2709506
3 miles S of city centre.
Public parkland course.
Pro Adrian Newboult; Founded 1932

Designed by Leeds City Council
18 holes, 4947 yards, S.S.S. 69
🏌 Welcome WD; book at WE.
[WD £7.75; WE £9.25.
🔄 Welcome by arrangement.
🍴 Limited.

8A 102 Moor Allerton
Coal Road, Wike, Leeds, W Yorks, LS17 9NH
☎ 0113 2661154, Fax 2371124, Pro 2665209, Sec 2661154, Rest/Bar 2682225
5 miles from Leeds off A61 Harrogate road.
Parkland course.
Pro Richard Lane; Founded 1923
Designed by Robert Trent Jones, Sr.
27 holes (3 x 9 loops), High: 6841. Lakes: 6470. Blackmoor: 6673 yards; S.S.S. High: 74. Lakes 72. Blackmoor: 73.
🏌 7.
🏌 Welcome by prior arrangement.
[WD £43; WE £67.
🔄 Welcome by prior arrangement; tee times reserved for groups of 12 or more; reductions Nov-March.
🍴 Full clubhouse facilities.
🛏 Club can provide list of recommended hotels.

8A 103 Moortown
Harrogate Road, Leeds, West Yorkshire, LS17 7DB
🌐 www.moortown-gc.co.uk
📧 secretary@moortown-gc.co.uk
☎ 0113 2681682, Fax 2680986, Pro 2683636, Sec 2686521, Rest/Bar 2688746
On A61 Harrogate road 1 mile past outer ring road.
Parkland course.
Pro Bryon Hutchinson; Founded 1909
Designed by Dr A MacKenzie
18 holes, 6995 yards off the blue, 6757 yards off the white, S.S.S. 73
🏌 Welcome by prior arrangement.
[WD£55; WE and BH £65.
🔄 Welcome by prior arrangement; day rates also available; terms on application.
🍴 Full clubhouse restaurant and bar facilities.
🛏 Harewood Arms and others in Leeds area.

8A 104 Normanton
Hatfeild Hall, Aberford Road, Stanley, Wakefield, WF3 4JP
📧 fhoulgate@freenet.co.uk
☎ 01924 200900, Fax 200009,

Pro 200900, Sec 377943,
Rest/Bar 200900
Off M62 Junction 30; A642 1,7 miles
towards Wakefield turn right.
Parkland course.
Pro Frank Houlgate; Founded 1903/1998
18 holes, 6205 yards, S.S.S. 71
⅃ 15.
♦ Welcome except Sun before
3.30pm.
⌁ WD £22; Sat £22.
⌔ Welcome WD by prior
arrangement.
⛾ Full facilities.
⌁ Oulton Hall.

8A 105 Northcliffe
High Bank Lane, Shipley, West
Yorkshire, BD18 4LJ
⚏ www.northcliffegolfclubshipley.
co.uk
✉ northcliffe@bigfoot.com
☎ 01274 584085, Fax 596731,
Pro 587193, Sec 596731,
Rest/Bar 584085
On A650 W of Bradford to Saltaire
roundabout.
Undulating parkland course.
Pro M Hillas; Founded 1920
Designed by James Braid/Harry
Vardon
18 holes, 6113 yards, S.S.S. 71
⅃ 6.
♦ Welcome by prior arrangement.
⌁ WD £20; WE £25.
⌔ Welcome by prior arrangement; full
day's catering and golf package; £40.
⛾ Full clubhouse facilities.
⌁ Bankfield Hotel, Bingley.

8A 106 Oakdale
Oakdale, Harrogate, Yorkshire, HG1
2LN
☎ 01423 567162, Fax 536030,
Pro 560510, Sec 567162,
Rest/Bar 502806
Turn into Kent Road from Ripon Road
in Harrogate.
Undulating parkland with panoramic
views.
Pro Clive Dell; Founded 1914
Designed by Dr A MacKenzie
18 holes, 6456 yards, S.S.S. 71
♦ Welcome.
⌁ Terms on application.
⌔ Welcome WD by prior
arrangement; catering packages by
arrangement; terms available on
application.
⛾ Full facilities except Mon
lunchtime.
⌁ Crown; Fern; Majestic; Studley;
Old Swan; Balmoral.

8A 107 The Oaks
Aughton Common, Aughton, York,
Yorkshire, YO42 4PG
⚏ www.theoaksgolfclub.co.uk
✉ oaksgolfclub@hotmail.com
☎ 01757 288577, Fax 289029,
Pro 288007 same no for tee booking,
Rest/Bar 288001
On the B1228 1 mile N of Bubwith.
Wooded parkland course with 6
lakes.
Pro Jo Townhill; Founded 1996
Designed by J Covey
18 holes, 6743 yards, S.S.S. 72
⅃ 6.
♦ Public welcome weekdays.
Members and their guests only at
weekends. Accommodation available.
⌁ WD £20.
⌔ Welcome WD by arrangement;
packages of golf and catering
available; from £28.
⛾ Full bar and catering service; à la
carte restaurant.
⌁ Loftsome Bridge; Ye Olde Red
Lion.

8A 108 Otley
West Busk Lane, Otley, W Yorks, LS21
3NG
⚏ www.oatley-golfclub.co.uk
✉ office@otley-golfclub.co.uk
☎ 01943 465329, Fax 850387
Off A6038 on the outskirts of the
market town of Otley between Leeds
and Bradford.
Parkland course.
Pro Steven Thomkinson; Founded 1906
18 holes, 6245 yards, S.S.S. 70
♦ Welcome except Sat.
⌁ WD £29; WE £36.
⌔ Welcome WD by prior
arrangement with Sec; packages by
arrangement with Sec; terms on
application.
⛾ Full clubhouse bar and catering
facilities.
⌁ Chevin Lodge, Otley; Jarvis
Parkway, Leeds; The Grove, Ilkley.

8A 109 Oulton Park
Pennington Lane, Rothwell, Leeds,
LS26 8EX
☎ 0113 2823152, Fax 2826290,
Pro 2823152, Rest/Bar 2826290
Off M62 Junction 30, take A642 to
Rothwell, left at 2nd roundabout.
Parkland course.
Pro Steve Gromett; Founded 1990
Designed by Peter Alliss & Dave
Thomas
27 holes, 6470 yards, S.S.S. 71
⅃ 22.

♦ Welcome by prior arrangement.
⌁ WD £10.15; WE £13.15
⌔ Welcome WD by arrangement; full
golf and catering packages available;
also a 3169 yards par 35 9-hole
course; terms available on
application.
⛾ Full clubhouse restaurant and bar
facilities.
⌁ 5-star Oulton Hall on site.

8A 110 Outlane
Slack Lane, Outlane, Huddersfield, W
Yorks, HD3 3YI
☎ 01422 374762, Fax 311789,
Sec 311789
From M62 take A640 to Rochdale, left
under the motorway through Outlane
village.
Moorland/parkland course.
Pro DM Chapman; Founded 1906
18 holes, 6015 yards, S.S.S. 70
♦ Welcome by prior arrangement.
⌁ WD £18; WE £28.
⌔ Welcome by prior arrangement;
package details available from Mrs
Caroline Hirst; terms available on
application.
⛾ Full clubhouse facilities.
⌁ Old Golf House, Outlane.

8A 111 Owston Park
Owston Lane, Doncaster, S Yorks,
DN6 8EF
⚏ www.foremostonline.com
☎ 01302 330821
5 miles off A19 near Doncaster.
9-hole play and play.
Founded 1988
Designed by Mike Parker
9 holes, 6148 yards, S.S.S. 71
⅃ Putting green.
♦ Welcome; pay and play.
⌁ WD £4.50; WE £4.75.
⌔ No facilities.
⛾ Very limited.

8A 112 Painthorpe House
Golf & Country Club, Painthorpe Lane,
Crigglestone, Wakefield, WF4 3HE
☎ 01924 255083, Fax 252022
Close to M1 Junction 39.
Undulating parkland course.
Founded 1961
9 holes, 4548 yards, S.S.S. 62
♦ Welcome; restrictions on Sun.
⌁ WD £5; WE £6.
⌔ Welcome by arrangement; terms
on application.
⛾ Extensive facilities including four
bars, two ballrooms and a function
room.

8A 113 Pannal
Follifoot Road, Pannal, Harrogate,
Yorkshire, HG3 1ES
🌐 www.pannalgolfclub.cwc.net
✉ pannalgolfclub@btconnect.com
☎ 01423 871641, Fax 870043,
Pro 872620, Sec 872628,
Rest/Bar 872629
Off A61 Leeds-Harrogate road 3 miles
S of Harrogate.
Moorland/parkland course.
Pro David Padgett; Founded 1906
Designed by Sandy Herd
18 holes, 6622 yards, S.S.S. 72
⚐ 12.
† Welcome by prior arrangement
only.
⚑ WD £40; WE £50.
☞ Welcome by prior arrangement;
catering can be arranged; terms on
application.
🍽 Full clubhouse bar and catering
facilities.
🛏 Majestic, Harrogate.

8A 114 Phoenix
Pavilion Lane, Brinsworth, Rotherham,
S Yorks, S60 5PB
☎ 01709 838182, Fax 383788
Course is one mile along the Bawtry
road turning from the Tinsley
roundabout on the M1.
Undulating meadowland course.
Pro M Roberts; Founded 1932
18 holes, 6182 yards, S.S.S. 69
⚐ 20 covered.
† Welcome.
⚑ Terms on application.
☞ Welcome WD by prior
arrangement; packages for golf and
catering available; from £24.
🍽 Full catering facilities.

8A 115 Phoenix Park
Phoenix Park, Dick Lane, Thornbury,
Bradford, W Yorks, BD3 7AT
☎ 01132 561694
Off A647 Bradford to Leeds road at
Thornbury roundabout.
Undulating parkland course.
9 holes, 4646 yards, S.S.S. 66
† Welcome WD only.
⚑ Terms on application.
☞ Welcome by prior arrangement;
terms on application.
🍽 Catering available by prior
arrangement.

8A 116 Pike Hills   ⚷
Tadcaster Road, Askham Bryan, York,
Yorks, YO2 3UW
☎ 01904 706566, Fax 700797,

Pro 708756, Sec 700797,
Rest/Bar 704416
On A64 4 miles W of York.
Parkland course.
Pro I Gradwell; Founded 1920/46
18 holes, 6146 yards, S.S.S. 69
† Welcome WD; only with member
at WE.
⚑ WD £18; WE £18.
☞ Welcome by prior arrangement;
packages include full catering and 36
holes of golf; £35.
🍽 Full clubhouse facilities.

8A 117 Pontefract & District
Park Lane, Pontefract, W Yorks, WF8
4QS
🌐 www.pdgc.cwc.net
✉ pdgc@cwcom.net
☎ 01977 792241, Fax 792241,
Pro 706806, Sec 792241,
Rest/Bar 798886
Course is on the B6134 off the M62
Junction 32.
Parkland course.
Pro Nicholas Newman; Founded 1904
18 holes, 6232 yards, S.S.S. 70
† Welcome WD; by prior
arrangement WE.
⚑ WD £25; WE £32.
☞ Welcome WD except Wed;
packages available; terms on
application.
🍽 Full facilities.
🛏 Red Lion; Wenbrdige House; Park
Side Inn.

8A 118 Pontefract Park
Park Road, Pontefract, W Yorkshire
☎ 01977 723490
Close to Pontefract racecourse 0.5
miles from M62.
Public parkland course.
9 holes, 4068 yards, S.S.S. 62
† Welcome.
⚑ WD £3.20; WE £3.20 (9 holes).
☞ None.
🍽 None.

8A 119 Queensbury
Brighouse Road, Queensbury,
Bradford, West Yorkshire, BD13 1QF
☎ 01274 882155, Pro 816864,
Sec 882155, Rest/Bar 882155
From the M62 Junction 26 take the
A58 towards Halifax for 3.5 miles
then turn to Keighley for three miles;
also via the A647, 4 miles from
Bradford.
Undulating parkland course.
Pro Dave Delaney; Founded 1923
9 holes, 5024 yards, S.S.S. 65

† Everyone welcome.
⚑ WD £15; WE £30.
☞ Welcome by prior arrangement;
packages available; function facilities;
terms on application.
🍽 Full bar and à la carte restaurant
service.
🛏 Novotel.

8A 120 Rawdon
Buckstone Drive, Rawdon, Leeds, W
Yorks, LS19 6BD
☎ 0113 2506040, Pro 2505017,
Sec 2506044
On A65 6 miles from Leeds turning left
at Rawdon traffic lights.
Undulating parkland course.
Pro Craig Shackelton; Founded 1896
9 holes, 5982 yards, S.S.S. 69
† Welcome WD.
⚑ Terms on application.
☞ Welcome WD by prior
arrangement; golf and catering
packages available; 3 all-weather and
4 grass tennis courts.
🍽 Full facilities except Mon.
🛏 Peas Hill; Robin Hood; Travel
Lodge.

8A 121 Renishaw Park
Golf House, Mill Lane, Renishaw,
Sheffield, S Yorks, S21 3UZ
☎ 01246 432044, Fax 432116,
Pro 435484, Rest/Bar rest ext 23
bar ext 22
1.5 miles W of the M1 Junction 30 on
the A6135.
Parkland course.
Pro J Oates; Founded 1911
Designed by Sir G Sitwell and Edward
Lutyens
18 holes, 6262 yards, S.S.S. 70
† Welcome by arrangement.
⚑ WD £23.50; WE £32.50
☞ Welcome by arrangement;
packages on application; WD day
ticket £34; WE day ticket £38.50; terms
on application.
🍽 Full clubhouse facilites.
🛏 Sitwell Arms.

8A 122 Richmond
Bend Hagg, Richmond, N Yorks, DL10
5EX
☎ 01748 825319, Fax 821709,
Pro 822457, Sec 823231,
Rest/Bar 825319
From A1 Scotch Corner follow the
Richmond road to lights in town; turn
right.
Parkland course; extended to 18 in
1892.

Pro Paul Jackson; Founded 1892
Designed by Frank Pennink
18 holes, 5886 yards, S.S.S. 68
⌘ Large practice area.
† Welcome, after 3.30pm on Sun.
⌐ WD £20; WE £25.
⌒ Welcome by prior arrangement;
reduced rates for groups of more than
24; packages available; from £18.
◉ Full bar and restaurant facilities
everyday.
⌐ Turf Hotel; Black Lion; Kings Head.

8A 123 Riddlesden ☎
Howden Rough, Riddlesden, Keighley,
W Yorks, BD20 5QN
☎ 01535 602148, Sec 607646
From A650 Bradford road turn into
Scott Lane.
Moorland course.
Founded 1927
18 holes, 4295 yards, S.S.S. 63
† Welcome.
⌐ WD £12; WE £16.
⌒ Welcome on WD by prior
arrangement; terms available on
application.
◉ Clubhouse facilities.
⌐ Dalesgate Hotel.

8A 124 Ripon City
Palace Road, Ripon, N Yorks, HG4
3HH
☎ 01765 601987, Pro 600411,
Sec 603640, Rest/Bar 603640
Course is on the A6108 one mile N of
Ripon.
Undulating parkland course.
Pro Tim Davis; Founded 1908
New 9 holes designed by ADAS
18 holes, 6120 yards, S.S.S. 69
† Welcome with handicap certs
preferred.
⌐ WD £20; WE £30.
⌒ Welcome by arrangement;
packages available for groups of more
than 20.
◉ Full clubhouse facilities.
⌐ Nags Head; Kirkgate House both
Thirsk.

8A 125 Robin Hood
Owston Hall, Owston, Nr Carcroft,
Doncaster, S Yorks, DN6 9JF
☎ 01302 722800, Fax 728885
6 miles N of Doncaster on B1220 off
the A19.
Parkland course; formerly Owston Park
GC.
Founded 1988/1996
Designed by W Adamson
18 holes, 6937 yards, S.S.S. 72

† Welcome.
⌐ WD £12; WE £14.
⌒ Welcome by prior arrangement;
full catering packages available for 12
or more players; free golf cart
available for groups of more than 20;
function room with facilities for 60-100
people.
◉ Full restaurant and bar facilities in
18th century clubhouse.
⌐ Accommodation and health suite
on site.

8A 126 Romanby
Yafforth Road, Northallerton, N Yorks,
DL7 0PE
☎ 01609 779988, Fax 779084,
Pro 779988, Sec 778855,
Rest/Bar 777824
Course is on the B6271 Northallerton-
Richmond road one mile NW of
Northallerton.
Parkland course.
Pro Tim Jenkins; Founded 1993
Designed by W Adamson
18 holes; 6663 yards, S.S.S. 72; plus 6
hole academy course
⌘ 12.
† Welcome.
⌐ WD £20; WE £25.
⌒ Welcome 7 days; Premier Tee and
Silver Tee packages available; from
£26.50.
◉ Full clubhouse bar and restaurant
facilities.
⌐ Golden Lion.

8A 127 Rother Valley
Mansfield Road, Wales Bar, Sheffield,
Yorks, S31 8PE
☎ 0114 2473000, Fax 2476000
Course is between Sheffield and
Rotherham off the M1 Junction 31;
follow the signs for Rother Valley
country park.
Parkland with water features.
Pro Jason Ripley; Founded 1996
Designed by M Roe/M Shattock.
18 holes, 6602 yards, S.S.S. 72
† Welcome.
⌐ WD £11 (£7.50 Mon); WE £16.
⌒ Welcome at all times; packages
include catering, golf and use of driving
range; par 3 course; £10-£30.
◉ Restaurant and bar facilities
available.

8A 128 Rotherham
Thrybergh Park, Doncaster Road,
Thrybergh, Rotherham, South
Yorkshire, S65 4NU
⌐ www.rotherhamgolf.co.uk

⌐ gerry@rotherhamgolf.plus.com
☎ 01709 850466, Fax 859517,
Pro 850480, Sec 850466,
Rest/Bar 850466
On A630 Doncaster to Rotherham
Road.
Parkland course.
Pro Simon Thornhill; Founded 1903
18 holes, 6324 yards, S.S.S. 70
† Welcome by arrangement with Pro
or Sec.
⌐ Terms on application.
⌒ Welcome except Wed by prior
arrangement with Sec; minimum 16;
discounts for groups of 40 or more;
snooker; terms on application.
◉ Full facilities.
⌐ The Courtyard; Moat House;
Limes; Brecon.

8A 129 Roundhay
Park Lane, Leeds, Yorks, LS8 2EJ
☎ 0113 2662695, Fax 2661686,
Pro 2661686, Sec 2662695,
Rest/Bar 2662695
4.5 miles from city centre on A58 to
Wetherby.
Parkland with mature trees.
Pro Jim Pape; Founded 1922
9 holes, 5322 yards, S.S.S. 65
† Municipal pay and play.
⌐ WD £8.50; WE £9.50.
⌒ Welcome by arrangement with Pro;
packages available on application;
from £8.50.
◉ Catering available in restaurant in
evenings Tues-Sat; bar.
⌐ Beechwood.

8A 130 Roundwood
Off Green Lane, Rawmarsh,
Rotherham, S Yorks, S62 6LA
☎ 01709 523471, Fax 523478
Course is off the A633 2.5 miles N of
Rotherham.
Parkland course.
Founded 1977
18 holes, 5713 yards, S.S.S. 67
† Welcome except WD mornings.
⌐ WD £12; WE £15.
⌒ Welcome WD by prior
arrangement; packages available;
terms on application.
◉ Bar facilities; catering Wed to Sat.

8A 131 Rudding Park ☎
Follifoot, Harrogate, N Yorks, HG3 1DJ
⌐ www.ruddingpark.com
⌐ golfadmin@ruddingpark.com
☎ 01423 872100, Fax 873011,
Pro 873400
Off A658 Harrogate by-pass 2 miles S

of Harrogate.
Parkland course.
Pro Mark Moore, Niel Moore, Rob Hobkinson; Founded 1995
Designed by Hawtree
18 holes, 6871 yards, S.S.S. 73
⚑ 18 covered.
† Welcome with handicap certs.
⌐ £22.50 Mon-Thurs, £27.50 Fri-Sun.
⌐ Welcome with prior arrangement; packages available; terms on application.
🍽 Full clubhouse facilities.
⌐ Rudding Park.

8A 132 Ryburn
The Shaw, Norland, Sowerby Bridge, W Yorks, HX6 3QP
☎ 01422 831355
3 miles S of Halifax.
Hilly moorland course.
Founded 1910
9 holes, 4907 yards, S.S.S. 65
† Welcome WD; WE by arrangement.
⌐ WD £14; WE 20.
⌐ Welcome by prior arrangement; terms on application.
🍽 Catering and bar facilities.
⌐ The Hobbit Inn.

8A 133 Sand Moor
Alwoodley Lane, Leeds, W Yorks, LS17 7DJ
☎ 0113 2685180, Fax 2685180, Pro 2683925, Sec 2685180, Rest/Bar 2681685/2692718
6 miles from centre of Leeds on the A61 N.
Undulating parkland/moorland course.
Pro Peter Tupling; Founded 1926
Designed by A MacKenzie
18 holes, 6429 yards, S.S.S. 71
† Welcome WD, except 12 noon-1.30pm, Tues 9.30am-10.30am and Thurs 8.30am-12 noon.
⌐ WD £32.
⌐ Welcome WD by prior arrangement; catering packages by arrangement; terms available on application.
🍽 Full facilities.
⌐ Harewood Arms; Parkway; Forte Crest.

8A 134 Sandhill
Middlecliffe Lane, Little Houghton, Barnsley, S72 0HW
☎ 01226 753444, Fax 753444, Pro 753444, Rest/Bar 755079
Off A635 Barnsley-Doncaster road

near Darfield.
Parkland course.
Founded 1993
Designed by John Royston
18 holes, 6257 yards, S.S.S. 70
⚑ 18 floodlit.
† Welcome.
⌐ WD £10; WE £13.
⌐ Welcome WD: not before 10am Sat or 12 noon Sun; packages available; terms on application.
🍽 Full clubhouse facilities available.
⌐ Ardsley Moat House.

8A 135 Scarborough North Cliff
North Cliffe Ave, Burniston Road, Scarborough, YO12 6PP
☎ 01723 360786, Fax 362134, Pro 365920
2 miles N of town centre on coast road.
Seaside/parkland course.
Pro Simon Dellor; Founded 1928
Designed by James Braid
18 holes, 6425 yards, S.S.S. 71
† Welcome except before 10am Sun.
⌐ WD £18; WE £22.
⌐ Welcome by prior arrangement with Sec; packages for groups between 8 and 40; catering packages by arrangement; terms available on application.
🍽 Full facilities.
⌐ Park Manor; Headlands.

8A 136 Scarborough South Cliff ♛
Deepdale Avenue, Scarborough, YO11 2UE
☎ 01723 360522, Fax 376969, Pro 365150, Sec 374737
1 mile S of Scarborough on the main Filey road.
Parkland/seaside course.
Pro Tony Skingle; Founded 1903
Designed by Dr A MacKenzie
18 holes, 6039 yards, S.S.S. 69
⚑ Large practice area.
† Welcome.
⌐ Prices on application.
⌐ Welcome WD and WE by prior arrangement; packages available; terms on application.
🍽 Full facilities.
⌐ Crown; St Nicholas; Southlands; Mount House.

8A 137 Scarcroft
Syke Lane, Scarcroft, Leeds, W Yorks, LS14 3BQ
🖳 www.starcroftgc.co.ukl

🖳 sececretery@starcroftgc.co.uk
☎ 0113 2892311, Pro 2892780, Sec 2892311, Rest/Bar 2892263
Off A58 Leeds to Wetherby road turning left at Bracken.
Parkland course.
Pro Darren Tear; Founded 1937
Designed by Robert Blackburn
18 holes, 6426 yards, S.S.S. 71
† Welcome; some WE restrictions.
⌐ WD £30; WE £40; party over 20 people £28.
⌐ Welcome by prior arrangement; packages available for all-day golf and catering for groups of 20 or more; £40.
🍽 Full clubhouse facilities.
⌐ Jarvis, Wetherby; Harewood Arms, Harewood.

8A 138 Scathingwell
Scathingwell Centre, Scathingwell, Tadcaster, Yorks, LS24 9PF
☎ 01937 557878, Fax 557090, Pro 557864
Course is on the A162 three miles from the A1 between Tadcaster and Ferrybridge.
Parkland course.
Pro Steve Footman; Founded 1993
Designed by I Webster
18 holes, 6771 yards, S.S.S. 72
† Welcome but prior booking essential.
⌐ WD £16; WE £18.
⌐ Welcome by prior arrangement; individual packages can be arranged; summer and winter packages available; terms on application.
🍽 Full clubhouse facilities.
⌐ Hilton, Garforth; Selby Fork Hotel.

8A 139 Selby
Mill Lane, Brayton, Selby, N Yorks, YO8 9LD
🖳 www.selbygolfclub.co.uk
🖳 selbygolfclub@hotmail.com
☎ 01757 228622, Fax 228785, Pro 228785, Rest/Bar 228590, 228226
3 miles SW of Selby; 1 mile W of A19 at Brayton village.
Links course.
Pro Andrew Smith; Founded 1907
Designed by JH Taylor & Hawtree Ltd, Donald Steel & Co
18 holes, 6374 yards, S.S.S. 71
† Welcome WD with handicap certs; WE with member.
⌐ WD £30 per round, £35 for day.
⌐ Welcome Wed, Thurs and Fri by prior arrangement; catering packages by arrangement; snooker; terms on application.

🍴 Full facilities.
🛏 Londesbro; Selby Fork Motel; The Owl.

8A 140 Serlby Park
Serlby, Doncaster, South Yorkshire, DN10 6BA
☎ 01777 818268, Sec 818268, Rest/Bar 818268
3 miles S of Bawtry.
Parkland course.
Founded 1904
Designed by Viscount Galway
9 holes, 5376 yards, S.S.S. 66
† Welcome only with member.
Ⅰ Guests with members only.
⚘ Welcome only by prior arrangement with Sec; terms on application.
🍴 Clubhouse facilities.
🛏 Crown, Bawtry; Mount Pleasant; Olde Bell, both Barnaby Moor.

8A 141 Settle
Buckhaw Brow, Settle, Yorks, BD24 0DH
🖳 www.settlegolfclub.com
☎ 01729 825288, Sec 825288, Rest/Bar 825288
Course is on Kendal Road one mile beyond town.
Parkland course.
Founded 1895
Designed by Tom Vardon
9 holes, 5414 yards, S.S.S. 68
† Welcome except Sun.
Ⅰ WD £12; WE £12.
⚘ Welcome by prior arrangement; terms on application.
🍴 Clubhouse facilities available for limited catering.
🛏 Falcon Hotel, Settle; Royal Oak, Settle.

8A 142 The Shay Grange Golf Centre
Long Lane, Off Bingley Road, Bradford, West Yorkshire, BD9 6RX
☎ 01274 491945, Fax 491547, Pro 491945
Course is off the A650 Bradford road at Cottingley.
Parkland course.
Pro Neil Reeves; Founded 1996
Designed by Tim Colclough
9 holes, 3380 yards, S.S.S. 58
Ⅰ 32.
† Pay and play.
Ⅰ WD £5; WE £7.
⚘ Welcome by prior arrangement; discounts available including golf and meals at nearby restaurant; from £10.

🍴 Limited.
🛏 Jarvis Bankfield.

8A 143 The Shipley
Beckfoot Lane, Cottingley Bridge, Bingley, W Yorks, BD16 1LX
🖳 www.shippleygc.co.uk
✉ professional@shippleygc.co.uk
☎ 01274 563674, Fax 567739, Pro 563674 ext 21, Sec 563674, Rest/Bar 563674 ext 22
On A650 6 miles N of Bradford.
Parkland course.
Pro JR Parry; Founded 1896
Designed by Colt, Alison and Dr MacKenzie
18 holes, 6235 yards, S.S.S. 70
Ⅰ Large practice area.
† Welcome except Tues before 3pm and Sat after 3.30pm.
Ⅰ WD £26, WE £29.
⚘ Welcome Wed, Thurs, Fri; packages available; terms on application.
🍴 Full clubhouse facilities available.
🛏 The Ramada Jarvis Bank Field Hotel.

8A 144 Silkstone
Field Head, Silkstone, Barnsley, S Yorks, S75 4LD
☎ 01226 7980328, Pro 790128
On A628 1 mile from M1.
Undulating meadowland.
Pro Kevin Guy; Founded 1893
18 holes, 6069 yards, S.S.S. 70
† Welcome WD.
Ⅰ Terms on application.
⚘ Welcome WD by prior arrangement; packages available; terms on application.
🍴 Full facilities except Mon.
🛏 Ardsley Moat House; Brooklands Motel.

8A 145 Silsden
High Brunthwaite, Silsden, Keighley, W Yorks, BD20 0NH
☎ 01535 652998, Sec 01943 864263
4 miles from Keighley on A6034 to Silsden, turn E at canal.
Moorland/meadowland course.
Founded 1913
14 holes, currently under development, 4870 yards, S.S.S. 64
† Welcome; WE restrictions.
Ⅰ Terms on application.
⚘ Terms on application.
🍴 Clubhouse facilities.
🛏 Steeton Hall.

8A 146 Sitwell Park
Shrogswood Road, Rotherham, Yorkshire, S60 4BY
☎ 01709 700799, Fax 703637, Pro 540961, Sec 541046, Rest/Bar 700799
From M1 Junction 33; take 2nd exit at roundabout until signposted; also from M18 Junction 1.
Parkland course.
Pro Nick Taylor; Founded 1913
Designed by Dr A MacKenzie
18 holes, 6209 yards, S.S.S. 70
† Welcome.
Ⅰ WD £24; WE £28.
⚘ Welcome by prior arrangement with the Secretary; discounts for parties of 30; terms available on application. Snooker and billiard tables.
🍴 Clubhouse facilities.
🛏 Campanile; Beefeater The Brecks.

8A 147 Skipton
Shortlee Lane, Off North-West By-Pass, Skipton, N Yorks, BD23 3LF
🖳 www.skiptongolfclub.co.uk
✉ enquries@skiptongolfclub.co.uk
☎ 01756 795657, Fax 796665, Pro 793922, Sec 795657
Course is on the A65 one mile N of Skipton.
Undulating parkland with panoramic views.
Pro Peter Robinson; Founded 1896
18 holes, 6076 yards, S.S.S. 69
Ⅰ 0.5 miles away.
† Welcome; some restrictions Tues and WE.
Ⅰ Terms on application.
⚘ Welcome WD by prior arrangement with Sec; packages available; snooker and reading rooms; £23.
🍴 Dining, banqueting and bar. Members and golfers only.
🛏 Hanover, Skipton; Devonshire Arms, Bolton Abbey; Stirk House, Gisburn.

8A 148 South Bradford
Pearson Road, Odsal, Bradford, BD6 1BJ
☎ 01274 679195, Pro 673346
From Odsal roundabout take Stadium Road and then Pearson Road.
Undulating meadowland course.
Pro Paul Cooke; Founded 1906
9 holes, 6076 yards, S.S.S. 69
† Welcome WD.
Ⅰ WD £16. 9 Hole course £10.
⚘ Welcome Tues-Fri by prior arrangement; terms available on application.

🎔 Full facilities except Mon.
🗫 Guide Post.

8A 149 South Leeds   𝕌
Gypsy Lane, Off Middleton Ring Road,
Leeds, W Yorks, LS11 5TU
☎ 0113 2700479, Pro 2702598,
Sec 2771676
Close to M1 Junction 45 and M62
Junction 28.
Undulating parkland course.
Pro Mike Lewis; Founded 1914
Designed by Dr A MacKenzie
18 holes, 5769 yards, S.S.S. 68
† Welcome WD; WE only with
member.
  Ⅰ WD £18; WE £9.
↺ Welcome by prior arrangement;
packages can be arranged depending
on numbers; terms on application.
🎔 Clubhouse facilities.
🗫 Oulton Hall; Leeds International
Hilton.

8A 150 Spaldington
Spaldington Lane, Howden, E Yorks,
DN14 7NG
☎ 01757 288262, Pro 01430 432484,
Rest/Bar 01430 432484
Take B1228 out of Howden towards
Bubwith and then head for
Spaldington.
Parkland course.
Pro A Pheasant; Founded 1995
Designed by PMS Golf
9 holes, 3482 yards, S.S.S. 29
🏌 20 floodlit.
† Welcome.
  Ⅰ WD £4; WE £4.
↺ Welcome.
🎔 Snacks.
🗫 The Wellington Hotel,Howden.

8A 151 Springhead Park
Willerby Road, Hull, East Yorkshire,
HU5 5JE
☎ 01482 656309/604968,
Sec 656958, Rest/Bar 656309
From A62 follow signs from Humber
Bridge to Beverley to major roundabout
and then signs to Willerby.
Parkland course.
18 holes, 6401 yards off the white,
S.S.S. 71
† Municipal course; open to the
public with a green fee ticket.
  Ⅰ WD £8.50; WE £10.50.
↺ Welcome by prior arrangement
with Sec; terms available on
application.
🎔 Clubhouse facilities.
🗫 Trusthouse Forte North Ferraby

8A 152 Springmill
Queens Drive, Osset, W Yorks
☎ 01924 272515
1 mile from Osset towards Wakefield.
Public parkland course.
9 holes, 2330 yards
† Welcome.
  Ⅰ Terms on application.

8A 153 Stocksbridge & District
30 Royd Lane, Townend, Deepcar,
Sheffield, Yorks, S36 2RZ
☎ 0114 2882003, Pro 2882779
Close to M1 Junction 36.
Moorland course.
Pro Tim Brookes; Founded 1924
18 holes, 5097 yards, S.S.S. 65
† Welcome WD.
  Ⅰ WD £26; WE £27.
↺ Welcome WD by prior
arrangement; packages include 36
holes of golf and all day catering; £25.
🗫 Tankersley Manor; The Wentworth;
Ardsley House; Hallam Towers;
Grosvenor.

8A 154 Sutton Park
Salthouse Road, Hull, Yorks, HU8 9HF
☎ 01482 374242, Fax 701428,
Pro 0614781
A165 E to Salthouse Road.
Parkland course.
Pro Dennis Taylor; Founded 1935
18 holes, 6296 yards, S.S.S. 70
🏌 32 (and 18 pitch and putt holes).
† Welcome by prior arrangement.
  Ⅰ Terms on application.
↺ Welcome by prior arrangement;
terms on application.
🎔 Bar facilities.

8A 155 Swallow Hall
Swallow Hall, Crockery Hill, York,
YO19 4SG
🖳 www.swallowhall.co.uk
✉ jtscores@hotmail.com
☎ 01904 448889, Fax 448219,
Sec 448889
Off A19 S of Selby; after 1.5 miles turn
left to Wheldrake.
Public parkland course.
Founded 1991
18 holes, 3092 yards, S.S.S. 56
🏌 7.
† Welcome.
  Ⅰ WD £9; WE £10.
↺ Welcome by arrangement.
🎔 Full catering facilities.

8A 156 Tankersley Park
High Green, Sheffield, S Yorks, S35 4LG

🖳 www.pgagolfshop.co.uk
✉ iankirk5@aol.com
☎ 0114 2468247, Fax 2455583,
Pro 2455583
From M1 Junction 35A entrance 400
yards.
Parkland course.
Pro Ian Kirk; Founded 1907
Designed by Hawtree
18 holes, 6212 yards, S.S.S. 70
† Welcome, booking at WE
essential.
  Ⅰ WD £26; WE £34.
↺ Welcome by prior arrangement on
WD; catering packages available;
terms on application.
🎔 Full catering facilities available;
bar. Not on Mondays.
🗫 Tankersley Manor; Norfolk Arms.

8A 157 Temple Newsam
Temple Newsam Road, Leeds, W
Yorks, LS15 OLN
☎ 0113 2645624, Pro 2647362
On A64 York road 5 miles from Leeds.
Then take A63.
Undulating parkland course.
Pro Adrian Newbold; Founded 1923
Designed by Lady Dorothy
36 holes, 6094 yards, S.S.S. 69
🏌 Practice area for 60 people.
† Welcome.
  Ⅰ Terms on application.
↺ Welcome by arrangement;
packages available; terms on
application.
🎔 Full facilities; carvery WE.
🗫 Windmill; Mercury.

8A 158 Thirsk & Northallerton
Thornton-&-Street, Thirsk, N Yorks,
YO7 4AB
☎ 01845 522170, Fax 525115,
Pro 526216, Sec 525115,
Rest/Bar 522170
Near A19 and A168 2 miles N of
Thirsk.
Parkland course.
Pro Robert Garner; Founded 1914/1997
Designed by W Adamson
18 holes, 6495 yards, S.S.S. 70
† Welcome WD; only with member
at WE.
  Ⅰ WD £20; WE £20.
↺ Welcome WD by prior
arrangement; catering packages
available; from £20.
🎔 Full clubhouse facilities.
🗫 Golden Fleece; Three Tuns.

8A 159 Thorne
Kirton Lane, Thorne, Doncaster, S

Yorks, DN8 5RJ
☎ 01405 815173, Fax 741899,
Pro 812084, Sec 812084
From M18 Junction 6 to Thorne;
signposted.
Parkland course.
Pro Edward Highfield; Founded 1980
Designed by Richard Highfield
18 holes, 5366 yards, S.S.S. 65
† Welcome.
Ⅰ WD £9; WE £10.
♫ Welcome by prior arrangement;
£50 deposit required which is refunded
on the day; terms on application.
🍽 Clubhouse facilities.
↪ Belmont.

8A 160 Tinsley Park
High Hazel Park, Darnall, Sheffield, S
Yorks, S9 4PE
☎ 0114 2037435, Rest/Bar 2610004
Course is on the A57 from Junction 33
on the M1.
Parkland course.
Pro APR Highfield; Founded 1921
18 holes, 6084 yards, S.S.S. 69
† Welcome.
Ⅰ WD £8.50; WE £10.00.
♫ Welcome by arrangement with the
local council.
🍽 Full facilities.
↪ Royal Victoria.

8A 161 Todmorden
Rive Rocks, Cross Stone Rd,
Todmorden, OL14 8RD
☎ 01706 812986, Fax 812986,
Sec 812986, Rest/Bar 812986
1.5 miles along Halifax road.
Moorland course.
Founded 1895
9 holes, 5902 yards, S.S.S. 68
† Welcome WD; WE by
arrangement.
Ⅰ WD £15; WE £20.
♫ Welcome WD by prior
arrangement.
🍽 Clubhouse facilities.
↪ Scaite Cliffe Hall; Brandschatter
Berghoff.

8A 162 Wakefield Golf Club
Woodthorpe Lane, Sandal, Wakefield,
WF2 6JH
☎ 01924 255104, Fax 242752,
Pro 255380, Sec 258778
Course is on the A61 three miles S of
Wakefield.
Parkland course.
Pro Ian Wright; Founded 1891
Designed by Alex Herd
18 holes, 6653 yards, S.S.S. 72

† Welcome by prior arrangement.
Ⅰ WD £27; WE £40.
♫ Welcome by application to Sec;
catering packages by arrangements;
snooker; terms on application.
🍽 Full facilities.
↪ Cedar Court; The Chasley.

8A 163 Waterton Park
The Balk, Walton, Wakefield, WF2 6QL
🖱 www.waterton.co.uk
☎ 01924 259525, Fax 256969,
Pro 255557, Rest/Bar 255855
Course is close to M1 Junction 39
following signs for Barnsley and A61;
left to Wakefield and then to Shay Lane.
Parkland on Waterton Hall, 26-acre
lake.
Pro Nick Wood; Founded 1995
Designed by S Gidman
18 holes, 6843 yards, S.S.S. 72; 73 for
women.
Ⅰ Practice range.
† Welcome as members' guests
only. Limited pay and play on WD.
Ⅰ Not available.
♫ None.
🍽 Bars and dining room in the
exclusive club house.
↪ Waterton Park.

8A 164 Wath
Abdy Lane, Rawmarsh, Rotherham, S
Yorks, S62 7SJ
☎ 01709 878609, Pro 878609
Off A633 in Wath, 7 miles N of
Rotherham.
Downland course.
Pro Chris Bassett; Founded 1904
† Welcome WD; only with a member
WE.
Ⅰ WD £16, £21 for the day.
♫ Welcome by prior arrangement;
special packages available for golf and
catering; terms on application.
🍽 Full facilities.
↪ Moat House, Rotherham.

8A 165 West Bowling
Newall Hall, Rooley Lane, Bradford, W
Yorks, BD5 8LB
☎ 01274 724449, Pro 728036,
Sec 393207
At Junction of M606 and Bradford ring
road.
Parkland course.
Pro Ian Marshall; Founded 1898
18 holes, 5769 yards, S.S.S. 68
† Welcome WD; restrictions at WE.
Ⅰ WD £22; WE £30.
♫ Welcome Wed, Thurs, Fri by
arrangement with the manager;

catering by arrangement; snooker;
terms on application.
🍽 Full facilities.
↪ Novotel; Norfolk Gardens; Guide
Post; Tong Village; Victoria.

8A 166 West Bradford
Chellow Grange Road, Haworth Road,
Bradford, W Yorks, BD9 6NP
☎ 01274 542767, Fax 482079,
Pro 542102
Course is off the B6144 three miles W
of Bradford.
Parkland course.
Pro Nigel Barber; Founded 1900
18 holes, 5723 yards, S.S.S. 68
† Welcome except before 9.30am
and between 12 noon-1.30pm.
Ⅰ WD £21; WE £21.
♫ Welcome by arrangement;
packages including catering and golf
with reduced green fees available;
terms on application.
🍽 Full clubhouse facilities.

8A 167 West End (Halifax)
Paddock Lane, Highroad Well, Halifax,
W Yorks, HX2 ONT
☎ 01422 353608, Fax 341878,
Pro 363294, Sec 341878,
Rest/Bar 369844
2 miles W of Halifax off Burnley-
Rochford road.
Parkland course.
Pro David Rishworth; Founded 1906
Designed by Members
18 holes, 5937 yards, S.S.S. 69
† Welcome by prior arrangement.
Ⅰ WD £21; WE £28.
♫ Welcome by prior arrangement
with Sec; packages available; from
£21.
🍽 Clubhouse facilities.
↪ Windmill Court, Halifax.

8A 168 Wetherby
Linton Lane, Wetherby, Yorks, LS22
4JF
☎ 01937 580089, Fax 581915,
Sec 580089, Rest/Bar 582527
Course is one mile W of A1 S of Linton
village.
Parkland course.
Pro David Padgett; Founded 1910
18 holes, 6235 yards, S.S.S. 70
† Welcome Mon and Tues
afternoons; all day Wed, Thurs, Fri.
Ⅰ WD £25.
♫ Welcome by prior arrangement;
packages available; discounts for
groups of 40; terms available on
application.

|●| Full clubhouse facilities.
⌐ Linton Springs; Jarvis Resort;
Wood Hall.

8A 169 **Wheatley**
Armthorpe Road, Doncaster, S Yorks,
DN2 5QB
📧 Wheatley.golfclub@virgin.net
☎ 01302 831655, Fax 812736,
Pro 834085
Close to Doncaster racecourse
following the ring road S; opposite
large water tower.
Undulating parkland; relocated 1933.
Pro Steve Fox; Founded 1913/1933
Designed by George Duncan
18 holes, 6405 yards, S.S.S. 71
† Welcome.
[WD £27; WE £38.
⌂ Welcome WD by prior arrangement;
day ticket (WD £25); catering by prior
arrangement; from £20.
|●| Full facilities.
⌐ Balmoral; Earl of Doncaster; Punches.

8A 170 **Whitby**
Sandsend Road, Low Straggleton,
Whitby, N Yorks, YO21 3SR
☎ 01947 602768, Fax 600660,
Pro 602719, Sec 600660
On A174 coast road between Whitby
and Sandsend.
Seaside course.
Pro Tony Mason; Founded 1892
18 holes, 6134 yards, S.S.S. 69
† Welcome by prior arrangement.
[WD £22; WE £28.
⌂ Welcome by prior arrangement;
winter and summer packages available
for groups of 8 or more; from £21.50.
|●| Full facilities.
⌐ Seacliff; White House; Arundell.

8A 171 **Whitwood**
Altofts Lane, Whitwood, Castleford, W
Yorks, WF10 5PZ
☎ 01977 604215, Pro 512835,
Rest/Bar 512835
Course is 0.5 miles towards Castleford
off M62 Junction 31.
Parkland course.
Pro Richard Golding; Founded 1986
Designed by Steve Wells (Wakefield
Council)
9 holes, 6282 yards, S.S.S. 70
† Welcome; booking system
available.
[WD £5.90; WE £8.
⌂ Welcome by arrangement with the
Pro; terms on application.
|●| Available at local inn.
⌐ Bridge Inn.

8A 172 **Willow Valley Golf &
Country Club**
Highmoor Lane, Clifton, Brighouse, W
Yorks, HD6 4JB
🖳 www.wvgc.co.uk
📧 golf@wvgc.co.uk
☎ 01274 878624, Fax 852805,
Pro 878624, Sec 878624,
Rest/Bar 878624
From M62 Junction 25 take A644 to
Brighouse; turn right at first
roundabout.
American parkland style course.
Pro Julian Howarth; Founded 1993
Designed by J Gaunt
18 holes and 9 holes, 7021 yards for
18 holes and 2039 yards for 9 holes,
S.S.S. 72
Ⅰ 24 floodlit.
† Welcome.
[WD £23; WE £28.
⌂ Welcome WD; packages available
for groups of 12 or more; from £32.00
|●| Full clubhouse facilities.
⌐ Forte Crest; Black Horse Inn;
Hartshead Moor.

8A 173 **Withernsea**
Chestnut Ave, Withernsea, E Yorks,
HU19 2PG
☎ 01964 612258, Sec 612078
25 miles E of Hull on main road to
Withernsea.
Seaside links course.
Pro G Harrison; Founded 1907
9 holes, 6207 yards, S.S.S. 72
† Welcome; after 2pm Sun.
[WD £10; WE £10.
⌂ Welcome by prior arrangement;
catering packages can be arranged;
from £10.
|●| Clubhouse facilities.
⌐ Kings Town Hotel, Headon.

8A 174 **Wombwell (Hillies)**
Wentworth View, Wombwell, Barnsley,
S Yorks, S73 0LA
☎ 01226 754433, Fax 758635, Sec
758635
4 miles SE of Barnsley.
Meadowland course.
Founded 1981
9 holes, 4190 yards, S.S.S. 60
Ⅰ Practice nets.
† Welcome.
[WD £6.30; WE £7.80.
⌂ Welcome by prior arrangement;
from £6.30.
|●| Bar service only.
⌐ Ardsley House.

8A 175 **Woodhall Hills**
Woodhall Road, Calverley, Pudsey, W
Yorks, LS28 5UN
☎ 0113 2564771, Sec 2554594
Take A647 Leeds-Bradford road to
Pudsey roundabout; follow signs to
Calverley; 0.25 miles past Calverley
Golf Club.
Parkland course.
Pro Warren Lockett; Founded 1905
18 holes, 6184 yards, S.S.S. 70
† Welcome.
[WD £20.50; WE £25.50.
⌂ Welcome by arrangement with
secretary/manager; golf and catering
packages available for groups of 20 or
more; from £31.
|●| Full clubhouse facilities available.
⌐ Cedar Court, Bradford.

8A 176 **Woodsome Hall**
Fenay Bridge, Huddersfield, W Yorks,
HD8 0LG
☎ 01484 602739, Fax 608260,
Pro 602034, Rest/Bar 602971
From either M62 Junction 24 or 26
towards Huddersfield then A629
towards Sheffield turning right at
Farnley Tyas/Honley signs.
Parkland course.
Pro Mike Higginbottom; Founded 1922
Designed by J Braid
18 holes, 6096 yards, S.S.S. 69
† Welcome except Tues.
[WD £30; WE £40.
⌂ Welcome by prior arrangement
except Tues and Sat; handicap certs
required; menus for catering packages
available from club; TV lounges;
halfway bar available; deposit required;
terms available on application.
|●| Full catering and bar facilities;
jacket and tie required.
⌐ Hanover International;
Huddersfield Hotel.

8A 177 **Woolley Park**   ♛
Woolley Park, New Road, Woolley,
Wakefield, W Yorks, WF4 2JS
🖳 www.woolleypark.co.uk
📧 info@woolleypark.co.uk
☎ 01226 380144, Fax 390295,
Pro 380144, Sec 382209,
Rest/Bar 380144
From Junction 38 on the M1 follow the
signs for Woolley Hall; from the A61
Wakefield to Barnsley road take the
Woolley signs from the crossroads.
Parkland course.
Pro Jon Baldwin; Founded 1995
Designed by M Shattock
18 holes, 6636 yards, S.S.S. 72
† Welcome.

ͳ Terms on application.
⟲ Welcome by prior arrangement; packages available; terms on application.
🍽 Clubhouse catering facilities available except Mon.
🛏 Hotel Saint-Pierre.

8A 178 Wortley
Hermit Hill Lane, Wortley, Sheffield, S35 7DF
☎ 0114 2885294, Fax 2888469, Pro 2886490, Sec 2888469, Rest/Bar 2885294
Course is off the A629 through Wortley village.
Undulating wooded parkland course.
Pro Ian Kirk; Founded 1894

18 holes, 6035 yards, S.S.S. 69
† Welcome by prior arrangement.
ͳ WD £27; WE £30.
⟲ Welcome Mon, Wed and Fri by prior arrangement; catering by arrangement except Mon; terms on application.
🍽 Clubhouse facilities available except Mon.
🛏 Ardsley Moat House; Brooklands, both Barnsley; Tankersley Manor.

8A 179 York Golf Club
Lords Moor Lane, Strensall, York, Yorks, YO5 5XF
🖥 www.yorkgolfclub.co.uk
☎ 01904 491840, Fax 491852,

Pro 490304, Sec 491840
3 miles N of A1237 York ring road from Earswick/Strensall roundabout.
Tree-lined heathland course.
Pro A Hoyle; Founded 1890
Designed by JH Taylor (1904)
18 holes, 6302 yards, S.S.S. 70
† Welcome by prior arrangement; with member at WE only. Visitors allowed on Sun.
ͳ WD £30.
⟲ Welcome except Tues am and Sat; packages can include 27 or 36 holes of golf; some Sun available; catering available; from £32.
🍽 Bar and catering facilities.
🛏 Accommodation guide sent on request.

8B
Northumberland, Durham, Cleveland, Tyne & Wear

Stephen Keppler is one end of the strange history of Seaton Carew. He looks like an extra out of 'Lock, Stock and Two Smoking Barrels', talks with a hybrid accent of cockney and the American deep south, earns a living as a club pro in Atlanta and made a splash by qualifying for the 2001 PGA where he only just missed the cut. His bizarre journey, via the British Walker Cup team, began when he won the Boys Amateur Championship at Seaton Carew in 1978.

At the other end of Seaton Carew's history is a Dr Duncan McCuaig from St Andrews who finding the local land reminiscent of his home course began biffing a ball around it. His activity led in 1874 to the foundation of the Durham and Yorkshire Golf Club, later renamed Seaton Carew.

It is a fine links with an industrial backdrop of chimneys and chemical plants. Donald Steel called the 17th green "as notable an instrument of torture as man can devise".

Hartlepool Golf Club, similarly threatened by the North Sea, and Cleveland, a club formed in the local Lobster Inn, are good neighbouring courses although some object to the rampant air pollution of the area.

There are several good courses to the west of Hartlepool, including Barnard Castle, defined by its becks and hills, and Bishop Auckland, a course built on Church of England land. But the most famous of them is Brancepeth Castle where Leonard Crawley, a former English Amateur Champion, golf correspondent and driver of large motor vehicles, was an admiring member.

On land that was once a deer park, Brancepeth presents many challenges, not least a wobbly bridge constucted by the Royal Engineers. Eight holes on the course are affected by ravines. The ninth hole, 200 plus yards across an exposed ravine, was described by Darwin as of "terrifying grandeur." At least the soul can find solace in views of the castle and the 12th century church of St Brandon.

Just south of Newcastle is Beamish Park, a parkland design influenced by Henry Cotton, and to the north of the city is the Northumberland. Lying largely within the rails of the racetrack the course is of sufficient quality to have hosted the English Amateur and the Women's Commonwealth. It is on the short side unless your golf ball repeatedly ricochets back over your head from the rails, in which instant it plays rather long.

To the west of Newcastle is Slaley Hall, a host of European tour events. The building has been modernised to create a pretty comfortable hotel, but the golf itself consists of a big course with a small character. Rather typical of its excess is the ninth hole which has a mass of features and a dearth of personality.

Heading further up the north east coast is Seahouses, a lovely meld of dunes, coves and marshland, and just before the Scottish border is Berwick-upon-Tweed. A fair links it is distinguished by views of Holy Island from amidst the dunes.

8B 1 Allendale

High Studdon, Allenheads Road,
Allendale, Hexham, Northumberland,
N47 9DH
☎ 01434 683926
On B6295 1.5 miles S of Allendale in
the direction of Allenheads.
Hilly parkland course.
Founded 1907/1992
Designed by Members/English Golf
Union/Sports Council
9 holes, 5044 yards, S.S.S. 65
♦ Welcome except August Bank
Holiday Mon.
⌊ Prices on application.
⟡ Welcome by arrangement;
corporate days welcome; catering by
arrangement; terms available on
application.
⦿ Clubhouse facilities available.
⌁ Kings Head; Hare & Hounds;
Allenheads.

8B 2 Alnmouth Golf Club

Foxton Hall, Lesbury, Alnmouth,
Northumberland, NE66 3BE
⌁ www.alnmouthgolfclub.com
✉ secretray@alnmouth.com
☎ 01665 830231, Fax 830992,
Pro 830043, Sec 830231,
Rest/Bar 830231
5 miles SE of Alnwick.
Parkland course.
Pro Lindsey Hardy; Founded 1869
Designed by HS Colt
18 holes, 6429 yards, S.S.S. 71
♦ Welcome Mon, Tues and Thurs;
Dormy House guests welcome at all
times.
⌊ WD £22-£30; WE £25-£35
⟡ Welcome Mon, Tues, Thurs; day
packages available; maximum groups
of 30; from £20.
⦿ Clubhouse catering facilities
available.
⌁ Foxton Hall has its own Dormy
Hall

8B 3 Alnmouth Village

Marine Road, Alnmouth,
Northumberland, NE66 2RZ
⌁ www.golfuk.co.uk
✉ golfingspence@aol.com
☎ 01665 830370, Fax 602096
On A1068 from Alnmouth.
Undulating links course.
Founded 1869
9 holes, 6078 yards, S.S.S. 70
⌊ Practice ground.
♦ Welcome; restrictions on
competition days.
⌊ WD £15, WE £20; Juniors £7.50.
⟡ Welcome with handicap certs;

catering packages by arrangement;
from £15.
⦿ Catering available except
Tues.
⌁ Marine House Hotel, Red Lion,
Hope and Anchor.

8B 4 Alnwick

Swansfield Park, Alnwick,
Northumberland, NE66 1AT
☎ 01665 602632, Sec 602499
From A1 S signposted to Willowburn
Ave and then into Swansfield Park
Road.
Founded 1907/1993
Designed by G Rochester/A Rae
18 holes, 6250 yards, S.S.S. 70
♦ Welcome by prior arrangement
with the starter.
⌊ WD £18-£25; WE and BH £20-
£25.
⟡ Welcome between April 1 and Oct
1 by prior arrangement; packages
available in season of unlimited golf
and full day's catering; minimum 4; £25
⦿ Full clubhouse facilities available.
⌁ White Swans; Royal Oak; Plough;
Hotspur.

8B 5 Arcot Hall

Dudley, Cramlington, Northumberland,
NE23 7QP
☎ 0191 236279, Fax 2170370
Course is 1.5 miles off the A1 near
Cramlington.
Parkland course; formerly at Benton,
Pro Graham Cant; Founded 1909/48
Designed by James Braid
18 holes, 6389 yards, S.S.S. 70
♦ Welcome WD; restrictions WE.
⌊ WD £26; WE £30.
⟡ Welcome by prior arrangement on
WD; packages available; from £26.
⦿ Lounge bar and restaurant
facilities.
⌁ Holiday Inn; Swallow, Gosforth
Park.

8B 6 Backworth

Backworth Welfare, The Hall,
Backworth, Shiremoor, NE27 OAH
☎ 0191 2681048, Sec 2581291
Course on the B1322 one mile from
the A19/A191 Junction at Shiremoor
crossroads.
Parkland course.
Founded 1937
9 holes, 5930 yards, S.S.S. 69
♦ Welcome WD except Tues 11am-
3pm; restrictions at WE.
⌊ WD £12; WE £16.
⟡ Welcome by prior arrangement

with Sec; packages can be negotiated
depending on numbers; terms on
application.
⦿ Full bar and restaurant facilities
available.
⌁ Rex; Park; Stakis Wallsend;
Grand.

8B 7 Bamburgh Castle

The Wynding, Bamburgh,
Northumberland, NE69 7DE
⌁ www.bamburghcastlegolfclub.org
✉ bamburghcastlegolfclub@
hotmail.com
☎ 01668 214378, Fax 214607,
Pro 214378, Sec 214321,
Rest/Bar 214378
Course is five miles E of the A1 via the
B1341 or the B1342 into Bamburgh
village.
Seaside course.
Founded 1896/04
Designed by George Rochester
18 holes, 5621 yards, S.S.S. 67
♦ Welcome by prior arrangement
except on competition days and BH.
⌊ WD £26.50 per round £32 per day.
WE £32.50 per round £37.50 per
round.
⟡ Welcome by prior written
arrangement with Sec; full catering
packages available, except Tues; from
£30.
⦿ Full catering available except
Tues.
⌁ Victoria; Mizen; Sunningdale; Lord
Crewe.

8B 8 Barnard Castle

Harmire Road, Barnard Castle, DL12
8QN
⌁ www.barneycastlegolf club.org
✉ pro@barnardcastlegolfclub.org.uk
☎ 01833 638355, Fax 695551,
Pro 631980, Rest/Bar 637237
Course is on the B6278 one mile N of
town signposted Middleton in Teesdale.
Parkland course.
Pro Darren Pearce; Founded 1898
Designed by AS Watson
18 holes, 6406 yards, S.S.S. 71
♦ Welcome by prior arrangement.
⌊ WD £20; WE £27.
⟡ Welcome WD by prior
arrangement; catering packages
available; from £18.
⦿ Restaurant and bar facilities.
⌁ Jersey Farm Hotel; Morris Arms

8B 9 Beamish Park

The Clubhouse, Beamish, Stanley, Co
Durham, DH9 0RH

www.Beamishparkgc.fsbuisness.
co.uk
☎ 0191 3701382, Fax 3702937,
Pro 3701984
From A1 take B693 towards Stanley
and follow the signs for Beamish
museum.
Tree-lined parkland course.
Pro Chris Cole; Founded 1907/50
Designed by Henry Cotton (part)/W
Woodend
18 holes, 6218 yards, S.S.S. 70
† Welcome by arrangement.
⌶ WD £16; WE £20.
⌒ Welcome by arrangement; on
application.
⏵ Full clubhouse facilities.
⏴ Coppy Lodge GH.

8B 10 Bedlingtonshire
Acorn Bank, Bedlington,
Northumberland, NE22 6AA
☎ 01670 822457, Fax 822087,
Pro 822087
Off A189 Ashington road 10 miles N of
Newcastle.
Parkland course.
Pro Marcus Webb; Founded 1972
Designed by Frank Pennink
18 holes, 6813 yards, S.S.S. 73
⌁ Practice ground.
† Welcome by arrangement.
⌶ WD £16; WE £22.
⌒ Welcome by prior arrangement
with secretary; packages can be
arranged; terms available on
application.
⏵ Full clubhouse facilities.
⏴ Swan Inn, Choppington; Half Moon
Inn, Stakeford; Holiday Inn, Seaton
Born.

8B 11 Belford   ☎
South Road, Belford, Northumberland,
NE70 7DP
☎ 01668 213433, Fax 213919,
Sec 213587, Rest/Bar 213433
Just off A1 midway between Alnwick
and Berwick on Tweed.
Parkland course.
Founded 1993
Designed by Nigel W Williams
9 holes, 6304 yards, S.S.S. 70
⌁ 6 indoor, 4 outdoor.
† Welcome.
⌶ WD £15; WE £18.
⌒ Welcome by prior arrangement;
some WE available; packages include
27 holes plus all-day catering; from
£23.
⏵ Full clubhouse facilities.
⏴ Blue Bell; Purdy Travel Lodge.

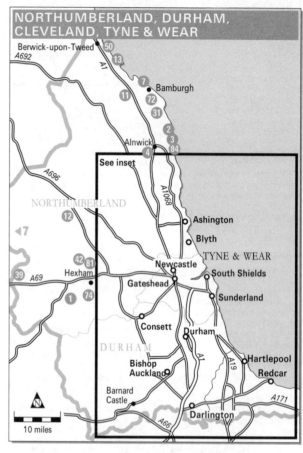

NORTHUMBERLAND, DURHAM, CLEVELAND, TYNE & WEAR

KEY		16	Bishop Auckland	33	Eaglescliffe
1	Allendale	17	Blackwell Grange	34	Elemore
2	Alnmouth	18	Blyth	35	Garesfield
3	Alnmouth Village	19	Boldon	36	George Washington County
4	Alnwick	20	Brancepeth Castle		Hotel & GC
5	Arcot Hall	21	Burgham Park	37	Gosforth
6	Backworth	22	Castle Eden & Peterlee	38	Hall Garth Golf & Country
7	Bamburgh Castle	23	Chester-le-Street		Club
8	Barnard Castle	24	City of Newcastle	39	Haltwhistle
9	Beamish Park	25	Cleveland	40	Hartlepool
10	Bedlingtonshire	26	Close House	41	Heworth
11	Belford	27	Consett & District	42	Hexham
12	Bellingham	28	Crook	43	High Throston
13	Berwick-upon-Tweed	29	Darlington	44	Hobson Municipal
	(Goswick)	30	Dinsdale Spa	45	Houghton-le-Spring
14	Billingham	31	Dunstanburgh Castle	46	Hunley Hall
15	Birtley	32	Durham City	47	Knotty Hill Golf Centre

8B 12 Bellingham Golf Club   ☎
Boggle Hole, Bellingham, Hexham,
Northumberland, NE48 2DT
www.bellinghamgolfcourse.co.uk.
Secretarybellinghamgc@

hotmail.co.uk.
☎ 01434 220530, Fax 220160,
Sec 220530, Rest/Bar 220152
Off the B6320 16 miles NE of Hexham
and the A69, on the outskirts of

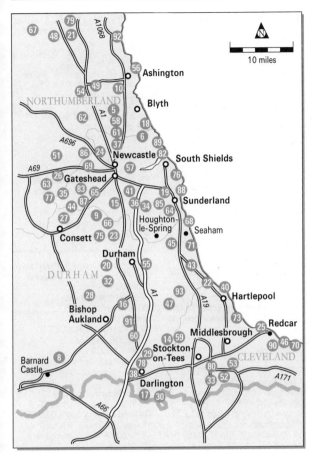

10 miles

48	Linden Hall	64	Ramside	80	Teesside
49	Longhirst Hall	65	Ravensworth	81	Tynedale
50	Magdalene Fields	66	Roseberry Grange	82	Tynemouth
51	Matfen Hall	67	Rothbury	83	Tyneside
52	Middlesbrough	68	Ryhope	84	Warkworth
53	Middlesbrough Municipal	69	Ryton	85	Wearside
54	Morpeth	70	Saltburn-by-the-Sea	86	Westerhope
55	Mount Oswald	71	Seaham	87	Whickham
56	Newbiggin-by-the-Sea	72	Seahouses	88	Whitburn
57	Newcastle United	73	Seaton Carew	89	Whitley Bay
58	Northumberland	74	Slaley Hall International	90	Wilton
59	Norton Golf Course		Golf Resort	91	Woodham Golf & Country
60	Oak Leaf Golf Complex	75	South Moor		Club
	(Aycliffe)	76	South Shields	92	Wooler
61	Parklands Golf Club	77	Stocksfield	93	Wyn (The Wellington)
62	Ponteland	78	Stressholme Golf Centre		
63	Prudhoe	79	Swarland Hall		

Bellingham.
Rolling parkland with natural hazards.
Founded 1893/1996
Designed by E Johnson/I Wilson (96)
18 holes, 6093 yards, S.S.S. 70

✒ 6 floodlit.
♦ Welcome; prior booking is
advisable.
▯ WD £20.00; WE £25.00.
⤤ Welcome every day by prior

arrangement; catering and golfing
packages available; from £17.50.
⦿❘ Full catering and bar facilities
available.
↩ George; Riviera and the Beaumont.

8B 13 **Berwick-upon-Tweed**
Goswick, Berwick-upon-Tweed,
Northumberland, TD15 2RW
⅗ www.goswicklinksgc.co.uk
✉ goswickgc@btconnect.com
☎ 01289 387256, Fax 387334,
Pro 387380
3.5 miles from A1; 5 miles S of
Berwick-upon-Tweed.
Links course.
Pro Paul Terras; Founded
1890/alterations1964
Designed by James Braid/F Pennink
18 holes, 6426 yards, S.S.S. 71
✒ Practice area
♦ Welcome; restrictions before
9.30am and between 12 noon-2pm at
WE.
▯ WD £25; WE £30.
⤤ Welcome WD & WE; packages
include full day's golf and catering for
minimum 10; prices on application.
⦿❘ Full clubhouse catering and bar
facilities.
↩ Blue Bell, Belford; Mizen Head,
Bamburgh; Haggerston Castle Holiday
Park.

8B 14 **Billingham**
Sandy Lane, Billingham, Cleveland,
TS22 5NA
✉ eddiedouglas@
billgolfclub.fsnet.co.uk
☎ 01642 533816, Fax 533816,
Pro 557060, Sec 533816,
Rest/Bar 554494
E of A19 near Billingham Town Centre.
Parkland course.
Pro Mike Ure; Founded 1967
Designed by Frank Pennink
18 holes, 6460 yards, S.S.S. 70
♦ Welcome.
▯ WD £25; WE £40. £15 WD with
member. £20 WE with a member.
⤤ Welcome by prior arrangement
with Sec; terms available on
application.
⦿❘ Full clubhouse facilities.
↩ Billingham Arms.

8B 15 **Birtley**
Birtley Lane, Birtley, Co Durham, DH3
2LR
☎ 0191 4102207, Sec 4102207,
Rest/Bar 4102207
Course is six miles S of Newcastle off

the A6127.
Parkland course.
Founded 1921
9 holes, 5660 yards, S.S.S. 67
† Welcome WD; with member at
WE.
Ⅰ WD £14.
⟳ Welcome WD by prior
arrangement; terms on application.
⦿ Bar facilities.
↩ George Washington County; local
B&Bs can be recommended.

8B 16 Bishop Auckland
High Plains, Durham Rd, Bishop
Auckland, Co Durham, DL14 8DL
⬡ www.bagc.co.uk
✉ @bagc.co.uk
☎ 01388 602198, Fax 607005,
Pro 661618, Sec 663648
0.5 miles N of town on Durham road.
Parkland course.
Pro David Skiffington; Founded 1894
Designed by James Kay
18 holes, 6399 yards, S.S.S. 71
† Welcome WD except Tues.
Ⅰ Prices on application.
⟳ Welcome by prior arrangement;
special packages for 20+ including 27
holes golf and all-day catering; prices
on application.
⦿ Full clubhouse facilities.
↩ The Castle; The Park Head.

8B 17 Blackwell Grange
Briar Close, Blackwell, Darlington, DL3
8QX
✉ Secretary@
blackwell-grange.demon.co.uk
☎ 01325 464464, Fax 464458,
Pro 462088, Sec 464458
1 mile S of Darlington on A66.
Parkland course.
Pro Joanne Furby; Founded 1930
Designed by Frank Pennink
18 holes, 5621 yards, S.S.S. 67
† Welcome.
Ⅰ WD £20; WE £30.
⟳ Welcome WD except Wed;
catering packages available; from £20.
⦿ Full clubhouse facilities.
↩ Blackwell Grange, Darlington.

8B 18 Blyth
New Delaval, Blyth, Northumberland,
NE24 4DB
✉ blythgc@lineone.net
☎ 01670 540110, Pro 356514,
Sec 540110
At W end of Plessey Road.
Parkland course.
Pro Andrew Brown; Founded 1905/1976

Designed by Hamilton Stutt & Co
18 holes, 6430 yards, S.S.S. 72
† Welcome WD.
Ⅰ WD £19; WE £24.
⟳ Welcome WD by prior
arrangement; 3 packages available for
society and company days; minimum
10; from £21.
⦿ Full clubhouse catering and bar
facilities.
↩ Large number in Whitley Bay.

8B 19 Boldon
Dipe Lane, East Boldon, Tyne & Wear,
NE36 0PQ
☎ 0191 5365835, Fax 5190157,
Sec 5365360
Course is on the A184 one mile E of
the A19/A1 Junction.
Parkland course.
Pro Sean Richardson/Phillip Carlaw;
Founded 1912
18 holes, 6338 yards, S.S.S. 70
† Welcome WD with restrictions;
after 3.30pm only at WE.
Ⅰ WD £18; WE £22.
⟳ Welcome by arrangement; catering
packages available; snooker; from £18.
⦿ Bar snacks and restaurant
facilities.
↩ Friendly.

8B 20 Brancepeth Castle ☏
Brancepeth Village, Durham, Co
Durham, DH7 8EA
⬡ www.brancepeth-castle-golf.co.uk
✉ brancepethcastle@btclick.com
☎ 0191 3780075, Fax 3783835,
Pro 3780183, Sec 3780075,
Rest/Bar 3783393
On A690 4 miles W of Durham; left at
the crossroads before Brancepeth.
Parkland course.
Pro D Howdon; Founded 1924
Designed by HS Colt
18 holes, 6375 yards, S.S.S. 71
† Welcome by prior arrangement.
Ⅰ WD£29; WE £30.
⟳ Welcome WD by prior
arrangement; special rates for groups
of more than 12 and 30; banqueting
facilities available; formal dinners can
be arranged; starter available; video
service for lessons; prices on
application.
⦿ Full clubhouse catering and bar
facilities; formal dinner and banquet
can be arranged.
↩ The Whitworth Hall Hotel;
Waterside GH, Royal Hotel, Durham.

8B 21 Burgham Park ☏
Near Felton, Morpeth, Northumberland,
NE65 8QP
☎ 01670 787898, Fax 787164,
Pro 787978, Sec 787898,
Rest/Bar 787501
6 miles N of Morpeth off the A1 at
Longhorsley road (C137).
Parkland course.
Pro S McNally; Founded 1994
Designed by A Mair
18 holes, 6751 yards, S.S.S. 72
Ⅰ 10.
† Welcome.
Ⅰ Terms on application.
⟳ Welcome except on competitions
days; catering packages available;
terms on application.
⦿ Full catering and bar facilities.
↩ Sun Inn, Warkworth; Blue Bell,
Belford.

8B 22 Castle Eden & Peterlee
Castle Eden, Hartlepool, Cleveland,
TS27 4SS
⬡ www.ceden-golf.co.uk
✉ derek.livingston@
btinternet.com
☎ 01429 836220, Fax 836510,
Pro 836689, Sec 836510,
Rest/Bar 836220
10 miles S of Sunderland; take slip
road off A19 towards Blackhall; 0.25
miles.
Parkland course.
Pro Peter Jackson; Founded 1927
Designed by Henry Cotton (back 9)
18 holes, 6282 yards, S.S.S. 70
† Welcome by prior arrangement.
Ⅰ WD £25; WE £35.
⟳ Golfing parties and societies
welcome. Contact Sec for information.
⦿ Full clubhouse facilities.
↩ Castle Eden Inn.

8B 23 Chester-le-Street
Lumley Park, Chester-Le-Street, Co
Durham, DH3 4NS
✉ clsgc@ukonline.co.uk
☎ 0191 3883218, Fax 3881220,
Pro 3890157, Sec 3883218
Close to A167 0.5 miles E of Chester-
le-Street close to Lumley Castle and
Durham CCC ground.
Parkland course.
Pro David Fletcher; Founded 1908
Designed by JH Taylor (original 9)/T
Ray
18 holes, 6437 yards, S.S.S. 71
† Welcome by prior arrangement.
Ⅰ WD £20; WE £25.
⟳ Welcome by prior arrangements;
coffee and catering available

depending on numbers; terms on application. Not WE.
🍽 Full clubhouse facilities.
🛏 Lumley Castle.

8B 24 City of Newcastle

Three Mile Bridge, Gosforth, Newcastle upon Tyne, NE3 2DR
☎ 0191 2851775, Fax 2840700, Pro 2855481
Course is on the B1318 three miles N of Newcastle.
Parkland course.
Pro Steve McKenna; Founded 1892
Designed by Harry Vardon
18 holes, 6528 yards, S.S.S. 71
† Welcome.
Ⅰ WD £24; WE £28.
⌁ Welcome by prior arrangement most days; packages application on request from £20.00.
🍽 Full clubhouse facilities.
🛏 Swallow, Gosforth Park.

8B 25 Cleveland Golf Club �™

Queen St, Redcar, Cleveland, TS10 1BT
☎ 01642 471798, Fax 471798, Pro 483462, Rest/Bar 481757
Off A174 following signs for Teeside and Redcar.
Links course.
Pro Craig Donaldson; Founded 1897
18 holes, 6707 yards, S.S.S. 72
† Welcome.
Ⅰ WD £20; WE £22.
⌁ Welcome; packages can be arranged depending on numbers; terms on application.
🍽 Clubhouse bar and catering facilities.
🛏 Regency; Park.

8B 26 Close House

Close House, Heddon-On-The-Wall, Northumberland
☎ 01661 852953, Sec 4886515, Rest/Bar 852255
Course is off the A69 nine miles W of Newcastle.
Parkland/woodland course.
Founded 1965
Designed by Hawtree
18 holes, 5606 yards, S.S.S. 67
† Members' guests only.
Ⅰ Terms on application.
⌁ Welcome WD by prior arrangement; packages available to include all-day catering; corporate days by arrangement.
🍽 Catering and bar facilities in the Mansion House.

🛏 Copthorne; Novotel, both Newcastle; Holiday Inn, Seaton Burn.

8B 27 Consett & District

Elmfield Road, Consett, Co Durham, DH8 5NN
☎ 01207 502186, Fax 505060, Pro 580210, Sec 505060
Course is on the A691 14 miles N of Durham.
Parkland course.
Pro Stuart Old; Founded 1911
Designed by Harry Vardon
18 holes, 6023 yards, S.S.S. 69
† Welcome by prior arrangement with Pro.
Ⅰ WD £17; WE £25.
⌁ Welcome by prior arrangement with Sec; all-day menu available for £10; from £17.
🍽 Full clubhouse facilities.
🛏 Royal Derwent; Raven.

8B 28 Crook

Low Job's Hill, Crook, Co Durham, DL15 9AA
☎ 01388 762427, Sec 767926, Rest/Bar 767926
On A690 9 miles W of Durham.
Parkland course, hilly in parts.
Founded 1919
18 holes, 6102 yards, S.S.S. 69
† Welcome by prior arrangement.
Ⅰ Prices on application.
⌁ Welcome WD by prior arrangement; packages on application; from £14.
🍽 Clubhouse facilities.
🛏 Helme Park.

8B 29 Darlington

Haughton Grange, Darlington, Co Durham, DL1 3JD
☎ 01325 355324, Fax 488126, Pro 484198, Sec 355324, Rest/Bar 355324
Between A1 and A66 at N end of Darlington.
Parkland course.
Pro Craig Dilley; Founded 1912
Designed by MacKenzie
18 holes, 6270 yards, S.S.S. 70
Ⅰ 9-acre practice.
† Welcome WD.
Ⅰ WD £20.
⌁ Welcome by prior arrangement; packages and special rates for larger groups; from £15.
🍽 Full clubhouse facilities.
🛏 White Horse; Kings Head, both Darlington; Eden Arms, Rushyford.

8B 30 Dinsdale Spa

Neasham Road, Middleton-St-George, Darlington, Co Durham, DL2 1DW
☎ 01325 332222, Fax 332297, Pro 332515, Sec 332297
Off the A67 near Teeside Airport midway between Middleton St George and Neasham.
Parkland course.
Pro Neil Metcalfe; Founded 1910
18 holes, 6090 yards, S.S.S. 69
Ⅰ Practice ground.
† Welcome when tee times allow.
Ⅰ WD £25; WE with member £15; second guest £17.50.
⌁ Welcome by prior arrangement with Sec; catering packages available; from £20.
🍽 Full clubhouse bar and catering facilities.
🛏 Croft Spa; Davenport.

8B 31 Dunstanburgh Castle ☙

Embleton, Elnwick, Northumberland, NE66 3XQ
🖧 www.dunstanburgh.co.uk
✉ golfclub@dunstanburgh.com
☎ 01665 576562, Fax 576562
7 miles NE of Elnwick off the A1; follow signs to Embleton.
Seaside links course.
Founded 1900
Designed by James Braid
18 holes, 6298 yards, S.S.S. 70
† Welcome.
Ⅰ WD £16; WE £20/£28 day ticket.
⌁ Welcome by prior arrangement; packages available; separate dining facilities; from £16.
🍽 Full clubhouse facilities.
🛏 Sportsmans Inn; Dunstanburgh Castle, both Embleton.

8B 32 Durham City ☙

Littleburn Lane, Langley Moor, Durham, DH7 8HL
☎ 0191 3780069, Pro 3780029
Course is off the A690 two miles SW of Durham.
Parkland course.
Pro Steve Corbally; Founded 1887
Designed by CC Stanton
18 holes, 6326 yards, S.S.S. 70
† Welcome by prior arrangement.
Ⅰ WD £24; WE £30.
⌁ Welcome WD; packages available; terms on application.
🍽 Full catering; limited service Mon.

8B 33 Eaglescliffe

Yarm Road, Eaglescliffe, Stockton-on-Tees, Cleveland, TS16 0DQ

☎ 01642 780098, Fax 780238, Pro 790122, Sec 780238, Rest/Bar 780238
On A135 Stockton to Yarm.
Undulating parkland course.
Pro Graeme Bell; Founded 1914
Designed by James Braid, modification by H Cotton
18 holes, 6275 yards, S.S.S. 70
Welcome.
WD £26-£35; WE £36-£50.
Welcome WD by prior arrangement; packages include 18 holes of golf and 3-course meal; prices on application.
Full clubhouse facilities.
Parkmore; Sunnyside; Clareville.

8B 34 **Elemore**
Easington Lane, Haughton le Spring, Tyne and Wear
☎ 0191 5173057, Fax 5173054, Sec 5173057, Rest/Bar 5173057
5 miles E of Durham City; W of Easington Lane.
Parkland course.
Founded 1994
Designed by Jonathan Gaunt
18 holes, 5947 yards, S.S.S. 69
Pay and play.
WD £9; WE £12.
Welcome by prior arrangement; terms on application.
Bar and function room.
Fox and Hounds, Hetton-le-Hole.

8B 35 **Garesfield**
Chopwell, Tyne And Wear, NE17 7AP
☎ 01207 561309, Fax 561309, Pro 563082, Sec 561309, Rest/Bar 561278
On B6315 to High Spen off A694 from A1 at Rowlands Gill.
Undulating wooded parkland course.
Pro David Race; Founded 1922
Designed by William Woodend
18 holes, 6458 yards, S.S.S. 72
Welcome .
Terms on application.
Welcome by prior arrangement except Mon and Sat; catering packages can be arranged with the steward; terms on application.
Full clubhouse facilities except Mon.
Towneley Arms, Rowlands Gill.

8B 36 **The George Washington County Hotel & CG** 𝕿
Stonecellar Road, Washington, Tyne and Wear, NE37 1PH
☎ 0191 4029988, Fax 4151166, Pro 4178346, Sec 4168341
Course is signposted from the A1 (M) and the A194.
Parkland course.
Pro David Patterson; Founded 1990
18 holes, 6604 yards, S.S.S. 72
20.
Welcome by prior arrangement; special rates for hotel guests.
WD £20; WE £20.
Welcome by prior arrangement; special rates for groups of more than 15; hotel packages; leisure club; pool; spa; terms on application.
Full clubhouse and hotel facilities.
105-bedroom George Washington Country Hotel on site.

8B 37 **Gosforth**
Broadway East, Gosforth, NE3 5ER
☎ 0191 2853495, Fax 2846274, Pro 2850553, Sec 2853495, Rest/Bar 2856710
Off A6125 3 miles N of Newcastle.
Parkland course with stream feature.
Pro Graeme Garland; Founded 1906
18 holes, 6024 yards, S.S.S. 69
Welcome by prior arrangement.
WD £24; WE £24.
Welcome WD by prior arrangement; catering packages available; discounts for groups of more than 12; from £24.
Full clubhouse facilities.
Swallow Gosforth Park; Novotel.

8B 38 **Hall Garth Golf & Country Club**
Coatham Mundeville, Nr Darlington, Co Durham, DL3 3LU
www.corushotels.co.uk/hallgarth
☎ 01325 320246, Fax 310083, Pro 300400, Sec 300400, Rest/Bar 300400
From A1 (M) Junction 59 take A167 towards Darlington; top of hill.
Parkland course.
Founded 1995
Designed by B Moore
9 holes, 6607 yards, S.S.S. 72
Welcome.
WD £8; WE £10.00.
Welcome; packages available; terms on application.
Bar and restaurant facilities on site; hotel on site.
Hall Garth, 16th century country house with leisure facilities.

8B 39 **Haltwhisle** 𝕿
Banktop, Greenhead, Via Carlisle, Cumbria, CA6 7HN
☎ 016977 47367, Fax 011434 344311, Sec 01434 344000, Rest/Bar 016977 47367
Off A69 N of Haltwhisle turn right at Greenhead.
Parkland course.
Founded 1967
Designed by Members
18 holes, 5660 yards, S.S.S. 69
Welcome except after 5pm Wed and Fri and before 3pm on Sun.
WD £12; WE £15.
Welcome by prior arrangement; packages include 27 holes of golf and all-day catering; from £20.
Bar and catering facilities available.
Greenhead Hotel.

8B 40 **Hartlepool**
Hart Warren, Hartlepool, Cleveland, TS24 9QF
www.hartlepoolgolclub.co.uk
☎ 01429 274398, Fax 274129, Pro 267473
Course is off the A1086 at N edge of Hartlepool.
Seaside links course.
Pro Graham Laidlaw; Founded 1906
Designed by James Braid (in part)
18 holes, 6215 yards, S.S.S. 70
Practice area.
Welcome; restricted to members' guests Sun.
WD £25; WE £36.
Welcome WD by prior arrangement; catering packages available from the steward; snooker; terms on application.
Full clubhouse facilities, except Mon.
Staincliffe; Marine; Travelodge.

8B 41 **Heworth**
Gingling Gate, Heworth, Tyne and Wear, NE10 8XY
☎ 0191 4962137, Sec 4699832
Course is close to the A1 (M) SE of Gateshead.
Parkland course.
Founded 1912
18 holes, 6404 yards, S.S.S. 71
Welcome but not before 10am at WE.
WD £15; WE £15.
Welcome by prior arrangement; catering packages by arrangement; dining room; from £15.
Bar and restaurant.
George Washington.

8B 42 Hexham ✆
Spital Park, Hexham, Northumberland,
NE46 3RZ
⚃ www.hexhamgolfclub.ntb.org.uk
✉ hexham.golf.club@talk21.com
☎ 01434 603072, Fax 601865,
Pro 604904, Sec 603072
Course is on the A69 one mile W of
Hexham.
Undulating parkland course.
Pro Martin Foster; Founded 1907
Designed by Harry Vardon
18 holes, 6301 yards, S.S.S. 70
♟ Practice ground.
⚠ Welcome by arrangement.
♟ WD £30; WE £40.
☼ Welcome except WE by
arrangement; packages available; from
£25.
✉ Clubhouse catering and bar.
⚀ Beaumont.

8B 43 High Throston
Hart Lane, Hartlepool, Cleveland, TS26
OUG
☎ 01429 275325, Sec 268071
From A19N take A179 to Hartlepool.
Parkland course with USGA standard
green.
Pro Graham Bell (available upon
request); Founded 1996
Designed by J Gaunt
18 holes, 6247 yards, S.S.S. 70
♟ Practice green and putting green.
⚠ Welcome.
♟ WD £16; WE and BH £19.
☼ Welcome by prior arrangement.
✉ Pies, coffee.
⚀ Raby Arms.

8B 44 Hobson Municipal
Burnopfield, Newcastle-upon-Tyne,
NE16 6BZ
☎ 01207 271605, Fax 271069,
Pro 271605, Sec 570189,
Rest/Bar 270941
On main Newcastle-Consett road
opposite Hobson Industrial estate.
Parkland course.
Pro JW Ord; Founded 1980
18 holes, 6403 yards, S.S.S. 71
⚠ Pay and play.
♟ WD £12; WE £16.
☼ Welcome by arrangement with the
Pro; packages available; terms on
application.
✉ Catering and bar facilities.
⚀ Towneley Arms.

8B 45 Houghton-le-Spring
Copt Hill, Houghton-le-Spring, Tyne
and Wear, DH5 8LU

☎ 0191 5847421, Fax 5840048,
Pro 5847421, Sec 5840048,
Rest/Bar 5841198
On B1440 Houghton-le-Spring to
Seaham Harbour road 0.5 miles from
Houghton-le-Spring.
Hillside testing; semi heathland.
Pro Kevin Gow; Founded 1908
18 holes, 6443 yards, S.S.S. 71
⚠ Welcome after 9am; WE
restrictions.
♟ WD £20-£30; WE £28-£33.
☼ Welcome by prior arrangement;
golf and catering packages available;
from £30.
✉ Catering and bar facilities
available.
⚀ White Lion; Ramside Hall; Rainton
Lodge.

8B 46 Hunley Hall ✆
Brotton, Saltburn-by-the-Sea, N Yorks,
TS12 2QQ
✉ enquiries@hunleyhall.co.uk
☎ 01287 676216, Fax 678250,
Pro 677444
Off A174 from Teesside to Brotton into
St Margaret's Way.
Meadowland.
Pro Andrew Brook; Founded 1993
Designed by J Morgan
27 holes, 6918 yards, S.S.S. 73
♟ 12 floodlit.
⚠ Welcome.
♟ WD £20; WE £30.
☼ Welcome Mon to Sat; packages for
18 and 27 holes of golf and for
catering available; terms on
application.
✉ Restaurant and bars; members
bar; spike bar; all-day catering
available.
⚀ Accommodation on site; 2 Star.

8B 47 Knotty Hill Golf Centre
Sedgefield, Stockton-on-Tees, TS21
2BB
⚃ www.knottyhillgolfcentre.co.uk
✉ khgc21@btopenworld.com
☎ 01740 620320, Fax 622227,
Sec 620320, Rest/Bar 620320
Course is on the A177 one mile from
Sedgefield, and four miles from the A1
(M) Junction 60.
Naturally undulating parkland course.
Founded 1991
Designed by C Stanton
♟ 21 bays.
⚠ All welcome. Grass tee area, 2
putting greens, 2 chipping areas &
practice bunker.
♟ WD £13; WE £13 prices for both
courses.

☼ Welcome WD; terms on
application.
✉ Full clubhouse facilities available.
⚀ Hardwick Hall, Sedgefields.

8B 48 Linden Hall
Linden Hall Hotel, Longhorsley,
Morpeth, Northumberland, NE65
8XF
☎ 01670 500011, Fax 500001
From A1 take A697 to Coldstream until
reaching Longhorsley; course half mile
on right.
Parkland course.
Pro David Curry; Founded 1997
Designed by J Gaunt
18 holes, 6846 yards, S.S.S. 73
♟ Practice range, 12 bays.
⚠ Welcome with handicap certs.
♟ WD £22.50; WE £27.50.
☼ Welcome by prior arrangement;
packages for golf and catering
available; corporate days arranged;
leisure club, gym in hotel; prices on
application.
✉ Grill room, conservatory and 2
bars.
⚀ Linden Hall on site.

8B 49 Longhirst Hall ✆
Longhirst Hall, Longhirst,
Northumberland, NE61 3LI
⚃ www.longhirstgolf.co.uk
✉ enquiries@longhirstgolf.co.uk
☎ 01670 791505, Pro 791768, Sec
862449, Rest/Bar 791505
From A1 take signs to Hebron Cockle
Park; after 2 miles at T junction turn
left and follow signs for Longhurst Hall;
2 miles N of Morpeth.
Parkland course.
Pro Graham Kent; Founded 1997
18 holes, 6572 yards, S.S.S. 72
♟ Practice.
⚠ Welcome.
♟ Seniors £20; juniors £10.
☼ Welcome by prior arrangement;
packages include golf, catering and, if
required, hotel and self-catering
accommodation; group and corporate
days can be arranged for any size.
✉ Full facilities in clubhouse and The
Hall.
⚀ Longhirst Hall 75-room hotel on
site and self-catering at Micklewood
Village on site.

8B 50 Magdalene Fields ✆
Berwick-upon-Tweed, Northumberland,
TD15 1NE
⚃ www.magdaleen-feilds.co.ukl
✉ mail@magdalenefields.co.uk

☎ 01289 306384, Fax 306384,
Sec 306130
5 minutes walk from centre of town in
direction of coast.
Seaside course with parkland fairways.
Founded 1903
18 holes, 6407 yards, S.S.S. 71
✝ Welcome by prior arrangement.
⌊ WD £18; WE £20.
⟲ Welcome WD; restrictions Sat and
Sun; catering packages available; from
£16.
⦿ Bar and restaurant.
⟿ Queen's Head, Berwick.

8B 51 Matfen Hall
Matfen Hall, Matfen, Near Newcastle
upon Tyne Northumberland, NE20
ORH
♨ www.matfenhall.com
▤ info@matfenhall.com
☎ 01661 886400, Fax 886055,
Pro 886400, Rest/Bar 886500
Just off B6318 Military road 15 miles W
of Newcastle.
Parkland course; Total yards 6534.
Pro John Harrison; Founded 1994
Designed by M James/A Mair/J Gaunt
18 holes, 6534 yards, S.S.S. 71
✍ Open air practice facilities
including short game area.
✝ Welcome.
⌊ Winter WD £15, WE £20; Summer
WD £27.50, WE £30.
⟲ Welcome by prior arrangement;
golf and catering packages available;
par 3 course; practice range; terms on
application. Society and Company calls
are welcome.
⦿ Full bar and restaurant facilities
available.
⟿ Matsen Country House Hotel.

8B 52 Middlesbrough
Brass Castle Lane, Marton,
Middlesbrough, TS8 9EE
♨ www.middlesbroughgolfclub.co.uk
▤ golf@brass45.fsbusinesss.co.uk
☎ 01642 311515, Fax 319607,
Pro 311766, Sec 311515,
Rest/Bar 316430
1 mile W of A172 5 miles S of
Middlesbrough.
Parkland course.
Pro Don Jones; Founded 1908
Designed by James Braid
18 holes, 6278 yards, S.S.S. 70
✍ 3 practice grounds and putting
green.
✝ Welcome except Tues and Sat.
⌊ Prices on application.
⟲ Welcome by prior arrangement;
packages of golf and catering available;

terms available on application.
⦿ Full facilities; restaurant service
available at 24 hours notice.
⟿ Blue Bell Hotel, Acklam.

8B 53 Middlesbrough Municipal
Ladgate Lane, Middlesbrough, TS5 7YZ
♨ www.middlesbrough.gov.uk
☎ 01642 315533, Fax 300726,
Pro 300720
Access to the course from the A19 via
the A174 to Acklam.
Undulating parkland course.
Pro Alan Hope; Founded 1977
Designed by Middlesbrough Borough
Council
18 holes, 6333 yards, S.S.S. 70
✝ Welcome but must arrange starting
time.
⌊ WD £10.90; WE £13.50, Twilight
£6.25; Winter WD £8; WE £10; Twilight
£5.
⟲ Welcome by prior arrangement;
terms on application.
⦿ Catering available; lunches.
⟿ Blue Bell.

8B 54 Morpeth
The Common, Morpeth, NE61 2BT
♨ www.morpethgolf.co.uk
☎ 01670 504942, Fax 504942,
Pro 515675, Sec 504942,
Rest/Bar 504942
On A197 1 mile S of Morpeth.
Parkland course.
Pro Martin Jackson; Founded 1906
Designed by Harry Vardon (1922)
18 holes, 6104 yards, S.S.S. 69
✍ Practice area.
✝ Welcome by prior arrangement
after 9.30am.
⌊ WD £22.50; WE £27.50.
⟲ Welcome WD by prior
arrangement with Sec; packages for
golf and catering available; terms on
application.
⦿ Snacks, bar lunches, dinner
available; no catering on Mon during
winter.
⟿ Waterford Lodge; Queens Head;
Linden Hall.

8B 55 Mount Oswald
Mount Oswald Manor, South Road,
Durham, Co Durham, DH1 3TQ
♨ www.mountoswald.co.uk
▤ information@mountoswald.co.uk
☎ 0191 3867527, Fax 3860975
On A1050 SW of Durham.
Partly wooded parkland course.
Founded 1924
18 holes, 6101 yards, S.S.S. 69

✝ Welcome; after 10am Sun.
⌊ Mon-Thurs £12.50; Fri-Sun and
BH £15.
⟲ Welcome by prior arrangement;
special rates for 12 or more; some WE
available; function room for 80; other
smaller private rooms; packages for
golf and catering; from £22.
⦿ Full clubhouse catering.
⟿ Three Tuns.

8B 56 Newbiggin-by-the-Sea Clubhouse
Newbiggin-by-the-Sea,
Northumberland, NE64 6DW
☎ 01670 817344, Fax 520236,
Pro 817833
Off A197 following signs for Newbiggin-
by-the-Sea from A189 from Newcastle.
Seaside links course.
Pro Marcus Webb; Founded 1884
18 holes, 6516 yards, S.S.S. 71
✍ Remote practice area.
✝ Welcome after 10am except on
competition days.
⌊ WD £16; WE £20.
⟲ Welcome by prior arrangement
with Sec; catering packages available.
⦿ Full clubhouse facilities.
⟿ Beachcomber.

8B 57 Newcastle United
60 Ponteland Road, Cowgate,
Newcastle-upon-Tyne,
Northumberland, NE5 3JW
♨ www.nujc.co.uk
▤ info@nujc.co.uk
☎ 0191 2864693, Fax 2864323,
Pro 2869998, Sec 2864323
2 miles W of the city centre.
Mooreland course.
Founded 1892
Designed by Tom Morris
18 holes, 6612 yards, S.S.S. 71
✝ Welcome WD; not on WE
competition days.
⌊ Prices on application. WD £18 per
day. Motorised buggies and bar meals
available. Special rates for societies.
⟲ Welcome by arrangement; catering
packages by arrangement; snooker;
terms available on application.
⦿ Bar and snacks.
⟿ Gosforth Park.

8B 58 Northumberland
High Gosforth Park, Newcastle upon
Tyne, Tyne and Wear, NE3 5HT
☎ 0191 2362498, Fax 2362490,
Rest/Bar 2362 2009
Off A1 5 miles N of Newcastle.
Parkland course.

Founded 1898
Designed by Members
18 holes, 6683 yards, S.S.S. 72
♱ Welcome by arrangement.
⏾ WD £35.
⏁ Very limited availability terms on application.
🍴 Full clubhouse facilities.
↩ Swallow Gosforth Park;Marriot.

8B 59 Norton Golf Course
Junction Road, Stockton-on-Tees, Cleveland, TS20 1SU
☎ 01642 676385, Fax 608467, Sec 674636, Rest/Bar 612452
From A177 2 miles N of Stockton roundabout.
Parkland course.
Founded 1989
Designed by T Harper
18 holes, 5855 yards, S.S.S. 71
♱ Public pay and play.
⏾ WD £10; WE £12.
⏁ Welcome by prior arrangement; packages available both for WD; bookings much be made more than 7 days in advance; from £16.
🍴 Full catering facilities.
↩ Swallow, Stockton.

8B 60 Oak Leaf Golf Complex (Aycliffe)
School Aycliffe Lane, Newton Aycliffe, Co Durham, DL5 6QZ
☎ 01325 310820, Fax 310820, Pro 310820, Sec 316040
Take A1 (M) to A68 and then turn into Newton Aycliffe; course on left.
Parkland course.
Andrew Waites
18 holes, 5818 yards off the white; 5308 yards off the yellow, S.S.S. 68 off the white; 66 off the yellow
⏾ Yes.
♱ Everyone welcome; no restrictions.
⏾ WD £9.50; WE £11.00; concessions for under-18s and over-60s. WD £6.50 WE £9.50.
⏁ Welcome at off-peak times; deposit required; sports and leisure complex; terms on application.
🍴 Bar and restaurant facilities available.
↩ Redworth Arms, Redworth; Eden Arms; Getna Hotel.

8B 61 Parklands Golf Club
High Gosforth Park, Newcastle-upon-Tyne, NE3 5HQ
☎ 0191 2364867, Fax 2363322, Pro 2364480, Sec 2364480,

Rest/Bar 2364480
Course is off the A1 three miles N of Newcastle.
Parkland course.
Pro Brian Rumney; Founded 1971
18 holes, 6060 yards, S.S.S. 69
⏾ 45 floodlit.
♱ Welcome.
⏾ WD £15; WE £18.
⏁ Welcome by prior arrangement; catering packages available; terms on application.
🍴 Bar and restaurant facilities available.
↩ Marriott Gosforth Park.

8B 62 Ponteland
Bell Villas, Ponteland, Newcastle-upon-Tyne, Tyne and Wear, NE20 9BD
☎ 01661 822689, Fax 860077, Pro 01661822689 ext 18, Sec 822689 ext 10,
Rest/Bar 822689 ext 21
On A696 2 miles N of Newcastle Airport.
Parkland course.
Pro Alan Robson-Crosby; Founded 1927
Designed by Harry Ferney
18 holes, 6524 yards, S.S.S. 71
♱ Welcome Mon-Thurs; Fri, Sat, Sun as members' guest.
⏾ WD £25.00; WE £10.00 per day with a member.
⏁ Welcome on Tues and Thurs; catering packages can be arranged; from £22.50.
🍴 Full clubhouse facilities.

8B 63 Prudhoe   ⛳
Eastwood Park, Prudhoe, Northumberland, NE42 5DX
☎ 01661 832466, Fax 830710, Pro 836188, Sec 832466,
Rest/Bar 832466
Course is on the A695 12 miles W of Newcastle.
Parkland course.
Pro John Crawford; Founded 1930
18 holes, 5862 yards, S.S.S. 69
♱ Welcome except on competition days.
⏾ Prices on application £20 per day.
⏁ Welcome WD by arrangement; terms on application.
🍴 Bar snacks and meals available.
↩ Beaumont, Hexham.

8B 64 Ramside
Ramside Hall Hotel, Carrville, Durham, DH1 1TD
☎ 0191 3869514, Fax 3869519, Pro 3869514, Sec 3869514,
Rest/Bar 3869514

On A690 Sunderland road 400m from A1 (M) Junction 62.
Parkland course; 3 x 9 loops.
Pro Robert Lister; Founded 1996
Designed by Stephen Marnoch Jonathan Gaunt
27holes/3 loops of 9 holes, 1-18 holes 6851 yards off the blue, S.S.S. 73 off the blue
⏾ 16.
♱ Welcome by prior arrangement. 3 x 9 loops: Bishops Cathedral; Cathedral Princess; Prince Bishops.
⏾ WD £28; WE £35.
⏁ Welcome by prior arrangement; full society and corporate packages available; terms on application.
🍴 Full bar and restaurant facilities; hotel restaurant and bar also.
↩ On site Ramside Hall.

8B 65 Ravensworth
Moss Heaps Wrekenton, Gateshead, Tyne and Wear, NE9 7UU
🖳 www.ravensworthgolfclub.co.uk
☎ 0191 4876014, Fax 4872843, Pro 4913475, Sec 4872843
Course is off the A1 two miles S of Gateshead.
Moorland/parkland course.
Pro Shaun Cowell; Founded 1906
18 holes, 5966 yards, S.S.S. 69
♱ Welcome.
⏾ Prices on application.
⏁ Welcome WD by prior arrangement; catering packages available; terms on application.
🍴 Full facilities available.
↩ Swallow Hotel, Gatehead.

8B 66 Roseberry Grange
Grange Villa, Chester-le-Street, Durham, DH2 3NF
☎ 0191 3700670, Fax 3702047, Pro 3700660, Sec 3702047
3 miles W of Chester-le-Street close to A1 (M) Junction.
Parkland course.
Pro Alan Hartley; Founded 1987
18 holes, 6023 yards, S.S.S. 69
♱ Welcome WD; by prior arrangement WE.
⏾ WD £11.50; WE £15; telephone booking essential.
⏁ Welcome; terms on application.
🍴 Full clubhouse facilities.
↩ Lumley Castle; Beamish Park.

8B 67 Rothbury
Old Race Course, Rothbury, Morpeth, Northumberland, NE65 7TR
☎ 01669 621271, Sec 620718

Off A697 at Weldon Bridge following the signs for Rothbury; 15 miles N of Morpeth.
Flat course alongside river.
Founded 1891
Designed by J B Radcliffe
9 holes, 5681 yards, S.S.S. 67
♱ Welcome WD; restrictions apply at WE.
⌊ WD £11; WE £16.
♉ Welcome WD by arrangement; catering packages available during the day; by arrangement for evening meals; bar closed between 3pm-7.30pm; reductions for larger groups; from £11.
⦿ Clubhouse facilities.
↵ Queens Head; Newcastle Hotel, both Rothbury.

8B 68 Ryhope
Leechmore Way, Ryhope, Sunderland, Durham, SR2 ODH
☎ 0191 5237333, Sec 5536373
Turn off the A19 at Ryhope village towards Hollycarrside.
Being re-designed.
Pro Brian and Roger Janes; Founded 1991
Designed by Sunderland Borough Council
16 holes, 6001 yards, S.S.S. 69
♱ Welcome.
⌊ WD £6, WE £7; £1 discount for over-60s; £2 discount for cheaper; £1 discount for ladies.

8B 69 Ryton ☛
Dr Stanners, Clara Vale, Ryton, Tyne and Wear, NE40 3TD
☎ 0191 4133253, Fax 4131642, Sec 4133737, Rest/Bar 4133737
Course is off the A695 signposted Crawcrook.
Parkland course.
Founded 1891
18 holes, 5950 yards, S.S.S. 69
♱ Welcome WD; by prior arrangement WE.
⌊ Prices on application.
♉ Welcome; discounts for groups of more than 16; WE available; catering packages; prices available on application.
⦿ Clubhouse facilities.
↵ Ryton County Club; Hedgefield; Marriott Gateshead.

8B 70 Saltburn-by-the-Sea
Hob Hill, Saltburn-by-Sea, Cleveland, TS12 1NJ
☎ 01287 622812, Fax 625988,

Pro 624653, Sec 622812
On A1268 1 mile from Saltburn.
Parkland course.
Pro Mike Nutter; Founded 1894
18 holes, 5897 yards off the white, S.S.S. 68, par 70 off the white
♱ Welcome; restrictions Sun and Thurs; limited Sat.
⌊ WD £22; WE £28.
♉ Welcome by prior arrangement; catering available except Mon; terms on application.
⦿ Full clubhouse facilities; limited Mon catering but could cater for larger parties on Mon.
↵ Royal Oak.

8B 71 Seaham
Dawdon, Seaham, Co Durham, SR7 7RD
☎ 0191 5812354, Pro 5130837, Sec 5811268
2 miles NE of the A19.
Heathland course.
Pro Glyn Jones; Founded 1911
Designed by Dr A MacKenzie
18 holes, 6017 yards, S.S.S. 67
♱ Welcome.
⌊ Prices on application.
♉ Welcome; terms available on application.
⦿ Full clubhouse facilities.

8B 72 Seahouses
Beadnell, Seahouses, Northumberland, NE68 7XT
☎ 01665 720794, Fax 721994, Sec 720794, Rest/Bar 720794
On the B1340 S of Seahouses village.
Links course; upgraded to 18 in 1976.
Founded 1913/1976
18 holes, 5462 yards, S.S.S. 67
♱ Welcome; groups of more than four must book in advance.
⌊ Prices on application.
♉ Welcome by prior arrangement everyday except Sun; packages for catering, golf and local hotels available; prices available on application.
⦿ Full catering service except Tues when limited food is available; full bar in summer.
↵ Sunningdale; Beadnell Towers; Sportsman; Blue Bell, Belford.

8B 73 Seaton Carew
Tees Road, Seaton Carew, Hartlepool, TS25 1DE
⌨ www.peatoncarewgolfclub.co.org.uk
☎ 01429 266249, Fax 261040, Pro 890660, Sec 261040

Course is off the A178 three miles S of Hartlepool.
Championship links course.
Pro Mark Rogers; Founded 1874
Designed by Duncan McCuaig
♩ Practice area.
♱ Welcome WD; WE restricted.
⌊ WD £30; WE £40.
♉ Welcome by prior arrangement; catering by arrangement; snooker; from £30.
⦿ Full facilities.
↵ Seaton; Staincliffe Marine.

8B 74 Slaley Hall International Golf Resort ☛
Slaley, Hexham, Northumberland, NE47 0BY
⌨ slaley.hall@devere-hotels.com
☎ 01434 673350, Fax 673152, Pro 673154
Off A69; 23 miles from Newcastle.
Wooded, heath and parkland course.
Pro Mark Stancer; Founded 1989
Designed by Dave Thomas
18 holes, 7021 yards, S.S.S. 74
♩ 1.
♱ Welcome WD by arrangement; hotel residents only at WE.
⌊ WD £65; WE £65.
♉ Welcome WD for groups of 9+ by arrangement with the golf office; residential groups may play WE; golf packages available through golf office; residential golf breaks from £110; customised golf days available; video analysis; corporate days; hotel has leiseire facilities and spa; from £45
⦿ Bar clubhouse.
↵ On site Slaley Hall.

8B 75 South Moor Golf Club ☛
The Middles, Craghead, Stanley, Co Durham, DH9 6AG
☎ 01207 232848, Fax 284616, Pro 283525, Sec 232848, Rest/Bar 232848
Off the A693 6 miles W of Chester-le-Street on B6532 1 mile S of Stanley.
Moorland course.
Pro Shaun Cowell; Founded 1923
Designed by Dr A MacKenzie
18 holes, 6445 yards, S.S.S. 71
♱ Welcome with handicap certs.
⌊ WD £15; WE £26.
♉ Welcome WD between 9.30am-11am and 2pm-3.30pm; WE between 10am-11am and 2pm-3.30pm; catering packages available; snooker table; from £15.
⦿ Full clubhouse facilities.
↵ Lambton Arms; Lumley Castle; South Causey; Harperley Hotel

8B 76 South Shields

Cleadon Hills, South Shields, Tyne and
Wear, NE34 8EG
⛳ www.ssgc.co.uk
📧 TheSecretary@southshield-
golf.freeserve.co.uk
☎ 0191 4560475, Fax 4568942,
Pro 4560110, Sec 4568942
Close to A19 and A1 (M) near Cleadon
Chimney.
Heathland links course.
Pro Gary Parsons; Founded 1893
Designed by McKenzie/Baird
18 holes, 6264 yards, S.S.S. 71
† Welcome.
[WD £20; WE £25.
⏱ Welcome by prior arrangement;
terms on application.
🍽 Clubhouse catering and bar
facilities available.
🛏 Sea Hotel.

8B 77 Stocksfield ☞

New Ridley, Stocksfield,
Northumberland, NE43 7RE
⛳ www.sgcgolf.co.uk
📧 info@sgcgolf.co.uk
☎ 01661 843041, Fax 843046
2 miles from Stocksfield on the New
Ridley Road, off the A695 Hexham-
Prudhoe Road.
Woodland/parkland course.
Pro David Mather; Founded 1913/80
Designed by Frank Pennink
18 holes, 6013 yards, S.S.S. 70
† Welcome except Wed and Sat.
[WD £25; WE £30.
⏱ Welcome by arrangement;
special packages with or without
catering for 18/27/36 holes available;
some reductions for larger groups;
from £18.
🍽 Full clubhouse facilities.
🛏 Beaumont, Hexha; Royal Derwent,
Allensford.

8B 78 Stressholme Golf Centre

Snipe Lane, Darlington, DL2 2SA
☎ 01325 461002
2 miles S of Darlington.
Parkland course.
Pro Ralph Gibens; Founded 1976
18 holes, 6229 yards, S.S.S. 71
🏌 15 bays; floodlit.
† Welcome.
[WD £11; WE £13.
⏱ Welcome by arrangement with
professional; terms on application.
🍽 Clubhouse facilities.
🛏 Blackwell Grange.

8B 79 Swarland Hall ☞

Coast View, Swarland, Morpeth,
Northumberland, NE65 9JG
☎ 01670 787010, Rest/Bar 787940
Course is one mile W of the A1 eight
miles S of Alnwick.
Parkland course.
Pro Wayne Tyrie; Founded 1993
18 holes, 6628 yards, S.S.S. 72
🏌 Practice.
† Welcome.
[WD £13; WE £18. Full Day £18
WD, WE £23.
⏱ Welcome; packages available for
golf and catering; 10 percent discount
for parties of more than 12; from £12
🍽 Full dining and bar facilities
available.
🛏 The Oaks Hotel, Alnwick.

8B 80 Teeside

Acklam Road, Thornaby, Stockton,
Cleveland, TS17 7JS
☎ 01642 676249, Fax 676252,
Pro 673822, Sec 616516
Off A1130 Thornaby-Acklam Road.
Parkland course.
Pro Ken Hall; Founded 1901
18 holes, 6535 yards, S.S.S. 71
† Welcome by arrangement; before
4.30pm WD after 11.30am WE.
[WD £26; WE £26.
⏱ Welcome WD by prior arrangement;
minimum group 10, max 35; from £20.
🍽 Full clubhouse facilities.
🛏 Swallow, Stockton; Golden Eagle,
Thornaby.

8B 81 Tynedale

Tyne Green, Hexham,
Northumberland, NE46 3HQ
☎ 01434 608154
From A69 Hexham road turn into
Countryside Park; course 0.5 miles on
S of river Tyne.
Parkland course.
Pro Ian Waugh; Founded 1907
9 holes, 5403 yards, S.S.S. 67
† Welcome; except before 11am Sun
[Prices on application.
⏱ Welcome by prior arrangement;
discounts for groups of more than 10;
prices on application.
🍽 Full clubhouse facilities.
🛏 Beaumont; County; Royal.

8B 82 Tynemouth

Spital Dene, Tynemouth, North
Shields, Tyne and Wear, NE30 2ER
☎ 0191 2574578, Fax 2595193,
Sec 2573381
On A695.

Parkland course.
Pro John McKenna; Founded 1913
Designed by Willie Park
18 holes, 6359 yards, S.S.S. 71
† Welcome WD after 9.30am; after
12.30pm Sun; limited Sat.
[WD £20; WE £20.
⏱ Welcome WD by prior arrangement;
catering packages available; terms
available on application.
🍽 Lunches, teas and snacks available.
🛏 Park.

8B 83 Tyneside

Westfield Lane, Ryton, Tyne and Wear,
NE40 3QE
☎ 0191 4132177, Fax 4132742,
Pro 4131600, Sec 4132742,
Rest/Bar 4138357
7 miles W of Newcastle off A695 S of
river.
Parkland course.
Pro Malcolm Gunn; Founded 1879
Designed by HS Colt (1910)
18 holes, 6033 yards, S.S.S. 69
🏌 Large practice area.
† Welcome.
[£25 pound WD & WE.
⏱ Welcome by prior arrangement;
reductions for groups of 18 or more;
catering packages available; prices on
application.
🍽 Full clubhouse catering and bar
facilities.
🛏 Ryton Park; Hedgefield Inn;
Copthorne, Newcastle; Marriott,
Gateshead; Ravensdene, Gateshead.

8B 84 Warkworth

The Links, Warkworth, Morpeth,
Northumberland, NE65 0SW
⛳ www.walkwordgolf.com.uk
☎ 01665 711596
Off A1068 at Warkworth; 10 miles N of
Morpeth.
Seaside links course.
Founded 1891
Designed by Tom Morris
9 holes, 5986 yards, S.S.S. 69
🏌 Practice.
† Welcome except Tues and Sat.
[WD £12; WE £20.
⏱ Welcome by prior arrangement;
catering packages available by
arrangement with stewardess; from £12.
🍽 Bar and catering facilities in
season; by arrangement in winter.
🛏 Warkworth House; Sun.

8B 85 Wearside

Coxgreen, Sunderland, Tyne and
Wear, SR4 9JT

☎ 0191 5342518, Fax 5346186,
Pro 5344269
Course is off the A183 towards
Chester-le-Street; turn right signposted
Coxgreen to a T junction; then turn left.
Meadowland/parkland course.
Pro Doug Brools; Founded 1892
18 holes, 6373 yards, S.S.S. 70
⚑ Practice + 4-hole par 3 practice
course.
† Welcome except on competition
days.
Ⅼ WD £20; WE £26.
♣ Welcome on application to Sec;
catering packages available; from £25.
🍴 Full clubhouse facilities.
💤 Seaburn.

8B 86 Westerhope
Whorlton Grane, Westerhoper,
Newcastle-upon-Tyne, NE5 1PP
☎ 0191 2867636, Pro 2860594,
Rest/Bar 2869125
On the B6324 5 miles W of Newcastle;
close to the Jingling Gate public house.
Wooded parkland course.
Pro N Brown; Founded 1941
Designed by Alexander Sandy Herd
18 holes, 6444 yards, S.S.S. 71
† Welcome.
Ⅼ Terms on application.
♣ Welcome by prior arrangement;
catering packages available; prices on
application.
🍴 Full clubhouse facilities.
💤 Airport Moat House; Holiday Inn;
Novotel, all Newcastle.

8B 87 Whickham
Hollinside Park, Whickham, Newcastle-
upon-Tyne, Tyne and Wear, NE16 5BA
✉ enquires@whickhamgolfclub.co.uk
☎ 0191 4887309, Fax 4881576,
Pro 4888591, Sec 4881576
Off the A1 at Whickham; follow signs
for Burnopfield, club 1.3 miles.
Parkland course.
Pro Graeme Lisle; Founded 1911
18 holes, 5878 yards, S.S.S. 68
† Welcome.
Ⅼ WD £20; WE £25.
♣ Welcome WD by arrangement with
Sec; discounts for larger groups;
catering packages; from £15.
🍴 Full catering facilities.
💤 Gibside Arms, Whickham; Beamish
Park; County; Copthorne; Derwent
Crossing, all Newcastle.

8B 88 Whitburn
Lizard Lane, South Shields, Tyne and

Wear, NE34 7AF
☎ 0191 5292144, Fax 5294944,
Pro 5294210, Sec 5294944
Off coast road mid-way between
Sunderland and South Shields.
Parkland course.
Pro David Stephenson; Founded 1932
18 holes, 5900 yards, S.S.S. 68
⚑ Practice area.
† Welcome WD; by prior
arrangement WE.
Ⅼ WD £20; WE £25.
♣ Welcome WD by prior arrangement;
restrictions Tues; limited availability WE;
discounts for groups of 11 or more;
catering packages available by prior
arrangement; from £20.
🍴 Full clubhouse facilities.
💤 Seaburn; Roker.

8B 89 Whitley Bay
Claremont Road, Whitley Bay, Tyne
and Wear, NE26 3UF
🖳 www.wbgolf.free-online.co.uk
✉ secretarywbgolf@
netscapeonline.co.uk
☎ 0191 2520180, Fax 2970030,
Pro 2525688, Rest/Bar 2520180
N of Town centre.
Simulated links course.
Pro Gary Shipley; Founded 1890
18 holes, 6529 yards, S.S.S. 71
† Welcome WD.
Ⅼ WD £22.
♣ Welcome by prior arrangement;
discounts available for larger groups;
catering packages available; from £30.
🍴 Clubhouse catering facilities.
💤 The Grand, Tynemouth; Park;
Windsor, both Whitley Bay; Stakis
Wallsend.

8B 90 Wilton
Wilton, Redcar, Cleveland, TS10 4QY
☎ 01642 465265, Fax 452730,
Pro 452730, Sec 465265,
Rest/Bar 465886
Off A174 Whitby-Redcar road through
Lazenby following signs for Wilton
Castle.
Parkland course.
Pro Pat Smillie; Founded 1952/66
18 holes, 6153 yards, S.S.S. 69
⚑ Under future development.
† Welcome if carrying handicap certs.
Ⅼ WD £22; WE £24.
♣ Mon, Wed and Fri and some
Sundays and BH. Catering on
arrangement with secretary.
🍴 Full clubhouse facilities.
💤 Post House, Thornaby; Marton
Way; Blue Bell, both Middlesbrough.

8B 91 Woodham Golf & ☎
Country Club
Burnhill Way, Newton Aycliffe, Durham,
DL5 4PN
☎ 01325 320574, Fax 315254,
Pro 315257, Rest/Bar 301551
Off the A167 to Woodham village in
Newton Aycliffe.
Parkland course.
Pro Ernie Wilson; Founded 1983
Designed by J Hamilton Stutt
18 holes, 6771 yards, S.S.S. 72
† Welcome by prior arrangement.
Ⅼ Winter fees all times £25.
♣ Welcome by prior arrangement;
some WE available; minimum 12
players; catering packages by
arrangement; buggy hire available;
practice area; from £15.
🍴 Full bar and restaurant facilities
available.
💤 Eden Arms, Rushyford.

8B 92 Wooler
Dod Law, Doddington, Wooler,
Northumberland, NE71 6EA
☎ 01668 281791
Course is East of the B6525 Wooler-
Berwick Rd; signposted from
Doddington Village.
Moorland course.
Founded 1976
Designed by Club Members
9 holes, 6372 yards, S.S.S. 70
† Welcome.
Ⅼ Terms on application.
♣ Welcome by prior arrangement
with Sec; catering can be arranged
terms on application.
🍴 Bar and Catering facilities available.
💤 Wheatsheaf; Black Bull; Ryecroft
Tankerville Arms.

8B 93 Wyne
Wynyard Park, Billingham, TS22 5QJ
☎ 01740 644399, Fax 644599
On A689 at Wynyard Park between A1
and A19.
Parkland course with mature
woodlands.
Pro David Whlea; Founded 1996
Designed by Hawtree & Son
18 holes, 7100 yards, S.S.S. 73
⚑ Floodlit driving range; practice
ground.
† Welcome.
Ⅼ Terms on application.
♣ Corporate days only; full corporate
golf day organisation and packages
available; terms on application.
🍴 Full restaurant and bar facilities.
💤 Club can supply list of local hotels.

SCOTLAND

9A

Lothian, Borders, Dumfries & Galloway

The Honourable Company of Edinburgh Golfers, otherwise known as Muirfield, has perhaps the most astonishing array of champions of any Open venue. The inclusive list reads Harry Vardon, James Braid (twice), Ted Ray, Walter Hagen, Henry Cotton, Gary Player, Jack Nicklaus, Lee Trevino, Tom Watson, Nick Faldo (twice) and, er, Alf Perry. Partly because it is flatter and greener than many links, Nicklaus considered Muirfield the fairest of all the Open courses.

Tell that to Tony Jacklin. In the third round of the 1972 Open, Trevino went on a run of birdies that included a thinned bunker shot on the sixteenth that hit the flag halfway up and fell down into the hole. In the final round Trevino made a complete mess of the seventeenth, said, "I've thrown it away" and then chipped in for a par. Jacklin played the hole classically, three putted from nowhere and was never the same man again.

The course is an unusual design in that the first nine are played clockwise round the boundary circle and the second nine are played mainly anti-clockwise around an inner ring. The venue of the 2002 Open, Muirfield has been voted the finest course in the world. It is the elite amongst an extraordinary little cluster of courses.

Gullane has three courses, Nos 1, 2 and 3, and a view of Muirfield. As long ago as 1650 the local weavers used to play matches against each other on Gullane Hill.

The No 1 is the premier course. The greens are almost beyond compare, as is the panoramic view from the seventh tee. Just up the road are Longniddry, Kilspindie and Luffane New. Luffane may be over one hundred years old, but in this part of the world that is considered ingenue. The course can be windy, but the smallish greens are exceedingly true.

Along the coast is North Berwick, one of the world's most venerable courses with old fashioned virtues like stone walls and redans. Furthest east in this extraordinary stretch of golfing terrain is Dunbar, with one of the meanest holes around. The par three sixteenth is called the Narrows. The name has something to do with the fact that it is 25 yards wide with an out of bounds wall to the left and a beach to the right.

Travelling inland the heart of the Borders has more to do with rugby than golf, but the Roxburghe is a new course that is fast establishing a reputation.

Around the capital itself Musselburgh was a regular home to the Open at the end of the nineteenth century, but has been somewhat superseded by Royal Musselburgh.

Bruntsfield Links – in fact it is parkland – is another historic Edinburgh course and Dalmahoy, the venue of the 1992 Solheim Cup, caters to all sorts of extravagant tastes including clay pigeon shooting and polo.

On the western side of the country, Portpatrick and Powfoot are fine golfing flankers either side of Southerness, a course designed by Mackenzie Ross whilst he was resurrecting Turnberry just after the war.

Almost opposite to Silloth-on-Solway on the other side of the firth, Southerness is a championship challenge that has hosted the Scottish Amateur. From the eighth where the golfer aims at the lighthouse there is a stretch of holes along the firth that culminates in the tough twelfth. Its green is so close to the edge that a hearty second can run through onto the beach.

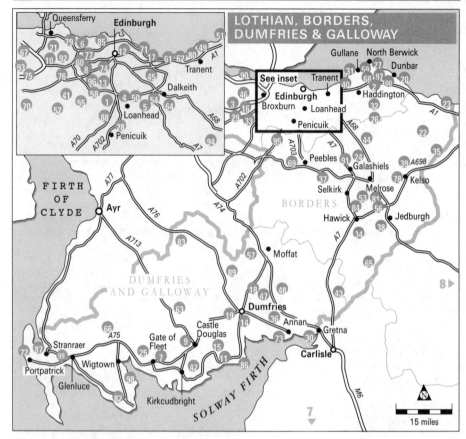

9A 1 **Baberton**
50 Baberton Avenue, Juniper Green,
Midlothian, EH14 5DU
☎ www.baberton.co.uk
✉ babertongolfclub@btinternet.com
☎ 0131 4534911, Fax 4534678,
Pro 4533555, Sec 4534911,
Rest/Bar 453 3361
On A70 5 miles W of central Edinburgh.
Parkland course.
Pro Ken Kelly; Founded 1893
Designed by Willie Park
18 holes, 6129 yards, S.S.S. 70
† Welcome by prior arrangement
with the secretary or club manager.
[Terms available on application to
the club.
⌲ Welcome by prior arrangement;
catering packages available; from £22.
⦿ Full clubhouse facilities.
⤵ Braid Hills, Edinburgh.

9A 2 **Bass Rock**
6 Harperdean Cottages, Harperdean,

Haddington, E Lothian, EH41 3SQ
☎ 01620 822082
[Club plays at North Berwick.

9A 3 **Bathgate**
Edinburgh Road, Bathgate, West
Lothian, EH48 1BA
☎ 01506 630505, Fax 636775,
Pro 630553, Rest/Bar 652232
Club lies two mins E of town centre
and station.
Parkland course.
Pro S Strachan; Founded 1892
Designed by Willie Park
18 holes, 6328 yards, S.S.S. 70
[Practice facilities.
† Welcome.
[WD £17; WE £33.
⌲ Welcome by prior arrangement; full
day's catering package £12.
⦿ Full clubhouse facilities.
⤵ Hillcroft; Dreadnought; Kaimpark;
Hilton, Livingston.

9A 4 **Braid Hills**
Braid Hills Approach, Edinburgh,
Midlothian, EH10 6JY
☎ 0131 4529408, Pro 4476666
Course is on the A702 from City
centre.
Hillside course with panoramic views.
Founded 1897
18 holes, 5865 yards, S.S.S. 68
† Welcome.
[WD £12; WE £14.
⌲ Welcome by prior arrangement; in
summer two courses (second course:
4832 yards, S.S.S 64); in winter they
amalgamate as one; from £12.
⦿ Clubhouse facilities.
⤵ Braid Hills.

9A 5 **Broomieknowe**
Golf Course Road, Bonnyrigg,
Midlothian, EH19 2HZ
☎ www.brommieknowe.com
✉ administrator@
broomieknowe.com

KEY		34	Hawick	68	North Berwick
1	Baberton	35	Hirsel	69	Peebles
2	Bass Rock	36	Hoddom Castle	70	Polkemmet Country Park
3	Bathgate	37	Innerleithen	71	Portobello
4	Braid Hills	38	Jedburgh	72	Portpatrick (Dunskey)
5	Broomieknowe	39	Kelso	73	Powfoot
6	Bruntsfield Links	40	Kilspindie	74	Prestonfield
7	Cally Palace Hotel	41	Kingsknowe	75	Pumpherston
8	Carrickknowe	42	Kirkcudbright	76	Ratho Park
9	Castle Douglas	43	Langholm	77	Ravelston
10	Cogarburn	44	Lauder	78	The Roxburghe
11	Colvend	45	Liberton	79	Royal Burgess Golfing
12	Craigentinny	46	Linlithgow		Society of Edinburgh
13	Craigmillar Park	47	Lochmaben	80	Royal Musselburgh
14	Crichton Royal	48	Lockerbie	81	St Boswells
15	Dalbeattie	49	Longniddry	82	St Medan
16	Deer Park Golf &	50	Lothianburn	83	Sanquhar
	Country Club	51	Luffness New	84	Selkirk
17	Duddingston	52	Marriott Dalmahoy	85	Silverknowes
18	Dumfries & County	53	Melrose	86	Southerness
19	Dumfries & Galloway	54	Melville	87	Stranraer
20	Dunbar	55	Merchants of Edinburgh	88	Swanston
21	Dundas Park	56	Minto	89	Thornhill
22	Duns	57	Moffat	90	Torphin Hill
23	Eyemouth	58	Mortonhall	91	Torwoodlee
24	Galashiels	59	Muirfield – Honourable	92	Turnhouse
25	Gatehouse-of-Fleet		Co of Edinburgh Golfers	93	Uphall
26	Gifford Golf Club	60	Murrayfield	94	Vogrie
27	Glen	61	Musselburgh	95	West Linton
28	Glencorse	62	Musselburgh Old Course	96	West Lothian
29	Greenburn	63	New Galloway	97	Whitekirk
30	Gretna	64	Newbattle	98	Wigtown & Bladnoch
31	Gullane	65	Newcastleton	99	Wigtownshire County
32	Haddington	66	Newton Stewart	100	Winterfield
33	Harburn	67	Niddry Castle		

☎ 0131 663 9317, Fax 6632152,
Pro 6602035, Rest/Bar 6637844
Club is off the A7 at the Eskbank Road
roundabout 5 miles from Edinburgh
Parkland course.
Pro Mark Patchett; Founded 1906
Designed by James Braid; Alterations
by Hawtree/Ben Sayer
18 holes, 6150 yards, S.S.S. 70
† Welcome.
Ⅰ WD £19; WE £25.
⌀ Welcome WD by prior
arrangement; day tickets available for
£28, catering available; group
discounts available.
🍽 Clubhouse facilities.
⌂ Dalhousie Castle.

9A 6 Bruntsfield Links
32 Barton Avenue, Davidsons Mains,
Edinburgh, EH4 6JH
☎ 0131 3361479, Fax 3365538,
Pro 3364050, Sec 3361479,
Rest/Bar 3362006
Off A90 Forth Bridge road 3 miles NW
of Edinburgh city centre; 6 miles from
the airport.
Mature parkland course with stunning
views of the Firth of Forth.
Pro Brian MacKenzie; Founded
1761/1898
Designed by Wille
Park/MacKenzie(22)/Hawtree(74)

18 holes, 6407 yards, S.S.S. 71
Ⅰ 6 bays.
† Welcome by prior arrangement
with Sec or Pro.
Ⅰ WD £42; WE £60.
⌀ Welocme with prior written
arrangement; packages available for
lunch, high tea or dinner in the club's
magnificent dining room; jacket and tie
required in clubhouse; from £40.
🍽 Full catering and Bar facilities
available.
⌂ Many in Edinburgh area.

9A 7 Cally Palace Hotel
Gatehouse Of Fleet, Castle Douglas,
Kirkcudbrightshire, DG7 2DL
🖳 www.callypalace.co.uk
🖂 info@callypalace.co.uk
☎ 01557 814 341, Fax 814 522
33 miles W of Dumfries on A75;
signposted from Gatehouse.
Parkland course.
Founded 1994
Designed by Tom Macaulay
18 holes, 5800 yards, S.S.S. par 70
† Hotel guests only.
Ⅰ Applicable to guests only.
🍽 Full hotel facilities.
⌂ On site Cally Palace.

9A 8 Carrickknowe
Glendevon Park, Edinburgh, EH12 5VZ
☎ 0131 337 1096
Opposite the Holiday Hotel on
Balgreen Road.
Parkland course.
Founded 1933
18 holes, 6055 yards, S.S.S. 68
† Welcome.
Ⅰ WD £10; WE £12.50.
⌀ Welcome.
🍽 No catering facilities.

9A 9 Castle Douglas
Abercromby Road, Castle Douglas,
Kirkcudbrightshire, Dumfries &
Galloway, DG7 1BA
☎ 01556 502801, Sec 502099
On A713 towards Ayr 400 yards from
the town clock.
Parkland course.
Founded 1905
9 holes, 5408 yards, S.S.S. 66
† Welcome.
Ⅰ WD £ 12; WE £12.
⌀ Welcome; bar meals can be
arranged; from £ 12.
🍽 Bar meals available.
⌂ Kings Arms; Imperial; Douglas Arms.

9A 10 Cogarburn
Newbridge, Midlothian, EH28 8NN
☎ 0131 3334110, Sec 3334110,
Rest/Bar 3334110
Close to Edinburgh Airport sliproad off
A8 Glasgow Road.
Parkland course.
Founded 1975
12 holes, 5070 yards, S.S.S. 64
† Welcome by prior arrangement
with Sec.
Ⅰ WD £12; WE £16.
⌀ Welcome by prior arrangement
with Sec; catering can be arranged in
new clubhouse; from £10.
🍽 Full catering and bar facilities
available.
⌂ Barnton; Royal Scot.

9A 11 Colvend
Colvend, Dalbeattie,
Kirkcudbrightshire, Dumfries &
Galloway, DG5 4PY
🖳 www.secretary@
colvendgolfclub.co.uk
🖂 secretary@colvendgolfclub.co.uk
☎ 01556 630398, Fax 630495,
Sec 610878, Rest/Bar 630398
On A710 Solway coast road 6 miles
from Dalbeattie.
Parkland course.

Founded 1905
Designed by Willie Fernie 1905;
D Thomas (1985); J Soutar extension
to 18 (1997)
18 holes, 5220 yards, S.S.S. 67
♦ Everyone welcome.
☂ WD £20; WE £20.
♨ Welcome by prior arrangement;
tee reservations require £5 per head
deposit; concession of £2 for groups of
10 or more; catering packages
available.
🍽 Full catering and bar facilities
available.
🛏 Cairngill; Clonyard; Baron's Craig;
Pheasant.

9A 12 **Craigentinny**
143 Craigentinny Ave, Edinburgh,
EH17 6RG
☎ 0131 5547501, Sec 6574815,
Rest/Bar 6524815
Club is one mile from Meadowbank
Stadium.
Links course.
Pro Tom Steele; Founded 1891
18 holes, 5179 yards, S.S.S. 66
♦ Public links course.
☂ WD £10.00; WE £11.50.
♨ Welcome by prior arrangement
with Council; details available on
application.
🍽 Catering facilities available at club.
🛏 Local hotels and guesthouses
within half a mile.

9A 13 **Craigmillar Park**
1 Observatory Road, Edinburgh,
Midlothian, EH9 3HG
🖥 craigmillerparkgc@lineone.net
☎ 0131 6670047, Fax 6620371,
Pro 6672850, Sec 6670047,
Rest/Bar 6672837
From A68 Princes Street turn right at
Cameron Toll; course 100 yards on
right.
Parkland course.
Pro Brian McGhee; Founded 1895
Designed by James Braid
18 holes, 5851 yards, S.S.S. 69
♦ Welcome WD and Sun after 2pm.
☂ WD £18.00, WE £25.
♨ Welcome WD by prior arrangement
with Sec; separate facilities; catering
packages available; from £18.
🍽 Full catering facilities.
🛏 Iona Hotel, Edinburgh.

9A 14 **Crichton Royal**
Bankend Road, Dumfries,
Dumfriesshire, DG1 4TH
☎ 01387 247894, Fax 257616,

Sec 247894, Rest/Bar 247894
1 mile from Dumfries near Crichton
Royal Hospital.
Wooded parkland course.
9 holes, 3084 yards
♦ Welcome by prior arrangement,
but must avoid competition days.
☂ £12.
♨ Welcome by advance notice; terms
on application.
🍽 Clubhouse facilities.

9A 15 **Dalbeattie**
Dalbeattie, Kirkcudbrightshire, DG5
4JR
☎ 01556 611421, Sec 610311
Course is 1 mile from Dalbeattie on the
B794 (Haugh of Urr road), 10 miles
SW of Dumfries.
Parkland course.
Founded 1894
9 holes, 5710 yards, S.S.S. 68
🏌 Practice range and putting green.
♦ Restrictions Mon, Wed, Thurs after
5 pm.
☂ £12 (day ticket £15).
♨ Welcome outside restricted
times.
🍽 Clubhouse facilities.
🛏 The Kings Arms, The Square
Dalbeattie.

9A 16 **Deer Park Golf &** ☎
Country Club
Golf Course Road, Camps Rigg,
Livingston, West Lothian, EH54 8AB
🖥 deerpark@muir/group.co.uk
☎ 01506 446699, Fax 435608,
Pro 446688
Leave M8 at Junction 3 and follow signs
to Knightsbridge; club is signposted.
Parkland course.
Pro Brian Dunbar; Founded 1978
Designed by Charles Lawrie
18 holes, 6192 yards, S.S.S. 72
♦ Everyone welcome.
☂ WD £24; WE £36.
♨ Welcome by prior arrangement
both WD and WE; catering packages
available; from £32.
🍽 Full clubhouse and country club
facilities.
🛏 Travel Lodge,Deer Park; Houston
House; Hilton.

9A 17 **Duddingston**
Duddingston Road West, Edinburgh,
Midlothian, EH15 3QD
🖥 www.duddingston-golf-club.com
☎ 0131 6611005, Fax 6614301,
Pro 6614301, Sec 6617688,
Rest/Bar 6617688

2 miles from city centre near A1 turning
right at Duddingstons crossroads.
Parkland course.
Pro Alastair McLean; Founded 1895
Designed by Willie Park Jnr
18 holes, 6473 yards, S.S.S. 72
♦ Welcome WD.
☂ WD £30.
♨ Welcome Tues and Thurs by prior
arrangement; catering packages can
be arranged; terms on application.
🍽 Full clubhouse facilities.
🛏 Many in Edinburgh.

9A 18 **Dumfries and County**
Edinburgh Road, Dumfries,
Dumfriesshire, DG1 1JX
🖥 www.dumfriesandcounty-gc.
fsnet.co.uk
🖥 dumfriesandcounty@
netscapeonline.co.uk
☎ 01387 253 585, Fax 253585,
Pro 268918, Sec 253585,
Rest/Bar 249921
On A701 Moffat to Edinburgh road 1
mile NE of town centre.
Parkland course; The Wee Yin; 90
yards, 14th.
Pro Stuart Syme; Founded 1912
Designed by James Braid
18 holes, 5928 yards, S.S.S. 68
♦ Welcome WD between 9.30am-
11am; 2pm-3.30pm; WE Sat; Sun after
10am.
☂ WD £26; WE £26.
♨ Welcome by prior arrangement
with pro; separate facilities; catering
packages available; from £26.
🍽 Club bat and dining room.
🛏 Cairndale; station; Moreig;
Balmoral; Edenbank.

9A 19 **Dumfries and Galloway**
2 Laurieston Avenue, Dumfries,
Dumfriesshire, DG2 7NY
☎ 01387 263848, Fax 263848,
Pro 256902, Sec 263848,
Rest/Bar 253582
On A75 W of Dumfries.
Parkland course.
Pro Joe Fergusson; Founded 1880
Designed by Willie Fernie
18 holes, 5803 yards, S.S.S. 68
♦ Welcome except competition days;
prior booking essential in summer.
☂ WD £25; WE £30.
♨ Welcome by prior arrangements;
catering packages available except
Mon; from £25.
🍽 Full facilities available; except Mon.
🛏 Cairndale; Station.

9A 20 Dunbar

East Links, Dunbar, East Lothian,
EH42 1LL
☎ 01368 862317, Fax 865202,
Pro 862086, Sec 862317,
Rest/Bar 862317
0.5 miles E of Dunbar; 30 miles E of
Edinburgh off A1.
Links course.
Pro Jackie Montgomery; Founded
1794/1856
Designed by Tom Morris
18 holes, 6426 yards, S.S.S. 71
† Welcome WD by prior arrangement
9.30am-12.30pm & 2pm onwards except
Thurs; WE 10am-12 noon and after 2pm.
↲ Terms upon application.
⌁ Welcome by prior arrangement WD;
catering packages available; from £30.
⦿ Full clubhouse facilities.
↵ Gruachan GH; Royal Mackintosh.

9A 21 Dundas Park

South Queensferry, West Lothian,
EH30 9SP
☎ 0131 3315603
Course is one mile south of S
Queensferry on the A8000.
Parkland course.
Founded 1957
9 holes, 6024 yards, S.S.S. 69
↲ Practice range.
† Welcome by arrangement.
↲ Terms on application.
⌁ Welcome by prior arrangement;
terms on application.
⦿ Snacks in clubhouse.

9A 22 Duns ☏

Harden Rd., Trinity Park, Duns,
Berwickshire, TD11 3HN
☎ 01361 882194, Sec 882717
Course is one mile W of Duns off the
A6105 Greenlaw – Duns road, taking
the junction signposted Longformacus.
Parkland/upland course.
Founded 1894/1921
Designed by AH Scott
18 holes, 6209 yards, S.S.S. 70
† Welcome.
↲ WD £14; WE £17.
⌁ Welcome by prior arrangement with
Sec; some WE tee-times available; all
day golf; limited clubhouse facilities but
snack meals can be arranged April –
October; from £15.
⦿ Full facilities.
↵ Barniken House.

9A 23 Eyemouth

The Clubhouse, Gunsgreenhill,
Eyemouth, TD14 5SF

✉ eyemouthgolfclub@global.net
☎ 01890 750551, Pro 750004
One mile off the A1 on the A1107 E of
Burmouth.
Seaside parkland course.
Pro Paul Terras; Founded 1884/1994
Designed by James Baine
18 holes, 6472 yards, S.S.S. 72
† Welcome any day.
↲ WD £20; WE £25.
⌁ Welcome by prior arrangement;
special catering packages available.
⦿ Full clubhouse facilities.
↵ Press Castle; Cul-Na-Sithe;
Dunlaverock House; Ship; Dolphin.

9A 24 Galashields ☏

Ladhope Recreation Ground,
Galashiels, Selkirkshire, TD1 2NJ
☎ 01896 753724, Sec 755525
On A7 to Edinburgh 0.5 miles N of
town centre.
Hilly parkland course.
Founded 1883
Designed by James Braid
18 holes, 5185 yards, S.S.S. 67
† Welcome.
↲ WD £16; WE £21.
⌁ Welcome by prior arrangement
with Sec; package deals available;
terms available on application.
⦿ Full clubhouse facilities.
↵ Abbotsford Arms; Kingsknowes;
Kings.

9A 25 Gatehouse-of-Fleet

Lauriseston Rd, Gatehouse-Of-Fleet
☎ 01644 450260, Sec 01557 450260
From A75 into Gatehouse-of-Fleet
follow signs for Laurieston; course 0.5
miles.
Parkland course with stunning views.
Founded 1921
9 holes, 5042 yards, S.S.S. 66
† Welcome. Membership available
(£90 per annum 2001 rate).
↲ WD £10; WE £10.
⌁ Welcome by prior arrangement;
local hotels can provide catering
arrangements; terms on application.
⦿ None at course.
↵ Masonic Arms; Murray Arms.

9A 26 Gifford Golf Club

Edinburgh Road, Gifford, Haddington,
East Lothian, EH41 4JE
🖳 www.giffordgolfclub.com
✉ secretray@
giffordgolfclub.fsnet.co.uk
☎ 01620 810 267, Sec 810267
On A1 4 miles from the market town of
Haddington.

Undulating parkland course in
Lammermuir foothills.
Founded 1904
Designed by Willie Watt
9 holes, 6255 yards, S.S.S. 70
† Welcome.
↲ WD £13, £20 day ticket; WE £13.
⌁ Welcome; discounts for larger
groups; from £10.
⦿ Full facilities at village hotels;
clubhouse.
↵ Goblin Ha'; Tweeddale Arms.

9A 27 Glen

East Links, Tantallon Terrace, North
Berwick, East Lothian, EH39 4LE
🖳 www.glengolfclub.co.uk
☎ 01620 892726, Fax 895288,
Pro 894596, Rest/Bar 892221
Signposted from A198 1 mile E of town
centre.
Seaside links course.
Founded 1906
Designed by James Briad
18 holes, 6094 yards, S.S.S. 69
† Welcome.
↲ WD £17; WE £23.
⌁ Welcome by prior arrangement;
catering packages available; from
£17.
⦿ Full clubhouse facilities.
↵ Marine; Belhaven; Golf.

9A 28 Glencorse

Milton Bridge, Penicuik, Midlothian,
EH26 0RD
☎ 01968 677189, Fax 674399,
Pro 676481, Rest/Bar 677177
On A701 Peebles road 9 miles S of
Edinburgh.
Parkland course with stream of 10
holes.
Pro C Jones; Founded 1890
Designed by Willie Park
18 holes, 5217 yards, S.S.S. 66
† Welcome; restrictions on comp
days.
↲ WD £20; WE £26.
⌁ Welcome Mon-Thurs and Sun
afternoon by prior arrangement;
packages for golf and catering also
available for parties of 10 or more;
from £18.
⦿ Full clubhouse catering and bar
packages.
↵ Royal Hotel, Pencuik.

9A 29 Greenburn

6 Greenburn Rd, Bridge Street,
Fauldhouse, Bathgate, West Lothian,
EH47 9HG
☎ 01501 771187, Rest/Bar 770292

4 miles S of M8 Junction 4 and 5.
Parkland/moorland course.
18 holes, 6046 yards, S.S.S. 70
⚑ Practice area.
† Welcome by prior arrangements;
WE 9am-10am and 2pm-3pm.
Ⓛ WD £17; WE £20.
↻ Welcome WD by prior
arrangement; catering packages
available; terms on application.
🍴 Full clubhouse facilities.
↩ Hillcroft.

9A 30 Gretna

Kirtle View, Gretna, Dumfriesshire,
DG16 5HD
☎ 01461 338464
Course is 0.5 miles W of Gretna on S
side of the A75; 1 mile from the
M74/A75 Junction.
Parkland course.
Founded 1991
Designed by Nigel Williams/Bothwell
9 holes, 6430 yards, S.S.S. 71
† Welcome except on competition
days.
Ⓛ WD £8: WE £10.
↻ Welcome by prior arrangement
catering packages by arrangement
terms on application.
🍴 Catering available by prior
arrangement.
↩ Many Hotels in local area.

9A 31 Gullane ♛

West Links Road, Gullane, East
Lothian, EH31 2BB
🖳 www.gullanegolfclub.com
☎ 01620 842255, Fax 842327,
Pro 843111
Leave the A1 S to the A198.
300-year-old seaside links course;
Open qualifying course.
Pro Jimmy Hume; Founded
1882/1898/1910
Course 1: 18 holes, 6466 yards, S.S.S. 71
Course 1: 18 holes, 6244 yards, S.S.S. 71
Course 3: 18 holes, 5252 yards, S.S.S. 48
† Welcome with handicap certs by
prior arrangement.
Ⓛ WD £60, WE £75 (Course 1); WD
£28, WE £33 (Course 2); WD £16, WE
£22 (Course 3).
↻ Welcome by prior arrangement;
corporate days can be arranged; also
conference day packages with exclusive
use of the first-class accommodation in
the Members' clubhouse for seminars
and conferences for groups of 12-24;
Heritage of Golf Museum; coaching
clinics; terms available on application.
🍴 Full clubhouse catering facilities in
the Members' clubhouse.

↩ Club can provide a list in Gullane,
North Berwick and Aberlady.

9A 32 Haddington

Amisfield Park, Whittinghame Drive,
Haddington, East Lothian, EH41 4PT
🖳 www.haddingtongolf.co.uk
☎ 01620 822727, Fax 826580,
Pro 822727, Sec 823627,
Rest/Bar 822727
Three quarters of a mile E of
Haddington just off the A1; 17 miles E
of Edinburgh.
Parkland course.
Pro John Sandilands; Founded 1865
18 holes, 6317 yards, S.S.S. 70
† Welcome, WE pre-booking essential.
Ⓛ WD £19; WE £25 Discounts for
group bookings of 8+.
↻ Welcome; full day's golf; catering
packages available in the season by
arrangement Oct-Mar; from £25.
🍴 Full catering and bar facilities Apr-
Sept.
↩ Plough, Maitlandfield,The George.

9A 33 Harburn

West Calder, West Lothian, EH55 8RS
☎ 01506 871131, Fax 870286,
Pro 871582, Sec 871131,
Rest/Bar 871256
Course is on the B7008 2 miles of West
Calder 5 miles from M8 Junction 4.
Parkland course.
Pro Stephen Mills.; Founded 1933
18 holes, 5921 yards, S.S.S. 68
† Welcome except on competition days.
Ⓛ WD £18; Fri £21; WE £23.
↻ Welcome except on competition
days; packages for Mon-Thurs; Fri, Sat
and Sun available including day's golf,
lunch and high tea; separate changing
facilities; from £35.
🍴 Full clubhouse facilities.
↩ Bankton House; Livingston Hilton.

9A 34 Hawick ♛

Vertish Hill, Hawick Golf Club House,
Hawick, Roxburghshire, TD9 0NY
☎ 01450 372293, Sec 374947
Just S of Hawick on A7.
Parkland course.
Founded 1877.
18 holes, 5933 yards, S.S.S. 69
⚑ Practice area.
† Welcome; restrictions until after
3.30pm on some Sats; not before
10.30am Sun.
Ⓛ WD £20; WE £20.
↻ Welcome by arrangement; catering
packages in season; separate facilities;
terms on application.

🍴 Full clubhouse facilities in summer.
↩ Kirkland; Mansfield House; Emsfield.

9A 35 Hirsel

Kelso Rd, Coldstream, Berwickshire,
TD12 4NJ
🖳 www.hustlegc.co.uk
▤ listed on site
☎ 01890 882678, Fax 882233,
Sec 882233
On A697 through Coldstream; golf club
is signposted.
Parkland course.
Pro Keith Lobben; Founded 1949
18 holes, 6111 yards, S.S.S. 70
⚑ Practice area.
† Welcome.
Ⓛ WD £20; WE £27.
↻ Welcome by prior arrangement;
catering and golf packages available;
more than 10 players must book in
advance; 2-10 must book up to 10
days in advance; no starts before
10am; terms on application.
🍴 Full clubhouse facilities.
↩ Tillmouth park; Collingwood Arms;
Cross Keys.

9A 36 Hoddom Castle

Hoddom, Lockerbie, Dumfriesshire,
DG11 1AS
☎ 01576 300251, Fax 300757,
Sec 300244, Rest/Bar 300727
Course is 3 miles from the A74 and 2
miles SW of Ecclefechan on the B752;
M74 Junction 6.
Pay and play inland course.
9 holes, 2274 yards, S.S.S. 33
† Welcome.
Ⓛ £9.
↻ Limited.
🍴 Snacks.

9A 37 Innerleithen

Leithen Water, Innerleithen,
Peeblesshire, EH44 6NL
☎ 01896 830951, Sec 830050,
Rest/Bar 830951
0.75 miles from town centre down
Leithen Road.
Heathland/parkland course.
Founded 1886
Designed by Willie Park
9 holes, 6056 yards, S.S.S. 69
† Welcome.
Ⓛ WD £11; WE £13.
↻ Welcome but groups of more than
six should book; maximum 42; from £11.
🍴 Facilities available by prior
arrangement.
↩ Corner House; Traquar Arms.

Gullane

In his poem about Gullane Hill in 1896, John Thomson wrote that playing golf at the famed links course was the perfect cure for both summer colds and winter coughs. Standing on some of the tees, with spectacular views of the majestic East Lothian scenery and beyond, it's difficult not to feel inspired.

Less than an hour's drive from Edinburgh, Gullane is not one course, but three. Each has its own special characteristics and each is so well-preserved and so well-drained, that neither winter greens nor winter tees are used, balls are played as they lie throughout the year and the greens, even in mid-January, are so slick that the slightest downhill tap can result in the ball shooting way past the hole.

Every time the Open Championship is played at nearby Muirfield, visible from the seventh tee, Gullane's premier course is used for qualifying. It is no surprise, therefore, that the par 71 Gullane One is the magnet for enthusiasts from all over the world even though the par 65 Gullane Three, with its more sympathetic yardage, is increasingly popular for senior citizens and is a third of the price.

Although golf has been played at Gullane for over 300 years, up until 1850 there were only seven holes. The course was extended with the invention of the gutta ball.

Gullane Golf Club now welcomes over 30,000 visitors a year, the 54 holes presenting a rare opportunity to play three adjacent courses on the same day in mid-summer.

The clover leaf shape of Gullane One means that, apart from the beginning and the end, the wind invariably blows at different angles and unlike many predominantly flat links courses, Gullane rises to 200 feet which provides a wonderful variation of uphill and downhill shots.

The opening hole, right beside the pro shop and twelfth century village church, quickly brings the course's many steep-faced traps into play – three of them protect the first green – but it is the second which provides the first real test of skill even at only 380 yards off the back tee. Slightly uphill with rising rough on each side of the fairway and a fearsome pin position, it plays its full length straight into the prevailing wind which one recent American visitor said could part the gates of Hell!

Few holes anywhere in Scotland provide a more spectacular view than the seventh which reveals the full glory of 'Gullane Hill' and 360 degrees of breathtaking scenery around the Firth of Forth. On a clear day, you can see for up to 40 miles in every direction including the city of Edinburgh and Arthur's Seat.

The second nine is considerably longer than the first, typified by the fifteenth, a bruising par five with a double dog-leg, six bunkers down the left and a fearsome green. The combination of wind and slope can make three putts seem like quite an achievement. The usually wind-assisted par four seventeenth is driveable despite its 390 yards, but it still takes an impressive blow to carry the cross-bunkers that lie 40 yards short of the green.

No visit to Gullane is complete without a visit to the club's museum, a trove of memorabilia and mementoes belonging to local historian, author and archivist Archie Baird. This unique collection provides a fascinating insight into the origins of golf and its various stages of development both in terms of equipment and heritage. If you're lucky, Archie will give you a running commentary. – **Andrew Warshaw**

9A 38 Jedburgh

Dunion Road, Jedburgh,
Roxburghshire, TD8 6LA
☎ 01835 863587
0.75 mile W of Jedburgh on Hawick
road.
Undulating parkland course.
Founded 1892
9 holes, 5555 yards, S.S.S. 67
♦ Welcome except on competition
days; WE booking advisable.
○ Terms on application.
○ Welcome with at least 2 weeks'
notice; catering and bar facilities
available between May and
September; from £12.
◙ Available in season.
↩ Royal; Jedforest.

9A 39 Kelso

Racecourse Rd., Kelso,
Roxburghshire, TD5 7SL
☎ 01573 223009, Sec 223259
1 mile N of Kelso inside National Hunt
Racecourse.
Flat parkland course.
Founded 1887
Designed by James Braid
18 holes, 6046 yards, S.S.S. 70
♦ Welcome.
○ WD £16; WE £20.
○ Welcome by prior arrangement;
includes all day golf; catering packages
available; notice needed for Mon or
Tues; from £20.
◙ Clubhouse facilities; closed Mon-
Wed in winter.
↩ Cross Keys; Queen's Head.

9A 40 Kilspindie

The Clubhouse, Aberlady, Longniddry,
East Lothian, EH32 0QD
☎ 01875 870216, Fax 870358,
Pro 870695, Sec 870358
Off A198 North Berwick road
immediately E of Aberlady; private road
leads to the club.
Seaside course.
Pro Graham Sked; Founded 1867
Designed by Ross & Sayers; Extended
by Willie Park
♦ Welcome by prior arrangement
with the club.
○ WD £25; WE £30.
○ Welcome by prior arrangement;
catering packages available; terms on
application.
◙ Full catering facilities with bar and
dining room.
↩ Kilspindie House.

9A 41 Kingsknowe

Lanark Road, Edinburgh, Midlothian,
EH14 2JD
☎ 0131 4411144, Fax 4412079,
Pro 4414030, Sec 4411145
On A70 on the SW ouskirts of
Edinburgh.
Undulating parkland.
Pro Andrew Marshall; Founded 1908
Designed by Alex Herd, James Braid,
JC Stutt
18 holes, 5979 yards, S.S.S. 69
♦ Welcome by prior arrangement
with Pro.
○ WD £21; WE £30.
○ Welcome by prior application to
sec; full day's golf and catering
available; separate changing; from £18.
◙ Full clubhouse catering and bar
facilities.
↩ Orwell Lodge; Edinburgh Post
House.

9A 42 Kirckcudbright

Stirling Crescent, Kirkcudbright,
Kirkcudbrightshire, DG6 4EZ
✉ kbtgolfclub@lineone.net
☎ 01557 330314, Rest/Bar 330314
Off A711 road from the A75 Dumfries-
Stanraer Road.
Parkland course.
Founded 1893
18 holes, 5739 yards, S.S.S. 69
♦ Welcome; some restrictions
Tues/Wed.
○ WD £18; WE £18.
○ Welcome by prior arrangement; full
day £23; from £18.
◙ Clubhouse facilities.
↩ Royal; Selkirk; Commercial.

9A 43 Langholm

Whitaside, Arkinholm Terrace,
Langholm, Dumfriesshire, DG13 0JR
☎ 013873 81247, Sec 80673
Off the A7 Edinburgh-Carlisle road in
centre of Langholm; follow signs to the
course.
Hillside course.
Founded 1892
9 holes, 5744 yards, S.S.S. 68
♦ Welcome.
○ WD £10; WE £10.
○ Welcome by prior arrangement;
catering available by prior
arrangement; £10.
◙ Clubhouse facilities.
↩ Eskdale; Buck; Crown.

9A 44 Lauder

Galashields Rd., Lauder, Scotish
border region, TD2 6RS

🖳 www.laudergolf.org.uk
✉ secretary@
laudergolfcourse.org.uk
☎ 01578 722526, Fax 722526
On A68 30 miles S of Edinburgh; 0.5
miles outside Lauder.
Parkland course.
Founded 1896
Designed by W. Park of Musselburgh
9 holes, 6002 yards, S.S.S. 70
♦ Welcome except before noon Sun
and 5.30pm-7.30pm Wed.
○ WD £10; WE £10.
○ Welcome by prior arrangement;
golf only available; from £10.
◙ Catering can be arranged with
local hotels.
↩ Lauderdale; Eagle; Black Bull.

9A 45 Liberton

Gilmerton Road, Edinburgh,
Midlothian, EH16 5UJ
☎ 0131 6643009, Fax 6660853,
Pro 6641056,
Rest/Bar 664 8580
Exit Edinburgh city by-pass at
Gilmerton A7 Junction; course 3 miles
towards city.
Parkland course.
Pro Ian Seith; Founded 1920
18 holes, 5306 yards, S.S.S. 66
♦ Welcome.
○ WD £17; WE £25.
○ Welcome WD by prior written
arrangement; 36 holes of golf, coffee,
lunch, high tea; max 40; £33.
◙ Full clubhouse facilities.

9A 46 Linlithgow   ☞

Braehead, Golf Course Rd, Linlithgow,
W Lothian, EH49 6QF
☎ 01506 671044, Fax 842764,
Pro 844356, Sec 842585
Approx 10 miles from Edinburgh on
M9.
Undulating parkland course.
Pro Steve Rossie; Founded 1913
Designed by Robert Simpson of
Carnoutsie
18 holes, 5729 yards, S.S.S. 68
Ⅰ Practice area.
♦ Welcome except Sat and
competition days.
○ WD £17 (£10 winter); WE £25
(£10 winter).
○ Welcome by arrangement with
Sec; catering packages available
except Tues, from £17.
◙ Full clubhouse facilities.
↩ Balcastle; Queens; Sommerton
House.

9A 47 Lochmaben
Castlehillgate, Lochmaben, Lockerbie,
Dumfriesshire, DG11 1NT
☎ 01387 810552
Course is 4 miles from the A74 at
Lockerbie on the A709 road to
Dumfries.
Parkland course.
Founded 1926
Designed by James Braid
18 holes, 5377 yards, S.S.S. 67
⏴ Practice area.
♦ Welcome; on competition days by
prior arrangements.
Ⅰ WD £18; WE £22.
⚐ Welcome by prior arrangement;
catering packages available; caddie
car hire; from £16.
⦿ Full clubhouse facilities.
⌁ Balcastle; Queens, Sommerton
House.

9A 48 Lockerbie ♛
Corrie Rd., Lockerbie, Dumfriesshire,
DG11 2ND
⛳ www.lockerbiegolf.com
☎ 01576 203363, Fax 203363,
Sec 203363, Rest/Bar 203363
Leave M74 at Lockerbie and course is
signposted.
Tree-lined parkland course with pond
in play on 3 holes.
Founded 1889
Designed by James Braid (original 9)
18 holes holes, 5463 yards, S.S.S. 67
♦ Welcome; prior booking is advisable.
Ⅰ WD £15; WE £18.
⚐ Welcome by prior arrangement; 36
holes of golf; morning coffee, light lunch;
evening meal (£30 Sat); from £27.
⦿ Full clubhouse facilities.
⌁ Queens; Kings; Ravenshill;
Dryfesdale.

9A 49 Longniddry
Links Road, Longniddry, East Lothian,
EH32 0NL
⛳ www.longniddirygolfclub.co.uk
✉ seceraty@
longnidderygolfclub.co.uk
☎ 01875 852141, Fax 853371,
Pro 852228, Sec 852141,
Rest/Bar 852 623
On B6363 in Longniddry village from
the A1.
Parkland and links course.
Pro John Gray; Founded 1921
Designed by Harry Colt
18 holes, 6260 yards, S.S.S. 70
⏴ Practice area.
♦ Welcome WD; WE by arrangement.
Ⅰ WD £35; WE £45.
⚐ Welcome by prior arrangement

and with handicap certs; catering
packages can be arranged with the
clubmaster; tee times between 9.30am
and 4pm; deposit of £10 per person
required; credit cards accepted; max
40; from £50 for two rounds.
⦿ Full clubhouse facilities.
⌁ Kilspindie house; Maitlandfield;
Greencraigs.

9A 50 Lothianburn ♛
Biggar Road, Edinburgh, Midlothian,
EH10 7DU
☎ 0131 4455067, Pro 4452288,
Rest/Bar 4452206
On A702 Biggar to Carlisle road, 200
yards from City by-pass at Lothianburn
exit.
Hilly course.
Pro Kurt Mungall; Founded 1893/1928
Designed by James Braid (1928)
18 holes, 5662 yards, S.S.S. 68
♦ Welcome WD up to 4.30pm; WE
with member.
Ⅰ WD £16.
⚐ Welcome WD by prior
arrangement with Sec; discounts
available for more than 16 in a party;
catering packages by prior
arrangement; from 13.
⦿ Clubhouse facilities.
⌁ Braid Hills.

9A 51 Luffness New
Aberlady, E Lothian, E32 0QA
☎ 01620 843114, Fax 842933,
Sec 843336, Rest/Bar 843376
1 mile outside Aberlady on the A198
Gullane road.
Links course.
Founded 1894
Designed by Tom Morris (1894)
18 holes, 6122 yards, S.S.S. 70
⏴ Practice range: 5-hole course.
♦ Welcome WD only.
Ⅰ WD £37.50.
⚐ Welcome WD by prior arrangement;
full day's golf £55; catering by prior
arrangement; from £35.
⦿ Smoke room; dining room; lunch
daily except Mon; high tea/dinner by
arrangements (min 10).
⌁ Marine, N Berwick; Golf, Greywalls
(Gullane).

9A 52 Marriott Dalmahoy
Kirknewton, Midlothian, EH27 8EB
⛳ www.leisure.dalmahoy@marriot
hotel.co.uk
☎ 0131 3358010, Fax 3353577,
Sec 33358010
Course is on the A71 seven miles W of

Edinburgh.
Rolling parkland course.
Pro Stuart Callan; Founded 1927
Designed by James Braid
2 x 18 holes; East: 6651 West: 5168
yards; S.S.S. East:72 West 68
⏴ Practice range, 12 bay all-weather
floodlit.
♦ Welcome WD and WE by prior
arrangement and with handicap certs.
Ⅰ WD £55 (East), £35 (West); WE
£75 (East), £45 (West).
⚐ Welcome WD by prior
arrangement, corporate days can be
organised; catering and residential
packages available; leisure facilities,
including indoor heated pool, spa,
sauna, tennis, gym, health and beauty
saloon; terms on application.
⦿ Facilities in the Long Weekend
Restaurant.
⌁ Marriot Dalmahoy.

9A 53 Melrose
Dingleton, Melrose, Roxburghshire
☎ 01896 822855, Sec 822758
2 miles N of St Boswell off the A68
Newcastle to Edinburgh Road; half a
mile S of Melrose.
Undulating wooded parkland course.
Founded 1880
9 holes, 5562 yards, S.S.S. 68
♦ Welcome WD; Sat very limited;
most Sundays available.
Ⅰ WD £16, WE £16.
⚐ Welcome by arrangement, catering
can be arranged; from £16.
⦿ Available by prior arrangement.

9A 54 Melville
South Melville, Lasswade, Midlothian,
EH18 1AN
☎ 0131 6638038, Fax 6540814,
Sec 6540224
Off the Edinburgh city by-pass on the
Galashiels A7 road.
Parkland course.
Pro Gary Carter; Founded 1995
Designed by P Campbell/G Webster
9 holes, 4310 yards, S.S.S. 62
⏴ 34 bays; 22 covered, 12 outdoor.
♦ WD £12; WE £16.
Ⅰ Mon-Thurs; minimum 10,
maximum 20, from £12.
⚐ Welcome by prior arrangement.
⦿ Snacks available.
⌁ Eskbank; Dalhousie Castle.

9A 55 Merchants of Edinburgh
Merchants Of Edinburgh, Craighill
Gardens, Edinburgh, Midlothian, EH10
5PY

☎ 01506 871933, Pro 4478709
Course is off the A701 S of Edinburgh.
Hilly parkland course.
Pro NEM Colquhoun; Founded 1907
18 holes, 4889 yards, S.S.S. 64
† Welcome WD before 4pm.
⌊ WD £15.
⚲ Welcome WD before 4pm by prior
arrangement Catering packages can
be arranged; from £15.
⚑ Available except Thurs; full bar.
⚲ Braid Hills.

9A 56 Minto
Minto Village, By Denhom, Hawick,
Roxburghshire, TD9 8SH
⚲ www.mintogolfclub.com
⚲ pat@mintogolfclub.freeserve.co.uk
☎ 01450 870220, Fax 870126,
Sec 375841
5 miles NE of Hawick leaving A698 at
Denholm.
Parkland course, new course for
season 2000.
Founded 1928
18 holes, 5453 yards, S.S.S. 67
⚑ Practice area and putting green.
† Welcome by prior arrangement.
⌊ WD £22; WE £27.50.
⚲ Welcome by prior arrangement;
packages available; from £22.
⚑ Full clubhouse facilities.
⚲ Contact the Scottish Tourist Board.

9A 57 Moffat   ♛
Coatshill, Moffat, Dumfriesshire, DG10
9SB
☎ 01683 220020
Leave A74 (M74) at Beattock; take A701
to Moffat for 1 mile; club is signposted.
Moorland course with tree plantations,
spectacular views.
Founded 1884
Designed by Ben Sayers
18 holes, 5263 yards, S.S.S. 67
† Welcome except Wed pm.
⌊ WD £18.50, WE £28.50.
⚲ Welcome by prior arrangement
except Wed; includes 2 rounds of golf,
morning coffee; snack lunch; evening
dinner; from £30.
⚑ Full clubhouse facilities.
⚲ Beechwood Country; Moffat
House; Annandale Arms; Balmoral;
Buchanan; Star.

9A 58 Mortonhall
231 Braid Road, Edinburgh,
Midlothian, EH10 6PB
⚲ www.mortonhallgc.co.uk
⚲ clubhouse@
mortonhallgc.sagehost.co.uk

☎ 0131 4476974, Fax 4478712,
Pro 4475185, Sec 4476974,
Rest/Bar 4472411
On A72 2 miles S of the city.
Moorland course.
Pro Douglas Horn; Founded 1892
Designed by James Braid and Fred
Hawtree
18 holes, 6502 yards, S.S.S. 72
† Welcome by prior arrangement.
⌊ £30; £40 for the day.
⚲ Welcome by prior arrangement;
catering packages available; terms on
application.
⚑ Bar and catering facilities available.
⚲ Braid Hills.

9A 59 Muirfield (Honourable Company Of Edinburgh Golfers)
Muirfield, Gullane, East Lothian,
EH31 2EG
☎ 01620 842123
Course is on the A198 to the NE of
Gullane.
Links course; staged 14 Open
Championships since 1892.
Founded 1744
Designed by Tom Morris
18 holes, 6970 yards, S.S.S. 73
† Welcome only Tue and
Thur.
⌊ WD £90.
⚲ Welcome on Tues and Thurs only
by prior arrangement; no more than
12 golfers allowed; must have
handicap certs; 18 handicap
maximum for men; terms available
on application.
⚑ Full catering and bar service
available (ladies may not lunch in
clubhouse).
⚲ Greywalls; Kilspindie House.

9A 60 Murrayfield
43 Murrayfield Road, Edinburgh, EH12
6EU
☎ 0131 337 3478, Fax 3130721,
Pro 3373479
2 miles W of city centre.
Parkland course.
Pro James Fisher; Founded 1896
18 holes, 5764 yards, S.S.S. 69
† Welcome only with member.
⌊ Terms on application.
⚲ Limited.
⚑ Bar snacks; dining room; meals
served daily except Mon.
⚲ Ellersly House; Murrayfield.

9A 61 Musselburgh
Monktonhall, Musselburgh, Midlothian,
EH21 6SA

☎ 0131 6652005, Fax 6657055,
Pro 6657055, Sec 6652005,
Rest/Bar 665 2005
On B6415 to Musselburgh from the
end of the A1 Edinburgh By-pass.
Parkland course.
Pro Fraser Mann; Founded 1938
Designed by James Braid
18 holes, 6614 yards, S.S.S. 73
† Welcome by prior arrangement.
⌊ WD £20; WE £25.
⚲ Welcome by prior arrangement;
catering packages available; terms on
application.
⚑ Bar and restaurant facilities available.
⚲ Kings; Manor; Woodside.

9A 62 Musselburgh Old Course
10 Balcarres Road, Millhill,
Musselburgh, Midlothian, EH21 7RG
☎ 0131 6656981
Course is seven miles E of Edinburgh
on the A199 at Musselburgh
racecourse.
Seaside links course.
9 holes, 5380 yards, S.S.S. 67
† Welcome WD, prior booking
essential.
⌊ Terms on application.
⚲ Welcome by prior arrangement;
terms on application.
⚑ Catering facilities.

9A 63 New Galloway
High Street, New Galloway, Castle
Douglas, Kirkcudbrightshire, DG7 3RN
⚲ www.nggc.com
☎ 01644 420737, Fax 450685,
Sec 450685
Course is of the A713 to New Galloway.
Moorland course.
Founded 1902
Designed by G Baillie
9 holes, 5006 yards, S.S.S. 67
† Welcome.
⌊ WD £12.50 WE £12.50.
⚲ Welcome by prior arrangement
with Sec; catering packages can be
organised from £10.
⚑ Bar and snack facilities available.
⚲ Kenmure Arms; Cross keys;
Kalmar.

9A 64 Newbattle
Abbey Road, Dalkeith, Midlothian,
EH22 3AD
☎ 0131 6631819, Pro 6601631,
Sec 6631819, Rest/Bar 6632123
On A7 7 miles SW of Edinburgh; taking
Newbattle exit at Eskbank roundabout.
Undulating parkland course.
Pro Scott McDonald; Founded 1935

18 holes, 6025 yards, S.S.S. 70
✝ Welcome WD up to 4pm.
✆ WD £17; WD £17.
✆ Welcome Mon-Fri by prior
arrangement between 9.30am and
4pm; catering packages available;
terms on application.
🍽 Full clubhouse facilities.
⌂ Lugton; Eskbank.

9A 65 Newcastleton ☫
Holm Hill, Newcastleton,
Roxburghshire, TD9 0QD
☎ 013873 75257
On A7 25 miles N of Carlisle; 10 miles
from Canonbie/Newcastleton Junction.
Hilly course.
Founded 1894
Designed by J Shade (74)
9 holes, 5748 yards, S.S.S. 68
✝ Welcome.
✆ WD £7; WE £8.
✆ Welcome by prior arrangement;
packages can be arranged with local
hotel; from £7.
🍽 Facilities at Liddlesdale Hotel.
⌂ Liddlesdale; Grapes.

9A 66 Newton Stewart ☫
Kirroughtree Avenue, Minnigaff, Newton
Stewart, Wigtownshire, DG8 6PF
☎ 01671 402172
Course is close to the A75 Carlisle-
Stranraer road; one mile from the town
centre.
Parkland/hill course.
Founded 1896/1992
18 holes, 5887 yards, S.S.S. 69
🏌 Practice range.
✝ Welcome.
✆ WD £21 (winter £10); WE £24
(winter £10).
✆ Welcome by prior arrangement;
catering by prior arrangement with the
steward; terms available on application.
🍽 Full clubhouse facilities available.
⌂ Glencalm; Crown.

9A 67 Niddry Castle
Castle Road, Winchburgh, Broxburn,
West Lothian, EH52 6RQ
🖥 www.niddrycastlegc.co.uk
☎ 01506 891097
Course is on the B9080 in centre of
village; five miles from the Newbridge
interchange.
Parkland course.
Founded 1982
Designed by Derek Smith
9 holes, 5518 yards, S.S.S. 67
✝ Welcome WD; by arrangement at
WE.

✆ WD £13; WE £19.
✆ Welcome WD by prior
arrangement; full catering packages by
arrangement; £12.
🍽 Full clubhouse facilities.
⌂ Tally-Ho, Winchburgh.

9A 68 North Berwick (see overleaf)
New Club House, Beach Road, North
Berwick, East Lothian, EH39 4BB
🖥 www.topweb.free-online.co.uk/mb
☎ 01620 895040, Fax 893274,
Pro 893233, Sec 895040,
Rest/Bar 894766
In North Berwick take the last left turn
before the town centre.
Links course.
Pro D Huish; Founded 1832
18 holes, 6420 yards, S.S.S. 71
✝ Welcome by prior arrangement.
✆ WD £42 WE £65.
✆ Welcome by prior arrangement;
catering packages can be arranged;
terms on application.
🍽 Full clubhouse catering facilities
available.
⌂ Marine Hotel; many B&Bs in the
area.

9A 69 Peebles
Kirkland Street, Peebles, Peeblesshire,
EH45 8EU
☎ 01721 720197, Sec 720099
Located on the NW side of Peebles off
A72; signposted; 23 miles S of
Edinburgh.
Undulating parkland course.
Founded 1892
Designed by James Braid; Alterations
by HS Colt
18 holes, 6160 yards, S.S.S. 70
✝ Welcome by prior arrangement
with the club.
✆ WD £18; WE £25.
✆ Welcome by prior arrangement
except on Sat; new clubhouse opened
in 1997; catering packages available
by arrangement; terms on application.
🍽 Full clubhouse facilities available.
⌂ Peebles Hotel Hydro; Park;
Kingsmuir; Greentree.

9A 70 Polkemmet Country Park
Park Centre, Polkemmet Country Park,
Bathgate, West Lothian, EH47 0AD
☎ 01501 743905, Rest/Bar 744441
Park is on the N side of the B766
midway between Harthill and Whitburn.
Parkland course.
Founded 1981
Designed by W Lothian District Council

9 holes, 6531 yards
✝ Welcome; no restriction.
✆ WD £4.75; WE £5.55.
✆ Welcome.
🍽 Bar and restaurant facilities available.
⌂ Eillcroft, Whitburn; Holiday Inn;
Dreadnought, both Bathgate.

9A 71 Portobello
Stanley Street, Edinburgh, Midlothian,
EH15 1JJ
☎ 0131 6694361
On A1 E of Edinburgh, off Milton Road.
Parkland course.
Founded 1826
9 holes, 4504 yards, S.S.S. 64
✝ Welcome.
✆ WD £4.50 WE £5.00.
✆ Welcome by prior arrangement.
⌂ Kings Manor.

9A 72 Portpatrick (Dunskey)
Golf Course Road, Portpatrick,
Stranraer, Wigtownshire, DG9 8TB
☎ 01776 810276, Fax 810811
Follow A77 or A75 to Stranraer and
then follow signs for Portpatrick; on
entering village turn right at the War
Memorial.
Links style clifftop course.
Founded 1903
Designed by Dunskey Estate/W M
Hunter of Prestwick
18 holes, 5908 yards, S.S.S. 68
🏌 Practice range.
✝ Welcome with handicap certs.
✆ WD £19; WE £22.
✆ Welcome by prior arrangement;
handicap certs required; catering
packages available; weekly tickets
£100; day rates; also Dinvin course:
1504 yards, par 3; from £8.
🍽 Full clubhouse facilities; meals
until 9pm daily.
⌂ Fernhill; Portpatrick; Downshire;
Harbour House.

9A 73 Powfoot
Cummertrees, Powfoot, Annan,
Dumfriesshire, DG12 5QE
🖥 www.powfoot.com
📧 bsutherland@
powfootgolfclub.fsnet.co.uk
☎ 01461 700276, Fax 700276,
Pro 700327, Sec 700276
Course is off the A75 road to
Annan/Dumfries taking the second
turning for Annan until signs for
Cummertrees and Powfoot on the
B724; 3 miles later sharp left after
railway bridge.
Links course.

North Berwick

North Berwick's tight fairways may not receive the full body massage and manicure enjoyed by others in Britain, but few links courses can touch the place in terms of history and heritage. Every year thousands of visitors converge on what is the thirteenth oldest golf club in the world.

Golf has been played for centuries on the same West Links piece of land and it is still used for Open qualifying. Only at St. Andrew's can you tread more ancient fairways in Scotland. These days the course is owned by the local council and is home to four separate clubs with a combined membership of 900. Green fees for visitors are £42 during the week and £65 at weekends.

Ben Sayers, one of golf's legendary players and club manufacturers, was one of North Berwick's favourite sons and his original workshop still stands in a fold in the rumpled ground by the first tee. Sayers played in 43 consecutive Open championships from 1880 to 1923 and taught, among others, King Edward V11 and, when he was Prince of Wales, George V.

To say North Berwick is stimulating would be an understatement, but it is best played during the balmier seasons. Winter tees and obligatory fairway winter mats are in play from December to February when the grass, which has to withstand over 40,000 rounds a year, is dormant.

North Berwick has an antiquated charm with all manner of walls, burns and yawning bunkers. Virtually every hole sets a different problem in terms of length, judgement, skill and direction. The more you play it, the more danger you discover. Anything sliced or pushed invariably ends up on the beach – not very encouraging when the tide is in – and underclubbing can prove fatal.

The second hole is the first real test of skill with the sea a mere two yards or so from the edge of the fairway to gobble up anything wayward off the tee. The seventh is a totally different test of strategy with a nasty looking burn right in front of the green that forces the mid to high handicapper to lay up with their second shot.

The ninth hole on the figure-of-eight course is one of the only places where the sea is not in view, but it's a lovely par five just the same. Left is soon out of bounds yet playing right makes the hole longer. The fourteenth is aptly named 'Perfection', with the sea on the left and a blind second shot – the only one on the course – to a green that stands ominously close to the beach.

It is followed by the 'Redan', named after a Crimean War battle, apparently because the shape of the bunkers are in the same formation as the opposing armies. The 192-yard par three is one of the most copied holes with a green that slopes right to left and front to back. Even with a solid tee shot average players are grateful for just three putts.

One feature of North Berwick is that there are deliberately no yardage markers since most of the members regard distance judgement as a traditional skill. Another outstanding feature is the excellent par three children's course for twelve-year-olds and under. Here adults must be accompanied by a child, or so the joke goes.

One small tip. If you decide to park your car down the side of the clubhouse, don't forget to pay the 50 pence insurance fee – any slice from the eighteenth fairway is potentially a shattering blow and it could be your window that gets picked out. – **Andrew Warshaw**

Pro Gareth Dick; Founded 1903
Designed by James Braid
18 holes, 6266 yards, S.S.S. 71
† Welcome except Sat and after
1pm on Sun.
Ⓛ WD £25; WE £27; BH £28.
⌁ Welcome by prior arrangement;
terms on application.
Ⓛ Full clubhouse facilities.
⌁ Powfoot Golf Hotel; Cairndale Hotel,
Dumfries, Imperial Hotel, Castle Douglas.

9A 74 Prestonfield
6 Priestfield Road North, Edinburgh,
Midlothian, EH16 5HS
⌁ www.prestonfield.co.uk
☎ 0131 667 9665, Pro 667 8597,
Sec 667 9665
Close to Commonwealth Games pool.
Parkland course.
Pro John McFarlane; Founded 1920
Designed by Peter Robertson
18 holes, 6212 yards, S.S.S. 70
† Welcome by arrangement.
Ⓛ WD £22; WE £33.
⌁ Welcome WD starting from 9.30am
and 2pm; catering packages available;
terms on application.
Ⓛ Full catering except Mon.
⌁ Prestonfield House; March Hall;
Rosehall.

9A 75 Pumpherston
Drumshoreland Road, Pumpherston,
Livingston, West Lothian, EH53 0LH
☎ 01506 432869
400 yards E of the village cross.
Undulating parkland course.
Founded 1895
9 holes, 5434 yards, S.S.S. 66
† Welcome with a member.
Ⓛ £4 with a member.
⌁ Welcome WD by prior arrangement;
max party 24; bar snack and meals to
order; terms on application.
Ⓛ Clubhouse facilities.

9A 76 Ratho Park
Ratho, Newbridge, Midlothian, EH28
8NX
☎ 0131 3331752, Fax 3331752,
Pro 3331406, Sec 3331752,
Rest/Bar 3332566
Adjacent to Edinburgh Airport 8 miles
W of Edinburgh.
Parkland course.
Pro Alan Pate; Founded 1928
Designed by James Braid
18 holes, 5900 yards, S.S.S. 68
† Welcome by prior arrangement
with the Pro.
Ⓛ WD £25; WE £35.

⌁ Welcome Tues, Wed, Thurs by
prior arrangement; packages for golf
and catering available for groups of 12
or more; terms available on application.
Ⓛ Full clubhouse bar and restaurant
facilities.

9A 77 Ravelston
24 Ravelston Road, Blackhall,
Edinburgh, Midlothian, EH4 5NZ
☎ 0131 3152486
From city centre turn left at Blackhall
Junction then across the crossroad
and turn right 100 yards further on.
Parkland course.
Founded 1912
Designed by James Braid
9 holes, 5200 yards, S.S.S. 65
† Welcome WD.
Ⓛ Wd £7.50.
⌁ Small groups welcome by prior
arrangement; from £15.
Ⓛ Snacks and bar facilities.
⌁ Garden Court Holiday Inn.

9A 78 The Roxburghe ⚭
Heiton, Kelso, Roxburghshire, TD5 8JZ
⌁ www.roxburgh.net
✉ golf@roxburgh.net
☎ 01573 450333, Fax 450611
On A698 between Jedburgh and Kelso.
Woodland/parkland course.
Pro Craig Montgomery; Founded 1997
Designed by Dave Thomas
18 holes, 7111 yards, S.S.S. 75
�𝖨 Practice range and short game area.
† Welcome by prior arrangement.
Ⓛ WD £50; WE £50.
⌁ Welcome by prior arrangement;
catering packages by prior arrangement.
Ⓛ Spikes bar; full facilities available
in hotel.
⌁ The Roxburghe Hotel (on site).

9A 79 Royal Burgess Golfing Society of Edinburgh
181 Whitehouse Rd, Edinburgh,
Midlothian, EH4 6BY
⌁ www.royalburgess.co.uk
✉ seceratery@royalburgess.co.uk
☎ 0131 3392075, Fax 3393712,
Pro 3396474, Sec 3392075,
Rest/Bar 3392012
Course is on the W side of Edinburgh
on the Queensferry road, 100 yards
from the Barnton Junction.
Parkland course.
Pro George Yuille; Founded 1735
Designed by Tom Morris
18 holes, 6494 yards, S.S.S. 71
† Welcome by prior arrangement; no
lady members.

⌁ By prior arrangement.
⌁ Welcome by prior arrangement;
catering by arrangement; terms
available on application.
Ⓛ Clubhouse lunches and bar snacks.
⌁ Barnton; Royal Scot.

9A 80 Royal Musselburgh
Royal Musselburgh Golf Club,
Prestongrange House, Prestonpans,
East Lothian, EH32 9RP
⌁ www.royalmusselburgh.co.uk
✉ royalmossuburghbtinternet.com
☎ 01875 810276, Fax 810276,
Pro 810139, Rest/Bar 813671
Course is on the B1361 North Berwick
Road.
Parkland course.
Pro John Henderson; Founded 1774
Designed by James Braid
18 holes, 6237 yards, S.S.S. 70
† Welcome by prior arrangement.
Ⓛ WD £22; WE £35.
⌁ Welcome WD except Fri
afternoons by prior arrangement;
catering can be arranged; £35 per day
for golf; from £20.
Ⓛ Full catering facilities available.
⌁ Marine Hotel; Golf Inn.

9A 81 St Boswells
Braeheads Road, St Boswells,
Melrose, Roxburghshire, TD6 0DE
☎ 01835 823527
Off the A68 in St Boswells.
Parkland course.
Founded 1899
Designed by William Park, altered by
John Shade (1956)
9 holes, 5250 yards, S.S.S. 66
† Welcome by prior arrangement.
Ⓛ WD £15; WE £15.
⌁ Welcome by prior arrangement if
more than six in party; catering can be
arranged in advanced; from £15.
Ⓛ Bar and light snacks available at
WE; other times by prior arrangement.
⌁ Buccleuch Arms.

9A 82 St Medan
Monreith, Newton Stewart,
Wigtownshire, DG8 8NJ
☎ 01988 700358
Off the A747 3 miles S of Port William
following the A714 from Newton
Stewart.
Links course.
Founded 1905
9 holes, 4454 yards, S.S.S. 63
† Welcome.
Ⓛ WD £12; WE £12.
⌁ Welcome by prior arrangement;

terms on application.
🏮 Clubhouse facilities.

9A 83 Sanquhar
Old Barr Rd, Sanquhar, Dumfriesshire,
DG4 6JZ
☎ 01659 50577, Sec 58181
Course is off the A76, 0.5 miles from
Sanquhar.
Parkland course.
Founded 1894
9 holes, 5594 yards, S.S.S. 68
🕴 Welcome.
ℂ WD £10; WE £12.
🖰 Welcome by arrangement; catering
by arrangement; snooker; bowls; darts;
from £10.
🏮 Clubhouse facilities.
🖈 Blackaddie; Glendyne; Nithsdale.

9A 84 Selkirk   ☏
The Hill, Selkirk, Selkirkshire, TD7 4NW
☎ 01750 20621, Pro 20621,
Sec 20621, Rest/Bar 20621
Course is 0.5 miles S of Selkirk on the A7.
Heathland course.
Founded 1883
Designed by Willie Park
9 holes, 5620 yards, S.S.S. 67
🕴 Welcome WD by prior
arrangement except Mon pm; WE by
prior arrangement.
ℂ Terms on application.
🖰 Welcome WD; some WE; catering
packages prior arrangement; terms on
application.
🏮 Bar open evenings and WE during
the summer; at other times by
arrangement.
🖈 Heatherlie; Woodburn; Glen all
Selkirk.

9A 85 Silverknowes
Silverknowes Road, Edinburgh,
Midlothian, EH4 5ET
☎ 0131 3363843
W end of Edinburgh off Cramond
Foreshore.
Municipal links course.
Founded 1958
18 holes, 6097 yards, S.S.S. 70
🕴 Welcome by prior arrangement.
ℂ WD £10.00; WE £12.50.
🖰 Welcome by prior arrangement;
terms on application.
🖈 Commodore, adjacent.

9A 86 Southerness
Southerness, Kirkbean, Dumfries,
Dumfriesshire, DG2 8AZ
🖳 www.southernessgolfclub.com

🖥 admin@southernessgc.
sol.co.uk
☎ 01387 880677, Fax 880644,
Sec 880677, Rest/Bar 880677
Course is on the A710 15 miles S of
Dumfries.
Links course on Solway firth.
Founded 1947
Designed by MacKenzie Ross
18 holes, 6566 yards, S.S.S. 73
🕴 Welcome by prior arrangement;
handicap certs required.
ℂ WD £35; WE £45.
🖰 Welcome by prior arrangement;
packages available; from £45.
🏮 Full catering facilities.
🖈 Cairndale; Clonyard; Cavens
House; Paul Jones Hotel.

9A 87 Stranraer
Stranraer, Chreachmore, Leswalt,
Stranraer, DG9 0LF
☎ 01776 870245, Fax 870445,
Sec 870445
On A718 to Kirkcolm 3 miles from
Stranraer.
Parkland/seaside course; on present
site since 1953.
Founded 1905/1953
Designed by James Braid
18 holes, 6308 yards, S.S.S. 72
🕴 Welcome except at members'
times; not before 9.15am or between
12.30pm-1.30pm and 5-6pm.
ℂ WD £20; WE £25.
🖰 Welcome by prior arrangement;
same restrictions apply as to visitors;
catering can be arranged; separate
locker rooms; terms on application.
🏮 Full catering and bar service
available.
🖈 North West Castle; Kelvin House;
Fernhill.

9A 88 Swanston   ☏
11 Swanston Road, Edinburgh,
Midlothian, EH10 7DS
☎ 0131 4452239, Fax 4452239,
Pro 4454002
S side of the city on the lower slopes
of Pentland Hills.
Hillside course.
Pro Richard Fyvie; Founded 1927
Designed by Herbert More
18 holes, 5004 yards, S.S.S. 65
🕴 Welcome WD; some WE restrictions.
ℂ WD £15; WE £20.
🖰 Welcome by prior arrangement;
catering and golf packages available;
from £15.
🏮 Full facilities.
🖈 Braid Hills.

9A 89 Thornhil
Blacknest, Thornhill, Dumfriesshire,
DG3 5DW
☎ 01848 330546, Pro 331779
Off A76 at Thornhill 14 miles N of
Dumfries.
Moorland/parkland course.
Pro James Davidson; Founded 1893
18 holes, 6085 yards, S.S.S. 70
🕴 Welcome by prior arrangement.
ℂ WD £22; WE £28.
🖰 Welcome by prior arrangement;
catering packages arranged through
the steward; terms on application.
🏮 Full clubhouse facilities.
🖈 George; Gillbank.

9A 90 Torphin Hill
Torphin Road, Edinburgh, Midlothian,
EH13 0PG
☎ 0131 4411100, Pro 4414061,
Sec 4414061
SW of Colinton Village.
Hilly course.
Pro Jamie Browne; Founded 1895
18 holes, 4580 yards, S.S.S. 67
🕴 Welcome except before 2pm at WE.
ℂ WD £12; WE £20.
🖰 Welcome WD by prior
arrangement; terms on application.
🏮 Clubhouse facilities.
🖈 Braid Hills.

9A 91 Torwoodlee   ☏
Edinburgh Road, Galashiels,
Selkirkshire, TD1 2NE
☎ 01896 752660
2 miles outside Galashiels on the main
Edinburgh Road.
Parkland course.
Pro R Elliot; Founded 1895
Designed by Willie Park (new layout,
John Gurner)
18 holes, 6087 yards, S.S.S. 68
🕴 Welcome by prior arrangement.
ℂ Terms on application.
🖰 Welcome by prior arrangement;
packages for golf and catering
available; from £20.
🏮 Full clubhouse facilities.
🖈 Kingsknowe; Galashiels; Burts,
Melrose.

9A 92 Turnhouse
154 Turnhouse Road, Edinburgh,
Midlothian, EH12 0AD
☎ 0131 3391014, Pro 3397701
Course is on the A9080 W of city near
the airport.
Parkland/heathland course.
Pro John Murray; Founded 1909
18 holes, 6153 yards, S.S.S. 69

✝ Welcome by arrangement WD only.
✉ WD £18.
🕗 Welcome by prior arrangement WD only; catering packages available everyday for 12 or more; terms on application.
🍽 Full facilities Mon-Sat, prior arrangement for Sun.
🛏 Royal Scot; Posthouse; Stakis.

9A 93 Uphall

Houston Mains, Uphall Golf Club, Uphall, West Lothian, EH52 6JT
☎ 01506 856404, Fax 855358, Pro 855553
On A899 200 yards W of Uphall; 0.5 miles from M8 Junction 3; 15 miles W of Edinburgh.
Tree-lined parkland course.
Pro Gordon Law; Founded 1895
18 holes, 5592 yards, S.S.S. 67
✝ Welcome by prior arrangement except on competition days.
✉ WD £14; WE £18.
🕗 Welcome by prior arrangement; catering packages available; snooker; disabled facilities; from £14.
🍽 Full bar and catering facilities available.
🛏 Houston House.

9A 94 Vogrie

Vogrie Estate Country Park, Gorebridge, Midlothian, EH23 4NN
☎ 01875 821716, Sec 8217986
Off A68 Jedburgh Road.
Parkland course.
Founded 1989
9 holes, 5060 yards, S.S.S. 66
✝ Public pay and play.
✉ Terms on application.
🕗 Welcome; some restrictions; terms on application.
🍽 Tea room in park.

9A 95 West Linton

Medwyn Road, West Linton, Peeblesshire, EH46 7HN
☎ 01968 660463, Pro 660256, Sec 660970, Rest/Bar 660589
Course is off the A702 at West Linton.
Moorland course.
Pro I Wright; Founded 1890

Designed by Braid/Millar/Fraser
18 holes, 6132 yards, S.S.S. 69
✝ Welcome WD and after 1pm on non-competition WE.
✉ Terms on application.
🕗 Welcome WD by prior arrangement with Sec; catering packages available; from £18.
🍽 Full clubhouse facilities.
🛏 Gordon Arms.

9A 96 West Lothian ℭ

Airngath Hill, Linlithgow, West Lothian, EH49 7RH
☎ 01506 826030, Fax 826030, Pro 825060
Take A706 from Linlithgow to Bo'ness for 2.5 miles, and then turn right to the golf club.
Parkland course.
Founded 1892
Designed by W Park (1892), J Adams (1923), F Middleton (1975)
18 holes, 6046 yards, S.S.S. 71
✝ Welcome WD; WE by prior arrangement.
✉ WD £17; WE £22.
🕗 Welcome WD and non-competition WE by prior arrangement; terms available on application.
🍽 Full clubhouse facilities available.
🛏 Richmond Park; Earl O'Moray.

9A 97 Whitekirk ℭ

Whitekirk, N Berwick, Lothian, EH42 1XS
✉ golf@whitekirk.u-net.com
☎ 01620 870300, Fax 870330
Course is mile and a half from North Berwick on the A198.
Links course.
Pro Paul Wardell; Founded 1995
Designed by Camuron St Claire
18 holes, 6526 yards, S.S.S. 71
⚑ Golf Academy; practice range.
✝ Welcome.
✉ WD £18/£30, WE £25/£40.
🕗 Welcome; £25/50 (special WD offers available).
🍽 Full clubhouse meals available.

9A 98 Wigtown & Bladnoch

Lightlands Terrace, Wigtown, Dumfries & Galloway, DG8 9EF

☎ 01988 403354
On A746 0.25 miles from town centre.
Parkland course.
Founded 1960
9 holes, 5462 yards, S.S.S. 67
✝ Welcome.
✉ WD £10; WE £10.
🕗 Welcome by prior arrangement; packages with local hotels; terms on application.
🍽 Clubhouse facilities.
🛏 Conifers Leisure Park.

9A 99 Wigtownshire County

Mains Of Park, Glenluce, Newton Stewart, Wigtownshire, DG8 0NN
☎ 01581 300420, Sec 300420, Rest/Bar 300420
On the A75 8 miles E of Stranraer.
Links course.
Founded 1894
Designed by G Cunningham/C Hunter
18 holes, 5843 yards, S.S.S. 68
✝ Welcome.
✉ WD £18.50; WE £20.50
🕗 Welcome by prior arrangement; discounts for groups of 10 or more; catering packages available; from £18.50.
🍽 Clubhouse facilities.
🛏 Glenbay; Kelvin, both Glenluce; North West Castle, Stranraer.

9A 100 Winterfield

North Road, Dunbar, East Lothian, EH42 1AU
☎ 01368 862280, Fax 863562, Pro 863562, Sec 863562, Rest/Bar 862280
Off A1 to Dunbar; club 0.5 miles from High Street.
Links course.
Pro Kevin Phillips; Founded 1935
18 holes, 5169 yards, S.S.S. 64
✝ Welcome; WE by prior arrangement.
✉ WD £15; WE £17.
🕗 Welcome by prior arrangement with Pro; packages available for 18 or 36 holes of golf plus catering; from £15.
🍽 Full clubhouse facilities.
🛏 Bayswell; Hillside; Goldenstones; Craigengelt; Royal Mackintosh.

9B

Strathclyde

It has been said, with only a slight exaggeration, that you can walk from Ayr to Glasgow without ever leaving a golf course. If there really was a fairway to heaven then it would lie on the Ayrshire coast where there are more great golf courses per square mile than anywhere else in the world.

At the southern end are the two courses at Turnberry of which the more famous is the Ailsa, although the Arran is not to be sniffed at. It is remarkable that there is any golf going on here at all. In the second world war the grass had become concrete airstrips used to train the RAF Coastal Command.

Turnberry was the scene of the 1977 Open when Tom Watson and Jack Nicklaus spent the final two rounds exchanging birdies on a hole-by-hole basis. It is also the setting of the most photographed scene in golf, the drive from the ninth tee set out on a rocky promontory. On a summer's evening Turnberry just makes you want to sigh.

Moving north to Ayr itself Belleisle is an excellent public course and rather more affordable than some of its more famous neighbours. But Prestwick feels like home. The venue of the first twelve Open Championships, Prestwick was the perfect host to the 2001 Amateur Championship.

Next up is Troon. A day here is rather pricey and the second course is something of an anticlimax, but the welcome is excellent and the marshals politely diligent in ensuring that the pace of play is maintained above a steady crawl.

After the 1973 Open here Lee Trevino said, "Someone once said that nobody 'murders' Troon. The way I played they couldn't even arrest me for second degree manslaughter." Eleven years earlier Jack Nicklaus, playing in his first Open, took a ten at the eleventh hole where a railway lurks behind the stone wall by the green. The second nine really can be that difficult.

North of Troon there is an extraordinary trio of courses that are literally next door to one another. At one end of Western Gailes a golfer can hit a shot over the railway onto Kilmarnock (Barassie) and at the other end he can knock it onto Glasgow Gailes. To the north are Irvine and Largs.

Barassie and Glasgow Gailes are used for Open Qualifying and in 1972 Western Gailes held the Curtis Cup. Lord Brabazon, a somewhat biased member, said, "If you have time play just three courses – Western Gailes, Prestwick and Turnberry."

Across the sea are Machrie on the Isle of Skye and Machrihanish on the Mull of Kintyre. Machrie is a testing links with the enticement of an after-round whisky by the peat fire. Machrinahish vies with Prestwick for the finest opening hole in Scottish golf. The golfer has to decide how much of the beach to carry with his drive, the beachcomber has to decide where to shelter. There is a sign warning, "Danger, First Tee Above, Please Move Along The Beach."

The grandest recent addition to golf in the region is Loch Lomond where Retief Goosen won the 2001 World Invitational a month after becoming US Open Champion and where Sergio Garcia was fined for being rather rude about the greens. The course does justice to its glorious surrounds, but it is rather exclusive. Even members are restricted to how often they can play and one was kicked out for ignoring his limitations.

9B 1 Airdrie
Rochsoles, Airdrie, Lanarkshire, ML6
0PQ
☎ 01236 762195, Pro 754360
Course is N of Airdrie on Glenmavis
road.
Parkland course.
Pro Jamie Carver; Founded 1877
Designed by James Braid
18 holes, 6004 yards, S.S.S. 69
† Welcome by letter of introduction.
[WD £15; WE £15.
⌂ Welcome WD by prior
arrangement with Sec; catering
packages can be arranged; snooker;
from £15.
⦿ Full clubhouse facilities.
⌁ Tudor; Kenilworth.

9B 2 Alexandra Park
Alexandra Park, Sannox Gdns,
Glasgow, G31 8SE
☎ 0141 5561294, Pro 7700519
Course is off the M8 before Blochairn.
Wooded parkland course.
Pro Alistair Baker; Founded 1818
Designed by Graham McArthur
9 holes, 4016 yards, S.S.S. 61
† Welcome.
[Terms on application.
⌂ Welcome.
⦿ None.
⌁ Millennium Hotel; Kelvin Park;
Stakis Ingram Hotel; Central;
Courtyard.

9B 3 Annanhill
Irvine Road, Kilmarnock, Ayrshire, KA1
3RT
☎ 01563 521644, Sec 525557
One mile N of Kilmarnock on the A71
Irvine Road.
Parkland course.
Founded 1957
Designed by J McLean
18 holes, 6269 yards, S.S.S. 70
† Welcome by prior arrangement.
[WD £12; WE £17.
⌂ Welcome by prior arrangement;
catering packages can be arranged in
advance; terms available on
application.
⦿ Full clubhouse facilities available.
⌁ Howard Park; Portman.

9B 4 Ardeer
Greenhead, Stevenston, Ayrshire,
KA20 4JX
☎ 01294 464542, Pro 601327,
Sec 465316
Follow A78 signs for Largs and
Greenock on High road by-passing
Stevenston; turn right in Kerelaw road
for course.
Parkland course.
Founded 1880
18 holes, 6409 yards, S.S.S. 71
† Welcome except Saturdays.
[WD £18; WE £30.
⌂ Welcome Sun-Fri; full day's golf
(£40 on Sun); discounted packages
available for groups of 12 or more;
discounted from £32.
⦿ Full clubhouse catering facilities
available.

9B 5 Auchenharvie Golf Complex
Moorpark Road West, Stevenston,
Ayrshire, KA20 3HU
☎ 01294 603103, Pro 603103,
Rest/Bar 469051
Take the A78 to Ardrossan, take A738
to Stevenson.
Parkland course.
Pro Bob Rodgers; Founded 1981
Designed by Michael Struthers
9 holes, 5203 yards, S.S.S. 65
⫶ Driving range floodlit.
† Welcome.
[WD £5.25; WE £6.80.
⌂ Welcome by prior arrangement;
from £5.25.
⦿ Clubhouse bar.
⌁ Redburn hotel.

9B 6 Ayr Belleisle
Belleisle Park, Doonfoot Road, Ayr,
Ayrshire, KA7 4DU
☎ 01292 441258, Fax 442632,
Sec 441258, Rest/Bar 442331
Follow the signs for Burns Cottage
Drive on the A719 1.5 miles S of Ayr.
Parkland course/on same site as Ayr
Seafield.
Pro David Gemmel; Founded 1927
Designed by James Braid & Stutt
18 holes, 6431 yards, S.S.S. 71
† Public pay and play.
[Prices on application.
⌂ Welcome; 7-day advance booking
system; catering by prior arrangement
in local hotels; separate locker room.
⦿ Facilities available.
⌁ Belleisle.

9B 7 Ayr Dalmilling
Dalmilling, Westwood Ave, Ayr,
Ayrshire, KA8 0QY
☎ 01292 263893, Fax 610543
On A77 1 mile N of Ayr near
racecourse.
Parkland course/meadowland.
Pro Philip Cheyney; Founded 1960
18 holes, 5724 yards, S.S.S. 67
† Welcome by prior arrangement.
[WD £13.50; WE £14.
⌂ Welcome by at least seven days'
prior arrangement; catering packages
involving snacks/lunches/high tea
available; terms available on
application.
⦿ Full clubhouse facilities available.

9B 8 Ayr Seafield
Belleisle Park, Ayr, Ayrshire, KA7 4DU
☎ 01292 441258, Fax 442632
Course is 1.5 miles S of Ayr on the
A719 following signs for Burns Cottage
Drive.
Parklands/seaside course; on same
site as Ayr Belleisle.
Pro David Gemmel; Founded 1927
Designed by J Braid
18 holes, 5481 yards, S.S.S. 68
⫶ Practice range.
† Welcome.
[WD £11; WE £11.
⌂ Welcome by prior arrangement;
seven-day booking system in
operation; catering can be arranged in
the local hotels; from £11.
⦿ Limited.
⌁ Belleisle.

9B 9 Ballochmyle
Ballochmyle, Mauchline, Ayrshire, KA5
6LE
☎ 01290 550469, Fax 553657
On B705 off A76 1 mile S of
Mauchline; following signs for
Ballochmyle Hospital.
Inland/parkland course.
Founded 1937
18 holes, 5972 yards, S.S.S. 69
† Welcome except Sat.
[Terms on application.
⌂ Welcome every day except Sat;
tee times available between 9am-10am
and 2pm-3pm WD; Sun 10am-
10.45am and 2.30pm-3.15pm; Catering
packages available; terms on
application.
⦿ Full clubhouse facilities.
⌁ Royal; Dumfries Arms.

9B 10 Balmore
Balmore, Torrance, Glasgow, G64 4AW
⌨ www.balmoregolfclub.co.uk
▤ secretary@
balmoregolfclub.co.uk
☎ 01360 620240, Sec 620284
6/7 miles N of Glasgow on A807 off
A803.
Parkland course.
Founded 1906

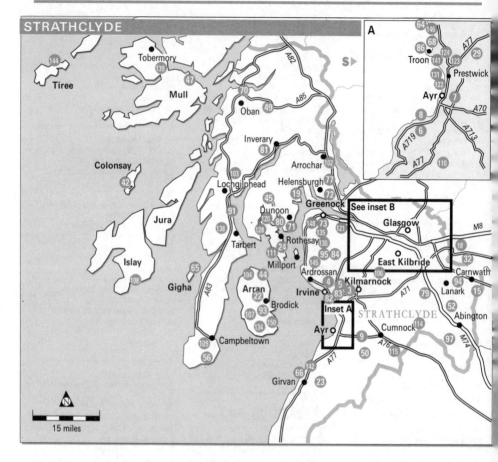

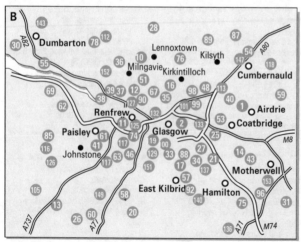

Designed by James Braid
18 holes, 5542 yards, S.S.S. 67
Ι Practice area.
† Welcome by introduction of a member.
Γ Terms on application.
◇ Terms on application.
|◉| Full clubhouse facilities.

9B 11 **Barshaw**

Barshaw Park, Glasgow Road, Paisley, Renfrewshire
☎ 0141 8892908
1 mile before Paisley Cross off the A737.
Meadowland course.
Founded 1920
18 holes, 5703 yards, S.S.S. 67
† Welcome.
Γ WD £7.70; WE £7.70; concessions apply.
◇ Limited.

KEY		31	Carluke	63	Fereneze	95	Largs	126	Ranfurly Castle
1	Airdrie	32	Carnwath	64	Gailes Golf Course	96	Larkhall	127	Renfrew
2	Alexandra Park	33	Cathcart Castle	65	Gigha	97	Leadhills	128	Rothesay
3	Annanhill	34	Cathkin Braes	66	Girvan	98	Lenzie	129	Rouken Glen
4	Ardeer	35	Cawder	67	Glasgow	99	Lethamhill	130	Routenburn
5	Auchenharvie Golf	36	Clober	68	Glasgow (Gailes)	100	Linn Park	131	Royal Troon
	Complex	37	Clydebank & District	69	Gleddoch Country Club	101	Littlehill	132	Ruchill
6	Ayr Belleisle	38	Clydebank Municipal	70	Glencruitten	102	Loch Lomond	133	Sandyhills
7	Ayr Dalmilling	39	Clydebank Overtoun	71	Gourock	103	Lochgilphead	134	Shiskine
8	Ayr Seafield	40	Coatbridge	72	Greenock	104	Lochranza	135	Skelmorlie
9	Ballochmyle	41	Cochrane Castle	73	Greenock Whinhill	105	Lochwinnoch	136	Strathaven
10	Balmore	42	Colonsay	74	Haggs Castle	106	Loudoun Gowf Club	137	Strathclyde Park
11	Barshaw	43	Colville Park	75	Hamilton	107	Machrie Bay	138	Tarbert
12	Bearsden	44	Corrie	76	Hayston	108	Machrie Hotel & Golf	139	Tobermory
13	Beith	45	Cowal	77	Helensburgh		Links	140	Torrance House
14	Bellshill	46	Cowglen	78	Hilton Park	109	Machrihanish	141	Troon Municipal
15	Biggar	47	Craignure	79	Hollandbush	110	Maybole	142	Turnberry Hotel
16	Bishopbriggs	48	Crow Wood	80	Innellan	111	Millport	143	Vale of Leven
17	Blairbeth	49	Dalmally	81	Inverary	112	Milngavie	144	Vaul
18	Blairhead Golf Course	50	Doon Valley	82	Irvine	113	Mount Ellen	145	West Kilbride
19	Blairmore & Strone	51	Douglas Park	83	Irvine Ravenspark	114	Muirkirk	146	Western Gailes
20	Bonnyton	52	Douglas Water	84	Kilbirnie Place	115	New Cumnock	147	Westerwood Hotel Golf
21	Bothwell Castle	53	Drumpellier	85	Kilmacolm	116	Old Course Ranfurly		& Country Club
22	Brodick	54	Dullatur	86	Kilmarnock (Barassie)	117	Paisley	148	Whinhill
23	Brunston Castle	55	Dumbarton	87	Kilsyth Lennox	118	Palacerigg	149	Whitecraigs
24	Bute	56	Dunaverty	88	Kirkhill	119	Pollok	150	Whiting Bay
25	Calderbraes	57	East Kilbride	89	Kirkintilloch	120	Port Bannatyne	151	Williamwood
26	Caldwell	58	East Renfrewshire	90	Knightswood	121	Port Glasgow	152	Windyhill
27	Cambuslang	59	Easter Moffat	91	Kyles of Bute	122	Prestwick	153	Wishaw
28	Campsie	60	Eastwood	92	Laglands	123	Prestwick St Cuthbert		
29	Caprington	61	Elderslie	93	Lamlash	124	Prestwick St Nicholas		
30	Cardross	62	Erskine	94	Lanark	125	Ralston		

🍴 Limited.
🍺 Water Mill; Brablock

9B 12 Bearsden
Thorn Road, Bearsden, Glasgow,
Lanarkshire, G61 4BP
☎ 0141 9422351, Sec 9422281,
Rest/Bar 9422351
1 mile N of Bearsden Cross on Thorn
Road.
Parkland course.
Founded 1891
9 holes, 6014 yards, S.S.S. 69
† Welcome only as the guest of a
member.
[Terms on application.
⌒ Welcome only by prior
arrangement; terms available on
application.
🍴 Full facilities.
🍺 Black Bull; Burnbrae.

9B 13 Beith
Threepwood Road, Beith, Ayrshire,
KA15 2JR
☎ 01505 503166, Fax 506814,
Sec 506814, Rest/Bar 503166
1st left southbound on Beith by-pass
A737.
Hilly parkland course.
Founded 1896
Designed by the Members
18 holes, 5625 yards, S.S.S. 68
† Welcome.
[WD £15; WE £20.

⌒ Welcome by written prior
arrangement; catering packages by
arrangement; from £15.
🍴 Full catering facilities.

9B 14 Belshill
Community Rd, Orbiston, Bellshill,
Lanarkshire, ML4 2RZ
☎ 01698 745124
Between Belshill and Strathclyde
country park close to M74 Junction 5
for the A725 Junction on the A8.
Parkland course.
Founded 1905
18 holes, 6315 yards, S.S.S. 70
† Welcome by prior arrangement
restricted Sat.
[March – October WD £18; WE £25
November to February WD £10 WE
£18.
⌒ Welcome by prior written
arrangement tee off after 1.30pm Sun;
all inclusive packages available for 18
and 36 holes; from £18.
🍴 Full catering facilities.
🍺 Bothwell Bridge; Moorings House;
Silvertrees.

9B 15 Biggar
The Park, Broughton Road, Biggar,
Lanarkshire, ML12 6QX
☎ 01899 220618, Pro 220319,
Sec 220566
Off the A702 0.5 miles from the town
centre.

Parkland course.
Founded 1895
Designed by Willie Park
18 holes, 5537 yards, S.S.S. 67
† Welcome by prior arrangement.
[WD £8; WE £14.
⌒ Welcome by prior arrangement;
packages for golf and catering may be
available in 1998; terms on
application.
🍴 Full clubhouse facilities available.
🍺 Elphinstone; Clydesdale; Tinto.

9B 16 Bishopbriggs
Brackenbrae Road, Bishopbriggs,
Glasgow, Lanarkshire, G64 2DX
🖧 www.scottishholidays.net
✉ bgcsecretary@dial.pipex.com
☎ 0141 7721810, Fax 7622532,
Pro ,Sec 7728938,
Rest/Bar 7721810
On A803 4 miles N of Glasgow turning
200 yards short of the Bishopbriggs
cross.
Parkland course.
Founded 1906
Designed by James Braid
18 holes, 6041 yards, S.S.S. 69
† Welcome by prior arrangement
with the club.
[Terms on application.
⌒ Welcome WD; apply to Secretary
at least 1 month in advance; terms on
application.
🍴 Catering facilities.

9B 17 Blairbeth

Blairbeth Golf Club, Fernbrae Avenue, Rutherglen, Glasgow, Lanarkshire, G73 4SF
☎ 0141 6343355, Sec 5697266
1 mile S of Rutherglen off Stonelaw Road.
Parkland course.
Founded 1910/57
18 holes, 5518 yards, S.S.S. 68
† Welcome either as a member's guest or by prior arrangement with the club.
[Terms on application.
⌂ Terms on application.
◉ Clubhouse facilities.
↵ Kings Park.

9B 18 Blairhead Golf Club

Ben Har Road, Schotts, Lanarkshire, ML7 5BJ
☎ 01501820431, Fax 1825868, Pro 1822658, Sec 1825868, Rest/Bar 1820431
Take M8 to Junction 5; then A7057 to Shotts; 1.5 miles to course.
Parkland course.
Pro John Strachan; Founded 1895
Designed by James Braid
18 holes, 6125 yards, S.S.S. 70
⌇ Practice range available.
† Welcome WD; Sat after 4.30pm and Sun by prior arrangement.
[WD £14 single round £22 full day; WE £16 single round £28 full day.
⌂ Welcome WD; full day's golf and catering included in packages; visitors' locker room; £30.
◉ Full clubhouse facilities. Please contact clubhouse for further information.
↵ Golden Circle; Bathgate; Travelodge Newhouse; Hillcroft Whitburn.

9B 19 Blairmore & Strone

Blairmore, By Dunoon, Argyll, PA23 8TJ
☎ 01369 840676
On A880 0.75 miles N of Strone and 5 miles N of Dunoon.
Undulating moorland and parkland course with panoramic views of the Clyde.
Founded 1896
Designed by J Braid
9 holes, 4224 yards, S.S.S. 62
† Welcome; some restrictions Sat and Mon evening.
[WD £8; WE £10.
⌂ Welcome by prior arrangement with Secretary; from £8.
◉ Bar facilities available in the Summer.

9B 20 Bonnyton

Kirtonmoor Road, Eaglesham, Glasgow, G76 0QA
☎ 01355 302781, Fax 303151, Pro 302256
1 mile S of Eaglesham; 10 miles S of Glasgow.
Moorland course.
Pro Kendal McWade; Founded 1957
18 holes, 6255 yards, S.S.S. 71
† Welcome by arrangement.
[Terms on application.
⌂ Welcome Mon and Thurs by prior arrangement; catering packages can be arranged; terms available on application.
◉ Full clubhouse facilities.
↵ The Hilton, East Kilbride.

9B 21 Bothwell Castle

Blantyre Road, Bothwell, Glasgow, Lanarkshire, G71 8PJ
☎ 01698 853177, Fax 854052, Pro 852052, Sec 854052
3 miles N of Hamilton on the A9071 from the M74 Junction 5.
Parkland course.
Pro Adam McCloskey; Founded 1922
18 holes, 6243 yards, S.S.S. 70
† Welcome WD 9.30am to 3.30pm.
[WD £22.
⌂ Welcome by written prior arrangement; catering packages by arrangement; from £22.
◉ Full clubhouse facilities.
↵ Silvertrees; Bothwell Bridge.

9B 22 Brodick

Brodick, Brodick, Isle of Arran, KA27 8DL
✉ peter@fatpro.freeserve.co.uk
☎ 01770 302349, Pro 302513
1 mile N of Pier.
Parkland/links course.
Pro Peter McCalla; Founded 1897
18 holes, 4736 yards, S.S.S. 64
† Welcome by prior arrangement.
[WD £18; WE £20.
⌂ Welcome by prior written arrangement; catering packages available; from £14.
◉ Full clubhouse facilities.

9B 23 Brunston Castle

Bargany, Dailly, By Girvan, Ayrshire, KA26 9RH
☎ 01465 811471, Fax 811545
Off the A77 at Girvan then on to B741 to Dailly.
Parkland course.
Pro Alan Reid; Founded 1992
Designed by Donald Steel

18 holes, 6681 yards, S.S.S. 73
⌇ 15 bays all floodlit.
† Welcome.
[Wd £26; WE £30.
⌂ Welcome by prior arrangement with the club Pro; package includes a full day's golf; company days; pro-ams; 10 per cent discount for larger groups; £5 per person deposit required; from £40.
◉ Full clubhouse facilities with restaurant.
↵ Brunston Castle Holiday Resort; Malin Court, Turnberry, Ardlochan Hotel, Maidens.

9B 24 Bute

Kingarth, Isle of Bute, Strathclyde
☎ 01700 504369, Sec 504369
In Stravanan Bay off A845 Rothesay-Kilchattan Bay road.
Links course.
Founded 1888
9 holes, 4994 yards, S.S.S. 64
† Welcome, but not before 12.30 pm on Sat.
[From £6; details available on application.
↵ Kingarth; St Blanes.

9B 25 Calderbraes

57 Roundknowe Road, Uddingston, Glasgow, Lanarkshire, G71 7TS
☎ 01698 813425
Close to start of M74; 4 miles from Glasgow.
Hilly parkland course.
Founded 1891
9 holes, 5186 yards, S.S.S. 67
† Welcome on WD.
[WD £18.
⌂ Welcome WD by prior arrangement; maximum 20; catering packages available; from £12.
◉ Full bar and catering facilities available.
↵ Redstones.

9B 26 Caldwell

Caldwell Golf Club, Uplawmoor, Glasgow, East Rangeshire, G78 4AU
☎ 01505 850329, Fax 850604, Pro 850616, Sec 850366
Off A736 5 miles SW of Barrhead; 12 miles NE of Irvine.
Moorland course.
Pro Stephen Forbes; Founded 1903
18 holes, 6228 yards, S.S.S. 70
† Welcome WD but advisable to check in advance.
[Terms on application.
⌂ Welcome WD except Thur by prior

arrangement; catering by arrangement; terms on application.
🍽 Clubhouse facilities.
⌁ Uplawmoor; Dalmeny Park.

9B 27 Cambuslang
30 Westburn Drive, Cambuslang, Glasgow, Lanarkshire, G72 7NA
☎ 0141 6413130, Sec 6413130, Rest/Bar 6413130
Off main Glasgow to Hamilton road at Cambuslang.
Parkland course.
Founded 1892
9 holes, 5942 yards, S.S.S. 69
† Welcome by written application to secretary, come with members.
Ⅰ Terms on application.
⌁ Apply in writing to secretary; catering by arrangement; terms on application.
🍽 Full clubhouse facilities.
⌁ Cambus Court.

9B 28 Campsie
Crow Road, Lennoxtown, Glasgow, G65 7HX
☎ 01360 310244, Pro 310920
Course is on the B822 to the N of Lennoxtown.
Hillside/parkland course.
Pro Mark Brennan; Founded 1897
Designed by W Auchterlonie
18 holes, 5509 yards, S.S.S. 67
† Welcome WD; WE by prior arrangement after 4 pm.
Ⅰ WD £12; WE £15.
⌁ Welcome by prior arrangement with Secretary; full day's golf; catering by prior arrangement; from £20.
🍽 Clubhouse facilities.
⌁ Glazert Country House Hotel, Lennoxtown.

9B 29 Caprington
Ayr Road, Caprington, Kilmarnock, Ayrshire, KA1 4UW
☎ 01563 523702
Course is on the Ayr road S of Kilmarnock.
Parkland course.
18 holes, 5781 yards, S.S.S. 68
† Welcome.
Ⅰ Terms on application.
⌁ Apply to secretary.
🍽 Clubhouse facilities.

9B 30 Cardross
Main Road, Cardross, Argyll Bute, Dunbartonshire, G82 5LB
🖳 www.cardross.com

✉ cardross@globalnet.co.uk
☎ 01389 841213, Fax 842162, Pro 841350, Sec 841754
On A814 to Helensburgh 18 miles from Glasgow.
Parkland course.
Pro Robert Farrell; Founded 1895
Designed by James Braid
18 holes, 6469 yards, S.S.S. 71
† Welcome WD.
Ⅰ WD £25.
⌁ Welcome WD By Prior Arrangement.
🍽 Full clubhouse facilities.
⌁ Cameron House; Kirkton House.

9B 31 Carluke
Mauldslie Road, Carluke, Lanarkshire, ML8 5HG
☎ 01555 770574, Pro 751053, Rest/Bar 771070
Access from both the M74 and the M8; from the M74 leave at Junction 7 and take the Lanark turn until the lights at Garron Bridge; then left on to the A71 and then on to the B7011; club is 2.5 miles.
Parkland course.
Pro Ricky Forrest; Founded 1894
18 holes, 5899 yards, S.S.S. 69
† Welcome WD 9am-4pm.
Ⅰ WD £23 but variable in the summer months.
⌁ Welcome by prior arrangement; maximum 24; from £23-£33.
🍽 Full clubhouse facilities.
⌁ Popinjay; Cartland Bridge.

9B 32 Carnwath
Carnwath Golf Club, 1 Main Street, Carnwath, Lanark, Lanarkshire, ML11 8JX
☎ 01555 840251
5 miles NE of Lanark.
Undulating parkland course.
Founded 1907
18 holes, 5953 yards, S.S.S. 69
† Welcome except Sat or after 4pm.
Ⅰ WD £22; WE £30.
⌁ Welcome WD except Tues and Thurs by prior arrangement; catering by arrangement; from £20.
🍽 Every day except Tues and Thurs.
⌁ Tinto, Symington.

9B 33 Cathcart Castle
Cathcart Castle Golf Club, Mearns Road, Clarkston, Glasgow, Lanarkshire, G76 7YL
☎ 0141 6389449, Fax 63817201, Pro 6383436

Course is on the B767 one mile from Clarkston.
Undulating parkland course.
Pro Stephen Duncan; Founded 1895
18 holes, 5832 yards, S.S.S. 68
† Tourists welcome by prior arrangement.
Ⅰ WD £30; WE £30.
⌁ Welcome Tuesdays and Thursdays by arrangement with secretary; day ticket £35; catering by prior arrangement; from £25.
🍽 Clubhouse facilities.
⌁ Redhurst; Macdonald; Busby.

9B 34 Cathkin Braes
Cathkin Road, Rutherglen, Glasgow, G73 4SE
☎ 0141 6346605, Pro 6340650, Sec 6346605
On B759 SE of Glasgow between A749 and B766.
Moorland course.
Pro Stephen Bree; Founded 1888
Designed by James Braid
18 holes, 6208 yards, S.S.S. 71
† Welcome WD.
Ⅰ WD £25.
⌁ Welcome WD by prior arrangement; packages from £25.
🍽 Full catering facilities.
⌁ Stuart ;Bruce; Burnside; Busby.

9B 35 Cawder
Cadder Road, Bishopbriggs, Glasgow, Lanarkshire, G64 3QD
☎ 0141 7727101, Pro 7727102, Sec 7725167
Course is off the A803 Glasgow-Kirkintilloch road 0.5 miles E of Bishopbriggs.
Parkland course.
Pro Ken Stevely; Founded 1933
Designed by Donald Steel (Cawder); James Braid (Keir)
Cawder: 18 holes, 6295 yards, S.S.S. 71; Keir: 18 holes, 5870 yards, S.S.S. 68
† Welcome WD by prior arrangement with secretary.
Ⅰ WD £26.
⌁ Welcome WD by prior arrangement with secretary; day ticket £33; catering packages by arrangement; from £26.
🍽 Full catering facilities.
⌁ Black Bull; Glazert Country House; Crow Wood House.

9B 36 Clober
Craigton Road, Milngavie, Glasgow, G62 7HP

www.clobergc@lineone.net
☎ 0141 9561685, Fax 9561416,
Pro 9566963, Sec 9561685,
Rest/Bar 956 1685
7 miles NW of Glasgow.
Parkland course.
Pro Campbell Elliot; Founded 1952
Designed by Lyle family
18 holes, 4963 yards, S.S.S. 66
† Welcome WD until 4pm.
Ⅰ WD £15.
⌕ Welcome WD by prior
arrangement; catering packages
available; terms available on
application.
🍴 Full clubhouse facilities.
⌕ Burnbrae, West Highland Gate.

9B 37 Clydebank & District
Hardgate Golf Club, Glasgow Road,
Hardgate, Clydebank, Dunbartonshire,
G81 5QY
☎ 01389 383832
Off A82 turning right at Hardgate; ten
miles W of Glasgow.
Parkland course.
Pro D Pirie; Founded 1905
Designed by Committee members
18 holes, 5825 yards, S.S.S. 68
† Welcome WD.
Ⅰ WD £15.
⌕ Welcome WD by prior
arrangement; terms available on
application.
🍴 Full clubhouse facilities.
⌕ West Hills; Boulevard; Radnor;
Duntugher; West Highways.

9B 38 Clydebank Municipal
Overtoun Road, Dalmuir, Clydebank,
G81 3RE
☎ 0141 9528698, Rest/Bar 9528698
Eight miles W of Glasgow.
Municipal parkland course.
18 holes, 5349 yards, S.S.S. 67
† Welcome except between 11am-
2pm at WE.
Ⅰ Terms on application.
⌕ Contact local district council; terms
on application.
🍴 Snack and cafe facilities available.
⌕ Radnor.

9B 39 Clydebank Overtoun
Overtoun Road, Clydebank,
Dunbartonshire, G81 3RE
☎ 0141 9526372
Course is five minutes from Dalmuir
station.
Municipal parkland course.
Pro Ian Toy; Founded 1928
18 holes, 5349 yards, S.S.S. 66

† Welcome.
Ⅰ WD £6.55; WE £7.
⌕ Welcome by arrangement; limited
facilities.
🍴 Café only.

9B 40 Coatbridge
Townhead Road, Coatbridge,
Lanarkshire, ML5 2HX
☎ 01236 421492
In Coatbridge town.
Public parkland course.
Pro George Weir; Founded 1971
18 holes, 6026 yards, S.S.S. 69
✂ Practice range, 18 bays floodlit.
† Welcome.
Ⅰ WD £5.10; £7.60.
⌕ Welcome by prior arrangement.
🍴 Full facilities.

9B 41 Cochrane Castle
Scott Avenue, Johnstone,
Renfrewshire, PA5 0HF
☎ 01505 320146, Fax 325338,
Pro 328465
Half a mile off Beith Road in Johnstone.
Parkland course.
Pro Alan Logan; Founded 1895
Designed by Charles Hunter of
Prestwick; altered by James Braid
18 holes, 6194 yards, S.S.S. 71
† Welcome WD; with member at WE.
Ⅰ WD £22 per round. £30.00 per day.
⌕ None.
🍴· Full clubhouse facilities available.
⌕ Bird in Hand; Lynnhurst, both
Johnstone.

9B 42 Colonsay
Isle of Colonsay, Argyll, PA61 7YP
www.colonsay.org.uk
☎ 01951 200316, Fax 200353,
Sec 200369
Two miles W of Scalasaig pier; car
ferry two-and-a-half hour journey from
mainland.
Natural machair course.
Founded 1880
18 holes, 4775 yards, S.S.S. 72
† Welcome.
Ⅰ WD £10; WE £10.
🍴 All facilities at Colonsay Hotel;
courtesy car provided to course.
⌕ The Colonsay Hotel.

9B 43 Colville Park
New Jerviston House, Merry Street,
Motherwell, Lanarkshire, ML1 4UG
☎ 01698 263017, Fax 230418,
Pro 265779, Sec 265378
One mile NE of Motherwell railway

station.
Parkland course.
Pro Alan Forrest; Founded 1923
Designed by James Braid
18 holes, 6265 yards, S.S.S. 70
† Welcome only as the guest of a
member.
Ⅰ WD £3; WE £3.
⌕ Welcome by written prior
arrangement; catering packages can
be arranged; maximum 36; £20.
🍴 Full clubhouse facilities available.
⌕ Old Mill; Moorings; Silvertrees.

9B 44 Corrie
Sannox, Isle of Arran, KA27 8JD
☎ 01770 810223
Seven miles N of Brodick on A84 coast
road.
Picturesque undulating course.
Founded 1892
9 holes, 3896 yards, S.S.S. 61
† Welcome except for some Thurs
and Sat afternoons.
Ⅰ Terms on application.
⌕ Welcome by prior arrangement;
catering by arrangement; maximum
normally 12.
🍴 Catering available in season April
until October.

9B 45 Cowal
Ardenslate Road, Kirn, Dunoon, Argyll,
PA23 8NN
www.cowalgolfclub.co.uk
☎ 01369 705673, Fax 705673,
Pro 702395, Sec 705673,
Rest/Bar 702426
From the Shore road turn up Kirn Brae.
Heath/parkland course.
Pro Russell Weir; Founded 1891
Designed by James Braid
18 holes, 6063 yards, S.S.S. 70
† Welcome.
Ⅰ WD £24; WE £34.
⌕ Welcome; packages include
transport, catering and 18 holes of golf;
from £38.
🍴 Full clubhouse catering available.
⌕ Local tourist office can provide
details.

9B 46 Cowglen
301 Barrhead Road, Glasgow,
Lanarkshire, G43 1EU
☎ 0141 6320556, Pro 6499401,
Rest/Bar 6496003
S side of Glasgow following signs for
Burrell Collection,M77 2mns from the
end of Barrhead Junction.
Undulating parkland course.
Pro Simon Payne; Founded 1906

18 holes, 5976 yards, S.S.S. 69
♦ Welcome on WD,competition free days.
⌐ WD £25.50.
⌐ Welcome by prior arrangement with secretary; catering packages available; from £22.
⦿ Clubhouse facilities.
⌐ Tinto, Thistle close to city centre.

9B 47 Craignure
Scallastle, Craignure, Isle of Mull, PA65 6AY
☎ 01680 812487
Course in one mile from Oban/Mill ferry terminal.
Links course built on estuary of Scallastle River.
Founded 1895/1979
9 holes, 5072 yards, S.S.S. 65
♦ Welcome on competition days.
⌐ Terms on application.
⌐ Welcome by arrangement; weekly ticket (from £45) available.
⦿ Limited clubhouse facilities.
⌐ Tinto.

9B 48 Crow Wood
Garnkirk House, Cumbernauld Road, Muirhead, Glasgow, G69 9JF
☎ 0141 7792011, Fax 7799148, Pro 7791943, Sec 7794954
Off A80 Stirling road midway between Stepps and Muirhead five miles N of Glasgow.
Parkland course.
Pro Brian Moffat; Founded 1925
Designed by James Braid
18 holes, 6261 yards, S.S.S. 71
♦ Welcome WD.
⌐ Prices on application.
⌐ Welcome WD only by prior arrangement; catering can be arranged.
⦿ Full clubhouse facilities.
⌐ Garfield House, Stepps; Crow Wood House, Muirhead; The Travel Lodge.

9B 49 Dalmally
'Orchy Bank', Dalmally, Argyll, PA33 1AS
☎ 01838 200370
Two miles W of Dalmally Village on A85.
Parkland course.
Founded 1987
Designed by C McFarlane Barrow
9 holes, 4514 yards, S.S.S. 63
♦ Welcome.
⌐ WD £10; WE £10.
⌐ Welcome by prior arrangement;

bar snacks and meals can be arranged; £8.
⦿ By prior arrangement; bar facilities.
⌐ Glen Orchy Lodge.

9B 50 Doon Valley
Hillside, Patna, Ayr, Ayrshire, KA6 7JT
☎ 01292 531607, Sec 550411
On A713 Ayr to Castle Douglas road ten miles S of Ayr.
Undulating parkland course.
Founded 1927
Designed by Course redesigned by E Ayrshire Council
9 holes, 5856 yards, S.S.S. 69
⌐ Practice area and practice green.
♦ Welcome WD; WE by arrangement.
⌐ WD £6.50; WE £ 6.50; concessions apply.
⌐ Welcome WD; WE by prior arrangement; day ticket for golf; catering available by arrangement.
⦿ Bar open evenings WD; all day WE.
⌐ Smithson Farm B&B; Parsons Lodge.

9B 51 Douglas Park
Hillfoot, Bearsden, Glasgow, G61 2JT
⌐ www.douglasparkgolfclub.net
☎ 0141 9422220, Pro 9421482
Course is six miles N of Glasgow adjacent to Hillfoot station off Milngavie road.
Undulating parkland course.
Pro DB Scott; Founded 1897
18 holes, 5962 yards, S.S.S. 69
♦ Welcome only as members' guests; occasional overseas visitors if course is quiet.
⌐ WD £22.
⌐ Welcome Wed and Thurs only; full day's golf £30; catering can be arranged.
⦿ Full catering and licensed bar available.
⌐ Burnbrae.

9B 52 Douglas Water
Ayr Road, Rigside, Lanark, ML11 9NY
☎ 01555 880361
Course is on the A70 seven miles SW of Lanark.
Undulating parkland course.
Founded 1922
Designed by Striking Coal Miners 1921
9 holes, 5890 yards, S.S.S. 69
♦ Welcome except on competition days.
⌐ Terms on application.
⌐ Welcome by prior arrangement

with secretary; terms available on application.
⦿ Very limited.

9B 53 Drumpellier
Drumpellier Ave, Coatbridge, Lanarkshire, ML5 1RX
⌐ www.drumpellier.com
☎ 01236 424139, Fax 428723, Pro 432971, Sec 428723
Course is on the A89 eight miles E of Glasgow.
Parkland course.
Pro David Ross; Founded 1894
Designed by W Fernie
18 holes, 6227 yards, S.S.S. 70
♦ Welcome WD.
⌐ Day ticket costs £30.
⌐ Welcome WD by prior arrangement; catering packages available.
⦿ Full clubhouse catering facilities.
⌐ Georgian.

9B 54 Dullatur
Glen Douglas Dirve, Dullatur, Glasgow, Lanarkshire, G68 0AR
☎ 012367 23230, Fax 27271
One and a half miles from Cumbernauld Village.
Parkland course.
Pro Duncan Sinclair; Founded 1896
Designed by J Braid
Antonine: 18 holes, 5940 yards, S.S.S. 69; Carrickstone: 18 holes, 6204 yards, S.S.S. 70
♦ Welcome except on comp days.
⌐ Available upon application.
⌐ Welcome except on competition days; catering packages available from £12.50; from £15.
⦿ Full clubhouse facilities available.
⌐ Castlecary House.

9B 55 Dumbarton
Broadmeadows, Dumbarton, Dunbartonshire, G82 2BQ
☎ 01389 765995, Sec 765995
Course is off the A82 fifteen miles NW of Glasgow.
Meadowland course.
Founded 1888
18 holes, 6017 yards, S.S.S. 69
♦ Welcome WD.
⌐ WD £25.
⌐ Welcome by arrangement; catering by arrangement; terms on application.
⦿ Full clubhouse facilities available.
⌐ The Abbots Ford Hotel & The Dumbuck Hotel.

9B 56 Dunaverty

Southend By Campbeltown,
Campbeltown, Argyll, PA28 6RW
☎ 01586 830677
Course is on the B842 ten miles S of
Campbeltown.
Undulating seaside course.
Founded 1889
18 holes, 4799 yards, S.S.S. 63
† Welcome.
£ From £13.
♪ Limited availability; strictly by prior
arrangement; day tickets start at £22
WD; £25.00 WE.
▮●▮ Snacks available.
↵ Argyll.

9B 57 East Kilbride

Chapelside Road, Nerston, Glasgow,
Lanarkshire, G74 4PF
☎ 013552 20913, Pro 22192,
Sec 47728
Course is in Nerston 10 miles SE of
Glasgow.
Parkland course.
Pro Willie Walker; Founded 1900/67
Designed by Fred Hawtree
18 holes, 6419 yards, S.S.S. 71
† Welcome WD by prior
arrangement with secretary.
£ WD £25.
♪ Welcome WD by prior written
arrangement; catering packages
available; pool room; from £20.
▮●▮ Full clubhouse facilities.
↵ Hilton; Bruce; Stuart; Crutherland
House.

9B 58 East Renfrewshire

Loganswell, Pilmuir, Newton Mearns,
Glasgow, Lanarkshire, G77 6RT
☎ 01355 500256, Pro 500206,
Sec 0141 333 9989,
Rest/Bar 500256
Course is on the A77 Glasgow to
Kilmarnock road two miles S of
Newton Mearns.
Moorland course.
Pro Gordon D Clarke; Founded 1922
Designed by James Braid
18 holes, 6097 yards, S.S.S. 70
▮ Free practice area.
† Welcome by arrangement with Pro.
£ WD £35 or £40 for a day ticket.
♪ Welcome Tues and Thurs by
arrangement with secretary; catering
and bar facilities by prior arrangement
with the clubhouse manager; from £30.
▮●▮ Full clubhouse facilities.

9B 59 Easter Moffat ☎

Mansion House, Plains, Airdrie,

Lanarkshire, ML6 8NP
☎ 01236 842289, Pro 843015,
Sec 842878
Two miles E of Airdrie on the old
Edinburgh-Glasgow road.
Moorland/parkland course.
Pro Graham King; Founded 1922
18 holes, 6240 yards, S.S.S. 70
† Welcome.
£ WD £20; no visitors WE.
♪ Welcome WD by prior
arrangement; day tickets £20; catering
by prior arrangement; from £15.
▮●▮ Clubhouse facilities.
↵ Tudor Hotel, Airdrie.

9B 60 Eastwood

Muirshield Loganswell, Newton
Mearns, Glasgow, G77 6RX
▤ secretary@
eastwoodgolfclub.demon.co.uk
☎ 01355 500280, Fax 500280,
Pro 500285, Sec 500280,
Rest/Bar 500261
On M77 from Glasgow; three miles S
of Newton Mearns.
Moorland/parkland course.
Pro Iain Darroch; Founded 1893
Designed by J Moon
18 holes, 5864 yards, S.S.S. 68
▮ Practice area.
† Welcome WD.
£ WD £24 £30 for full day.
♪ Welcome WD by prior
arrangement; catering packages by
arrangement; from £24.
▮●▮ Clubhouse facilities.
↵ Redhurst, Fenwick.

9B 61 Elderslie

63 Main Road, Elderslie, Johnstone,
Renfrewshire, PA5 9AZ
♨ www.elderleegolfclub.net
▤ annanderson@
eldersleegolfclub.freeserve.co.uk
☎ 01505 323956, Fax 344346,
Pro 320032, Sec 323956,
Rest/Bar 322835
On A737 between Paisley and
Johnstone.
Undulating parkland course.
Pro Rickey Bowen; Founded 1909
Designed by James Braid
18 holes, 6175 yards, S.S.S. 70
† Welcome WD.
£ WD £24; £32 for two rounds.
♪ Welcome Mon, Wed and Fri by
prior arrangement; day ticket £32;
catering by arrangement; snooker;
from £20.
▮●▮ Full clubhouse facilities.
↵ The Glasgow Airport.

9B 62 Erskine

Bishopton, Renfrewshire, PA7 5PH
☎ 01505 862302, Pro 862108
Off Erskine Toll Bridge and turn left
along B815 for 1.5 miles.
Parkland course.
Pro Peter Thomson; Founded 1904
18 holes, 6241 yards, S.S.S. 70
† Welcome if introduced by or
playing with a member.
£ Terms on application.
♪ Welcome by prior arrangement;
catering by prior arrangement only;
terms on application.
▮●▮ Meals served to members or their
guests only.
↵ Erskine; Crest.

9B 63 Fereneze

Fereneze Avenue, Barrhead, Glasgow,
Lanarkshire, G78 1HJ
☎ 0141 8811519, Fax 8817149,
Pro 8807058, Sec 8817149
9 miles SW of Glasgow near Barrhead
station.
Moorland course.
Pro Stuart Kerr; Founded 1904
18 holes, 5962 yards, S.S.S. 71
† Welcome by prior arrangement or
with member.
£ Terms on application.
♪ Welcome WD only by prior
arrangement; catering by arrangement;
terms available on application.
▮●▮ Full clubhouse facilities available;
WD evening meals by prior
arrangement.
↵ Dalmeny Park.

9B 64 Gailes Golf Course and Range

Killemont, Bearsden, G61 2TW
♨ www.glasgowgailes-golf.com
☎ 01294 311258
From Glasgow – M77/A77 S, A71 to
Irvine, straight off at next junction
Harbourside, signposted from there.
Flat.
18 holes, 7000 yards
† Yes.
£ WD £42 per round, £50 per day;
WE £55 per round, £60 per day.
♪ Yes.
▮●▮ Yes.
↵ Thistle Hotel, Irvine.

9B 65 Gigha

Isle of Gigha, PA41 7AA
☎ 01583 505254
Ferry from Tayinloan takes 20 minutes;
course is half a mile N from Gigha
Post Office.

Parkland course.
Founded 1988
Designed by Members
9 holes, 5042 yards, S.S.S. 65
† Welcome.
Ⅼ WD £10; WE £10.
⌂ Welcome; day ticket £10; meals and bar at Gigha Hotel; from £10.
❙❍❙ Meals and bar available at the Gigha Hotel.
⌁ Gigha; Tayinloan.

9B 66 Girvan
Girvan, Ayrshire, KA26 9HW
☎ 01465 714346, Rest/Bar 714272
Course is off the A77 Stranraer to Ayr road.
Seaside links/parklands course.
Founded pre 1877
Designed by James Braid
18 holes, 5064 yards, S.S.S. 64
Ⅰ Practice area.
† Welcome by prior arrangement.
Ⅼ Prices on application.
⌂ Welcome by prior arrangement; catering available.
❙❍❙ Catering by arrangement.
⌁ Turnberry Hotel.

9B 67 Glasgow
Killermont, Bearsden, Glasgow, Lanarkshire, G61 2TW
☎ 0141 9421713, Fax 9420770, Pro 9428507, Sec 9422011
6 miles NW of Glasgow near Killermont Bridge taking the A81 or A806.
Parkland course.
Pro Jack Steven; Founded 1787/1905
Designed by Tom Morris Snr
18 holes, 5968 yards, S.S.S. 69
† Welcome by prior arrangement.
Ⅼ WD £42; WE £42.
⌂ None.
❙❍❙ Lunches and high teas by application.
⌁ Grosvenor; Burnbrae; Black Bull; Pond.

9B 68 Glasgow (Gailes)
Gailes, By Irvine, Ayrshire, KA11 5AE
☎ 01294 311258, Fax 0141 9422011, Pro 01294 311561, Sec 0141 942 2011, Rest/Bar 01294 311258
2 miles S of Irvine on A78.
Championship seaside links.
Pro Jack Steven; Founded 1787/1892
Designed by Willie Park, Jnr
18 holes, 6513 yards, S.S.S. 72
† Welcome by prior arrangement

with secretary or if introduced by a member.
Ⅼ WD £42; WE £47.
⌂ Welcome by prior arrangement with secretary only; WD day tickets £52; catering by prior arrangement; from £42.
❙❍❙ Full clubhouse facilities.
⌁ Hospitality Inn, Irvine; Marine, Troon.

9B 69 Gleddoch Country Club
Old Greenock Road, Langbank, Port Glasgow, Renfrewshire, PA14 6YE
☎ 01475 540304, Fax 540459, Pro 540704
M8 to Greenock; first turning to Langbank Houston on B789.
Parkland/moorland course.
Pro Keith Campbell; Founded 1975
Designed by Hamilton Stutt
18 holes, 6357 yards, S.S.S. 71
† Welcome by arrangement with Pro.
Ⅼ WD £30; WE £40; day tickets start at £40.
⌂ Welcome; catering packages by arrangement; terms on application.
❙❍❙ Clubhouse facilities.
⌁ Glenddoch House.

9B 70 Glencruitten
Glencruitten Road, Oban, Argyll, PA34 4PU
☎ 01631 562868, Pro 564115, Sec 564604
1 mile from the town centre.
Parkland course.
Founded 1910
Designed by James Braid
18 holes, 4250 yards, S.S.S. 63
† Welcome.
Ⅼ WD £17; WE £18.
⌂ Welcome by prior arrangement; discounts available.
❙❍❙ Full clubhouse facilities.
⌁ Royal hotel; Calodoen Hotel.

9B 71 Gourock
Cowal View, Gourock, Renfrewshire, PA19 1HD
☎ 01475 631001, Pro 636834
2 miles uphill from Gourock station.
Moorland course.
Pro Graham Clarke; Founded 1896
Designed by Henry Cotton
18 holes, 6408 yards, S.S.S. 72
Ⅰ Small practice area.
† Welcome by prior arrangement with Pro shop.
Ⅼ WD £20; WE £27.
⌂ Welcome by prior arrangement;

day tickets available WD £27; WE £29; catering by prior arrangement.
❙❍❙ Bar lunches and high teas; dinners by arrangement.
⌁ Gantock.

9B 72 Greenock
Forsyth Street, Greenock, Renfrewshire, PA16 8RE
☎ 01475 720793, Sec 791912
1 mile SW of the town on the main road to Gourock on the A8.
Moorland course.
Pro Paul Morrison; Founded 1890
Designed by James Braid
27 holes, 5838 yards, S.S.S. 69
† Welcome by prior arrangement with secretary.
Ⅼ Terms on application.
⌂ Welcome by prior arrangement with secretary.
❙❍❙ Full clubhouse facilities.
⌁ Tontine.

9B 73 Greenock Whinhill
Beith Road, Greenock, Renfrewshire, PA16 9LN
☎ 01475 724694, Pro 721064
Off Largs Road.
Parkland course.
Founded 1911
Designed by W Fernie
18 holes, 5504 yards, S.S.S. 68
† Welcome.
Ⅼ WD £6.50; WE £6.50.
⌂ None welcome.
❙❍❙ By prior arrangement.
⌁ Stakis Gantock.

9B 74 Haggs Castle
70 Dumbreck Road, Glasgow, Lanarkshire, G41 4SN
☎ 0141 4270480, Fax 4271157, Pro 4273355, Sec 4271157
Course is close to Junction 1 off the M77.
Parkland course.
Pro J McAlister; Founded 1910
Designed by Peter Alliss & Dave Thomas
18 holes, 6464 yards, S.S.S. 71
† Welcome on WD by prior arrangement.
Ⅼ WD £30.
⌂ Welcome WD only by arrangement with secretary; catering by arrangement; terms on application.
❙❍❙ Full clubhouse facilities.
⌁ Shenbrooke Castle, Pollockshields.

9B 75 Hamilton
Riccarton, Ferniegair, Hamilton,
Lanarkshire, ML3 7UE
☎ 01698 282872, Pro 282324,
Sec 459537
Off A74 between Larkhall and Hamilton.
Parkland course.
Pro Maurice Moir; Founded 1892
Designed by James Braid
18 holes, 6264 yards, S.S.S. 70
⚐ Practice area.
† Welcome on WD by prior
arrangement.
[WD £30 (18 holes); £40 day ticket.
⚐ By arrangement with secretary;
catering packages by arrangement;
terms on application.
🏴 Clubhouse facilities.

9B 76 Hayston
Campsie Road, Kirkintilloch, Glasgow,
Lanarkshire, G66 1RN
☎ 0141 7761244, Fax 7769030,
Pro 7750882, Sec 7750723
7 miles N of Glasgow.
Parkland course.
Pro Steve Barnett; Founded 1926
Designed by James Braid
18 holes, 6042 yards, S.S.S. 70
⚐ Practice area.
† Welcome by prior arrangement on
WD only.
[Available upon application.
⚐ Welcome Tues and Thurs by prior
arrangement; day tickets from £30;
maximum 24; catering by arrangement;
from £20.
🏴 Full clubhouse facilities.
🏴 Kincaid House.

9B 77 Helensburgh
25 East Abercromby Street,
Helensburgh, Dunbartonshire, G84 9JD
☎ 01436 674176, Fax 671170,
Pro 675505
Follow A82 to Helensburgh; signposted
in town.
Moorland course.
Pro David Fotheringham; Founded 1893
Designed by James Braid
18 holes, 6104 yards, S.S.S. 70
† Welcome WD.
[WD £20.
⚐ Welcome by prior arrangement;
includes food and golf; from £35.
🏴 Full clubhouse dining facilities.
🏴 Commodore, Helensburgh;
Camerous House, Balloch.

9B 78 Hilton Park
Stockiemuir Road, Milngavie, Glasgow,
G62 7HB

☎ 0141 9565124, Fax 9564657,
Pro 9565125, Sec 9564657,
Rest/Bar 9565124
On A809 8 miles N of Glasgow.
Moorland course.
Pro Billy McCondichie; Founded 1927
Designed by James Braid
36 holes, 6054/5497 yards, S.S.S.
70/73
† Welcome WD by prior
arrangement.
[WD £24, £32 full day.
⚐ Welcome WD; day rate of approx.
£30; catering by arrangement; from £20.
🏴 Full catering facilities available.
🏴 Kirkhouse; County Club.

9B 79 Hollandbush
Acretophead, Lesmahagow, Lanark,
Lanarkshire, ML11 0JS
🖳 www.hollandbushgolfclub.co.uk
✉ mail@hollandbushgolfclub.co.uk
☎ 01555 893484, Fax 893484,
Pro 893646, Sec 893484,
Rest/Bar 893546
Off Junction 9 M74 at Lesmahagow
and Coalburn.
Parkland course on edge of moorland.
Founded 1954
Designed by K Pate/J Lawson
18 holes, 6318 yards, S.S.S. 70
⚐ Practice range available.
† Public municipal course.
[WD £8.20; WE £9.30.
⚐ Welcome.
🏴 Full clubhouse facilities but not on
Mon.
🏴 Shawlands; Popinjay.

9B 80 Innellan
Knockamillie Road, Innellan, Argyll
☎ 01369 830242
4 miles S of Dunoon.
Parkland course.
Founded 1891
9 holes, 4878 yards, S.S.S. 63
† Welcome anytime except Mon
evening.
[Terms on application.
⚐ Welcome by prior arrangement;
catering by arrangement; terms on
application.
🏴 By prior arrangement.
🏴 Esplanade; Slatefield; Rosscalm.

9B 81 Inverary
Inverary, Argyll
☎ 01499 302508
SW corner of town on Lochgilphead
Road.
Parkland course.
Founded 1993

Designed by Watt Landscaping
9 holes, 5700 yards, S.S.S. 68
† Welcome except competition days.
[WD £10; WE £10.
⚐ Welcome by prior arrangement;
golf only; catering available by special
arrangement with local hotels; from
£10.
🏴 None.
🏴 Loch Fynn; Great Inn.

9B 82 Irvine
Bogside, Irvine, Ayrshire, KA12 8SN
☎ 01294 275979, Pro 275626
On the road from Irvine to Kilwinning,
turn left after Ravespark academy and
carry straight on for 0.5 miles over the
railway bridge.
Links course.
Pro Keith Erskine; Founded 1887
Designed by James Braid
18 holes, 6408 yards, S.S.S. 73
† Welcome; but not before 3pm at
WE.
[WD £30; WE £45.
⚐ Welcome by prior arrangement
with secretary; catering packages by
prior arrangement; from £30.
🏴 Full clubhouse facilities.
🏴 Hospitality Inn; Golf Hotel.

9B 83 Irvine Ravenspark
13 Kidsneuk Lane, Irvine, Ayrshire,
KA12 8SR
☎ 01294 271293, Pro 276467
On A78 midway between Irvine and
Kilwinning.
Municipal parkland course.
Pro Peter Bond; Founded 1907
18 holes, 6429 yards, S.S.S. 71
† Welcome; not before 2.30pm on
Sat.
[WD £9; WE £13.
⚐ Welcome WD; by prior
arrangement; from £15.50.
🏴 Full clubhouse facilities.
🏴 Thistle; Annfield; Redburn; Golf Inn.

9B 84 Kilbirnie Place
Largs Rd, Kilbirnie, Ayrshire, KA25 7AJ
☎ 01505 683398, Sec 684444
On the main Largs Road on the
outskirts of Kilbirnie.
Parkland course.
Founded 1922
18 holes, 5517 yards, S.S.S. 69
† Welcome WD.
[WD £15 WE £20.
⚐ Welcome by prior arrangement;
from £18.
🏴 Full facilities.
🏴 Ryan.

9B 85 Kilmalcolm
Porterfield Road, Kilmacolm,
Renfrewshire, PA13 4PD
▩ secretary@
kilmalcolmgolf.sagehost.co.uk
☎ 01505 872139, Fax 874007,
Pro 872695
From M8 Glasgow airport follow the
main signs to Irvine; turn off second
junction and follow A761 to Kilmalcolm.
Moorland course.
Pro Iain Nicholson; Founded 1890
Designed by James Braid
18 holes, 5961 yards, S.S.S. 69
† Welcome; prior booking essential
for WE.
⌊ WD £20.50; WE £20.50 will be
changing.
⟡ Welcome WD by prior
arrangement; packages and prices
depend on numbers; terms on
application.
⦿ Full clubhouse facilities.
⌁ Many in Glasgow, Renfrew and
Paisley.

9B 86 Kilmarnock (Barassie)
Hillhouse Road, Troon, Ayrshire, KA10
6SY
⛬ www.kbgc.co.uk
▩ barrasiegc@lineone.net
☎ 01292 313920, Fax 318300,
Pro 313920, Sec 313920,
Rest/Bar 313920
Course is two miles N of Troon directly
opposite Barassie railway station.
Championship links course.
Pro Gregor Howie; Founded 1887
Designed by Matthew M Monie
27 holes, 6484 yards, S.S.S. 74
† Welcome WD except Wed; not
before 8.30am or between 12.30pm –
1.30pm.
⌊ WD start at £50, WE £60.
⟡ Welcome WD except Wed by
arrangement; catering can be arranged
in advanced with club caterer; dining
room; television lounge; also 9-hole
course available, 2888 yards, par 34.
⦿ Full clubhouse dining and bar;
jacket and tie must be worn in dining
room.
⌁ South Beach; Prestland House,
both Troon.

9B 87 Kilsyth Lennox
Tak-Ma-Doon, Kilsyth, Glasgow,
Lanarkshire, G65 0HX
☎ 01236 824115, Sec 823213
Course is on the A80 12 miles from
Glasgow.
Moorland/parkland course.
Founded 1907

18 holes, 5912 yards, S.S.S. 70
† Welcome by prior arrangement
with secretary or starter.
⌊ WD £14; WE £16.
⟡ Welcome by arrangement with
secretary; from £16.
⦿ Clubhouse facilities.

9B 88 Kirkhill
Greenlees Road, Cambuslang,
Glasgow, Lanarkshire, G72 8YN
☎ 0141 6413083, Fax 6418499,
Pro 6417972, Sec 6418499,
Rest/Bar 6413083
Follow East Kilbride road from
Burnside, take first turning on left past
Cathkin by-pass roundabout.
Meadowland course.
Pro Duncan Williamson; Founded 1910
Designed by James Braid
18 holes, 5900 yards, S.S.S. 70
† Welcome by arrangement.
⌊ WD £20; WE £22.
⟡ Welcome by prior arrangement;
catering by prior arrangement with
caterer; from £15.
⦿ Full facilities by prior arrangement;
snacks and bar meals available.
⌁ Kings Park; Burnside; Stuart;
Bruce.

9B 89 Kirkintilloch
Todhill, Campsie Road, Kirkintilloch,
Glasgow, G66 1RN
☎ 0141 7761256, Fax 7752424,
Sec 7752387
1 mile from Kirkintilloch on road to
Lennoxtown.
Parkland course.
Founded 1895
Designed by James Braid
18 holes, 5860 yards, S.S.S. 69
† Welcome with letter of introduction.
⌊ WD £18; WE £18.
⟡ Welcome by prior arrangement;
day ticket from £28; catering by
arrangement; from £18.
⦿ Clubhouse facilities; restrictions
Mon and Tues.
⌁ Garfield, Stepps.

9B 90 Knightswood
Lincoln Avenue, Knightswood, G13
☎ 0141 959 6358
From city centre go W along Great
Western Road through Knightswood
past the cross an then left into Lincoln
Avenue.
Flat parkland course.
Founded 1920
9 holes, 5586 yards, S.S.S. 64
† Welcome, except Fri morning.

⌊ WD £3.40; WE £3.40.
⟡ Welcome with same restrictions as
visitors; from £6.50.
⦿ Limited.
⌁ Charing Cross Tower Hotel, The
Grovesnor

9B 91 Kyles of Bute ℭ
The Moss, Kames, Tighnabruaich,
Argyll, PA21 2EE
☎ 01700 811603, Sec 811603
Course is on the B3836 on the road
from Dunoon to Tighnabruaich, B8000
to Millhouse.
Undulating moorland course.
Founded 1907
9 holes, 4748 yards, S.S.S. 64
† Welcome all times except Wed
evenings and Sun 9.30am – 1pm.
⌊ WD £8 per day WE £10 per day.
Annual membership £70.
⟡ Welcome by arrangement with
secretary.
⦿ Snacks when available.
⌁ Royal; Kames; Kilfenan.

9B 92 Laglands
Auldhouse Road, East Kilbride,
Glasgow, Lanarkshire, G75 9DW
☎ 01352 48172, Sec 0141 6442623
Course is three miles SE of East
Kilbride.
18 holes, 6202 yards, S.S.S. 70
† Welcome.
⌊ Terms on application.
⟡ Terms on application.

9B 93 Lamlash
Lamlash, Isle of Arran, KA27 8JU
☎ 01770 600296, Fax 600296,
Sec 600272
Course is three miles S of pier terminal
at Brodick.
Undulating heathland course.
Founded 1889
Designed by W Auchterlonie/W Fernie
18 holes, 4640 yards, S.S.S. 64
⌇ Practice putting green.
† Welcome.
⌊ £12 but this is only available after
4pm; Day ticket WD £16, WE £20.
⟡ Welcome; full catering available.
⦿ Full clubhouse facilities.
⌁ Glenisle; Lilybank; Marine.

9B 94 Lanark
The Moor, Whitelees Rd, Lanark, S
Lanarkshire, ML11 7RX
☎ 01555 663219, Fax 663219,
Pro 661456
Take A73 or A72 to Lanark; turn left in

town for Whitelees road.
Moorland course.
Pro Alan White; Founded 1851
Designed by T Morris
18 holes, 6306 yards, S.S.S. 71
✝ Welcome WD; with member at
WE.
𝄞 WD £26. Full day £40.
↻ Welcome by prior arrangement on
WD; larger groups welcome Mon-
Wed; maximum of 12 people Thurs &
Fri; catering by arrangement; from
£24.
🍽 Full clubhouse facilities.
↵ Cartland Bridge; Popinjay; Tinto.

9B 95 Largs
Irvine Rd, Largs, Ayrshire, KA30 8EU
⚏ www.largsgolfclub.co.uk
✉ secretery@largsgolfclub.co.uk
☎ 01475 673594, Fax 673594,
Pro 686192, Sec 673594
Course is on the A78 one mile S of
Largs.
Parkland/woodland course.
Pro Kenneth Docherty; Founded 1891
18 holes, 6115 yards, S.S.S. 71
✝ Welcome by arrangement.
𝄞 WD £30 per round, £40 per day;
WE £40.
↻ Welcome Tues and Thurs by prior
arrangement; packages available for
18 and 36 holes of golf plus catering;
from £30.
🍽 Full clubhouse facilities.
↵ Priory House; Haylie; Queens.
Moorings Hotel.

9B 96 Larkhall
Burnhead Rd, Larkhall, Lanarkshire,
NLI9 3AA
☎ 01698 881113
Take M8 to Larkhall exit then head SW
on B7019.
Municipal parkland course.
9 holes, 6423 yards, S.S.S. 71
✝ Welcome.
𝄞 WD £3.50; WE £3.80.
↻ Welcome by prior arrangement;
limited catering is available; from
£3.50.
🍽 Bar.

9B 97 Lead Hills
Leadhills, Bigagr, Lanarkshire, ML12
6XR
☎ 01659 74324
On B797 in Leadhills village 6 miles
from A74 at Abingdon.
Moorland course, highest in Scotland.
Founded 1935
9 holes, 4100 yards, S.S.S. 62

✝ Welcome.
𝄞 Details available on request.
↻ Welcome catering organised in
local hotel; from £5.
🍽 Local Hotel.
↵ Hopetoun Arms.

9B 98 Lenzie
19 Crosshill Rd, Lenzie, Glasgow, G66
5DA
✉ scotdavidson@
lenziegolfclub.demon.co.uk
☎ 0141 7761535, Pro 7777748,
Sec 7761535, Rest/Bar 7761535
10 miles NE of Glasgow; leave M8 at
Stirling Junction then head for
Kirkintilloch.
Parkland course.
Pro J McCallum; Founded 1889
18 holes, 5984 yards, S.S.S. 69
✝ Welcome by prior arrangement.
𝄞 WD £18.
↻ Welcome by prior arrangement
with the club Secretary; catering
packages available by prior
arrangement; professional can assist
on society days with golf clinic etc,
from £28.
🍽 Full clubhouse facilities available.
↵ Moddiesburn; Garfield; Stepps.

9B 99 Lethamhill
Cumbernauld Rd, Glasgow, G33 1AH
☎ 0141 7706220, Fax 7700520,
Pro 7707135, Sec 7706220
On A80 adjacent to Hogganfield Loch.
Municipal parkland course.
Pro Gary Mctagart
18 holes, 5836 yards, S.S.S. 70
✝ Welcome.
𝄞 WD £7.70; WE £7.70.
↻ Welcome.
🍽 Burger van.

9B 100 Linn Park
Simsall Rd, Glasgow, G44 5EP
☎ 0141 6375871
Off M74 S of Glasgow.
Public parkland course.
Founded 1925
Designed by Glasgow Parks
18 holes, 5005 yards, S.S.S. 65
✝ Welcome.
𝄞 Details upon application.
↻ Welcome by prior application from
£5.50.
🍽 Clubhouse facilities available.

9B 101 Littlehill
Auchinairn Rd, Bishopbriggs, Glasgow,
G74 1UT

☎ 0141 7721916, Sec 770 0519
3 miles N of city centre.
Public parkland course.
Founded 1924
Designed by James Braid
18 holes, 6228 yards, S.S.S. 70
✝ Welcome.
𝄞 WD £6; WE £6; concessions apply.
↻ Apply to Council for full details.
🍽 Clubhouse facilities available;
except Mon; no catering on summer
WE.

9B 102 Loch Lomond
Rossdhu House, Luss by Alexandria,
Dunbartonshire, G83 8NT
⚏ www.lochlomond.com
☎ 01436 655555, Fax 655500
On the A82 on the W bank of Loch
Lomond.
Championship parkland course
Scottish Open.
Pro Colin Campbell; Founded 1994
Designed by Tom Weiskopf and Jay
Morrish
18 holes, 7060 yards, S.S.S. 72
✝ Private; as the guest of a member
only.
𝄞 WD £150; WE £150.
↻ None.
🍽 First-class clubhouse facilities
available.
↵ Cameron House.

9B 103 Lochgilphead
Blarbuie Rd, Lochgilphead, Argyll,
PA31 8LE
☎ 01546 602340
Follow signs for Argyll and Bute
Hospital from the centre of
Lochgilphead.
Hilly parkland course.
Founded 1891/1963
Designed by Dr Ian MacCammond
9 holes, 4484 yards, S.S.S. 63
✝ Welcome.
𝄞 WD £10; WE £10.
↻ Welcome; weekly ticket of £30
reductions for groups registered with
the club: from £10.
🍽 Bar facilites.
↵ Stag Argyll.

9B 104 Lochranza
Lochranza, Isle of Arran, KA27 8HL
☎ 01770 830273, Fax 830600
Course is in Lochraza opposite
distillery.
Grassland course with rivers/trees 3
holes on seashore.
Founded 1991
Designed by Iain M Robertson

18 holes, 5654 yards, S.S.S. 70
♦ Welcome between April and Late
October.
ℂ WD £12 WE £12 concessions
apply.
♢ Welcome by prior arrangement day
ticket £15 available packages can
include accomodation, meals ferry,
distillery visit and golf from £10.
🍽 Snacks available.
↩ Hotel/Guest house packages
available.

9B 105 Lochwinnoch
Burnfoot Rd, Lochwinnoch,
Renfrewshire, PA12 4AN
⌗ www.lochwinnochgolf.co.uk
✉ admin@lochwinnochgolf.co.uk
☎ 01505 842153, Fax 843668,
Pro 843029, Sec 842153,
Rest/Bar 842153
On A760 10 miles S of Paisley.
Parkland course.
Pro Gerry Reilly; Founded 1897
18 holes, 6025 yards, S.S.S. 71
♦ Welcome WD before 4pm.
ℂ WD £20; WE £20.
♢ Welcome by prior arrangement
WD; catering packages available.
Please contact course secretary for
details.
🍽 Clubhouse facilities.
↩ Lindhurst.

9B 106 Loudoun Golf Club
Galston, Ayrshire, KA4 8PA
✉ secretary@loudgowf.sol.co.uk
☎ 01563 821993, Fax 820011,
Sec 821993, Rest/Bar 820551
On A71 5 miles E of Kilmarnock.
Parkland course.
Founded 1909
18 holes, 6016 yards, S.S.S. 68
♦ Welcome WD only by prior
arrangement.
ℂ WD £20 per round.
♢ Welcome WD by prior
arrangement; catering packages can
be arranged; from £11.
🍽 Full catering facilities.
↩ Loudoun Mains; Newmilns; Fox
Bar Kilmarnock.

9B 107 Machrie Bay Golf Club
Machrie, Isle of Arran, KA27
⌗ www.twemsleywaitrose.com
☎ 01770 850232, Sec 850247
9 miles W of Brodick.
Links course.
Founded 1900
Designed by William Fernie
9 holes, 2200 yards, S.S.S. 62

✐ Practice area.
♦ Welcome.
ℂ WD £25; WE £25.
♢ Welcome by prior arrangement.
🍽 Full clubhouse and hotel catering
and bar facilities with à la carte
restaurant.

9B 108 Machrie Hotel and Golf Links
Port Ellen, Isle of Islay, Argyll, PA42
7AN
☎ 01496 302310, Fax 302404,
Sec 302212
Ferry from Kennacraig (2hrs) or plane
from Glasgow (30 mins).
Traditional links course.
Founded 1891
Designed by Wille Campbell/Donald
Steel
18 holes, 6250 yards, S.S.S. 70
♦ Welcome residents recieve
discounts.
ℂ WD£35.
♢ Welcome by prior arrangment; day
rates available; also accomodation and
golf packages can be arranged; hotel
can also advise on air packages from
Glasgow; conference facilities; own
beach; Salmon and Trout fishing
snooker from £20.
🍽 Full clubhouse catering and bar
facilities with à la carte restaurant.
↩ Machrie Bay Hotel.

9B 109 Machrihanish
Machrihanish, Campbeltown, Argyll,
PA28 6PT
☎ 01586 810213, Fax 810221
Course is five miles W of
Campbeltown on the B843.
Natural links course.
Pro Ken Campbell; Founded 1876
Designed by Tom Morris
18 holes, 6225 yards, S.S.S. 71
♦ Welcome by prior arrangement.
ℂ WD £30; WE £40.
♢ Welcome by prior arrangement
with club Pro; some WE available;
catering by prior arrangement; some
air packages available;
accommodation packages also on
offer.
🍽 Full clubhouse facilities.
↩ See club for details

9B 110 Maybole
Memorial Park, Maybole, Ayrshire,
KA19
☎ 01292 616666
Course is nine miles S of Ayr on main
Stranraer road.

Hillside course with splendid views.
Founded 1905
9 holes, 5304 yards, S.S.S. 66
♦ Welcome.
ℂ Available upon application.
♢ Welcome.
↩ Many available in local area;
Abbotsford.

9B 111 Millport
Golf Rd, Millport, Isle of Cumbrae,
KA28 0HB
⌗ www.secretary@millport.co.uk
✉ millportgolfclub.co.uk
☎ 01475 530311, Fax 530306,
Pro 530305, Sec 530306,
Rest/Bar 530311
10 mins ferry crossing from Largs in
Ayrshire; 4 miles from the Ferry
Terminal.
Heathland course.
Pro Haldane Lee; Founded 1888
Designed by James Braid
18 holes, 5828 yards, S.S.S. 69
✐ Practice area.
♦ Welcome.
ℂ WD £20; WE £25.
♢ Welcome by prior arrangement;
catering packages by arrangement.
🍽 Full facilities.

9B 112 Milngavie
Laighpark, Milngavie, Glasgow, G62
8EP
☎ 0141 9561619;, Fax 9564252
Off A809 NW of Glasgow; club can
provide detailed directions.
Moorland course.
Founded 1895
Designed by J Braid
18 holes, 5818 yards, S.S.S. 68
♦ Welcome on WD by prior
arrangement.
ℂ WD £22.
♢ Welcome by prior arrangement;
packages ranging from £9 can be
arranged including 4-course dinner;
from £20.
🍽 Full clubhouse facilities available.
↩ Black Bull; Burnbrae; both
Milngavie.

9B 113 Mount Ellen
Johnstone Rd, Johnstone House,
Gartcosh, Glasgow, G69 8EY
☎ 01236 872277, Fax 872249
From M8 N and A89 take B752 N to
Gastosh on to B804 in direction of
Glenboig.
Parkland course.
Pro Iain Bilsborough; Founded 1905
18 holes, 5525 yards, S.S.S. 67

† Welcome WD only.
[WD £16.
⟳ Welcome by prior arrangement; terms on application.
⦿ Full clubhouse facilities.
⌁ Garsfield Housel; Stepps; Moodiesburn House; Moodiesburn.

9B 114 Muirkirk
Cairn View, Muirkirk, Strathclyde, KA18 3QW
☎ 01290 661556, Fax 661556, Sec 661556
13 miles W of Junction 12 on M74 on A70.
Pay and play.
Founded 1991
9 holes, 5366 yards, S.S.S. 67
† Welcome at all times.
[£8.00 seniors £5, juniors £3.
⟳ Societies welcome at WE by arrangement with secretary.
⦿ Limited.
⌁ The Coachouse Inn, and various B&Bs.

9B 115 New Cumnock
Lochill, New Cumnock, Ayrshire, KA18 4BQ
☎ 01290 338848
On the A76 1 mile to the NW of New Cumnock.
Parkland course.
Founded 1901
Designed by W Fernie
9 holes, 5332 yards, S.S.S. 68
† Welcome; tickets available from the Loch side Hotel next to the course.
[From £8 adult day £6 for children; £4 winter price £8 standard.
⟳ None.
⦿ Limited; Loch side Hotel next door.
⌁ Lochside Hotel.

9B 116 Old Course Ranfurly
Ranfurly Place, Bridge of Weir, Renfrewshire, PA11 3DE
⌂ www.oldranfurly.com
✉ seretary@oldranfurly.com
☎ 01505 613612, Fax 613214, Pro 613612, Sec 613214, Rest/Bar 613612
Course is five miles W of Glasgow Airport.
Heathland course.
Pro Derek McIntosh; Founded 1905
Designed by W Park Jnr
18 holes, 6061 yards, S.S.S. 70
† Welcome by prior arrangement WD; as the guest of a member only at WE.
[WD £20.
⟳ Welcome by written prior

arrangement WD; day ticket of £30 available; from £20.
⦿ Full clubhouse facilities available.
⌁ Normandy; Renfrew; Glyn Hill Paisley.

9B 117 Paisley
Braehead, Paisley, PA2 8TZ
⌂ www.paisleygc.com
✉ paisleygc@onetel.net.uk
☎ 0141 8843903, Fax 8843903, Pro 8844114, Rest/Bar 8842292
Leave M8 Junction 27 follow signposts for Paisley town centre. Turn left at Canal Street Station and follow road for 1.5 miles. Turn right at Glenburn road and left into Braehead Road. Golf club is at top of hill.
Moorland course.
Pro Gordon Stewart; Founded 1895/1951
18 holes, 6466 yards, S.S.S. 72
† Welcome WD before 4pm.
[WD £18 per round, £32 per day ticket. Members and their guests welcome at WE.
⟳ Welcome by prior arrangement WD; day ticket £32; golf and catering package can be provided.
⦿ Full clubhouse facilities available.

9B 118 Palacerigg
Palacerigg Country Park, Cumbernauld, G67 3HU
⌂ www.palacerigggolfclub.co.uk
✉ palacerigg_golfclub@lineone.net
☎ 01236 734969, Fax 721461, Pro 721461
Take A80 to Cumbernauld and follow signs for Country Park.
Wooded parkland course.
Pro John Murphy; Founded 1974
Designed by Henry Cotton
18 holes, 6444 yards, S.S.S. 71
† Welcome.
[WD £5.10; WE £7.40.
⟳ Welcome WD by prior arrangement; range of packages available; full day's golf and catering; from £25.
⦿ Full clubhouse facilities available; restrictions Mon/Tues.
⌁ Castlecarry; Moodiesburn; Cumbernauld Travel Inn.

9B 119 Pollok ⛿
90 Barrhead Road, Glasgow, G43 1BG
⌂ www.pollok.gc@lineone.net
✉ pollock.gc@lineone.net
☎ 0141 6321080, Fax 6491398, Sec 6324351, Rest/Bar 6321080
Course lies four miles S of the city of

Glasgow off M77 Junction 2 on B736.
Wooded parkland course.
Founded 1892
18 holes, 6257 yards, S.S.S. 70
† Welcome WD; gentlemen only.
[WD £32.
⟳ Welcome by prior arrangement with the Secretary, £32 per day Mon-Fri, £40 Sat and Sun.
⦿ Full clubhouse catering facilities.
⌁ Albany; Macdonald.

9B 120 Port Bannatyne ⛿
Bannatyne Mains Rd, Port Bannatyne, Isle of Bute, PA20 0PH
☎ 01700 504544
Course is two miles N of Rothesay on the Isle of Bute above the village of Port Bannatyne.
Hilly seaside course.
Founded 1912
Designed by James Braid
13 holes, 5085 yards, S.S.S. 65
† Welcome.
[WD £8; WE £10.
⟳ Welcome by prior arrangement; reductions for groups of 30-39 to £10; for more than 40.
⌁ New clubhouse. Ardmory House; Royal; Ardbeg.

9B 121 Port Glasgow
Devol Farm Industrial Estate, Port Glasgow, Inverclyde, PA14 5XE
☎ 01475 704181
On M8 towards Greenock SW of Glasgow in the town of Port Glasgow.
Undulating course.
Founded 1895
18 holes, 5712 yards, S.S.S. 68
† WD until 3.55pm; WE by introduction after 4pm Sat.
[WD £15, day pass £20.
⟳ Welcome by prior arrangement on non-competition days; catering by prior arrangement; terms available on application.
⦿ Clubhouse facilities.
⌁ Clune Brae; Star.

9B 122 Prestwick (*see overleaf*)
2 Links Rd, Prestwick, Ayrshire, KA9 1QG
⌂ www.prestwickgc.co.uk
✉ bookings@prestwickgc.co.uk
☎ 01292 477404, Fax 477255
1 mile from Prestwick Airport adjacent to Prestwick station.
Links course; hosted first Open Championship in 1860.
Pro Frank Rennie; Founded 1851

Designed by Tom Morris
18 holes, 6544 yards, S.S.S. 73
† Welcome by arrangement.
▯ WD £85; day ticket £125.
⌂ Welcome by prior arrangement;
terms on application.
|● Full clubhouse facilities; dining
room men only; Cardinal room.
↙ Parkstone; Fairways; Golf View;
North Beach.

9B 123 Prestwick St Cuthbert
East Rd, Prestwick, Ayrshire, KA9
2SX
☎ 01292 477101, Fax 671730
Take A77 to Whitletts roundabout and
then follow signs for Heathfield Estate.
Parkland course.
Founded 1899
Designed by Stutt & Co
18 holes, 6470 yards, S.S.S. 71
† Welcome WD but booking
essential; only with member at WE.
▯ WD and WE £22.
⌂ Welcome by prior arrangement;
day ticket £30; meal packages can be
arranged with prior notice from £10.50;
from £22.
|● Full clubhouse facilities.
↙ St Nicholas; Golf.

9B 124 Prestwick St Nicholas
Grangemuir Rd, Prestwick, Ayrshire,
KA9 1SN
☎ 01292 477608
From Prestwick town centre take the
road to Ayr; turn right at Grangemuir
road Junction; proceed under railway
bridge to course.
Links course.
Founded 1851/1892
Designed by C Hunter & J Allan
18 holes, 5952 yards, S.S.S. 69
† Welcome WD and Sun afternoon;
prior booking essential.
▯ WD £30; WE £35.
⌂ Welcome WD and some Sun
afternoons by prior arrangement;
catering by prior arrangement; from
£30.
|● Full clubhouse refurbishment
completed spring 1998.
↙ Parkstone.

9B 125 Ralston
Strathmore Ave, Ralston, Paisley,
Renfrewshire, PA1 3DT
☎ 0141 8821349, Fax 8839837,
Pro 8104925, Rest/Bar 8821470
Course is off the main Paisley to
Glasgow road.
Parkland course.

Pro Colin Monroe; Founded 1904
18 holes, 6029 yards, S.S.S. 63
† With members only on WD.
▯ WD £18.
⌂ Welcome by prior arrangement;
catering by arrangement; terms on
application.
|● Full clubhouse facilities.
↙ Abbey.

9B 126 Ranfurly Castle
Golf Road, Bridge of Weir,
Renfrewshire, PA11 3HN
⌨ www.ranfurlycastle.com
☎ 01505 612609, Fax 610406,
Sec 612609
From the M8 take the Irvine road to
Bridge of Weir; turn left at Prieston
road and at top of the rise the
clubhouse is on right.
Spacious heathland course.
Pro Tom Eckford; Founded 1889
Designed by Andrew Kirkaldy & Willie
Auchterlonie
18 holes, 6284 yards, S.S.S. 71
† Welcome WD.
▯ WD £25.
⌂ Welcome weekdays except
Wednesdays. £25 per round. £35 per
day.
|● Full clubhouse bar and restaurant
service.
↙ Glynhill; Renfrew; Stakis Glasgow
Airport.

9B 127 Renfrew
Blythswood Estate, Inchinnan Rd,
Renfrew, PA4 9EG
☎ 0141 8866692, Fax 8861808
Leave the M8 at Junction 26 then take
the A8 to Renfrew turning to the club at
the Normandie Hotel.
Parkland course.
Pro Steven Thomson; Founded 1894
Designed by John Harris
18 holes, 6818 yards, S.S.S. 73
† Visitors are welcome.
▯ WD £35.00.
⌂ Welcome Mon Tues and Thurs by
arrangement; catering by arrangement;
day ticket £35.
|● Full clubhouse bar and catering
facilities.
↙ Dean Park; Glynhill; Normandie
Hotel.

9B 128 Rothesay
Canada Hill, Rothesay, Isle of Bute,
PA20 9HN
✉ thedougals@tinyworld.co.uk
☎ 01700 503554, Fax 503554,
Pro 503554, Sec 503780,

Rest/Bar 502244
30 minutes by steamer from Wemyss
Bay.
Undulating parkland/moorland course.
Pro Jim Dougal; Founded 1892
Designed by James Braid/Ben Sayers
18 holes, 5419 yards, S.S.S. 66
† Visitors most welcome. Prior
arrangement advised at weekends.
▯ Terms on application.
⌂ Welcome by prior arrangement;
catering by prior arrangement; from
£15.
|● Full clubhouse facilities in the
season April-October.
↙ Club will supply comprehensive list
of local hotels.

9B 129 Rouken Glen
Stewarton Rd, Thornliebank, Glasgow,
G46 7UZ
☎ 0141 6387044
5 miles S of Glasgow.
Parkland course.
Pro Kendal McReid; Founded 1922
18 holes, 4800 yards, S.S.S. 64
▯ Practice range, 18 bays floodlit.
† Welcome.
▯ Terms on application.
⌂ Welcome by prior arrangement;
terms on application.
|● Snacks.
↙ The MacDonalds.

9B 130 Routenburn
Largs Ayrshire, KA30 8SQ
☎ 01475 673230, Pro 687240
1 mile N of Largs turning left at first
major turning on the Greenock road.
Seaside hill course.
Pro Greig McQueen; Founded 1914
Designed by James Braid
18 holes, 5680 yards, S.S.S. 68
† Welcome WD by prior
arrangement.
▯ WD £12; WE £18.
⌂ Welcome WD by prior
arrangement; catering packages by
prior arrangement; terms on
application.
|● Full facilities except Thurs.
↙ Queens Hotel Brisbourne Hotel.

9B 131 Royal Troon
Craigend Rd, Troon, Aryshire, KA10
6EP
⌨ www.golf@royaltroon.com
✉ bookings@royaltroon.com
☎ 01292 311555, Fax 318204,
Pro 313281, Rest/Bar 317578
3 miles from A77 and Prestwick
Airport.

Prestwick

The home of the first twelve Open Championships, Prestwick is either a favourite course in Britain or an insoluble puzzle. It is a short course by modern standards, thought to lack the infrastructure these days necessary to accommodate the vast hordes who gather at an Open Championship. But its fascination never wanes.

Running down the side of the first hole is a railway line. At the 2001 Amateur Championship one unfortunate golfer from South Africa deposited two balls onto the tracks. Rich enough to employ a man to carry his bag he obviously did not consider himself wealthy enough to lose two golf balls. The unfortunate caddie was sent to retrieve them. As the train inevitably whizzed by, the bag toter scrambled back over the wall followed by some frothy local invective from the driver. Further up the same hole there is a graveyard over which stands a derelict kirk, a remaining wall pointing to the heavens in the shape of the arrow. On glancing across at so ominous a sign, the caddie decided to hurry on to the tee of the second rather than push his luck any further.

The eventual winner of the 2001 Championship was Michael Hoey from Ireland. He had the ability to play the occasional tee shot so low that you would be hard pushed to describe the ball as airborne. He never quite mastered Prestwick, but he knew enough about the game to get on pretty well with it.

Much in accordance with local expectation, the American challenge never fathomed the local dialect required to play the course and disappeared soon after it had arrived. Prestwick is about as far removed from target golf as it is possible to be.

The course is rich with history. The story goes that a local monk decided to settle an argument with the Lord of Culzean over a round of golf. If the monk finished the loser he was to forfeit his nose. Never would victory smell sweeter.

Prestwick is crammed with holes that would offend the likes of Scott Hoch, but that delight the locals. At the third hole the golfer must carry the huge Cardinal bunker, stiffened with railway sleepers, that spans the width of the fairway. The par three fifth, the Himalayas, is a blind shot played over a colossal dune with discs set into the face to indicate – or approximate – the direction required.

The tenth hole, at 450 yards, uphill at the finish and usually into the wind, is as hard a par four as you are likely to find. It heads towards the sea where golfers head lemming-like after running into double figures on the hole.

The fifteenth must be the narrowest drive in golf, a tiny spine of land intent on kicking off the ball into the rough on either side. Those with the courage and curiosity to make it as far as the seventeenth must clear not only 'the Alps' with their blind second shot, but also the vast Sahara bunker that fronts the green. The powers that be have been kind enough to cut a set of eight steps into the front of the bunker, making lunch at least a distant possibility.

The course exudes variety and history, a wonderful test of shot making and brainpower. — **Mark Reason**

Championship links course; host of 1997 Open.
Pro Brian Anderson; Founded 1878
Designed by Willie Fernie/James Braid
18 holes, 7079 yards, S.S.S. 73
♦ 12.
† Mon, Tues and Thurs only; maximum handicap 20.
↕ WD £150 (incl lunch).
⟳ Welcome by prior arrangement; price includes lunch and coffee; also Portland course: 18 holes 6274 yards par 71; £95 for two rounds.
⦿ Full bar and restaurant service.
⟿ Marine; Piersland House.

9B 132 Ruchill
Brassey Street, Maryhill, Glasgow
☎ 0141 7700519, Pro 7707135, Sec 7706220
From Glasgow city centre,100 yards off M8, Junction 12.
Municipal parkland course.
Pro G Taggart; Founded 1928
18 holes, 5836 yards, S.S.S. 68
♦ Practice pitch and putt.
† Public.
↕ Pay and play.
⟳ Contact city council.

9B 133 Sandyhills
223 Sandyhills Rd, Glasgow, G32 9NA
☎ 0141 7631099, Sec 7780787
E side of Glasgow from Tollcross road turn left at Killin Stand right into Sandyhills Road.
Parkland course.
Founded 1905
18 holes, 6237 yards, S.S.S. 70
† Welcome by prior arrangement.
Terms on application.
⟳ Welcome by prior arrangement; catering packages available; terms on application.
⦿ Full clubhouse catering facilities available.
⟿ Hilton; Moat House; Marriott all in Glasgow.

9B 134 Shiskine
Blackwaterfoot, Isle of Arran, KA27 8HA
☎ 01770 860226, Fax 860205, Pro 860226
Course is 300 yards off the B880 in Blackwaterfoot.
Seaside course with magnificent views.
Founded 1896
Designed by Willy Ferney
12 holes, 2990 yards, S.S.S. 42
† Welcome; handicap certs required in July and August period.

↕ WD £13; WE £16.
⟳ Welcome by prior arrangement with club manager; packages available with Kinloch Hotel accommodation and golf; day tickets available (WD £18; WE £25); also weekly and fortnightly tickets; tennis and bowls.
⦿ Tea room lunches high teas from April-October; bar at Kinloch Hotel 500 yards away.
⟿ Kinloch Hotel.

9B 135 Skelmorlie
Skelmorlie, Ayrshire, PA17 5ES
☎ 01475 520152
1 mile from Wemyss Station.
Parkland/moorland course.
Founded 1891
Designed by James Braid
18 holes, 5104 yards, S.S.S. 65
† Welcome by prior arrangement except Sat.
↕ Terms on application.
⟳ Welcome by prior arrangement except Sat catering by prior arrangement terms available on application.
⦿ Full clubhouse facilities.
⟿ Haywood.

9B 136 Strathaven
Overton Avenue, Glasgow Road, Strathaven, ML10 6NL
✉ manager@
strathavengolfclub.fsbusiness.co.uk
☎ 01357 520421, Fax 520539, Pro 521812, Sec 520421, Rest/Bar 520421
On A723 East Kilbride road on outskirts of the town.
Tree-lined undulating parkland course.
Pro Matt McCrorie; Founded 1908
Designed by William Fernie of Troon
Extended to 18 holes by JR Stutt
18 holes, 6250 yards, S.S.S. 71
† Everyone welcome weekdays. Not weekends.
↕ WD until 4pm £25 per round. WD £35 per day.
⟳ Welcome Tues by prior arrangement with Sec; catering by prior arrangement; club can organise morning coffee hot and cold snacks lunches high teas and dinners; Packages start from £11.
⦿ Full clubhouse facilities available.
⟿ Strathaven; Springvale.

9B 137 Strathclyde Park
Mote Hill, Hamilton, Lanarkshire, ML3 6BY
☎ 01698 429350, Pro 285511

1.5 miles from M74 close to Hamilton Ice rink.
Public parkland course.
Pro William Walker
9 holes, 6350 yards, S.S.S. 70
♦ Practice range available.
† Welcome.
↕ WD £3.30 WE £3.90.
⟳ Welcome; catering by prior arrangement; from £3.
⦿ Catering by prior arrangement.
⟿ Travelodge.

9B 138 Tarbert
Kilberry Rd, Tarbert, Argyll, PA29 6XX
☎ 01880 820565
1 mile from A83 to Campbeltown from Tarbert on B8024.
Hilly seaside course.
9 holes, 4460 yards, S.S.S. 63
† Welcome by prior arrangement.
↕ From £8.
⟳ Welcome WD; day ticket for £15; from £10.
⦿ Full clubhouse facilities available.
⟿ Stonefield Castle; West Loch.

9B 139 Tobermory
Erray Rd, Tobermory, Isle of Mull, PA75 6PR
✉ tobgolf@mull.fsbusiness.co.uk
☎ 01688 302338, Fax 302140
Signposted in Tobermory.
Cliff top heathland course with views over Sound of Mull.
Founded 1896
Designed by David Adams (1935)
9 holes, 4890 yards, S.S.S. 64
♦ Practice range and net.
† Welcome; advance booking system.
↕ Terms on application.
⟳ Welcome by prior arrangement by calling (01355) 806271; catering packages by prior arrangement; from £16.
⦿ Full clubhouse facilities available.

9B 140 Torrance House
Strathaven Rd, East Kilbride, G75 0QZ
☎ 01355 249720, Sec 248638
Course is on the A726 on the outskirts of E Kilbride travelling South to Strathaven.
Municipal parkland course.
Founded 1969
Designed by Hawtree and Sons
18 holes, 6476 yards, S.S.S. 71
♦ Practice range 1 mile from club.
† Welcome; advance booking system.
↕ Terms on application.

⟲ Welcome by prior arrangement by calling 01355 80627; catering packages by prior arrangement from £16.
🍽 Full clubhouse facilities available.

9B 141 **Troon Municipal**
Harling Drive, Troon, Ayrshire, KA10 6NE
🏴 www.golfsouthairshine.co.uk
☎ 01292 312464, Fax 312578, Pro 315566
100 yards from the railway station.
Links course.
Pro Gordon Mckenley; Founded 1905
Darley: 18 holes, 6360 yards, S.S.S. 71
Lochgreen: 18 holes, 6822 yards, S.S.S. 72; Fullerton: 18 holes, 4689 yards, S.S.S. 63
Ⅰ Practice areas available.
† Welcome.
Ⅰ Terms on application.
⟲ Welcome by prior arrangement; catering by arrangement; terms on application.
🍽 Full clubhouse facilities.
⌁ Anchorage Hotel; Marine Hotel; South Beach Hotel.

9B 142 **Turnberry Resort**
Turnberry Hotel, Turnberry, Ayrshire, KA26 9LT
🏴 www.turnberry.co.uk
✉ monty.tunberry@westin.com
☎ 01655 331000, Fax 331706, Pro 334043, Sec 331000, Rest/Bar 331000
On A77 15 miles SW of Ayr.
Championship seaside links.
Pro David Fleming; Founded 1897
Designed by MacKenzie Ross (Ailsa)
18 holes, 6976 yards, S.S.S. 72
Ⅰ 12 long game 4 short game.
† Booking essential.
Ⅰ WD £80; WE £80. Subject to variation in April 2002.
⟲ Only welcome if society is resident in the hotel.
🍽 Full clubhouse restaurant and bar; first-class hotel facilities.
⌁ Turnberry Hotel Golf Courses & Spa.

9B 143 **Vale of Leven**
Northfield Rd, Bonhill, Alexandria, Dumbartonshire, G83 9ET
☎ 01389 752351
Off A82 Glasgow to Dumbarton road at signs marked Bonhill & Alexandria.
Moorland course with views of Loch and Ben Lomond.
Pro Gordon Brown; Founded 1907

---

18 holes, 5162 yards, S.S.S. 66
† Welcome except Sat.
Ⅰ WD £17; WE £21.
⟲ Welcome by prior arrangement; catering packages by prior arrangement with club caterers.
🍽 Full clubhouse and bar facilities available.
⌁ Balloch; Duck Bay Marina; Lomond Park; Tullichewan.

9B 144 **Vaul**
Scarinish, Isle of Tiree, Argyll, PA77 6XH
☎ 01879 220729
On the E end of the Island 3 miles from the pier and 5 miles from the airport; 40-minute flight from Glasgow; 50 miles W of Oban by ferry.
Links course.
Founded 1920
9 holes, 5674 yards, S.S.S. 68
† Welcome.
Ⅰ WD £5; WE £5.
⟲ Welcome by prior arrangement; weekly and fortnightly tickets available; from £10.
🍽 Catering at Lodge Hotel.
⌁ Lodge; Glassary GH; Kirkapol GH.

9B 145 **West Kilbride**
33-35 Fullerton Drive, Seamill, W Kilbride, Ayrshire, KA23 9HT
🏴 www.westkilbride.com
✉ golf@westkilbride.com
☎ 01294 823911, Fax 829573, Pro 823042, Rest/Bar 823128
On A78 Androssan to Largs road at Seamill.
Flat seaside links course alongside Firth of Clyde.
Pro Graham Ross; Founded 1893
Designed by Tom Morris
18 holes, 6452 yards, S.S.S. 70
Ⅰ Practice area.
† Welcome WD after 9.30am.
Ⅰ WD £38.
⟲ Welcome Tues and Thurs only by prior arrangement; catering to be arranged in advance with the caterer; from £38.
🍽 Full clubhouse facilities.
⌁ Seamill Hydro.

9B 146 **Western Gailes**
Gailes, Irvine, Ayrshire, KA11 5AE
🏴 www.westerngails.com
✉ enquiries@westerngails.com
☎ 01294 311357, Fax 312312
Course is on the A78 five miles N Troon.
Championship links; Open qualifying course.

Founded 1897
18 holes, 6714 yards, S.S.S. 73
Ⅰ Practice area.
† Welcome WD except Thurs, Tues.
Ⅰ WD £85. incl lunch; £90 Sun.
⟲ Welcome by prior arrangement WD except Thurs and Tues; day tickets from £115; catering by arrangement.
🍽 Clubhouse catering and bar.
⌁ The Thistle.

9B 147 **Westerwood Hotel** ⓣ
St Andrews Drive, Cumbernauld, G68 0EW
✉ westerwood@morton-hotel.com
☎ 01236 457171, Fax 738478, Pro 725281, Sec 725281
Signposted off the A80 13 miles from Glasgow.
Parkland course.
Pro Allen Tate; Founded 1989
Designed by Seve Ballesteros and Dave Thomas
18 holes, 6616 yards, S.S.S. 72
Ⅰ Practice range available.
† Welcome.
Ⅰ WD £13.50; WE £15.
⟲ Welcome by prior arrangement; packages available; hotel leisure facilities; residents discounts; from £22.50.
🍽 Full clubhouse catering facilities available.
⌁ Westerwood Hotel on site.

9B 148 **Whinhill**
B1Eith Road, Greenock, Renfrewshire
☎ 01475 724694, Sec 724694
Just outside Greenock on old Largs road.
Parkland course.
18 holes, 5434 yards, S.S.S. 68
† Welcome.
Ⅰ Terms on application.
⟲ None.
🍽 Small clubhouse for members only.

9B 149 **Whitecraigs**
72 Ayr Rd, Giffnock, G46 6SW
✉ wcraigsgc@aol.com
☎ 0141 6394530, Fax 616 3648, Pro 6392140, Rest/Bar 6391795
Course is on the A77 seven miles S of Glasgow.
Parkland course.
Pro Alistair Forrow; Founded 1905
18 holes, 6013 yards, S.S.S. 70
† Welcome on WD but booking is essential.
Ⅰ WD £40; including coffee high tea and light snacks.
⟲ Welcome Wed only; catering by

arrangement; day tickets from £50; from £35.
🍽 Full clubhouse facilities available.
🛏 The Redhurst hotel.

9B 150 **Whiting Bay**
Golf Course Rd, Whiting Bay, Isle of Arran, KA27 8QT
☎ 01770 700487
8 miles S of Brodick.
Undulating heathland course.
Founded 1895
18 holes, 4405 yards, S.S.S. 63
† Welcome.
⌐ WD £13; WE £17; after 4pm all rounds are £10.
⌐ Welcome by prior arrangement with Sec; discounts available for groups of 10 or more; from £13.
🍽 Clubhouse catering and bar facilities.
🛏 Cameronia; Grange House; Kiscadale; Royal.

9B 151 **Williamwood**
Clarkston Rd, Netherlee, Glasgow, G44 3YR
📧 secretary@ williamwoodgc.fsnet.co.uk
☎ 0141 6371783, Fax 5710166

5 miles S of Glasgow.
Wooded parkland course.
Founded 1906
Designed by James Braid
18 holes, 5878 yards, S.S.S. 69
⌡ Practice area.
† Welcome.
⌐ WD £27, day pass £37.
⌐ Welcome WD by arrangement; catering by arrangement; terms on application.
🍽 Full clubhouse facilities available.
🛏 Redhurst Clarkston; The Tinto Firs, Giffnock.

9B 152 **Windyhill**
Baljaffray Rd, Bearsden, Glasgow, G61 4QQ
🖥 www.windyhill.co.uk
☎ 01419422349, Fax 9425874, Pro 9427157, Sec 9422349
1 mile N of Bearsden.
Parkland course.
Pro Chris Duffy; Founded 1908
Designed by James Braid
18 holes, 6254 yards, S.S.S. 70
⌡ Practice area.
† Welcome WD.
⌐ WD £20.
⌐ Welcome by prior arrangement;

discounts available for larger groups; catering available by arrangement; £20.
🍽 Full bar and restaurant facilities.
🛏 Jury's Pond Hotel Glasgow, Travel Lodge.

9B 153 **Wishaw**
55 Clelend Road, Lower Main Street, Wishaw, Lanarkshire, ML2 7PH
📧 craig.innes@virgin.net
☎ 01698 372869, Fax 9425874, Pro 9427157, Sec 520421, Rest/Bar 860688
Course is 15 miles SE of Glasgow; five miles from the M74 Motherwell Junction.
Parkland course.
Pro Stuard Adair; Founded 1897
Designed by James Braid
18 holes, 6100 yards, S.S.S. 69
⌡ Practice range available.
† Welcome WD until 4pm; not Sat and by prior arrangement Sun.
⌐ Prices on application.
⌐ Welcome WD; Sun only by special arrangement; day's golf; catering packages by prior arrangement.
🍽 Full clubhouse facilities available.
🛏 Commercial Hotel.

9C

Tayside, Central Region, Fife

If Ayrshire is heavenly then Fife is sacred ground. On that note there has been a great deal of blaspheming about St Andrews in recent years along the lines that modern equipment has emasculated it and the longer players can just blast left most of the way round. There is something in this, but should anyone be lucky or persuasive enough to get a start time on the Old Course after dawn, they will hardly turn it down.

Fortified by finnan-haddock, Henry Longhurst used to regard the journey to St Andrews as the most romantic rail journey in the world. But these days Leuchars is as far as you can get. Longhurst wrote an article beseeching Barbara Castle not to close St Andrews station. It ended "You can't let them do it, Barbara. You can't, really," until he was forced to add the postscript, "Sadly, and as ultimate proof that nothing is sacred in this world, she did."

Nicklaus said that there were three types of Open, one in Scotland, one in England and one at St Andrews. However much technology has changed it, the Old Course is still sacred ground, but the New, the Dukes, the Eden and the Jubilee all also take a fair bit of playing.

A fifteen-minute drive along the coast, a new course has sprung up called Kingsbarns. The British tried to build one there, but failed, so the Americans supplied the necessary initiative instead. They have made a brilliant job of it. There are some breathtaking holes along the coast, some wicked greens, an impressive clubhouse and an absence of exclusivity. All in all it must be the best new course in Britain.

Further round the coast, Leven and Lundin links are the sort of neighbours we would all like to have and Crail is an old friend of many. To the north of St Andrews, Scotscraig is a brutally hard course with some ferocious bunkers.

Inland Ladybank is a much more soothing proposition amidst the gorse and pines, as is Buchanan Castle, over towards Glasgow. Buchanan Castle was the home to the belligerent Ryder Cup golfer Eric Brown who won all his singles matches in the fifties while everyone around him was failing. Typically he described another course in the region as "a bloody goat track, but a sporty one."

The course was Crieff and from it you can see Gleneagles where the 2014 Ryder Cup will be played. It is a beautiful spot amidst the Grampians and the Trossachs and has three courses, the Kings, the Queens and the Monarch.

Those with a taste for scenery and elevated tees will enjoy Gleneagles.

Dundee's leading course is probably Downfield. Blairgowrie, Glenbervie, King James VI and Montrose are all worth noting in the region, but it is Montrose's neighbour to the south that bestrides them like a colossus. Plonked on a harsh piece of land open to the weather Carnoustie welcomes visitors and then spends several hours berating them about the quality of their golf.

The final three holes must represent one of the most daunting finishes in the world. The 16th is 230 yards to a small heavily bunkered green, the 17th fairway is an island amidst the twists of the Barry Burn and the eighteenth is mon dieu et sacre bleu. Since his collapse at the 1999 Open, Jean van de Velde has returned to play the hole in a mere five strokes – with a putter.

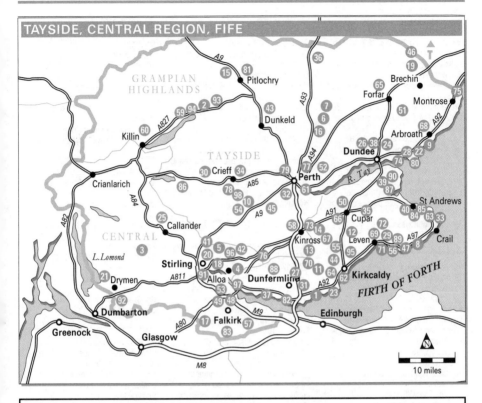

TAYSIDE, CENTRAL REGION, FIFE

KEY		21	Buchanan Castle	40	Duke's Course (St	60	Killin	81	Pitlochry
1	Aberdour	22	Buddon Links		Andrews)	61	King James VI	82	Pitreavie (Dunfermline)
2	Aberfeldy	23	Burntisland	41	Dunblane New	62	Kinghorn	83	Polmont
3	Aberfoyle	24	Caird Park	42	Dunfermline	63	Kingsbarn Links	84	St Andrews
4	Alloa	25	Callander	43	Dunkeld & Birnam	64	Kirkcaldy	85	St Andrews Bay
5	Alva	26	Camperdown	44	Dunnikier Park	65	Kirriemuir	86	St Fillans
6	Alyth		(Municipal)	45	Dunning	66	Ladybank	87	St Michaels
7	Alyth Strathmore	27	Canmore	46	Edzell	67	Leslie	88	Saline
8	Anstruther	28	Carnoustie Golf Links	47	Elie Sports Club	68	Letham Grange	89	Scoonie
9	Arbroath	29	Charleton	48	Falkirk	69	Leven	90	Scotscraig
10	Auchterarder	30	Comrie	49	Falkirk Tryst	70	Lochgelly	91	Stirling
11	Auchterderran	31	Cowdenbeath	50	Falkland	71	Lundin	92	Strathendrick
12	Balbirnie Park	32	Craigie Hill	51	Forfar	72	Lundin Ladies	93	Strathtay
13	Ballingry	33	Crail Golfing Society	52	Glenalmond	73	Milnathort	94	Taymouth Castle
14	Bishopshire	34	Crieff	53	Glenbervie	74	Monifieth	95	Thornton
15	Blair Atholl	35	Cupar	54	Gleneagles Hotel	75	Montrose Links Trust	96	Tillicoultry
16	Blairgowrie	36	Dalmunzie	55	Glenrothes	76	Muckhart	97	Tulliallan
17	Bonnybridge	37	Dollar	56	Golf House	77	Murrayshall	98	Whitemoss
18	Braehead	38	Downfield	57	Grangemouth	78	Muthill		
19	Brechin	39	Drumoig Hotel and	58	Green Hotel	79	North Inch		
20	Bridge of Allan		Golf Course	59	Kenmore Golf Course	80	Panmure		

Balbirnie Park Golf Club

A fine example of the best in traditional parkland design, with a par of 71,
6200 yards - a challenge for golfers of all abilities.

Balbirnie Park, Markinch, by Glenrothes, Fife KY7 6NE
Tel: **01592 612095**   Fax: **01592 612383**

9C 1 Aberdour
Seaside Place, Aberdour, Fife, KY3 0TX
☎ 01383 860688, Fax 860050, Pro
860256, Sec 860080
In Aberdour village on coast route to
Burntisland.
Parkland/seaside course with views of
River Forth.
Pro Gordon McCallum; Founded 1896
Designed by Peter Robertson & Joe
Anderson
18 holes, 5460 yards, S.S.S. 66
✝ Welcome by prior arrangement.
[Mon-Sat: £17; Sun: £24.
✎ Welcome except Sat by prior
arrangement; day ticket from £28;
catering by arrangement with the
clubmaster; maximum parties of 24 on
Sun; from £17.
⬤ Full clubhouse catering.
⌂ Woodside.

9C 2 Aberfeldy
Taybridge Rd, Aberfeldy, Perthshire,
PH15 2BH
☎ 01887 820535
Follow signs from A9 at Ballinluig
through the centre of Aberfeldy for
Weem and first right at Wades Bridge.
Parkland course.
Founded 1895
Designed by Souters
18 holes, 5283 yards, S.S.S. 66
✝ Welcome.
[WD £14; WE £14.
✎ Welcome by prior arrangement;
catering by arrangement; terms on
application.
⬤ Full facilities.
⌂ Palace; Crown, both Aberfeldy.

9C 3 Aberfoyle
Braeval, Aberfoyle, Stirlingshire, FK8
3UY
☎ 01877 382493, Sec 382638
1.5 miles from Aberfoyle on the main
Stirling road.
Parkland course.
Founded 1890
Designed by James Braid
18 holes, 5218 yards, S.S.S. 66
✝ Welcome; some restrictions at WE.
[Terms on application.
✎ Welcome by prior arrangement;
restrictions on numbers; from £12.
⬤ Full clubhouse facilities.
⌂ Rob Roy Motor Inn; Forth Inn.

9C 4 Alloa
Schawpark, Sauchie,
Clackmannanshire, FK10 3AX

▣ alloagolf@
schawpark.fsbusiness.co.uk
☎ 01259 722745
On the A908 1 mile N of Alloa; 8 miles
E of Stirling.
Undulating parkland course.
Pro Bill Bennett; Founded 1891
Designed by James Braid
18 holes, 6229 yards, S.S.S. 71
[2 practice areas.
✝ Welcome.
[Prices on application.
✎ Welcome WD by arrangement;
catering available by prior arrangement;
snooker room; from £23.
⬤ Full clubhouse facilities.
⌂ Harviestoun; Royal Oak; Dunmar
House; Claremont Lodge.

9C 5 Alva
Beauclerc St, Alva, Clackmannanshire,
FK12 5LH
☎ 01259 760431
Course is on the A91 Stirling to St
Andrews road; follow signs for Alva
Glen as the club car park is at
entrance to Glen Hillside.
Sloping fairways/plateau greens.
Founded 1901
9 holes, 4846 yards, S.S.S. 64
✝ Welcome.
[Terms on application.
✎ Welcome by prior arrangement;
facilities limited; no pro shop no
equipment for hire; terms on application.
⬤ Bar snacks only; clubhouse open for
7pm each night and from noon at WE.
⌂ Alva Glen.

9C 6 Alyth
Pitcrocknie, Alyth, Perthshire, PH11 8HF
☎ 01828 632668, Fax 633491,
Pro 632411, Sec 632268
Course is one mile SE of Alyth on the
B954.
Parkland course with views over Angus
& Perthshire.
Pro Tom Melville; Founded 1894
18 holes, 6205 yards, S.S.S. 71
✝ Welcome by prior arrangement.
[WD £22; WE £33.
✎ Welcome by prior arrangement;
catering available by arrangement; Pro
can assist with golf clinics; day and
weekly tickets; from £22.
⬤ Full clubhouse facilities.
⌂ Lands of Loyal; Alyth; Lossett.

9C 7 Alyth Strathmore
Leroch, Alyth, Perthshire, PH11 8NZ
⬚ www.strathmoregolf.com
▣ enquiries@strathmoregolf.com

☎ 01828 633322
Course is five miles E of Blairgowie on
the A926.
Founded 1996
18 holes, 6454 yards, S.S.S. 72
[10 floodlit bays and practice area.
✝ Welcome; pay and play.
[Terms on application.
✎ Welcome; corporate days
available.
⬤ Full clubhouse facilities.
⌂ Lands of Loyal; Alyth; Lossett.

9C 8 Anstruther   ✆
Marsfield, Shore Rd, Anstruther, Fife,
KY10 3DZ
☎ 01333 310956, Fax 312283,
Sec 312283
Turn off main road at Craw's Nest Hotel.
Seaside course.
Founded 1890
9 holes, 4588 yards, S.S.S. 63
✝ Welcome.
[WD £12; WE £15.
✎ None.
⬤ Snacks and lunches.
⌂ Craw's Nest.

9C 9 Arbroath
Elliot, Arbroath, Angus, DD11 2PE
☎ 01241 872069, Pro 875837
Take A92 from Dundee N and turn right
2 miles before Arbroath.
Seaside links course.
Pro Lindsay Ewart; Founded 1903
Designed by James Braid
18 holes, 5856 yards, S.S.S. 69
✝ Welcome; not before 9.30am WE.
[WD £18; WE £24.
✎ Welcome by prior arrangement;
catering by arrangement; terms on
application.
⬤ Full clubhouse facilities.
⌂ Seaforth; Cliffburn; Viewfield.

9C 10 Auchterarder
Orchil Rd, Auchterarder, Perthshire,
PH3 1LS
☎ 01764 662804, Fax 662804,
Pro 663711
Course is off the A9 next to Gleneagles
Hotel.
Wooded heathland course.
Pro Gavin Baxter; Founded 1892
Designed by Bernard Sayers
18 holes, 5775 yards, S.S.S. 68
✝ Welcome by prior arrangement or
with a member.
[POA.
✎ Welcome by prior arrangement
with Sec; catering and golf packages
by arrangement.

|●| Full catering and bar facilities available.
↝ Cairn Lodge; Colliearn House; Duchally.

9C 11 Auchterderran
Woodend Rd, Cardenden, Fife, KY5 0NH
☎ 01592 721579
Course is on the main Lochgelly to Glenrothes road at the N end of Cardenden.
Parkland course.
Founded 1904
9 holes, 5250 yards, S.S.S. 66
† Welcome, but prior booking advisable.
⌞ From £9.
⌁ Welcome by arrangement; catering by prior arrangement; from £9.
|●| Bar and snacks facilities available; meals cooked to order.
↝ Bowhill; Central.

9C 12 Balbirnie Park
Markinch, Glenrothes, Fife, KY7 6NR
▤ craigfdonnerley@aol.com
☎ 01592 612095, Fax 612383, Pro 752006, Sec 752006
2 miles E of Glenrothes off A92 on A911.
Scenic parkland course.
Pro Craig Donnerley; Founded 1983
18 holes, 6210 yards, S.S.S. 70
✐ Practice area.
† Welcome by arrangement.
⌞ WD £27; WE £33.
⌁ Welcome by prior arrangement; catering packages by arrangement; terms on application.
|●| Full clubhouse; all-day catering.
↝ Balbirnie House.

9C 13 Ballingry
Lochore Meadows Country Park, Crosshill, By Lochgelly, Ballingry, Fife, KY5 8BA
▤ frs@lmcp.fsnet.co.uk
☎ 01592 414300
W of M90 between Lochgelly and Ballingry.
Parkland course.
Founded 1981
9 holes, 6484 yards, S.S.S. 71
† Welcome.
⌞ WD £8.60 (18) £5.40 (9); WE £11.20 (18) £7.60 (9).
⌁ Welcome by prior arrangement; angling, wind-surfing; terms on application.
|●| Catering in café in park centre.
↝ Navitie House.

9C 14 Bishopshire
Kinnesswood by Kinross, Tayside, Tayside, KY13
☎ 01592 780203
Course is three miles E of Kinross off the M90.
Upland course.
Founded 1903
Designed by W. Park
10 holes, 4784 yards, S.S.S. 64
† Welcome.
⌞ Terms on application.
⌁ Limited by arrangement; catering by arrangement or at local hotels; from £6.
|●| Available at the Lomond Hotel 400 yards away.
↝ Lomond; Scotlandwell Inn.

9C 15 Blair Atholl
Blair Atholl, Perthshire, PH18 5TG
☎ 01796 481407, Fax 481751
Course is on the A9 five miles N of Pitlochry.
Parkland course.
Founded 1896
9 holes, 5710 yards, S.S.S. 68
† Welcome except competition days.
⌞ WD £15; WE £17.
⌁ Welcome by prior arrangement; catering by arrangement; from £13.
|●| Clubhouse facilities.
↝ Atholl Arms; Tilt.

9C 16 Blairgowrie
Perthshire, PH10 6LG
⊞ www.blairgowrie-golf.co.uk
▤ admin@blairgowrie-golf.co.uk
☎ 01250 872622, Fax 875451, Pro 873116, Sec 872622
1 mile S of Blairgowrie off the A93; 15 miles N of Perth.
Heathland course with pine, silver birch, bloom.
Pro Charles Dernie
Designed by Thomas/Alliss
Landsdown: 18 holes, 6590 yards, S.S.S. 73, Rosemount: 18 holes, 6802 yards, S.S.S. 74
† Welcome by prior arrangement; some restrictions apply Wed, Fri and WE.
⌞ Prices on application.
⌁ Welcome with same restrictions as visitors; catering packages by arrangement; also 9-hole Wee course, 2327 yards, par 32, designed by Old Tom Morris in 1889; terms on application.
|●| Full clubhouse facilities.
↝ Kinloch House; Moorfield House; Altamount House; Angus; Royal.

9C 17 Bonnybridge
Larbert Rd, Bonnybridge, Stirlingshire, FK4 1NY
☎ 01324 812822
Course is on the B816 three miles W of Falkirk.
Undulating moorland course.
Founded 1925
9 holes, 6128 yards, S.S.S. 70
† Welcome with a member or by letter of introduction.
⌞ WD £16; WE £16.
⌁ None.
|●| Meals at WE; bar facilities; limited in winter.
↝ Royal.

9C 18 Braehead
Cambus, by Alloa, Clackmannanshire, FK10 2NT
⊞ www.only-golf.co.uk
☎ 01259 722078, Fax 214070, Pro 722078, Sec 725766, Rest/Bar 725766
On A907 Stirling-Alloa Road about 1.5 miles W of Alloa.
Parkland course.
Founded 1891
18 holes, 6086 yards, S.S.S. 69
✐ Practice range.
† Everyone welcome.
⌞ WD £18; WE £24. summer rate WD £10: WE £12 winter rate, discounts for group bookings.
⌁ Welcome all week by prior arrangement; catering packages by arrangement; from £24 per day.
|●| Full catering facilities.
↝ Royal Oak; Dunmar House.

9C 19 Brechin Golf and Squash Club ♛
Trinity, by Brechin, Angus, DD9 7PD
☎ 01356 622383, Pro 625270
1 mile outside Brechin on the A90 road to Aberdeen.
Rolling parkland course.
Pro Stephen Rennie; Founded 1893
18 holes, 6096 yards, S.S.S. 70
✐ Practice range.
† Welcome; restrictions Sat and Sun 10am-12 noon & 2.30pm-4.30pm.
⌞ WD £15; WE £20.
⌁ Welcome WD by prior arrangement; packages for eight or more include all catering and 2 rounds of golf; £26.
|●| Full clubhouse facilities.
↝ Northern Hotel.

9C 20 Bridge of Allan
Sunnlaw, Bridge of Allan, Stirlingshire
☎ 01786 832332

3 miles N of Stirling.
Undulating course; one of toughest par 3s in Scotland.
Founded 1895
Designed by Old Tom Morris
9 holes, 5120 yards, S.S.S. 65
♦ Welcome WD and Sun.
[WD on application.
☞ By prior arrangement; terms on application.
|●| Bar facilities.
⌁ Royal.

9C 21 Buchanan Castle

Drymen, Glasgow, G63 0HY
📧 buchanancastle@sol.co.uk
☎ 01360 660307, Fax 660993,
Pro 660330, Sec 660307,
Rest/Bar 660369
Course is on the A811 Glasgow to Aberfoyle road; entrance just before Drymen.
Secluded parkland course with stunning views.
Pro Keith Baxter; Founded 1936
Designed by James Braid
18 holes, 6059 yards, S.S.S. 69
/ Practice range.
♦ Welcome by arrangement.
[WD £30; WE £30.
☞ Welcome Thurs and Fri by prior arrangement; full day's golf £40; catering by arrangement with Club master; from £30.
|●| Full clubhouse facilities.
⌁ Buchanan Arms; Winnock Hotel.

9C 22 Buddon Links

Links Parade, Carnoustie Angus, Tayside, DD7 7JE
🖳 www.carnoustiegolflinks.co.uk
☎ 01241 853249, Fax 852720,
Pro 411999, Sec 853789
10 miles E of Dundee on A92.
Links course.
Pro Lee Vannett
Designed by Alan Robertson, Old Tom Morris
18 holes, 6941 yards, S.S.S. 73
/ Nets.
♦ Welcome; some weekend restrictions.
[£80.
☞ By arrangement.
|●| Contact local clubs.

9C 23 Burntisland

Burntisland, Fife, KY3 9LQ
☎ 01592 873247, Fax 874093,
Pro 873116
Course is on the B923 0.5 miles E of Burntisland.

Parkland course.
Pro Paul Wytrazek; Founded 1897
Designed by J Braid
18 holes, 5965 yards, S.S.S. 70
♦ Welcome except competition days.
[WD £17; WE £25; concessions apply for juniors.
☞ Welcome except on comp days; contact manager for starting times; £5 per head deposit; catering packages by arrangement; terms on application.
|●| Full clubhouse bar and catering: facilities 8am-8pm.
⌁ Inchview; Kingswood.

9C 24 Caird Park

Mains Loan, Dundee, Tayside, DD4 9BX
☎ 01382 453606, Sec 438871
Course is reached via Kingsway to the NE of the town.
Parkland course.
Pro Jack Black; Founded 1926
18 holes, 6352 yards, S.S.S. 70
♦ Public.
[Available on request.
☞ Book through Dundee City Council leisure and parks dept; terms on application.
|●| By prior arrangement; bar and lounge facilities.
⌁ Swallow; Kingsway.

9C 25 Callander

Aveland Rd, Callander, Perthshire, FK17 8EN
☎ 01877 330090, Fax 330062,
Pro 330975
Course is off the A84 at the E end of Callander.
Parkland course.
Pro Allen Martin; Founded 1890
Designed by Tom Morris (1890); Redesigned by W Fernie
18 holes, 5151 yards, S.S.S. 66
/ Small practice range.
♦ Welcome by prior arrangement.
[POA.
☞ Welcome by prior arrangement; catering packages by arrangement; from £26 for a day ticket.
|●| Full catering facilities.
⌁ Abbotsford Lodge; Myrtle Inn; Dreadnought.

9C 26 Camperdown (Municipal)

Camperdown Park, Dundee, Tayside, DD2 4TF
☎ 01382 623398
At Kingsway Junction of the Coupar-Angus Road.
Parkland/wooded course.

Pro Roddy Brown; Founded 1959
Designed by Eric Brown
18 holes, 6561 yards, S.S.S. 72
♦ Welcome; pay and play.
[WD £15; WE £15.
☞ Welcome by prior arrangement; on application; from £15.
|●| Clubhouse facilities.
⌁ The Swallow. Travel Lodge (directly outside).

9C 27 Canmore

Venturefair Ave, Dunfermline, Fife, KY12 0PE
☎ 01383 724969
Course is on the A823 one mile N of Dunfermline.
Undulating parkland course.
Pro David Gemmel; Founded 1897
18 holes, 5432 yards, S.S.S. 66
♦ Welcome WD; Sat after 4pm; not on competition days.
[WD £15 and £20 for a day ticket; WE £20 and £30 for a day ticket.
☞ Welcome by prior arrangement; catering and day rates by arrangement; from £12.
|●| Full clubhouse facilities.
⌁ Several in Dunfermline.

9C 28 Carnoustie Golf Links

Links Parade, Carnoustie, Angus, DD7 7JE
🖳 www.carnoustiegolflinks.co.uk
📧 administrator@carnoustiegolflinks.co.uk
☎ 01241 853789, Fax 852720,
Pro 853789, Sec 853789
Course is on the A930 12 miles NE of Dundee.
Open Championship links.
Pro Lee Vannet; Founded 1842
Designed by A Robertson; Tom Morris; James Braid
Three 18-hole courses, 6941 yards, S.S.S. 75
♦ Welcome by prior arrangement; WE restrictions.
[WD up to £80; WE up to £80. In April only £40 WD and WE.
☞ Welcome by prior arrangement; catering by arrangement; also Burnside course: 18 holes 6020 yards; £25 per round. Buddon links: 18 holes, 5420 yards; £20 per round.
|●| Full clubhouse facilities.

9C 29 Charleton

Colinsburgh, Fife, KY9 1HG
☎ 01333 340505, Fax 340583
0.5 miles W of Colinsburgh on B942.
Parklands course.

CARNOUSTIE GOLF LINKS

LINKS PARADE, CARNOUSTIE DD7 7JE, ANGUS

CHAMPIONSHIP COURSE: This world-renowned links course is famous for it's tough finish. True certainly, but each and every hole is capable of asking questions even professional golfers may not have answers to.
One thing is for certain, a birdie or even a par here will give you a great deal of satisfaction on a course Ernie Els described as one of the top three links courses in the world.

THE BURNSIDE: This is a shorter but tighter test of golf. With small greens, five short holes and a par four 17th that would not be out of place on any Championship venue, this is a course that many golfers would love to have as their home one.

BUDDON LINKS: This is a shorter alternative to the other two courses. Unlike them the Barry Burn isn't much of a threat here, instead two ponds which come into play at four holes, provide the interest – and the danger! An ideal course to play with either of the other two to make a perfect few days days golfing.

VISITORS WELCOME. Green Fees: Championship £80, Burnside £25, Buddon £20. SPECIAL APRIL/MAY OFFERS. Phone for details.
Telephone: 01241 853789; Fax: 01241 852720. e-mail: administrator@carnoustiegolflinks.co.uk www.carnoustiegolflinks.co.uk

---

Pro Andy Huddon; Founded 1994
Designed by Johnny Salversson
18 holes, 6152 yards, S.S.S. 70
⚐ 12 bays.
† Welcome; pay and play course.
⚑ WD £20; WE £24; day tickets. WD £32.00; WD £38.00.
⚡ Rates for groups of 15 or more.
🍴 Restaurant; bar.
⚓ Victoria hotel.

9C 30 **Comrie**
Laggan Braes, Comrie, Perthshire, PH6 2LR
☎ 01764 670055
On A85 7 miles W of Crieff; course signposted from village.
Founded 1891
9 holes, 6040 yards, S.S.S. 70
† Welcome; restrictions after 4.30pm Mon and Tues.
⚑ WD details on application.
⚡ Welcome by arrangement; catering by arrangement; from £10.
🍴 Light refreshments; coffee; teas.
⚓ Royal; Comrie; Mossgiel GH; Langower GH.

9C 31 **Cowdenbeath**
Seco Place, Cowdenbeath, Nr Dunfermline, Fife, KY4 8PD
☎ 01383 511918, Sec 513709
6 miles E of Dunfermline.
Parkland course.
Founded 1990/1998
18 holes, S.S.S. 71
⚐ Practice range.
† Welcome.
⚑ WD £7; WE £8.
⚡ Welcome by arrangement; catering by prior arrangement; from £7.
🍴 Bar and snacks available.
⚓ Halfway House; Kingseat.

9C 32 **Craigie Hill** ☎
Cherrybank, Perth, Perthshire,

PH2 0NE
📧 chgc@fairieswell.freeserve.co.uk
☎ 01738 624377, Pro 622644
1 mile W of Perth with easy access from A9 and M90.
Hilly course.
Pro Ian Muir; Founded 1909
Designed by W Ferne and J Anderson
18 holes, 5386 yards, S.S.S. 67
† Welcome; bookings required on Sun.
⚑ Terms on application.
⚡ Welcome WD and some Sun by prior arrangement; catering by arrangement; from £15.
🍴 Full facilities. Not Mon.
⚓ Lovat.

9C 33 **Crail Golfing Society**
Balcomie Clubhouse, Fifeness, Crail, KY10 3XN
🖳 www.golfagent.com/clubsites/criel
📧 crialgolfs@aol.com
☎ 01333 450686, Fax 450416, Pro 450960, Sec 451414, Rest/Bar 450278
Course is 11 miles SE of St Andrews on the A917. Seventh oldest club in world; moved from Sauchope in 1895.
Links course
Pro Graeme Lennie; Founded 1786/1895
Designed by Tom Morris
† Welcome.
⚑ WD £30; WE £35.
⚡ Full catering facilities.
🍴 Full service with views over course and N Sea.
⚓ Club can supply detailed list.

9C 34 **Crieff** ☎
Perth Rd, Crieff, Perthshire, PH7 3LR
☎ 01764 652397, Fax 653803, Pro 652909
Course is on the A85 on the E edge of Crieff.
Parkland ferntower course.
Pro David Murchie; Founded 1891

Designed by Old Tom Morris/R Simpson (1914)/J Braid (1924)/J Stark & J Freeman (1980)
27 holes, 6450 yards, S.S.S. 72
† Welcome.
⚑ WD from £23; WE from £30. June, July, August, Sept WD £26, WE £35.
⚡ Welcome; catering by arrangement; from £20.
🍴 Full clubhouse facilities.
⚓ Crieff Hydro; Murray Park; Foulford Inn.

9C 35 **Cupar** ☎
Hilltarvit, Cupar, KY15 5JT
📧 secretraty@cupargolfclubfreeserve.co.uk
☎ 01334 653549, Fax 653549
25 miles on Ceres Rd; SE outskirts of Cupar; 9 miles from St Andrews.
National Trust parkland course; oldest 9-hole course in country.
Founded 1855
Designed by Alan Robertson
9 holes, 5074 yards, S.S.S. 65
† Welcome except Sat.
⚑ WD £15; WE £15.
⚡ Welcome; discounts available; private room; catering by arrangement; from £12.
🍴 Snacks and meals.
⚓ Eden House.

9C 36 **Dalmunzie**
Spittal of Glenshee, Blairgowrie, Perthshire, PH10 7QG
🖳 www.welcome.to/dalmunzie
📧 dalmunzie@aol.com
☎ 01250 885226, Fax 885226, Rest/Bar 885224
On A93 Blairgowrie to Braemar Rd; 18 miles N of Blairgowrie.
Hilly upland course.
Founded 1922
Designed by Alister MacKenzie
9 holes, 4070 yards, S.S.S. 60
† Everyone welcome.

⌊ WD £10; WE £10.
⟳ Welcome by arrangement; discounts of 10 per cent for more than 10 on WD; terms available on application.
▮◉▮ Facilities in hotel.
⌂ Dalmunzie House.

9C 37 **Dollar**
Brewlands House, Dollar, Clackmannanshire, FK14 7EA
☎ 01259 742400
In Dollar signposted 0.5 miles off A91. Hillside course; 2nd Brae is 97 yards.
Founded 1890
Designed by Ben Sayers
18 holes, 5242 yards, S.S.S. 66
♦ Welcome except competition days.
⌊ WD £12; WE £20.
⟳ Welcome by prior arrangement; packages (WD £30 WE £35) include 36 holes of golf and full day's catering; maximum 36.
▮◉▮ Full clubhouse facilities.
⌂ Castle Campbell Hotel.

9C 38 **Downfield**
Turnberry Ave, Dundee, Tayside, DD2 3QP
✉ downfieldgc@aol.com
☎ 01382 825595, Fax 813111, Pro 889246
Follow Kingsway to A923; right into Faraday St then first left to Harrison Road; left at Dalmahoy Drive and sharp left to club.
Championship parkland course; Qualifying course for 1999 Open.
Pro Kenny Hutton; Founded 1932
Designed by CK Cotton
18 holes, 6803 yards, S.S.S. 73
♦ Welcome WD; restrictions at WE.
⌊ Terms on application.
⟳ Welcome by arrangement; special packages available for golf and catering; terms on application.
▮◉▮ Full clubhouse facilities.
⌂ Gourdie Croft; Swallow both Dundee; Invercarse Hotel.

9C 39 **Drumoig Hotel and Golf Course**
Leuchars, St Andrews, Fife, KY16 0BE
♨ www.drumoigleisure.com
✉ drumoig@sol.co.uk
☎ 01382 541800, Fax 542211
From Forth Rd bridge exit M90 at Junction 2A Follow A92 to Glenrothes then remain on this road following signs for Tay Bridge when you reach Forgan roundabout go right onto the St Andrews road. Drumoig is down the hill

on the left hand side.
Parkland course.
Founded 1996
18 holes, 6376 yards, S.S.S. 70
⌿ Onsite practice facility.
♦ Welcome all week.
⌊ WD £28; WE £33.
⟳ Special rates for 8 or more.
▮◉▮ Full facilities.

9C 40 **The Duke's Course** ♘
(St Andrews)
St Andrews, Fife, Scotland, KY16 9SP
♨ www.oldcoursehotel.co.uk
☎ 01334 474371
Five minutes drive from the centre of St Andrews.
Classic Scottish parkland course.
Founded 1995
Designed by Peter Thomson
18 holes, 7271 yards, S.S.S. 75
⌿ 10 bays and practice area.
♦ Welcome.
⌊ £50 – £55.
⟳ Welcome any time.
▮◉▮ Clubhouse facilities include bar restaurant and Boardroom for private dining and meetings.
⌂ Old Course Hotel Golf Resort & Spa.

9C 41 **Dunblane New**
Perth Rd, Dunblane, Stirlingshire, FK15 0LJ
☎ 01786 823711
Course is six miles N of Stirling on the old A9 at the Fourways roundabout.
Parkland course.
Pro Bob Jamieson; Founded 1923
18 holes, 5957 yards, S.S.S. 69
♦ Welcome WD; restrictions at WE.
⌊ Terms on application.
⟳ Welcome Mon, Thurs and Fri by prior arrangement; catering packages by arrangement; tennis and squash adjacent; terms available on application.
▮◉▮ Full clubhouse facilities.
⌂ Dunblane Hydro; Stirling Arms.

9C 42 **Dunfermline**
Pitfirrane, Crossford, Dunfermline, Fife, KY12 8QW
☎ 01383 723534
On S of A994 2 miles W of Dunfermline on the road to the Kincardine Bridge.
Parkland course.
Pro Steven Craig; Founded 1887
Designed by JR Stutt & Sons
18 holes, 6126 yards, S.S.S. 70
♦ Welcome WD between 10am-12noon and 2pm-4pm; Sun but not Sat.

⌊ WD from £20; WE from £25.
⟳ Welcome WD by arrangement; day ticket WD from £30; Sun from £35; catering by arrangement; snooker; from £20.
▮◉▮ Bar and restaurant facilities.
⌂ Keavil; Pitfirran Arms; The Maltings.

9C 43 **Dunkeld & Birnam**
Fungarth, Dunkeld, Perthshire, PH8 0HU
☎ 01350 727524, Fax 728660
Course is on the A923 one mile N of Dunkeld.
Heathland course with panoramic views.
Founded 1892
9 holes, 5322 yards, S.S.S. 67
♦ Welcome.
⌊ WD £11; WE £16.
⟳ Welcome by prior arrangement; catering packages by prior arrangement; from £11.
▮◉▮ Full bar and catering facilities.
⌂ Royal Dunkeld; Stakis Dunkeld House Resort.

9C 44 **Dunnikier Park**
Dunnikier Way, Kirkcaldy, Fife, KY1 3LP
☎ 01592 261599
Leave A92 at Kirkcaldy West roundabout and join B981 for 1 mile.
Parkland course.
Pro Gregor Whyte; Founded 1963
Designed by R Stutt
18 holes, 6601 yards, S.S.S. 72
♦ Welcome; invitation needed for clubhouse.
⌊ Terms on application.
⟳ Welcome by prior arrangement with Sec; catering packages by arrangement; terms on application.
▮◉▮ Full catering facilities.
⌂ Dunnikier House; Dean Park.

9C 45 **Dunning**
Rollo Park, Dunning, Perth, PH2 0RG
☎ 01764 684747, Sec 684212
Off A9 9 miles SW of Perth.
Parkland course.
Founded 1952
9 holes, 4836 yards, S.S.S. 63
♦ Welcome except on WE.
⌊ WD £14 £16 WE.
⟳ Welcome WD and most Sun; WD price £14; from £10.
▮◉▮ Soft and hot drinks in clubhouse; meals by prior application; also in village hotels.
⌂ Kirks Hotel and Dunham Hotel.

9C 46 Edzell

High St, Edzell, by Brechin, Angus,
DD9 7HT
✉ secretary@
edzellgolfclub.demon.co.uk
☎ 01356 648235, Fax 648094,
Pro 648462, Sec 647283
Take B996 off the A90 at the N end of
the Brechin by-pass.
Parkland course.
Pro Alastair Webster; Founded 1895
Designed by Bob Simpson
Practice range, driving range, 9
bays, floodlight.
Welcome.
WD £24; WE £30.
Welcome; some restrictions; by
prior arrangement with Sec; catering
by prior arrangement; driving range;
terms available on application.
Full clubhouse bar and restaurant
facilities.
Glenesk; Panmure both Edzell.

9C 47 Elie Sports Club

Elie, Fife, KY9 1AS
☎ 01333 330955, Sec 330508,
Rest/Bar 331132
Course is on the A917 10 miles S of St
Andrews.
Seaside course.
Pro Robin Wilson; Founded 1900
Designed by James Baird
9 holes, 4160 yards, S.S.S. 64
Six covered bays & six outdoor
bays.
Welcome.
Day ticket WD £10; WE £10.
Welcome by prior arrangement;
packages available; terms on
application.
Clubhouse facilities.
Old Manor; Lundin Links; Victoria
Hotel.

9C 48 Falkirk

136 Stirling Rd, Camelon, FK2 7YP
☎ 01324 611061, Fax 639573
On A9 1.5 miles N of Falkirk.
Parkland course.
Founded 1922
Designed by James Braid
18 holes, 6230 yards, S.S.S. 70
Welcome WD; not Sat.
WD £15.
Welcome WD and Sun by prior
arrangement; catering by arrangement;
£30.
Full clubhouse facilities.
Stakis Park Hotel.

9C 49 Falkirk Tryst

86 Burnhead Rd, Larbert, FK5 4BD
☎ 01324 562415, Fax 562091,
Pro 562091, Sec 562054
On A88 5 miles N of Falkirk close to
the A9 Falkirk-Stirling road.
Links course.
Pro Steven Dunsmore; Founded 1885
18 holes, 6053 yards, S.S.S. 69
Welcome WD by prior
arrangement.
WD £22.
Welcome WD by prior
arrangement; catering packages by
arrangement; from £22.
Full facilities.
Stakis Park; Airth Castle; Airth;
Plough; Stenhousemuir; Commercial
Larbert.

9C 50 Falkland

The Myre, Falkland, Cupar, Fife, KY15
7AA
☎ 01337 857404
In the Howe of Fife near to Freuchie
and Auchtermuchty.
Parkland course.
Founded 1976
9 holes, 5140 yards, S.S.S. 65
Welcome except on competition
days.
WD £5; WE £8.
Welcome by prior arrangement;
packages available; terms on
application.
Full facilities during summer;
restricted in winter.
Hunting Lodge.

9C 51 Forfar

Cunninghill, Arbroath Rd, Forfar,
Angus, DD8 2RL
✉ forfargolfclub@uku.co.uk
☎ 01307 462120, Fax 468495,
Pro 465683
From A90 to Forfar centre; course is
one mile E of town on the A932
Arbroath road.
Parkland course.
Pro Peter McNiven; Founded 1871
Designed by James Braid
18 holes, 6052 yards, S.S.S. 69
Welcome by prior appointment.
Terms on application.
Welcome between 10am-11.30am
and 2.30pm-4pm except Sat morning;
day tickets available; catering by
arrangement; from £16.
Full clubhouse facilities available.
Chakelbank Forfar.

9C 52 Glenalmond

Glenalmond, Perthshire, Tayside
☎ 01738 880270
Moorland course; part of Glenalmond
Trinity College.
Founded 1923
9 holes, 4801 yards, S.S.S. 68
Members only.
Terms on application.

9C 53 Glenbervie

Stirling Rd, Larbert, Stirlingshire, FK5
4SJ
☎ 01324 562983, Fax 551504,
Pro 562725
M876 Junction 2 left on to A9; club 300
yards.
Parkland course.
Pro John Chilles; Founded 1932
Designed by James Braid
18 holes, 6423 yards, S.S.S. 71
Welcome WD.
WD £32.
Welcome Tues and Thurs by prior
arrangement; packages for 18/36 holes
of golf and catering; from £44.
Full clubhouse facilities.

9C 54 Gleneagles Hotel

Auchterarder, Perthshire, PH3 1NF
☎ 01764 662231
Halfway between Perth and Stirling on
the A9.
Inland links/moorland course.
18 holes, 6471 yards, S.S.S. 69
Practice range for members and
residents only.
Welcome.
WD from £75 and up to £100.
Reduced rates for residents.
Welcome; catering packages by
arrangement; also 9-hole par 3 course;
country club for residents; health spa;
clay target shooting school; equestrian
centre; terms on application.
Full clubhouse bar and grill
facilities; full hotel restaurant
conference centre and bars.
Gleneagles Hotel.

9C 55 Glenrothes

Golf Course Rd, Glenrothes, Fife, KY6
2LA
☎ 01592 758686
Leave M90 at Junction 3; A92 for
Glenrothes; follow signs for Whitehill
Industrial Estate.
Parkland course.
Founded 1958
Designed by JR Stutt
18 holes, 6444 yards, S.S.S. 71
Welcome.

⌶ Available on request.
⌁ Welcome by prior arrangement; catering available by arrangement with steward; groups of 12-40 only; day tickets available; terms on application.
⦿⌶ Full bar and catering facilities.
⌁⌐ Holiday Inn; Rescobie Hotel.

9C 56 Golf House
Elie, Leven, Fife, KY9 1AS
⌷ sandy@
golfhouseclub.freeserve.co.uk
☎ 01333 330327, Fax 330895, Pro 330955, Sec 330301, Rest/Bar 330327
Course is on the A915 12 miles S of St Andrews.
Links course; Ladies club: Elie & Earlsferry GC.
Pro Robin Wilson; Founded 1875
18 holes, 6241 yards, S.S.S. 70
⌶ 3 Driving range bays and practice green.
† Welcome after 10am; ballot in July & August; no Sun visitors May-Sept.
⌶ WD £38, £50 per day; WE £48, £60 per day.
⌁ Welcome except in July and August; day rates.
⦿⌶ Full catering and bar.
⌁⌐ Craw's Nest Anstruther.

9C 57 Grangemouth
Polmonthill, by Falkirk, Stirlingshire, FK2 0YE
☎ 01324 503840, Pro 503040, Rest/Bar 711500
M9 Junction 4; follow signs to Polmonthill.
Parkland course.
Pro Greg McFarlane; Founded 1973
Designed by Sportwork
18 holes, 6314 yards, S.S.S. 70
† Welcome.
⌶ WD £14; WE £17.50.
⌁ Welcome by prior arrangement; catering by prior arrangement; from £14.00.
⦿⌶ Clubhouse facilities available.
⌁⌐ Inchrya; Grange; Lea Park.

9C 58 Green Hotel
2 The Muirs, Kinross, KY13 7AS
⊹ www.green-hotel.com
⌷ golf@green-hotel.com
☎ 01577 863407, Fax 863180, Pro 865125, Sec 863407, Rest/Bar 862237
Course is opposite Green Hotel.
Parkland course.
Pro Stuart Gerraghy; Founded 1991
Designed by Sir David Montgomery
18 holes, 6438 yards, S.S.S. 72
† Welcome.

⌶ WD £27; WE £37.00.
⌁ Welcome; catering in hotel or clubhouse by arrangement.
⦿⌶ Full facilities at hotel and clubhouse.
⌁⌐ Green Hotel.

9C 59 Kenmore Golf Course ☡
Kenmore, Aberfeldy, Perthshire, PH15 2HN
⊹ www.taymouth.co.uk
⌷ info@taymouth.co.uk
☎ 01887 830226, Fax 830211, Pro 830226, Sec 830226, Rest/Bar 830775
On A827 through Kenmore village.
Slightly undulating parkland course.
Pro Alex Marshall; Founded 1992
Designed by R Menzies and Partners
9 holes, 6052 yards, S.S.S. 69
† Welcome.
⌶ WD £13; WE £14.
⌁ Welcome by arrangement; catering packages available; £20.
⦿⌶ Full service.
⌁⌐ Kenmore.

9C 60 Killin ☡
Killin, Perthshire, FK21 8TX
☎ 01567 820312
W end of Loch Tay on A827 Killin to Aberfeldy road.
Parkland course; 5th/14th is The Dyke 96 yards.
Founded 1913
Designed by John Duncan of Stirling
9 holes, 5016 yards, S.S.S. 65
† Welcome.
⌶ WD £12; WE £12.
⌁ Welcome by prior arrangement; full packages available; minimum 8; from £12.
⦿⌶ Full catering and bar facilities.
⌁⌐ Bridge of Lochay; Killin; Clachaig.

9C 61 King James VI
Moncreiffe Island, Perth, Perthshire, PH2 8NR
⊹ www.kingjamesVI.co.uk
☎ 01738 625170, Fax 445132, Pro 632460
In the centre of the River Tay; access by footpath from Tay Street or Shore Road.
Parkland course; one of only two courses on river island in the world.
Pro A Coles; Founded 1858/1897
Designed by Tom Morris
18 holes, 6038 yards, S.S.S. 68
⌶ Practice ground, putting green, nets.
† Welcome by prior arrangement but not Sat.

⌶ Terms on application.
⌁ Welcome by prior arrangement with the Pro; catering by arrangement; from £18.
⦿⌶ Full facilities.
⌁⌐ Salutation; Royal George; Isle of Skye.

9C 62 Kinghorn
Macduff Crescent, Kinghorn, Fife, KY3 9RE
☎ 01592 890345
Off A92 3 miles W of Kirkcaldy.
Undulating links course.
Founded 1887
Designed by layout recommended by Tom Morris
18 holes, 5166 yards, S.S.S. 66
† Welcome.
⌶ WD £9; WE £12.
⌁ Welcome by prior written arrangement; groups of 12-30; catering packages by arrangement; from £9.
⦿⌶ Full catering facilities.
⌁⌐ Kingswood; Longboat.

9C 63 Kingsbarns Links
Kingsbarns, Fife, KY16 8QD
⊹ www.kingsbarns.com
⌷ info@kingsbarns.com
☎ 01334 460860, Fax 460877, Rest/Bar 460867
6 miles SE of St Andrews on the A917.
Links course.
Pro David Scott; Founded 2000
Designed by Kyle Phillips
18 holes, 6174 yards
⌶ Driving range with complimentary balls.
† Pay and play – book in advance.
⌶ £125 (June-Nov).
⌁ Welcome by appointment.
⦿⌶ Full Catering facilities and Bar.
⌁⌐ Hotels in Crail & St Andrews.

9C 64 Kirkcaldy
Balwearie Rd, Kirkcaldy, Fife, KY2 5LT
☎ 01592 260370, Fax 203258, Pro 203258
On A92 at W end of town.
Parkland course.
Pro A Mckay; Founded 1904
Designed by Tom Morris
18 holes, 6038 yards, S.S.S. 69
† Welcome; some restrictions Sat.
⌶ WD £16; WE £22.
⌁ Welcome by prior arrangement; restrictions Sat; day rates and catering packages available; from £16.
⦿⌶ Full clubhouse facilities.
⌁⌐ Parkway Hotel; Dunnikier House.

9C 65 Kirriemuir

Northmuir, Kirriemuir, Angus, DD8 4LN
🖳 www.kirriemuirgc@aol.com
☎ 01575 573317, Fax 574608,
Sec 572144
N of Kirriemuir and accessible from
A90 Dundee-Aberdeen road.
Parkland course.
Pro Karyn Dallas; Founded 1908
Designed by James Braid
18 holes, 5510 yards, S.S.S. 67
† Welcome WD.
 POA.
⟲ Welcome by prior arrangement;
day tickets available; catering and
hospitality packages available; £5 pp
deposit required; from £16.
🍽 Full catering packages.
⤳ Airlie Arms; Thrums: Castleton
Park; Chapelbank.

9C 66 Ladybank

Annsmuir, Ladybank, Fife, KY15 7RA
☎ 01337 830320, Fax 831505,
Pro 830725, Sec 830814
In Ladybank off A914 between
Glenrothes and Dundee.
Heathland course.
Pro Martin Gray; Founded 1879
Designed by Tom Morris
18 holes, 6601 yards, S.S.S. 72
† Welcome WD and some Sun by
arrangement; handicap certs required.
 WD £30; WE £35. April to Oct WD
£35, day ticket £45.
⟲ Welcome WD by prior arrangement
with the club Pro; catering packages
available; names and handicaps of all
players required 7 days before arrival;
dining room for 70; from £30.
🍽 Full clubhouse bar and catering
facilities.
⤳ Club can provide a list of local
hotels.

9C 67 Leslie

Balsillie, Leslie, Fife, KY6 3EZ
☎ 01592 620040
Leave M90 at Junctions 5 or 7; Leslie
11 miles.
Undulating course.
Founded 1898
9 holes, 4940 yards, S.S.S. 64
† Welcome.
 WD £8.50; WE £10.50.
⟲ Welcome by arrangement; catering
by arrangement; from £8.50.
🍽 Clubhouse facilities.
⤳ Greenside; Rescobie.

9C 68 Letham Grange Resort ☏

Colliston, by Arbroath, Angus, DD11 4RL

🖳 www.lethamgrange.co.uk
🖳 lethamgrange@sol.co.uk
☎ 01241 890377, Fax 890725,
Pro 890377
Follow Letham Grange signs in
Arbroath from Dundee-Arbroath road.
Parkland course.
Pro Steven Moir; Founded 1987
Designed by Donald Steel
2 x 18 holes, 6968 yards, S.S.S. 73
 Practice facilities.
† Welcome; some restrictions at WE.
 WD £35 WE £40 (Old); WD £18,
WE £22.50 (Glens); combination rates
available from £40.
⟲ Welcome by prior arrangement;
catering packages available; contact
Ben Greenhill at club; from £25.
🍽 Full clubhouse facilities.
⤳ 4-star Letham Grange.

9C 69 Leven

PO Box 14609, Links Rd, Leven, Fife,
KY8 4HS
☎ 01333 426096, Fax 424229,
Sec 424229, Rest/Bar 426096
Enter Leven on A915 from Kirkcaldy
and follow signs to the Beach.
Seaside links course.
Founded 1820
18 holes, 6436 yards, S.S.S. 70
† Welcome; not before 9.30am WD;
10.30am WE.
 WD £28; WE £30.
⟲ Welcome by prior arrangement;
catering packages by arrangement;
snooker table; from £28.
🍽 Full catering facilities.
⤳ Calodoenon hotel.

9C 70 Lochgelly

Cartmore Road, Lochgelly, Fife, KY5
9PB
☎ 01592 780174, Pro 782589,
Rest/Bar 780174
On A910 2 miles NE of Cowdenbeath.
Parkland course.
Pro Martin Goldie; Founded 1896/1911
18 holes, 5454 yards, S.S.S. 67
† Everyone welcome.
 WD £12; WE £23 for a full day.
⟲ Welcome by prior arrangement;
terms on application.
🍽 By arrangement only. Always
available.

9C 71 Lundin

Golf Rd, Lundin Links, leven, KY8 6BA
🖳 www.lundingolfclub.co.uk
☎ 01333 320202, Fax 329743,
Pro 320051, Sec 320202,
Rest/Bar 320202

On seaward side of the village on East
Neuk Coast Road from Kirkcaldy.
Seaside links course.
Pro David Webster; Founded 1868
Designed by James Braid
18 holes, 6394 yards, S.S.S. 71
† Welcome between 9am-3.30pm
Mon-Thurs; 9am-3pm Fri; after 2.30pm
Sat; availability during seasons.
 WD £32; WE £40.
⟲ Welcome by prior arrangement
with Sec; WD ticket of £37; catering
packages by arrangement; from £29.
🍽 Full facilities.
⤳ The old Manor; The Lundin Links;
The Crusoe.

9C 72 Lundin Ladies

Woodielea Road, Lundin Links, Fife,
KY8 6AR
🖳 lundinladies@madasafish.com
☎ 01333 320832, Sec 320832
10 miles East of Kirkcaldy on A915 on
N side of road in village of Lundin
Links.
Parkland course.
Founded 1891
Designed by James Braid
9 holes, 4730 yards, S.S.S. 67
† Visitors welcome including men.
Green fees may vary between summer
and winter.
 Terms on application.
⟲ Block bookings available except
Wed April-August; contact clubhouse
for further information.
🍽 Tea and Coffee available.
⤳ Lundin Links; Old Manor Hotel.

9C 73 Milnathort

South St, Milnathort, Kinross, KY13 9XA
🖳 milnathortgolf@ukgateway.net
☎ 01577 864069
1 mile N of Kinross leaving M90 at
Junction 6(N)/Junction 7(S).
Undulating course with trees.
Founded 1910
9 holes, 5993 yards, S.S.S. 69
 Practice range.
† Everyone welcome.
 WD £12; WE £14.
⟲ Welcome by prior arrangement;
catering by arrangement with
clubmaster; from £16.
🍽 Clubhouse facilities.
⤳ Jolly Beggars; Thistle; Royal.

9C 74 Monifieth

Medal Starters Box, Princes St,
Monifieth, Angus, DD5 4AW
☎ 01382 532678, Fax 535553,
Pro 532945

5 miles E of Dundee on coast.
Links course.
Pro Ian McLeod; Founded 1850
18 holes, 6655 yards, S.S.S. 72
⌇ Practice range.
⸙ Welcome.
⌣ WD £30; WE £36.
⟳ Welcome; composite tickets available with Ashludie Course (18 holes, 5123 yards, par 68).
⦿ Clubhouse facilities.
⤳ Panmure packages available; Woodlands.

9C 75 Montrose Links Trust ⚋
Traill Drive, Montrose, Angus, DD10 8SW
⌁ www.montroselinks.co.uk
✉ jsnboyd@aol.com or secretary@montroselinks.co.uk
☎ 01674 672634, Fax 671800
Turn off Dundee-Aberdeen A90 at Brechin and take A935 to Montrose.
Links course.
Pro Jason Boyd; Founded 1562
Designed by Willly Park Jnr
36 holes, 6533 yards, S.S.S. 72
⌇ Practice area.
⸙ Welcome; but not before 2.30pm Sat or 10am on Sun.
⌣ Medal course £32 a round WD, £42 a day and £38 for a composite day, WE £36-£50 for the day and £44 for the comps Broom Field course, 4850 yards, par 66 S.S.S. 63. Green fees £16 WD and £18 WE.
⟳ Welcome by prior arrangement; same restrictions as for visitors; facilities available at the 3 clubs adjacent to courses (Montrose Caledonia GC 01674 672313; Montrose Mercantile GC 672408; Royal Montrose 672376); also Broomfield course.
⦿ Catering available at member clubs.
⤳ Park Hotel; Links.

9C 76 Muckhart
Drumburn Rd, Muckhart, by Dollar, Clackmannanshire, FK14 7JH
☎ 01259 781423, Fax 781544,
Pro 781493
Off A91 6 miles E of Alloa; S of Muckhart; signposted.
Heathland course on rising ground.
Pro Keith Salmoni; Founded 1908/1971
27 holes, 6034 yards, S.S.S. 69
⌇ Practice area.
⸙ Welcome.
⌣ WD £20; WE £25.
⟳ Welcome; catering by arrangement; £10 addition for playing 9-hole course.
⦿ Full catering and bar facilities.
⤳ Glenfargh.

9C 77 Murrayshall
Murrayshall Country House Hotel, Scone, Perthshire, PH2 7PH
⌁ www.murrayshall.co.uk
✉ info@murrayshall.co.uk
☎ 01738 554804, Fax 552595,
Pro 554804, Rest/Bar 551171
On A94 Cupar-Angus road 4 miles from Perth by Scone.
Parkland course.
Pro Alan Reid; Founded 1981
Designed by J Hamilton Stutt
18 holes, 6441 yards, S.S.S. 72
⌇ 18,11 of which are covered.
⸙ Everyone welcome.
⌣ WD £27; WE £30.
⟳ Welcome; packages by arrangement; from £22.
⦿ Full facilities and hotel bar and restaurants.
⤳ Murrayshall on site.

9C 78 Muthill
Peat Road, Muthill, by Crieff, Perthshire, PH5 2DA
✉ muthillgolfclub@lineone.net
☎ 01764 681523, Fax 681557,
Sec 681523
From Crieff course is on right before Muthill at Bowling Green.
Undulating parkland course.
Founded 1911
Designed by members
9 holes, 4700 yards, S.S.S. 63
⸙ Everyone welcome.
⌣ WD £15; WE £18.
⟳ Welcome but booking essential.
⦿ Meals but no bar.
⤳ The Village Inn.

9C 79 North Inch
35 Kinnoull Street, Perth, PH1 5GD
☎ 01738 476476, Fax 475210,
Pro 636481
N of Perth adjacent to Gannochy Trust Sports Complex.
Tree-lined course running alongside river.
Pro Stewart Gow
18 holes, 5178 yards, S.S.S. 65
⸙ Welcome.
⌣ WD £4.20; WE £5.25.
⟳ Welcome by prior arrangement; some summer restrictions apply.
⦿ Catering at Bell's Sports Complex.

9C 80 Panmure
Burnside Road, Barry, Carnoustie, DD7 7RT
⌁ www.panmuregolfclub.co.uk
✉ secretary@panmuregolfclub.co.uk

☎ 01241 855120, Fax 859737,
Pro 852460, Sec 855120,
Rest/Bar 853120
Off A930 2 miles W of Carnoustie.
Seaside course.
Pro Neil MacKintosh; Founded 1845
18 holes, 6317 yards, S.S.S. 71
⌇ Practice range.
⸙ Welcome except Tues am and Sat before 4pm.
⌣ WD £45; WE £45 or £60 per day.
⟳ Welcome by arrangement; catering packages by arrangement; day ticket £60.
⦿ Full facilities.
⤳ Carlogie; Panmure; Station; Woodlands,Carnoustie Hotel.

9C 81 Pitlochry
Golf Course Rd, Pitlochry, Perthshire, PH16 5QY
☎ 01796 472792
A9 to Pitlochry then via Atholl Rd, Larchwood Rd to Golf Course road.
Hill course.
Pro George Hampton; Founded 1908
Designed by Willie Fernie of Troon; Modernised by Major C Hut
18 holes, 5811 yards, S.S.S. 69
⸙ Welcome by arrangement with the Pro. Terms on application.
⌣ Welcome by arrangement; catering by arrangement with Steward; terms on application.
⦿ Full clubhouse facilities.

9C 82 Pitreavie (Dunfermline)
Queensferry Rd, Dunfermline, Fife, KY11 5PR
☎ 01383 722591, Fax 722591,
Pro 723151
M90 N of Forth Road Bridge; 3rd exit signposted Dunfermline; club 3 miles.
Parkland course.
Pro Paul Brookes; Founded 1922
Designed by Dr A MacKenzie
18 holes, 6032 yards, S.S.S. 69
⌇ Practice area.
⸙ Welcome.
⌣ WD £19; WE £26.
⟳ Welcome; catering by arrangement; terms on application.
⦿ Full clubhouse facilities.
⤳ Pitbauchlie House; King Malcolm.

9C 83 Polmont ⚋
Manuelrigg Maddiston, by Falkirk, Stirlingshire, FK2 0LS
☎ 01324 711277, Fax 712504,
Sec 713811
4 miles S of Falkirk 1st right after Fire Brigade HQ.

Undulating parkland course.
Founded 1904
9 holes, 6092 yards, S.S.S. 69
♦ Welcome except on Sat.
Ⓛ WD £8; WE £14.
⟳ Welcome by prior arrangement;
catering by arrangement with Sec;
from £14.
🍽 Clubhouse facilities.
⌂ Inchrya Grange; Polmont.

9C 85 **St Andrews Bay**
Kingask, St Andrew s, Fife, KY16 8PN
🖧 www.standrewsbay.com
📧 info@standrewsbay.com
☎ 01334 472664
A917 from St Andrews to Crail. 2 miles
on left.
Flat course.
18 holes, over 7000 yards, S.S.S. 72;
36 hole, opening July 2002
♦ Yes.
Ⓛ £30 over winter, going into season.
⟳ Yes.
🍽 1 restaurant/buffet à la carte, bar
with light meals all day.
⌂ On site.

9C 86 **St Fillans**
South Loch Earn Rd, St Fillans,
Perthshire, PH6 2NJ
🖧 www.st-fillans-golf.com
☎ 01764 685312, Fax 685312,
Sec 685300
On A85 at E end of the village.
Parkland course.
Founded 1903
Designed by W Auchterlonie
9 holes, 6043 yards, S.S.S. 69
♦ Welcome.
Ⓛ WD £14; WE £18.
⟳ Welcome by arrangement;
maximum 16; catering by arrangement;
from £24.
🍽 Catering facilities; no bar.
⌂ Achray; Four Seasons; Drummond
Arms.

9C 87 **St Michaels**   ℂ
Leuchars, Fife, KY16 0DX
📧 stmichaelsgc@btclick.com
☎ 01334 839365, Fax 838666
5 miles from St Andrews on main road
to Dundee.
Undulating parkland course.
Founded 1903
18 holes, 5802 yards, S.S.S. 68
♦ Welcome except before 12 noon
on Sun.
Ⓛ WD £22; WE £22.
⟳ Welcome by written prior
arrangement; restrictions apply on

Sun; 36 holes of golf and full catering.
🍽 Full facilities.
⌂ St Michaels Inn; many in St
Andrews.

9C 88 **Saline**
Kinneddar Hill, Saline, Fife, KY12 9LT
☎ 01383 852591
Course is five miles NW of
Dunfermline.
Hillside course.
Founded 1912
9 holes, 5304 yards, S.S.S. 66
♦ Welcome except Sat.
Ⓛ WD £9; WE £11.
⟳ Welcome WD and Sun only;
maximum 24; catering packages by
prior arrangement; terms on
application.
🍽 Full catering.
⌂ Saline Castle; Campbell;
Pitbauchly.

9C 89 **Scoonie**
North Links, Leven, Fife, KY8 4SP
🖧 www.scooniegolfclub.com
☎ 01333 307007, Fax 307008,
Sec 307007, Rest/Bar 307007
10 miles SW of St Andrews.
Parkland course.
Founded 1951
18 holes, 4979 yards, S.S.S. 65
♦ Welcome by arrangement with
Secretary except Sat, or via the website.
Ⓛ WD on application.
⟳ Welcome by appointment with
Secretary; groups of 12-30; catering by
arrangement; terms on application.
🍽 Full clubhouse facilities.
⌂ Caledonian.

9C 90 **Scotscraig**
Golf Rd, Tayport, Fife, DD6 9DZ
📧 scottscraig@scottishgolf.com
☎ 01382 552515, Fax 553130,
Pro 552855
On B946 3 miles from S end of Tay
Road Bridge.
Links course.
Pro Stuart Campbell; Founded 1817
18 holes, 6550 yards, S.S.S. 72
♦ Welcome WD and by prior
arrangement at WE.
Ⓛ WD £35; WE £40.
⟳ Welcome by prior arrangement;
packages by arrangement; day tickets
WD £40; WE £45; from £30.
🍽 Full catering facilities.
⌂ Seymour; Scores; Rusacks; Russell.

9C 84 **St Andrews**
St Andrews Links Management
Committee, Pilmour Cottage, St
Andrews, Fife, KY16 9JA
☎ 01334 466666, Fax 477036,
Pro 475757, Sec 475757, Bar/Rest
473107
60 miles north of Edinburgh via
A91 to St Andrews; turning to
course is on the left before the
town; by rail to Leuchars on
Edinburgh-Dundee main line.
Ⓛ Apply for details.
⟳ Welcome; terms on application.
🍽 Clubhouse facilities and in
local hotels.
⌂ Full range in St Andrews from
B&B to international standard.

Old Course
18 holes, 6566 yards, S.S.S. 72
Most famous Championship links
in the world.
Founded 1400
Designed by Nature and
Tom Morris, A Robertson,
A MacKenzie
♦ Welcome with handicap certs;
no play on Sun.

Balgove Course
9 holes, 1530 yards
Founded 1974
♦ Welcome; children under 16
reduced prices.
Ⓛ WD £7; WE £7.

Eden Course
18 holes, 6112 yards, S.S.S. 70
Founded 1914
Designed by HS Colt
♦ Public.

Jubilee Course
18 holes, 6805 yards, S.S.S. 72
Founded 1897/1989
Designed by J Angus/ Donald
Steel (1989)
♦ Welcome.

New Course
18 holes, 6604 yards, S.S.S. 72
Founded 1895
Designed by Old Tom Morris
♦ Welcome.

Strathtyrum Course
18 holes, 5094 yards, S.S.S. 65
Founded 1993
Designed by Donald Steel
♦ Welcome.

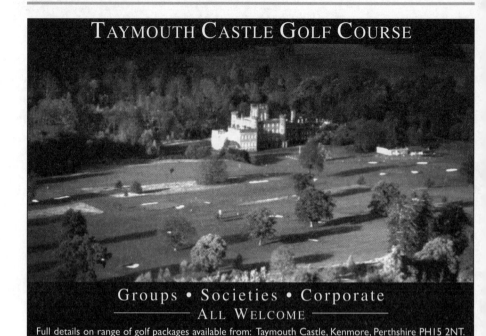

9C 91 Stirling
Queens Rd, Stirling, Stirlingshire, FK8 3AA
☎ 01786 46 4098
On A811 1 mile W of town.
Parkland course.
Pro Ian Collins; Founded 1869
Designed by J Braid/H Cotton
18 holes, 6438 yards, S.S.S. 71
⚑ Practice area.
† Welcome WD; some WE restrictions.
� WD £28; WE £28; £40 for day ticket.
⌖ Welcome WD by prior arrangement; day ticket £40; catering by arrangement; pool table.
⦿ Full clubhouse facilities.
⤳ Golden Lion.

9C 92 Strathendrick
Glasgow Rd, Drymen, Stirlingshire, G63 0AA
✉ marrisonpe@aol.com
☎ 01360 660695, Fax 600567,
Sec 600567
Off A811 1 mile S of Drymen; 17 miles NW of Glasgow.
Hilly moorland course.
Founded 1901
9 holes, 4982 yards, S.S.S. 64
† Welcome WD 8.30am-2.30pm

May-Sept.
� WD £12.
⌖ Limited access by prior arrangement; terms on application.
⦿ None.
⤳ Buchanan Arms; Winnock.

9C 93 Strathtay
Lyon Cottage, Strathtay, Perthshire, PH9 0PG
☎ 01887 840211
4 miles W of Ballinlug on A827.
Inland course.
9 holes, 4082 yards, S.S.S. 63
† Welcome; restrictions May-Sept on Sun afternoons and Mon evenings.
� £10.
⌖ Welcome by prior arrangement; packages available; from £20.
⦿ Full clubhouse facilities.
⤳ Kenmore.

9C 94 Taymouth Castle
Kenmore, by Aberfeldy, Tayside, PH15 2NT
☎ 01887 830228, Fax 830228,
Rest/Bar 830397
Course is 5 miles W of Aberfeldy on the A827.

Parkland course.
Pro Gavin Dott; Founded 1923
Designed by James Braid
18 holes, 6066 yards, S.S.S. 69
† Welcome.
☽ WD £22 WE £26.
⌖ Welcome.
⦿ Full clubhouse facilities.
⤳ Kenmore.

9C 95 Thornton
Station Road, Thornton, Fife, KY1 4DW
🖧 www.thorntongolfclubfife.co.uk
✉ johntgc@ic24.net
☎ 01592 771111, Fax 774955,
Sec 771111, Rest/Bar 771161
1 mile off the A92 road at the Redhouse roundabout midway between Kirkcaldy and Glenrothes.
Parkland course.
Founded 1921
Designed by Members
18 holes, 6155 yards, S.S.S. 69
† Welcome.
☽ Midweek round £17; midweek day £27; WE round £25; WE day £35.
⌖ Welcome; catering packages by arrangement.
⦿ Full clubhouse facilities; new clubhouse opened in Dec 1995.

⤷ Crewn, Thornton; Rescobie; Albany both Glenrothes; Royal Dean Park both Kirkcaldy.

9C 96 **Tillicoultry**
Alva Road, Illicoultry, FK13 6BL
▤ Tilligc@stirling,.co.uk
☎ 01259 750124
9 miles E of Stirling on the A91.
Undulating parkland course.
Founded 1899
Designed by Peter Robertson
9 holes, 5358 yards, S.S.S. 66
† Welcome by arrangement.
 WD £12; WE £18.
⟳ Welcome by arrangement with Sec; catering by prior arrangement; terms on application.
🍽 Restaurant and bar facilities.

9C 97 **Tulliallan**
Alloa Rd, Kincardine on Forth, FK10 4BB
⤷ www.tulliallan-golf-club.co.uk
▤ enquires@tulliallangc.f9.co.uk
☎ 01259 730396, Pro 730798,
Sec 730396, Rest/Bar 733952 bar,
733953 restuarant
0.5 miles N of the Kincardine Bridge on the Alloa road.
Parkland course.
Pro Stephen Kelly; Founded 1902
18 holes, 5965 yards, S.S.S. 69
† Welcome by arrangement.
 WD £16; WE £20.
⟳ Welcome by prior arrangement except Sat; day tickets WD: £29.50; WE: £38; WD maximum group of 40; Sun max group of 24; from £20; catering available with booking in advance.
🍽 Full clubhouse facilities.
⤷ Powfoulis Manor.

9C 98 **Whitemoss**
Whitemoss Road, Dunning, Perthshire, PH2 0QX
☎ 01738 730300, Fax 774955
1 mile off the A9; 2 miles past the Gleneagles Hotel.
Parkland course.
Founded 1994
Designed by IGolf
18 holes, 5995 yards, S.S.S. 69
† Welcome by arrangement.
 WD £15; WE £18.
⟳ Welcome by prior arrangement; Catering packages available by prior arrangement; catering packages available by prior arrangement; day tickets £25.
🍽 Full facilities.
⤷ Colon Hotel, The Smiddy Haugh.

Highlands, Grampian

When Tom Watson pitched up at Royal Dornoch in 1981, he intended to play eighteen holes, pack his bag and move on. Unable to tear himself away he played a second and then a third round before declaring, "This is the most fun I have had playing golf in my whole life." That is not a bad endorsement from a man who two years later would win his fifth Open Championship.

In 2002 Royal Dornoch celebrates its 125th anniversary although there are records of golf being played on the links as early as 1616. Donald Ross, the most famous of all American golf architects, was the pro and head greenkeeper here for a while and touches of his style linger on.

The most famous hole is the fourteenth hole called 'Foxy', a double dog leg with a tilting green, but void of bunkers. Harry Vardon called it "the most memorable hole in golf".

The fact that Dornoch is further north than Moscow might deter some, but it is easily accessible from Inverness airport and not as cold as you might think. Remoteness and tranquillity are part of the charm unless you are unlucky enough to be around when Guy Ritchie and Madonna are having one of their bashes.

Andrew Carnegie, of steel and music hall fame, was reputedly asked to play at Dornoch. The club has a shield in his name. But legend has it that he thought he ought to learn to play the game first so he had Skibo constructed, a course that was redesigned by Donald Steel at the start of the nineties. It is now the Carnegie Club, a fine course, but prohibitively expensive. At these prices you would think that it had hosted twenty Opens.

Other notable courses at the northern extremity of Scotland are Brora, where a midnight competition is held in June, Tain, a heather and links course that offers good value, and Golspie, a course full of underfoot variety.

Back through Inverness on the south side of the Moray Firth is Nairn where the 1999 Walker Cup was held. Colin Montgomerie won the 1987 Scottish Amateur here and named his design company accordingly. The likes of Willie Whitelaw and Harold McMillan were staunch advocates of the course and area. It is not the longest links in the world, but the glassy greens will find out anyone who has been a victim of their putter.

Inland of Inverness, close to the shores of Loch Ness, is Boat of Garten. The course is a test of accuracy and concentration as the mind is apt to be distracted by the beauty of the Cairngorms and River Spey.

East of Nairn lies Moray, the Old is better than the New, with views over the Firth, and Cruden Bay, formerly a golfing resort in the days of the railway. The eyes should be getting sore from beauty by this time.

The Balgownie course at Royal Aberdeen with its valleyed fairways between the dunes was described by Bernard Darwin as "much more than a good golf course – a noble links." Founded in 1780 it is one of the oldest clubs in the world, although the game was played much earlier than that. The Aberdeen register of 1565 lists golf as 'an unlawful amusement'. The nearby Kings Links is another historic setting. A public course, its reasonable green fees ensure a brisk trade. Just down the coast Murcar is at least a patch on Royal Aberdeen and not dissimilar in lay out.

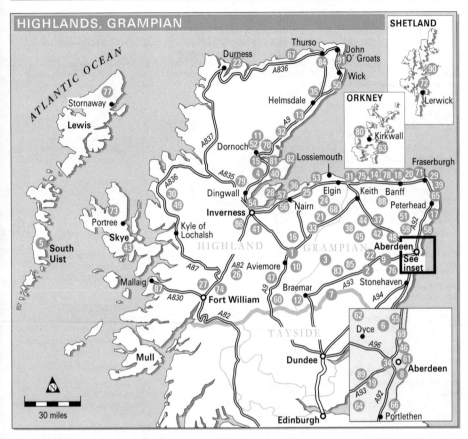

HIGHLANDS, GRAMPIAN

KEY		19	Deeside	37	Huntly	56	Nairn	75	Spey Bay
1	Abernethy	20	Duff House Royal	38	Insch	57	Nairn Dunbar	76	Stonehaven
2	Aboyne	21	Dufftown	39	Inverallochy	58	Newburgh-on-Ythan	77	Stornoway
3	Alford	22	Dunecht House	40	Invergordon	59	Newmachar	78	Strathlene
4	Alness	23	Durness	41	Inverness	60	Newtonmore	79	Strathpeffer Spa
5	Askernish	24	Elgin	42	Inverurie	61	Northern	80	Stromness
6	Auchmill	25	Forres	43	Isle of Skye	62	Oldmeldrum	81	Tain
7	Ballater	26	Fort Augustus	44	Keith	63	Orkney	82	Tarbat
8	Balnagask	27	Fort William	45	Kemnay	64	Peterculter	83	Tarland
9	Banchory	28	Fortrose and	46	King's Links	65	Peterhead	84	Thurso
10	Boat of Garten		Rosemarkie	47	Kingussie	66	Portlethen	85	Torphins
11	Bonar Bridge & Ardgay	29	Fraserburgh	48	Kintore	67	Reay	86	Torvean
12	Braemar	30	Gairloch	49	Lochcarron	68	Rothes	87	Traigh Golf Course
13	Brora	31	Garmouth & Kingston	50	Lybster	69	Royal Aberdeen	88	Turriff
14	Buckpool (Buckie)	32	Golspie	51	McDonald	70	Royal Dornoch	89	Westhill
15	Carnegie Club	33	Grantown-on-Spey	52	Monk's Walk	71	Royal Tarlair	90	Whalsay
16	Carrbridge	34	Hazlehead	53	Moray	72	Shetland	91	Wick
17	Cruden Bay	35	Helmsdale	54	Muir of Ord	73	Skeabost		
18	Cullen	36	Hopeman	55	Murcar	74	Spean Bridge		

9D 1 Abernethy
Nethybridge, Inverness-Shire, PH25 3EB
www.abernethygolfclub.com
info@abernethygolfclub.com
01479 821305, Fax 821305,
Sec 872479
On B970 Grantown-on-Spey to Boat of
Garten road.
Undulating course with views of Spey
valley.
Founded 1893
9 holes, 4986 yards, S.S.S. 66
Practice green.
Welcome with restrictions applying
on Sun.
WD £13; WE £16.
Welcome by arrangement with
Sec; packages available; terms on
application.
Full clubhouse facilities in
season.
Nethybridge; Mountview;
Heatherbrae.

9D 2 Aboyne
Formaston Park, Aboyne,
Aberdeenshire, AB34 5HP
www.aboynegolf.com
aboynegolf@btinternet.com
013398 86328, Fax 87592,
Pro 86328, Sec 87078,
Rest/Bar 86328
Course is off the A93 from Aberdeen;
take first turning on right after entering
village.
Undulating parkland course.
Founded 1883
18 holes, 5944 yards, S.S.S. 68
Welcome.
WD £19; WE £23.
Welcome by prior arrangement
except Sun; day tickets available (WD
£25, WE £30); catering packages by
arrangement between April and
October; from £12.
Full facilities during summer.
Charleston; Huntly Arms.

9D 3 Alford   ☎
Montgarrie Road, Alford, AB33 8AE
www.golf.alford.co.uk
golf@alford.co.uk
019755 62178, Fax 62178,
Sec 62178, Rest/Bar 62178
On A944 in the village of Alford 25
miles W of Aberdeen.
Parkland course.
Founded 1982
Designed by David Hurd
18 holes, 5483 yards off the white,
S.S.S. 65
Welcome; some restrictions on
club comp days.

WD £13; WE £20.
Welcome by prior arrangement;
day tickets available (WD £19; WE
£26); shotgun starts can be organised
for a minimum of 50 players; catering
packages by prior arrangement; from
£13.
Full clubhouse facilities available.
Kildrummy Castle; Forbes Arms.

9D 4 Alness   ☎
Ardross Rd, Alness, Ross-Shire
01349 883877
Course is on the A9 10 miles N of
Dingwall.
Founded 1904
Designed by John Sutherland
18 holes, 5000 yards, S.S.S. 64
Welcome except 4.30pm-7.30pm
Mon.
Terms upon application.
Welcome by prior arrangement;
catering by prior arrangement; terms
on application.
By prior arrangement.
Commercial Hotel.

9D 5 Askernish
Lochboisdale, Askernish, South Uist,
Western Isles, HS81 5SY
01878 700298
Take the ferry from Oban to
Lochboisdale; course is 5 miles N of
Lochboisdale.
Links course; most Western course in
Scotland.
Founded 1891
Designed by Tom Morris
18 holes, 5042 yards, S.S.S. 67
Welcome.
WD £10; WE £10.
Welcome; terms available on
application.
By prior arrangement.
Lochboisdale Hotel.

9D 6 Auchmill
Bonny View road, Auchmill, AB16 7FQ
01224 715214
5 miles N of Aberdeen.
Municipal parkland course.
18 holes, 5560 yards, S.S.S. 69
Welcome.
On application.
Only with prior arrangement
through Council.
Limited.

9D 7 Ballater   ☎
Victoria Road, Ballater, Aberdeenshire,
AB35 5QX

013397 55567, Fax 55057,
Pro 55658
42 miles W of Aberdeen on the A93.
Heath/parkland course.
Pro Billy Yule; Founded 1892
Designed by James Braid/H Vardon
18 holes, 6112 yards, S.S.S. 69
Welcome by arrangement.
Terms on application.
Welcome by arrangement; catering
and day rates; from £18.
Bar and catering facilities.
Club can provide comprehensive list.

9D 8 Balnagask
St Fitticks Rd, Balnagask, Aberdeen
01224 876407, Sec 871286,
Rest/Bar 871286
2 miles SE of the city.
Municipal seaside course.
Founded 1903
Designed by Hawtree & Son
18 holes, 6065 yards, S.S.S. 69
Practice ground and 9-hole pitch
and putt.
Welcome.
WD £9; WE £11.25.
Welcome by prior arrangement
with the council.
By arrangement with the council.
Caledonian.

9D 9 Banchory
Kinneskie Rd, Banchory,
Kincardineshire, AB31 5TA
crighton@
banchorygolf club.uk.org
01330 822365, Fax 822491,
Pro 822447
Course is 100 yards off the A93 the
main Aberdeen to Braemar road.
Parkland course; 16th hole Doo'cot is
88 yards.
Pro David Naylor; Founded 1905
18 holes, 5781 yards, S.S.S. 68
Welcome; all times bookable.
WD £20 (18 holes) day ticket £27;
WE £23 (18 holes).
Welcome; catering packages by
prior arrangement; terms on
application.
Full catering lounge and dining
room facilities.
Burnett Arms; Tor-na-coille;
Banchory Lodge.

9D 10 Boat of Garten
Inverness-Shire, PH24 3BQ
www.boatgolf.com
boatgolf@enterprise.net
01479 831282, Fax 831523,
Rest/Bar 831731

2 miles E of A9 30 miles S of Inverness.
Heathland course.
Pro James Ingram; Founded 1898
Designed by James Braid
18 holes, 5866 yards, S.S.S. 69
⚐ Practice area.
♦ Welcome WD 9.30am-6pm; WE 10am-4pm.
⌷ WD £25; WE £30.
⌁ Welcome by prior arrangement; day tickets available; catering by arrangement; separate changing rooms available.
⍾ Full clubhouse facilities.
⌐ The Boat; Craigard.

9D 11 Bonar Bridge & Ardgay
Market Stance, Migdale Rd, Bonar Bridge, Sutherland, IV24 3EJ
☎ 01863 766199, Fax 766738
Off A836 at Bonar Bridge 0.5 miles up Migdale Rd; 12 miles W of Dornoch.
Parkland course.
Founded 1904
9 holes, 5284 yards, S.S.S. 63
♦ Welcome.
⌷ WD £12; WE £12.
⌁ Welcome WD by prior arrangement; terms available on application.
⍾ Clubhouse facilities in season.

9D 12 Braemar ☎
Cluniebank Rd, Braemar, Aberdeenshire, AB35 5XX
☎ 013397 41618, Sec 01224 704471, Rest/Bar 013397 41618
Signposted from the village centre; turn left opposite Fife Arms Hotel.
Parkland course.
Founded 1902
Designed by Joe Anderson
18 holes, 4935 yards, S.S.S. 64
♦ Welcome.
⌷ WD £14; WE £17.
⌁ Welcome; packages include 36 holes of golf and catering; from £20; WE £32.
⍾ Full clubhouse facilities.
⌐ Invercauld Arms; Fife Arms; Moorfield House.

9D 13 Brora
43 Golf Rd, Brora, Sutherland, KW9 6QS
⌂ www.highlandescape.com
✉ seceratary@broragolf.co.uk
☎ 01408 621417, Fax 622157
On A9 N of Inverness; turn right over bridge in centre of Brora.
Traditional links course.

Founded 1891
Designed by James Braid
18 holes, 6110 yards, S.S.S. 69
⚐ Practice range.
♦ Welcome.
⌷ WD £25; WE £30.
⌁ Welcome by prior arrangement; on application; from £20.
⍾ Clubhouse facilities.
⌐ Royal Marine; Links.

9D 14 Buckpool (Buckie)
Barhill Rd, Buckie, Banffshire, AB56 1DU
☎ 01542 832236
Turn off the A98 at Buckpool.
Links course.
Founded 1933/65
Designed by Hawtree & Taylor
18 holes, 6257 yards, S.S.S. 70
♦ Welcome.
⌷ WD £15; WE £20.
⌁ Welcome by prior arrangement; packages include 36 holes of golf with full catering; WE discounts for groups of more than 10.
⍾ Full clubhouse facilities.
⌐ Marine Buckie.

9D 15 Carnegie Club
Skibo Castle, Dornoch, Sutherland, IV25 3RQ
⌂ www.carnegieclub.co.uk
✉ info@carnegieclubs.com
☎ 01862 894600, Fax 894601
Take A9 towards Wick from Inverness; first left after Dornoch Bridge signposted Meikle Ferry North; continue for 1 mile and turn right at Green Sheds.
Championship links course; new 9-hole parkland course (members course).
Pro David Thompson; Founded 1994
Designed by Donald Steel
18 holes, 6671 yards, S.S.S. 72
⚐ Driving range bays.
♦ WD by arrangement only.
⌷ Prices on application.
⌁ WD only; includes soup, sandwiches and house wine.
⍾ Full facilities in the club.
⌐ Morangie House; Mansfield House, both Tain; Royal Golf; Burghfield, both Dornoch.

9D 16 Carrbridge ☎
Inverness Rd, Carrbridge, Inverness-shire, PH23 3AU
☎ 01479 841623, Sec 841201
Off A9 25 miles S of Inverness.
Parkland course/heathland course.

Founded 1980
Designed by local enthusiasts
9 holes, 5402 yards, S.S.S. 68
♦ Welcome.
⌷ WD £12; WE £13.
⌁ Limited to small groups. Tea coffee and snacks; from April-October.
⌐ Contact Carrbridge Tourist Association.

9D 17 Cruden Bay
Aulton Rd, Cruden Bay, Peterhead, Aberdeenshire, AB42 7ON
⌂ www.crudenbaygolfclub.co.uk
✉ cbaygc@aol.com
☎ 01779 812285, Fax 812945, Pro 812414
Course is off the A90 10 miles from Peterhead; or from Aberdeen off the A90 and then the A975.
Championship links course.
Pro Robbie Stewart; Founded 1899
Designed by Tom Morris & Archie Simpson
27 holes, 6395 yards, S.S.S. 72
⚐ Practice range; 10 covered bays.
♦ Welcome; restrictions until after 9.30am Mon; after 10.30am Tues and at WE (Main); Welcome (St Olaf).
⌷ WD £50, WE £60 (Main); WD £15, WE 15, £20 (St Olaf).
⌁ Welcome WD except Wed by prior arrangement; handicap certs needed; minimum 16 players; catering by prior arrangement; from £25 (Main); welcome (St Olaf).
⍾ Full clubhouse facilities.
⌐ Club can provide list.

9D 18 Cullen
The Links, Cullen, Buckie, Banffshire, AB56 4UU
☎ 01542 840685, Fax 841977
Off the A98 at the W end of the town on the Moray Firth coastline.
Traditional links course with natural rock landscaping.
Founded 1879.
Designed by Tom Morris (original 9 holes); Charles Neaves
18 holes, 4610 yards, S.S.S. 62
♦ Welcome WD; some restrictions on WE and July/August.
⌷ Terms on application.
⌁ Welcome by prior arrangement; restrictions on Wed and Sat; day tickets available; catering packages by arrangement; from £10.
⍾ Clubhouse catering and bar.
⌐ Cullen Bay; Royal Oak; Bayview; Three Kings; Grant Arms; Seafield Arms; Waverley.

9D 19 Deeside

Golf Rd, Bieldside, Aberdeen,
Aberdeenshire, AB15 9DL
✉ ddc@bieldside28.freeserve.co.uk
☎ 01224 869457, Rest/Bar 861792
Course is on the A93 three miles W of
Aberdeen.
Parkland course.
Pro FJ Coutts; Founded 1903
18 holes, 5971 yards, S.S.S. 70
† Welcome after 9am WD and 4pm
Sat; letter of introduction needed.
Ⓛ WD £40; WE £55.
⟳ Welcome Thurs only by
arrangement; catering packages by
arrangement; terms available on
application.
🍽 Full facilities.
⌁ Cults; Bieldside Inn.

9D 20 Duff House Royal

The Banyards, Banff, Banffshire, AB45
3SX
🖱 www.theduffhouseroyalgolfclub.
co.uk
✉ duff_house_royal@btinternet.co.uk
☎ 01261 812062, Fax 812224,
Pro 812075, Sec 812062,
Rest/Bar 812062
On A98.
Parkland course.
Pro R Strachan; Founded 1909
Designed by Dr A & Major CA
MacKenzie
18 holes, 6161 yards, S.S.S. 70
† Welcome except before 11am and
between 12.30pm-3.30pm WE and in
July/August.
Ⓛ WD £18; WE £24.
⟳ Welcome by prior arrangement;
catering and day packages by
application; terms on application.
🍽 Full facilities.
⌁ Banff Springs; County; Fife Lodge.

9D 21 Dufftown

Tomintoul Road, Dufftown, Keith,
Banffshire, AB55 4BX
🖱 www.speyside.moray.org/
Dufftown/Golfclub
✉ marion_dufftowngolfclub@
yahoo.com
☎ 01340 820325, Fax 820325,
Sec 820325, Rest/Bar 820325
On B9009 1 mile S of Dufftown.
Moor/parkland course.
Founded 1896
Designed by A Simpson
18 holes, 5308 yards, S.S.S. 67
† Welcome.
Ⓛ £12 per round; £15 for the day.
⟳ Welcome by prior arrangement;
discounts for groups of more than 12;

catering by prior arrangement; from £12.
🍽 Full clubhouse facilities.
⌁ Fife Arms; Craigellachie.

9D 22 Dunecht House

Dunecht, Skene, Aberdeenshire, AB3
7AX
☎ 01224 511634
Course on B994 to Dunecht.
Inland wooded course.
Founded 1925
9 holes, 6270 yards, S.S.S. 70
† Members only.
Ⓛ Terms on application.

9D 23 Durness   ☏

Balnakeil, Durness, Sutherland, IV27
4PN
✉ mackenziedurness@aol.com
☎ 01971 511364, Fax 511321
57 miles NW of Lairg on A838; turn left
in village square.
Links/parkland course.
Founded 1988
Designed by F Keith; L Ross; I
Morrison
9 holes, 5555 yards, S.S.S. 69
† Welcome.
Ⓛ Terms on application.
⟳ Welcome; terms available on
application.
🍽 Clubhouse facilities.
⌁ Cape Wrath; Parkhill; Rhiconich.

9D 24 Elgin

Hardhillock, Birnie Road, Elgin, Moray,
IV30 8SX
🖱 www.elgingolfclub.com
✉ secretary@elgingolfclub.com
☎ 01343 542338, Fax 542341,
Pro 542884, Sec 542338,
Rest/Bar 542338
On A941 Birnie road, 1 mile S of Elgin
town centre.
Parkland course.
Pro Kevin Stables; Founded 1906
Designed by John MacPherson
18 holes, 6411 yards, S.S.S. 71
Ⓛ 16.
† Everyone welcome.
Ⓛ £26 per day any day of the week.
⟳ Welcome by prior arrangement
with Sec David Black; discounts for
larger groups; full catering available.
🍽 Clubhouse bar and catering.
⌁ Sunnihill; Laichmoray; Eight
Acres; Mansion House.

9D 25 Forres   ☏

Muiryshade, Forres, IV36 2RD
🖱 www.forresgolfclub.fsnet.co.uk

✉ sandy@forresgolfclub.fsnet.co.uk
☎ 01309 672250, Fax 672250,
Pro 672250, Sec 672250,
Rest/Bar 672949
On A96 26 miles E of Inverness; 1 mile
S of Forres.
Parkland course.
Pro Sandy Aird; Founded 1889
Designed by James Braid
18 holes, 6141 yards, S.S.S. 69
† Welcome by prior arrangement
with the Professional.
Ⓛ WD £24; WE £24.
⟳ Welcome by prior arrangement;
maximum number 60; terms on
application.
🍽 Full clubhouse facilities.
⌁ Ramnee.

9D 26 Fort Augustus

Markethill, Fort Augustus, Inverness-
shire, PH32 4DT
☎ 01320 366660
0.75 miles S of Fort Augustus on A82.
Moorland course.
Founded 1905
Designed by Dr Lean
9 holes, 5452 yards, S.S.S. 67
† Welcome.
Ⓛ WD £10; WE £10.
⟳ Welcome by prior arrangement; on
application; from £8.
🍽 Limited.
⌁ Lovat Arms; Richmond House.

9D 27 Fort William

North Rd, Torlundy, Inverness-shire,
PH33 6SN
☎ 01397 704464, Fax 705893
On A82 2 miles N of Fort William.
Parkland course.
Founded 1975
Designed by JR Stutt
18 holes, 6217 yards, S.S.S. 71
† Welcome.
Ⓛ WD £15; WE £15.
⟳ Welcome by arrangement; golf
packages only; no catering; £15.
🍽 Bar snacks available.
⌁ Milton; Moorings.

9D 28 Fortrose & Rosemarkie

Ness Rd East, Fortrose, Ross-shire,
IV10 8SE
🖱 www.fortrosegolfclub.co.uk
✉ secretary@fortrosegolfclub.co.uk
☎ 01381 620529, Fax 621328
Off A832 to Fortrose off the A9 at Tope
roundabout.
Links course on headland; stunning
views.
Founded 1888

Designed by James Baird
18 holes, 5883 yards, S.S.S. 69
† Welcome.
⌊ WD £20; WE £25.
⌃ Welcome by prior arrangement
with Sec; day tickets available (WD
£30, WE £35); from £20.
⊖ Clubhouse facilities.
⌐ Royal; Kinkell House.

9D 29 Fraserburgh ⌖
Philnorth, Fraserburgh, Aberdeenshire,
AB43 8TL
⌁ www.fraserburghgolfclub.net
✉ fburghgolf@aol.com
☎ 01346 516616, Pro 517898,
Sec 516616, Rest/Bar 518287
S of first roundabout when entering
Fraserburgh and then first right.
Links course.
Founded 1881
Designed by James Braid
27 holes, 6278 yards, S.S.S. 70
† Everyone welcome.
⌊ WD £15; WE £25.
⌃ Welcome by prior arrangement;
catering packages by arrangement;
also 9-hole course, 4800 yards, par 64;
from £15.
⊖ Bar and dining room facilities
available.
⌐ Royal; Tufted Duck, both
Fraserburgh.

9D 30 Gairloch
Gairloch, Ross-shire, IV21 2BE
✉ secretary@
gairlochgc.freeserve.net
☎ 01445 712407
On A832 60 miles W of Inverness.
Seaside course with stunning views;
7th hole An Dun, is 91 yards.
Founded 1898
Designed by Captain AW Burgess
9 holes, 4514 yards, S.S.S. 64
⌇ Practice area with bunker.
† Welcome.
⌊ WD £15; WE £15.
⌃ Welcome by prior arrangement;
weekly ticket: £49; by prior
arrangement; refreshments.
⊖ Clubhouse facilities.
⌐ Gairloch; Myrtle Bank Millcroft; Old
Inn, Creag Mor.

9D 31 Garmouth & Kingston ⌖
Spey St, Garmouth, Fochabers,
Morayshire, IV32 7NJ
✉ garmouthgolfclub@aol.com
☎ 01343 870388, Fax 870388
3 miles N of A96 at Mosstodloch cross
roads.

Links/parkland course.
Founded 1932
Designed by George Smith
18 holes, 5935 yards, S.S.S. 69
† Welcome by prior arrangement.
⌊ Terms on application.
⌃ Welcome by prior arrangement;
catering by arrangement; games room;
terms on application.
⊖ Bar and dining room facilities.
⌐ Garmouth; Gordon Arms
Fochabers.

9D 32 Golspie
Ferry Rd, Golspie, Sutherland, KW10
6ST
☎ 01408 633266
On A9 to Golspie.
Links course.
Founded 1889
Designed by James Braid
18 holes, 5890 yards, S.S.S. 68
† Welcome.
⌊ WD £20; WE £20.
⌃ Welcome by prior arrangement;
day tickets: WD £25; WE £25;
discounts for groups; catering by
arrangement; from £20.
⊖ Bar and catering facilities.
⌐ Stags Head; Golf Links; Ben
Bhraggie; Sutherland Arms.

9D 33 Grantown-on-Spey
Golf Course Rd, Grantown-on-Spey,
Morayshire, PH26 3HY
⌁ www.grantononspeygolfclub.co.uk
☎ 01479 872079, Fax 873725
On NE of town signposted off the
Grantown-Nairn/Forres road.
Parkland/woodland course.
Pro James Macpherson; Founded 1890
Designed by James Braid
18 holes, 5710 yards, S.S.S. 68
⌇ Practice range.
† Welcome except before 10am at
WE.
⌊ WD £20; WE £25.
⌃ Welcome by prior arrangement
except before 10am at WE; catering by
arrangement; from £20.
⊖ Full bar and catering facilities.
⌐ Culdearn House; Garth; Muckrach
Lodge.

9D 34 Hazlehead
Hazlehead Park , Aberdeen, AB15 8BD
☎ 01224 910711, Sec 310711
Course is four miles NW of the city
centre.
Municipal moorland courses.
Pro Alistair Smith
18 holes, 6304 yards, S.S.S. 68

† Welcome.
⌊ WD £9; WE £25.
⌃ Apply to council; 2 other courses;
18 holes 6045 yards S.S.S. 68; 9holes'
2770 yards S.S.S. 34 terms on
application.
⊖ Available nearby.
⌐ Treetops; Belverdere Queens.

9D 35 Helmsdale
Golf Rd, Helmsdale, Sutherland, KW8
6JA
☎ 01431 821324
Off A9 in village of Helmsdale.
Moorland course.
Founded 1895
9 holes, 3720 yards, S.S.S. 60
† Welcome.
⌊ Terms on application.
⌃ Welcome by application.
⊖ None.
⌐ Navidale; Bridge; Belgrave.

9D 36 Hopeman Golf Club
Hopeman, Moray, IV30 5YA
✉ hopemangc@aol.com
☎ 01343 830578, Fax 830152
On B9012 7 miles N of Elgin.
Seaside links-type course.
Founded 1906
Designed by Charles Neaves
18 holes, 5590 yards, S.S.S. 67
† Welcome except some Sat
competition days.
⌊ WD £15; WE £20; concessions
apply.
⌃ Welcome by prior arrangement
with Sec; catering packages by
arrangement; pool table; terms
available on application.
⊖ Full catering facilities.
⌐ Station.

9D 37 Huntly
Cooper Park, Huntly, Aberdeenshire,
AB54 4SH
⌁ www.huntleygc.co.uk
✉ huntleygc@tinyworld.co.uk
☎ 01466 792643, Pro 794181
On A96 0.5 miles from the town centre
through school arch.
Parkland course.
Pro Sendy Aird; Founded 1892
18 holes, 5399 yards, S.S.S. 66
† Welcome.
⌊ WD £15; WE £20.
⌃ By arrangement with Sec; catering
by arrangement; snooker; darts; terms
on application.
⊖ Clubhouse facilities.
⌐ Commercial; Station.

9D 38 **Insch**
Golf Terrace, Aberdeenshire
☎ 01464 820363
Off A96 28 miles NW of Aberdeen.
Parkland course with water hazards
extended 1997.
18 holes, 5395 yards, S.S.S. 67
† Welcome.
⌇ Terms on application.
⌁ By arrangement with Sec; catering
by arrangement; snooker darts terms
on application.
◉ Clubhouse facilities.
⌇ Commercial; Station.

9D 39 **Inverallochy**
White Link Inverallochy, Nr
Fraserburgh, AB43 8XY
☎ 01346 582000, Sec 582324
4 miles SE of Fraserburgh.
Seaside links course.
Founded 1888
18 holes, 5101 yards, S.S.S. 65
† Welcome by prior arrangement
except before 10am at WE.
⌇ WD £12; WE £15. Winter WD £8,
WE £10.
⌁ Welcome by prior arrangement;
catering by arrangement; terms on
application.
◉ Catering and licensed bar.
⌇ Tufted Duck.

9D 40 **Invergordon**   ☎
King George St, Invergordon, Ross-
shire, IV1 0BD
☎ 01349 852715
Course is off the B817 from the A9 to
Invergordon.
Parkland course; extended to 18 holes
1996.
Founded 1893
Designed by J Urquhart; Extended by
A Rae 1996
18 holes, 6030 yards, S.S.S. 69
⌿ Practice area.
† Welcome.
⌇ WD £15; WE £15; £20 per day.
£10 in winter.
⌁ Welcome by prior arrangement with
Clubhouse manager;day ticket £15;
catering by arrangement; from £12.
◉ Bar and bar meals service.
⌇ Kincraig; Marine.

9D 41 **Inverness**
Culcabock Rd, Inverness, IV2 3XQ
⌁ www.invernessgolfclub.co.uk
✉ igc@freeuk.com
☎ 01463 233422, Fax 239882,
Pro 231989, Sec 239882,
Rest/Bar 233422

1 mile W of A9 near Raigmore
Hospital.
Parkland course.
Pro Alistair Thomson; Founded 1883
Designed by James Braid
18 holes, 6256 yards, S.S.S. 70
† Welcome; restrictions on Sat comp
days.
⌇ WD £29.00 per round; £39.00 per
day.
⌁ Welcome by prior arrangement;
limited; terms on application.
◉ Full restaurant and bar.
⌇ Marriot; Craigmonie; Inverness
Thistle.

9D 42 **Inverurie**
Blackhall Rd, Inverurie, AB51 1JB
✉ administrator@inveruriegc.co.uk
☎ 01467 624080, Fax 621051,
Pro 620193, Sec 624080
17 miles W of Aberdeen off the A96.
Slightly wooded parkland course.
Pro Mark Lees; Founded 1923
Designed by G Smith and JM Stutt
18 holes, 5711 yards, S.S.S. 68
† Welcome.
⌇ WD £14; WE £18.
⌁ Welcome by prior arrangement;
some discounts for larger groups;
catering packages by arrangement;
from £14.
◉ Full bar and catering.
⌇ Strathburn; Kintore Arms.

9D 43 **Isle of Skye**
Sconser, Isle of Skye, IV48 8TD
☎ 01478 650414
On A87 between Skye Bridge and
Portree.
Parkland course.
Founded 1964
Designed by Dr F Deighton
9 holes, 4677 yards, S.S.S. 64
† Welcome.
⌇ Terms on application.
⌁ Welcome by arrangement with
Sec; discounts for groups of 15 or
more; from £10.
◉ By arrangement.
⌇ Sligachan Hotel.

9D 44 **Keith**
Fife Park, Keith, Banffshire, AB55 3DF
☎ 01542 882469
A96 to Keith; course 0.5 miles.
Parkland course.
Founded 1965
18 holes, 5802 yards, S.S.S. 68
† Welcome.
⌇ Terms on application.
⌁ Welcome by prior arrangement;

day tickets available; catering packages
by arrangement; pool table; from £10.
◉ Clubhouse facilities.
⌇ Fife Arms; Grampian; Royal; Ugie
House, all in Keith.

9D 45 **Kemnay**
Monymusk Road, Kemnay,
Aberdeenshire, AB51 5RA
☎ 01467 642225, Fax 643715,
Sec 643746, Rest/Bar 642060
On A96 15 miles N of Aberdeen; turn
on to B994.
Parkland course.
Pro Ronnie McDonald; Founded
1908
Designed by Greens of Scotland Ltd
(new Course)
18 holes, 5903 yards, S.S.S. 70
† Welcome except on competition
days.
⌇ WD £17; WE £19.
⌁ Welcome by prior arrangement;
day tickets available; catering by
arrangement; from £17.
◉ Full clubhouse facilities available.
⌇ Park Hill Lodge; Grant Arms;
Burnett Arms.

9D 46 **King's Links**
Golf Rd, King's Links, Aberdeen, AB24
5QB
☎ 01224 632269
Close to Pittodrie Stadium in the E of
the city.
Municipal seaside course.
18 holes, 6384 yards, S.S.S. 71
† Welcome.
⌇ Terms on application.
⌁ Welcome by prior arrangement; day
tickets (WD £20, WE £25); reductions
for 20 or more golfers; from £16.
◉ Clubhouse facilities.
⌇ Silverfjord; Scot House.

9D 47 **Kingussie**
Gynack Rd, Kingussie, Inverness-
shire, PH21 1LR
☎ 01540 661600, Fax 662066,
Rest/Bar 661374
Off A9 and turn in to club at Duke of
Gordon Hotel.
Scenic hilly course.
Founded 1891
Designed by Vardon & Herd
18 holes, 5555 yards, S.S.S. 67
† Welcome.
⌇ WD £16; WE £18.
⌁ Welcome by prior arrangement;
day tickets (WD £20, WE £25);
reductions for 20 or more golfers; from
£16.

⦿ Clubhouse facilities.
◞ Silverfjord; Scot House.

9D 48 Kintore ⬧
Balbithan Rd, Kintore, Inverurie,
Aberdeenshire, AB51 0UR
☎ 01467 632631, Fax 632995
Off A96 12 miles N of Aberdeen.
Undulating moorland course.
Founded 1911
18 holes, 6019 yards, S.S.S. 69
⌿ Practice nets.
† Welcome except Mon & Wed
4.30pm-6pm and after 4.30pm Fri.
⌐ Terms on application.
◔ Welcome by prior arrangement;
catering by arrangement; day tickets
available; terms available on
application.
⦿ Full clubhouse facilities.
◞ Toryburn; Thainstone.

9D 49 Lochcarron
East End, Lochcarron
☎ 01520 722229
0.5 miles E of Lochcarron.
Parkland/links course.
Founded 1908
9 holes, 3578 yards, S.S.S. 60
† Welcome except Sat 2-5pm.
⌐ WD £7.50; WE £7.50.
◔ Welcome by prior arrangement
only; catering by arrangement at
village hotel; weekly ticket £20; from
£7.50.
⦿ No clubhouse facilities; catering at
local hotels.
◞ Rockvilla Hotel.

9D 50 Lybster
Main St, Lybster, Caithness, KW3 6BL
☎ 01593 721308, Sec 721316
On A9 13 miles S of Wick.
Moorland course; smallest in Scotland.
Founded 1926
9 holes, 3796 yards, S.S.S. 62
† Welcome; honesty box.
⌐ WD £8; WE £8.
◔ Welcome except Sat evening (club
comp).
◞ The Port and Arms Hotel.

9D 51 McDonald
Hospital Rd, Ellon, Aberdeenshire,
AB41 9AW
☎ 01358 720576, Fax 720001,
Pro 722891, Rest/Bar 723741
Course is off the A90 16 miles N of
Aberdeen.
Parkland course.
Pro Ronnie Urquhart; Founded 1927

18 holes, 5991 yards, S.S.S. 70
† Welcome by prior arrangement.
⌐ WD £15; Sat £18; Sun £18.
◔ Welcome by prior arrangement;
day tickets available (WD £20, Sat
£24, Sun £30); from £14.
⦿ Full clubhouse facilities.
◞ Buchan Hotel; New Inn; Station
Hotel.

9D 52 Monk's Walk, Skibo Castle
The Carnegie Club, Skibo Castle,
Dornoch, Sutherland, IV25 3RQ
⌨ www.carnegieclub.co.uk
✉ skibo@carnegieclubs.com
☎ 01862 894600
Up A9, over Dornoch bridge, turn left
towards Clashmore.
Flat links course.
† Yes, Mon-Fri.
⌐ £130 for 18 holes + lunch.
◔ Yes, still £130 pp.
⦿ Yes.
◞ Skibo Castle.

9D 53 Moray
Stotfield Rd, Lossiemouth, Moray, IV31
6QS
⌨ www.moraygolf.co.uk
✉ secretary@moraygolf.co.uk
☎ 01343 812018, Fax 815102,
Pro 813330
At Lossiemouth turn off from A96, 6
miles N of Elgin, on the coast.
Links course.
Pro Alistair Thomson; Founded 1889
Designed by Tom Morris
2x18 holes, old 6617 new 6004 yards,
S.S.S. new 69 old 73
⌿ Large practice range, private
driving range nearby.
† Welcome by arrangement.
⌐ WD £25; WE £30 (New); WD £35
WE £45 (Old).
◔ Welcome by prior arrangement;
some discounts available for larger
groups; day tickets WD £25, WE £30
(New); WD £35, WE £45 (Old); from
£30.
⦿ Full clubhouse facilities.
◞ Stotfield; Skerry Brae.

9D 54 Muir of Ord
Great North Rd, Muir of Ord, Ross-
shire, IV6 7SX
⌨ www.golfhighland.co.uk
✉ muirgolf@supanet.com
☎ 01463 870825, Fax 871867
15 miles N of Inverness.
Moorland/parkland course with links-
type fairways.

Founded 1875
Designed by James Baird
18 holes, 5557 yards, S.S.S. 68
† Welcome but not before 11am at
WE and on competition days.
⌐ WD £18; WE £20.
◔ Welcome by prior arrangement;
discounts available for groups of more
than 15; daily and weekly tickets
available; snooker and pool tables;
from £14.
⦿ Bar and catering facilities.
◞ Ord Arms; Priory.

9D 55 Murcar ⬧
Bridge Of Don, Aberdeen,
Aberdeenshire, AB23 8BD
⌨ www.murcar.co.uk
✉ murcar-golf-club@lineone.net
☎ 01224 704354, Fax 704354,
Pro 704370, Rest/Bar 705345
On A92 3 miles from Aberdeen on road
to Fraserburgh.
Seaside course.
Pro Gary Forbes; Founded 1909
Designed by Archie Simpson
18 holes, 6241 yards, S.S.S. 71
⌿ Practice area.
† Welcome; restrictions Sat until
3pm; Sun & Tues am; Wed pm, but
can play between 2pm-4pm on Wed.
⌐ WD £45, day ticket £65; WE £55;
day ticket £75.
◔ Welcome WD with prior
arrangement with Sec; daily tickets
from £65; catering packages by
arrangement; also 9-hole course with a
par of 35.
⦿ Full clubhouse facilities.
◞ Mill of Mundurno.

9D 56 Nairn (see overleaf)
Seabank Rd, Nairn, IV12 4HB
✉ bookings@nairngolfclub.cou.uk
☎ 01667 453208, Fax 456328,
Pro 452787, Rest/Bar 452103
Off A96 at Nairn Old Parish Church.
Championship links;1990 Walker Cup
venue.
Pro Robin Fyfe; Founded 1887
Designed by Tom Morris; James Braid;
A Simpson
18 holes, 6745 yards, S.S.S. 72
⌿ Practice range.
† Welcome by prior arrangement.
⌐ WD £70; WE £70.
◔ Welcome by prior arrangement;
handicap certs required; catering
packages by arrangement; £60.
⦿ Full clubhouse facilities.
◞ Golf View; Newton; Altonburn;
Windsor hotel.

Nairn

Shortly after staging the 1999 Walker Cup, Nairn Golf Club celebrated its 112th anniversary making it something of an upstart in the long and colourful history of Scottish golf. But rarely will you find a more spectacular seaside course or better greens that even in mid-winter are true and well preserved.

Nairn also has the reputation of one of the driest and most temperate climates in Britain. When much of Scotland is saturated by rainfall and gripped by freezing temperatures, Nairn can be positively balmy. Because of this micro-climate, winter greens, unavoidable at many courses, are used on average only three weekends a year.

The course, first put on the golfing map in 1895 when all the leading players of the day competed for what was then an exceptional purse of twenty pounds, was reshaped in the closing years of the last century and then modified over a decade by five-times Open champion James Braid.

It was Braid who, in 1923, reported: "The putting greens were always the outstanding feature of the course and still fully maintain their excellence. The texture and turf and the character of the greens are unrivalled." The same could be said now, partly because some of the courses landing areas are roped off early in the year – except for competition play – as an act of preservation.

As with so many Scottish courses, anecdotes abound at Nairn. Garfield is perhaps the most frequently discussed of these, a cat that resided in the gorse bushes between the third green and the fourth tee. It enjoyed the generosity of the locals who would carry tubs of cat food in their bags. Sadly Garfield is no more, which at least allows for full concentration at the 144-yard par three fourth, with bunkers left and right of a pin often cruelly placed tight to the sea on this kidney-shaped green.

The fifth is even more intimidating, the toughest of drives, with the sea close on the right, and two bunkers left. It is a great hole, but if it is length that turns you on, then the seventh takes some beating. With the prevailing wind in their faces and from the championship tee, even some of the best amateur players cannot make the carry over bushes and heather required to reach the fairway.

The eighth, on the other hand, proves that you don't need distance to make a good hole. It's relatively short, but the approach has to land on a green that looks and plays like an inverted saucer.

The thirteenth is the hardest hole on the course and has drawn praise from countless American architects looking for a stroke index one to copy. As if trouble on both sides of the fairway after a drive towards a frighteningly large bunker isn't enough, an undulating green protected by bunkers on both sides nearly always leaves a fast and awkward putt.

If Nairn were to have a signature hole, it would probably be the fourteenth with its gorgeous views over the Moray Firth to the Black Isle beyond. It may only be a par three, but you are playing from a raised tee, where anything from a driver to a medium iron is needed depending on the wind direction. The green is conspicuous by a large adjacent gully and can reduce a wobbly putter to tears.

Nairn has done its best in recent years to move from its early exclusive character to relaxed informality. One of the first entries in the club's suggestion book was that women should only be allowed into the clubhouse when the thermometer reached freezing point. Thankfully times have changed. — **Andrew Warshaw**

9D 57 Nairn Dunbar
Lochloy Rd, Nairn, IV12 5AE
🏠 www.nairndunbar.com
✉ davidtorrance@
nairndunbargolfclub.fsnet.co.uk
☎ 01667 452741, Fax 456897,
Pro 453964
0.5 miles E of Nairn on A96.
Links course.
Pro D Torrance; Founded 1899
18 holes, 6712 yards, S.S.S. 73
⚐ 300 yard practice facility.
† Welcome.
⚑ WD £35; WE £43.
⚒ Welcome but booking essential.
Group rates are negotiable.
🍽 Full clubhouse facilities available.
⚐ Golf View; Links; Claymore.

9D 58 Newburgh-on-Ythan
Beach Road, Newburgh,
Aberdeenshire, AB41 6BE
🏠 www.newborough-on-ythan.co.uk
✉ secretary@newborough.co.uk
☎ 01358 789058, Fax 788104
From A90 12 miles N of Aberdeen to
A975 to Newburgh.
Links course; new 9 holes added 1996.
Founded 1888/1996
Designed by Greens of Scotland
(Aberdeen)
18 holes, 6162 yards, S.S.S. 72
⚐ One progress.
† Welcome.
⚑ Terms available on application.
⚒ Welcome by prior arrangement; full
day's golf and catering packages
available; terms available on
application.
🍽 New clubhouse opened in July
1999.
⚐ Udny Arms; Ythan Hotel.

9D 59 Newmachar   ♛
Swailend, Newmachar, Aberdeen,
AB21 7UU
☎ 01651 863002, Fax 863055,
Pro 863222
12 miles N of Aberdeen off A947
Aberdeen-Banff road.
Parkland course.
Pro Gordon Simpson; Founded 1990
Designed by Dave Thomas
Hawkshill: 18 holes, 6623 yards,
S.S.S. 73
Swailend: 18 holes, 6388 yards, S.S.S. 70
⚐ Practice range 12 bays.
† Welcome but handicap certs are
required.
⚑ WD £30 WE £40 (Hawkshill); WD
£15 WE £20 (Swailend).
⚒ Welcome by prior arrangement; from
£30 (Hawkshill); from £15 (Swailend).

🍽 Full clubhouse facilities available.
⚐ Dunavon House; Kirkhill; Marriott
Dyce.

9D 60 Newtonmore
Golf Course Rd, Newtonmore,
Highland, PH20 1AT
🏠 www.newtonmoregolf.com
✉ secretary@newtonmoregolf.com
☎ 01540 673328, Pro 673611
2 miles S of Newtonmore off the A9.
Parkland course.
Pro Bob Henderson; Founded 1893
Designed by James Braid
18 holes, 6057 yards, S.S.S. 69
† Welcome.
⚑ WD £17; WE £18.
⚒ Welcome by prior arrangement
with Sec; day tickets available; catering
packages by arrangement; pool table;
from £15.
🍽 Full clubhouse facilities; except
Tuesdays, exceptions made for large
parties.
⚐ Glen; Balavil Sports; Lodge;
Mains.

9D 61 Northern
Golf Rd, Kings Links, Aberdeen, AB24
5QB
☎ 01224 636440, Fax 622679
E of City. Down at the sea.
Municipal seaside course.
18 holes, 6270 yards, S.S.S. 69
⚐ 18 all floodlit.
† Welcome.
⚑ POA.
⚒ Welcome by arrangement; terms
on application.
🍽 Full facilities at WE; by
arrangement WD.

9D 62 Oldmeldrum   ♛
Kirk Brae, Oldmeldrum, Aberdeenshire,
AB51 0DJ
☎ 01651 872648, Fax 873555,
Pro 873555, Sec 872648,
Rest/Bar 872648
On A947 from Aberdeen.
Parkland course; extended to 18 holes
in 1994.
Pro Hamish Love; Founded 1885
18 holes, 5988 yards, S.S.S. 69
† Welcome by prior arrangement.
⚑ WD £14; WE £20.
⚒ Welcome by prior arrangement
with pro; catering packages by
arrangement; from £14.
🍽 Full facilities.
⚐ Meldrum House; Meldrum Arms;
Redgarth; Cromlet Hill B&B.

9D 63 Orkney
Grainbank, Kirkwall, Orkney, KW15
1RD
☎ 01856 872457
W boundary of Kirkwall.
Parkland course.
Founded 1889
18 holes, 5411 yards, S.S.S. 67
† Welcome.
⚑ WD £15; WE £15 per day in
summer. in winter £5 per day.
⚒ Welcome; day's golf; snacks and
meals can be arranged at lunchtime
during the summer; games room; from
£10.
🍽 Full clubhouse facilities.

9D 64 Peterculter   ♛
Oldtown, Burnside Rd, Peterculter,
Aberdeen, AB14 0LN
🏠 www.petercultergolfclub.co.uk
✉ info@petercultergolfclub.co.uk
☎ 01224 735245, Fax 735580,
Pro 734994, Rest/Bar 735245
Take the A93 to Royal Deeside into
Peterculter turning left before Rob Roy
Bridge.
Undulating scenic parkland course on
banks of River Dee.
Pro Dean Vannet; Founded 1989
Designed by E Lappin/Greens of
Scotland
18 holes, 5947 yards, S.S.S. 69
† Welcome.
⚑ WD £12; WE £16.
⚒ Welcome WD by prior
arrangement; day tickets (WD £18, WE
£21); catering by prior arrangement;
from £12.
🍽 Full clubhouse facilities.
⚐ Golden Arms.

9D 65 Peterhead   ♛
Craigewan Links, Peterhead,
Aberdeenshire, AB42 1LT
✉ phdgc@freenetname.co.uk
☎ 01779 472149, Fax 480725,
Sec 480725, Rest/Bar 472149
On A92 and A975 30 miles N of
Aberdeen.
Seaside links course.
Founded 1841
Designed by Willie Park and James
Braid
18 holes, 6173 yards, S.S.S. 71
† Welcome; some Sat restrictions
apply.
⚑ WD £18 per round, £24 per day;
WE £22 per round, £30 per day. In
winter, WD £13.50 per day, WE
£16.50. 9-hole course: £10 for adults,
£5 for juniors.
⚒ Welcome by arrangement with

Royal Dornoch

Long before a golf club was formed at Dornoch in 1877, the game was played along the seashore and frowned upon by the authorities because they wanted the local subjects to practise a different sort of marksmanship. Good soldiers were needed more than good golfers.

Today Royal Dornoch, which has staged both the Amateur and Scottish Amateur, is rated among the best courses in the world. It has a deserved reputation as one of the hidden gems of the game, being far removed from Scotland's main centres of population and, until the last 30 years, relatively inaccessible.

Dress code is more flexible than at many elite clubs, though if you get caught with your hat on in the bar, it will cost you a round of drinks. Most people aren't warned until they are standing at the counter!

In terms of romance and scenery, it is simply unique with a local population of just 1,200 and a mesmerising flow of holes, contours and colours. Prince Andrew and Ben Crenshaw are among the honorary members, while Tom Watson, who headed north for a quick practice round before winning the third of his five Opens at Muirfield, ended up playing three times in a day. He called it "the most enjoyment I've ever had on the golf course."

Royal Dornoch is fun yet also a supreme test of skill and concentration for your average handicapper, which is one reason why certificates are required: 24 maximum for men, 39 for women. Is this a rare example of men being discriminated against by a golf club?

American golfers love the peacefulness and serenity of Dornoch despite being forced either to carry their bags or use trollies. Only two buggies are provided, each for players with a proven medical ailment.

After a relatively uncomplicated opening hole, the par three second is a killer round the green, which is 45 yards from front to back, surrounded by steep bankings and two monster bunkers with horribly deep faces. Watson said that the second to the second at Dornoch was the hardest shot he had ever played.

Although Dornoch is a haven of tranquility most of the time and one of the few links courses where you can see the sea from every hole, it does have one off-putting factor. Every few minutes fighter jets roar overhead, threatening your concentration as they fly in and out of the nearby bombing base in a constant stream of training exercises.

Dornoch has no official signature hole, but the seventh, looking back along the beach and the North Sea where dolphins frolic, has arguably the best view while the fourth, a 427-yard par four, has a landing area off the tee of only about 30 yards, the drive having to carry rough, bunkers and hollows.

The famous fourteenth is a double dog-leg and the only hole without a single bunker. Instead, the ultra thin green is 48 yards wide, but only 24 yards deep and sits across the line of play. No wonder the hole is named 'Foxy'.

Dornoch is generally fair, rewards good shots and won't have you searching for a ball that you swear was sweetly and accurately struck. There is a downside, however. You can easily go round without losing a single ball, only to discover you haven't played anywhere near your handicap.

Hitting fairways is relatively straightforward, but at Dornoch pitching and chipping is everything. You are just as likely to be faced by a fifty-yard chip as a five-yard chip because of the size and speed of the greens. Just ask Tom Watson.

— Andrew Warshaw

Royal Dornoch Golf Club

Golf Road, Dornoch, Sutherland IV25 3LW

The Championship Course, rated 9th amongst Britain's top courses is a links of rare subtlety in a splendid setting. The second 18 hole links course, **The Struie**, provides a fresh quality challenge.

Office Tel: **(01862) 810219**
Secretary Tel: **(01862) 811220**
Fax: **(01862) 810792**
E-mail: **rdgc@royaldornich.com**
Web site: **http://www.royaldornoch.com**

Sec; restrictions Sat; catering packages by arrangement; also 9-hole course, 2400 yards, S.S.S. 60; from £16.
Clubhouse with full facilities.
Palace; Waterside Inn.

9D 66 Portlethen ♛
Badentoy Rd, Portlethen, Aberdeenshire, AB12 4YA
info@portlethengc.fsnet.co.uk
☎ 01224 781090, Fax 781090, Pro 782571, Rest/Bar 782575
Course is on the A90 six miles S of Aberdeen.
Parkland course.
Pro Muriel Thomson; Founded 1989
Designed by Donald Steel
18 holes, 6670 yards, S.S.S. 72
Welcome WD 9.30am-3pm; not Sat; Sun after 1pm.
WD £15; WE £22.
Welcome by prior arrangement with admin dept; catering packages available; pool table and buggy hire; from £14.
Full clubhouse facilities.
Travel Inn.

9D 67 Reay ♛
The Clubhouse, Reay, by Thurso, Caithness, KW14 7RE
☎ 01847 811288
11 miles W of Thurso.
Seaside links course.
Founded 1893
18 holes, 5884 yards, S.S.S. 68
Welcome except competition days.
Available upon application.
Welcome by prior arrangement with Sec; catering by prior arrangement; from £15.
Full clubhouse facilities.
Forss House Forss; Park Hotel; Thurso; Melvich Hotel.

9D 68 Rothes
Blackhall, Rothes, Aberlour, Banffshire, AB38 7AN
☎ 01340 831443, Fax 831443, Sec 831617, Rest/Bar 831443

10 miles S of Elgin on A941 at S end of the town.
Parkland course.
Founded 1990
Designed by John Souter
9 holes, 4972 yards, S.S.S. 65
Everyone welcome.
WD £12; WE £15.
Welcome by prior arrangement; packages for golf and catering can be arranged; terms available on application.
Full bar and restaurant facilities.
Ben Aigen; Eastbank; Craigellachie Hotel Graigellachie.

9D 69 Royal Aberdeen *(see overleaf)*
Links Road, Bridge of Don, Aberdeen, AB23 8AT
www.royalaberdeengolf.com
admin@royalaberdeengolf.com
☎ 01224 702571, Fax 826591, Pro 702221
2 miles N on the main road from Aberdeen on the A90 to Fraserburgh.
Seaside links course.
Pro R MacAskill; Founded 1780
Designed by Robert Simpson and James Braid
18 holes, 6372 yards, S.S.S. 71
Welcome WD; WE restrictions.
WD £55; WE £65.
Welcome by prior arrangement WD; day ticket £75; also Silverburn shorter course for high handicappers, 4066 yards; from £55.
Dining room; lounge and bar.
Atholl; Marcliffe; Udny Arms.

9D 70 Royal Dornoch
Golf Rd, Dornoch, Sutherland, IV25 3LW
www.royaldornoch.com
☎ 01862 810219, Fax 810792, Pro 810902, Sec 811220, Rest/Bar 810371
Course is 45 miles N of Inverness off the A9.
Championship links course.
Pro A Skinner; Founded 1877
Designed by Tom Morris; John Sutherland; George Duncan
36 holes, 6514 yards, S.S.S. 73

Welcome with handicap certs.
WD £57; WE £65.
Welcome by prior arrangement; handicap certs required; catering by prior arrangement; and combination tickets with Struie course also available; from £57.
Full clubhouse facilities.
Club can provide a list of local hotels GH and B&Bs.

9D 71 Royal Tarlair
Buchan St, Macduff, Aberdeenshire, AB44 1TA
www.royaltarliar.co.uk
info@royaltarliar.co.uk
☎ 01261 832897, Fax 833455
Course is on the A98 48 miles from Aberdeen.
Parkland course.
Founded 1923
Designed by George Smith
18 holes, 5866 yards, S.S.S. 68
Welcome.
£15 round. Per day £20.
None.
Full catering and bar.
Highland Haven; Banff Springs.

9D 72 Shetland
Dale, Gott by Lerwick, Shetland Is
☎ 01595 840369
3 miles N of Lerwick.
Undulating moorland course.
Founded 1891
Designed by Fraser Middleton
18 holes, 5776 yards, S.S.S. 69
Welcome.
WD from £12; WE from £12.
Welcome by arrangement; weekly tickets available; from £12.
Bar and snacks.
Lerwick; Grand; Queens.

9D 73 Skeabost
Skeabost Bridge, Isle of Skye, IV51 9NP
☎ 01470 532322
40 miles from Kyle of Lochalsh.
Parkland course.
Founded 1984
9 holes, 3224 yards, S.S.S. 60
Welcome.

Royal Aberdeen

Founded in 1790, the Royal Aberdeen club, or Balgownie Links as the actual course is named, is widely recognised as possessing one of the finest outward nines in the world. Year after year, some of golf's most knowledgeable architects come to look and learn.

With only 350 members and a traditional gentlemanly clubhouse, Royal Aberdeen is a classic old-style golf club of log fires and whisky. It disregards pub-type accessories such as pool tables or one-armed bandits. It is enough to have a natural links course that meanders out through a valley and back along a plateau.

Although the course runs essentially out and back along the North Sea shore, individual holes switch direction subtly, changing the angle of the wind and bringing variety and balance to a testing examination of golf at any level.

What makes the outward nine so special is the blend of holes, with some of the tees placed on the landward side, others on the seaward side, plus the wonderful dune formations, good greens and stunning views.

After an opening hole conspicuous by two well-positioned bunkers that can play havoc with club selection, the golfer is faced by the longest hole on the course. The second is a classic par five at 507 yards that was simply meant to be a golf hole and nothing else. Stand on the tee and watch how the fairway stretches through the dunes. An accurate drive is essential. Then try to thread your second up through the valley. If you negotiate that, a tricky pitch awaits you to a green guarded by bunkers right and left.

The third is a strong par three from an elevated tee on the seaward side and any high handicappers who manage to carry the bunker on to the green deserve considerable praise. Don't be deceived by the fifth that, although relatively short at 290 off the yellow tees, has a strategically positioned bunker to prevent players slamming their tee shot with a driver.

The wind plays such a big part here that the golf course is always shifting. "You can never go out there and think you can hit a certain club on a certain hole," said Royal Aberdeen professional Ronnie MacAskill.

"The golf course changes all the time. The slightest breeze makes the course very angry and it tests you right from the word go which makes the outward nine so interesting. You have to be right on the ball, if you'll excuse the pun. I've been here for 27 years and every time I go out, the course throws up a new challenge."

If you get to the turn with your confidence intact, you shouldn't have too many problems coming back. No par fives await you, but beware the blind drive on the tenth where anyone who overshoots the green is left with an awkward downhill chip or putt. The eighteenth is a superb finishing hole with an elevated tee into a bunkered valley followed by an elevated green.

Because Royal Aberdeen is on a sand base and drains quickly, winter rules normally apply for just two months of the year, with only frost forcing closure. When that happens, play invariably switches to the club's second, far shorter Silverburn course - part links, part parkland - which is a fair test in itself.

Although the whirr of helicopters flying to and from the North Sea oil rigs have become a regular and not always welcome feature at Balgownie, most players have managed to adapt over the years. Besides, the choppers provide an additional excuse for that bad round! — **Andrew Warshaw**

WD £10; WE £10.
🍽 Bar and restaurant in the hotel
April-Oct.
🛏 Skeabost (26 beds).

9D 74 **Spean Bridge**
Station Rd, Spean Bridge, Fort William,
PH34 4EU
☎ 01397 704954
Course is eight miles N of Fort William
on the A82.
Inland course.
9 holes, 2203 yards, S.S.S. 63
† By arrangement only.
£8.
🏌 By arrangement only.

9D 75 **Spey Bay**
Spey Bay, Fochabers, Moray,
IV32 7PJ
☎ 01343 820424
Turn off the A96 near Fochabers
Bridge follow the B9104 Spey Bay
road to coast.
Links course.
Founded 1907
Designed by Ben Sayers
18 holes, 6092 yards, S.S.S. 69
🏌 Practice range.
† Welcome but booking advisable on
Sundays.
WD £10; WE £13.
🏌 Welcome by application; day
packages available; tennis;
petanque; putting; terms available on
application.
🍽 Full facilities; meals and bar all
day; bar lunches in winter.
🛏 Spey Bay.

9D 76 **Stonehaven**   ☾
Cowie, Stonehaven, Aberdeenshire,
AB39 3RH
☎ 01569 762124, Fax 765973
N of Stonehaven on A92; signposted at
the mini roundabout near the Leisure
Centre.
Parkland course on cliffs overlooking
Stonehaven Bay.
Founded 1888
Designed by A Simpson
18 holes, 5103 yards, S.S.S. 65
† Welcome except before 4pm Sat
and on competition days.
WD £15; WE £20.
🏌 Welcome WD and Sun; catering
available by prior application to
Secretary; terms available on
application.
🍽 Full facilities. everyday except
Mondays.
🛏 Heugh; County; Station; Crown.

9D 77 **Stornoway**
Castle Grounds, Stornoway, Isle of
Lewis, HS2 0XP
☎ 01851 702240
0.5 miles outside Stornoway in the
grounds of Lews Castle.
Parkland course.
Founded 1890
Designed by JR Stutt
18 holes, 5252 yards, S.S.S. 66
† Welcome except on Sun.
Terms on application.
🏌 Welcome by prior written
arrangement with Secretary; special
rates available by application; from £12.
🍽 Bar and bar snacks.
🛏 Caberfeidh; Royal; Seaforth.

9D 78 **Strathlene**   ☾
Portessie, Buckie, Banffshire, AB56
2DJ
🖥 www.scottishholidaysstrathgolf@
aol.com
☎ 01542 831798, Fax 831798,
Pro 831798, Sec 831798
Off the Elgin-Banff coast route 2 miles
E of Buckie Harbour.
Undulating moorland/seaside course.
Pro Brian Slorach; Founded 1877
Designed by Alex Smith
18 holes, 5977 yards, S.S.S. 69
🏌 Practice range.
† Welcome except before 9.30am
and between 12 noon-2pm at WE.
Terms on application.
🏌 Welcome by prior arrangement;
catering by arrangement; day and
weekly tickets available; terms on
application.
🍽 Full facilities; one bar and meals.
🛏 St Andrews.

9D 79 **Strathpeffer Spa**
Strathpeffer, Ross-shire, IV14 9AS
☎ 01997 421219
5 miles N of Dingwall.
Upland course.
Founded 1888
Designed by W Park
18 holes, 4813 yards, S.S.S. 64
† Welcome except before 10am Sun.
Available on application.
🏌 Welcome by prior arrangement;
packages available for golf and
catering.
🍽 Full facilities.
🛏 Ben Wyvis; Highland; Holly
Lodge.

9D 80 **Stromness**
Ness, Stromness, Orkney, K16 3DU
☎ 01856 850772

Situated at the S end of town bordering
Hoy Sound.
Parkland course.
Founded 1890
18 holes, 4762 yards, S.S.S. 63
† Welcome.
WD £12; WE £12.
🏌 Welcome; catering packages by
arrangement; tennis; pool table; darts
and bowls; terms available on
application.
🛏 Stromness; Royal.

9D 81 **Tain Golf Club**   ☾
Chapel Road, Tain, Ross-shire, IV19
1JE
🖥 www.tain-golfclub.co.uk
📧 info@tain-golfclub.co.uk
☎ 01862 892314, Fax 892099,
Sec 892314, Rest/Bar 892314
35 miles N of Inverness on A9; 0.25
miles from Tain.
Links course.
Founded 1890
Designed by Tom Morris
18 holes, 6404 yards, S.S.S. 71
† Everyone welcome.
WD £30 per round, £36 per day;
WE £36 per round, £46 per day.
🏌 Welcome by prior arrangement;
discount of 20% for groups; catering by
arrangement; terms available on
application.
🍽 Full facilities.
🛏 Morangie; Mansfield House both
Tain; Royal; Carnegie Lodge bot Tain.

9D 82 **Tarbat**
Rock Cottage, Rock Field Village,
Portmahomack, Ross-Shire,
IV20 1SL
📧 christina@
portmahomack.fsnet.co.uk
☎ 01862 871486
9 miles E of Tain on the B9165 off the
A9.
Seaside links course.
Founded 1909
Designed by J. Sutherland
9 holes, 5082 yards, S.S.S. 65
🏌 Practice ground.
† Welcome; some restrictions on Sat.
Day ticket: WD £12; WE £12.
🏌 Welcome by prior arrangement
with Sec; catering by arrangement;
local hotels provide full meal and bar
service.
🍽 Limited facilities; see local hotels.
🛏 Castle; Caledonian; Oyster
Catcher.

9D 83 Tarland
Aberdeen Rd, Tarland, Aboyne,
Aberdeenshire, AB34 4YN
☎ 01339 881413
5 miles NW of Aboyne; 30 miles W of
Aberdeen.
Parkland course.
Founded 1908
Designed by Tom Morris
9 holes, 5875 yards, S.S.S. 68
† Welcome.
Ⅰ WD £12; WE £15.
⟳ Welcome by prior arrangement;
terms on application.
❘●❘ Full facilities June-Sept; otherwise
by arrangement.
↙ Aberdeen Arms; Commercial.

9D 84 Thurso
Newlands Of Geise, Thurso,
Caithness, KW14 7XF
☎ 01847 893807
2 miles SW from centre of Thurso on
B870.
Parkland course.
Founded 1893
Designed by W Stuart
18 holes, 5853 yards, S.S.S. 69
Ⅰ Practice net and indoor beginners
net.
† Welcome.
Ⅰ Terms on application.
⟳ Welcome by prior arrangement;
terms on application.
❘●❘ Full facilities.
↙ Park Hotel.

9D 85 Torphins
Bog Rd, Torphins, Aberdeenshire,
AB31 4JU
☎ 01339 882115, Sec 882402
Signposted in village; 6 miles W of
Banchory on A980.
Parkland course with Highland views.
Founded 1896
9 holes, 4738 yards, S.S.S. 63
† Welcome.
Ⅰ WD £10 WE £12.
⟳ Welcome by prior arrangement.
❘●❘ Full facilities at WE.
↙ Learney Arms.

9D 86 Torvean
Glenurquhart Rd, Inverness,
Inverness-shire, IV3 8JN
☎ 01463 225651, Fax 225651,

Pro 711434, Rest/Bar 236648
On A82 Fort William road approx
1 mile from Inverness town centre.
Municipal parkland course.
Founded 1962
Designed by T Hamilton
18 holes, 5784 yards, S.S.S. 68
† Welcome; tee bookings advisable.
Ⅰ WD £14.10; WE £16 aprox, call to
confirm, winter rates will apply.
⟳ Welcome by arrangement with
Highland Council.
❘●❘ Town Hall.
↙ Inverness; terms on application.
Meals by arrangement. Lochness.

9D 87 Traigh Golf Course
Traigh, Arisag, by Mallaig, Arsaig,
Inverness-Shire, PH39 4NT
☎ 01687 450337, Sec 450645
On the A830 Fort William to Mallaig road.
Links course.
Founded 1995
Designed by John Salvesen
9 holes, 4912 yards, S.S.S. 65
† Welcome.
Ⅰ Terms on application.
❘●❘ Clubhouse snacks.
↙ Arisaig Hotel: Arisaig House; Marine;
Glas na Cardoch; West Highland.

9D 88 Turriff   ☎
Rosehall, Turriff, Aberdeenshire, AB53
4HD
🖳 www.terriffgolfclub.freeonline.co.uk
☎ 01888 562982, Fax 568050,
Pro 563025, Sec 562982,
Rest/Bar 562982
On B9024 1 mile up Huntly road.
Meadowland/parkland course.
Pro John Black; Founded 1896
18 holes, 6107 yards, S.S.S. 69
Ⅰ Practice ground.
† Welcome except before 10am WE;
handicap certs required.
Ⅰ WD £18; WE £22.
⟳ Welcome by arrangement with
Sec; day tickets available (WD £20,
WE £27); from £16.
❘●❘ By prior arrangement.
↙ Union; White Heather. Bamff Strings.

9D 89 Westhill
Westhill Heights, Aberdeenshire, AB32
6RY
🖳 wgolfclub@aol.com

☎ 01224 740159, Fax 740159,
Pro 740159, Sec 742567,
Rest/Bar 743361
Course is on A944 6 miles from
Aberdeen.
Undulating parkland/moorland course.
Pro George Bruce; Founded 1977
Designed by Charles Lawrie
18 holes, 5849 yards, S.S.S. 69
Ⅰ Practice green.
† Welcome except Sat.
Ⅰ WD £14; WE £20.
⟳ Welcome WD and Sun by prior
arrangement; catering packages by
special arrangement; terms on
application.
❘●❘ Bar facilities.
↙ Broadstreik Inn; Westhill Inn.

9D 90 Whalsay
Skaw Taing, Island of Whalsay,
Shetland, ZE2 9AL
☎ 01806 566483
At N end of Island.
Moorland course.
Founded 1975
18 holes, 6009 yards, S.S.S. 68
† Welcome; restrictions on
competition days.
Ⅰ WD £10; WE £10.
⟳ Welcome by prior arrangement;
packages available; terms on
application.
❘●❘ Bar and catering facilities
available.
↙ Hotels on Shetland.

9D 91 Wick
Reiss, Wick, Caithness, KW1 4RW
☎ 01955 602726, Sec 602935
Course is on the A9 three miles north
of Wick.
Links course.
Founded 1870
Designed by McCulloch
18 holes, 5976 yards, S.S.S. 70
† Welcome.
Ⅰ WD £15; WE £15.
⟳ Welcome by prior arrangement
catering by prior arrangement.
❘●❘ Bar an limited catering facilities
available.
↙ Mackays.

It has been claimed that the Blorenge and the river Usk are "the purple headed mountain and the river running by" of Cecil Alexander's hymn 'All things bright and beautiful'. Although it's more likely that Alexander wrote the words in her native Ireland, you can understand how the myth of Wales arose.

The Monmouthshire, with views of the Blorenge and the Usk, Royal St Davids and Aberdovey on the West coast, Nefyn and District, perched on the cliffs, Cradoc and Llandrindod Wells, at the foothills of the Brecon Beacons and Cambrian Mountains, Ashburnham, overlooking Carmarthen Bay, the list just goes on and on. Wales has a preponderance of spectacularly beautiful golf courses.

Darwin described Aberdovey as "the course that my soul loves best in the world." A few miles to the north, Royal St Davids nestles in the shadow of Harlech castle and Snowdon. Actually, 'nestle' is not really a word that many associate with St Davids. When people stagger in after grappling with gale force winds and a sequence of gargantuan dunes, after a struggle to even reach some of the fairways, the language is a bit fresher than 'nestle'. It has been said that St David's is the hardest par 69 in the world and not many would disagree.

Royal Porthcawl, the host of the 1995 Walker Cup, has the reputation of being Wales's top course. It is quite some accolade because there are so many to choose from. Not so very far from Porthcawl, Southerndown is a wonderful anachronism.

There is a fascinating variety of holes, right from the contradictory opening par four of short yardage and long carries, that goes up a hill without an apparent end. The course is very well mowed by sheep, although the recycled material they leave behind can cause awkward lies. And being in Wales, there are superb views, this time of the Bristol Channel.

Celtic Manor, the new, flash kid on the block, has done a great deal to promote golf in Wales after being awarded the 2010 Ryder Cup. But the decision had more to do with rewarding a sponsor of the European Tour than favouring a great golf course.

Of Wales's golfing hotels, many people have a soft spot for St Pierre, the first post-war championship course to be built in Britain. It is incredible now to think that the cost of the construction, the land and the manor house (where the crown jewels were stashed during the Battle of Agincourt) was just £30,000. It has many childhood memories for me, but then it is that sort of place. Wasn't it here that Bernhard Langer climbed up a tree to play a chip shot onto the green?

Wales is full of myth. At the Glamorganshire the card says "slow play is deplored". It was here that between the wars a member won a bet by taking 68 minutes to play eighteen holes. We all fancy we could do that, but could we score 63 in the process.

Tenby, the oldest constituted club in Wales, Borth & Ynslas, Conwy, Prestatyn, Pyle & Kenfig, Pennard, they all have courses worth the playing and stories worth the telling.

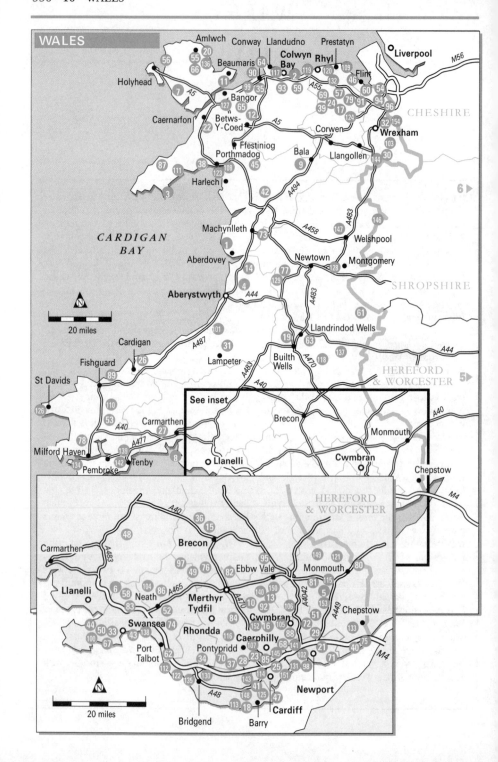

Aberdovey

Aberdovey is not the toughest links in Britain, but if offered only one course on which to play for the rest of your life, you might just choose Aberdovey. It is full of change and intrigue to challenge the single figure handicapper and it is kind to older golfers who can no longer manage huge carries to the fairways. There is magic here.

Maybe it is the scenery, which isn't dramatic on the grand scale, but a gentle blend of dunes, hills and water. Maybe it is the railway that runs alongside and promises great adventures by steam train. Maybe it is the sheep that still graze on the course. Maybe it is the ghost of Bernard Darwin. Whatever it is, you can't miss the magic.

Darwin's uncle first brought golf to this piece of land along with nine flowerpots to hole out in. Over the ensuing years Bernard saw many changes to the club, which now has a room named after him, but he never fell out of love with it. He wrote, "About this one course in the world I am a hopeless and shameful sentimentalist and I glory in my shame."

When Darwin was asked to nominate his favourite individual eighteen holes for a cigarette promotion, his sixteenth was Aberdovey's 288-yard par four. A smoker of Churchman's No.1 had a one in eighteen chance of getting a cigarette card in his packet with a map and Darwin's description of the hole on it.

The sixteenth runs beside the railway line and these days tempts the long hitters to go for the carry over some rough humps to a raised green. The alternative is to lay up with a mid iron, but still face quite an intimidating second shot if the wind is blowing. In response to an angry train

driver who had just been pinged by his drive, one living member said, "If you had been on time, I'd have missed you."

There are many superb holes here. The start has three bewitching par fours and a famous par three called 'Cader'. This was once the site of a monstrous bunker with sleepers and a periscope with which to spot the fate of the ball, but both have sadly passed away. The par three twelfth to an elevated green overlooking Cardigan Bay is a wondrous hole - when the south westerly is blowing it takes a lot of courage to hang your ball out over water and sand that you know are there, but can't see. From there it is a straight strong finish of fours and fives as you turn towards the hills beyond the Dovey Estuary.

The Welsh Amateur hasn't been held here since 1966, when the local farmers only agreed to remove their cattle from the course at the very last minute. The farmers had to be bought off after blaming the club for the loss of some sheep on the railway line. For most competitions the animals stay. When one competitor asked for a ruling after his ball landed in a cowpat, the Welsh Golfing Union official is reputed to have imposed a two-shot penalty because the ball was in motion.

The amiable members say that they don't want too many good things to be heard about their club in case they are overrun, but secretly they rather like showing people around, including royalty. It takes the Duke of York one hour and six minutes to travel from London to Aberdovey. But he does have a helicopter. Bernard Darwin's romantic train journey took a little longer. — **Mark Reason**

Abersoch Golf Club

Golf Road, Abersoch, Pwllheli, Gwynedd LL53 7EY
Office tel: 01758 712636   Pro shop: 01758 712622   Fax: 01758 712777
www.abersochgolf.co.uk

Abersoch Golf Course is a picturesque Links and parkland course with far-reaching breathtaking views across Cardigan Bay and the Snowdonian mountains, with mature trees and water hazards, providing a challenge for golfers of all standards. Designed in 1908 by the great Harry Vardon - six time winner of the Open Championship, the course has since been extended to 18 holes. Built on a spacious sixty-acre site adjoining the beach - all the greens are constructed on sand to ensure optimum conditions for golfers in all conditions. With a sheltered position and a mild climate, Abersoch is the ideal course all year round. To make your visit as comfortable as possible, we also have a full catering service, all-day bar facilities and special golfing weekend breaks including accommodation. Enjoy a warm welcome at Abersoch!

---

10 1 Aberdovey
Station Road, Aberdovey, Gwynedd,
LL35 0RT
🏌 www.aberdoveygolf.co.uk
☎ 01654 767493, Fax 767027, Pro
767602, Sec 767493, Rest/Bar 767210
On A493 W of Aberdovey, adjacent to
station.
Links course.
Pro John Davies; Founded 1892
18 holes, 6445 yards, S.S.S. 71
⚐ Practice area.
✝ Welcome with handicap certs.
Ⅰ WD £30; WE £37.50.
⚑ Welcome by prior arrangement;
handicap certs needed; terms on
application.
🍽 Clubhouse facilities.
⌂ Trefeddian; Bodfor; Plas Penhelig;
Brodawell.

10 2 Abergele & Pensarn   ♛
Tan-Y-Gopa Rd, Abergele,
Denbighshire, LL22 8DS
☎ 01745 824034, Fax 824034,
Pro 823813, Sec 824034, Rest/Bar
826716
A55 at Abergele/Rhuddlan exit;
through town; first left past the police
station.
Parkland course.
Pro IR Runcie; Founded 1910
Designed by Hawtree & Sons
18 holes, 6526 yards, S.S.S. 72
✝ Welcome by arrangement.
Ⅰ Terms on application.
⚑ Welcome by arrangement;
members have priority until 10.15am
and until 2pm in the afternoon; 27
holes of golf, light lunch, 3-course
meal; terms on application.
🍽 Full clubhouse facilities.
⌂ Kinmel Manor; Colwyn Bay; Dol
Hyfryd.

10 3 Abersoch   ♛
Golf Road, Abersoch, Gwynedd,

LL53 7EY
🏌 www.abersochgolf.co.uk
☎ 01758 712622, Fax 712777
6 miles from Pwlheli; first left through
the village.
Seaside links course.
Pro Alan Jones; Founded 1907
Designed by Harry Vardon
18 holes, 5671 yards, S.S.S. 68
✝ Welcome with handicap certs.
Ⅰ WD £20; WE £24.
⚑ Welcome by prior arrangement.
🍽 Full facilities.
⌂ Deucoch; Carisbrooke.

10 4 Aberystwyth   ♛
Bryn-Y-Mor Road, Aberystwyth,
Ceredigion, SY23 2HY
🖂 aberystwythgolf@talk21.com
☎ 01970 615104, Fax 626622,
Pro 625301, Sec 615104, Rest/Bar
615104
N end of the promenade behind the
seafront hotels; access road adjacent
to cliff railway; 1 mile from the town
centre.
Undulating meadowland course.
Professional on site; Founded 1911
Designed by Harry Vardon
18 holes, 6119 yards, S.S.S. 71
✝ Welcome; some WE restrictions. 2
Practice grounds & putting green.
Ⅰ WD £18.50; WE £22.50.
⚑ Welcome by prior arrangement;
packages available.
🍽 Bar and restaurant facilities.
⌂ Apply to Sec for details.

10 5 Alice Springs
Court Wyndermere, Bettws Newydd,
Usk, Monmouthshire, NP15 1JY
☎ 01873 880708, Fax 881075, Pro
880914, Sec 880708
3 miles N of Usk and 8 miles N of
Abergavenny on B4598.
Parkland course.
Pro Mike Davis; Founded 1986

Designed by Keith R. Morgan
Monnow Course: 18 holes; Usk
Course: 18 holes, Monnow Course:
5544; Usk Course: 5953, S.S.S.
Monnow Course: 69; Usk Course: 70
✝ Welcome; book at any time- Mon
to Sun.
Ⅰ WD £15; WE £17.
⚑ Welcome by prior arrangement;
packages available; driving range.
🍽 Full catering and bar facilities;
phone before arrival; terms on
application.
⌂ Cwrt Bleddybn; The Three
Salmons Hotel, Usk; The Rat Trap.

10 6 Allt-y-Graban
Allt-Y-Graban Rd, Pontlliw, Swansea,
W Glam, SA4 1DT
☎ 01792 885757/883279
From M4 Junction 47 take the A48 to
Pontlliw.
Parkland course.
Founded 1993
Designed by FG Thomas
9 holes, 4453 yards, S.S.S. 63
⚐ Practice green.
✝ Welcome.
Ⅰ 18 holes WD £8.50; WE £9.50.
⚑ Welcome; minimum 10; catering by
arrangement; from £6.
🍽 Clubhouse facilities.
⌂ Forest Motel; The Fountain Inn.

10 7 Anglesey   ♛
Station Road, Rhosneigr, Gwynedd,
LL64 5QX
🏌 www.theangleseygolfclub.com
🖂 info@theangleseygolfclub.com
☎ 01407 810219, Fax 811202, Pro
811202, Sec 811202, Rest/Bar 810219
8 miles SE of Holyhead; on A4080 off
A5 between Gwalchmai and
Bryngwran.
Links course with dunes and heather.
Pro P Lovell; Founded 1914
18 holes, 6300 yards, S.S.S. 68

✝ Welcome.
⌐ Terms on application.
♻ Welcome by prior arrangement; packages and reductions available for more than 10 players; terms on application.
🍴 Clubhouse bar and catering facilities.
🛏 Treaddur Hotel; Trecastell; Maelog Lake; Gadleys Country House; Eryl Mor.

10 8 Ashburnham
Cliff Terrace, Burry Port, Carmarthenshire, SA16 0HN
☎ 01554 832269, Fax 832269, Pro 833846, Sec 832269, Rest/Bar 832466
4 miles from Llanelli; 9 miles from M4.
Championship links.
Pro RA Ryder; Founded 1894
2 x 18 holes, Championship: 6936; Medal: 6627 yards, S.S.S.
Championship course:74; Medal course:73
✝ Welcome by prior arrangement.
⌐ WD £27.50 per round; WE £32.50 per round.
♻ Welcome WD by prior arrangement.
🍴 Full facilities except Mondays.
🛏 Ashburnham; Stradey Park Hotel; Diplomat Hotel.

10 9 Bala Golf Club ⚭
Penlan, Bala, Gwynedd, LL23 7YD
☎ 01678 520359, Fax 521361, Pro 520359, Sec 520359, Rest/Bar 520359
Off the main Bala-Dolgellau road.
Upland course with spectacular views.
Pro Tony Davies; Founded 1973
10 holes, 4791 yards, S.S.S. 64
✝ Welcome; some WE restrictions.
⌐ WD £12; WE £15.
♻ Welcome by prior arrangement; terms on application.
🍴 Bar with snacks available.
🛏 The Plas Coch Hotel, special packages available.

10 10 Bargoed
Heolddu, Bargoed, CF81 9GF
☎ 01443 830143, Fax 830608
Pro 836411, Sec 830608
10 miles north of Caerphilly.
Part moorland/mountain course.
Founded 1912
18 holes, 6049 yards, S.S.S. 70
✝ Welcome WD; with member only at WE.

⌐ WD £18. With a member only at weekends.
♻ Welcome by prior arrangement.
🍴 Bar facilities and evening meals.
🛏 Meas Manor; Park; Baverstocks.

10 11 Baron Hill
Beaumaris, Anglesey, N Wales, LL58 8YW
🖳 www.baronhill.co.uk
✉ golf@baronhill.co.uk
☎ 01248 810231, Fax 810231, Sec 810231, Rest/Bar 810231
A545 from Menai Bridge to Beaumaris; Turn left on entering Beaumaris.
Heathland course.
Founded 1895
9 holes, 5596 yards, S.S.S. 68
✐ 1 practice net, 1 practice green.
✝ Welcome by arrangement with Secretary or steward; club competitions on Sundays. Ladies day Tue morning.
⌐ WD £15; WE £15.
♻ Welcome by prior arrangement; bar and catering packages available; terms on application.
🍴 Clubhouse facilities.
🛏 Bull's Head; Bishop's Gate; Bulkeley.

10 12 Betws-y-Coed
The Clubhouse, Betws Y Coed, Gwynedd, LL24 0AL
☎ 01690 710556, Sec 710556, Rest/Bar 710556
Off A470 or A5 opposite Midland Bank in village centre.
Parkland course.
Founded 1971
9 holes, 4998 yards men's course, 4427 yards women's course, S.S.S. 64
✝ Everyone welcome.
⌐ Summer: WD £10-15; WE £20. Winter WD £10 WE and bank holidays £15 winter.
♻ Welcome by prior arrangement; catering and bar packages available; terms on application.
🍴 Full clubhouse facilities.
🛏 Glen Aber; Gwydir; Waterloo. Royal Oak.

10 13 Blackwood
Lon Pennant, Cwmgelli, Blackwood, Gwent, NP12 1EL
☎ 01495 223152, Sec 222121, Rest/Bar 223152
Course is 0.25 miles N of Blackwood on the A4048 Blackwood-Tredegar road.

Parkland course.
Founded 1914
9 holes, 5304 yards, S.S.S. 66
✝ Welcome WD; with a member at WE.
⌐ WD £14; WE £18.
♻ Welcome by prior arrangement; terms on application.
🍴 Bar and catering facilities.
🛏 Maes Manor.

10 14 Borth and Ynyslas. ⚭
Borth, Dyfed, Ceredigion, SY24 5JS
🖳 www.borthgolf.co.uk
✉ secretary@borthgolf.co.uk
☎ 01970 871202, Fax 871202, Pro 871557, Sec 871202, Rest/Bar 871202
8 miles S of Macynlleth; 4 miles N of Aberystwyth on A487.
Links course.
Pro JG Lewis; Founded 1885
Designed by H Colt
18 holes, 6116 yards, S.S.S. 70
✝ Welcome by arrangement.
⌐ WD £25 per day; WE £29.
♻ Welcome; minimum 8 in summer, 6 in winter; catering packages available; from £10.
🍴 Bar and catering facilities.
🛏 Black Lion, Talybont; Belle View, Marine Hotel, Aberystwyth; Ynyshir Hall.

10 15 Brecon
Newton Park, Llanfaes, Brecon, Powys, LD3 8PA
☎ 01874 622004
50 yards, from A40 on W of town.
Parkland course.
Founded 1902
Designed by J Braid
9 holes, 5256 yards, S.S.S. 66
✝ Welcome.
⌐ WD £10; WE £10.
♻ Welcome by arrangement; catering packages available; terms on application.
🍴 Catering facilities available.
🛏 Peterstone Court.

10 16 Bryn Meadows Golf & Country Club.
Maesycwmmer, Ystrad Mynach, Caerphilly, CR82 7SN
🖳 www.brynmeadows.co.uk
☎ 01495 225590, Fax 228272, Pro 221905, Sec 225590, Rest/Bar 225590
Off A469 15 miles from Cardiff.
Parkland course.
Pro Bruce Hunter; Founded 1973
Designed by E Jefferies & B Mayo
18 holes, 6156 yards, S.S.S. 70

✝ Welcome.
▯ WD £15; WE £25.
☄ Welcome WD by arrangement;
special golf packages; function rooms;
new gym; indoor pool; Jacuzzi; pool
table.
🍽 Full facilities; bar and à la carte
restaurant.
🛏 On site hotel Bryn Meadows.

10 17 Bryn Morfydd Hotel ♛
Llanrhaeadr, Denbighshire, Clwyd,
LL16 4NP
🖥 www.brynmorfyddhotel.co.uk
☎ 01745 890280, Fax 890488
Off A525 between Denbigh and Ruthin.
Founded 1982/92
Designed by Alliss/Thomas (Duchess
course)
Dukes course:18; Duchess course: 9
holes, Dukes course: 5800; Duchess
course: 2000 yards, S.S.S. Dukes
course: 68; Duchess course: 27
▯ Practice nets and putting green.
✝ Welcome.
▯ WD £15; WE £20.
☄ Welcome by arrangement;
packages available; from £25.
🍽 Full clubhouse and hotel facilities.
🛏 3-star hotel on site.

10 18 Brynhill
Port Rd, Barry, S Glam, CF62 8PN
☎ 01446 735061, Fax 733660, Pro
733660, Sec 720277
M4 Junction 33 take signs for Barry
and Cardiff Airport on to the A4050.
Undulating meadowland course.
Pro Peter Fountain; Founded 1921
Designed by GK Cotton
Summer: 18; Winter: 18 holes,
Summer: 5884; Winter: 5732 yards,
S.S.S. Summer: 70; Winter: 69
✝ Welcome except Sun; handicap
certs may be required.
▯ WD £20; WE £25.
☄ Welcome WD by prior
arrangement; from £17.
🍽 Bar and catering facilities; lunches,
afternoon teas and dinners.
🛏 Mount Sorrel; International;
Copthorne.

10 19 Builth Wells
Golf Clubs Road, Builth Wells, Powys,
LD2 3NF
🖥 www.builthwellsgolfclub.co.uk
📧 builthwellsgolfclub1@
btinternet.com
☎ 01982 553296, Fax 551064,
Pro 551155, Sec 553296, Rest/Bar
553296

On A483 Builth-Llandovery road just
after River Irfon bridge on outskirts of
Builth.
Parkland course; no par 5s.
Pro Simon Edwards; Founded 1923
18 holes, 5376 yards, S.S.S. 67
✝ Welcome with handicap certs.
▯ WD £17; WE £23.
☄ Welcome; packages and
reductions; terms on application.
🍽 Clubhouse bar and catering.
🛏 Pencerrig House; Caerberis
Manor; Greyhound Hotel; Cedars GH.

10 20 Bull Bay ♛
Bull Bay, Amlwch, Anglesey, LL68 9RY
🖥 www.bullbaygc.co.uk
📧 ian@bullbaygc.co.uk
☎ 01407 830960, Fax 832612, Pro
831188, Rest/Bar 830213
On A5025 via Benllech and course is 1
mile beyond Amlwch.
Clifftop heathland course, most
northern course in Wales.
Pro John Burns; Founded 1913
Designed by Herbert Fowler of Walton
Heath
18 holes, 6276 yards, S.S.S. 70
▯ Practice area and putting green.
✝ Welcome by prior arrangement.
▯ WD £20; WE £25.
☄ Welcome; meals can be provided
🍽 Clubhouse facilities.
🛏 Trecastell; Bull Bay; Lastra Farm
Hotel.

10 21 Caerleon
Broadway, Caerleon, Newport, Gwent,
NP18 1AY
☎ 01633 420342, Fax 420342,
Pro 420342, Sec 420342,
Rest/Bar 420342
3 miles from M4 Junction 25 for
Caerleon.
Parkland course.
Pro M Phillips; Founded 1974
Designed by Donald Steel
9 holes, 5800 yards, S.S.S. 68
▯ Practice range 12 Bays floodlit.
✝ Everyone welcome.
▯ WD: 18 holes £6.20; 9 holes
£4.15; WE: 18 holes £7.70; 9 holes
£5.20.
☄ Welcome by arrangement; terms
on application.
🍽 Snacks and bar.
🛏 Priory.

10 22 Caernarfon Golf Club ♛
Royal Town of
Aberforeshore, Llanfaglan, Gwynedd,
LL54 5RP

🖥 www.caernarfongolfclub.co.uk
📧 caerngc@talk21.com
☎ 01286 673967, Fax 672535,
Pro 678359, Sec 673783
A470 from A55 at Caernarfon towards
Porthmadog; at new road bridge turn
right, club 1.5 miles.
Parkland course.
Pro Aled Owen; Founded 1907/1981
18 holes, 5891 yards, S.S.S. 68
✝ Welcome.
▯ WD £18; WE £22.
☄ Welcome; special rates for 10 or
more players; full facilities available;
terms on application.
🍽 Full catering and bar facilities.
🛏 Celtic Royal; Seiont Manor; Bryn
Eisteddfod; Erw Fair all Caernarfon;
Eryl Mor.

10 23 Caerphilly
Pencapel, Mountain Rd, Caerphilly,
CF83 1HJ
☎ 029 20883481, Fax 20863441, Pro
2086 9104, Sec 20863441
On A469 7 miles from Cardiff; 250
yards from rail and bus stations.
Steep wooded mountainside course.
Pro Joel Hill; Founded 1905
Designed by Fernie (original 9)
18 holes, 5944 yards, S.S.S. 70
▯ Practice green and bunkers.
✝ Welcome WD; WE only with a
member.
▯ WD £20.
☄ Limited numbers, by prior
arrangement only.
🍽 Bar and dining room.
🛏 Mount; Greenhill; Moat House;
Cedar Tree.

10 24 Caerwys 9 of Clubs
Caerwys, Mold, Flintshire, CH7 5AQ
☎ 01352 720692, Fax 01691 777793
1.5 miles S of the A55 midway
between St Asaph and Holywell.
Undulating parkland course.
Founded 1988
Designed by Eleanor Barlow
9 holes, 3080 yards, S.S.S. 60
✝ Welcome.
▯ Terms on application.
☄ Welcome by prior arrangment.
🍽 Light refreshments.

10 25 Cardiff
Sherborne Ave, Cyncoed, Cardiff,
CF23 6SJ
📧 cardiff.golfclub@virgin.net
☎ 029 20753320, Fax 20680011,
Pro 20754772, Sec 20753320
3 miles N of Cardiff, 2 miles W of

Pentwyn, on A48(M) M4 Junction 29.
Undulating parkland course.
Pro Terry Hanson; Founded 1922
18 holes, 6013 yards, S.S.S. 70
♦ Welcome.
I WD £35; WE £40.
⟲ Welcome by prior arrangement;
Thurs only; terms on application;
snooker room available.
🎱 New clubhouse facilities.
⌐ Post House, Pentwyn.

10 26 Cardigan
Gwbert-on-Sea, Cardigan, Ceredigion,
SA43 1PR
⌐ www.cardigangolf.sagenet.co.uk
☎ 01239 612035, Fax 621775, Pro
615359
3 miles N of Cardigan.
Links/parkland course with view of
River Teifi.
Pro C Parsons; Founded 1895
Designed by Hawtree
18 holes, 6687 yards, S.S.S. 72
♦ Welcome.
I WD £20; WE and BH £25.
⟲ Welcome by prior arrangement;
packages and catering available;
satellite TV; pool table; squash courts;
discounts available, please contact sec
for details.
🎱 Clubhouse facilities.
⌐ Cliff Hotel; Gwbert Hotel.

10 27 Carmarthen   ☎
Blaenycoed Rd, Carmarthen,
Carmarthenshire, SA33 6EH
⌐ www.cumlaingolfclub.com
✉ johnathanseccgc@aol.uk
☎ 01267 281214, Fax 281493,
Pro 281493, Sec 281588
4.5 miles N of town.
Upland course.
Pro Pat Gillis; Founded 1907
Designed by JH Taylor
18 holes, 6245 yards, S.S.S. 71
♦ Welcome; ladies day Tues.
I Winter: WD £15; WE £20;
Summer: WD £20; WE £25.
⟲ Welcome WD; packages and
discounts available; terms on
application.
🎱 Full clubhouse facilities.
⌐ Falcon; Ivy Bush; Forge Motel.

10 28 Castell Heights
Blaengwynlais, Caerphilly, Mid-
Glamorgan, CF8 1NG
☎ 029 20886666, Fax 20863243,
Sec 20861128
4 miles from M4 Junction 32 on the
Tongwynlais-Caerphilly road.

Mountainside course.
Pro Sion Bebb; Founded 1982
9 holes, 5376 yards, S.S.S. 66
I Practice range; 6 bays.
♦ Welcome; dress codes apply.
I WD £5.50; WE £5.50.
⟲ Welcome by arrangement; phone
Sec.
🎱 Bar and bar snacks.
⌐ The Friendly Hotel.

10 29 The Celtic Manor Resort ☎
Coldra Woods, Newport, NP18 1HQ
⌐ www.celtic-manor.com
✉ postbox@celtic-manor.com
☎ 01633 413000, Fax 412910,
Pro 410312, Sec 410310,
Rest/Bar 413000
M4 Junction 24 just 5 minutes from the
Severn Bridge.
Three championship courses in 1400
acres of panoramic undulating
parkland course.
Pro Scott Patience; Founded 1995
Designed by Robert Trent-Jones Jnr
(Wentwood Hills 1999) & Robert Trent-
Jones Snr (Roman Road 1995 Coldra
Woods 1996)
Wentwood Hills: 7403 yards, par 72,
S.S.S. 77 (PGA European Tours venue
– Wales open); Roman Road: 18
holes, 6685 yards, par 69, S.S.S. 72;
Coldra Woods: 4001 yards, par 39
I The Golf School: two-tier floodlit
driving range, coaching with video
graphics; short play areas; practice
range. Superb clubhouse with luxury
locker rooms.
♦ Everyone welcome.
I Wentwood Hills Mon-Thu £55 Fri,
Sat, Sun £60. Roman Road Mon-Sun
£37. Coldra Woods £16 Mon-Sun.
Prices are for 18 holes.
⟲ Welcome by prior arrangement;
corporate and society packages
available.
🎱 4 restaurants on site. 3 bars, also
full catering facilities available.
⌐ 400 – room 32 suite 5-star hotel
with 1500-delegate Convention Centre.

10 30 Chirk   ☎
Chirk, Nr Wrexham, Flintshire, LL14
5AD
⌐ www.jackbarker.com
✉ chirkgolf@lineone.net
☎ 01691 774407, Fax 773878, Pro
774407, Sec 774407, Rest/Bar 774243
Course is five miles S of Wrexham just
off the A5.
Parkland course; 2 holes greater than
600 yards.
Pro Mark Maddison; Founded 1991

18 holes, 7045 yards, S.S.S. 73
I Practice range, 15 undercover
floodlit bays; practice bunker.
♦ Everyone welcome.
I Terms on application.
⟲ Welcome; full clubhouse facilities;
terrace; buggies; driving range; also 9-
hole Mine Rock course par 3.
🎱 Clubhouse facilities; spike bar;
restaurant; snacks and meals.
⌐ Golden Pheasant, Glyn Cieriog;
The Royal Hotel Llangollen.

10 31 Cilgwyn
Llangybi, Lampeter, Ceredigion, SA48
8NN
☎ 01570 493286
Course is 4 miles N of Lampeter on
the A485.
Parkland course.
Founded 1905/1977
9 holes, 5309 yards, S.S.S. 67
♦ Welcome.
I WD £10: WE £15.
⟲ Welcome minimum of 10 players
bar and restaurant packages available
from £8.
🎱 Clubhouse facilities.
⌐ Falcondale; Black Lion both
Lampeter.

10 32 Clay's Golf Centre
Bryn Estyn Road, Wrexham, LL13 9UB
☎ 01978 661406, Fax 661417,
Pro 661406, Sec 661406,
Rest/Bar 661416
From A483 Wrexham-Chester road
take A534 for Nantwich and Wrexham
Industrial Estate; 2 miles turn to golf
centre.
Parkland course; new 9-hole pitch and
putt course.
Pro D Larvin; Founded 1991
Designed by RD Jones
18 holes, 5794 yards, S.S.S. 68
I 16.
♦ Welcome all times.
I WD £14; WE £19.
⟲ Welcome by prior arrangement;
minimum 12; deposit required; practice
balls; 18-27 holes of golf; light lunch; 3-
course dinner; terms on application.
🎱 Full catering facilities available.
⌐ Cross Lane, Marchweil; Holt
Lodge, Wrexham.

10 33 Clyne
118/120 Owls Lodge Lane, Mayals,
Swansea, SA3 5DP
✉ clynegolfclub@supanet.com
☎ 01792 401989, Fax 401078,
Pro 402094, Sec 401989,

Rest/Bar 403534
From the M4 to Swansea; exit for
Mumbles at Blackpill, head for Gower
and then take first right into Owls
Lodge Lane.
Moorland course.
Pro Johnathan Clewett; Founded 1920
Designed by HS Colt/Harris
18 holes, 6334 yards, S.S.S. 71
⚑ Practice area.
† Welcome with handicap certs.
[WD £25; WE £30.
⚐ Welcome WD except Tues;
catering packages and reductions for
more than 20 players; from £20.
◖◎◗ Clubhouse facilities.
⌐ Marriott, Swansea; St Anne's,
Mumbles.

10 34 Coed-y-Mwstwr Golf Club
The Club House, Coychurch, Near
Bridgend, CF35 6AF
🖳 www.coed-y-mwstwr.co.uk
▤ coed-y-mwstwr@lineone.net
☎ 01656 862121, Fax 864934,
Sec 864934
From M4 Junction 35 turn towards
Bridgend and then into Coychurch.
Parkland course.
Founded 1994
Designed by Chapman Warrel
9 holes, 6144 yards, S.S.S. 70
⚑ 2.
† Welcome with handicap certs;
dress codes apply.
[Prices on application.
⚐ Welcome by prior arrangement;
packages available; terms on
application.
◖◎◗ Clubhouse facilities.
⌐ Coed-y-Mwstwr.

10 35 Conwy (Caernarvonshire)
Beacons Way, Morfa, Conwy,
Gwynedd, LL32 8ER
☎ 01492 593400, Fax 593363, Pro
593225, Sec 592423, Rest/Bar 593400
Just off A55 at Conwy.
Links course.
Pro Peter Lees; Founded 1890
18 holes, 6647 yards, S.S.S. 72
† Welcome with handicap certs
standard golf dress code.
[Winter WD £17 WE £20; Summer
WD £24 WE £30; juniors £9 all yr.
⚐ Welcome with prior arrangement
through Sec; catering available winter
package coffee and biscuits 18 holes of golf
and 3 course meal WD £20 WE £25;
summer packages also available; snooker
room; dartboards; function room; Pro is a
commentator.
◖◎◗ Clubhouse facilities.

⌐ Royal; Esplanade; The
Risborough; all Llandudno; The
Castlebank; Conway.

10 36 Cradoc
Penoyre Park, Cradoc, Brecon, Powys,
LD3 9LP
🖳 www.cradoc.co.uk
▤ secretary@cradoc.co.uk
☎ 01874 623658, Fax 611711,
Pro 625524, Sec 623658,
Rest/Bar 624396
Take B 4520 road to Upper Chapel
past Brecon Cathedral and turn left to
Cradoc village.
Parkland course.
Pro Richard W Davies; Founded 1967
Designed by C.K.Cotton
18 holes, 6301 yards, S.S.S. 72
⚑ 12.
† Welcome by prior arrangement.
[WD £20; WE £25.
⚐ Welcome by prior arrangement
with secretary; packages available;
terms on application.
◖◎◗ Clubhouse facilities available.
⌐ Peterstone Court; Llangoed Hall;
Castle of Brecon; Lansdown; The
George Hotel.

10 37 Creigiau
Llantwit Road, Creigiau, Cardiff, CF15
9NN
▤ manager@creigiaugolf.co.uk
☎ 029 20890263, Fax 20890706,
Pro 20891909, Sec 20890263,
Rest/Bar 20891243/20891900
4 miles NW of Cardiff towards Llantrisant.
Parkland course.
Pro Ian Luntz; Founded 1926
18 holes, 6063 yards, S.S.S. 70
⚑ Practice area for members only.
† Welcome WD except Tues (ladies
day) when prior booking is required;
members only at weekends.
[WD £30.
⚐ Welcome by prior arrangement;
min 20 max 40.
◖◎◗ Bar and full catering facilities.
⌐ Friendly Hotel; Miskin Manor; Park;
Royal; Angel; Hilton; St Davids; Celtic
Manor.

10 38 Criccieth
Ednyfed Hill, Criccieth, Gwynedd, LL52
0PH
☎ 01766 522154, Pro 522154,
Sec 523385, Rest/Bar 522154
On A497 4 miles from Portmadoc;
turn right past Memorial Hall; course
0.5 miles.
Meadowland course.

Founded 1904
18 holes, 5787 yards, S.S.S. 68
† Welcome.
[WD £13/16; WE £18.
⚐ Welcome by prior arrangement.
◖◎◗ bar and catering facilities.
⌐ George IV; Bron Eifion; Marine;
Lion.

10 39 Denbigh
Henllan Rd, Denbigh, LL16 5AA
▤ secretary@
denbighgolfclub.fsbbusiness.co.uk
☎ 01745 816669, Fax 814888, Pro
814159, Sec 816669, Rest/Bar 816664
Course is 0.5 mile from Denbigh on the
B5382.
Parkland course.
Pro Mike Jones; Founded 1922
Designed by John Stockton
18 holes, 5712 yards, S.S.S. 68
† Welcome by prior arrangement.
[WD £24 for day, £18 per round;
WE £30, for day, £24 per round.
⚐ Welcome; packages and catering
available; call for details.
◖◎◗ Clubhouse facilities available.
⌐ Talardy Park; Oriel House both St
Asaph.

10 40 Dewstow
Caerwent, Monmouthshire, NP26 5AH
🖳 www.dewstow-golf-club.co.uk
▤ johnharris@btconnect.com
☎ 01291 430444, Fax 425816,
Pro 430444, Sec 430444,
Rest/Bar 430444
Off A48 between Newport and
Chepstow.
Parkland course/Valley course.
Pro Johnathan Skeuse; Founded
1988
2 x 18 holes, 6176 yards, S.S.S. 69
Park course/70 Valley course
⚑ Practice range, 26 bays floodlit
and covered.
† Everyone welcome.
[WD £16; WE £19 summer rates.
Various deals in winter. Please consult
professional shop for details.
⚐ Welcome WD; some restrictions at
WE; packages available; from £20.
◖◎◗ Full bar and restaurant facilities.
⌐ Beaufort; Old Course.

10 41 Dinas Powis
Golf House, Old Highwalls, Dinas
Powis, CF64 4AJ
☎ 029 20512727, Fax 20512727, Pro
20513682, Rest/Bar Bar 20512157
Rest 20514128
Centre of Dinas Powys, 5 miles from

Cardiff.
Parkland course; 90 yards 7th.
Pro Gareth Bennett; Founded 1914
18 holes, 5872 yards, S.S.S. 69
🏌 Practice area.
† Welcome with handicap certs;
dress codes apply.
🍴 WD £25; WE £30.
↳ Welcome by prior arrangement
and with handicap certs; terms on
application.
🍴 Clubhouse facilities.
🛏 Many in Cardiff.

10 42 Dolgellau ☂

Pencefn Road, Dolgellau, Gwynedd,
LL40 2ES
🖳 www.dolgellaugolf.com
☎ 01341 422603, Fax 422603,
Sec 422603, Rest/Bar 422603
0.5 miles N of Dolgellau.
Parkland course.
Founded 1911
9 holes, 4671 yards, S.S.S. 63
🏌 Practice range; club and trolley hire.
† Always welcome.
🍴 WD £15; WE £18; two-for-one
vouchers.
↳ Welcome by prior arrangement;
catering packages available; from £13.
🍴 Clubhouse facilities.
🛏 Royal Ship Hotel, Dolgellau.

10 43 Earlswood

Jersey Marine, Neath, West
Glamorgan, SA10 6JP
☎ 01792 321578, Pro 816159,
Sec 812198
Signposted off B 4290 road off the
A483 Neath-Swansea road.
Parkland course.
Pro Mike Day; Founded 1993
Designed by Stan Gorvett
18 holes, 5174 yards, S.S.S. 68
† Everyone welcome.
🍴 WD £8; WE £8.
↳ Welcome by prior arrangement; £8
per person standard rate for groups.
🍴 By arrangement with secretary.
🛏 The New Tower Hotel.

10 44 Fairwood Park

Blackhills Lane, Upper Killay,
Swansea, SA2 7JN
☎ 01792 297849, Fax 297849,
Pro 299194, Sec 297849,
Rest/Bar 203648
Turn into Blackhills Lane opposite
Swansea Airport.
Parkland championship course.
Pro Gary Hughes; Founded 1969
Designed by Hawtree&Co

18 holes, 6754 yards, S.S.S. 73
† Welcome by prior arrangement.
🍴 WD £25; WE £30.
↳ Welcome by prior arrangement;
terms on application.
🍴 Clubhouse facilities.
🛏 Winston Hotel Bishopston;
Langrove Hotel, Parkmill; Hillcrest,
Mumbles.

10 45 Ffestiniog

Clwb Golff Ffestiniog, Y Cefn,
Ffestiniog, Gwynned
☎ 01766 762637
On the B4391 1 mile from Ffestiniog.
Scenic mountain course.
Founded 1893
9 holes, 5032 yards, S.S.S. 65
† Welcome; some WE restrictions.
🍴 WD £10; WE £10.
↳ Welcome by prior arrangement.
🍴 Clubhouse facilities by
arrangement; bar.
🛏 Abbey Arms; The Pengwren.

10 46 Flint

Cornist Park, Flint, Flintshire, CH6 5HJ
🖳 slwflint@aol.com
☎ 01352 732327, Fax 811885
Course is one mile S from the centre
of Flint.
Parkland course.
Founded 1965
Designed by H Griffith
9 holes, 5980 yards, S.S.S. 69
† Welcome.
🍴 WD £10; WE £10. Closed on
Sundays to non-members.
↳ Welcome WD by arrangement; up
to 27 holes of golf.
🍴 3-course meal from £12.
🛏 Clubhouse facilities. The Mountain
Park View Hotel Flint; Springfield Halkyn.

10 47 Glamorganshire

Lavernock Rd, Penarth, CF64 5UP
🖳 glamgolf@btconnect.com
☎ 029 20701185, Fax 20701185,
Pro 20701 7401, Sec 2070 1185
5 miles SW of Cardiff just off M4
Junction 33.
Parkland course.
Pro Andrew Kerr-Smith; Founded 1890
Designed by W East & T Simpson
18 holes, 6056 yards, S.S.S. 70
🏌 Practice ground with net buggies
and clubs for hire.
† Welcome by arrangement; dress
codes apply.
🍴 WD £35; WE £40.
↳ Welcome Thurs and Fri only;
catering packages available;

reductions for more than 20; from £25.
🍴 Clubhouse facilities.
🛏 Walton House Hotel; Raisdale both
Penarth.

10 48 Glynhir

Glynhir Rd, Llandybie, Ammanford,
Carmarthenshire, SA18 2TF
☎ 01269 850472, Fax 851365, Pro
851010, Sec 851365
3.5 miles from Ammanford; off A483
towards Llandello.
Parkland course.
Pro Duncan Prior; Founded 1967
Designed by FW.Hawtree
18 holes, 6026 yards, S.S.S. 70
🏌 Covered, 4 bay driving range
† Welcome except Sun with
handicap certs.
🍴 WD £16; WE £22.
↳ Welcome by arrangement; Tues
and Fri; terms on application.
🍴 Clubhouse facilities.
🛏 The Mill at Glynhir (next to
course); Cawdor Arms; White Hart Inn;
Plough Inn all Llandello.

10 49 Glynneath

Penycraig, Glynneath, SA11 5UH
🖳 www.glynneathgolfclub.co.uk
🖳 neil.evans9@lineone.co.uk
☎ 01639 720452
From A465 road at Glynneath take
B4242 for 1.5 miles to
Pontneathvaughan.
Parkland and wooded hilltop course.
Pro Neil Evans
Designed by Cotton
18 holes, 5656 yards, S.S.S. 68
† Welcome; no restrictions.
🍴 WD £15; WE £20.
↳ Welcome; catering and bar snacks
available.
🍴 Clubhouse facilities.
🛏 Baverstock; Tynewydd Hotel,
Penderyn.

10 50 Gower

Cefn Goleu, Three Crosses, Gowerton,
Swansea, SA4 3HS
🖳 www.gowergolf.co.uk
🖳 deggmorgan@aol.co.uk
☎ 01792 872480, Fax 872480, Pro
879905, Sec 872480, Rest/Bar 872480
Follow the A484 towards Gowerton
and then take the B4295 to
Penclawdd; after one mile turn to
Three Crosses.
Parkland course with lakes.
Pro Alan Williamson; Founded 1995
Designed by Donald Steel
18 holes, 6441 yards, S.S.S. 71

Welcome.

⌐ Terms on application.

⌐ Welcome by prior arrangement; maximum 100; from £12.

⦿ Bar and catering facilities available.

⌐ The Mill at Glynhir; Winston Bishopston.

---

10 51 Greenmeadow

Treherbert Road, Croesyceiliog, Cwmbran, Gwent, NP44 2BZ

☎ 01633 869321, Fax 868430

Off A4042 5 miles N of M4 Junction 26.

Parkland course.

Founded 1978

18 holes, 6078 yards, S.S.S. 70

⌐ Practice range; 26 bays covered and floodlit.

Welcome.

⌐ Terms on application.

⌐ Welcome by prior arrangement; packages available; professional clinics; tennis courts; private function rooms.

⦿ Full clubhouse catering facilities.

⌐ Parkway; Commodore.

---

10 52 Grove

South Cornelly, Nr Porthcawl, Mid Glamorgan, CF33 4RP

⌐ www.grovegolf-porthcawl.co.uk

☎ 01656 788771, Fax 788414, Pro 788300, Sec 788771, Rest/Bar 788771

Off M4 Junction 37 near the Glamorgan Heritage Coast at Porthcawl.

Parkland course with water features.

Pro Leon Warne; Founded 1997

18 holes, 6128 yards, S.S.S. 70

Welcome; bookings essential.

⌐ Terms on application.

⌐ Welcome by prior arrangement.

⦿ Bar and restaurant; function rooms.

⌐ Green Acre Motel,17 bedrooms all ensuite, indoor pool, restaurants, bars with beautiful views over the welsh hills.

---

10 53 Haverfordwest ☏

Arnolds Down, Haverfordwest, Pembrokeshire, SA61 2XQ

⌐ www.haverfordwestgolf. homestead.com

☎ 01437 763565, Fax 764143, Pro 768409

1 mile E of Haverfordwest on A40.

Parkland course.

Pro Alex Pile; Founded 1904

18 holes, 5966 yards, S.S.S. 69

Welcome by prior arrangement.

⌐ POA.

⌐ Welcome by arrangement; catering

packages available; terms on application.

⦿ Bar; bar snacks and dining room.

⌐ Mariners.

---

10 54 Hawarden

Groomsdale Lane, Hawarden, Deeside, Flintshire, CH5 3EH

☎ 01244 531447, Fax 536901, Pro 520809

Off A55 at Ewloe towards Hawarden; Groomsdale Lane opposite police station after playing fields.

Undulating parkland course.

Pro Alec Rowlands; Founded 1911/1950

18 holes, 5894 yards, S.S.S. 68

Welcome; members comp day Sat.

⌐ WD £18; Sun £25.

⌐ Welcome by prior arrangement with Sec.

⦿ Bar and full catering facilities; meals by arrangement.

⌐ St David's Park, Ewloe.

---

10 55 Henllys Hall

Beaumaris, Anglesey, Gwynedd, LL58 8HU

☎ 01248 810412, Fax 811511

4 miles from A55.

Parkland course with Snowdonia views and water features.

Pro Peter Maton; Founded 1997

Designed by Roger Jones

18 holes, 6098 yards, S.S.S. 71

⌐ Practice area.

Welcome by prior arrangement.

⌐ Terms on application.

⌐ Welcome by prior arrangement; catering and hotel packages; terms on application; sun room; fitness centre; tennis court; swimming pool; leisure centre (under construction).

⦿ Full hotel facilities; bar and restaurant.

⌐ Henllys Hall on site.

---

10 56 Holyhead ☏

Trearddur Bay, Holyhead, Anglesey, LL65 2YI

☎ 01407 763279, Fax 763279, Pro 762022, Rest/Bar Bar 762119 Rest 765113

A55 to Holyhead, carry on to roundabout, 1 mile from Treardur Bay.

Undulating heathland.

Pro Steve Elliott; Founded 1912

Designed by James Braid

18 holes, 6060 yards, S.S.S. 70

⌐ Practice range 0.5 miles away; 10 bays.

Welcome; book in advance.

⌐ Terms on application.

⌐ Welcome by arrangement.

⦿ Full bar and catering facilities.

⌐ On site dormy house hotel; Treardurr Bay; Anchorage; Beach.

---

10 57 Holywell ☏

Brynford, Nr Holywell, Flintshire, CH8 8LQ

✉ holywell_golf_club@lineone.net

☎ 01352 713937, Fax 07092369597, Pro 710040

From A55 at Holywell exit take A5026 then take Brynford signs.

Natural moorland/links type course around quarries.

Pro Matt Parsley; Founded 1906

18 holes, 6164 yards, S.S.S. 70

⌐ Practice area and buggies for hire.

Welcome; dress codes apply.

⌐ WD £18; WE £23.

⌐ Welcome by arrangement with Sec; catering packages available; snooker; reduced rates for groups of 20; from £15.

⦿ Full catering facilities and bar.

⌐ Club can recommend hotels.

---

10 58 Inco

Clydach, Swansea, W Glamorgan, SA6 5EU

☎ 01792 844216, Rest/Bar 841257

Course is two miles N of the M4 Junction 45.

Parkland course with river and trees featured.

Founded 1965

18 holes, 6064 yards, S.S.S. 69

⌐ Practice green, practice nets.

Welcome.

⌐ Terms on application.

⌐ Welcome by prior arrangement.

⦿ Catering by arrangement.

---

10 59 Kinmel Park Golf Complex

Bodelwyddan, Denbighshire, LL18 5SR

☎ 01745 833548

Just off A55 between St Asaph and Abergele.

Parkland course.

Pro Peter Stebbings; Founded 1988

Designed by Peter Stebbings

9 holes, 3100 yards, S.S.S. 58

Pay and play.

⌐ WD £4; WE £4.50.

⌐ Welcome; Peter Stebbing's Golf Academy; snack bar and refreshments; terms on application.

⦿ Bar.

10 60 Kinsale

Llanerchymor, Holywell, Flintshire, CH8 9DX
☎ 01745 561080
Off A548 coast road at turning for Maes Pennant.
Parkland course.
Pro Alan Norwood; Founded 1994
Designed by Ken Smith
9 holes, 6005 yards, S.S.S. 70
❚ Practice range, 12 Bays floodlit.
† Welcome; pay and play.
❚ WD and WE: 9 holes £7.50; 18 holes £11.00; special price for juniors every day but Sun.
⟂ Welcome by arrangement.
◉ Full clubhouse facilities.
⌐ Kinsale Hall.

10 61 Knighton ♛

The Ffrydd, Knighton, Powys, LD7 1DL
☎ 01547 528646, Fax 529284
SW of Knighton off the A488 Shrewsbury-Llandrindod Wells road at junction with A4113.
Upland course.
Founded 1913
Designed by Harry Vardon
9 holes, 5338 yards, S.S.S. 66
† Welcome; advised to book in advance for weekends.
❚ WD £10; WE £12.
⟂ Welcome by prior arrangement; terms on application.
◉ Clubhouse facilities.
⌐ Red Lion; Knighton Hotel.

10 62 Lakeside

Water St, Margam, Port Talbot, SA13 2PA
☎ 01639 899959, Rest/Bar 883486
0.5 miles from M4 Junction 38 off A48 to Margam Park.
Parkland course.
Pro M Wootton; Founded 1992
Designed by M Wootton/DT Thomas
18 holes, 4580 yards, S.S.S. 63
† Welcome.
❚ WD £9.50; WE £9.50.
⟂ Welcome except Sun; golf and meal; £15.
◉ Catering available.
⌐ Twelve Knights; Seabank; Esplanade.

10 63 Llandrindod Wells ♛

Llandrindod Wells, Powys, LD1 5NY
♨ www.lwgc.co.uk
✉ secretary@lwgc.co.uk
☎ 01597 822010, Fax 823873, Pro 822247, Sec 823873, Rest/Bar 822010
Signposted in the town.

Moorland course.
Pro Phil Davies; Founded 1905
Designed by Harry Vardon
18 holes, 5759 yards, S.S.S. 69
❚ Practice green.
† Welcome.
❚ Prices on application.
⟂ Welcome by prior arrangement with Sec; terms on application.
◉ Clubhouse facilities.
⌐ Metropole; Montpellier; Griffin House; Penybont; Pencerrig.

10 64 Llandudno (Maesdu)

Hospital Rd, Llandudno, Gwynedd, LL30 1HU
☎ 01492 876016, Fax 871570, Pro 875195, Sec 876450
A55 to Conwy-Deganwy exit, then A546 to clubhouse.
Parkland course.
Pro Simon Boulden; Founded 1915
Designed by Tom Jones
18 holes, 6545 yards, S.S.S. 72
❚ Practice range, clubs and buggies for hire.
† Welcome by arrangement.
❚ WD £25; WE £30.
⟂ Welcome everyday; maximum 36 at WE; 50 in week; no concessions; from £25.
◉ Catering and bar facilities.
⌐ Royal; Esplanade; Risboro.

10 65 Llanfairfechan

Llannerch Road, Llanfairfechan, Conwy, LL33 0EB
☎ 01248 680144, Sec 680524
Course is south of the A55 in Llanfairfechan.
Parkland course.
Founded 1972
9 holes, 3119 yards, S.S.S. 57
❚ Practice nets.
† Welcome.
❚ WD £10; WE £10. All day
⟂ Welcome by prior arrangement; catering by arrangement; terms on application.
◉ Some catering and bar facilities evenings and weekends.
⌐ Split Willow.

10 66 Llangefni (Public)

Llangefni, Anglesey, LL77 8YQ
☎ 01248 722193, Pro 722193
On the outskirts of Llangefni towards Amlwch.
Parkland course.
Pro Paul Lovell; Founded 1983
Designed by Hawtree & Sons
9 holes, 1467 yards, S.S.S. 28

† All Welcome.
❚ WD £3.20; WE £3.50; children and OAPs £1.80 & WE £2.00.
⟂ Welcome by prior arrangement.
◉ In local café.

10 67 Llangland Bay

Llangland Bay, Swansea, SA3 4QR
♨ www.langllandbaygolfclub.com
✉ golf@llanglandbay.sagehost.co.uk
☎ 01792 361721, Fax 361082, Pro 366186, Sec 361721, Rest/Bar 366023
Take Junction 42 of M4 heading west towards Swansea. Take A483 to Swansea. From Swansea take the main road to Mumbles. Follow signs to Caswell and Langland from Mumbles.
Seaside parkland course.
Pro Mark Evans; Founded 1904
Designed by various designers
18 holes, 5857 yards, S.S.S. 69
† Everyone welcome.
❚ Terms on application.
⟂ Welcome by prior arrangement; maximum 36; catering packages available by prior arrangement; winter packages available; terms on application. Handicap certificates essential.
◉ Clubhouse facilities except Mondays.
⌐ Llangland Court; St Annes Hotel.

10 68 Llanishen

Cwm, Heol Hir, Lisvane, Cardiff, CF14 9UD
☎ 029 20755078, Fax 20755078, Pro 20755076, Sec 20755078
5 miles N of Cardiff 1 mile N of Llanishen.
Parkland course.
Pro RA Jones; Founded 1905
18 holes, 5296 yards, S.S.S. 66
† Welcome WD; WE only with a member.
❚ WD £24; WE £12.
⟂ Welcome Thurs afternoons; packages available with catering; from £18.
◉ Clubhouse facilities.
⌐ Cardiff Bay; Angel; Manor House; New House.

10 69 Llannerch Park

North Wales Golf Range and Course, St Asaph, Denbighshire, LL17 0BD
☎ 01745 730805, Pro 730805
On A525 between St Asaph and Trefnant.
Parkland course.
Pro Michael Jones; Founded 1988

9 holes, 1587 yards, S.S.S. 30
🏌 14.
🚶 Public pay and play.
🏌 WD £3.00; WE £3.00.
🏌 Societies welcome. Pre
arrangement for groups would be
appreciated.
🍴 Refreshments.
🛏 The Oriel House, The Trefnant
Hotel,The Bryn Glas.

10 70 Llantrisant & Pontyclun
Off Ely Valley Road, Talbot Green, Mid-
Glam, CF72 8AL
📧 lpgc@barbox.net
☎ 01443 222148, Pro 228169, Sec
224601, Rest/Bar 222148
M4 Junction 34 then A4119 to Talbot
Green.
Parkland course.
Pro Mark Phillips; Founded 1927
18 holes, 5950 yards, S.S.S. 67
🚶 Welcome except Sun; terms on
application.
🏌 WD £20; WE £25.
🏌 Welcome; menus available at all
times; from £15.
🍴 Bar and restaurant facilities.
🛏 Miskin Manor.

10 71 Llanwern
Tennyson Avenue, Llanwern, Newport,
NP6 2DY
☎ 01633 412029, Fax 412209, Pro
413233, Sec 412029, Rest/Bar 413278
1 mile form M4 jct 24.
Parkland course.
Pro Stephen Price; Founded 1928
18 holes, 6177 yards, S.S.S. 69
🚶 Welcome.
🏌 WD non-members £25 guests of
member £15.
🏌 Welcome Wed, Thurs, Fri with
prior arrangment; reduced rates golf
and catering for more than 20; terms
on application.
🍴 Catering available.
🛏 Stakis Country Court; Hilton
Nationall Holiday Inn; Travel Inn Celtic
Mabnor.

10 72 Llanyrafon
Llanfrechfa Way, Cwmbran, NP44 8HT
☎ 01633 874636
S to Pontypool off the M4 Junction 26.
Parkland course.
Pro Dave Woodman; Founded 1981
9 holes, 2566 yards, S.S.S. 54
🏌 Practice area.
🚶 Welcome.
🏌 WD £3.10; WE £3.60; under 16s
and over 60s: WD £2.20 WE £2.30.

🏌 Welcome by arrangement.
🍴 Refreshments.

10 73 Machynlleth
Newtown Road, Machynlleth, Powys,
SY20 8DU
☎ 01654 702000
0.5 miles out of town on the A480
Newtown road.
Parkland course.
Founded 1905
Designed by James Braid
9 holes, 5726 yards, S.S.S. 67
🏌 Practice area and putting green.
🚶 Welcome; Thurs 12-3 ladies; Sun
8-11.30 men.
🏌 WD £12; WE £15.
🏌 Welcome; 10% reduction for
groups of 8 or more; terms on
application. Catering available on
application to the secretary in writing.
🍴 Clubhouse facilities.
🛏 Wynnstay Plas Dolguog.

10 74 Maesteg
Mount Pleasant, Neath Rd, Maesteg,
CF34 9PR
☎ 01656 732037, Pro 735742, Sec
734106
Adjacent to B4282 main Maesteg to
Port Talbot road 0.5 miles from
Maesteg.
Hilltop course with forest views down
the valley.
Pro Christopher Riley; Founded 1912
Designed by James Braid (1945)
18 holes, 5939 yards, S.S.S. 69
🏌 Practice ground.
🚶 Welcome.
🏌 WD £17; WE £20.
🏌 Welcome by prior arrangement.
🍴 Bar meals available.
🛏 Heronstone, Bridgeend; Abervon,
Port Talbot; Greenacres GH, Maesteg.

10 75 Marriott St Pierre ♛
Hotel Golf & CC
St Pierre Park, Chepstow,
Monmouthshire, NP6 6YA
🖥 www.marriott.com
📧 reservations.stpierre@
marriotthotels.co.uk
☎ 01291 625261, Fax 629975,
Pro 635205, Sec 625261,
Rest/Bar 625261
Course is two miles from Chepstow on
the A48.
Parkland course.
Pro Craig Dun; Founded 1962
Designed by Bill Cox
18 holes on championship course, 18
holes on amateur course, 6538

champ/5569 amat yards, S.S.S. 68
amat/74 champ
🏌 13.
🚶 Everyone welcome.
🏌 Terms on application.
🏌 Welcome WD; WE residents only;
catering packages available; function
rooms available; terms available on
application.
🍴 Long Weekend Café Bar; The
Orangery restaurant.
🛏 On site Marriott hotel.

10 76 Merthyr Tydfil
(Cilsanws), Cloth Hall Lane, Cefn
Coed, Merthyr Tydfil, Mid-Glam, CF48
2NU
☎ 01685 723308
Course is two miles N of Merthyr on
Cilsanws Mountain in Cefn Coed.
Mountain top heathland course.
Founded 1908
18 holes, 5622 yards, S.S.S. 69
🚶 Welcome except on Sun
competition days.
🏌 WD £10; WE £15.
🏌 Welcome by prior arrangement;
meals available; terms available on
application.
🍴 Clubhouse facilities.
🛏 Mount Dolu Lodge.

10 77 Mid-Wales Golf Centre
Maesmawr, Caersws, Nr Newtown,
Powys
☎ 01686 688303
6 miles W of Newtown.
Farmland course.
Founded 1992
Designed by Jim Walters
9 holes, 2554 yards, S.S.S. 54
🏌 Practice range 12 bays floodlit, 8
covered.
🚶 Welcome.
🏌 WD £7; WE £9.
🏌 Welcome by prior arrangement.
🍴 Light snacks and bar.
🛏 Maesmawr Hall.

10 78 Milford Haven
Woodbine House, Hubberston, Milford
Haven, SA73 3RX
🖥 www.mhgc.co.uk
☎ 01646 692368, Fax 697870,
Pro 697870, Sec 697822,
Rest/Bar 692368
0.75 miles W of town on road to Dale.
Meadowland course.
Pro Dylwn Williams; Founded 1913
Designed by David Snell
18 holes, 6035 yards, S.S.S. 70
🏌 4.

† Everyone welcome.
 Ⅼ WD £15; WE £20.
 ♂ Welcome at all times; terms on application.
 🍽 Restaurant and bar facilities.
 ↵ Lord Nelson; Sir Benfro; Little Haven.

10 79 Mold
Cilcain Rd, Pantymwyn, Mold, Flintshire, CH7 5EH
 ⤴ www.moldgolfclub.co.uk
 ✉ info@moldgolfclub.co.uk
 ☎ 01352 741513, Fax 741517, Pro 740318, Sec 741513, Rest/Bar 741513
3 miles from Mold; leave on Denbigh road; turn left after 400 yards(next to bluebell public house) and follow road for 2.5 miles.
Undulating parkland course.
Pro Mark Jordan; Founded 1909
Designed by Hawtree
18 holes, 5528 yards, S.S.S. 67
† All welcome including weekends.
 Ⅼ WD £18; WE £20.
 ♂ Welcome by prior arrangement; catering packages by arrangement.
 🍽 Full facilities.
 ↵ Bryn Awel.

10 80 Monmouth ♛
Leasebrook Lane, Monmouth, Monmouthshire, NP25 3SN
 ☎ 01600 712212
Signposted from the Monmouth-Ross on Wye (A40) road.
Undulating parkland course.
Pro Brian Gurling; Founded 1896
18 holes, 5698 yards, S.S.S. 69
𝄃 Practice area.
† Welcome anytime except Sun morning before 11.30am.
 Ⅼ WD £17.50; WE £20.
 ♂ Welcome by prior arrangement with the secretary; packages available; from £18.
 🍽 Clubhouse facilities.

10 81 Monmouthshire
Llanfoist, Abergavenny, Monmouthshire, NP7 9HE
 ✉ secretary@monmouthshire-g-c.sagehost.co.uk
 ☎ 01873 852606, Fax 852606, Pro 852532
2 miles SW of Abergavenny.
Parkland course; three successive par 5s.
Pro Brian Edwards; Founded 1892
Designed by James Braid
18 holes, 5978 yards, S.S.S. 70

† Welcome by arrangement.
 Ⅼ WD £30; WE £35.
 ♂ Welcome Mon and Fri by prior arrangement; for groups of 16-35 £25; 36+ £20; terms on application.
 🍽 Full clubhouse facilities.
 ↵ The Bear Hotel, Creek Howell; The Manor, Creek Howell.

10 82 Morlais Castle
Pant, Dowlais, Merthyr Tydfil, Mid-Glamorgan, CF48 2UY
 ☎ 01685 722822, Fax 722822, Pro 388700, Sec 373271, Rest/Bar 722822
Follow signs for Brecon Mountain Railway.
Moorland course.
Pro H Jarrett; Founded 1900
18 holes, 6320 yards, S.S.S. 71
𝄃 Practice ground; buggies and clubs for hire.
† Welcome anytime.
 Ⅼ WD £16; WE £20.
 ♂ Welcome WD by prior arrangement with Sec.
 🍽 Full catering and bar facilities in new clubhouse.
 ↵ Treganna; Travel Lodge.

10 83 Morriston ♛
160 Clasemont Rd, Morriston, Swansea, SA6 6AJ
 ☎ 01792 771079, Fax 795628, Pro 772335, Sec 796528
3 miles N of Swansea city centre on A4067.
Parkland course.
Pro Darryl Rees; Founded 1919
18 holes, 5755 yards, S.S.S. 68
𝄃 Practice area.
† Welcome.
 Ⅼ WD £18; WE £30.
 ♂ Welcome by prior arrangement only.
 🍽 Lunches and bar facilities available.
 ↵ The Holiday Inn; Dolphin; Forest Motel; Jarvis.

10 84 Mountain Ash ♛
The Clubhouse, Cefn Pennar, Mountain Ash, Mid-Glam, CF45 4DT
 ☎ 01443 472265, Fax 479459, Pro 478770
Off A470 Cardiff to Abercynon road at Mountain Ash; follow signs to Cefn Pennar.
Mountain heathland course.
Pro Marcus Wills; Founded 1908
18 holes, 5553 yards, S.S.S. 67
† Welcome.

 Ⅼ WD £15; WE £18.
 ♂ Welcome; special packages available from secretary; terms on application.
 🍽 Clubhouse facilities.
 ↵ Baverstocks, Aberdare.

10 85 Mountain Lakes ♛
Blaengwynlais, Nr Caerphilly, Mid-Glam, CF83 1NG
 ✉ info@golfclub.co.uk
 ☎ 029 20861128, Fax 20863243, Pro 20886666, Sec 20861128, Rest/Bar 20886686
4 miles from M4 Junction 32 on Tongwynlais-Caerphilly road.
Mountain-Parkland course.
Pro S Bebb; Founded 1989
Designed by B Sandow/J Page
18 holes, 6343 yards, S.S.S. 73
𝄃 Practice range, 15 bays.
† Welcome.
 Ⅼ WD £18; WE £18.
 ♂ Welcome by prior arrangement; terms on application; from £19.
 🍽 Restaurant and bar facilities.
 ↵ New Country House.

10 86 Neath
Cadoxton, Neath, SA10 8AH
 ☎ 01639 643615, Pro 633693
2 miles from Neath in Cadoxton.
Mountain course.
Pro EM Bennett; Founded 1934
Designed by James Braid
18 holes, 6490 yards, S.S.S. 72
† Welcome WD.
 Ⅼ WD £20.
 ♂ Welcome by arrangement with Sec; terms on application.
 🍽 Full clubhouse facilities.
 ↵ Castle Neath.

10 87 Nefyn & District
Morfa Nefyn, Pwllheli, Gwynedd, LL53 6DA
 ✉ nefyngolf@tesco.net
 ☎ 01758 720966, Fax 720476, Pro 720102, Rest/Bar Bar 720218 Rest 721626
1 mile W of Nefyn; 18 miles W of Caernarfon.
Seaside clifftop course on Llyn Peninsula.
Pro John Froom; Founded 1907
26 holes, 6548 yards, S.S.S. 71
𝄃 Practice area.
† Welcome by prior arrangement; handicap certs preferred; dress codes apply.
 Ⅼ WD £26, day pass £33; WE £31, day pass £38.

Welcome by prior arrangement except for 2 weeks in August; 10 per cent reduction for groups of 12 or more; snooker table; terms on application.
Full clubhouse facilities; restaurant and bar.
Nanhoron Nefyn; The Linksway, Morfa Nefyn.

10 88 Newport
Great Oak, Rogerstone, Newport, Gwent, NP1 9FX
☎ 01633 892643, Fax 896676, Pro 893271, Sec 892643, Rest/Bar 894496
3 miles from Newport M4 Junction 27 on B4591.
Parkland course.
Pro Paul Mayo; Founded 1903
18 holes, 6431 yards, S.S.S. 71
Welcome by prior arrangement.
WD £30; WE £40.
Welcome Wed; Thurs; Fri and some Sun; handicap certs required; discounts available at off-peak times; from £30.
Full clubhouse facilities.
Celtic Manor, Newport.

10 89 Newport (Pembs)
Newport, Pembrokeshire, SA42 0NR
☎ 01239 820244
Follow signs for Newport Sands from Newport.
Seaside course.
Pro Julian Noott; Founded 1925
Designed by James Braid
9 holes, 5815 yards, S.S.S. 68
Driving bays (2 open and 2 covered).
Welcome.
Terms on application.
Welcome by prior arrangement; terms on application.
Full bar and restaurant facilities.
Self-catering flats on site.

10 90 North Wales ☎
72 Bryniau Rd, West Shore, Llandudno, Gwynedd, LL30 2DZ
www.northwales.uk.com/nwgc
golf@nwgc.freeserve.co.uk
☎ 01492 875325, Fax 873355, Pro 876878, Rest/Bar 875342
2 miles from A55 on A546 Llandudno/Deganwy road.
Links course.
Pro Richard Bradbury; Founded 1894
Designed by Tancred Cummins
18 holes, 6287 yards, S.S.S. 71
Welcome.

WD £26; WE and BH £36.
Welcome with handicap certs; practice area and snooker; terms on application.
Full bar and restaurant facilities.
Many in Llandudno.

10 91 Northop Country ☎
Park Golf Club
Nr Chester, Flintshire, CH7 6WA
☎ 01352 840440
Off A55 at Northop/Connahs Quay exit; entrance is on slip road.
Parkland course.
Pro Matthew Pritchard; Founded 1994
Designed by John Jacobs
18 holes, 6735 yards, S.S.S. 73
Driving range.
Welcome by prior arrangement.
WD £30; WE £35.
Welcome by arrangement WD; catering packages available; corporate days arranged; tennis; gym; sauna.
Full restaurant facilities; bar; terrace.
St Davids Park Ewloe.

10 92 Oakdale
Llwynon Lane, Oakdale, Gwent, NP12 0NF
hole19@callnet.com
☎ 01495 220044
M4 Junction 28 then A467 to Crumlin and B4251 to Oakdale.
Parkland course.
Founded 1990
Designed by Ian Goodenough
9 holes, 2688 yards, S.S.S. 56
Practice range, 18 bays floodlit.
Welcome.
WD £5; WE £5 (second 9 £3); basket of range balls £1.30.
Welcome by prior arrangement.
Snacks in clubhouse.
The Mace Manor.

10 93 Old Colwyn
Woodland Avenue, Old Colwyn, Clwyd, LL29 9NL
☎ 01492 515581, Sec 515581, Rest/Bar 515581
Off A55 at Old Colwyn exit towards Old Colwyn.
Undulating meadowland course.
Founded 1907
Designed by James Braid
9 holes, 5263 yards, S.S.S. 66
Welcome WD; by prior arrangement at WE.
WD £10; WE £15.
Welcome by arrangement; reductions for 10 or more players;

menus by arrangement; terms on application.
Full clubhouse facilities.
Bodelwyddan Castle has reduced rates for golfers; Lyndale.

10 94 Old Padeswood
Station Rd, Padeswood, Mold, Clwyd, CH7 4JL
www.oldpadeswood.co.uk
☎ 01244 547701, Pro 547401, Sec 547401, Rest/Bar 547701
On A5118 between Penyfford and Mold close to A55.
Meadowland course in valley.
Pro Tony Davies; Founded 1933/1978
Designed by Arthur Joseph
18 holes, 6685 yards, S.S.S. 72
Practice range par 3 course.
Welcome.
WD £20; WE £25.
Welcome WD; restaurant; bar; also par 3 course; from £20.
Full clubhouse facilities.
Many in Chester Wrexham and Mold.

10 95 Old Rectory Hotel And Conference Centre
Llangattock, Crickhowell, Powys, NP8 1PH
www.theoldrectoryhotelcrichowell. co.uk
ftu@ theoldrectoryhotelcrichowell.co.uk
☎ 01873 810373
A40 to Crickhowell.
Parkland course.
Founded 1968
9 holes, 2600 yards, S.S.S. 54
Welcome.
WD £7.50; WE £7.50.
Terms on application; bars meals and restaurant available.
Bar and restaurant.
On site hotel; 20 en suite rooms.

10 96 Padeswood & Buckley ☎
The Caia, Station Lane, Padeswood, Mold, Flintshire, CH7 4JD
padeswoodgc@compuserve.com
☎ 01244 550537, Fax 541600, Pro 543636, Sec 550537, Bar 550537 Rest 546072
Off Penyfford-Mold road A5118 at Old Padeswood turning; club 50 yards further on.
Parkland course alongside River Alyn.
Pro DV Ashton; Founded 1933
Designed by Heap and Partners
18 holes, 5888 yards, S.S.S. 69
Welcome; members only at

weekends; dress codes apply.
⌊ WD £20 per round or £25 per day.
summer April-October Sat £25 per
round. £13 per person per round
weekdays.
⌁ Welcome WD; packages include
28 holes of golf; coffee on arrival.
◉ Light lunch and dinner; prices on
application; full clubhouse facilities and
restaurant.
⌁ St David's Park; Ewloe; Beaufort
Park; New Brighton.

10 97 Palleg
Palleg Rd, Lower Cwmtwrch, Swansea
☎ 01639 842193
Course is off the Swansea-Brecon
road.
Meadowland course.
Pro Sharon Roberts; Founded 1930
Designed by CK Cotton
9 holes, 6418 yards, S.S.S. 72
† Welcome with handicap certs WD;
with member at WE.
⌊ WD £13.
⌁ Welcome by prior arrangement;
terms on application.
◉ Clubhouse facilities.
⌁ Y Stycle Upper Cwmtwrch; Dab-
Yr-Ogof Caves; Abercrane; Goufch
Arms B and B.

10 98 Parc Golf Club
Church Lane, Coedkernew, Newport,
Gwent, NP1 9TU
☎ 01633 680933, Fax 680955,
Pro 680933, Sec 681011,
Rest/Bar 681011
M4 Junction 28; on to A48 towards
Cardiff for 1.5 miles.
Parkland course.
Pro Darren Griffiths; Founded 1989
Designed by B Thomas & T Hicks
18 holes, 5619 yards, S.S.S. 68
⌲ Extensive tuition by Darren
Griffiths, Russell Jones and Barry
Thomas. Practice range; 38 bays
floodlit and carpeted; buggies and
clubs for hire.
† Welcome WD; WE by prior
arrangement.
⌊ WD £15; WE £17.
⌁ Welcome by arrangement.
◉ Full facilities; bar restaurant;
function room; conference suite.
⌁ Coach & Horses; Travel Lodge
both Castleton.

10 99 Penmaenmawr �
Conway Old Rd, Penmaenmawr,
Conwy, LL34 6RD
☎ 01492 623330

3 miles W of Conwy on A55 to
Dwygyfylchi.
Undulating parkland course.
Founded 1910
9 holes with 18 tees, 5350 yards,
S.S.S. 66
⌲ Practice area.
† Welcome except Sat.
⌊ WD £12; Sun £18.
⌁ Welcome by prior arrangement;
inclusive package of 27 holes including
lunch and dinner; from £25.
◉ Bar and restaurant.
⌁ Caerlyr Hall.

10 100 Pennard
2 Southgate Rd, Southgate, Swansea,
W Glamorgan, SA3 2BT
☎ 01792 233131, Fax 234797, Pro
233451, Sec 233131, Rest/Bar 233131
8 miles W of Swansea via A4067 and
B4436.
Undulating seaside course.
Pro Mike Bennett; Founded 1896
Designed by J Braid
18 holes, 6231 yards, S.S.S. 72
⌲ Practice area; no buggies allowed
on course; trolleys and clubs for hire.
† Welcome; dress codes apply (no
jeans or trainers) on course and in
clubhouse.
⌊ WD £27; WE £35.
⌁ Welcome by prior arrangement;
minimum group 12; snooker; from £20.
◉ Bar snacks; lunches and evening
meals.
⌁ Osborne; Winston; Nicholaston;
Cefn Goleua; Fairy Hill.

10 101 Penrhos Golf & CC �
Llanrhystud, Nr Aberystwyth,
Cardiganshire, SY23 5AY
⌁ www.penrhosgolf.co.uk
✉ info@penrhos.co.uk
☎ 01974 202999, Fax 202100
9 miles S of Aberystwyth on A487; take
Llanrhystud turning on to B4337. signs
from village.
Parkland course.
Pro Paul Diamond; Founded 1991
Designed by Jim Walters
18 holes and 9-hole academy course,
6641 yards, S.S.S. 72
⌲ 3 bays and teeing off area.
† Welcome except Sun am.
⌊ WD £20; WE £25.
⌁ Welcome by arrangement; catering
packages available; £18-£40.
◉ Full clubhouse facilities.
⌁ On site motel; 15 en suite rooms;
Marine; Conrah Country both
Aberystwyth; Plas Morfa Llanon.

10 102 Peterstone Golf & Country Club
Peterstone Wentloog, Cardiff, CF3 2TN
⌁ www.peterstonelakes.com
✉ peterstone_lakes@
yahoo.com
☎ 01633 680009, Fax 680563,
Pro 680075, Sec 680009,
Rest/Bar 680009
Take A48 towards Cardiff from M4
Junction 28 turning left to Marshfield;
course 2.5 miles.
Links/parkland course.
Pro Darren Clark; Founded 1990
Designed by Bob Sandow
18 holes, 6555 yards, S.S.S. 72
† Welcome.
⌊ WD £16.50; WE £22.50.
⌁ Welcome Mon-Fri; full packages;
corporate days; photographs; starter;
half-way house; on-course competition;
presentation evenings; terms on
application.
◉ Full bar and restaurant facilities;
Fairways restaurant.
⌁ Wentloog; Travelodge; Moat
House.

10 103 Plassey
The Plassey Golf Course, Eyton,
Wrexham, LL13 0SP
⌁ www.plasseygolf.co.uk
☎ 01978 780020, Fax 781397
4 miles SE of Wrexham signposted
from A483.
Parkland course.
Pro Simon Ward; Founded 1992
Designed by K Williams
9 holes, 2434 yards, S.S.S. 32
† Pay and play; telephone first.
⌊ WD £7; WE £8 for 9 holes. WD £7;
WE £12 for 18 holes.
⌁ Unlimited access; terms on
application. Practice area restricted to
members.
◉ Full facilities.
⌁ Cross Lanes Hotel.

10 104 Pontardawe
Cefn Llan, Pontardawe, Swansea, SA8
4SH
☎ 01792 863118, Fax 830041,
Pro 830977
From M4 Junction 45 take A4067 to
Pontardawe.
Moorland course.
Pro Gary Hopkins; Founded 1924
18 holes, 6038 yards, S.S.S. 70
⌲ Practice green.
† Welcome WD with handicap certs.
⌊ WD £18.
⌁ Welcome by arrangement; prices
vary depending on numbers; catering

by arrangement.
🍽 Full clubhouse facilities.
🛏 Pen-yr-Alt.

10 105 Pontnewydd
West Pontnewydd, Cwmbran, Gwent,
NP44 1AB
☎ 01633 482170
Follow signs for West Pontnewydd or
Upper Cwmbran; W slopes of
Cwmbran.
Meadowland course.
Founded 1875
14 holes, 5353 yards, S.S.S. 67
† Welcome WD; WE as guest of a
member.
⌐ WD terms on application.
⌐ Welcome by prior arrangement;
terms on application.
🍽 Limited.
🛏 Parkway; Commodore.

10 106 Pontypool   ℭ
Lasgarn Lane, Trevethin, Pontypool,
Gwent, NP4 8TR
☎ 01495 763655, Pro 755544
Off A4042 at St Cadoc's Church in
Pontypool.
Mountain course.
Pro James Howard; Founded 1919
18 holes, 5963 yards, S.S.S. 69
† Welcome by arrangement.
⌐ WD £20; WE £24.
⌐ Welcome by prior arrangement;
packages available; terms on
application.
🍽 Full catering facilities except Mon.
🛏 Holiday Inn-Pontypool; Three
Salmons; Glyn-yr-Avon both Usk;
Parkway, Cwnbran.

10 107 Pontypridd
Ty-Gwyn, Ty-Gwyn Road, The
Common, Pontypridd, Mid-Glam, CF37
4DJ
☎ 01443 402359, Fax 491622,
Pro 491210, Sec 409904,
Rest/Bar 402359
12 miles NW of Cardiff E of Pontypridd
off A470.
Mountain course.
Pro Wade Walters; Founded 1905
Designed by Bradbeer
18 holes, 5881 yards, S.S.S. 66
† Welcome with handicap certs.
⌐ Terms on application.
⌐ Welcome by arrangement with the
Pro; packages available; terms on
application.
🍽 Clubhouse facilities.
🛏 Lechwen Hall; The Millfield Hotel.

10 108 Porthmadog
Morfa Bychan, Porthmadog, Gwynedd,
LL49 9UU
☎ 01766 512037, Fax 514638,
Pro 513828, Rest/Bar 512037
1 mile W of Porthmadog High Street
after turning towards Black Rock Sands.
Parkland/links course.
Pro Pete Bright; Founded 1902
Designed by James Braid
18 holes, 6363 yards, S.S.S. 71
† Welcome by arrangement.
⌐ WD £20; WE £26.
⌐ Welcome by prior arrangement;
discounts for groups of more than 16;
catering available; terms on
application.
🍽 Clubhouse facilities.
🛏 Tydden Llwyn; Sportsmans.

10 109 Prestatyn
Marine Rd East, Prestatyn,
Denbighshire, LL19 7HS
🖳 www.prestatyngc.co.uk
✉ prestatyngc@freenet.co.uk
☎ 01745 854320, Fax 888327,
Pro 852083, Sec 888353
Off A548 coast road to Prestatyn.
Championship links.
Pro ML Staton; Founded 1905
Designed by S Collins
18 holes, 6808 yards, S.S.S. 73
⌐ Practice areas.
† Welcome except Sat and Tues
morning.
⌐ WD £25; WE £30.
⌐ Welcome except Sat and Tues am
by prior arrangement; 27 holes; lunch
and dinner.
🍽 Clubhouse facilities.
🛏 Talardy St Asaph; Traeth Ganol;
Sands; Prestatyn; Craig Park; Dyserth.

10 110 Priskilly Forest Golf Club
Castlemorris, Haverfordwest,
Pembrokeshire, SA62 5EH
🖳 www.priskillyforest.co.uk
✉ jevans@priskillyforest.co.uk
☎ 01348 840276, Fax 840276
On B4331 towards Mathry off A40 at
Letterstone.
Picturesque mature parkland course.
Founded 1992
Designed by J.Walters
9 holes, 5874 yards, S.S.S. 69
⌐ Practice area.
† Welcome.
⌐ Prices on application.
⌐ Welcome by arrangement; limited
catering facilities.
🍽 Licensed bar and tea rooms.
🛏 Priskilly Forest GH on site.

10 111 Pwllheli
Golf Rd, Pwllheli, Gwynedd, LL53 5PS
☎ 01758 612520, Fax 701644,
Sec 701644
Turn into Cardiff Road in town centre;
bear right at the first fork; course
signposted.
Parkland/links course.
Pro John Pilkington; Founded 1900
Designed by Tom Morris; extended
James Braid
18 holes, 6200 yards, S.S.S. 69
⌐ Practice ground.
† Welcome.
⌐ WD £22; WE £27.
⌐ Welcome most days by prior
arrangement.
🍽 Full facilities.
🛏 Caeau Capel; Nefyn; Bryn
Eisteddfod Clynnogfawr; Nanhoron
Morfa.

10 112 Pyle & Kenfig
Waun-Y-Mer, Kenfig, Bridgend, S
Wales, CF33 4PU
🖳 www.pyleandkenfiggolfclub.
co.uk
✉ secretary@
pyleandkenfidgolfclub.co.uk
☎ 01656 783093 and 771613,
Fax 772822, Pro 772446
M4 Junction 37 in direction of
Porthcawl, call for directions.
Links/downland course.
Pro Robert Evans; Founded 1922
Designed by H Colt
18 holes, 6741 yards, S.S.S. 73
⌐ Practice area.
† Welcome.
⌐ WD £35; WE £35.
⌐ Welcome by arrangement; prices
vary according to numbers; terms on
application.
🍽 Full bar and catering facilities.
🛏 Fairways; Atlantic; Seabank.

10 113 Radyr
Drysgol Rd, Radyr, Cardiff, CF15 8BS
🖳 www.radyrgolf.co.uk
✉ manager@radyrgolf.co.uk
☎ 029 20842408, Fax 20843914,
Pro 20842476, Sec 20842408,
Rest/Bar 20842408
4 miles from M4 Junction 32; 8 miles
from Cardiff.
Parkland course.
Pro R Butterworth; Founded 1902
18 holes, 6078 yards, S.S.S. 70
† Welcome by prior arrangement.
⌐ WD £38; WE £38.
⌐ Welcome with prior arrangement;
catering packages available; separate
facilities for parties of 35-40; dining

room for 125+; terms on application.
🍽 Full dining and bar facilities.
🛏 Quality Inn.

---

10 114 RAF St Athan
Clive Road, St Athan, Vale Of
Glamorgan, CF62 4jd
📧 sec@stanthangolfclub
☎ 01446 751043, Fax 751862
First right after St Athan village on
Cowbridge road.
Parkland course.
Founded 1976
9 holes, 6542 yards, S.S.S. 72
⛳ Practice green.
🏌 Welcome except Sun.
🎫 WD £12; Sat £16.
🖊 Welcome by arrangement with
Sec.
🍽 Full facilities available; except
Mon.

---

10 115 Raglan Parc 🅲
Parc Lodge, Raglan, Monmouthshire,
NP5 2ER
📧 golf@raglanparcfreeserve.co.uk
☎ 01291 690077, Fax 690075, Pro
0778680-7629, Sec 690077, Rest/Bar
690077
0.5 miles from Raglan at junction of
A40 and A449.
Undulating parkland course.
Pro Gareth Gage; Founded 1994
18 holes, 6604 yards, S.S.S. 72
🏌 Welcome; booking advisable.
🎫 WD £15; WE £18.
🖊 Welcome by prior arrangement.
🍽 Light lunch and 3-course meal;
from £25; Bar snacks and light meals.
🛏 The Beaufort; The Country Court;
Travelodge.

---

10 116 Rhondda
Golf House, Penrhys, Mid-Glamorgan,
CF43 3PW
☎ 01443 433204, Fax 441384,
Pro 441385, Sec 441384,
Rest/Bar 433204
On Penrhys road between Rhondda
Fach and Rhondda Fawr.
Mountain course.
Pro Gareth Bebb; Founded 1910
18 holes, 6205 yards, S.S.S. 70
⛳ 22.
🏌 Welcome WD; restrictions WE.
🎫 WD £15; WE £20.
🖊 Welcome by arrangement;
function room available; terms on
application.
🍽 Full clubhouse bar and catering
facilities.
🛏 Heritage Park.

---

10 117 Rhos-on-Sea
Penrhyn Bay, Llandudno, Conwy, LL30
3PU
☎ 01492 549100, Pro 548115
From A55 take Old Colwyn exit and
follow coast road to Penrhyn Bay;
course is between Rhos-on-Sea and
Llandudno.
Pro Mike Macara; Founded 1899
Designed by JJ Simpson
18 holes, 6064 yards, S.S.S. 69
🏌 Welcome.
🎫 WD £10; WE £20.
🖊 Welcome everyday but only by
prior arrangement; catering terms on
application; from £10.
🍽 Full clubhouse facilities.
🛏 On site dormy house hotel.

---

10 118 Rhosgoch 🅲
Rhosgoch, Builth Wells, Powys, LD2
3JY
🖱 www.rhosgoch-golf.co.uk
☎ 01497 851251, Fax 851251,
Sec 851251, Rest/Bar 851251
Off B4594 at turning to Clyro, between
Erwood and Kington.
Parkland course.
Founded 1984
Designed by Herbie Poore
9 holes, 4995 yards, S.S.S. 66
🏌 Everyone welcome.
🎫 WD £8; WE £10.
🖊 Welcome by prior arrangement;
terms on application.
🍽 Bar and snacks.
🛏 Clyro Court, The Swan Hotel, The
Kilvert Hotel.

---

10 119 Rhuddlan
Meliden Rd, Rhuddlan, Denbighshire,
LL18 6LB
🖱 www.rhuddlangolfclub.co.uk
📧 golf@rhuddlangolfclub.fsnet.
co.uk
☎ 01745 590217, Fax 590472,
Pro 590898, Sec 590217,
Rest/Bar 591978
Course is off the A55 three miles N of
St Asaph.
Parkland course.
Pro Andrew Carr; Founded 1930
Designed by Hawtree&Co
18 holes, 6471 yards, S.S.S. 71 off the
whites, 70 off the yellows
🏌 Welcome; only with a member on
Sun.
🎫 WD £24; Sat £30.
🖊 Welcome WD by arrangement.
🍽 Lunch and dinner daily; bar
facilities.
🛏 Plas Elwy; Kinmel Manor
(packages available for both).

---

10 120 Rhyl
Coast Rd, Rhyl, Denbighshire, LL18
3RE
☎ 01745 353171, Fax 353171,
Pro 353171
1 mile from station on A548 Prestatyn
road.
Seaside links course.
Pro Tim Leah; Founded 1890
9 holes, 6220 yards, S.S.S. 70
⛳ Practice area.
🏌 Welcome.
🎫 WD £20; WE £25.
🖊 Welcome by prior arrangement;
discount of 20 per cent for parties of
more than 20 players; full catering
packages available; snooker; from £1.
🍽 Full catering facilities.
🛏 Grange; Marina; Garfields.

---

10 121 The Rolls of Monmouth
The Hendre, Monmouth,
Monmouthshire, NP25 5HG
🖱 www.therolesgolfclub.co.uk
📧 enquiries@therolesgolfclub.
co.uk
☎ 01600 715353, Fax 713115,
Sec 715353, Rest/Bar 715353
4 miles NW of Monmouth on the
B4233.
Parkland course.
Founded 1982
Designed by Urbis Planning
18 holes, 6733 yards, S.S.S. 73
🏌 All welcome by arrangement.
🎫 Prices on application.
🖊 Welcome by prior arrangement;
special offers on Mon.
🍽 Lunch 18 holes; prices on
application; full catering facilities
available.
🛏 Riverside.

---

10 122 Royal Porthcawl
Rest Bay, Porthcawl, Mid Glam, CF36
3UW
🖱 www.royalporthcawl.com
📧 royalroyalporthcawl@
cs.com
☎ 01656 782251, Fax 771687, Pro
773702, Rest/Bar 782251
M4 Junction 37 and follow signs for
Porthcawl/Rest bay.
Championship Links course.
Pro Peter Evans; Founded 1891
Designed by Charles Gibson
18 holes, 6685 yards, S.S.S. 74
⛳ Practice range.
🏌 Welcome Mon pm, Tues, Thurs,
Fri. Handicap Certs requires.
🎫 WD £55 – £65; WE £65 – £75.
🖊 Welcome by arrangement
restaurant and bar facilities.

Royal Porthcawl

Donald Steel put it rather well. "It can represent the best and the worst, heaven and hell. However, few courses reward the good old fashioned virtues of control and flight better than Porthcawl."

Tiger Woods will know exactly what Steel is on about. In 1995, Royal Porthcawl became the first club in Wales to host the Walker Cup. Woods was on the American team. In the opening round of singles, Woods was up against Gary Wolstenholme who in the modern idiom is about as short as it is possible to be.

Wolstenhome cheerfully admits that he never tires of relating the tale of his victory over Woods. He says, "You can win matches by intimidating your opponent if you keep hitting fairways and greens the whole time. The famous win against Tiger was an example."

Standing on the eighteenth tee the pair were all square. After the drives, as usual Tiger was way out in front. Wolstenholme had a five-wood left down to the green. Woods had a seven-iron. Wolstenholme found the edge of the green, Woods tugged his shot out of bounds in the direction of the clubhouse. "Great Britain and Ireland wins the match, one up." As Steel observed and Wolstenholme confirmed, Porthcawl rewards the man who can control his ball.

Yet the course had rather humbler origins than its modern reputation might suggest. Founded in 1891, it consisted of nine holes on a piece of land called Lock's Common. The golfers shared it with cattle and needed the permission of the local parish vestry to use the land.

Eventually eighteen holes were completed nearer to the shoreline although, despite its setting, Royal Porthcawl is not a typical links course. The good news is that there is a lack of the huge sandhills that cause so much grief at places like Ballybunion. The bad news is that there is an absence of huge sandhills, allowing the wind to tear across the course unchecked.

The par five fifth was considered by Henry Cotton to be one of the great holes in golf. It is not overly long at 476 yards, but the second or third shot is uphill to a green generous in its length and wretchedly parsimonious in its width. A boundary wall flanks the green to the left and there is a large grassy knoll and a cavernous bunker to the right. If you are lucky enough to find the green, but unlucky enough to be beyond the pin, you will need to attach crampons to the golf ball in order to make it stop.

The opening trio of holes are amongst the best in golf, each one a par four, each one posing different questions, each one threatening the same result - a ball on the beach. It is possible to see the ocean from every one of Porthcawl's eighteen holes, but it is only at the start that the view is a threatening one.

Royal Porthcawl is a bewitching combination of links and moorland golf, of rolling fairways and undulating greens. — **Mark Reason**

Royal St David's

God and man must have stayed up very late together and drunk an awful lot of coffee in order to knock up a backdrop of Snowdonia, Cardigan Bay and Harlech Castle. The set designers have done Royal St David's proud.

Visually it is an awesome golf course. It also requires a great deal of playing. David Huish, the professional at North Berwick, called it, "the most difficult par 69 in the world." One of the problems is that it is not a traditional out and back links. There are pockets of holes facing in all directions. So whatever the direction of the wind it will slap you in the face somewhere on the course.

The finish to Royal St David's - with the exception of the eighteenth which some consider a rather mundane par three, an overstated view because of what precedes it - is majestic. The fifteenth is a superb par four of over four hundred yards influenced on both sides by some lowering dunes. The sixteenth tee is the highest on the course. A spectacular drive is inevitable and if well hit will leave a shortish second that is hard to gauge. The seventeenth, reflecting some of the holes in the second half of the front nine, curiously relies on a more heathland nature for its protection. Just to complicate things further each of the three holes points in a different direction.

The founding fathers of the course were Harold Finch-Hatton, an exotic boomerang-wielding adventurer and brother to the Finch-Hatton of 'Out of Africa' fame, and William Henry More, who would become one of the finest club secretaries the game has ever known. Among his many sensible dicta are, "Cultivate the arithmetical skill and memory of a ready-money bookmaker - without his repartee...And when the handicap lists are up rejoice exceedingly if there be general grumbling. You may rest assured that justice has been done."

More had many hurdles to overcome through the years. David Lloyd George, in the days when he was Chancellor of the Exchequer, was accused by one member of having failed to pay his green fee. Earlier in its history the club was premature in assuming the royal preface and was ticked off by the palace who did not confer the status for another twelve years.

But perhaps most bizarre of all was the instigation of a local rule on account of the original greenkeeper's bibulous nature. Because the aforementioned was often to be found comatose from drink and stretched out in a pink hunting jacket on various parts of the course, it was decided that a ball coming to rest near his figure could be dropped two club lengths away without penalty.

Perhaps More's greatest contribution was to make a phone call to facilitate Robert Graves's commission with the Royal Welch Fusiliers. It was through this association that Graves, a reluctant member who resigned from the golf club and gave up the game because "I found it made for my temper", came to write 'Goodbye To All That'.

At times the more recent members can understand Graves's frustration with the game. There is a crow about that has a habit of making off with golf balls. Even more serious are the drainage problems. The club lost several weeks of golf a year or so ago due to waterlogged ground, but steps are in hand to remedy the situation.

David Morkill, the current in the line of articulate secretaries, explains a new drainage project that seems to involve American mud, the Archimedes screw and half the contents of Tracey Island. He seems to have everything in hand.

Come rain or shine, Royal St David's is worthy of its monarchial and canonised status. — **Mark Reason**

🍽 Full restaurant and bar facilities.
⌂ Club has own Dormy house from £45 pp Atlantic; Fairways.

10 123 Royal St David's
Harlech, Gwynedd, LL46 2UB
🖳 www.royalstdavids.co.uk
☎ 01766 780203, Fax 781110,
Pro 780857, Sec 780361,
Rest/Bar 780203
On the A496 Lower Harlech road under the Castle.
Championship links.
Pro John Barnett; Founded 1894
18 holes, 6571 yards, S.S.S. 74
♦ Welcome; booking essential.
⌊ WD £35; WE £40.
⌀ Welcome; booking essential; 10 per cent reduction for more than 40 players; £5 deposit per player 2 months before visit; from £30.
🍽 Full catering facilities.
⌂ Rum Hole; St David's both Harlech.

10 124 Ruthin Pwllglas ⌤
Ruthin Pwllglas, Ruthin, Denbighshire, LL15 7AR
☎ 01824 702296
On A494 2.5 miles S of Ruthin; right fork before Pwllglas village.
Parkland/meadowland course.
Pro Michael Jones; Founded 1906
Designed by David Lloyd Rees
10 holes, 5418 yards, S.S.S. 66
♦ Welcome.
⌊ WD £12.50; WE £18.00.
⌀ Welcome by prior arrangement.
🍽 Bar and catering facilities by prior arrangement.
⌂ Ruthin Castle; The Whitstay; The Anchor; The Manor House; The Eagles.

10 125 St Andrews Major
Coldbrook Rd East, Nr Cadoxton, Barry, S Glamorgan, CF6 3BB
☎ 01446 722227
From M4 Junction 33 follow signs to Barry and Cardiff Airport turn left to Sully.
Parkland course.
Founded 1993
Designed by MRM Leisure
18 holes, 5862 yards, S.S.S. 70
⌁ 12 Bay driving range, floodlit.
♦ Welcome pay and play course.
⌊ £16.
⌀ Welcome packages available 18 holes and 2 course meal £20.
🍽 Full bar and restaurant facilities; Sun lunches.
⌂ Copthorne; The International; Mount Sorrell; Travel Lodge.

10 126 St David's City
Whitesands, St David's, Pembrokeshire, SA62 6PT
☎ 01437 721751
Course is two miles W of St David's following the signs for Whitesands Bay.
Links course; most westerly Welsh course.
Founded 1902
9 holes, 5582 yards, S.S.S. 70
♦ Welcome; some restrictions Fri pm.
⌊ Day tickets: WD £15 (winter £10); WE £15 (winter £10).
⌀ Welcome by arrangement.
🍽 At the Whitesands Bay Hotel adjacent to course.
⌂ Whitesands Bay; Old Cross; St Nons; Warpool Court.

10 127 St Deiniol
Pen Y Bryn, Bangor, Gwynedd, LL57 1PX
✉ secretary@ stdeiniol.fsbusiness.co.uk
☎ 01248 353098, Pro 353098, Sec 370792, Rest/Bar 353098
From A5/A55 intersection follow A5122 for 1 mile to E of Bangor.
Undulating parkland course; views of Menai and Snowdonia.
Founded 1906
Designed by James Braid
18 holes, 5654 yards, S.S.S. 67
♦ Welcome; phone in advance for weekends.
⌊ WD £14; WE £18.
⌀ Welcome by appointment; packages vary; terms on application.
🍽 Full clubhouse facilities; no catering Mon by prior arrangement.
⌂ Eryl Mor.

10 128 St Giles ⌤
Pool Rd, Newtown, Powys, SY16 3AJ
☎ 01686 625844
1 mile E of Newtown on A483.
Riverside/parkland course.
Pro DP Owen; Founded 1895
⌁ Practice putting area.
♦ Welcome.
⌊ Terms on application.
⌀ Welcome by arrangement; packages include refreshments.
🍽 Clubhouse facilities with bar and restaurant.
⌂ Elephant and Castle.

10 129 St Idloes
Penrallt, Llanidloes, Powys, SY18 6LG
☎ 01686 412559, Pro 412559,

Sec 650712, Rest/Bar 412559
Off A470 at Llanidloes; 1 mile down B4569.
Undulating course; superb views from hill plateau.
Founded 1906
Designed by Members
9 holes, 5540 yards, S.S.S. 66
♦ All welcome, ring for information.
⌊ WD £12.50; WE £15.50.
⌀ Welcome; packages available; terms on application.
🍽 Clubhouse facilities.
⌂ Mount Inn; Unicorn; Lloyds; also lots of B&Bs.

10 130 St Mary's Hotel
St Mary's Hill, Pencoed, S Glamorgan
☎ 01656 860280, Sec 861100
Off Junction 35 of M4.
Parkland courses.
9 holes, 2426 yards, S.S.S. 34
♦ Welcome by prior arrangement.
⌊ By negotiation.
⌀ Welcome; packages available.
Country club; floodlit driving range.

10 131 St Mellons
St Mellons, Cardiff, CF3 8XS
☎ 01633 680401, Fax 681219,
Pro 680101
Close to M4 Junctions 28 (W); 30 (E).
Parkland course.
Pro Barry Thomas; Founded 1964
18 holes, 6275 yards, S.S.S. 70
♦ Welcome WD; members only at WE.
⌊ WD £32.
⌀ Welcome Tues and Thurs; packages vary according to numbers; terms on application.
🍽 Clubhouse facilities.
⌂ St Mellons Hotel; Travel lodge.

10 132 St Melyd
The Paddock, Prestatyn, Denbighshire, LL19 9NB
🖳 www.stmelydgolf.co.uk
✉ info@stmelydgolf.co.uk
☎ 01745 854405, Fax 856908,
Sec 854405, Rest/Bar 854405
On A547 on the main Prestatyn to Meliden road.
Undulating parkland course.
Pro Andrew Carr; Founded 1922
9 holes, 5839 yards, S.S.S. 68
♦ Welcome except Thurs (Ladies day) and Sat.
⌊ WD £18; WE and BH £22.
⌀ Welcome except Thurs and Sat; 18 holes and 3-course meal £24.
🍽 Full facilities except Tues.
⌂ Nant Hall; Graig Park.

10 133 Shirenewton Golf Club
Shirenewton, Nr Chepstow, Gwent,
NP6 6RL
✉ lee.paget@aol.com
☎ 01291 641642, Fax 641472,
Pro 641471, Sec 641471,
Rest/Bar 641642
Off M4 take A48 towards Newport, on
reaching Chirk take road to
Shirenewton (2.5 miles).
Parkland course.
Pro Lee Pagett; Founded 1995
Designed by M Weeks/Tony Davies
18 holes, 6607 yards, S.S.S. 72
⚐ Practice range.
✝ Welcome.
✧ WD £15; WE £18.
✧ Welcome by prior arrangement.
🍴 Full facilities.
✧ On site.

10 134 South Pembrokeshire
Military Rd, Pembroke Dock,
Pembrokeshire, SA72 6SE
☎ 01646 621453, Fax 621453,
Pro 621453, Sec 621453,
Rest/Bar 621453
Main A477 road from Carmarthen to
Pembroke dock; 100 yards after town
boundary sign turn right to Pembroke.
Parkland course.
Pro A Hall; Founded 1970
18 holes, 6100 yards, S.S.S. 72
⚐ 6.
✝ Welcome.
✧ WD £15; WE £20.
✧ Welcome by prior arrangement;
catering packages available; some
discounts for larger groups; from £16.
🍴 Clubhouse facilities.
✧ Coach House; Cleddau Bridge;
Kings Arms.

10 135 Southerndown
Ogmore-by-Sea, Bridgend, CF32 0QP
✉ www.southerndowngolfclub.com
✉ southerndowngolf@btconnect.com
☎ 01656 880476, Fax 880317,
Pro 880326, Sec 880476,
Rest/Bar 880326
4 miles from Bridgend on the coast
road to Ogmore-by-Sea.
Links/downland course.
Pro Denis McMonagle; Founded 1906
Designed by W Herbert Fowler
18 holes, 6417 yards, S.S.S. 72
✝ Welcome.
✧ WD £30; WE £40.
✧ Welcome WD by prior
arrangement; handicap certs required.
🍴 Full facilities.
✧ Sea Lawns; Sea Bank; Heronston;
Great House.

10 136 Storws Wen
Brynteg, Anglesey, LL78 8JY
☎ 01248 852673, Fax 853843,
Pro 852673, Sec 852673,
Rest/Bar 852673
2 miles from Benllech on B5108;
course is 1.5 miles on right before the
California Hotel.
Parkland course.
Pro Jonathan Kelly; Founded 1996
Designed by K Jones
9 holes, 5002 yards, S.S.S. 65
✝ Welcome.
✧ WD: 9 holes, £10; 18 holes £13;
WE: 9 holes £13; 18 holes £18.
✧ Welcome by arrangement;
packages available.
🍴 Clubhouse facilities.
✧ Fully furnished self-catering
accommodation on site; Bryntiyon;
Glanrafon; Bay Court; California.

10 137 Summerhill Golf Club ✵
Hereford Road, Clifford, Hay-on-Wye,
HR3 5EW
☎ 01497 820451, Pro 820451,
Sec 820451, Rest/Bar 820451
On B4352 from Hay towards toll
bridge.
Parkland course.
Pro Andy Gealy; Founded 1994
9 holes, 5858 yards, S.S.S. 70
✝ Welcome.
✧ Terms on application.
✧ Welcome by prior arrangement;
private function room; catering
packages.
🍴 Full facilities.
✧ Kilvert; Swan.

10 138 Swansea Bay
Jersey Marine, Neath, W Glamorgan,
SA10 6JP
☎ 01792 812198, Pro 816159,
Sec 814153, Rest/Bar 812198
From A483 take B4290 to Jersey
Marine.
Links course.
Pro Mike Day; Founded 1892
18 holes, 6605 yards, S.S.S. 73
✝ Welcome with handicap certs;
dress code applies.
✧ WD £16; WE £22.
✧ Welcome by arrangement;
packages by arrangement; terms on
application.
🍴 Full clubhouse facilities.
✧ Many in Swansea area.

10 139 Tenby
The Burrows, Tenby, Pembrokeshire,
SA70 7NP

✉ www.tenbygolfclub.co.uk
✉ tenbygolfclub@
netscapeonline.co.uk
☎ 01834 842978, Fax 842978,
Pro 844447, Sec 842978
On A477 to Tenby, W of town.
Championship links course.
Pro Mark Hawkey; Founded 1888
18 holes, 6224 yards, S.S.S. 71
⚐ Practice area.
✝ Welcome with handicap certs.
✧ WD £26; WE £32.
✧ Welcome by arrangement; catering
packages by arrangement.
🍴 Full facilities.

10 140 Tredegar and Rhymney
Cwmtysswg, Rhymney, NP22 3BQ
✉ golfclub@
tredegarandrhymney.fsnet.co.uk
☎ 01685 840743, Sec 843400,
Rest/Bar 840743
On B4256 1.5 miles from Rhymney.
Undulating mountain course.
Founded 1921
18 holes, 5332 yards, S.S.S. 67
✝ Welcome.
✧ Prices on application.
✧ Welcome except Sun am.
🍴 Bar and snacks; meals by prior
arrangement.
✧ Red Lion Tredegar.

10 141 Tredegar Park
Parc-Y-Brain Road, Rogerstone,
Newport, NP10 9TG
✉ secretary.tpgc@breathemail.net
☎ 01633 895219, Fax 897152,
Pro 894517, Sec 894433
Near the 14 locks canal centre.
Parkland course.
Pro M Morgan; Founded 1923
Designed by James Braid
18 holes, 6564 yards, S.S.S. 72
⚐ Practice ground; clubs for hire.
✝ Welcome with handicap certs and
member.
✧ WD £15; WE £20.
✧ Welcome by prior arrangement;
minimum group 16; from £35.
🍴 Restaurant and bar facilities.
✧ Rising Sun.

10 142 Trefloyne
Trefloyne Park, Penally, Tenby,
Pembrokeshire, SA70 7RG
✉ www.walesholidays.co.uk/trefloyne
☎ 01834 842165, Fax 841165,
Pro 841165
Off A4139 Tenby to Pembroke road at
Penally.
Parkland course.

Pro S Laidler; Founded 1996
18 holes, 6635 yards, S.S.S. 71
⚑ Practice ground; buggies and
clubs for hire.
† Welcome.
▯ WD £21; WE £26.
⚑ Welcome by prior arrangement;
clubhouse facilities; minimum 8.
🍽 Catering by arrangement; light
refreshments; licensed bar.

10 143 Vale of Glamorgan
Hensol Park, Hensol, S Glamorgan,
CF7 8JY
☎ 01443 665899, Rest/Bar 667800
From M4 Junction 34 follow signs to
Pendoylan.
Parkland course.
Pro Peter Johnson; Founded 1993
Designed by P Johnson
18 + 7 holes, 6401 yards, S.S.S. 71
⚑ Practice range, 20 floodlit bays;
buggies and clubs for hire; tuition.
† Welcome WD; with member at
WE; standard dress.
▯ WD £30.
⚑ Welcome by arrangement with
Adrian Davies; full society packages;
function room; Vale of Glamorgan
health and racket club; computer
analysis; £25-£39.
🍽 Full clubhouse facilities and bar;
Hotel restaurant 'Lakes Brasserie' and
'Hogan's Bar'.
⚑ On site hotel 143 rooms.

10 144 Vale of Llangollen
The Club House, Holyhead Road,
Llangollen, Denbighshire, LL20 7PR
☎ 01978 860613, Fax 860906,
Pro 860040, Sec 860906,
Rest/Bar 860613
1.5 miles E of Llangollen on the A5.
Parkland course set on valley floor.
Pro David Vaughan; Founded 1908
Designed by Members
18 holes, 6656 yards, S.S.S. 73
⚑ Practice area.
† Welcome with handicap certs.
▯ WD £25; WE £30.
⚑ Welcome WD; 30 holes of golf with
club catering; from £25.
🍽 Clubhouse facilities.
⚑ Bryn Howel; Tyn-y-Wew; Wild
Pheasant All Llangollen.

10 145 Virginia Park
Virginia Park, Caerphilly, Mid-Glam,
CF8 3SW
✉ cwithy@fsnet.co.uk
☎ 02920 863919, Pro 850650
In centre of town next to Caerphilly

recreation centre.
Parkland course.
Pro Peter Clark; Founded 1992
9 holes, 4772 yards, S.S.S. 66
† Welcome.
▯ WD: 9 holes £7.50 18 holes £14;
WE: 9 holes £7.50.
⚑ Welcome by arrangement.
🍽 Full bar and refreshments.

**10 146 Welsh Border Golf
Complex**
Bulthy Farm, Bulthy, Middletown, Nr
Welshpool, Powys, SY21 8ER
☎ 01743 884247, Fax 884247,
Sec 884247, Rest/Bar 884247
Via A458 Shrewsbury/Welshpool road
following sign from Middletown.
Parkland course.
Pro Andy Griffiths; Founded 1991
Designed by Andrew Griffiths
2 separate 9-hole courses, 6012 yards,
S.S.S. 69
⚑ 10.
† Welcome; dress codes apply for
Long course.
▯ Long: WD £10 WE £10; short £6.
⚑ Welcome by prior arrangement.
🍽 Bar and restaurant facilities.
⚑ Rowton Castle; Bulthy Farm.

10 147 Welshpool ⚌
Golfa Hill, Welshpool, Powys, SY21
9AQ
☎ 01938 850249
On the A458 out of Welshpool towards
Dolgellau.
Hilly course.
Founded 1931
Designed by James Braid
18 holes, 5708 yards, S.S.S. 70
† Welcome.
▯ WD £12.50 WE £15.50.
⚑ Welcome by prior arrangement;
WD packages available from £18.
🍽 Clubhouse facilities.
⚑ Gorfa; Royal Oak Both Welshpool.

10 148 Wenvoe Castle
Wenvoe, Cardiff, CF5 6BE
☎ 029 2059 1094, Fax 20594371,
Pro 20593649, Sec 20594371,
Rest/Bar 20591094
Follow Signs for Cardiff Airport from
M4 Junction 33.
Parkland course.
Pro J Harris; Founded 1936
Designed by J Braid
18 holes, 6422 yards, S.S.S. 71
⚑ Two practice facilities; putting
green.
† Welcome WD only.

▯ WD £24.
⚑ Welcome WD; special rates for 16
or more.
🍽 Clubhouse facilities.
⚑ The Copthorne.

10 149 Wernddu Golf Centre ⚌
Old Ross Rd, Abergavenny,
Monmouthshire, NP7 8NG
☎ 01873 856223, Fax 852177
1.5 miles NE of Abergavenny on
B4521 off A465.
Parkland course; 18th is 615 yards.
Pro Alan Ashmead; Founded 1992
Designed by G Watkins/A Ashmead
18 holes, 5413 yards, S.S.S. 67
⚑ Practice range, 26 bays floodlit.
† Welcome.
▯ WD £15; WE £15.
⚑ Welcome; maximum 24; terms on
application; from £14.
🍽 Bar snacks.
⚑ Great George.

10 150 West Monmouthshire
Golf Road, Nantyglo, Gwent, NP3 4QT
☎ 01495 310233, Fax 311361,
Pro 310233, Sec 310233,
Rest/Bar 310233
A465 Heads of Valley road, western
valley A467 to Semtex roundabout;
follow Winchestown signs.
Mountain heathland course; highest in
England and Wales.
Founded 1906
18 holes, 6300 yards, S.S.S. 69
† Welcome; with member Sun.
▯ WD £15; Sat £15.
⚑ Welcome WD by prior
arrangement; package includes meals;
from £20.
🍽 Full clubhouse facilities available.
⚑ Nearby Guest Houses available.

10 151 Whitchurch (Cardiff)
Pantmawr Rd, Whitchurch, Cardiff,
CF14 7TD
✉ whitchurch@golfclub14.
fsnet.co.uk
☎ 029 20620958, Fax 20529860,
Pro 20614660, Sec 20620985,
Rest/Bar 20529893/20529877
Along A470 towards Cardiff from M4
Junction 32.
Parkland course.
Pro Eddie Clark; Founded 1915
18 holes, 6321 yards, S.S.S. 71
† Welcome; guests of members only
at WE. Welcome if no major
competitions.
▯ WD £35; WE £40.
⚑ Welcome Thurs; reductions for

groups over 60 and between 24-40; minimum 24; 24-40 £22; 41-60 £25; 61+ £28.
🍽 Full clubhouse facilities available.
🛏 Quality Inn; Friendly Hotel; Masons Arms.

10 152 **Whitehall**
The Pavilion, Nelson, Treharris, Mid-Glam, CF46 6ST
☎ 01443 740245
Off A470 at Treharris and Nelson exit.
Mountain course.
Founded 1922
Designed by local enthusiasts
9 holes, 5666 yards, S.S.S. 69
† Welcome WD; with captain's permission at WE.
ℑ WD £15; WE £20.
↻ Welcome by arrangement with Sec; catering packages by arrangement.

🍽 Clubhouse facilities.
🛏 Llechwen Hall, Pontypridd.

10 153 **Woodlake Park** ♔
Glascoed
Pontypool, Monmouthshire, NP4 0TE
🖳 www.woodlake.co.uk
🖳 golf@woodlake.co.uk
☎ 01291 673933, Fax 673811
3 miles W of Usk overlooking Llandegfedd reservoir.
Undulating parkland course.
Pro Adrian Pritchard; Founded 1993
Designed by MJ Wood/HN Wood
18 holes, 6284 yards, S.S.S. 72
ℑ Practice range, nets available.
† Welcome WD; with booking at WE.
ℑ WD £22.50; WE £30.
↻ Welcome by prior arrangement; catering and golf packages available; snooker; pool table; from £20.
🍽 Full clubhouse bar and restaurant

facilities.
🛏 Three Salmons; Rat Trap; New Court and Greyhound Inn all Usk.

10 154 **Wrexham**
Holt Road, Wrexham, N Wales, LL13 9SB
☎ 01978 261033, Fax 364268, Pro 351476, Sec 364268, Rest/Bar Bar 261033; Rest 358705
Course is two miles NE of Wrexham on the A534.
Sandy parkland course.
Pro Paul Williams; Founded 1906/1924
Designed by James Braid
18 holes, 6233 yards, S.S.S. 70
† Welcome with handicap certs.
ℑ WD £22; WE £27.
↻ Welcome WD except Tues, 27 holes of golf, coffee on arrival, light lunch, evening meal; £35.
🍽 Full clubhouse catering facilities.

"When the world was moulded and fashioned out of formless chaos, this must have been the bit over – a remnant of chaos." Thackeray could have been writing about the view of the Giant's Causeway from the fifth green at Royal Portrush or, still upset by his shanked tee shot, he could have been attempting to define golf.

Portrush is a severe test of driving and by the time the golfer reaches the aptly named Purgatory and Calamity Corner, he can be broken on its wheel.

In 1951 it became the only Irish club to have hosted an Open Championship, when Max Faulkner's victory preceded a drought of British winners that would last until Tony Jacklin's win in 1969.

Harry Colt considered the course his masterpiece and Darwin wrote that the famous architect had built himself a monument more enduring than brass.

Fred Daly, Ireland's only Open Champion to date, caddied here in his youth and Joe Carr, the most loved of Irish golfers, stood on the ninth tee ten up with ten to play in the final of the Amateur Championship. Christy O'Connor called it the sort of course he would love to go back to again and again.

On the other side of Belfast is Royal County Down, a course that Old Tom Morris laid out at a cost "not to exceed four pounds". Is it better than Portrush? Is Monet better than Manet? Is Rupert Brooke better than Wilfred Owen? Are these pointlessly subjective questions? County Down often finishes higher in the polls simply because it is regarded as the more beautiful course.

The course is situated in the shadow of the Mountains of Mourne and lined with heather and gorse and huge sand dunes. Tom Watson said that the first eleven holes were the finest consecutive holes of links golf that he had ever played. The modernists are not fond of the amount of blind shots that they are required to play, but then they also tend to complain if they have a bad lie in a bunker or if the texture of the sand isn't quite to their liking.

Royal Portrush and Royal County Down are the great courses of Northern Ireland, but there are also plenty of good ones. Portstewart and Castlerock are close by Portrush on the northern coast. In early days Portstewart went against the usual golfing trend by banning a railway station in order to discourage the vulgar hordes. It is more welcoming these days and will soon become the second club in Ireland to have 54 holes. Castlerock is a difficult exposed links with a famous fourth called 'leg of mutton' with an out of bounds on either side and a stream across.

In Belfast itself are Balmoral, the home club of Daly, Shandon Park, host to the Gallaher Ulster Open in the sixties, Malone, a parkland course re-sited in the sixties, and Belvoir Park, where Philip Walton won the Irish Professional Championship in his great Ryder Cup year of 1995.

County Down has the most courses in Northern Ireland. Clandeboye has 36 holes, a championship course and wonderful views over the Irish Sea and Belfast Lough, Bangor is yet another Braid design, Ardlass begins almost on the edge of a cliff and Warrenpoint is the home club of Ronan Rafferty.

County Tyrone is surprisingly devoid of golf courses given its size but it does boast Dungannon, the home club of Darren Clarke, and Omagh, a fine course on the river Drumragh. Between Tyrone and Down, County Armagh has one or two decent parkland courses of which perhaps the pick is Portadown by the river Bann.

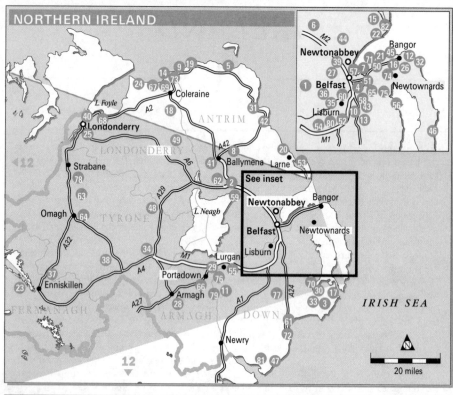

KEY

1	Aberdelghy	16	Blackwood	33	Downpatrick	50	Kirkistown Castle	67	Portstewart

1 Aberdelghy
2 Allen Park
3 Ardglass
4 Ashfield
5 Ballycastle
6 Ballyclare
7 Ballyearl Golf and
   Leisure Centre
8 Ballymena
9 Ballyreagh
10 Balmoral
11 Banbridge
12 Bangor
13 Belvoir Park
14 Benone Par 3
15 Bentra

16 Blackwood
17 Bright Castle
18 Brown Trout
19 Bushfoot
20 Cairndhu
21 Carnalea
22 Carrickfergus
23 Castle Hume
24 Castlerock
25 City of Derry
26 Clandeboye
27 Cliftonville
28 County Armagh
29 Craigavon
30 Crossgar
31 Cushendall
32 Donaghadee

33 Downpatrick
34 Dungannon
35 Dunmurry
36 Edenmore Golf Course
37 Enniskillen
38 Fintona
39 Fortwilliam
40 Foyle
41 Galgorm Castle
42 Garron Tower
43 Gilnahirk
44 Greenisland
45 Helen's Bay
46 Holywood
47 Kilkeel
48 Killymoon
49 Kilrea

50 Kirkistown Castle
51 The Knock
52 Lambeg
53 Larne
54 Lisburn
55 Lurgan
56 Mahee Island
57 Mallusk
58 Malone Golf Club
59 Massereene
60 Mount Ober
61 Mourne
62 Moyola Park
63 Newtownstewart
64 Omagh
65 Ormeau
66 Portadown

67 Portstewart
68 Radisson Roe Park Hotel
69 Rathmore
70 Ringdufferin
71 Royal Belfast
72 Royal County Down
73 Royal Portrush
74 Scrabo
75 Shandon Park
76 Silverwood
77 Spa
78 Strabane
79 Tandragee
80 Temple
81 Warrenpoint
82 Whitehead

11 1 Aberdelghy Golf Club
Aberdelghy, Bells Lane, Lambeg,
Lisburn, Co. Antrim, BT27 4QH
☎ 028 92662738, Fax 92603432
Off the main Lisburn road at Bells Lane
in Lamberg.
Parkland course.
Pro Ian Murdoch; Founded 1986
18 holes, 4139 yards, S.S.S. 62
♦ Welcome except Sat am.
☾ WD £10; WE £12.
⌐ Welcome except Sat am.

🍴 Snacks available.
⌐ Forte Post House.

11 2 Allen Park
45 Castle Rd, Antrim, Co Antrim, BT41
4NA
☎ 01489 429001
Inland course.
18 holes, 6683 yards, S.S.S. 70
♦ Welcome.
☾ Terms on application.

⌐ Packages available; terms on
application.
🍴 Full bar and restaurant facilities
available.

11 3 Ardglass
Castle Place, Ardglass, Co Down,
BT30 7TP
☎ 028 44841219, Fax 44841841
On B1 7 miles from Downpatrick; 30
miles S of Belfast.

Seaside course.
Pro Philip Farrell; Founded 1896
18 holes, 6065 yards, S.S.S. 69
† Welcome WD; Sun afternoon.
Ⅰ WD £22; WE £28.50.
⟳ Welcome by prior arrangement WD and Sun am; packages on application; £15.
⦿ Full facilities.
⌁ Burrendale; Slieve Danard; Burford Lodge GH.

11 4 Ashfield
Freeduff, Cullyhanna, Co Armagh
☎ 028 30868180
Parkland course.
Founded 1990
18 holes, 5620 yards, S.S.S. 67
† Welcome.
Ⅰ WD £10; WE £12.
⟳ Terms on application.
⦿ Clubhouse facilities.

11 5 Ballycastle
Cushendall Road, Ballycastle, Co Antrim, BT54 6QP
☎ 028 20762536, Fax 20769909, Pro 20762506
On A2 between Portrush and Cushendall.

Mixture of parkland, links and heath.
Pro Ian McLaughlin; Founded 1890
18 holes, 5757 yards, S.S.S. 70
† Welcome by prior arrangement; some WE restrictions.
Ⅰ WD £20; WE £28.
⟳ Welcome by prior arrangement; WE restrictions; terms on application.
⦿ Full clubhouse facilities.
⌁ Marine.

11 6 Ballyclare
25 Springvale Rd, Ballycare, BT39 9JW
☎ 028 93322696, Fax 93322696, Rest/Bar 93342352
1.5 miles N of Ballyclare at Five Corners.
Parkland course.
Founded 1923
Designed by Tom McCauley
18 holes, 5745 yards, S.S.S. 71
Ⅰ Practice range.
† Welcome.
Ⅰ WD £16; WE £22.
⟳ Welcome by prior arrangement; minimum 20 players; catering by arrangement; snooker; from £14-£18.
⦿ Bar and restaurant service.
⌁ Country House; Dunadry Inn; Chimney Corner; Five Corners B&B;

Fairways B&B.

11 7 Ballyearl Golf and Leisure Centre
585 Doagh Rd, Newtownabbey, Belfast, BT36 8RZ
☎ 028 90848287, Fax 90844896, Pro 90840899,
Rest/Bar 90843401
1 mile N of Mossley off B59.
Public parkland course.
9 holes, 2306 yards, S.S.S. 27
Ⅰ Practice range, driving range, 27 bays, fully floodlit.
† Welcome.
Ⅰ WD £5.00 (non-members); WE £5.80 (non-members) 2 x 9, junior price WD £2.90, WE £4.60. OAP £2.30 WD and £2.70 WE.
⟳ Terms on application. ·
⦿ No facilities.
⌁ Corrs Corner; Motel; Chimney Corner.

11 8 Ballymena
128 Raceview Rd, Ballymena, DT42 4HY
☎ 028 25861487, Pro 25861652, Rest/Bar 25861207
2.5 miles E of the town on the A42 to

Brough Shane and Carnlough.
Heathland/parkland course.
Founded 1903
18 holes, 5299 yards, S.S.S. 67
⚑ Practice area.
† Welcome except Tues and Sat.
Ⓛ WD £17; WE £22.
⟳ Welcome by prior arrangement
with the Hon Secretary.
🍴 Full clubhouse bar and restaurant.

11 9 Ballyreagh
Glen Rd, Portrush, Antrim, BT56 8LX
☎ 01265822028
In Portrush.
9 holes, 2800 yards, S.S.S. 33
† Welcome.
Ⓛ £9.00.
⟳ Limited.

11 10 Balmoral
518 Lisburn Rd, Belfast, BT9 6GX
☎ 028 90381514, Fax 90 666759,
Pro 90667747, Sec 90381514,
Rest/Bar 90668540
2 miles S of Belfast city centre;
immediately beside the King's Hall on
the Lisburn road opposite Balmoral
Halt station.
Parkland course.
Pro Geoff Blakeley; Founded 1914
18 holes, 6276 yards, S.S.S. 70
† Welcome except Sat and after
3pm Sun.
Ⓛ WD £20; WE £30.
⟳ Welcome by prior arrangement
Mon and Thurs; special packages are
available.
🍴 Full clubhouse bar and restaurant.
⌕ Forte Crest; Europa; Plaza; York;
Balmoral; Beechlawn.

11 11 Banbridge ☎
116 Huntly Rd, Banbridge, Co Down,
BT32 3UR
⌨ www.info@branbridge-
golf.freeserve.co.uk
☎ 028 40662211, Fax 40669400,
Pro 40626189, Rest/Bar 40662342
1 mile N of Bainbridge.
Parkland course.
Founded 1913
18 holes, 5590/5341/4987 yards,
S.S.S. 67
⚑ Driving range available through the
Pro shop.
† Welcome; dress code.
Ⓛ WD £15; WE £20.
⟳ Welcome by prior arrangement;
must be GUI recognised societies;
catering by arrangement; from £12.
🍴 Lounge and bar facilities available.

⌕ Banneille House; Bellmount Hotel;
Downshire Arms.

11 12 Bangor ☎
Broadway, Bangor, Co Down, BT20
4RH
📧 bgcsecretary@aol.com
☎ 028 91270922, Fax 91453394,
Pro 9146 2164
0.75 miles S of town centre.
Parkland course.
Pro Michael Bannon; Founded 1903
Designed by James Braid
18 holes, 6410 yards, S.S.S. 71
⚑ Practice green.
† Welcome except Sat; ladies have
priority Tues.
Ⓛ WD £25; WE £30. that includes
£0.75 insurance charge.
⟳ Welcome by prior arrangement
except Tues and Sat; catering by
arrangement; £20 + catering.
🍴 Full bar and catering facilities.
⌕ Marine Court; Royal.

11 13 Belvoir Park
73 Church Rd, Newtownbreda, Belfast,
BT8 7AN
⌨ www.belverparkgolfclub.com
📧 info@belvoirparkgolfclub
☎ 028 90491693, Fax 9064 6113,
Pro 9064 6714, Rest/Bar 90642817
4 miles from Belfast off the Ormeau
road.
Parkland course.
Pro Maurice Kelly; Founded 1927
Designed by HS Colt
18 holes, 6516 yards, S.S.S. 71
⚑ Practice range.
† Welcome. prior bookings.
Ⓛ WD £33; WE £38.
⟳ Only 6 per month permitted by
prior arrangement with the club
Secretary.
🍴 Full facilities supplied by Brian
McMillan.
⌕ La Mon House; Stormont.

11 14 Benone Par 3 Course
53 Benone Ave, Benone, Limarvady,
Derry, BT49 0IQ
☎ 01504750555
10 miles N of Limarvady on A2.
Inland course.
9 holes, 1447 yards
† Pay and play.
Ⓛ £4.00.

11 15 Bentra
1 Slaughterford Rd, Whitehead, Co
Antrim, BT38 9TG

☎ 028 93378996, Rest/Bar 353666
5 miles N of Carrickfergus on Larne rd.
Municipal parkland course.
Founded 1842
9 holes, 6084 yards, S.S.S. 68
⚑ Practice range 200 yards 10 bays.
† Pay and play.
Ⓛ WD £8; WE £11.
⟳ Welcome; tee times can be
reserved.
🍴 Bar snacks at Bentra roadhouse.

11 16 Blackwood
150 Crawfordsburn Rd, Clandeboye,
Bangor, BT19 1GB
☎ 028 91852706, Fax 91853785
On A2 towards Bangor from Belfast
turn to Newtonards; course 1.5 miles.
Parklands.
Pro Justin Parsons; Debbie Hanna;
Founded 1994
Designed by Simon Gidman
18 holes, 6392 yards, S.S.S. 70
⚑ Practice range 25 Floodlit Bay.
† Welcome; pay and play.
Ⓛ WD £19; WE £25.
⟳ Welcome by prior arrangement.
🍴 Bar snacks and restaurant.
⌕ Clanyboyde Lodge.

11 17 Bright Castle
14 Coniamstown Rd, Bright, Co Down,
BT30 8LU
☎ 028 44841319
5 miles S of Downpatrick.
Parkland course; 16th hole, par 6 is
735 yards.
Founded 1970
Designed by Arnold Ennis
18 holes, 7143 yards, S.S.S. 74
⚑ Brand new clubhouse due for
completion Spring 2002.
† Welcome.
Ⓛ WD £11; WE and BH £14.
⟳ Welcome by prior arrangement;
catering by arrangement.
🍴 Catering facilities.
⌕ Abbey Lodge.

11 18 Brown Trout
209 Agivy Road, Aghadowey, Nr
Coleraine, Co Londonderry, BT51 4AD
📧 bill@browntroutinn.com
☎ 028 70868209, Fax 70868878
7 miles S of Coleraine on the
intersection of A54 & B66.
Parkland course.
Pro Ken Revie; Founded 1973
Designed by Bill O'Hara Snr
9 holes, 5510 yards, S.S.S. 68
† Welcome.
Ⓛ WD £10; WE £15.

⟳ Welcome by prior arrangement; catering packages by prior arrangement; private room for meals and presentations; accommodation for small groups; society rates from £7.
🍴 Full catering and bar facilities.
🛏 Brown Trout Country Inn on site.

11 19 **Bushfoot**
50 Bushfoot Rd, Portballintrae, Co Antrim, BT57 8RR
☎ 028 20731317, Fax 20731852,
Sec 20731317,
Rest/Bar 20732588
4 miles E of Portrush on the coast.
Seaside links course.
Founded 1890
9 holes, 5914 yards, S.S.S. 68
† Welcome except on competition days (Tue and Sat). Practice ground available.
[WD £15; WE £20.
⟳ Welcome by prior arrangement; function room; snooker room.
🍴 Restaurant and Bar.
🛏 Bay View Hotel; Port Ballintrae.

11 20 **Cairndhu**
192 Coast Rd, Ballygally, Larne, Co Antrim, BT40 2QG
✉ ciarndhu@globalgolf.com
☎ 028 28583324
4 miles N of Larne on the Glens of Antrim coast road.
Parkland course.
Pro Bob Walker; Founded 1928
Designed by John S.F. Morrison
18 holes, 6700 yards, S.S.S. 69
† Welcome.
[WD £20.00; Sat £30.00; Sun-£25.00.
⟳ Welcome by prior arrangement; discounts for groups of 20 or more; from £15.
🍴 Clubhouse facilities.
🛏 Highways; Londonderry Arms; Ballygally Holiday Apartments.

11 21 **Carnalea**
Station Rd, Bangor, Co Down, BT19 1EZ
☎ 028 91270368, Fax 91273989,
Pro 91270122, Sec 91270368
1.5 miles from Bangor adjacent to Carnalea station.
Parkland course on shore of Belfast Lough.
Pro Thomas Loughran; Founded 1927
18 holes, 5574 yards, S.S.S. 67
† Welcome; Sat after 2.30pm.
[WD £16.50; WE £21.
⟳ Welcome except Sat; catering by

arrangement; from £20.
🍴 Bar and restaurant facilities.
🛏 Royal; Marine Court; Crawfordsburn Inn.

11 22 **Carrickfergus**
35 North Rd, Carrickfergus, Co Antrim, BT38 8LP
✉ carrickfergusgc@talk21.com
☎ 028 93 363713, Fax 363023,
Pro 351803, Rest/Bar 362203
Odd A2 9 miles NE of Belfast on the North Rd; 1 mile from Shore Road.
Parkland/meadowland course.
Pro Mark Johnson; Founded 1926
18 holes, 5623 yards, S.S.S. 68
† Welcome except Sat.
[Terms on application.
⟳ Welcome WD by arrangement.
🍴 Full facilities.
🛏 Coast Road; Dobbins; Glenavna; Quality Inn.

11 23 **Castle Hume**   ⟳
Castle Hume, Blake Road Enniskillen, Co Fermanagh, BT93 7ED
🖳 www.castlehume.co.uk
☎ 028 66 327077, Fax 327076
5 miles from Enniskillen on the Donegal road.
Parkland course.
Pro Gareth McShea; Founded 1991
18 holes, 6525 yards, S.S.S. 72
† Welcome.
[WD £15; WE £20.
⟳ Welcome; minimum group of 12; discounted fees for groups 12 or more: WD £12; WE £18.
🍴 Bar and restaurant.
🛏 Innishbeg Cottages.

11 24 **Castlerock**
65 Circular Rd, Castlerock, Co Londonderry, BT51 4TJ
☎ 028 70848215, Fax 70849440,
Pro 70848314, Sec 70848314
Off A2 6 miles W of Coleraine.
Links course.
Pro Robert Kelly; Founded 1901
Designed by Ben Sayers
18 holes, 6737 yards, S.S.S. 72
† Welcome; arrange with Pro.
[WD £30; WE £40.
⟳ Welcome by prior arrangement; catering by prior arrangement; from £25.
🍴 Full catering facilities.
🛏 Golf Hotel.

11 25 **City of Derry**
49 Victoria Rd, Londonderry, BT47 2PU

☎ 028 71346369, Fax 71310008,
Pro 71311496
On main Londonderry-Strabane road three miles from Craigavon Bridge.
Parkland course; also 9-hole pay and play Dunhugh course.
Pro Michael Docherty; Founded 1912
18 holes, 6429 yards, S.S.S. 71
𝙸 Practice range.
† Welcome WD before 4.30pm; WE by prior arrangement.
[WD £20; WE £25.
⟳ Welcome WD; limited WE availability.
🍴 Full facilities.
🛏 Everglades; Broomhill House; White Horse Inn; Waterfoot.

11 26 **Clandeboy Ava**
Tower Rd, Conlig, Newtownards, Co Antrim, BT23 3PN
🖳 www.clandeyboyglofclub.com
✉ contact@cgc-ni.com
☎ 028 91271767, Fax 91473711,
Pro 91271750, Rest/Bar 91473706 & 91270992
In village of Conlig off the Belfast-Bangor road at Newtonards.
Parkland course.
Pro Peter Gregory; Founded 1933
Designed by Baron von Limburger
36 holes, 5755 yards, S.S.S. 68 & 71
† Welcome; Sat restrictions.
[WD £22; WE £27.50; (Ava); WD £27.50; WE £33 (Dufferin).
⟳ Welcome WD except Thurs; packages include golf and food; from £20-£35 (Ava); from £30-£40 (Dufferin).
🍴 Full clubhouse dining and bar facilities.
🛏 The Clandeboy lodge; Marine Court Hotel.

11 27 **Cliftonville**
44 Westland Rd, Belfast, BT14 6NH
☎ 028 90744158, Pro 90228585,
Sec 90746595,
Rest/Bar 744158
From Belfast take Antrim road for two miles then turn into Cavehill Rd and left again at Fire Station.
Parkland course.
Pro Robbie Hutton; Founded 1911
9 holes, 5706 yards, S.S.S. 70
𝙸 Practice range.
† Welcome except Tues afternoon and Sat.
[WD £13; WE £16.
⟳ Welcome by arrangement with secretary J M Henderson.
🍴 Bar and Catering facilities.
🛏 Lansdowne Court.

11 28 County Armagh ♋
The Demesne, Newry Rd, Armagh, Co
Armagh, BT10 1EN
📧 info@golfarmagh.co.uk
☎ 028 37522501, Fax 37525861,
Pro 37525864
Off Newry Rd 0.25 miles from the city.
Parkland course.
Pro Alan Rankin; Founded 1893
18 holes, 6212 yards, S.S.S. 69
⌇ Practice range.
† Welcome except 12 noon-2pm Sat;
12 noon-3pm Sun.
⌇ WD £15; WE £20.
⌀ Welcome by arrangement except
Sat.
🍽 Full facilities except Mon.
⌁ Charlemont Arms; Drumshill
House.

**11 29 Craigavon Golf Ski
Centre**
Turmoyra Lane, Silverwood, Lurgan,
Co Armagh, BT66 6NG
☎ 028 38326606, Fax 38347272,
Pro 38326606, Sec 38326606,
Rest/Bar 38326606
Playing facilities at Craigavon.
Founded 1984. Off Junction 10 of M1
motorway.
Parkland course.
Pro Des Paul; Founded 1984
39 holes, 6188 yards for 18 holes,
S.S.S. 72
⌇ 16 covered bays 8 open bays
pitching practice area.
† Everyone welcome.
⌇ Mon-Fri adult £13.50, WE adult
£17; junior/OAP Mon-Fri £4.00; WE
£5.00.
⌀ Local rules will apply.
🍽 Cafe open 7 days per week.
Society meals available.

11 30 Crossgar
231 Derryboye Rd, Crossgar, Co.
Down, BT30 9DL
☎ 028 44831523
From Belfast 5 miles S of Saintfield
close to town of Crossgar.
Parkland course.
Founded 1993
Designed by John Cuffey
9 holes, 4538 yards, S.S.S. 63
† Welcome.
⌇ WD £10; WE £11. (9-hole £6 WD;
£7 WE).
⌀ Welcome by prior arrangement;
from £9.
🍽 Small restaurant and bar.
⌁ Millbrook Lodge, Abbey Lodge.

11 31 Cushendall ♋
Shore Road, Cushendall, Ballymena,
Co Antrim, BT44 0QG
☎ 028 21771318, Sec 21758366,
Rest/Bar 21771318
On main Antrim coast road 25 miles N
of Larne.
Parkland course.
Founded 1937
Designed by Daniel Delargy
9 holes, 4384 yards, S.S.S. 63
† Welcome; start sheet on Thurs.
⌇ WD £13; WE £18.
⌀ Welcome on application to
secretary Mr S McLaughlin; catering
packages available in summer; from
£10.
🍽 Full catering in summer; bar
facilities.

11 32 Donaghadee
84 Warren Rd, Donaghadee, Co Down,
BT21 0PQ
📧 deegolf@freenetname.co.uk
☎ 028 91888697, Fax 91888891,
Pro 91882392, Sec 91883624
6 miles S of Bangor on the coast road.
Part links and inland course.
Pro Gordon Drew; Founded 1899
18 holes, 5570 yards, S.S.S. 69
† Welcome by prior arrangement.
⌇ WD £22; WE £25.
⌀ Welcome Mon, Wed, Fri by prior
arrangement; discounts for groups of
24 or more catering packages
available by arrangement; from £20.
🍽 Clubhouse facilities.

11 33 Downpatrick
43 Saul Rd, Downpatrick, Co Down,
BT30 6PA
☎ 028 44615947, Pro 44615167
23 miles SE of Belfast off A24 and A7.
Parkland course.
Founded 1930
Designed by Hawtree & Sons
18 holes, 6299 yards, S.S.S. 69
† Welcome; some WE restrictions.
⌇ WD £15; WE £20.
⌀ Welcome by prior arrangement.
🍽 Full facilities.
⌁ Denvir; Abbey Lodge.

11 34 Dungannon ♋
34 Springfield Lane, Mullaghmore,
Dungannon, Co Tyrone, BT70 1QX
☎ 028 87722098, Fax 87727338
0.5 miles from Dungannon on
Donaghmore road.
Parkland course.
Founded 1890
18 holes, 6046 yards, S.S.S. 69

† Welcome; restrictions Tues
(ladies day).
⌇ WD £18; WE £22.
⌀ Welcome by prior arrangement
except Tues and Sat.
🍽 Full facilities.
⌁ Glengannon Hotel; Oaklin Hotel.

11 35 Dunmurry
91 Dunmurry Lane, Dunmurry, BT17
9JS
☎ 028 90610834, Fax 90602540,
Pro 90621314, Sec 90620834,
Rest/Bar 621402
Follow signs for Dunmurry from the
M1; turn left at first traffic lights.
Parkland course.
Pro J Dolan; Founded 1905
Designed by TJ McAuley
18 holes, 6080 yards, S.S.S. 69
† Welcome by prior arrangement.
⌇ WD £23; WE £33.
⌀ Welcome WD by written
arrangement; packages available; from
£16.
🍽 Full clubhouse facilities.
⌁ Beech Lawn.

11 36 Edenmore Golf Course
Edenmore House, 70 Drumnabreeze
Rd, Maralin, Co. Armagh, BT67 0RH
☎ 028 92611310, Fax 92613310
M1 from Belfast to Junction 5 for Moira
to Maralin.
Parkland course.
Founded 1992
Designed by Frank Ainsworth
18 holes, 6244 yards, S.S.S. 71
† Welcome except Sat am; priority
for members before 2pm on Sat.
⌇ WD £13; WE £16.
⌀ Welcome by prior arrangement;
packages on request; private dinners
for groups of 25-80.
🍽 Restaurant available WD only.
⌁ White Gables.

11 37 Enniskillen ♋
Castlecoole, Enniskillen, Co
Fermanagh, BT74 6HZ
🖳 www.home.btclick.com/
enniskillen.golf
📧 enniskillen.golf@btclick.com
☎ 028 66325250
1 mile from Enniskillen off Tempo Rd.
Parkland course.
Founded 1896
Designed by Dr Dixon & George
Mawhinney/TJ McAuley
18 holes, 6189 yards, S.S.S. 69
† Welcome.
⌇ WD £15; WE and BH £18.

Welcome by arrangement; catering by arrangement with the steward; snooker.
Full catering and bar facilities.
Fort Lodge; Ashbury; Killyhevlin; Railway; Belmore Court.

11 38 Fintona
Ecclesville Demesne, Fintona, Co Tyrone, BT78 2BJ
028 82841480, Fax 82841480, Pro 82840777
9 miles SW of Omagh.
Parkland course.
Founded 1904
9 holes, 5866 yards, S.S.S. 70
Welcome WD.
WD £15; guests of members £10.
Welcome by prior arrangement; packages available; groups of more than 20 £10; under 20 £15.
Full facilities on request.
Silver Birches.

11 39 Fortwilliam
8A Downview Ave, Belfast, B15 4EZ
028 90370770, Fax 9037 1891, Pro 9037 0980, Rest/Bar 90376798
3 miles from Belfast off Antrim road.
Parkland course.
Pro Peter Hanna; Founded 1891
Designed by Butchart
18 holes, 5973 yards, S.S.S. 69
Welcome.
WD £22; WE £29.
Welcome by prior arrangement; discounts for groups of more than 15; catering packages available by arrangement; from £18.
Clubhouse facilities.
Lansdowne Court; Chimney Corner.

11 40 Foyle
12 Alder Road, Londonderry, Co Londonderry, BT48 8DB
028 71352222
2 miles N of Londonderry off Culmore road.
Parkland course.
Pro Kieran McLoughlin; Founded 1994
Designed by F Ainsworth
18 holes, 6678 yards, S.S.S. 71
Practice range 19 bays covered and floodlit.
Welcome.
WD £11; WE £14.
Welcome; bookings taken 12 months in advance; discount for groups of 14 or more; packages with hotels and catering available; also 9-hole par 3 course; from £12.

Restaurant and bar facilities.
Waterfoot Hotel & CC; Whitehorse Inn.

11 41 Galgorm Castle
Galgorm Rd, Ballymena, BT42 1HL
0126646161
On outskirts of Ballymena off A42.
Parkland course.
Designed by S Gidman; Founded 1997
18 holes, 6736 yards, S.S.S. 72
Welcome by prior arrangement.
WD £19; WE £25.
Packages; corporate days.
Full clubhouse facilities.
Galgorm Manor.

11 42 Garron Tower
St Macnissi's College, Carnlough, Co Antrim, BT44 0JS
028 28885202
Playing facilities at Cushendall and Ballycastle Golf Clubs.
Founded 1968

11 43 Gilnahirk
Manns Corner, Upper Braniel Rd, Gilnahirk, Castlereagh, Belfast, BT5 7TX
028 90448477
3 miles from Belfast off Ballygowan road.
Public moorland course.
Pro Kenneth Gray; Founded 1983
9 holes, 5924 yards, S.S.S. 68
Welcome.
WD: 18 holes £8.50, 9 holes £5; WE: 18 holes £10, 9 holes £6.
Welcome by prior arrangement.
No catering facilities.

11 44 Greenisland
156 Upper Rd, Carrickfergus, Co Antrim, BT38 8RW
028 90862236, Rest/Bar 90862236
8 miles N of Belfast; 2 miles from Carrickfergus.
Parkland course.
Founded 1894
Designed by C Day
9 holes, 5624 yards, S.S.S. 69
Everyone welcome.
WD £12; WE £18.
Welcome by prior arrangement; on application; from £12.
Full clubhouse facilities.

11 45 Helen's Bay
Golf Rd, Helen's Bay, Bangor, Co

Down, BT19 1TL
pclarke@helensbaygc.com
028 91852601, Fax 91852815, Sec 91852815, Rest/Bar 91852601
4 miles W of Bangor off the B20; next to Crawfordsburn Country Park.
Parkland course on shores of Belfast Lough.
Founded 1896
9 holes, 5181 yards, S.S.S. 67
Welcome except Tues and Sat; restrictions Thurs pm and Fri summer am.
WD £17; Fri, Sun and BH £20.
Welcome by prior arrangement Sun, Mon, Wed, Thurs morning and Fri; Minimum 10 Maximum 40; private room for dining or presentations; catering packages available; from £12.
Full bar and restaurant facilities.

11 46 Holywood
Nuns Walk, Demesne Rd, Holywood, Co Down, BT18 9LE
028 90423135, Fax 90425040, Pro 90425503, Rest/Bar 9042138
On A2 6 miles E of Belfast.
Undulating course.
Pro Paul Gray; Founded 1904
18 holes, 6028 yards, S.S.S. 68
Welcome except Sat.
WD £15; Sun £20.
Welcome except Thurs, Sat and BH.
Bar and catering facilities.

11 47 Kilkeel
Mourne Park, Kilkeel, Co Down, BT34 4LB
028 4762296, Fax 91765095
3 miles W of Kilkeel; 45 miles S of Belfast.
Parkland course.
Pro Eddie Hackett; Founded 1948/1993
Designed by Lord Justice Babbington
18 holes, 6615 yards, S.S.S. 72
Practice range close to course.
Welcome by prior arrangement.
WD £16; WE £20.
Welcome by arrangement; catering on application; from £14.
Full clubhouse facilities.
Kilmurey Arms; Cronfield Arms; Slieve Danard; Burrendale.

11 48 Killymoon
200 Killymoon Rd, Cookstown, Co Tyrone, BT80 8TW
028 86763762, Pro 86763460, Rest/Bar 86762254
Off A29 0.5 miles S of Cookstown.
Parkland course.
Pro Gary Chambers; Founded 1889

Designed by Hugh Adair
18 holes, 5486 yards, S.S.S. 69
† Welcome except Sat after 4pm.
[WD £21; WE £25.
⌂ Welcome except Thurs and Sat by prior arrangement; rates negotiable.
⦿ Full facilities.
⌐ Glenavon; Greenvale; Royal.

11 49 Kilrea
38 Drumagarner Rd, Kilrea, Co Londonderry
☎ 028 70821048
0.5 miles from Kilrea Village on Maghera road.
Parkland course.
Founded 1919
9 holes, 4514 yards, S.S.S. 62
† Welcome except after 4.30pm Tues and Wed and Sat pm.
[WD £10; WE £12.50.
⌂ Welcome by prior arrangement; limited catering; from £10.
⦿ Limited.
⌐ Port Neal Lodge.

11 50 Kirkistown Castle   ✆
142 Main Rd, Cloughey, Co Down, BT22 1JA
⛳ www.kcgc.org
☎ 028 42771233, Fax 4277 1699, Pro 427 71004
A20 from Belfast to Kircubbin; follow signs to Newtonards and Portaferry; then B173 to Cloughey.
Links course.
Pro John Peden; Founded 1902
Designed by B Polley
18 holes, 5616 yards, S.S.S. 70
† Welcome.
[WD £18.75; WE £25.75.
⌂ Welcome WD by prior arrangement; packages for groups of 16 or more.
⦿ Full facilities.
⌐ Portaferry.

11 51 The Knock
Summerfield, Upper Newtownards Rd, Dundonald, BT16 2QX
☎ 028 90482249, Fax 90483251, Pro 90483825, Sec 90483251
4 miles E of Belfast off the Upper Newtonards road.
Parkland course.
Pro Gordon Fairweather; Founded 1895
Designed by Cole, Mckenzie & Allison
18 holes, 6435 yards, S.S.S. 71
⌁ Practice green.
† Welcome every day except Sat.
[WD £20; WE £25.
⌂ Welcome Mon and Thurs;

discounts for groups of more than 40; catering packages; from £18.
⦿ Full bar and restaurant facilities.
⌐ Stormont; Clandeboye; Strangford.

11 52 Lambeg
Aberdelghy, Bells Lane, Lambeg, Lisburn, Co Antrim, BT27 4QH
☎ 028 92662738
Off the main Lisburn road at Bells Lane in Lambeg.
Parkland course.
Pro Ian Murdoch; Founded 1986
18 holes, 4528 yards, S.S.S. 62
† Welcome except Sat am.
[WD £10; WE £12.
⌂ Welcome except Sat am.
⌐ Hotels in Belfast.

11 53 Larne
54 Ferris Bay Rd, Islandmagee, Larne, BT40 3RT
☎ 028 43724234
From Belfast N to Carrickfergus and 6 miles from Whithead; from Larne S along the coast road to Islandmagee.
Seaside course.
Founded 1894
Designed by Babington
9 holes, 6288 yards, S.S.S. 69
† Welcome except Sat.
[WD £8; WE £15.
⌂ Welcome except Sat.
⦿ Full clubhouse facilities available.
⌐ Magheramorne House.

11 54 Lisburn
68 Eglantine Rd, Lisburn, Co Antrim, BT27 5RQ
☎ 028 92677216, Fax 9260 3608, Pro 9267 7217, Rest/Bar 92662186
Take Springfield roundabout exit from M1 in direction of Hillsborough.
Parkland course.
Pro Blake Campbell; Founded 1905/1973
Designed by Hawtree & Sons
18 holes, 6647 yards, S.S.S. 72
† Welcome WD before 3pm; Sat after 5.30pm; Sun with member.
[WD: Adult £25 Juvenile £12.50; WE: Adult £30 Juvenile £15.
⌂ Welcome Mon and Thurs before 3pm; discounts for groups of 20 or more before 12.30; from £25.
⦿ Clubhouse facilities available.

11 55 Lurgan
The Demesne, Lurgan, Co Armagh, BT67 9BN
☎ 028 38322087, Fax 38325306,

Pro 38321068
Centre of Lurgan off Windsor Avenue past park and down road between Park Lake and Brownlow House.
Parkland course.
Pro Des Paul; Founded 1893
Designed by Frank Pennink
18 holes, 6257 yards, S.S.S. 70
† Welcome except Sat; Tues Ladies day; Wed competition day; visitors permitted certain times; restrictions Fri pm; best to ring in advance.
[WD £15; WE £20.
⌂ Welcome by prior arrangement as guest policy; discounts for groups of 50 or more; catering packages available; from £15.
⦿ Restaurant and lounge bar.
⌐ Ashburn; Silverwood; Carngrove; Seagoe.

11 56 Mahee Island
Comber, Newtownards, Co Down, BT23 6ET
☎ 028 17541234
Turn left 0.5 miles from Comber off Comber to Killyleagh road.
Parkland/seaside course.
9 holes, 5590 yards, S.S.S. 68
† Welcome; restrictions Sats only.
[WD £10; WE £15.
⌂ Welcome WD except Mon; Sun available; catering by prior arrangement; from £10.
⦿ By prior arrangement; no bar.

11 57 Mallusk
Newtownabbey, Co Antrim, BT36 2RF
☎ 028 90843799, Fax 321647
From Belfast on A8 to Antrim; course just before Chimney Corner Hotel.
Founded 1992.
9 holes, 4686 yards, S.S.S. 64
† Welcome except Sat before 11.30am.
[WD £6.50; WE £9.
⌂ Welcome by prior arrangement.
⦿ None.
⌐ Chimney Corner.

11 58 Malone Golf Club
240 Upper Malone Rd, Dunmurry, Belfast, BT17 9LB
✉ manager@malonegolfclub.co.uk
☎ 028 90612695, Fax 90431394, Pro 90614917, Sec 90612758, Rest/Bar 614916/612695
5 miles from Belfast city centre
Parkland course.
Pro Michael McGee; Founded 1895
Designed by Fred Hawtree/Comdr. J Harris

18 holes, 6599 yards, S.S.S. 71
♱ Welcome; start sheet operates Wed pm.
Ⅰ WD: non-members £33 guests of members £15; WE: non-members £38 guests of members £17.
⚘ Welcome Mon and Thurs by prior arrangement; catering packages by prior arrangement; also Edenderry course: 9 holes 3160 yards par 72; £32.
|●| Full clubhouse catering and bar facilities.

11 59 Massereene
51 Lough Rd, Antrim, Co Antrim, BT41 4DQ
⌨ www.massereene.com
✉ info@massereene.com
☎ 028 94428096, Fax 94487661, Pro 94464074, Rest/Bar 94428101
1 mile S of town; 3.5 miles from Aldergrove Airport.
Parkland course.
Pro Jim Smyth; Founded 1895
Designed by F.W. Hawtree
18 holes, 6604 yards, S.S.S. 72
♱ Welcome WD and WE; Fri Ladies day; Sat restrictions.
Ⅰ WD £25; WE £30.
⚘ Welcome by prior arrangement; from £20.
|●| Full facilities.
⌐ Dunadry.

11 60 Mount Ober   ⚭
24 Ballymaconaghy, Knockbracken, Belfast, BT8 4SB
☎ 028 90795666, Fax 90705862, Pro 90701648, Sec 90401811
Off Four Winds roundabout.
Parkland course.
Pro G Loughrey/S Rourke; Founded 1985
18 holes, 5391 yards, S.S.S. 68
Ⅰ Practice range floodlit bays.
♱ Welcome except Sat.
Ⅰ WD £12.
⚘ Welcome except Sat; catering packages; function rooms; 10 percent discount in Pro shop; from £11.
|●| Full clubhouse facilities.
⌐ La Mon House; Stormont Hotel.

11 61 Mourne
36 Golf links Rd, Newcastle, Co Down, BT33 0AN
☎ 01936723889
Playing facilities at Royal Co Down.

11 62 Moyola Park
Shanemullagh, Castledown,

Magherafelt, Co Londonderry, BT45 8DG
☎ 028 79468468, Fax 946826, Pro 79468830, Rest/Bar 79468270
Course is off the A6 Belfast/Derry road – at Magherfelt roundabout.
Mature parkland course.
Pro Vivian Teague; Founded 1976
Designed by Don Patterson
18 holes, 6491 yards, S.S.S. 71
♱ Welcome by arrangement.
Ⅰ WD £17; WE £25.
⚘ Welcome by prior arrangement only; discounts available; packages by arrangement; from £17.
|●| Clubhouse facilities.
⌐ Rural College; Glenavon Hotel.

11 63 Newtownstewart
38 Golf Course Rd, Newtownstewart, Co Tyrone, BT78 4HU
⌨ www.globalgolf.com/m.newtownstewart
✉ newtown.stewart@lineone.net.
☎ 028 81661466, Pro 81662242
2 miles SW of Newtownstewart on B84.
Parkland course.
Founded 1914
Designed by Frank Pennink
18 holes, 5341 yards, S.S.S. 69
Ⅰ Practice range; buggies hire and club hire available at the golf shop.
♱ Welcome.
Ⅰ WD £12; WE £17.
⚘ Welcome if affiliated to the GUI; catering packages by arrangement; special society packages from £15 WD £20 WE (meal inclusive).
|●| Bar and restaurant facilities.
⌐ Mellon Country Inn, Silverburch.

11 64 Omagh
83a Dublin Road, Omagh, Co Tyrone, BT78 1HQ
☎ 028 8224 1442/82243160, Fax 82243160, Rest/Bar 82243160
On A5 about 1 mile from town centre.
Parkland course.
Founded 1910
18 holes, 5650 yards, S.S.S. 70
♱ Welcome WD and WE; Tues Ladies day.
Ⅰ WD £12 WE £18.
⚘ Welcome WD and WE by prior arrangement.
|●| Clubhouse facilities.
⌐ Silverbirch; Hawthorne House.

11 65 Ormeau
50 Park Rd, Belfast, BT7 2FX
☎ 028 90641069, Fax 90640250, Pro 90640999, Sec 90640700

Adjacent to Ormeau road alongside Ravenhill Rd and Park Rd.
Parkland course.
Pro Bertie Wilson; Founded 1892
9 holes, 4862 yards, S.S.S. 65
♱ Welcome; Sat members only.
Ⅰ WD £9; WE £11.
⚘ Welcome mainly Thurs and Sun; packages available.
|●| Full bar and catering facilities available.
⌐ Stormont Hotel.

11 66 Portadown
192 Gilford Rd, Portadown, Craigavon, Co Armagh, BT63 5LF
☎ 028 38355356, Pro 38334655, Rest/Bar 38355356
3 miles from Portadown on Gilford road.
Parkland course.
Pro Paul Stevenson; Founded 1908
18 holes, 5649 yards, S.S.S. 70
♱ Welcome by arrangement; members only Tues (ladies) and Sat (men).
Ⅰ WD £17; WE £ 22.
⚘ Welcome by prior written arrangement; green fees from £16; catering packages by prior arrangement; snooker squash and indoor bowls available for members.
|●| Bar and restaurant facilities.

11 67 Portstewart
117 Strand Road, Portstewart, Co Londonderry, BT55 7PG
⌨ www.portstewartgc.co.uk
✉ bill@portstewartgc.co.uk
☎ 028 70832015, Fax 70834097, Pro 70832601, Sec 70832015, Rest/Bar 70834543
4 miles W of Portrush.
Links course.
Pro Alan Hunter; Founded 1894
18 holes, 6779 yards, S.S.S. 73
♱ Welcome WD on application.
Ⅰ Strand: WD £60 WE £80; Riverside: WD £12 WE £17; Old: WD £10 WE £14.
⚘ Welcome WD by prior booking.
|●| Full facilities in season. Limited facilities on Mondays.

11 68 Radisson Roe Park
Roe Park, Limavady, Co Derry, BT49 9LB
☎ 028 77760105
Course is on the A2 Londonderry-Limavady road 16 miles from Londonderry.
Parkland course.

Pro Seamus Duffy; Founded 1993
18 holes, 6309 yards, S.S.S. 71
⚐ Practice range 10 covered floodlit
bays.
† Welcome.
�Ⅰ WD £20; WE £20.
⟳ Welcome by prior arrangement;
catering packages; from £15.
🍽 Restaurant and bar facilities.
⌁ Radisson Roe Park Hotel on site.

11 69 Rathmore
Bushmills Rd, Portrush, BT56 8JG
☎ 028 70822996, Fax 70822996,
Rest/Bar 70822285
Playing facilities at Royal Portrush.
Founded 1947.
Links.
18 holes, 6273 yards
† Details on request.
Ⅰ WD £30; WE £35.
⟳ Details on request.
⌁ Magherabuoy House; Royal Court.

11 70 Ringdufferin
Ringdufferin Rd, Toye, Killyleagh, Co
Down, BT30 9PH
✉ 1125@dial.pipex.com
☎ 028 44828812, Fax 44828812,
Sec 44828812,
Rest/Bar 44828812
2 miles N of Killyleagh on the Comber
road.
Parkland course.
Pro Roy Skillen; Founded 1992
Designed by F Ainsworth
18 holes, 5113 yards, S.S.S. 66
† Everyone welcome.
Ⅰ 9 holes: WD £6 WE £7; 18 holes:
WD £9 WE £10.
⟳ Welcome; catering by
arrangement; from £6.
🍽 Clubhouse facilities.

11 71 Royal Belfast
Station Rd, Craigavad, Holywood, Co
Down, BT18 0BP
⌨ www.royalbelfast.co.uk
☎ 028 90428165, Fax 90421404,
Pro 90428586, Rest/Bar 90397792
2 miles E of Holywood on A2.
Parkland course.
Pro Chris Spence; Founded 1881
Designed by HC Colt/Donald Steel
(1988)
18 holes, 6306 yards, S.S.S. 71
⚐ Practice area with two bay shed
for bad weather.
† Welcome except Wed or Sat
before 4.30pm.
Ⅰ WD £40 WE £50.
⟳ Welcome by arrangement.

🍽 Full facilities.
⌁ Culloden.

11 72 Royal County Down
Newcastle, Co Down, BT33 0AN
✉ golf@royalcountydown.org
☎ 028 43723314, Fax 4372 6281
On A24 30 miles S of Belfast.
Links course.
Pro Kevan Whitson; Founded 1889
Designed by Tom Morris Senior
36 holes, 7037 and 4708 yards, S.S.S.
74 and 63
† Welcome WD except Wed; other
days by prior arrangement.
Ⅰ Championship: WD £90 WE £100;
Annesley: WD £18; WE £28.
⟳ Welcome by arrangement with Sec
for the Annsley links.
🍽 Full clubhouse facilities.

11 73 Royal Portrush
Bushmills Rd, Portrush, Co Antrim,
BT56 8JR
☎ 028 70822311, Fax 70823139
1 mile from Portrush off A1.
Championship links; 1951 Open
course.
Pro Gary McNeil; Founded 1888
Designed by H.S. Colt
18 holes, 6818 yards, S.S.S. 73
† Welcome WD between 9.10am-
11.50am; Mon between 9.20am-
11.50am.
Ⅰ Wed and Fri after 2pm; restrictions
at WE. WD £70; WE and BH £80.
⟳ None.
🍽 Local hotels can provide meals.

11 74 Scrabo
233 Scrabo Rd, Newtownards, Co
Down, BT23 4SL
✉ scrabogc@compuserve.com
☎ 028 91812355, Fax 91822919,
Pro 91817848, Sec 91812355,
Rest/Bar 91815048
Off A20 10 miles E of Belfast; near
Scrabo Tower.
Hilly parkland course.
Pro Paul McCrystal; Founded 1907
18 holes, 5699 yards, S.S.S. 71
† Welcome WD except Wed.
Ⅰ WD £15; WE £20.
⟳ Welcome any day except Sat; not
in June; from £13.
🍽 Full bar and restaurant.
⌁ Strangford Arms; George; La Mon
House.

11 75 Shandon Park
73 Shandon Park, Belfast, BT5 6NY

☎ 028 90793730, Fax 90402773,
Pro 90797859
3 miles from city centre via Knock dual
carriageway.
Parkland course.
Pro Barry Wilson; Founded 1926
Designed by Brian Carson
18 holes, 6282 yards, S.S.S. 70
† Welcome WD and Sun.
Ⅰ WD £22; WE £27.
⟳ Welcome Mon and Fri only by prior
arrangement; reductions available for
groups of more than 24 and 40.
🍽 Meals and bar snacks.
⌁ Stormont.

11 76 Silverwood
Tormoyra Lane, Silverwood, Lurgan,
Co Armagh, BT66 6NG
☎ 028 38326606, Fax 38347272
Playing facilities at Craigavon off M1
roundabout ar Largon.
Founded 1984
18 holes, 6188 yards, S.S.S. 72
⚐ Putting green.
† Welcome.
Ⅰ Terms on application.
⟳ Welcome.
🍽 Cafe.

11 77 Spa
20 Grove Rd, Ballynahinch, Co Down,
BT24 8PN
☎ 028 97562365, Fax 974158
0.5 miles from Ballynahinch; 11 miles S
of Belfast.
Wooded parkland course.
Founded 1907/1987
Designed by F Ainsworth
18 holes, 6469 yards, S.S.S. 72
† Welcome except Sat.
Ⅰ WD £15; WE £20.
⟳ Welcome except Sat; discounts for
parties of more than 16; catering
packages by arrangement. No
reduction on Sun.
🍽 Full clubhouse facilities.
⌁ White Horse; Millbrook.

11 78 Strabane
Ballycolman, Strabane, Co Tyrone,
BT82 9PH
✉ strabgc@aol.com
☎ 028 71382007, Fax 7188 6514,
Sec 71382007,
Rest/Bar 71382271
1 mile from Strabane on Dublin road
beside church and schools.
Parkland course.
Founded 1908
Designed by Eddie Hackett
18 holes, 5854 yards, S.S.S. 69

Royal County Down

There can't be many championship courses around the world that Jack Nicklaus hasn't played but, until the summer of 2001, Royal County Down was one of them. For some reason the great man had never made it to Northern Ireland, but when he was invited to play in the Senior Open British Championship, his curiosity got the better of him. So it was that Nicklaus, Arnold Palmer and Gary Player teed it up on a misty July morning – an appropriate triumvirate for a course so steeped in history.

And he was not disappointed. Despite the odd grumble about the number of blind holes, he proclaimed it "a great golf course". "You can't take risks," he added. "You just have to hang in there and be defensive."

Founded in 1889, Royal County Down is a links in the finest tradition, evolving naturally out of the dune landscape and described by the late Peter Dobereiner as "thrilling, even without a club in your hand". With its splendidly old-fashioned clubhouse, it has clung to its history, changing little since Harry Vardon made a few changes before the First World War.

Since then it has played host to 15 Irish Open Amateur Championships, two British Open Amateurs, two Home Internationals and, in 1968, the Curtis Cup. More recently the Senior British Open came to town as part of a three-year deal beginning in 2000.

The first three holes follow the shores of Dundrum Bay to a towering sandhill and offer a daunting challenge. The fourth is the first of four short holes, played from a lofty tee and requiring an intimidating 200-yard shot to a smallish green fortified by grassy swales and bunkers.

There are two fine dog-leg holes, the fifth and thirteenth, and arguments abound as to which is the better. The challenge at both is positioning the tee shot, at the fifth to have sight of the green and at the thirteenth to reach through the neck of the valley to overcome the dog-leg.

The sixth, with its tiny green, leads on to the second of the par threes at the seventh, the green falling away to a large bunker on the left. The 429-yard eighth requires not only a well-positioned tee shot, but a pinpoint second into a narrow green sloping away to trouble on either side. The ninth tee shot is blind, but what you don't see from the tee is compensated by what greets you at the brow of hill - surely one of golf's great views.

The tenth is the third short hole and, with the eleventh and twelfth, leads northwards to the dog-legged thirteenth with its green set in a amphitheatre of gorse. The fourteenth, the last short hole, is played from a raised tee into a well-bunkered green 200 yards away.

The course then heads home. The fifteenth requires two demanding strokes – a slight dog-leg and a green guarded by gorse on the left and a heather hollow on the right. The sixteenth is a short par four played over a valley. Most will go for the green and look for a birdie and, while this is feasible, the impetuous can be tempted to their doom.

The last two holes continue towards the clubhouse with the par five eighteenth providing a thrilling finale. Re-structured by Donald Steel in 1998, it is a marvellous challenge for even the best players – fair when played sensibly, but quick to punish the impulsive.

Located at Newcastle in the south of County Down, the club is accessible from all parts of Ireland and the UK, with Belfast International Airport just an hour's drive away. Accommodation is plentiful but, if you want to be good to yourself, stay at the excellent Slieve Donard Hotel just a short hop from the club. — **Simon Hart**

✝ Welcome WD; WE by arrangement.
⌇ WD £15; WE £17.
🌣 Welcome by arrangement with Sec.
🍽 Full facilities by arrangement only.
⬒ Fir Trees Hotel.

---

11 79 **Tandragee**　　　　　　**ⵞ**
Market Hill Rd, Tandragee, Co Armagh, BT62 2ER
🖳 www.tandagree.co.uk
✉ office@tandagree.co.uk
☎ 003553841272, Fax 38840664,
Pro 38841761, Sec 38841272,
Rest/Bar 76338841763
On B3 in Tandragee on the A27.
Parkland course.
Pro Paul Stevenson; Founded 1922
Designed by F. Hawtree
18 holes, 5747 yards, S.S.S. 71
✝ Welcome WD 10.30am-2pm and WE after 3pm.
⌇ WD £15; WE £20.
🌣 Welcome by prior arrangement; catering by prior arrangement; from £15.
🍽 Full bar and restaurant facilities.
⬒ Carngrove; Seagoe; Bannview.

11 80 **Temple Golf and Country Club**
60 Church Rd, Boardmills, Lisburn, Co Down, BT27 6UP
🖳 www.templegolf.com
✉ info@templegolf.com
☎ 028 92639213
On main Ballynahinch road out of Belfast.
Parkland course.
Founded 1994
9 holes, 5451 yards, S.S.S. 66
⌇ Practice area.
✝ Welcome except Sat am in summer.
⌇ WD £10; WE £14.
🌣 Welcome by arrangement; from £16.
🍽 Full facilities.
⬒ Ivanhoe; Millbrook.

---

11 81 **Warrenpoint**
Lower Dromore Rd, Warrenpoint, Co Down, BT34 3LN
✉ warrenpointgolfclub@tog21.com
☎ 028 41753695, Fax 41752918,
Pro 41752371, Rest/Bar 41752219
5 miles from Newry on Warrenpoint road.

Parkland course.
Pro Nigel Shaw; Founded 1893
18 holes, 6161 yards, S.S.S. 70
✝ Welcome by prior arrangement.
⌇ WD £20; WE £27.
🌣 Welcome by prior arrangement.
🍽 Full facilities.
⬒ Canal Court.

---

11 82 **Whitehead**
McCrea's Brae, Whitehead, Co Antrim, BT38 9NZ
☎ 028 93370820, Fax 93370825,
Pro 93370821, Sec 93370820,
Rest/Bar 93370822(bar)
933370823 (restaurant)
On the Co Antrim coast between Larne and Carrickfergus.
Parkland course.
Pro Colin Farr; Founded 1904/1975
Designed by AB Armstrong
18 holes, 6050 yards, S.S.S. 69
✝ Welcome WD; WE With a member.
⌇ WD £116; WE £21.
🌣 Welcome WD anytime and Sun 10.30an-12 noon by prior arrangement; catering by prior arrangement with chef.
🍽 Full clubhouse facilities.
⬒ Coast Road, The Quality Inn.

REPUBLIC OF IRELAND

12

Ireland is a glutton for golf. Already stuffed full of great courses, it has spent the last few years attracting the likes of Arnold Palmer, Bernhard Langer, Christy O'Connor Jnr, Greg Norman, Peter McEvoy, Des Smyth, Philip Walton and Jack Nicklaus to build several more. A sensible way to give an idea of the choice involved is to start in the north-west corner and sweep anti-clockwise around the country.

Donegal offers Ballyliffin, described by Nick Faldo as "the most natural golf course ever", Rosapenna and Donegal, where just the names of the Blue Stack Mountains and the Valley of Tears hint at the enchantment of the place. County Sligo has been described by Tom Watson as "a magnificent links" and Enniscrone by an admiring architect as "the last site for a great links development in the British Isles."

Westport is one of the most beautiful spots in Mayo and a venue for the Irish Close Championship, whilst in Galway Connemara has just been upgraded to championship standard and Galway Bay is that strange hybrid called 'parkland by the sea'.

Lahinch on the spectacular coast of Clare has been described as 'the Irish St Andrews' and is a favourite of Phil Mickelson. There is less going on by the sea in Limerick so instead they took the water inland and dumped gallons of it to create a 14-acre lake at the Adare Golf Club.

Like the country as a whole Kerry is spoiled for choice. Ballybunion has two monumental courses to the north; Tralee is a Palmer design with an open front nine and dune laden back nine in 'Ryan's Daughter' country; and from the legendary links of Waterville they say that you can see Boston on a clear day. In the midst of them all is Killarney, inspired by an aristocratic figure who was usually known simply as Castlerosse. He had a tree plonked in the middle of the fifteenth green to attract publicity and declared, "When anyone sees Killarney, even if he is the basest heretic, he must believe in God."

Cork has Bantry Bay, the ruggedly splendid Old Head of Kinsale and Fota Island.

Tramore is a championship venue in Waterford and Rosslare has just been reinforced against the elements to give Wexford a course of comparative stature.

Wicklow is the home of Pat Ruddy, the sort of bloke who gives golf courses a good name even in the circles of the most seethingly politically correct. This charming man is responsible for The European and was also persuaded to take a hand in the design of Druids Glen.

Huddled together in the arms of Dublin are Royal Dublin, the home club of Christy O'Connor; Portmarnock, of whose incomparable greens Darwin said, "Even on a raw Easter time they demand that the ball should be soothed rather than hit towards the hole"; Portmarnock Links "where nothing is overlooked but the sea"; and The Island, described by Darren Clarke as "a fantastic links which tests every club in the bag".

The final stop around the coastal tour is County Louth, a secluded gem at the mouth of the River Boyne.

In truth some of Ireland's latest additions to the inland scene are a bit contrived in comparison. The K Club, Kilkea Castle and Mount Juliet are mighty designs and mightily designed. Even Tullamore, one of the country's best inland courses, has not escaped the designer fashion of recent times.

REPUBLIC OF IRELAND

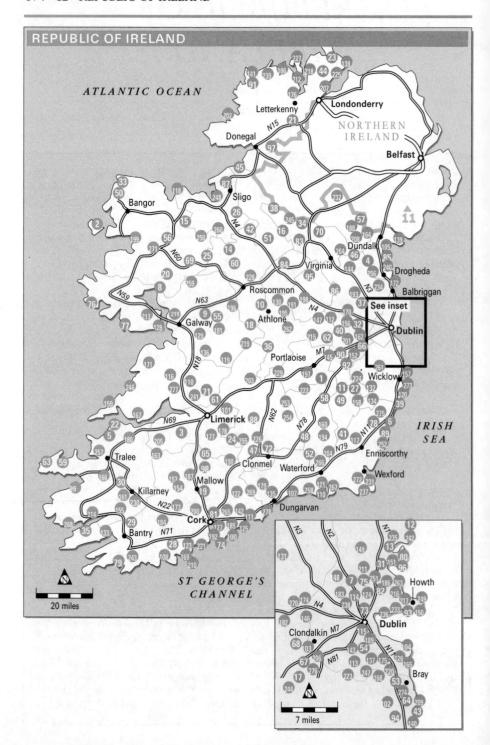

ATLANTIC OCEAN

Letterkenny
Londonderry

NORTHERN
IRELAND

Donegal

Belfast

Bangor
Sligo

Galway
Roscommon
Athlone
Virginia
Dundalk
Drogheda
Balbriggan

See inset
Dublin

Portlaoise
Wicklow

Limerick

Tralee
Clonmel
Waterford
Enniscorthy
Wexford

Killarney
Mallow

Cork
Dungarvan

Bantry

ST GEORGE'S
CHANNEL

IRISH
SEA

20 miles

Clondalkin
Dublin
Howth

Bray

7 miles

KEY					
1	Abbeyleix	59	Castlegregory Golf and Fishing Club	115	Elm Park
2	Achill Island	60	Castlerea	116	Ennis
3	Adare Golf Club	61	Castletroy	117	Enniscorthy
4	Ardee	62	Castlewarden Golf & Country Club	118	Enniscrone
5	Ardfert			119	Esker Hills Golf & Country Club
6	Arklow	63	Ceann Sibeal (Dingle)	120	The European Club
7	Ashbourne	64	Charlesland	121	Faithlegg
8	Ashford Castle	65	Charleville	122	Fermoy
9	Athenry	66	Cill Dara	123	Fernhill
10	Athlone	67	City West Hotel	124	Forrest Little
11	Athy	68	Clane	125	Fota Island
12	Balbriggan	69	Claremorris	126	Foxrock
13	Balcarrick	70	Clones	127	Frankfield
14	Ballaghaderreen	71	Clonlara	128	Galway
15	Ballina	72	Clonmel	129	Galway Bay Golf & Country Club
16	Ballinamore	73	Clontarf	130	Glasson G & CC
17	Ballinascorney	74	Cobh	131	Glebe
18	Ballinasloe	75	Coldwinters	132	Glencullen
19	Ballininamona	76	Connemara	133	Glengarriff
20	Ballinrobe	77	Connemara isles	134	Glenmalure
21	Ballybofey & Stranorlar	78	Coollattin	135	Gold Coast Golf and Leisure
22	Ballybunion	79	Coosheen	136	Gort
23	Ballyhaunis	80	Corballis	137	Grange
24	Ballykisteen Golf & Country Club	81	Cork	138	Greencastle
		82	Corrstown	139	Greenore
25	Ballyliffin	83	County Cavan	140	Greystones
26	Ballymote	84	County Longford	141	Gweedore
27	Baltinglass	85	County Louth	142	Harbour Point
28	Bandon	86	County Meath (Trim)	143	Hazel Grove
29	Bantry Bay	87	County Sligo	144	Headfort
30	Beaufort	88	County Tipperary Golf & Country Club	145	Heath
31	Beaverstown			146	Hermitage
32	Beech Park	89	Courtown	147	Highfield
33	Belmullet	90	Craddockstown	148	Hollystown
34	Belturbet	91	Cruit Island	149	Hollywood Lakes
35	Berehaven	92	Curragh	150	Howth
36	Birr	93	Deer Park Hotel	151	The Island Golf Club
37	The Black Bush	94	Delgany	152	The K Club
38	Blacklion	95	Delvin Castle	153	Kanturk (18 holes)
39	Blainroe	96	Donabate	154	Kanturk (9 holes)
40	Bodenstown	97	Donegal	155	Kenmare
41	Borris	98	Doneraile	156	Kilcock
42	Boyle	99	Dooks	157	Kilcoole
43	Bray	100	Douglas	158	Kilkea Castle
44	Buncrana	101	Dromoland Castle	159	Kilkee
45	Bundoran	102	Druids Glen	160	Kilkenny
46	Cabra Castle	103	Dublin Mountain	161	Killarney Golf Club
47	Cahir Park	104	Dun Laoghaire	162	Killeen
48	Callan	105	Dundalk	163	Killeline
49	Carlow	106	Dunfanaghy	164	Killin Park
50	Carne Golf Links	107	Dungarvan	165	Killiney
51	Carrickmines	108	Dunmore	166	Killorglin
52	Carrick-on-Shannon	109	Dunmore East Golf & Country Club	167	Kilrush
53	Carrick-on-Suir			168	Kilternan Golf & Country Club
54	Castle	110	East Clare		
55	Castle Barna	111	East Cork	169	Kinsale
56	Castlebar	112	Edenderry	170	Knockanally Golf & Country Club
57	Castleblayney	113	Edmondstown		
58	Castlecomer	114	Elm Green		

171	Lahinch Golf Club	228	Roscommon
172	Laytown & Bettystown	229	Roscrea
173	Lee Valley	230	Ross
174	Leixlip	231	Rosslare
175	Leopardstown Golf Centre	232	Rossmore
176	Letterkenny	233	Royal Dublin Golf Club
177	Limerick	234	Royal Tara Golf Club
178	Limerick County Golf & Country Club	235	Rush
179	Lismore	236	St Annes
180	Listowel	237	St Helen's Bay
181	Loughrea	238	St Margaret's Golf & Country Club
182	Lucan	239	St Patricks
183	Luttrellstown Castle	240	Seapoint
184	Macroom	241	Shannon
185	Mahon	242	Skerries
186	Malahide	243	Skibbereen & West Cabbery
187	Mallow	244	Slade Valley
188	Mannan Castle	245	Slieve Russell Golf & Country Club
189	Milltown		
190	Mitchelstown	246	Spanish Point
191	Moate	247	Stackstown
192	Monkstown	248	Strandhill
193	Moor-Park	249	Sutton
194	Mount Juliet	250	Swinford
195	Mount Temple	251	Swords
196	Mountbellew	252	Tara Glen
197	Mountrath	253	Templemore
198	Mullingar	254	Thurles
199	Mulranny	255	Tipperary
200	Muskerry	256	Townley Hall
201	Naas	257	Tralee
202	Narin & Portnoo	258	Tramore
203	Nenagh	259	Tuam
204	New Ross	260	Tubbercurry
205	Newcastle West	261	Tulfarris Hotel & Country Club
206	Newlands		
207	North West	262	Tullamore
208	Nuremore	263	Turvey Golf & CC
209	Old Conna	264	Virginia
210	Old Head Links	265	Water Rock
211	The Open Golf Centre	266	Waterford
212	Otway	267	Waterford Castle Golf & Country Club
213	Oughterard		
214	Parknasilla	268	Waterville Golf Links
215	Portarlington	269	West Waterford
216	Portmarnock	270	Westmanstown
217	Portmarnock Hotel and Golf Links	271	Westport
		272	Wexford
218	Portsalon	273	Wicklow
219	Portumna	274	Woodbrook
220	Powerscourt	275	Woodenbridge
221	Raffeen Creek	276	Woodlands
222	Rathdowney	277	Woodstock
223	Rathfarnham	278	Youghal
224	Rathsallagh House		
225	Redcastle		
226	Rockwell		
227	Rosapenna		

Beechwood, The Grange, Malahide, Co. Dublin

12 1 **Abbeyleix**
Stradbally Rd, Abbeyleix, Co Laois
☎ 00353 502 31450
Course is situated 0.5 miles off Main Street.
Parkland course; Founded 1895.
9 holes, 5626 yards, S.S.S. 68
♦ Welcome.
↿ Terms on application.
♢ Welcome.
↙ Hibernian; Killeshin; Montague; Globe House.

12 2 **Achill Island**
Keel Achill, Co Mayo
☎ 00353 98 43456
Via Castlebar or Westport.
Seaside course.
Founded 1952
Designed by P Skerrit
9 holes, 5378 yards, S.S.S. 66
♦ Welcome.
↿ Terms on application.
🍴 Full clubhouse facilities available.
↙ Atlantic; McDowalls; Slievemore; Strand; Gray's GH.

12 3 **Adare Golf Club**
Adare Manor, Adare, Co Limerick
⌨ www.adaremanor.ie
✉ adaremanor@aol.com
☎ 00353 61 396566, Fax 396124, Sec 396204
10 miles from Limerick on the Killarney Road. Adare dual carriageway, and follow to golf course.
Parkland course built round castle and friary ruins.
Founded 1995
Designed by Robert Trent Jones Sr
18 holes, 7138 yards, S.S.S. 69
♦ Welcome WE with member or by prior arrangement.
↿ 9-hole €65 (residents €55); 18-hole: €110, residents €80.
♢ Welcome by prior arrangement; catering packages can be supplied; see website for hotel packages.
🍴 Clubhouse facilities available.
↙ Adare Manor hotel.

12 4 **Ardee**
Town Parks, Ardee, Co Louth
☎ 00353 41 6853227, Fax 6856137, Pro 68 56747
0.25 miles N of town on Mullinstown Road.
Parkland course.
Pro Scot Kirkpatrick; Founded 1911
Designed by Eddie Hackett
18 holes, 5500 yards, S.S.S. 69
⌁ Practice Range.

♦ Welcome WD.
↿ WD €35 Sat €50.
♢ Welcome Mon-Sat by prior arrangement.
🍴 Full facilities available.

12 5 **Ardfert**
Sackville, Ardfert, Tralee
☎ 00353 66 7134744
15 miles N of Tralee on R551.
Parkland course.
9 holes
♦ Welcome.
↿ 9-hole €15; 18-hole; €23.
♢ Limited but welcome.

12 6 **Arklow**
Abbeylands, Arklow, Co Wicklow
☎ 00353 402 32492,
Fax 91604
Signposted from town centre after turning at bridge.
Links course.
Founded 1927
Designed by Hawtree & Taylor
18 holes, 5604 yards, S.S.S. 69
⌁ Practice range; practice bunkers and nets.
♦ Welcome by arrangement.
↿ WD €40.
♢ Welcome by prior arrangement; Welcome WD and Sat morning; deposit of required; catering packages.
🍴 Bar and restaurant facilities.
↙ Arklow Bay.

12 7 **Ashbourne**
Archerstown, Ashbourne, Co Meath
✉ ashgc@iol.ie
☎ 00353 1 8352005, Fax 8352561, Rest/Bar 835 2005
On N2 12 miles from Dublin.
Parkland course with water features.
Founded 1991
Designed by Des Smyth
18 holes, 5872 yards, S.S.S. 70
⌁ Practice area.
♦ Welcome.
↿ WD €35; WE €45.
♢ Welcome WD; golf and catering packages available; terms on application.
🍴 Full bar and restaurant service.
↙ Ashbourne House.

12 8 **Ashford Castle**
Cong, Co Mayo
⌨ www.ashford.ie
✉ ashford@ashford.ie
☎ 00353 92 46003
27 miles N of Galway on shores of

Lough Corrib.
Parkland course.
Pro Tom Devereux; Founded 1972
Designed by Eddie Hackett
9 holes, 4506 yards, S.S.S. 70
♦ Residents only.
↿ Terms on application.
♢ Welcome by prior arrangement with pro.
🍴 Bar facilities.
↙ Ashford Castle; packages available.

12 9 **Athenry**
Palmerstown, Oranmore, Co Galway
✉ athenrygc@eircom.net
☎ 00353 91 794466
5 miles from Athenry off N6 Galway-Dublin road.
Parkland course.
Pro Raymond Ryan; Founded 1902
Designed by Eddie Hackett
18 holes, 6200 yards, S.S.S. 70
♦ Welcome except Sun.
↿ WD €26; WE €32.
♢ Welcome by prior arrangement.
🍴 Full bar and catering facilities.

12 10 **Athlone**
Hodson Bay, Athlone, Co Roscommon
☎ 00353 902 92073, Fax 94080
3 miles N of Athlone on the Roscommon Road.
Parkland course; All Ireland finals course 1998.
Pro Martin Quinn; Founded 1892
Designed by J McAllister
18 holes, 5935 yards, S.S.S. 71
♦ Welcome; some restrictions Tues and Sun.
↿ WD €27; WE €30.
♢ Welcome by prior arrangement; discount for groups of more than 40; catering packages available; terms on application.
🍴 Full clubhouse facilities.
↙ Hodson Bay; Prince of Wales; Shamrock; Royal Hoey.

12 11 **Athy**
Geraldine, Athy, Co Kildare
☎ 00353 507 31729, Fax 34710
On T6 2 miles N of Athy.
Undulating parkland course.
Founded 1906
18 holes, 5500 yards, S.S.S. 69
♦ Welcome WD.
↿ Terms on application.
♢ Welcome Sat mornings. 9am–1pm.
🍴 By arrangement with the steward.
↙ Lenster Arms Hotel, Kilkea Castle.

12 12 Balbriggan
Blackhall, Balbriggan, Co Dublin
☎ 00353 1 8412229, Fax 8413927,
Sec 8412229, Bar 8412173
0.75 miles S of Balbriggan on the N1
Dublin-Belfast Road.
Parkland course.
Founded 1945
Designed by R Stilwell; J Paramour
18 holes, 5922 yards, S.S.S. 71
† Welcome WD except Tues.
[WD €32.
⌁ Welcome by prior arrangement
with Sec; discounts for more than 30
players; from €31.
⦿ Full clubhouse facilities.

12 13 Balcarrick
Corballis, Donabate, Co Dublin
☎ 00353 1 8436228, Rest/Bar 843
6957
Founded 1972
18 holes, 6362 yards, S.S.S. 73
† Welcome.
[WD €32; WE €40.

12 14 Ballaghaderreen
Aughalista, Ballaghaderreen, Co
Roscommon
☎ 00353 907 60295
3 miles from Ballaghaderreen.
Parkland course.
Founded 1937
9 holes, 5363 yards, S.S.S. 67
† Welcome.
[€15 per day.
⌁ Welcome by prior arrangement.
⦿ Bar and snack facilities.

12 15 Ballina
Mossgrove, Shanaghy, Ballina, Co
Mayo
☎ 00353 96 21050
On the outskirts of Ballina on the
Bonniconlon Road.
Parkland course.
Founded 1910
Designed by Eddie Hackett
18 holes, 6103 yards, S.S.S. 69
† Welcome.
[WD €25; WE €32.
⌁ Welcome; reductions for groups of
12 or more; from €20 WD and €27
WE.
⦿ Full clubhouse facilities.
⌐ Downhill; Bartra House.

12 16 Ballinamona
Mourne Abbey, Mallow, Cork
☎ 00353 22 29314
Founded 1997.

Founded 1997
9 holes, 3110 yards, S.S.S. 110
† Welcome.
[Terms on application.

12 17 Ballinamore
Creevy, Ballinamore, Co Leitrim
☎ 00353 78 44346
1.5 miles NW of Ballinamore.
Parkland course.
Founded 1939
Designed by Arthur Spring
9 holes, 4782 yards, S.S.S. 68
† WD welcome; WE phone in
advance.
[Terms on application; group rates
available.
⦿ Bar facilities.

12 18 Ballinascorney
Bohernabreena, Tallaght, Co Dublin
☎ 00353 1 451 2082
10 Miles SW of Dublin.
Parkland course.
Founded 1971
18 holes, 5648 yards, S.S.S. 67
† WD Welcome; WE phone in
advance.
[WD €25; WE €35; group rates
available.
⦿ Bar facilities.

12 19 Ballinasloe
Rossgloss, Ballinasloe, Co Galway
▤ Ballinasloegolfclub@eire.com.net
☎ 00353 905 42126, Fax 42538
2 miles off the N6 on the Portumna
Road.
Parkland course.
Pro Nigel Howley/Shane O'Grady;
Founded 1894
Designed by Eddie Connaughton
18 holes, 5865 yards, S.S.S. 70
[Practice area.
† Welcome Mon-Sat.
[WD €29; WE €25. Group rate:
€20.
⌁ Welcome Mon-Sat; catering
packages.
⦿ Bar and restaurant facilities.
⌐ Haydens; East County; Gullanes.

12 20 Ballinrobe
Cloona Castle, Ballinrobe, Co Mayo
▤ bgcgolf@iol.ie
☎ 00353 92 41118, Fax 41889, Sec
09241118, Rest/Bar 42090
30 miles from Galway. 6 miles from
Ashford Castle Hotel.
Parkland course set in beautiful
scenery.

Founded 1895
Designed by Eddie Hackard
18 holes, 5540 yards, S.S.S. 73
[5 bays.
† Welcome; some restrictions on
Sun.
[Terms on application.
⌁ Welcome WD by arrangement;
catering packages by arrangement;
fishing can be organised; terms on
application.
⦿ Bar and restaurant facilities.

12 21 Ballybofey & Stranorlar
Stranorlar, Ballybofey, Co Donegal
☎ 00353 74 31093
Course is signposted off the Strabane-
Ballybofey Road; 14 miles from
Strabane.
Parkland course.
Founded 1957
Designed by PC Carr
18 holes, 5437 yards, S.S.S. 69
† Welcome.
[Terms on application.
⌁ Welcome by prior arrangement;
terms on application.
⦿ Bar facilities; meals by
arrangement.

12 22 Ballybunion *(see overleaf)*
Sandhill Rd, Ballybunion, Co Kerry
☎ 00353 68 27146, Fax 27387
20 miles N of Tralee.
Traditional links course.
Pro Brian O'Callaghan; Founded 1893
Designed by Simpson McKenna
2 x 18 holes, 6593 yards, S.S.S. 72
† Welcome WD; limited at WE.
[WD and WE: €110 (Old), €75
(Cashen).
⌁ Ring Sec to find out information.
⦿ Full catering facilities.
⌐ Club can provide detailed list;
some golf packages available.

12 23 Ballyhaunis
Coolnaha, Ballyhaunis, Co Mayo
☎ 00353 907 30014
Course is two miles from Ballyhaunis
on the N83.
Parkland course.
Pro David Carney; Founded 1929
9 holes, 5413 yards, S.S.S. 68
† Welcome Mon-Sat; with member
Sun.
[Terms on application.
⌁ Welcome Mon-Sat by prior
arrangement; reductions for groups of
more than 20; from €20.
⦿ Full catering facilities available.
⌐ Cill Aodain; Belmont.

Ballybunion

Standing on the first tee of the Old Course there is nothing particularly intimidating about the drive until your eye wanders slightly to the right.

Lurking over the wall is a graveyard, not exactly the background you would choose for your opening blow. The only less auspicious sporting introduction is the cemetery just below one of Austria's ski jumping ramps.

Situated on a remote spot of the West of Ireland coast, the Old Course at Ballybunion can be a fearsome place when the wind begins to freshen up off the Atlantic. The locals refer to this wind as the 'Ballybunion whisper' which is a bit like describing Ben Elton as a softly spoken master of comic subtlety.

The geology of this part of Kerry can be just as intimidating. The colossal dunes at Ballybunion tend to run across the fairways rather than alongside them. They present such fearsome sentinels that Christy O'Connor Senior said, "When the wind blows, anyone who breaks 70 here is playing better than he is able to play."

Sergio Garcia found out what he meant during the final round of the 2000 Murphy's Irish Open. Having strolled round to a 66 in serene conditions the previous day, the Spaniard finished with a rather windy 77. Standing on the seventeenth tee, Garcia's compatriot Jose Maria Olazabal had been moved to snap his driver in two and place the offending pieces in an adjacent rubbish bin.

Many will sympathise with him, but even those who fail to finish with their full complement of clubs will be moved by Ballybunion's beauty. The American Herbert Wind, writing in the 'New Yorker', called Ballybunion "the finest seaside course I have ever seen." His words seem to have inspired cohorts of Americans to descend upon the course each year. Numbered amongst them is Bill Clinton, who has a habit of turning up on an almost yearly basis, blocking the roads for miles around and engendering in the locals a rare mix of reverence, affection and contempt.

On being asked whether she would still refer to Clinton as President on his arrival, one of the local ladies said, "'Mr Clinton' is as good as he's going to get. I don't like the man." Others obviously do like the man judging from the statue in the town centre.

The eleventh and fifteenth holes at Ballybunion knock Clinton's statue into a cocked hat. The eleventh has an elevated tee from which the golfer can see the angry Atlantic Ocean threatening to create a few more widows. The long second shot needs to be threaded between two enormous dunes that guard the green. It is an awesome sight matched only by the 228-yard fifteenth, the second of consecutive short holes.

Tom Watson, who was the millennium captain of the club, said, "After playing Ballybunion for the first time, a man would think that the game of golf originated there. There is a wild look to the place."

Ballybunion has a second course that is nearly as good. Indeed some prefer it. Its architect Robert Trent Jones said, "When I first saw the piece of land chosen I was thrilled beyond words." It would be hard to find a finer thirty-six holes anywhere in the world. — **Mark Reason**

12 24 Ballykisteen Golf & Country Club
Ballykisteen, Co Tipperary
☎ www.tipp.ie/ballykgc.htm
☎ 00353 62 33333
3 miles from Tipperary on the Limerick Road. 20 mins from Limerick city.
Parkland course.
Founded 1994
Designed by Des Smyth
18 holes, 6765 yards, S.S.S. 73
✠ Floodlight driving range, 12 bays.
✝ Welcome booking advisable.
☖ Terms on application.
☼ Welcome.
◉ Bar and restaurant.

12 25 Ballyliffin
Ballyliffin, Carndonagh P.O, Co Donegal
☎ www.Ballyliffingolfclub.com
☎ 00353 77 76119, Fax 76672
8 miles from Buncrana.
Seaside links course.
Founded 1947
39 holes, 6612 yards, S.S.S. 72
✝ Welcome.
☖ WD €38; WE €42.
☼ Welcome by prior arrangement; terms on application.
◉ Bar snacks and meals.

12 26 Ballymote
Carrigans, Ballymote, Co Sligo
☎ 00353 71 89059, Rest/Bar 83089
Course is off the N4 15 miles S of Sligo Town.
Parkland course.
Founded 1993
9 holes, 5302 yards, S.S.S. 65
✝ Welcome.
☖ Terms on application.
☼ Welcome; discount for groups of more than 20.
◉ At local restaurant.
☞ Sligo Park; Tower Hotel Sligo; Noreen Mullen GH; Eileen Cahill GH.

12 27 Baltinglass
Baltinglass, Co Wicklow
☎ 00353 508 81350, Sec 81031
40 miles S of Dublin.
Parkland course.
Founded 1928
Designed by Dr WG Lyons; Hugh Dark and Col. Mitchell
9 holes, 5554 yards, S.S.S. 69
✝ Welcome.
☖ WD €16; WE €20.
☼ Three welcome per month; terms on application.
◉ By arrangement.

☞ Carlow.

12 28 Bandon
Castlebernard, Bandon, Co Cork
☎ 00353 23 41111, Fax 44690
2 miles W of Bandon.
Parkland course.
Pro Paddy O'Boyle; Founded 1909
18 holes, 5663 yards, S.S.S. 69
✝ Welcome by prior arrangement.
☖ WD €30; WE €35.
☼ Welcome between March and October on WD.
◉ Except Wed and Sat; catering packages available. Full bar and catering facilities.

12 29 Bantry Bay ☪
Donemark, Bantry, Co Cork
☎ info@bantrygolf.com
☎ 00353 27 50579
2 km NW of Bantry on the Killarney Road.
Clifftop parkland course with views of Bantry Bay/Beara.
Pro Finbar Condon; Founded 1975
Designed by E Hackett & C O'Connor Jnr
18 holes, 5910 yards, S.S.S. 72
✝ Welcome WD 8.30am-4.30pm; by arrangement WE and BH.
☖ Oct-Mar €35; June-Sept €40.
☼ Welcome by prior arrangement; catering packages available.
◉ Full catering facilities.
☞ West Lodge; Bantry Bay; Reendesert; Ballylickey Manor; Seaview.

12 30 Beaufort ☪
Churchtown, Beaufort, Killarney, Co Kerry
☎ www.globalgolf.com
☎ beaufortgc@eircom.net
☎ 00353 64 44440, Fax 44752
7 miles W of Killarney off the N72.
Parkland course.
Pro Hugh Duggan; Founded 1995
Designed by Arthur Spring
18 holes, 6605 yards, S.S.S. 72
✝ Welcome.
☖ WD €45; WE €55.
☼ Welcome; discounts available for groups.
◉ Full bar and catering.
☞ Europe; Great Southern; Dunloe Castle.

12 31 Beaverstown
Beaverstown, Donabate, Co Dublin
☎ www.beaverstown.com

☎ info@beaverstown.com
☎ 00353 1 8436439, Fax 84350539, Rest/Bar 84351371
15 miles N of Dublin; 3 miles from Dublin Airport.
Parkland course.
Founded 1984
Designed by Eddie Hackett
18 holes, 5972 yards, S.S.S. 72
✠ Practice nets.
✝ Welcome WD and some Sat.
☖ WD €50; WE €65.
☼ Welcome by prior arrangement; terms on application.
◉ Full facilities.
☞ Dunes.

12 32 Beech Park
Johnstown, Rathcoole, Co Dublin
☎ 00353 1 4580522, Fax 4588365
3km from Rathcoole village off the Naas dual carriageway.
Parkland course.
Founded 1974
Designed by Eddie Hackett
18 holes, 5762 yards, S.S.S. 70
✝ Welcome Mon, Thurs and Fri; only with a member at WE.
☖ WD €38.
☼ Welcome Mon, Thurs and Fri; catering packages available.
◉ Full bar and catering.
☞ Green Isle; City West; Bewleys; Ambassador.

12 33 Belmullet
Carne, Belmullet, Co Mayo
☎ 00353 97 82292, Sec 81136
1.5 miles W of Belmullet.
Seaside links course.
Founded 1925
Designed by Eddie Hackett
18 holes, 6058 yards, S.S.S. 72
✝ Welcome.
☖ March-Oct €40; Nov-Feb €25.

12 34 Belturbet
Erne Hill, Belturbet, Co Cavan
☎ 00353 4995 22287, Sec 22498
0.5miles on the Cavan Road from Belturbet.
Parkland course.
Founded 1950
9 holes, 5347 yards, S.S.S. 65
✝ Welcome.
☖ Terms on application.
☼ Welcome by prior arrangement.
◉ Full facilities.

12 35 Berehaven
Millcove, Castletownbere, Co Cork

⊟ beregolfclub@aircom.net
☎ 00353 27 70700
On the main Castletownbere Road 20
miles W of Glengarriff.
Links course.
Founded 1906/1993
9 holes, 4759 yards, S.S.S. 65
♦ Welcome.
⌊ Terms on application.
⌂ Details of special rates available
on application, tennis, fishing,
swimming sailing available.
⦿ Clubhouse facilities.

12 36 Birr
The Glenns, Birr, Co Offaly
☎ 00353 509 20082
2.5 miles W of Birr on the Banagher
Road.
Parkland course.
Founded 1893
18 holes, 5748 yards, S.S.S. 69
♦ Welcome; must book at WE.
⌊ WD €23; WE €32.; details of
seasonal offers available on
application.
⌂ Welcome by prior arrangement;
discounts available depending on
numbers; catering packages available;
terms on application.
⦿ Full catering facilities.
⟿ Dooleys; County.

12 37 Black Bush
Thomastown, Dunshaughlin, Co Meath
⚏ www.iol.ie\blackbush
☎ 00353 1 8250021, Fax 8250400
0.5 miles E of Dunshaughlin on
Ratoath Road.
Parkland course.
Pro Shane O'Grady; Founded 1987
Designed by Robert Brown
27 holes, 6434 yards, S.S.S. 70
⌇ Practice range. Driving range, 5
bays, floodlit.
♦ Welcome.
⌊ WD €26; WE €32 (including Fri).
⌂ Welcome WD; catering packages
available; also 9-hole course; terms on
application.
⦿ Full catering facilities.

12 38 Blacklion
Toam, Blacklion, Co Cavan
☎ 00353 72 53024
Off the Sligo-Enniskillen Road at
Blacklion.
Parkland course.
Founded 1962
Designed by Eddie Hackett
9 holes, 5605 yards, S.S.S. 69
♦ Welcome.

⌊ Terms on application.
⌂ Welcome by arrangement.
⦿ Full facilities.

12 39 Blainroe
Blainroe, Co Wicklow
⊟ blainrowgolfclub@eaircom.net
☎ 00353 404 68168, Fax 69369, Pro
66470
3 miles S of Wicklow on coast road.
Seaside course.
Pro John Macdonald; Founded 1978
Designed by Hawtree & Sons
18 holes, 6070 yards, S.S.S. 72
♦ Welcome by prior arrangement.
⌊ WD €41; WE €53.
⌂ Welcome by prior arrangement;
catering packages available.
⦿ Full clubhouse facilities.

12 40 Bodenstown
Bodenstown, Sallins, Co Kildare
☎ 00353 45 897096
5 miles N of Naas.
Parkland course.
Founded 1973
36 holes, 6321 yards, S.S.S. 73
♦ Welcome; members only on Old
Course at WE.
⌊ WD and WE €17.
⌂ Welcome by prior arrangement.
⦿ Full catering facilities.

12 41 Borris
Deer Park, Borris, Co Carlow
☎ 00353 503 73143
16 miles from Carlow off the Dublin
Road.
Parkland course.
Founded 1902
9 holes, 5596 yards, S.S.S. 69
♦ Welcome.
⌊ WD and WE: €20.
⌂ Welcome; terms on application.
⦿ Bar and catering facilities
available.
⟿ Lord Bagenal; Seven Oaks;
Newpark.

12 42 Boyle
Knockadoo Brusna, Boyle, Co
Roscommon
☎ 00353 79 62594
2 miles S of Boyle on the N61
Roscommon Road.
Parkland course.
Founded 1911/1972
Designed by Eddie Hackett
9 holes, 4914 yards, S.S.S. 66
♦ Welcome.
⌊ Available on application.

⌂ Welcome by prior arrangement;
discounts and catering packages
available.
⦿ Full bar and catering facilities.
⟿ Forest Park; Royal.

12 43 Bray
Ravenswell Rd, Bray, Co Wicklow
☎ 00353 1 2862484
Off the L29 from Dublin.
Parkland course.
Founded 1897
9 holes, 5782 yards, S.S.S. 70
♦ Welcome WD except Mon.
⌊ WD €30.
⌂ Welcome by prior arrangement;
must be affiliated to GUI.
⦿ Limited facilities.

12 44 Buncrana
Buncrana, Co Donegal
⊟ buncranagc@aircom.net
☎ 00353 77 62279
Parkland course.
9 holes, 4250 yards, S.S.S. 62
♦ Welcome.
⌊ Available on application.
⌂ Mon-Thurs by prior arrangement,
especially WE.
⦿ Under refurbishment.

12 45 Bundoran
Bundoran Golf Club, Bundoran, Co
Donegal
⚏ www.bundorangolfclub.com
☎ 00353 72 41302, Fax 42014
22 miles N of Sligo.
Links/parkland course.
Pro David Robinson; Founded 1894
Designed by Harry Vardon
18 holes, 5688 metres, S.S.S. 70
♦ Welcome by arrangement. Book
for weekends.
⌊ WD €30; WE €40.
⌂ Welcome by prior arrangement.
⦿ Limited on course to snacks; by
arrangement. Hotel on site for meals.
⟿ Great Northern on course;
Holyrood; Addingham; Fox's Lair;
Marlborough; Atlantic.

12 46 Cabra Castle
Kingscourt, Co Cavan
⚏ www.cabracastle.com
⊟ cabrach@iol.ie
☎ 00353 4296 67030
6 miles S of Carrickmacross.
Parkland course.
Founded 1977
9 holes, 5308 yards, S.S.S. 68
♦ Welcome; only with a member on

Sun. Free golf if hotel resident.
⌂ Terms on application.
⟳ Welcome by prior arrangement except Sun. WE packages available.
|○| Full facilities.
⌐ Cabra Castle Hotel.

12 47 Cahir Park
Kilcommon, Cahir, Co Tipperary
☎ 00353 52 41474
1 mile S of Cahir on Clogheen Road.
Parkland course.
Founded 1965
Designed by Eddie Hackett
18 holes, 5446 yards, S.S.S. 69
† Welcome; by prior arrangement at WE.
⌂ WD and WE: €25.
⟳ Welcome on Sat by prior arrangement; catering packages can be arranged with 72 hours notice; terms on application.
|○| Bar facilities.

12 48 Callan
Geraldine, Callan, Co Kilkenny
⌐ www.callanglfclub.com
◧ info@callangolfclub.com
☎ 00353 56 25136, Fax 25949
10 miles S of Kilkenny; 1 mile from Callan.
Parkland course.
Pro John Odwyer; Founded 1929
Designed by Des Smyth
18 holes, 6450 yards, S.S.S. 70
† Welcome.
⌂ WD €25.
⟳ Welcome WD and Sat am by prior arrangement.
|○| Full bar facilities, catering available
⌐ The Old Charter House.

12 49 Carlow
Deerpark, Dublin Rd, Carlow, Co Carlow
⌐ www.carlowgolfclub.com
◧ carlowgolfclub@tint.ie
☎ 00353 503 31695, Fax 40065
1 mile from Carlow station off Naas to Dublin Road.
Undulating parkland.
Pro Andrew Gilbrit; Founded 1899
Designed by Tom Simpson
18 holes, 5844 yards, S.S.S. 71
† Welcome.
⌂ WD €44; WE €57.
⟳ Welcome WD by arrangement.
|○| Full catering facilities.

12 50 Carne Golf Links
Carne, Belmullet, Co Mayo

◧ carngolf@iol.ie
☎ 00353 97 82292, Fax 81477
1.5 miles W of Belmullet.
Seaside links course.
Founded 1925
Designed by Eddie Hackett
18 holes, 6058 yards, S.S.S. 72
† Welcome.
⌂ March-Oct €40; Nov-Feb €25.

12 51 Carrickmines
Golf Lane, Carrickmines, Dublin 18
☎ 00353 1 2955972
8 miles S of Dublin.
Heath/parkland course.
Founded 1900
9 holes, 6103 yards, S.S.S. 69
† Welcome except Wed and Sat.
⌂ WD €33; WE €38.
⟳ None.
|○| Limited.

12 52 Carrick-on-Shannon
Woodbrook, Carrick-on-Shannon, Co Roscommon
☎ 00353 79 67015
3 miles W of Carrick on N4.
Parkland course.
Founded 1910
Designed by Eddie Hackett
9 holes, 5545 yards, S.S.S. 68
† Welcome.
⌂ Terms on application.
⟳ Welcome by prior arrangement with Sec.
|○| Full bar and catering facilities.

12 53 Carrick-on-Suir
Garravoone, Carrick-on-Suir, Co Tipperary
☎ 00353 51 640047
15 miles from Waterford.
Parkland course.
Founded 1939
Designed by Edward Hackett
18 holes, 6061 yards, S.S.S. 71
† Welcome Wed and WE; booking advisable.
⌂ WD €26; WE €30; reduced rates if with a member; group rates available.
⟳ Welcome; catering packages; private rooms; group discounts.
|○| Full catering facilities.
⌐ Carraig.

12 54 Castle
Woodside Drive, Rathfarnham, Dublin
◧ leslie@castlegolfclub-dublin.com
☎ 00353 1 4904207, Fax 4920264
Turn left after Terenure and take

second right.
Parkland course.
Pro David Kinsella; Founded 1913
Designed by HS Colt
18 holes, 6024 yards, S.S.S. 69
† Welcome WD, booking advisable.
⌂ WD €56.
⟳ Welcome by prior arrangement only.
|○| Full facilities.

12 55 Castle Barna
Daingean, Co Offaly
⌐ www.castlebarna.ie
◧ info@castlebarna.ie
☎ 00353 506 53384, Fax 53077
7 miles S of N6 at Tyrellspass. Stay on the main Tullamore/Edendairy Road.
Parkland course.
Founded 1993
Designed by A Duggan
18 holes, 6200 yards, S.S.S. 69
⌿ Practice putting green.
† Welcome; restrictions Sun am.
⌂ WD €15; WE €20.
⟳ Welcome by arrangement, society special available, ring for info.
|○| Coffee shop and restaurant.
⌐ The Sports Man Inn, Tullamore Court, The Bridge House Hotel.

12 56 Castlebar
Rocklands, Castlebar, Co Mayo
☎ 00353 94 21649
1.25 miles from town centre.
Parkland course.
Founded 1910
18 holes, 5698 yards, S.S.S. 70
† Welcome WD.
⌂ Terms on application.
⟳ Welcome by prior arrangement.
|○| By arrangement.

12 57 Castleblayney
Onomy, Castleblayney, Co Monaghan
☎ 00353 42 9749485
Almost in Castleblayney town centre.
Parkland course.
Founded 1984
Designed by Bobby Browne
9 holes, 4923 yards, S.S.S. 66
† Welcome.
⌂ Available upon application.
⟳ Welcome by prior arrangement.
|○| Full facilities.
⌐ Glencarn; Central.

12 58 Castlecomer
Drumgoole, Castlecomer, Co Kilkenny
◧ castlecomergolf@aircom.net
☎ 00353 56 41139

On N7 10 miles N of Kilkenny.
Parkland course.
Founded 1935
Designed by Pat Ruddy
9 holes, 5923 yards, S.S.S. 71
✴ Practice area.
† Welcome Mon-Sat by prior
arrangement.
⌞ WD and WE: €20.
♂ Welcome except Sun.
🍽 By prior arrangement.

**12 59 Castlegregory Golf and
Fishing Club**
Stradbelly, Castlegregory, Kerry
☎ 00353 66 7139444
2 miles W of Castlegregory.
9-hole links.
Founded 1989
Designed by Arthur Spring
9 holes, 5842 yards, S.S.S. 68
✴ Practice area.
† Welcome.
⌞ Terms on application.
♂ Welcome by prior arrangement.
🍽 Limited Club facilities.

12 60 Castlerea
Clonalis, Castlerea, Co Roscommon
☎ 00353 907 20068
On main Dublin-Castlebar Road.
Parkland course.
Founded 1905
9 holes, 4974 yards, S.S.S. 66
† Welcome.
⌞ Terms on application.
♂ Welcome by prior arrangement;
catering packages by arrangement.

12 61 Castletroy
Castletroy, Co Limerick
☎ 00353 61 335753, Fax 335373,
Pro 330450
Course is 3 miles from Limerick on the
N7.
Parkland course.
Pro Kevin Bennis; Founded 1937
18 holes, 5802 yards, S.S.S. 71
† Welcome by prior arrangement.
⌞ WD €32; WE €40.
♂ Welcome by prior arrangement;
€25.
🍽 Full catering facilities.
◄ Castletroy Park; Kilmurry Lodge.

**12 62 Castlewarden Golf &
Country Club**
Castlewarden, Straffan, Co Kildare
☎ 00353 1 4589254
Between Rathcoole and Kill.
Moorland course.

Founded 1989
Designed by Tommy Halpin;
Redesigned: RJ Browne (1992)
18 holes, 6008 yards, S.S.S. 71
✴ Practice area.
† Welcome Mon, Thurs and Fri.
⌞ Mon-Thurs am €25, pm €33.50;
WE €33.50.
♂ Welcome Mon, Thurs, Fri and
some Sat mornings.
🍽 Full facilities.

12 63 Ceann Sibeal (Dingle)
Ballyferriter, Dingle, Co Kerry
⌨ www.dingle-golf.com
✉ dinglegc@iol.ie
☎ 00353 66 915 6255, Fax 6409
1.5 Mile from Ballyferriter, 9 miles from
Dingle.
Traditional links.
Pro Dermot O'Connor; Founded 1924
Designed by Eddie Hackett (1972)/
Christy O'Connor (1988)
18 holes, 6696 yards, S.S.S. 72
† Welcome.
⌞ Winter €25; Spring €38; Summer
€50.
♂ Welcome; catering packages by
arrangement; terms on application.
🍽 Full bar and restaurant service.
◄ Skellig; Benners.

12 64 Charlesland
Greystones, Co Wicklow
⌨ www.charlesland.com
☎ 00353 1 2874350, Fax 2874360
Off the N11 Dublin-Wexford Road at
Delgarny turning.
Parkland course.
Pro Pete Duignam; Founded 1992
Designed by E Hackett
18 holes, 6169 metres, S.S.S. 72
† Welcome.
⌞ Mon-Thurs €44, €32 before
10am; W €57.
♂ Welcome by prior arrangement;
discounts for group bookings; terms on
application.
🍽 Full facilities.
◄ La Touche; Charlesland.

12 65 Charleville
Smiths Rd, Ardmore, Charleville, Co
Cork
⌨ www.charlegolf.com
✉ charlevillegolf@eircom.net
☎ 00353 63 81257, Fax 81274, Pro
21269
On main road from Cork to Limerick.
Parkland course.
Founded 1909
27 holes, 6430 yards, S.S.S. 70

† Welcome by prior arrangement.
⌞ Terms on application.
♂ Welcome except Sun by prior
arrangement.
🍽 Bar and restaurant service
available.

12 66 Cill Dara
Kildare, Co Kildare
☎ 00353 455 21433, Fax 22945
1 mile E of Kildare.
Moorland course.
Pro Mark Bouyle; Founded 1920
9 holes, 5738 yards, S.S.S. 70
† Welcome.
⌞ Terms on application.
♂ Welcome by prior arrangement;
catering packages available.
🍽 Clubhouse facilities.
◄ Corragh Lodge.

12 67 City West Hotel
City West Country House Hotel,
Saggart, Dublin
☎ 00353 1 4010900, Fax 4010945
Off M50 at M7 for S of Ireland at City
West Business Park.
Parkland course.
Designed by Christie O Connor
18 holes, 6691 yards, S.S.S. 70
† Welcome.
⌞ WD 38; WE €45. Residents: WD
€32; WE €38.
♂ Welcome, packages available.
Hotel and conference facilities.
🍽 Full catering facilities.

12 68 Clane
Clane, Co Kildare
☎ 00353 1 6286608
Playing facilities at Clongowes.
Founded 1976
9 holes
† Welcome except Sun.
⌞ Terms on application.
♂ Welcome WD by prior
arrangement; catering packages by
arrangement.
🍽 By arrangement.

12 69 Claremorris
Rushbrook, Castlemagarett,
Claremorris, Co Mayo
☎ 00353 94 71527, Sec 71868
1.5 miles from Claremorris on Galway
Road.
Parkland course.
Founded 1917
9 holes, 5600 yards, S.S.S. 69
† Welcdome except Sun.
⌞ WD €23; WE €25.

⌖ Welcome WD by prior arrangement; catering packages by arrangement.
๏ By arrangement.

12 70 Clones
Hilton Park, Clones, Co Monaghan
☎ 00353 47 56017
3 miles from Clones.
Parkland course.
Founded 1913
9 holes, 5206 yards, S.S.S. 67
⚑ Welcome.
⌖ WD and WE: €20.
⌖ Welcome by prior arrangement with the secretary; catering by arrangement.
๏ Clubhouse facilities.
⚑ Lennard Arms; Creighton; Hibernian; Riverdale.

12 71 Clonlara
Clonlara Golf and Leisure, Clonlara, Co Clare
☎ 00353 61 354141, Fax 342288
Course is 7 miles NE of Limerick on the Corbally-Killaloe Road.
Woodland/parkland course.
Founded 1993
12 holes, 5187 yards, S.S.S. 69
⚑ Welcome; pay and play.
⌖ Mon-Thurs €13; Fri-Sun and BH €15. Students over 16 €10, under €8. OAP €10. Discounts do not apply Fri-Sun or BH.
⌖ Welcome by prior arrangement; discounts for groups of 20 or more; tennis; sauna; games room; fishing; terms on application.
๏ Bar facilities; catering by order.
⚑ Self-catering accommodation on site.

12 72 Clonmel
Lyreanearla, Mountain Rd, Clonmel, Co Tipperary
☎ 00353 52 21138, Fax 24050, Pro 24050
3 miles from Clonmel.
Parkland course.
Pro Robert Hayes; Founded 1911
Designed by Eddie Hackett
18 holes, 5845 yards, S.S.S. 71
⚑ Welcome.
⌖ WD €30; WE €35 (with member €25).
⌖ Welcome from April to October; terms on application.
๏ Full clubhouse facilities available.
⚑ Clonmel Arms; Minella; Hearns; Hanora's Cottage.

12 73 Clontarf
Donnycarney House, Malahide Rd, Co Dublin
⅛ www.indigo.ie
✉ info.cgc@indigo.ie
☎ 00353 1 8331892, Fax 8831933, Pro 8331877, Rest/Bar 8331520
2.5 miles NE of city centre off Malahide Road.
Parkland course.
Pro Mark Callan; Founded 1912
18 holes, 5317 yards, S.S.S. 67
⚑ Welcome.
⌖ WD €38; WE €50.
⌖ Welcome Tues or Fri; packages include catering.
๏ Full clubhouse facilities available.
⚑ Caftfe Castle.

12 74 Cobh
Ballywilliam, Cobh, Co Cork
☎ 00353 21 4812399, Fax 66915 6409
1 mile E of Cobh.
Public parkland course.
Pro Dermot O'Connor; Founded 1987
Designed by Bob O'Keeffe
9 holes, 4366 yards, S.S.S. 63
⚑ Welcome WD; by prior arrangement WE.
⌖ €16.
⌖ Welcome Mon-Sat.
๏ Bar facilities.

12 75 Coldwinters
Newtown House, St Margaret's, Co Dublin
☎ 00353 1 8640324
On M50 Ballymun exit, then the Noel exit, for 1.5 miles come to a T junction turn left.
Parkland course; also 9-hole course 2163 metres par 31.
Pro Roger Yates; Founded 1993
18 holes, 5973 yards, S.S.S. 69
⚐ 23 bays, floodlit and undercover.
⚑ Welcome; pay and play.
⌖ Terms on application.
⌖ Welcome by prior arrangement.
๏ Coffee shop on site.
⚑ Many in Dublin.

12 76 Connemara Championship Links
Ballyconneely, Clifden, Co Galway
⅛ www.westcoastlinks.com
✉ links@iol.ie
☎ 00353 95 23502, Fax 23662
Signposted from Clifden.
Links course.
Pro Hugh O'Neill; Founded 1973
Designed by Eddie Hackett

27 holes, 6611 yards, S.S.S. 73
⚐ Practice area.
⚑ Welcome.
⌖ WD €45; WE €50, low season WD €30, WE €32.
⌖ Welcome; minimum parties of 20; catering packages available; terms on application.
๏ Full bar and restaurant facilities.
⚑ Rock Glen; Abbey Glen; Foyles; Alcock & Brown; Ballinahynch.

12 77 Connemara Isles
Annaghuane, Connemara, Connemara, Galway
☎ 00353 91 572498, Fax 572214
5 miles W of Costello.
Links.
9 holes, 5168 yards, S.S.S. 67
⚑ Welcome.
⌖ Terms on application.
๏ Full facilities in thatched clubhouse.

12 78 Coollattin
Coollattin, Shillelheh, Co Wicklow
☎ 00353 55 29125, Fax 29125
12 miles SW of Aughrim.
Parkland course.
Founded 1922
18 holes, 6148 yards, S.S.S. 69
⚑ Welcome WD.
⌖ WD €30; WE €40.
⌖ Welcome WD by prior arrangement.
๏ Bar and snacks; meals by arrangement.

12 79 Coosheen
Coosheen, Schull, Co Cork
☎ 00353 28 28182
1 mile E of Schull.
Seaside parkland course.
Founded 1989
Designed by Daniel Morgan
9 holes, 4020 yards, S.S.S. 58
⚑ Welcome.
⌖ WD and WE: €16.
⌖ Welcome; from €16.
๏ Full bar and restaurant.
⚑ East End; West Cork; Westlodge.

12 80 Corballis
Dunabate, Co Dublin
✉ corballis@golfdublin.com
☎ 00353 1 8436583
N of Dublin on Belfast Road.
Links course.
Founded 1971
Designed by City Council
18 holes, 49951 yards, S.S.S. 64

Co. Sligo Golf Club

Invariably known as Rosses Point, Co. Sligo Golf Club is another of those diamonds that decorate the west coast of Ireland, forever brilliant and usually understated, but still a priceless gem.

It has inspired the celebrated poet William Butler Yeats to rhapsodise its charm and Tom Watson rarely misses a chance to play the course whenever he is in Britain to play in the Open Championship. Even the Manchester United's Sir Alex Ferguson played here recently.

Watson does not just want to practice on a links course, he is captivated by the challenge of the 18 holes on the Rosses Point peninsula and is constantly warmed by the welcome and hospitality of the area.

Peter Alliss has said, "Rosses Point stands right at the very top of the list of Irish golf courses."

It is also one of the oldest, having been established in 1894. There were changes along the way, but the present links were laid out in 1927 by one of the most famous golf course architects of all, Harry S Colt.

Watson is not the only famous golfer to make pilgrimages to the course that lies just four miles from the town of Sligo. Legends such as Walter Hagen, Bobby Locke, Henry Cotton and Nick Faldo have all passed by and gone away talking about the majesty of the course and the surrounding area.

The whole area is dominated by the unusual mountain, Benbulben, which has a remarkable similarity to Table Mountain in Cape Town, South Africa. Right by the course there is a sweeping bay with three delightful beaches. It would be hard to imagine a more inviting place to play.

Teeing the ball up on the first hole provides the player with a fair start, straight with a slight uphill climb to an elevated tee. The magic truly begins to unfold on the second green, usually reached with a relative short iron second shot. The need to concentrate on the putter must be interrupted by the panorama.

The view is of a vast sweep, taking in the awesome Benbulben with the rolling Atlantic down below. An inviting downhill drive awaits on the third tee where the attractiveness is no less.

Moving on there are plateau greens and fiendishly placed bunkers and if ever a hole was designed to trap the unwary it must be the seventh which looks straightforward until the ball-grabbing gremlins who lurk in the stream that runs across the front of the green get to work.

That stream reappears on the next hole, a dog-leg that has been the subject of many photographs, paintings and sketches. The tenth and eleventh take the player closest to Benbulben, but the golfer is already well on his way to Tom Watson's favourite hole, the fourteenth.

This is a testing par four at the best of times, but if the wind is blowing, it becomes a daunting challenge for even the most consistent shot-maker. Something similar can be expected on the fifteenth that demands a tee shot to be carried over some wild dunes close to the shore. As Joe Carr said, "It is not possible to scramble successfully at Rosses Point: the right golf shots have to be played."

The finish is tough, but by then either exhilaration or despair will have set in. Rosses Point cannot fail to affect the emotions over its entire 6,645 yards. The fairways are considered the most undulating in Ireland, but it was from the third tee that Yeats poured all the charm of the view into his immortal words.

Rosses Point has Atlantic weather, which means a rain-suit, umbrella and change of clothing should always be handy. But, no downpour could detract from the joy of playing Rosses Point. — **Jim Mossop**

† Public pay and play.
Ⅰ WD €14; WE €18.
⌂ By arrangement.
⑩ Snack facilities.
↩ Waterside Hotel.

12 81 Cork
Little Island, Cork, Co Cork
☎ 00353 21 4353451, Fax 4353410
5 miles E of Cork City off N25.
Parkland/heathland course.
Pro Peter Hickey; Founded 1888
Designed by Alister MacKenzie
18 holes, 6119 yards, S.S.S. 72
† Welcome.
Ⅰ WD €70; WE € 80.
⌂ Packages by arrangement from €50 WD; €55 WE.
⑩ Bar and catering facilities.
↩ Ashbourne House; Silver Springs; Jurys.

12 82 Corrstown
Corrstown, Kilsallaghan, Co Dublin
⚑ www.corrstowngolfclub.com
✉ corrstown@eircom.net
☎ 00353 1 8640533, Pro 8643322
10 minutes from Dublin Airport; access from Swords Rd and Ashbourne Rd.
Parkland course.
Pro Pat Gittens; Founded 1992
Designed by E B Connaughton
27 holes, 5584 yards, S.S.S. 72
† Welcome Mon-Fri; after 1pm WE.
Ⅰ WD €35; WE €45.
⌂ Welcome by prior arrangement.
⑩ Full bar and catering facilities.
↩ Forte Crest; Great Southern, both Dublin Airport; Forte Posthouse, Swords Road.

12 83 County Cavan
Arnmore House, Drumelis, Cavan, Co Cavan
☎ 00353 4943 31541, Fax 31541, Pro 31388
1 mile from Cavan on the Killeshandra Road.
Parkland course.
Pro Ciaran Carroll; Founded 1894
Designed by E Hackett
18 holes, 5634 yards, S.S.S. 70
† Welcome.
Ⅰ Terms on application.
⌂ Welcome; restrictions Wed and Sun.
⑩ Full catering facilities.
↩ Farnham Arms; Kilmore.

12 84 County Longford
Glack, Longford

☎ 00353 43 46310, Fax 47082
E of Glack off the Dublin-Sligo N4 Rd.
Undulating parkland course.
Founded 1894
Designed by E Hackett
18 holes, 5494 yards, S.S.S. 67
† Welcome.
Ⅰ Terms on application.
⌂ Welcome by prior arrangement.
⑩ Clubhouse catering facilities.

12 85 County Louth
Baltray, Drogheda, Co Louth
☎ 00353 4198 81530, Fax 81531, Pro 81536
5 miles NE of Drogheda.
Links course.
Pro Paddy McGuirk; Founded 1892
Designed by Tom Simpson
18 holes, 6783 yards, S.S.S. 72
† Welcome by prior arrangement.
Ⅰ WD €80; WE €100.
⌂ Welcome by prior arrangement; catering packages by arrangement;
⑩ Full bar and catering facilities.
↩ Boyn Valley.

12 86 County Meath (Trim)
Newtownmoynagh, Trim, Co Meath
☎ 00353 46 31463
3 miles from Trim on the Longwood Road.
Parkland course.
Founded 1898
Designed by Eddie Hackett
18 holes, 6503 yards, S.S.S. 72
† Welcome; restrictions Thurs, Sat and Sun.
Ⅰ Terms on application.
⌂ Welcome Mon-Sat by prior arrangement.
⑩ Full bar and catering facilities.

12 87 County Sligo
Rosses Point, Co Sligo
⚑ www.countysligogolfclub.ie
✉ cosligo@iol.ie
☎ 00353 71 77134, Fax 77460, Pro 77171, Sec 77186, Rest/Bar 77186
5 miles N of Sligo.
Links course.
Pro Jim Robinson; Founded 1894
Designed by Colt & Alison
27 holes, 6043 yards, S.S.S. 72
Ⅰ Practice area.
† Welcome; Between 11.40 and 1pm at WE.
Ⅰ €55 Mon-Thur; €70 Fri, Sat and Sun.
⌂ Welcome by prior arrangement; special rates and packages for 20 or more players.

⑩ Full clubhouse facilities.
↩ Tower Hotel; Sligo Park; Yeats Country Hotel.

12 88 County Tipperary Golf & Country Club
Dundrum, Co Tipperary
✉ dundrumh@iol.ie
☎ 00353 62 71717, Fax 71718, Pro 71717
6 miles W of Cashel.
Parkland course.
Founded 1993
Designed by Philip Walton
18 holes, 6955 yards, S.S.S. 72
† Welcome.
Ⅰ WD €38; WE €45.
⌂ Welcome; information about group discounts available upon request.
⑩ Full catering and bar facilities.
↩ Dundrum House on site.

12 89 Courtown
Kiltennel, Gorey, Co Wexford
☎ 00353 55 25166
Leave N11 at Gorey following the Road to Courtown Harbour.
Parkland course.
Pro John Coone; Founded 1936
Designed by Harris & Associates/Henry Cotton
18 holes, 5898 yards, S.S.S. 71
† Welcome; some restrictions Tues and WE.
Ⅰ May-Sept WD €36, WE €42; Oct-Apr WD €30, WE €36.
⌂ Welcome by prior arrangement with secretary/manager; reductions for groups of more than 20.
⑩ Full catering and bar facilities.
↩ Marlfield; Courtown; Bayview.

12 90 Craddockstown
Craddockstown, Naas, Co Kildare
☎ 00353 45 97610
Parkland course.
Founded 1983
18 holes, 6134 yards, S.S.S. 72
† Welcome.
Ⅰ Available upon application.

12 91 Cruit Island
Kincasslagh, Letterkenny, Co Donegal
☎ 00353 75 43296
6 miles from Dungloe opposite the Viking House Hotel.
Links course.
Founded 1986
9 holes, 4860 yards, S.S.S. 64
† Welcome by prior arrangement.
Ⅰ Terms on application.

◔ Welcome by prior arrangement
Mon-Fri & Sat morning.
◉ Full clubhouse facilities available.
⌕ Standhouse; Keadeen.

12 92 Curragh
Curragh, Co Kildare
☎ 00353 45 441714, Fax 441714,
Sec 441238
2 miles SE of Newbridge.
Parkland course.
Pro Gerry Burke; Founded 1883
Designed by David Ritchie
18 holes, 6035 yards, S.S.S. 71
† Welcome by prior arrangement.
⌁ WD €25; WE €30.
◔ Welcome by prior arrangement
Mon-Fri & Sat morning.
◉ Full clubhouse facilities available.
⌕ Standhouse; Keadeen.

12 93 Deer Park Hotel
Deer Park Hotel, Howth, Co Dublin
☎ 00353 1 8322624, Fax 8326039
9 miles E of the City centre.
Parkland course; 2 x 9-hole courses;
12-hole pitch+putt.
Founded 1973
Designed by Fred Hawtree
18 holes, 6770 yards, S.S.S. 71
† Welcome; restrictions Sun am.
⌁ Terms on application.
◔ Welcome WD by prior
arrangement; catering packages
available by prior arrangement;
function rooms.
◉ Full restaurant and bar facilities.
⌕ Deer Park on site.

12 94 Delgany   ⟊
Delgany, Co Wicklow
☎ 00353 1 2874536, Fax 2873977,
Pro 2874697
Off N11 1 mile past Glenview Hotel.
Parkland course.
Pro Gavin Kavanagh; Founded 1908
Designed by H Vardon
18 holes, 5480 yards, S.S.S. 68
⌁ Practice area.
† Welcome.
⌁ WD €38.
◔ Welcome by prior arrangement;
from €38.
◉ Full bar and catering facilities.
⌕ Glenview; Delgany Inn.

12 95 Delvin Castle
Delvin Castle, Delvin, Westmeath
☎ 00353 44 64315
On N52 in the village of Delvin. Mature
parkland with lakes.

Mature parkland with lakes.
Founded 1995
Designed by J Day
18 holes
† Welcome; restrictions Wed and
Sun.
⌁ Available upon request.
◔ Welcome by prior arrangement.
◉ Full bar and catering service
available.

12 96 Donabate   ⟊
Donabate, Balcarrick, Co Dublin
⌂ www.donabategolfclub.ie
☎ 00353 1 8436346, Fax 8435012
1 mile N of Swords on the Dublin-
Belfast Road.
Parkland course.
Pro Hugh Jackson; Founded 1925
27 holes, 6534 yards, S.S.S. 73
† Welcome WE with a member.
⌁ WD €40; WE €45.
◔ Welcome by prior arrangement.
◉ Clubhouse catering facilities.
⌕ Watersite Hotel; The Bracken
Court Hotel.

12 97 Donegal
Murvaghy, Laghey, Co Donegal
⌂ www.donegalgolfclub.ie
▤ info@donegalgolfclub.ie
☎ 00353 73 34054, Fax 34377
8 miles from Donegal on the
Ballyshannon Road.
Links course.
Founded 1960/73
Designed by Eddie Hackett
18 holes, 6547 yards, S.S.S. 75
⌁ Practice range, large practice
ground.
† Welcome.
⌁ Mon-Thurs €40; Fri-Sun and BH
€55.
◔ Welcome by prior arrangement;
discounts for more than 16 golfers;
snooker.
◉ Full bar and restaurant facilities.
⌕ Sandhouse.

12 98 Doneraile
Doneraile, Co Cork
☎ 00353 22 24137
Off T11 28 miles from Cork; 9 miles
from Mallow.
Parkland course.
Founded 1927
9 holes, 5055 yards, S.S.S. 67
† Welcome.
⌁ Terms on application.
◔ Welcome by prior arrangement.
◉ Full clubhouse facilities available.

12 99 Dooks
Glenbeigh, Co Kerry
⌂ www.dooks.com
▤ office@dooks.com
☎ 00353 6697 68205, Fax 68476
On the N70 between Killonglin and
Glenbeigh.
Links course.
Founded 1889
Designed by Eddie Hackett/Donald
Steel
18 holes, 6071 yards, S.S.S. 68
† Welcome.
⌁ WD and WE: €40; advisable to
book for WE.
◔ Welcome by prior arrangement;
from €30.
◉ Full clubhouse facilities.
⌕ Towers; Bianconi.

12 100 Douglas
Douglas, Co Cork
☎ 00353 21 895297
3 miles from Cork; 0.5 miles past
Douglas village.
Parkland course.
Founded 1909
18 holes, 5664 yards, S.S.S. 69
† Welcome; reservations needed at
WE.
⌁ Terms on application.
◔ Welcome by prior arrangement
before start of the season.
◉ Catering facilities.

12 101 Dromoland Castle
Newmarket-on-Fergus, Co Clare
⌂ www.tormolland@eircom.ie
▤ Dromoland@eircom.ie
☎ 00353 61 368444, Fax 368498
14 miles from Limerick on N18 and 6
miles from Shannon on N19.
Parkland course.
Pro Philip Murphy; Founded 1963
Designed by Wigginton
18 holes, 6098 yards, S.S.S. 71
⌁ Practice area.
† Welcome.
⌁ Residents €45; Indiv WD €50,
WE €60; group 12 WD €40, WE €45.
◔ Welcome by prior arrangement;
catering packages available; leisure
spa and health studios and swimming
pool.
◉ Full clubhouse facilities.
⌕ Clare Inn; Oakwood Arms;
Limerick Inn.

12 102 Druids Glen
Newtonmountkennedy, Co Wicklow
☎ 00353 1 2873600, Fax 2873699,
Pro 2873211

Signposted on N11 from Dublin taking Newtonmountkennedy/Glengalaugh junction.
Parkland course; European Tour venue.
Pro Eamonn Darcy; Founded 1993
Designed by T Craddock & P Ruddy
18 holes, 7026 yards, S.S.S. 73
⌇ Practice range, practice facilities and 3-hole academy.
† Welcome.
⌶ WD and WE: €125.
⌁ Welcome every day by prior arrangement; minimum 20 players; catering packages by arrangement; from €82.50.
⦿ Full clubhouse bar and restaurant facilities.
⊸ The Druids Glen Marriot.

12 103 **Dublin Mountain**
Gortlum, Brittas, Co Dublin
☎ 00353 1 4582622
Undulating parkland course.
Founded 1993
18 holes, 5433 yards, S.S.S. 69
† Welcome.
⌶ Terms on application.
⌁ Terms on application.
⦿ Clubhouse facilities.

12 104 **Dun Laoghaire**
Eglinton Park, Tivoli Rd, Dun Laoghaire, Co Dublin
✉ dlgc@iol.ie
☎ 00353 1 2803916, Fax 2804868, Pro 2801694, Sec 2803916
7 miles S of Dublin; 0.5 miles from Ferry port.
Parkland course.
Pro Vincent Carey; Founded 1910
Designed by HS Colt
18 holes, 5298 yards, S.S.S. 68
† Welcome except Thurs and Sat.
⌶ WD and WE: €50.
⌁ Welcome by prior arrangement with the manager; discounts for groups of 30 or more; from €45.
⦿ Full clubhouse facilities.
⊸ Royal Marine; Rochestown; Killiney Castle.

12 105 **Dundalk**
Blackrock, Dundalk, Co Louth
☎ 00353 4293 21731, Fax 22022
2 miles S of Dundalk taking the coast Road to Blackrock.
Parkland course.
Pro James Cassidy; Founded 1904
Designed by Dave Thomas & Peter Alliss
18 holes, 6160 yards, S.S.S. 72

† Welcome.
⌶ WD and WE: €45.
⌁ Welcome by prior arrangement; catering packages by arrangement;
⦿ Bar and restaurant facilities available.
⊸ Fairway.

12 106 **Dunfanaghy**
Dunfanaghy, Letterkenny, Co Donegal
☎ 00353 74 36335
On N56 from Letterkenny 0.5 miles E of Dunfanaghy.
Seaside links course.
Founded 1904
Designed by H Vardon
18 holes, 5006 yards, S.S.S. 66
† Welcome but notice is essential.
⌶ WD €22; WE €27.
⌁ Welcome by prior arrangement; discounts for groups of more than 12 and 20; from €17 and €20 at WE.
⦿ Full clubhouse facilities available.
⊸ Arnolds; Carrig Rua; Port-n-Blagh; Shandon.

12 107 **Dungarvan**
Knocknagranagh, Dungarvan, Co Waterford
☎ 00353 58 43310, Fax 44113, Pro 44707
2.5 miles E of Dungarvan on the N25 Waterford to Rosslare Road.
Parkland course.
Pro David Hayes; Founded 1924/1993
Designed by Maurice Fives
18 holes, 6785 yards, S.S.S. 73
⌇ Practice range 1 mile.
† Welcome; booking needed at WE.
⌶ WD €28; WE €35.
⌁ Welcome by prior arrangement; catering packages available.
⦿ Full clubhouse facilities available.
⊸ Clonea Strand; Gold Coast; Lawlors; Park.

12 108 **Dunmore**
Dunmore House, Muckross, Clonakilty, Co Cork
⌲ www.dunmorehousehotel.com
☎ 00353 23 33352, Fax 34686
Signposted 3 miles from Clonakilty.
Hilly Open course.
Founded 1967
Designed by E Hackett
9 holes, 4464 yards, S.S.S. 61
† Welcome. Except Sun and BH.
⌶ Details upon request.
⌁ Welcome by prior arrangement.
⦿ Bar and restaurant facilities in Dunmore House.

12 109 **Dunmore East Golf & Country Club** ⛳
Dunmore East, Co Waterford
⌲ www.dunmore-golf.com
✉ dunmoregolf@eircom.net
☎ 00353 51 383151, Fax 383151
10 miles from Waterford in the village of Dunmore East.
Seaside parkland course.
Pro James Nash; Founded 1993
Designed by William Henry Jones
18 holes, 6655 yards, S.S.S. 71
† Welcome.
⌶ WD €21; WE €26.
⌁ Welcome by prior arrangement; terms on application.
⦿ Full clubhouse facilities.
⊸ Ivory Lodge; Dunmore Holiday Villas; Haven.

12 110 **East Clare**
Coolreigh, Bodyke, Co Clare
✉ eastclaregolfclub@tinet.ie
☎ 00353 61 921322, Fax 921717
15 miles E of Ennis.
Parkland course.
Founded 1992
Designed by A Spring
18 holes, 5922 yards, S.S.S. 71
† Welcome.
⌶ WD €25; WE €30.
⌁ Welcome; discounts for groups of 25 or more – call for details.
⦿ Bar and restaurant.
⊸ None.

12 111 **East Cork**
Gortacrue, Midleton, Co Cork
☎ 00353 21 4631687, Fax 4613695, Pro 463 3667
Leave Cork to Waterford road at Midleton; course is 2 miles on the Fermoy Road.
Pro Don MacFarlane; Founded 1970
Designed by Edward Hackett
18 holes, 5774 yards, S.S.S. 67
† Welcome with prior booking.
⌶ WD and WE: €25.
⌁ Welcome by prior arrangement; minimum 10 players.
⦿ Full clubhouse facilities.
⊸ Commodore; Middleton Park; Garryvoe.

12 112 **Edenderry**
Kishawanny, Edenderry, Co Offaly
☎ 00353 405 31072, Fax 33911
6 miles from Enfield.
Parkland course.
Founded 1947
Designed by E Hackett
18 holes, 6029 yards, S.S.S. 72

✝ Welcome.
⌇ WD €30; WE €35 (€18 with member).
↻ Welcome except Thurs and Sun.
🍽 Clubhouse facilities.
↵ Wells; Tullamore Court.

12 113 Edmondstown
Edmondstown Rd, Rathfarnham, Dublin 16
🔗 www.edmondstowngolfclub.ie
✉ info@edmondstowngolfclub.ie
☎ 00353 1 4932461, Fax 4933152, Pro 4941049, Sec 4931082, Rest/Bar 493 2461, 4933205
8 miles SW of City centre.
Parkland course.
Pro Andrew Crofton; Founded 1944
Designed by Mcevoy Cooke
18 holes, 6113 yards, S.S.S. 71
⚑ Practice ground.
✝ Welcome but it is advisable to make reservations.
⌇ WD €55; WE €65.
↻ Welcome; terms on application.
🍽 Full facilities.
↵ Many in Dublin.

12 114 Elm Green
Castleknock, Dublin
🔗 www.golfdublin.com
☎ 00353 1 8200797
15 mins from Dublin Airport.
Public course.
Pro Arnold O'Connor; Founded 1992
18 holes, 6013 yards, S.S.S. 66
⚑ 25 bays.
✝ Welcome.
⌇ WD €65; WE €75.
↻ Welcome.
🍽 Limited.
↵ Local pubs available.

12 115 Elm Park
Nutley Lane, Donnybrook
☎ 00353 1 2693438
2 miles from City centre.
Parkland course.
Founded 1925
Designed by Fred Davies
18 holes, 5355 yards, S.S.S. 68
✝ Welcome by prior arrangement.
⌇ Terms on application.
↻ Welcome Tues.
🍽 Full facilities.

12 116 Ennis
Drumbiggle, Ennis, Co Clare
☎ 00353 6568 29211, Fax 41848, Pro 20690, Sec 24074
1 mile from town centre.

Parkland course.
Pro Martin Ward; Founded 1912
18 holes, 5592 yards, S.S.S. 69
✝ Welcome.
⌇ WD and WE: €30.
↻ Welcome by prior arrangement; minimum group 10.
🍽 Full clubhouse facilities.
↵ Auburn Lodge; Old Ground; West County.

12 117 Enniscorthy
Knockmarshal, Enniscorthy, Co Wexford
☎ 00353 54 33191
1 mile from town on the Newross-Waterford Road.
Parkland course.
Pro Martin Sludds; Founded 1926
Designed by E. Hackett
18 holes, 6115 yards, S.S.S. 72
✝ Welcome by prior arrangement.
⌇ Mon-Thurs €25; Fri-Sun €34.
↻ Welcome by prior arrangement with group rates available; terms on application.
🍽 Full facilities.
↵ Murphy Floods.

12 118 Enniscrone
Enniscrone, Co Sligo
☎ 00353 96 36297
7 miles from Ballina.
Championship links course.
Pro Charlie McGoldrick; Founded 1918/31
Designed by E Hackett
18 holes, 6720 yards, S.S.S. 72
⚑ Practice area.
✝ Welcome by prior arrangement.
⌇ WD €45; WE €60.
↻ Welcome by prior arrangement; minimum 12; catering packages by arrangement.
🍽 Full bar and catering.
↵ Downhill, Ballina; Atlantic; Benbulbow; Castle, all in Enniscrone.

12 119 Esker Hills G & CC
Tullamore, Co Offaly
🔗 www.eskerhillsgolf.com
✉ info@eskerhillsgolf.com
☎ 00353 506 55999, Fax 55021
2.5 miles W of Tullamore.
Undulating parkland course.
Founded 1996
Designed by C O'Connor Jnr
18 holes, 6618 yards, S.S.S. 70
✝ Welcome.
⌇ WD €27; WE €37.
↻ Welcome by arrangement; terms on application.

🍽 Coffee shop facilities.
↵ The Bridge House Hotel.
Tullamore Court.

12 120 The European
Brittas Bay, Co Wicklow
🔗 www.theeuropeanclub.com
✉ info@theeuropeanclub.com
☎ 00353 404 47415, Fax 47449
37 S of Dublin on N11.
Links course.
Founded 1993
Designed by Pat Ruddy
20 holes, 7089 yards, S.S.S. 72
⚑ Practice range, practice ground.
✝ Welcome by prior arrangement.
⌇ WD and WE: €100 pp per round; €150 pp per day.
↻ Welcome by prior arrangement; minimum group 24.
🍽 Full clubhouse facilities.
↵ Tinakilly House; Grand, Wicklow; Arklow Bay.

12 121 Faithlegg
Faithlegg Golfclub, Co. Waterford
☎ 00353 51 382241
6 miles from Waterford city centre on the banks of the Suir.
Parkland course.
Pro John Julie; Founded 1993
Designed by Patrick Merrigan
18 holes, 6674 yards, S.S.S. 72
⚑ Practice area.
✝ Welcome.
⌇ Mon-Thurs €22 before 9am and €35 after; Fri-Sun €50.
↻ Welcome by prior arrangement; packages available; terms on application.
🍽 Full bar and restaurant facilities.

12 122 Fermoy
Corrin, Fermoy, Co Cork
☎ 00353 25 31472
2 miles from Fermoy off Cork-Dublin Road.
Undulating parkland course.
Founded 1893
Designed by Commander Harris
18 holes, 5795 yards, S.S.S. 70
✝ Welcome WD.
⌇ Terms on application.
↻ Welcome WD and Sat am.
🍽 By arrangement.

12 123 Fernhill
Carrigaline, Co Cork
☎ 00353 21 373103
Parkland course.
Founded 1994

The European Club

Local legend has it that Pat Ruddy drove a JCB digger onto a stretch of grass, scrubland and sandhills in 1987 and didn't come home until 1993 when the golfing masterpiece known as The European Club was completed.

Now the course that Pat built ranks as one of the most formidable links courses in the British Isles. All it lacks is a history, but to play it you would never realise that The European is so young. Ruddy gave it character the moment he had the vision as he first spied the stretch of land.

Ruddy is one of golf's gentle eccentrics. The game is his passion, humour his currency. He has designed other courses, owned and edited golf magazines and played the game for the sheer enjoyment.

As he said of The European, "Rugged dunes, deep bunkers and sea breezes, fast running fairways, large, undulating greens that invite the pitch-and-run approach and acres of tall, waving marram grass. This is the very essence of golf - as it was at the beginning and was always meant to be."

The Ruddy family run The European and do so with a genuine friendliness because the creator believes that the game should be fun, courses should not be crowded, the game should be played leisurely with everything about the place conducted in a 'spirit of simplicity.'

There is nothing simple about the links themselves. Pat has invested time and money into giving Ireland a course on which any one of the 18 holes might be ranked as a signature hole anywhere else.

Numerous books have placed The European high on its lists. Good reasons for such a ranking include the par three second. At 160 yards it should on paper present few problems, but in reality it can be something of a monster.

Tee and green are elevated. The green is guarded by bunkers and sand dunes on three sides and bang in front is a bunker that may well be the deepest in all Ireland and beyond. When the wind blows, club selection is likely to involve anything from a 3-wood upwards.

The front bunker's face climbs 15 feet and is banked with old railway sleepers. Play out sideways, is the usual advice. Survive that and you have done well, but there are many more difficulties ahead.

Mastering the seventh (stroke one) represents the ultimate challenge. It is a par four of 435 yards and the 200 yard carry over deep grass from the tee brings an immediate moment of anxiety. A shot straying right flies out of bounds and there is trouble on the left.

Hitting the fairway is a good start, but by no means the end of the worrying. Many visitors would be glad of a bogey five as they contemplate a long-iron or fairway wood shot to a green that is almost completely bunkered on the left and has out of bounds and a stream on the right.

Gary Player has lent his name to the eleventh (a par four of 385 yards). It is not long, but accuracy off the tee is vital, such is the trouble on the way to the slightly elevated green. Walk away with a par and brace yourself for the twelfth, another par four, this time measuring 420 yards.

Miss the narrow fairway on the right and the outcome will most likely be an unplayable lie on the beach. There is much more to delight the golfer at this gem of a course.

The European is worth finding and is easy to locate. Take the main Rosslare road south from Dublin until you come to the sign-posts for Brittas Bay, turn left at Jack White's Inn and follow the road until you hit the beach. — **Jim Mossop**

18 holes
† Welcome.
 Terms on application.
 Terms on application.

12 124 Forrest Little
Forest Little, Cloghran, Co Dublin
 www.forrestlittle.com
 00353 1 8401763, Fax 8401000
0.5 miles beyond Dublin Airport on the
Dublin-Belfast Road, take first left.
Parkland course.
Pro Tony Judd; Founded 1940
Designed by Fred Hawtree
18 holes, 5865 yards, S.S.S. 70
† Welcome WD.
 Terms on application.
 Welcome, normally Mon and Thurs
afternoon.
 Full bar snacks and restaurant.

12 125 Fota Island
Fota Island, Carrigtwohill, Co Cork
 00353 21 4883700, Fax 4883713,
Pro 4883710
Take N25 E from Cork City towards
Waterford and Rosslare; after 9 miles
take the exit for Cobh/Fota, course 0.5
miles.
Pro Kevin Morris; Founded 1993
Designed by Peter McEvoy and Christy
O'Connor Jnr
18 holes, 6927 yards, S.S.S. 73
† Welcome.
 WD €65; Fri-Sun €90.
 Group rates for min of 20 available
on application; from €50.
 Full facilities.
 Midleton Park; Ashbourne House;
Jury's Cork.

12 126 Foxrock
Torquay Rd, Dublin, Co Dublin
 00353 1 2893992, Fax 2894943,
Pro 2893414
About 6 miles from Dublin; turn right off
T7 just past Stillergan on the
Leopardstown Road then left into
Torquay Road.
Parkland course.
Founded 1893
9 holes, 5667 yards, S.S.S. 69
† Welcome Mon-Wed am, Thurs, Fri
and Sun with a member.
 €40, €15 with a member.
Welcome Mon and Thurs.
 Snacks.

12 127 Frankfield
Frankfield, Douglas, Co Cork
 00353 21 363124

10 miles S of Cork.
Parkland course.
Founded 1984
9 holes, 4621 yards, S.S.S. 65
† Welcome.
 Terms on application.
 Lunches.

12 128 Galway
Blackrock, Salthill, Co Galway
 00353 91 522033, Fax 529783,
Pro 523038
3 miles W of Galway.
Tight tree-lined parkland course.
Pro Don Wallace; Founded 1895
Designed by A MacKenzie
18 holes, 5832 yards, S.S.S. 71
† Welcome.
 WD €35; WE €45.
 Welcome WD by prior
arrangement; catering packages by
arrangement.
 Full catering facilities.
 Salthill; Galway Bay; Jameson's;
Spinnaker.

12 129 Galway Bay Golf &
Country Club   ₢
Renville, Oranmore, Co Galway
 00353 91 790500
From Galway take the coast road
through Oranmore; course is
signposted from there.
Founded 1993
Designed by Christy O'Connor Jnr
18 holes, 7190 yards, S.S.S. 72
 Practice range; practice bays.
† Welcome if carrying handicap
certs.
 Apr-Oct: Mon-Thurs €55, Fri-Sun
€60, Nov- March: Mon-Thurs €25,
Fri-Sun €32.
 Welcome by prior arrangement;
group rates available for groups of
over 20.
 Restaurant; spikes bar; bar.

12 130 Glasson Golf & CC
Glasson, Athlone, Co Westmeath
 00353 902 85120
6 miles N of Athlone on the N55.
Parkland course.
Founded 1994
Designed by C O'Connor
18 holes, 7120 yards, S.S.S. 72
† Welcome.
 Terms on application.
 Welcome by prior arrangement;
catering packages by arrangement.
 Full clubhouse facilities.

12 131 Glebe
Kildalkey Rd, Trim, Meath
 00353 46 31926
1 mile from Trim.
Parkland pay and play course.
18 holes, 6466 yards, S.S.S. 73
† Welcome.
 Terms on application.
 By arrangement.
 Snacks available.

12 132 Glencullen
Glencullen, Co Wicklow
 00353 1 2940898
4 miles from Kilternan; follow signs for
Johnny Fox's pub.
9 holes, 5400 yards, S.S.S. 69
† Welcome.
 Terms on application.
 Snack facilities.

12 133 Glengarriff
Glengarriff, Co Cork
 00353 27 63150
On T65 55 miles W of Cork.
Seaside course.
Founded 1936
9 holes, 4094 yards, S.S.S. 66
† Welcome.
 Terms on application.
 Welcome by prior arrangement;
discounts depending on group size.
 Full facilities.
 Self-catering lodge
accommodation on site.

12 134 Glenmalure
Greenane, Rathdrum, Co Wicklow
 00353 404 46679, Fax 46679
2 miles W of Rathdrum.
Parkland course.
Founded 1993
Designed by Pat Suttle
18 holes, 5850 yards, S.S.S. 66
† Welcome.
 WD €25; WE €35.
 Welcome by prior arrangement;
discounts depending on group
numbers.
 Full facilities.
 Glenmalure Pines self catering
lodge accomodation beside site.

12 135 Gold Coast Golf   ₢
Ballinacourty, Dungarvan, Co
Waterford
 00353 58 44055, Fax 44055,
Rest/Bar 42249
Located 3 miles from Dungarvan.
Parkland course by the sea.
Founded 1939. Amended 1997

Designed by Maurice Fives
18 holes, 6171 yards, S.S.S. 72
🏌 Practice range.
† Welcome by prior arrangement.
┐ WD €30; WE €40.
↺ Welcome by prior arrangement;
discounts depending on size of group
and date of visit.
🍽 Full facilities.
↭ Gold Coast Hotel; Gold Coast
Holiday Homes; Clonea Strand.

12 136 Gort

Castlequarter, Gort, Co Galway
☎ 00353 91 632244
Off Kilmacduagh Road.
Parkland course.
Founded 1924/1996
Designed by C O'Connor Jnr
18 holes, 5939 yards, S.S.S. 71
† Welcome; some restrictions Sun
morning.
┐ WD €22; WE €26.
↺ Welcome by prior arrangement;
deposit required in advance; catering
packages available.
🍽 Lunches and snacks available.
↭ Sullivans Gort.

12 137 Grange

Rathfarnham, Dublin
☎ 00353 1 4932889, Fax 4939490,
Pro 4932299, Sec 493 9490
7 miles S from city.
Parkland course.
Founded 1910
Designed by James Braid
18 holes, 5517 yards, S.S.S. 69
† Welcome WD except Tues and
Wed afternoon.
┐ WD €57.
↺ Welcome Mon and Thurs by prior
arrangement.
🍽 Full facilities.

12 138 Greencastle

Greencastle, Moville, Co Donegal
☎ 00353 7 781013
On L85 23 miles NE of Londonderry
through Moville.
Public seaside course.
Founded 1892
Designed by Eddie Hackett
18 holes, 5211 yards, S.S.S. 67
† Welcome.
┐ WD €20; WE €26.
↺ Welcome by prior arrangement.
🍽 Bar and catering facilities.

12 139 Greenore

Greenore, Co Louth

☎ 00353 4293 73678
15 miles out of Dundalk on the Newry
Road.
Wooded seaside semi links course.
Founded 1896
Designed by Eddie Hackett
18 holes, 6647 yards, S.S.S. 71
🏌 Driving range.
† Welcome by prior arrangement.
┐ WD €33; WE €45.
↺ Welcome by arrangement.
🍽 Full facilities.
↭ Apply to club.

12 140 Greystones

Greystones, Co Wicklow
⁂ www.greystonesgc.com
✉ seceratery@greystonesgc.com
☎ 00353 1 2874136, Fax 2873749,
Pro 2875308, Rest/Bar 2876624
N11 out of Dublin towards Wexford.
Parkland course.
Pro Karl Holmes; Founded 1895
Designed by Paddy Merrigan.
18 holes, 5322 yards, S.S.S. 69
† Welcome Mon, Tue, Fri
┐ WD €33; WE €38.
↺ Welcome by arrangement.
🍽 Full facilities.
↭ La Touche.

12 141 Gweedore

Derrybeg, Letterkenny, Co Donegal
☎ 00353 7 531140
L82 from Letterkenny or T72 from
Donegal.
Seaside course.
Designed by Eddie Hackett
9 holes, 6150 yards, S.S.S. 69
† Welcome.
┐ Details available upon application.
↺ Welcome at WE.
🍽 Lunches at WE.

12 142 Harbour Point

Little Island, Cork, Co Cork
☎ 00353 21 4353094, Fax 4354408,
Pro 4883710
6 miles E of Cork.
Parkland course.
Pro Brendan McDaid; Founded 1991
Designed by Paddy Merrigan
18 holes, 6063 yards, S.S.S. 72
† Welcome.
┐ WD €34; WE €38.
↺ From €30.
🍽 Full facilities.
↭ John Barley Corn; Ashbourne
House; Midleton Park; Fitzpatricks
Silver Springs.

12 143 Hazel Grove

Mt Seskin Rd, Jobstown, Tallaght,
Dublin
☎ 00353 1 4520911
On the Blessington Road 2.5 miles
from Tallaght.
Parkland course.
Founded 1988
Designed by Jim Byrne
11 holes, 5030 yards, S.S.S. 67
🏌 Practice area.
† Welcome except Tue and Sun
morning.
┐ Terms on application.
↺ Welcome by prior arrangement;
maximum 50 players; Sat morning
maximum 40; catering packages
available.
🍽 Bar function room.
↭ Abberly Court.

12 144 Headfort

Kells, Co Meath
☎ 00353 46 40146, Fax 49282, Pro
40639, Rest/Bar 419440
N3 from Dublin on Cavan route.
Parkland course.
Pro Brendan McGovern; Founded
1928
Designed by Christy O'Connor Jnr
36 holes, 5973 yards, S.S.S. 71
† Welcome.
┐ WD €35.00; WE €40.00. New
course: €50.00.
↺ Welcome by prior arrangement;
catering package by arrangement.
🍽 Full facilities.
↭ Headfort Arms.

12 145 Heath

The Heath, Portlaoise, Co Laois
☎ 00353 502 46533, Fax 46866,
Pro 46622
4 miles NE of Portlaoise off the main
Dublin to Cork/Limerick Road.
Heathland course.
Pro Eddie Doyle; Founded 1930
18 holes, 5721 yards, S.S.S. 70
🏌 Practice range.
† Welcome WD; WE by prior
arrangement.
┐ Terms on application.
↺ Welcome by prior arrangement.
🍽 Full facilities.

12 146 Hermitage

Lucan, Co Dublin
☎ 00353 1 6268049, Pro 6268072
8 miles from Dublin; 1 mile from Lucan.
Parkland course.
Pro Simon Byrne; Founded 1905
Designed by Eddie Hackett

18 holes, 6051 yards, S.S.S. 71
♱ Welcome WD.
⌊ WD €70; WE €80.
⟡ Welcome WD by arrangement; five golf and meal packages; latest tee time 1.45pm; from €70.
⦿ Full clubhouse catering facilities.
⌁ Finnstown; Bewley; Spa; Morans Red Cow; Green Isle.

12 147 Highfield
Carbury, Co Kildare
☎ 00353 405 31021
In Carbury.
Parkland course.
Pro Peter O'Hagan; Founded 1992
18 holes, 5707 yards, S.S.S. 72
⫫ 5 bays.
♱ Welcome.
⌊ WD €20; WE €30.
⟡ Welcome; booking is advisable.

12 148 Hollystown
Hollystown, Dublin 15, Co Dublin
☎ 00353 1 8207444
8 miles off N3 Dublin-Cavan road at Mulhuddart or off the main N2 Dublin-Ashbourne road at Ward.
Parkland course.
Founded 1993
18 holes, 6303 yards, S.S.S. 72
⫫ Practice ground, driving range.
♱ Welcome.
⌊ WD €25; WE €35.
⦿ Coffee shop.

12 149 Hollywood Lakes ⟐
Hollywood, Ballyboughal, Co Dublin
⌁ www.hollywoodlakesgolf.com
☎ 00353 1 8433406, Fax 8433002
15 minutes N of Dublin Airport via N1 and R129 to Ballyboughal.
Parkland course.
Pro Mel Flanagan; Founded 1991
Designed by Mel Flanagan
18 holes, 6246 yards, S.S.S. 72
⫫ Practice range; practice bar
♱ Welcome except Sat and Sun before 1.00; booking advisable.
⌊ WD €30; WE €35.
⟡ Welcome by prior arrangement; reductions for larger groups; catering packages by arrangement; early bird rates between 8am and 10am Mon-Fri; from €15.
⦿ Full facilities.
⌁ Grove; Grand; Airport.

12 150 Howth
Carrickbrack Rd, Sutton, Dublin 13
⌁ www.howthgolfclub.ie

✉ secretary@howthgolfclub.ie
☎ 00353 1 8323055, Fax 8321793
Situated on Howth Head to the NE of Dublin.
Heathland course.
Pro John McGuirk; Founded 1912
Designed by James Braid
18 holes, 5614 metres, S.S.S. 69
⫫ Practice ground.
♱ Welcome WD except Wed.
⌊ WD and WE: €50.
⟡ Welcome WD except Wed; reductions on numbers over 10 by arrangement.
⦿ Bar snacks, full catering for groups by arrangement.
⌁ Marine; Bailey Court.

12 151 The Island Golf Club
Corballis, Donabate, Co Dublin
⌁ www.theislandgolfclub.com
✉ islandgc@iol.ie
☎ 00353 1 8436462, Fax 8436860,
Sec 843 6462
Leave N1 1 mile beyond Swords at Donabate signpost, then L91 for 3 miles and turn right at sign.
Traditional links course.
Pro Kevin Kelleher; Founded 1890
Designed by F Hawtree & Eddie Hackett (over last 30yrs)
18 holes, 6800 yards, S.S.S. 73
⫫ Practice facilities.
♱ Welcome by prior arrangement.
⌊ All time €100.
⟡ Welcome by prior arrangement.
⦿ Full facilities.

12 152 The K Club
Kildare Hotel & Country club, Straffan, Co. Kildare
☎ 00353 1 601 7300, Fax 6017399
22 miles from Dublin via N7 Naas Road.
Parkland course.
Pro Ernie Jones; Founded 1991
Designed by Arnold Palmer
18 holes, 7159 yards, S.S.S. 74
⫫ Practice range available.
♱ Welcome by prior arrangement.
⌊ Apr-Oct €245; Nov-Mar €110.
⟡ Welcome groups of 16 or more; catering packages by arrangement.
⦿ Full clubhouse facilities, bar, coffee shop.
⌁ Kildare Hotel & Country Club on site, 5-star.

12 153 Kanturck – 18 Holes
Fairyhill, Kanturck, Co Cork
☎ 00353 29 50534, Sec 0872 217510

1 mile from Kanturck via Fairyhill Road
Parkland course.
Founded 1973
Designed by Richard Barry
18 holes, 5721 yards, S.S.S. 70
♱ Welcome but prior arrangement is advisable.
⌊ WD €15; WE €20.
⟡ Welcome by prior arrangement with the seretary; catering packages by arrangement through the secretary; group rates available.
⦿ Full facilities.
⌁ Duhallow Park; Assolas.

12 154 Kanturck – 9 Holes
Fairy Hill, Kanturck, Cork
☎ 00353 29 47238, Fax 50534
Course is three miles SW of Kanturck on the R579.
Founded 1974
9 holes, 6026 yards, S.S.S. 69
♱ Welcome.
⌊ Terms on application.
⦿ Bar and catering facilities.

12 155 Kenmare
Killowen Rd, Kenmare, Co Kerry
⌁ www.kenmaregolfclub.com
☎ 00353 64 41291, Fax 42061
Off the N22 Cork to Killarney Road and then on to the R569.
Parkland course on the mouth of a river.
Pro Charlie McCarthy; Founded 1903
Designed by Eddie Hackett
18 holes, 6000 yards, S.S.S. 69
♱ Welcome but booking will be necessary on weekends.
⌊ Details available on application.
⟡ Welcome by prior arrangement; minimum 18 players; catering by arrangement.
⦿ Only snacks are available; restaurant next door.
⌁ Park; Kenmare Bay; Sheen Falls.

12 156 Kilcock
Gallow, Kilcock, Co Meath
☎ 00353 1 6284074
2 miles N of Kilcock.
Parkland course.
Founded 1985
Designed by Eddie Hackett
18 holes, 5801 yards, S.S.S. 70
♱ Welcome WD; WE by prior arrangement.
⌊ WD €20; WE €25.
⟡ Welcome by prior arrangement.
⦿ Bar snacks.

12 157 Kilcoole
Kilcoole, Co Wicklow
✉ adminkg@aircom.net
☎ 00353 1 2872066, Fax 2010497
21 miles S of Dublin on coast.
Parkland course.
Founded 1992
Designed by Brian Williams
9 holes, 5278 Men. Ladies 5082 yards, S.S.S. 69
♣ Welcome except Sat and Sun am.
↑ Terms on application.
♪ Welcome by prior arrangement.
⛶ Full bar and catering facilities.
↩ Latouche; Glen View.

12 158 Kilkea Castle ♛
Castle Dermot, Co Kildare
✉ kilkeagolfclub@eircom.net
☎ 00353 503 45555, Fax 45505
40 miles from Dublin.
Parkland course.
Founded 1994
Designed by McDadd & Cassidy
18 holes, 6097 metres, S.S.S. 71
↑ Welcome; by booking only.
↑ Mon–Thurs €39 Fri–Sun and BH €45.
♪ Welcome by prior arrangement; terms on application.
⛶ Full facilities.
↩ Kilkae Castle Hotel.

12 159 Kilkee ♛
East End, Kilkee, Co Clare
☎ 00353 6590 56048
400 yards from town centre.
Links and Meadowland course.
Founded 1896
Designed by McAlister
18 holes, 5537 yards, S.S.S. 69
↑ Welcome.
↑ Terms on application.
♪ Welcome by prior arrangement; restrictions in July and early August; catering packages by arrangement.
⛶ Full facilities.

12 160 Kilkenny
Glendine, Kilkenny, Co Kilkenny
☎ 00353 56 65400
1 miles NW of Kilkenny off the Castlecorner Road.
Parkland course.
Founded 1896
18 holes, 5857 yards, S.S.S. 70
↑ Welcome.
↑ WD €35; WE €40.
♪ Welcome but booking is essential.
⛶ Clubhouse facilities.

12 161 Killarney Golf Club
Mahoney's Point, Killarney, Co Kerry
☎ 00353 64 31034, Fax 33065
2 miles W of Killarney on the N70.
Parkland and lakeside course.
Pro Tony Covemy; Founded 1939
Designed by Sir Guy Campbell & Henry Longhurst
54 holes, 6474 yards, S.S.S. 73
↑ Welcome by prior arrangement.
↑ WD and WE: €70.
♪ Welcome with prior arrangement and handicap certificates essential; discounts for groups of 20 or more.
⛶ Full clubhouse facilities.
↩ Club can provide a detailed list.

12 162 Killeen
Kill, Co Kildare
☎ 00353 45866003
N7 to Kill village then head to Straffan.
Parkland course.
Founded 1991
18 holes, 4989 yards, S.S.S. 70
↑ Welcome.
↑ WD €25; WE €32.
♪ Welcome.
⛶ Full bar and catering.

12 163 Killeline
Cork Road, Newcastle West, Co Limmerick
☎ 00353 69 61600
Cork road on the edge of Newcastle West.
Parkland course.
Founded 1993
Designed by Kevin Dorian
18 holes, 6720 yards, S.S.S. 72
↑ Welcome.
↑ Terms on application.
♪ Welcome at all times by arrangement; catering packages available.
⛶ Full facilities. Bar and restaurant.
↩ Courtney Lodge (very close); Rathkeale House; Devon Inn.

12 164 Killin Park
Killin Park, Dundalk
☎ 00353 42 9339303
3 miles NW of Dundalk on Castledown Road.
Founded 1991
18 holes, 3322 yards, S.S.S. 65
↑ Welcome.
↑ WD €18; WE €23.
♪ Welcome by prior arrangement.
⛶ Snacks and bar.
↩ The Derryhale

12 165 Killiney
Ballinclea Rd, Killiney, Co Dublin
✉ killineygollf@aircom.iecom.net
☎ 00353 1 2852823, Fax 2852861, Pro 2856294
3 miles from Dun Laoghaire.
Parkland course.
Pro Paddy O Biol; Founded 1903
9 holes, 5655 yards, S.S.S. 70
↑ Welcome but booking is essential.
↑ WD and WE: €38.
♪ Welcome on most days, but prior arrangement is necessary.
⛶ Full clubhouse facilities.
↩ Killiney Castle; Killiney Court.

12 166 Killorglin
Steelroe, Killorglin, Co Kerry
☎ 00353 6697 61979
On the N70 Tralee Road 3km from the bridge at Killorglin.
Parkland course.
Pro John Gleeson; Founded 1992
Designed by Eddie Hackett
18 holes, 6467 yards, S.S.S. 71
↑ Welcome.
↑ Terms on application.
♪ Welcome; terms on application.
⛶ Full clubhouse facilities.
↩ Bianconi Inn; Riverside House; Grove Lodge; Fairways B&B; Laune Bridge; Fern Rock.

12 167 Kilrush
Parknamoney, Kilrush, Co Clare
🖥 www.kirushgolfclub.com
✉ info@kilrushgolfclub.com
☎ 00353 6590 51138, Fax 52633, Sec 087 623 7557
0.5 miles from Kilrush on N68 from Ennis.
Parkland course.
Pro Sean O'Connor; Founded 1934
Designed by Dr A Spring (extended in 1994)
18 holes, 5986 yards, S.S.S. 70
↑ Welcome.
↑ WD €25; WE €30.
♪ Welcome by prior arrangement; discount terms on application.
⛶ Full clubhouse facilities available all year round.
↩ Halpins; Stella Maris; Bellbridge.

12 168 Kilternan Golf & Country Club
Kilternan Hotel, Enniskerry Road, Co Dublin
☎ 00353 1 2955559, Fax 2955670
On N11 S of Dublin.
Hilly parkland course.
Pro Gary Headley; Founded 1988

Designed by E Hackett
18 holes, 4952 yards, S.S.S. 66
⚑ Driving nets, practice, putting
green. Buggies and trolleys available.
✝ Welcome.
Ⅰ WD €25; WE and BH €32.
⚲ Welcome by prior arrangement;
leisure club; tennis courts; workout
studios.
🍽 Full facilities in hotel.
🛏 Kilternan Hotel on site; golf
packages available.

12 169 Kinsale
Farrangalway, Kinsale, Cork
☎ 00353 21 772197, Pro 773258
3 miles N of Kinsale on Cork Road. 3
miles NE of Kinsale.
Parkland course.
Pro Ger Broderick; Founded 1912
Designed by J Kenneally
18 holes, 6609 yards, S.S.S. 72
✝ Welcome.
Ⅰ Terms on application.
⚲ Welcome by prior arrangement;
restricted to 11.30am-1.30pm only at
WE; catering by arrangement.
🍽 Full clubhouse facilities.
🛏 Actons; Trident; Blue Haven.

12 170 Knockanally Golf & Country Club
Donadea, North Kildare
✉ golf@knocknally.com
☎ 00353 458 69322
3 miles off the main Dublin-Galway
Road between Kilcock and Enfield.
Parkland course.
Pro Martin Dassie; Founded 1985
Designed by Noel Lyons
18 holes, 6424 yards, S.S.S. 72
✝ Welcome.
Ⅰ WD €28.00; WE €40.00.
⚲ Welcome by prior arrangement
everyday.
🍽 Full clubhouse facilities.
🛏 The John's Town House Hotel.

12 171 Lahinch Golf Club
Lahinch, Co Clare
🖧 www.lahinchgolf.com
✉ info@lahinchgolf.com
☎ 00353 6570 81003, Fax 81592
34 miles from Shannon Airport.
Seaside course.
Pro Robert McCavery; Founded 1892
Designed by JD Harris/Donald Steel
(Castle); Old course designed by Tom
Morris (1892), redesigned by Dr A
MacKenzie
Castle: 18 holes, 5138 yards, S.S.S. 70;
Old: 18 holes, 6633 yards, S.S.S. 71

✝ Welcome.
Ⅰ Terms on application.
⚲ Welcome but booking is essential;
especially for Sun.
🍽 Full facilities.

12 172 Laytown & Bettystown
Bettystown, Co Meath
☎ 00353 41 27563, Fax 28506, Pro
28793, Sec 27170
45 miles N of Dublin Airport.
Links course.
Pro Robert Browne; Founded 1909
18 holes, 5668 yards, S.S.S. 69
✝ Welcome by prior arrangement.
Ⅰ Terms on application.
⚲ Welcome WD and some Sat;
terms on application.
🍽 Full bar and catering facilities.

12 173 Lee Valley   ₢
Clashanure, Ovens, Co Cork
☎ 00353 21 7331721, Fax 7331695,
Pro 331758
On main Cork-Killarney Road. M22.
Parkland course.
Pro John Savage; Founded 1993
Designed by Christy O'Connor Jnr
18 holes, 6715 yards, S.S.S. 72
✝ Welcome by prior arrangement.
Ⅰ April-Oct: WD €44, WE €54; Nov-
March: WD €30, WE €38. Early Bird -
April-Oct before 10.00am - €30.
⚲ Welcome by prior arrangement.
🍽 Full clubhouse facilities.
🛏 Blarney Park; Farran House.

12 174 Leixlip
Leixlip, Co Kildare
☎ 00353 1 6244978, Sec 6246185
Off N4 past Lucan.
Parkland course.
Founded 1994
Designed by E Hackett
18 holes, 6068 yards, S.S.S. 70
✝ Welcome.
Ⅰ Details upon application.
⚲ Welcome by prior arrangement;
discounts for large groups.
🍽 Clubhouse facilities.
🛏 Becketts; Springfield; Spa.

12 175 Leopardstown Golf Centre
Foxrock, Dublin
☎ 00353 1 2895341, Fax 2892569
5 miles S of Dublin.
Parkland course.
Pro Michael Allen, Steven O'Donnell
18 holes, 5384 yards, S.S.S. 66
⚑ 50 indoor and 50 outdoor.

✝ Welcome.
Ⅰ Terms on application.
⚲ Welcome, but booking in advance
is essential.
🍽 Café and restaurant facilities.

12 176 Letterkenny
Barnhill, Letterkenny, Co Donegal
☎ 00353 7421150
On T72 2 miles N of Letterkenny.
Parkland course.
Founded 1913
Designed by E Hackett
18 holes, 6239 yards, S.S.S. 71
✝ Welcome.
Ⅰ Terms on application.
⚲ Welcome by arrangement.
🍽 Bar and snacks available; meals
by prior arrangement.

12 177 Limerick
Ballyclough, Co Limerick
🖧 www.limerickgc.com
☎ 00353 61 415146, Fax 319219,
Pro 412492, Rest/Bar 414083
Course is south of the city on the
Fedamore Road.
Parkland course.
Pro Lea Hurrington; Founded 1891
18 holes, 5938 yards, S.S.S. 71
✝ Welcome before 4pm WD except
Tues.
Ⅰ €50.
⚲ Welcome Mon, Thu, Fri Morning.
🍽 Full facilities.
🛏 Feltcourse Hotel.

12 178 Limerick County Golf   ₢ & Country Club
Bellyneety, Co Limerick
☎ 00353 61 351881
5 miles S of Limerick towards
Bruff/Kilmallock.
Parkland course.
Founded 1994
Designed by Des Smyth
18 holes, 6191 yards, S.S.S. 72
⚑ Practice range; driving range and
golf school.
✝ Welcome.
Ⅰ WD €33; WE €45.
⚲ Welcome; deposit required; from
€25.
🍽 Full facilities.
🛏 Castleray Park; Woodlands; Jury's.

12 179 Lismore
Lismore, Co Waterford
☎ 00353 58 54026
0.5 miles from Lismore on the Killarney
Road.

Parkland course.
Founded 1965
Designed by Eddie Hackett
9 holes, 5291 yards, S.S.S. 67
† Welcome; some Sun reserved.
ɪ Details available upon application.
↻ Welcome by arrangement; terms on application.
⦿ Clubhouse facilities.

12 180 **Listowel**
Feale View, Listowel, Kerry
☎ 00353 68 21592
In village of Listowel.
Parkland course.
9 holes, S.S.S. 70
† Welcome.
ɪ Terms on application.
⦿ Snack bar facilities.

12 181 **Loughrea**
Loughrea, Co Galway
☎ 00353 91 841049
On L11 1 mile N of Loughrea.
Meadowland course.
Founded 1924
Designed by Eddie Hackett
18 holes, 5176 yards, S.S.S. 68
† Welcome.
ɪ €20 daily.
↻ Welcome by prior arrangement.
⦿ Clubhouse facilities.

12 182 **Lucan**
Celbridge Rd, Lucan, Co Dublin
✉ lucangolf@eircom.net
☎ 00353 1 6280246, Fax 6282929, Sec 6282106
Take the N4 from Dublin and turn off at Celbridge.
Parkland course.
Founded 1897
Designed by E Hackett
18 holes, 5994 yards, S.S.S. 71
† Welcome. Mon, Tues and Fri. Other times with member.
ɪ WD and WE: €40.
↻ Welcome by arrangement.
⦿ Full bar and restaurant service.
↩ Springfield, the Lucan Spa.

12 183 **Luttrellstown Castle** ₢
Castleknock, Dublin 15
⌨ www.luttrellftown.ie
✉ enquiries@luttrellftown.ie
☎ 00353 1 8089988, Fax 8089989
Leave N1 at M50 intersection following southbound signs; exit M50 at Castleknock.
Parkland course.
Pro Graham Campbell; Founded 1993

Designed by Dr Nick Bielenberg/ Edward Connaughton
18 holes, 7000 yards, S.S.S. 73
ɪ Yes.
† Welcome.
ɪ WD €80; WE €85.
↻ Welcome; special rates negotiable for groups; terms available on application.
⦿ Full clubhouse facilities.
↩ Liffey Valley; Kildaire Hotel & CC; Conrad International; on-site accommodation in 2 courtyard apartments. Plus 14 bedrooms in private castle.

12 184 **Macroom**
Lackaduv, Macroom, Co Cork
✉ mcroomgc@iol.ie
☎ 00353 26 41072, Fax 41491
On main Cork/Killarney road on the outskirts of the town.
Parkland course.
Founded 1924
Designed by J Kennealy (new 9 holes)
18 holes, 5586 yards, S.S.S. 70
† Welcome; some WE restrictions apply.
ɪ Details upon application.
↻ Welcome by prior arrangement between March-October.
⦿ Full facilities.
↩ Castle.

12 185 **Mahon**
Clover Hill, Blackrock, Co Cork
☎ 00353 21 294280
2 miles SE of Cork.
Municipal parkland course.
Founded 1980
18 holes, 4217 yards, S.S.S. 62
† Welcome WD; WE by prior arrangement.
ɪ WD €18; WE €19.
⦿ Bar snacks; lunch and dinner by arrangement.

12 186 **Malahide** ₢
Beechwood, The Grange, Malahide, Co Dublin
⌨ www.malahidegolfclub.ie
☎ 00353 1 8461611, Fax 8461270, Pro 8460002
8 miles N of Dublin; 1 mile S of Malahide.
Parkland course.
Pro John Murray; Founded 1892/1990
Designed by Eddie Hackett
27 holes, 6066 yards, S.S.S. 72
† Welcome Mon, Thurs, Fri and Sat up to 9.30.
ɪ WD €50; WE €85.

↻ Welcome Mon, Thurs, Fri and Sat morning; discounts available; catering by arrangement; from €40.
⦿ Full bar and restaurant facilities available.
↩ Grand Hotel; Portmarnock Links.

12 187 **Mallow**
Ballyellis, Mallow, Co Cork
✉ Golfmall@golfree.indigo.ie
☎ 00353 22 21145, Fax 42501, Pro 43424
1.5 km from Mallow on the Killanvullen Road.
Parkland course.
Pro Sean Conway; Founded 1892/1947
Designed by Commander JD Harris
18 holes, 5960 yards, S.S.S. 72
† Welcome, but booking is advisable for weekends.
ɪ WD €32; WE €38; booking required for tee-off time.
↻ Welcome WD by prior arrangement; packages available.
⦿ Full clubhouse facilities.
↩ Longueville House; Hibernian.

12 188 **Mannan Castle**
Donaghmoyne, Carrickmacross, Co Monaghan
☎ 00353 4296 63308, Fax 63195
4 miles NE of Carrickmacross on the Crossmaglen Road.
Parkland course.
Founded 1994
Designed by F Ainsworth
9 holes, 6008 yards, S.S.S. 71
† Welcome.
ɪ WD €20; WE €30.
↻ Welcome WD and Sat mornings.
Clubhouse facilities.

12 189 **Milltown**
Lower Churchtown Rd, Milltown, Co Dublin
☎ 00353 1 4976090, Fax 4976008
3 miles S of the city centre via Ranelagh village.
Parkland course.
Pro John Harlet; Founded 1907
Designed by FE Davies
18 holes, 5638 yards, S.S.S. 69
† Welcome except Tues and Sat; with a member on Sun.
ɪ €80 WD only; booking required.
↻ Welcome by prior arrangement; catering packages by prior arrangement; private function room.
⦿ Bar and restaurant facilities.
↩ Berkeley Court; Jury's; Herbert Park; Montrose.

12 190 Mitchelstown

Mitchelstown, Co Cork
☎ 00353 25 24072
1 mile from Mitchelstown off the N1
Dublin to Cork Road.
Parkland course.
Founded 1908
Designed by David Jones
18 holes, 5148 yards, S.S.S. 67
† Welcome.
↳ Details available upon application.
♻ Welcome except Sun; catering
packages available.
🍽 Full facilities.

12 191 Moate

Aghanargit, Moate, Co Westmeath
☎ 00353 902 81271, Fax 81267
On Dublin-Galway Road.
Parkland course.
Pro Paul Power; Founded 1900
Designed by B Browne (1993
extension)
18 holes, 5752 yards, S.S.S. 70
⚑ Practice area.
† Welcome.
↳ WD €20; WE €25 (€6 with
member).
♻ Welcome except after 12.30pm at
WE; catering packages available;
visitors locker room.
🍽 Full bar and catering facilities.
↳ Grand.

12 192 Monkstown

Parkgariffe, Monkstown, Co Cork
☎ 00353 21 4841376, Sec 841376
11 miles E of Cork; turn right off the
Rochestown Road at the Rochestown
Inn.
Parkland course.
Pro Matt Murphy; Founded 1908/71
Designed by Peter O'Hare/Tom Carey
18 holes, 5669 yards, S.S.S. 70
⚑ Practice ground.
† Welcome.
↳ Terms on application.
♻ Welcome by prior arrangement.
🍽 Restaurant and bar facilities
available.
↳ Rochestown Park.

12 193 Moor-Park

Mooretown, Navan, Co Meath
☎ 00353 46 27661
Parkland course.
Founded 1993
18 holes, 5600 yards, S.S.S. 69
† Welcome.
↳ Terms on application.
🍽 Limited snack bars.

12 194 Mount Juliet

Thomastown, Co Kilkenny
🖳 www.moutjuliet.com
🖂 info@mountjulius.ie
☎ 00353 56 24455, Fax 24522, Pro
73063
Course is signposted in Thomastown
off the main Dublin-Waterford Road.
Parkland course.
Pro Brendan McDermott; Founded
1992
Designed by Jack Nicklaus
18 holes, 7112 yards, S.S.S. 74
⚑ Practice ground with driving bays
and 18-hole putting course.
† Welcome by prior arrangement.
↳ WD €135; WE €150.
♻ Welcome by prior arrangement;
minimum 20 people; Mon-Thurs €100;
Fri, Sat, Sun: €110.
🍽 Full facilities.
↳ Mount Juliet.

12 195 Mount Temple

Mount Temple Village, Moate, Co
Westmeath
☎ 00353 902 81545, Fax 81957
4 miles off the main N6 Dublin-Galway
route in Mount Temple Village.
Combination of links and parkland
course.
Founded 1991
Designed by Robert J Brown and
Michael Dolan
18 holes, 5872 yards, S.S.S. 71
⚑ Practice range; 3-hole practice
area.
† Welcome; by arrangement at WE.
↳ WD €25; WE €32.
♻ Welcome by prior arrangement;
terms on application.
🍽 Catering and wine licence; pub
100 yards.
↳ Hudson Bay; Prince of Wales;
Royal Hoey; Shamrock Lodge;
Bloomfield House.

12 196 Mountbellew

Shankhill, Mountbellew, Co Galway
☎ 00353 905 79259
Course is on the T4 28 miles E of
Galway.
Undulating meadowland course.
Founded 1929
18 holes, 5214 metres, S.S.S. 66
⚑ Practice area.
† Welcome.
↳ Details available upon application.
♻ Welcome by prior arrangement;
terms on application.
🍽 Catering by arrangement; snacks.
↳ The Malthouse.

12 197 Mountrath

Knockinina, Mountrath, Co Laois
☎ 00353 502 32558
0.5 miles off the main Dublin-Limerick
Road.
Undulating parkland course.
Founded 1929
18 holes, 5536 metres, S.S.S. 69
† Welcome; some WE restrictions.
↳ WD and WE: €20.
♻ Welcome WD by prior
arrangement; discounts for larger
groups; terms on application.
🍽 Full clubhouse facilities available.
↳ Killeshin; Montague; Leix Co;
Grants; Racket Hall.

12 198 Mullingar

Belvedere, Mullingar, Co Westmeath
☎ 00353 44 48366, Pro 41499
3.5 miles from Mullingar on the N52.
Parkland course.
Pro Mr John Burns; Founded 1894
Designed by James Braid
18 holes, 6468 yards, S.S.S. 70
† Welcome.
↳ WD €32; WE €38.
♻ Welcome by prior arrangement;
packages available; terms on
application.
🍽 Full clubhouse facilities.

12 199 Mulranny

Mulranny, Westport, Co Mayo
☎ 00353 98 36262
15 miles from Westport.
Links course.
Founded 1968
9 holes, 6255 yards, S.S.S. 69
† Welcome.
↳ Terms on application.
♻ Welcome by prior arrangement.
🍽 Full clubhouse facilities available.
↳ Many in Westport.

12 200 Muskerry

Carrigrohane, Co Cork
☎ 00353 21 385297
7 miles W of Cork near Blarney.
Parkland course.
Founded 1897
18 holes, 5786 yards, S.S.S. 71
† Welcome WD except Wed
afternoons; Thurs mornings and after
3.30pm Fri.
↳ Terms on application.
♻ Welcome by prior arrangement.
🍽 Full facilities.

12 201 Naas

Kerdiffstown, Naas, Co Kildare

⅏ www.naasgolfclub.ie
☎ 00353 458 74644, Fax 96109
Between Johnstown and Sallins.
Parkland course.
Founded 1886
Designed by Arthur Spring
18 holes, 5660 yards, S.S.S. 69
† Welcome Mon, Wed, Fri and Sat.
⌖ WD €27; WE €35.
⟲ Welcome Mon, Wed, Fri and Sat morning.
🍽 Bar; meals by prior arrangement only.
⌁ The Ambassador Killanahee, Habour View, Red House, Johnstown Inn.

12 202 Narin & Portnoo
Portnoo, Co Donegal
✉ narimportnoo@eircom.net
☎ 00353 75 45107, Fax 45107
From Donegal via Ardara.
Links seaside course.
Founded 1930
18 holes, 5396 metres, S.S.S. 69
† Welcome; some summer restrictions.
⌖ WD €25; WE €30.
⟲ Welcome by prior arrangement.
🍽 Snacks and full bar facilities.
⌁ The Lake House Hotel

12 203 Nenagh Golf Club ☏
Beechwood, Nenagh, Co Tipperary
☎ 00353 67 31476
4 miles E of Nenagh.
Parkland course.
Founded 1892
Designed by Alister MacKenzie (original 9); E Hackett (additional 9)
18 holes, 5491 yards, S.S.S. 68
⌁ Practice range; large practice ground.
† Welcome but by prior arrangement at WE.
⌖ Details available on application.
⟲ Welcome by prior arrangement.
🍽 Full facilities.

12 204 New Ross
Tinneranny, New Ross, Co Wexford
☎ 00353 514 21433, Fax 20098
1 mile from town centre off Waterford Road.
Parkland course.
Founded 1905
18 holes, 5751 yards, S.S.S. 70
† Welcome; some Sun restrictions.
⌖ Terms on application.
⟲ Welcome by arrangement; no group discounts available.
🍽 Clubhouse facilities.

12 205 Newcastle West
Ardagh, Co Limerick
☎ 00353 69 76500
Off N21 2 miles beyond Rathkeale.
Parkland course.
Founded 1939/94
Designed by Arthur Spring
18 holes, 6317 yards, S.S.S. 72
† Welcome.
⌖ Available on application.
⟲ Welcome with prior arrangement; catering packages by arrangement.
🍽 Bar and restaurant.
⌁ Courtenay Lodge; Rathkeale House; Devon Inn.

12 206 Newlands
Clondalkin, Dublin
☎ 00353 1 4593157, Pro 4593538
6 miles from city centre.
Parkland course.
Founded 1926
Designed by James Braid
18 holes, 5696 yards, S.S.S. 70
† Welcome.
⌖ WD and WE: €55.
⟲ Welcome WD.
🍽 Full facilities.

12 207 North West
Lisfannon, Fahan, Co Donegal
☎ 00353 77 61715
2 miles S of Buncrana.
Seaside links course.
Pro Caseamus McBriarty.; Founded 1892
18 holes, 5759 yards, S.S.S. 69
† Welcome.
⌖ Available upon request.
⟲ Welcome by prior arrangement WD and WE in the summer.
🍽 Bar and restaurant.
⌁ Gateway Hotel.

12 208 Nuremore
Carrickmacross, Co Monaghan
☎ 00353 4296 61438
1 mile S of Carrickmacross.
Parkland course.
Founded 1964
Designed by Eddie Hackett
18 holes, 6246 yards, S.S.S. 74
† Welcome.
⌖ WD €30; WE €37.
⟲ Welcome by prior arrangement.
🍽 Clubhouse and hotel facilities.

12 209 Old Conna
Ferndale Road, Bray, Co Dublin
⅏ www.oldconnor.com
☎ 00353 1 2826055, Fax 2825611,

Pro 2720022
12 miles from Dublin.
Parkland course.
Founded 1977
Designed by Eddie Hackett
18 holes, 5590 yards, S.S.S. 72
† Welcome but booking advisable.
⌖ €45. Discounts before 9:30am on WD and for those who with members.
🍽 Bar and full meal service.
⌁ The Royal Hotel, The Killiney Court.

12 210 Old Head Links
Kinsale, Co Cork
☎ 00353 21 778444
20 miles S of Cork. Clifftop setting on Atlantic promontory.
Founded 1996
Designed by J Carr/R Kirby
18 holes, 7200 yards, S.S.S. 72
† Welcome.
⌖ Terms on application.
⟲ Welcome by prior arrangement.
🍽 Bar and light meals; full restaurant service.

12 211 The Open Golf Centre
Newtown House, St Margaret's, Co Dublin
☎ 00353 1 8640324
4 miles from Dublin; adjacent to Dublin Airport.
Parkland course.
Pro Robin Machin; Founded 1993
Designed by Martin Hawtree
27 holes, 6570 yards
⌁ Practice range 15 bays.
† Welcome.
⌖ WD €16; WE €24.
⟲ Welcome by prior arrangement; from €16.
🍽 Full facilities.
⌁ Forte Crest.

12 212 Otway
Saltpans, Rathmullan, Co Donegal
☎ 00353 74 58319
15 miles NE of Letterkenny by Lough Swilly.
Links course.
Founded 1893
9 holes, 4234 yards, S.S.S. 60
† Welcome.
⌖ Terms on application.
⟲ Welcome.
⌁ Fort Royal; Rathmullan House; Pier Hotel.

12 213 Oughterard
Gortreevagh, Oughterard, Co Galway

Portmarnock Golf Club

There is more than a hint of romance in a paragraph contained in the Portmarnock Golf Club's centenary (1894-1994) guide. It contains every nuance of this great, traditional Irish links when it says: "On Christmas Eve 1983, WC Pickeman and George Ross rowed from Sutton to the Portmarnock peninsula. They were seeking the site for a golf links. They liked what they found and one year later the formal opening of Portmarnock Golf Club took place. Could they have imagined how their simple venture would have developed during the following years?"

It is not clear why Pickeman was known by his initials, but he was clearly his own man since he went into print to offer the following advice: "Don't forget at all times to talk as loudly as possible both on the links and in the clubhouse. It commands attention. And although many may consider you a cad others will accept you at your own valuation."

Like the founder father, Portmarnock Golf Club is full of character and characters as it quietly dominates a small peninsula with water on three sides - no two successive holes playing in the same direction - spectacular views and constant teasing by the vagaries of the wind.

From the back tees the course stretches more than 7,000 yards, but there are compensations in the beautiful tranquillity of the place, the flora and fauna and the view from any part of the course.

There is knee-deep rough to frustrate the wild hitter, but even from there the panorama is therapeutic. To the south there is the Hill of Howth, to the east there are the sand hills above the sea and out to the Lambay Islands.

The west offers the sheltered inlet of the sea and to the north there are the famous Mountains of Mourne.

The course, eight miles from Dublin, is a regular winner of magazine awards - best this, best that - and is the true test of a shot-maker and while the visitor may not have to fly the ball distances that took the likes of Seve Ballesteros, Bernhard Langer, Ian Woosnam, Jose-Maria Olazabal and Ben Crenshaw to wins in the Irish Open, he will still find 6,600 yards a serious examination.

The course has some celebrated holes, with the fourteenth and fifteenth dueling for the accolades although the fifth (a par four of 407 yards) was always regarded by Harry Bradshaw, for 40 years the club professional and runner up in the 1949 British Open, as the best on the course.

Henry Cotton described the fourteenth as the best hole in golf and Arnold Palmer insists that the fifteenth is the best par three in the world. The fourteenth, a par four, is played towards the sea along a gently turning fairway. The narrow green sits on a plateau and is protected by two tricky bunkers. Humps and hillocks abound and a seriously precise approach shot is required.

Crenshaw shares Palmer's opinion of the fifteenth hole which has an out-of-bounds beach running along the length of the hole from the right. Darwin wrote, "I know of no greater finish in the world than the last five holes at Portmarnock."

Portmarnock would make a perfect Ryder Cup course and many people, particularly in Ireland, were disappointed that the match did not go there in 1993, two years after it held the Walker Cup. Sad to say Britain lost with Paul McGinley and Padraig Harrington failing to score a point between them in the match.

There is so much to commend Portmarnock. Its location is perfect for visitors to Dublin. The birds, grasses and flowers make it an environmentalist's dream and the nineteenth hole is a place of rich, warm, welcoming, Irish hospitality.
— **Jim Mossop**

☎ 00353 91 82131
1 mile from Oughterard on N59.
Mature parkland course with elevated greens.
Founded 1973
Designed by Hawtree/Hackett
18 holes, 6089 yards, S.S.S. 69
† Welcome.
[Terms on application.
⌂ Welcome WD.
🍽 Bar snacks; full à la carte menu.

12 214 **Parknasilla**
Parknasilla, Sneem, Co Kerry
☎ 00353 64 45122
2 miles E of Sneem on the Ring of Kerry Road.
Undulating seaside course.
Pro Miles Watt; Founded 1974
9 holes, 4652 yards, S.S.S. 65
† Welcome.
[Terms on application.

12 215 **Portarlington**
Garryhinch, Portarlington, Co Offaly
☎ 00353 502 23115
On L116 between Portarlington and Mountmellick.
Parkland course.
Founded 1909
18 holes, 6004 yards, S.S.S. 71
† Welcome.
[WD €20; WE €25.
⌂ Welcome; from WD€ 20; WE €27.
🍽 Bar and restaurant facilities.
🛏 East End Hotel.

12 216 **Portmarnock** ☏
Portmarnock, Co Dublin
🖥 www.portmarnockgolfclub.ie
✉ secretary@portmarnockgolfclub.ie
☎ 00353 1 8462968, Pro 8462634, Rest/Bar 8461400 and 8462794
From Dublin along the coast road to Baldoyle and on to Portmarnock.
Seaside links course.
Pro Joey Purcell; Founded 1894
Designed by WC Pickeman and George Ross
27 holes, 6497 yards, S.S.S. 75
† Welcome.
[WD €130; WE €160.
⌂ Welcome Mon, Tues, Thu and Fri by prior arrangement.
🍽 Full facilities.
🛏 The Portmarnock Hotel, The Grand Hotel.

12 217 **Portmarnock Hotel & Golf Links**
Strand Road, Portmarnock, Co Dublin
☎ 00353 1 846 0611, Fax 846 1077
On road out of Portmarnock, on right just before coast road to Malahide.
Seaside links.
Pro Paul Cuddy; Founded 1995
Designed by Bernhard Langer
18 holes, 6500 yards, S.S.S. 71
† Welcome.
[Apr-Oct €100; Nov-Mar €60 WD, €85 WE; residents €80 summer; €52 winter.
⌂ Accommodation and golf packages available.
🍽 Bar and restaurant.
🛏 Hotel on site.

12 218 **Portsalon**
Portsalon, Fanad, Co Donegal
☎ 00353 74 59459
Course is 20 miles north of Letterkenny.
Seaside links course.
Founded 1891
Designed by Mr Thompson of Portrush
18 holes, 5880 yards, S.S.S. 68
† Welcome by prior arrangement.
[WD €23; WE €30.
⌂ Welcome by prior arrangement; from €12.50.
🍽 Full facilities.
🛏 Fort Royal; Rathmullan House; Pier Hotel.

12 219 **Portumna**
Ennis Rd, Portumna, Co Galway
✉ enquire at jfhines@eir.com.net
☎ 00353 509 41059, Fax 41798, Pro 941051
1.5 miles from Portumna on Ennis Road.
Parkland course.
Pro Richard Clarke; Founded 1913
Designed by Eddie Carrington
18 (extra 2 in development) holes, 5474 yards, S.S.S. 71
⫝ Practice area.
† Welcome.
[€25.
⌂ Welcome by prior arrangement with Sec; special packages available; terms on application.
🍽 Restaurant and bar.
🛏 Shannon Oaks.

12 220 **Powerscourt**
Powerscourt Estate, Enniskerry, Co Wicklow
☎ 00353 1 2046033, Fax 2761303
12 miles south of Dublin just off N11 in Enniskerry.
Parkland course.
Pro Paul Tompson
Designed by Peter Macevoy
18 holes, 7063 yards, S.S.S. 72
† Welcome.
[Summer €100; Winter €90 (WD and WE).
⌂ Welcome by arrangement WE and WD.
🍽 Full bar and restaurant facilities.
🛏 Hotel facilities. Powerscourt.

12 221 **Raffeen Creek**
Ringaskiddy, Co Cork
☎ 00353 21 378430
1 mile from Ringaskiddy ferry.
Seaside/parkland course with water.
Founded 1988
Designed by Eddie Hackett
9 holes, 5098 yards, S.S.S. 68
† Welcome WD; WE afternoon only.
[Terms on application; concessions apply.
⌂ Welcome by arrangement.
🍽 Bar food.

12 222 **Rathdowney**
Rathdowney, Portlaoise, Co Laois
☎ 00353 505 46170, Fax 46065
Off the N7 in Rathdowney.
Parkland course.
Founded 1930
Designed by Eddie Hackett
18 holes, 5894 yards, S.S.S. 71
† Welcome; some Sun restrictions apply.
[WD €20; WE €25.
⌂ Welcome by prior arrangement with the secretary; bar and catering packages by prior arrangement; from €20.
🍽 Clubhouse facilities.
🛏 Leix Co; Woodview GH.

12 223 **Rathfarnham**
Newtown, Rathfarnham
☎ 00353 1 4931201, Fax 4931561
Course is two miles from Rathfarnham.
Parkland course.
Pro Brian O'Hara; Founded 1899
Designed by John Jacobs
9 holes, 5833 yards, S.S.S. 70
† Welcome WD except Tues and WE.
[WD and WE: €30.
⌂ Welcome by prior arrangement.
🍽 Lunch and dinners by prior arrangement.
🛏 Free Rock.

12 224 Rathsallagh Golf and County Club
Dunlavin, Co Wicklow
🖥 info@rathsallagh.com
☎ 00353 45 403316, Fax 403295
Course is 32 miles SW of Dublin.
Parkland course.
Founded 1994
Designed by Peter McEvoy and Christy O'Connor Jnr
18 holes, 6160 yards, S.S.S. 71
† Welcome.
Ⅰ Jan-March: Mon-Thurs €40, Fri-Sun €50; April-Oct: Mon-Thurs €55; Fri-Sun €70.
⌕ Welcome by arrangement.
🍴 Full function room, bar and restaurant, full catering facilities.

12 225 Redcastle
Redcastle, Moville, Co Donegal
☎ 00353 77 82073
Parkland course.
Founded 1983
9 holes, 6152 yards, S.S.S. 70
† Welcome.
Ⅰ WD €20; WE €26.
⌕ Welcome, but booking essential.
🍴 Full bar and restaurant.

12 226 Rockwell
Rockwell College, Cashel, Co Tipperary
☎ 00353 62 61444
Parkland course.
Founded 1964
9 holes, 3782 yards, S.S.S. 60
† Welcome by arrangement.
Ⅰ Terms on application.
⌕ Terms on application.
🍴 Limited facilities.

12 227 Rosapenna
Rosapenna Hotel, Downings, Co Donegal
🖳 www.rosapenna.ie
☎ 00353 74 55301, Fax 55128
25 miles from Letterkenny.
Links course.
Pro Don Patterson; Founded 1893
Designed by Tom Morris (1893); redesigned by Braid & Vardon
18 holes, 6271 yards, S.S.S. 71
† Welcome.
Ⅰ WD €40; WE €45.
⌕ Welcome, but must have handicap certificates.
🍴 Full hotel bar and restaurant facilities.
🛏 Rosapenna Hotel (4-star) on site.

12 228 Roscommon
Mote Park, Roscommon, Co Roscommon
☎ 00353 903 26382
Course is 0.25 miles from Roscommon Town.
Parkland course.
Founded 1904/1996
Designed by Eddie Connaughton
18 holes, 6040 yards, S.S.S. 70
† Welcome except Tues and Sun.
Ⅰ Dec-Feb: €15; March-Nov: €25.
⌕ Welcome by prior arrangement; catering by arrangement.
🍴 Full bar and restaurant facilities available.
🛏 Abbey; Royal; Regans; Gleesons.

12 229 Roscrea
Derryvale, Roscrea, Co Tipperary
☎ 00353 505 21130, Fax 23410
2 miles E of Roscrea on N7.
Parkland course.
Founded 1892
Designed by A. Spring
18 holes, 5708 yards, S.S.S. 70
† Welcome.
Ⅰ WD €15; WE €20.
⌕ Welcome by prior arrangement; group discounts available.
🍴 Bar and restaurant facilities.
🛏 Rackette Hall Hotel; Grants Hotel.

12 230 Ross
Ross Rd, Killarney, Kerry
🖳 www.rossgolfclub.com
☎ 00353 64 31125, Fax 31860
0.5 miles from Killarney.
Parkland course with water features.
Pro Alan O'Mara; Founded 1995
Designed by Roger Jones
9 holes, 3300 yards, S.S.S. 72
† Welcome.
Ⅰ Terms on application.
⌕ Welcome.
🍴 Full clubhouse facilities with spectacular views.
🛏 The Gleneagle.

12 231 Rosslare
Rosslare Strand, Co Wexford
🖳 www.iol.ie/~rgolsclb/
🖥 office@ruslaregolf.com
☎ 00353 53 32203, Fax 32263, Pro 32032, Sec 32203, Rest/Bar 32113
6 miles from the Rosslare ferry terminal; 10 miles S of Wexford.
Seaside links course.
Pro Johnny Young; Founded 1905/1992
Designed by Hawtree & Taylor (Old); Christy O'Connor Jnr (New)

18 for old and 12 for the new holes, 6577 yards, S.S.S. 72
† Welcome.
Ⅰ WD €35; WE €50.
⌕ Welcome by prior arrangement; catering packages by arrangement.
🍴 Full clubhouse facilities.
🛏 Kelly's Resort.

12 232 Rossmore
Rossmore Park, Cootehill Road, Monaghan, Co Monaghan
☎ 00353 47 81316, Pro 71222, Sec 81316
1.5 miles on the Cootehill Road out of Monaghan town.
Parkland course.
Founded 1916
Designed by Des Smyth
18 holes, 5507 yards, S.S.S. 68
† Welcome.
Ⅰ WD €25; WE €32.
⌕ Welcome; discounts are available for larger groups.
🍴 Full bar and restaurant facilities.
🛏 Four Seasons.

12 233 Royal Dublin
North Bull Island, Dollymount
🖳 www.theroyaldublingolfclub.com
🖥 kenealy@theroyaldublingolfclub.com
☎ 00353 1 8336346, Fax 8336504, Pro 8336477, Sec 833 6346, Rest/Bar 8333370 and 8337153
NE from Dublin along the Coast Road to Bull Wall across the wooden bridge.
Links course.
Pro Leonard Owens; Founded 1885
Designed by HS Colt
18 holes, 6330 yards, S.S.S. 73
† Welcome except Wed and Sat before 4pm.
Ⅰ WD €100; WE €115.
⌕ Welcome but must book a year in advance; catering by prior arrangement.
🍴 Full clubhouse facilities, bar and restaurant.
🛏 Marine; Hollybrook; Howth Lodge.

12 234 Royal Tara
Bellinter, Navan, Co Meath
🖳 www.royaltaragolfclub.com
🖥 theroyaltaragolfclub@ie
☎ 00353 46 25244, Fax 25508, Pro 26009, Sec 25508
Off N3 30 miles N of Dublin.
Parkland course.
Pro Adam Whiston; Founded 1906
Designed by Des Smyth Golf Design
27 holes, 6400 yards, S.S.S. 71

† Welcome by arrangement.
 WD €35; WE €40.
 Welcome Mon, Thurs, Fri and Sat by arrangement.
 Full bar and catering facilities.
 "The Adrboyne, New Grange.

12 235 Rush
Rush, Co Dublin
☎ 00353 1 8437548
Off the Dublin-Belfast Road at Blakes Cross.
Links course.
Founded 1943
9 holes, 5598 yards, S.S.S. 69
† Welcome WD only.
 €29.
 Welcome by prior arrangement.
 Full facilities.

12 236 St Annes
North Bull Island, Dollymount
 www.stanneslinksgolf.com
 info@stanneslinksgolf.com
☎ 00353 1 8336471, Fax 8334618,
Pro 8336471, Sec 833 6471
5 miles N of Dublin City.
Links course.
Pro Paddy Skerritt; Founded 1921
Designed by Eddie Hackett
18 holes, 5669 metres, S.S.S. 69
 Practice area.
† Welcome, except Sun.
 WD €45; WE €60.
 Welcome; group rates available.
 Full facilities.
 Marine; St Lawrence; Forte Posthouse; Grand; Sutton Castle.

12 237 St Helen's Bay ℭ
St Helen's, Kilrane, Rosslare Harbour, Co Wexford
☎ 00353 53 33234, Fax 33803
5 minutes from the Rosslare ferry-port in the village of Kilrane.
Links/parkland course mixture.
Founded 1993
Designed by Philip Walton
18 holes, 6091 yards, S.S.S. 72
† Welcome.
 Terms on application.
 Welcome by prior arrangement; packages available; tennis; accommodation on site; terms on application.
 Full clubhouse, dining and bar facilities.
 Great Southern; Rosslare; Devereux; Ferrycarrig.

12 238 St Margaret's Golf & Country Club
St Margaret's, Co Dublin
 www.margrette.net
 reservations@stmargetes.net
☎ 00353 1 8640400, Fax 8640289
4 miles W of Dublin Airport.
Parkland course.
Pro David O'Sullivan; Founded 1992
Designed by Ruddy & Craddock
18 holes, 6919 yards, S.S.S. 73
† Welcome.
 April-Oct: Mon-Wed €60; Thurs and Sun €70; Fri-Sat €75; Nov-March: Mon-Wed €45; Thurs and Sun €55; Sat €65.
 Welcome by prior arrangement; corporate days available.
 2 bars and 2 restaurants.
 Forte Crest; Grand Malahide.

12 239 St Patricks
Hotel Carrigart, Carrigart, Donegal
 www.carrigarthotel.com
☎ 00353 74 551141, Fax 55250
Seaside links course.
Founded 1996
Designed by E Hackett & Joanne O'Herne
36 holes, 7046 yards, S.S.S. 72
† Welcome.
 Welcome by prior arrangement, short notice is fine.
 Carrigart (full facilities with views across Sheephaven Bay).

12 240 Seapoint ℭ
Termonfeckin, Co Louth
 www.seapointgolfclub.com
☎ 00353 4198 22333, Fax 22331, Rest/Bar 98810
In Termonfeckin off the N1 Dublin to Drogheda Road.
Championship links course.
Pro David Carroll; Founded 1993
Designed by Des Smyth; Declan Branigan
18 holes, 7100 yards, S.S.S. 74
 Driving range with a large practice ground.
† Welcome.
 Mon-Thurs €30; Fri €38; WE: €50.
 Welcome WD by arrangement; discounts for larger groups.
 Bar and restaurant facilities.
 Boyne Valley Neptune Hotel.

12 241 Shannon
Shannon Airport, Co Clare
☎ 00353 61 471849, Fax 471507
0.5 miles from Shannon Airport.

Woodland/parkland course.
Founded 1966
18 holes, 6186 yards, S.S.S. 72
† Welcome; WE booking advisable.
 WD €35; WE €45.
 Welcome by prior arrangement.
 Bar snacks and meals.

12 242 Skerries
Haccketstown, Skerries, Co Dublin
☎ 0035 1 490925, Sec 491567
N of Dublin Airport off the Belfast Road.
Parkland course.
Pro Jimmy Kinsella; Founded 1906
18 holes, 6081 yards, S.S.S. 72
† Welcome.
 WD €40; WE €45.
 Welcome on Mon and Thurs by prior arrangement; terms on application.
 Full facilities.
 Trusthouse Forte; Dublin Airport.

12 243 Skibbereen & West
Licknavar, Skibbereen, Co Cork
☎ 00353 28 21227
2 miles from Skibbereen on the Baltimore Road.
Parkland course.
Founded 1905
Designed by Eddie Hackett
18 holes, 6069 yards, S.S.S. 68
† Welcome with handicap certs.
 Terms on application.
 Welcome by prior arrangement.
 Full clubhouse facilities.
 West Cork; Eldon; Casey's; Baltimore Harbour; Celtic Ross.

12 244 Slade Valley
Lynch Park, Brittas, Co Dublin
☎ 00353 1 4582183
8 miles W of Dublin off M7.
Undulating parkland course.
Founded 1970
Designed by WD Sullivan and D O'Brien
18 holes, 5337 yards, S.S.S. 68
† Welcome WD; WE with a member.
 WD €25; WE €40.
 Welcome by prior arrangement with Sec.
 Full WE facilities.
 Green Isle; Downshire House.

12 245 Slieve Russell Golf & Country Club
Ballyconnell, Co Cavan
☎ 00353 49 26444, Fax 26474
90 miles NW of Belfast.

Parkland course.
Founded 1992
Designed by Paddy Merrigan
18 holes, 6413 yards, S.S.S. 74
♦ Welcome; book in advance.
୮ Terms on application.
⌒ Welcome by prior arrangement.
⦿ Full facilities.

12 246 Spanish Point
Spanish Point, Miltown Malbay, Co Clare
☎ 00353 6570 84198
2 miles from Milton Malbay; 8 miles
from Lahinch.
Seaside course.
Founded 1896
9 holes, 3574 yards, S.S.S. 58
♦ Welcome.
୮ Terms on application.
⌒ Welcome; booking is strongly
recommended.
⦿ Light snacks only.

12 247 Stackstown
Kellystown Road, Rathfarnham
▤ stackstowngc@aircom.net
☎ 00353 1 4941993, Pro 4944561
Take exit 13 off the M50 follow the
road to Leopards Town and
ticknockabout 1 mile.
Hilly course with panoramic views.
Founded 1976
18 holes, 5789 yards, S.S.S. 71
♦ Welcome WD; WE by prior
arrangement.
୮ WD €30; WE €38.
⌒ Welcome by prior arrangement.
⦿ Full bar and restaurant.

12 248 Strandhill
Strandhill, Co Sligo
☎ 00353 71 68188, Fax 68811
5 miles W of Sligo.
Links course.
Founded 1932
18 holes, 5516 yards, S.S.S. 68
♦ Welcome; booking is
recommended.
୮ WD €35; WE €45.
⌒ Welcome by prior arrangement;
from €35.
⦿ Full facilities.
↩ Ocean View; Tower.

12 249 Sutton
Cush Point, Sutton, Dublin 13
▒ www.suttongolfclub.org
▤ suttongc@indigo.ie
☎ 00353 1 8322965, Fax 8321603,
Pro 8321703
7 miles NE of city centre.

Seaside links course.
Pro Nicky Lynch; Founded 1890
9 holes, 5226 yards, S.S.S. 67
♦ Welcome; restrictions Tues and
Sat.
୮ WD €35; WE €45.
⌒ Welcome by prior arrangement.
⦿ Full restaurant. Conference
facilities.
↩ The Marine.

12 250 Swinford
Brabazon Park, Swinford, Co Mayo
☎ 00353 94 51378
1 km S of Swinford on the Kiltimagh
Road.
Parkland course.
Founded 1922
9 holes, 5542 yards, S.S.S. 70
♦ Welcome.
୮ €15 per day.
⌒ Welcome except Sun; special
packages available; from €15.
⦿ Full catering; lounge bar.
↩ Cill Aodain; Breaffy; Welcome Inn.

12 251 Swords
Balheary Ave, Swords, Dublin
☎ 00353 1 8909819, Fax 8901303
5 mins from Swords centre.
Parkland course.
18 holes
♦ Welcome.
୮ Terms on application; pay and play.
⦿ Snack bar.

12 252 Tara Glen
Ballymoney, Courtown, Co Wexford
☎ 00353 55 25413
Parkland course.
Founded 1993
9 holes
♦ Welcome by prior arrangement.
୮ Terms on application.
⌒ Welcome by prior arrangement.
⦿ Bar.

12 253 Templemore
Manna South, Templemore, Co
Tipperary
☎ 00353 504 31400, Fax 31913
0.5 miles S of town centre off the N62.
Parkland course.
Founded 1972
9 holes, S.S.S. 70
♦ Welcome.
୮ WD €15; WE €20.
⌒ Welcome. Catering can be
arranged; terms on application.
⦿ Limited but available by prior
arrangement.

↩ Templemore Arms; Grants; Anner;
Hayes; Munster.

12 254 Thurles
Turtulla, Thurles, Co Tipperary
☎ 00353 504 21983, Fax 24647
1 mile from Thurles towards the main
Cork-Dublin road.
Parkland course.
Pro Sean Hunt; Founded 1944
Designed by J McAllister
18 holes, 6465 yards, S.S.S. 71
♦ Practice range 200 yards from
club.
♦ Welcome except Sun.
୮ €25; with members €12.50.
⌒ Welcome except Sun.
⦿ Full facilities.
↩ Anner; Hayes, Monstrouw Hotel.

12 255 Tipperary
Rathanny, Tipperary
▤ tipperarygolfclub@eircom.net
☎ 00353 62 51119, Fax 52132
1 mile from the town on the Glen of
Aherlow Road.
Parkland course.
Founded 1896
18 holes, 6300 yards, S.S.S. 71
♦ Driving range adjacent.
♦ Welcome; some Sun restrictions
apply.
୮ WD €20; WE €25.
⌒ Welcome by prior arrangement.
⦿ Bar and full restaurant facilities.
↩ Royal, Tipperary; Aherlow House
Hotel; Glen Hotel.

12 256 Townley Hall
Townley Hall, Tullyallen, Drogheda, Co
Louth
☎ 00353 4198 42229
Parkland course.
Founded 1994
18 holes, 4978 yards
♦ Welcome.
୮ Details available upon application.

12 257 Tralee
West Barrow, Ardfert, Co Kerry
▒ www.traleegolfclub.com
▤ info@traleegolfclub.com
☎ 00353 6671 36379, Fax 36008
8 miles West from Tralee on the
Churchill Road.
Links course.
Pro David Power; Founded 1896/1984
Designed by Arnold Palmer Design
18 holes, 6192 metres, S.S.S. 73
♦ Welcome.
୮ €110.

⌒ Welcome by prior arrangement; discounts available for larger groups.
🍴 Full restaurant, bar and clubhouse facilities.
🛏 Mount Brandon; Grand; Abbeygate.

12 258 Tramore
Newtown Hill, Tramore, Co Waterford
🖳 www.tranmoregolfclub.com
✉ tragolf@iol.ie
☎ 00353 51 386170, Fax 390961, Rest/Bar 381247/386583
Course is 7 miles S of Waterford on coast road.
Parkland course.
Pro Derry Kiely; Founded 1894
Designed by Tibbett (1936/37)
18 holes, 6055 yards, S.S.S. 72
⌁ Local one.
† Welcome; prior booking is advisable.
⌇ WD €40; WE €45.
⌒ Welcome by prior arrangement.
🍴 Catering and bar facilities.
🛏 Grand; Majestic; O'Sheas.

12 259 Tuam
Barnacurragh, Tuam, Co Galway
☎ 00353 93 28993, Fax 26003
1 mile outside Tuan on the Athenwy Road.
Parkland course.
Pro Larry Smyth; Founded 1907
Designed by E Hackett
18 holes, 6045 yards, S.S.S. 71
⌁ Practice range.
† Welcome.
⌇ €23; €15 with member.
⌒ Welcome by prior arrangement except on Sat afternoon and Sun; discounts for groups of more than 20; deposit of €65 required; catering by arrangement; from €15.
🍴 Full clubhouse bar and restaurant facilities.
🛏 Imperial.

12 260 Tubbercurry
Ougham, Tubbercurry, Co Sligo
☎ 00353 71 85849
0.5 miles from town on the Ballymote Road.
Parkland course.
Founded 1991
Designed by Eddie Hackett
9 holes, 5490 yards, S.S.S. 69
† Welcome; Sun by arrangement.
⌇ Details on application.
⌒ Welcome except Sun; discounts available; catering by arrangement; from €15.

🍴 Full bar and restaurant facilities.
🛏 Conleys.

12 261 Tulfarris Hotel & Country Club
Blessington, Co Wicklow
☎ 00353 45 64612
6 miles from Blessington off N81.
Parkland course.
Founded 1989
Designed by Eddie Hackett
9 holes, 5612 yards, S.S.S. 69
† Welcome; some Sun restrictions.
⌇ Terms on application.
⌒ Welcome by prior arrangement; terms on application.
🍴 Restaurant and bar facilities.

12 262 Tullamore
Brookfield, Tullamore, Co Offaly
☎ 00353 506 21439
3.5 miles S of Tullamore off the R451 to Kinnity from the N52.
Parkland course.
Founded 1886
Designed by James Braid
18 holes, 6434 yards, S.S.S. 70
† Welcome but prior booking is advisable.
⌇ WD €32; WE €40.
⌒ Welcome by prior arrangement; terms on application.
🍴 Full bar and restaurant facilities.

12 263 Turvey Golf & CC
Turvey Ave, Donabate, Dublin
☎ 00353 1 8435179
18 holes
† Welcome.
⌇ Terms on application.
🍴 Snack bar.

12 264 Virginia
Virginia, Co Cavan
🖳 www.bichotels.com
☎ 00353 49 8548066
50 miles N of Dublin on the main Dublin-Cavan Road.
Meadowland course.
Founded 1946
9 holes, 4139 metres yards, S.S.S. 62
† Welcome.
⌇ WD and WE: €15.
⌒ Welcome by prior arrangement.
🍴 Hotel on site.
🛏 Park Hotel.

12 265 Water Rock
Midleton, Cork
☎ 00353 21 613499, Fax 633150

5 mins from Midleton.
Parkland course.
18 holes, 6223 yards, S.S.S. 70
† Welcome.
⌇ Terms on application.
🍴 Clubhouse facilities.

12 266 Waterford
Newrath, Waterford, Co Waterford
☎ 00353 51 876748, Fax 853405, Pro 856568
On N9 from Dublin 1 mile from Waterford or N25 from Rosslare.
Parkland course.
Founded 1912
Designed by Cecil Barcroft and Willie Park
18 holes, 5722 yards, S.S.S. 70
† Welcome.
⌇ Terms on application.
⌒ Welcome by arrangement with secretary/manager; terms on application.
🍴 Full clubhouse facilities available.
🛏 Jury's; Tower; Granville; Bridge.

12 267 Waterford Castle Golf & Country Club
The Island, Ballinakill, Co Waterford
☎ 00353 51 871633
2 miles from Waterford on the Dunmore East Road.
Parkland course on island in River Suir.
Founded 1993
Designed by Des Smyth and Declan Brannigan
18 holes, 6303 yards, S.S.S. 73
† Welcome by arrangement.
⌇ Mon-Thurs €41; Fri-Sun €49; except Jan-March and Aug: €38/€45.
⌒ Welcome by arrangement.
🍴 Clubhouse facilities.

12 268 Waterville Golf Links
Ring of Kerry, Waterville, Co Kerry
☎ 00353 66 74102
1 mile W of Waterville half-way through the Ring of Kerry.
Links course.
Pro Liam Higgins; Founded 1901/1972
Designed by E Hackett
18 holes, 7184 yards, S.S.S. 74
⌁ Practice range open to green fee paying players and members.
† Welcome.
⌇ WD €125 (4-8pm €63): WE €125.
⌒ Welcome by prior arrangement; discount 10% for 20 or more players; from €110.
🍴 Full clubhouse facilities.
🛏 Waterville House; Butler Arms; Bay View.

12 269 West Waterford ☏
Coolcormack, Dungarvan, Co Waterford
☎ 00353 58 43216, Fax 44343
3 miles W of Dungarvan off the N25 on
the Aglish Road.
Parkland course.
Founded 1993
Designed by Eddie Hackett
18 holes, 6802 yards, S.S.S. 74
† Welcome.
[WD €26; WE €32.
♢ Welcome everyday by prior
arrangement.
⦿ Full clubhouse facilities available
everyday.
↷ Lawlors; Park; Clonea Strand.

12 270 Westmanstown
Clonsilla, Dublin 15
☎ 00353 1 8205817, Fax 8205858,
Sec 0862446296
Course is off the Dublin Road in Lucan
village 1.25 miles following the signs
for Clonsilla.
Parkland course.
Founded 1988
Designed by Eddie Hackett
18 holes, 5826 yards off the blue, 5613
yards off the white, 4900 yards for
ladies, S.S.S. 70
† Welcome but booking is essential
at WE. Cheaper with a member €15.
[WD €35; WE €40.
♢ Welcome by prior arrangement.
⦿ Full clubhouse facilities available.
↷ The Spa Hotel, Westcounty, Travel
Lodge.

12 271 Westport
Carrowholly, Westport, Co Mayo
☎ 00353 98 25113, Fax 27217
2 miles from Westport.
Parkland course.
Founded 1908
Designed by Hawtree & Son
18 holes, 6959 yards, S.S.S. 73
† Welcome.
[Terms on application.
♢ Welcome by prior arrangement;
special packages available; terms on
application.
⦿ Lounge bar and dining facilities
available.

12 272 Wexford
Mulgannon, Wexford
☎ 00353 53 42238, Pro 46300, Sec

44611
In Wexford town.
Parkland course.
Founded 1960
Designed by J. Hamilton Stutt & Co
(original); Des Smyth (new)
18 holes, 5578 yards, S.S.S. 70
† Welcome; restrictions Wed
evening and Thurs.
[WD €26; €WE 32.
♢ Welcome by prior arrangement;
discounts for larger groups; terms on
application.
⦿ Bar and snacks.

12 273 Wicklow
Dunbur Rd, Wicklow, Co Wicklow
☎ 00353 404 67379, Pro 66122
On L29 32 miles from Dublin.
Seaside course.
Founded 1904
18 holes, 5695 yards, S.S.S. 70
† Welcome but booking for WE is
strongly advisable.
[WD and WE: €35.
♢ Welcome by prior arrangement.
⦿ Full clubhouse facilities.

12 274 Woodbrook
Dublin Rd, Bray, Co Wicklow
⌨ www.woodbook.ie
✉ woodbrook@
internetireland.ie
☎ 00353 1 2824799, Fax 2821950
Course is 11 miles south of Dublin on
the N11.
Parkland course.
Pro William Kinselle; Founded 1921
18 holes, 5996 yards, S.S.S. 71
⚑ Practice area.
† Welcome by arrangement; booking
essential for WE.
[Oct-March: €40; April-Sept: WD
€75, WE and BH €85.
♢ Welcome Mon, Thurs and Fri by
prior arrangement.
⦿ Full clubhouse facilities.
↷ The Royal Hotel, The Glen View.

12 275 Woodenbridge
Woodenbridge Golf Club, Arklow, Co
Wicklow
☎ 00353 402 35202, Fax 35754
45 miles S of Dublin on N11 to Arklow.
Parkland course.
Founded 1884
Designed by Patrick Merrigan

18 holes, 6400 yards, S.S.S. 70
⚑ Practice ground.
† Welcome except Thurs and Sat.
[Terms available upon application.
♢ Welcome WD by prior
arrangement.
⦿ Full clubhouse facilities.

12 276 Woodlands
Coill Dubh, Naas, Co Kildare
☎ 00353 45 860777
On outskirts of Naas.
Parkland course.
Founded 1985
18 holes, 5202 yards, S.S.S. 71
† Welcome but booking is normally
needed for weekends.
[WD €16; WE €20.
♢ Welcome with prior arrangement.
⦿ Bar food available and catering on
request.

12 277 Woodstock
Woodstock House, Shanaway Road,
Ennis, Co Clare
⌨ www.slh.com
☎ 00353 65 6829463,
Fax 6820304
In Ennis.
Parkland course.
Founded 1993
Designed by Dr Arthur Spring.
18 holes, 5879 yards, S.S.S. 71
† Welcome.
[WD €35; WE €40.
♢ Welcome by prior arrangement;
terms of group rates on application.
⦿ Club house catering facilities; bar
food available.
↷ Woodstock House Hotel.

12 278 Youghal
Knockaverry, Youghal, Co Cork
☎ 00353 24 92787, Fax 92641,
Pro 92590
On N25 between Rosslare and Cork.
Parkland course.
Pro Liam Burns; Founded 1898
Designed by Commander Harris
18 holes, 5646 yards, S.S.S. 70
† Welcome.
[WD €25; WE €32.
♢ Welcome by prior arrangement.
⦿ Full clubhouse facilities available.
↷ Walter Raleigh; Devonshire Arms.

INDEX